Nutrition, Health, and Safety for Young Children

Promoting Wellness

Joanne Sorte

Oregon State University

Inge Daeschel

Oregon State University

Carolina Amador

Community Health Centers of Benton and Linn Counties

D1282009

PEARSON

Boston   Columbus   Indianapolis   New York   San Francisco   Upper Saddle River
Amsterdam   Cape Town   Dubai   London   Madrid   Milan   Munich   Paris   Montréal   Toronto
Delhi   Mexico City   São Paulo   Sydney   Hong Kong   Seoul   Singapore   Taipei   Tokyo

Vice President and Editorial Director: Jeffery W. Johnston
Executive Editor: Julie Peters
Editorial Assistant: Pamela DiBerardino
Development Editor: Jon Theiss
Executive Field Marketing Manager: Krista Clark
Executive Product Marketing Manager: Christopher Barry
Marketing Assistant: Elizabeth Mackenzie-Lamb

Program Manager: Megan Moffo
Project Manager: Janet Domingo
Manufacturing Buyer: Carol Melville
Art Director: Diane Lorenzo
Media Project Manager: Michael Goncalves
Editorial Production and Composition Services: Lumina Datamatics, Inc.

Credits and acknowledgments borrowed from other sources and reproduced, with permission, in this textbook appear on the appropriate pages within the text.

Every effort has been made to provide accurate and current Internet information in this book. However, the Internet and information posted on it are constantly changing, so it is inevitable that some of the Internet addresses listed in this textbook will change.

Photo credits appear here and on page: Howard Shooter/Dorling Kindersley Limited; alexskopje/Fotolia; 2xSamara.com/Fotolia; Glayan/Shutterstock; Suzanne Clouzeau/Pearson Education; arek_malang/Shutterstock; DragonImages/Fotolia; Mat Hayward/Fotolia; Richard Green/Alamy; Andy Crawford and Steve Gorton/Dorling Kindersley, Ltd; Vitalinka/Shutterstock; Michaeljung/Shuttterstock; Marmaduke St. John/Alamy; Paul Vasarhelyi/Shutterstock; ia_64/Fotolia; ChiccoDodiFC/Fotolia

Library of Congress Cataloging-in-Publication Data
Names: Sorte, Joanne, author. | Daeschel, Inge, author. | Amador, Carolina, author.
Title: Nutrition, health, and safety for young children : promoting wellness / Joanne Sorte, Oregon State Unviersity; Inge Daeschel, Oregon State University; Carolina Amador, Community Health Centers of Benton and Linn Counties.
Description: Third Edition. | Boston : Pearson, [2017]
Identifiers: LCCN 2015035807 | ISBN 9780133956764 (pbk.)
Subjects: LCSH: Children—Health and hygiene—Textbooks. | Children—Nutrition—Textbooks.
Classification: LCC RJ101 .S655 2017 | DDC 618.92—dc23
LC record available at http://lccn.loc.gov/2015035807

16 2021

ISBN-13: 978-0-13-395676-4
ISBN-10:   0-13-395676-8

I extend loving appreciation to my parents, Jean and Burrell Godard; to the many children who educated me along the way; and to Bruce, our children, their spouses, and our grandchildren: Cascade, Matt, Caden, Finley, Jerry, Misty, Isabelle, Nathaniel, and Sally, who have taught me many things about nutrition, health, and safety and the joys of playing outdoors.

Joanne sorte

I would like to extend my thanks to my husband Mark and our four children and their spouses/significant others, Ariel and David, Lea and Kyle, Kimberly and Dylan, and Devin, for their love and support throughout the writing of this book and through all of life's joys and challenges. A special thanks to my parents Elmar and Christina Frodden and my sisters Christina Anderson and Kerrin Hutz. And finally my eternal gratitude to the WIC, public health, EMS, and hospital staff whose efforts on my behalf place them in the category of heroes!

Inge daeschel

I extend genuine appreciation to all children, each of whom bring wisdom, courage, and joy to the world. I also would like to extend an extra special thanks to my family: Scott, Lucia, Oscar, and Felix, who bring me great peace, joy, and awe.

Carolina amador

We would like to acknowledge two professionals who made contributions to the nutrition chapters: Lauren Au, R.D., of the University of California, Berkeley and Samantha Ramsay, R.D.N., L.D., of the University of Idaho.

ABOUT THE AUTHORS

Joanne Sorte has worked as an early childhood professional for over 40 years. She received a Bachelor of Arts degree in Child Development and Family Life and a Master of Science degree in Human Development and Family Sciences from Oregon State University. She began her early childhood professional experiences as a home visitor for the Home Base program in Yakima, Washington; directed a preschool program for Lower Columbia College in Longview, Washington; and worked as a family services coordinator for Head Start. She then taught for 27 years as a Senior Instructor for the College of Public Health and Human Sciences at Oregon State University. During this time, she also served as Director of the Child Development Laboratory, developing a blended early education preschool program model in which children from low-

From Left: Joanne Sorte, Inge Daeschel, and Carolina Amador

income families participate through support of the Oregon Head Start Prekindergarten Program, along with children who have special developmental needs and children from the general community. She directed the practicum experience for students majoring in child development, supervised graduate students, and facilitated research on child development and wellness. She has coauthored an intervention program for preschool settings with Inge Daeschel, called "Health in Action: 5 Steps to Good Health." Recently retired, she continues to enjoy assisting early childhood settings in partnering with families to improve children's health and wellness.

Inge Daeschel is a licensed and registered dietitian who is a board-certified specialist in pediatric nutrition. She received her Bachelor of Science Degree in Foods and Nutrition Science at Plattsburgh State University in New York. She completed her dietetic internship at Massachusetts General Hospital in Boston and received her Master of Science degree in Nutrition Science from the University of Tennessee, Knoxville. She worked at Duke University Medical Center, first as pediatric dietitian clinician and later as assistant chief clinical dietitian. This position was instrumental in developing her interest in helping families understand the nutritional needs of their children.

She and her family relocated to Oregon, where she worked at the Corvallis Clinic. and Later she accepted a faculty position as an instructor for the College of Public Health and Human Sciences at Oregon State University where she was Health and Nutrition Services Coordinator of the OSU Child Development Laboratory and the OSU Oregon Head Start Prekindergarten Program. Currently, Inge is a nutrition consultant who provides services to WIC, Early Head Start, and two Head Start programs, including the OSU Child Development Laboratory. Her expertise in feeding children is based on personal as well as professional experience that she gained from raising four children, including one with multiple food allergies. She has coauthored with Joanne Sorte an intervention program called "Health in Action: 5 Steps to Good Health," which promotes wellness by providing focused messages that address nutrition and physical activity in early childhood programs.

Carolina Amador, M.D., M.P.H. is a board-certified general pediatrician. She received a Bachelor of Education degree in Speech Pathology at the University of Georgia in Athens. She earned her medical degree from the Medical College of Georgia in Augusta and completed her residency in pediatrics at West Virginia University in Morgantown. She worked as Chief Resident in Pediatrics at West Virginia University, where she developed a lactation clinic as well as a focus on advocacy for breast-feeding mothers. She has a master's degree in Public Health from the University of Washington in Seattle with a focus on maternal and child health. She moved with her husband to Corvallis, Oregon, and has worked as a general pediatrician for 12 years. She is currently employed by a community health center that serves a large percentage of Hispanics and migrant workers. During these years as a general pediatrician, she has developed professional interests in childhood obesity prevention, health disparities, and Latino health. She has been involved in community events and organizations advocating for children's health, including the Oregon State University Oregon Head Start Prekindergarten Program Health Services Advisory Committee, the Benton County Healthy Weight and Lifestyle Coalition, the Benton County Oral Health Coalition, and the Breastfeeding Coalition of Benton County. Throughout her years of education and medical practice, she has participated in several international health experiences in Ecuador, Honduras, Uganda, and Malawi.

PREFACE

This is an exciting and innovative time to be an early childhood educator. There is widespread and enthusiastic confirmation that early childhood professionals play a crucial role in children's early education and development by helping to establish the foundations of wellness to support young children now and in the future. With this strong support for the value of the early years comes a call to make high-quality care and education accessible to all children. Teachers are expected to learn and use teaching strategies that will help all children attain wellness and be ready for success in school, and more than ever before, early childhood teachers are held accountable for children's progress in learning. It is a time of innovation and evolution.

NEW TO THIS EDITION

- **Fully digital text format** is now available for use with face-to-face, online, and hybrid classes, extending the nutrition, health, and safety message to future teachers. The Pearson Enhanced eText is the only ebook to include:
  - **Check Your Understanding quizzes** have been added to follow each chapter section. Students can link to an electronic multiple choice or short answer quiz to check their understanding of important topics. Students receive immediate feedback, allowing them to review the material before moving on, which helps ensure that learning outcomes are achieved.
  - **End-of-Chapter Quizzes** connect students to multiple choice questions that measure their understanding of the chapter's learning outcomes. Immediate feedback clarifies the correct response and includes a brief rationale to help students understand important concepts.
  - **Videos** are included again with this edition, but the variety is expanded.

- **Chapters have been streamlined, revised, and rearranged** to provide a better flow of topics and information, enhancing instruction and improving student understanding. Chapters 15 and 16 (from the second edition) have been switched to present child abuse and neglect within the context of safety promotion and to complete the study of wellness with the exploration of emergency management and response.
- **Terminology used to explore nutrition concepts is more accessible** for students. New nutrition guidelines, including the Institute of Medicine 2010 guidelines for vitamin D, are discussed. References are more current to reflect current evidence-based practices for feeding young children.

- **Discussion of health practices is enhanced** for relevance to teachers, including aspects of health screenings, descriptions of common infectious diseases, and classroom management strategies to improve health and wellness for children with special health care needs. In addition, a focus on social and emotional health in early childhood adds to the overall message of attaining mental health and wellness.
- **Safety chapters** have been revised to improve clarity and reduce redundancy. Basic first aid procedures are ordered in a user-friendly fashion. Recognition of the many forms of violence that children experience are discussed, and strategies are offered to help teachers address these negative experiences through compassionate and empowering classroom practices.
- **New content.** In this third edition of *Nutrition, Health,* and *Safety for Young Children*, you are invited to explore the wide range of challenges that teachers of young children face today, including the following:
  - An increasingly diverse population of young learners.
  - More identified food allergies.
  - Concern about childhood obesity.
  - Increasing numbers of children who are not immunized against disease.
  - Children with special health care needs being served in classrooms.
  - New kinds of threats to children's safety.
  - Emergency management planning.
  - Increased awareness of the need to develop healthy environments and use sustainable practices in early childhood settings.

This edition explores these challenges by helping students understand the interrelationships among nutrition, health, and safety and discover strategies to share their knowledge with children and their families.

SCOPE AND PURPOSE OF THIS BOOK

This practical text provides today's students with a comprehensive understanding of the nutrition, health, and safety needs of young children from birth into school age. In-text examples, case scenarios, and questions promote thinking about professional situations and give students a glimpse into the everyday contemporary classroom environment. These concrete illustrations and common examples prepare teachers to serve diverse populations of young children in family child care, child care centers, preschools, and elementary school settings.

The intention is to provide students with a strong understanding of wellness concepts, equipping them to implement healthful practices and teach young children ways to contribute to their own wellness. These skills emerge as students gain insight into the basic approaches used to enhance children's well-being:

- **Partner with children and families and with nutrition, health, and safety professionals to promote wellness in young children.** Students learn that they will work within a network of support to meet children's nutrition, health, and safety needs.

- **Implement and model appropriate wellness practices.** Students will be able to design and use practices that are fitting for children's age and developmental capabilities, that are in tune with children's developmental, health, and language needs, and that are responsive to family cultural practices.
- **Recognize the important contributions of nutrition, health, and safety to children's learning and overall well-being.** Students will be ready to:
  - Provide wholesome nutrition that promotes optimal growth, development, and learning.
  - Attend to children's individual health needs and implement healthful classroom practices that build wellness habits to last a lifetime.
  - Establish environments and implement practices that ensure children's physical and emotional safety, creating the foundations that inspire exploration, creativity, and discovery.

Students are invited to join the team of early childhood professionals who cherish the important early years of growth and development and who celebrate each child's potential for a healthy, happy, and productive future. The following pages describe what is new to this edition and how this text helps students to understand, see, and teach wellness concepts.

- Through anecdotes, cases, and authentic examples, the authors use a story-telling approach that helps **contextualize** wellness concepts for students. Chapter-opening **scenarios** reveal common situations involving teachers, children, and their families grappling with nutrition, health, and safety issues. These scenarios are woven through each chapter to illustrate the teacher's role.
- The text promotes **culturally responsive** teaching of nutrition, health, and safety concepts, including content about vegetarian, religious, and cultural diets and ways to work with children and families from diverse backgrounds.
- A unique chapter on **children's mental health** explores current thinking about children's emotional health needs. (See Chapter 12.)
- Pedagogical features reinforce concepts and terminology: Learning Outcomes, key terms and glossary definitions, predictable Check Your Understanding quizzes at the end of major sections (digital only), end-of-chapter Reviews, Quizzes (digital), and Application items.

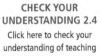

CHECK YOUR UNDERSTANDING 2.4

Click here to check your understanding of teaching English language learners about nutrition.

Chapter Quiz

 Click here to check your understanding of the foundations of optimal nutrition.

- Topical features in each chapter—**Nutrition Notes, Safety Segments, Policy Points,** and **Health Hints**—introduce readers to current issues in health, safety, and nutrition to create awareness and develop effective practices.

NUTRITION NOTE   Fats for Infants

Fat is an important nutrient for infants and toddlers who have high energy needs because of their rapid growth. These young children have a small stomach capacity and can meet their nutritional needs for growth and development only by eating calorie-dense fats. The fat intake requirement of infants is greater than at any other time in life, with infants needing 45% to 55% of their calories from fat.

Fats serve not only as a[n] aid in the absorption of t[...] and K. Fat is also a source of [...] vital in supporting optimal br[...] infants. It is very important [...] and toddlers to recognize the[...] development.

Sources: "Low Fat Diets for Babies," Hassink, S. G., *American Academy of Pediatrics,* 2012, HealthyChildren.org at http://www.he[...] /feeding-nutrition/pages/Low-Fat-Diets-For-Babies.aspx; "Dietary (n-3) Fatty Acids and Brain Development," by S. M. Innis, 2007, J[...] "Lipid Requirements of Infants: Implications for Nutrient Composition of Fortified Complementary Foods," by R. Uauy and C. Castillo, 200[...] 2962S–2972S.

SAFETY SEGMENT   Keep Children Safe from Multivitamin[...]

The Dietary Reference Intakes (DRIs) provide guidance on the amount and types of essential nutrients individuals need to consume to maintain a healthy diet. Sometimes children may not eat as well as they should. Families may consider giving multivitamins to their children to make sure nutrition goals are met. Should children take multivitamins? Most healthy children do fine without dietary supplementation. Their needs are less than those of adults, and they may be consuming foods that are fortified, such as breakfast cereals and juices.

Teachers should direct families with concerns to discuss the use of multivitamins with their doctor or dietitian. If they

are advised to take multivitamin[...] are designed for children. Careg[...] how they are dispensed. Many [...] like candy, and children who t[...] at risk.

The American Academy of [...] Nutrition and Dietetics agree tha[...] ments (except for vitamin K in n[...] for breast-fed infants, non–breas[...] drink less than 32 ounces of fo[...] needed for most healthy childre[...] nutrient needs with foods rather [...]

POLICY POINT
Supporting Policy Changes That Impact Obesity

Many teachers feel a strong need to advocate for change in their school or community to fight the obesity epidemic. To start, they need information to "shake things up." To influence decision makers, they need information that relates specifically to their state.

of obesity and discusses what each state is doing to address the obesity epidemic. Another website that provides state-by-state data on the food environment is the USDA's Economic Research Service website, which includes the Food Environment Atlas and Food Desert Locator. This website provides state and county information that relates to a community's ability to access nutritious

---

HEALTH HINT   High-Fructose Corn Syrup: Are There Health Risks?

Does high-fructose corn syrup (HFCS) increase the risk of obesity and the chronic diseases associated with obesity because of the way it is metabolized? Does it cause heart disease, diabetes, and accumulation of damaging fat in the liver? Some studies suggest that this is the case, although research has had conflicting results. HFCS is used in food products such as soft drinks, canned fruits, and processed desserts because it remains stable in acidic foods and drinks, is less expensive than sugar, and comes from a reliable and plentiful U.S. crop: corn. This type of corn syrup was originally called HFCS to distinguish it from regular corn syrup, which is 100% glucose. However, it is similar in composition to sucrose (table sugar) and honey in that it contains about 42% to 55% fructose, whereas sugar contains 50% fructose and honey contains about 49%.

There are various hypotheses as to why HFCS may contribute to obesity. Originally correlations were made that linked the rise of obesity to a time frame that also saw an increased use of HFCS in foods and beverages. Although this may seem plausible, it doesn't necessarily show cause and effect. For example, added sugars from all sources, particularly when combined with solid fats, have been linked to obesity and other related health concerns. Another theory suggests that fructose may impact appetite regulation in a negative way. When glucose is absorbed, it triggers the release of the hormones insulin and leptin and suppresses the production of ghrelin—hormonal

responses that inhibit appetite. This does not occur when fructose is absorbed. There is speculation that this may lead to overeating. However, some confusion surrounds studies that focus on pure fructose versus HFCS. It is important to remember that because sugar has about the same amount of fructose as HFCS, cutting back on sugar naturally reduces fructose in the diet. The American Academy of Nutrition and Dietetics evaluated numerous studies related to high-fructose corn syrup and consistently found little evidence that high-fructose corn syrup differed from sugar in how it affects metabolism, hunger, satiety, and calorie intake (American Academy of Nutrition and Dietetics, 2012b).

Can evidence-based recommendations be made about high-fructose corn syrup? Not yet because research is still ongoing.

In the meantime, teachers can take a judicious approach to high-fructose corn syrup and all added sugars by:

- Not offering soft drinks to young children.
- Serving fresh fruit instead of canned fruit, especially fruits packed in heavy syrup.
- Avoiding excessive use of processed desserts, snack bars, and sweets.
- Encouraging a diet higher in fiber content, which is a natural way to decrease HFCS and other fructose-containing sugars in the diet and promote satiety.

HELPS STUDENTS TO *SEE* WELLNESS CONCEPTS ... AND *APPLY* THEM

Pearson Education

CLASSROOM CONNECTION

Watch this video about Walk to School Day and Bike to School Day, collaborative efforts between a school and community. What are some other school and community activities that provide children with opportunities to increase their physical activity?

- **Videos** are embedded directly into pages of the Pearson eText via margin notes. These allow students to immediately see examples of wellness practices in action and learn from them.

- Nutrition chapters 2–7 are thoughtfully written to break down complex content using clear language, diagrams, and frequent classroom examples.

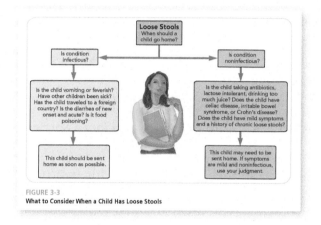

FIGURE 3-3
What to Consider When a Child Has Loose Stools

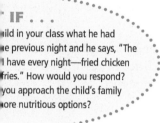

IF . . .

ild in your class what he had e previous night and he says, "The I have every night—fried chicken ries." How would you respond? you approach the child's family ore nutritious options?

- Reflective **What If ...** situations place students in the classroom to think about how they would solve day-to-day challenges related to nutrition, health, and safety. Many of these What If... margin notes ask readers to consider **Ethical questions**, in keeping with NAEYC's Code of Ethical Conduct.

- **Progressive Programs & Practices** features allow students to view wellness topics through the experience of early childhood professionals who are addressing issues and concerns in their communities.

PROGRESSIVE PROGRAMS & PRACTICES

A National School Garden and Farm to School Service Progra

By Debra Eschmeyer, FoodCorps, Inc.

FoodCorps is a national nonprofit organization, through AmeriCorps, that seeks to combat childhood obesity, food insecurity, and diet-related disease while training the next generation of farmers and public health leaders. Service members invest a year of paid public service conducting nutrition education; building and tending school gardens; and sourcing local food for school meals in high-obesity, limited-resource communities.

Children at risk for obesity and children facing food insecurity are, ironically, often the same. FoodCorps addresses the root cause of both: lack of access to healthy food. In keeping with the directives of the National Prevention Council, FoodCorps is not a response to obesity's symptoms, but a strategic plan to build community-based school environments that make healthy choices the norm, not the exception.

Under the Edward M. Kennedy Serve America Act signed into law in 2009, AmeriCorps is slated to triple in size by 2017. FoodCorps leverages federal funds and partners with local groups to provide schools with the people power needed to change their food environments. And it does so without burdening already

In the first year of service, 50 service members taught more than 50,000 children, built or restored 500 school and community gardens, recruited 1,700 volunteers to help improve school food, and harvested 11,000 pounds of garden-fresh produce for food-insecure children and families. Beyond the statistics, the service members' stories—of salsa taste tests and broccoli biology lessons and local food and farmer days in the school lunchroom—are inspiring. Meanwhile, there is a protection of green space, renewal of vacant lots and concrete schoolyards, and revival of vibrant economies for farmers and food producers.

"We get very excited to eat things we usually don't like, like broccoli, spinach, peas, and carrots . . . we grew it, so we like it a lot more."—Eva, age 10

"This is the first time I'm ever trying it (broccoli). My mom usually tries to get me to eat it, but I'm going to give it a shot today."—middle school student in Des Moines, Iowa

"See?! I like every fruit and vegetable there is! And I eat all of it!"

"The kohlrabi is just a hit," said Christopher Chemsak, FoodCorps service member. "They love to pull it out of the ground

- The theme of being a good **role model** to children is emphasized throughout.

HELPS STUDENTS *TEACH* WELLNESS CONCEPTS TO CHILDREN

- **Your Role in Children's Wellness** establishes the importance of integrating nutrition, health, and safety concepts throughout learning activities and in the daily curriculum. A suggested activity plan format supports students who need to create learning activities in a practicum or field experience.

- **Teaching Wellness curriculum lesson activities** are provided in each chapter. The activities are presented in developmentally appropriate ways for infants and toddlers, preschoolers, and school-age children. Some of these can be viewed in videos.

- The content of the text aligns with **NAEYC** professional preparation and program standards.

SUPPORT MATERIALS FOR INSTRUCTORS

The following resources are available for instructors to download from www.pearsonhighered.com. Instructors select Instructor Resources, enter the author or title of this book, select this particular edition of the book, and then click on the "Resources" tab to log in and download textbook supplements.

Instructor's Resource Manual (0-13-402704-3)

The revised Instructor's Resource Manual provides chapter-by-chapter tools to use in class. In-class activities, discussion questions, and additional resources will reinforce key concepts and applications and keep students engaged.

Test Bank (0-13-402743-4)

These multiple-choice, true-false, and essay questions tied to each chapter provide instructors with a variety of assessment items to evaluate student understanding of chapter content. An answer key is included.

PowerPoint™ Slides (0-13-402693-4)

The PowerPoint slides include key concept summarizations, diagrams, and other graphic aids to enhance learning. They are designed to help students understand, organize, and remember core concepts and theories.

TestGen™ (0-13-402698-5)

TestGen is a powerful test generator that instructors install on a computer and use in conjunction with the TestGen test bank file for the text. Assessments, including equations, graphs, and scientific notation, may be created for both print and online testing.

TestGen is available exclusively from Pearson Education publishers. Instructors install TestGen on a personal computer (Windows or Macintosh) and create tests for classroom testing and for other specialized delivery options, such as over a local area network or on the Web.

The tests can be downloaded in the following formats:

- TestGen Testbank file—PC
- TestGen Testbank file—MAC
- TestGen Testbank—Blackboard 9 TIF
- TestGen Testbank—Blackboard CE/Vista (WebCT) TIF
- Angel Test Bank (zip)
- D2L Test Bank (zip)
- Moodle Test Bank
- Sakai Test Bank (zip)

Acknowledgments

We extend our thanks to the many reviewers whose valuable feedback and insights helped shape and enhance our manuscript: Maria Abercrombie, Chattahoochee Technical College; Shannon M. Bracamonte, New Mexico State University; Lisa Fuller, Cerro Coso Community College; Constance Gassner, Ivy Tech Community College; and Rachelle Powell, North Lake College.

We especially appreciate the students, children, and families of the Child Development Laboratory Preschool at Oregon State University and to the teachers and staff for their expert insight and advice.

We extend special appreciation to the staff of the Community Health Centers of Benton and Linn Counties for enthusiastically serving underprivileged children in our community and for always offering their time and energy to advocate for children and their families.

Finally, we thank our editor, Julie Peters, and project manager, Doug Bell, whose encouragement, expertise, and support made this book possible.

BRIEF CONTENTS

CONTENTS

PART 3 Promoting Healthful Practices 275

SPECIAL FEATURES

Safety Segments

Policy Points

PART

1

PROMOTING WELLNESS

1   Your Role in Children's Wellness

CHAPTER 1

Your Role in Children's Wellness

After reading this chapter, you should be able to:

1. Define wellness and describe how nutrition, health, and safety work together for children's health and well-being.
2. Identify and discuss factors that influence children's wellness.
3. Describe how children learn and discuss the strategies used to develop a wellness curriculum.
4. Explain why it is beneficial to partner with families and community members to promote children's wellness.

CASE STUDY It is lunchtime at Kaylee's family child care program. After completing her associate degree in early childhood development, Kaylee opened her family child care program as a way to work in her field while enjoying her two young children. The children wash their hands and gather in the kitchen for lunch. Kaylee serves Dominique his "burrito" in small tortilla pieces with spoonfuls of refried beans and grated cheese. As she serves the older children, she gives Nancy a burrito without cheese because she has a milk allergy. Then Kaylee sits down to eat with the children. "Beans!" says Dominique. Kaylee and the children cheer for Dominique's new word.

Across town, Hector is carrying out the recyclables and trash from the preschool class. As he walks to the side of the building, Hector thinks about Zach, a child who

attends in a wheelchair. Zach has a muscle-wasting disease that will continue to worsen. But it is Zach's cheerful spirit that sticks in Hector's mind. Today Zach asked if whales can live under the ice at the North Pole. Hector doesn't know the answer to this question, so he decides to stop at the library on his way home to find a book about whales that he and Zach can explore.

In another community, Sharina and Amelia walk through the children's play yard carrying clipboards, each with a safety checklist. They are helping with a review of the play areas as part of a tribal health initiative to increase children's participation in active play. They make notes about the hard-packed ground under the play structures and watch as some children throw bark chips over the fence. They begin to develop ideas for recommendations to improve the play environment.

This is an exciting time to be an early childhood professional! Research on growth and development continues to emphasize the importance of the early years in setting the stage for a child's future capacity to learn. The important role that teachers play in guiding children's development is being given renewed attention and recognition. Teachers are second only to families in developing the context of healthful nutrition, health, and safety that surrounds the children they serve. Teachers participate in this process by providing care and education in a variety of settings: family child care, center-based child care, kindergarten, after-school care, evening child care, and more. Because care and education are intricately intertwined during the early years, we refer to all those who provide care and education to young children as *early childhood teachers*.

Early childhood teachers have much in common. In the opening scenario, each teacher demonstrates special enjoyment of very young children and knowledge of child development. Each participates willingly in the full spectrum of responsibilities associated with caring for children, including individualized planning, daily tasks, and classroom management. Each actively embraces the intriguing challenge of providing purposeful experiences to advance children's learning while keeping them safe. Central to these efforts are each child's nutrition, health, and safety. This chapter describes the links between nutrition, health, and safety; offers information about important influences on children's well-being; explores current issues in nutrition, health, and safety; and discusses the important ways that teachers contribute to the development and potential of young children by teaching wellness concepts.

BUILDING THE FOUNDATIONS FOR CHILDREN'S WELLNESS

Families, early childhood educators, and community members alike envision communities in which wellness is a goal for all people. **Wellness** is a positive state of health and well-being often described by words such as *healthy, happy*, and *thriving*. Wellness emerges from healthful practices such as consuming a nutritious diet, exercising, and sleeping well. Achieving wellness requires access to resources, including sufficient food, immunizations, health care, and safe environments. The early childhood years are an important period for building the foundations for wellness. Learning the healthful practices that lead to wellness during the early years is crucial to children's ability to attain optimal development and establish the capacity to learn.

wellness
a positive state of health and well-being

Understanding the Interrelationships Between Nutrition, Health, and Safety

The foundation of healthy growth, development, and wellness are established through the building blocks of nutrition, health, and safety. Each makes a specific contribution to the child's ability to grow and thrive.

- *Nutrition* encompasses the relationship between the nutrients that are eaten, digested, and absorbed and the way they contribute to growth and health. A child's **diet**, or the foods and beverages consumed to nourish and support the body and its processes, must meet the child's nutritional demands during the active early years for the child to grow appropriately. Serving safe and healthy food is a common responsibility of early childhood teachers.

diet
the foods and beverages consumed to nourish and support the body and its processes

- *Health* focuses on physical and mental well-being and the absence of disease. It is achieved through a variety of healthful practices that seek to prevent and minimize illness or disease. Teachers contribute to children's health in many ways, such as encouraging families to obtain childhood immunizations and by teaching children how and when to wash their hands.
- *Safety* centers on keeping children from harm. Safety is increased through practices that reduce the likelihood of injury or exposure to environmental toxins. Teachers promote safety by creating safe environments, implementing appropriate procedures, and supervising children's safe interactions.

The interrelationships between these factors become evident as the healthful benefits of one influences the positive outcomes in the others and as gaps or challenges in one area negatively affect the others. For example:

- For foods to be healthful, they must be stored, prepared, and served in a sanitary manner.
- When children consume safe and healthful foods, their bodies are provided with the nutrients needed for optimal development, including learning. A healthy diet also improves the child's ability to fend off illness and to recover from illness and injury when they occur.
- Healthy children grow strong and are capable of playing in coordinated and safe ways. Children who are healthy and well nourished are ready to be more attentive in the learning setting and are better able to learn about safety rules and ways to stay healthy through appropriate health practices, including eating healthy foods.

Some aspects of the interrelationship are complex. For example, child nutrition impacts the risk for disease in adulthood (Faulk & Dolinoy, 2011; Simopoulos & Milner, 2010). From the moment of conception, a child's diet is thought to trigger a predisposition, or tendency, to good or poor health by influencing how specific genes are expressed (*Nutrition and the Epigenome*, 2012). Pregnancy and prenatal development, early childhood, puberty, and old age are all times when diet can influence gene function, creating a positive or negative impact on health (Dolinoy, Das, Weidman, & Jirtle, 2007). Factors such as a mother's diet and rate of weight gain during pregnancy, the birth weight of the infant, and the infant's diet may predict risk for chronic disease in adulthood. It is thought that these factors trigger *epigenetic changes* (changes that have an external rather than a genetic origin) in gene expression that increase the likelihood the child will develop obesity, diabetes, heart disease, or cancer as an adult (Dolinoy et al., 2007; Simopoulos & Milner, 2010; Wang et al., 2012).

Early childhood teachers generally recognize the important relationships between nutrition, health, and safety and implement classroom practices to foster positive development. They know that children need to learn healthy practices during early development. Teachers also:

- Share an important responsibility with families to provide the best nutrition possible for infants and children, helping to meet the child's immediate nutritional needs while at the same time protecting the child from future chronic disease.
- Promote positive health practices and may be instrumental in identifying gaps in a child's health services by providing information and referrals to families.
- Work to ensure children's safe experiences in the early childhood setting.

The importance of decisions such as these demonstrate that the impact teachers have on children's lives is momentous. Each teacher in the opening scenarios embraces the goals of nutrition, health, and safety in the context of their early childhood program. Kaylee adapts a nutritious lunch to fit the needs of children according to their age and special dietary needs. Hector looks beyond Zach's health concerns and responds to Zach's curiosity by bringing new books into the classroom for exploration and learning. Sharina and Amelia review the playground for safety concerns and identify needed equipment to encourage appropriate active play. In order to put wellness approaches into action teachers keep aware of current trends and issues that impact nutrition, health, and safety services in early childhood programs.

A healthy, thriving child is ready to explore and learn.

Junial Enterprises/Fotolia

Recognizing Trends That Affect Nutrition Services

Renewed attention is being given to the critical role good nutrition plays in preventing disease and promoting health during the early years of development. Current trends and guidelines that influence children's nutritional well-being focus on preventing overweight and obesity and redefining children's diets to support good health.

The Obesity Epidemic

The number of children in the United States who are **overweight** or **obese** has increased at an alarming rate since the 1970s, labeling the situation an *obesity epidemic*. As shown in Figure 1-1, the obesity rate grew from 5% in the 1970s among

overweight
an excess of body fat that may lead to obesity; measured by a body mass index score in the 85th to 95th percentile

obese
a medical condition related to the excess accumulation of body fat that may have an adverse effect on health; measured by a body mass index score that is higher than the 95th percentile

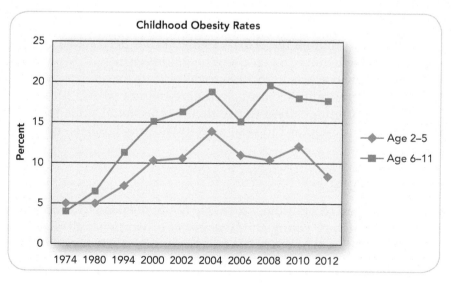

FIGURE 1-1

Trends in Childhood Obesity

Source: Based on: Ogden, C. and Carroll, M. (2010). Prevalence of Obesity Among Children and Adolescents: United States, Trends 1963–1965 Through 2007–2008. National Center for Health Statistics (NCHS) Health E-Stat. Ogden, C., Carroll, M., Kit, B., & Flegal, K. (2012) Prevalence of obesity in the United States, 2009–2010. NCHS data brief, no 82. Hyattsville, MD: National Center for Health Statistics. Centers for Disease Control and Prevention. (2014). Childhood Obesity Facts. Prevalence of Childhood Obesity in the United States, 2011–2012.

2- to 5-year-olds (4% for 6- to 11-year-olds) to as high as nearly 14% in 2004 (19% for 6- to 11-year-olds (Centers for Disease Control and Prevention [CDC], 2014). Between 2004 and 2012, the obesity rate dropped significantly for children ages 2 to 5 to 8.4%, with a relatively smaller decrease to 17.7% for 6- to 11-year olds (CDC, 2014; Ogden & Carroll, 2010; Ogden, Carroll, Kit, & Flegal, 2012), Robert Wood Johnson Foundation [RWJF], 2015).

While the recent decrease in the obesity rate shows a positive trend, the concern persists for the 12.7 million children under the age of 19 who have obesity. Serious health consequences are associated with being overweight or obese at such a young age. This concern is especially significant for low-income preschool-age children, who are most at risk. Of those children, 1 in 7 is identified as having obesity. The incidence also varies according to racial and ethnic group. In 2011, the highest incidence of obesity was identified among Hispanic (22.4%) and non-Hispanic black (20.2%) youth, with lower rates among non-Hispanic white (14.1%) and non-Hispanic Asian (8.6%) youth (CDC, 2013; CDC, 2014).

A variety of factors are associated with the increase in obesity among children. Trends in family eating behaviors include eating more snacks; eating meals away from home; and eating larger portion sizes, which include high amounts of sugar, fats, and calories (Let's Move, 2012). Lifestyle factors have led to less physical activity as people are increasingly engaged in sedentary activities such as sitting while watching television and playing computer games, which leads to less energy expenditure (American Psychological Association, 2012; Council on Communications and Media, 2011). In early childhood settings, children are spending more time at table activities and less time playing actively outdoors (Sorte & Daeschel, 2006). These trends have tipped the scales, resulting in more children who have overweight or obesity.

The small reduction in obesity rates in some areas is a positive trend. States that report declines in obesity rates also report that they have taken steps to address the obesity epidemic by, for example, requiring wellness policies in schools and early childhood settings and planning community initiatives to encourage walking and bicycling. However, even though the obesity epidemic has been widely publicized, some believe that it is too harsh to focus attention on this issue with young children. Many states have not taken action to include requirements for offering healthy food or ensuring physical activity in licensed child care centers (CDC, 2014). Even so, teachers are in an important position to use their professional skills to encourage healthy eating habits and regular physical activity, putting children on course for healthy development.

Redefining Children's Diets

Among health authorities, recognition is growing about the need to address the specific nutritional needs of very young children and to promote healthful eating habits during the early childhood years. A variety of resources have been developed to help teachers and families contribute to children's health now and in the future.

Dietary Guidelines for Americans, 2015 The U.S. Department of Health and Human Services and the USDA promote good nutrition practices for the general population through the *Dietary Guidelines for Americans, 2015* (U.S. Department of Health and Human Services & U.S. Department of Agriculture, 2015). The guidelines promote healthy diets for individuals 2 years of age and older, including those at risk for chronic disease. The goal is to guide people to achieve and maintain a healthy weight, improve health, and prevent disease. The guidelines form the foundation for federal food and nutrition policies and educational initiatives.

Dietary Reference Intakes (DRIs) The National Academy of Medicine develops scientifically based guidelines called the *Dietary Reference Intakes* as a guide for good nutrition. The DRIs provide guidelines for nutrient intake for vitamins, minerals, and calorie-containing nutrients that are important for healthy development. They also serve as the foundation for food guidelines in the U. S. and Canada (National Academy of Medicine, 2015).

MyPlate MyPlate is the symbol developed by the USDA to help Americans visually understand what proportion of their meals should come from each of the five food groups (fruits, vegetables, grains, protein, and dairy) (U.S. Department of Agriculture, 2011). MyPlate conveys the key messages of the Dietary Guidelines for Americans in a simple, easy-to-understand format. This helps families and teachers understand how to construct meals to support and maintain children's health and to promote the development of good eating habits.

Feeding Children A variety of organizations, including the USDA child nutrition programs such as the Child and Adult Care Food Program (CACFP) and the National School Lunch Program (NSLP), Head Start, and the National Association for the Education of Young Children (NAEYC), offer specific guidelines about feeding young children. The guidelines provide information for creating a positive nutritional environment for young children. They describe the roles and responsibilities of teachers and families, provide directives to ensure that food is clean and safe, consider how food is presented to young children, and confirm the child's right to choose what and how much to eat from the foods that are offered. These guides help teachers to establish the foundation for optimal nourishment, a vital component of good health. The *Progressive Programs and Practices* feature describes an initiative designed to address obesity in young children by providing training for early childhood educators.

Understanding Current Issues That Impact Children's Health

There is general awareness that health and well-being are founded on the prevention and treatment of illness, yet many children continue to have insufficient access to basic health care services. Current efforts are focusing on ways to address this problem. These include identifying the indicators of well-being, exploring disparities in health care, understanding the role of children's mental health, and addressing the needs associated with including children with significant health concerns in early childhood classrooms.

Indicators of Well-Being

Since 1997, agencies across the federal government have collaborated through the Federal Interagency Forum on Child and Family Statistics to compile a report on the well-being of children and families: *America's Children in Brief: Key National Indicators of Well-Being* (Federal Interagency Forum on Child and Family Statistics [FIFCFS], 2012). These indicators provide insight into the challenges that must be addressed to ensure that each child has the opportunity for healthful development. Some important indicators for health are discussed next.

PROGRESSIVE PROGRAMS & PRACTICES

Training Teachers in Healthy Practices

By Tracy Moran and Tom Browning, Erikson Institute and Illinois Action for Children

Recently, new standards were recommended for Chicago's center-based child care centers to reduce childhood obesity and improve overall health. The new standards included serving children reduced-fat milk and reducing sweetened beverage consumption, limiting screen time, and increasing daily physical activity.

To help with implementing the new regulations, local organizations[1] collaborated to develop training seminars for early child care providers. They invited a small group of early childhood providers to brainstorm ideas and talk about managing challenges related to health and wellness. Topics that evolved included finding ways to motivate child care providers to be healthier role models, challenges with accessing and affording healthy foods, high-crime activity in neighborhoods, and perceived apathy of parents. Providers made many suggestions for promoting physical activity, such as having relay races with plastic eggs on spoons, bowling using partially filled water bottles as bowling pins, taking a walk to learn about nature, and giving each child a magnifying glass and letting the children explore the outdoor environment. From this conversation, a curriculum was designed to positively influence providers' knowledge and behaviors regarding nutrition, physical activity, health, and overall child well-being.

Then for nine months, five trainers conducted 87 trainings engaging more than 1,000 participants. Training locations were selected to ensure broad participation. Large numbers of participants agreed to implement the new standards. Over half of the providers reported meeting the standards prior to the training,

with the exception of the milk standard. Twenty-eight percent of providers rated the reduced-fat milk standard as the most difficult to implement due to perceived cost increases or expected disagreement from children and/or parents.

Lindsey Samples

According to child care provider Maria Salazar, "I started to implement the change from 2% to 1% milk in my day care. I was afraid when I started, but the children have assimilated and taken to the change easily. I have the children stand while putting together a puzzle so that they can be more active throughout the day. They are sleeping better because they are now tired. I also participate in the activities with the children and I love it."

[1]Including The Otho S.A. Sprague Memorial Institute, Erikson Institute, Illinois Action for Children, the Chicago Department of Public Health and the Consortium to Lower Obesity in Chicago Children

Health Insurance Health insurance coverage is an important indicator of whether families can access preventive care and treatment for their child if the child is sick or injured. In 2010, 7.3 million children ages 0 to 17 (nearly 10% of the age group) had no form of health insurance at some time during the year (FIFCFS, 2012). Without health care insurance, families are more likely to forgo preventive health care due to its high cost and may delay obtaining medical treatment until an illness is in an advanced stage.

Access to a Usual Medical Provider Families who have an identified and accessible source for health care services (sometimes called a *medical home*) are more likely to obtain the preventive and treatment services needed to ensure good health. In the absence of a usual medical provider, families may obtain services at an emergency room or another source where medical records and familiarity with the child's health history are not available. In 2010, 5% of children did not have a usual medical provider (FIFCFS, 2012).

Oral Health Oral health care, including regular brushing and professional dental care, is an important indicator of general health. Although yearly checkups are recommended for children over the age of 1, many children do not have access to a dentist. In 2010, 48% of children ages 2 to 4, and 15% of children ages 5 to 17 had not seen a dental care provider in the past year (FIFCFS, 2012). This is of particular concern as cavities are the most common illness in childhood. Untreated oral health needs negatively impact children's health and ability to learn and thrive.

Childhood Immunizations Preventive health care includes obtaining vaccinations for preventable diseases. In 2013, 70% of children ages 19 to 35 months received the recommended immunizations. This leaves 30%, or more than 8 million children, without protection from preventable diseases (Centers for Disease Control and Prevention, 2014).

Oral health is a critical component of health and well-being

Disparities in Health Care

Disparities in health care refers to the situation in which some individuals or groups of children are disproportionately at risk for disease and do not have adequate access to health care. Children living in poverty, those who are a member of a minority group, and those being raised by very young parents have the highest risk for health disparities. Poor children typically have less access to health insurance and most often do not have a usual health care provider. They also tend to suffer more often from oral health care problems and are less likely to be immunized.

Children's Mental Health

The incidence of mental health problems among young children, such as not being able to cope and function in social settings, is considered to be at a crisis level in the United States today. The majority of these concerns are not addressed due to a lack of access to mental health services, the stigma associated by some to the potential diagnosis of mental illness, and the limited number of mental health consultants with expertise in serving very young children (World Health Organization, 2014). Unresolved mental health concerns introduce risk factors for disease and injury and limit children's opportunity to lead normal lives.

Inclusion of Children with Significant Health Concerns

More children with special health concerns such as asthma, food allergies, and diabetes are participating in early childhood classrooms than ever before. In 2011, more than 9% of children under the age of 17 were diagnosed with asthma (7 million), and nearly 5% of children had significant food allergies (Bloom, Cohen, & Freeman, 2011). Many children who have unidentified health needs, such as iron deficiency, obesity, or other health conditions also participate in children's programs. Teachers need to be prepared to accommodate children with significant health concerns. In the opening scenario, Hector demonstrated his comfort with managing Zach's needs. With this confidence he was able to look beyond Zach's health challenge and focus on teaching.

Identifying Emergent Issues in Child Safety

Children's wellness is directly related to the steps taken to prevent injury and increase safety in the home and early childhood setting. Emergent issues related to children's safety include managing security in children's settings, implementing regulatory guidelines, and planning for disasters.

Security Management

In recent years, more attention has been given to addressing security in early childhood settings. Children's programs are located in a variety of spaces throughout communities. Some are situated in neighborhoods that introduce particular safety challenges. Families want programs to explain how security practices will ensure that only authorized people will be able to take the child from the setting. Custody issues between divorced parents are often part of this concern. While most programs have some method for controlling entry to the early childhood spaces, not all choose to address safety risks by installing coded entry locks or other security devices. Deliberations about this issue continue as families and teachers explore their worries about whether security devices ultimately increase children's safety and whether they unduly detract from the comfortable family-friendly environments that are the hallmark of early childhood settings.

Regulatory Guidelines

The regulations that govern licensed child care and education settings continue to evolve to address newly identified risks to children's safety. Standards for maximum group size, adult-to-child ratios, rules for supervision of children, and steps for screening staff and volunteers for criminal backgrounds are periodically reviewed to ensure that they adequately address child safety needs and improve the quality of care in the setting.

There is also growing scrutiny of environmental health and the products used in construction of children's facilities, toys, and play materials. Restrictions are being put in place related to use of hazardous chemicals in paints and insect sprays in children's environments. The U.S. Consumer Product Safety Commission publishes toy safety regulations. One example related to toy safety is described in the following *Safety Segment*.

Emergency Management Planning

Disasters and emergency events of the past decade have increased awareness of the need for emergency management planning for programs serving young children. Emergencies from natural causes such as severe weather, as well as human-made disasters such as chemical spills or purposeful attacks, unfortunately have come to the forefront of safety management planning. Coupled with the increasing numbers of children in part- and full-day education settings, it is necessary

SAFETY SEGMENT   Laws Governing Toy Safety

The Consumer Product Safety Improvement Act of 2008 prohibits the sale of toys that contain lead-based products or various chemicals (for example, *phthalates*) present in some plastics. Manufacturers must prove compliance with the law, which requires testing by independent labs to prove that every accessible toy component meets the guidelines. The laws governing toy safety aim to remove dangerous products present in children's play things.

Source: *Consumer Product Safety Improvement Act, as Amended H.R. 2715, Public Law 112–128 (August 12, 2011 Version)*, retrieved March 23, 2015, from www.cpsc.gov /businfo/cpsa.pdf.

to make plans to respond appropriately when children's safety is threatened. Greater attention is needed to ensure that teachers and children's programs link with their communities to address the full scope of emergency management planning.

Promoting Wellness Through National Initiatives

Early childhood teachers, families, health professionals, and policy makers are joining together to promote wellness for young children through policies and national initiatives. These efforts are based on public health approaches that seek to bring citizens together around disease prevention and intervention. Individuals are encouraged to learn and practice positive health behaviors, and the community is charged with taking responsibility for establishing policies and practices that promote individual and community wellness. Several national initiatives promote these interests, providing examples of ways citizens and the government work together to address the health and wellness needs of all people.

Healthy People 2020

Healthy People 2020 is the newest wave of an initiative established to improve the health and well-being of people across the country. The initiative's goals are to help people of all ages to:

- Attain longer lives free of preventable disease, disability, injury, and premature death.
- Achieve health equity, eliminate disparities, and improve the health of all groups.
- Create social and physical environments that promote good health for all.
- Promote quality of life, healthy development, and healthy behaviors across all life stages.

(U.S. Department of Health and Human Services [HHS], 2012).

To reach these goals, *Healthy People 2020* identifies 600 objectives within 42 topic areas. Topics that relate to the care and education of young children include those listed in Figure 1-2. The initiative invites individuals and organizations to integrate the goals into their daily lives. In this way, the project generates multiple approaches to improving the health of young children and their families.

FIGURE 1-2 *Healthy People 2020* **Topics That Aim to Improve Children's Nutrition, Health, and Safety**

- Access to Quality Health Services
- Clinical Preventative Services
- Environmental Quality
- Injury and Violence
- Maternal and Child Health
- Mental Health
- Nutrition, Physical Activity, and Obesity
- Oral Health
- Reproductive and Sexual Health
- Social Determinants of Health
- Substance Abuse
- Tobacco

Source: *Healthy People 2020* by the U.S. Department of Health and Human Services, retrieved April 2015, from WWW.healthypeople.gov/2020/.

The Healthy, Hunger Free Kids Act of 2010

This legislation sets policy for federal child nutrition programs such as the National School Lunch Program, the School Breakfast Program, and the Child and Adult Care Food Program. It directs the USDA to increase access to healthy foods for low-income children, address childhood obesity by requiring schools and participating children's programs to offer healthier food options, and expand support for breastfeeding through the WIC program. The Act represents a federal commitment to providing better access to healthy foods, educating children to make healthy food choices, and teaching children healthy habits that can improve their health for a lifetime (USDA Food & Nutrition Service, 2012).

National Call to Action to Promote Oral Health

oral health
all aspects of dental, gum, and mouth health

This initiative is implemented by the U.S. Department of Health and Human Services under the leadership of the U.S. Surgeon General. It identifies oral health (which includes all aspects of dental, gum, and mouth health) as critical to general health and recognizes the need to address the disabling effects of craniofacial birth defects (U.S. Department of Health & Human Services (HHS), 2003). The U.S. Surgeon General describes unmet oral health needs as a "silent epidemic" affecting vulnerable people, including poor children and those of racial and ethnic minority groups (HHS, 2003). Action steps focus on encouraging partners to increase understanding of the importance of oral health and to implement strategies to address the barriers that limit access to oral health care.

Healthy Child Care America

Healthy Child Care America is an initiative coordinated by the American Academy of Pediatrics that brings together Maternal and Child Health and the Office of Child Care around a shared vision to improve children's education, health, and safety in child care (American Academy of Pediatrics [AAP], 2007). The initiative's vision aims to:

- Increase access to preventive health services.
- Ensure safe physical environments.
- Promote a medical home for all children. (AAP, 2007)

Healthy Child Care America serves as a resource for families, early childhood educators, and health professionals encouraging collaborative efforts to support children so that they enter school healthy and ready to learn.

National Health and Safety Performance Standards for Child Care

The National Resource Center for Health and Safety in Child Care and Early Education is a program of the HHS's Maternal and Child Health Bureau. The goal is to promote health and safety in out-of-home child care settings nationwide. The center provides a resource for families and child care providers called *Caring for Our Children: National Health and Safety Performance Standards: Guidelines for Out-of-Home Child Care Programs*. A sample of the resources that promote health and safety in out-of-home care is listed in Figure 1-3. The performance standards were established in collaboration with the American Academy of Pediatrics and the American Public Health Association. The standards guide teachers who work directly with young children, state agencies who license early childhood programs, and those who develop child care and education policies.

FIGURE 1-3 **Health and Safety Resources Provided by the National Resource Center for Health and Safety in Child Care and Early Education**

- Guides for families, including selecting child care and indicators of quality early childhood programs
- Guidance publications, such as *Caring for Our Children: National Health and Safety Performance Standards: Guidelines for Out-of-Home Child Care Programs*, that provide standards for typical and special care situations, such as caring for children with special developmental needs, transporting children in child care, and administering medications
- Web-based resources such as *Healthy Kids Healthy* Care
- Links to child care information
- Responses to frequently asked questions
- State licensing information

Sources: American Academy of Pediatrics, American Public Health Association, National Resource Center for Health and Safety in Child Care and Early Education. 2011. *Caring for our children: National health and safety performance standards; Guidelines for early care and education programs* (3rd ed.). Elk Grove Village, IL: American Academy of Pediatrics; Washington, DC: American Public Health Association. Also available at nrckids.org.

Education Programs that Interface with Health and Wellness Initiatives

Health and wellness can significantly impact children's success and achievement in school. To reinforce this connection, several education-focused efforts have been initiated. These include the programs discussed next:

- *Elementary and Secondary Education Act (ESEA)* Originally established as the *War on Poverty*, and now called the *No Child Left Behind Act*, the goal is to reduce the school achievement gap that exists between children raised in poverty and those raised in households with more abundance (U.S. Department of Education, 2015).

- *Common Core State Standards Initiative* This Initiative promotes use of a set of common standards in English Language Arts/Literacy and Mathematics that outline what children should know and be able to do upon completion of each grade (K–12), and aim to ensure that high school graduates have the skills they need to be ready to enter college or careers (National Governors Association Center for Best Practices (NGA Center) & Council of Chief State School Officers (CCSSO), 2015).

- *Partnership for 21st-Century Skills* This effort works to provide students graduating from high school with the skills they will need to be capable of succeeding in rigorous higher-education coursework and prepared to compete in the 21st-century global workforce (The Partnership for 21st Century Skills, 2011).

Although early childhood education is not a formal partner in these efforts, many of the elements align well with the early childhood developmental approach that builds children's capacities to become self-directed learners capable of contributing to their own well-being.

WHAT IF . . .
one of your relatives asked you about your plans to be a prekindergarten teacher? What could you tell them about the national initiatives that you would be a part of as an early childhood educator?

CHECK YOUR UNDERSTANDING 1.1

Click here to check your understanding of the foundations of children's wellness.

FACTORS THAT INFLUENCE CHILDREN'S WELLNESS

Many factors affect children's well-being and ability to learn. Some add interest and richness to children's experiences, while others may put children at risk for poor development. Some influences have a general or overarching impact, while others encompass trends that are causing changes in how nutrition, health, and safety are addressed in early childhood classrooms. These influences can be complex and are important for teachers to consider. Teachers have the capacity to enhance the positive potential of desirable influences. They also have the opportunity to mediate or reduce the damaging effects of negative influences, helping children gain the capacity for success that they may not otherwise achieve.

Considering the Contexts in Which Children Grow and Develop

Children do not grow and develop in isolation, nor are teachers the only people concerned about children's healthy growth and development. Children's wellness is heavily influenced by the *contexts*, or settings, in which they live. These contexts include the environment and circumstances that surround the child and affect the child's experiences. Urie Bronfenbrenner's (1979) ecological systems theory helps explain how the contexts that surround children—and the systems of interaction among the people in those settings—impact children's health and well-being. This theory considers the child as developing within a nested series of surrounding contexts and systems, each connecting and interacting with the others. Figure 1-4 depicts the child encircled by four types of contexts and systems.

FIGURE 1-4

Bronfenbrenner's Ecological Systems Theory Describes the Contexts That Influence Child Development

- *Microsystem:* This system includes the environments that immediately surround the child, such as the home, the early childhood setting, and school. Safe and nurturing aspects of this environment positively affect children's health and well-being, whereas hunger or dangers in the environment may interrupt healthy development.

- *Mesosystem:* This system encompasses the connections and interactions that take place in the microsystem. Nurturing parenting and positive relationships with the teacher are examples of positive influences on children's development, whereas domestic violence or disagreements among parents and teachers can negatively affect children's well-being.

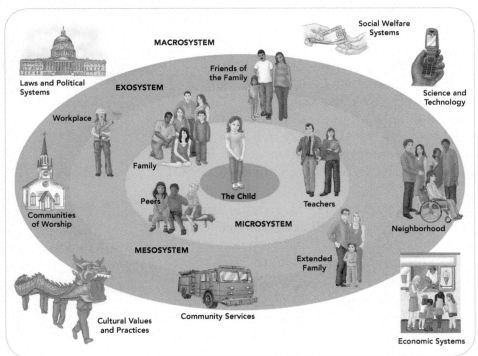

- *Exosystem:* This system involves the people and places that provide indirect influences on the child's development, such as the extended family or neighborhood. Children's wellness is enhanced through the support of extended family members and safe neighborhoods, but it is negatively affected by disagreements among the extended family or unsafe neighborhoods.

- *Macrosystem:* This system addresses the influences of the larger social, cultural, political, and economic contexts that provide support for child development or that challenge children's ability to grow and thrive. Children's wellness is supported when the society provides access to health care and high-quality early childhood education. Conversely, children's well-being may be threatened in times of economic depression due to reduction in resources such as reduced access to health care (Bronfenbrenner, 1979).

Early childhood teachers have responsibilities that intersect with all levels of these contextual systems. Teachers have direct responsibility for creating and managing the early childhood setting (microsystem). They establish important connections between the early childhood setting and the child's home (mesosystem) by building relationships where families and teachers share knowledge and ideas about how to best promote the child's development.

Finally, teachers extend their professional skills and responsibilities to the larger systems that affect children (the exosystem and macrosystem) by advocating for the needs of children at school board meetings or community planning commissions and by championing the development of policies and local, state, and national initiatives that aim to improve outcomes for young children.

Pearson Education

CLASSROOM CONNECTION

Watch this video of two girls, each drawing and answering questions about her neighborhood. Notice how each child is able to express what she likes best about her neighborhood. Think about the detail the older child uses in describing how laws are developed and how one law was used in her neighborhood.

Understanding the Overarching Challenges to Children's Wellness

Numerous dynamics have a widespread impact on children's wellness. These include multicultural factors, diverse family structures, poverty, living conditions, environmental issues, and food insecurity. All are examples of dynamics that influence children's development across the spectrum of nutrition, health, and safety services, and are topics educators consider when teaching young children.

Multicultural Classrooms

Early childhood class groups continue to become more diverse and multicultural. The number of children of Hispanic heritage is growing fastest in nearly all parts of the country. It is anticipated that by 2050, more than half of America's children will be Hispanic or Asian or will be of two or more races (Federal Interagency Forum on Child and Family Statistics [FIFCFS], 2013). It is also estimated that 22% of children nationwide speak a home language other than English. These numbers vary depending on the region, with rates as high as 34% of children in the West and as low as 12% in the Midwest. This information is important because many children who have difficulty communicating in English face challenges in learning and being successful in their future work settings. Figure 1-5 provides a visual depiction of the diverse racial composition of children under age 18 in the United States today.

Greater cultural and ethnic diversity also brings more variety in family child-rearing practices. Examples include diet, food choices, dress, hygiene, comfort with health practices, levels of physical activity, expectations for boys and girls, and other aspects such as how sleeping arrangements are managed at home and how

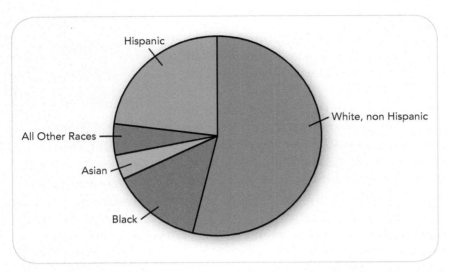

FIGURE 1-5
Racial and Ethnic Composition Among Children Under Age 18 in the United States (2010)
Source: Based on: *America's Children in Brief: Key National Indicators of Well-Being, 2011,* Demographic Background, by the Federal Interagency Forum on Child and Family Statistics, 2010, retrieved from www.childstats.gov /americas children/demo.asp.

napping is arranged in the classroom. Teachers need to know that perspectives on children's nutrition, health, and safety vary among the families they serve.

Teachers themselves have beliefs and expectations that are rooted in their own cultural or ethnic perspectives, which may impact how and what they teach in the classroom. To best take advantage of multicultural richness and to ensure that all children have the support they need to succeed in school, teachers must be competent in embracing cultural diversity and implementing strategies that support teaching of all children. Finding ways to invite conversation about diverse approaches and practices and knowing how to negotiate differing perspectives are important opportunities for new discoveries that will improve teacher skills and enhance children's learning opportunities.

Diverse Family Structures

Family structures continue to evolve and change, becoming increasingly complex. Notions of the traditional family no longer reflect the home lives of young children today. Family arrangements include various combinations of adults caring for children, such as children raised by teenage mothers, single parents, grandparents, or same-sex parents. Some children join families through adoption or live temporarily in foster care placements. Others divide their time between the homes of their divorced parents or are members of blended families created through remarriage. Each context offers unique supports and challenges to child rearing.

Families are the most important teachers of young children, yet some family structures may put children at risk for poor developmental outcomes. For example, children born to unmarried mothers may be at risk for low birth weight, infant mortality, and the negative effects of poverty (FIFCFS, 2012). Children who join families through adoption, or who have a parent who is imprisoned, may experience loss, grief, or the problems associated with separation from a parent (Allard & Greene, 2011; Glaze & Maruschak, 2010).

Children benefit when teachers get to know each family as a unique group. Understanding a family's strengths and challenges helps teachers plan school experiences that assist children toward more positive outcomes.

Poverty

Poverty is a significant threat to children's well-being. In 2011, 22% of children under the age of 18 were living in poverty (FIFCFS, 2013). Nearly 10% of children lived in homes whose family income was less than half the national poverty level, the highest rate since 1994. The poverty numbers are nearly three times higher among black and Hispanic children than white non-Hispanic children. Overall, many children are encountering poverty's challenges.

The impacts of poverty are particularly disturbing because poverty is a contributor to nearly every negative influence on children's wellness. Children raised in poverty are more likely to experience poor health outcomes. Families living in poverty must make difficult choices, such as paying rent or purchasing food. Low-cost housing is often substandard and is more likely to have environmental hazards such as lead-based paint. Children may be malnourished because families are compelled to select low-cost foods rather than make nutritious purchases. Families may not be able to afford preventive or necessary health care. As a result, children living in poverty are more likely to experience cognitive, behavioral, and social-emotional problems that get in the way of learning. This can lead to lower educational attainment and increased unemployment across their lifetime.

A Matter of ETHICS

Imagine that you want to have the children in your class make "community soup," an activity for which each child is usually asked to bring in a food to contribute to the soup. Making a food contribution might be difficult for some of the low-income families in your class. How might you arrange this activity in a way that respects the dignity and worth of each child and family?

Housing and Homelessness

Families with young children often struggle to find affordable and safe housing. Nearly 46% of households with children in the United States face problems such as inadequate or crowded housing that costs more than 30% of the family's household income (FIFCFS, 2013). Inadequate housing suggests all manner of deficiencies, including those that put children at risk, such as older homes that contain dangerous lead-based products or housing that is located in unsafe neighborhoods.

Many low-income families (18%) face severe housing problems because their housing costs more than 50% of the family's monthly income (FIFCFS, 2013). When housing costs require such a large portion of the family income, the family struggles to meet other basic needs, including food and health care. The frequency of moves among these families is especially high, as families who have trouble making rent payments often look for opportunities to save money by finding less expensive housing.

Severe housing problems make family life very stressful. They increase family mobility; cause irregular school attendance, which interrupts learning and social connections; and may lead to homelessness. In 2011, 149,000 children were homeless (FIFCFS, 2013). Early childhood teachers must build relationships quickly and work purposefully to reinforce learning opportunities for children who experience such disruptions.

Environmental Health and Safety

Environmental impacts on children's health and wellness are being considered more closely as information about the potential for negative effects are identified. Due to their small size, high rate of growth, and close interaction with their surroundings, young children are particularly at risk from the effects of environmental toxins. Exposure to lead in the environment is associated with learning and behavior problems, and contaminants in water can lead to health issues, including gastrointestinal illnesses. In urban settings, children may be at risk from industrial and vehicle contaminants, while in rural settings, children may be at risk from agricultural sprays.

Air quality is also being closely studied. Air pollutants, including ozone, solid particulates and liquid droplets, sulfur dioxide, and nitrogen dioxide, are known to increase asthma and respiratory problems (FIFCFS, 2013). High levels of carbon monoxide in the air reduce the blood's ability to transport oxygen, which can lead to health problems. In 2012, 67% of children lived in counties where air pollution was above allowable levels (FIFCFS, 2014). In addition, secondhand tobacco smoke can lead to increased respiratory problems, pneumonia, asthma, and sudden infant

Hunger may get in the way of children being able to focus and learn.

death syndrome (SIDS) (FIFCFS, 2013). Because of the overall negative impacts, the U.S. Surgeon General has stated that there is no risk-free exposure to secondhand smoke.

Food Insecurity

The USDA reports that more than 22% of children ages 0 to 17 years live in households that are classified as experiencing *food insecurity* (FIFCFS, 2014). In 2014, nearly one in six households reported that they were experiencing food hardship, or food insecurity (Food Research and Action Center [FRAC], 2015). Food insecurity refers to not having access to enough food at all times to maintain an active healthy life. Families faced with food insecurity often make changes in their diets by reducing the variety, quality, and desirability of the foods they obtain (Coleman-Jensen, Gregory, & Singh, 2014; Douglas-Hall & Chau, 2008). Many rely on community emergency food sources such as food banks or social service agencies to supplement the family's access to food.

Food insecurity puts children at risk for poor diets and related health concerns. Hunger can easily get in the way of children being able to focus and learn. For this reason, teachers should look for signs that children are hungry and ask children, "Did you have breakfast today?" This cues teachers to assist families in accessing community resources and the school's lunch program. Many early childhood programs participate in the Child and Adult Care Food Program, which offers guidance and monetary reimbursement for providing children with healthy food.

Advocating for Children's Wellness

Nutrition, health, and safety are crucial to children's wellness, their ability to learn, and ultimately their ability to develop to their full potential. Teachers, therefore, must be advocates for addressing negative influences on children's development and promoters for supporting children's wellness. One way teachers begin is by making a commitment to professionalism. This commitment goes beyond the concept of "do no harm" in that it encourages teachers to purposefully take action to improve children's health and well-being. It means being intentional about the choices made when planning environments and implementing activities for children. It also means using evidence-based practices rather than making choices based on myths or "the way it's always been done."

Making a commitment to professionalism encompasses the expectation that teachers develop the *dispositions* (the values, beliefs, and attitudes) that promote positive outcomes in the children they teach. Dispositions that are of particular importance in teaching include the values of fairness and equity and the belief that all children can learn. Teachers demonstrate these values every day through their words and interactions with children and families.

The decisions and actions of teachers are guided by the NAEYC *Code of Ethical Conduct and Statement of Commitment* (2011). The *Code* articulates the dispositions, values, beliefs, and attitudes held by professional teachers of young children. It guides teachers to recognize and defend early childhood as a valuable

POLICY POINT

Advocating for Healthy Child Development Supports Strong Communities

Policies that support healthful child development are founded on scientific research and emerge from the belief that all children can learn. The publications and resources of the Center on the Developing Child at Harvard University help to promote this understanding by reinforcing the concept that healthy growth and development are the foundation for strong communities and economic prosperity and that science can be used to enhance child well-being. The mission statement of the Center on the Developing Child presents the notion that equalizing opportunities for all children is essential to creating the responsible and productive citizens on which society depends. Early childhood teachers are important advocates for the development of policies designed to address the issues that put children at risk for failure in school. Research-based practices help to "close the gap between what we know and what we do to support positive life outcomes for children" (Center on the Developing Child, 2007).

Source: The President and Fellows of Harvard College. 2012. The Center on the Developing Child. Retrieved online April 2012 at: http://developingchild.harvard.edu/.

and vulnerable stage of life, while understanding that children develop within the embrace of their families, and respecting the dignity and worth of each individual child (NAEYC, 2011).

The *Code* is also a beginning point for becoming an advocate for children and families. Being an advocate means supporting actions that promote the well-being of children, such as backing initiatives to provide more healthful meals in schools and supporting efforts to provide safe parks and outdoor areas where children can play and families can socialize. Being an advocate is an endeavor that develops over the years. This commitment to professionalism unfolds as early childhood practitioners learn to take on leadership roles in their program and community and work alongside professionals in nutrition, health, and safety to improve children's well-being. The *Policy Point* describes the importance of advocating for healthy child development.

Within the classroom, teachers express their commitment to professionalism by recognizing the importance of wellness in the learning process. They put this commitment into action by learning all they can about nutrition, health, and safety and by putting this knowledge into practice by teaching children the behaviors and activities that lead to wellness.

CHECK YOUR UNDERSTANDING 1.2

Click here to check your understanding of factors that influence children's wellness.

TEACHING CHILDREN WELLNESS CONCEPTS

While the trends that affect children's nutrition, health, and safety are studied and addressed at national and local levels, important activities that contribute to children's wellness take place in the early childhood classroom. Teaching children wellness concepts is exceptionally rewarding because early childhood is a time when children develop the capacity to use their learning "tools." Their innate curiosity and motivation to explore make young children capable of learning healthful behaviors and being participants in promoting their own wellness. This sets them on a healthy course for the future. To help children reach these desired outcomes, teachers must understand how children learn, know how to use purposeful teaching approaches, and be ready with a "toolbox" of ideas to implement a wellness-focused curriculum.

Understanding How Children Learn

During the *early childhood years*, birth through age 8, many physical and emotional changes occur. Children gain strength, coordination, and control over movement. Complex skills such as walking and speech emerge, and the intricacies of social and emotional development play out as children develop trust and attachment to caregivers. Language blossoms, and cognitive problem-solving skills are tested and refined. This wealth of growth and maturation is founded on healthy brain development, encouraged through teaching approaches that help children construct knowledge, and reinforced by knowledge of the commonly recognized domains of development.

Early Brain Development

At birth the brain is a relatively immature organ. Even so, the newborn child has nearly 100 billion *neurons*, or brain cells, that are ready to assist with growth and development. Children's ability to learn and ultimately to function in society depends on the success of the brain to develop a complex system of neural connections. This brain growth and development is stimulated by experiences and interactions.

As children experience new information, the neurons reach out to one another, interacting and building a network of highly sophisticated connections that link the various parts of the brain. During the infant and toddler years, the brain focuses on organizing the information provided by the sensory systems of sight, touch, taste, smell, and hearing. From age 3 onward, brain development is highly directed toward growing and refining the neural connections. These links influence all aspects of children's functioning and ability to learn, such as recognizing the sounds that form language, coordinating movement, recognizing shapes and letters, and developing the ability to manipulate math functions, control behavior, and manage social interactions (Fox, Levitt, & Nelson, 2010; Massachusetts Institute of Technology, 2006; National Institute of Mental Health, 2011).

An important part of the process of evolving brain cell connections is a process called brain *plasticity*. Plasticity refers to the brain's ability to be flexible and change when new information expands or replaces previous knowledge. It allows for the modification of existing neural connections. For example, young children may first learn to call all four-sided figures a square. With experience they learn to focus on the length of the sides, and the angles of the corners to distinguish a rectangle or trapezoid. The original understanding of what makes a square remains, while new experiences stimulate new neural connections and new understandings. Brain plasticity provides for these modifications and is a crucial part of the child's ability to learn.

Children who are provided rich opportunities to use their five senses and to touch and explore develop highly complex webs of neural connections that support future learning. Figure 1-6 depicts how the brain's complex network of connections evolves through interaction and experience. Brain cell connections that are used again and again establish the channels for managing information and making sense of experiences and learning. Practicing skills is a primary way of reinforcing these brain cell connections. In this way, experience and learning build the "architecture" of the child's brain (Center on the Developing Child, 2007).

Children who are deprived of learning opportunities or who experience chronic stress or toxic environments show diminished neural development in areas of their brains, especially the areas that control learning and behavior (National Scientific Council on the Developing Child, 2006). A recent study reports that children from lower-income families (where deprivations and stress may be common) have a smaller brain surface area in the regions that support language, executive functions, and spatial skills (Noble et al., 2015). Chronic negative experiences result in brain cell connections being closed off or "pruned away" (Hawley, 2000). The consequence is a "use it or lose it" process. Connections that are not used are pruned away to allow the brain to be more efficient. In sum, the experiences children have (or don't have) during the formative early childhood years establish the child's capacity to learn and set the course for future development.

Constructing Knowledge

Learning occurs when children act on things and interact with people. It unfolds as children follow their interests, select the toys and materials that intrigue them, and practice and repeat skills that are exciting to them. Providing freedom to explore allows children to test new ideas, repeat routines to reinforce existing knowledge, take in information at their own pace, and come to understand new ways of using information. This interactive process is called *play*. Play is the context within which children construct the knowledge base that supports their understanding of the world (Piaget, 1929).

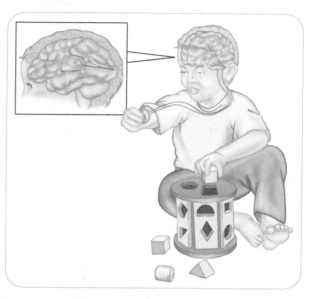

FIGURE 1-6

Exploration and Experience Build the Architecture of the Brain

Social interactions and language are important parts of this learning process. The ideas that children share as they talk about what they are doing and the ideas and directions that they give each other keep them engaged and pique their interest in the learning opportunity. Teachers and families also use social interactions and language to help children focus on the significant aspects of an activity and make meaning from what they have experienced. For example, teachers offer new vocabulary or ask questions that focus children's attention on what they are doing. With a 2-year-old, the teacher might say, "See how the soap bubbles wash off your hands? That is the way we wash germs away too!" Or with a 7-year-old, a teacher might say, "You were running fast at recess. Is your heart pumping quickly? Can you feel how you are breathing hard? Why does your body react this way after running?" The teacher's involvement helps the child notice and think about aspects of the activity. The questions encourage the child to wonder, predict, and offer ideas. Important social aspects of culture are also communicated and practiced through social interaction and language (Vygotsky, 1962).

Teachers guide the learning process by structuring experiences that are familiar and interesting to the child and that offer challenges just beyond the child's current level of understanding and ability. This process is called *scaffolding*. Just as scaffolding equipment provides a framework of support during a construction project, scaffolding in teaching refers to providing the series of supports that allow a child to move into new levels of understanding and higher levels of skill. Figure 1-7 depicts the steps involved in scaffolding using the example of a cooking activity.

Exploring in the Developmental Domains

Learning in young children, infants through preschool age, is commonly described as occurring in four developmental areas or *domains*. These include physical, cognitive, language, and social-emotional domains. Each domain fosters growth through the contributions of particular learning systems.

STEP	SCAFFOLDING APPROACH	WHAT A TEACHER MIGHT DO AND SAY
7	**Introduce a new activity.** Building on the previous task, introduce a slightly more challenging activity. Repeat the scaffolding steps.	Offer a next-step baking activity. Say for example, "It looked like you enjoyed baking biscuits today. Tomorrow the baking center will have a recipe for tortillas. You can let me know if you need any help getting started."
6	**Observe the children continuing the activity.** Watch how each child proceeds with the task without support.	Continue to be physically near. Watch to ensure each child is proceeding successfully.
5	**Reduce participation gradually.** Observe how the children proceed with less help.	Watch and respond if a child has questions or asks for help. "Yes, it is normal for the dough to be sticky. Try sprinkling on a spoonful of flour and using the flat part of your hands and fingers to mix at this point. Does that help with cutting the biscuits? Let me know when your pan of biscuits is ready to bake."
4	**Let children lead—but stay engaged.** Follow each child's interest and efforts. Offer explanations and supportive suggestions as needed.	Offer encouragement: "I see you are measuring. You are right, Step Two says one tablespoon of baking powder." Do you see the straight area at the top of the container? How can you use it to make sure to measure just one tablespoon of baking powder? That's it!
3	**Describe the task at hand.** Verbalize what the children are doing. Identify the materials and how they can be used. Ask questions about the task.	Point to the step-by-step recipe cards. Say, "Here are the steps. First get all the things you need: bowl, measuring spoons, stirring spoon, and biscuit cutter. Now measure the flour into your bowl. Yes, one cup of flour."
2	**Become involved.** Ask the children what they are doing. Request permission to watch and help.	Ask, "Are you getting ready to bake biscuits? Can I help you get started?"
1	**Observe children at work.** Become aware of what each child is working on. Use your knowledge of the child's strengths, interests, and needs.	Watch the children who are working at the biscuit-making activity. Notice the children who are moving materials around but do not know how to begin.

FIGURE 1-7

Steps in Scaffolding Children's Learning

Source: Bodrova, E., & Leong, D. J. (2006). *Tools of the mind: The Vygotskian approach to early childhood education* (2nd ed.). Upper Saddle River, NJ: Prentice Hall.

Physical Development Physical development includes overall physical health as well as growth and development of the muscle systems. It includes the large muscles of the arms, legs, and whole body used to accomplish movement such as running, as well as the small muscles of the hands, fingers, wrist, toes, and eyes used to accomplish manipulation tasks such as writing and reading. Learning in the physical domain focuses on:

- Developing muscle strength, control, and stamina to accomplish safe and purposeful movement, such as a baby holding its head up or a child pouring a cup of milk.
- Integrating movement to accomplish a new skill, such as a toddler learning to stand, a preschooler learning to ride a tricycle, or a school-age child learning to dribble a basketball.
- Coordinating movement to accomplish complex tasks, such as focusing the eyes and using hand movements to string a bead, put on clothes, or toss a ball through a hoop.

Cognitive Development Cognitive development involves learning to understand and make meaning from the world. It includes the maturation of the sensory systems that form the basis of perception and the skills to use this information to learn. Cognitive development includes:

- Developing memory, such as learning to wash one's hands before sitting down for a snack.
- Using problem-solving skills, such as learning to match shapes.
- Thinking logically, such as knowing that a cat is small and an elephant is big.
- Using symbols, such as understanding gestures, reading signs, drawing, and writing.

Language Development This domain involves understanding and using language and other forms of communication to gather and exchange information and ideas. It includes:

- Listening and speaking.
- Using language to express needs and to make social connections, such as asking for help to reach a toy or asking for a turn at the swing.
- Building the foundations for literacy skills such as reading and writing.

Social-Emotional Development Social-emotional development involves building the skills needed to interact, work, and play successfully with others. This area encompasses how children learn about the world and their place in it. Social-emotional development means:

- Learning to build trusting and caring relationships with others.
- Identifying and expressing feelings in appropriate ways: "I miss my mom, but I know she'll come back after work."
- Developing the ability to make choices, take responsibility for one's actions, and be capable of solving problems in social settings: "OK, you be the red guy and I'll be the blue guy. Next time I get red."

Learning across the developmental domains is highly interrelated. That is, successful learning in one domain affects, and is also dependent on, successful learning in the other domains. For example, fine motor skills help children manipulate small blocks. As children build, they are able to explore concepts of size comparison and balance, which enhances cognitive development.

Competency in the language domain allows a child to communicate with others, building friendships that promote social-emotional development. Skills acquired through maturation and experiences in the developmental domains also set the foundation for successful learning in the kindergarten core curriculum areas, including early literacy and mathematics, science, art, social science, health, and well-being. Teachers consider these interrelated aspects as they plan learning activities.

Inspiring a Positive Approach to Learning

Each child has his or her own style of learning. Understanding each child's learning style and supporting the child to develop strategies to successfully navigate various learning settings are important ways teachers help children develop a positive approach to learning, including attributes such as:

- Motivation and curiosity—to explore and discover.
- Confidence—to engage in the learning process.
- Focus—to pay attention and notice the details of the lesson.
- Persistence—to keep trying.
- Adaptability—to retain and use new information and concepts in new settings.

Activities that spark children's interest invite them to interact with materials and to process ideas and concepts at their own pace, thus reinforcing positive perceptions about learning.

Planning with Purpose

Teaching is an interactive process that requires purposeful and intentional planning, making it more than a gathering of interesting activities that children enjoy. Informed decisions must be made about how to assemble the indoor and outdoor environments and how to present activities to optimize learning and help children learn desired concepts. It is this purposeful approach that characterizes high-quality teaching and is associated with greater academic gains among young children when they enter kindergarten (Howes et al., 2008). Purposeful teaching is based on a commitment to use evidence-based practices. It includes following developmentally appropriate practices, applying a variety of teaching strategies, and providing culturally relevant experiences.

Using Evidence-Based Practices

Effective practitioners need to know and understand the interventions and practices that are most successful in providing for children's nutrition, health, and safety. These are called *evidence-based practices*. They include approaches that are credible and reliable in creating positive change, such as improving a skill, promoting knowledge, or achieving a specific outcome. Reputable sources for evidence-based practices regarding children's nutrition, health, and safety include the National Institutes of Health, Office of the Surgeon General, American Dietetic Association, American Academy of Pediatrics, and Consumer Product Safety Commission. Guidance from credible sources such as these, prepares teachers to know what to do, how to do it, and why.

A familiar evidence-based approach for early childhood education forms the basis for **developmentally appropriate practice (DAP)** outlined by the NAEYC

developmentally appropriate practice (DAP)
a teaching approach that addresses the child's age and maturity, the child's individual characteristics, and the context in which the child grows and develops

(Copple & Bredekamp, 2009). DAP guides teachers to consider three important aspects as they establish environments and effective teaching approaches to best meet children's needs:

- The age-related characteristics of children, which allow teachers to predict the activities and experiences that will promote children's development.
- Individual child characteristics learned through observations and interactions with each child, which inform the teacher about the child's strengths, interests, and approaches to learning.
- The social and cultural contexts in which the children live, which help teachers plan meaningful and relevant experiences for children (Copple & Bredekamp, 2009).

Staying informed about evidence based approaches such as DAP, helps teachers align with the practices that are supported by professional consensus. This assists teachers to avoid following approaches that are based heavily on opinion and personal preference.

Planning wellness goals for nutrition is a good example of a topic that must be based on sound evidence based practices. Nearly everyone has an opinion about food and what constitutes a healthful diet. Many cultural values are related to food with respect to what is eaten and how it is prepared, and families may follow a variety of dietary practices. Teachers focus on promoting information and behaviors that are commonly understood to advance health and well-being. Focusing the message on basic evidence based practices can help bridge differing points of view. For example, the wellness concept of "Food should be clean and carefully prepared" is a practice that everyone would value. Established health and nutrition practices recognize that germs and potential toxins can be found on unwashed fruits and vegetables. Focusing the nutrition wellness lessons on evidence-based concepts gives teachers confidence that the nutrition message is credible.

Another aspect of evidence-based practice is the purposeful teaching cycle, as depicted in Figure 1-8. This approach puts teachers in the role of research investigators. For the evidence-based approach to be successful, it needs to be applied in a way that interests children and fits their readiness to learn. As the activities are presented, teachers constantly observe how children participate in and respond to the wellness lessons. Adjustments are made if children are struggling to understand a concept or if they are not showing interest in the activity. Observation and evaluation guide teachers to follow up on activities that children especially enjoy, allowing children's questions and ideas to extend the lesson. This brings the teaching process full circle.

FIGURE 1-8

Essential Elements in Teaching Wellness

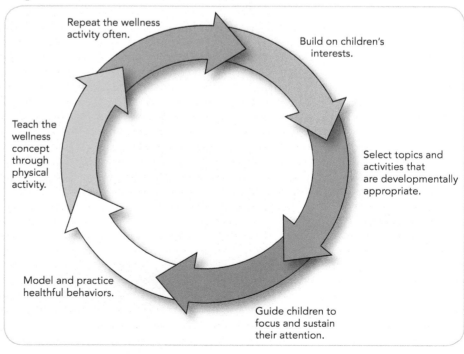

Repeat the wellness activity often.

Build on children's interests.

Teach the wellness concept through physical activity.

Select topics and activities that are developmentally appropriate.

Model and practice healthful behaviors.

Guide children to focus and sustain their attention.

CLASSROOM CONNECTION

Watch this video to learn more about developmentally appropriate practices (DAP). Listen to the description of the aspects that guide the teacher's understanding of DAP: age appropriateness and individual appropriateness. Why is using DAP an important approach to teaching?

Engaging in Developmentally Appropriate Practices

The purposeful teaching plan puts developmentally appropriate practices into action. Because children are most able to learn when the activities and experiences are appropriate for their age, stage of development, and individual maturity level, DAP approaches match tasks with the child's level of understanding and skill to scaffold the learning experience appropriately (Copple & Bredekamp, 2009; Piaget, 1929). Infants, toddlers and preschoolers, and early elementary age groups each have a unique developmental readiness to learn.

Infants Babies ages birth to 18 months learn foremost through sensory exploration and movement. Piaget (1929) calls this the *sensorimotor period*. Touching toys, bringing a toy to the mouth and exploring its sensations, and moving arms, legs, hands, head, and torso are a baby's method of learning and discovery. Increasing coordination and motor skill development such as rolling over, crawling and walking, and recognizing an *object's permanence* (the continued existence of an object even though it is out of sight) are examples of the ways learning is demonstrated. Teaching infants wellness concepts involves:

- Providing safe opportunities for babies to freely explore using their sensory and motor skills, such as placing toys within reach of the infant's hands and feet.
- Introducing healthful routines, including washing the baby's hands before eating and after diapering.
- Modeling safe interactions, such as guiding the baby to touch another child with gentle motions.

Toddlers and Preschoolers Children ages 16 months to 5 years of age tend to use their intuitive curiosity as the motivation and method for learning. These children explore without preconceived notions. They use their sensory and motor capabilities to touch and manipulate and explore uses of toys, and begin to organize newly discovered information. For example, a toddler may attempt to sit on a doll house–sized chair, showing awareness of the purpose of the toy, but not yet recognizing the disparity of her size compared with the size of the toy chair. A preschooler may use a block as part of a road for a toy truck or in other play as a cellphone.

Children in this age group begin to organize their understanding by using increasingly complex spoken language. They also begin to use symbols to represent ideas, such as drawing pictures of themselves with their family. Piaget (1929) called this the *preoperational period* in recognition of the child's need to experience the environment in order to begin the process of understanding it. Wellness activities for toddlers and preschoolers are promoted by:

- Providing ample opportunity for children to explore their ideas by manipulating materials such as real and toy foods and utensils and dramatizing wellness scenarios in dramatic play

Interacting with real food is a good way for children to learn about healthy eating.

settings such as getting a shot or receiving a bandage "to stop the blood from the accident."

- Offering planned activities that guide children to learn nutrition, health, and safety rules, such as washing their hands before eating or sitting down to eat to avoid choking.
- Using language to support understanding of wellness concepts: "Closing the gate keeps everyone safe" and "Covering your mouth when you cough keeps your friends healthy."

WHAT IF . . .

you were assigned to teach 2-year-old toddlers instead of the 3-year-old preschoolers you normally teach? What aspects of children's nutrition would you explore to prepare yourself to feed toddlers appropriately?

Early Elementary-Age Children Children ages 5 to 8 learn best when they can explore ideas in real and tangible ways. Providing actual experiences helps this age group to grasp the facts of an idea. For example, using blocks to explore the math concepts of addition and subtraction helps to ground the concept of quantity in real terms. Collecting the classroom's paper garbage for a week helps children to visualize how much paper is used and clarifies the importance of recycling much more than simply talking about recycling. Planned wellness activities that are rich with hands-on opportunities are important for teaching this group, which Piaget (1929) termed the *concrete operations period*. Wellness activities for elementary school children include:

- Offering individualized activities, such as having children keep a diary of all the foods they have eaten for the day.
- Guiding small group activities, such as inviting children to use a safety checklist to identify any potential dangers in the classroom.
- Identifying healthful alternatives to less healthy activities, such as snacking on apples instead of potato chips.

Because learning emerges in different ways for different age groups, teachers must establish approaches to teaching about wellness that are not just a simplified form of activities that are used with older age groups, but activities that are developmentally appropriate. Figure 1-9 provides an example of a wellness curriculum that shows how each age group is capable of learning about fruits and vegetables according to the children's developmental readiness.

Employing a Variety of Teaching Strategies

Educators use a variety of methods when teaching, but variety does not mean random or haphazard. It refers instead to using a range of evidence-based approaches to engage children's interest and. Some commonly used teaching strategies are described next.

- *Child-selected play*—allows children to be self-directed. Children are free to choose the activities that are of interest to them and to play at that activity until they are ready to make a change. In this approach, wellness lessons are presented through the materials provided. For example, placing a large plastic model of teeth, a large toothbrush, and fluffy soap bubbles in the sensory table invites children to "practice" brushing teeth, thus exploring a beneficial oral health practice.
- *Teacher-directed activities*—are presented and lead by the teacher. These activities are structured by the teacher who focuses on teaching a specific skill or involving children in a prescribed process. For example, the teacher may lead a group of children through the steps of taking cover in an earthquake drill or on the proper way to cover a cough. Teacher-directed activities also teach the general skills of listening, responding, and following directions.

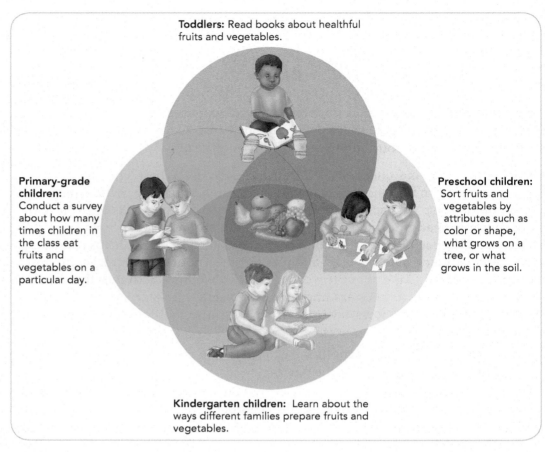

Toddlers: Read books about healthful fruits and vegetables.

Primary-grade children: Conduct a survey about how many times children in the class eat fruits and vegetables on a particular day.

Preschool children: Sort fruits and vegetables by attributes such as color or shape, what grows on a tree, or what grows in the soil.

Kindergarten children: Learn about the ways different families prepare fruits and vegetables.

FIGURE 1-9

Planning a Wellness Curriculum to Fit Children's Developmental Capabilities

- *Infusing wellness topics across the curriculum*—ensures that children will come into repeated contact with the wellness message. In this approach, the environment is set up so that the wellness message is presented in various ways in each of the common developmental domains. Figure 1-10 describes how teachers might plan a variety of activities around a wellness concept.

- *Hands-on exploration*—allows children to use all of their sensory capabilities and innovative ideas to inspect, touch, manipulate, taste, smell, shake, weigh, and poke. This approach provides opportunity for children to experience, internalize, and understand all manner of lessons that would not otherwise be available to them. Talking about the temperature of an ice cube is one approach, but this does not convey the concept of cold with nearly the impact that holding an ice cube provides.

- *Process-oriented activities*—engage children to freely use materials without the expectations associated with creating a final product. The focus here is on the process rather than the end product. For example, Sue offers a variety of craft supplies for children to choose and use as they wish. Wilson offers bike helmets, knee pads, and other safety-oriented sporting equipment in the preschool's dramatic play area. He allows the children to become familiar with the props and use them to develop their own play themes.

FIGURE 1-10   Infusing Wellness Messages Across the Curriculum

Cognitive Development

- Match real fruits and vegetables to colored construction paper to discover a food rainbow. (Art)
- Conduct cooking activities to sample a variety of foods. Sample the same food prepared in different ways: fresh, juiced, sauced. (Science)
- Create a picture list of different foods. Have children mark the foods they like. Identify most and least liked. (Math)

Physical Development

- Play sorting games using small manipulative toys; define variety; sort matching items; then sort to create groups with variety (no matches). (Fine motor; Math)
- Paint a class mural of foods on butcher paper placed on the wall. (Art)
- Hop to music. Stop the music and ask each child, "What is your favorite: fruit, vegetable, dairy, grain?" (Health and well-being)

Social-Emotional Development

- Read the book and provide props for children to dramatize the story *The Very Hungry Caterpillar* (E. Carle). (Literacy)
- Ask parents for ideas about field trips to places where food is grown, processed, or sold. (Social Studies)
- Invite families to come to school to talk about foods from their family tradition. (Social Science)

Language Development

- Provide a fresh fruit, vegetable, or grain. Ask small groups of children to talk about the food and make a list of different words to describe that food. (Literacy)
- Have children interview their families to learn about each person's favorite foods. (Social Science)
- Create a classroom chart of all the different foods the children eat for a week. (Social Science)

Wellness Concept

- Eat a variety of foods every day.

- *Project learning*—involves children in exploration of topics that emerge from their interests and questions, and that evolve across a period of time until the children determine that the exploration is complete. This approach builds on children's initial curiosity, which helps them be invested in the topic. It supports children's participation in their own learning and teaches the steps of inquiry and persistence. The teacher's role is to nudge thinking by helping children formulate their questions and identify where they can search out the answers. Explorations could include an in-depth study of insects, creating a group collage of 100 leaves, or exploring how apples get from a farm to the children's lunch table.
- *Incidental learning*—occurs when a learning opportunity unexpectedly emerges. The teacher takes advantage of the chance to teach a concept. For example, after noticing a child watching the birds at the bird feeder outside the window, the teacher might talk about the foods that birds eat to stay healthy and then relate the idea to foods that children eat to grow strong and healthy.

Including Culturally Relevant Approaches

To be most effective, wellness activities should be compatible with the child's family and cultural experiences. The NAEYC (2011) points out that providing links and continuity between home and school helps to support learning.

Knowledge of each family's approaches to nutrition, health, and safety guides teachers to create culturally appropriate wellness activities. For example, learning to serve one's self an appropriate portion during family-style meal service at preschool is one way of practicing healthful eating behaviors. However, a child might be confused by this lesson if the practice at home is for an adult to serve the child.

Some families believe that children should eat all that has been served, whereas the classroom approach may be to encourage but never force children to eat. Engaging in conversations about such topics helps teachers and families find ways to explore wellness practices in ways that are compatible for both school and home.

Children who are English language learners often benefit from learning new concepts in their home language before or alongside learning them in English. The familiarity of the home language adds credibility to the message and ensures that children fully understand complex issues. This is especially important when teaching safety skills, such as staying away from poisonous products, using playground equipment safely, or not playing near traffic. Teachers need the support of families and language resource personnel to ensure that each child in the class has access to important wellness information in the language he or she understands best.

Designing a Wellness Curriculum

An effective wellness program is established by identifying appropriate wellness messages, including nutrition, health, and safety themes; addressing local wellness needs; drafting activity lesson plans; and ensuring that the plans allow all children to be included.

Identifying Developmentally Appropriate Wellness Messages

Most teachers naturally teach children about the importance of eating healthy foods, washing their hands, covering coughs to prevent the spread of germs, and standing back from traffic and crossing the street with an adult. These are *wellness messages*, or lessons that children are capable of understanding, and when practiced, they can become habits that contribute to the child's health and well-being.

Formally designed health and safety goals have been established to help guide the development of a comprehensive program of wellness activities for young children. Wellness goals for children include these examples of capabilities that children will learn to demonstrate (American Association for Health Education, 2007):

- Describe how to prevent communicable disease by showing how to cover coughs.
- Show how friends can influence health behaviors through dramatic play.
- Identify community helpers who are health providers (doctor, dentist, nurse).
- Demonstrate healthy ways to express needs and feelings by giving a puppet show.
- Give an example of a health-related decision (I am hurt, hungry, or sleepy).
- Recognize a healthy activity, such as drinking water or brushing teeth.
- Demonstrate a safe behavior, such as sitting and chewing carefully while eating.
- Tell others about a healthy behavior, such as telling their family that being active is good.

Examples of appropriate wellness messages that encompass the concepts of nutrition, health, and safety are presented in Figure 1-11.

In addition, some wellness messages may be needed to address safety aspects specific to the community. For example, while avoiding germs is an important wellness concept for all children, staying away from the ocean is an important safety concept for children who live along the coast and learning to ride the subway safely

---

FIGURE 1-11 Sample Wellness Messages

Nutrition
- Food helps our bodies grow strong and be healthy.
- Our bodies need a variety of foods every day.
- Only eat the food that our family or teachers serve us.
- Drink water every day.

Health
- Germs can make you sick.
- Cover our coughs to keep from spreading germs.
- Wash hands to get rid of germs.
- Parents, doctors, and dentists can help if you get sick.

Safety
- Stay away from things that are hot.
- Follow the rules to keep safe.
- Go to a parent or teacher if you need help.
- Hold hands and cross the street with an adult.

---

is important for children who live in large cities. The wellness curriculum should be planned to include activities that address such local issues.

Reviewing Activities for Safety

Teachers use the planning process to evaluate each activity for appropriateness and safety. This is especially important when trying new ideas that have been gathered from curriculum resources, including the Internet. Each idea needs to be assessed with the specific group of children in mind. Some examples in this review process include:

- Considering the credibility of the curriculum resource: Is the source reputable? Is the source selling something?
- Thinking about the message being promoted: Is the message appropriate for the class? Can the message be adapted to better fit the needs of the children?
- Studying each activity for potential dangers: Are the materials used safe and appropriate? Should any adaptations be made to improve safety?
- Imagining how the activity will be set up: Are there potential dangers related to the ways children will be involved?
- Anticipating how the activity will be supervised to ensure safety: Is a teacher needed within an arm's length to direct the activity, or can children interact with the materials under general supervision?

Thinking about safety issues during the planning process is an important step in presenting safe and appropriate wellness activities.

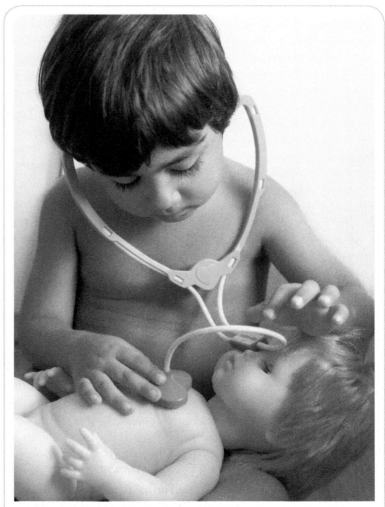

elisabetta figus/Fotolia

Providing safe props supports children's exploration of wellness messages.

Drafting Activity Lesson Plans

Writing a lesson plan is a step in purposeful planning. The writing process helps to ensure that the activities are relevant, organized, and developmentally appropriate, and guides the educator to clarify each activity's learning purpose. It helps confirm that the plan is thought through from start to finish. Lesson plans typically include components and actions such as those listed below.

- *Teaching wellness message.* Capture the overall concept in a short summary statement.
- *Learning outcome.* Identify what children will know and be able to do after participating in the planned activities.
- *Vocabulary focus.* List the words that may be new to the children and that should be defined and explained by the teacher.
- *Safety watch.* Describe the safety issues that must be considered when presenting the activity and include ways to address them.
- *Target age group.* Identify the age group for which the activity is appropriate.
- *Goal.* State the age and developmentally appropriate skill the children will be able to show or the information the children will be able to talk about as a result of the activity. Use a phrase such as *children will be able to* … and verbs such as *demonstrate, show, tell,* and *explain.* Activity goals describe a step in the process of achieving the overall learning outcome.
- *Materials.* List the materials needed to conduct the activity.
- *Activity plan.* Explain what the teacher will do to prepare and teach the activity. Describe the steps of what the children will do.
- *How to adjust the activity.* Describe ways to adjust the activity to meet the needs of all children, such as those who are English language learners and children who have special developmental or health needs. Give ideas for supports, such as offering adaptive scissors for a child with motor skill challenges or revising a recipe for a child who has a food allergy.
- *Did you meet your goal?* Draft questions to guide reflection about whether the children achieved the desired goal. Can they show the desired skill or talk about the focus information? Use these observations to recognize aspects of the activity that worked well and those that need to be changed next time.

Written lesson plans demonstrate how each activity contributes to the overall wellness program. Figure 1-12 provides an example of a wellness activity plan using this approach.

Including All Children: The Individuals with Disabilities Education Act

Many children with developmental challenges participate in today's early childhood classrooms. This has not always been the case. Before the initiation of federal laws ensuring the rights of children with disabilities to a free and appropriate public education, only one in five children with disabilities received services to address their early education needs. In 1975, Congress enacted the Education for All Handicapped Children Act (Public Law 94-142) enabling young children across the nation to receive *early intervention* (for children birth through age 2) and *special education* services (for children ages 3 to 21). These services work to prepare children and youth for further education, employment, and independent living. Since that time, the law has been reauthorized, most recently with the Individuals with

FIGURE 1-12 Sample Wellness Activity Lesson Plan

Teaching wellness message: All living things need water.

Learning outcome: Children will learn that their bodies need water to be healthy and grow.

Vocabulary focus: water, oxygen, sweat, nutrients, active play, less active play, thirsty.

Safety watch: Conduct the activity in an open area where children can move safely. Ensure there is space around each child, and monitor that children keep from bumping one another. Supervise the serving of water for cleanliness.

Target age group: Preschool and elementary.

Goal: Children will be able to name the times when it is important to drink water.

Materials: A variety of picture cards showing children engaged in active play (sports, hiking, playing on playground), and less active play (reading, making a puzzle, building with blocks), cups, cold water.

Activity Plan: Gather children in a space where they can move freely. Introduce the activity by talking about how our bodies need water to make healthy blood (so our brains can get the oxygen we need to think); it lets our bodies sweat so we can cool down; it helps with digestion so our bodies get the nutrients we need to grow. Talk about times when your body might get thirsty and you need to drink water (when you wake up in the morning after a long night's sleep, at meal times, when it is hot, and before, during, and after you play hard). Give examples of times when it is less likely that your body will get thirsty (less active play like reading, painting, playing with trucks). After this kind of play it is not as likely that your body will get thirsty, so it is not so important to drink water. Now introduce the game. Show the children the picture cards. Guide them to jump up if they see a picture showing children playing actively (when it is important to drink water) and sit down if they see a picture card showing children being less active (when it is less important to drink water). After children have learned the game, invite one of the children to show the cards. When you are done playing ask the children to sit down and offer them a cup of cold water. Remind them that the body needs water to do its work and to grow. It is especially important to drink water before, during, and after active play.

How to adjust the activity: Prepare to support English language learners by creating a teacher cue card with the words for "jump up" and "sit down" in the children's home languages. Include phonetic spelling to assist with pronunciation as needed. Make adjustments to include children with special developmental needs, such as changing the physical response to stretching arms up when it is important to drink water, and down when it is not so important, or ask the children to suggest a response where everyone can participate. Repeat the directions at intervals for children who need reminders. Allow children to watch if they are uncomfortable responding. Repeat the game at transition or group times so children will become familiar with the concept.

Did you meet your goal? Can you observe each child responding appropriately to the picture cards? Are children able to identify times when it is important to drink water?

Disabilities Education Act (IDEA) of 2004. The IDEA has four main objectives (U.S. Department of Education, 2007):

- To ensure a free and appropriate public education for all children with disabilities.
- To protect the rights of children with disabilities.
- To support states to provide special education services.
- To ensure that early intervention programs are effective.

Currently more than 200,000 infants and toddlers and their families receive early intervention services and 6.5 million children and youth receive special education services each year (U.S. Department of Education, 2015). The majority of these children participate in classrooms with their typically developing peers.

Early childhood teachers participate with families, physicians, and others in identifying children who may be eligible to receive services through the IDEA.

Children with observable developmental delays are referred to the local education agency (LEA), which has the responsibility to provide early intervention and special education services. The LEA conducts assessments to determine the nature of the child's developmental delay and to ascertain if the disability hinders the child's educational progress. Children may be identified for service based on hearing, vision, speech, orthopedic or other health impairments, autism, pervasive developmental delay, or other learning disabilities.

When children are identified for special education services, families, teachers, and special education professionals work together to create an *individualized family services plan (IFSP)* for infants and children birth through age 2 or an *individualized education program (IEP)* for children 3 to 21 years of age. These plans describe the child's disability, including how it affects the child's learning. Goals are listed to promote and track the child's educational progress, and plans are made to select an early childhood placement that offers the least restrictive and most appropriate environment.

The IFSP or IEP is a resource for teachers. It helps teachers identify accommodations that may be needed in the classroom, such as special scissors to support children with fine motor delay, adaptive chairs for children with orthopedic impairments, or open floor plans and furniture arrangements for children who move with a wheelchair. In some cases, children are assigned a special education assistant who supports the child's inclusion in the classroom. Specialized instructional approaches may also be required to support children's learning, including wellness concepts. Early intervention therapists can offer ideas for teachers about ways to adapt activities to support children's participation and understanding of the wellness message.

Accessing Supports for Teachers

Many resources are available to provide ideas about wellness topics to explore with young children. Children's literature, curriculum books and Internet resources, and professional development trainings are some familiar resources for teachers.

Children's Literature

Children's books provide a wonderful way to introduce wellness topics. The colorful presentation and engaging characters focus children's attention on specific messages, such as what foods to eat for good health, what happens when you visit the doctor or dentist, and how to stay safe. In response to the growing interest in teaching children wellness concepts, authors and vendors offer picture books on a variety of nutrition, health, and safety topics. As always, teachers need to review these resources to ensure that the message is reflective of current trends in wellness and that the presentation is developmentally appropriate. Teachers often create a list of their favorite books for teaching particular topics, adding to it when new resources are discovered. A beginning list of children's literature is offered in Figure 1-13. Other lists of appropriate children's literature for wellness topics can be found on the NAEYC and American Dietetic Association websites.

Curriculum Books and Internet Resources

Curriculum books and the Internet provide ready access to a variety of activity ideas and directions for implementing wellness lessons for young children. It is important for teachers to assess the activity ideas, weighing them against the

---

FIGURE 1-13   Children's Literature to Support the Wellness Curriculum

Nutrition

The Very Hungry Caterpillar (E. Carle)
Eating the Alphabet: Fruits & Vegetables from A To Z (L. Ehlert)
Bread Bread Bread (A. Morris & L. Heyman)
Everybody Cooks Rice (N. Dooley)
My Whole Food ABC's (D. Richard)
I Will Never Not Ever Eat a Tomato (L. Child)
Drink More Water (C. Dalton)
Let's Read About Food (C. Klingel)
Dinosaurs Alive and Well; A Guide to Good Health (L. Krasny Brown & M. Brown)
Munching: Poems About Eating (L. Bennett Hopkins)
The Bugabees: Friends with Food Allergies (A. Recob)

Health

Como Cuidar Mis Dientes/Taking Care of My Teeth (T. Debezelle)
Those Mean Nasty Dirty Downright Disgusting but Invisible Germs (J. A. Rice)
Why I Sneeze, Shiver, Hiccup, & Yawn (M. Berger)
My Amazing Body: A First Look at Health and Fitness (P. Thomas)
Germs Are Not for Sharing (E. Verdick & M. Heinle)
Bear Feels Sick (K. Wilson & J. Chapman)
Sleep Is for Everyone (P. Showers)
Cuts, Breaks, Bruises, and Burns: How Your Body Heals (J. Cole)
Today I Feel Silly and Other Moods That Make My Day (J. Curtis)
I Feel Happy and Sad and Angry and Glad (M. Murphy)
Everybody Has Feelings: Todos Tenemos Sentimientos (C. Avery)

Safety

The Allergy Buddy Club; The Green Apple Tales Series on Food Safety (Rice-Andrea)
Safety on the Playground; Safety on the School Bus; Safety Around Strangers (L. Raatma)
Franklin's Bicycle Helmet (E. Moore)
Stop Drop and Roll (M. Cuyler)
Dinosaurs, Beware! A Safety Guide (M. Brown)
Never Talk to Strangers: A Book About Personal Safety (I. Joyce)
Safety First; Series (J. Mattern)
Arthur's Fire Drill (M. Brown)
No Dragons for Tea: Fire Safety for Kids (and Dragons) (J. Pendziwol)

developmental capabilities of the class and making any needed adaptations. Figure 1-14 provides examples of teacher resources that are particularly suited for a wellness program.

Professional Development Training

Commitment to continuing education is a quality of successful teachers. A report of the National Academy of Medicine and the National Research Council (NAM & NRC, 2015) confirms that early childhood educators have a great responsibility for children's health, development, and learning. The report promotes the belief that early childhood educators should be afforded the respect given to teachers of older children, while also highlighting the need for early childhood educators to have the evidence-based skills and competencies that lead to educational excellence.

FIGURE 1-14   Teacher Resources to Support Wellness Curriculum Development

Nutrition
- The USDA's Choose MyPlate for Preschoolers.
- USDA/ARS Children's Nutrition Research Center at Baylor College of Medicine. Nutrition Information and Sites Just for Kids.
- Kalich, K., Bauer, D., & McPartlin, D. (2009). *Early sprouts: Cultivating healthy food choices in young children.* Redleaf Press.
- USDA Agriculture Library, Food and Nutrition Information Center, Lifestyle Nutrition.
- The National Dairy Council's Nutrition Explorations.

Health
- SPARK Early Childhood Physical Activity Program and SPARK K–6 Physical Activity Program.

- Kids Health in the Classroom. The Nemours Foundation.
- National Association of Sport & Physical Education.
- Smith, C. J., Hendricks, C. M., & Bennett, B. S. *Growing, growing strong: A whole health curriculum for young children* (rev. ed.). Redleaf Press.

Safety
- Feigh, A. *I can play it safe.*
- O'Brien-Palmer, M. *Healthy me: Fun ways to develop good health and safety habits.*
- Safe Kids USA.
- National Resource Center for Health and Safety in Child Care and Education.
- U.S. Consumer Products Safety Commission.

CHECK YOUR UNDERSTANDING 1.3

Click here to check your understanding of teaching children wellness concepts.

Accessing professional development opportunities, attending seminars and workshops, and participating in in-service training are all ways to build the professional skills needed to be an effective teacher.

Membership in the National Association for the Education of Young Children, the nation's largest professional association for those who work with and advocate for children and families, is an important resource for professional development. NAEYC membership connects teachers to a multitude of resources and information that are directly applicable to the education of young children. The NAEYC conferences are popular venues for learning and exchanging ideas about teaching young children.

PARTNERING WITH FAMILIES AND THE COMMUNITY

Creating partnerships with families and community members is an important aspect of the wellness initiative. Parents, who are the first teachers of the young child, have much to share about how their child learns and what goals they have for their child in the early childhood setting. Community members bring expertise to add to the plan. Teachers also want to share the important outcomes they are fostering as children participate and learn in the early childhood classroom. Working together, families, community members, and teachers create a team to implement mutual goals for children's wellness through curriculum development and reinforcing wellness concepts at home and school.

Collaborating in Curriculum Development

Creating a partnership with families and community members helps ensure that the wellness curriculum is part of a broader community of health and wellness efforts.

Partnering with Families

Inviting families to participate in the development of the wellness program is an ideal way to gather a variety of relevant ideas. Often wellness topics emerge from the questions and challenges family's face, such as how to encourage children to eat vegetables, or brush their teeth. Families are uniquely able to offer suggestions that reflect their culture, and to provide ideas about how to adapt activities to address children's special developmental needs or health challenges.

Participation can occur through group meetings or by inviting families to post ideas on the program or school Facebook page, contribute to a school blog, or e-mail their ideas to be added to a bulletin board display. These approaches offer a forum for gathering ideas and discussing conflicting points of view, and provide an opportunity for the teacher to present program or school policies. The familiarity inspired by such discussions contributes to strong parent and teacher relationships. It may encourage family members to volunteer to participate in presenting the wellness activities and expands the idea that everyone shares in the responsibility of teaching children about healthful practices.

Engaging with Community Resources

Community health care professionals are important partners when designing a wellness-oriented curriculum. Medical providers, dietitians, dental hygienists, and other community health providers bring information about current health issues and goals for promoting healthful behaviors. When invited to be part of wellness team, they are often willing to come to the classroom to talk with children and families, offer tours of their health facility, or provide training for teachers and families. This broadens the impact of the wellness effort.

Convening an Advisory Committee

Some early childhood settings create a health services advisory committee, made up of parents, teachers, and community health providers, to discuss program health and wellness practices and to offer advice about program policies and procedures. The committee members share their ideas and expertise and, in turn, gain a better understanding of the important roles that the early childhood program and teachers play in providing for children's health and wellness. Engaging with families and community partners builds a network of understanding and advocacy for the value of health and wellness during the early childhood years.

Reinforcing Wellness Concepts at Home and School

The collaborative relationship built between the teacher and families increases the likelihood that wellness concepts taught at school will be reinforced at home. Communication and role modeling are important elements of this collaboration.

Communicating About Wellness Goals

School-to-home communication is an important part of creating a partnership around wellness. Sharing the wellness messages being studied at school may introduce new information for the families or serve as a reminder to practice the healthful behaviors at home. Also, when families know what wellness topics are being discussed at school, they can reinforce the ideas at home and encourage their child

Joanne Sorte

FIGURE 1-15

Children's Art Creates a Wellness Newsletter for Everyone to Enjoy

to show or talk about what they have learned. Figure 1-15 provides an example of ways children's artwork can share a wellness message being explored in the classroom.

Communicating with families about the topics covered in the wellness curriculum is good practice, but is also necessary. Some topics have the potential to raise concerns or frighten children. For example, even a carefully presented lesson about evacuating the classroom for a fire drill may introduce worries in children who are mature enough to recognize that a fire could happen and that fire is very dangerous. Ongoing communication helps families know when such activities are being discussed, so they can watch for signs of worry and comfort children with the knowledge that the family and safety workers will take care of them.

Sharing Community Health Information

Teachers are important resources for families. They keep attuned to common and emergent community health issues, such as food safety alerts, new immunization requirements, and product safety issues, and are well positioned to pass this information along. Having a plan to communicate wellness information is helpful, such as establishing a special bulletin board for important news or creating a family e-mail list. These outreach efforts demonstrate the teacher's commitment to child well-being, assist families in developing networks of support, and guide them to the services children may need.

Providing Guidance When Needed

Sometimes teachers provide guidance for families when there is concern for a child's unmet nutrition, health, safety, or educational need. Building a strong relationship helps make discussions of special issues a natural part of the teacher-parent relationship. Engaging in sensitive health discussions may be difficult, but it is an important part of the teacher-parent relationship. The *Health Hint* offers guidance for teachers when they need to share difficult concerns with parents.

HEALTH HINT   Talking with Families About Children's Health

Sometimes teachers need to communicate concerns about a child's health. When talking with families, remember to:

- Be sensitive; know that most parents care about their child's health.
- Communicate respectfully.

- Be prepared to state your concerns carefully and simply.
- Recognize family challenges.
- Assist with creating strategies for improvement.
- Be a positive member of the child's support network.
- Be aware of resources in the community to which you can refer the family.

Being Healthful Role Models

Children learn by watching others, including their family and teachers. That means that these important role models need to know about wellness practices, and have a healthful attitude and physical energy. In this way children see how you put your healthy ideas into practice. Here are ways to set a good example for children (American Academy of Pediatrics, 2007):

- Eat well and stay active.
- Get regular health checkups and recommended vaccinations.
- Join a smoking cessation program if you smoke.
- Ensure positive experiences with food and eating; sit together at meals.
- Participate in physical activities with children. Dance, be active, and play together.
- Model healthful behaviors: wash hands, cover coughs, stay home when ill.

Healthy role modeling enhances wellness activities in the classroom. For example, when teachers demonstrate how to use tongs to serve apple slices, children recognize this as the appropriate way to serve food. When teachers bend and stretch vigorously during musical games, children learn to participate enthusiastically too. When adults wash their hands after sneezing, children see that adults practice the health behaviors that they expect of children. Being a healthful role model demonstrates that wellness habits are something you do, not just talk about. The *Nutrition Note* provides ideas about ways adults model healthful eating.

Making the commitment to be a healthful role model for young children is one way teachers align with the high standards of the teaching profession. This effort calls on early childhood teachers to be willing to reflect on their current practices, that is, to identify personal strengths to enhance further and areas in which additional professional development is needed. The self-inventory in Figure 1-16 offers a guide for developing professional competencies in nutrition, health, and safety for young children. Successful educators are open to new ideas and approaches that will improve their capacity to be healthful role models as they promote children's abilities to grow and thrive.

CHECK YOUR UNDERSTANDING 1.4

Click here to check your understanding of partnering with families and the community.

NUTRITION NOTE   Adults Are Important Models for Healthful Eating

The American Dietetic Association tracks eating practices as a measure of diet trends. A recent survey revealed that adults have increased consumption of these healthy foods in the past five years:

- Whole grains.
- Fruits and vegetables.
- Fish and chicken.
- Foods with health-related benefits such as berries and omega-3 rich foods.

Overall, more adults report that they "have a good attitude toward diet and exercise" and that they "are doing all they can to eat healthfully." This is a promising trend for the health and well-being of both adults and children. Families and teachers who model eating nutritious foods and other healthful eating practices, encourage children's acceptance of wholesome foods and teach positive eating habits. This contributes to children's wellness.

Source:*Nutrition and You: Trends 2011: Report of Results,* presented at the American Dietetic Association Food and Nutrition Conference and Exposition, September 24, 2011.

FIGURE 1-16   Self-Inventory for Wellness Practices

How much do you know about your own health and well-being? How much do you know about the nutrition, health, and safety practices of young children, from birth to age 8?

Personal Practices	Always	Sometimes	Never	Reflections and Comments
I eat vegetables and/or fruits at every meal.				
I drink skim or 1% milk and choose low-fat cheeses.				
Half of the grains I eat are whole grains.				
I am overweight.				
I feel rested when I wake up each day.				
I smoke.				
I get at least 150 minutes of cardiovascular exercise every week.				
I wash my hands with soap and water after I use the bathroom.				
I eat fast food.				
My vaccinations are up to date.				
I have a primary care physician or a "medical home."				
I get a flu shot each year.				
I have a dental checkup at least once each year.				
I wear a seat belt and avoid talking on a cell phone or text messaging when I drive.				
I follow bicycle safety rules when I am riding on the road.				
I wash fresh fruits and vegetables before I eat them.				
I get 8 hours of sleep most nights.				
When I teach children I dress appropriately so I am comfortable playing outdoors with them.				
I recognize signs of illness and stay home when I am ill.				
I develop friendships and enjoy socializing and laughing with others.				
I have friends/family with whom I can consult when I have concerns.				

FIGURE 1-16   Self-Inventory for Wellness Practices (*Continued*)

Young Children's Wellness Practices	I Was Aware of This	I Was Somewhat Aware of This	I Was Not Aware of This	Reflective Questions and Things I Want to Learn About
The medical field recommends that, ideally, infants should be exclusively breast-fed for the first 4 to 6 months.				
It is recommended that adults replace infants' use of a bottle and nipple with a cup after 12 months of age.				
Children age 2 and older should drink skim or 1% milk unless they are underweight.				
Children should be served fruits and/or vegetables at meal and snack times.				
Children should be offered but not forced to eat any food including a "no thank-you bite."				
Fresh fruit should be served rather than juice because it adds fiber to the diet.				
Breakfast is a very important meal and enhances learning.				
Children should have their first dental visit by their first birthday.				
Families are children's first teachers, but teachers can have tremendous influence over young children's health and well-being.				
Being outside in cold weather does not, by itself, give a child a cold.				
Play promotes cognitive development.				
Building relationships with nurturing adults promotes children's development.				
Children should be physically active every day.				
TV viewing should be limited to 1 to 2 hours or less per day and children under age 2 should not view TV at all.				
Even very young children can learn ways to keep safe.				

SUMMARY

- Children's wellness (the positive state of health and well-being) is established on the interrelated foundations of nutrition, health, and safety. A focus on wellness has inspired a variety of national initiatives that seek to address challenges to children's well-being.

- Many factors influence children's wellness, including the contexts in which children grow and develop. Teachers are called to embrace their professional responsibilities by working to improve children's health and wellness outcomes in the educational setting.

- Understanding the impacts of early brain development on the child's ability to construct knowledge guides teachers to use purposeful and developmentally appropriate strategies to design and implement a wellness curriculum suitable for young children.

- Teachers build strong relationships with families and community health and wellness personnel, gleaning ideas and expertise for the development of the school's wellness approaches. These connections also create partners who recognize the importance of advocating for children's health and wellness.

Never before has the value of the early learning years been recognized with such enthusiasm and intensity. Teachers offer significant contributions to the health and vitality of children, families, and communities, making it an exciting time to be a teacher of young children. This text guides teachers in understanding the interrelationship of nutrition, health, and safety. It also provides background information so that teachers feel confident in their ability to create learning environments and teaching approaches that will make a significant contribution long after children have grown beyond the early childhood years.

Chapter Quiz

 Click here to check your understanding of Chapter 1, Promoting Wellness.

Discussion Starters

1. Consider the term *wellness*. Make a list of words that describe wellness to you. What would wellness look like in a young child? Describe how nutrition, health, and safety contribute to your interpretation of wellness. Share your list and reflections with others.

2. Reflect on the complex influences that impacted the nutrition, health, and safety of children in the community where you grew up. How would you describe the typical family in your home community? Were resources available to assist families who had needs? What community services benefited you during your early development?

3. Identify wellness topics that would be especially important to teach children in the community where you live and explain why. Describe a wellness message that would be appropriate for these children and discuss some of the teaching strategies and activities you would use to teach your identified wellness message.

4. Consider the cultural diversity present in your community. What aspects of each tradition would contribute to the plans for teaching children about nutrition, health, and safety wellness? What community partners would you invite to help create an appropriate wellness curriculum for young children?

Practice Points

1. Gather more information about the Common Core Standards Initiative. What aspects of this approach are relevant to teachers of children ages birth through age 9? What are some of the concerns being voiced about adapting the Common Core Standards for early childhood education?

2. Identify an issue in your community that challenges children's wellness. Investigate the topic to learn about the scope or size of the problem and talk with others to learn what is being done to address the issue. Summarize your findings in a one page report to share with others.

3. Select a wellness message related to each of the foundations of wellness: nutrition, health, and safety. Brainstorm a list of topics and activities that could be used to teach each message. Identify one wellness message and draft a lesson plan for a particular age group. Work with a teacher to implement one of your activities and reflect on its effectiveness.

4. Contact a child care program, Head Start, a school, or a community health agency to learn if they implement a health or wellness curriculum for young children. Ask how parents and community members are involved in the wellness activities. Learn about any challenges, successes, or lessons learned from their effort. Prepare a one page summary of what you have learned and share it with the school or agency you contacted.

Web Resources

Healthy Child Care America

National Association for the Education of Young Children

National Scientific Council on the Developing Child

U.S. Department of Education, Building the Legacy: IDEA 2004

Key Terms

developmentally appropriate practice (DAP)

diet
obese
oral health

overweight
wellness

PART 2

PROMOTING GOOD NUTRITION

CHAPTER 2

The Foundations of Optimal Nutrition

learning outcomes

After reading this chapter, you should be able to:

1. Discuss nutritional issues that impact children and how they relate to the changing food environment.
2. Define *malnutrition* and discuss nutrition issues that lead to under- and overnutrition.
3. Discuss the recommended guidelines that promote healthful eating and how to use them in the early childhood education settings.
4. Describe diverse ethnic educational resources that contribute to healthful diets in the early childhood setting.

CASE STUDY Luisa arrives early at preschool with **3-year-old Gabriella.** They have just come from a doctor's appointment where Luisa learned that Gabriella is overweight and has iron-deficiency anemia. This means Gabriella does not have enough iron in her blood for healthy development. Luisa is upset and explains to her daughter's preschool teacher, Cecilia, that she can't understand why Gabriella, who is eating enough to become overweight, isn't getting enough iron.

As Cecilia reviews the materials she has about children's nutrition, she remembers that Gabriella receives a vegetarian diet when she is at preschool and that Gabriella is enthusiastic about drinking milk and eating cheese and yogurt. The next day Cecilia shows Gabriella's mother a website that discusses the iron content of foods. Luisa realizes that Gabriella is not eating many of the iron-rich foods listed and decides to add more of these to her child's diet. She also recognizes that some of Gabriella's favorite foods, the dairy products, are rich

in calcium and vitamin D, but are not very good sources of iron.

Cecilia says that she will explore whether the preschool lunch can be changed to offer more iron-rich foods in place of some of the cheese entrées that are being served as part of Gabriella's vegetarian diet. Cecilia copies the information about iron-rich foods and provides Luisa with the telephone number of the local Women, Infants, and Children program where she can get more nutritional advice. Luisa leaves the classroom feeling much more positive about the situation and appreciates the collaborative support provided by Cecilia.

Life cannot exist without nutrition. From the moment babies are fed their first meal, the nutrients they consume affect their growth, development, and well-being. **Nutrients** are substances found in foods that are essential requirements of life and are necessary for survival and growth. **Nutrition** refers to the relationship between the nutrients found in foods and their influence on the human body. The nutritional environments to which children are exposed both before birth and throughout their early childhood years influence health across the life span (Bernal & Jirtle, 2010; Faulk & Dolinoy, 2011; Nutrition and the epigenome, 2012).

Teachers play an important role in creating environments that support children's nutritional health (Academy of Nutrition and Dietetics, 2011; Kenney, Henderson, Humphries, & Schwartz, 2011). Some teachers plan menus, select foods, and manage food preparation and service in the early childhood setting. In settings for older children, teachers are typically much less engaged in direct food service, but are equally involved in recognizing the important health impacts of good nutrition on children's ability to participate, to pay attention to lessons, and to learn.

In the chapter-opening case scenario, Cecilia, a busy teacher, takes time to discuss Luisa's concerns about her child's nutrition. When Cecilia learns that Gabriella has a nutritional deficit, she helps Luisa to discover ways to address her child's nutritional needs both at home and at school. Cecilia demonstrates a basic knowledge of nutrition and recognition of the resources that are available to support appropriate planning for children's diets. Her knowledge about the significance of nutrition to good health and learning makes an important contribution.

This chapter introduces the science of nutrition and provides an overview of current nutrition issues faced by children and their families. This prepares teachers to recognize and address the diet concerns of young children. Important standards and evidence-based recommendations that form the basis for nutrition guidelines for feeding infants, toddlers, preschoolers, and early primary school-age children are also discussed. This basic nutrition knowledge equips teachers to do the following:

- Understand how nutrition impacts children.
- Identify food sources of nutrients.
- Recognize the components of a healthful diet.
- Plan healthful menus.
- Use the various education and nutrition information guidelines.
- Develop personal eating habits that influence teachers' health and enhance their ability to serve as role models for children.
- Recognize creditable sources of nutrition information.

This chapter also presents a summary of food guidance systems created for different populations to better understand the rich diversity of ethnic foods served to young children and how they contribute to a healthful diet.

UNDERSTANDING HOW NUTRITION AFFECTS CHILDREN

Optimal nutrition provides children with the building blocks they need for healthful growth and development. Providing optimal nutrition for children in the early childhood setting relies on teachers who have an appropriate understanding of the components of good nutrition and recognition of the factors that sidetrack families from providing the foods that children need for healthful growth and development.

Identifying Optimal Nutrition

Optimal nutrition refers to the best possible nourishment for children. It is based on access to an appropriate amount and combination of foods in the diet, including

nutrients
substances found in foods that are essential requirements of life and are necessary for survival and growth

nutrition
refers to the relationship between the nutrients found in foods and their influence on the human body

David Kostelnik/Pearson Education, Inc

Teachers who work with parents to understand and support the optimal nutrition of young children help them acquire the nutritional building blocks needed to thrive.

dairy products, grains, fruits, vegetables, meats, and beans. Consuming these foods provides children with essential nutrients such as proteins and important vitamins and minerals. Optimal nutrition includes eating foods that provide phytochemicals and antioxidants, which are natural compounds found in fruits and vegetables that may protect against disease. It also entails eating the right combination of carbohydrates, fats, and proteins so that the needs of growth are balanced with physical activity. Too little energy from food means that children will not grow adequately; too much energy from food means that children will face problems with obesity.

In the early childhood setting, optimal nutrition means eating healthful meals that meet the standards that are set by government and health agencies and that are offered in appropriate ways and at times of the day to support children's energy needs. It includes carefully selected snacks, the types of foods served at school events, and the recipes used in cooking activities. Finally, good nutrition is reinforced by teachers who serve as role models for healthy eating by eating nutritious meals *with* children.

phytochemicals
natural compounds found in plants that may protect against disease and support good health

antioxidants
natural compounds found in plants that may protect cells from damage and thereby decrease the risk of cancer

Collaborating with Families

Most parents are genuinely concerned about how their children eat and have a strong commitment to the types of foods they serve at home. Factors such as family socioeconomic status, rural versus urban living, family lifestyle, ethnicity, and religious traditions influence the foods families give their children to eat. The early childhood program may be the family's first experience entrusting others with feeding their children and their first exposure to food provided in a group setting. Parents want to know what their child will be eating and want to participate in ensuring that their child is cared for appropriately. Teachers such as Cecilia understand these concerns. They invite parents to share important information about the child's needs. They are also prepared to describe the menus and ways foods are offered to children to help parents become confident in the teacher's ability to provide for their child's well-being appropriately.

Children come to early childhood classes with unique nutritional needs that are influenced by their age, activity level, genetics, and sometimes the presence of disease or illness. Teachers such as Cecilia accommodate the nutritional needs and special dietary requirements of each child in their classes and establish a common ground with families to ensure that the meals served are safe, nutritious, tasteful, and acceptable. Creating collaborative relationships with families to meet children's nutritional requirements sets a tone that supports good health and fosters positive food experiences.

Teachers are also important resources for parents when it comes to feeding young children. The early childhood years provide a window of opportunity for establishing habits that lead to a lifetime of healthful eating and wellness (Academy of Nutrition and Dietetics, 2011). During these years, children explore flavors and textures and develop comfort and familiarity with foods that are frequently served. They begin to establish preferences for these familiar foods, including how they are prepared and served. They learn to appreciate the variety of foods offered, which becomes a standard for what they expect when meals are served in the future. They develop confidence that food will be available to them and that they can trust their families and teachers to satisfy their hunger.

WHAT IF . . .

a child joined your class who was identified as very underweight and both parents were developmentally delayed? How would you address the nutritional needs of this child and ensure that the family understood how to meet the child's needs at home too?

Teachers support the development of good eating habits by establishing predictable schedules for meals in a relaxed and comfortable environment. Teachers help families learn to advocate for children's optimal nutrition by encouraging parents to urge schools and early child care programs to serve nutritious foods and to promote physical activity to support good health. For example, when school budget cuts result in decisions that eliminate physical education programs, teachers can provide families with the guidance they need to communicate their opinions effectively with school authorities. Teachers can direct interested families to participate in school wellness committees so that parents have input into the nutrition and physical activity standards established for their schools.

Recognizing Challenges to Nutrition

Teachers and parents play an important role in shaping the health of young children. They teach children about food and nutrition and must be able to address childhood nutrition issues such as occurred in Gabriella's case. To be prepared to manage this complex responsibility effectively, teachers must be able to recognize aspects of the changing food environment that challenge children's diets and learn about ways to work with families to ensure that children have the opportunity to experience optimal nutrition.

During the past 30 years, there has been a shift in the way Americans eat. These changes represent challenges to good nutrition and have the potential to compromise children's health.

Disappearing Family Meals

Meals that are prepared at home and served and consumed by the family are important to children's nutrition. Children eat more fruits, vegetables, whole grains, and calcium-rich foods and less soda and fried foods when meals are prepared at home (Adams, 2011; Larson et al., 2013). In addition, family meals help children develop a sense of family connection and social support that helps them do well in school (Academy of Nutrition and Dietetics, 2012). However, sit-down family meals are not occurring consistently in the home setting. Recent survey data show that 17% of families with children 5 years of age or younger eat three or less meals together per week as a family and that only 28% of family meal occasions include children (Murphy, 2012; Sloan, 2012). Further, some parents are preparing separate meals for children based on their preferences and then preparing a second meal for themselves (Sloan, 2012). Children also skip meals such as breakfast or dinner on occasion and rely on snacks to fill the gap (Academy of Nutrition and Dietetics, 2011). The good news and perhaps a sign of the economic times is that the percentage of families eating meals at home increased from 52% to 73% in 2010 (Academy of Nutrition and Dietetics, 2011).

David Kostelnik/Pearson Education, Inc.

Teachers who take time to address the nutritional concerns of children in their programs create a bond of trust.

It appears that more families are eating at home, but they are not always eating together. The disadvantage of preparing separate food for children based on their preferences and not eating meals together as a family is that it limits children's opportunity to learn about and try new foods and decreases the opportunity for the adults in children's lives to act as role models.

Using Convenience Foods

Families who choose to eat at home often look for convenient and quick-to-prepare foods. One reason for this is the time constraints that working parents experience. Over 50% of families have dual incomes, and 5.2% of all women employed hold more than one job. In addition, 76% of employed women are mothers with children under age 6 (U.S. Department of Labor U.S. Bureau of Labor Statistics, 2014). These families are strapped for time and often resort to quick mealtime solutions when feeding their children. For example, 58% of consumers surveyed indicate that time was the most important criterion for selecting what foods to purchase (Sloan, 2012). Another factor influencing the preparation of family meals is that many individuals lack basic cooking skills and have not learned how to "cook from scratch" (Jarratt & Mahaffie, 2007). Those parents who report that they do have good cooking skills often still choose to use convenience foods, which have become a normal part of many meals prepared for children (Chenhall, 2010). Prepackaged, heat and serve, and frozen foods can offer convenience but often at a nutritional cost. Many can be high in fat, sugar, and sodium content and may lose a portion of beneficial nutritive properties such as vitamins and fiber during processing.

The reliance on convenience food is also evident in the lunches children bring from home. Children's lunches often include prepackaged lunch meals, store-bought cookies, chips, or soft drinks. Home-packed lunches often do not provide the variety of fruits, vegetables, whole grains, and dairy products needed to support good nutrition in young children (Hubbard et al., 2014; Sweitzer et al., 2010; Sweltzer, Briley, & Robert-Grey, 2009). Teachers who understand nutrition requirements can provide helpful nutrition education to families to ensure that home-packed lunches are nutritious. Figure 2-1 provides menu ideas that can be shared with families on how to prepare safe and healthy meals for the lunch boxes of preschool and school-age children.

Eating Away from Home

Busy families sometimes rely on meals provided by fast-food restaurants. Children are attracted to fast-food establishments because of the exciting environment and promotional toys that are offered. Parents are attracted to the low-cost menu items. However, families may not always recognize the high nutritional price they pay for these quick meal solutions. Children who eat fast food receive larger portions than they would consume at home, and fewer options for

---

FIGURE 2-1   Healthy Lunch Box Ideas for Preschoolers and School-Age Children

Monday:
Turkey with cold roasted sweet potato slices on whole grain bread*
Orange Wedges
Zucchini and summer squash sticks

Tuesday:
Peanut butter and banana on a whole grain sandwich thin**
Low-fat cottage cheese with chives (to use as dip)
Red and green pepper strips

Wednesday:
Sliced low-fat cheese, leafy dark green lettuce rolled up on a whole grain tortilla

Sliced mangoes and strawberries
Broccoli florets

Thursday:
Tuna salad in a whole grain pita with spinach leaves
Kiwi slices
Carrot match sticks

Friday:
Lentil soup with shredded low-fat cheese***
Whole grain corn bread square
Sliced melon
Diced tomatoes and cucumbers
(All meals served with non-fat milk)

*Keep cold foods safe: Lunches should be packed in an insulated box or a bag with an icepack and refrigerated upon arrival at school.
**Replace with sunflower seed butter if peanut allergies are a concern.
***Keep hot foods safe: Soups and leftover casseroles can be sent to school cold with an ice pack and heated up or can be kept in an insulated container such as a thermos that will keep it appropriately hot. Temper the container or thermos with hot water before placing hot food inside.

---

fruits, vegetables, and milk are available. Fast-food meals also tend to be high in sodium and higher in total fat (including the less healthy saturated and trans fats). In addition, children drink more soft drinks when eating at restaurants. Soft drinks are nutrient-poor and energy-dense meaning that they contain no nutrients and provide extra calories because they are full of sugar. This is especially problematic because when soft drinks are consumed, they often contribute to lower-quality diets (Piernas, Mendez, Ng, Gordon-Larsen, & Popkin, 2014). Researchers have shown that eating frequently at fast-food restaurants can lead to obesity and living close to fast-food restaurants increases the likelihood of eating more fast food (Boone-Heinonen et al., 2011; U.S. Food and Drug Administration, 2013; Krukowski, Eddings, & West, 2011). The Patient Protection and Affordable Care Act of 2010 is a law that requires nutrition labeling of menu items for chain restaurants and similar retail food establishments with 20 or more locations and vending machines that aid families in making healthier food choices when eating out (U.S. Food and Drug Administration, 2013).

In spite of increasing awareness about an obesity epidemic and the recent challenging economic times, families' reliance on fast food for quick, inexpensive meals continues. For example, McDonald's Corporation (2012) reported a 7.5% increase in sales in the United States in the last quarter of 2011 (McDonald's Corporation, 2012). Teachers may observe families dropping off children with a fast-food breakfast or offering them a fast-food meal or snack when picking

Because of time and cost, fast food is a convenient and inexpensive way to feed busy families. What are the consequences for today's children?

Ministr-84/Shutterstock

WHAT IF . . .

you ask a child in your class what he had for dinner the previous night and he says, "The same thing I have every night—fried chicken and French fries." How would you respond? How might you approach the child's family to discuss more nutritious options?

them up at the end of the day. While supervising children at play, teachers may observe play themes such as this one:

Meredith, a preschool teacher, notices Tristan playing in the drama play area. He sits in a chair outside the playhouse and leans toward the "window." In an official tone he orders, "A hamburger and fries!" When Tristan's not ordering fast food at play, he frequently asks Meredith if they are going to have a hamburger and fries at lunch. Later, Tristan's mother tells Meredith that she is worried about Tristan's weight. After talking with Meredith, Tristan's mother decides to limit trips for fast-food meals and to prepare more meals at home.

Struggling with Food Affordability

The economy has left many parents struggling to purchase sufficient food to meet the needs of their families. Many family wage earners have lost jobs and remain unemployed. Others who have found positions may be earning lower wages. Another compounding problem is the increasing cost of food (Food Research and Action Center, 2012). All these factors contribute to the difficulties families face putting adequate food on the table. Being able to afford food has become a problem for some middle-class as well as low-income families. Some families who are on the edge of poverty do not qualify for the Supplemental Nutrition Assistance Program (SNAP or formerly the Food Stamp Program) or other nutrition assistant programs available to lower-income families. Participation in SNAP rose to 15% of the U.S. population (Coleman-Jensen, Gregory, & Singh, 2014). Economizing strategies used by families in all income ranges when purchasing food include buying less healthy foods, including fewer fruits and vegetables and less dairy, meat, poultry, and fish. In 2013, estimates indicated that close to 10% of U.S. children live in food-insecure households (Coleman et al., 2014). Teachers who are aware of these trends can connect families to child nutrition programs and community resources that provide emergency food assistance.

Identifying New Wellness Opportunities

Emerging interest in wellness has created a heightened awareness around food production and nutrition practices. Many families are paying special attention to the foods they serve, and school settings are focusing on wellness policies.

Growing Interest in Sustainable Food Practices

Some families have made a gradual shift in how they think about food they purchase for their children. Many families are interested in supporting sustainable food practices such as:

- Choosing pesticide- or hormone-free food that is processed minimally.
- Selecting foods that are grown and produced locally, which reduces pollution.
- Buying fair trade products (Sloan, 2012).

Some families, such as Gabriella's, are environmental vegetarians who choose a vegetarian lifestyle because they believe the production of animal foods is not sustainable. Parents who select organic or sustainable foods or both may bring this preference to the school setting. They may confront teachers with food requests that are difficult to fulfill in an institutional food service setting where food costs and availability must be factored into menu planning. These situations present an opportunity for collaboration with families. Together teachers and families can explore the challenges of meeting new requests and identify opportunities for change. New ideas offered by concerned parents can be the motivating factor for improving menus and providing a fresh look at established mealtime routines.

WHAT IF . . .
you were approached by a parent who tells you that his family eats only organic food and requests a "natural foods diet" for his child? How would you respond?

Increasing Interest in Wellness in the School Environment

Children spend a significant amount of time in early childhood settings and at school, where they may eat breakfast, lunch, and an afternoon snack. As a result, they consume a sizable portion of their daily food intake in the education setting (Story, 2009). Health authorities and parents have become increasingly interested in promoting wellness in settings that serve young children, which could lead to improvements in the diets offered.

A major shift in the school food environment can be credited to the Healthy, Hunger-Free Kids Act of 2010. This act provides additional funding to improve access to healthy foods and represents the first increase in reimbursement rates above cost-of-living increases to programs in over 30 years (U.S. Department of Agriculture, Food and Nutrition Service, 2012c). The bill improves the nutritional standards of all foods served at schools, including school meals, vending machines, à la carte lunch items, and foods sold at school stores. It also updates and improves wellness policies and helps advance the use of local foods by assisting communities in developing farm to school connections and establishing school gardens. See the Progressive Programs & Practices feature, *A National School Garden and Farm to School Program*, to see how schools can obtain help changing school environments and implementing school gardens while at the same time addressing childhood obesity and food insecurity. These positive changes to the school food environment have an impact on the quality of diets offered to children in schools.

CHECK YOUR UNDERSTANDING 2.1
Click here to check your understanding of the nutritional issues that impact children and examples of the changing food environment.

UNDERSTANDING MALNUTRITION

Negative nutritional trends affect the food environment both at home and in the school setting. In fact, the overall quality of the diet consumed by children in the United States does not meet national dietary standards and recommendations for maintaining good nutritional status. When children's diets do not contain the right combination of nutrient-rich foods, malnutrition can develop. Malnutrition refers to an imbalance in the diet of one or more vital nutrients that support appropriate growth and development. The two types of imbalance are:

- **Undernutrition**, in which children do not consume enough calories, protein, or other nutrients.
- **Overnutrition**, in which children consume an excess of nutrients required for normal growth, development, and metabolism (Shine Dyer & Rosenfeld, 2011).

In the opening case scenario, Gabriella faces both aspects of malnutrition: iron-deficiency anemia due to insufficient iron intake and obesity due to too many calories in the diet. Researchers suggest that undernutrition and overnutrition can occur simultaneously when children eat foods low in nutrients such as iron, but high in calories (Cepeda-Lopez, Aeberli, & Zimmerman, 2010). Gabriella is not alone. Researchers, using a survey tool to assess quality of U.S. diets called

malnutrition
an imbalance of one or more vital nutrients in the diet that support appropriate growth and development, resulting in undernutrition or overnutrition

undernutrition
a type of malnutrition in which individuals do not consume sufficient calories, protein, or other nutrients to meet their bodies' needs

overnutrition
a type of malnutrition in which individuals consume too many calories

PROGRESSIVE PROGRAMS & PRACTICES

A National School Garden and Farm to School Service Progra

By Debra Eschmeyer, FoodCorps, Inc.

FoodCorps is a national nonprofit organization, through AmeriCorps, that seeks to combat childhood obesity, food insecurity, and diet-related disease while training the next generation of farmers and public health leaders. Service members invest a year of paid public service conducting nutrition education; building and tending school gardens; and sourcing local food for school meals in high-obesity, limited-resource communities.

Children at risk for obesity and children facing food insecurity are, ironically, often the same. FoodCorps addresses the root cause of both: lack of access to healthy food. In keeping with the directives of the National Prevention Council, FoodCorps is not a response to obesity's symptoms, but a strategic plan to build community-based school environments that make healthy choices the norm, not the exception.

Under the Edward M. Kennedy Serve America Act signed into law in 2009, AmeriCorps is slated to triple in size by 2017. FoodCorps leverages federal funds and partners with local groups to provide schools with the people power needed to change their food environments. And it does so without burdening already overtaxed teachers, administrators, or school lunch budgets.

Tapping into the groundswell of interest in food, farming, and health, emerging leaders are recruited for a year of public service. Serving under the direction of partner organizations in public schools, service members implement a three-ingredient recipe for healthy kids:

1. Knowledge: teach children what healthy food is and where it comes from
2. Engagement: create hands-on opportunities to grow fresh food in school gardens and engage parents, volunteers, teachers, and business leaders in the school food environment
3. Access: work with local farmers to bring high-quality food into the school cafeteria

Because of this grassroots approach, the solutions FoodCorps service members foster remain durable, even after management of their projects is passed to new service members and eventually to the community itself.

In the first year of service, 50 service members taught more than 50,000 children, built or restored 500 school and community gardens, recruited 1,700 volunteers to help improve school food, and harvested 11,000 pounds of garden-fresh produce for food-insecure children and families. Beyond the statistics, the service members' stories—of salsa taste tests and broccoli biology lessons and local food and farmer days in the school lunchroom—are inspiring. Meanwhile, there is a protection of green space, renewal of vacant lots and concrete schoolyards, and revival of vibrant economies for farmers and food producers.

"We get very excited to eat things we usually don't like, like broccoli, spinach, peas, and carrots . . . we grew it, so we like it a lot more."—Eva, age 10

"This is the first time I'm ever trying it (broccoli). My mom usually tries to get me to eat it, but I'm going to give it a shot today."—middle school student in Des Moines, Iowa

"See?! I like every fruit and vegetable there is! And I eat all of it!"

"The kohlrabi is just a hit," said Christopher Chemsak, FoodCorps service member. "They love to pull it out of the ground and say, 'Can we cut this up?' I think it's harvesting something they helped grow. The kids get so excited about carrots with the green leafy stems still attached on top that they fight over them. They take pride in having been a part of the growing and harvesting process, which is really the most beautiful part to me, when I can help them reconnect with the direct source of their food."

Mykola Velychko/Fotolia

© FoodCorps, Inc., 2012

the Healthy Eating Index 2005, found that although meat and grain food groups were consumed in recommended amounts, fruits, vegetables, and milk are still lacking in U.S. diets. The survey also found that people are still eating too much sodium, saturated fat, and calories from solid fats and added sugars (Reedy, Krebs-Smith, & Bosire, 2010). Although educational leaders, school districts, and individual schools have made moderate progress improving the healthy eating environment in schools, children still do not meet national dietary guidelines (Kraak, Story, & Wartella, 2012). For example, the third School Nutrition Dietary

Assessment Study found that children, when evaluated separately from the total population, are not eating enough fruits, vegetables, dairy products, and whole grains and are consuming too many high-calorie, low-nutrient-containing foods and beverages (Story, 2009). This highlights the need and supports Healthy People 2020's goals to improve fruit, vegetable, whole-grain, and low-fat milk intake and to decrease foods that are high in added sugar, sodium, and solid fats in the diets of young children (U.S. Department of Health and Human Services, 2012). Teachers become part of the solution to this nutritional paradox by understanding the difference between undernutrition and overnutrition and helping families address some of the more common conditions that may occur due to these aspects of malnutrition.

Recognizing Undernutrition

Although diets in the United States include an abundance of food for many people, the nutritional well-being of children can be compromised by nutrient deficiencies, or undernutrition. Undernutrition may be the result of poor dietary choices, serious illness, or lack of financial resources to provide sufficient amounts of healthful foods.

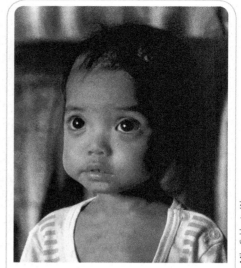

Mike Goldwater/Alamy

Identifying undernutrition requires looking beyond the child's height and weight. Consider the child's living conditions and economic situation and whether the child has a history of medical or psychological problems.

Insufficient Calorie Intake

Some infants and children do not consume sufficient calories to grow properly. They often appear significantly thinner or smaller compared with other infants and children of the same age. Physicians follow growth by measuring weight, length or height, and head circumference and comparing these measurements to standard growth charts. If children vary significantly from established growth patterns, they may be diagnosed with failure to thrive, a condition in which a child's growth rate slows down or comes to a halt. Infants or children with failure to thrive experience a drop-off in the rate of weight gain first, followed over time by a faltering of growth in height.

failure to thrive
a condition in which the growth rate slows down or comes to a halt; may be due to an underlying medical condition such as heart, lung, or digestive problems or related to psychological, social, or financial problems within the family

Sometimes growth failure can be related to psychological, social, or financial problems within the family. Undernutrition can occur in families who:

- Experience emotional problems.
- Experience economic problems such as unemployment or homelessness.
- Are involved in substance abuse.
- Lack knowledge about appropriate feeding.
- Use poor feeding techniques or have established a poor feeding relationship with their child (Johns Hopkins Children's Center, 2012a, 2012b).

When undernutrition is recognized, teachers work in conjunction with health care providers and families to provide nutrition support to children who are not growing properly. Specially prepared infant formulas, supplemental high-calorie beverages, and nutritious high-calorie snacks may be prescribed. If the problem is **psychosocial**, teachers can help families access appropriate support services such as those provided by doctors, dietitians, social workers, or qualified mental health advisers. A psychosocial concern refers to psychological or social factors that affect a child's well-being. For example, if a mother does not interact well

psychosocial
refers to psychological and social factors that affect well-being

with her baby because of postpartum depression and therefore doesn't respond appropriately to her baby's hunger cues, a psychosocial feeding problem can result.

supplemental food programs
federal food programs that provide nutrition assistance for at-risk populations such as children, low-income families, and the elderly

Teachers can refer parents to supplemental food programs (federal food programs that provide nutrition assistance) such as the Special Supplemental Nutrition Program for Women, Infants, and Children, more commonly known as the WIC program. WIC serves low-income women, infants, and children up to age 5 by providing nutritious foods to supplement their diets (U.S. Department of Agriculture, Food and Nutrition Service, 2012b). In addition, food resources can be obtained from the Supplemental Nutrition Assistance Program (SNAP), formerly called the Food Stamp Program, which helps low-income families buy food (U.S. Department of Agriculture, Food and Nutrition Service, 2012a).

Iron-Deficiency Anemia

iron-deficiency anemia
a common single-nutrient deficiency of iron that results in the body making fewer red blood cells with less hemoglobin than normal; causes sleepiness, impaired growth and development, and increased risk of infection in young children

Iron-deficiency anemia is a condition in which, due to lack of iron in the diet, a person's body does not make enough healthy red blood cells to accomplish the goal of transporting oxygen in the bloodstream. It is one of the more common nutrient deficiencies among children in the United States (U.S. National Library of Medicine, National Institutes of Health, 2010). Researchers estimate that approximately 9% of children 1 to 3 years of age are iron deficient and that toddlers of Hispanic descent have an even higher incidence of 13.9% (Baker, Greer, & The Committee on Nutrition, 2010).

WHAT IF . . .
you suspected that a child in your class was not getting sufficient food due to the family's economic difficulties? How would you address this issue with the family? What food resources in your community would you recommend to them?

The signs of iron deficiency include sleepiness, irritability, difficulty concentrating, pale skin, headache, brittle nails, a sore tongue, and problems with memory and learning (Fretham, Carlson, & Georgieff, 2011; U.S. National Library of Medicine, National Institutes of Health, 2010). In addition, when children are deficient in iron, their immune system is less able to fight off infections, leading to illness and decreased school attendance. Of greatest importance is the association of iron-deficiency anemia with cognitive, socioemotional behavioral, and motor skill developmental delays (Georgieff, 2011). When young children do not receive enough iron in their diet, the development of the central nervous system may be significantly delayed and brain development may also be compromised (Baker, Greer, & The Committee on Nutrition, 2010; Beard, 2008). A window of opportunity may be available when these adverse effects can be corrected. The window, however, is age- and time-sensitive. If left untreated, the health concerns associated with iron-deficiency anemia may be irreversible (Baker et al., 2010; Beard, 2008).

Children ages 1 to 3 are at higher risk for iron deficiency if they are:

- younger
- of Hispanic descent
- born prematurely
- overweight or obese
- from low-income families
- consume milk, a beverage that is low in iron to the exclusion of iron-rich solid foods (Baker et al., 2010; Brotanek, Gosz, Weitzman, & Flores, 2008; Fretham, Carlson, & Georgieff, 2011; Queen Samour & King, 2012; Ziegler, 2011)

In the opening case scenario, Gabriella faces three risk factors for iron deficiency. She is overweight and is of Hispanic descent. In addition, Gabriella consumes a diet that is low in iron content due to her vegetarian food choices. She prefers cheese and milk products instead of iron-rich beans, peas, lentils, and leafy green vegetables. For Gabriella, the risk factors compound, resulting in her iron deficiency.

Teachers are in a good position to watch for the symptoms of iron deficiency. Teachers affiliated with Head Start programs are more likely to be aware of children who have low iron levels because of the Head Start–mandated requirement that medical and nutritional screens be conducted. These screenings often include an evaluation of children's iron status.

Vitamin D and Health

Historically, researchers focused on the role of vitamin D in preventing **rickets**, a nutritional deficiency caused by a lack of vitamin D. **Vitamin D** is a nutrient that can be obtained from dietary sources but is also produced in the skin in the presence of sunlight. A severe deficiency of vitamin D can affect the absorption of calcium and phosphorus, which in turn causes bones to form improperly, resulting in severe skeletal deformities. With the discovery of the beneficial role of vitamin D came the clear understanding of how to cure this form of undernutrition. The public health initiative that resulted in adding vitamin D to milk in the 1930s appeared to have effectively eradicated vitamin D deficiency in the United States (National Institutes of Health, Office of Dietary Supplements, 2011). However, it has been recognized in more recent years that low vitamin D status is still a problem in the United States, (Holick, 2010; Queen Samour & King, 2012). In addition, health authorities now understand that vitamin D has many functions in the body and is needed for more than just bone health. For example, vitamin D may play a role in the prevention of cancer, heart disease, infectious diseases, and autoimmune disorders (National Institutes of Health, Office of Dietary Supplements, 2011; Queen Samour & King, 2012). Children most likely to be impacted are babies who were exclusively breast-fed without vitamin D supplementation in the past six months; children who immigrated from Asia, Africa, and the Middle East; and children who are not exposed to sufficient sunlight especially if they live in a temperate climate, use sunscreen, and/or are dark-skinned and obese children (Holick, 2010; National Institutes of Health, Office of Dietary Supplements, 2011). The dietary recommendation for vitamin D was tripled by the Institute of Medicine in 2010 (Institute of Medicine, 2011).

Teachers can contribute to children's health and reduce the risk of vitamin D deficiency in young children by ensuring that children are offered vitamin D–fortified milk or vitamin D and calcium–fortified soy milk at meal and snack times instead of juice or soft drinks. Other foods to encourage that are good sources of vitamin D include fortified yogurt, fortified cereals, and fortified fruit juices. Salmon, tuna, and sardines are naturally rich sources of vitamin D (National Institutes of Health, Office of Dietary Supplements, 2011).

Addressing Undernutrition

In the United States, several program serve the nutritional needs of children:

- National School Lunch Program
- School Breakfast Program

rickets
a nutritional deficiency caused by a lack of vitamin D; can cause bones to form improperly, resulting in severe skeletal deformities

vitamin D
a nutrient (fat-soluble vitamin) that aids in calcium absorption; can be obtained from dietary sources such as fortified milk and yogurt, but can also be produced in the skin in response to sunlight

Thomas Perkins/Fotolia

Selecting cereal, milk, and orange juice fortified with vitamin D gives an excellent boost to children's diets.

- Child and Adult Care Food Program
- Summer Food Service Program
- Fresh Fruit and Vegetable Program (U.S. Department of Agriculture, Economic Research Service, 2011)

Both the National School Lunch Act (1946) and the School Breakfast Program (1966) were enacted by Congress to help protect against dietary deficiency diseases and to improve the nutrition of low-income children (Story, 2009). The goals of the Healthy Hunger-Free Kids Act of 2010 include improving access to and enhancing the nutrition standards of these programs. As previously mentioned, other government-sponsored nutrition programs that families can be linked to in the community include the Special Supplemental Nutrition Program for Women, Infants, and Children (WIC), which provides meal packages for pregnant and postpartum women and children as well as nutrition services to almost half of all infants born in the United States, and the Supplemental Nutrition Assistance Program (SNAP) (U.S. Department of Agriculture, Economic Research Service, 2011). Other nutrition networks that can support the nutritional needs of low-income families include food pantries, soup kitchens, and emergency food assistance programs. These programs act as a nutrition safety net for young children. Teachers need to be knowledgeable about these resources and understand the importance of addressing any form of undernutrition that is identified so that they can help families access resources, as Cecelia did in the opening case scenario.

Recognizing Overnutrition

Consuming excessive calorie-rich foods also plays a role in the quality of diet and health of young children. Overnutrition is a form of malnutrition caused by an imbalance of calories consumed when compared with calories needed for growth and activity. Overnutrition causes children to become overweight or obese. Today's changing nutrition environment and more sedentary lifestyles are factors in overnutrition that have resulted in an epidemic of obesity in young children. In fact, obesity is the number-one form of malnutrition in the United States today. Among preschool children ages 2 to 5, obesity increased from 5.0% to 12.1% during 1976 to 1980 and 2009 to 2010 and from 6.5% to 18% among those ages 6 to 11. Overall, about 12.5 million children ages 2 to 19 are obese in the United States (Odgen, Carroll, & Centers for Disease Control and Prevention, 2010; Ogden, Carroll, Kit, & Flegal, 2012).

Identifying Obesity in Children

Obesity is identified and defined based on measurements of children's heights and weights that are plotted on growth charts. Conducting height and weight screenings during the beginning of a program's year can help screen for children who are underweight or overweight and obese. The Centers for Disease Control and Prevention (CDC) provides growth charts to assist in screening and identifying children who are at risk for overweight and obesity from ages 2 to 20. The charts show percentile curves that represent the range of distribution of heights and weights typical in young children in the United States (Centers for Disease Control and Prevention, 2010).

In children over age 2, another criterion used to determine appropriate rate of growth is the body mass index (BMI). BMI assesses body weight relative to height to

body mass index (BMI) a calculation that evaluates weight in relation to height to assess whether an individual is obese or underweight. In young children, BMI is also a measure of growth. It is calculated by dividing the weight of a person by the height squared determine the risk for overweight or obesity. The CDC makes it easy for teachers to calculate and plot BMIs for individual children and by class with their online BMI tool for schools (see the Web Resources listing at the end of the chapter). Figure 2-2 shows different BMI measurements for a 5-year-old boy. This figure illustrates how BMIs are used to identify underweight, healthy weight, overweight, and obese children.

For infants and toddlers under age 2, growth is evaluated by monitoring weight, length, and weight relative to length using the World Health Organization (WHO) growth charts, which better reflect growth in infancy (Centers for Disease

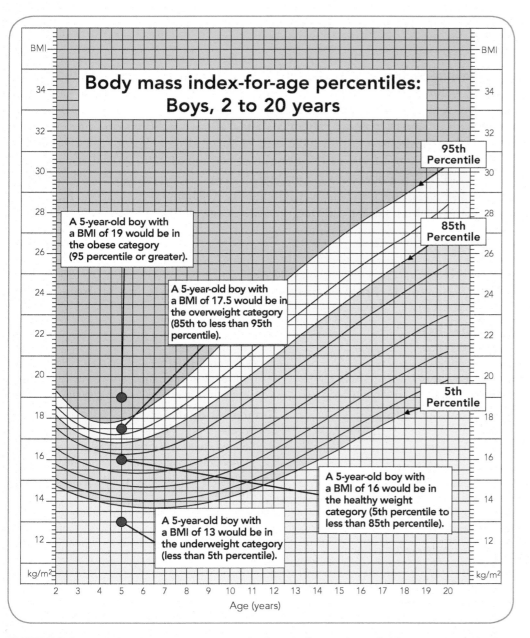

FIGURE 2-2   What Is the BMI? This growth chart indicates how children are identified as obese, overweight, healthy weight, and underweight using the BMI calculation.

Source: Based on *Healthy Weight: Assessing Your Weight: About BMI for Children and Teens*, by the Centers for Disease Control and Prevention, 2012, retrieved from http://www.cdc.gov/healthyweight/assessing/bmi/childrens_bmi/about_childrens_bmi.html.

Control and Prevention, 2010). These measurements should be recorded regularly throughout the year to ensure that proper growth is occurring. (Growth charts are discussed in more detail in Chapter 9.)

If excessive weight gain is identified, sharing this information with parents can set a course for change and obesity prevention. In dealing with weight issues in young children, an "ounce of prevention is truly worth a pound of cure" because children who are obese when they are young are more likely to grow up to be overweight and obese adults. A fat baby is no longer regarded as a healthy baby, and children do not always grow out of their "baby fat."

The Health Consequences of Obesity

sleep apnea
a sleep disorder in which a person's breathing pauses during sleep

Being overweight or obese during childhood is of great concern because of the immediate as well as long-term health consequences. Obese children suffer from problems such as **sleep apnea** (a sleep disorder in which a person's breathing pauses during sleep) and asthma, and they are at risk for diabetes. These conditions can interfere with learning and contribute to a higher incidence of absenteeism (Spruyt & Gozal, 2012; U.S. National Library of Medicine, National Institutes of Health, 2012; University of Washington, 2012). Being obese at a young age and over a long period of time can have a significant adverse impact on health and longevity (Olshansky et al., 2005). Figure 2-3 summarizes the health risks for children who are overweight or obese.

FIGURE 2-3   Health Problems Associated with Obesity in Children

Heart-related risks:
High blood cholesterol levels
High blood pressure
Increased risk of heart attack or stroke as adults

Endocrine-related risks:
Insulin resistance
Type 2 diabetes

Cancer-related risks:
Breast cancer
Colon cancer
Cancer of the esophagus
Kidney cancer

Gastrointestinal-related risks:
Nonalcoholic fatty liver disease
Gall bladder disease

Lung-related risks:
Asthma
Obstructive sleep apnea syndrome (a sleep disorder in which there are frequent breathing interruptions during sleep)

Orthopedic-related risks:
Bow legs
Slipped capital femoral epiphysis (the ball of the thigh bone slips off the thigh bone)
Arthritis

Mental health-related risks:
Depression
Low self-esteem
Face social stigmatization and discrimination

Sources: U.S. Department of Health and Human Services, The Surgeon General's Vision for a Healthy and Fit Nation. Rockville, MD: U.S. Department of Health and Human Services, Office of the Surgeon General, 2010. http://www.surgeongeneral.gov/library/obesityvision/obesityvision2010.pdf; Policy Statement: Prevention of Pediatric Overweight and Obesity, American Academy of Pediatric Committee on Nutrition, 2003 reaffirmed 2007, Pediatrics 112(2): 424–430; U.S. Department of Health and Human Services, National Institutes of Health National Cancer Institute Fact Sheet: Obesity and Cancer Risk Fact Sheet: National Cancer Institute, 2012. Retrieved from http://www.cancer.gov/about-cancer/causes-prevention/risk/obesity/obesity-fact-sheet.

Unfortunately, the health-related consequences of obesity can become self-perpetuating. Consider this scenario:

> *At age 8, Colin was significantly obese. During his third-grade year, he developed diabetes, a medical condition of high blood sugar often linked to obesity. Colin experienced considerable trouble concentrating and paying attention in class, and he ultimately had to see a doctor for managing his blood sugar. Colin missed school, and when he was able to return, he had to manage his blood sugar with medication. If Colin forgot to take his medication with a meal, he would become tired and get headaches. Although his teacher tried to help him catch up with class assignments, his diabetes symptoms sometimes made it hard for him to progress in his schoolwork.*

In this scenario, Colin's obesity caused both health and learning problems.

The Psychosocial Impact of Obesity

Children who are obese often experience low self-esteem, depression, and poor peer interactions (Nevin-Folino, 2008). Children who are obese face stigmatizing attitudes by the adults who care for them, such as health professionals, teachers, PE teachers, and parents, as well as their peers. The impact of the negative stereotyping and marginalization by their peers is particularly painful for obese children and can become apparent in preschoolers as early as age 3. Students become sensitized to obesity, preferring non-obese friends and attributing negative personality traits such as laziness and sloppiness to obese children (O'Dea & Eriksen, 2010; Schwimmer, Burwinkle, & Varni, 2003). Teachers should be particularly attuned to the challenges faced by children who are overweight and obese whose struggles with self-esteem increase as they mature.

A Matter of ETHICS

You have overheard a teacher being critical of the family of an obese boy. The teacher believes that the child's health is in jeopardy and that this fact is being ignored by his parents. You also notice that the teacher tries to limit the portions the child is served while he is at preschool. What is your responsibility in this situation? What are the ethical responsibilities that this teacher has ignored in her interactions with the family and child?

The Role of Inadequate Physical Activity

Lack of sufficient physical activity contributes to the other side of the coin of obesity—inadequate **energy expenditure** (the amount of calories burned), which compounds the problem of overnutrition. Maintaining a healthy weight requires a fine balance between calorie intake and energy expenditure. Some practices in early childhood and school settings may contribute to inadequate physical activity among young children, such as:

energy expenditure
the amount of energy or calories used by the body during rest and physical activity

- Providing little space for safe indoor or outdoor active play.
- Offering insufficient opportunities for physical activity in daily programming.
- Devoting most of the school day to academic achievement, at the cost of time for exercise.
- Neglecting training of teachers in after-school programs who are able to promote and model physical activity.
- Withholding recess as a form of punishment or as a means to have children catch up on assignments.
- Eliminating physical education classes due to funding constraints.

Teachers are in a good position to encourage activity in young children by increasing the amount of time in the daily schedule devoted to outside play and incorporating physical activity into daily routines as follows:

- Plan walking field trips and scavenger hunts in the community.
- Include a physical activity center during self-select time.

Pearson Education

CLASSROOM CONNECTION

Watch this video about Walk to School Day and Bike to School Day, collaborative efforts between a school and community. What are some other school and community activities that provide children with opportunities to increase their physical activity?

- Provide activities using portable playground equipment such as balls and hoops.
- Plan school events with a physical activity theme, such as a field day, sock hop dance, walk or bike to school day, walking club, parent–child activity night.
- Offer fund-raisers that encourage physical activity such as a jog-a-thon, fun run, or family walking obstacle course.
- Promote noncompetitive sports so that all children—regardless of skill level and ability—want to participate.
- Plan time for both structured and unstructured play.
- Integrate physical activity into lesson plans (Lee, Srikantharajah, & Mikkelsen, 2010).

The National Association for Sport and Physical Education (NASPE) is a professional organization and national authority on physical education, sports, and physical activity. The NASPE has established general physical activity guidelines for children in two main age divisions: birth to age 5 and ages 5 to 12 (see Web Resources). These age-specific physical activity recommendations give teachers parameters to consider as they strive to achieve physically active environments for the children in their care. Important standards are listed for each age group. It is recommended that toddlers (1- to 2-year-olds) receive 30 minutes of structured physical activity each day and that preschoolers (3- to 4-year-olds) get 60 minutes. Toddlers and preschoolers should participate in at least 60 minutes or more of unstructured play per day as well. NASPE also recommends that, unless sleeping, young children should not be sedentary for more than 60 minutes at a time.

Guidelines are also offered on how to promote the physical activity of infants by creating safe settings that do not limit movement, but do stimulate babies to explore their environment (National Association for Sport and Physical Education, 2009). The NASPE website provides links to excellent resources that help teachers incorporate physical activity into the early childhood education setting.

food insecurity
the lack of access to enough food to prevent hunger at all times due to lack of financial resources

Food Insecurity and Obesity

Food insecurity, or consistently having too little food to eat due to financial constraints, can predispose low-income children to overweight and obesity. Although it seems contradictory, hunger and obesity can exist side by side. The rationale behind this association is not completely understood; however, food insecurity can lead to less expensive, less healthy food choices that are limited in variety. In addition, children who do not have a consistent source of food may overeat when food is available. Low-income families often must choose high-fat, energy-dense, inexpensive food to maximize their calories per dollar spent. They also face additional risk factors for obesity, such as limited access to healthy and affordable foods and lack of safe and accessible recreational facilities, parks, and walking trails that support physical activity (Food Research and Action Center, 2011).

Andersen Ross/Getty Images

Inactive lifestyles contribute to the rising incidence of obesity.

Teachers need to understand that children who are obese and who eat larger than normal serving sizes may be reacting to the stress of food insecurity. Teachers should consider how they might support these children who struggle with the stigma of obesity and poverty. Here is how one teacher approached the situation:

Vanessa, a preschool teacher, carefully supervises Kimberly during mealtime, especially when oranges are on the menu. Kimberly, who is overweight, frequently serves herself more orange wedges than the one-half orange portion planned for each child. This became a problem during the family-style meal service when the other children at the table did not get their share of oranges. Vanessa, who was concerned about Kimberly's weight, mentioned this behavior to Kimberly's father, Mark. Mark explained that the family could not afford to buy fresh fruit very often and admitted that Kimberly had never had oranges before coming to school. Vanessa recognized that Kimberly's family was suffering from food insecurity. During the meal service, she showed Kimberly how to count out her portion. Then she arranged for Kimberly to have more oranges wedges after everyone was served, if she wanted them.

Addressing Obesity

Helping children learn healthful eating habits and encouraging enjoyment of physical activity are two ways teachers can promote a proactive approach to the challenges of the obesity epidemic. It is important for educators to stay abreast of evidence-based approaches to achieve these goals. Teachers and their early childhood programs are partners with families and communities in promoting healthy lifestyles for children. Classroom approaches that help teachers be proactive in addressing the concerns of obesity include the following:

- Provide an environment that supports wellness, such as offering nutritious meals and providing space and equipment for physically active play.
- Integrate nutrition concepts into program curriculum and activities. For example children can study different kinds of beans, learn how whole-grain bread is made, and participate in growing a vegetable garden.

POLICY POINT

Supporting Policy Changes That Impact Obesity

Many teachers feel a strong need to advocate for change in their school or community to fight the obesity epidemic. To start, they need information to "shake things up." To influence decision makers, they need information that relates specifically to their state.

The Oregon Health & Science University, with support from the U.S. Department of Health and Human Services, developed a website called the Data Resource Center for Child and Adolescent Health. This resource offers state-by-state data on the incidence of obesity and discusses what each state is doing to address the obesity epidemic. Another website that provides state-by-state data on the food environment is the USDA's Economic Research Service website, which includes the Food Environment Atlas and Food Desert Locator. This website provides state and county information that relates to a community's ability to access nutritious foods and participate in physical activity, the incidence of food insecurity, and other socioeconomic information. These powerful facts can provide the impetus teachers need to support change that improves the wellness of young children.

Source: *Childhood Obesity Action Network, State Obesity Profiles*, by the National Initiative for Children's Healthcare Quality, the Child Policy Research Center, and the Child and Adolescent Health Measurement Initiative, 2009, retrieved on April 6, 2012, from the website *Your Food Environment Atlas*, U.S. Department of Agriculture Economic Research Service, 2010.

CHECK YOUR UNDERSTANDING 2.2
Click here to check your understanding of nutrition issues that lead to under- and overnutrition in children.

- Introduce games that promote physical activity, such as "Duck, Duck, Goose" and "Four Square."
- Invite parents to help plan menus, to share ideas about nutrition activities and games, and to promote these wellness approaches at home.
- Be a good wellness role model. Eat with pleasure the healthful meals served to children. Model enjoyment of physical activity and participate in active games with the children.

Teachers who have insight into the challenging and changing nutrition environment in the United States have the tools necessary to formulate a plan for protecting the health and well-being of young children in their care. See the *Policy Point* for information on supporting policy changes that impact obesity.

USING RECOMMENDED STANDARDS TO GUIDE HEALTHY EATING

Knowledge of nutrition is crucial in supporting good health in adults and children alike. Teachers and parents select and plan a healthy diet for the children in their care and therefore must understand the components of food that contribute to a balanced diet. Researchers and experts in the field of nutrition have established guidelines and standards to ensure that teachers know how to plan appropriate menus and serve foods that support healthy development.

Understanding Dietary Reference Intakes

Dietary Reference Intakes (DRIs)
a listing of daily estimated nutrient requirements; used to assess diets for adequacy at the nutrient level

The Dietary Reference Intakes (DRIs) established by the Institute of Medicine of the National Academies are one of the important standards used to guide development of a healthful diet. They establish evidence-based reference values that specify the amount of nutrients needed in the diets of adults, children, and population groups to maintain good health (Committee to Review Dietary Reference Intakes for Vitamin D Food and Nutrition Board & Institute of Medicine of the National Academies, 2011; Otten, Pitzi-Hellwig, & Meyers, 2006). The nutrients reviewed within the DRI guidelines include those that are considered essential nutrients because they either cannot be made in the body or cannot be made in sufficient quantities to meet the body's needs; consequently, the nutrients must be consumed in the diet.

The DRIs form the basis for diet recommendations made by health and government authorities. They are used as a foundation for the development of public policies that address the health and wellness of children in the United States. For example, the *Dietary Guidelines for Americans, 2010* and the MyPlate base their diet recommendations on meeting the nutrient goals established by the DRIs. In addition, the National School Lunch Program and the School Breakfast Program have updated their standards for meal planning to reflect the DRIs and Dietary Guidelines for Americans (U.S. Department of Agriculture, Food and Nutrition Service, 2012c). The DRIs are the guiding force when researchers assess the nutritional quality of children's diets. Studies that link iron-deficiency anemia to insufficient iron intake could not draw these conclusions without the DRIs, the yardstick for healthy diets. To understand the DRIs, it is helpful to become familiar with how the nutrients are divided into different categories, as discussed next.

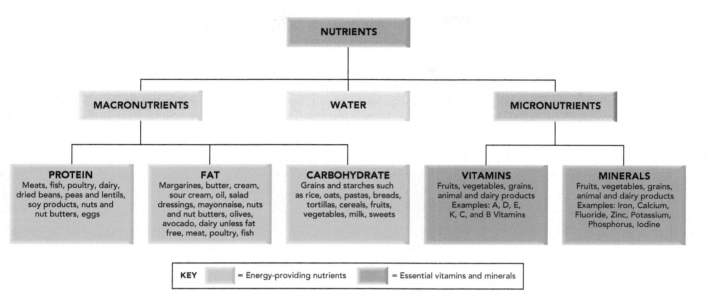

FIGURE 2-4
Classification of Nutrients

Classification of Nutrients

Nutrients are classified into six major categories: protein, fat, carbohydrates, vitamins, minerals, and water (Figure 2-4). Food provides energy or calories from proteins, fats, and carbohydrates (macronutrients) and essential nutrients such as vitamins and minerals (micronutrients).

Macronutrients Proteins, fats, and carbohydrates are macronutrients that are needed in large amounts in the diet. Carbohydrates and fats are predominantly used as sources of fuel for the body. Proteins can also be used as fuel; however, they are preferentially used to regulate body processes and serve as building blocks for body structures such as muscles, organs, and blood.

The balance of macronutrients in the diet as well as the total amount provided by the diet is very important. Too many calories from the macronutrients will cause excessive weight gain, whereas too little may result in insufficient growth. Macronutrients are found in the typical foods children consume during a day. For example, a tuna sandwich served at lunch contains protein (in the tuna), carbohydrates (in the bread), and fat (in the mayonnaise). Most foods are a combination of macronutrients. Bread contains mostly carbohydrates, but does have some protein, and its fat content can vary considerably, as in the case of a high-fat croissant. The milk served at mealtime is also a combination of protein, fat, and carbohydrates unless the milk is fat-free.

Micronutrients The micronutrients include vitamins and minerals. The body requires micronutrients in much smaller amounts than macronutrients, but they are essential for children to thrive. It is with the assistance of micronutrients that energy from the macronutrients can be processed. Micronutrients promote growth and development. Each micronutrient has a unique role. Micronutrients are found in all different types of foods, but some foods have a higher concentration of certain micronutrients. For example, milk is a natural source of calcium and is fortified with vitamin D, whereas citrus fruits and strawberries are high in vitamin C. Food that contains a significant amount of micronutrients per calorie of food consumed

macronutrients
nutrient category that includes protein, fats, and carbohydrates; they are the energy- or calorie-providing nutrients and are needed in large amounts in the diet

carbohydrates
macronutrients in the form of sugars and starches that provide the body with energy

fats
macronutrients that provide the most concentrated source of energy for the body; also used to cushion the organs and to insulate the body

proteins
essential macronutrients that function as the building blocks for body structures such as muscles and organs; can also be used as a source of energy when necessary

micronutrients
nutrient category that includes vitamins and minerals that are required in much smaller amounts than macronutrients, but are essential because the body cannot synthesize them and will not function properly without them. Children will not thrive without these nutrients in spite of sufficient calorie intake

vitamins
an organic or carbon-containing class of essential micronutrients that are not made in the body or in sufficient amounts to support the body's needs and therefore must be obtained from the diet

minerals
an inorganic or non–carbon-containing class of micronutrients that are required in small amounts and must be obtained from the diet

is called nutrient dense. For example, a fresh fruit cup with strawberries, blueberries, and bananas served with nonfat light yogurt and a slice of whole-grain toast is more nutrient dense than a couple of doughnuts or croissants for breakfast in the morning.

Water Water is essential for survival because all systems in the body need water to carry on life processes. Water transports nutrients in the bloodstream and flushes the body of wastes. It helps the body maintain proper temperatures through perspiration. Children obtain water from the beverages they drink, but also get water from foods they eat, such as fruits and vegetables.

Components of the Dietary Reference Intakes

The DRIs include five component parts. The first four components establish recommendations for consuming micronutrients. The fifth component establishes guidelines for the macronutrients (Otten et al., 2006). The components are as follows:

- *Recommended Dietary Allowances (RDAs)*
- *Adequate Intakes (AIs)*
- *Estimated Average Requirements (EARs)*
- *Tolerable Upper Intake Levels (ULs)*
- *Acceptable Macronutrient Distribution Ranges (AMDRs)*

Young children up to age 3 have a higher AMDR for fats than do older children and adults. This is because they have smaller stomachs and a rapid rate of growth, both of which result in a need for higher-calorie foods. This influences diet recommendations such as serving whole milk to most children up to age 2 and then switching to skim or 1% milk for children older than 2 years of age (see the *Nutrition Note*).

Some parents, in an effort to provide healthful diets to young children, restrict foods that have higher fat contents. Teachers can share with families that restricting fat excessively in young children's diets can negatively impact their rate of growth. For example, a teacher noticed that a 14-month-old in her program was not gaining weight as well as in the past. In a discussion with her mother, the teacher learned the baby was weaned from breast milk to rice milk when her daughter turned

---

NUTRITION NOTE   Fats for Infants

Fat is an important nutrient for infants and toddlers who have high energy needs because of their rapid growth. These young children have a small stomach capacity and can meet their nutritional needs for growth and development only by eating calorie-dense fats. The fat intake requirement of infants is greater than at any other time in life, with infants needing 45% to 55% of their calories from fat.

Fats serve not only as a source of energy, but also as an aid in the absorption of the fat-soluble vitamins A, D, E, and K. Fat is also a source of *essential fatty acids*, which are vital in supporting optimal brain growth and development in infants. It is very important for adults who care for infants and toddlers to recognize the important role fat plays in early development.

Sources: "Low Fat Diets for Babies," Hassink, S. G., *American Academy of Pediatrics*, 2012, HealthyChildren.org at http://www.healthychildren.org/English/ages-stages/baby/feeding-nutrition/pages/Low-Fat-Diets-For-Babies.aspx; "Dietary (n-3) Fatty Acids and Brain Development," by S. M. Innis, 2007, *Journal of Nutrition*, *137*(4): 855–859; and "Lipid Requirements of Infants: Implications for Nutrient Composition of Fortified Complementary Foods," by R. Uauy and C. Castillo, 2003, *Journal of Nutrition*, *133*(9): 2962S–2972S.

1 year old. A referral to a dietitian revealed that rice milk was not an ideal choice because of its low fat and protein content. A switch back to whole milk resulted in an improved rate of weight gain.

Other families may worry about picky eaters who make limited food choices and wonder if they are getting enough nutrients. They may wonder if giving them multivitamins is appropriate. The *Safety Segment* describes the importance of using caution when offering multivitamins. Teachers, when asked, should refer concerned parents to their health care providers for recommendations about multivitamin use.

In summary, the DRIs reflect a variety of goals established by nutrition experts. These goals include ensuring that diets are adequate but not excessive in nutrient content and are protective of long-term health. Although teachers may not need to refer often to the DRIs, being familiar with them (and recognizing the science behind such resources) reminds teachers of the importance of nutrition and diet to healthy growth and development.

Evaluating Daily Values and Reading Food Labels

Another nutrient-based guidance system is one that teachers see every day: the **daily values (DVs)**, which are located on the label of almost all foods purchased and consumed. Daily values indicate what percentage of the daily recommended amount of a nutrient is met when a portion of a food is consumed. For example, a label may show that a serving of food meets 20% of the daily recommended amount of iron. This means that 80% more iron must be consumed in other foods to meet the total daily value. The total daily value is based on a 2,000-calorie diet. Figure 2-5 shows an example of DVs displayed on a food label.

The daily values were established as a standard for measuring the contribution of a food item or supplement to the diet. The daily values are different from the DRIs in that they are not as age- and gender-specific. Instead, they represent what has been determined to be the average intake range of most people in the

daily values (DVs)
dietary reference values that are used on food labels and represent the requirements of an "average" individual, unlike Dietary Reference Intakes, which have reference values that represent different age and gender categories

---

SAFETY SEGMENT   Keep Children Safe from Multivitamin Overdoses

The Dietary Reference Intakes (DRIs) provide guidance on the amount and types of essential nutrients individuals need to consume to maintain a healthy diet. Sometimes children may not eat as well as they should. Families may consider giving multivitamins to their children to make sure nutrition goals are met. Should children take multivitamins? Most healthy children do fine without dietary supplementation. Their needs are less than those of adults, and they may be consuming foods that are fortified, such as breakfast cereals and juices.

Teachers should direct families with concerns to discuss the use of multivitamins with their doctor or dietitian. If they are advised to take multivitamins, they should select ones that are designed for children. Caregivers should be careful about how they are dispensed. Many multivitamins look and taste like candy, and children who take too many put themselves at risk.

The American Academy of Pediatrics and the Academy of Nutrition and Dietetics agree that vitamin and mineral supplements (except for vitamin K in newborn infants and vitamin D for breast-fed infants, non–breast-fed infants, and children who drink less than 32 ounces of formula or milk per day are not needed for most healthy children and that it is better to meet nutrient needs with foods rather than in pill form.

Sources: *Vitamin D: On the Double*, Healthychildren.org, American Academy of Pediatrics, 2012, at http://www.healthychildren.org/English/healthy-living/nutrition/pages /Vitamin-D-On-the-Double.aspx; *Pediatric Nutrition Handbook*, 6th edition, edited by R. Kleinman, 2009, Elk Grove, IL: American Academy of Pediatrics; *Position of the American Dietetic Association: Nutrient Supplementation* by the Academy of Nutrition and Dietetics, 2005, *Journal of the American Dietetic Association, 109*(12): 2073–2085.

The nutrient content of a product cannot be assessed without knowing its serving size and how many servings are in a box.

Divide fat calories by total calories × 100 to get %fat calories. Healthy diets aim for more foods that have 30% calories or less from fat.

Information on fat and cholesterol content is particularly important for those concerned about heart health or weight. *Trans* fat and saturated fats and cholesterol should be kept as low as possible. Remember that just because a food announces its *trans* fat free does not mean it is low in saturated fats.

The sodium content of U.S. diets tends to be higher than desirable. A food is considered low sodium if it has 140 mg or less per serving.

The total carbohydrate figure includes fiber and sugar. The sugar includes natural sugars as well as added. This product is higher than some because it is a cereal with raisins. Look for foods that are rich in fiber. High fiber is 5 g or more per serving.

Children and adults should consume a diet rich in these nutrients. This product has been fortified and is a good source of iron. The DV for iron is 18 mg. At 25% this cereal provides 4.5 mg of iron per serving. 5% or less of DV is low and 20% or more is high in a particular nutrient.

Here are the standard intakes by which the %DV is derived. The complete list of the standard nutrients content for a 2,000-calorie diet can be found at: www.fda.gov/Food/ResourcesForYou/Consumers/NFLPM/ucm274593.htm

Ingredients are listed from highest to lowest concentration. Allergy information is provided.

Nutrition Facts

Serving Size 1 cup (59g/2.1 oz)
Servings per Container About 12

Amount per Serving		Cereal
Calories		190
Calories from fat		15

	% Daily Values*
Total Fat 1.5g	2%
Saturated fat 0g	0%
Trans fat 0g	0%
Cholesterol 0mg	0%
Sodium 350mg	15%
Potassium 360mg	10%
Total Carbohydrate 45g	15%
Dietary fiber 7 g	28%
Sugars 19g	
Other carbohydrates 19g	
Protein 5g	
Vitamin A	10%
Vitamin C	0%
Calcium	2%
Iron	25%

*Daily Values are based on a 2,000 calorie diet. Your daily values may be higher or lower depending on your calorie needs

	Calories	2000	2500
Total fat	Less than	65g	80g
Sat fat	Less than	20g	25g
Cholesterol	Less than	300mg	300mg
Total carbohydrates		300g	350g
Fiber		25g	30g

Ingredients: Whole wheat, bran, sugar, raisins
CONTAINS: WHEAT

FIGURE 2-5

Sample Label for a High-Fiber Cereal

Sources: U.S. Food and Drug Administration, updated 2012. Retrieved from http://www.fda.gov/Food/ResourcesForYou/Consumers/ucm266853.htm; Eating Healthier and Feeling Better Using the Nutrition Facts Label U.S. Food and Drug Administration Appendix A: Definitions of Nutrient Content Claims, updated 2011. Retrieved from http://www.fda.gov/Food/GuidanceComplianceRegulatoryInformation/GuidanceDocuments/FoodLabelingNutrition/FoodLabelingGuide/ucm064928.htm.

United States. The requirements for children ages 4 and older, teenagers, adults, and the elderly were examined and averaged into one set of values. That is, the daily values are designed for an "average" person; they are a "one-size-fits-all" recommendation. This approach is appropriate to meet the needs of most people; however, some individuals may need less than the DV-recommended amounts of nutrients and some might need more. Infants and young children, for example, need less than the daily value on a typical food label. Because infants and children have lower nutrient needs than the daily value listed for a 2,000-calorie diet, teachers need to recognize that meeting 100% daily value is not a goal for them. Rather, daily values can best be used to understand the nutritional composition of a food. For example, a food that contains 5% or less of the daily value is low in a particular nutrient. If it contains 20% or more of a nutrient, it is considered a high source of that nutrient (U.S. Food and Drug Administration, 2012).

Food Label Requirements

In 1990, the Nutrition Labeling and Education Act (NLEA) established clear food labeling requirements. The content of labels must now include:

- *Serving size and servings per container:* Listed in both the U.S. system of measurement (1/2 cup) and metric amounts (120 mL) or in amounts commonly consumed (6 crackers).
- *Nutrient amounts per serving:* Includes calories, fat calories, total fat, trans fats and saturated fats, cholesterol, sodium, potassium, total carbohydrates, fiber, sugar, and protein (**trans fats** are a type of unhealthy fat found in food; they can promote heart disease).
- *Nutrients: as a percentage (%) of daily values:* Includes total fat, trans fats, saturated fats, cholesterol, sodium, total carbohydrate, fiber, vitamin A, vitamin C, calcium, and iron.
- *Ingredients:* Listed in order of highest to lowest concentration.
- *Warnings:* Lists possible allergens (briefly discussed in next section).
- *Nutrition claims:* Uses a standardized approach, such as what constitutes "low fat" or "high fiber" (see Table 2-1).

trans fat
a type of unhealthy dietary fat that is created when oils are partially hydrogenated; when found in food, they can promote heart disease

TABLE 2-1 Understanding Nutrient Content Claims

Nutrient	Per Serving
SODIUM	
Sodium free	Less than 5 mg
Very low sodium	35 mg or less
Low sodium	140 mg or less
Reduced sodium	25% lower than regular
CALORIES	
Calorie free	Less than 5 calories
Low calorie	40 calories or less
Reduced	25% lower than regular
FAT	
Fat free	Less than 0.5 g
Low fat	3 g or less
CHOLESTEROL	
Cholesterol free	Less than 2 mg
Low cholesterol	20 mg or less
SATURATED FAT	
Saturated fat free	Less than 0.5 g
Low saturated fat	1 g or less
Reduced saturated fat	25% less than regular
TRANS FAT	
Trans fat free	Less than 0.5 g
FIBER	
High fiber	5 g or more

Source: Appendix A: Definitions of Nutrient Content Claims: Guidance for Industry: A Food Labeling Guide U.S. Food and Drug Administration, 2011, retrieved April 9, 2012, from http://www.fda.gov/Food/GuidanceComplianceRegulatoryInformation/GuidanceDocuments/FoodLabelingNutrition/FoodLabelingGuide/ucm064911.htm.

WHAT IF . . .

a parent informed you that she did not want her healthy child to consume any foods with peanuts? How would you negotiate a common ground with the parent and the child who might object to having to eat something different from what the other children in the class get to eat?

Overall, the information provided on food labels helps consumers determine how the food contributes to the daily total nutritional intake and how a food's nutritional content compares with that of other foods. Teachers are likely to use label-reading skills when they comparison-shop, looking for nutrient-rich foods to use in any type of food preparation for children, whether for lunches, snacks, or food-related school activities.

Reading Labels for Food Allergens

The Food Allergen Labeling and Consumer Protection Act, approved in 2004 and initiated in 2006, mandates that eight major foods or food groups—milk, eggs, fish, crustacean shellfish, tree nuts, peanuts, wheat, and soybeans—be included on the food label to help people with food allergies recognize products they may need to avoid.

Special Labeling for Infant/Toddler Foods

The FDA and USDA have established slightly different labeling regulations for foods such as infant cereals and baby foods that are targeted toward children under the age of 2 and children ages 2 to 4. For example, labels may not contain information about fats and cholesterol. These regulations were developed in recognition of the specific nutrient needs of very young children. Special labeling for children's foods ensures that adults who care for children avoid making the mistake of inadvertently restricting certain nutrients such as fat and cholesterol that are needed for young children to grow properly (U.S. Food and Drug Administration, 2011b, 2011c).

Label reading is an important skill for teachers who may be gatekeepers for the types of food schools purchase for their meal service or foods uses for cooking activities. Label reading helps teachers to:

- Make decisions about the nutritional contribution of different foods.
- Ensure that children get foods that are rich in healthful vitamins, minerals, and fiber.
- Select foods low in saturated fats, trans fats, and cholesterol (if over age 2).
- Avoid foods that are high in sodium.
- Select appropriate foods for children with food allergies or sensitivities, cultural food preferences, and special diets.

Using the *Dietary Guidelines for Americans, 2010*

The *Dietary Guidelines for Americans, 2010* is a collaborative effort of the Department of Health and Human Services (HHS) and the USDA (U.S. Department of Health and Human Services & U.S. Department of Agriculture, 2011). The guidelines are issued every five years to address the needs of people 2 years of age and older, offering recommendations for the general public as well as special populations such as children, the elderly, and pregnant women. The key points of the current dietary guidelines are described in Figure 2-6.

The dietary guidelines provide overall lifestyle recommendations that include dietary guidance and recommendations for physical activity. In addition, the guidelines promote the development of healthy eating patterns that support achieving and maintaining a healthy weight. The principles of food safety are also

FIGURE 2-6 *Dietary Guidelines for Americans, 2010*

Overarching Goals

1. Maintain calorie balance over time to achieve and sustain a healthy weight.
2. Focus on consuming nutrient-dense foods and beverages.

Key Recommendations

1. Balance calories to manage weight.
   - Improve eating and physical activity behaviors.
   - Control total calorie intake to manage body weight.
   - Increase physical activity and reduce sedentary behaviors.
   - Maintain appropriate calorie balance at each stage of life.
2. Reduce certain foods and food components.
   - Reduce sodium intake to less than 2,300 mg and for those over 51 years of age, and those of any age who are African Americans or who have hypertension, diabetes, or chronic kidney disease, reduce sodium intake to 1,500 mg.
   - Consume less than 10% of calories as saturated fat by replacing with monounsaturated and polyunsaturated fats.
   - Consume less than 300 mg per day of dietary cholesterol.
   - Keep *trans* fatty acids as low as possible.
   - Reduce the intake of calories from solid fats and added sugars.
   - Limit the intake of foods that contain refined grains especially those that contain added sugars, solid fats, and sodium.
   - If alcohol is consumed it should be consumed in moderation.
3. Increase certain foods and food components.
   - Increase vegetable and fruit intake.
   - Increase variety of vegetables (orange, red, dark green vegetables and beans/peas).
   - Consume at least half of all grains as whole grains.
   - Increase fat-free or low-fat milk and milk products.
   - Choose a variety of protein foods (seafood, lean meats, poultry, eggs, beans and peas, soy products, and unsalted nuts and seeds).
   - Increase the use of seafood by choosing it to replace some meat or poultry in the diet.
   - Use oils to replace solid fats where possible.
   - Choose foods that provide more potassium, dietary fiber, calcium, and Vitamin D in the diet.
4. Build healthy eating patterns.
   - Select an eating pattern that meets nutrient needs over time at an appropriate calorie level.
   - Account for foods and beverages consumed and assess how they fit within a total healthy eating pattern.
   - Follow food safety recommendations when preparing and eating foods.

Source: Dietary Guidelines for Americans, 2010, by the U.S. Department of Health and Human Services and the U.S. Department of Agriculture, 2011 retrieved April 11, 2012 http://www.health.gov/dietaryguidelines/dga2010/DietaryGuidelines2010.pdf.

stressed (U.S. Department of Health and Human Services & U.S. Department of Agriculture, 2011).

The dietary guidelines highlight that consuming nutritious foods, rather than supplements, is the foundation for good health. They also stress the importance of making smart choices from all food groups to obtain the most nutrients per calorie consumed. Figure 2-7 provides guidelines for selecting foods that are nutrient dense in relation to their calorie content, such as whole grains, fruits, vegetables, nonfat or low-fat milk and low-fat dairy products, lean meats, poultry, seafood, beans, peas, nuts, and seeds. Nutrient-dense foods are high in vitamin and mineral content compared with their calorie content. Select unprocessed foods lower in sodium, solid fat, and added sugar content. Consider how the dietary guidelines with their focus on nutrient-dense foods were put to use by Kerrin in her family child care program:

nutrient-dense foods foods that are high in vitamin and mineral content while relatively low in calorie content

> Kerrin decided to review the Dietary Guidelines before writing the menus for her child care program. She thought she was doing very well because she chose many nutrient-dense fruits and vegetables for her menu. She realized, however, that the guidelines recommended that at least half of the grains offered to children be whole grains. She decided to take steps to

Pearson Education

CLASSROOM CONNECTION

Early childhood educators use literature to help children learn about different cultures. As you watch this video, think about children's books that describe cultural differences in food, eating, and mealtimes. Which of these books are offered in languages other than English?

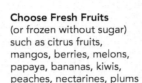

Choose Fresh Fruits (or frozen without sugar) such as citrus fruits, mangos, berries, melons, papaya, bananas, kiwis, peaches, nectarines, plums

Choose Fresh Vegetables (or frozen without sauces) such as dark green and deep orange vegetables as well as tomatoes; red, green, and yellow peppers; red cabbage

Select Whole, Basic, Unprocessed Foods

Select Lean Cuts of Meat, Skinless Poultry and Fish, and Use More Alternative Protein Sources such as dried beans, peas and lentils, soy products, and nuts or nut butters

Select Low-Fat Dairy Products such as skim or 1% milk (age 2 and older), low-fat cheeses and plain yogurt with fresh fruit

Select Whole Grains such as oats, brown rice, whole grain breads, rolls and cereals, barley, corn tortillas

FIGURE 2-7

Components of a Nutrient-Dense Diet

increase the whole-grain portions offered on her menus. After Kerrin exposed the children to the new food items through taste testing, she switched to whole-grain bread products, brown rice, and whole-grain cereals. She also decided to combine nutrient-dense foods such as chicken stir fry over brown rice and sweet potato muffins, yogurt, and berry smoothies. These changes were implemented progressively and enhanced the nutritional quality of the menu and were well received by the children because they were involved in the taste testing.

Together the Dietary Guidelines and the DRIs are the primary contributors to the policies that guide federally supported child nutrition programs. These guidelines can also be used more directly by teachers for:

- Planning menus.
- Implementing good nutrition and health education activities and lessons (see the *Teaching Wellness* feature).
- Developing parent education programs.
- Selecting topics for newsletters, posters, and bulletin board displays.
- Making healthy decisions about what to eat and how to plan their own active lifestyle to enhance health.

Overall, the primary goal of the dietary guidelines is to promote and protect the health of the current and future generations of U.S. citizens. Everyone plays a role in achieving this goal, including individuals, families, teachers, and health care professionals, as well as policy makers (U.S. Department of Health and Human Services & U.S. Department of Agriculture, 2011).

LEARNING OUTCOME   **Children will experience the sensory aspects (touch, smell, taste) of fruits and vegetables.**

Vocabulary focus: Touch, smell, taste, texture, odor, fragrance, flavor, names of foods, vitamins, minerals, fiber, names of rainbow colors.

Safety watch: Be aware of children's food allergies or restrictions; avoid serving these foods. Prepare foods appropriately to ensure food safety and to avoid potential for choking. Monitor for cleanliness and safety as children participate.

INFANTS AND TODDLERS

- **Goal:** Babies who are eating finger foods and toddlers will touch, smell, and taste fruits and vegetables.
- **Materials:** Paper or plastic cups, plate or tray, fruits and vegetables (such as bananas, berries, oranges, green beans, zucchini, squash, carrots, potatoes).
- **Activity plan:** Cook firm vegetables until soft enough to pierce with a fork. Cut foods into tiny pieces no larger than ¼ inch. For babies and toddlers, offer foods one at a time based on the child's feeding plan. Offer familiar foods first and then add new foods to explore. Place a small portion of cut-up food on a tray or plate. Cover the food with a cup turned upside down. Show the child that a food is under the cup. Encourage the child to pick up the cup and discover the food underneath. Show the child that it is OK to touch the food. Describe touching, smelling, and tasting the food, such as, "This is a fruit called banana. Let's touch it." Pretend to touch the banana and say, "It is soft. Let's smell the banana." Pretend to smell the food and say, "The banana smells good! Let's taste the banana!"

Pretend to taste the food and say, "The banana tastes sweet!" Next time try a different food.

- **How to adjust the activity:** To support children who are learning English, create picture cards depicting the food to be explored. Include the name of the food in English as well as the child's home language (also spelled out phonetically for all children if needed). Say the name of the food in both English and the home language. Support children with special developmental needs by guiding their hands as they touch the food and moving the food to the child with your clean and gloved hand. Provide ample time for touching and smelling according to the child's needs and never force children to taste the food. Reinforce each child's effort by remarking, "You are getting to know about fruits and vegetables by smelling, touching, and tasting these foods. That is a good way to learn."
- **Did you meet your goal?** Did the child explore—touch, smell, and taste—the offered foods?

PRESCHOOLERS AND KINDERGARTNERS

- **Goal:** Children will explore the texture, smell, and flavor of various fruits and vegetables and learn about why these foods are good for them.
- **Materials:** The children's book *Eating the Alphabet: Fruits & Vegetables from A to Z*, by Lois Ehlert; six fresh fruits and vegetables depicted in the book, six cups, foil, serving bowl, small plates, spoons, napkins, a serving tray, paper towels.
- **Activity plan:** Select six foods and cut them into bite-size pieces. Place a small spoonful of each food in a cup, cover with foil, and poke a few small holes in the foil with a fork. Place the remaining portion of each food in serving bowls. Set everything on a tray. Cover the serving bowls with paper towels so that the foods are a mystery. Invite children to gather for the activity. Explain that there are many fruits and vegetables—enough for each letter of the alphabet. Read the children's book. Encourage children to name the fruits and vegetables as you read. Teach children by saying, "Fruits and vegetables are good for our bodies. Eating a variety of fruits and vegetables helps us feel good and gives our bodies the energy we need to stay healthy so that we can run and play and our bodies grow strong." Name a fruit or vegetable from the book and ask children to jump high if they have tried the food that was named. Vary the movement each time a new food is named. Invite children to gather at a table. Ask them to smell the foods

that are hidden in the foil-covered cups and try to identify them by the smell. Then ask the children to remove the foil to discover the food inside the cup. Uncover and pass the serving bowls of foods. Invite children to serve themselves a piece of each food. Encourage them to describe the texture, smell, and flavor of each food. Identify which food is a fruit and which is a vegetable. Encourage children's efforts by saying, "You are really exploring these fruits and vegetables using your senses to touch, smell, and taste them." Reinforce why these foods are important to eat.

- **How to adjust the activity:** Use picture cards with the food names included in English and the other home languages of children in the class. Repeat the name of each food in all languages spoken by children in the class. Reinforce the message by using gestures as you speak to communicate touching, smelling, and tasting the foods. Be aware that some children may have an aversion to touching certain foods or textures. Provide time for children to explore. Ensure that each child can readily reach the cups to smell; then serve the foods to taste them. Do not force children to touch, smell, or taste.
- **Did you meet your goal?** Are children able to describe the texture, odor, and flavor of each food? Can the children describe why eating fruits and vegetables is important?

(continued)

- **Goal:** Children will learn that a healthy meal includes a "half plate" of fruits and vegetables. They will be able to identify a color combination of fruits and vegetables that is very healthy (rich in vitamin A) and describe why fruits and vegetables are an important part of the diet.

- **Materials:** MyPlate Mini Poster (refer to the MyPlate website for more information), picture or poster showing many fruits and vegetables, construction paper for each color of the rainbow (red, orange, yellow, green, blue, purple), magazine pictures depicting brightly colored fruits and vegetables (or stickers of fruits and vegetables), small white paper plate, crayons or marking pens, scissors, glue.

- **Activity plan:** Gather children together and show them the MyPlate Mini Poster. Briefly review the different food groups. Point out that the poster shows that a healthy meal includes enough fruits and vegetables to fill half the plate. Describe the benefits of these foods by saying, "Fruits and vegetable are very high in vitamins, minerals, and fiber. These are all important for the body to grow." Explain that a very healthy group of fruits and vegetables includes those that are dark green, orange, or red, such as spinach, broccoli, mangos, papayas, cantaloupe, carrots, sweet potatoes, red peppers, and tomatoes. Invite the children to make a rainbow placemat using the colored construction paper. Provide a small paper plate to glue to the placemat. Ask the children to fill half of their plate with pictures of fruits and vegetables for each color of the rainbow by cutting and pasting pictures, drawing a picture of a food, or writing in the name of the food or food group with a marker of the food group's color. Remind them to be sure to include some dark green and orange or red foods.

- **How to adjust the activity:** Label a piece of construction paper for each color of the rainbow with the name of the color in English as well as the home languages of the children in the class. Name the colors of the rainbow in all languages. Prepare the craft activity to suit the developmental needs of children in the class. Allow ample time for children to work. Offer adaptive scissors, glue sticks or tape, previously cut out pictures, or stickers depicting fruits and vegetables to assist all children in being successful.

- **Did you meet your goal?** Are children able to fill their half of their plate with a rainbow of fruits and vegetables? Did they include dark green, orange, or red choices? Can they describe why fruits and vegetables are healthy foods?

Using the Choose MyPlate Food Guidance System

The MyPlate icon is the USDA's replacement for the MyPyramid Food Guidance System. The MyPlate recommendations are more easily understood because the visual illustration of a place setting that includes an image of a plate divided into four color-coded sections (purple for protein, red for fruits, orange for grains, green for vegetables, and a blue side dish for dairy) shows not only what to eat, but also the proportions recommended. For example, the fruits and vegetables portion takes up half of the plate (Figure 2-8).

The goal of MyPlate, like its predecessor the MyPyramid, is to combine the specific nutrient recommendations of the DRIs and the general messages of the *Dietary Guidelines for Americans, 2010* and translate them into practical guidelines for building a healthy diet. The MyPlate system helps individuals achieve personal health and nutrition goals and offers recommendations and strategies for young children ages 2 to 5, children ages 6 to 11, and adults (U.S. Department of Agriculture, 2012). The system focuses on the importance of both diet and physical activity to enhance health and is individualized for different age categories of children. For example, Figure 2-9 illustrates sample 1,400-calorie meal and snack patterns that meet the nutritional needs of 4-year-old boys and girls who- are active 30 to 60 minutes per day.

The MyPlate guidance system offers a solution to healthy eating that is personalized and easy to understand. According to the USDA, the overall goals of the MyPlate system are to encourage adults and children to:

- Balance calories by enjoying foods but eating less and avoiding oversized portions.
- Increase in the diet healthy foods such as whole grains, vegetables, fruits, and fat-free or low-fat dairy products.

FIGURE 2-8
ChooseMyPlate

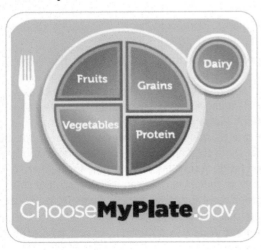

Source: U.S. Department of Agriculture's ChooseMyPlate, USDA, 2012, retrieved April 17, 2012, from http://www .choosemyplate.gov/index.html.

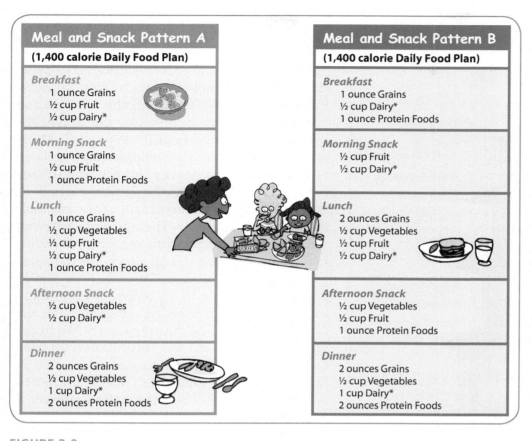

Meal and Snack Pattern A

FIGURE 2-9
1,400-Calorie Meal and Snack Patterns for Preschoolers
Source: USDA ChooseMyPlate, retrieved April 17, 2012, from http://www.choosemyplate.gov/downloads/1400cals.pdf.

- Reduce foods that are higher in sodium, added sugar, and solid fats, such as highly salted processed foods, cakes, cookies, candies, sweetened soft drinks, and high-fat meats such hot dogs, bacon, and sausage (U.S. Department of Agriculture, 2012).

Other resources available on the MyPlate website include a 10 Tips Nutrition Education Series, educational materials, and lessons that support nutrition and physical activities messages in the classroom setting.

ETHNIC FOOD GUIDANCE SYSTEMS

The U.S. population is becoming increasingly multicultural. Consequently, teachers must be responsive to the cultural influences on children's diets as well as other aspects of school life. Various resources are available to support teachers as they become familiar with the food guidance systems from other countries. For example, Figure 2-10 illustrates an example of a Chinese food guide. Other examples of food guidance systems that are from different countries or that represent different ethnic groups can be found in the Web Resource section. Many of the recommendations are similar to those of the USDA food guidance system in that eating a variety of nutritious foods in appropriate portions is encouraged. Figure 2-11 shows how the MyPlate can be modified to accommodate typical food choices for a sampling of ethnic groups.

CHECK YOUR UNDERSTANDING 2.3
Click here to check your understanding of the recommended guidelines that promote healthful eating and how to use them in the early childhood education settings.

Fats and
Oils, 25g

Milk and
Milk Products, 100g
Bean and
Bean Products, 50g

Meat and Poultry,
50–100g
Fish and Shrimp, 50g
Eggs, 25–50g

Vegetables, 400–500g
Fruits, 100–200g

Cereals, 300–500g

China

FIGURE 2-10
A Food Guide Pagoda from China
Source: Based on an illustration from the Chinese Nutrition Society, http://www
.cnsoc.org/asp-bin/EN/?page=8&class=42&id=149.

WHAT IF . . .

a parent from an Asian culture expressed
concern that there were not enough menu
items that appealed to her child? For example,
the parent noticed that rice was not offered
very often. How would you respond?

Providing Bilingual Educational Materials

The MyPlate website provides many of its materials in Spanish, including its 10 Tips Nutrition Education Series. Although the MyPyramid approach has been archived by the USDA, the information shared is still very valid. Many educational materials are available in translated versions that help convey important nutrition concepts. For example, the Pyramid has been translated into 20 different languages available on the MyPlate website. These materials are versatile tools that teachers can use when educating families on nutrition-related topics. The Canadian government publishes *Canada's Food Guide*, which is available in 18 different languages, including 7 Native American languages (Health Canada, 2011). The Southeastern Michigan Dietetic Association has information on food choices in the MyPyramid format for a variety of cultural groups (Southeastern Michigan Dietetic Association, 2004). This information, presented in English, helps teachers understand traditional ethnic food choices. The National Agricultural Library, USDA has an excellent link to resources for understanding cultural and ethnic foods practices and nutrition recommendations for educators (see Web Resources).

Teaching English Language Learners

Appropriate teaching practices guide how nutrition concepts are presented for all children, with special consideration given to those who are English language learners. Strategies that promote understanding of the nutrition message include the following:

- Have children learn by participating in hands-on activities such as cooking activities and taste tests.
- Use a range of foods, recipes, and food preparation and cooking methods to reflect a variety of cultural approaches.
- Base the activity on a bilingual children's picture book with a focus on nutrition.
- Use visuals such as real food, food models, or pictures of food whenever presenting a verbal message.
- Speak clearly. Show and explain concepts in more than one way.
- Invite parents and others to visit the class to demonstrate a nutrition concept, to engage children in a cultural food tradition, and to be role models promoting the value of cultural diversity.
- Plan field trips to local businesses such as ethnic supermarkets, restaurants, and bakeries to experience how traditional foods are made.

FIGURE 2-11 Modifying MyPlate for a Sampling of Ethnic Groups

Ethnic Group	Vegetables	Fruits	Grains	Protein	Dairy
Mediterranean	Eggplant, artichokes, squash, tomatoes, grape leaves, onions, mushrooms, okra, cucumbers, greens	Grapes, dates, figs, persimmons, pomegranate, lemons, grapefruit	Rice, bulgur, couscous, freekeh (green wheat), pasta, pita bread, pilaf, risotto	Seafood, poultry, lamb, beef, pork, nuts, fava beans, legumes, seeds	Yogurt, cheese, (feta, ricotta), milk
Navajo	Carrots, celery, corn, green beans, hominy, Navajo spinach, onion, potatoes, chili peppers, spinach, squash, squash blossoms, tomatoes	Apples, apricots, avocados, bananas, cantaloupe, casabas, grapes, kiwi, Navajo melon, raisins, sumac and juniper berries, watermelon, wax currant, wolfberry, yucca bananas	Alkaad (cake), blue corn bread, mush and dumplings, fry bread, kneel down bread, tortillas, whole grain bread	Mutton, deer, elk, fish, prairie dog, poultry, pork, deer, rabbit, pinon nuts, squash seeds, tumble mustard seeds, pinto beans	Milk, goats milk, cheese
Vietnamese	Artichoke, asparagus, broccoli, cabbage, carrots, cauliflower, corn, cucumbers, dauhu, eggplant, garlic, gia, green beans, leeks, mang, mung beans, onions, potatoes, raumuong (water spinach), squash, sweet potatoes, tomatoes	Mangosteen, dragon fruit, persimmons, banana, carambola, grapes, guava, jejube, lemon, lit chi, coconut, lychee, mango, orange, pandeo, papaya, pineapple, watermelon	Banh trang (rice paper wrapper) cellophane noodles, cha gio (egg roll), mein, mung beans, vermicelli, rice, rice noodles, xoi (sweet rice dish)	Beef, chicken, crab, duck, pork, shrimp, squid, fish. Eggs, tofu	Milk (valued but not traditional)

Sources: Mediterranean Grains: "The History and Healthful Preparation of Four Old and Emerging Varieties," by Nour El-Zibdeh, *Today's Dietitian* 12 (6) 36, 2010; Mediterranean Fruits, FruitsInfo.com, 2012. http://www.fruitsinfo.com/mediterranean_fruits.htm; Navajo Food, 2011. http://navajo-arts.com/food-navajo.html; Indiana's Food for the Hungry, Modifying the Food Pyramid: Mexican American, Puerto Rican, Navajo, Jewish http://www.cfs.purdue.edu/safefood/nutrition/modifypyramid4.html; Modifying the Food Pyramid: African American, Asian Indian, Chinese American, Vietnamese American http://www.cfs.purdue.edu/safefood/nutrition/modifypyramid3.html; Vietnamese family health: What we eat to grow.http://vietfamilyhealth.org/nutrition/Nutrition_WhatWeEat_Online.pdf. (All sources retrieved April 15, 2012.)

Teachers who promote healthful eating from a multicultural perspective need to challenge themselves to explore new ideas and ways of planning appropriate and healthful menus for young children. They should also educate themselves about the nutrition traditions of alternative cultures. The resources that guide teachers and families with important nutritional information provide the structure to guide decision making about the selection and presentation of foods. However, the foods selected and the lessons taught about nutrition evolve from the teacher's knowledge of the needs of all children in the group, including their cultural traditions. This highlights the important role that teachers play in selecting and serving healthful foods in the early childhood setting and in presenting nutrition wellness activities that assist all children in learning valuable nutrition lessons.

CHECK YOUR UNDERSTANDING 2.4

Click here to check your understanding of teaching English language learners about nutrition.

SUMMARY

- The changing food environment has resulted in less time spent sharing family meals and more reliance on fast foods, restaurant dining, and convenience foods, which have negatively impacted the quality of children's diets. In spite of many positive trends, including more sustainable food practices and improvements in school meals, children's diets still fall far below the recommendations for fruit, grain, and dairy groups and are higher in fat and sodium content than advised by the *Dietary Guidelines for Americans* (Wood & Child and Nutrition Division, Food and Nutrition Service, 2008).

- Malnutrition is the imbalance of one or more nutrients in the diet that support appropriate growth and development. Consuming too few or too many nutrients negatively impacts learning and development and may have lifelong health consequences. In addition, overconsuming food coupled with decreased physical activity has resulted in an obesity epidemic among young children that threatens their long-term health and wellness. Recognizing nutritional problems during the early years offers the opportunity for modifications to be made to improve children's health outcomes. This positive contribution involves teachers, families, and health care providers.

- The food guidance systems are important resources that help teachers create an environment that fosters good nutrition and health. The Dietary Reference Intakes, which are established levels of nutrient requirements, and the daily values found on food labels provide specific information on nutrient requirements to help guide food selection and menu planning. The *Dietary Guidelines for Americans, 2010* provides general advice on nutrition and physical activity. The MyPlate educational tool takes the guesswork out of healthful eating by providing simple-to-use guidance on how to construct a nutrient-dense, high-quality diet. Teachers can use this information to establish classroom practices that promote good health and wellness in young children as well as to guide their own personal health goals.

- The food guidance systems are adaptable to a variety of ethnic food practices, and many are available in languages other than English so that increasingly teachers have tools they need to overcome language barriers and to protect the health of all children in their care.

Chapter Quiz

 Click here to check your understanding of the foundations of optimal nutrition.

Discussion Starters

1. Explain how food insecurity can lead to obesity. How can teachers help alleviate food insecurity if they identify this problem in children's families?
2. How can teachers address the obesity epidemic in their programs?
3. How can teachers implement the principles of the *Dietary Guidelines for Americans, 2010* and the MyPlate food guidance system in their classrooms? How would you do this for toddlers, preschoolers, and school-age children?

Practice Points

1. Monica is exactly 4 years old. She weighs 48 pounds and is 44 inches tall. Using the CDC BMI website listed in the Web Resources section, calculate her BMI. Today is 1/1/present year. Her birth is 1/1/present year – 4. Using the growth chart (available on the CDC growth chart website listed in the Web Resources section) determine the percentile for her height, weight, and BMI. What weight classification would you give her? What does this tell you about Gabriella?

2. Suppose you were like Gabriella and consumed a vegetarian diet and wanted to assess whether your iron intake was sufficient. Refer to the MyPlate website for more information. What changes might you make to the meals below to improve your iron intake?

Breakfast:	1 flour tortilla with 2 ounces of cheese
	½ cup orange juice
	1 cup milk, 2%
Snack:	1 cup milk, 2%
	¼ cup teddy graham crackers
Lunch:	1 slice whole-wheat bread with 1 ounce of cheese
	1 cup tomato soup
	1 sliced kiwi
	1 cup of milk, 2%
Snack:	1 apple
Dinner:	½ cup rice, white
	2 ounces cheese
	1 cup salad with 1 tablespoon Italian dressing
	1 flour tortilla
	1 cup apple juice

3. Refer to the breakfast cereal food label shown in Figure 2-5. Explain three nutritional qualities that make this a healthy food choice. What might you be concerned about?

Web Resources

American Academy of Pediatric Nutrition: *What Every Parent Needs to Know*,

CDC Growth Charts and BMI Calculator

ChooseMyPlate.gov

Data Resource Center for Child and Adolescent Health, Childhood Obesity State Report Cards

Dietary Guidelines for Americans, 2010

Institute of Medicine of the National Academy, Dietary Reference Intakes

National Association for Sport and Physical Education

The Food and Nutrition Information Center of the National Agricultural Library of the USDA, 2011

USDA Food and Nutrition Information Center Dietary Guidance; Ethnic/Cultural Food Pyramids, 2011

Your Food Environment Atlas (USDA)

Key Terms

Antioxidants

Body mass index (BMI)

Carbohydrates

Daily Values (DVs)

Dietary Reference Intakes (DRIs)

Energy expenditure

Failure to thrive

Fats

Food insecurity

Iron-deficiency anemia

Macronutrients

Malnutrition

Micronutrients

Minerals

Nutrient-dense foods

Nutrients

Nutrition

Overnutrition

Phytochemicals

Proteins

Psychosocial

Rickets

Sleep apnea

Supplemental food programs

Trans fats

Undernutrition

Vitamin D

Vitamins

CHAPTER 3

The Science of Nutrition

learning outcomes

After reading this chapter, you should be able to:

1. Define nutrition science.
2. Identify the steps in the process of digestion.
3. Identify how nutrients are absorbed and how teachers can help children with common digestive conditions such as constipation and lactose intolerance.
4. Describe the function of the macronutrients (carbohydrates, proteins, and fats) and the food groups in which they are found.
5. Define the function of the micronutrients (vitamins and minerals) and their interactions in supporting the growth, development, and health of infants and children.
6. Summarize how the knowledge of nutrients can be used to plan healthful diets for young children and teach them nutrition concepts.

CASE STUDY

Jamal is a 5-year-old kindergartner who is noticeably large for his age. During health screening day, his teacher, Tonya, notices that his weight is in the 95th percentile range when plotted on standard growth charts. In his backpack, she puts a notice for his family with his height and weight measurements. As she thinks about Jamal, it occurs to her that since the first day of school, he has frequently complained of being tired, has been irritable, and often has difficulty concentrating in class due to his hunger. She wonders if there is a connection to his increased weight gain.

The next day Jamal's mother, Aiesha, tells Tonya that she has scheduled an appointment with the doctor. She tells Tonya that she suspects his increase in weight is related to his blood sugar and that he frequently drinks sugar-sweetened beverages, including soda and energy drinks.

A couple of weeks later, Aiesha shares important news with Tonya. Jamal has been to a specialist where tests revealed that he has diabetes. Aiesha was told that diabetes is a disease where there are high levels of sugar in the blood. Aiesha was also told that the cornerstone to his treatment is diet.

Aiesha asks Tonya if the school will be able to provide Jamal with healthy, balanced meals. Tonya explains that to accommodate children with special diets, a table is available where children may sit together and get assistance from lunchroom staff. Perhaps Jamal may want to join this group at mealtime.

Tonya then calls the director of food services about the need for a balanced diet. She also notes that the classroom parents rotate bringing yogurt for snacks. Aiesha agrees to bring in a couple boxes of yogurt to have on hand for Jamal. After her discussion with Tonya, Aiesha feels confident that her son will receive appropriate and appealing meals at school and that he will begin to have a balanced diet to help with his diabetes.

DEFINING NUTRITION SCIENCE

Nutrition science is the study of how food provides nourishment to support the growth, maintenance, and repair of the human body. Understanding the science of nutrition helps teachers learn about healthful eating for themselves and the children in their care. The responsibility of feeding young children is important because they are nutritionally vulnerable and dependent on adults to make choices and provide for them. For example, infants and children need more calories for their size compared with adults because they are growing. When they are not consuming the right types and amounts of food, nutritional problems can develop quickly. If children face the additional stress of an illness or a disorder such as diabetes, the nutritional concerns can increase significantly.

This chapter explains why the substances found in food are necessary for good health. You will learn how the body digests and absorbs food to generate the energy needed to function. We discuss disorders that young children might experience as their bodies digest and absorb food and beverages so that you will feel prepared to handle a variety of feeding challenges. You will learn why different food groups are important to maintain a healthful diet, and you will learn about the role of the *essential macronutrients* (carbohydrates, protein, and fats) and *micronutrients* (vitamins and minerals). Finally, you will learn the fundamentals needed to teach young children about nutrition and to support those who have digestive disorders.

nutrition science
the study of how foods provide nourishment to support the growth, maintenance, and repair of the human body

CHECK YOUR UNDERSTANDING 3.1
Click here to check your understanding of nutrition science.

UNDERSTANDING THE PROCESS OF DIGESTION

To understand why specific foods are needed in the diet, we need to start at the beginning and look at what happens to food once it is consumed. The overall goal of eating is to take the nutrients in food and transport them through the body, where they are used to maintain body functions. The nutrients found in food are essential for young children because they:

- Provide energy.
- Are necessary for growth.
- Repair and maintain the body.
- Regulate body processes.
- Affect how genes are expressed.

How does digestion work? Teachers who understand this process will have a better understanding of why nutrients and balanced diets are so important for infants and young children. This knowledge helps in developing strategies to ensure that all children are well nourished.

The Digestion Process

Digestion is the mechanical and chemical breakdown of foods into smaller nutrient components, making the nutrients available for absorption. Multiple steps take place when the cereal with milk served for breakfast is turned into the fuel children

digestion
the mechanical and chemical breakdown of foods into smaller nutrient components to make them available for absorption

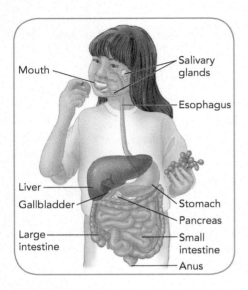

FIGURE 3-1

The Digestive System

gastrointestinal tract
the mouth, esophagus, stomach, and small and large intestines; part of the body where foods are digested and changed to nutrients in anticipation of being absorbed

need to start the day. The process takes place in the digestive system, which is made up of the **gastrointestinal tract** and other organs that aid in digestion. This multiple-organ system is the gateway for all nutrients into the body.

The gastrointestinal tract is like a long, tube-shaped conveyor belt with food pushed along the length of it by the wavelike contractions of the intestinal muscles. As Figure 3-1 illustrates, food undergoes both mechanical and chemical changes within the digestive tract to ready it for absorption, which occurs predominantly in the small intestine.

As food moves along this conveyor belt, it is chopped, churned, and mixed with enzymes, acids, and mucus, which slowly change it into smaller absorbable substances. Attached to the gastrointestinal tract are accessory organs such as the salivary glands, liver, and pancreas. These organs secrete a variety of components that also aid in the digestion process (see Table 3-1).

The Mouth

The start of all digestive action takes place in the mouth. The mechanical process of chewing physically breaks down food into small pieces. This allows saliva (spit) to begin its work. Saliva released from the salivary glands contains digestive **enzymes**, which start the chemical breakdown of food. Enzymes are proteins that speed up chemical reactions. Saliva keeps the tongue moist so that taste buds can work more effectively. The moist chewed-up food forms a mass, which is pushed to the back of the mouth by the tongue, ready to be swallowed. The teacher's role in this first step of digestion is to

TABLE 3-1   The Parts of the Gastrointestinal Tract and Their Functions

	Accessory Organs	Chemical Secreted	Functions
Mouth	Teeth	None	Mechanically chop food into small pieces.
	Tongue	Lingual lipase	The tongue moves food around in the mouth. Fat digestion begins.
	Salivary glands	Saliva, enzyme amylase	Saliva moistens foods; carbohydrate breakdown begins.
Esophagus	None	None	Provides passageway from mouth to stomach.
Stomach	None	Gastric juices that include:	The stomach acts as a holding unit for food as it is churned and mixed, and it produces secretions.
		Acids	Create an acidic environment so that enzymes can work.
		Enzyme pepsin	Causes protein breakdown.
		Mucus	Binds and mixes food; protects stomach.
Small intestine		Intestinal juices and mucus	Secretions cause the chemical breakdown of proteins, fats, and carbohydrates to substances that can be absorbed; protects and lubricates the intestine.
	Liver and gallbladder	Bile	Bile emulsifies fats and helps in fat breakdown.
	Pancreas	Pancreatic juices	Juices cause chemical breakdown of proteins, fats, and carbohydrates to substances that can be absorbed.
Large intestine, rectum, and anus	None	None	Absorb water; store and eliminate stools.

Sources: Based on NIH NIDDK Your Digestion System and How it Works, retrieved July 13, 2015, at http://www.niddk.nih.gov/health-information/health-topics/Anatomy/your-digestive-system/Pages/anatomy.aspx; *Williams' Essentials of Nutrition and Diet Therapy* (pp. 188–194) by E. D. Schlenker, 2007, St. Louis, MO: Mosby Elsevier.

decide the types of foods to offer children that match their ability to chew. This reduces the risk of choking.

Textures of Foods

Textures of food play a role in children's ability to chew and swallow. This ability depends on the child's age and whether the child has conditions that interfere with chewing. For example, infants who are learning to swallow their first nonliquid foods are offered puréed textures. This provides a gradual introduction of new textures to manage. By around 10 months, teeth begin to appear and side-of-the-mouth chewing develops. Foods with more texture are well received at this time. Food textures may need to be altered for children who have difficulty chewing because of motor development delays. The *Teaching Wellness* feature provides an activity that will help children understand how their mouth helps jump-start the process of digestion.

Digestion begins in the mouth and proceeds through multiple steps before the food that is consumed can be used for energy.

enzymes
proteins produced by the body's cells to speed up chemical reactions

Protecting Teeth

Foods provide both dental risks and benefits. These risks and benefits need to be considered when selecting foods in order to protect the teeth. Although foods provide the nutrition needed to strengthen teeth, some foods can cause dental decay. Dental decay occurs when various plaque-forming bacteria turn the carbohydrates that children eat into acid. This acid causes the loss of calcium from the teeth, resulting in decay.

Protecting teeth starts as soon as they erupt. For infants, this means that babies should not be put to bed with bottles filled with beverages such as milk, infant formula, fruit juice, or fruit drink or allowed to access a filled bottle or sippy cup all day (American Dental Association, 2014). Ongoing, repeated exposure to the sugars contained in these beverages puts infants at risk for baby bottle tooth decay. Baby bottle tooth decay is the development of early dental cavities that is extensive and particularly damaging to the front teeth, although any teeth can be involved.

Untreated dental decay can cause suffering and pain and affect the ability to eat, speak (impaired language development), and concentrate in the school setting (Centers for Disease Control and Prevention Division of Oral Health, 2014). Nutritional factors that increase the risk of dental decay include a high intake of fruit juices and soft drinks; delayed weaning from the bottle; access to toddler cups throughout the day; and the intake of sticky foods such as raisins, granola bars, and carbohydrate foods (for example, bread, crackers, and cookies) that get stuck in the teeth. These factors result in prolonged exposure of the tooth surface to the acids that cause tooth decay.

By contrast, the foods that protect teeth include milk and yogurt. These dairy products may be helpful in neutralizing acids produced by bacteria in the mouth and provide calcium, phosphorus, and magnesium, which help to build strong teeth in young children (Mayo Clinic, 2014). Fluoride found in fluoridated water is another nutrient that protects teeth by making tooth enamel strong and preventing bacteria from making acids that

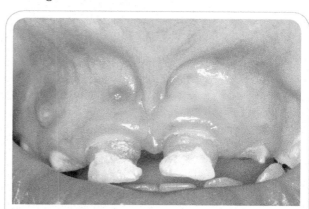

Teaching families about infant dental hygiene and the risks of putting babies to bed with bottles can help prevent baby bottle tooth decay.

LEARNING OUTCOME   **Children will gain an understanding of how tasting and chewing food begins the digestion process.**

Safety watch: Be aware of children's food allergies or restrictions. Adjust foods that are used as needed. Monitor for cleanliness in food activities.

OLDER INFANTS AND TODDLERS

- **Goal:** Children will explore moist and dry foods and learn about chewing foods to make them easier to swallow.
- **Materials:** A plate for each child, chopped plums, unsalted saltine crackers.
- **Safety watch:** Cut the plum into pieces no larger than ¼ inch. Supervise eating. Offer a sip of water if the cracker is too dry for the child to chew and swallow.
- **Vocabulary focus:** Plum, cracker, taste, chew, moist, swallow.
- **Activity plan:** For infants who are eating solid foods and for toddlers, offer a plate with small pieces of a fresh plum and an unsalted cracker. Encourage the child to pick up a piece of food and taste it. Name the food and say words to add interest, such as "That is a plum. Does it taste sweet? Sour? Is it smooth and moist in your mouth?" or "Does the cracker feel dry in your mouth?" Describe the process of chewing. Say, "The cracker is crunchy. You are using your teeth to chew the cracker to make it easy to swallow. When you chew, the cracker gets wet and soft so that you can swallow it. You are tasting and chewing. This is how we help our food be ready to swallow." Talk about chewing and swallowing at meal times.
- **How to adjust the activity:** Offer familiar foods first. Create support cards with the names of the tasting foods and the vocabulary words in the child's home language. If needed, spell out each word phonetically to assist with pronunciation. Ensure that all children are able to pick up the offered foods. Allow children time to explore the foods. Encourage but do not force children to taste the foods.
- **Did you meet your goal?** Did the children explore the offered food by chewing and tasting? Did they hear you talk about chewing the food to make it easier to swallow?

PRESCHOOLERS AND KINDERGARTNERS

- **Goal:** Children will learn that digestion starts in the mouth as food is chewed and mixed with saliva.
- **Materials:** Large model of teeth, the book *The Very Hungry Caterpillar* by Eric Carle, snack supports: plates, napkins, plastic knives, washed bananas (in the peel), stick pretzels, raisins, broccoli, peanut butter (or whipped light cream cheese if there are peanut allergies), cups, milk in small pitchers.
- **Safety watch:** Supervise children as they create their caterpillar snack to ensure cleanliness and safety.
- **Vocabulary focus:** Teeth, saliva, swallow, digestion.
- **Activity plan:** Gather children. Read *The Very Hungry Caterpillar.* As you read, invite the children to name the foods the caterpillar eats. Help children recognize that the caterpillar grows larger as he eats. When finished, summarize that eating healthy food helps all living things grow and develop. Explain that like the caterpillar, we use our teeth to bite and chew foods. We have teeth for biting, grinding, and chewing. Show these teeth on the model and discuss how the teeth have different shapes for their different purposes. Describe that we use our tongues to move food as we chew. "Our saliva, the moisture our mouth makes, helps the food become soft and slippery as we chew so that we can swallow the food. These are steps in digestion that happen in our mouths."

    Invite children to create a hungry caterpillar for snack. Provide each child with a plate, a knife, and half of a banana. Pass small bowls filled with the other snack-building foods. Guide children to peel the banana,

place it on their plate, and cut it into five pieces. Describe the steps to spread one side of each banana piece with peanut butter (or cream cheese) and stick the pieces together. Use the peanut butter (or cream cheese) to stick two raisins to the front banana to represent eyes. Show children how to stick the pretzel sticks into the sides of each banana piece to represent legs and place two into the front piece to represent antennae. Place a piece of broccoli in front of the caterpillar to "eat." Take a picture of children with their caterpillar snack. Pass cups and milk and invite children to eat their caterpillar snack. As you eat, talk about biting, chewing, and swallowing the different foods. Help children identify the foods that take more or less chewing before they are ready to swallow. Say, "We chew food so that it is easy to swallow. The food that is chewed goes into our stomach and helps us feel full. It gives us energy to play, think, and grow."

- **How to adjust the activity:** For English learners, use the model teeth to demonstrate biting and chewing food while describing what is happening in English (and alternative languages if possible). Create prompt cards for the focus vocabulary words in the home languages of children in the class. Be purposeful to ensure that each child has a chance to name a food the caterpillar in the book eats—in English or their home language. Support children with mobility challenges to create the caterpillar snack. Offer tongs, short-handled plastic knives, or other tools to help all children be successful. Provide time for children to eat their "caterpillar" snack.

- **Did you meet your goal?** Can children explain what happens in the mouth to start digestion?

SCHOOL-AGE CHILDREN

- **Goal:** Children will learn that digestion is the way the body breaks down food so that it can use the food's nutrients and that digestion starts in the mouth and continues in the stomach.
- **Materials:** Saltine crackers, mirror, bowl of quick-oats oatmeal, cups, spoons, pitchers with warm water, bowl of raisins.
- **Safety watch:** Supervise for safety and cleanliness as children use the mirror and mix and mash the oatmeal.
- **Vocabulary focus:** Saliva, digestion, stomach, vitamins, minerals, fiber.
- **Activity plan:** Describe how digestion starts in the mouth and continues in the stomach. Offer each child a saltine cracker. Ask them to chew for 30 seconds but not swallow the cracker. Pass a mirror around and ask them to inspect the cracker mash in their mouths. When everyone has had a turn, ask the children to continue chewing and swallowing their cracker. Talk about what happened in their mouths while they chewed—their teeth crushed the cracker and their mouth's made saliva, or "spit," to help the cracker mash be soft and wet enough to swallow. Explain that when we chew and swallow food, we begin the first stage of digestion. Ask children to imagine what it feels like to swallow the cracker without moisture in their mouths! Now offer each child a spoon and cup and guide them to serve themselves two heaping spoonfuls of dry quick oats. Ask them to taste a spoonful of dry oats. Is it easy to eat? *Now guide and then pour* ¼ cup of warm water over the oats in their cup and use their spoon to mash and stir the mix. Ask the children to inspect and describe the mash made in their "stomach mixer" cups. Explain that the stomach uses the same mixing and mashing actions to continue the digestion process until the food is a soft wet mash that helps the body get ready to absorb the nutrients in food (say the words *vitamins, minerals,* and *fiber*) when it moves from the stomach into the rest of the body. Pass a bowl of raisins and invite children to mix in some raisins and eat their "stomach mixer" snack.

    Summarize that our teeth crush the food, our saliva moistens the foods and makes it easier to swallow, and our stomachs do the next step of mixing and mashing so that our bodies can get the food energy it needs for us to play, work, think, and grow.

- **How to adjust the activity:** Provide picture card prompts for the steps of the activity to guide English learners and children who may need frequent reminders of the directions. Offer a bowl or a cup with a handle to provide greater stability for a child with motor coordination challenges.
- **Did you meet your goal?** Can children explain the purpose of digestion? Are they able to identify what happens in the mouth and stomach during the process of digestion?

damage teeth (Centers for Disease Control and Prevention, 2013). Well water and bottled water may not be good sources of fluoride. The xylitol found in some sugar-free gums, mints, and toothpastes is also effective in reducing the incidence of cavities by decreasing bacteria in the mouth and helping to strengthen teeth (Hirsch, Edelstein, Frosh, & Anselmo, 2012). Teachers help children protect their teeth by teaching them the basics of oral hygiene, including teeth brushing as part of their daily routine. Teachers are also important resources for families. For example, they can provide guidance to help children receive needed dental services, as described in this example:

Three-year-old Devin attends the Head Start program. Although he attends school regularly, he is often irritable and tired. He does not smile, and he does not eat well. One day his teacher, Lea, notices that Devin has a swollen cheek. She is concerned and asks Devin to let her look in his mouth. She sees that Devin's front teeth are visibly decayed, but he says that a back tooth is hurting him.

Pearson Education

CLASSROOM CONNECTION

Watch this video of a teacher who reads *The Very Hungry Caterpillar* to children and provides the snack-making learning activity described below.

WHAT IF . . .

you needed to plan the menu for your family child care program, which serves infants through preschool-age children? What modifications in texture might you need to take into consideration? How will you ensure that modified foods are appealing to all age groups?

Lea calls Devin's mother, Andrea, and learns that Devin still takes a bottle to bed. Lea tells Andrea that she thinks Devin is suffering from painful cavities. She strongly encourages Andrea to schedule an emergency dental exam. She helps her locate a dentist who will provide the service at a reduced cost for children enrolled in the Head Start program. The exam reveals that two of Devin's teeth are infected. Devin receives extensive dental treatment. When it is completed, Lea notices that he has an entirely different demeanor. He is happy, smiles, eats with enthusiasm, and is ready to learn.

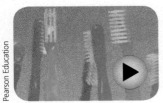

Pearson Education

CLASSROOM CONNECTION

Watch this video of Super Smile Day, a special event held at a school. Notice the different activities for both children and families to promote oral health. What other activities might you include?

dysphagia
a disorder characterized by the inability to swallow foods or liquids easily

gastroesophageal reflux (GER)
reflux of stomach contents into the esophagus

Swallowing and the Esophagus

Next in the process of digestion is swallowing. After the mass of chewed food is swallowed, it enters the esophagus, a tube that connects the mouth to the stomach. The food mass is pushed by wavelike contractions to the stomach.

Swallowing Difficulties

Swallowing food is a simple process that occurs without effort for most individuals. However, the process of chewing and swallowing uses a multitude of muscles and must be synchronized with breathing. Some children have a condition called **dysphagia**, which is the inability to swallow foods or liquids easily. Many conditions are associated with dysphagia, such as prematurity, developmental disabilities, cerebral palsy, and Down syndrome.

Teachers and families need to be aware that swallowing difficulties can result in significant feeding challenges. Feeding times may be prolonged, and the child may choke, cough, or gag, which is unpleasant and frightening for the child and requires the extra attention of teachers. Teachers often become part of a team, which includes families, health care professionals, and early intervention staff, to work together to achieve the goals of safe eating and good nutrition. Figure 3-2 provides a checklist for teachers who work with children who have swallowing disorders.

Reflux

Sometimes infants and children experience difficulty keeping food in the stomach, causing spitting up or **gastroesophageal reflux (GER)**. As many as 67% of 4-month-old

---

FIGURE 3-2   Teacher's Checklist: Caring for Children with Swallowing Disorders

❑ **Positioning:** Does the child need special positioning and an adaptive feeding chair? The correct position is essential in promoting safe swallowing during feeding.

❑ **Oral aversion:** Is the child involved in a desensitization program to help him overcome aversion to flavors, textures, consistencies, and temperatures of foods? What is the teacher's role?

❑ **Nutrition plan:** Is a modification of food consistency needed? Does special menu planning need to happen before the child can come to school? Are supplements required?

❑ **Adaptive feeding equipment:** Does the child need tube feeding equipment, positioning seats, or special cups, plates, bottles, nipples, or plates?

❑ **Skill building:** Are there exercises that focus on developing oral motor skills and or adaptive swallowing skills? What are the teacher's responsibilities?

Source: Based on *Pediatrics Nutrition Handbook*, 6e, edited by R. Kleinman, 2009, Elk Grove, IL: American Academy of Pediatrics Committee on Nutrition.

infants with GER spit up at least once a day after a feeding (Campanozzi et al., 2009). Often called "happy spitters," these infants grow well and do not experience any pain or compromise to their growth. The spitting up usually resolves by 12 to 14 months without any negative consequences (Reuter-Rice & Bolick, 2012). Teachers can help reduce some of the symptoms infants experience by supporting the baby in an upright position during and after feeding. Suggestions for managing digestive conditions are listed in Table 3-2.

TABLE 3-2 Common Childhood Disorders of the Gastrointestinal Tract

Disorder	Symptoms	Nutrition Risk Factors	Tips for Teachers*
Celiac disease	Gas, bloating, abdominal pain, and diarrhea or constipation, poor appetite, fatigue, weight loss.	Poor growth, malabsorption, anemia, increased risk for osteoporosis.	Pay close attention to diet. Avoid food with gluten, such as wheat, barley, rye, and oats (unless the oats are gluten-free). Meet with families, teachers, and food service staff to review diet and label reading and discuss use of gluten-free products.
Constipation	The painful passage of stool that is hard and dry.	Poor appetite.	*Infants with constipation:* Refer family to health care professional for advice. *Children with constipation:* Encourage them to gradually consume more foods high in fiber (fruits, vegetables, whole grains), drink sufficient fluids, and be physically active.
Diarrhea	Watery stools that occur three or more times per day, cause stomach cramping, and are not explained by change in diet.	Dehydration. *Signs of dehydration:* dry mouth and tongue, decreased amount of dark-colored urine, or in infants and toddlers, a decrease in the number of wet diapers, dry skin, crying without tears, and excessive sleepiness.	Infants and children who are sick with diarrhea should be sent home. Maintaining adequate hydration is important. Upon the return to school, offer a regular diet and avoid excess juice and high-fat foods.
Gastroesophageal reflux disease (GERD)	Occurs when stomach contents back up into the esophagus (spitting up or vomiting).	Poor growth, food refusal, difficulty eating.	Thickened formula may be recommended. Feed and keep infants in an upright position (at least 30 minutes after a meal). Avoid overfeeding, tight diapers, and car seat positioning.
Lactose intolerance	Noninfectious diarrhea, gas, and bloating caused by the inability to break down lactose, the sugar found in milk.	Children on a lactose-free diet may need calcium and vitamin D supplementation if unable to tolerate any dairy products.	Limit or restrict milk products based on individual tolerance. Substitute lactose-free milk or fortified soy milk in the school setting.
Swallowing disorders	Coughing, choking, or gagging during feedings.	Malnutrition, aspiration (getting food or liquids into the lungs), pneumonia, and difficult mealtime behavior.	Assessment of oral motor capabilities by a speech or an occupational therapist to provide guidelines on positioning, food consistency, etc. Include written guidelines in the IFSP or IEP. Very important to use feeding chair that supports the swallowing process.
Vomiting	The forceful emptying of the stomach's contents through the mouth.	Dehydration (see signs of dehydration listed for diarrhea).	Children who experience two or more incidences of vomiting within the previous 24 hours should be sent home. Maintain adequate hydration. Upon return to school, offer regular diet but avoid excess juice and high-fat foods.

*Children identified with a special health condition that warrants a modification in diet or special feeding technique require written instructions from the child's parents/guardians and health care provider. Teachers can consult with a registered dietitian. When children are sick, teachers should not hesitate to call their parents/guardians. Young children can get very sick quickly, and teachers may need to call health care providers.

Sources: American Academy of Pediatrics, American Public Health Association, National Resource Center for Health and Safety in Child Care and Early Education. 2011. *Caring for Our Children: National Health and Safety Performance Standards; Guidelines for Early Care and Education Programs,* 3rd edition. Elk Grove Village, IL: American Academy of Pediatrics; Washington, DC: American Public Health Association; Also available at http://nrckids.org. Kleinman, R. (Ed.). (2009). *Pediatric Nutrition Handbook* (6th ed.). Elk Grove Village, IL American Academy of Pediatrics; Digestive Diseases: A–Z List of Topics and Titles, National Digestive Diseases Information Clearinghouse, retrieved April 29, 2012, from http://digestive.niddk.nih.gov/ddiseases/a-z.asp; The Academy of Nutrition and Dietetics, Pediatric Nutrition Care Manual, 2011. Digestive Topics A–Z, The North American Society of Pediatric Gastroenterology and Hepatology and Nutrition, http://www.naspghan.org/wmspage.cfm?parm1=444.

CHECK YOUR UNDERSTANDING 3.2

Click here to check your understanding of digestion and what teachers can do to support digestion.

The Stomach

Once food reaches the stomach, it is mixed with stomach acids, secretions, and enzymes, which begin to break down the protein in the food. The stomach's role is to squeeze and churn the food and move it further along the digestive tract. Although food generally flows from the stomach to the small intestine, sometimes it comes back up when children vomit. Whereas reflux is usually burping of stomach contents, vomiting is a more violent event.

The first question that may come to mind for teachers when they are considering a vomiting episode is "Should this child go home?" Vomiting can be caused by gastrointestinal infections or other factors such as allergies, medications, overeating, and motion sickness. Schools and preschools have policies about illness that are shared with families through parent handbooks or preschool websites. The National Resource Center for Health and Safety in Child Care and Early Education (American Academy of Pediatrics, American Public Health Association, National Resource Center for Health and Safety in Child Care and Early Education, 2011) recommends that if children have two or more episodes of vomiting within 24 hours, they should be sent home. In practice, because it is often difficult for a teacher to know how often a child has vomited within a 24-hour period, parents are called. A decision as to whether a child should go home is made based on the child's history of illness, the incidence of similar illnesses in the classroom, and the possibility of a noninfectious source of illness such as twirling too long on the tire swing.

UNDERSTANDING THE PROCESS OF ABSORPTION

absorption
the transport of nutrients from the small intestine into the circulatory system

The transport of nutrients from the gastrointestinal tract into the body is called **absorption**. The primary site of absorption is the small intestine. When food has been broken into smaller units, it is ready to be transported into the body via the circulatory system.

The Small Intestine

villi
located on the surface of the folds of the small intestine; is where absorption takes place

microvilli
located on the surface of the villi, further expanding the surface area to enhance absorption of nutrients

When the stomach has completed churning and breaking food into smaller pieces, it releases it into the small intestine. The small intestine is an approximately 20-foot-long tube where most of the nutrients are absorbed (U.S. National Library of Medicine, National Institutes of Health, 2014). To accomplish this, the inside of the small intestine has a series of folds that are lined with **villi**. The finger-like villi are, in turn, lined with **microvilli** so that the total area involved in absorption is larger in size than a tennis court (Shills, Shike, Ross, Caballero, & Cousins, 2006).

Intestinal enzymes, acids, bile, and pancreatic juices further digest the major nutrients, breaking down carbohydrates, proteins, and fats and making them ready for absorption. When the nutrients are finally small enough to be absorbed, they enter the circulatory system (National Institute of Diabetes and Digestive and Kidney Diseases, National Institutes of Health, 2013). Once in the circulatory system, they are transported to various cells of the body. Table 3-3 shows the food

TABLE 3-3 Macronutrient Sources and the Breakdown Products of Digestion

Macronutrient	Selected Sources	Primary Breakdown Products	Role of Nutrient
Protein	Meats, beans, fish, poultry, yogurt, eggs	Amino acids	Growth and repair; can be used as energy if necessary
Fats	Oil, butter, mayonnaise, salad dressing	Fatty acids and glycerol	Stored energy source. Aids absorption of vitamins A, D, E, K
Carbohydrates	Grain products, fruits, vegetables, milk	Simple sugars: fructose, glucose, and galactose	Body's main energy source

sources and final breakdown products of carbohydrates, protein, and fats. The products that are not absorbed by the small intestine are collected in the large intestine.

The Large Intestine

The large intestine is the last section of the digestive system. Its primary role is to absorb water and some minerals and vitamins from the products not absorbed in the small intestine. Anything that cannot be digested, such as fiber, collects in the rectum until it is expelled via the anus as a bowel movement.

Understanding Problems Related to Absorption

Providing children with a variety of foods from each of the food groups at mealtime is the best way to ensure a healthy, balanced diet. However, children can face nutritional problems in spite of eating a good diet if they have trouble with absorption. These problems can be significant enough to impact a child's growth and development. Understanding factors that impact nutritional health ensures that teachers can effectively care for children with health concerns. Children who are physiologically comfortable will be more apt to learn. Parents feel confident leaving their child in the care of a teacher who understands and is able to respond to their child's unique needs.

Understanding Malabsorption

When the small intestine's lining becomes damaged, it is difficult to absorb nutrients. This condition is called malabsorption and can happen in a number of different circumstances. Diet-related conditions of malabsorption can often be modified by changes in diet.

Lactose Intolerance One of the enzymes in the small intestine is called *lactase*. Lactase helps digest the sugar in milk, called *lactose*. In comparison to a milk protein allergy, which is an immune response that triggers serious and sometimes life-threatening symptoms, children who are lactose intolerant simply do not make sufficient lactase. When they consume too many dairy foods or beverages with lactose, they develop gas, bloating, and diarrhea (Queen Samour & King, 2012).

The degree of lactose intolerance varies among individuals. Some children who are lactose intolerant may be able to tolerate up to a cup of milk or yogurt per day. Yogurt with active live cultures and aged cheese are generally better tolerated

malabsorption
occurs when damage to the small intestine's lining results in difficulty absorbing nutrients, leading to diarrhea and sometimes weight loss

lactose intolerant
term used to define an individual who experiences gas, bloating, and diarrhea because of an inability to break down the lactose found in milk

than milk. Infants who are lactose intolerant can do well with either a lactose-free or soy formula. The incidence of lactose intolerance is also higher in certain ethnic populations. For example, it is estimated that 20% of African American, Asian, and Hispanic children under the age of 5 have some evidence of lactose malabsorption (Queen Samour & King, 2012). Teachers and parents should clarify a feeding plan for children with lactose intolerance. It is also important for teachers to understand the effects of lactose intolerance and recognize how they may affect a child. For example:

> *Jesse, a third grader, requests a pass to the restroom about a half hour after lunch. He is gone for 15 minutes. When he returns to the classroom, the substitute teacher is upset. She assumes Jesse had simply wasted time in the bathroom and halls. Jesse turns beet red and emphatically states, "I was using the bathroom!" He explains: "The only thing I did wrong was drink chocolate milk. I really like it, but it doesn't like me. It gives me a stomachache." A quick look at his health files confirms lactose intolerance.*

WHAT IF . . .

the family of a toddler with lactose intolerance in your program was inconsistent in restricting lactose. This was causing the child to have periodic bouts of diarrhea that were affecting potty training. How would you discuss this subject with the parents?

The symptoms of lactose intolerance can be quickly resolved by avoiding foods high in lactose content. Milk is a high-lactose food. Using lactose-reduced milk or vitamin D and calcium–enriched soy milk in place of regular milk will solve most children's problems. A conversation with families helps teachers understand the degree of lactose sensitivity. Other dairy products such as yogurt, cheese, and ice cream also contain lactose and may or may not need to be eliminated depending on the degree of sensitivity. Less obvious sources of lactose that teachers need to consider include pancake or cake mixes, processed meats, and boxed potato products.

Diet-Related Diarrheas Diarrhea can be caused by factors such as viruses and bacteria, but sometimes children eat or drink something that triggers diarrhea. Diarrhea is characterized by watery stools that occur with increased frequency and stomach cramping.

Certain foods can cause diarrhea in young children. For example, many foods contain sugar alcohols (a type of sugar substitute) that are not completely digested and absorbed by the body. Sugar-free gum, candy, and cookies may contain sugar alcohols. These foods pass into the large intestine and are fermented by bacteria, which can cause diarrhea when children eat too much of them.

Other causes of diarrhea include the following (American Academy of Nutrition and Dietetics, 2011; Ball, Bindler, & Cowen, 2010):

- Excess juice consumption, particularly apple and pear juices.
- Consumption of drinks with caffeine, such as tea and soft drinks.
- Diets that are excessively high in fiber.
- Overfeeding.
- The introduction of new foods that the child does not tolerate.

When a child has a bout of diarrhea, teachers must review the symptoms, consider the classroom incidence of diarrhea, and obtain family input before deciding whether to send a child home. Sometimes it is unclear whether a child is ill. Loose stools are not always indicative of a major gastrointestinal

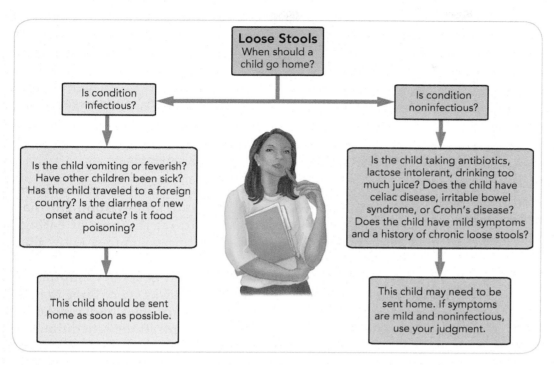

FIGURE 3-3
What to Consider When a Child Has Loose Stools

illness; they could instead indicate a mild change in stool patterns. Figure 3-3 provides guidance in determining when to send children home if they have loose stools.

Diarrhea that is caused by viruses or bacteria may also be accompanied by vomiting. This combination creates a more critical condition because dehydration can occur.

Understanding Constipation

Sometimes too much water is absorbed in the large intestine and constipation occurs. Constipation is the painful passage of stools that are hard and dry. This problem sometimes happens when children feel shy about using the bathroom at the early childhood or school programs or develop a fear of pain from passing hard stool because of problems with constipation in the past. Some children with special health care needs can be prone to constipation because of abnormal anatomy or function of the intestinal tract, low muscle tone, medications, or inability to communicate needs (Yang, Lucas, & Feucht, 2010). Constipation in young children can be caused by lack of fiber in the diet, such as consuming too many refined (white) grains, inadequate fluid intake, and insufficient physical activity. When the amount of fiber in the diet is insufficient, the waste products of digestion and absorption move more slowly through the large intestine and, consequently, more water is reabsorbed, causing drier stools. Adding fiber and water to the diet allows for easier passage of stools. Physical activity also stimulates the movement of stool through the gastrointestinal tract.

A Matter of ETHICS

Sometimes potty training can be challenging for families. The expectations of parents might exceed the abilities of the child. What would you do if you believed a young child in your program was having problems with constipation because of potty training pressure from parents? What would you do if you witnessed a parent berating a child for soiling a diaper or for refusing to use the toilet when asked? What is your ethical responsibility to this child and what is the overriding principle in the NAEYC code of ethical conduct that should direct your decisions on managing this situation?

WHAT IF . . .

your class had an early lunch period right before recess and you observed on more than one occasion your third-grade students rushing through lunch and throwing away food so that they could get outside to play? How would you resolve the problem?

**CHECK YOUR
UNDERSTANDING 3.3**
Click here to check your understanding absorption and problems related to absorption in young children.

Teachers can help prevent constipation by providing children with:

- Opportunities to drink water with and between meals, especially on warm days.
  - Sufficient time for physical activity.
    - Nutritious foods rich in fiber, such as fruits and vegetables.
    - Easy access to toilet facilities.

Aiding Digestion and Absorption

To ensure that children receive the most nutrition from their foods, teachers must create an environment that enhances and supports the natural rhythms of eating. Children feel confident about eating when they know that meals will be presented within a reasonable time frame and include foods they enjoy. The stomach generally empties in two to four hours. Planning meals and snacks every three to four hours is appropriate for most children. In fact, the Child and Adult Care Food Program (CACFP) requires specific mealtime scheduling so that meals are not served too close together or too far apart.

The sight, aromas, and taste of food can be very important to children. These factors stimulate the production of saliva and gastric juices and can contribute to muscular activity of the gastrointestinal tract, inducing hunger pains. It is essential to provide appealing meals that stimulate the senses and whet the appetite to ensure adequate intake. For some low-income families, the meals provided at school are the best chance for their children to eat healthy, balanced meals. Making sure desirable, appetizing foods are served supports a healthy diet.

Emotional upset can interfere with digestion. This occurs because under stress, the body makes fewer digestive enzymes. In addition, the wavelike movements of the gastrointestinal tract that move food along are limited by stress. For these reasons, meals should be provided in a calm environment with limited distractions. To avoid stress and anger at mealtimes, plan enough time so that children can eat in a relaxing manner. In the elementary school setting, the timing of meals before outside breaks can result in a rush to finish eating. Planning sufficient time for meals as well as outdoor play provides the best balance for health and nutrition.

THE FUNCTION OF MACRONUTRIENTS: CARBOHYDRATES, PROTEINS, AND FATS

Through the process of digestion, food is converted into components that can be readily absorbed. The macronutrients (carbohydrates, proteins, and fats) are needed in large amounts because they supply energy. This energy is used for physical activity and the repair and replacement of cells as well as for growth and development in children. In this section, we discuss energy as well as the composition of food and macronutrients. This information will help you put into focus the rationale behind diet recommendations for young children.

Understanding Energy

Food provides energy for the body. Food energy is measured in the form of calories. A **calorie** represents the amount of energy released from food when it is metabolized by the body. Different macronutrients provide different amounts of calories. The calories per gram of protein, fats, and carbohydrates are as follows:

- Protein   4 calories
- Carbohydrates   4 calories
- Fats   9 calories

Children need energy to run and play as well as to maintain body functions such as breathing and pumping blood. The energy released from these nutrients when they are metabolized provides the fuel needed by the body.

calorie
a unit of measurement of the amount of energy that is released from food when it is metabolized by the body

Nutrient Composition of Foods

Food is a complex mixture of carbohydrates, proteins, fats, vitamins, and minerals. When children drink a glass of low-fat milk, they are consuming protein, fat, and carbohydrates. The meat in a roast beef sandwich contains protein and fats, whereas the whole-grain bread contains some protein but mostly carbohydrates, as illustrated in Figure 3-4. The mayonnaise on the sandwich is predominantly fat, whereas the lettuce and tomato have small amounts of carbohydrates. When children eat a piece of fruit, they are consuming carbohydrates.

Foods can be grouped together based on similar nutrient composition. The MyPlate system uses these food groups to explain healthy meal choices (U.S. Department of Agriculture, 2015). Understanding the composition of food can be helpful when working with children who require special diets. For example, when planning meals for children with diabetes, such as Jamal, teachers should understand the sources of carbohydrates in the diet. Eating an appropriate amount from each food group ensures that the body has sufficient energy, vitamins, and minerals to sustain life. Achieving the right balance between calories consumed and calories burned is one of the primary goals of healthy eating.

FIGURE 3-4
Macronutrients

Releasing or Storing Energy

The metabolism of nutrients is a balancing act in which energy is being released for immediate use or stored so that it is available at a later time. This releasing and storing occurs simultaneously from the moment of conception to the end of life. For example, when children play basketball, they use energy to contract their muscles, move their body, pump blood, breathe faster, and perspire to keep cool. When they stop for a snack of orange wedges, they use energy to digest and absorb the oranges. At the same time, energy is also being used to maintain and repair the body and build muscles as they exercise. Growth will continue to occur even while children play basketball, provided there is enough energy available in the diet. If children eat more oranges than they need immediately for fuel, energy will be stored in the liver, muscles, and fat cells for later use.

The releasing and storing of energy cannot be accomplished without the presence of vitamins, minerals, and water.

Milk, meat, and whole-wheat bread are a combination of macronutrients, whereas mayonnaise is mainly fat and fruits are mostly carbohydrates.

Determining Energy Needs

Children's energy (calorie) needs change as they grow and vary depending on how old they are, whether they are boys or girls, and what size they are. Calorie needs also vary according to children's level of activity. Physically active children have greater energy needs than do classmates who watch television or play video games. The amount of energy children need depends on many variables; however, a closer evaluation of energy needs by health care professionals may be needed when children are underweight or overweight.

Children have high calorie needs in relation to their size because of the energy requirements for growth. The Dietary Reference Intakes (DRIs) list the calorie requirements of children by age (see Web Resources) (Otten, Pitzi-Hellwig, & Meyers, 2006). Teachers who feed children must take into consideration their differing needs for calories and serve age-appropriate portion sizes. Providing healthful diets and an environment that supports physical activity ensures that the balance of using and storing energy is maintained and that proper growth and excess weight gain is avoided.

Carbohydrates

Carbohydrates provide the body's most abundant source of energy. They are found in grains, fruits, vegetables, milk products, and sweets. Cultures throughout the world rely on carbohydrates to provide their predominant source of nourishment. Each culture's carbohydrate choice is based on geography, terrain for farming, and cultural traditions. For example, rice is the staple crop in most Asian countries, whereas corn is the staple crop in many Latin American countries. Plant sources of carbohydrates are important because they provide an ongoing source of glucose. Glucose, a simple sugar, is the common fuel for all cells and the only source of energy for the brain. The different types of carbohydrates, which include simple sugars and complex carbohydrates, are illustrated in Figure 3-5.

Sugars

Six different sugars play a role in children's diets. They are divided into two groups based on whether they occur as a single sugar unit or are bonded together as two units.

monosaccharides
the simplest type of sugar consisting of single sugar units, including glucose, fructose, and galactose

Monosaccharides The simplest type of sugar consisting of single sugar units are **monosaccharides**. They include glucose, fructose, and galactose. Glucose and fructose occur naturally in foods such as fruits and honey. Galactose is a simple sugar made by animals and is found in the milk they produce. All sugars and starches must be broken down to monosaccharides via digestion to be absorbed and metabolized in human cells (Goodman, 2010; Sizer & Whitney, 2011).

disaccharides
sugars that contain two single sugar units that are bonded together. They include sucrose, lactose, and maltose

Disaccharides Two single sugar units, when bonded together, are called **disaccharides**. They include sucrose, lactose, and maltose. Table sugar is sucrose. It consists of fructose and glucose units that are bonded together. Lactose is milk sugar. It consists of galactose and glucose sugar units. Maltose consists of two glucose units.

Conflicting Role of Sugar in the Diets of Young Children Teachers and families often have very strong preferences about whether sugar should be included in the

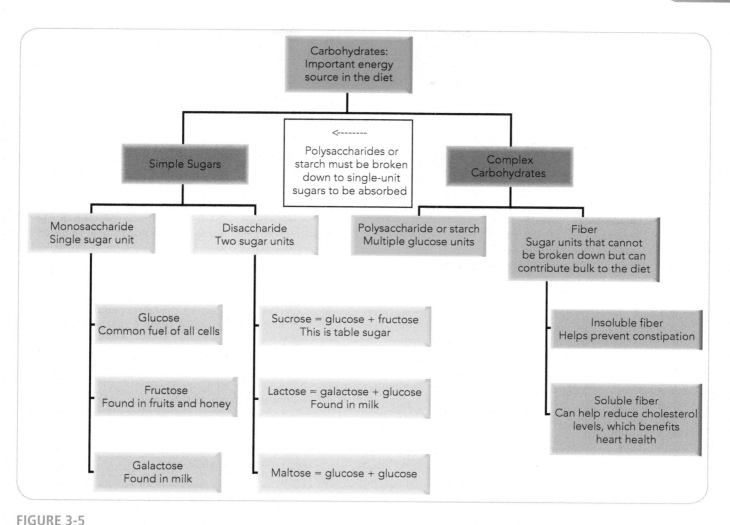

FIGURE 3-5
Types of Carbohydrates

diets of young children. Teachers must make judgments about how to manage these concerns, as described in the following scenario:

> *Hallie, a teacher in a kindergarten/first-grade blended class, has a parent who believes that graham crackers contain too much sugar and should not be offered as a snack in class. Another parent has complained because Hallie does not allow cupcakes to be served for celebrations such as birthdays. A third parent does not permit her child to eat canned fruit at snack time because it contains high-fructose corn syrup. Each parent has strong feelings about sugar. Hallie tries to accommodate their preferences while at the same time considering the school's policies.*

Opinions about sugar can be put into perspective by reviewing the recommendations of health authorities and federal guidelines. The Institute of Medicine's DRIs recommend that sugar not exceed 25% of total calories (Otten et al., 2006). Health concerns exist about the increased use of added sugars in the diets of young children as discussed in the *Health Hint* (American Academy of Nutrition and Dietetics, 2012b).

The body does not distinguish between a unit of glucose obtained by drinking a soda versus a unit of glucose obtained by

WHAT IF . . .
other teachers in your school offered candy as a reward to children who are staying on task? What type of nonfood methods might you suggest as an alternative to motivate students?

HEALTH HINT High-Fructose Corn Syrup: Are There Health Risks?

Does high-fructose corn syrup (HFCS) increase the risk of obesity and the chronic diseases associated with obesity because of the way it is metabolized? Does it cause heart disease, diabetes, and accumulation of damaging fat in the liver? Some studies suggest that this is the case, although research has had conflicting results. HFCS is used in food products such as soft drinks, canned fruits, and processed desserts because it remains stable in acidic foods and drinks, is less expensive than sugar, and comes from a reliable and plentiful U.S. crop: corn. This type of corn syrup was originally called HFCS to distinguish it from regular corn syrup, which is 100% glucose. However, it is similar in composition to sucrose (table sugar) and honey in that it contains about 42% to 55% fructose, whereas sugar contains 50% fructose and honey contains about 49%.

There are various hypotheses as to why HFCS may contribute to obesity. Originally correlations were made that linked the rise of obesity to a time frame that also saw an increased use of HFCS in foods and beverages. Although this may seem plausible, it doesn't necessarily show cause and effect. For example, added sugars from all sources, particularly when combined with solid fats, have been linked to obesity and other related health concerns. Another theory suggests that fructose may impact appetite regulation in a negative way. When glucose is absorbed, it triggers the release of the hormones insulin and leptin and suppresses the production of ghrelin—hormonal

responses that inhibit appetite. This does not occur when fructose is absorbed. There is speculation that this may lead to overeating. However, some confusion surrounds studies that focus on pure fructose versus HFCS. It is important to remember that because sugar has about the same amount of fructose as HFCS, cutting back on sugar naturally reduces fructose in the diet. The American Academy of Nutrition and Dietetics evaluated numerous studies related to high-fructose corn syrup and consistently found little evidence that high-fructose corn syrup differed from sugar in how it affects metabolism, hunger, satiety, and calorie intake (American Academy of Nutrition and Dietetics, 2012b).

Can evidence-based recommendations be made about high-fructose corn syrup? Not yet because research is still ongoing.

In the meantime, teachers can take a judicious approach to high-fructose corn syrup and all added sugars by:

- Not offering soft drinks to young children.
- Serving fresh fruit instead of canned fruit, especially fruits packed in heavy syrup.
- Avoiding excessive use of processed desserts, snack bars, and sweets.
- Encouraging a diet higher in fiber content, which is a natural way to decrease HFCS and other fructose-containing sugars in the diet and promote satiety.

Sources: American Academy of Nutrition and Dietetics. (2012). Position of the Academy of Nutrition and Dietetics: Use of nutritive and nonnutritive sweeteners, *Journal of the Academy of Nutrition and Dietetics, 112*(3), 739–757; International Food Information Council Foundation, 2011. *Questions and Answers about Fructose*, Food Insight; White, J. S. (2008). Straight talk about high-fructose corn syrup: What it is and what it ain't. *American Journal of Clinical Nutrition, 88*(6), pp. 1716S–1721S; Lustig, R. H. (2010). Fructose: Metabolic, hedonic, and societal parallels with ethanol. *Journal of the American Dietetic Association 110*(9), 1307–1321; Elliot, S., Keim, N., Stern, J., Teff, K., & Havel, P. (2002). Fructose, weight gain, and the insulin resistance syndrome. *American Journal of Clinical Nutrition, 76*, 911–922.

eating a slice of whole-grain bread when it comes to metabolizing that glucose for energy. However, teachers need to consider other concerns related to the inclusion of foods that contain sugar. For example, a soda is full of sugar and excess calories, whereas the slice of whole-grain bread is rich in fiber, vitamins, and minerals. Eating foods high in sugar content such as sugar-sweetened beverages, sweets, and sweetened grain products may displace needed nutrients in the diet of young children and therefore compromise diet quality (American Academy of Nutrition and Dietetics, 2008). For example, children who consume chocolate chip cookies during a midmorning cooking activity may not eat their lunch of turkey sandwiches with milk, apples, and carrot sticks. Consequently, they will get fewer of the recommended nutrients that are important for growth and development. Other concerns about food high in added sugars are that they are usually higher in energy density and lower in essential nutrients and dietary fiber (American Academy of Nutrition and Dietetics, 2012b). There is also strong evidence that drinking sugar-sweetened beverages contributes to overweight and obesity in children (U.S. Department of Agriculture, 2010). In addition, frequent exposure to sugary, sticky foods and sweetened beverages is linked to an increase in dental cavities (Roberts & Wright, 2012).

Sugar occurs naturally in foods such as fruit and milk. Sugar content of food can be identified using the nutrition facts label, which indicates the total grams of sugar in a product. However, because this includes naturally occurring sugar such as that contributed by fruit and milk, it is challenging to identify how much is added sugar. This requires looking at the list of ingredients for words that mean added sugar, such as:

- high-fructose corn syrup or corn sweeteners
- words that contain "ose": fructose, dextrose, glucose, maltose, sucrose
- brown sugar
- honey
- molasses
- evaporated cane juice
- fruit juice concentrate

It important to remember that ingredients are listed from highest to lowest concentration on the label. So a food item at the beginning of the list that has added sugars or lists several types of added sugar may contain more added sugar than is desirable.

Taken together, there is concern when children's diets exceed the recommended level for sugar intake. For this reason, schools are taking steps to reduce children's intake of high-calorie soft drinks at school, as discussed in the *Policy Point*.

POLICY POINT

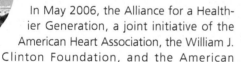

Reducing High-Calorie Soft Drink Consumption in Schools

In May 2006, the Alliance for a Healthier Generation, a joint initiative of the American Heart Association, the William J. Clinton Foundation, and the American Beverage Association, announced new school beverage guidelines that voluntarily remove high-calorie soft drinks from all U.S. schools starting in the 2009–2010 school year.

Although guidelines for preschool programs are not available, the recommendations for children in primary school allow the following:

- Bottled water.
- Up to 8 ounces of milk or juice.
- Regular or flavored milk or a USDA acceptable soy milk alternative that is fat-free or low-fat and provides up to 150 calories per serving.
- 100% juice that provides up to 120 calories per 8-ounce serving and 10% of the daily value for three vitamins and/or minerals.

These guidelines have become the standard of practice for the soft drink beverage industry and will be used as a basis for establishing contract arrangements with elementary, middle, and high school programs. They are applicable to the school setting, including before- and after-school programs and include all beverages sold outside the context of school breakfast and school lunch programs (vending machines, snack carts, à la carte menu items).

These guidelines do not cover sporting events, school plays, and so on, where parents are present or are selling soft drinks as boosters. They do not supersede state legislation, school district policies, or local initiatives, which may be more restrictive. For example, schools may choose not to allow sugar-sweetened soft drinks at school plays or other after-school events that include parents.

This initiative has been a step in the right direction in that it shows that both schools and industry are making a concerted effort to reduce the intake of calorie-rich, nutrient-poor beverages. Has the initiative been effective? The American Beverage Association states that these guidelines, including those established for middle schools and high schools, have resulted in an 88% reduction in beverage calories shipped to schools since 2004. These guidelines, as well as school wellness policies, appear to be having an impact.

Sources: American Beverage Association & the Alliance for a Healthier Generation. (2009). *School Beverage Guidelines*. Retrieved May 6, 2012, from http://www.ameribev .org/nutrition-science/school-beverage-guidelines/the-guidelines/; American Beverage Association. (2011). News Releases: School Beverage Guidelines. Retrieved May 6, 2012, from http://www.ameribev.org/nutrition-science/school-beverage-guidelines/news-releases/; Terry-McElrath, Y. M., O'Malley, P. M., & Johnston, L. D. (2012). Factors affecting sugar-sweetened beverage availability in competitive venues of US secondary schools. *Journal of School Health, 84*(1), 44–55.

The complex carbohydrates found in dietary sources include starch and fiber.

The goal is for children to consume sugar in moderation and within the context of an otherwise healthful diet. Teachers set the tone in the classroom for healthful eating by raising the level of awareness among parents as well as children. For this reason, many children's settings limit foods that are perceived as "sweets." Healthful food choices can include foods that are sweet tasting. However, teachers should select foods with nutritionally redeeming qualities such as sweet potato or carrot muffins; zucchini bread made with whole grains; oatmeal raisin cookies; and plain low-fat yogurt served with ripe strawberries, raspberries, or blackberries. Overall, the goal for children and their families is to learn a mindful and moderate approach to eating.

Complex Carbohydrates

Complex carbohydrates are the second category of carbohydrates. They include two different types: starch and dietary fiber. The *starches*, also called **polysaccharides**, consist of multiple glucose sugars linked together in chains. Breaking down starches into simple sugars (glucose) through the digestive process makes them available for absorption in the small intestine.

polysaccharides
complex carbohydrates that consist of multiple glucose sugars linked together in chains. Also called starch

Fiber is a type of carbohydrate that cannot be used as energy because humans lack the digestive enzymes to break it down. However, dietary fiber does provide significant health benefits. The recognized health benefits depend on the type of fiber being consumed: insoluble or soluble (American Academy of Nutrition and Dietetics, 2012a).

Insoluble Fiber A type of fiber that comes from the structural components of plant cell walls and does not dissolve in water is referred to as **insoluble fiber**. Wheat bran, rice bran, whole-wheat breads, crackers, cereals, and the seeds in berry fruits are examples of this insoluble fiber. Eating foods with insoluble fiber aids digestion. Insoluble fiber acts like a sponge to draw water into the stool. Softer, bulkier stools move through the gastrointestinal tract more quickly, which helps children maintain regular bowel habits and avoid constipation.

insoluble fiber
a type of dietary fiber that does not dissolve in water. It comes from the structural components of plant cell walls and is found in wheat bran, rice bran, whole-wheat breads, crackers, cereals, and the seeds in berry fruits. This type of fiber prevents constipation

soluble fiber
a type of dietary fiber that readily mixes with water to form gels. It gives foods a thickened consistency and is found in oatmeal, oat bran, and beans. It can bind with cholesterol, thus inhibiting cholesterol absorption, which can protect against heart disease

Soluble Fiber A fiber that readily mixes with water, forming gels and giving foods a thickened consistency, is called **soluble fiber**. Oatmeal, oat bran, and beans are examples of soluble fiber sources (American Academy of Nutrition and Dietetics, 2012a). Soluble fiber offers significant health benefits. It also delays stomach emptying, making children feel full longer, and may aid in weight control.

Whole grains are a type of carbohydrate in which all parts of the grain, including the germ, endosperm, and bran, are consumed. For example, oatmeal, brown rice, and whole wheat are examples of whole grains. Whole grains are healthy for children because they are rich in fiber, vitamins, and minerals and contain naturally occurring phytonutrients that reduce the risk for cancer, diabetes, and heart disease and promote healthy weight management and gastrointestinal health (Jonnalagadda et al., 2011).

Adding more fiber to early child care program menus can be easily accomplished with a few simple adjustments in food selection that focus on whole grains and more fresh fruits and vegetables, while also including children in taste-testing the new menu items. Figure 3-6 shows examples of both a high-fiber and low-fiber breakfast.

Breakfast A	Fiber (grams)		Breakfast B	Fiber (grams)
½ cup Raisin bran	5.5		½ cup Puffed rice	0.2
1 cup milk, skim	0		1 cup milk, skim	0
Whole-grain bread	2.2		White bread	0.6
1 Tbsp peanut butter	1		1 Tbsp cream cheese	0
1 cup strawberries	3.3		1 cup orange juice	1.0
Total	**12 grams**			**1.8 grams**

FIGURE 3-6 A High-Fiber and Low-Fiber Breakfast

Source: U.S. Department of Agriculture (updated 2011). National Nutrient Data Base for Standard Reference. Retrieved May 6, 2012, from http://ndb.nal.usda.gov/.

Proteins

Proteins are the basis of life in humans. Without proteins, the body cannot grow, reproduce, or repair itself. Proteins are organic compounds that contain carbon, hydrogen, oxygen, and nitrogen. Proteins are essential in all life processes and are particularly important to young children because they are growing.

Defining the Function of Proteins

Proteins have three primary roles: growth and repair of the body, regulation of the processes within the body, and energy:

1. *Proteins are necessary for growth and repair.* Proteins form structures in the body such as skin, bones, organs, and muscles. Insufficient protein during growth can impede brain development and function (Otten et al., 2006). Proteins consumed in the diet are digested into amino acids, which when absorbed are used to make body protein that needs to be replaced.

2. Proteins control body functions. This is managed through a system of regulatory processes. Enzymes, hormones, antibodies, and red blood cells are just a sampling of the protein-based components that help the body maintain vital functions. When children fight off a cold, antibodies (a type of protein found in the blood that fights infections) come to their rescue. When they eat lunch, protein-based enzymes break down the food for digestion and absorption. The multitude of uses for protein in the body explains why it is so important for children to have sufficient amounts in their diet.

3. Proteins can be used for energy if necessary. Protein, however, is a fuel of last resort because of its importance in other body functions such as growth and development. Too much protein in the diets of children is not stored as protein, but instead is converted into body fat.

WHAT IF . . .

a parent believed that his overweight child needed to follow a low-carbohydrate diet? What are the disadvantages of such a diet for young children? How would you handle this diet request?

Eggs, lean meat, poultry, and beans are excellent sources of protein in the diet.

Tetra Images/Getty Images

Understanding Amino

amino acids
biological compounds that act as the building blocks for all proteins

Amino Acids acids are the biological compounds that act as building blocks for all proteins. Twenty different amino acids combine in innumerable ways to build the vast array of proteins found in humans. The process for converting dietary protein into human protein is as follows:

1. Plant or animal protein is consumed.
2. Protein is broken down into amino acids in the small intestine.
3. Amino acids are absorbed and recombined in different sequences according to the type of human protein needed (such as skin cells, hormones, muscle).

Essential, Nonessential, and Conditionally Essential Amino Acids How well children are able to build proteins for their body depends on whether the right amount and type of amino acids are available. Amino acids can be categorized based on the need to have them provided in the diet:

- Essential amino acids: the nine amino acids the body cannot make. It is "essential" that these amino acids be provided by the diet.
- Nonessential amino acids: the five amino acids the body can readily make.
- Conditionally essential amino acids: amino acids the body is sometimes able to make, but sometimes must be provided by the diet in times of illness or stress (Otten et al., 2006; U.S. National Library of Medicine National Institutes of Health, 2013).

complementary protein
proteins that are low in different amino acids but can be combined to provide enough total essential amino acids to form all the amino acids necessary to build human protein

The Quality of Protein All the essential amino acids must be available in the diet to make the body's protein. If a particular essential amino acid is low in the diet, the body will make protein only until it runs out of this amino acid in spite of the fact that other amino acids are readily available. Similar to missing a link in a chain, if one link is missing, the chain cannot be put together.

When a food is low in a particular amino acid, that amino acid is called the limiting amino acid. The presence or absence of a limiting amino acid determines the quality of the protein:

- *High-quality protein:* Protein that comes from animal sources has all the essential amino acids or links needed to make human protein chains. These are called high-quality proteins and include milk, eggs, cheese, meats, fish, and poultry. All protein from animal sources is high-quality except gelatin. Soy protein is also a source of high quality protein.
- *Lower-quality protein:* Some foods provide lower-quality proteins because they do not contain much protein or have a limiting amino acid. For example, fruits and many vegetables are generally not good sources of protein. Other foods of plant origin can add significant amounts of protein to the diet but are limiting in an amino acid. For instance, grains are low in some amino acids and legumes are low in others. However, if they are combined over the course of the day, enough essential amino acids are available to make the necessary links to form the proteins needed by the body (Sizer & Whitney, 2011). These foods are said to contain **complementary protein** because, in combination, they provide all the amino acids necessary to build human protein.

Thinkstock/Getty Images

Some of children's favorite foods consist of complementary proteins.

Traditionally, people from all cultures have learned to match foods that provide complementary proteins. Examples include:

- Red beans and rice.
- Peanut butter and whole-grain bread.
- Bean burritos.
- Falafel (made from chick peas) and whole-wheat pita.
- Hummus (chick peas and ground sesame seeds) and whole-wheat crackers.
- Tofu or other soy products and rice.

Supplementing a lower-quality protein (one with a limiting amino acid) with small amounts of high-quality animal protein will result in a complete protein combination that provides all the essential amino acids, such as adding cheese to a beans dish.

Defining Protein Requirements

The Dietary Reference Intakes for protein requirements change as children grow. For example, children's protein needs are 13 grams per day for 1- to 3-year-olds and 19 grams for 4- to 8-year-olds (Otten et al., 2006). To put this into perspective, 1 cup of milk has about 8 grams of protein on average, a 1-ounce serving of meat/poultry provides 7 grams of protein, and a slice of bread from the grain group provides about 3 grams of protein. Totaled together, 18 grams is enough to meet just about all the protein needs of young children. The typical U.S. diet provides ample protein. The Child and Adult Care Food Program (CACFP) requires 1.5 ounces of protein to be served for lunch for 3- to 5-year-olds. This represents about 10 grams of protein. To get a sense of what this portion represents, visualize half of a deck of cards. Although this may seem like a small portion, for a child, it provides more than enough protein.

Fats

Fats are the most concentrated source of calories in the diet. Although too much fat is not beneficial because of its link to obesity, there is a role for healthful fats in children's diets. Fats provide **essential fatty acids** (linoleic acid and alpha-linolenic acid) that cannot be made by the body and must be obtained from the diet. Essential fatty acids are needed for normal growth and development (Simopoulos, 2011). They also help control inflammation and blood clotting and are important in promoting good vision and maintaining a healthy immune system (Birch et al., 2010; Linus Pauling Institute at Oregon State University, 2014; U.S. National Library of Medicine & National Institutes of Health, 2015). Lack of essential fatty acids in infants may impact brain development and can result in learning problems (U.S. National Library of Medicine & National Institutes of Health, 2015). Fats help with the absorption of the fat-soluble vitamins A, D, E, and K and provide a concentrated source of energy to support growth in infants and young children (Otten et al., 2006). Fats also add flavor and satiety to foods.

Types of Dietary Fat

Dietary fats are often referred to as "good" fats and "bad" fats. Good fats reduce the risk of heart disease and are called unsaturated fats. They include **polyunsaturated fats** and **monounsaturated fats**, and both reduce the risk for heart disease by

essential fatty acids
a type of fatty acid that cannot be made by the body and must be obtained from the diet; needed for growth and for maintaining a healthy immune system

polyunsaturated fats
unsaturated fats with two or more double bonds in their chemical structure that come predominantly from plant sources (such as corn oil and safflower oil) are liquid at room temperature and reduce the risk of heart disease

monounsaturated fats
unsaturated fats with one double bond in their chemical structure (such as olive oil and canola oil) that also come from plant sources are liquid at room temperature and reduce the risk of heart disease

omega-3 fatty acids
polyunsaturated fats that are found in fish and plant oils such as canola and flaxseed oil; protect against heart disease

saturated fats
fats found predominantly in animal sources that are solid at room temperature and detrimental to heart health

trans fatty acids
fats formed during the process of hydrogenation, when liquid oils are made solid, and are especially harmful to heart health

dietary cholesterol
a fatlike, waxy substance that is found in foods of animal origin and plays a role in the risk for heart disease when consumed in excess

lowering blood cholesterol levels and decreasing inflammation (Weber & Noels, 2011). The polyunsaturated fats include two types: omega-6 fatty acids and omega-3 fatty acids. Corn oil, safflower oil, and seeds are rich in omega-6 fatty acids, whereas fattier fish such as salmon, tuna, mackerel, and sardines as well as plant oils such as canola, soybean, and flaxseed oils are rich in omega-3 fatty acids (American Academy of Nutrition and Dietetics, 2012a).

The "bad" dietary fats are increase the risk of heart disease. They include the saturated fats and trans fatty acids. Saturated fats come predominantly from animal sources, but also include coconut oil, palm oil, and palm kernel oil. Trans fatty acids are formed during food processing when liquid oils are made solid through the process of hydrogenation. Although both types of fat increase the risk of heart disease, trans fatty acids are especially harmful (American Heart Association, 2014a). Dietary cholesterol is a fatlike substance that is found in foods of animal origin. Cholesterol is also made in the body. Increased levels of cholesterol in the bloodstream are associated with the risk for heart disease. Although eating a diet high in cholesterol-containing foods is linked to elevated blood cholesterol levels, the impact is not as significant as that caused by trans fats and saturated fats. Table 3-4 lists types of dietary fats and dietary cholesterol, fats, their dietary sources, and their impact on the risk for heart disease.

Dietary Fats and Health

The health impact of dietary fats is linked to how cholesterol and fats are transported in the blood. Just as oil and vinegar don't mix, neither do fats, cholesterol, and blood. To transport fat and cholesterol to where they are needed in the body, the liver packages them in a lipoprotein "coating." One of the lipoproteins that transports cholesterol in the blood is low-density lipoprotein (LDL), also commonly called LDL cholesterol or "bad" cholesterol. Elevated LDL cholesterol levels in the bloodstream are a marker for heart disease. LDL deposits cholesterol within the artery walls, which accumulates, causing the formation of a plaque. These deposits are made of cholesterol and other fatty compounds that clog the

low-density lipoprotein (LDL)
a class of lipoprotein that transports cholesterol in the bloodstream; when elevated, it can increase the risk of heart disease

TABLE 3-4   Types and Sources of Dietary Fats and Dietary Cholesterol

Types of Fat or Cholesterol	Example of Dietary Sources	How They May Impact Risk for Heart Disease
Polyunsaturated fats	Corn oil, safflower oil, sunflower oil, soybean oil	Reduce
Omega-3 fatty acids	Flax oil, canola oil, soybean oil, fatty types of fish	Reduce
Omega-6 fatty acids	Fattier fish such as salmon, tuna, mackerel, herring, trout, and sardines and canola oil, flaxseed and flaxseed oil, walnuts and walnut oil, corn, safflower, sunflower, and soybean oils	Reduce
Monounsaturated fats	Olives, avocados, olive oil, canola oil, peanut oil, nuts and seeds	Reduce
Saturated fats	Cheese, meats, poultry, cream, butter, ice cream, palm oil, palm kernel oil	Increase
Trans fats	Stick margarine, vegetable shortening, some commercial baked goods such as pastries and doughnuts, commercially fried foods such as French fries	Increase
Dietary cholesterol	Cheese, meats, poultry, milk, butter, eggs, liver	Increase

Sources: Harris, W. S., Mozaffarian, D., Rimm, E., et al. Omega-6 fatty acids and risk for cardiovascular disease: A science advisory from the American Heart Association Nutrition Subcommittee of the Council on Nutrition, Physical Activity, and Metabolism; Council on Cardiovascular Nursing; and Council on Epidemiology and Prevention. *Circulation*, 2009 (updated 2011), retrieved from http://my.americanheart.org/professional/General/Omega-6-Fatty-Acids-in-the-Hierarchy-of-Cardiovascular-Protection_UCM_433122_Article.jsp. Harvard School of Public Health, 2012. The Nutrition Source Fats and Cholesterol: Out with the Bad, In with the Good, retrieved from http://www.hsph.harvard.edu/nutritionsource/what-should-you-eat/fats-and-cholesterol/. Mayo Clinic, 2011. Dietary fats: Know which types to choose, retrieved from http://www.mayoclinic.com/health/fat/NU00262. *Dietary Reference Intakes: The Essential Guide to Nutrient Requirements*, 2006, by the National Academy of Sciences, courtesy of the National Academies Press, Washington, DC.

arteries in a process called atherosclerosis, which can increase the risk for a heart attack (Harvard School of Public Health, 2015). In addition, atherosclerosis can trigger inflammation, which may further contribute to heart disease (Ridker, 2012).

Another common lipoprotein is high-density lipoprotein (HDL). This is called the "good cholesterol" because the higher the levels, the lower the risk for heart disease. HDL picks up excess cholesterol in the circulatory system and brings it back to the liver, where it can be excreted.

The key to a heart-healthy lifestyle is to:

- Substitute healthy dietary fats (polyunsaturated and monounsaturated) for unhealthy fats (trans fat and saturated fats).
- Limit the amount of cholesterol consumed.
- Maintain a healthy weight.
- Exercise regularly.

high-density lipoprotein (HDL) a class of lipoprotein that transports excess cholesterol from the bloodstream back to the liver, where it is excreted; associated with lower risk for heart disease

---

NUTRITION NOTE   The Role of Trans Fats and Saturated Fats in Children's Diets

As of January 1, 2006, the U.S. Food and Drug Administration requires that trans fats be listed on food labels. Why might this create problems in children's diets? With the initiation of this labeling law, food companies have had to find replacements for trans fats. There has been concern that trans fat might be replaced with saturated fats, which, like trans fats, stimulate the production of LDL (bad cholesterol). A recent study compared the composition of 5,000 U.S. cookie and cracker products before and after the trans fat law was implemented. The use of partially hydrogenated vegetable oil (a source of trans fats) in chip products did decrease without a corresponding increase in saturated fat content. However, that was not the case with cookie products, where sometimes trans fats were replaced with saturated fats such as palm oil and palm kernel oil. Although many food manufacturers have made favorable changes in the types of fats used in commercially prepared food items, it is still important that teachers look for both trans fat and saturated fat content when checking the labels. Review the food label shown here to compare the fat composition of various types of desserts.

Compare Desserts! *
Keep an eye on Saturated Fat, Trans Fat, and Cholesterol!

Granola Bar ±	Sandwich Cookies ±	Cake, Iced and Filled ±
Nutrition Facts	**Nutrition Facts**	**Nutrition Facts**
Serving Size 1 bar (33g)	Serving Size 2 cookies (28g)	Serving Size 2 cakes (66g)
Servings Per Container 10	Servings Per Container 19	Servings Per Container 6
Amount Per Serving	Amount Per Serving	Amount Per Serving
Calories 140 Calories from Fat 45	**Calories** 130 Calories from Fat 45	**Calories** 280 Calories from Fat 140
% Daily Value*	% Daily Value*	% Daily Value*
Total Fat 5g 8%	**Total Fat** 5g 8%	**Total Fat** 16g 25%
Saturated Fat 1g ⇐ 5%	Saturated Fat 1g ⇐ 5%	Saturated Fat 3.5g ⇐ 18%
Trans Fat 0g ⇐	Trans Fat 1.5g ⇐	Trans Fat 4.5g ⇐
Cholesterol 0mg ⇒ 0%	**Cholesterol** 0mg ⇒ 0%	**Cholesterol** 10mg ⇒ 3%
Saturated Fat : 1g	Saturated Fat : 1g	Saturated Fat : 3.5g
+ *Trans* Fat : 0g	+ *Trans* Fat : 1.5g	+ *Trans* Fat : 4.5g
Combined Amt.: 1g	Combined Amt.: 2.5g	Combined Amt.: 8g
Cholesterol: 0% DV	Cholesterol: 0% DV	Cholesterol: 3% DV

*Nutrient values rounded based on FDA's nutrition labeling regulations.
± Values for total fat, saturated fat, and trans fat were based on the means of analytical data for several food samples from Subramaniam, S., et al., "Trans, Saturated, and Unsaturated Fat in Foods in the United States Prior to Mandatory Trans-Fat Labeling," *Lipids* 39, 11–18, 2004. Other information and values were derived from food labels in the marketplace.

Sources: Van Camp, D., Hooker, N. H., & Lin, C. J. (2012). *Changes in Fat Contents of US Snack Foods in Response to Mandatory* Trans *Fat Labeling.* Public Health Nutrition, 15, 1130–1137. doi: 10.1017/S1368980012000079; *Trans Fat Now Listed with Saturated Fat and Cholesterol on the Nutrition Facts Label*, by the U.S. Food and Drug Administration, updated 2011, retrieved May 16, 2012, from http://www.fda.gov/food/ingredientspackaginglabeling/labelingnutrition/ucm274590.htm; Mozaffarian, D., & Jacobsen, M. F. (2010). *Correspondence: Food Reformulations to Reduce Trans Fatty Acids. New England Journal of Medicine*, 362, 2037–2039.

Teachers should understand that the biggest influence on blood cholesterol levels is the mix of fats in the diet—more so than the amount of cholesterol found in foods. The *Nutrition Note* takes a look at the role of saturated and trans fats in children's diets.

Implications of Dietary Fats in Children's Diets

Thinking about heart disease in infants and young children may seem premature. However, as teachers plan what they should feed young children, they must consider the foods that will foster children's healthful growth and development. They also need to consider the importance of nutrition as it relates to disease prevention. It has been estimated that as many as 50% of primary school–age children have one or more risk factors for heart disease (Reed, Warburton, & McKay, 2007). Furthermore, children may inherit a genetic predisposition to elevated blood cholesterol levels.

The type of fat consumed in the diet plays an important role in supporting the health of all children. Consequently, as teachers plan meals and cooking activities, they should focus on the use of healthy fats. For example, when making biscuits with children, teachers should select a recipe that uses vegetable oil instead of shortening and when using margarine, they should select a brand that does not have trans fatty acids.

Remember, however, that during infancy and the toddler years, restricting fat and cholesterol is not advised by health care professionals because of the calories these children need for growth. The position of the American Academy of Pediatrics and Institute of Medicine of the National Academies is that young children should make a gradual transition from receiving 50% of their calorie needs from fat during infancy to 30% to 35% during the ages of 2 to 3 (American Academy of Pediatrics, Hassink, S., 2014; Otten et al., 2006). By the time children are ages 4 and older, a diet more closely aligned with the adult requirements of 25% to 35% is recommended (American Heart Association, 2014b).

Summary of the Role of Macronutrients

The goal of a healthful diet is to achieve a beneficial balance of macronutrients. Foods are a combination of proteins, fats, and carbohydrates. When children eat foods in a manner that supports MyPlate recommendations, they are ensured balanced diets that contain an appropriate percentage of calories from carbohydrates, fats, and proteins. The diet will have sufficient protein for the growth and repair of the body. It will have enough fat to meet calorie needs, but not too much, thereby decreasing the risk of heart disease and obesity. It will have ample carbohydrates to meet energy needs and provide sufficient fiber for good health.

Now that you have learned about macronutrients, let's turn to a discussion of micronutrients.

CHECK YOUR UNDERSTANDING 3.4

Click here to check your understanding of macronutrients and their role in children's nutrition.

THE FUNCTION OF MICRONUTRIENTS: VITAMINS AND MINERALS

Vitamins and minerals are components in food that are required in small amounts to sustain body processes. They are referred to as *micronutrients*. Vitamins and minerals are needed to release and utilize the energy found in protein, fats, and carbohydrates. They help transport oxygen, fight infections, build body structures such as bones and teeth, and keep the body working efficiently and in good repair.

Vitamins and minerals may also play an important role in preventing chronic diseases such as high blood pressure, heart disease, stroke, and cancer (Drake, 2011; U.S. Department of Health and Human Services & U.S. Department of Agriculture, 2015). The goal of all nutrient guidance systems is to encourage the intake of a varied and balanced diet, thereby ensuring that children consume the micronutrients needed to sustain health.

Vitamins

The body requires 13 essential vitamins, as listed in Table 3-5. Vitamins are organic compounds found predominantly in the foods we eat. The exceptions are vitamin D, which can be made by the body when the skin is exposed to sunlight, and vitamin K, which is produced by microorganisms in the gastrointestinal tract (Sizer & Whitney, 2011). Vitamins are essential. Without them, we cannot process and use energy from the proteins, fats, and carbohydrates we consume. Vitamins can be categorized into two groups: water-soluble and fat-soluble.

Water-Soluble Vitamins

The water-soluble vitamins include all the B vitamins and vitamin C. These vitamins dissolve in water and are absorbed directly into the bloodstream. Unlike fat-soluble vitamins, water-soluble vitamins cannot be stored in any significant amount in the body. Therefore, the B vitamins and vitamin C should be consumed on a daily basis. Because excess water-soluble vitamins are excreted in urine, the risk for toxicity from overconsumption is low.

water-soluble vitamins vitamins that dissolve in water and are therefore not stored in the body (B vitamins and vitamin C)

Water-soluble vitamins often act as coenzymes, or partners that help enzymes, to regulate all types of body processes, including those that produce energy (Anderson & Young, 2012). For example, the B vitamins act as coenzymes in the metabolism of proteins, fats, and carbohydrates.

coenzymes compounds that help enzymes in their activities and are used in processes that release energy

Fat-Soluble Vitamins

The fat-soluble vitamins include vitamins A, D, E, and K. These vitamins dissolve in fat and are stored in the body until needed. This means that they do not need to be consumed every day. The absorption of fat-soluble vitamins is enhanced by fat in the diet. For example, vitamin A in a fresh spinach salad is absorbed better when the salad is eaten with an oil-based salad dressing.

fat-soluble vitamins vitamins that dissolve in fat and are therefore stored in the body (vitamins A, D, K, and E)

Because fat-soluble vitamins are stored, children are less likely to develop a deficiency of these vitamins. However, they are at more risk for toxicity if overconsumption occurs.

Minerals

Minerals are substances that originate from the earth. Minerals come from plants and animal foods and from water. The minerals in the ground are absorbed by plants and become part of the food chain. Like vitamins, minerals initiate and regulate processes within the body. They are essential for growth because they are part of body structures such as bones and teeth.

Minerals are divided into two groups, the macrominerals and the microminerals, based on how much is required in the diet:

- **Macrominerals:** calcium, phosphorus, magnesium, sodium, chloride, sulfate, and potassium. The requirement for macrominerals is 100 mg/day or more.

macrominerals minerals needed in larger amounts (100 mg/day or more)

TABLE 3-5   Vitamins

	Functions	Good Food Sources*	Symptoms of Excess Intake	Symptoms of Deficiency
WATER SOLUBLE				
Thiamin (B_1)	Helps metabolize carbohydrates and some amino acids for energy. Is necessary for the normal functioning of the heart and nervous system.	Enriched, fortified, or whole-grain products such as breads and cereals, wheat germ, pork, ham, liver, legumes, and nuts and fortified meat substitutes.	None reported.	Symptoms include appetite loss, weight loss, mental changes, muscle weakness, heart failure, and nerve problems. Leads to beriberi.
Riboflavin (B_2)	Helps metabolize protein, fat, and carbohydrates for energy and is needed for growth and red blood cell production.	Animal protein such as meat, liver, eggs, and milk products; enriched bread and fortified cereals; and green leafy vegetables.	None reported.	Sore throat, mouth, and tongue with cracks at the corners of mouth.
Niacin (B_3)	Helps metabolize carbohydrates, protein, and fat for energy. Is beneficial for the digestive system and skin.	Animal protein such as meat, liver, poultry, fish, milk products, and eggs; enriched, fortified, or whole-grain products such as breads and cereals; and legumes.	None reported from dietary sources. Niacin used as a medication to improve blood fat levels can cause flushing and liver injury.	Leads to pellagra: symptoms include rash, vomiting, diarrhea, bright red tongue, depression, apathy, and memory loss.
Pyridoxine (B_6)	Helps metabolize proteins and maintains blood sugar levels by releasing glucose from stored glycogen, helps make the hemoglobin found in red blood cells.	Meat, fish, poultry, starchy vegetables, bananas, livers, fortified soy-based meat substitutes, and cereals.	Neurologic disorders and numbness.	Convulsions, loss of weight, depression, confusion, skin problems, and microcytic anemia.
Pantothenic acid	Helps metabolize proteins, fats, and carbohydrates for energy and synthesize fatty acids.	Poultry, meat, fish, eggs, broccoli, milk and yogurt, potatoes, whole grains, and legumes.	None reported.	Deficiency is rare.
Biotin	Helps metabolize proteins, fats, and carbohydrates for energy.	Widely available in foods, especially liver, egg yolk, milk, avocado, yeast, and meat.	None reported.	Deficiency is rare but can be associated with eating a large amount of raw egg whites (egg whites have avidin, which binds with biotin). Skin conditions, loss of appetite, depression, and hair loss.
Folate or folic acid	Involved in protein metabolism, red blood cell formation, and DNA and new cell synthesis.	Liver, leafy green vegetables, beans, legumes, seeds, fortified breads and cereals, and citrus fruits and juice.	Excess masks vitamin B12 deficiency, which can cause neurologic damage.	Macrocytic anemia, poor growth, and swollen tongue. Women who are deficient have increased risk of giving birth to infants with neural tube defects.
Vitamin B_{12}	Involved in the metabolism of fatty acids and amino acids. Helps form red blood cells and maintains the central nervous system.	Found in animal foods, meat, fish, poultry, cheese, milk, eggs, and fortified soy products.	None reported.	Leads to anemia and neurologic problems, depression, confusion, and dementia.
Vitamin C	Involved in collagen formation. Improves wound healing, resistance to infection, and iron absorption.	Fruits and vegetables: especially citrus fruits, tomatoes, potatoes, kiwi fruit, peppers, broccoli, and strawberries.	Increased incidence of kidney stones, gastrointestinal distress.	Leads to scurvy: symptoms include bleeding gums, decreased wound healing, easy bruising, and swollen and painful joints.

(Continued)

TABLE 3.5 Vitamins (*Continued*)

	Functions	Good Food Sources*	Symptoms of Excess Intake	Symptoms of Deficiency
FAT SOLUBLE				
Vitamin A	Important for normal vision, growth, immune function, formation of skin and mucous membranes, gene expression and reproduction, and bone growth.	There are two types: *Preformed:* liver, dairy products, fish, and fortified margarine. *Carotenoids:* orange fruits and vegetables (carrots, sweet potatoes, cantaloupe) and dark green vegetables.	Toxicity only from preformed vitamin A: nausea, vomiting, headache, dizziness, blurred vision, and lack of muscular coordination; excessive intake during pregnancy leads to birth defects.	Night blindness, blindness, poor growth, and impaired resistance to infection.
Vitamin D	Aids in the absorption and raises the levels of calcium and phosphorus in the blood, which promotes bone maintenance and formation.	Can be made in the skin in the presence of sunlight. *Food sources:* fatty fish, fortified milk, orange juice and cereals, and infant formula. Breast milk is not a rich source; therefore, supplementation is recommended in exclusively breast-fed infants.	High blood levels of calcium, calcification of soft tissues such as kidneys, blood vessels, nausea, vomiting, and poor appetite.	Leads to faulty bone growth and rickets in children and under-mineralized bones in adults.
Vitamin E	Acts as an antioxidant protecting cell membranes and is involved in immune function.	Vegetable oils, whole grains, wheat germ, fortified cereals, nuts, green leafy vegetables, meats, poultry, fish, and eggs.	None reported with naturally occurring vitamin E; excessive supplementation can lead to impaired blood clotting.	Very rare but can lead to nerve and muscle damage, vision problems, and weakened immune system and in premature infants hemolytic anemia.
Vitamin K	Involved in blood clotting and bone metabolism.	Produced by gastrointestinal tract bacteria. Dark green leafy vegetables, broccoli, vegetable oils, and margarine.	None reported.	Rare, but when it does occur, it can lead to impaired blood clotting. Vitamin K does not cross the placenta effectively; therefore, infants are provided vitamin K supplementation at birth.

*Breast milk and formula are good sources of vitamins unless indicated otherwise.

Sources: *Dietary Reference Intakes: The Essential Guide to Nutrient Requirements*, edited by J. J. Otten, J. Pitzi-Hellwig, and L. D. Meyers, 2006, Washington, DC: National Academies Press; *An Evidence-Based Approach to Vitamins and Minerals-Health Benefits and Intake Recommendations*, 2nd edition, by J. Higdon and V. J. Drake, 2012, New York: Thieme Publishing Group; Medline Plus: Vitamins, *U.S. National Library of Medicine National Institutes of Health*, 2012. Retrieved from http://www.nlm.nih.gov/medlineplus/ency/article/002399.htm; Vitamin and Mineral Fact Sheets, 2011, Office of Dietary Supplements, National Institutes of Health. Retrieved from http://ods.od.nih.gov/factsheets/list-VitaminsMinerals/; *Manual of Pediatric Nutrition*, 4th edition, edited by K. M. Hendricks and C. Duggan, 2005, Hamilton, Ontario: B. C. Decker, Inc.; and *Pediatric Nutrition Handbook*, 6th edition, edited by R. Kleinman, 2009, Elk Grove, IL: American Academy of Pediatrics.

- **Microminerals:** iron, zinc, iodine, fluoride, selenium, manganese, copper, chromium, molybdenum, and cobalt. The requirement for microminerals is 15 mg/ day or less (Mahan, Escott-Stump, & Raymond, 2012).

Table 3-6 illustrates the role of selected macrominerals and microminerals and describes the symptoms that children might exhibit if their bodies do not have enough or receive too much of these important nutrients.

A subcategory of the macrominerals includes the **electrolytes**. Electrolytes such as chloride, potassium, and sodium play an important role in helping to regulate fluids in and out of the body's cells. These minerals also help transmit nerve impulses by sending messages to the brain for muscles to contract and relax. During gastrointestinal upset, diarrhea and vomiting can cause a loss of electrolytes and water. This can quickly result in dehydration. **Dehydration** is the dangerous lack of water in the body that can occur when insufficient fluids are consumed or when the body experiences excessive loss of fluids through vomiting and diarrhea.

microminerals
minerals needed in smaller amounts (15 mg/day or less)

electrolytes
a subcategory of minerals that help regulate fluid movement in and out of the body's cells and help transmit nerve impulses

dehydration
a dangerous lack of water in the body due to not drinking enough or losing too much through perspiring, vomiting, and/or diarrhea

TABLE 3-6 Selected Minerals

	Functions	Good Food Sources	Symptoms of Excess Intake	Symptoms of Deficiency
MACROMINERALS				
Calcium	Is a component of bones and teeth; important for growth; involved in blood clotting, nerve impulse, muscle contractions.	Milk and milk products, sardines, clams, oysters, tofu, kale, broccoli, greens, calcium-fortified orange juice, and soy milk.	Decreases absorption of other minerals, impairs kidney function.	Increases risk of fractures and osteoporosis.
Phosphorus	Involved in the formation of bones and teeth and in energy metabolism, is important in growth and maintenance of tissues, maintains acid–base balance of body fluids, is part of cell membranes and genetic materials of cell.	Dairy foods, meat, fish, and almost all other foods.	Blood levels can become elevated when kidneys are not functioning well or when calcium regulation is dysfunctional.	Rare.
Magnesium	Involved in bone health and a plethora of enzymatic reactions, including those involved in energy metabolism, protein synthesis, and maintenance of blood sugar levels. Involved in the contraction and relaxation of muscles.	Green leafy vegetables, whole grains, nuts, legumes, and tofu.	None from food sources. Excess supplementation can cause diarrhea, severe hypotension, confusion, muscle weakness, difficulty breathing, and irregular heartbeat.	Rare: hypocalcemia, muscle cramps and seizures, loss of appetite, nausea, vomiting, fatigue, and weakness.
Sodium and chloride	Maintains fluid balance, regulates blood pressure, is involved in the function of nerves and muscles.	Salt, cured and processed foods; condiments such as soy sauce, ketchup, and steak sauce.	High blood pressure in salt-sensitive individuals, which is a risk factor for heart disease, stroke, and kidney disease.	Rare: Extreme exercise in hot temperatures can cause sodium depletion with symptoms of confusion, headache, vomiting, and seizure.
Potassium	Maintains fluid balance and regulates blood pressure. Is involved in the function of nerves and muscles, maintains heartbeat.	Fruits and vegetables.	Blood levels can become elevated when kidneys are not functioning well (hyperkalemia), which can lead to muscle weakness, temporary paralysis, and cardiac arrhythmia.	Hypokalemia (low blood potassium) can occur in people who are taking diuretics or who have severe vomiting or diarrhea, which can lead to fatigue, muscle weakness, stomach pain, and, if severe, cardiac arrhythmias.
MICROMINERALS				
Iron	Involved in the transport of oxygen as part of red blood cells and helps with energy metabolism and is needed for growth, reproduction, and immune function.	Meat, poultry, fish, fortified breads and cereals, beans, peas, and lentils.	Acute toxicity, gastrointestinal distress. Accidental overdose of supplements containing iron is the largest cause of fatal poisoning in children under the age of 6.	Iron-deficiency anemia, weakness, pale skin, delayed cognitive development, increased risk of infection, fatigue, and irritability.
Zinc	Is essential for growth and development and plays a role in wound healing and immune response. It impacts the senses of taste and smell.	Red meats, liver, eggs, dairy products, some seafood, vegetables, whole grains, and fortified breakfast cereals.	Excess supplementation may cause diarrhea, stomach cramps, and vomiting; can suppress the immune system.	Slow growth, poor appetite, slow wound healing, loss of hair, infections, and problems with sense of taste and smell.
Iodine	Is an essential component in thyroid hormones, which regulate enzymes and metabolic processes.	Seafood, iodized salt, and processed foods that use iodized salt.	Thyroiditis, thyroid suppression.	Goiter, mental retardation, cretinism, hypothyroidism, and delay in growth and development.

(Continued)

TABLE 3.6 Selected Minerals (*Continued*)

	Functions	Good Food Sources	Symptoms of Excess Intake	Symptoms of Deficiency
Fluoride	Is necessary for the health of teeth and bones. Protects against dental caries.	Fluoridated water.	Enamel and skeletal fluorosis.	Dental decay.
Selenium	Functions as a coenzyme and acts as an antioxidant.	Meat, organ meats, seafood, cereals, dairy products, and fruits and vegetables depending on the selenium content of the soil in which they were grown.	Hair and nail brittleness and gastrointestinal disturbances, rash, fatigue, nervous system abnormalities, and garlic breath.	Enlarged heart, impaired immune system.

Sources: *Dietary Reference Intakes: The Essential Guide to Nutrient Requirements*, edited by J. J. Otten, J. Pitzi-Hellwig, and L. D. Meyers, 2006, Washington, DC: National Academies Press; *An Evidence-based Approach to Vitamins and Minerals: Health Benefits and Intake Recommendations*, 2nd edition, by J. Higdon and V. J. Drake, 2012, New York: Thieme Publishing Group; Medline Plus: Minerals, *U.S. National Library of Medicine National Institutes of Health*, 2012. Retrieved from http://www.nlm.nih.gov/medlineplus/minerals.html; Vitamin and Mineral Fact Sheets, 2011, Office of Dietary Supplements, National Institutes of Health. Retrieved from http://ods.od.nih.gov/factsheets/list-VitaminsMinerals/; *Manual of Pediatric Nutrition*, 4th edition, edited by K. M. Hendricks and C. Duggan, 2005, Hamilton, Ontario: B. C. Decker, Inc.; and *Pediatric Nutrition Handbook*, 6th edition, edited by R. Kleinman, 2009, Elk Grove, IL: American Academy of Pediatrics.

A diet high in sodium content is not recommended for young children. High sodium intake is associated with high blood pressure in salt-sensitive individuals. The *Dietary Guidelines for Americans, 2010* emphasizes the importance of not eating too much salt (U.S. Department of Health and Human Services & U.S. Department of Agriculture, 2015).

Water

The macronutrients and micronutrients receive a great deal of attention in the discussion of a healthy diet. Little attention, however, is given to the importance of water in the diet. Adults cannot survive more than three to five days without water; young children, even fewer days. Water accounts for about 60% of the adult's body composition and 78% of the infant's body (U.S. Geological Survey, 2014). Water performs myriad functions:

- Water regulates body temperature through perspiration.
- Water transports nutrients and oxygen as a component of blood.
- All chemical reactions of the body take place in water.
- Water helps to remove waste products from the body (Sizer & Whitney, 2011).

Decreases in the water content of the body can have immediate consequences. Individuals feel tired, experience headaches, and find it difficult to concentrate. Insufficient water can lead to dehydration and death.

Because of their higher water composition, infants and children are more sensitive to fluctuations in water status. Diarrhea, vomiting, and fever can quickly lead to dehydration. Providing a liquid rehydration solution such as Pedialyte can restore fluid and electrolytes. Teachers must make sure that infants and children are

WHAT IF . . .

you noticed that your program's menu frequently offered a combination of high-sodium menu items such as a ham sandwich served with a pickle and canned soup? What recommendations might you make? What are some healthier food options?

Offering water at routine times helps children maintain a healthy fluid balance.

Rob Byron/Fotolia

WHAT IF . . .

you were taking your class on a walking field trip and the day turned out to be unseasonably warm? How would you ensure that each child had access to enough water?

well hydrated, especially on warm days when children are active. Child care centers, family day care homes, at-risk afterschool programs, and shelters participating in CACFP must have water readily accessible for children during the day (Oregon Department of Education, 2012; U.S. Department of Agriculture, 2014). An added advantage to providing children with water is the fluoride (in fluoridated communities), a mineral that protects teeth from the risk of dental decay.

Important Vitamins and Minerals for Children

All vitamins are important for children to consume. However, vitamins involved in growth need special consideration. Oftentimes vitamins and minerals work in concert to provide the combination of nutrients needed to perform important roles in the body.

The Teamwork of B Vitamins

The B vitamins work together in important body processes. As discussed earlier, protein is used to produce enzymes that jump-start and speed up the chemical reactions that occur in the body, sometimes by a factor of a million or more (Berg, Tymoczko, & Stryer, 2010). To do this, the enzymes must join with the molecules involved in a reaction. Coenzymes support them in this role. The B vitamins, in addition to other roles, often act as coenzymes in metabolic processes, assisting in the release of energy from the macronutrients. Some of the B vitamins also prevent certain types of anemia. Folic acid helps prevent neural tube defects.

Vitamin A

Vitamin A is generally recognized for its role in vision. The old wives' tale that carrots are good for the eyes is true. Vitamin A, found in carrots, sweet potatoes, and dark leafy green vegetables, will not correct near- or farsightedness, but this vitamin is required for vision. Vitamin A is needed to make a pigment of the eye that is very sensitive to light and aids vision. In addition to its role in vision, vitamin A also supports growth of bones and the overall body and helps maintain a healthy immune system.

Children in developing countries throughout the world still experience deficiencies in vitamin A and the resulting blindness and increased risk of severe infection or death that occurs if left untreated. The World Health Organization estimates that 250,000 to 500,000 vitamin A–deficient children become blind every year and half of them die within 12 months of becoming blind (World Health Organization, 2015). Vitamin A deficiency is usually not a problem in the United States, but it can occur in children who experience malabsorption. For example, a child with celiac disease is more likely to be at risk for vitamin A deficiency. Figure 3-7 lists sources of vitamin A that appeal to children.

Vitamin A toxicity is a more likely concern in the United States. This can be caused by well-meaning parents who over-supplement or provide more than the Tolerable Upper Intake Levels (UL) of vitamin A. This is of particular concern because the U.S. food supply consists of many vitamin-fortified foods

Eating a variety of rich-colored fruits and vegetables provides vitamins and minerals.

Vanessa Davies/Dorling Kindersley Limited

FIGURE 3-7   Child-Friendly Sources of Vitamin A

- **Infants:** pureed peaches, apricots, mangoes, or commercially prepared pureed carrots, sweet potatoes, and squash.
- **Toddlers:** milk, eggs, shredded cheese, diced cooked carrots, mashed sweet potatoes with crushed pineapple, diced peaches, mango or apricot yogurt parfait, diced cantaloupe, steamed broccoli with cheese sauce, vegetable soups made with peas, carrots, sweet potatoes, and/or spinach, pumpkin custard.

- **Preschoolers and older:** milk, eggs, cheese, carrot sticks, carrot raisin salad, spinach and grapefruit salad, sweet potato, pumpkin, or carrot muffins or bread, homemade baked sweet potato fries, mango or peach smoothie, raw broccoli or red pepper strips with low-fat dip, homemade cream of spinach or kale soup, cantaloupe slices, peas and carrots, cottage cheese with cubed peaches, mangos or papaya, salad with dark green leafy lettuces, baked sweet potato, apricots, frozen homemade fruit pops made with peach or apricot nectar.

and beverages. In addition, children who mistake chewable or "gummy" style multivitamins for candy are also at risk for toxicity. Too much vitamin A can cause skin rashes, loss of appetite, problems with bones, liver damage, and even death (Higdon & Drake, 2012). Because vitamin A is one of the fat-soluble vitamins, excess amounts are stored in the liver, which increases the risk of toxicity.

Vitamin D, Calcium, Phosphorus, and Magnesium

Vitamin D is required for healthy bone development, as are the minerals calcium, phosphorus, and magnesium. Calcium, phosphorus, and magnesium also play a key role in the structure of teeth. These three minerals account for 98% of the body's mineral content (Kleinman, 2009). They are priority nutrients for children because of their importance for bone growth and maintenance. Vitamin D stimulates the intestinal absorption of calcium and phosphorus. Vitamin D is synthesized in the skin through exposure to sunlight. Certain factors can limit this synthesis. For example, children who are dark-skinned, are obese, or use sunscreen make less vitamin D.

A vitamin D deficiency can cause rickets, a condition that results in the softening of bones in young children. Teachers can influence the consumption of these important bone-building nutrients by offering milk and dairy products and other foods that are good sources of vitamin D, calcium, phosphorus, and magnesium. The intake of these nutrients can be increased in children's diets in the following ways:

- Offer cold cereal with milk.
- Prepare hot cereal and cream soups with milk instead of water.
- Offer vitamin D–fortified regular or Greek yogurt.
- Substitute calcium and vitamin D–fortified soy milk or orange juice when children have a milk allergy or are lactose intolerant.
- Make smoothies using milk, yogurt, and fruit.
- Offer fatty fish such as tuna, sardines, and salmon.

Iron and Vitamin C

Iron and vitamin C are another important vitamin and mineral team that are linked together in function. Lack of iron in children's diets results in iron-deficiency anemia, which is a particular concern among older babies and toddlers as they transition from breast milk and formula to solids. Because the consequences of iron-deficiency anemia are linked to adverse effects on both motor and cognitive

Pearson Education

CLASSROOM CONNECTION

In this video, a teacher describes foods that will be served during a school's Southeast Asian lunch. What strategies does she use to discourage children's negative comments and increase their respect for culturally different foods?

nonheme iron
a type of iron that is not readily absorbed by the body; found in plants

heme iron
a readily absorbed form of iron found in meats

WHAT IF . . .

a mother in your program was her breastfeeding 6-month-old and wanted you to provide cow's milk to the baby while in your care whenever she did not have a sufficient amount of pumped breast milk available? What would you advise?

CHECK YOUR UNDERSTANDING 3.5

Click here to check your understanding of micronutrients and their role in supporting the growth, development, and health of infants and children.

FIGURE 3-8   Food Combinations That Support Iron Absorption

Vitamin C and Nonheme Iron Combinations
orange wedges and enriched cereal
salsa and burritos
tomato sauce and chili beans
sliced strawberries and a peanut butter on whole-wheat sandwich
kiwi and orange tossed spinach salad

Meat and Nonheme Iron Combinations
ham and pea soup
pork and baked beans
ground beef and bean burrito

---

development, teachers must understand dietary strategies for making the most of the iron found in children's diets (Kleinman, 2009).

The iron content of a food does not reflect the amount of iron that will be absorbed. Studies show that plant sources of iron (nonheme iron), such as beans, peas, lentils, and green leafy vegetables, are not as well absorbed as the animal sources of iron (heme iron) found in meats, poultry, eggs, and fish (Higdon & Drake, 2012).

Certain dietary strategies, however, can help balance meals for better iron absorption. Vitamin C, for example, enhances the absorption of nonheme iron. Figure 3-8 provides some nutritious ideas for pairing iron with vitamin C–rich foods. In addition, just a little bit of meat in a meal containing nonheme iron will enhance overall iron absorption (Hurrell & Egli, 2010). A bean and beef burrito, for example, is a food combination that promotes nonheme iron absorption. Foods can also impede iron absorption. For example, diets that have a very high fiber content and the tannins found in tea can inhibit iron absorption.

Teachers can ensure that young children start off on the right foot when it comes to iron intake by following suggestions such as these recommended by the American Academy of Pediatrics Committee on Nutrition (Dee et al., 2008; Kleinman, 2009).

- Introduce iron-fortified infant cereal or strained meats around 6 months of age.
- Supplement iron for those breast-fed infants who are not able to consume enough iron from foods.
- Do not feed infants younger than 12 months regular cow, goat, or soy milk.
- Avoid serving young children excessive amounts of milk, which can decrease their appetite for high-iron foods.

IMPLEMENTING NUTRITION SCIENCE

Teachers need to understand the food guidance standards such as the Dietary Reference Intakes and the USDA's Choose *MyPlate* from Chapter 2 and basic nutrition information from this chapter for several reasons:

- Meeting children's nutritional needs.
- Understanding how diet recommendations impact personal health.
- Understanding nutrition across the array of cultural food preferences as they plan snacks and meals.
- Understanding the nutrition principles they are teaching.

Meeting the Nutritional Needs of Children

Teachers who understand the principles of nutrition have a stepping stone to knowing what to feed children and how to address their nutritional concerns. Teachers can best understand how to meet children's needs by evaluating each child's nutrition and health histories with attention directed to:

- Evidence of overnutrition or undernutrition.
- Health conditions that impact nutrition, such as celiac disease or diabetes.
- The need for special diets.
- Food likes and dislikes.
- Cultural food preferences.

This type of information used in conjunction with the above-mentioned resources helps teachers plan healthful menus and address the nutritional needs of all children in their care. See the Progressive Programs & Practices feature *Helping Hungry Children Through the Weekend* to see how teachers and volunteers collaborate to address a nutritional concern of children identified in their community.

Promoting Personal Health

Teachers work hard and must cope with stress and the time constraints of their profession. In addition, teachers have the added responsibility of making sure children are kept safe while in their care. When teachers don't eat well, exercise, and get enough sleep, they compromise their own resiliency. Teachers need to take care of themselves so that they can provide optimal care and education for children. Teachers who exercise and eat healthfully promote their own wellness and are prepared to be vital educators and positive role models for children.

Understanding Cultural Food Choices

Understanding cultural food preferences and belief systems regarding food choices is an important part of providing nutritional care for children. Minimizing personal cultural biases and preconceived opinions is important in effective communication. For instance, infants starting solids in the United States rely on infant cereals, strained meats, and fruits and vegetables as first foods. They then gradually transition to foods with more texture. Infants from Hispanic families are more likely to be introduced to foods such as rice, soups, tortillas, and beans as early as 6 to 12 months of age (Mennella, Ziegler, Briefel, & Novak, 2006). This is a cultural difference rather than a "wrong way" of feeding infants.

Showing respect for a culture while providing nutritional care creates a collaborative approach between teachers and parents that ultimately benefits the child. Understanding basic nutrition principles helps teachers promote healthful diets that explore and honor cultural preferences. Here is how one teacher puts this philosophy into action:

Miguel, a 24-month-old, is a selective eater and does not like many of the foods Brittany offers at her family child care program. Brittany asks Miguel's mother, Diana, what foods Miguel enjoys. Diana tells Brittany that Miguel's favorite dish at home is caldo de pollo. Brittany is not familiar with the ingredients, so Diana explains the recipe for the

WHAT IF . . .

you were a teacher of a kindergarten/first-grade blended class and planned to teach about dairy products? What nutrition concepts do you think are appropriate for this age? How would you modify the lesson to take into consideration the age range of children in the classroom?

PROGRESSIVE PROGRAMS & PRACTICES

Helping Hungry Children Through the Weekend

By Jennifer Moore and Todd Morrone, Food4Kids Backpack Program of North Florida, Inc.

One in four children in Alachua County, Florida, are affected by poverty and live in food-unstable (food-insecure) households despite the resources of free and reduced-price lunch/breakfast, afterschool snacks, food stamps, and other programs that target hunger.

The Food4Kids Backpack Program of North Florida, Inc., targets children who are "chronically hungry" and at risk of not receiving food over the weekend when other resources are not available. Teachers, staff, and administration at participating schools can refer children to the program when they witness regularly exhibiting behaviors or symptoms of chronic hunger such as:

- Stealing or hoarding food.
- Rushing food lines Monday morning and quickly eating all food served.
- Being excessively tardy and/or absent.
- Being extremely thin.
- Being unable to concentrate.

HaywireMedia/Fotolia

After parental consent is obtained, all school-age children in the home are provided with the equivalent of seven meals each weekend. Every Friday, a rolling backpack full of child-friendly nonperishable food items are discreetly distributed to the enrolled student. Allergies, homelessness, or lack of electricity are taken into consideration and adjustments are made as needed. The empty backpack is returned to school on Monday to be refilled for the next weekend.

How It Works: Food4Kids is run completely by volunteers and partners with the school to identify and distribute the backpacks to the recipients. Each school is assigned a coordinator to manage the program at the school and work closely with the staff and volunteers to follow the program model. The schools as well as the local food bank provide storage space. Volunteers transport food supplies monthly and pack food weekly, and a local television network donates public service announcements to help increase community awareness and support. Community organizations organize food drives, while businesses serve as official drop-off locations for food donations and display information to their patrons. Some businesses and churches have dedicated employees, members, and resources to help support a school. Girl Scout troops have initiated food drives and collected items to donate. Marketing concepts such as the ability to sponsor a child, host a food drive, or volunteer time and talent have been created to provide a variety of ways to participate.

chicken and vegetable soup. Later that week, Brittany serves caldo de pollo for lunch and all the children, including Miguel, enjoy the nutritious food.

Teaching Nutrition Concepts

Understanding nutrition science helps teachers effectively teach nutrition concepts, and teaching nutrition concepts is no longer an option when it comes to good health. For example, the California Department of Education believes nutrition is so important that it has drafted nutrition competencies for children prekindergarten through grade 12 (California Department of Education, 2014). These competencies are aligned with the national and state health education standards. Eight overarching nutrition competencies relate to understanding basic nutrition concepts, analyzing nutrition influences, assessing valid nutrition information, and using strategies for practicing and promoting nutrition-enhancing behaviors. The competencies offer suggestions on how these goals will be met for the various grade levels. For example, the first competency, entitled *Essential nutrition concepts*, includes content standards for kindergartners, three of which are listed below:

1. Know the six nutrient groups and the functions
   - Identify foods of plant origin
   - Classify plant foods such as fruits, vegetables, and grains
   - Identify the variety of foods of animal origin
2. Know nutrition and health guidelines
   - Name a variety of health foods and explain why they are necessary for energy and good health
   - Identify a variety of healthy snacks
   - Describe tools used to measure servings of food
3. Identify the physiological process in digestion, absorption, and metabolism of nutrients
   - Describe food by using senses: taste, touch, sight, smell, and sound (California Department of Education, 2014).

This example highlights the growing expectation for teachers to present activities and lessons that teach developmentally appropriate nutrition concepts that can be reinforced across grade levels and shows another way in which the understanding of nutrition science promotes effective teaching.

CHECK YOUR UNDERSTANDING 3.6

Click here to check your understanding of why it is important for teachers to know about nutrition and nutritional needs.

SUMMARY

- Nutrition science is the study of how food provides nourishment to the body to support its growth, maintenance, repair, and reproduction. The consequences of poor nutrition are evident in both immediate and long-term health.
- Teachers may find that understanding the science of nutrition is enhanced by an awareness of how food is digested, absorbed, and metabolized. It can also help teachers in discussions about snacks, meals, and eating with children and family members.
- The energy-providing *macronutrients* include protein, fats, and carbohydrates.
- Vitamins and minerals are *micronutrients* that sustain body processes and are needed to release and utilize the energy found in protein, fats, and carbohydrates.
- Water is a vital nutrient. It transports nutrients and oxygen as a component of blood, and all chemical reactions of the body take place in water.
- Teachers who learn the principles of nutrition are able to translate recommendations into healthful meals and snacks for children and choose healthful diets for themselves. They are also able to take cultural food differences into account when planning snacks and meals. Providing children with hands-on activities to learn about chewing, digestion, and basic nutrition concepts helps them make healthful food choices.

Chapter Quiz

 Click here to check your understanding of Chapter 3, The Science of Nutrition.

Discussion Starters

1. Imagine that the parents of children in your classroom have complained that the school's food menu has too many solid fats, added sugars, and processed high-sodium foods and not enough fiber. How would you address this issue? Whom would you involve in this conversation?

2. The process of digestion involves the mechanical and chemical breakdown of food. What are some examples of the mechanical breakdown of food? What are some examples of chemical breakdown? What are the breakdown products of the macronutrients?

3. Select from its website one of the eight overarching nutrition competencies developed by researchers at the UC Davis Center for Nutrition in Schools. Select a specific content area within the competency. Explain how you would teach a concept and what levels of expectations you might have for kindergarten and third-grade children.

Practice Points

1. What would happen if a child in your program had diarrhea? How would you decide whether she should go home or stay at school? What foods or beverages should she avoid until she feels better and no longer has diarrhea?

2. A 3-year-old who has celiac disease is going to start school soon. Plan a lunch menu and snack menu for his first day at school.

3. Develop a Teaching Wellness lesson for a third-grade class that teaches a concept from the competency and content area you selected for question 3 in the Discussion Starters.

Web Resources

California Department of Education Nutrition Competencies for California's Children

Celiac Disease Foundation

Celiac Sprue Association

Dietary Reference Intakes

National Digestive Diseases Information Clearinghouse

Key Terms

Absorption

Amino acids

Calorie

Coenzymes

Complementary protein

Dehydration

Dietary cholesterol

Digestion

Disaccharides

Dysphagia

Electrolytes

Enzymes

Essential fatty acids

Fat-soluble vitamins

Gastroesophageal reflux (GER)

Gastrointestinal tract

Heme iron

High-density lipoprotein (HDL)

Insoluble fiber

Lactose intolerant

Low-density lipoprotein (LDL)

Macrominerals

Malabsorption

Microminerals

Microvilli

Monosaccharides

Monounsaturated fats

Nonheme iron

Nutrition science

Omega-3 fatty acids

Polysaccharides

Polyunsaturated fats

Saturated fats

Soluble fiber

Trans fatty acids

Villi

Water-soluble vitamins

CHAPTER 4

Feeding Infants

After reading this chapter, you should be able to:

1. Describe the importance of balancing a nurturing and supportive feeding relationship while optimizing infants' nutrient needs.
2. Describe how to feed infants from birth to 6 months of age.
3. Describe how to feed infants ages 6 months to 1 year and facilitate the progression of solid foods.
4. Discuss concerns and methods for feeding infants with special needs.
5. Reinforce cultural influences on feeding practices for infants through the first year.

CASE STUDY Amelia, a family child care provider, has just been introduced to baby Manuel. His mother Lucia is dropping him off at Amelia's house for the first time. Manuel is 3 months old and accepts a bottle but still prefers to feed from the breast. Manuel's mother wishes she could continue breastfeeding but is not sure how she can continue nursing while going back to work. Lucia has many questions for Amelia because she is concerned about Manuel's transition to family child care. After dropping off Manuel, Lucia asks Amelia if she can talk with her when she picks up Manuel because she has questions about introducing solids foods and identifying a feeding routine.

As demonstrated in the opening case scenario, teachers and families need to work together to plan a successful transition to child care, and to communicate about children's nutritional needs. In this chapter, we explore feeding practices for infants, including ways to create positive eating experiences. We focus on feeding issues that sometimes arise during specific developmental stages, and offer strategies to support the optimal nourishment of infants during critical times of growth and development. However, not every infant can adapt to the standard approach to feeding; thus, flexibility and accommodations may be needed for babies with special needs. We also provide information on the influence of cultural food practices. Teachers should be sensitive to cultural differences, and they should be prepared to manage the different nutritional needs of infants from various cultural backgrounds.

THE BALANCE OF NURTURE AND NUTRIENTS

feeding relationship the relationship between the infant and the caregiver during eating occasions in which the caregiver responds to infant's feeding cues, uses appropriate feeding practices, and offers good nutrition

Infants need a nurturing feeding relationship and appropriate nutrition in order to grow and thrive. The **feeding relationship** between infants and their caregivers is an important contributor to successful growth and development. A good feeding relationship is established when caregivers are responsive to infants' feeding cues of hunger and satiation. For example, during the first few months of life infants should be fed on demand (Holmes, 2013). When an infant is hungry, he or she will cry. A caregiver who responds to the infant by providing food is developing the infant's trust, which will impact later eating behaviors. Effective feeding practices and good nutrition are fostered with a caring relationship, which is critical during the rapid growth in the first months after birth.

Through their senses of touch, site, and smell, infants learn about the world around them. Verbal and tactile stimulation such as holding, talking to, and smiling at an infant encourages cognitive (or intellectual) and emotional development. Responding to infants' senses reinforces the feeding relationship, which can support young children's willingness to eat a variety of foods later on. Appropriate infant feeding involves the feeding relationship, and the food offered to children. Both must be considered to optimize infants' growth and development.

Visual and tactile interaction is critical for cognitive and emotional development of the infant.

An infant should be fed according to his or her physical and cognitive development. How the infant develops both physically and cognitively is influenced by a number of factors. From the beginning, the health of the infant's mother during pregnancy impacts the developing fetus (Kleinman, 2009; Retnakaran et al., 2012). An undernourished mother during pregnancy can put the infant at nutritional risk during the first few months of life and often impacts how the infant is fed. An infant born prematurely or an infant born with special health care needs may require unique feeding strategies. Furthermore, an infant's physical development as well as cognitive indicators throughout the first year of life will determine the frequency of meals, the amount of food offered, when solid foods are introduced, the type of solid foods introduced, and how the child progresses to adult foods. Teachers have a key role in working with families to establish the feeding relationship and to provide good nutrition. In this chapter, we discuss the approach to feeding infants in two age categories: birth to 6 months of age and 6 to 12 months of age.

CLASSROOM CONNECTION

An increasing amount of research identifies the important relationship between nutrition and infant brain development. As you watch this video, consider the potential negative effects of poor nutrition in infancy.

FEEDING INFANTS: THE FIRST 6 MONTHS

The first 6 months of life are a time of significant growth and development. At birth, infants do not have a fully developed gastrointestinal tract, immune system, nervous system, or brain (Kleinman, 2009). Good nutrition is essential to support the continued development of these vital systems. By around 5 months of age, most infants have doubled their birth weight. By the end of the first year, birth weight is increased by approximately 200% and length by 50% (Mahan, Escott-Stump, & Raymond, 2012). The size of the brain doubles by age 1 and triples by age 6, reaching 93% of its adult size (Perneczky et al., 2010; Sinclair & Dangerfield, 1998). To achieve this rapid rate of growth and provide needed support for optimal brain development, a sufficient supply of calories and nutrients is needed.

CHECK YOUR UNDERSTANDING 4.1

Click here to check your understanding of the role of nurture and nutrients in the support of infants' growth and development.

While a sufficient supply of calories and nutrients are needed for infant's growth, caregivers must be reminded that *infants need only breast milk or formula for the first 4 to 6 months of life*. Breast milk and formula are the only food sources infants need because they are specifically suited to the infant's developing body. Giving food sources other than breast milk or formula can have dire consequences. In addition, on-demand feeding is critical to ensure that infants get enough calories. On-demand feeding is defined as providing food at the time, frequency, and amount determined by the infant. Due to infants' small stomachs, they typically consume only a low volume (2 to 4 ounces) of breast milk or formula at each feeding. So that they get enough calories, infants require frequent feedings. Breast milk is ideal because it is easily and quickly digested and provides ideal proportions of essential nutrients. We will discuss both breast milk and formula in feeding infants.

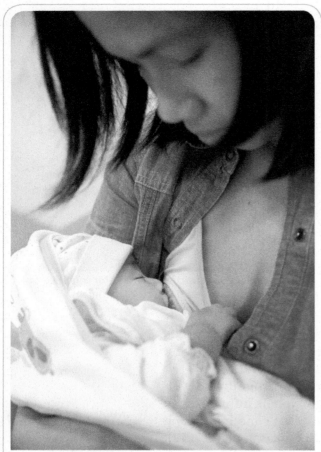

Breastfeeding is considered the gold standard for nourishing the infant.

The Breast-Fed Infant

Breast milk is the gold standard for the nourishment of infants because it contains the perfect combination of nutrients to support optimal growth and development. In some situations, however, the use of breast milk is not recommended—for example, mothers who are HIV positive, are taking illegal drugs, or are taking certain prescribed medications (Kleinman, 2009). Unlike formula, the nutrient content of breast milk changes over time to meet the maturing infant's needs. When fed exclusively to babies, breast milk will support growth until 6 months of age (Kleinman, 2009; Queen Samour & King, 2012), and thereafter should be continued along with complementary foods (American Academy of Pediatrics, 2012; The World Health Organization, 2011).

Benefits of Breast Milk

Breast milk is the recommended infant food of choice by a number of health organizations including the American Academy of Pediatrics, the World Health Organization, and the Academy of Nutrition and Dietetics (formerly the American Dietetic Association) (Eidelman, Schandler, & American Academy of Pediatrics, 2012; World Health Organization, 2011; American Dietetic Association, 2009). Breast milk offers unique nutritional and non-nutritional benefits that protect and promote the optimal growth and development of infants (Eidelman et al., 2012).

Nutritional Benefits

The nutritional benefits of breast milk are significant. The type of fat found in breast milk is easily absorbed by the baby, and its composition appears to be ideally suited to promote brain and vision development (Kleinman, 2009). The protein composition of breast milk is more easily digested than that of formula, and it provides the right amount to promote growth. The type of iron in breast milk is more readily

WHAT IF . . .

While you were feeding a 2-month-old baby a bottle of breast milk, the mother arrived at the program and wanted to nurse the baby instead? How would you respond to this request? Could this feeding be counted as a reimbursable meal in the Child and Adult Care Food Program? How might you get a definitive answer?

absorbed, and breast milk contains enzymes that help in the absorption of fats, carbohydrates, and protein.

Immunological and Other Health Benefits

Breast milk can keep infants from getting sick because it provides many immunological benefits. **Colostrum**, the first milk produced by the nursing mother, is rich in protective components. These components include antibodies that help prevent illness and infection. After the first week, colostrum is no longer produced, but breast milk continues to provide antibodies; in addition, it contains good bacteria that promote a healthy gastrointestinal track that can reduce the infant's risk of allergies and intolerances. Furthermore, the type of milk sugar in breast milk (called oligosaccharides) helps to establish and promote the growth of a beneficial microbial population (Li et al., 2012), which can lessen the risk of infection from harmful bacteria and the development of allergies (University of Illinois College of Agricultural, Consumer and Environmental Sciences, 2012). Other benefits of breast milk include the reduced risk of diseases such as asthma and diabetes as well as a decreased risk for common childhood illnesses—ear infections, respiratory infections, and gastroenteritis (commonly known as the "stomach flu": vomiting and diarrhea) (American Academy of Pediatrics, 2012f; World Health Organization, 2013). Breastfeeding may reduce, by about 15% to 25%, the chance of infants becoming overweight or obese, and the longer the mother nurses, the greater the protective effect (Koletzko et al., 2009). Figure 4-1 shows the decreased

colostrum
the first milk produced by the nursing mother; it is rich in antibodies and other protective components to help keep infants healthy

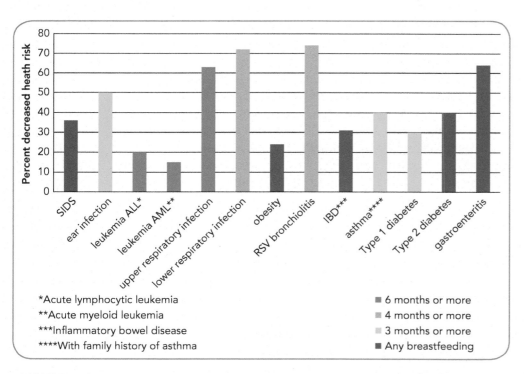

*Acute lymphocytic leukemia
**Acute myeloid leukemia
***Inflammatory bowel disease
****With family history of asthma

- 6 months or more
- 4 months or more
- 3 months or more
- Any breastfeeding

FIGURE 4-1

The Percent Decreased Health Risk Related to Duration of Exclusive Breastfeeding

Sources: Based on American Academy of Pediatrics. (2012). "Policy Statement Breastfeeding and the Use of Human Milk," *Pediatrics*, 129(3), pp. e827–e841 (doi: 10.1542/peds.2011-3552); Ip, S., Chung, M., Raman, G., Chew, P., Magula, N., DeVine, D., Trikalinos, T., & Lau, J. (2007). *Breastfeeding and maternal and infant health outcomes in developed countries*. Rockville, MD: Agency for Healthcare Research and Quality; (Evidence Reports/Technology Assessments, No. 153.) from http://www.ahrq.gov/downloads/pub/evidence/pdf/brfout/brfout.pdf; American Academy of Pediatrics. (2012). "Executive Summary: Breastfeeding and the Use of Human Milk," *Pediatrics*, 129(3), pp. 600–603.

risk of illness for a variety of health conditions (related to the duration of breast-feeding). The reduced occurrence of illness is particularly important for working mothers and their employers.

Cognitive and Emotional Benefits

Breast-fed infants, particularly those born prematurely, perform better on IQ tests administered later in childhood and have overall improved cognitive performance than children who do not receive breast milk in infancy (Guxens et al., 2011; Isaacs et al., 2010; Kramer et al., 2008). In addition, breastfeeding may protect against developmental delays and support the attainment of gross motor skills and language development (Dee, Li, Lee, & Grummer-Strawn, 2007).

Other Benefits to Breastfeeding

Teachers directly benefit from having breast-fed infants in their care. Breast-fed infants are less likely to have colds, ear infections, urinary tract infections, and diarrhea. An additional benefit is that the Child and Adult Care Food Program (CACFP), a child nutrition program designed to reimburse programs to offset the cost of nutritious meals, supports breastfeeding. The CACFP provides reimbursement to programs for breast milk that is fed to infants in a bottle, thereby reducing costs to programs that might otherwise need to purchase formula. A claim to CACFP for reimbursement cannot be made, however, if the breastfeeding mother nurses the baby while at the child care setting (U.S. Department of Agriculture, Food and Nutrition Service, 2000). Figure 4-2 summarizes some of the healthy components of breast milk compared with commercial infant formula.

Rates of Breastfeeding

In the United States, breastfeeding rates continue to rise. The Centers for Disease Control Breastfeeding Report Card for 2014 reported 79% of infants started breastfeeding in 2011. This percentage is still below the target of 81.9% established by *Healthy People 2020* (Centers for Disease Control and Prevention, 2011b). While the rate of breastfeeding is improving, the number of women who are exclusively breastfeeding (no solids, no water, and no other liquids) their infant at 3 months of age is only 34%, which is well below the target goal. Lower rates of breastfeeding initiation in the United States occur more frequently among mothers who are non-Hispanic black women, mothers who are of lower socioeconomic status, mothers who are under the age of 20, and/or women who are unmarried (Centers for Disease Control and Prevention, 2011b).

Cultural Influences on Breastfeeding Practices

Cultural perspectives can influence whether women breast-feed their infants and for how long (Fischer & Olson, 2014). Foreign-born Hispanic women living in the United States are more likely to initiate breastfeeding and breast-feed longer than Hispanic mothers who have spent all of their lives in the United States (Gill, 2009; Sparks, 2011). Although, non-Hispanic black women have lower rates of breastfeeding initiation in the United States; however, in recent year this group has improved (McDowell, Wang, & Kennedy-Stephenson, 2008). While

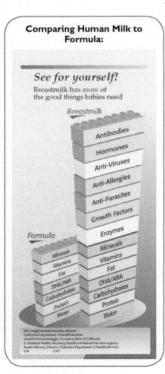

FIGURE 4-2
The Beneficial Qualities of Breast Milk
Source: Used courtesy of the WIC Supplemental Nutrition Branch of the California Department of Health Services.

breastfeeding is promoted in the United States, the culture may reflect the maternal perception that breastfeeding is an option rather than the norm for feeding infants.

Specific cultural and religious beliefs can have both positive and negative influences on breastfeeding practices among nursing women. A number of examples are provided in the following text. Religious guidance encourages Islamic women to breast-feed their infants for two years (Shaikh & Ahmed, 2006). However, the traditional garb worn by Islamic women can decrease their exposure to the sun, lowering vitamin D status in mothers and thus reducing vitamin D in their breast milk for infants (Allali et al., 2006; Haggerty, 2011). During the month of Ramadan, fasting is practiced by Muslims from sunup to sundown. Although religious guidance exempts breastfeeding women, some choose to fast for spiritual reasons in spite of their recognition that it can impact milk supply, and can lead to more supplemental feedings (Al-Oballi Kridli, 2011). Some Hispanic mothers believe that breast milk can be negatively affected by situations that precipitate strong anger (*coraje*) or shock (*susto*) in their lives. They may choose not to breast-feed or to stop breastfeeding for fear the milk will be harmful to the baby. Asian mothers may believe that "vital energy" is required for the production of breast milk and that when the body is "imbalanced," the mother's milk can become unhealthy for the baby (Pak-Gorstein et al., 2009). Native American populations have a high rate of breastfeeding initiation, but exclusively breastfeeding and continuing to breast-feed decreases more rapidly than in other ethnic groups except for the African American population (Chapman & Perez-Escamilla, 2012). In recent years, resurgence in traditional values and in a connection to the spirituality of the Native American culture has increased the importance of breastfeeding and as a result breastfeeding rates has increased (Centers for Disease Control and Prevention, 2011a). However, cultural disparity in breastfeeding continues to exists, and effort to support breastfeeding in different cultures is needed (Chapman & Perez-Escamilla, 2012). Figure 4-3 from the U.S. Department of Health and Human Services, Office on Women's Health shares the practical benefits of breastfeeding that can resonate for any mother who is considering whether to breastfeed. Regardless of the cultural background, when promoting breastfeeding, it is important to consider the influence of extended family members such as grandmothers, aunts, and fathers. Support from family can enhance successful changes in infant feeding practices, including initiation of breastfeeding (Dellwo, Houghton, & Graybeal, 2001; Horodynskia, Calcaterab, & Carpenter, 2012).

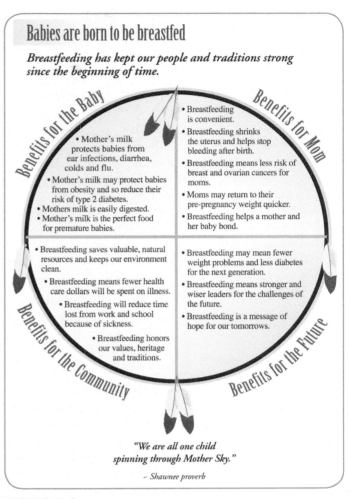

FIGURE 4-3

A Breastfeeding Guide for American Indians and Alaska Native Families

Source: U.S. Department of Health and Human Services, Office on Women's Health, An Easy Guide to Breastfeeding for American Indians and Alaska Native Families, retrieved January 1, 2015, from http://www.womenshealth.gov/publications/our-publications/breastfeeding-guide/breastfeedingguide-nativeamerican-english.pdf.

Carla Mestas/Pearson Education, Inc.

Family members such as fathers influence mothers' feeding decisions.

Teachers who learn about the cultural perspectives of breastfeeding are better able to understand and support the establishment of healthful feeding practices. Child care providers should foster close communication about the care of infants and approach varying beliefs and practices with sensitivity and respect. Teachers who include family members in interactive and supportive discussions about breastfeeding may increase the length of time or even likelihood that mothers choose to breast-feed.

Supporting Breastfeeding Mothers

Organizations and legislation support breastfeeding practices. The WHO emphasizes the role of caregivers in supporting breastfeeding mothers who return to work (World Health Organization, 2010; World Health Organization & UNICEF, 2003). On their Breastfeeding Report Card, the Centers for Disease Control and Prevention evaluates a state's child care regulations that support breastfeeding based on the National Resource Center for Health and Safety in Child Care and Early Education best care standards (Centers for Disease Control and Prevention, 2011a; National Resource Center for Health and Safety in Child Care and Early Education, University of Colorado Denver, 2011). From this work, the Patient Protection and Affordable Care Act was passed by Congress and signed by President Obama in 2010. Health insurance reform legislation under Section 4207 requires employers to provide break time and a private place other than a bathroom for nursing mothers to express breast milk, for as long as one year after a child's birth (United States Breastfeeding Committee, 2011). This act also ensures breastfeeding women are given the support and counseling they need from trained health care providers such as lactation consultants, and that they are given breastfeeding equipment such as breast pumps. These services are provided because research has demonstrated that breastfeeding is an effective preventive step to protect the health of mothers and their infants (U.S. Department of Health and Human Services, 2012). Child care centers are an important part of the nursing mother's support system. The National Association for the Education of Young Children as well as other health authorities provide specific guidelines on how to support breastfeeding in early childhood settings (National Association for the Education of Young Children, 2012). A sample program policy in support of breastfeeding is presented in the *Policy Point* feature. Creating a policy reinforces the program's commitment to families and outlines the responsibilities of teachers and other program staff.

Teachers can have a key role in supporting the breastfeeding mother. Women who have a sense of "confident commitment" are more likely to be successful in breastfeeding (Avery, Zimmermann, Underwood, & Magnus, 2009). Teachers who share in the care of infants can offer positive support for this commitment.

The first step in supporting breastfeeding mothers may occur before babies are enrolled. Teachers should talk with the family about their decision to breast-feed and find out when the child will begin to attend the child care center. Breastfeeding support is particularly important for mothers who are returning to work (Mirkovic, Perrine, Scanlon, & Grummer-Strawn, 2014) and dealing with new schedules, lack of sleep, and obstacles in the work environment. The decision to return to work

POLICY POINT

Supporting Breastfeeding in the Early Childhood Settings

Sunshine Child Care Center recognizes the nutritional and health benefits of breastfeeding, and is committed to supporting mothers who want to breast-feed or provide expressed breast milk for their infants. To promote and support this philosophy, the center offers a comfortable, culturally attuned environment that adheres to the following policy:

1. Mothers will be provided a private place to breast-feed or pump breast milk that has access to a comfortable chair, a water supply for hand washing, and an electrical outlet.

2. Mothers will be allowed to keep pumped breast milk in the center's refrigerator. All breast milk will be stored in clean containers and labeled with infant's name and the date milk was expressed.

3. All staff will be trained on the breastfeeding policy, including the appropriate handling of breast milk. The information used to establish proper handling of breast milk will come from the following resources, all of which can be found online:

The American Academy of Pediatrics (AAP)

Centers for Disease Control and Prevention (CDC)

Caring for Our Children: National Health and Safety Performance Standards (CFOC)

NAEYC recommendations (as outlined in Health Standard 5.B.09)

4. The storage of breast milk will follow the *most* recent recommendations of AAP, CDC, CFOC, and NAEYC.

Storage and handling recommendations:

- Expressed breast milk will be used within 24 hours.
- Breast milk will be discarded if not used within 48 hours.
- Breast milk that will not be used within 24 hours will be frozen.
- Breast milk will be thawed in the refrigerator. It should not be microwaved, which can create hot spots that may burn baby's mouth and destroy some of the beneficial qualities of breast milk.
- Thawed breast milk will be stored no more than 24 hours.
- Frozen breast milk will be stored no more than 3 months at 0°F (−18°C).
- Thawed breast milk will not be refrozen.
- Any breast milk that has set out over an hour or that has been fed to an infant will be discarded.
- Milk from a bottle that was partially consumed will *not* be saved.

5. All staff will receive training on how to sensitively coordinate infant feeding with the breastfeeding mother's work schedule.

- Staff will help ease mother and baby's transition to work by developing a feeding plan.
- Staff will try not to feed baby just before mother arrives.
- Staff will try not to waste breast milk.

6. Breastfeeding will be supported and promoted by sharing information for mothers and posting flyers that highlight the child care center's commitment to breastfeeding. The policy will be made available to parents in the parent handbook.

7. The program director will be responsible for maintaining and updating the policy and ensuring that compliance standards are met.

Sources: Storing and Preparing Expressed Breast Milk, by American Academy of Pediatrics, 2014, retrieved January 1, 2015, from http://www.healthychildren.org/English/ages-stages/baby/breastfeeding/Pages/Storing-and-Preparing-Expressed-Breast-Milk.aspx; Centers for Disease Control and Prevention, Proper Handling and Storage of Human Breast Milk, 2010, retrieved January 1, 2015, from http://www.cdc.gov/breastfeeding/recommendations/handling_breastmilk.htm; Academy for Early Childhood Program Accreditation: Standard 5: NAEYC Accreditation Criteria for Health Standard, by the National Association for the Education of Young Children, 2014, retrieved January 1, 2015, from http://www.naeyc.org/files/academy/file/AllCriteriaDocument.pdf; Model Health Breastfeeding Promotion and Support Policy for Child Care Programs, by Public Health: Seattle and King County, 2014, retrieved January 1, 2015, from http://www.kingcounty.gov/healthservices/health/child/childcare/modelhealth.aspx.

does not tend to influence breastfeeding initiation, but it often impacts the duration, as women stop breastfeeding upon returning to work (Ogbuanu, Glover, Probst, Liu, & Hussey, 2011).

The teacher's next step in supporting a breastfeeding mother is to share the center's breastfeeding policy. Teachers can explain how the child care center provides a comfortable and private place to nurse and how the center will work with the mother to accommodate her feeding schedule. Teachers should reinforce the open door policy that allows the mother to come to the center to feed her child (for example, during lunch breaks) to maintain her milk supply. Child care centers also should be aware of the state and local policies and provide families with information to reinforce how those policies are followed.

Another step for teachers to use in supporting a breastfeeding mother is to share information with parents about transitioning from the breast to bottle. Teachers should encourage parents to start early but not too early. For the first four weeks of life, infants are mastering the skill of feeding from the breast. Introducing a bottle too early can hinder the development of this skill. The ideal time is when the child is 4 to 6 weeks old and when the infant has demonstrated competency in feeding through consistent feedings and proper growth. Once parents have offered a bottle, they should be consistent in offering a bottle every day or every other day. If the infant will not take a bottle from the mother, another family member can feed the infant from the bottle. Avoid offering the bottle when the infant is too hungry or upset. Teachers can reinforce to parents that an infant's comfort in feeding from a bottle can take time and may be a gradual transition.

Teachers also can help breastfeeding mothers by linking pregnant and nursing mothers to community organizations and resources that promote and support breastfeeding. For example, teachers can provide parents with phone numbers for various resources: a lactation consultant; a dietitian; the county Women, Infants, and Children (WIC) office; and La Leche League. Many organizations are available and offer information, guidance, and tools to manage breastfeeding challenges.

> **WHAT IF . . .**
> you were caring for a breast-fed infant who was crying and hungry but you knew the mother was due to arrive within a half hour and liked to breast-feed when she got there? How would you manage this situation?

Safe Handling of Breast Milk

Teachers must take special precautions to handle, store, and serve breast milk safely. Teachers should always wash their hands before handling breast milk. Breast milk is not considered to be body fluid but rather food by the CDC, so universal precautions such as wearing gloves when handling breast milk are not necessary and it can be safely stored in a refrigerator like other foods (Centers for Disease Control and Prevention, 2010). Breast milk should be provided in clean containers such as sturdy plastic bags designed for storing breast milk. Breast milk stored in soiled containers should not be accepted. Containers should be clearly labeled with the baby's name and the date the milk was expressed.

> **WHAT IF . . .**
> you noticed that a bottle of breast milk in the refrigerator had not been labeled with the date it was expressed by the mother who dropped it off? What would you do?

When the infant arrives at the child care setting, the breast milk should be stored in the refrigerator immediately until the baby is ready for a feeding. Refer to the *Policy Point*, which includes storage and handling guidelines for breast milk. By using safe handling techniques, breastfeeding mothers and caregivers of breast-fed infants can maintain the quality of expressed breast milk and the health of the baby.

Breast Milk Composition

Breast milk is not a standard product. The first breast milk produced when the infant is born, called colostrum, is pale to bright yellow in color. Mature breast milk (produced after the first week or two) can vary in color depending on the fat content of the milk and the foods or supplements the mother consumes. The fat in breast milk will rise to the top of the storage container. The amount of fat varies depending on how much fore milk and hind milk is expressed. Fore milk is the watery, nutrient-rich milk that is first released when the baby begins to nurse. Hind milk is nutrient rich in fat and calories and is secreted at the end of nursing or expressing breast milk. When an infant is fed from a bottle, gently shaking the bottle of breast milk ensures that the fat is redistributed in the milk and made available to the infant. Because breast milk is nutrient dense but a mother's supply may be limited at the child care setting, mothers should be encouraged to express and save breast milk in small 2-oz volumes as well as larger volumes to give child care providers an option when the infant shows signs of varying levels of hunger. This helps prevent the waste of this valuable food.

fore milk
the watery, nutrient-rich breast milk that is first released when the baby begins to nurse or the mother first expresses breast milk

hind milk
the breast milk that is nutrient rich in fat and calories and is secreted at the end of nursing or expressing breast milk

Nutrients to Consider in Breastfed Infants

Although breast milk is a perfect form of nutrition designed to meet the needs of most healthy infants, some dietary considerations when using breast milk require special attention as the infant matures.

Vitamin D Breast milk is not a rich source of vitamin D, an important vitamin that enhances calcium absorption and facilitates the building of strong bones and teeth. Vitamin D is produced in the body when skin is exposed to sun. However, infants and young children who have minimum exposure to sunlight and who are dark-skinned could be at risk for low levels of vitamin D. Therefore, the AAP recommends providing 400 IU vitamin D supplements for all breastfeeding infants (American Academy of Pediatrics, 2011).

Vitamin B$_{12}$ A lack of vitamin B$_{12}$ can be a concern for infants of breastfeeding mothers who are vegan (vegetarians who do not consume any foods of animal origin, including dairy products and eggs). Vegan mothers are encouraged to take vitamin B$_{12}$ supplements (Roed, Skovby, & Lund, 2009).

Iron Prior to birth, babies store iron in the liver, and iron in breast milk is easily absorbed through 6 months of age. But by 6 months of age (or earlier in premature infants), an infant's iron reserves are depleted. Insufficient iron can negatively impact growth and cognitive development. For these reasons, at 6 months of age it is important to introduce iron-rich foods such as iron-fortified cereal to supplement the infant's dietary intake of iron from breast milk (Przyrembel, 2012). Introducing whole cow's milk at this age is not recommended because it can cause intestinal bleeding, which also increases the risk of anemia (Kleinman, 2009).

Zinc Zinc is an important mineral for growth and a well-functioning immune system. Zinc in breast milk is easily absorbed and meets the needs of infants until about 6 months of age. The older breastfed infant's need for zinc can be met with zinc-fortified cereals and strained meats (American Academy of Pediatrics, 2012e; Kleinman, 2009).

Note that the infant's need for iron and zinc coincides with the typical introduction of solid foods between 4 and 6 months of age. Infants should not be given solid foods before this time. Offering solids foods before 4 to 6 months of age does not provide nutritional benefit and can harm the infant's developing gastrointestinal tract and does not help a child sleep through the night. However, delaying introduction of solids can result in suboptimal intake of these nutrients, minimize diversity of the diet, and hinder preference for textured foods.

The Formula-Fed Infant

Some babies receive their nutrition through formula, which is a manufactured product used as a substitute for breast milk. Although breast milk is the best form of nourishment, formula will support baby's growth and development. Mothers may choose to use infant formula for several reasons. Women in the United States who are infected with HIV or have active tuberculosis should not breast-feed (Mahan et al., 2012). Although mothers can take many medications while they are nursing, some are unsafe and negatively impact the baby, resulting in the need to use formula. Women may choose not to breast-feed for other reasons, such as limited time, breast infections, or personal preference. Regardless of mothers' choice to feed their infants—through breastfeeding, infant formula feeding, or some combination of the two—they should be supported in their decision.

Types of Infant Formula

Like breast milk, infant formula is designed to meet the nutrient needs of infants until 6 months of age. A variety of infant formulas are available, and infant formulas may differ in the type of carbohydrate, protein, and fat they contain. Several of the different types of infant formula are discussed next.

Modified Cow's Milk–Based Formulas Modified cow's milk is the most commonly used commercial formula. It is composed of cow's milk that has been altered to provide less protein, more fat, and carbohydrates in an easily digested form. Some cow's milk formulas are lactose-free, to support the feeding of the rare infant who is lactose intolerant. This product is not appropriate for infants who are allergic to milk because it contains cow's milk protein.

Soy-Based Formulas Soy-based products were developed in the 1960s for infants who were lactose intolerant or allergic to cow's milk. The substitution of soy formula for infants with a cow's milk allergy is currently less accepted because 30% to 64% of infants who do not tolerate cow's milk formula also are unable to tolerate soy formula. In addition, 10% to 14% of infants with a cow's milk protein allergy go on to develop a soy milk protein allergy (Bhatia & Greer, 2008; Queen Samour & King, 2012). Families who follow a vegetarian diet may choose to use soy-based formulas.

Hypoallergenic Formulas Hypoallergenic formulas contain protein that has been broken down into smaller components, making them easier to absorb and less likely to cause an allergic response. These products were developed for children with cow's milk or soy allergies and for infants who have gastrointestinal or liver disease that result in problems with absorption.

There are two types of hypoallergenic formulas. The extensively hydrolyzed formulas have the protein broken down into amino acids and small peptides, whereas the amino acid–based or elemental formulas are designed for extremely sensitive infants and contain only amino acids. These formulas are very expensive and are only selected with careful consideration by health care providers or registered dietitian nutritionists.

Other Formulas Premature formulas are designed to support the increased nutritional needs of the premature infant. They provide higher calories, more protein, and increased levels of some vitamins and minerals per ounce compared with standard formulas (Queen Samour & King, 2012). Although premature infants may benefit from additional nutrients, the more concentrated nutrient content must be closely monitored to prevent gastrointestinal problems. Therefore, formula that deviates from standard mixing directions on the label must have a prescription from a health care provider or registered dietitian nutritionist. Follow-up infant formulas are intended to meet the needs of older infants and toddlers (9 to 24 months) who have begun to eat solids but may not be eating enough to meet all of their nutritional requirements. The AAP states that although these products are nutritionally adequate, they do not have a significant advantage over breast milk or formula in combination with a healthy diet (Kleinman, 2009).

All infant formulas undergo scrutiny by the U.S. Food and Drug Administration (FDA). The vitamin and mineral content of formula is standardized based on FDA regulations that specify the nutrient level requirements to ensure all formulas fed to infants are safe and nutritionally complete (Food and Drug Administration, 2011). Infant formula selection is based on what is most appropriate for the baby, and infants should receive the same type and form of formula in the child care setting that is used in the home setting.

Formula Intolerance

Formula intolerance occurs when infants have adverse reactions related to the formula they are consuming. Teachers need to keep families informed when babies show signs of excessive gas, bloating, diarrhea, abdominal pain, vomiting, excessive crying, rash, or allergic symptoms.

formula intolerance results when infants have undesirable symptoms related to the formula they are consuming

Recognizing when babies are unable to tolerate their formula can be challenging. Normal infant behavior includes crying, vomiting, gas, and diarrhea. Often well-meaning mothers will switch formulas in an attempt to solve these perceived problems. However, switching formulas may be unnecessary and could result in expensive changes that may not be warranted (Berseth, Mitmesser, Ziegler, Marunycz, & Vanderhoof, 2009). Teachers can reassure families about normal infant behavior and direct them to health care providers if they have concerns about formula intolerance.

Forms of Infant Formula

Infant formula is available in three forms:

- *Ready-to-feed:* This is usually the most expensive form and requires no preparation.
- *Canned concentrate:* This formula requires water to be added to a concentrate.
- *Powdered:* This is the least expensive form of formula and requires a powder to be mixed with water.

A child care program may have a policy of only offering ready-to-feed formulas if this is mandated by state licensing requirements or if they do not have adequate space for formula preparation.

Safe Preparation of Infant Formula

Safe and sanitary procedures must be used when preparing infant formula. Formula and water must be measured following the manufacturer's directions. Inaccurate measurements can lead to dangerous problems. If formula is prepared with too much water, it will be too low in calories and nutrients to meet the needs of the baby, resulting in poor growth. If the formula is too concentrated, diarrhea and dehydration can result, which places a toll on the infant's kidneys. Guidelines for preparing formula will vary depending on the form used (ready-to-feed, liquid concentrate, or powder).

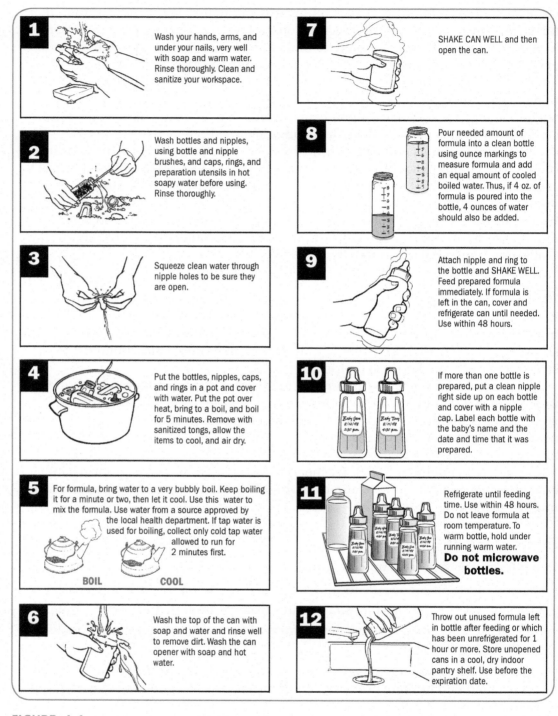

1 Wash your hands, arms, and under your nails, very well with soap and warm water. Rinse thoroughly. Clean and sanitize your workspace.

2 Wash bottles and nipples, using bottle and nipple brushes, and caps, rings, and preparation utensils in hot soapy water before using. Rinse thoroughly.

3 Squeeze clean water through nipple holes to be sure they are open.

4 Put the bottles, nipples, caps, and rings in a pot and cover with water. Put the pot over heat, bring to a boil, and boil for 5 minutes. Remove with sanitized tongs, allow the items to cool, and air dry.

5 For formula, bring water to a very bubbly boil. Keep boiling it for a minute or two, then let it cool. Use this water to mix the formula. Use water from a source approved by the local health department. If tap water is used for boiling, collect only cold tap water allowed to run for 2 minutes first.
BOIL   COOL

6 Wash the top of the can with soap and water and rinse well to remove dirt. Wash the can opener with soap and hot water.

7 SHAKE CAN WELL and then open the can.

8 Pour needed amount of formula into a clean bottle using ounce markings to measure formula and add an equal amount of cooled boiled water. Thus, if 4 oz. of formula is poured into the bottle, 4 ounces of water should also be added.

9 Attach nipple and ring to the bottle and SHAKE WELL. Feed prepared formula immediately. If formula is left in the can, cover and refrigerate can until needed. Use within 48 hours.

10 If more than one bottle is prepared, put a clean nipple right side up on each bottle and cover with a nipple cap. Label each bottle with the baby's name and the date and time that it was prepared.

11 Refrigerate until feeding time. Use within 48 hours. Do not leave formula at room temperature. To warm bottle, hold under running warm water. **Do not microwave bottles.**

12 Throw out unused formula left in bottle after feeding or which has been unrefrigerated for 1 hour or more. Store unopened cans in a cool, dry indoor pantry shelf. Use before the expiration date.

FIGURE 4-4

Preparation Checklist for Standard Liquid Concentrated Iron-Fortified Infant Formula (using glass or hard plastic bottles)*

*Directions for the preparation of ready-to-feed and powdered infant formula can also be found on this website.

Source: USDA Infant Nutrition and Feeding: A Guide for the use of WIC and CSF programs, WIC Works Resource System, 2009, retrieved January 1, 2015, from http://www.nal.usda.gov/wicworks/Topics/FG/Chapter4_InfantFormulaFeeding.pdf.

If powdered formula is used, it is important to use the scoop provided in the can because scoops vary in size. In addition, powdered formula cannot be sterilized; thus, proper food safety handling procedures should be followed. Figure 4-4 provides general guidelines for preparing formula using standard liquid concentrated formula.

The National Resource Center for Health and Safety in Child Care and Early Education is a valuable resource for child care settings. An online book on health and safety standards with policies and procedures is provided titled *Caring for Our Children: National Health and Safety Performance Standards: Guidelines for Out-of-Home Child Care Programs*, Third Edition (American Academy of Pediatrics, American Public Health Association, and National Resource Center for Health and Safety in Child Care and Early Education, 2011). The World Health Organization also provides guidelines for the safe preparation of powdered infant formula in child care settings. See resources at the end of the chapter.

> ## A Matter of ETHICS
>
> You observe your coworker and friend preparing powdered infant formula haphazardly without carefully measuring powder or water. When you question her about it, she responds that this is how she made formula for her daughter and she never had a problem. You want to go to your director, but you worry about getting your friend in trouble. She is a single parent who really needs her job. How would you handle this? What risks are involved with this practice? Section III of the NAEYC Code of Ethical Conduct discusses the Ethical Responsibilities to Colleagues. What is your responsibility to your coworker and to your employer? What is your ethical responsibility to the infants in your program?

Understanding the Feeding Relationship

One of the many pleasures in caring for children is feeding young infants. This is an important time for teachers and infants to connect one-on-one in a relaxed and comfortable setting. Designate a special place to feed infants such as a comfortable chair that allows you to enjoy the time socializing with the baby. Looking into infants' eyes and allowing them to gaze back at you builds positive bonds of trust and appreciation. It is during this interaction that teachers learn to recognize the feeding cues babies give to indicate when they are hungry or full.

On-Demand Feeding

Infants should always be fed on demand. It is not appropriate to impose a feeding schedule on infants in a child care setting unless this has been authorized by a health care professional for medical reasons. On-demand feeding fosters optimal growth and development and is reinforced when adults respond appropriately to infant feeding cues (Holmes, 2013).

Feeding Cues

Teachers should be able to recognize feeding cues so they can satisfy the needs of the infant. Although developmentally infants share common traits, they also exhibit a variety of individual characteristics, making each feeding relationship unique. Infants are born with the instinctual ability to cry when they are hungry. However, babies cry for a variety of reasons, and the caregiver must learn to identify the underlying reason the baby is crying. Adults who fail to provide food for an infant who is hungry can hinder the child's emotional development.

Signs of Hunger and Satiety

Successfully reading hunger and satiety (fullness) cues can reduce infants' stress and enhance the feeding relationship. Some infants who are not fed in a timely manner become overly frustrated, and when they receive

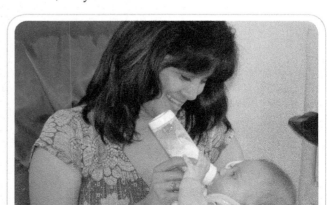

A close feeding relationship between teacher and child enhances the baby's growth and development.

Carla Mestas/Pearson Education, Inc.

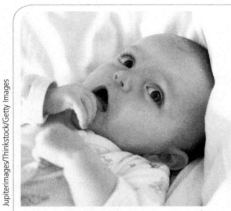 

Recognizing babies' early signs of hunger prevent them from having to use later signs of hunger and crying.

the breast or bottle they may sputter or gulp air. This can lead to gas, stomach distention, spitting up, and even more crying. Early response to infants' cues of hunger and fullness can prevent this reaction. Thus, teachers must rely exclusively on an infant's behavior to determine if the child is hungry or full. Table 4-1 provides a list of common behaviors associated with hunger and fullness in infants.

Babies' fullness cues should not be disregarded in an effort to have them finish a bottle or clean a plate. This can cause infants to fuss and struggle. If the conflict persists, it will likely result in poor eating habits (over- or undereating) and compromise the feeding relationship (Hurley & Black, 2011). For example, adults' lack of sensitivity to infants' fullness cues can result in overfeeding, setting the stage for excess weight gain and obesity (Black & Aboud, 2011; Hurley, Cross, & Hughes, 2011; Worobey, Lopez, & Hoffman, 2009). With time and experience as well as input from families, teachers and infants settle into a routine and an effective feeding relationship ensues. The *Teaching Wellness* feature provides examples of ways in which teachers can help older infants and young children identify their signs of hunger and fullness.

TABLE 4-1   Understanding Hunger and Fullness Cues in Infants

Hunger Cues	Fullness Cues
EARLY CUES	
Alert and looking at caregiver	Stops sucking
Increased arm and leg motions	Seals lips together
Mouthing lips, fingers, or fists	Turns face away
Rooting	Spits out or plays with nipple
Grunting sounds	Falls asleep
Opens mouth wide	Limbs are relaxed
Fussing	
Making sucking motions with the mouth	
Reaching to mother or the breast	
LATE CUES	
Appears tense	Baby arches back and turns face away
Frantic crying	Baby gets irritable with repeated attempts to offer bottle
Trembling	Crying

Sources: Infant feeding, 2012, California Department of Public Health, retrieved January 1, 2015, from http://www.cdph.ca.gov/programs /NutiritionandPhysicalActivity/Documents/MO-NUPA-InfantFeedingGuidelines.pdf; *Infant Nutrition and Feeding: A Guide for Uses in the WIC and CSF Programs*, by the National Agricultural Library, 2009, retrieved January 1, 2015, from http://www.nal.usda.gov/wicworks/Topics/FG/Contents.pdf; and *Child of Mine: Feeding with Love and Good Sense*, by Ellyn Satter, 2000, Boulder, CO: Bull Publishing Company.

Feeding Infants from a Bottle

Teachers must follow best practice when feeding infants from a bottle. Teachers should not put infants in a crib with a bottle. Bottle-propping puts babies at risk for choking, earaches, and dental caries. It also decreases time spent in bonding and socializing. Instead, teachers should feed one baby at a time so they can easily and quickly interpret and be responsive to feeding cues.

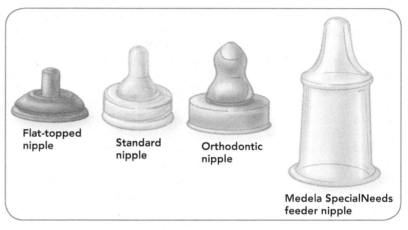

Infants prefer formula or breast milk that is warm, but this is not necessary. The USDA Food and Nutrition Service, in its infant nutrition and feeding guide, provides guidance for caregivers who feed infants breast milk or formula from a bottle (U.S. Department of Agriculture, 2009) (see Web Resources). Teachers should wash their hands before feeding infants. Babies should be held comfortably, positioned so their heads are held higher than their trunks and they are facing the teacher to prevent choking and promote social interaction. The bottle should be tilted so the milk moves into and fills the nipple. Keeping the nipple full prevents the infant from swallowing excessive air. Families can select nipples based on infant preference or need as illustrated in Figure 4-5.

FIGURE 4-5

Examples of Different Types of Nipples

Periodically, babies need to take a break to be burped. This is accomplished by the teacher holding the baby upright against the teacher's shoulder and gently patting the baby's back until air has been expelled. Feeding and burping should be comfortably paced and not rushed. Feeding continues until babies provide cues they are full. Some spitting up after a feeding is normal. However, projectile vomiting or vomiting of large volumes of breast milk or formula may indicate the need to recommend the family consult with a health care provider.

Communicating with Parents

Communicating with parents is an important teacher responsibility (Johnson, Ramsay, Armstrong Shultz, Branen, & Fletcher, 2013). A baby's behavior cannot be fully understood unless it is put into the context of the child's most recent experiences. For example, it is important for parents to share information such as how well the baby is sleeping at night, when the baby was last fed and changed, and whether the baby is teething. Teachers cannot effectively read the signs of the infant if they don't know "what's up."

Similarly, teachers need to share information such as what and how much the infant eats and the frequency of diaper changes so the family feels informed. One way to ensure detailed communication is to send home a note with families at the end of each day. Another effective communication approach is to use a notebook with a section for writing comments back and forth between the teacher and family.

WHAT IF . . .

you had a mother who was consistently behind schedule when dropping off her infant and frequently left without sharing important details such as when her baby was last fed? How might you ensure better communication?

How Often and How Much to Feed a Baby

Babies usually develop a routine for eating that is influenced by their weight, age, whether they receive breast milk or formula, and whether they are eating solids.

TEACHING WELLNESS   I Feel Hungry, I Feel Full

LEARNING OUTCOME   Children will be able to communicate when they are hungry and when they are full.

Vocabulary focus: Hungry, full, stomach, tummy

Safety watch: Ensure foods are prepared and served appropriately, such as serving puréed fruits and vegetables for young infants and small mashed pieces for older infants. Choose foods that avoid children's food allergies and restrictions.

INFANTS

- **Goal:** Babies will learn the concepts of hungry and full through the use of baby sign motions.
- **Materials:** Age-appropriate baby foods; sign language glossary that includes terms for *full* (bend elbow and hold hand and arm straight across the body; keep hand and arm parallel and lift up under the chin) and *hungry* (shape hand as if holding a cup; place hand on upper chest with palm facing chest and slide it downward).
- **Activity plan:** While preparing and during the meal, ask, "Are you hungry? Is your tummy hungry? Do you want to eat?" Use sign language hand motions for *hungry* and make motions toward your own tummy. Allow baby to

help self-feed. When the baby stops eating (closes mouth, turns away head, or acts disinterested in eating) ask, "Are you full?" while making the sign for feeling *full*. Do this routinely before and after mealtimes. Add a new sign motion for *thirsty*.

- **How to adjust the activity:** Adapt the vocabulary words to a child's home language when giving the sign motions. Reinforce the activity frequently.
- **Did you meet your goal?** Can you observe the infant attending to your words and motions as you talk and make the signs for hungry and full?

In general, breastfed newborns tend to eat every 1½ to 3 hours, or about 8 to 12 times per day, for the first six weeks. By the time they are 4 to 6 months old, they consume greater volumes of breast milk, and feedings gradually decrease to five or more feedings per day (Kleinman, 2009). Newborns receiving formula typically need 8 to 12 feedings per day, although some will be hungry less often because formula takes longer to digest compared with breast milk. By 4 to 6 months, the number of formula feedings decreases to 5 to 8 bottles per day (although it can sometimes be more) as infants mature and are able to hold greater volumes in their stomachs (Queen Samour & King, 2012). With the introduction of solid foods, infants begin to need less breast milk or formula.

While guidelines on the frequency and amount infants should be fed are available, providers must be reminded to feed on demand. In addition, infants experience growth spurts, at which time the demand for formula or breast milk may increase. Table 4-2 provides information on the typical feeding expectations for infants illustrating the wide range of feedings per day and the amount of breast milk or formula consumed.

The expectations for infant meal quantities, outlined by the CACFP through the U.S. Department of Agriculture are from the USDA website, demonstrates the range of breast milk and formula intake on a per meal basis. The CACFP provides this information as a guideline for meeting reimbursement requirements. The CACFP supports on demand feeding by allowing flexibility in the time the feeding occurs (when the baby is hungry) and how much is offered (feed until the baby is full).

Inappropriate Infant Feeding Practices

At times, teachers may learn that families are not feeding infants in appropriate ways. Teachers can take the opportunity to gather resources and educate families about safe and healthy feeding practices. The family's health care provider and a

TABLE 4-2   Feeding Guidelines for Infants

Age	Approximate Number and Volume of Feedings (Breast Milk or Formula) per Day[a]	
	Number of Feedings/Day	Amount(oz)/Feeding[b]
0–4 mo	8–12	2–6
4–6 mo	4–8	6–8
6–8 mo	3–5	6–8
8–12 mo	3–4	6–8

[a]Formula and breast milk contain the same amount of calories per ounce; therefore, expressed breast milk's range of intake is comparable to that of formula.

[b]Recommendations do not include the introduction and amounts of solid foods to offer infants. See USDA Website for the CACFP Infant Meal Plan, which provides solid food recommendations.

Sources: American Academy of Nutrition and Dietetics, *The Pediatric Nutrition Care Manual*, 2012; and Queen Samour, P., & King, K., *Pediatric Nutrition*, 4th edition, 2012. Boston: Jones and Bartlett Learning.

registered dietitian nutritionist are valuable resources. The following sections illustrate some of the common poor feeding practices.

Adding Cereal to the Bottle

Sometimes adults add cereal to formula or breast milk with the misunderstanding that it will increase a baby's likelihood to sleep through the night. This is not the case, and it can be harmful because cereal in the bottle can lead to choking (Nemours, 2012) and increase the risk of acquiring allergies (American Academy of Pediatrics, 2012d). Putting cereal in the bottle may result in excessive caloric intake, putting the baby at risk for overweight and obesity (American Academy of Pediatrics, 2012g). If bottles containing formula (including those with added cereal) are given to infants when they are put to bed, the formula can pool in the mouth and create an ideal environment for cavity-causing bacteria (National Institute of Dental and Craniofacial Research & National Institute of Health, 2011).

Mothers may not recognize cereal as a solid food and may receive pressure from grandparents or other family members about feeding decisions (Heinig et al., 2006). The *Nutrition Note* discusses the influence of grandparents in feeding infants and offers suggestions on how teachers can collaborate with grandparents to support healthful infant feeding practices.

Finishing the Bottle

Adults may encourage a baby to finish the bottle to avoid wasting formula or breast milk. This disrupts the infant's ability to self-regulate food intake and alters responsiveness to internal cues of hunger and satiety, putting them at risk for developing obesity (Ruowei, Scanlon, May, Rose, & Birch, 2014). The infant's feeding cues should be respected. When the baby is full, the feeding is stopped and the extra formula or breast milk is discarded.

Using Honey in the Bottle or on the Pacifier

The inappropriate feeding practice of putting honey in a baby's bottle can have severe outcomes. A serious

Putting the baby to bed with a bottle increases the risk of cavities and choking. It also is a missed opportunity for socializing.

Jupiterimages/Thinkstock/Getty Images

Carla Mestas/Pearson Education, Inc.

Adults can reinforce internal cues by stopping feeding when the infant shows signs of fullness.

infantile botulism
a serious illness that results from ingesting *Clostridium botulinum* spores that release a deadly toxin in the gastrointestinal tract

foodborne illness called infantile botulism can occur in infants as a result of consuming honey (Division of Communicable Disease Control, Center for Infectious Diseases, California Department of Public Health, 2011). This illness occurs because infants' digestive systems are not fully developed. This allows the *C. botulinum* spores to grow and eventually release a potent toxin causing illness. This rare foodborne illness can cause a progression of symptoms that lead to paralysis and death if not identified early and treated.

Avoiding honey is imperative until after the baby's first birthday (American Academy of Pediatrics, 2012c). This includes foods to which honey has been added, such as yogurt with honey. Teachers can create awareness of the risk by providing parents access to resources. The California Department of Public Health's Infant Botulism Treatment and Prevention Program has created a website and brochure that explains the risk factors associated with this rare but deadly food poisoning (Division of Communicable Disease Control, California Department of Public Health, 2010).

Offering Alternative Milks

Families should not feed their babies with a product other than breast milk or infant formula. Milk produced by cows should not be served until a baby has reached 12 months of age. Consuming cow's milk can lead to iron-deficiency anemia and can cause gastrointestinal upset and intestinal blood loss in some infants. Cow's milk is too high in protein, sodium, and potassium for infants, which puts stress on the kidneys. Finally, cow's milk is not supplemented with vitamins and minerals that babies need (Kleinman, 2009; Queen Samour & King, 2012).

Goat's milk should not be used for the same reasons. Goat's milk is very low in folic acid, which can lead to a form of anemia (Queen Samour & King, 2012). Alternative vegetarian beverages designed for consumption by adults, such as soy beverages, rice beverages, and other vegetarian milk substitutes, are not acceptable for infants. These beverages may be too low in fat, and they are not supplemented appropriately to meet the vitamin and mineral needs of infants. The protein content of rice milks and other vegetarian milk substitutes, except soy milk, is low, and malnutrition has been reported in infants fed these types of beverages (U.S. Department of Agriculture, 2009). Teachers can offer guidance if parents suggest the use of alternative milks before a baby reaches his or her first birthday.

CHECK YOUR UNDERSTANDING 4.2

Click here to check your understanding of feeding infants from birth to 6 months of age.

FEEDING THE INFANT: 6 MONTHS TO THE FIRST BIRTHDAY

complementary foods
any foods or beverages introduced to babies' diets in addition to breast milk or formula

Between 6 and 12 months of age, babies' bodies and diets undergo a significant transformation. The maturation of the gastrointestinal tract allows the infant's diet to evolve from the exclusive intake of liquids to the consumption of adult-like solid foods. Babies are gradually exposed to a myriad of aromas, flavors, and textures that come with the introduction of complementary foods. Complementary foods are any foods or beverages introduced to babies' diets that are in addition to breast milk or formula.

NUTRITION NOTE   Grandparents and Infant Feeding Decisions

Parents have the ultimate responsibility for making decisions regarding the care and feeding of their infants. Grandparents play a wonderful and important role in the lives of their grandchildren, but sometimes they can exert significant influence on feeding decisions, especially when parents are young or inexperienced. Many grandparents share child-rearing responsibilities and are involved in dropping off and picking up children.

Grandparents have a natural interest in the child's well-being, but they may not be aware that guidelines for feeding infants have changed since they were parents. For example, grandparents may have introduced solids before 4 months of age, which has been shown to be harmful to infants. Grandparents may believe a heavy baby is a healthy baby and force infants to finish a bottle rather than respond to the infant's internal cues. Grandmothers may not be supportive of breastfeeding if they did not breast-feed themselves. Parents may make appropriate decisions about feeding that are not supported by grandparents, creating tension that can spill into the early childhood setting.

Teachers must respect boundaries and recognize that unless grandparents have legal custody or guardianship of their grandchildren; the parents have the final say about what to feed their children. However, teachers can help by creating a strong bond of communication among all family members involved in the infant's care. Teachers can provide sources of information for grandparents such as:

- Grandparents Play an Important Role available at http://lovingsupport.nal.usda.gov/content/grandparents-play-important-role
- A Special Message for Grandparents available at http://health.mo.gov/living/families/wic/wiclwp/pdf/R_WIC_Grandparents.pdf

North Dakota State University Education and Extension Service also has a handout entitled "Seniors and Food Safety: When Grandparents Take Care of Grandchildren." See the North Dakota State University publications website for more information.

These messages also help guide grandparents to be part of the infant's support team:

✓ Learn and follow new child care practices and recommendations, especially those that relate to infant feeding.

✓ Support the infant's family in their efforts to provide the best nutritional options for your grandchildren.

✓ Follow infant hunger and fullness cues. Allow infants to decide when they want to eat and how much.

✓ Give infants the gift of a healthful diet. As they begin their transition from breast milk or formula to solids, offer only nutritious foods and beverages.

✓ Spoil your grandbabies by giving them loving attention instead of rewarding them with food.

✓ Share the message of good nutrition with other family members.

Introducing Complementary Foods

As infants grow, their need for additional vitamins and minerals requires the introduction of additional foods and beverages. However, the ideal time for infants to start complementary foods has been a topic of ongoing discussion among different health organizations (Kleinman, 2009). Introducing solids too early can result in increased risk for choking, eczema, and food allergies. Early introduction of solids may displace the valuable nutrients found in breast milk and formula, thus interfering with proper growth (Grummer-Strawn et al., 2008; U.S. Department of Agriculture, 2009). Early introduction of solids is associated with an increased risk of developing obesity (Huh, Rifas-Shiman, Taveras, Oken, & Gillman, 2011; Dattilo et al., 2012). Many professional organizations recommend exclusive breastfeeding for around the first 6 months of life and adding solids when the baby is 6 months old (Academy of Nutrition and Dietetics, 2012; American Academy of Pediatrics, 2012; World Health Organization, 2011).

The "window of opportunity" for introducing complementary foods and advancing flavors and

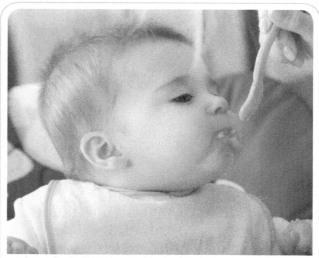

Babies should begin eating when they demonstrate developmental signs of readiness, usually between 4 and 6 months of age.

Igor Stepovik/123RF

textures occurs somewhere between 4 and 6 months of age through 10 months of age. Providing a gradual transition in food textures during this time decreases the risk of rejection of foods with more texture and consistency at a later date (Butte et al., 2004; Coulthard, Harris, & Emmett, 2009). Infants who are exposed to a variety of foods and textures are more accepting of new textures and new foods compared with those infants who are not (Blossfied, Collins, & Delahunty, 2007). For example, offering a baby puréed commercial infant bananas first, then well-mashed ripe bananas, and finally ripe bananas cut up into ¼-inch pieces is an example of a progression of textures. If this advance in texture does not occur, as babies get older, they may refuse more lumpy textures and have more long-term feeding problems (Coulthard et al., 2009). Ultimately the decision to start complementary foods is linked to the infant's nutritional needs and developmental signs of readiness. Teachers and families should use signs of infant readiness as guidelines when considering the introduction and progression of solid foods in babies' diets.

Linking Developmental Skills to Feedings

Transitioning from liquids to puréed solids, from puréed solids to textured foods, and then to the self-feeding of table foods are all eating achievements linked developmental milestones. Infants are born with the instinctual skills that help them survive. They know to turn reflexively toward the breast or bottle when their mouth or cheek is brushed by the nipple (rooting reflex) and will begin to suck when something touches the roof of their mouth (sucking reflex). When the lips are touched, the tongue comes out of the mouth (tongue thrust reflex). These reflexes help to ensure that infants can latch onto a bottle or breast. In addition, infants possess a gag reflex, which is activated when food is placed in the back of the mouth and results in the ejection of the food.

Infants' development and growth can help determine when to initiate semisolid foods. Solid food introduction occurs when infants develop the oral motor skills to consume semisolid foods safely (Queen Samour & King, 2012). The tongue thrust and gag reflexes gradually start to diminish. The transition through textures should coincide with infants' developmental progress from being able to keep food in their mouth, moving it around with their tongues, and then using an up-and-down chewing motion. Initial signs of readiness include the ability to sit with support and to indicate hunger by opening the mouth and leaning in or to indicate fullness by closing the mouth and leaning away (Academy of Nutrition and Dietetics, 2012; Queen Samour & King, 2012). Just like any other milestone, the developmental readiness for starting solid foods has an age range, and although some infants may be ready to eat solids earlier (around 4 to 5 months), in general, most will be ready to start complementary feedings at around 6 months of age (Cattaneo et al., 2011). Delaying the introduction of complementary food beyond the age of about 26 weeks may increase the risk of nutritional insufficiency, particularly for children from low-income families (Przyrembel, 2012). Compared with first-time parents, teachers may have more experience feeding infants, and thus their role is to help families learn to recognize the signs of developmental readiness.

Table 4-3 provides helpful information for determining the types of foods to introduce based on

Cascade Sorte and Matt Bracken

Infants progressively develop feeding skills. This infant has mastered the palmer grasp and has moved on to begin working on the pincer grasp by using his thumb and index finger to pick up an individual oat cereal ring.

TABLE 4-3 Infant Feeding Guidelines: Birth to 12 Months

Age Range	Development Feeding Characteristics	Key Recommendations	Infant Feedings
Birth to around 6 months	Instinctual reflexes present at birth through around 5 months include: • rooting reflex • suck-swallow-breathe reflex coordinates breathing with feeding • gag reflex when food is placed in the back of the mouth • tongue thrust occurs when lips are touched that allows sucking but not swallowing from a spoon or cup	1. Exclusively breast-feed for the first 6 months. 2. Begin transition to solids when infants exhibit readiness skills.	Breast milk and/or formula
	Infants develop readiness skills for the introduction of solids (around 4–6 months) that include: • ability to hold head up and sit with support • put fingers in mouth • open mouth to receive food • move food in the mouth with tongue to aid in swallowing • remove food from spoon with lips • indicate hunger by moving toward food and fullness by turning head away • tongue thrust and gag reflex start to diminish	1. A traditional first solid food is infant cereal, which provides iron and zinc 2. Introduce single-ingredient new foods and wait 3–5 days before introducing another new food to observe for allergic reactions 3. Do not offer juice or water as all the liquid that baby needs comes from breast milk or formula 4. Do not offer honey through the first year of life due to the risk of botulism foodborne illness	Fortified infant cereal, puréed vegetables, meats, and fruits

Around 6 to 12 months	Infants continue to develop feeding skills that support the introduction of solids with more textures (around 6–9 months) such as:
	• sits unsupported
	• is able to position food in the mouth and move food between jaws for chewing
	• uses an up-and-down chewing motion
	• begins to reach for food and feed self
	• takes food off spoon readily
	• drinks from a cup with some spilling
		1. Breastfeeding recommended for at least the first year of life
		2. Infant moves through 4 stages of textures:
		  • Puréed
		  • Mashed (puréed with a few lumps)
		  • Chopped (more lumpy)
		  • Small pieces of soft food (no more than ¼-inch thick)
		3. Be sure infants have mastered one texture before moving to another
		4. Infants should begin to drink liquids from a cup
		5. Do not add sugar, salt, spices, gravies, or butter to infant foods
			Introduce a variety of healthy foods of appropriate transitional texture such as meats, cereals, vegetables, fruits, eggs and fish, beans, tofu, cottage cheese, plain yogurt, rice, and noodles

	Infants begin to master chewing and take more of a role in self feeding (around 9–12 months): • begins to use a rotary motion for chewing food • is able to move food from side to side of mouth • mashes food using the tongue and jaw • uses the thumb and finger in a pincher grasp to pick up food • self-feeds finger foods • starts to use a spoon to self-feed • curves mouth around a cup	1. Introduce finger foods. 2. Offer a variety of new foods during this window of opportunity. 3. If a new food is rejected, offer it again. It can take numerous tries before an infant accepts a food.	Introduce a variety of healthy foods of appropriate transitional texture such as meats, cereals, vegetables, fruits, eggs and fish, beans, tofu, cottage cheese, plain yogurt, rice, and noodles

Sources: American Academy of Pediatrics, 2012, Ages and Stages: Switching to Solid Foods from healthychildren.org. American Academy of Pediatrics, American Public Health Association, National Resource Center for Health and Safety in Child Care and Early Education, 2011; Caring for our children: National health and safety performance standards; *Guidelines for Early Care and Education Programs*. 3rd edition. Elk Grove Village, IL: American Academy of Pediatrics; Washington, DC: American Public Health Association. Also available at http://nrckids.org. *Pediatric Nutrition Handbook*, 6th edition, edited by R. E. Kleinman, 2009, Elk Grove Village, IL: American Academy of Pediatrics; "The Start Healthy Feeding Guidelines for Infants and Toddlers," by N. Butte, K. Cobb, J. Dwyer, W. Graney, and K. Rickard, 2004, *The Journal of the American Dietetic Association, 104*(3), 442–454; *Infant Nutrition and Feeding: A Guide for Use in the WIC and CSF Programs*, 2009; U.S. Department of Agriculture, Food and Nutrition Service, Special Supplemental Nutrition Program for Women, Infants and Children, 2009, Washington, DC: U.S. Department of Agriculture from http://wicworks.nal.usda.gov/infants/infant-feeding-guide; and Key Changes in WIC Recommendations, 2009, California WIC program from http://www.cdph.ca.gov/programs/wicworks /Documents/NE/WIC-NE-InfantFeedingGuidelines-ComparisonOfInfantFeedingRecommendations.doc.

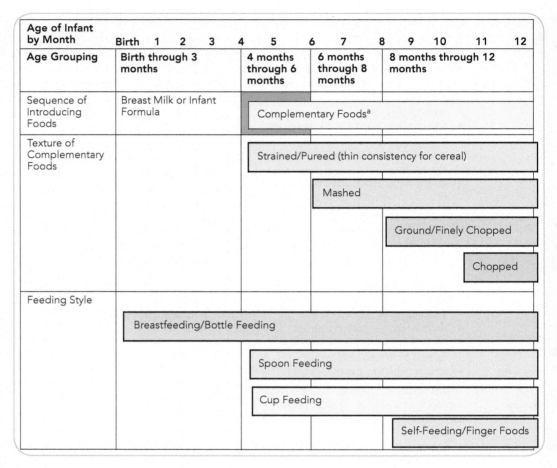

FIGURE 4-6

Relationships Between the Introduction of Complementary Foods and the Transition in Texture and Feeding Styles

Special note: represents the age range when most infants are developmentally ready to begin consuming complementary foods. The American Academy of Pediatrics section on breastfeeding recommends exclusive breastfeeding for the first six months of life. The AAP Committee on Nutrition recommends that in developed countries, complementary foods may be introduced between ages 4 and 6 months. This is a population-based recommendation, and the timing of introduction of complementary foods for an individual infant may differ from the recommendation.

aComplementary foods include infant cereal, fruits, vegetables, and meats and other protein-rich foods modified to a texture appropriate for the infant's developmental readiness.

Source: From *Infant Nutrition and Feeding: A Reference Handbook for Nutrition and Health Counselors in the WIC and CSF Programs*, National Agricultural Library, 2008, retrieved September 20, 2009, from http://www.nal.usda.gov/wicworks/Topics /Infant_Feeding_Guide.html#guide.

developmental milestones. Figure 4-6 offers guidance on the sequencing of food in relation to food textures and feeding skills.

Understanding What to Feed Infants

Research does not support the introduction of complementary foods in any specific order. However, the American Academy of Pediatrics recommends fortified infant cereals as important first foods because they introduce key nutrients, iron and zinc, which are important minerals in the diets of breastfed infants (Kleinman, 2009). Teachers can share with families the benefits of introducing fortified cereals in their babies' diets especially when the babies are breast-fed.

Single-ingredient foods should be introduced into infants' diets one at a time with a wait period of three to five days before introducing the next new food. This way, if an allergy develops, it is easier to identify the food that caused it (Kleinman, 2009). For example, after introducing rice cereal and offering it successfully, an infant might then progress to another cereal. Once all of the cereals have been introduced, meats might be a logical next step for breastfed infants. Commercially prepared yogurt desserts or smoothies, should not be offered because they often contain added sugar in the form of concentrated fruit juice and other ingredients such as rice flour. Infant dinners contain a variety of mixed ingredients that make it difficult to determine the food source that triggers an allergic reaction. The CACFP does not reimburse for baby food combination dinners or dessert baby foods, and the WIC program only offers single-ingredient baby food in its infant meal packages, although combinations of single ingredients such as apple-banana are allowed (Oregon Department of Education, 2009; U.S. Department of Agriculture, Food and Nutrition Service, 2012b). A notebook or chart checklist system in which parents communicate the acceptability of a new food to the caregiver can be helpful. Figure 4-7 provides an example.

WHAT IF . . .

you had limited experience with babies and were assigned to provide care in an infant class? What questions or worries might you have about feeding babies? What resources could you turn to for advice?

FIGURE 4-7 Infant Food Checklist

Baby's name _____

General guidelines to remember:

- Introduce the new food.
- Offer it for approximately 3 to 5 days before introducing another new food.
- Watch for signs of allergic reaction.
- Remember: Babies do not need fat, sugar, spices, or salt added to foods.

Check the appropriate boxes when you want your baby's teacher to begin a new food at school that the baby has been exposed to at home and tolerates.

Infant Cereal

☐ Rice cereal   ☐ Barley cereal   ☐ Oatmeal

Strained Meats/Poultry

☐ Strained chicken   ☐ Strained turkey   ☐ Strained beef or veal

Strained Vegetables

☐ Green beans   ☐ Sweet potatoes   ☐ Peas

☐ Squash   ☐ Carrots   ☐ Spinach

Strained Fruits

☐ Peaches   ☐ Prunes   ☐ Guava

☐ Applesauce   ☐ Apricots   ☐ Papaya

☐ Pears   ☐ Mango   ☐ Prunes

☐ Bananas

☐ Finger foods _____

_____

_____

Avoid Introducing Fruit Juice Early

Fruit juice should not be offered to infants before 6 months of age because it can replace other foods, including breast milk or formula. If juice is given to babies after they reach 6 months of age, it should be 100% juice, limited to no more than 4 ounces per day and introduced in a cup rather than a bottle. Excess juice intake can increase the risk for excessive weight gain and dental caries, and it can lead to diarrhea, gas, abdominal distention, and diaper rash. Water is not necessary in most situations before infants are 6 months of age because their fluid needs are met by breast milk or formula. Once solids are introduced to the diet or when days are hot, small amounts of water can be offered to infants with advice from their physicians (American Academy of Pediatrics, 2012b).

Home-Prepared Baby Food

Some caregivers choose to make home-prepared baby food. This is an acceptable alternative that can be cost-effective and offers increased flexibility with ingredients and textures; however, the available time caregivers have to make home-prepared baby food and food safety are important considerations. Home-prepared infant foods should be made from fresh ingredients with no added salt or sugar, cooked until soft and tender, puréed, and stored promptly. Figure 4-8 provides guidelines on preparing and storing baby food. The *Health Hint* describes some of the precautions to consider when preparing infant foods.

Understanding How to Feed Solids to Infants

An important goal for teachers and families is to create a feeding experience that continues to foster the feeding relationship. Feed babies at a pace that is

---

Making your own baby food is easy

Homemade baby food is good for your baby. It will help your baby get used to the foods your family eats, and you always know what is in it!

Did you know that you can help your baby get a good start with solids using the foods and utensils you already have home?

Try these simple steps:

1 You will need a clean fork, potato masher, food processor or blender.

2 To make sure your fresh fruits and vegetables are clean and safe, scrub them, peel off the skin and remove stems, pits and seeds.

3 Prepare meats by removing bones, skin and visible fat.

4 Cook hard or tough foods until soft.

5 Cool to room temperature.

6 Mash, purée or blend food by adding small amounts of cooking water, breast milk, or formula until mixture is smooth.

Even if you like foods sweet or salty, your baby will prefer the natural flavor of foods—avoid adding sugar, salt or syrups to baby's food.

> Never use honey in your baby's food- honey can make your baby very sick.

Keeping your baby food safe

The safest way to feed your baby is to put the amount of food your baby will eat into a small bowl. Throw away anything that is left over in the bowl.

Feeding your baby directly from the container will cause the food to spoil quickly.

Storing

- If you have any baby food leftover, you can store it in the refrigerator for up to two days in a container with a tight-fitting lid.

- If you want to keep your baby food longer, you can then put the container in the freezer.

- One good way to store baby food in individual portions is to freeze it in an ice cube tray. Once it is frozen, transfer the cubes to a plastic bag and return them to the freezer.

FIGURE 4-8

Making Baby Food

Source: Used with permission from the Oregon WIC program www.healthoregon.org/WIC.

HEALTH HINT   Is Homemade Baby Food Always Best?

Many families and early childhood teachers enjoy preparing baby food from fresh ingredients. They like the idea of knowing exactly what the infant is eating. They may make this choice because they prefer organic ingredients, have an abundance of fresh produce from home gardens, or want to save money. Making baby food is a healthful choice; however, adults who care for young children must be aware that chemicals can be present in the home-prepared baby food. For example, nitrates are found in some foods and water. Infants who consume unsafe levels of nitrates develop a type of anemia known as "methemoglobinemia" or "blue baby syndrome." Babies younger than 3 to 6 months of age are particularly susceptible. Formula and baby food prepared with well water contaminated with high levels of nitrates can be the source of toxic levels. Families and child care settings with wells should check the nitrate level in their well water, and vegetables with high nitrate content should not be given to children in excess amounts. Commercially prepared baby foods are monitored for nitrate content and do not pose a risk. In addition, infants do not receive high levels of nitrates in breast milk regardless of a mother's diet.

Sources: Basic Information About Nitrate in Drinking Water by U.S Environmental Protection Agency, 2012, from http://water.epa.gov/drink/contaminants/basicinformation/nitrate.cfm; "Vegetable-borne Nitrate and Nitrite and the Risk of Methaemoglobinaemia," by Thomas Chan, 2011, *Toxicology Letters*, 200(1), 107–108; *Infant Nutrition and Feeding: A Guide for Use in the WIC and CSF Programs* by U.S. Department of Agriculture, Food and Nutrition Service, Special Supplemental Nutrition Program for Women Infants and Children, 2009, from http://wicworks.nal.usda.gov/infants/infant-feeding-guide; Starting Solid Foods, by the American Academy of Pediatrics, 2008, from http://www.aap.org/bookstore/brochures/br_solidfoods_2008_sample.pdf; "Drinking Water from Private Wells and Risks to Children" by Walter J. Rogan, Michael T. Brady, the Committee on Environmental Health, and the Committee on Infectious Diseases, *Pediatrics*, 2009, 123(6), e1123–e1137 (doi: 10.1542/peds.2009-0752);

comfortable for them. When feeding infants solid foods, consider the following practical recommendations:

- The teacher's hands should be washed before preparing and serving the meal, and the infant's hands should be washed before eating.
- Teachers should have space identified for feeding infants that includes high chairs with removable trays that can be easily sanitized.
- Babies should have specifically assigned and labeled high chairs.
- Babies should be placed in a high chair when fed unless they have special needs or disabilities. Sitting up straight with feet supported promotes proper swallowing and helps reduce the risk of choking.
- Teachers should use plastic-coated baby spoons and have extra spoons available to allow the infant to hold his or her own spoon while feeding.
  - Food should be placed on the tip of the spoon to make it easier to access and swallow and begin by mixing a small amount of cereal into breast milk or formula and gradually increase texture.
- Teachers should always prepare food in a small bowl for serving. Don't feed babies directly from a jar because this will contaminate the baby food.
  - Do not force children to finish food in the bowl. Stop feeding when the infant shows signs of being full.
- Teachers should always supervise the baby in the high chair. Never leave the baby unattended.
- Teachers need to remember babies have small stomachs and, therefore, require small but frequent meals and snacks.

The CACFP provides other helpful guidelines on suggested meals and snack routines for infants (search the USDA Website for CACFP Meal Pattern Requirements for Infants and Children).

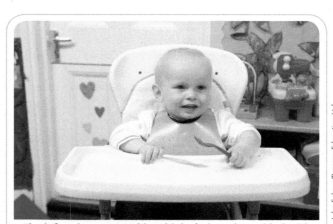

The infant is supported in a high chair and provided with spoons to foster the development of self-feeding.

Jules Selmes/Pearson Education Ltd

Feeding the Older Infant

From 6 months to 1 year of age, infants are transitioning from puréed foods to modified adult foods over an amazingly short period of time. Caregivers can foster the development of infants' oral and self-feeding skills. By offering developmentally appropriate foods and providing verbal and physical guidance, caregivers can optimize children's development at mealtimes.

Offering Finger Foods

palmer grasp
the developmental ability of infants to pick up items with the heel of the palm and four fingers

pincer grasp
the developmental ability of infants to pick up items using the thumb and forefinger

The introduction of finger foods gives infants an opportunity to practice their fine motor skills. Finger foods can be introduced into diets when infants can sit up, have developed the palmer grasp (the ability to pick up items with the heel of the palm and four fingers), and then later have developed the pincer grasp (the ability to pick up items using the thumb and forefinger) and can bring this food to their mouth. In addition, oral motor skills such as using the jaw to mash foods and moving food side to side in the mouth are indicators that babies are ready to eat finger foods. This generally occurs between 7 and 8 months of age. Finger foods should be soft enough for babies to chew using their gums and should be offered in sizes and shapes that prevent infants from choking. Examples of finger foods are listed in Figure 4-9.

Reducing the Risk of Choking

When planning meals for infants, it is imperative to consider whether the food prepared might pose a choking risk. Although Chapter 7 discusses choking risks in young children and provides a list of high-risk foods to avoid, this section addresses the specific choking concerns of infants. All foods offered to an infant should be cut into pieces no larger than ¼ inch in diameter. Because infants are new eaters and are developing oral motor skills at different rates, teachers should continually monitor and evaluate their chewing and swallowing skills (NAEYC—Academy for Early Childhood Program Accreditation, 2012).

FIGURE 4-9   Examples of First Finger Foods

Fruits: Remove skin, seeds, or pits

- Diced or mashed ripe banana
- Diced ripe peaches, plums, or pears
- Diced mango or papaya or melon
- Diced canned fruits packed in their own juice, such as peaches, pears, or apricots

Vegetables

- Cooked and diced sweet or white potatoes, peas, and lima beans
- Cooked and diced broccoli or cauliflower
- Soft cooked and diced zucchini and summer squash

Grains and starches

- Toast wedges or plain soda crackers
- Soft cooked pasta
- Cereal rings

Protein foods

- Shredded or small cubes of cheese (¼ to ½ inch depending on age)
- Tender pieces of chicken or turkey cut into pea-sized pieces and served with gravy

Note: Only foods ¼ inch diameter or smaller should be offered.

Food items used for teething can pose a risk too. For example, chicken bones, raw carrots, frozen bananas, bagels, and whole apples are not recommended. The following foods have characteristics that cause concern for choking in infants:

- Slippery round or circular foods, such as grapes and cooked carrots.
- Easy-to-inhale foods such as sunflower seeds, peanuts, raisins, popcorn, and corn kernels.
- Sticky, chewy foods such as peanut butter, fruit leathers, and gummy candy.
- Firm food that can wedge in the throat such as hot dogs, whole bananas, and bagels.
- Hard, dry foods such as pretzels and chips (Mayo Clinic, 2011).

As older infants advance their eating skills, textured foods can be mixed with softer foods to aid in swallowing. For example, adding puréed carrots to rice, puréed sweet potatoes to finely diced turkey, or puréed peaches to alphabet pasta provides healthful, easy-to-swallow combinations.

Teachers can reduce the risk of choking by ensuring that infants are fed in a calm environment with limited distractions. For example, wiping off infants' faces before they swallow their last bite or putting food in their mouths while they are crying or laughing places babies at risk for choking. Likewise, medications for teething pain should not be applied before meals because gums, mouth, and throat can become numb. This can make swallowing more difficult. Teachers should sit and eat with infants at mealtimes to ensure safety.

Teachers may experience family members who don't support or understand the risks of specific foods. For instance, a parent might say, "Oh, my baby does fine with grapes. She knows how to chew them" or "I always give him popcorn, and he never chokes on it." Teachers have a responsibility to inform families of inappropriate feeding practices that put young infants at risk for choking.

Child care settings should establish policies, including a descriptive list of prohibited foods that prevent choking hazards from being served in the child care center.

WHAT IF . . .

while unpacking a home-prepared lunch for an 11-month-old you discovered a choking hazard (a cold hot dog packed in a baggie) as part of the meal. What would you do? What other concerns might you have about serving a hot dog to this infant?

Introducing Foods That Are Low in Nutritional Quality

Sometimes adults who care for infants introduce solids that are low in nutritional quality or foods that are high in calories in relation to the nutrients they offer. A better choice is to offer foods that have **high nutrient density**. Nutrient density describes foods with a high percentage of nutrients per serving size, but they are not excessively high in calories. For example, mashed bananas are nutrient dense because they are a rich source of vitamin C, potassium, and fiber and are low in fat and salt. Single-ingredient puréed infant foods are nutrient dense. Infants in the United States are often exposed to foods of minimal nutritional value such as French fries, candy, cookies, and cake.

high nutrient density describes foods with a high percentage of nutrients per serving size, but they are not excessively high in calories

Introducing these foods could replace nutrient dense foods and expose infants to excess amounts of sodium and calories. Families need positive reinforcement and guidance in helping their infants establish healthful eating habits. Teachers play an informative role in helping families navigate the introduction of solid foods and encouraging the introduction of age-appropriate soft-cooked and puréed or mashed whole foods such as fruits, cooked vegetables, and meats and poultry. Program policies and CACFP guidelines set the tone for early childhood settings and create a nutritional ambiance that can positively impact how families view food.

Infants Learning About Food and Eating

Eating is a learning process. Infants learn about food if they are allowed to explore it. This involves looking, touching, poking, squishing, smelling, and tasting food. Through these explorations, infants are learning how to move food in their mouth, to chew, and to swallow. Allowing babies to self-feed also is a learning experience. Avoid forcing children to eat foods. Babies can be cautious about new foods, and it may require numerous exposures before a new food is accepted. Adults must be understanding and patient as new foods are introduced and to respect the baby's cues for hunger, fullness, and enjoyment.

Teachers play a role in helping children to learn about foods. Continually offering infants a wide variety of foods increases their exposure to different foods. In addition, modeling good eating behaviors positively influences children's eating because babies and children learn from what they see teachers do and what they hear teachers say. Consider the following scenario:

Mary is in charge of the infant class. She takes a sip of the soft drink she has sitting on her desk. Jeremy, an 11-month-old, points to her can of soft drink but Mary says, "No, this is not for you, Jeremy." Jeremy starts crying just as Rosalie, his mother, comes in to pick him up. Mary explains why Jeremy is crying. Rosalie replies, "Well, I always share my soft drink with him. He loves it." What can Mary say?

Michelle D. Milliman/Shutterstock

Babies should be allowed to fully experience the food they are offered. Let them play with the food. The feel of the food as well as the taste and smell of the food all contribute to babies' learning experiences.

CHECK YOUR UNDERSTANDING 4.3

Click here to check your understanding of feeding infants from 6 months to 1 year of age.

FEEDING INFANTS WITH SPECIAL HEALTH CARE NEEDS

Infants with health-related conditions sometimes face significant feeding challenges that can impact growth and development. These conditions may include developmental disorders and physical disabilities. Teachers and families, as well as health care professionals, form a team to help infants acquire eating skills and behaviors that support good nutrition with sufficient calories for optimal growth.

Infants with Feeding Problems

feeding problems
developmental disorders related to the mouth

Infants with developmental delays may not always be effective eaters. Feeding problems become apparent as they struggle with nursing or bottle feedings and perhaps fail to gain weight appropriately. **Feeding problems** are defined by the American Academy of Pediatrics as developmental disorders related to the mouth (Kleinman, 2009). Feeding problems related to the swallowing process are identified in infants who have difficulty consuming liquids and who cough or choke during meals. Infants who gag on foods that need to be chewed and have a strong preference for smooth or crunchy foods but have no problems with liquids also show symptoms of a feeding problem (Kleinman, 2009).

oral hyposensitivity
an oral motor condition in which infants have less feeling in the mouth

Feeding problems can be either sensory or motor-based (Kleinman, 2009). For example, some babies may have issues with oral sensitivity. Infants with **oral hyposensitivity** have less feeling in the mouth, and therefore, are less conscious of where food is once it is placed inside their mouths. Oral hypersensitivity, on the other hand, describes a condition in which infants are overly aware of foods placed in or near their mouths. For these babies, food brought near or into the mouth can cause a gag or bite-down reflex. These conditions can make mealtimes challenging for both baby and caregiver (Yang, Lucas, & Feucht, 2010). Babies with oral motor delays may have difficulties chewing due to weak jaw muscles. They also may have problems moving food around in the mouth due to uncoordinated tongue movement, which can result in choking, gagging, and labored eating (Kleinman, 2009; Yang, Lucas, & Feucht, 2010). Teachers who suspect feeding issues or have concerns about an infant's ability to consume solids should confer with the family and recommend consultation with the family's health care provider.

oral hypersensitivity
an oral motor condition in which infants are overly aware of foods placed in or near their mouths

oral motor delay
a developmental delay that can result in weak oral muscles and tongue movement

Feeding Premature Infants

Premature infants, defined as infants who are born before 37 weeks of gestation, may have special feeding needs. Premature infants should receive breast milk if possible. Compared with formula, breast milk offers immunological protection and improved developmental outcomes. In premature infants (but not necessarily near-term infants), expressed breast milk can be fortified with special milk fortifiers to meet the higher protein, vitamin, and mineral requirements of growth (Academy of Nutrition and Dietetics, 2012; Kleinman, 2009). Premature infants who are not breast-fed require formulas that are specified for premature infants to meet the infants' higher nutrient needs.

If families want teachers to prepare the formula in any way that deviates from standard mixing directions on the label or to add fortifiers to breast milk, the child care setting should have a written policy that requires a prescription from the health care provider with a clearly written recipe. As the infant develops, teachers should rely on the guidance of the family and their health care provider on when to introduce solid foods for premature infants. As a rule, the introduction of solids for these infants should be based on developmental readiness, which may need to be based on the baby's due date or corrected age as opposed to date of birth. A baby's corrected age is the number of weeks the baby was born early subtracted from his or her current age in weeks. For example, an infant who enters a child care setting when he is 3 months old but was 3 weeks premature would have a corrected age of 9 weeks of age. Generally infants who are premature begin solids when they demonstrate signs of developmental readiness around 4 to 6 months corrected age (Academy of Nutrition and Dietetics, 2012).

corrected age
the number of weeks a baby is born early subtracted from the baby's current age in weeks

Feeding Infants with Cleft Lip and Cleft Palate

Cleft lip and cleft palate are birth defects of the lip and mouth that contribute to particularly complex swallowing problems. During the first few weeks of pregnancy, the sides of the lip and mouth begin developing and eventually come together. In some cases, the sides of the mouth or lips do not fuse properly, creating a cleft palate or cleft lip or both. A cleft lip is generally not problematic for babies because they can still suck and swallow. A cleft palate, however, consists of an opening in the roof of the mouth. Babies born with a cleft palate may not be able to suck successfully and are at increased risk of poor intake (Academy of Nutrition and Dietetics, 2012). The use of special bottles can allow formula or breast milk to be squeezed into the infant's mouth. Elongated nipples also can be used to help with sucking and swallowing (see Figure 4-5, the Medela Special Needs Feeder

cleft lip
a birth defect in which the lip does not grow together

cleft palate
a birth defect that consists of an opening in the roof of the mouth

FIGURE 4-10

Position for Feeding a Baby with Cleft Lip or Cleft Palate

CHECK YOUR UNDERSTANDING 4.4

Click here to check your understanding of feeding infants with special health care needs.

nipple). Figure 4-10 illustrates how to position a baby with cleft lip or cleft palate when feeding. Feeding in the upright position prevents breast milk or formula from getting in the infant's nose.

A cleft lip is surgically closed at about 6 weeks to 3 months of age, and a cleft palate is repaired at about 9 to 12 months; therefore, caregivers should make sure infants are well nourished prior to surgery (Academy of Nutrition and Dietetics, 2012). Children with cleft lip and palate can be fed an adequate diet with the use of a few simple strategies such as those outlined in Figure 4-11. Sometimes infants born with cleft lip and cleft palate require alternative feeding strategies. See the Progressive Programs & Practices feature that shows how an early Head Start program supports the family of an infant with significant feeding challenges.

FEEDING INFANTS FROM DIFFERENT CULTURES

The introduction of solids into the diets of infants is an important and celebrated event in many cultures. For example, one of children's first rites of passage in the Hindu religion is *annaprashana*. This ceremony celebrates the baby's first taste of solid food, a sweet rice dish prepared with milk. The baby sits in the lap of a family member and is fed the rice dish in a celebratory event that includes family and friends (Rajendran, 2011). Families of the Jewish faith may also participate in a weaning celebration. This is a family affair that occurs at home and can include a religious blessing and songs. Someone other than the mother, such as the father, a sibling, or a grandfather, has the honored role of feeding the baby solids for the first time (Diamant, 2005). In the United States, families might honor the start of feeding solids in a more casual way by taking photos of their baby's first bite of solid food and writing an entry about the event in the child's baby book or blog.

In general, most cultures have traditional first foods that include some type of grain mixed with water, broth, or milk to create a gruel or porridge that is fed to infants (Katz, 2003). Asian families, for example, may prepare congee, a thick rice-based soup to which a variety of ingredients can be added, such as tiny pieces of meat or fish (Kittler, Sucher, & Nelms, 2012; Ramachandran, 2004). Hispanic

---

FIGURE 4-11   Tips for Teachers: Feeding an Infant with a Cleft Lip or Cleft Palate

- Have parents demonstrate the use of special feeding equipment. If an elongated nipple with flexible bottle is used, practice squeezing the bottle in the sink to get an idea of the correct rate of flow.
- Have parents present the first time you feed the infant.
- Feed infants in an upright position to prevent milk from going up into the nose and ear canals (see Figure 4-10).
- Select a comfortable seat and try to reduce distractions. Infant feeding may take longer.
- Pay extra attention to burping because more air may be swallowed while feeding.
- Be supportive of the mother who pumps and feeds the baby breast milk.
- Remember: The progression of solids in babies with cleft lip or cleft palate is the same as comparably aged infants.

PROGRESSIVE PROGRAMS & PRACTICES

Caring for Caden

By Pam Woitt, Home Based Educator (HBE), and Madeleine Sprague, RD, Kidco Early Head Start, Albany, Oregon

Jessica and Robyn were 17 and 18 years old, respectively, and still seniors in high school when their baby, Caden, was born. Taking care of an infant can be challenging for teenagers but even more so for Jessica and Robyn, as Caden was born with cleft palate and Pierre Robin syndrome. With Pierre Robin, the lower jaw is smaller than a normally developed jaw, and Caden's tongue would fall back into his throat. He could not swallow and had difficulty breathing.

Caden spent three weeks in the hospital. A feeding tube was put in his nose to help him receive nutrition and to help with his breathing. Before Caden was sent home from the hospital, Robyn and Jessica were trained on how to replace the tube and how to use a special bottle to feed Caden.

Many people would be intimidated by the special care Caden needed, but Robyn and Jessica did what needed to be done. They jumped right in and fed Caden, changed the tubes, and went back to their schooling. Robyn started back to school full-time, and Jessica was able to get a tutor to come and work with her a few days a week. Both were committed to graduating on time.

Jessica had enrolled in Early Head Start during her seventh month of pregnancy, and the Home Based Educator (HBE) provided weekly home visits. These visits focused on preparation for parenthood, prenatal health concerns, the relationship with her partner, and the birth process. After Caden was born, the home based educator continued to offer support and helped connect the parents with resources in Portland. The parents signed up for and were able to receive SSD for Caden. The HBE informed them about the Ride Line transportation service to help get them back and forth to doctors' visits. These parents used all resources available to them.

Robyn and Jessica worked very hard to keep up with their studies and kept in frequent contact with their school counselors. They kept all their scheduled home visits with the HBE, and they never hesitated to ask questions. With the help of the HBE, they filled out five scholarship applications. They received all five scholarships in addition to a few they hadn't even applied for. Robyn

didn't just graduate; he overcame having to take extra classes to make up for those that didn't transfer from his previous school and raised his GPA in the process. Jessica was able to complete all her classes working with the tutor. Graduation was a very proud moment for their friends and family!

Patrick Walton/Pamela Walton Photography

Robyn said that Early Head Start was important in helping them fulfill their goals because the HBE believed in them; offered support by educating them on parenthood, child development, and nutrition; and provided encouragement and connections for taking care of a child with a disability.

Caden is now 18 months old and recently had jaw distraction surgery to bring out his lower jaw, had surgery to fix his cleft palate, and had his feeding tube removed. He is able to eat regular food. All this took place during Robyn and Jessica's first year of college. They kept up with their studies and managed Caden's appointments. Robyn recently earned his driver's license, and they no longer need the assistance of Ride Line.

Robyn and Jessica are great examples that when you have and use the support of family and community, you can accomplish anything!

---

families may choose to offer bean broth with small pieces of soaked tortilla, mashed beans, rice, and broth-based soups (Mennella, Ziegler, Briefel, & Novak, 2006). In the United States, rice, barley, and oatmeal are commercial baby cereals that are offered as traditional first foods.

The different cultural practices in feeding infants point out the need for teachers to understand and respect the basis of food choice in different cultural groups. At the same time, teachers have an important responsibility to ensure the safety and nutritional quality of foods offered at their child care setting. Both families and teachers share a common goal, which is to support the optimal health and development of the infants in their care.

CHECK YOUR UNDERSTANDING 4.5

Click here to check your understanding of feeding infants from different cultures.

SUMMARY

- Good nutrition during infancy is instrumental to growth and development. Infants who receive too much or too little nourishment can suffer immediate and long-term consequences.
- Breastfeeding is the preferred choice of feeding and should be supported in child care settings. Although breast milk is the ideal source of nutrition, formula can provide an alternative food source for infants that will support their growth. Infants should be introduced to solid foods between 4 to 6 months of age to help meet their needs for dietary sources of zinc and iron.
- When feeding infants breast milk, formula, or solid foods, teachers need to develop a supportive feeding relationship. Teachers need to be sensitive to feeding cues and recognize signs of hunger and fullness. A nurturing relationship between teachers and infants creates a climate of understanding and trust, which in turn supports effective feeding.
- Teachers should feed infants on-demand during the infant's first six months of life and allow infants to dictate when and how much they eat. Teachers also should promote healthful eating habits by routinely exposing infants to a wide variety of nutritious foods and modeling good eating habits. Teachers encourage infants to experience healthful eating by permitting them to use all their senses when they eat: see, touch, smell, taste, and even play with food during meals and snack times.
- Teachers have an important responsibility to work with families and their health care providers to accommodate infants with special needs. Teachers also must make conscientious efforts to understand different cultural practices related to feeding infants. Continued close communication between teachers and families is the cornerstone of collaborative care and facilitates the optimal nourishment of infants.

Chapter Quiz

 Click here to check your understanding of Chapter 4, Feeding Infants.

Discussion Starters

1. How would you support a nursing mother who is returning to work but has a job with an inflexible schedule and a boss who is unsympathetic to the mother's breast feeding goals?
2. A mother is hearing contradictory advice from friends, relatives, and health care professionals about introducing solid foods to her infant. How would you help this mother without adding to the confusing advice she has already received?
3. A mother is feeding her infant a cultural dish that contains honey. How do you manage this situation in a culturally sensitive way while considering the safety of her infant?

Practice Points

1. Baby Matt is 6 months old. He is currently being exclusively breastfed. His mother Jenna is wondering how to begin solids. Jenna asks Fran for advice. List the questions you might ask Jenna as you gather information for developing a feeding plan.

2. Using CACFP meal patterns for infants, found by searching the USDA website for CACFP meal patterns, design a menu for a 10-month-old infant.

3. Your child care center does not have a policy on choking hazards. Draft a policy on choking hazards and provide a list of foods you would prohibit.

Web Resources

American Academy of Pediatrics

Centers for Disease Control and Prevention: Breastfeeding

Infant Nutrition and Feeding: A Guide for Use in the WIC and CSF Programs

La Leche League

National Resource Center for Health and Safety in Child Care and Early Education

World Health Organization (WHO) Safe preparation, storage and handling of powdered infant formula: Guidelines

Key Terms

Cleft lip

Cleft palate

Colostrum

Complementary foods

Corrected age

Feeding problems

Feeding relationship

Fore milk

Formula intolerance

High nutrient density

Hind milk

Infantile botulism

Oral hypersensitivity

Oral hyposensitivity

Oral motor delays

Palmer grasp

Pincer grasp

CHAPTER 5

Feeding Toddlers, Preschoolers, and School-Age Children

learning outcomes

After reading this chapter, you should be able to:

1. Define the nutritional needs of toddlers and discuss how to manage eating issues typical of this age group.

2. Describe characteristics of preschool children's diets and factors that enhance how preschoolers learn about food and nutrition.

3. Explain how to create a quality nutritional environment for school-age children that supports the dietary guidelines and enhances the goals of the school lunch program.

CASE STUDY

Laura, a teacher in the toddler class, is concerned about Michaela, an 18-month-old who attends her child care program. Michaela is a petite child who was born four weeks premature and has a history of poor growth. Her mother, Hanna, has strong ideas about what and how much Michaela should eat. She insists that Laura make sure Michaela eats all of her lunch. She tells Laura, "Unless I watch her like a hawk, she won't eat, and the doctor says she needs to gain weight." Laura has tried a variety of ways to get Michaela to eat. Michaela is often resistant, and mealtimes have become stressful. Laura is concerned that sometimes the only nourishment Michaela will consume is her milk.

The situation comes to a head when Michaela, in a fit of frustration, throws her lunch plate to the floor. Laura, with Hanna's enthusiastic agreement, requests a meeting with their program's dietitian, Christina, who oversees their food service. Christina knows that using forceful techniques for getting children to eat during mealtimes often backfires. She commends both Hanna's and Laura's efforts on behalf of Michaela to provide her with a healthful diet, but points out the missing link for success—allowing Michaela to decide what she is going to eat and how much. Hanna is worried that this approach won't work, but she agrees to a trial period. At first, Michaela eats less, but as she sees that both her mother and teacher are not pressuring her to eat, she begins to feel free to explore her food. Michaela is still not a big eater, but things are improving. Mealtimes are less stressful, and Hanna is pleased that her relationship with her daughter is better because they are no longer battling about food.

Children undergo tremendous growth and developmental change during their first year of life. They enter the toddler years having completed the transition from a liquid-based diet to a variety of solid foods, having established self-feeding, and having developed vocabulary and communication skills around food. Their nutritional needs are in transition too. Toddlers, preschoolers, and school-age children are not growing as rapidly as infants. Therefore, their eating style changes from a somewhat indiscriminant ingestion of calories to a more selective mode of eating, in which preference plays an increasingly important role. Preschoolers are advancing the complexity of foods they consume because better chewing skills allow them to eat most foods found in adult diets, as long as they are modified to prevent choking. School-age children learn to make independent food choices and put into practice the eating habits they acquired when younger.

This chapter focuses on the nutritional requirements unique to three age groups: toddlers, preschoolers, and school-age children up to age 8 years. We review child nutrition programs that are implemented in the school setting and discuss how they set the stage for healthy diets. We also describe methods for managing the unique challenges that can complicate feeding and impact children's nutritional status. Finally, we provide strategies for using the classroom and cafeteria environments to support healthful nutrition messages. These approaches foster wholesome nutrition habits, providing children with a lifelong foundation of healthful eating.

FEEDING TODDLERS

Feeding toddlers (children from 12 to 36 months of age) is different from feeding infants. Infants' easy acceptance of food often changes when they become toddlers. Appetites that were once consistent in infants become sporadic and selective in toddlerhood. In addition, toddlers establish their autonomy by asserting themselves at mealtimes. Toddlers, like Michaela, are often ready and willing to do battle about what they will and will not eat. The wise caregiver remains neutral, does not over-react, and continues to offer nutritious foods in a supportive manner.

According to the Academy of Nutrition and Dietetics (2014), caregivers should:

- Allow toddlers to explore foods as they become increasingly independent in their food choices.
- Promote pleasure and success while eating.
- Avoid succumbing to unreasonable demands.

Caregivers are responsible for providing a variety of healthful foods that meet the nutritional needs of toddlers. To accomplish these goals, teachers need to understand the nutritional requirements of toddlers, recognize characteristics of toddler diets, and know how to feed toddlers in culturally appropriate ways.

Division of Responsibility in Feeding

Before addressing children's nutrient needs, caregivers must understand and follow the division of responsibility. Responsibility for healthful eating is shared between teachers and children. Teachers are responsible for *what* children eat, *when* they eat, and *where* they eat. Children are responsible for *whether* they eat and *how much* they eat (Satter, 2008). Children's responsibility relies on their innate ability to select and eat the amount of food needed to maintain growth and a healthful weight (Satter, 2008).

When teachers take over the child's responsibility negative repercussions may result. Children may overeat or display defiance and not eat enough. Children should not feel pressured to try a new food. Teachers may be surprised to learn that this means not requiring children to take a "no thank-you bite", "two bites", or to clean their plate. Allowing children to regulate their own food intake preserves the feeding relationship and helps children become competent eaters. Competent eaters are children who feel positive about foods and eating, are able to accept an increasing variety of different foods, and understand their internal food cues. Competent eaters know when they are hungry and when they are full (Satter, 2008).

In the opening case scenario, Hanna and Michaela had not established a division of feeding responsibility because Hanna did not trust Michaela to eat enough. In her well-intentioned goal of trying to get Michaela to eat, Hanna applied pressure and was met with resistance. Laura contributed to the problem by taking on Hanna's role as food enforcer. With input from the dietitian, Laura and Hanna were able to pull out of the food battle and allow Michaela the freedom of choice. Figure 5-1 provides a summary of how teachers can support the division of feeding responsibility in the early childhood and school settings.

A Matter of ETHICS

At your half-day preschool program, you observe a parent who arrives early for pickup specifically to observe how much her child eats at lunch. You notice that as soon as the parent appears, the child tends to slow down and stop eating. Generally the child eats as other children do—some days more and some days less—and is growing according to growth charts. This parent is concerned about the child getting the "right" foods to eat. You believe this pattern of pressure related to feeding may be going on at home too. The NAEYC Code of Ethical Conduct discusses the ethical responsibility of families. How do you support the parent and bring about the goals of communication, cooperation, and collaboration between classroom and home? The Code stresses the importance of providing parents access to the child's classroom, but in this case, you think it might be interfering with the child's meal. How would you navigate through this sensitive situation?

Understanding the Nutritional Needs of Toddlers

Toddlers need the same variety in their diets as adults. They have made the transition from strained infant foods to soft table foods. To address these changes, some

---

FIGURE 5-1   Division of Responsibility in Feeding

Teachers' Responsibilities: What, When, and Where

- Provide young children with structure when eating meals.
- Meals should be routine and include snacks in between meals.
- Meals and snack should be consumed in a designated area.
- Avoid menu substitutions or "short-order cooking" unless there is a medical reason.
- Serve family-style meals with the teacher socializing and modeling healthful eating.
- Avoid food or drinks between meals or snacks except for water.
- Minimize distractions so teachers and young children can enjoy eating together.

Children's Responsibility: How Much and Whether

- Allow children to self-serve while assisting them to take what they will realistically eat. Do not restrict how much they eat except as it relates to fair distribution of food between all children at the table. There should be enough food available, however allow them to have more of available food if they want it.
- Avoid the "no thank you", "two-bite rule", or the requirement to clean the plate, bite which is a control tactic that interferes with food acceptance because it takes away the child's joy in mastering a new food and puts pressure on the child.
- Let children decide what they would like to eat.
- Let children decide how much they want to eat from the food adults have put on the table.

adjustments to texture and size of pieces need to be made so that foods are easy and safe for toddlers to eat. As the amount of solid food eaten increases and begins to provide more of the nutrient needs of the toddler, the role of milk in the diet decreases. However, breast-feeding still has an important role, so teachers should support the mother who chooses to continue to breast-feed after one year, called **extended breastfeeding**.

Balancing Toddler Diets

The quality of toddlers' diets will vary from day to day based on their changing appetites and developing food preferences. Caregivers can enhance the likelihood of toddlers eating well by planning meals that include a variety of wholesome foods. Fruits and vegetables in an assortment of rich colors are more likely to add nutrients such as vitamins A and C, potassium, and fiber to the diet.

The child is being allowed to follow the Division of Responsibility. He is deciding **how much** or **whether** to serve himself. Adults can provide guidance and support. Their job is to decide **what** is offered and **when** the food is offered.

Carla Mestas/Pearson Education

Meats, poultry, and fish are rich sources of iron and zinc, and dairy products are excellent sources of vitamin D and calcium. A balanced diet for toddlers includes high-iron foods as well as fruits and vegetables rich in vitamin C, which aids in iron absorption.

extended breastfeeding the practice of mothers who continue to nurse their toddlers after 1 year of age

Understanding Portion Sizes for Toddlers

Children's appetites should dictate portion size. One rule of thumb to use when deciding how much to serve at meals is that children need about 1 tablespoon of food from each food group per year of age (Academy of Nutrition and Dietetics, 2012; Ramsay, Branen, & Johnson, 2012). The Child and Adult Care Food Program (CACFP) is a federally funded program that provides specific guidance regarding appropriate portion sizes for toddlers. Figure 5-2 provides a sample menu for toddlers using the CACFP guidelines for children ages 1 to 2. Menu planning is discussed in more detail in Chapter 6.

> **WHAT IF . . .**
> you weren't feeling hungry but when you sat down, someone served you a mixing bowl full of cooked rice and broccoli. How would you feel? How do you think toddlers feel when very large servings are offered to them?

Teachers are often surprised at the small portions recommended for children. Usually these amounts are sufficient for most children; however, the CACFP recommendations describe minimum portions, and some children may require or desire more food. It is important to serve enough food so that children feel satisfied. In the opening case scenario, Michaela's mother, Hanna, was concerned about her daughter eating enough. Laura could show Hanna examples of the normal portion sizes for toddlers to reinforce reasonable expectations for consumption.

The CACFP is intended to ensure that young children are offered a variety of nutrient dense foods to optimize growth and development. Food group requirements and specific portion amounts must be presented. In an effort to ensure the CACFP is in alignment with the *Dietary Guidelines for Americans, 2010*, the USDA requested the Institute of Medicine evaluate the program. Initial recommendations are offered in the report *Child and Adult Care Food Program Aligning*

Ariel Daeschel

Toddlers do best when they are provided an array of healthful foods and offered in a supportive manner. Allow toddlers to feed themselves but offer assistance when needed.

FIGURE 5-2   Sample Breakfast, Lunch, and Snack Menu Using CACFP Guidelines for Toddlers

MEAL	PORTION SIZE
Breakfast	
Oatmeal	¼ cup
Mixed berries	¼ cup
Milk, whole	½ cup
Lunch	
Milk, whole	½ cup
Simmered diced turkey with au jus	1 ounce (the size of a small matchbox)
Mashed sweet potatoes	2 tablespoons
Diced kiwi	2 tablespoons
Whole-grain bread	½ slice
Trans-fat-free margarine	½ teaspoon
Afternoon Snack	
Pizza muffin:	
Whole-wheat English muffin	¼ muffin
with tomato sauce and	1 tablespoon
cheese, shredded	½ ounce
Water	

Dietary Guidance for All and include larger servings and greater variety from vegetable and fruit groups (Committee to Review Child and Adult Care Food Program Meal Requirements & Institute of Medicine, 2011); other revisions include requirements for low-fat milk products and milk substitutes.

Recognizing Characteristics of Toddlers' Diets

Teachers who care for toddlers must make decisions about what foods are nutritious and safe for children to eat. Even when teachers do not plan the menus, they are responsible for setting the environment and supporting children at mealtimes (Branen & Fletcher, 2015). This includes considering the textures and consistency of food served, timing meals appropriately, and understanding the impacts of development on children's diets and eating capabilities.

Modifying Food Textures and Consistency

The textures and consistencies of food need to be adjusted for toddlers, especially when they begin to master table foods. Meats, poultry, and other foods need to be chopped into pieces no larger than ¼ inch in diameter for children 1 to 2 years of age and ½ inch in diameter for toddlers 3 to 5 years of age (National Association for the Education of Young Children, 2012). Soft, easy-to-mash foods should be offered. Extra sugar, salt, and spices are not necessary.

Ariel Daeschel

Teachers need to evaluate the eating skills of children and make decisions about the appropriateness of food served. This 9-month-old child has no problem managing thinly sliced zucchini sticks.

Adults must support children to transition to more advanced textures. While children are developing their taste preference, they also are developing their texture preferences. Reinforcing and offering children different textures (for example, smooth, lumpy, and mushy) can help children develop preferences for various textures in addition to different flavors.

Timing of Meals

Toddlers have small stomachs. However, they are ready to shift from on-demand feeding to scheduled meals. Offering three meals plus snacks every two to three hours provides toddlers ample opportunity to refuel. This routine is supportive of toddlers' variable appetites. In fact, meals and snacks should be at least two hours but no more than three hours apart (Academy of Nutrition and Dietetics, 2015; National Association for the Education of Young Children, 2012). This is helpful information to share with families. In the opening case scenario, Laura can reassure Hanna about her daughter's eating habits and explain toddlers' need for frequent meals and snacks. This way Hanna will know that even if Michaela doesn't consume very much at a mealtime, she will soon have another opportunity to eat at snack time.

Understanding Impacts of Development

Children's developmental skills influence their ability to navigate biting, chewing, and swallowing certain foods. For example, a 14-month-old toddler will have different eating skills than a 19-month-old. The 19-month-old may have no problems managing thinly cut zucchini sticks, whereas the 14-month-old will do better if the zucchini is steamed and cut into small pieces. Toddlers' willingness to eat also changes as they grow and develop. This willingness is impacted by a variety of factors, including the child's growth rate, preference for "sameness," and changes in the child's perceptions of taste.

Decrease in Growth Rate A toddler's rate of growth is slower than it is during the infant period. Because of this, the child's food intake decreases. This natural decrease in eating is sometimes seen as having a poor appetite or being picky.

The Need for "Sameness" Toddlers are busy maturing, developing, changing, and learning many new skills. Sometimes routine foods provide comfort and security during times of rapid change and development (Zero to Three, n.d.). Toddlers may be less likely to try new foods.

Changing Taste Perceptions Taste buds are located on the roof of the mouth, the cheeks, and the tongue. Research suggests there are variations in the ability to taste bitter. Some children may taste bitter more strongly; and in general, children have a greater number of taste buds compared with adults. Therefore, their food preferences are not within their control (Hayes et al., 2015; Nova, 2009; Schwartz, Issanchou, & Nicklaus, 2009). Spinach, broccoli, Brussel sprouts, cabbage, and grapefruit have flavors that may be too strong for some toddlers. In addition, more tactile children demonstrate a greater aversion to new foods, indicating the possibility of more extreme sensory characteristics in certain children that could impact food intake (Nederkoom, Jansen, & Havermans, 2015). Teachers need to be patient and understand that eating patterns are influenced by a toddler's stage of development.

Understanding Challenges in Feeding Toddlers

Toddlers experience significant developmental transitions as they strive to establish their independence. They are increasingly mobile and may occasionally show their autonomy through challenging behavior. "No" may become a well-used word in their vocabulary. Teachers recognize that these responses are natural expressions as toddlers begin to learn to make their own decisions, and they often show up at mealtimes. Teachers are better able to help promote positive eating habits if they recognize and anticipate potential feeding challenges and are prepared to address them.

Selective Eaters

selective eaters
children who make limited
food choices

Selective eaters are children who accept a limited variety of foods, eat small portions, and may not be interested in eating. This eating pattern is sometimes called picky or finicky. Selective eating, however, is relatively common in the toddler age group and is considered normal.

Before labeling children as selective eaters, teachers should reflect on normal toddler eating behavior and recognize that children's previous eating patterns are undergoing changes as they mature. Some selective eaters limit food choices to such an extent that teachers may become concerned about the nutritional adequacy of the child's diet. The best way to determine whether the problem is a significant issue is to assess the child's growth patterns using a growth chart. If children are growing at a normal rate, then they are getting sufficient calories to grow and develop in spite of their selective eating habits. For many toddlers choosy eating is a temporary phase. For a few, it can become a long-term pattern that may require intensive intervention using a team approach that includes a health care provider, registered dietitian nutritionist, families, and teachers (Davis, Cocjin, Mousa, & Hyman, 2010; Harding, Faiman, & Wright, 2010; Zero to Three, n.d.).

Food Neophobia

food neophobia
term used to describe fear
of new foods

Food neophobia refers to fear of new foods. Toddlers are often suspicious of new foods. This fear may be an adaptive behavior that has historically protected young children from eating poisonous substances (Monneuse, Hladik, Simmen, & Pasquet, 2011). Children may inherit their fear of new foods from their relatives (Cooke, Haworth, & Wardle, 2007; Kaar, Buti, & Johnson, 2014; Knaapila et al., 2007; Knaapila et al., 2011).

Despite children's food neophobia, if they are introduced to a variety of new foods early on and are given ample exposure to foods, it can help overcome their hesitations. Teachers understand that various and repeated exposures to any new concept help children to learn. The same holds true for learning to accept new foods. Young children must be exposed to new foods numerous times before they are confident enough to eat them (Satter, 2012a). Toddlers also benefit from having role models (parents, teachers, and particularly peers) who demonstrate pleasure in eating a variety of foods (Johnson, van Jaarsveld, & Wardle, 2011; O'Connell, Henderson, Luedicke, & Schwartz, 2012).

Another strategy is to offer new foods along with foods toddlers already like. This takes the pressure off the toddler because there is something available that he or she likes to eat. The toddler is able to try the new food without the pressure of hunger. Figure 5-3 provides additional ideas to help remove pressure while giving toddlers time to learn and get used to new foods or previously rejected foods.

FIGURE 5-3   Strategies for Encouraging the Selective Eater

Strategies for the eating challenge "I don't like vegetables!"

- Seat the child next to a child or teacher who likes vegetables.
- Offer vegetables as a first course: salad or vegetable sticks or vegetable soup.
- Add vegetables to foods: grated carrots to spaghetti sauce or zucchini or pumpkin to quick bread.
- Provide enjoyable opportunities to explore foods: classroom gardens, taste tests, cooking activities.
- Serve vegetables with condiments: low-fat ranch dressing or yogurt.
- Serve vegetables in child friendly ways: make a smoothie using fruits and vegetables.
- Minimize strong cooking odors that detract from the enjoyment of eating vegetables like overcooked broccoli.

Strategies for the eating challenge "I don't like meat!"

- Add meat to combination dishes: chicken stir fry, beef, and bean burrito.
- Offer protein alternates: peanut butter, beans, peas and lentils, tofu, tempeh, and eggs.
- Offer fork-tender meats such as braised beef or pork or chicken stew.

- Serve meats with condiments: catsup, barbeque sauce, salsa, low-fat cheese.

Strategies for the eating challenge "I don't like milk!"

- Serve milk cold and with a straw.
- Provide yogurt or low fat cheese as calcium rich alternatives.
- Serve calcium and vitamin D-fortified soy milk.
- Use milk in meal preparation: Use milk in hot and cold cereals, cream soups, or smoothies.

Strategies for the eating challenge "I refuse to eat a meal!"

- Ask the child to sit at the table and visit with the group; allow children to eat the amount they want (even if the amount is nothing).
- Do not offer alternatives to the meal (except for required special diets).
- Do not offer any food until the next snack or meal time.

Strategies for the eating challenge "I will only eat certain favorite foods (food jag)"

- Continue to offer the basic program menu food items.
- Avoid rewards for eating particular foods.
- Be patient. Food jags usually go away.

Food Jags

A **food jag** occurs when toddlers select a very limited number of favorite foods to eat and reject all others, including foods they liked in the past. Sometimes a well-loved favorite will suddenly no longer have appeal and another food will take its place. Teachers and families who recognize a food jag should try to focus on what the children are still eating rather than focusing on what they are no longer eating. It may become evident that although the child's food selections are limited, there may be three or four choices from each food group that the child still accepts. Teachers should not draw attention to this eating behavior because it may prolong the food jag. As in the case of the selective eater, teachers should continue to offer a variety of foods from each of the food groups.

Teachers may be concerned about conflicts with CACFP recommendations and reimbursement guidelines when children experience food jags and refuse to eat a particular food group. The *Policy Point* discusses how to navigate the CACFP when children are selective eaters or are experiencing a food jag.

Families and teachers may also become concerned that the quality of the child's diet is inadequate. Families who are concerned about a prolonged food jag can obtain advice and reassurance from the child's health care provider or a registered dietitian nutritionist.

food jag
the persistent eating of a limited number of favorite foods for a period of time

WHAT IF . . .
you had a toddler in your classroom who refused to sit at the table for breakfast? What if your program director was pressuring you to have all the children sit down together so that the meals could be counted for CACFP reimbursement? How would you handle this?

POLICY POINT

The Child and Adult Care Food Program and the Picky Eater

Children's programs can obtain CACFP reimbursement only if all of the required food groups, including fat-free or low-fat (1%) milk, are offered at each meal. Teachers may be concerned that to receive reimbursement, children must consume foods from all food groups. That is not the case. As long as the appropriate foods are offered, programs are permitted to count the meals as reimbursable. But what if a child can't drink milk?

- If a child has a medical reason for not drinking milk, such as lactose intolerance or milk allergy, a health authority can provide documentation that allows the program to make an appropriate substitution with non-dairy beverages that are nutritionally equivalent to milk and still receive CACFP reimbursement.

- If the child simply doesn't like milk, programs can still claim a reimbursement if the milk was offered but refused.

- If, however, families request that no milk be served and ask that juice be offered instead, the program cannot get CACFP reimbursement for that meal.

- If a child prefers and a family requests whole or 2% milk, the program cannot claim reimbursement for meals in which the higher-fat milk is offered. What about the child who refuses to eat a meal?

- If the child sits down and is offered a meal but chooses not to eat, the program can still receive reimbursement for this meal.

- If the child refuses to sit down at the table for a meal, the program cannot receive reimbursement.

Weaning from the Bottle

Children should wean from the bottle to reduce the risk of dental cavities and to avoid a lag in the development of appropriate feeding skills. The American Academy of Pediatrics recommends weaning children from a bottle by 12 to 15 months of age (Kleinman, 2009). Teachers can help support weaning by collaborating with families and making sure a consistent message is sent to toddlers both in the home and child care setting. Figure 5-4 provides strategies teachers and families can use to support the weaning process.

FIGURE 5-4   Strategies for Weaning from the Bottle

When:

Offer formula or breast milk from a cup starting at 6 months and begin the weaning process by around 12 months.

How:

1. Select one meal or snack time to introduce a cup. Use the cup at this meal for 1 week. Discuss with parents which meal to start substituting a cup for a bottle.
2. Every week substitute a cup for a bottle at another meal. Coordinate with parents which meal and what type of cup to use.
3. Assist the child to hold the cup and sip the liquid (the cup should not be filled to the top).
4. A toddler may still need assistance with self-comfort measures. Offer alternatives such as a pacifier, stuffed animal, and extra hugs and cuddles.
5. A consistent approach should be used at home and in the child care setting.

Source: Based on UCSF Benioff Children's Hospital FAQ Baby Bottle Weaning. Copyright 2002–2012 by the Regents of the University of California at http://www.ucsfbenioffchildrens.org/education/baby_bottle_weaning/.

Switching to Whole Milk

Infants require breast milk or formula during their first year of life. Once they reach their first birthday, they are ready to make the transition from formula to whole milk. The CACFP and Women, Infants, and Children (WIC) programs recommend that toddlers receive whole milk until 2 years of age (U.S. Department of Agriculture Food and Nutrition Service, 2011a; U.S. Food and Drug Administration Food and Nutrition Service, 2009). Fat-free, 1%, and 2% milk may be too low in fat content to support an adequate rate of weight gain and growth and should be offered only if recommended by a physician. The fat and cholesterol in whole milk may support neurological development and aids in vitamin A and D absorption. However, low-fat milk is encouraged after 2 years of age (Andreyeva, Luedicke, Henderson, & Schwartz, 2014) . The *Health Hint* describes some of the questions health authorities raise regarding the type of milk that should be offered to toddlers.

The child care provider is pouring milk in a pitcher for children to serve themselves.

Suzanne Clouzeau/Pearson Education

Exploring Cultural Differences in Feeding Toddlers

Teachers, families, and the children who attend early childhood programs come from a wide array of cultural backgrounds. Teachers who are familiar with their own cultural perceptions and seek out information and knowledge about other cultures are better able to understand and support the differences in family eating habits. For example, people eat food with their hands in Bangladesh, India, Nepal, and Pakistan, whereas people in Asian countries use chopsticks and spoons (Luitel, 2006). Some cultures sit on the floor to eat meals or serve themselves from a communal bowl. Understanding family eating practices helps teachers recognize these influences on toddlers' feeding skills and behaviors at mealtimes.

WHAT IF . . .
a 2-year-old child from India in your class wouldn't use eating utensils during mealtimes? What would you do?

Nutrition practices in food selection can vary as well. In China, Korea, Japan, and Southeast Asia and in Western African cultures, milk is not used as a beverage and is used minimally in cooking (Ishige, 2012; Maritz, 2011). In Hispanic cultures, milk is often considered an ideal food and it is believed that children cannot drink too much. Weaning from the bottle is often delayed, putting Hispanic children at risk for iron-deficiency anemia (Brotanek, Schroer, Valentyn, Tomany-Korman, & Flores, 2009).

Teachers need to use culturally sensitive approaches when discussing family food practices. Teachers also should support healthful traditional food practices and find ways to incorporate diverse foods in the children's menu at school. This can be accomplished by planning

Children's cultural practices may influence how they eat and serve themselves at meals.

Thinkstock/Getty Images

HEALTH HINT   The Fat Content of Milk: What's Best for Children?

The general consensus among health authorities is that when children reach 2 years of age, the fat content of the milk they consume should be gradually decreased from whole milk (4% butterfat content) to fat-free milk. This goal is promoted in an effort to introduce a heart-healthful diet and to prevent obesity in children. But recommendations become less clear for toddlers between 1 and 2 years of age. Issues under consideration include the following:

- Some health authorities discourage lower-fat (2% or 1%) or fat-free milk for children between 1 and 2 years of age because fat and cholesterol in a child's diet are beneficial for central nervous system development and provide adequate calories for growth.

- The American Academy of Pediatrics and the National Heart, Lung, and Blood Institute suggests 2%, 1%, or fat-free milk can be offered to children ages of 1 and above depending on a child's rate of growth, appetite, other

sources of fat in the diet and the nutrient density of other foods consumed, and the child's risk for obesity and heart diseases.

- The American Heart Association, whose mission is focused on preventing coronary artery disease, also advises 2% milk for children after age 1.

- The CACFP (in accordance with the requirements established by the Healthy Hunger Free Kids Act of 2010) allows only fat-free or low-fat (1%) milk to be served to children aged 2 and older. Children between 1 and 2 years, however, are served whole milk.

- The WIC program also provides whole milk to children between 1 and 2 years of age.

Teachers should follow the guidelines provided by governmental agencies and the recommendations of the USDA Food and Nutrition Service and be open to individualizing practices for toddlers if advised by the child's health care provider and in collaboration with families.

Sources: *Dietary Guidelines for Americans*, 2010, by the U.S. Department of Health and Human Services and U.S. Department of Agriculture, 2011, retrieved February 12, 2015, from http://www.cnpp.usda.gov/dietary-guidelines-2010; "Dietary Recommendations for Children and Adolescents: A Guide for Practitioners: Consensus Statement from the American Heart Association," by the American Heart Association, 2005, *Circulation*, 112(13), pp. 2061–2075 updated online September, 2014, at http://www.heart.org/HEARTORG/GettingHealthy/Dietary-Recommendations-for-Healthy-Children_UCM_303886_Article.jsp; "Expert Panel on Integrated Pediatric Guideline for Cardiovascular Health and Risk Reduction" 2012, *Pediatrics*, 129(4), pp. s1–s44 by the American Academy of Pediatrics from http://pediatrics.aappublications.org/content/129/4/e1111.full.pdf+html; "The Start Healthy Feeding Guidelines for Infants and Toddlers," by N. Butte et al., 2004, *Journal of the American Dietetic Association*, 104, pp. 442–454; and "Lipid Screening and Cardiovascular Health in Childhood," by S. R. Daniels, F. R. Greer, and the Committee on Nutrition, 2008, *Pediatrics*, 122(1), pp. 198–208.

Pearson Education

CLASSROOM CONNECTION

Watch this video and think about this teacher's use of hands-on and sensory experiences in teaching children about nutrition. How does she include English language learners in the lesson?

menus to include foods that reflect cultural preferences or special cultural occasions, and by planning social events such as potlucks where families can share special cultural dishes to promote cultural awareness.

Understanding the Teacher's Role in Promoting Healthful Eating Habits

The foremost nutrition goal for feeding toddlers is to establish a foundation of eating habits that supports immediate growth and long-term health (Ogata & Hayes, 2014). Teachers can achieve this goal by linking developmental skills to feeding skills and by being good role models.

Setting the Mealtime Environment

Teachers play a significant role in ensuring children have positive experiences around mealtimes. Adults are responsible for setting the mealtime environment to include the physical as well as emotional setting at the table. Adults can support children's physical environment by using appropriate child-sized equipment (tables, chairs, utensils, plates, and serving bowls). Adults must consider the emotional environment that includes child–child and teacher–child interactions.

Family-Style Service

Optimal practice at mealtimes is to follow **family-style service** where children at the table are offered foods from common serving bowls that are passed to each child (Branen & Fletcher, 2015; Dipti, Speirs, McBride, Donovan, & Chapman-Novakofski, 2014). Family-style service may better support children's self-regulation when given guidance and support by adults (Savage, Haisfield, Fisher, Marini, & Birch, 2012), may minimize waste (Branen & Fletcher, 1997), and may foster physical and verbal development. By having a teacher sit and eat with the children at the table, the children can be supported through guidance and intentional direction.

family-style service
the mealtime practice where children are offered food in common serving bowls that are passed to children for self-service

Linking Developmental Skills to Feeding Skills

Teachers develop a keen understanding of child development. They understand that children develop eating skills at different rates. Being attuned to children's development helps teachers make decisions about what and how to feed toddlers. Table 5-1 describes the link between physical, social–emotional, and intellectual development in accordance with approaches to feeding toddlers. The *Teaching Wellness* feature provides specific examples of ways teachers can help children experience new foods while they learn about nutrition.

Teachers as Role Models

Toddlers seek to imitate the adults in their lives. This means teachers are important role models, and children are watching and emulating what you eat (Natale et al., 2014). Teacher behaviors influence the choices they make. In addition, modeling pleasant interactions during mealtime introduces toddlers to appropriate eating behaviors. Providing opportunities for toddlers to self-feed and self-serve promotes competence and accomplishment.

Teaching Toddlers About Nutrition

Toddlers are curious and learn best when abstract concepts are a part of everyday tangible experiences. Some of the diverse ways toddlers learn about food and eating occur when they are exposed to healthful colorful meals rich in aromas, tastes, and textures. Mealtime in the classroom provides opportunities for toddlers to practice fine motor skills, such as spreading, pouring, and grasping foods with tongs. Mealtime also is an important time to introduce diverse foods and familiar foods prepared in different ways. Helping with cleanup fosters self-help skills as children put dishes into a tub and wipe their place at the table after they eat.

   Classroom activities provide opportunities for children to have direct hands-on experiences with food-related topics. Activities that introduce toddlers to nutrition concepts include simple food preparation

Children learn about food through dramatic play. This little boy has learned about food safety and is appropriately wearing gloves while pretending to handle fresh produce.

Cascade Sorte and Matt Bracken

TABLE 5-1   Developmental Influences on Toddlers' Eating and Relevant Teacher Strategies

Development Physical	Feeding Strategies for 12- to 24-Month-Olds
Toddlers' rate of growth decreases.	Toddlers are more selective and eat less than infants. Offer variety and age-appropriate portions.
They tend to eat frequently throughout the day.	Smaller frequent meals are more common. Snacks are desirable and necessary. Avoid daylong access to bottles or toddler cups filled with calorie-containing beverages. This can cause problems with dental decay and decrease appetite for food.
They begin to walk by 12–15 months.	Attention span can be short as toddlers practice new motor skills. Distractions should be kept to a minimum. They are expending calories as they move and grow, and adequate calorie intake is important.
Most can hold a cup and feed themselves with a spoon, but they still spill on occasion.	Toddlers should be allowed to self-feed but assistance should be available when they need it. Offer finger foods and other options that will stay on a spoon (for example, yogurt, cottage cheese, oatmeal).
Social–Emotional	
Toddlers want to be more independent.	Allow them to select what they want to eat. Offer choices but not too many. They may refuse a food. Do not pressure toddlers about which food to eat or force food intake. It may take numerous exposures before they are ready to try it. Allow them to practice eating skills and to select age-appropriate foods from a healthful array offered by caregivers.
Frustration can occur when they try activities they can't quite do yet, which leads to temper tantrums.	Provide gentle guidelines for mealtime behavior. Never feed a crying child. Offer meals that are easy for toddlers to eat to promote feelings of success rather than frustration (for example, green peas can be mashed to make them easier to eat).
They become aware of their possessions, and sharing can be challenging.	Each child should have his or her own high chair and, when old enough to sit at the table, his or her own space and place setting. Family-style meal service helps toddlers learn to take turns and share food from a common serving bowl.
Remembering rules is still not possible.	In a positive manner, remind children about mealtime rules such as washing hands, sitting down together, and not licking the serving spoon.
They are developing a sense of self and start to feel emotions such as pleasure, jealousy, affection, pride, and shame.	Help them to feel proud of their eating skills. Do not offer blame when spills occur. Recognize eating skill achievements such as "You are learning to drink from a cup."
They become more fearful as they begin to learn about the world.	Toddlers may be afraid to try new foods. Offer food without pressure. It takes many exposures before toddlers will accept a new food or a previously rejected food. Offer a new food along with a food they like.
They benefit by having routines and schedules.	There should be a schedule for when and how meals and snacks are served. Mealtime procedures should follow a typical beginning, (middle) eating, and ending sequence of events.
Cognitive	
Toddlers are curious and eager.	Offer many different types of foods with various flavors, textures, tastes, and smells. Allow them to touch, taste, squeeze, drop, and experience the food. Food may go in the mouth and out again. Allow children enough time to discover the different qualities of foods by allowing time for touching, smelling, and tasting it. Toddlers learn through these exploratory activities.
When they want something, they will point to it.	Be responsive to toddlers' communication attempts. When they point at a food, verbalize their request: "You are pointing at the yogurt. Do you want yogurt?" Teaching basic sign language can help toddlers communicate when they are hungry and when they are full.
They can identify familiar objects or pictures by name and begin to use two-word sentences.	Identify foods, eating utensils, and other toddlers sitting at the table by their names to facilitate language skill development. Read children's books that have themes in which children can identify different types of food. Use typical words associated with mealtimes, such as *please* and *thank you*.
They begin to use items for their intended function.	Demonstrate for toddlers how to use spoons and forks. Assist them when they drink beverages from a cup. Offer them a napkin to wipe their face.
Toddlers are very active.	Toddlers cannot sit for very long. Mealtimes vary but 20–30 minutes provides time for eating while not stretching mealtime beyond toddlers' limits. Do not allow toddlers to leave the table with food (either in their mouth or in their hand) because this can pose a choking risk.

Sources: The National Network for Child Care–NNCC, by C. Malley, 1991. University of Connecticut Cooperative Extension System, *Toddler Development (Family Day Care Facts* series). Amherst, MA: University of Massachusetts, retrieved July 16, 2012, from N.C. Division of Child Development and Early Education, 2008; Infant–Toddler Foundations, retrieved February 12, 2015, from http://ncchildcare.dhhs.state.nc.us/pdf_forms/dcd_infant_toddler_early_foundations.pdf; American Academy of Pediatrics, 2011. Ages and Stages Developmental Milestones 12 months, retrieved February 12, 2015, from HealthyChildren.org; and Medline Plus, 2010. *Toddler Development*, retrieved February 12, 2015, from http://www.nlm.nih.gov/medlineplus/ency/article/002010.htm.

TEACHING WELLNESS Will I Like What's Good for Me?

LEARNING OUTCOME   **Children will accept a variety of foods.**

Vocabulary focus: Try, sample, taste, flavor, taste-test, variety, nutritious, food groups.

Safety watch: Ensure foods are prepared and served appropriately for the age group and the child's abilities, such as serving puréed fruits and vegetables for young infants or small mashed pieces for older infants to ensure that children can manage food and to prevent choking. Choose foods that avoid children's food allergies and restrictions. Supervise children closely during the tasting and monitor for cleanliness and safety.

OLDER INFANTS AND TODDLERS

- **Goal:** Older infants will practice selecting and tasting different fruits and vegetables.
- **Materials:** Three or four fruits and vegetables of different colors prepared appropriately, such as mashed bananas or creamed corn (yellow), cut-up soft peaches or mangoes (orange), mashed peas or soft-cooked cut-up string beans (green), cut-up strawberries or watermelon, cooked mashed beets (red), mashed blueberries (blue); plates with small divisions.
- **Activity plan:** The teacher's and child's hands should be washed before beginning. Conduct the activity when

the child is calm and ready to explore. Place a small portion of each food in serving bowls and allow children to self-serve onto a divided plate. Encourage the child to explore and taste the foods. Demonstrate tasting the foods. Name the food and talk about the taste and color. Encourage tasting, but do not force. Allow the child to spit out the food as desired. Reinforce all efforts to explore and taste.

- **Did you meet your goal?** Did the child explore, choose, and taste a variety of foods?

PRESCHOOLERS AND KINDERGARTNERS

- **Goal:** Children will explore different forms of tomatoes and foods made from tomato products, choose products to taste, and identify which ones they like.
- **Materials:** The book *I Will Never Not Ever Eat a Tomato* by Lauren Child; tomatoes of different types (grape, pear, or cherry; Roma; traditional) cut into small pieces (to avoid choking hazard); tomato-based foods (ketchup, salsa, tomato soup, spaghetti sauce); serving bowls; serving spoons; tasting spoons; napkins; large sheet of paper; marking pens.
- **Activity plan:** Set up a tomato taste-testing center. Place each type of tomato and tomato food in a serving bowl. Place the sheet of paper on the wall or table. Draw columns on the paper and label one column for each tomato product. Invite the children to taste each food by letting

children serve themselves a small portion onto their plate. Talk about the foods and ask the children to describe the flavors. Guide the children to place an X in the column for each tomato and tomato food they like. At group time, gather the children and read the book. Talk about the themes in the book and reinforce the notion of exploring new tastes and flavors. Talk about the tomato taste-test and review the children's "votes" for each of the tomato foods. Identify the foods that more children liked. Ask the children to explain what they liked about the tomato foods. Ask the children to name four foods made from tomatoes.

- **Did you meet your goal?** Did children explore and taste different tomato products?

SCHOOL-AGE CHILDREN

- **Goal:** Children will be able to name the food groups, identify the variety of foods they eat and sort foods into the food groups, and describe what makes foods more nutritious or less nutritious.
- **Materials:** The book *MyPlate and You* by Gillia Olson; red, green, orange, purple, and blue construction paper; markers; scissors; glue; white paper plates; MyPlate poster; magazines with pictures of foods.

- **Activity plan:** Gather children together and introduce the concept of food groups and MyPlate. Read the book and review the MyPlate poster. Identify the different food groups and describe the qualities of foods that make them more nutritious or less nutritious. Nutritious foods are rich in vitamins, minerals, and fiber and low in fat. Less nutritious foods are often high in added fat, salt, or sugar and can be low in vitamins and minerals and high in calories.

Talk about the importance of eating a variety of foods for a healthful diet. Invite children to cut construction paper into shapes that replicate the MyPlate division of food groups and glue them onto a paper plate. (Another option is to provide real food from each food group.) Guide children to write the name of each food group on its section on their "MyPlate." Invite children to cut out pictures from magazines or draw pictures of foods they like and glue them onto the correct food group section. Talk about the goal of showing the variety of foods the child eats from each food group. Ask children to show their "MyPlate" and tell others about the different foods they eat. If some food groups include only one (or few) foods, encourage the children to suggest ideas of other foods that the child could try to increase the variety of foods enjoyed in that food group.

- **Did you meet your goal?** Can children name the food groups, match foods to the appropriate group, and describe what makes a food more nutritious or less nutritious?

This child can identify and write the names of the five foods groups.

Inge Daeschel

CHECK YOUR UNDERSTANDING 5.1

Click here to check your understanding of the nutritional needs of toddlers.

Pearson Education

CLASSROOM CONNECTION

Watch this video to see how to promote healthy eating with children by using hands-on activities with food.

tasks that allow them to stir, cut soft foods, pour ingredients into a bowl, wash fruits and vegetables, and knead dough. These experiences allow toddlers to taste, smell, and touch different foods. Children's books with food-related themes, dramatic play with food props, and creative activities that include food topics are appropriate ways to teach toddlers about foods and nutrition.

FEEDING PRESCHOOLERS

During the eager-to-please preschool years, children experience a decreased rate of growth that can result in unpredictable eating behaviors. Children's body fat naturally decreases as they leave the toddler years and enter the preschool years. This means preschool children's appetites, like those of toddlers, can be sporadic. Preschool children may eat well one day but less the next day. As their experience with foods expands, they also develop distinct preferences. To support preschoolers in their efforts to develop positive eating habits, teachers need to understand the nutritional needs and characteristics of the diets of this age group, understand how to create positive mealtime experiences, and teach children healthful nutrition concepts.

Understanding the Nutritional Needs of Preschool Children

Preschool-age children rely on a high-quality diet to support growth and development. The goal is to balance their nutrient needs with their calorie requirements and energy expenditure. This is best accomplished by providing a variety of foods rich in tastes, colors, and textures while establishing habits that promote an active lifestyle. Teachers can find dietary advice about feeding preschool-age children from several sources. These include the federal government's MyPlate food guidance system (see Figure 5-5), which offers health and nutrition information for preschoolers; the CACFP; and the *Dietary Guidelines for Americans, 2010* (U.S. Department of Agriculture, 2012a; U.S. Department of Agriculture, Food and Nutrition Service, 2011b; U.S. Department of Health and Human Services & U.S. Department of Agriculture, 2011). Each of these sources encourages the provision of a variety of foods from each of the five food groups. The MyPlate food guidance system offers the following selected messages:

FIGURE 5-5
MyPlate
Source: http://www.choosemyplate
.gov/print-materials-ordering/graph-
ic-resources.html.

- Balance calories to manage weight. For preschoolers, this means preventing obesity by maintaining healthy eating habits and an active lifestyle and reducing sedentary behaviors such as spending too much time in front of the TV or computer.

- Reduce foods that are high in salt, added solid fats, and sugars. Preschool-age children are learning healthy eating habits. Foods such as cakes, cookies, pies, candy, ice cream, soft drinks and high-fat meats like regular ground meat, hotdogs, bacon, sausage, and fried chicken are foods for occasional consumption. When planning menus or selecting snacks, choose foods lower in salt.

- Encourage a variety of colorful fruits and vegetables, offer whole grains and switch to fat-free or low-fat (1%) milk. See Figure 5-5, which illustrates these messages in the MyPlate icon.

Teachers play a very important role in helping children to learn about food. Exposing children to a variety of nutritious foods sets the tone for healthy eating across their life span. Most of the nutrient needs of preschoolers are being met, although potassium, vitamin E, and fiber are sometimes below recommended requirements (Butte et al., 2010). The U.S. Department of Agriculture also indicates that potassium, fiber, calcium, and vitamin D are nutrients of concern in American diets (U.S. Department of Health and Human Services & U.S. Department of Agriculture, 2011). However, the content of meals served in child care centers and family child care programs is still often high in saturated fats, added sugars, and foods high in salt content (Ball, Benjamin, & Ward, 2008; Benjamin Neelon, Vaughn, Ball, McWilliams, & Ward, 2012; Dwyer, Butte, Deming, Siega-Riz, & Reidy, 2010). Programs that participate in CACFP, particularly those that are Head Start programs, are more likely to provide more nutritious options (more fruits, vegetables, whole grains; less sweets, sweetened beverages, and snack-type foods) compared with those sites that are not participating in CACFP (Ritchie et al., 2012). Both CACFP and Head Start programs have standards and requirements in place that offer guidance to teachers regarding healthy diet and result in more nutritious meals. (Zuercher & Kranz, 2012).The USDA provides sample menus for meals and snacks that are appropriate for preschool-age children (Figure 5-6). They also share healthy eating tips and offer easy-to-understand posters that include the MyPlate icon and important nutrition messages.

Recognizing Characteristics of Preschool Children's Diets

Preschool-age children have developed many eating skills and are able to eat most of the foods adults eat. They enjoy socializing at mealtimes and are eager to participate in serving themselves. They develop confidence as they master tasks such

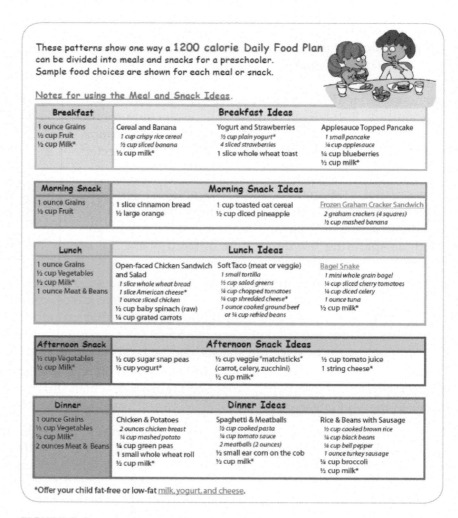

These patterns show one way a **1200 calorie Daily Food Plan** can be divided into meals and snacks for a preschooler. Sample food choices are shown for each meal or snack.

Notes for using the Meal and Snack Ideas.

Breakfast	Breakfast Ideas		
1 ounce Grains ½ cup Fruit ½ cup Milk*	Cereal and Banana *1 cup crispy rice cereal* *½ cup sliced banana* *½ cup milk**	Yogurt and Strawberries *½ cup plain yogurt** *4 sliced strawberries* *1 slice whole wheat toast*	Applesauce Topped Pancake *1 small pancake* *¼ cup applesauce* *¼ cup blueberries* *½ cup milk**

Morning Snack	Morning Snack Ideas		
1 ounce Grains ½ cup Fruit	1 slice cinnamon bread ½ large orange	1 cup toasted oat cereal ½ cup diced pineapple	<u>Frozen Graham Cracker Sandwich</u> *2 graham crackers (4 squares)* *½ cup mashed banana*

Lunch	Lunch Ideas		
1 ounce Grains ½ cup Vegetables ½ cup Milk* 1 ounce Meat & Beans	Open-faced Chicken Sandwich and Salad *1 slice whole wheat bread* *1 slice American cheese** *1 ounce sliced chicken* *½ cup baby spinach (raw)* *¼ cup grated carrots*	Soft Taco (meat or veggie) *1 small tortilla* *½ cup salad greens* *¼ cup chopped tomatoes* *¼ cup shredded cheese** *1 ounce cooked ground beef or ¼ cup refried beans*	<u>Bagel Snake</u> *1 mini whole grain bagel* *¼ cup sliced cherry tomatoes* *¼ cup diced celery* *1 ounce tuna* *½ cup milk**

Afternoon Snack	Afternoon Snack Ideas		
½ cup Vegetables ½ cup Milk*	½ cup sugar snap peas ½ cup yogurt*	½ cup veggie "matchsticks" (carrot, celery, zucchini) ½ cup milk*	½ cup tomato juice 1 string cheese*

Dinner	Dinner Ideas		
1 ounce Grains ½ cup Vegetables ½ cup Milk* 2 ounces Meat & Beans	Chicken & Potatoes *2 ounces chicken breast* *¼ cup mashed potato* *¼ cup green peas* *1 small whole wheat roll* *½ cup milk**	Spaghetti & Meatballs *½ cup cooked pasta* *¼ cup tomato sauce* *2 meatballs (2 ounces)* *½ small ear corn on the cob* *½ cup milk**	Rice & Beans with Sausage *½ cup cooked brown rice* *¼ cup black beans* *¼ cup bell pepper* *1 ounce turkey sausage* *¼ cup broccoli* *½ cup milk**

*Offer your child fat-free or low-fat <u>milk, yogurt, and cheese.</u>

FIGURE 5-6

MyPlate Sample Menu Meal Pattern for Preschoolers

Source: http://www.choosemyplate.gov/downloads/PatternA1200cals.pdf.

as spreading jam on a slice of bread and pouring milk from a small pitcher into a cup. As teachers promote these skills, various aspects of the preschool diet need to be considered to ensure children receive safe and nutritious meals. The textures and consistencies of foods still play a part in the preschool diet. Using appropriate scheduling of meals, paying attention to portion sizes, and establishing approaches that encourage children to accept new foods are important when feeding preschool children.

Food Textures and Consistencies

Preschool children have completed the teething process and are ready to eat most solid foods. But chewing and swallowing skills are still developing, so special attention must be given to foods that could represent a choking hazard. Foods that are difficult to chew, such as meats, still need to be cut into pieces that are ½ inch in diameter or smaller to avoid choking. Round cherry tomatoes and grapes, because of their shape, present a choking risk. However, by chopping fresh tomatoes or quartering grapes, this risk is avoided. Cutting raw vegetables such as carrots into thin strips makes them easier for children to bite and chew safely.

Supervision at mealtime is crucial. To decrease the risk of choking, teachers may need to remind preschool children to stay seated when they eat.

Scheduling Meals and Snacks

Preschool children become accustomed to eating meals and snacks at predictable times. As with toddlers, providing three meals and three snacks at intervals of every two to three hours provides active preschoolers with a consistent energy source throughout the day. Snacks should be planned to provide important nutrients and should be low in added fat and sugars. For example, a corn, bean, and salsa dip served with whole-grain corn tortillas provides a rich assortment of nutrients compared with cookies and a fruit punch drink.

Bagel
Calorie difference: 210 calories

3-inch diameter
140 calories

6-inch diameter
350 calories

Cheeseburger
Calorie difference: 257 calories

333 calories

590 calories

Soda
Calorie difference: 165 calories

6.5 ounces
85 calories

20 ounces
250 calories

French Fries
Calorie difference: 400 calories

2.4 ounces
210 calories

6.9 ounces
610 calories

Avoiding Portion Distortion

Teachers may unknowingly offer children larger portions than desirable in an effort to make sure children have sufficient food for growth. This is problematic and potentially unhealthy. Children consume more calories when large portions are offered, especially as they enter the preschool years (Burger, Fisher, & Johnson, 2011; Fisher, Liu, Birch, & Rolls, 2007; Piernas & Popkin, 2011). When children are allowed to serve themselves they choose smaller portions and may consume as much as 25% fewer calories (Orlet Fisher, Rolls, & Birch, 2003). Providing the opportunity for preschool children to serve themselves through family-style meal service, with guidance from teachers, puts a focus on their internal hunger and fullness cues that may help prevent excess calorie intake, thereby reducing the risk of obesity. Using child-sized plates and bowls also prevents portion distortion. (See Figure 5-7 for examples of how portions have increased in recent years).

FIGURE 5-7
Portion Distortion
Adapted from: http://www.nhlbi
.nih.gov/health/educational/wecan
/portion/menuview.htm#slide1.

Understanding the Teacher's Role in Creating a Positive Mealtime Experience

As previously described, a positive mealtime experience enhances children's comfort and offers a relaxed environment for eating and trying new foods. Similar to supporting toddlers, teachers help create this positive environment for preschoolers by creating a comfortable space and establishing routines that children can be a part of. Mealtimes should be considerate of cultural traditions and should encourage visiting and conversation. Teachers are important role models during mealtimes.

Arranging the Mealtime Environment

A comfortable physical environment supports meal service and enhances the eating experience. Space for children to eat should be adequate without being crowded. Chairs and tables should be child-sized so children can sit comfortably and focus on eating. Silverware, cups, plates, and serving utensils should be sized to match children's motors skills (American Dietetic Association, 2011).

The environment should be free of hazards such as food-warming units, electrical cords, and large containers of hot foods. Tables should be properly sanitized before and after use. The food served should be visually appealing and prepared in such a way as to promote children's success when eating. The setting can be decorated with a changing array of posters or food-related displays that convey nutrition messages, while adding color and interest to the space.

Establishing Comfortable Routines

Teachers set the tone for mealtimes by establishing routines that convey appropriate expectations and help the meal service flow easily and enjoyably. Children learn to predict their responsibilities and tasks, which provide them with a sense of security and comfort about mealtime. For example, children can wash their hands, help set the table, serve themselves family style, and help with cleanup.

Considering Cultural Traditions

Mealtimes are important for nourishing children, but they also convey social and cultural values. Mealtime practices vary across different social groups in the way children participate, the timing of meals, the items served, and the sequence of food presentation. Children obtain cultural knowledge about food and eating by their active observation and participation in mealtime routines and socialization (Ochs & Shohet, 2006). Teachers should be aware that children's cultural traditions and experiences may differ from the practices in the classroom setting. In the United States, a cultural norm at mealtimes is that everyone sits down together before anyone starts to eat. In China, however, older generations are often served before younger generations, and in formal social occasions, children may be excluded until older adults are finished eating (Ochs & Shohet, 2006).

Encouraging Conversation

Another very important aspect of meals is the opportunity they provide for language development. Talking and visiting during mealtime helps children learn new vocabulary and how to listen and tell stories (Fishel, 2010). Children acquire command of culturally relevant knowledge, and conversation contributes to language and cognitive skills that support children's ability to learn to read and write (Snow & Beals, 2006). Teachers encourage visiting by actively listening to children, restating and elaborating on what children have said, and asking probing questions during mealtime conversations:

- "Oh, you went to the zoo with your family this weekend. What sorts of things did you see and do at the zoo?"
- "Tell us about your new baby brother."
- "Tell us about that game you were playing outside today."

Supporting Children's Internal Cues of Hunger and Fullness

Infants and toddlers are generally in tune with their internal cues for hunger and satiety. They eat when they are hungry and stop when they are full (Fox, Devaney, Reidy, Razafindrakoto, & Ziegler, 2006). Children are born with this innate ability. It's like an internal thermostat that regulates their intake. If caregivers trust and respect this ability, children who are typically developing will eat just the right amount of food. As children enter their preschool years, however, they are more easily influenced by environmental cues such as the presence of desirable food, the time of day, and the portion size (Burger et al., 2011; McConahy, Smiciklas-Wright,

Mitchell, & Picciano, 2004; Rolls, Engell, & Birch, 2000). Because they are eager to please, they can be influenced by caregivers' verbal communication at mealtimes that either support or override their "thermostat," or self-regulation of food intake. When teachers use comments that validate children's expressions of hunger and fullness, they support children's sensitivity to calories consumed and reinforce their innate self-regulation skills (Ramsay et al., 2010). If teachers disregard children's fullness or hunger cues, problems can arise. For example, if caregivers encourage children to eat more, there is a possibility that children will eat in the absence of hunger, which can contribute to eating more calories than they need (Birch, Fisher, & Davison, 2003; Satter, 2012c). Alternatively, if families or teachers pressure less compliant children to eat more food, some may "dig in their heels," leading to greater resistance to eating, mealtime battles, and possibly poor weight gain (American Dietetic Association, 2011; Satter, 2012b). Also, rigidly restricting the amount and type of food a child consumes because of health reasons or concerns about weight can lead to the exact opposite eating behavior—overconsumption of calories (Satter, 2012c; Tan & Holub, 2011).

Consider the teacher who says to a child asking to be excused at the end of a meal, "Dylan you can't be full. You hardly touched your lunch. Finish your meal, or you can't leave the table." This teacher does not acknowledge a child's satiety. Over time, this punitive approach may diminish a child's ability to self-regulate food intake (Frankel et al., 2012). A teacher who asks "Dylan, does your tummy feel full? If so, you can leave the table" helps the child to evaluate satiety before leaving the table.

Teachers and caregivers who are aware of these influences may, through thoughtful conversation, role modeling, and insightful interactions, help children maintain their ability to recognize hunger and satiety cues and successfully self-regulate their food intake (Frankel et al., 2012). Table 5-2 provides examples of mealtime phrases that may either override or support children's self-regulation of energy intake. Recognizing children's hunger and satiety cues reinforces the division of feeding responsibilities approach, which specifies that teachers and parents are responsible for the what, where, and when of feeding children while children are responsible for how much and whether to eat (Satter, 2012c).

WHAT IF . . .
a child in your class often puts more on his plate than he can eat? What strategy might you use to address this situation?

TABLE 5-2 Supporting Children's Self-Regulation of Food Intake

Phase of the meal	Comments that can override children's internal self-regulation cues (Not supportive)	Comments that support children's internal self-regulation cues (Supportive)
Beginning of the meal	Take one of each item. You need to take a carton of milk. That's not enough. You need to take more.	Are you hungry? How much would you like? Are you thirsty? Would you like some milk? There is more if you are hungry.
During the meal	Take at least three bites, and then you can go outside. You eat when I tell you to eat! That's it? Drink some more milk. You want some more? You can go play once you eat your chicken and broccoli.	Are you feeling full? Is your tummy telling you it's time to eat? There is more milk in the pitcher if you are still thirsty. You can have more if you are still hungry. If you are full, you can leave the table.
At the end of the meal	Lunchtime is over. A clean plate is a happy plate. You want more? I think you have had enough.	Is your tummy full? Are you too full to eat the rest of the food on your plate? There is more in the bowl if you are still hungry.

Sources: S. A. Ramsay, L. J. Branen, J. Fletcher, E. Price, S. L. Johnson, M. Sigman-Grant, 2010, "'Are you done?' child care providers' verbal communication at mealtimes that reinforce or hinder children's internal cues of hunger and satiation," *Journal of Nutrition Education and Behavior*, 42(4), 265–270 and L. A. Frankel, S. O. Hughes, T. M. O'Connor, T. G. Power, J. O. Fisher, and N. L. Hazen, 2012. "Parental influences on children's self-regulation of energy intake: Insights from developmental literature on emotion regulation," *Journal of Obesity*, vol. 2012, Article ID 327259. doi:10.1155/2012/327259.

Being a Good Role Model

Preschool children watch and copy the behaviors of their teachers—a reminder of the importance of being a good role model. Teachers are role models for children when they sit and eat with them and consume the same foods the children are served (Branen & Fletcher, 2015; Natale et al., 2014). This encourages children to try new foods and learn about healthy eating habits (American Dietetic Association, 2011; Erinosho, Hales, McWilliams, Emunah, & Ward, 2012). An important aspect of modeling for preschool children involves helping children learn to make decisions about food by providing opportunities for children to serve themselves and choose what and how much they eat. It is important for teachers to remember that forcing a child to eat a food can create food aversions. Even teachers trying to be good role models may not be able to eat all the foods that are offered because of food restrictions, allergies, previous negative experiences, or preferences. Consider this situation:

Mac, a 68-year-old retiree, volunteers three days a week in a Head Start classroom. He confesses to the teacher, Mindy, that he finds eating lunch with the children a challenge. Mindy is surprised because the children generally interact well with Mac during mealtimes. He quickly reassures her that it isn't the children he finds challenging; it's eating the vegetables! He says vehemently, "I just can't eat cabbage, broccoli, or cauliflower. I know I should be a better role model, but my mother forced me to eat them when I was a kid and I just can't do it." Mindy reassures him that no one, including volunteers, is pressured to eat something he or she doesn't like.

Children may notice that a teacher does not eat a certain food and ask why. If teachers do not eat certain foods because of health conditions, this should be explained to the child. For example, a teacher with a food allergy may say, "My doctor helped me to learn that my body cannot accept eating peanuts. This is only true for some people, not everyone." Food restrictions related to cultural or religious practices can be explained by stating, "In my culture, we choose not to eat cheese." When teachers do not like a food that is served, they might respond by saying in a neutral way, "I don't care for broccoli when it is cooked. I like it better raw." These examples are a reminder that teachers are people too.

Being a good role model is not always easy, and teachers must learn how to navigate situations where their personal preferences challenge their ability to be the perfect role model. Sharing information simply and clearly and modeling how to try and eat as many foods as possible communicate an attitude of being open to new flavors and experiences.

Teaching Preschoolers About Nutrition

Preschoolers are full of questions and want to master new experiences. The most effective learning opportunities are those in which children are active participants. Nutrition concepts should be integrated into the daily routine and include hands-on activities (Lyn, Evers, Davis, Maalouf, & Griffin, 2014). Certain themes can teach children a breadth of information about nutrition.

Learning About the Origins of Food

Preschool children may not have a clear understanding of where food comes from. When asked, they may say that food comes from the kitchen, restaurant, or grocery store. Concepts such as what the origin of food is, how seeds grow into plants, where

LEARNING OUTCOME   Children will be able to communicate when they are hungry and when they are full.

Vocabulary focus: Hungry, eat, full, finish, stomach growling.

Safety watch: Ensure foods are prepared and served appropriately for the age group and the child's abilities. Choose foods that avoid children's food allergies and restrictions.

TODDLERS, PRESCHOOLERS, AND KINDERGARTNERS

- **Goal:** Children will be able to describe the signs of hunger and fullness.
- **Materials:** The children's book *Lunch* by Denise Fleming, three or four fruits and vegetables that are referred to in the book (watermelon, blueberries, peas, carrots), flat trays filled with paint (offering the colors of the selected foods), large mural-sized sheet of white paper, tubs with warm water, paper towels.
- **Activity plan:** Place the paper on the floor with the paint trays near one end and the tubs of water and towels at the other end. Gather the children and talk about how it feels to be hungry and full. Demonstrate the sign language hand motions. Ask children to describe how they feel when they are hungry (stomach rumbles and makes noise, mouth waters) and full (stomach feels tighter and bigger; no more growling and rumbling). Tell them it is important to learn to recognize their body's cues of hunger and fullness. Read the book *Lunch*. Talk about how the mouse feels at the begin-

ning of the book and at the end of the book. Use the sign language terms for *hungry* and *full*. Talk about the colors of the foods and describe how the foods help the body. Invite children to remove their shoes and socks. One at a time, ask each child to identify his or her favorite food on the tray. Guide the child to step in the tray with paint that matches the color of the favorite food and then walk across the paper just as the mouse does in the book. Hold the child's hand to prevent the child from slipping. Engage the other children by asking them to count the child's steps. Help the child wash and dry his or her feet and put socks and shoes on (an assistant is helpful here). Use clean water to wash each child's feet. While eating lunch together, remind the children of the feelings associated with hunger and fullness. Summarize that it is good to "listen" to our body as it "tells" us when we are hungry and when it is time to stop eating

- **Did you meet your goal?** Can children describe the cues for hunger and fullness?

SCHOOL-AGE CHILDREN

- **Goal:** Children will be able to identify the signs of hunger and fullness and describe the basic steps of digestion.
- **Materials:** The book *Chewy, Gooey, Rumble, Plop* by Steve Alton, stethoscopes.
- **Activity plan:** Plan the activity in the morning. Gather the children and read the book. Talk about why we eat food and what happens to food once it's eaten. Review the basic steps in digestion presented in the book. Discuss how the body sends signals when it is time to eat and when it is time to stop eating. Have children think about these signals and explain how it feels to be hungry and full. Identify three areas of the room: "hungry," "not hungry or full,"

and "full." Direct the children to think about how they feel right now and to go to that area. Ask children in the "hungry" area what it is that makes them feel they are hungry (how do they feel?). Ask why they might be feeling that way. Introduce the idea that being hungry can make it hard to concentrate at school. Ask children in other areas to describe how they feel and to explain why they may not be feeling hungry. Summarize why it is important to pay attention to the body's signals for hunger and fullness.

- **Did you meet your goal?** Can children identify and describe hunger and fullness signs? Can they describe the basic steps of digestion?

Ariel Willey

This toddler shows she is hungry by reaching and crying. She is happy when she receives her food and uses sign language to indicate when she is full.

Ariel Daeschel

Ariel Daeschel

Ariel Daeschel

Inkev Getty Images

Field trips extend the learning to real-life situations.

milk comes from, how food gets from the farm to the table, or how grains of wheat become loaves of bread may be new. Teachers can introduce these concepts in many ways, such as through field trips, school gardens, and classroom cooking activities.

Field Trips Taking preschoolers outside the classroom extends learning to real-life situations and experiences. Field trips, because of their novelty, often create memorable moments that enhance knowledge about food. A trip to the dairy barn, milk processing plant, and grocery store shows children the sequence of steps involved in getting milk from the farm to the table. Tasting different types of milk (whole, low-fat, skim, or goat's milk) while discussing the nutrients they contain and their health benefits is meaningful because children get to experience a lesson through multiple senses.

School Gardens School or classroom gardens provide an opportunity for children to experience the surprise and delight of pulling a carrot out of the ground or picking and shelling a fresh pea for the first time. Children are better able to develop a clear picture of the origin of food when they plant seeds, watch them grow, tend to the plants, and then have the pleasure of eating what they produced. School gardens have

Erika Landorf-Kelly, Pearson Education, Inc.

Children are learning about food in a school garden.

PROGRESSIVE PROGRAMS & PRACTICES

Gardens as Learning Environments

By Vanessa Thompson, Head Start of Lane County, Oregon

Head Start of Lane County is the leading birth-to-five early childhood program in Lane County, Oregon. Our mission is "Ensuring our youngest children have a solid foundation for life." We do this by promoting school readiness by focusing on the health, education, nutrition, and social needs of young children. Gardens are an extension of our learning environments. With some inspiration and tools, children can be practicing pre-math, science, and literacy skills while playing outside in the garden (counting, measuring, sorting, classifying, labeling, and documenting, to name a few).

We created low-maintenance gardens at all sites, despite challenges such as concrete, vandalism, and weeds. When school is out of session, enthusiastic staff members assume garden maintenance responsibilities, such as watering and harvesting, as part of the agency's wellness program.

According to teacher Jan Olguin, "When children are involved in the growing of vegetables, they eat more of them!"

Children plant year-round. In the fall, they plant fava beans, clover, and oats. In the spring, they pull up the clover crop and plant carrots, radishes, peas, and other vegetables. Indoor planting also occurs to allow children to witness root growth, to cut the grass they grew, and to take marigolds home to plant after they grow larger.

Ariel Willey

the potential to support children's healthy eating behaviors and increase physical activity (Wells, Myers, & Henderson, 2014). See the *Progressive Programs & Practices* feature that describes how a Head Start program implements classroom gardens.

Classroom Cooking Activities Cooking activities teach many concepts and are of great interest to children because they get to sample what they made. Literacy is promoted as children view simply illustrated directions and sequential steps. Math skills are practiced through measuring and weighing foods. Science concepts are introduced as children see how ingredients interact when they are mixed together. The origin of a food item is enhanced when children experience the steps of food preparation. For example, making corn tortillas by grinding dried corn, mixing, and baking offers an opportunity to study where the corn was grown and how it was dried.

Activities That Support Nutrition Education

Activities that teach children about food and nutrition are popular in the preschool classroom. Themes can be reinforced by offering related activities at various learning centers. Pizza is an example of a food that uses products from each food group. The following activities relate to pizza, a five-food-group food.

- *Dramatic play props for an Italian restaurant:* chef's hat; aprons; pizza delivery boxes; pizza pans; plastic pizza cutters; checkered tablecloth; plastic food models of pizza, spaghetti, salad, milk.
- *Math props:* a cash register and play money.

WHAT IF . . .

you wanted to extend the pizza theme by planning a manipulative activity and a game that promoted large motor skills? What activities would you develop?

CHECK YOUR UNDERSTANDING 5.2

Click here to check your understanding of the nutritional needs of preschoolers.

- *Literacy props:* menu, paper to record "pizza orders," telephone to receive take-out orders.
- *Creative materials to "make" pizza:* colored paper to cut and paste to make paper pizzas with a tan crust, green and red peppers, brown mushrooms, yellow pineapple, cheese and black olives.
- *Science exploration center with ingredients to make pizza:* whole-wheat flour, yeast, salt, warm water, measuring cups and spoons, bowls, pizza sauce, and toppings.

FEEDING SCHOOL-AGE CHILDREN

It is "Sock Hop" dance night for the children of Locust Grove School and children are having a fantastic time at this 1950s-style event. The Parent–Teacher Association (PTA) has obtained donations for the cake-walk contest. Soft drinks, cotton candy, and buttered popcorn are available for all to eat. The PTA is also selling candies and gift wrap as a fund-raiser. Anne, a teacher and member of the School Health Advisory Council, is supervising the dance. She is exasperated by the amount of food with little nutritional value at the dance. She wonders how she will be able to convey her health and nutrition concerns to other staff and families; then she comes up with a great idea. She will invite a member of the PTA to join the School Health Advisory Council. This will help create a connection between these groups who have the best interests of kids in common.

Primary school-age children become captains of their own ships when it comes to eating. They are now in a larger environment and experience less supervision at mealtimes. A school cafeteria is rife with activity; and throwing away parts of a packed lunch or choosing not to select or eat certain components of a school lunch menu are decisions that primary school-age children can make. Here is where they practice all the nutrition-related decision-making skills they learned in their home and early childhood programs.

In spite of this newfound freedom, teachers continue to have important responsibilities to positively influence children's ideas and decisions about food. Teachers need to understand the nutritional needs of this age group and recognize the characteristics of diets that support growth and development. They also need to understand how to create a positive nutritional environment and know how to teach nutrition and wellness concepts.

Understanding the Nutritional Needs of School-Age Children

School-age children's rate of growth is slow compared with infancy and preschool years. Their nutrient requirements increase with their increasing size and are reflected by larger portions in the CACFP food guidance system's recommendations. Children are able to accommodate longer time periods between meals.

The school-age years are a time when children's food choices are increasingly influenced by peer groups and media advertising. Maintaining a steady rate of growth can be hampered by societal influences such as decreased opportunities for physical activity, increased time in front of TVs and computers, increased exposure to foods of minimal nutritional value, and snack items that can lead to excess weight gain. Understanding these influences helps teachers understand the challenges that children face related to eating and being active.

Recognizing Characteristics of School-Age Children's Diets

School-age children have usually worked out the kinks of eating and experience fewer food-related feeding problems compared with toddlers and preschoolers. During this time, children become more responsible for selecting their own foods. If they are not pressured, school-age children can manage their internal hunger and satiety cues sufficiently to support growth and maintain normal weight. This success relies on an environment that supports healthful eating and avoids pressures related to food acceptance. Teachers contribute to this positive environment by being alert to the timing of meals and recognizing the importance of breakfast and the school lunch program.

Timing of Meals

A pattern of three meals with three snacks per day is still advised for school-age children. In most kindergarten and first-grade classroom settings, children consume snacks in the morning. By the time children are in second and third grade, the morning snack is discontinued. Teachers should be sensitive to the hunger cues among children in their classroom to determine whether to plan snacks as part of the morning routine. The type of snack is important. If snacks take the place of meals such as breakfast or dinner, they often are higher in added sugar and solid fat and lower in vitamins and minerals (American Dietetic Association and the American Dietetic Association Foundation, 2011; Fisher et al., 2015). Teachers who serve nutrient dense snacks that are low in solid fat and sugar, such as fruits, vegetables, low-fat dairy foods, and whole grains, make a positive contribution to children's nutrient needs and act as role models for children and their families. Healthy midmorning snacks may help children concentrate, improve memory, and fill in nutrient gaps by providing vitamins, minerals, proteins, and calories for growth and development (Benton & Jarvis, 2007; Martinez & Shelnutt, 2010; Muthayya et al., 2007).

The Importance of Breakfast

Some school-age children eat breakfast at home, whereas others participate in the School Breakfast Program. Other children may skip breakfast because of hectic family lifestyles, early morning time constraints, or the family's lack of familiarity with the School Breakfast Program. An estimated 20% of children are breakfast skippers (Deshmukh-Taskar et al., 2010). Eating breakfast boosts children's intake of key vitamins and minerals, improving the chances children will meet their daily nutrient requirements (Food Research & Action Center, 2010; Rampersaud, 2009). Children who skip breakfast may be more at risk for obesity because by the time they are able to eat, they are so hungry they may make poor choices and overeat (Coppinger, Jeanes, Hardwick, & Reeves, 2012; Deshmukh-Taskar et al., 2010). In addition, prolonged fasts, which occur when the breakfast meal is skipped, may increase the insulin response to food offered later in the day, promoting fat storage and weight gain (Rampersaud, Pereira, Girard, Adams, & Metzl, 2005).

School Breakfast Program The School Breakfast Program (SBP) is a child nutrition program administered by the federal Food and Nutrition Service that offers cash subsidies from the USDA for every meal served by participating school districts (U.S. Food and Drug Administration, 2012d). Thanks to the Healthy Hunger-Free Kids Act and input from experts at the Institute of Medicine, standards for both the SBP and National School Lunch Program (NSLP) have recently been improved. Participating schools must provide breakfasts that align with the most recent dietary guidelines and the Dietary Reference Intakes to promote healthy meals consistent with the latest evidence-based research (U.S. Food and Drug Administration, 2012a).

The SBP is an important core child nutrition program that becomes even more valuable during difficult economic times when families may not be able to afford meals for their children. Some children are not hungry when they first wake up. The SBP gives them another opportunity to eat a nutritious meal a little later in the morning (Food Research & Action Center, 2010). The SBP and NSLP are available free of charge to children whose family income is 130% or less than the federal poverty level. A reduced-price option also is available to families whose income is between 130% and 185% of the established federal poverty level (U.S. Food and Drug Administration, 2012d). This makes the SBP accessible to many children and families.

WHAT IF . . .
you noticed a child who consistently was coming to school hungry in the morning due to limited financial resources at home? How would you address this problem?

Impact of Breakfast on Learning Breakfast is a significant meal not only because it helps children maintain a balanced diet, but also because it can impact learning. Studies show that children who eat breakfast experience benefits such as:

- Increased math and reading scores.
- Improved speed and memory in cognitive tests (Centers for Disease Control and Prevention, 2012; Food Research & Action Center, 2010; Rampersaud, 2009).
- Improved school behavior and attentiveness, which supports the overall educational environment.

Children who do not eat breakfast are at a disadvantage academically. Teachers need to share this important information with families and help them explore options for providing morning meals for their school-age children.

Providing School Lunch

Lunch is usually the largest meal offered when children are at school. Thus, the NSLP plays a major role in children's diets.

National School Lunch Program The National School Lunch Program (NSLP) is a core child nutrition program offered by the USDA Food and Nutrition Service that provides nutritious lunches for children attending school. The Healthy, Hunger-Free Kids Act, 2010 resulted in an important reform for the NSLP. Like the SBP, to receive federal subsidies, school lunches must align with the most recent dietary guidelines and DRIs (U.S. Food and Drug Administration, 2012a). The recent changes to the school lunch program standards and how they are now more closely aligned with the dietary guidelines is shown in Table 5-3. School lunches must provide nutritious meals that keep fat at 30% of total calories or less and are reduced in sodium, saturated fat, and *trans* fat content. Daily calories offered at lunch must fall into a 550–650 minimum and maximum range. This supports the Dietary Guidelines goal of balancing calories to manage weight and prevent obesity (National Food Service Management Institute, 2012).

Like the School Breakfast Program, the NSLP is available free of charge to children whose family income is 130% or less than the federal poverty level and at reduced price to families whose incomes are between 130% and 185% of the

TABLE 5-3 Aligning the National School Lunch Program with the Dietary Guidelines for Americans

Dietary Guidelines Recommendations	National School Lunch Program Requirements (Kindergarten Through Grade 5)
Maintain calorie balance over time to achieve and sustain a healthy weight	Weekly average calorie range for lunch: 550–650
Food and food components to reduce: • Reduce sodium to 1500 mg • Reduce saturated fat to 10% or less, cholesterol to 300 mg or less, and trans fats and calories from solid fats • Limit added sugars	Menu planning requirements: • Sodium content in school lunches will be reduced to less than or equal to 640 mg. • Weekly average of saturated fat content must be less than 10%. Food labels should indicate zero trans fat per serving. Milk must be fat-free or 1%. • Serve unflavored milk; 100% full-strength juice may be served but cannot exceed half the fruit requirement per week. No snack-type fruit product such as fruit drops, leather, or strips. Frozen fruit cannot contain added sugar.
Food and food components to increase: • Increase vegetable and fruit intake • Increase whole grains • Choose a variety of lean protein foods	Menu planning requirements: • There is a weekly requirement of legumes and dark green, red/orange, starchy, and other vegetables. Vegetable and fruit requirement per lunch is increased from ½ cup to 1¼ cup. • All grains must be whole grains. • Lean meats, seafood, poultry, beans/peas, yogurt, tofu, nut butters, and nuts. Daily minimum and weekly ranges established.
Build healthy eating patterns: • Choose foods that provide calcium, vitamin D, potassium, and dietary fiber, nutrients of concern in U.S. diets • Remember that beverages count	Meal planning requirements: • Follow above-mentioned meal-planning requirements. • Water must be made available to children. Juice is limited to half the fruit requirement per week and must be 100% fruit juice. Milk must be fat-free or 1% and unflavored.

Sources: The University of Mississippi National Food Service Management Institute, 2012. *The New Meal Pattern Training Participant Guide* retrieved February 12, 2015, from http://nfsmi.org /documentlibraryfiles/PDF/20120627021105.pdf; U.S. Department of Agriculture, 2012. Final Rule Nutrition Standards National School Lunch and School Breakfast Programs, retrieved February 12, 2015, from http://www.fns.usda.gov/cnd/governance/legislation/dietaryspecs.pdf.

established federal poverty levels. The USDA also provides a variety of other programs to support the nutritional health and wellness of school-age children:

- *Team Nutrition:* This program provides technical support and training for food service employees at school, as well as nutrition education opportunities for children and teachers (U.S. Department of Agriculture Food and Nutrition Service, 2012b).

- *HealthierUS School Challenge:* This program promotes and recognizes positive change in school nutrition and health environments. It provides guidelines for improving nutrition and physical activity in the school setting. When schools comply with these recommendations, they are recognized with a monetary award and are certified as Bronze, Silver, Gold, or Gold of Distinction Schools (U.S. Department of Agriculture Food and Nutrition Service, 2012a). In 2010, First Lady Michelle Obama incorporated the HealthierUS School Challenge into her Let's Move initiative.

- *Let's Move:* The goals of the Let's Move program were established with the intent to solve the childhood obesity epidemic within a generation. Through integrated strategies, this initiative aims to put children on the path to good health by providing support, resources, and action steps to families, caregivers, schools, community leaders, chefs, and health care providers. Let's Move encourages the development of environments that support healthy nutrition and physical activity choices (Let's Move, 2010). *Chefs Move to Schools* is part of the *Let's Move* initiative that partners chefs with schools and school personnel to help in providing menu ideas, providing culinary training, and teaching children about healthy meals (Chefs Move to Schools, 2012).

★ **What is a Recess Before Lunch Policy?**

Where students go to recess first, then eat lunch.

Montana schools are reaping the benefits:

★ Improved student behavior on the playground, in the cafeteria and the classroom.

★ Students waste less food and drink more milk. This leads to increased nutrient intake.

★ Improved cafeteria atmosphere.

★ Children are more settled and ready to learn.

★ **Tips For Getting Started:**

★ Build support within your community and school staff.

★ Realize that adapting the schedule is a work in progress.

★ Develop a hand washing routine.

★ Schedule adequate time for students to eat (at least 25-30 minutes.)

★ Decide where to store cold lunches for easy access.

★ Take care of lunch money prior to recess.

★ Practice this new routine with the students. Spend as much time in the lunchroom as possible during first few weeks.

★ Be committed, even through a trial period, to stick with it. Expect some resistance.

FIGURE 5-8

Benefits of Recess Before Lunch

Source: Used with permission from http://opi.mt.gov/Programs /SchoolPrograms/School_Nutrition /MTTeam.html, Montana Team Nutrition Program, Montana State University and School Nutrition Programs, Office of Public Instruction, Helena, Montana, 2012.

- *Summer Food Service/Seamless Summer Programs:* These programs continue to provide nutritious school lunches throughout the summer break in communities where 50% or more of the children served are eligible for free or reduced meals year-round, ensuring low-income children have access to nutritious meals (U.S. Department of Agriculture Food and Nutrition Service, 2012).

- *Farm to school programs:* The Healthy, Hunger-Free Kids Act of 2010 established this program to improve children's access to locally grown and produced foods via regional farmers and other producers. Grant awards provide funding to support these efforts as well as hands-on educational and experiential activities that include school gardens, field trips to local farms, and cooking classes (U.S. Food and Drug Administration Food and Nutrition Service, 2012).

Teachers make a positive impact on children's nutrition and the wellness climate of schools by endorsing and participating in initiatives such as these.

School Lunch: Before or After Recess?   The predominant practice in primary schools is to eat lunch and then participate in outdoor recess. Yet research shows children who eat lunch after recess eat better, waste less food, and behave better (Montana Team Nutrition Program, 2009; Rainville, Wolf, & Carr, 2006). Many children rush through lunch to go outside to play. For children from low-income families, this can mean missing a vital opportunity for a nutritious meal. Teachers may consider advocating for offering lunch after recess if they notice children are coming back from recess hungry (Figure 5-8).

Understanding the Teacher's Role in Creating a Quality Nutrition Environment

Increased concern about the health of children in the United States due to increasing rates of childhood obesity and decreasing rates of activity have led to a greater awareness of the need to provide more healthful meals, more physical activity, and foods that are produced and purchased in more sustainable ways. This has led to the development of a school wellness movement. These initiatives have been supported by a number of recently enacted programs and initiatives that place a high degree of importance on good nutrition and physical activity.

School Wellness Policy

In 2004, the Child Nutrition and WIC Reauthorization Act required schools to establish a school wellness policy by January 2006. This law has shifted the focus of food service from providing not only adequate nutrient intake, but also meals that promote healthful eating habits in an effort to prevent chronic diseases such as obesity, diabetes, high blood pressure, heart disease, and stroke. As a result, federally sponsored school nutrition programs have made major strides to revamp their menus to address the new health and nutrition guidance systems. The Healthy, Hunger-Free Kids Act of 2010, expands the role of wellness policies in school districts. The act encourages the participation of physical education teachers and school health personnel in the development, implementation, and review of wellness policies and requires a system of evaluation and public updates on the content and degree of compliance to goals of the wellness policies (U.S. Food and Drug Administration Food and Nutrition Service, 2015).

The school wellness policy must address physical activity for improving the health climate of the school setting. The importance of physical education classes, recess, and before- and after-school opportunities to participate in sports activities are reemphasized. Figure 5-9 summarizes the requirements for establishing physical activity goals that must be included in the school wellness policy. Nutrition and physical activity are two sides of the same coin; without one or the other, children's health and wellness are compromised.

In addition, school wellness policies must address the provision of food that occurs outside the realm of traditional school food service. For example, food is commonly available at after-school programs and school social and sporting events. Food is often used as a reward in the classroom setting as well. Teachers, administrators, and parents need to develop policies that are supportive of healthy eating. The *Nutrition Note* gives an example of how teachers can avoid using food as a reward to reinforce behavior or reward academic achievement in the classroom setting. Guidelines from the Food and Nutrition Service for establishing policies that address these issues are offered in Figure 5-9 and can help teachers envision how they can foster good nutrition in all settings of the school environment.

Children with Special Needs All children are entitled to wellness. Some children with special developmental or health needs may experience challenges that make achieving wellness particularly relevant. Some may have conditions that predispose them to being underweight, whereas others will be more prone to obesity.

Teachers must communicate with families and health care providers to determine how to best meet children's goals for healthful weight. Some children may follow special diets to manage health conditions. On occasion, attending to these medical needs can compromise the overall quality of the child's diet. For example, meeting the nutritional needs for calcium in a child with a milk, egg, and soy allergy may prove difficult. Children on gluten-free diets may not be offered enough variety at school to ensure they eat enough. Teachers cannot make medical recommendations, but they can encourage collaboration among families, school nutrition personnel, registered dietitian nutritionists, and health care providers to ensure children's special nutritional needs have been addressed appropriately.

Children from Culturally Diverse Backgrounds Promoting wellness goals benefits all children but may be particularly important for children from diverse cultural backgrounds. Some ethnic groups suffer disproportionately more from chronic health conditions related to nutrition and obesity. For example, when using body

FIGURE 5-9   School Wellness Sample Policy Guidelines

Physical Activity Goals

- Students are given opportunities for physical activity:
  - during the school day through PE classes.
  - during daily recess periods for elementary school students.
  - through the integration of physical activity into the academic curriculum.
  - through a range of before- and/or after-school programs such as intramurals, interscholastic athletics, and physical activity clubs.
- Schools are required to:
  - work with the community to create ways for students to walk, bike, etc. safely to and from school.
  - encourage parents and guardians to support their children's participation in physical activity, to be physically active role models, and to include physical activity in family events.
  - provide training to enable teachers, and other school staff to promote enjoyable, lifelong physical activity among students.

Nutrition Education and Promotion Goals

- Students in grades pre-K-12 receive nutrition education that is:
  - interactive and teaches the skills they need to adopt healthy eating behaviors.
  - offered in the school dining room as well as in the classroom, with coordination between the foodservice staff and teachers.
  - consistent in the nutrition messages throughout schools, classrooms, cafeterias, homes, community, and media.
  - integrated into the health education or core curricula (e.g., math, science, language arts).
  - provided by staff who have nutrition education appropriate training.
- Schools will:
  - use district health education curriculum standards and guidelines that include both nutrition and physical education.
  - link nutrition education activities with the coordinated school health program.
  - conduct nutrition education activities and promotions that involve parents, students, and the community.

Goals for All Foods and Beverages Available During the School Day

- The school district will set guidelines for foods and beverages:
  - in a la carte sales in the food service program on school campuses.
  - sold in vending machines, snack bars, school stores, and concession stands on school campuses.
  - sold as part of school-sponsored fundraising activities.
  - served at parties, celebrations, and meetings during the school day.
- The school district makes decisions on these guidelines based on nutrition goals, not on profit making.

Goals for Other School-Based Activities

- The school district provides an environment that:
  - is a clean, safe, enjoyable meal environment for students.
  - provides enough space and serving areas to ensure all students have access to school meals with minimum wait time.
  - includes drinking fountains available so that students can get water at meals and throughout the day.
  - encourages all students participate in school meals program and protect the identity of students who eat free and reduced price meals.
  - ensures an adequate time for students to enjoy eating healthy foods with friends in schools.
  - schedules recess for elementary schools before lunch so that children will come to lunch less distracted and ready to eat.
  - prohibit the use of food as a reward or punishment in schools.
  - will not deny student participation in recess or other physical activities as a form of discipline or for classroom make-up time.
- The school district ensures:
  - all schools' fundraising efforts are supportive of healthy eating.
  - school or district-owned physical activity facilities open for use by students outside school hours.

(Continued)

FIGURE 5-9   School Wellness Sample Policy Guidelines (*Continued*)

- encourage parents, teachers, school administrators, students, foodservice professionals, and community members to serve as role models in practicing healthy eating and being physically active, both in school and at home.
- encourage all students to participate in school meals programs.

- a system is in place for informing and updating the public including parents of the content and implementation of wellness policy goals.
- a method of periodically assessing and reporting progress made in achieving the goals of the school wellness policy and that there are designated school official(s) that are responsible for ensuring wellness policy goals are achieved.

Sources: Based on Local School Wellness Policy, 2012, by USDA Food and Nutrition Service, retrieved July 28, 2011, from http://www.fns.usda.gov/tn/healthy/wellnesspolicy_requirements.html; Local School Wellness Policy Requirements, 2004, by USDA Food and Nutrition Service, retrieved July 28, 2012, from http://www.fns.usda.gov/tn/healthy/wellnesspolicy2004_requirements.html.

mass index as an indicator, the incidence of obesity is estimated at 31.2% among American Indian/Native Alaskan children, 22% for Hispanics, 20.8% for blacks, 15.9% for whites, and 12.8% in Asians (Anderson & Whitaker, 2009). Efforts to promote wellness among all children must be addressed in culturally appropriate ways. Strategies include:

- Communicating school wellness goals, policies, and educational materials in the home languages of children attending the school.
- Incorporating healthful ethnic dishes in the school menu.
- Providing translation services at parent education seminars.

The Cafeteria as a Learning Lab

Part of the technical assistance offered to schools to support the implementation of school wellness policies is access to resources that help teachers learn about and effectively convey nutrition and health messages. This includes taking advantage

NUTRITION NOTE   Avoid Using Food as a Reward

Rewarding children with food to reinforce behavior or to reward academic achievement is not good practice. Negative consequences of using food as a reward include:

- Creating value for the food being used for reward: Children begin to think "This candy must be very special if my teacher uses it to get me to do something."
- Encouraging children to eat when they are not hungry and creating a link between food and behavior rather than food and hunger: This promotes a pattern of children rewarding or comforting themselves with food and predisposes them to obesity in the future.
- Sabotaging children's diet: Children may be less likely to eat a healthy lunch or snack.

- Promoting eating between meals and snack times: This increases the risk for obesity and dental caries.
- Exposing children to high-fat and -sugar, low-vitamin and mineral foods: This creates a taste for these foods.

More effective and healthful ways to acknowledge positive behaviors include:

- Assigning children a leadership opportunity, such as passing out books or leading a song.
- Allowing children to choose the story at group time.
- Offering a walk with the teacher.
- Providing an extra five minutes of outside playtime.

of the school cafeteria as a learning lab. Resources, educational materials, and ideas to support nutrition education in the cafeteria are provided by the *Healthy Meals Resource System* (U.S. Food and Drug Administration, 2012c). Activities that use the cafeteria as a learning center include:

- Offering taste tests of new foods and recipes.
- Displaying food sculptures.
- Conducting nutrition poster contests.
- Providing cafeteria kitchen tours.
- Preparing healthful recipes.
- Inviting important guest visitors to promote good nutrition and physical activity.

Understanding the Teacher's Role in Promoting Healthful Eating Habits

Teachers continue to be an important influence in supporting good eating habits in school-age children. They enhance their influence by sharing nutrition information with families and advocating for the children in their care.

Communicating with Families

Teachers and school administrative staff have responsibilities to share nutrition and health information that supports healthful eating in the home environment. This can be accomplished by providing nutrition and health-related articles in school newsletters or on the school menus sent home with children. Schools can post the lunch menu on the school website and provide nutrient analysis for menu items. Information about carbohydrate content for children with diabetes and alternative menu options for children with special nutritional needs or preferences also can be provided. Teachers and schools can sponsor family events that promote physical activity and create a partnership approach to helping school-age children eat healthy and be active.

The school cafeteria becomes a learning lab when children are exposed to nutrition-related activities such as creating food sculptures.

Samantha Ramsay

Teachers as Advocates

Teachers are important advocates for healthy school environments. They promote healthful nutrition and wellness among school-age children by advocating for nutritious menus and supporting the school breakfast and lunch programs. Teachers continue to serve as role models for healthful eating and physical activity behaviors. Eating school lunches with children and participating in physically active games and events during recess send important messages to young children. Participating in school committees that support healthy eating and physical activity provides opportunities for teachers to advocate for policies and programs that fit the developmental learning of school-age children while fostering healthy habits that contribute to children's health and wellness.

Helping Families Access Nutrition Services

Sometimes children have nutritional needs that cannot be solved easily. Families may need to consult with health care providers and registered dietitian nutritionists who have expertise in the field of nutrition. The scrutiny of children's weight by health care authorities in the face of the obesity epidemic has brought the issue of overweight into the spotlight for many families (see Chapter 3 for a discussion on obesity). Families may turn to teachers with their concerns. Teachers can direct families to appropriate health care providers and support their recommendations.

The focus on the obesity epidemic has revealed another health care concern relating to weight: eating disorders. Eating disorders represent an extreme dysfunction in eating habits that develop gradually and can negatively impact the growth, development, and health of children (Kleinman, 2009; Mahan, Escott-Stump, & Raymond, 2012). Two commonly recognized types of eating disorders include anorexia nervosa and bulimia nervosa. **Anorexia nervosa** is caused by a distortion of body image and is characterized by the severe restriction of food intake resulting in significant weight loss. **Bulimia nervosa** entails binge eating followed by purging activities such as vomiting, using laxatives, or exercising excessively. Although eating disorders are typically considered an adolescent issue, more young children are being identified with eating disorders at earlier ages (Mahan et al., 2012; Pinhas, Morris, Crosby, & Katzman, 2011). These are psychological disorders that result in medical complications that can be life threatening (Queen Samour & King, 2012). Teachers should support nutritious diets to promote good health and avoid focusing on weight or appearance when discussing healthful eating with children. For example, it is appropriate to comment on healthful food choices such as, "It's great to see you drinking water instead of soda"; on the other hand, it's detrimental to state, "If you drink that soft drink, you're going to get fat." It is paramount that children develop a positive body image. An approach that avoids rigid restrictions of any food teaches children how to eat well with enjoyment.

anorexia nervosa
an eating disorder involving severe restriction of food intake resulting in significant and sometimes life-threatening weight loss

bulimia nervosa
an eating disorder involving periods of binge eating followed by purging activities such as vomiting, using laxatives, or exercising excessively

Teaching School-Age Children About Nutrition

The school-age years are an important time for teaching children about nutrition and wellness. The 2004 Child Nutrition and WIC Reauthorization Act focuses on nutrition education by requiring school wellness policies to include a systematic approach to nutrition education. Figure 5-9 provides a summary of the components of the school wellness policy that addresses the requirements for providing nutrition education in schools.

Nutrition education needs to be integrated into all aspects of the school environment. Nutrition messages should be incorporated into math, reading, and health curricula. Teachers may be concerned that teaching nutrition will require a new curriculum and take time from the daily schedule to teach a new subject, but this perspective requires a shift in mind-set (Huber, 2009). Any lesson plan can integrate physical activity and nutrition concepts. Refer to Figure 5-10 and consider how nutrition concepts can be interwoven into the unit on herbs and leafy greens. Many helpful resources are available, such as the U.S. Department of Agriculture National Agricultural Library's Curricula and Lesson Plans website .

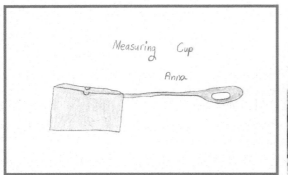

Measuring Cup

Anna

How To Make Caprese Salad

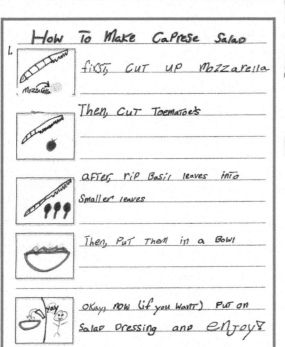

1. first CUT UP Mozzarella

Then, Cut Toematoe's

After, rip Basil leaves into Smaller leaves

Then, Put Them in a Bowl

Okay, now (if you want) Put on Salad Dressing and enjoy

FIGURE 5-10
Incorporating Nutrition Education into Primary-Grade Curricula

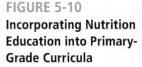

Ask me About Basil

Basil

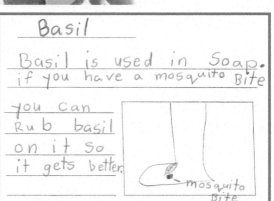

Basil is used in Soap. if you have a mosquito Bite you can Rub basil on it so it gets better.

mosquito Bite

how to Transplant a herb

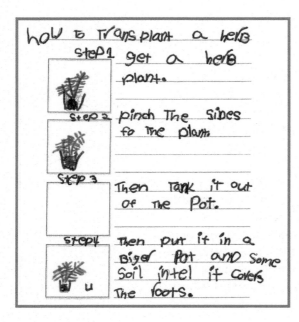

step 1 get a herb plant.

step 2 pinch The sides fo The plant

step 3 Then Tank it out of The Pot.

step 4 Then put it in a Biger Pot and Some Soil intel it covers The roots.

Facts about basil

* basil Truns black When you Cut it With a metal Knife * Basil is an herb * Basil Soap smals like genger * Basil is used in Pizza, Pesto, and Pasta * Some basil stems are long * Did you know! Basil Can't be Very Wet to survive.

Teaching Basic Nutrition Concepts

A useful curriculum for teaching basic nutrition concepts to school-age children is the USDA's ChooseMyPlate website, which has nutrition tips, recipes, information, and lesson plans for the MyPlate food guidance system. The goals of the lessons are to introduce the concept of food groups and teach students how to identify the foods they eat in their diets. Understanding these basic nutrition concepts helps children categorize foods and understand the role of food in maintaining good health.

Using an Integrated Nutrition Curriculum

Many nutrition and health curricula support an integrated approach to learning. For example, the North Carolina Nutrition Education and Training Program developed an integrated curriculum called *Food for Thought*. Lesson plans are available for kindergarten through grade 5 on nutrition-related topics. These lessons focus on integrating healthy eating and physical activity with math and English language arts. The lesson plans include objectives, teacher resources, and teacher input sections that help teachers organize their nutrition lessons.

Another curriculum called *Cooking with Kids* addresses goals established by a local student nutrition advisory council to improve school food. The bilingual curriculum introduces the concepts of food and culture through taste testing and cooking lessons. The cafeteria participates by serving *Cooking with Kids* recipes throughout the school year. The cooking lessons focus on preparing recipes from five different regions of the world. Each lesson begins by using a map to identify where the recipe originated and then provides the history of the foods and how they are grown, as well as the nutritional contributions of the ingredients used in preparing the recipe. Teachers have access to a tremendous amount of resources as they strive to promote nutrition and health messages in the school environment.

Teaching About Sustainable Nutrition

Sustainable nutrition is the consumption of food that is grown in such a way as to protect the environment. Sustainable nutrition practices focus on encouraging the use of foods that have had minimal processing, packaging, and transportation, thereby decreasing the energy used in their production. Careful sustainable growing practices are used to protect soil and water resources. Teachers can integrate sustainability concepts throughout the nutrition lessons they teach and relate these ideas to the school environment as well as the community at large.

CHECK YOUR UNDERSTANDING 5.3

Click here to check your understanding of the nutritional needs of school-age children.

SUMMARY

- The diets of toddlers and preschool-age children are in transition as eating skills develop. Children learn about foods through experience and repeated exposures. A varied and balanced diet is important to promote positive eating habits and to help children explore and accept a wide range of foods. Toddlers are busy acquiring new eating skills. Teachers support these efforts by understanding toddlers' nutritional requirements and knowing how to feed them to address selective eating as toddlers learn about eating.

- Preschool-age children have mastered many new eating skills and do well with routinely scheduled meals and snacks. The division of feeding responsibility helps preschool children learn to become autonomous eaters. This is supported by teachers who understand feeding responsibilities: Children choose *whether they eat* and *how much*, whereas teachers are responsible for *what*, *when*, and *where* children eat. Teachers need to understand general nutrition concepts and be familiar with the food guidance systems that support appropriate feeding practices such as the Child and Adult Care Food Program and the USDA's MyPlate for preschoolers and children.

- Children in kindergarten through elementary grades are still growing at a steady pace and need healthy, balanced diets that meet their growth needs. Teachers need to advocate for each child to receive breakfast at home or school and to support the school lunch program. School-age children have more freedom than younger children to make their own decisions when eating at school, so nutrition education, eating practices, and physical activity continue to be important. Teachers are important advocates for school-age children. As advocates, teachers contribute to school wellness policies by encouraging healthful practices related to food and physical activity across the school environment and in all school-related activities. Teachers continue to be powerful role models for children of all ages.

Chapter Quiz

Click here to check your understanding of Chapter 5, Feeding Toddlers, Preschoolers, and School-Age Children.

Discussion Starters

1. Describe how you would encourage a toddler who is a selective eater and has multiple food allergies to broaden his food choices. How would you approach an older child who is average weight but doesn't eat much lunch?

2. Outline plans for a field trip to help preschool children learn where bread comes from. Where would you take the group? On what aspects of bread production would you focus?

Practice Points

1. Using the CACFP guidelines for toddlers by searching for USDA CACFP guidelines on the web and plan menus for a breakfast, a lunch, and a snack.

2. Create a math activity for preschool-age children that integrates nutrition and sustainability concepts.

3. Using MyPlate and the Dietary Guidelines for Americans as resources, develop a school wellness policy for an elementary school. Would your policy suit the needs of a school that serves predominantly low-income families or families with a Hispanic or Native American cultural tradition? Explain.

Web Resources

CDC Local Wellness Policy Tools and Resources

ChooseMyPlate

Cooking with Kids Curriculum

Ellyn Satter's Division of the Responsibilities of Feeding

Feeding Young Children in Group Settings

Food and Nutrition Information Center: Toddler Nutrition and Health Resource List

Let's Move

North Carolina Division of Public Health: Eat Smart Move More: Food for Thought Curriculum

School Health Guidelines to Promote Healthy Eating and Physical Activity: Recommendations and Reports

USDA Local School Wellness Policy

Zero to Three

Key Terms

Anorexia nervosa

Bulimia nervosa

Extended breastfeeding

Family-style service

Food jag

Food neophobia

Selective eaters

CHAPTER 6

Menu Planning

learning outcomes

After reading this chapter, you should be able to:

1. Explain how to plan healthful meals using nutrition goals, evidence-based practices, and food budgeting.
2. Describe menu planning requirements and resources for child care settings.
3. Explain the procedure for building a menu.
4. Discuss strategies for managing young children's special dietary considerations.

CASE STUDY Jeanine places a set of old menus on her kitchen table and begins the process of planning a new set of menus for the upcoming week. Feeding 3- to 5-year-olds has its challenges. Every week she plans menus, shops, and prepares food for a group that includes one finicky eater, a child who is allergic to milk, another who is overweight, and one who for religious reasons does not eat pork. Included in the mix is a 3-year-old vegetarian whose well-intentioned mother makes many menu suggestions that Jeanine tries to accommodate even though it puts a strain on her food budget. Jeanine participates in the Child and Adult Care Food Program, a federal child nutrition program that provides funding to offset the cost of meals and snacks. This helps, but completing the paperwork to meet the program's reimbursement requirements is time-consuming.

Jeanine wants to plan nutritious meals, but with so many things to consider she worries children won't eat the food she prepares. Her goals are to plan nutritious menus that are appealing to children, meet families' expectations, and fit her food budget.

Translating diet guidelines can be challenging. Jeanine struggles with the weekly planning of healthful menus for a small group of young children who have a wide range of nutritional needs. How would you feed a group of 3- to 5-year-old children nutritious meals that meet all of their needs? To do so, you need a plan.

In this chapter, we describe a systematic way to develop appropriate menus. We begin by discussing the resources available for developing menus that meet quality recommendations and are appealing to children. We discuss how to establish and promote broad program-wide nutrition-related wellness goals through effective menu planning. We detail a step-by-step procedure for writing and implementing menus and define strategies for purchasing, storing, and preparing foods to keep menus cost effective. All of this work is for naught, however, if children don't eat what is offered. To address this, we discuss strategies that support children as they explore new foods. We also provide tactics for adapting menus for children with special dietary needs and religious or cultural preferences. This information will help you plan menus that support growth and development in young children.

HEALTHFUL MENU PLANNING

The menu is the foundation of health in the child care setting. Developing a healthful, cost-effective menu requires an understanding of nutrition goals, evidence-based nutrition practices, and food budgeting. The task of menu planning may seem daunting, but a good menu can save time and money, and—as with any other skill—developing a menu becomes easier with practice. Menu planning is made simpler by using a three-phase approach:

- *Phase 1:* Understand child nutrition and food program requirements.
- *Phase 2:* Write menus using a step-by-step approach.
- *Phase 3:* Adapt menus to support special dietary needs or food preferences.

The **first phase of menu planning includes understanding specific program requirements**. Teachers need to be aware of existing nutrition, licensing, and funding directives when planning menus in early childhood settings. For example, the *Dietary Guidelines for Americans* and the Dietary Reference Intakes (DRI) are food guidance systems that form the foundation for federal food program recommendations, including the Child and Adult Care Food Program, the National School Lunch Program, and the School Breakfast Program (Institute of Medicine, 2008; Murphy, Yaktine, Suitor, & Moats, 2011; U.S. Department of Agriculture, Food and Nutrition Service, 2012b).

The **second phase of menu planning includes the steps used to write and implement menus.** This is a creative process in which teachers are encouraged to take into consideration the flavors, textures, colors, and aromas of foods when designing menus that appeal to children as well as expose them to new flavors and textures.

The **third phase of menu development focuses on how to adapt menus to support alternative or special diets** so that all children, regardless of health concerns or cultural preferences, receive a healthy balanced diet. These three phases of menu planning provide teachers with an approach to create healthful, appealing menus that are easy to use and cost-effective.

CHECK YOUR UNDERSTANDING 6.1

Click here to check your understanding of healthful meals, nutrition goals, and evidence-based practices.

PHASE 1: UNDERSTANDING REQUIREMENTS FOR MENU PLANNING

Young children rely on their families and teachers to ensure they are offered nutritious foods. Planning healthy meals that appeal to children and accommodate their needs is so important in early childhood settings that a variety of established requirements must be met for licensed programs and those funded by state or federal agencies. Failure to provide healthy menus may jeopardize children's nutritional needs and may put the children's program or school at risk for having its license revoked or funding rescinded. Therefore, early childhood educators must:

- Understand menu planning;
- Identify guidelines and how to apply them;
- Develop a system to organize and access resources.

These steps prepare teachers for menu writing. However, teachers first must consider their specific program and the role they play in the menu planning process.

Identifying the Teacher's Role

The teacher's role in menu planning varies in early childhood settings. Most settings offer snacks and meals or supervise children as they eat food brought from home. Teachers who work in large child care centers and primary school settings generally are not responsible for writing menus. Such organizations usually rely on foodservice professionals to plan menus. In contrast, teachers in family child care settings and small child care centers are often involved in menu planning.

Although teachers may not always be directly involved in preparing menus, an understanding of the concepts and requirements for menu planning helps teachers reinforce healthful eating practices for children and their families. The menu is a focal point for teaching children about foods. Teachers can be advocates and supporters of healthful eating by eating healthfully themselves. They can provide information about the food at the child care setting and share with families the menu guidelines they follow for health and food safety.

Understanding Menu Planning Resources

Many resources are available to guide menu planning for young children. Health organizations offer diet guidelines based on evidence-based research. Food safety guidelines are often regulated through various licensing requirements. These guidelines direct the food choices teachers make in planning menus. A successful menu is appealing to children and is in compliance with food safety and nutrition guidelines. Examples of the different types of authorities, agencies, and programs that provide menu oversight are found in Table 6-1.

Federally Funded Food and Nutrition Programs with Menu Planning Systems

Three child nutrition programs provide the template for menu planning in early childhood settings: the Child and Adult Care Food Program, which guides menu planning for prekindergarten programs and the National School Lunch Program and the School Breakfast Program, which guide menu planning for schools. Each offers information on how to prepare menus that meet the federally assisted meal program requirements for reimbursement.

The Child and Adult Care Food Program (CACFP)

The CACFP is a federal child nutrition assistance program funded by the Food and Nutrition Service of the USDA. The CACFP aims to increase the quality and affordability of early childhood programs by providing funds for healthy meals and snacks. Participating programs can provide nutritious meals to children from low-income

TABLE 6-1 Menu Planning Resources

Types of Authorities	Types of Agencies	Types of Programs
Health authorities	Government agencies, health care organizations	Maternal and Child Health Bureau American Public Health Association American Academy of Pediatrics U.S. Department of Agriculture and the Department of Health and Human Services • Dietary Guidelines for Americans • ChooseMyPlate.gov Academy of Nutrition and Dietetics American Medical Association
Licensing authorities	State child care licensing agencies, Food and Drug Administration, Public Health Service, state public health divisions, county health departments	National Resource Center for Health and Safety in Child Care and Early Education Local, state, and federal regulators who inspect programs that are involved in food service using the FDA Food Code, which contains food safety rules
Accreditation authorities	National agencies that set professional standards for early childhood education programs	National Association for the Education of Young Children (NAEYC) National Association for Family Child Care (NAFCC) National Early Childhood Program Accreditation (NECPA) National After School Association (NAA)
Funding authorities	Administration for Children and Families, Office of Head Start, Federal or state agencies that provide funding for early childhood education programs and child nutrition programs	Child and Adult Care Food Program (CACFP) National School Lunch Program (NSLP) School Breakfast Program (SBP) After School Snack Program (ASSP) Federal and State Head Start and Early Head Start Programs

Sources: Based on *Caring for Our Children: National Health and Safety Performance Standards: Guidelines for Out-of-Home Child Care Programs*, 3rd ed., by American Academy of Pediatrics, American Public Health Association, and National Resource Center for Health and Safety in Child Care, 2011, Elk Grove, IL: American Academy of Pediatrics; Food Code, 2009 updated 2011; and Health.gov, the Office of Disease Prevention and Health Promotion, Office of the Assistant Secretary for Health, Office of the Secretary, U.S. Department of Health and Human Services, Office of Disease Prevention and Health Promotion, 2015, from health.gov.

families (U.S. Department of Agriculture, Food and Nutrition Service, 2015b). Child care settings participating in CACFP can receive reimbursement for either two meals and one snack per day or one meal and two snacks if certain eligibility criteria are met.

Eligibility for Participation Licensed or approved nonprofit public or private child care centers, Head Start programs, family child care homes, after-school programs, and homeless shelters are eligible to participate in the CACFP. For-profit child care programs may be eligible to participate in the CACFP if 25% of the children enrolled qualify for free or reduced-price meals or subsidized child care payments. All children enrolled in Head Start are eligible for free meals regardless of family income level (U.S. Department of Agriculture, Food and Nutrition Service, 2015b).

To receive CACFP reimbursement, participating programs must maintain accurate records, including menus planned, foods purchased and served, and numbers of children who ate each meal, called a point-of-service meal count. The CACFP reimbursement is paid directly to programs. Many child care settings, unlike primary school settings, do not charge separately for meals. The amount of reimbursement to programs is determined using guidelines based on the household income of each enrolled child. The classification of families' income does not reflect what families are charged, but rather the amount of reimbursement the program receives from the CACFP funding authority.

Benefits of CACFP CACFP helps offset food and food service administrative expenses. The CACFP authority provides yearly training for teachers to learn about food group amounts for infants and children and menu planning for young children.

Even programs that do not participate in the CACFP find the CACFP guidelines provide an excellent framework for drafting menus.

CACFP Program Requirements The CACFP has specific food requirements for infants and young children. Also called **meal patterns**, these are the food groups, or components, and amounts to be offered at breakfast, lunch, supper, and snack for infants and children. The meal patterns outline the food groups, or **components**, that need to be offered and the amounts of each food required to qualify as a CACFP-approved breakfast, lunch, supper, or snack. The food group components include milk, grains/breads, meats/meat alternatives, and fruits/vegetables. CACFP portions represent the minimum portion to serve, but more food can be offered if children show signs of hunger. Very active children and older children may need larger portions to satisfy their hunger. Sufficient food should be available; however, consistently offering portions that are too large encourages children to eat more and could impact overweight (Nicklas, Liu, Stuff, Fisher, Mendoza, & O'Neil, 2013). Table 6-2 illustrates CACFP meal patterns available for children in three different age categories (ages 1–2, 3–5, and 6–12). It can be reviewed in more detail by searching online for "USDA CACFP meal patterns," which will provide current CACFP guidelines and a free downloadable handbook.

meal patterns
food groups, or components, and amounts offered at breakfast, lunch, supper, and snack for infants and children

components
term used by the CACFP to describe food groups; includes milk, grains/breads, meats/meat alternatives, and fruits/vegetables

TABLE 6-2 CACFP Meal Pattern Requirements for Children

Food Components	Ages 1–2	Ages 3–5	Ages 6–12[1]
BREAKFAST: SELECT ALL THREE COMPONENTS FOR A REIMBURSABLE MEAL			
1 milk			
fluid milk	½ cup	¾ cup	1 cup
1 fruit/vegetable			
juice,[2] fruit and/or vegetable	¼ cup	½ cup	½ cup
1 grains/bread[3]			
bread or	½ slice	½ serving	1 slice
cornbread or biscuit or roll or muffin or	½ slice	½ serving	1 serving
cold dry cereal or	¼ cup	⅓ cup	¾ cup
hot cooked cereal or	¼ cup	¼ cup	½ cup
pasta or noodles or grains	¼ cup	¼ cup	½ cup
LUNCH OR SUPPER: SELECT ALL FOUR COMPONENTS FOR A REIMBURSABLE MEAL			
1 milk			
fluid milk	½ cup	¾ cup	1 cup
2 fruits/vegetables			
juice,[2] fruit and/or vegetable	¼ cup	½ cup	¾ cup
1 grains/bread[3]			
bread or	½ slice	½ serving	1 slice
cornbread or biscuit or roll or muffin or	½ slice	½ serving	1 serving
cold dry cereal or	¼ cup	⅓ cup	¾ cup
hot cooked cereal or	¼ cup	¼ cup	½ cup
pasta or noodles or grains	¼ cup	¼ cup	½ cup

(continued)

TABLE 6-2 CACFP Meal Pattern Requirements for Children (Continued)

Food Components	Ages 1–2	Ages 3–5	Ages 6–12[1]
1 meat/meat alternate			
meat or poultry or fish[4] or	1 ounce	1½ ounces	2 ounces
alternate protein product or	1 ounce	1½ ounces	2 ounces
cheese or	1 ounce	1½ ounces	2 ounces
egg[5] or	½	¾	1
cooked dry beans or peas or	¼ cup	⅜ cup	½ cup
peanut or other nut or seed butters or	2 Tbsp.	3 Tbsp.	4 Tbsp.
nuts and/or seeds or	½ ounce	¾ ounce	1 ounce
yogurt[6]	4 ounces	6 ounces	8 ounces
SNACK: SELECT TWO OF THE FOUR COMPONENTS FOR A REIMBURSABLE SNACK			
1 milk			
fluid milk	½ cup	½ cup	1 cup
1 fruit/vegetable			
juice,[2] fruit and/or vegetable	½ cup	½ cup	¾ cup
1 grains/bread[3]			
bread or	½ slice	½ slice	1 slice
cornbread or biscuit or roll or muffin or	½ serving	½ serving	1 serving
cold dry cereal or	¼ cup	⅓ cup	¾ cup
hot cooked cereal or	¼ cup	¼ cup	½ cup
pasta or noodles or grains	¼ cup	¼ cup	½ cup
1 meat/meat alternate			
meat or poultry or fish[4] or	½ oz.	½ oz.	1 oz.
alternate protein product or	½ oz.	½ oz.	1 oz.
cheese or	½ oz.	½ oz.	1 oz.
egg[5] or	½	½	½
cooked dry beans or peas or	⅛ cup	⅛ cup	¼ cup
peanut or other nut or seed butters or	1 Tbsp.	1 Tbsp.	2 Tbsp.
nuts and/or seeds or	½ oz.	½ oz.	1 oz.
yogurt[6]	2 oz.	2 oz.	4 oz.

[1]Children age 12 and older may be served larger portions based on their greater food needs. They may not be served less than the minimum quantities listed in this column.
[2]Fruit or vegetable juice must be full-strength. Juice cannot be served when milk is the only other snack component.
[3]Breads and grains must be made from whole-grain or enriched meal or flour. Cereal must be whole-grain or enriched or fortified.
[4]A serving consists of the edible portion of cooked lean meat or poultry or fish.
[5]One-half egg meets the required minimum amount (one ounce or less) of meat alternate.
[6]Yogurt may be plain or flavored, unsweetened or sweetened.

Source: From USDA Food and Nutrition Service Child and Adult Care Food Program at http://www.fns.usda.gov/cnd/care/programbasics/meals/meal_patterns.htm.

Meal pattern requirements for infants are very specific. They outline the minimum amounts of breast milk or formula and other appropriate infant foods that must be offered to meet CACFP guidelines. The infant meal patterns present the progression of foods offered to infants over the first year of life. They also offer guidelines about how much breast milk or formula infants generally consume. For guidance on infant meal patterns from birth through 11 months of age, access the online CACFP resources by searching online for "USDA CACFP meal patterns from birth through 11 months of age," which will provide current CACFP guidelines and a free downloadable handbook.

CACFP guidelines are continually reviewed and updated. Recently, recommendations have been made to improve nutrition and reduce childhood obesity (IOM, 2011; USDA, 2015a). For example, skim or low-fat milk (1%) must be served to children once they reach age 2 and drinking water must be readily accessible for children during the day, and especially at mealtimes (Middleton, Henderson, & Schwartz, 2013). Offering more whole grains; dark green, orange, and red vegetables; and less sodium is recommended (U.S. Department of Agriculture, Food and Nutrition Service, 2015b).

nutrient dense foods
foods that are high in vitamin and mineral content while relatively low in calorie content

creditable food
food that meets CACFP guidelines and is eligible for reimbursement

noncreditable food
food that does not meet CACFP guidelines and when served in place of a creditable component makes a meal or snack ineligible for reimbursement

CACFP Creditable Foods Offering **nutrient dense foods** is a priority of the CACFP. For example, CACFP guidelines recommend that foods from the grain group be either enriched or whole grains. If a food does not meet CACFP specifications, it is not considered a **creditable food**. A creditable food meets CACFP guidelines and is eligible for reimbursement. A **noncreditable food** does not meet CACFP guidelines and is not eligible for reimbursement. An example of a noncreditable food in the milk group is yogurt, which does not meet the standard of identity for fluid milk; however, it can be credited as a food choice in the meat/meat alternate group. Some but not all soy milks meet nutrient standards that allow them to be creditable as a milk substitute. When child care settings use noncreditable food items in place of creditable foods or make mistakes in menu planning, they cannot claim reimbursement for that meal. Figure 6-1 shows two lunch meals. The meal on the right does not meet CACFP standards because juice was served at lunch instead of the required milk.

The National School Lunch Program (NSLP) and School Breakfast Program (SBP)

The NSLP and SBP are USDA programs designed to improve children's health and well-being by providing access to nutritious meals. All public and private schools and residential child care institutions are eligible to participate in the NSLP program if they agree to offer a nonprofit school lunch program that meets all federal regulations and is available to all children (U.S. Department of Agriculture, Food and Nutrition Service, 2012b). The NSLP and SBP are managed by each state's education authority.

nutrient targets
requirements for the amounts of nutrients and dietary components to be provided by school meals

meal requirements
include standards for menu planning and identify what is offered and must be selected by students

Primary grade school teachers are unlikely to plan menus. However, they should be aware of the type of menu planning system in place at their school so that they can support and promote positive eating habits. Teachers who support the NSLP and SBP can reinforce a healthful school nutrition environment and enhance opportunities for nutrition education.

Nutrient targets, the requirements for the amounts of nutrients and dietary components to be provided by school meals have been established by the Institute of Medicine, and provide the scientific basis for developing meal standards (IOM, 2011). **Meal requirements** include standards for menu planning and identify what is *offered* and what must be *selected* by students. Recommendations for daily and weekly requirements provide the establishment of minimum and maximum calorie ranges for meals offered to children based on different age group categories. Nutrition goals include reducing sodium content of meals; keeping saturated fat content of meals to less than 10%; offering more dark green, orange, and red vegetables; and requiring labeled foods to contain zero

FIGURE 6-1
CACFP Standards Require Milk Be Provided with Breakfast and Lunch

grams of *trans* fats per serving (Stallings, Suitor, & Taylor, 2010). For details on the National School Lunch Standards, search online typing "National School Lunch Meal Standards."

Head Start/Early Head Start Programs

Head Start is another federal agency administered by the Office of Head Start (OHS), the Administration for Children and Families (ACF), and the U.S. Department of Health and Human Services (U.S. Department of Health and Human Services, Administration for Children and Families, 2011). Head Start and Early Head Start grantees are guided by the **Head Start Performance Standards**, federal regulatory guidelines that provide oversight on all aspects of Head Start and Early Head Start program administration. Menus in Head Start settings must meet CACFP guidelines and Head Start standards for menu planning. A section in the Head Start Performance Standards entitled *Child Nutrition* outlines the standards that relate to program nutrition services (Head Start Performance Standards Title 45, Volume 4, U.S.C. Section 1304.23, 1998). A few are summarized below:

Head Start Performance Standards
federal regulatory guidelines that provide oversight on all aspects of Head Start and Early Head Start program administration

- All children's nutritional needs must be met, including children with special diets and children with disabilities.
- Programs must serve foods that broaden a child's food experience, including cultural and ethnic foods.
- One-third of a child's daily nutritional needs must be met in part-day programs and one-half to two-thirds in full-day programs.
- Programs must participate in the CACFP, and portion sizes must meet CACFP guidelines.
- Foods served must be high in nutrients and low in fat, sugar, and salt.

Head Start Performance Standards support CACFP requirements and provide meals that are closely aligned to the *Dietary Guidelines for Americans*.

USDA Schools/Child Nutrition Commodity Program

The Food and Nutrition Service of the USDA manages the distribution of **commodity foods** through the USDA Schools/Child Nutrition Commodity Program (U.S. Department of Agriculture, Food and Nutrition Service, 2015b). Commodity food, also called USDA foods, are foods the federal government has legal authority to purchase from American farmers and are used in child nutrition programs. The food is made available to state agencies and Indian Tribal Organizations and is distributed through a variety of venues including the CACFP. Early childhood programs participating in CACFP are eligible to receive these foods. Commodity foods typically include some fresh but predominantly canned and frozen fruits, fruit juices, and vegetables; frozen or canned meats; poultry and tuna fish; cheese; dry and canned beans; peanut butter; vegetable oils; rice; pasta products; flour; cornmeal; and oats (U.S. Department of Agriculture, Food and Nutrition Service, 2015b). Programs using commodity foods should have a list of these foods on hand when planning menus.

commodity foods
foods the federal government has legal authority to purchase from American farmers and are used in child nutrition programs

Organizing Resources

Remembering the many details of menu planning is not necessary if resources are well organized and accessible. In the opening case scenario, Jeanine recognizes the need to improve her approach to writing menus. She starts by using a notebook to compile recommendations and regulations for meal service and menu planning. She also creates a computer folder to organize her electronic resources. She finds it helpful to review and refer to these resources while she drafts her menus. For example:

- A bookmark to the USDA's MyPlate (U.S. Department of Agriculture, 2015b).
- A copy of the *Dietary Guidelines for Americans* (U.S. Department of Health and Human Services & U.S. Department of Agriculture, 2015).
- Position paper of the Academy of Nutrition and Dietetics, *Benchmarks for Nutrition Programs in Child Care Settings* (American Dietetic Association, 2011b).
- State licensing guidelines for food preparation and service.
- CACFP guidelines (U.S. Department of Agriculture, Food and Nutrition Service, 2015) and handbook: *Nutrition and Wellness Tips for Young Children: Provider Handbook for the Child and Adult Care Food Program*, 2012.
- Special Supplemental Nutrition Program for Women, Infants, and Children (WIC) Works Resource System, which provides guidelines for feeding children from infancy to age 5, information on ethnic foods, and food preparation advice including thrifty recipes (WIC Works Resource Team, 2010).

Teachers who are drafting menus for their Head Start program might also include:

- Head Start Performance Standards for Nutrition (U.S. Department of Health and Human Services Food and Nutrition Service & Administration for Children and Families, 2009).

A program serving infants and toddlers may include:

- The USDA's Infant Nutrition and Feeding: A Guide for Use in the WIC and CSF Programs (U.S. Department of Agriculture, 2009).

A teacher in a large child care center involved in menu planning may include:

- A copy of the National Association for the Education of Young Children (NAEYC) Health Standards 5A (*Promoting and Protecting Children's Health and Controlling Infectious Disease*) and 5B (*Ensuring Children's Nutritional Well-Being*), which provide standards for feeding infants, food safety, timing of meals and snacks, and guidance on foods that cause choking (National Association for the Education of Young Children, 2015).
- The contact number for a registered dietitian nutritionist who can evaluate menus if the program does not participate in the CACFP.

In her menu planning, Jeanine uses the USDA's Choose MyPlate website and the Healthy Eating for Preschoolers Daily Food Plan for Preschoolers (Figure 6-2) (U.S. Department of Agriculture, 2012). She reviews the CACFP meal patterns to learn which food group components need to be offered at breakfast and lunch. She also learns that variety is important, especially when serving fruits and vegetables. She understands that nonfat or low-fat milk is a requirement for children age 2 and over, and she reviews guidelines that explain how to determine which grains qualify as whole grains (Murphy et al., 2011).

Jeanine learns from the Academy of Nutrition and Dietetics' position paper titled *Benchmarks for Nutrition Programs in Child Care Settings*, which references Head Start Performance Standards, that children in part-day programs (four to seven hours) should be served meals that meet one-third of their daily nutrient needs, whereas

WHAT IF . . .

you were not responsible for menu planning in your preschool program but noticed that the portions provided were often very large? What concerns might you have? What resources would you use to learn about appropriate portion sizes for the children?

Healthy Eating  Daily Food Plan

Use this Plan as a general guide.

- These food plans are based on average needs. Do not be concerned if your child does not eat the exact amounts suggested. Your child may need more or less than average. For example, food needs increase during growth spurts.

- Children's appetites vary from day to day. Some days they may eat less than these amounts; other days they may want more. Offer these amounts and let your child decide how much to eat.

Food group	2 year olds	3 year olds	4 and 5 year olds	What counts as:
Fruits	1 cup	1–1½ cups	1–1½ cups	**½ cup of fruit?** ½ cup mashed, sliced, or chopped fruit ½ cup 100% fruit juice ½ medium banana 4-5 large strawberries
Vegetables	1 cup	1½ cups	1½–2 cups	**½ cup of veggies?** ½ cup mashed, sliced, or chopped vegetables 1 cup raw leafy greens ½ cup vegetable juice 1 small ear of corn
Grains Make half your grains whole	3 ounces	4–5 ounces	4–5 ounces	**1 ounce of grains?** 1 slice bread 1 cup ready-to-eat cereal flakes ½ cup cooked rice or pasta 1 tortilla (6" across)
Dairy Protein Foods	2 ounces	3–4 ounces	3–5 ounces	**1 ounce of protein foods?** 1 ounce cooked meat, poultry, or seafood 1 egg 1 Tablespoon peanut butter ¼ cup cooked beans or peas (kidney, pinto, lentils)
Choose low-fat or fat-free	2 cups	2½ cups	2½ cups	**½ cup of dairy?** ½ cup milk 4 ounces yogurt ¾ ounce cheese 1 string cheese

FIGURE 6-2

Healthy Eating for Preschoolers Daily Food Plan

Source: *Health and Nutrition Information for Preschoolers*. USDA ChooseMyPlate.gov, 2012.

those in full-day programs (eight hours or more) should receive at least one-half to two-thirds of their daily requirements (American Dietetic Association, 2011b; U.S. Department of Health and Human Services Food and Nutrition Service & Administration for Children and Families, 2008). She also notes that she does a good job of meeting other recommended benchmarks in her child care program, such as using low-fat cheese and avoiding foods high in sugar or salt. Jeanine decides to check the website of the National Resource Center for Health and Safety in Child

Care and Early Education to refresh her memory on national and state health and safety performance standards. She is reminded that in her home state, she is required to participate in a food safety course to obtain a food handler's card and that her menus should follow CACFP guidelines.

RESOURCES AND STRATEGIES TO PROMOTE HEALTHFUL EATING HABITS THROUGH MENU PLANNING

Early childhood education programs influence many aspects of children's lives. For example, the early childhood setting can be a means of preventing and improving overweight and obesity in children (Hesketh & Campbell, 2010; Llargues et al., 2011; Vos & Welsh, 2010). Child care regulations for obesity prevention were reviewed in an effort to strengthen regulations nationally (National Resource Center for Health and Safety in Child Care and Early Education, University of Colorado Denver, 2011). Menus should be planned to meet not only the nutrient requirements of meals, but also the dietary practices that protect children's health, especially as it relates to obesity prevention. Strategies used to plan menus that optimize children's health and to prevent obesity are described below.

Offering Children More Fruits and Vegetables

Fruits and vegetables are rich in vitamins, minerals, and fiber and, with a few exceptions, are low in fat and always cholesterol-free. Consequently, eating fruits and vegetables can lead to a lower total fat, saturated fat, and cholesterol intake and a higher intake of nutrients protective against heart disease, high blood pressure, obesity, and certain cancers (American Dietetic Association, 2004; Annema, Heyworth, McNaughton, Iacopetta, & Fritschi, 2011; Flock & Kris-Etherton, 2011; Liu, 2003; U.S. Department of Agriculture Nutrition Evidence Library, 2010). Adding more fruits and vegetables to menus may create the dilemma of how to get children to eat them.

Enticing Children to Eat More Fruits and Vegetables The flavor of foods is the primary basis by which young children decide whether to eat or drink something (Harvard School of Public Health, 2011b). Children respond to certain tastes differently than adults. Infants and young children tend to like sweet-tasting foods more than adults do, and adults prefer bitter-tasting foods more often than children do (Beauchamp & Mennella, 2011; Harvard School of Public Health, 2011b). Infants, tend to be more accepting of new foods compared with toddlers or preschoolers (Schwartz, Chabanet, Lange, Issanchou, & Nicklaus, 2011), and around 2 years of age, children begin to demonstrate selective eating behaviors that may continue through early childhood (Birch & Anzman-Frasca, 2011). Flavor learning may be time-sensitive, in which infants and young children, if exposed frequently to new foods such as fruits and vegetables, learn to like their flavors and eat more of them (Beauchamp & Mennella, 2011; Forestell & Mennella, 2007). Teachers and families can partner in making sure that when infants are young, they are exposed to and are repeatedly offered a wide variety of fruits and vegetables, and in appealing ways (Correia, O'Connell, Irwin, & Henderson, 2014), thereby creating an acceptance that will last into older years (Birch & Anzman-Frasca, 2011; Guidetti & Cavazza, 2008; Satter, 2011). Adults also may recognize children prefer fruits over vegetables and they can be assured that fruit offers similar nutrients as vegetables (Ramsay et al., 2014). However, all fruit and vegetables should be offered to children continually to reinforce variety of intake and to provide repeated exposure to foods without forcing children to eat them.

Menu Planning Strategies to Include More Fruits and Vegetables Teachers can use a variety of strategies in menu planning to increase children's interest in fruits and vegetables. Consider these tactics:

- Consider flavors, textures, and smells when offering fruit and vegetables that appeal to children. For example, overcooked broccoli has a less desirable texture and aroma than raw broccoli.
- Offer visually appealing fruits and vegetables. Offer salads with many colors instead of plain iceberg lettuce (but prepare all fruits and vegetables appropriately to prevent choking hazards).
- Offer various forms of fruits and vegetables. Fresh, frozen, canned, and dry varieties all count toward good nutrition.
- Plan menu items into which shredded, pureed, or chopped vegetables and/ or fruits can be added to foods, such as pizza, spaghetti, chili, meatloaf, quick breads, and muffins.
- Offer fruits and vegetables using different methods of preparation (for example, shredded carrots, steamed carrots, mashed carrots, carrot soup, or carrot muffins).
- Offer menu items that combine various vegetables or fruits, such as soups, stir-fried vegetables, or fruit salads.
- Introduce a new fruit or vegetable frequently and offer it with familiar foods. Realize that children may need numerous exposures before they accept a food.
- Use classroom cooking activities to introduce children to new fruits and vegetables.
- Offer dips with fruit and vegetables to increase the likelihood that children will try them.
- Offer a variety of fruit and vegetables when planning menus to enhance nutrition.

  ✓ Offer a fruit or vegetable rich in vitamin C daily (citrus fruits, kiwis, strawberries, mangoes, red peppers, and tomatoes).
  ✓ Include dark green, orange, and red vegetables on the menu often (broccoli, spinach, kale, collard greens, carrots, sweet potatoes, winter squashes, tomatoes, and red peppers).
  ✓ Include more protein and fiber-rich legumes on the menu (such as black beans, garbanzo beans, kidney beans, lentils, pinto beans, soy beans, and split peas).
  ✓ Include potatoes on the menu, which compared with potato chips, is a more desirable food choice.

These strategies support children in trying more fruits and vegetables. However, the best approach, which is easy and costs next to nothing, is for *teachers and families to eat fruits and vegetables at mealtimes too*. Modeling, especially with enthusiasm, is a very effective strategy for improving children's willingness to try new foods (American Dietetic Association, 2011b; Guidetti & Cavazza, 2008).

Nutrient dense foods have a high nutrition content relative to calories. Many nutrient dense foods have undergone minimal food processing and have few ingredients added to them that detract from a healthful diet.

volff/Fotolia

Select Nutrient Dense Foods That Are Rich in Dietary Fiber Whole grains, legumes, fresh fruits, and vegetables are rich in nutrients including dietary fiber. Fiber has health-promoting qualities and reduces the risk of some chronic diseases. For example, certain types of fiber are effective at preventing constipation whereas other types of fiber help reduce cholesterol levels. **Whole grains** contain all parts of the grain kernel, including the bran, endosperm, and germ, after the grain is milled (Figure 6-3). They are rich in essential vitamins, minerals, and fiber. They also contain high levels of antioxidants, which are helpful in reducing the risk for cancer, heart disease, and other diseases (Carlsen et al., 2010; Harvard School of Public Health, 2011a). In contrast, **refined grains** have had the bran and germ removed in the milling process, which reduces the fiber and nutrient content. Examples of refined grain products include white bread, pasta, and white rice.

whole grains
grains that contain all parts of the grain kernel, including the bran, endosperm, and germ, after the grain is milled

refined grains
grains that have had the bran and germ removed during the milling process, which reduces the fiber and nutrient content

When purchasing whole-grain products, look for items that list the "whole-grain" ingredient first on the ingredient list or that state they are 100% whole grain. A grain food that contains the FDA-approved health claim "Diets rich in whole grain foods and other plant foods and low in total fat, saturated fat, and cholesterol may reduce the risk of heart disease and some cancers" on the label is another indication that the product is a significant source of whole grain and qualifies the grain as an acceptable choice for Child Nutrition Programs such as the CACFP (Murphy et al., 2011). The *Dietary Guidelines for Americans*, advises at least half the total number of recommended servings of grains consumed should be whole grains (U.S. Department of Health and Human Services and U.S. Department of Agriculture, 2015). The NSLP requirements recommend all whole grains (U.S. Department of Agriculture, Food and Nutrition Service, 2012a).

Choose Foods Naturally Low in Sodium Eating too many foods high in salt or sodium can be a risk factor for high blood pressure. Highly processed foods are often high in sodium content. The *Dietary Guidelines for Americans* recommends Americans, including children, consume 2300 mg of sodium or less per day (U.S. Department of Health and Human Services & U.S. Department of Agriculture, 2015). Selecting fresh fruits and vegetables, fresh meat, fish, and poultry instead of cured options and limiting high-sodium condiments or choosing lite varieties such as soy sauce, salad dressings, and pickles are good strategies for planning healthful menus.

Menu Planning Strategies to Include Nutrient Dense Foods Adding nutrient dense foods to program menus may require revising current menus. Strategies for adding more nutrient dense foods to menus include:

- Using more whole-grain breads, English muffins, bagels, and whole-grain corn tortillas.
- Using side dishes such as brown rice, bulgur, and whole-wheat pasta.
- Using whole-grain cooked and cold cereals for breakfast and snacks.
- Offering fresh, plain, frozen vegetables or low-sodium canned vegetables.
- Offering a variety of fresh fruits and canned fruit in lite syrup in place of juice.
- Offering fresh or frozen meat, fish, or poultry.
- Offering homemade soups to which barley, brown rice, or legumes have been added.
- Offering vegetarian meals such as salads with kidney beans, vegetarian chili, frijoles with whole-grain tortillas, or hummus with whole-grain pita bread.

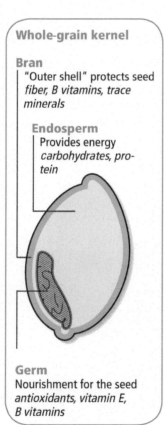

Whole-grain kernel

Bran
"Outer shell" protects seed
fiber, B vitamins, trace minerals

Endosperm
Provides energy
carbohydrates, protein

Germ
Nourishment for the seed
antioxidants, vitamin E, B vitamins

FIGURE 6-3
Components of a Whole Grain

Source: HealthierUS School Challenge Whole Grains Resource guide.

The goal of adding nutrient dense foods to the menu is to increase options that appeal to children's taste, fit into the program's budget, and work within the kitchen's food preparation capacity.

Limiting Solid Fats and Extra Fats When Planning Menus

Young children are growing and have high calorie needs. Fats are part of a healthful diet. However, a diet high in solid fats, including saturated fats and *trans* fats, may increase heart disease risk. Frequently eating high-fat foods such as fried foods and foods prepared with heavy sauces or gravy can result in excess calorie consumption and an unhealthy rate of weight gain (U.S. Department of Health and Human Services & U.S. Department of Agriculture, 2011).The menu should be planned to achieve a balance between low-fat and high-fat foods. In addition, the menu should emphasize more healthful monounsaturated fats than saturated fats. Several strategies help to accomplish this include:

- Offer only nonfat and low-fat milk (age 2 and older).
- Offer low-fat dairy products such as low-fat cheeses and fat-free yogurts.
- Use more heart-healthy oils, including olive, canola, and peanut oils, and select foods that contain heart-healthy fats such as avocados, nuts (modified to prevent choking), and seed butters.
- Use broth-based soups instead of cream-based soups.
- Use oven-baked sweet potato fries made from fresh potatoes tossed with a small amount of olive oil.
- Avoid the trans fatty acids found in some margarines, shortenings, crackers, cookies, pies, doughnuts, some chips, and fried fast foods.
- Offer heart-healthy fish such as tuna, salmon, and sardines.

> **WHAT IF . . .**
> you wanted to introduce nutrient dense foods into children's diets? What nutrient dense foods might appeal to young children?

Creating Menus That Support Sustainability

Interest in sustainability is growing and has relevance to menu planning and food service. **Sustainable practices** are practices that meet current needs without compromising the ability of future generations to meet their needs (United Nations Department of Social and Economic Affairs Division for Sustainable Development, 2009). Sustainability also encompasses the interconnectedness of human and natural systems. The following sections discuss sustainable practices in relation to menu planning and food service.

sustainable practices practices that meet current needs without compromising the ability of future generations to meet their needs

Using Locally Grown Produce

One way to support sustainability when planning menus is to purchase foods that are grown locally. Identify and purchase from growers located within the state or growers who are within a 400-mile radius of the program (Martinez et al., 2010). Choose to purchase food from growers who use sustainable agricultural practices that are environmentally friendly and socially responsible (that is, soil and water conservation, pesticide reduction, and wildlife habitat conservation). Select foods produced in environments that support safe and fair working conditions and that provide healthy and humane care of livestock (Allen, Benson, Shuman, & Skees-Gregory, 2011).

> **WHAT IF . . .**
> you wanted to support sustainability in early childhood settings? How would you approach this goal? How might teachers' sustainability practices influence young children?

Recycling and Composting

Recycling and composting are practices that contribute to sustainability. For example, establishing recycling stations in classrooms or cafeterias for milk cartons is a good way for children to participate in recycling activities and learn about the phases of production that end with recycling. Programs and schools can consider purchasing composting units used to compost cafeteria food waste. Children can see how compost changes over time and how it can be used to enrich gardens.

Planting School Gardens

A school garden is an excellent way to contribute to sustainability, while offering a range of other learning opportunities. Planting a garden provides opportunities to discuss climate, weather, soil, growing practices, insects, growing cycles, and food. When children tend gardens, they are physically active, which reinforces health goals. Eating homegrown fruits and vegetables helps children learn where food comes from and inspires them to try the fruits and vegetable they helped to grow.

At Sunnyside Environmental School, an inner-city school located in Portland, Oregon, every grade level has its own garden. The first- and second-grade classes create a "snacking" garden of vegetables that can be picked and eaten for immediate gratification (Anderson, 2009). The school's focus integrates academics with hands-on learning about horticulture, outdoor education, and the environment; giving inner-city children an opportunity to learn in the natural setting. The *Teaching Wellness* feature discusses planning a school garden with children of different ages. In addition, see the Progressive Programs & Practice feature that shows how schools in Berkeley, California, embrace school gardens.

Partnering with Children and Families as Resources for Menu Planning

Obtaining ideas from children, their families, and other program staff is an important resource for menu planning. Teachers have the opportunity to observe meal service in the classroom. By noticing children's response to menu items and the amount of food left on their plates, teachers can note trends in food preferences and eating habits. This insight can be used to develop or revise menus to enhance food acceptance. The *Health Hint* describes the partnership between teachers, families, and children in planning menus. Whether teachers are creating a brand-new menu or revising a menu, input from these sources can be invaluable.

Having resources easily accessible helps teachers such as Jeanine streamline their menu writing, create a menu that successfully meets the nutrient needs of young children, and supports the reimbursement requirements for federally funded child nutrition programs.

CHECK YOUR UNDERSTANDING 6.2
Click here to check your understanding of the requirements of menu planning and resources for child care settings.

PHASE 2: WRITING MENUS

With an understanding of the requirements for children's menus and knowledge of resources about how to plan healthful meals, teachers are ready to make decisions about the menu. The following discussion provides six steps for writing menus:

1. Gather Tools for Menu Planning
2. Prepare to Write the Cycle Menu

LEARNING OUTCOME   **Children will be able to describe how seeds planted in the ground grow into the vegetables we eat.**

Safety watch: Be aware of children's allergies and avoid known allergens as you interact with the garden and foods. Monitor children closely as they interact with the tools and activities. Ensure that children wash their hands after participating.

INFANTS AND TODDLERS

- **Goal:** Babies and toddlers will experience the look, color, smell, and feel of a vegetable garden.
- **Materials:** Identify a nearby vegetable garden or establish a program garden area, using strollers and vegetable examples (carrots, potatoes, green beans, lettuce leaves).
- **Vocabulary focus:** Garden, vegetables, brown, earth, green, leaves, smell, touch, carrot, potato, bean, tomato.
- **Activity plan:** Walk with infants and toddlers through the garden at different times during the growing season. Talk about what you see in the vegetable garden. Encourage children to look, touch, and smell appropriate aspects of the garden. Talk about the colors of the garden and the smell of recently turned dirt. Smell and touch the leaves of appropriate plants. Watch as water is used to sprinkle the garden. Describe the names of vegetables that grow in a garden. Serve an appropriate garden vegetable for a snack and talk about how the food grows from the earth.

- **How to adjust the activity:** Prepare vocabulary cards for the vocabulary words in English and the home languages of children in the group. Assist all children to explore the garden appropriately through sight, smell, and touch.
- **Did you meet your goals?** Can you observe babies and toddlers looking at and reaching out to touch the plants? Do toddlers repeat the names of the smells, textures, and vegetables grown in the garden?

PRESCHOOLERS, KINDERGARTNERS, AND SCHOOL-AGE CHILDREN

- **Goal:** Children will plant a Native American Three Sisters Garden and understand the steps of planting and growing foods.
- **Materials:** A 4' × 6' (or larger) gardening bed in a sunny area, child-sized gardening tools (a shovel, hoe, rake, watering can, wheelbarrow), seeds (corn, squash, and pole beans), access to water, the children's book *Corn Is Maize: The Gift of the Indians* by Aliki, the resource book *Native American Gardening: Stories, Projects and Recipes for Families* by Michael Caduto and Joseph Bruchac.
- **Vocabulary focus:** corn, maize, squash, beans, soil, seeds, germinate, sprout, harvest.
- **Activity plan:** Prepare a garden area for planting. Use the book *Native American Gardening* listed above and read an account of the tale of the Three Sisters found online. www.ncmuseumofhistory.org/collateral/articles/F05. legend.three.sisters.pdf.

  Gather the children and read the book *Corn Is Maize*. Describe how the Native Americans traditionally planted corn, beans, and squash together and called these the "three sisters." Explain to the children that the Native Americans learned that these three plants help each other grow. The corn provides shade for the small bean plants and becomes the poles for the beans as they grow. The beans add nutrients back into the earth. The squash makes a shady ground cover that helps the soil retain moisture. The prickly spines on the squash leaves keep away animals that like to eat corn. Talk about what is needed for seeds to grow: soil to grow in; water for the seeds to drink; and sunlight, which provides the food for growth. Working with small groups, invite children to use their hoes to make a circular mound of dirt about 18 inches across the bottom tapering to 10 inches across the top. Level off the top so that it makes a flat circle. Plant six corn seeds in each quarter of the circle, about 6 inches apart. Pat the soil and keep it evenly moist while the corn seeds begin to grow. When the corn has grown to about 6 inches in height, plant eight pole bean seeds around the edge of the circle about halfway down the mound. Finally, plant six squash seeds around the lower edge of the mound. Pat the soil over the seeds. Wash hands when done. During the growing season, work with the children to keep the soil evenly moist while these seeds germinate and to tend the garden by pulling weeds. Provide an ear of corn, several fresh beans, and a squash for children to open and study.

- **How to adjust the activity:** Create picture cards depicting each of the foods that are planted. Tape on a seed for each food and include the name of the food in English and each home language of children in the class. Make adjustments, such as providing a trowel with a large handle for a child who struggles to grip or placing a large piece of plywood over the soil for a firm surface so that children who travel in a wheelchair can move into the garden area. Take photos of all children participating at different points of the planting and growing process and post the photos to reinforce the steps of planting and growth.
- **Did you meet your goals?** Did children participate in planting and caring for the garden? Are children able to identify the steps in planting and growing food?

- **Goal:** Children will plant a Native American Three Sisters Garden and describe the steps of planting and growing foods and explain how to use them to plan a healthful menu.
- **Materials:** Gardening materials and resource book as described above, lined paper, pencils, recipe books.
- **Vocabulary focus:** soil, seeds, germinate, sprout, harvest, recipe, menu.
- **Activity plan:** Involve children in planting a Three Sisters Garden at school as described above. Read the stories in the book *Native American Gardening*, such as "The Bean Woman" or "Onenha, The Corn." During the growing season, assist children in creating and keeping a weekly garden journal describing the planting, tending, and growing process: what they do to tend the garden and what they observe. In preparation for harvest, guide children in researching recipes that include corn, beans, and squash

and create a menu that meets CACFP guidelines. Print out the selected recipes, invite the children to illustrate them, and include the recipes with their garden journal to take home at the end of the growing season.

- **How to adjust the activity:** Assist children who are learning English by posting pictures of gardening, planting, tending, and harvesting activities labeled in English. Encourage children with special developmental needs by providing adaptive pencils or pens, providing journal pages on clipboards for easier control, and offering ample time and support to create journal entries. Ensure that the garden area is accessible to children who travel by wheelchair. Consider a raised bed garden for easier access if indicated.
- **Did you meet your goals?** Did children participate in planting and tending the garden? Are children able to describe how seeds grow into plants that produce food? Can they plan a healthful menu using corn, beans, and squash?

3. Create a Budget for Menus
4. Build the Menu
5. Use Meal Service to Enhance Menu Acceptance
6. Manage Foods from Home

PROGRESSIVE PROGRAMS & PRACTICES

The Edible Schoolyard

By Kyle Cornforth, Martin Luther King, Jr. Middle School, Berkeley, CA

Martin Luther King, Jr. Middle School in Berkeley, California, is invested in promoting student wellness. The school board in Berkeley has an innovative wellness policy whose aim is to promote student and family health through education, garden and cooking classes, nutritious school meals, and core academic content in the classroom. Every student receives a comprehensive education about food and wellness that has three main pillars: a nine-week course focused on a variety of food-related topics; a nutrition services program providing healthy, seasonal meals prepared from scratch; and hands-on lessons in a garden and kitchen classroom at the Edible Schoolyard Berkeley.

The nutrition course "What's On Your Plate?" was developed by King Teachers for all sixth-grade students. The course is an interactive and hands-on approach to food science, nutrition, and other healthy lifestyle concepts. One objective of this course is to make students more aware of what they are eating—sugar in sodas, fat in chips, and portion sizes in fast food. The course encourages making healthy choices in the cafeteria through weekly tastings prepared by nutritional services. It also encourages students to try new foods through tastings of seasonal fruits and vegetables.

King Middle School also promotes wellness through the food served in the cafeteria. Meals are prepared from scratch from produce that is mostly local and/or organic, including meat, baked goods, and beverages. Importantly, the cafeterias in Berkeley operate on a balanced budget—income from students being served universal breakfasts and from students purchasing lunches pays for the ingredients and the labor it takes to produce school meals that are not only good for student health, but also good for the health of the wider economy and community.

The Edible Schoolyard Berkeley hosts the garden and kitchen program at King Middle School. The mission of the Edible Schoolyard Berkeley is to teach essential life skills and support academic learning through hands-on classes in a 1-acre organic garden and kitchen classroom. Students are taught the skills necessary to growing, tending, and harvesting food and preparing and eating fresh, seasonal, nutritious meals. In addition, classes at the Edible Schoolyard Berkeley are connected to classroom lessons and standards; students come to the garden and kitchen to deepen their learning about world cultures, ancient technologies, and life science concepts. The Edible Schoolyard Berkeley curriculum is fully integrated into the school day and teaches students how their choices about food affect their health, the environment, and their communities.

HEALTH HINT   Building Health in the Classroom and at Home Through Menu Planning

Harnessing children's and families' interest and energy can be empowering for both children's programs and families. Strategies to accomplish a home-school health partnership include:

- Matching menu offerings with curriculum activities in the classroom. For example, focus on including milk, yogurt, and low-fat cheese on the lunch menu and explore where dairy foods come from by taking a trip to a dairy.
- Asking children to offer ideas for menu items. Encourage them to name favorite fruits, vegetables, grains, dairy products, and meats and those they would like to try.

- Inviting families to participate in a menu review committee. Involving families in the development of menus invites them to contribute ideas and recipes that reflect their culture and individual or family eating practices.

Through a menu planning partnership, children, families, and teachers learn about food preferences, gain knowledge of family cultural and eating practices, and discuss the health benefits of certain foods. Families learn about food and health by working with teachers who are adhering to menu guidelines and requirements. When families are part of a menu planning partnership, they are empowered with the knowledge they need to make nutritious food choices at home that support good health for the entire family.

Step 1: Gather Tools for Menu Planning

The first step is to organize and review the resources discussed in the previous section. Other useful resources are:

- Old menus and cost analysis of the menus, if available.
- Menu templates (see Figure 6-4).
- A list of foods that reflects the food preferences of culturally diverse populations within the program (see Table 6-3).
- A list of the special diets and food allergies of children in your care.

FIGURE 6-4   Sample CACFP-Compatible Menu Template

Week 1	Monday	Tuesday	Wednesday	Thursday	Friday
Breakfast Milk Fruit/Vegetable Bread/Grain Meat/Meat Alternate (optional)					
Lunch Milk Meat/Meat Alternate Fruit/Vegetable (either two of one or one of each) Bread/Grain					
Snack **(any two components)** Milk Fruit/Vegetable Bread/Grain Meat/Meat Alternate					

TABLE 6-3 Culturally Diverse Food Preferences

Culture	Protein Sources	Grain Sources	Fruit and Vegetable Sources
Asian	Fish, pork, poultry, shellfish, dried beans, tofu, nuts	Rice, cereals, breads, noodles	Cabbage, kimchee, hot peppers, fruit juice
African American	Pork, ham, beef, fish, legumes, dried beans, peas	Rice; cereals; breads; biscuits; corn products such as hush puppies, corn-bread, grits	Greens such as collard greens, kale, cabbage, turnips, beets, onions, okra, succotash, carrots, potatoes, yams, sweet potatoes, corn, peaches, melons, apples, bananas
Middle Eastern	Beef, lamb, chicken, lentils, chick peas, pistachios, almonds, fish, black beans, yogurt	Couscous, millet, pita, rice, bulgur	Onions, spinach, cucumbers, artichokes, potatoes, green beans, cabbage, eggplant, okra, squash, olives, figs, apples, apricots, plums, grapes, melons, bananas, tangerines, lemons
Mexican	Beans, poultry, beef, pork, eggs, goat, fish, shellfish, chorizo, menudo	Rice, tortillas (corn and flour), breads	Tomatoes, jicama, yams, cactus, salsa, chilies, sweet potatoes, squash, onions, corn, tomatillos, guava, mango, bananas, oranges, cherimoya, limes

Sources: Based on *Cultural Diversity*, by the National Food Service Management Institute, 2002 and *Ohioline, Food: Cultural Diversity-Eating in America, 2010* Ohio State University, College of Food, Agriculture, and Environmental Sciences, retrieved March 29, 2015, from http://ohioline.osu.edu/lines/food.html.

- Recipes and recipe templates (from the program's previously used recipes, USDA website, etc.).
- A list of commodity foods.
- Price lists for suppliers of local grocers.
- A grocery shopping list template.

Once these tools have been gathered, teachers are ready to schedule a block of uninterrupted time to plan menus.

Step 2: Prepare to Write the Cycle Menu

cycle menu
a menu that offers a variety of foods every day, is planned for a week or longer, and repeats itself

The **cycle menu** offers a variety of foods every day, is planned for a week or longer, and then repeats itself. The menu items are offered in the same order as the previous cycle. A repeating four- to six-week cycle menu is often used in early childhood settings and schools. Cycle menus are time and cost effective. Establishing a cycle menu creates a system for shopping and food preparation. Cycle menus can be created to incorporate seasonal foods. For example a four- to six-week cycle can be offered in the summer to use seasonal produce such as watermelon, peaches, and berries. A winter cycle menu may include foods such as oranges, apples, and carrots. Cycle menus can be easily adjusted to reflect holidays or other special events.

Menus include a balance of familiar well-accepted foods with new food options that broaden taste experiences. For example, Jeanine decides to improve her menu planning practices by switching to a four-week cycle menu. Although the cycle menu initially takes time to write, in the long run, it saves her time and effort once it is complete. She plans to include some of the favorite foods she has used in the past, but will expand the menu to offer a greater variety of fruits, vegetables, and whole grains.

Step 3: Create a Budget for Menus

The menu should provide safe, healthful, and appealing meals to young children, and it directs the cost of meal service. For example, a menu that includes entirely fresh fruits and vegetables may cost more than one that relies on fresh, canned, and frozen produce. The way to understand the impact of these costs to the overall operation of an early childhood program is to develop a **budget**. A budget is the financial reserves available for purchasing, preparing, and serving foods. It is an itemized summary of expected food service–related expenses matched to the estimated income to cover these expenses. The menu must stay within the constraints of the budget allotted for food service expenses.

budget
the financial reserves available for purchasing, preparing, and serving foods

Determining Income Sources for Menu Implementation

The income to support food service operations costs comes from a variety of sources depending on the funding structure. These sources include:

- Family fees for care and education.
- Child care subsidies for eligible low-income children.
- CACFP reimbursements for meal service.
- Public school district funding.
- Grants such as Head Start funds provided for programs that serve low-income families (Oliveira, 2005).

Sufficient funds are needed to implement an early childhood food program, including the costs of food and equipment and the salaries of food service staff. The percentage of income needed is estimated to range from 6% to 19% of the total budget (Oliveira, 2005). If the costs for food service exceed 19% of the total program income, the menu, food purchasing, and food preparation practices should be reviewed to control costs.

Using Cost Control Strategies

Cost control strategies consider all aspects of food program expenses. Besides direct food purchasing expenses, other costs related to food service include the use of disposable supplies (napkins, straws, dish detergent) and durable items (dishes, silverware, cooking utensils, and food service equipment). Sometimes a very simple change can make a significant difference. For example, consider the following situation:

Sunshine Preschool food service staff must wear hairnets during food service. One of the teachers noticed that sometimes employees would use as many as three or four hairnets each day. She talked with the program's food service manager, who reviewed the kitchen supplier's catalog and found that each hairnet cost about 25 cents. The program was spending at least $5 per day on hairnets, whereas the cost of institution caps was $16 each. With the switch to caps instead of hairnets, the program would recoup the expense in two weeks and achieve a cost savings.

A budget for purchasing foods for classroom and program activities is important. A teacher may want to offer an activity that teaches children how orange juice is made using fresh oranges. A cooking activity may form the basis of a family meeting, or refreshments may be served at a family social or staff meeting. Procedures should be in place to communicate the budget available for these activities.

Guidelines also are needed to ensure teachers communicate with food purchasers in a timely manner so adjustments can be made to the weekly shopping list and avoid last-minute purchasing.

The USDA publication *Building Blocks for Fun and Healthy Meals—A Menu Planner for the Child and Adult Care Food Program* recommends the following strategies to help contain food service costs:

- Keep food records, especially related to food costs.
- Be a bargain hunter when it comes to buying foods:
  - ✓ Purchase locally and know what's in season.
  - ✓ Use commodity foods when available.
  - ✓ Shop from a grocery list and use coupons.
  - ✓ Shop at large discount stores.
  - ✓ Compare the cost of packaged items with the cost to purchase in bulk.
  - ✓ Purchase reusable food service supplies rather than disposable when possible. (This strategy can support sustainability as well as budget goals.)
  - ✓ Prevent food waste through spoilage by using proper storage strategies.
- Use **standardized recipes**. Standardized recipes are tested recipes that leave less room for error.
- Aim to prepare exactly what is needed to avoid excess leftovers and costly substitutions if food runs out and helps to ensure CACFP guidelines are met so full reimbursement can be claimed.

standardized recipes recipes that have been tested for quality, accuracy, and yield, which results in consistent, predictable food products

Step 4: Build the Menu

Deciding on menu choices and serving sizes requires the planner to consider the age and nutritional needs of children in the program. For example, will the menu serve older infants and toddlers as well as preschool-age children? Can food items be altered to accommodate the younger eaters? How will food be apportioned? Can the menu accommodate children on special diets? These types of questions guide menu development.

Selecting the Breakfast Menu

Foods traditionally offered at breakfast contribute significantly to the total day's intake of vitamins, minerals, and fiber; and can enhance the quality of a child's diet. Breakfast foods include fortified cereals; enriched and whole-grain breads; fruits; and protein foods such as eggs, cheese, and milk. When breakfast is skipped it is very difficult to make up these nutrients at other meals (Affenito, 2007; Hoyland, Dye, & Lawton, 2009). When breakfast is consumed, children show an increase in cognitive function, attention, and memory (Hoyland, Dye, & Lawton, 2009). Children who eat breakfast also may be more likely to maintain a healthful weight (Rampersaud, 2008). In spite of its many benefits, not all programs offer breakfast because it is assumed that children have eaten before coming to school. Instead, many programs offer a midmorning snack. Programs eligible to participate in the CACFP may find it cost effective to switch from offering a morning snack to offering breakfast. The reimbursement for the breakfast meal is larger than the morning snack, and with a few changes in the menu, the switch can be easily accomplished.

The breakfast menu can be constructed following CACFP guidelines. Selections are made from the three required components: milk, fruits/vegetables, and starches/grains. A meat/meat alternate component can be offered but is considered optional. Teachers can offer menu items such as whole-grain fortified cereals and whole-grain breads and items that increase the variety of fruits and vegetables served, especially those rich in vitamins A and C such as oranges, grapefruits, strawberries, kiwis, melons, mango, and tomatoes. Breakfast foods that are high in solid fats, *trans* fat, and added sugar and sodium such as bacon, sausage, sweetened cereals, and breakfast pastries and doughnuts should be avoided. Milk service (nonfat or low-fat) is required by the CACFP; therefore, menus will include fresh, frozen (unsweetened), or canned fruits (packed in its own juice) instead of juice for breakfast. Offering whole fruits or vegetables is desirable whenever possible. Figure 6-5 provides a breakfast

FIGURE 6-5 Sample Breakfast Menu for 3- to 5-Year Olds

Spring Menu					
Week 3 of 6	**Monday**	**Tuesday**	**Wednesday**	**Thursday**	**Friday**
Breakfast **Milk** **Fruit/Vegetable** **Starch/Grain** **Meat/meat alternate which is optional at breakfast**	milk, nonfat strawberries Wheat Chex® yogurt, nonfat	milk, nonfat kiwi red peppers whole-grain bread scrambled egg	milk, nonfat applesauce blueberries oatmeal	milk, nonfat banana oat rings cereal	milk, nonfat tomatoes black beans orange slices corn tortilla cheddar cheese
Required portions	¾ c milk ½ c strawberries ⅓ c cereal ½ c yogurt	¾ c milk ¼ c kiwis ¼ c peppers ½ slice bread ¾ of an egg	¾ c milk ¼ c applesauce ¼ c blueberries ¼ c oatmeal	¾ cup milk ½ banana ⅓ cup cereal	¾ c milk ⅛ c tomatoes ⅛ c black beans ¼ of an orange ½ tortilla ½ oz cheese, lowfat
SPECIAL DIRECTIONS	Hull and slice strawberries and serve on top of yogurt.	Peel and slice kiwi. Prepare eggs with peppers following standardized recipe.	Add applesauce to oatmeal to sweeten. Sprinkle blueberries on top.	Bananas can be sliced and served on top of cereal.	Prepare bean and cheese burrito following standardized recipe. Slice oranges.
TOTAL AMOUNT OF FOOD TO SERVE PER CLASS BASED ON A 20-CHILD CLASS	1 gal of milk 10 c of berries 7 c of cereal 10 c of yogurt	1 gal of milk 5 c kiwis 5 c of peppers 10 slices of bread 15 eggs	1 gal of milk 5 c of blueberries 5 c of applesauce 5 c of oatmeal	1 gal of milk 10 bananas 7 c cereal	1 gal of milk 5 c of tomatoes 5 c of beans 5 oranges 10 corn tortillas 10 oz of cheese
Special diets: 1 lactose-free diet in Room 115	Substitute soy milk for nonfat milk and soy yogurt for regular yogurt.	Substitute soy milk for nonfat milk.	Substitute soy milk for nonfat milk.	Substitute soy milk for nonfat milk.	Substitute soy milk for nonfat milk. Substitute beans for cheese.
1 no strawberries in Room 117	Substitute apple for strawberries.				

template that includes a one-week menu for preschool-age children. This template provides guidance on portions to be served to meet CACFP requirements as well as information on the amount of food needed to serve a class of 20.

Selecting the Lunch Menu

The lunch meal is the largest meal offered at most programs and contributes significantly to children's overall energy and daily nutrient intake. The main entrée is often selected first because this menu item tends to be the most expensive menu item. The following considerations are useful when planning a cycle menu for lunch:

- How often should a particular entrée be served during the menu cycle?
- If an entrée is offered more than once a month, how can the side dish be changed to ensure variety?
- How often will hot versus cold entrées be served? During the summer, sandwiches and chef's salads might be well received, whereas stews and soups may be preferred during the winter months.

commercially prepared entrée
a processed main course item to which ingredients may have been added

If a **commercially prepared entrée** (a processed main course item to which ingredients may have been added) is chosen for the menu, it must be identified by the Child Nutrition (CN) Labeling Program. This is a voluntary federal program that supports labeling disclosure for the Child Nutrition Programs (U.S. Department of Agriculture, Food and Nutrition Service, 2011c). A CN label is required by the CACFP on foods that contribute to the meat/meat alternate component of the menu for reimbursable meals. A CN label clearly identifies how a product can be counted in the CACFP meal component requirements (Figure 6-6). The CN label communicates how much is needed of a processed product to meet protein equivalents when planning meals that adhere to CACFP requirements.

After the entrée is selected, side dishes such as starches/grains, fruits, and vegetables need to be chosen. Side dishes contribute to the menu's balance both in nutrition and sensory appeal. Variety in the selection of the side dishes is important to ensure children get all the nutrients they need for good health. The flavors and textures in a meal should be varied and complementary. Menu selections should represent food components that look appealing as evidenced by a variety of colors, shapes, and sizes. Figure 6-7 shows two different planned lunches. The contrast of colors in Lunch 2 is more likely to increase the appetite in both children and teachers. This is desirable because it is much easier for teachers to model good eating behaviors when they enjoy the meal.

FIGURE 6-6   A Sample Child Nutrition (CN) Label

—— CN ——

CN   This 3.00 oz serving of raw beef patty provides when, cooked 2.00 oz equivalent meat for Child Nutrition Meal Pattern Requirements. (Use of this logo and statement   CN authorized by the Food and Nutrition Service, USDA 05-84.)

—— CN ——

Source: From *Building Blocks for Fun and Healthy Meals—A Menu Planner for the Child and Adult Care Food Program*, by the U.S. Department of Agriculture, Food and Nutrition Service, 2000, retrieved March 25, 2015, from http://www.fns.usda.gov/building-blocks-fun-and-healthy-meals.

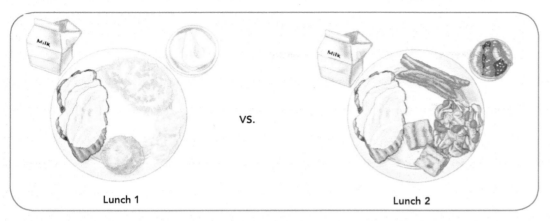

VS.

Lunch 1   Lunch 2

FIGURE 6-7   **Variety and Contrast in Flavor, Texture, and Visual Appeal Inspire a Good Appetite**

Side dishes such as the starches/grains and fruits and vegetables can often be used to introduce children to new foods. Young children who may be leery of unfamiliar foods do better when new foods are offered with familiar favorites. Offering a variety of foods, including new foods, as side dishes exposes children to new foods with less pressure to eat them. Ensuring children are offered new side dishes with an entrée or a side dish they like, is the best way to support children to develop an interest in new foods. The *Nutrition Note* describes ways to build children's interest in new foods.

Grains/Starches A variety of starch or grain side dishes on a menu is important. For example, if whole-wheat spaghetti is offered one day, offer whole-wheat tortilla tacos at the next meal. Starch or grain sides on the menu should include a variety of whole-grain breads, brown rice, whole-wheat or corn tortillas, and quinoa to maintain children's interest.

Fruits and Vegetables A variety of fruits and vegetables should be offered on the menu as well. This includes varying the way the fruits and vegetables are prepared and served. Some vegetables prepared appropriately to prevent choking hazards, such as broccoli, cauliflower, spinach, carrot sticks, and pepper strips, may be better accepted if they are served with low-fat dip. If shopping occurs once a week, perishable fresh produce should be offered early in the weekly menu and frozen or canned produce can be offered later. Some flexibility may be needed; for example, if the bananas are green on Monday and the kiwi fruit is hard on Tuesday, they should be used later in the week.

Beverage selections also are important to the nutritional value of meals. The beverages that meet the requirements for CACFP reimbursement are milk for breakfast and lunch and either milk or 100% fruit juice (but not both) for a snack. CACFP-acceptable milk alternatives such as certain soy milks should be available for children who are lactose intolerant or allergic to milk; a note from a health care provider is needed for reimbursement. The CACFP also requires that children have unlimited access to water throughout the day. Water also should be available for events such as walking trips, field days, and family social events. Children need to stay hydrated in the winter months when heavy clothing and strenuous outdoor activities coupled with heated inside environments can increase the need for fluids.

WHAT IF . . .

you were planning the side dishes to accompany a spaghetti entrée for lunch? What type of nutrient dense foods (fruits, vegetables, whole grains) and beverages would you select?

NUTRITION NOTE   Building Interest in New Foods

Children are enthusiastic about cooking activities, and it can be fun to taste the results of their cooking projects. Cooking with children provides opportunities to teach about foods: where food comes from; how food smells, tastes, and feels; and how to prepare different kinds of food. Cooking also engages children in activities that develop their motor skills as they use their arms, hands, and fingers. Children have different developmentally appropriate levels of "kitchen skills." Understanding children's skill levels helps teachers direct students to activities that help them feel successful. Kitchen skills for different age categories of children are provided in the table below.

Cooking Skills	1-year-olds	2-year-olds	3-year-olds	4- to 5-year-olds
Listening: Learns when you talk about the steps and identifies the ingredients and utensils used to prepare a recipe	X	X	X	X
Smelling, tasting, and feeling: Experiences food by smelling, tasting, and touching ingredients	X	X	X	X
Practices by doing: Plays with pots, pans, plastic bowls, and large spoons	X	X	X	X
Washing: Can scrub produce and wipe tops of cans and tabletops	X	X	X	X
Tearing: Pulls apart lettuce and bread into pieces	X	X	X	X
Dipping: Can dunk fruit and vegetable pieces into dips	X	X	X	X
Pouring: Pours liquids into mixtures and stirs ingredients together	With assistance	X	X	X
Kneading: Can knead dough	With assistance	X	X	X
Spreading: Is able to use a knife to spread peanut butter on bread	With assistance and use child-appropriate knife	Use child-appropriate knife	X	X
Peeling: Can use a peeler with carrots or potatoes	With assistance peeling basic foods	Can peel basic foods	Can peel basic foods	X
Mashing: Can mash soft fruits and vegetables	X	X	X	X
Measuring: Measures ingredients using spoons and cups		With adult assistance	With adult assistance	X
Rolling and cutting: Can use a rolling pin and a cookie cutter	With assistance	With adult assistance	X	X

Sources: *Cooking with Preschoolers* by Kids Health from Nemours, retrieved March 29, 2015, from http://kidshealth.org/parent/growth/learning/cooking_preschool.html ?tracking=P_RelatedArticle.

Selecting Snacks for the Menu

WHAT IF . . .

you were planning snacks for your program? What types of healthy and appealing snacks might you consider for infants, toddlers, preschoolers, and school-age children?

Snacks provide nutrients children miss at mealtimes. The CACFP requires snack menus include two components from any of the four food groups (milk, fruits/vegetables, cereals/grains, and protein/protein alternate) to meet reimbursement requirements. Although 100% fruit juice may be served as part of a healthy snack, priority should be given to fresh fruits and vegetables, which provide added fiber and nutrients and are more likely to help children feel full longer. Figure 6-8 provides examples of easy-to-prepare, child-friendly snacks that include at least two food groups.

FIGURE 6-8   Nutritious Snack Combinations

Low-fat cheese and whole-grain crackers
Peanut butter on thin sliced apples
Whole-grain cold cereal with banana and 1% milk
Whole-grain waffles topped with applesauce
Whole-grain English muffin mini pizza
Baked sweet potato wedges with sliced turkey strips

Low-fat cheese quesadilla topped with chopped tomato salsa
Whole-grain raisin bread with sliced low-fat Swiss cheese
Banana dipped in yogurt and crushed cereal
Turkey and low-fat cheese rollup served with carrot match sticks
Fruit salad topped with vanilla yogurt and low-fat granola cereal

Note: Cheese, although a dairy product, is considered a meat/protein alternate when counting food components for CACFP. Also, only two components in any combination are required for snacks.

Transitioning to New or Updated Menus

Once the cycle menu for breakfast, lunch, and snacks has been completed, a systematic evaluation of the menu is conducted to ensure requirements have been met. Figure 6-9 provides a checklist for reviewing the menus and determining whether they are ready to be implemented. All teachers involved in food preparation and

FIGURE 6-9   Sample Menu Evaluation Checklist

Sunshine Preschool Program
Date: 4/1/2012
Menu planner: Maren
Age of students: 3- to 5-year-olds
Are food components/food groups being met?

❑ Breakfast
  ❑ Milk component (nonfat or low-fat)
  ❑ Fruit or nonstarchy vegetable component (no juice)
  ❑ Bread/grain group
  ❑ Optional items: Meat/meat alternate component, trans fatty acid-free margarine, jam, jelly, low-fat cream cheese

❑ Lunch
  ❑ Meat/meat alternate component
  ❑ Fruit component: no juice
  ❑ Vegetable component: (1/2 cup total combined with fruit)
  ❑ Bread/grain component
  ❑ Milk component (nonfat or low-fat)
  ❑ *Optional foods*: salad dressing, low-fat vegetable dip, mayonnaise, salsa, ketchup

❑ Snacks contain two components of four components and focus on variety.
❑ At least half the grains are whole grains.
❑ There is wide variety within the components groups especially within the fruit/vegetable group.
  Dark green vegetables are offered frequently (at least two times per week).

Orange/red vegetables are offered frequently (at least three times per week).
Legumes are offered at least once per week (or can count as meat alternate).
At least three different fruits and five different vegetables are offered weekly

❑ Menus contain a variety of flavors, contrasting colors, shapes, textures, temperatures, and forms.
❑ Menus are culturally appropriate.
❑ Menus are able to accommodate special diets.
❑ Menus reflect input from children, parents, and staff.
❑ Menus support sustainability when possible (local seasonal foods, foods from program garden).
❑ Special occasions are represented.
❑ Menu items can be accommodated by the food preparation staff, equipment, and facilities.
❑ Menu items are foods appropriate for the age group.
❑ Recipes are available.
❑ Breakfast, lunch, and snack menu items avoid repetition of foods on any given day.
❑ Nutritional goals that support dietary guidelines and recommendations are met.
❑ A fresh fruit or raw vegetable is offered daily.
❑ A good source of vitamin C is offered each day.
❑ At least four different entrees are offered each week and they are moderate in fat content.
❑ Two or more sources of iron are offered each day.
❑ Water is available and accessible throughout the day.

Sources: Based on USDA Child and Adult Care Food Program Center Manual, Oregon Department of Education, updated 2009, retrieved March 29, 2015, from http://www.ode.state.or.us/search/page/?id=3285 and Committee to Review Child and Adult Care Food Program Meal Requirements, Food and Nutrition Board, Child and Adult Care Food Program: Aligning Dietary Guidance for All, 2010, retrieved March 29, 2015, from http://books.nap.edu/openbook.php?record_id=12959.

CLASSROOM CONNECTION

As you watch this video, consider how school meals provide children with opportunities to try new foods and learn about foods in different cultures.

service should participate in the menu review at this point. A food service employee might recognize a potential problem with equipment or food storage. A cook might recognize a food preparation procedure that takes more time than necessary. This input provides the opportunity to revise the menu plan as needed before it is put into use.

Purchasing food may involve a bit of trial and error as amounts of food needed for new recipes are estimated and tried. Opportunities to try new recipes before they are used in the new menu can be helpful, but may require additional time. The transition to the new menu can be eased by:

- Notifying families of the new menu in advance.
- Modeling an adventuresome attitude for the new menu and foods offered.
- Observing children's reaction to new menu options.

Through careful planning, the new menu can set the tone for healthy eating habits and have a beneficial impact on the nutritional status of children and teachers alike.

Step 5: Use Meal Service to Enhance Menu Acceptance

WHAT IF . . .

you observed that children were disinterested in the menu offerings because the menus were the same every week? What suggestions would you make to the director of food services for your program? What resources could you use to support your point of view?

Learning to eat is a developmental process. Infants are entirely dependent on adults to provide what is best for them nutritionally. As children mature, the teacher's role shifts from making food decisions for children to supporting them as they strive to achieve eating independence. This is accomplished by supporting children's development of food preferences (taste and texture), eating skills, and by providing an environment in which children are able to make their own healthful food selections within the context of the nutritious options provided by a well-planned menu.

Supporting the Development of Eating Skills

The menu creates opportunities for children to gain eating and self-feeding skills. Finger feeding is an important developmental stage in learning to self-feed. As children learn to manipulate a spoon and fork, the menu must reflect foods prepared in ways children can manage. Eating oatmeal with a spoon is a good first step, but peas may be too challenging for toddlers and preschoolers to eat with a fork. Thus, teachers should allow children to use their fingers as needed.

When planning menus for a wide range of ages (infants to preschoolers), the adaptability of foods served should be considered. Teachers should allow children to feed themselves as much as they are able, as well as allow for messiness. Spills are to be expected and should be treated in an unconcerned manner. Teachers can provide verbal and physical assists by reading children's cues. Planning meals that challenge children to learn new skills without frustration is an extra dimension in menu planning.

Use of age-appropriate equipment is important to support menu acceptance and enhance children's mealtime experience. Eating utensils, tables, and chairs should be age-appropriate in size. Children should be able to sit with their feet touching the ground. The table should be at a comfortable height, and there should be ample room at the table for children to maneuver. The room should be at a pleasant temperature with good lighting, and distractions (such as loud noises or the television) should be eliminated.

CLASSROOM CONNECTION

Watch this video to see preschoolers transitioning to lunch. What strategies do the teachers use to transition children from the activity to the meal?

Enhancing the Social Experience and Social Environment for Children

Mealtimes should be relaxed and enjoyable. Teachers create this comfortable atmosphere by establishing guidelines for acceptable eating behavior. This includes offering meals on a schedule and allowing enough time so meals are not rushed. Interruptions during mealtime should be minimal. Parents picking up children after lunch should be encouraged to avoid entering the room until meal service is done. If there is a television in the family child care home, it should not be on during meal service. Teachers should not be talking on the phone during meal service but rather at the table interacting with children. Social behaviors such as eating etiquette should be introduced and reinforced, such as washing hands before eating, helping to set the table, waiting until everyone is seated before beginning to eat (if age appropriate), and helping with cleanup after the meal. However, teachers should remember that children are learning about eating etiquette and it may take time to master these skills. Mealtimes are important social times as children talk and visit with each other and their providers.

CLASSROOM CONNECTION
Watch this video that shows a group of preschoolers eating lunch. What strategies do the teachers use to create a mealtime environment that is comfortable for children?

Selecting a Type of Meal Service

Meal service can be accomplished in a variety of ways in the early childhood or school setting, including the following:

- *Family-style meal service (best practice)* involves placing foods and beverages in serving containers on the table. Children serve themselves, choosing what and how much they will eat. In this approach, teachers sit with children to model appropriate eating behaviors, to assist with meal service when needed, and to encourage conversation (Connecticut State Department of Education, Bureau of Health/Nutrition, Family Services and Adult Education, 2010).

- *Cafeteria-style meal service* entails children making food choices while moving through a cafeteria line. Children select what they want to eat, but they do not determine the amount. This style of service is common in the primary school setting.

- *Restaurant-style meal service* involves portioning food out on plates before it is served to children at the table.

Regardless of the type of meal service, teachers should sit with children, modeling healthy eating practices and encouraging social interactions. Family-style meal service is the best practice, and it provides a comfortable and nonthreatening way to introduce new foods. It provides opportunities for teachers to model how children may serve themselves and gives children time to decide what to select based on their preferences. Children find the assurance they need to try new foods by observing what other children and teachers are eating. Family-style meal service allows children to make their selections based on how hungry they feel. To reinforce internal cues, teachers can cue children to their hunger and fullness (Ramsay et al., 2010) and encourage children to take smaller portions with the knowledge that they can serve themselves more if they are still hungry (Connecticut State Department of Education, Bureau of Health/Nutrition, Family Services and Adult Education, 2010). Family-style meal service also helps children practice fine motor skills as they dish out foods and pour beverages. Children learn to make choices, take turns, share, and "not lick the spoon."

Step 6: Managing the Menu and Other Occasions When Food Is Brought from Home

Many children's programs ask families to provide the food for snacks or have children bring lunches from home. Part of the challenge when children bring food from home is the inconsistency in what is provided and how it impacts the program's nutrition. For example, what should teachers do if families send soda pop in their children's lunch boxes or perishables that may pose a food safety risk? Developing policies and procedures for home-prepared meals helps establish a partnership with families to support a healthful eating environment.

One helpful resource is the NAEYC's standards for program accreditation. The NAEYC recommends that foods brought from home to be shared with other children must consist of whole fruits or commercially prepared packaged foods (NAEYC, 2012). Home-baked items may be delicious and healthful, but they can pose food safety risks if appropriate food preparation and storage practices are not followed. Children with allergies also are put at risk when there is no list of ingredients to which teachers can refer.

It is important to communicate with families the goals for maintaining the safety of food brought from home and the kinds of food allergies or food restrictions that could be present in the group. A sample policy is described in the *Policy Point*. Reviewing the food-from-home policies with families before children start the program and providing a list of acceptable foods, helps families make healthful choices for foods they send from home.

WHAT IF . . .

a parent arrived at school with a plate of homemade cupcakes to celebrate his child's birthday? How would you handle this? How would you draft a program policy to address this issue?

CHECK YOUR UNDERSTANDING 6.3

Click here to check your understanding of building menus.

POLICY POINT

Sample Policy for Foods Brought from Home

To manage food safety and to reduce the risk of exposing children to certain allergens, the policy of this program is that all food served to children will be provided by the program. Food from home is not allowed.

Exceptions will be provided as follows:

1. *To address special dietary needs due to a medical condition that cannot be accommodated by the program's menu (for example, multiple food allergies).*

   - A note is required from the medical provider.
   - The note must explain the medical condition and the necessary diet restrictions.

2. *To respond to religious dietary restrictions that cannot be accommodated by the program's menu.*

   - A note from the parent is required to be on file.
   - The note will list the foods the child cannot eat.

When lunch is brought from home because of medical or religious reasons noted above, families will be encouraged to support the health goals of the program by providing a balanced meal. The program will provide milk or a milk substitute.

   - Because the program cares for children with peanut and nut allergies, no foods made from peanut or nut products should be brought into the center.
   - No soft drinks, candy, chips, or sugary desserts such as cupcakes are allowed.
   - For safety, food must be brought to school in a lunch box or brown bag that has an ice pack to keep food appropriately chilled. The lunch box or brown bag should be labeled with the child's name and date and will be stored in the refrigerator located in the kitchen until meal service.
   - The program will provide the family with the Child and Adult Care Food Program guidelines for snacks and lunches to assist in planning healthful food-from-home meals.

Source: *Standard 5: Health Topic 5.B: Ensuring Children's Nutritional Well-Being, Criterion 5.B.02 and Criterion 5.B.05*, 2009, Washington, DC: National Association for the Education of Young Children.

PHASE 3: CREATING MENUS THAT SUPPORT ALTERNATIVE OR SPECIAL DIETS

Some children cannot consume the standard infant formula or the typical menu offered at a program or school. They may have food allergies or special medical conditions, or the family may have cultural, religious, or philosophical beliefs that require a special diet. Acting in partnership with families, teachers, food service staff, and administrative staff is important in order to find ways to accommodate children's special diet needs.

Planning menus to accommodate children with special diets is especially crucial for children who have food allergies.

Planning Menus for Children with Food Allergies

Managing special diets can be challenging, especially when children must follow allergen-restricted diets. An estimated 8% of children in the United States have food allergies (Gupta et al., 2011). Each classroom is likely to have one or two children with food allergies.

Understanding Food Allergies

Food allergies occur when the body's immune system responds inappropriately to the exposure of typically harmless proteins found in certain foods. Once these proteins are identified as foreign bodies, or allergens, the body produces defense molecules called immunoglobulin E (IgE) antibodies. After the initial response, the body is sensitized to the allergen. When the offending food is consumed again, IgE antibodies defend the body from the allergen "invaders" and cause white blood cells to release chemicals, including histamine, into the bloodstream. These chemicals cause the myriad of symptoms associated with allergies (Nemours, 2011; U.S. National Library of Medicine, the National Institutes of Health, 2010). Symptoms can include hives; rash; swelling of the mouth, tongue and throat; red and tearing eyes; wheezing; difficulty breathing; coughing; shortness of breath; trouble swallowing; vomiting; diarrhea; and anaphylaxis (Food Allergy Anaphylaxis Network, 2011; NIAID-sponsored expert panel et al., 2010). Anaphylaxis is a severe life-threatening reaction that can lead to a drop in blood pressure, loss of consciousness, and death if untreated. Some children, however, experience other food disorders that are not IgE-mediated that result in an assortment of delayed symptoms that occur hours or days after exposure, making identification of a food allergy more challenging (Berni Canani, Di Costanzo, & Troncone, 2011).

anaphylaxis
a life-threatening reaction that can lead to a drop in blood pressure, loss of consciousness, and death if untreated

FIGURE 6-10
Epinephrine Injector

The only way to prevent allergic reactions is to avoid the offending food (NIAID-sponsored expert panel et al., 2010). Special menu decisions must be made to omit foods that contain allergens from the diet of children with a particular food allergy. Teachers need to be prepared to manage a reaction to a severe food allergy in the event an accidental exposure occurs. A food allergy action plan, which must be developed by the family and the health care provider for emergency response, identifies symptoms and specifies how to treat the allergic reaction in case of an emergency (see the Food Allergy and Anaphylaxis Network (FAAN) Web Resource). Epinephrine is the product used most often to manage anaphylaxis, and it is administered by injection (Figure 6-10).

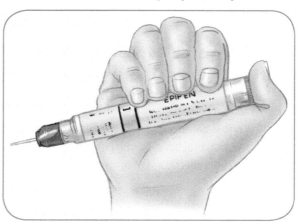

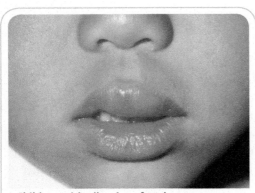

Dr. P. Marazzi/Science Source

Children with allergies often have symptoms such as hives, a rash, and swelling of the mouth and throat.

Teachers must remember to have a plan for the care of other children while they provide care for a child experiencing an allergic reaction. Feeding children with allergies is a serious responsibility. The consequences of making a mistake with their diet can be life threatening. Families must share information about children's allergies with teachers and food service staff before the child attends the program. This provides time to make appropriate adjustments to the menu. Food products are used in a variety of ways in early childhood programs. Teachers must be aware of times when an allergen exposure might occur. If everyone involved in food service is informed about a child's food allergy, the likelihood of a food service error is reduced. The *Safety Segment* provides an example of how one preschool program communicates about special diet requirements for children with food allergies. Teachers should listen to children who have life-threatening allergies, because very young children often are well aware of what they can and cannot eat.

Infants with Food Allergies

Allergies may begin to appear in infants when solid foods are introduced and they are exposed to new foods. Foods should be introduced one at a time, waiting three to five days before the next new food is offered. In this way, if allergy symptoms develop, it is easier to identify the offending food (Kleinman, 2009). Families should provide teachers with a list of foods that have been introduced successfully. Menus planned for infants emerge from the list of tolerated foods. If a food allergy is identified, the offending food is eliminated from the infant's diet.

FIGURE 6-11
Example of Labeling Special Diet Items

The family should approve the menu, and with the family's consent, the child's diet should be posted where it is easily accessible in areas where food is prepared, offered, and used for other activities (*Standard 5: Health Topic 5.B: Ensuring Children's Nutritional Well-Being, Criterion 5.B.05* (NAEYC, 2012)). Food labels should be read carefully. Foods purchased for infants should be single-ingredient foods to prevent inadvertent exposure to an allergen. Exclusive breastfeeding until infants are 4 to 6 months of age may offer protection from the development of food allergies (Ferdman, McClenahan, & Falco, 2010; NIAID-sponsored expert panel et al., 2010). For infants who are offered formula, extra care is needed when preparing the formula to avoid cross-contamination. Strategies to avoid cross-contamination include the following:

- Formula should be prepared in specifically identified containers, using specific mixing utensils.
- Bottles should be cleaned with specific bottle brushes and thoroughly rinsed.
- Special hypoallergenic formulas should be labeled so bottles are not inadvertently given to the wrong infant. The label on the formula should be double-checked before the infant is fed.

Toddlers, Preschoolers, and Primary-Grade Children with Food Allergies

The challenge in planning menus for children with food allergies is ensuring the foods offered are allergen-free while still meeting nutritional recommendations. In addition, it is important to create enough variety so children do not become bored with the substitutes offered. Food for young children should be

A Matter of ETHICS

A child in your program has a severe nut allergy, and you ask families not to bring nut products into your program. A mother of a child who enjoys peanut butter and jelly sandwiches for lunch complains that her child's rights are being ignored. What is the best course of action to resolve this ethical dilemma?

SAFETY SEGMENT   Communicating About Allergy Diets

Special diets need careful planning. Foods need to be handled safely to avoid cross-contamination, and the foods need to be distributed to the correct child. Good communication and safety checks along the way help prevent food "accidents." Below is an example of the steps involved in managing peanut allergies.

Sunshine Preschool receives food through an agreement with a vendor. The vendor is the local school district's food service. Food is prepared off-site and sent via heated and chilled carts to the preschool program. One classroom has two children severely allergic to peanuts. What can the teacher do to ensure that the children are safe from potentially life-threatening allergens?

1. *School district food service:* The teacher or preschool dietitian contacts the school district kitchen that provides food for the center. Information about a child's food allergy is communicated prior to the child attending the class. A peanut-free menu is requested, and all labels and recipes are checked for peanut-containing products. The school district kitchen ensures that containers and packaging for peanut-free diets are labeled.

2. *The preschool:* The preschool decides to eliminate peanuts or peanut products from the menu. Staff members and families are asked not to bring peanut products to school. A list of children who are on special diets includes the two children with peanut allergies. This list is posted on the kitchen bulletin board, and each teacher is given a copy. Staff is oriented not to make any substitutions for the peanut-free diet without prior approval from the dietitian. Staff members receive training on how to administer a rescue medication via an epinephrine injector.

3. *The classroom:* Assistant teachers are assigned to be in charge of serving and supervising service of special diets. The assistant teacher is asked to sit with the children who have food allergies at mealtime. Children with special diets are served first. A Food Allergy Emergency protocol is developed by the child's health care provider and is posted in the classroom near the phone so that all staff has the knowledge of what to do and who to call in case of an emergency.

Checklist for Managing Food Allergies in the Classroom

Activities or lesson plans:

☐ Do any cooking activities use foods with potential allergens?

☐ Are food items with potential allergens used in other activities (sensory tables with corn meal, pasta, or rice; pastas used for sorting and stringing; made-from-scratch play dough)?

Field trips:

☐ Are allergen-free foods available for lunch and snacks?

☐ Does the emergency kit include children's medications (epinephrine injector) and an up-to-date Food Allergy Action Plan?

☐ Does everyone know who is carrying the child's medication?

☐ Does someone have a cell phone?

Lunchroom procedures:

☐ Is there a plan to ensure that the child receives the correct food from food service?

☐ What practices are used to remove all traces of allergens during cleanup?

☐ Are kitchen staff informed and trained on food allergies?

☐ Is there sufficient supervision of the child with allergies during meal service to ensure that the correct food is selected and served and that children are not sharing food?

Social events:

☐ Are foods with allergens coming into the classroom from outside sources for classroom celebrations, picnics, etc.?

Teacher's absence:

☐ Is there a plan in place to ensure allergen safety when the teacher is absent?

☐ Is backup staff trained to supervise food service for children with allergies?

Classroom environment:

☐ Does more than one class use the same classroom (morning and afternoon classes)?

☐ Are both teachers aware of the allergies of each other's students?

prepared and served to avoid cross-contamination. Food purchased for children with allergies should be labeled with the child's name and date and properly stored. In addition, special diet items must be labeled when served so children receive the correct allergen-free foods (Figure 6-11). Menus for children with allergies should be approved by families and posted so all staff members involved know that children with special diets will be served. During meal service, young children should be supervised so they do not inadvertently consume other children's food. School-age children should be cautioned about sharing lunches.

When the menu is carefully planned to accommodate food allergies and food service safety checks are a routine part of food service and preparation, teachers minimize the risk of accidental exposure to food allergens.

Planning Menus for Children with Diabetes

Children with diabetes have special dietary needs that require close coordination between families and teachers. Meals and snacks must meet children's nutritional needs and help to maintain appropriate blood sugar levels (Siminerio et al., 2014). Teachers who have children with diabetes in the class need specialized training by a diabetes educator about the effects of physical activity, diet, and insulin on blood glucose levels. They also must be trained in the treatment of diabetes emergencies (American Diabetes Association, 2011a; Siminerio et al., 2014).

Understanding Type 1 and Type 2 Diabetes

Type 1 diabetes
a condition in which the body cannot produce insulin to get glucose from the bloodstream into the cell

Type 2 diabetes
a condition in which insulin is produced by the body but the cell receptors do not function and glucose from the blood stream cannot be taken up by the cell, often associated with overweight and obesity

There are two types of diabetes: **Type 1** and **Type 2**. Both result in elevated blood sugar levels, but the cause of these conditions is very different. In children with Type 1 diabetes, the cells in the pancreas that make insulin are not functioning; therefore, insulin injections are required. Children who have Type 2 diabetes still make insulin; however, receptors in the cells are not functioning, which is often associated with overweight and obesity (National Diabetes Education Program, 2011). A visual explanation of the differences between Type 1 and Type 2 diabetes can be observed by viewing the flash animations at the Kids Health website. (In a search engine, type "Kids Health video What happens in type 1 diabetes?")

Understanding the Diet for Type 1 Diabetes

The amount of carbohydrate-containing foods served at mealtime and snack time is very important for children. Carbohydrates (starches/grains, fruits, milk, and sweets) in a diet are broken down to glucose during digestion. These carbohydrate foods must be balanced throughout the day and in accordance with insulin injections. Regular meals and snacks with balanced carbohydrate foods help prevent high or low blood sugar levels.

meal plan
a diet guidance tool developed by health care professionals such as registered dietitian nutritionists to help children with diabetes and their families know what amount of carbohydrates they should eat and when to manage blood sugar levels

Diets for children with Type 1 diabetes vary depending on the child's age and calorie requirements. Teachers will know how much to offer based on the child's **meal plan**. A child's meal plan is developed and reviewed by health care professionals such as registered dietitian nutritionists to help children with diabetes. This individualized plan reflects the child's personal and cultural food preferences (American Dietetic Association, 2011a). The family receives the meal plan instructions and is typically the resource for communicating the meal plan to the teacher. In addition, management of all aspects of a child's diabetes, including diet, is outlined in the Diabetes Medical Management Plan and the 504 Plan (see Web resources). To accommodate children who have diabetes, families need to:

- Provide and review the child's meal plan and snack schedule.
- Provide instructions on what to do when food is offered at classroom parties or other special events.
- Provide the supplies needed to treat low blood sugar reaction, such as a source of glucose (simple carbohydrate).

For their part in accommodating children with diabetes, teachers need to:

- Learn the carbohydrate content of foods offered on the menu and understand the portions that are allowed per the child's meal plan.
- Provide families with information on portion sizes and calorie, carbohydrate, and fat content of meals served at school.
- Ensure regular mealtimes. If a meal is delayed, a backup plan for providing food is necessary to prevent the child with Type 1 diabetes from having a low blood sugar reaction.
- Review foods planned for special events and receive approval from families about the particular food items and amounts that should be offered.
- Plan appropriate foods for meals away from the program, such as picnics and field trips.
- Develop strategies and obtain guidance from families on what to do if a child refuses to eat.
- Obtain training and guidance on what foods to feed or medication to administer if the child's blood sugar levels get too low.
- Make provisions in case the teacher is absent. A substitute teacher must be trained in diet and diabetes management (American Diabetes Association, 2012).

WHAT IF . . .

a child in your class had diabetes and the lunch meal was late? You wonder whether you should provide an emergency snack to the child with diabetes while the other children continue to wait. How would you manage this?

Teachers may be called on to check children's blood sugar levels, make decisions about the amount of food to serve based on the child's blood sugar level, and administer insulin. All information pertaining to these types of decisions is included in the Diabetes Medical Management Plan and the 504 Plan.

Understanding the Diet for Type 2 Diabetes

The overall goals of diet therapy for children with Type 2 diabetes are similar to the goals for children with Type 1 diabetes, which include providing a nutritious diet that minimizes elevations in blood sugar levels by focusing on the carbohydrate content of meals. However, lifestyle changes that promote healthy weight and encourage physical activity also are very important objectives (American Dietetic Association, 2011a; National Diabetes Education Program, 2011). Children with Type 2 diabetes are often treated with lifestyle changes first; however, sometimes they need oral medications and insulin to control blood sugar levels.

Planning Menus for Children Who Are Overweight or Obese

A healthful menu accommodates children who are overweight unless a physician has determined that a specially structured diet is a medical necessity (Academy of Nutrition and Dietetics, 2012). Only a select group of children with significant obesity-related health issues require a multidisciplinary obesity care team. In this case, families may provide more specific diet recommendations from their health care team (Academy of Nutrition and Dietetics, 2012; Skelton & Beech, 2011).

A child's blood sugar level is monitored by pricking the finger and using a glucose meter to determine whether his or her blood sugar is within the acceptable range.

Bochkarev Photography/Shutterstock

Strategies for managing overweight or obesity among children also address prevention. Attention is given to improving health rather than focusing on weight. This protects both the physical and social/emotional well-being of young children (August et al., 2008; Weight realities division of the Society of Nutrition Education, Center for Weight and Health, U.C. Berkeley, 2003). The American Academy of Pediatrics, the Academy of Nutrition and Dietetics, and the USDA recommend the following evidence-based nutrition practices for preventing and treating overweight and obesity:

- Limit sugar-sweetened beverages, soft drinks, and juice at mealtime and snack time.
- Offer sufficient fruits and vegetables at mealtime and snack time.
- Offer breakfast daily.
- Offer appropriate portion sizes at mealtime and snack time.
- Limit calorie-dense and high-fat foods at mealtime and snack time.
- Serve nonfat or low-fat milk to children age 2 and older (American Dietetic Association, 2010a; Davis et al., 2007; U.S. Department of Agriculture, 2010).

Planning Menus for Children with Special Health Care Needs

Children with disabilities or special health care needs may have special diet requirements and may be at increased risk for nutritional problems. For example, children may have unique feeding concerns, such as problems with chewing and swallowing. This highlights the need for careful discussion of menus and adjustments that may be needed to ensure the child's dietary needs are well understood. Directions for meeting the child's nutrition and feeding needs in the classroom setting should be obtained from the child's health care provider and registered dietitian nutritionist.

tube feedings
a method of feeding in which a liquid supplement is fed via a tube that goes into the stomach or small intestine

In some situations, teachers may require specialized training. For example, if a child requires **tube feedings**, teachers must be trained in tube feeding administration. With tube feeding, a liquid supplement is fed via a tube that enters the stomach or small intestine. This method is used when a child is not able to eat solid foods or the amount that can be eaten is insufficient in volume for the child to achieve adequate nutritional intake. Training is provided by a qualified health care professional. A medical statement must be on file documenting the need for the special diet and describing the recommended feeding practices. Figure 6-12 is a sample form that can be used for any child requiring a special diet (Food and Nutrition Service & United States Department of Agriculture, 2001).

Many factors should be considered when adapting menus for children with special health and diet needs. Children with special needs may have varying requirements for calories to maintain an appropriate rate of growth. Some children may find it difficult to eat enough calories to support growth because of increased calorie requirements, oral-motor problems, or developmental delay of feeding skills; whereas other children may face increased risk for obesity due to poor muscle tone or decreased physical activity. Some children may experience reflux, diarrhea, or constipation (Samour & King, 2012). Table 6-4 provides a summary of some nutritional health concerns of children with special health care needs.

Adjustments to the way food is offered also may be needed. These include:

- *Food texture:* Food may need to be ground or puréed.
- *Food consistency:* A commercial thickener may need to be added to liquids.

FIGURE 6-12 Eating and Feeding Evaluation: Children with Special Needs

PART A			
Student's Name		Age	
Name of School	Grade Level	Classroom	

Does the child have a disability? If yes, describe the major life activities affected by the disability.	Yes	No
Does the child have special nutritional or feeding needs? If Yes, complete Part B of this form and have it signed by a licensed physician.	Yes	No
If the child is not disabled, does the child have special nutritional or feeding needs? If Yes, complete Part B of this form and have it signed by a recognized authority.	Yes	No

If the child does not require special meals, the parent can sign at the bottom and return the form to the school food service.

PART B
List any dietary restrictions or special diet.
List any allergies or food intolerances to avoid.
List foods to be substituted.
List foods that need the following change in texture. If all foods need to be prepared in this manner, indicate "All." Cut up or chopped into bite size pieces: Finely ground: Pureed:
List any special equipment or utensils that are needed.
Indicate any other comments about the child's eating or feeding patterns.

Parent's Signature	Date:
Physician or Medical Authority's Signature	Date:

From *Accommodating Children with Special Dietary Needs in School Nutrition Programs—Guidance for Food Service Staff*, p. 34, 2001, Alexandria, VA: USDA Food and Nutrition Service, retrieved March 29, 2015, from http://www.fns.usda.gov/cnd/Guidance/special_dietary_needs.pdf.

- *Special equipment:* Special equipment such as a feeding chair or special plate and eating utensils may be necessary.
- *Commercial supplements:* Supplements used to boost calorie intake or for tube feeding may be necessary.
- *Calorie level:* High-calorie or low-calorie foods may be needed.
- *Mealtimes:* More time may be needed for consuming meals.

Families, the child's medical team, and early intervention specialists are good resources for guidance about managing children's eating concerns. During

TABLE 6-4 Nutritional Concerns of Select Health Care Conditions

Special Health Care Condition	Impact on Eating and Diet	Impact on Growth/Nutritional Status/Overall Health	Implications for Teachers
Attention deficit hyper-activity disorder (ADHD)	Medications can decrease appetite.	Some children experience weight loss or reduced growth rate.	Provide high-calorie, nutrient dense foods. Offer three meals with three snacks.
Autism spectrum disorder	Difficulty with changes in routine, including mealtimes. Medications can interact with nutrients and impact nutritional status. Limited food acceptance due to sensitivities related to taste, texture, odor, and temperature of foods.	Some children experience weight loss or reduced growth rate. Some families try special diets (e.g., gluten- and milk-free diet) with restrictions that can increase the risk of inadequate intake.	Provide a routine schedule for mealtimes with three meals and three snacks. Introduce new foods with foods that are liked. Avoid distractions. If weight is low, provide high-calorie, nutrient dense foods.
Cerebral palsy	Oral motor problems can result in prolonged feeding time and decreased food intake. Medications can interact with nutrients and impact nutritional status.	Children may experience inadequate calorie intake, resulting in poor growth. Calorie needs can be higher with hypertonia/spasticity, resulting in decreased weight, or can be lower with hypotonia, resulting in increased weight gain. Constipation is common.	May need specialized feeding equipment, adjustment in food textures or tube feedings, extra time for feeding. If underweight, provide high-calorie, nutrient dense foods. If overweight, provide lower calorie, nutrient dense foods. Provide fiber-rich foods and adequate liquids.
Down syndrome	Poor suck in infancy. Short stature results in decreased energy needs.	At risk for poor growth initially but increased risk later for obesity. Constipation is common.	Watch for adequate growth the first year and later provide low-calorie, fiber-rich foods, adequate liquids, and physical activity.
Fetal alcohol syndrome	Poor suck and difficult to feed.	Children may experience inadequate calorie intake, resulting in poor growth.	Provide high-calorie, nutrient dense foods. Offer three meals with three snacks. Tube feeding may be needed.
Epilepsy and seizure disorder	Medications can interact with nutrients and impact nutritional status.	Constipation can occur.	Offer nutrient dense foods rich in fiber and adequate liquids. Some children may need special diets for seizure control that are coordinated with family and health care providers.
Muscular dystrophy	Muscle weakness can lead to chewing and swallowing problems that result in prolonged feeding time and decreased food intake.	Children may experience inadequate calorie intake, resulting in poor growth. Sometimes obesity occurs when ability to walk is reduced, resulting in decreased calorie needs. Appetite can be increased due to medication.	May need specialized feeding equipment, adjustment in food textures or tube feedings, and extra time for feeding. If underweight, provide high-calorie, nutrient dense foods. If overweight, provide lower calorie, nutrient dense foods.
Spina bifida	Swallowing problems may develop allergy to latex.	Sometimes obesity occurs when ability to walk is reduced, resulting in decreased calorie needs. Constipation can occur.	If overweight, provide lower-calorie, nutrient dense foods. If there is a latex allergy, avoid bananas, kiwi, water chestnuts, and avocados.

Sources: *Journal of the American Dietetic Association*, 2010, *110*(2). Position of the American Dietetic Association: Providing Nutrition Services for People with Developmental Disabilities and Special Health Care Needs; *Pediatric nutrition in chronic diseases and developmental disorders: Prevention, assessment and treatment*, 2nd ed., edited by S. W. Ekvall, & V. K. Ekvall, 2005, New York: Oxford University Press; *Pediatric nutrition care manual*, American Dietetic Association, 2011, https://www.nutritioncaremanual.org; and Bagnell, A., & Davies, T. (2008). *Muscular dystrophy campaign: Nutrition and feeding*, http://www.muscular-dystrophy.org/.

mealtimes, teachers should observe children with special eating concerns carefully, watching for chewing, swallowing, and other eating problems. The NAEYC (National Association for the Education of Young Children, 2012) recommends that staff keep a daily record documenting the type and amount of food consumed by children with special needs and provide this information to families. Any concerns should be shared because children may need to be referred to a feeding clinic that offers the services of a physician, a registered dietitian nutritionist, and an occupational or speech therapist.

Planning Menus for Children Following a Vegetarian Diet

A vegetarian diet is a diet in which the child does not consume animal or fish products; rather, the primary source of protein comes from plant foods. Teachers need to understand different types of vegetarian diets and which diet a child follows to provide menu substitutions appropriately. Table 6-5 describes four types of vegetarian diets and the foods that are avoided and consumed.

Infants with Vegetarian Diets

The age of a child influences vegetarian menu planning decisions. A vegetarian diet can safely meet the nutritional needs of infants. At first, infants are breastfed or provided regular formula. Soy formula is an option for infants whose families avoid all animal sources of food including milk. Solid foods are introduced gradually, following the same guidelines recommended for nonvegetarian infant diets. In place of meat or poultry protein sources, eggs, dairy products such as cottage cheese and yogurt, and protein-rich vegetable foods such as puréed legumes, tofu, and soy yogurts are offered. Infant cereal is particularly beneficial, especially for breast-fed infants, because it is rich in iron and zinc, nutrients generally found in meat products. Nut or peanut butter is a good vegetarian food, but it should not be given by the spoonful to children younger than 4 years of age due to the risk of choking (U.S. Department of Agriculture, 2015c). Bread and peanut butter can form a glob in the roof of the mouth, which can make it difficult to swallow and is a risk for choking.

Toddler, Preschool, and Primary-Grade Children with Vegetarian Diets

Young children whose vegetarian diet includes milk, other dairy products, and eggs receive a diet that supports growth. It can be more challenging to meet the nutrient needs of children on vegan diets. Sometimes the fiber content of a plant-based vegan diet provides so much bulk that children become full before their nutrient needs are met. One way to ensure sufficient calories and protein for growth is to provide nutrient- and calorie-dense foods. Food products that increase calories in the diet include nut butters (assuming there are no allergies), oils, and avocado. Whole soy milk should be offered for toddlers from age 1 until 2 years of age rather than fat-free or low-fat soy milk, and it should be fortified with calcium and vitamin D. The CACFP provides guidelines for acceptable soy milks that more closely align

TABLE 6-5 Types of Vegetarians

Type of Vegetarian	Avoids	Consumes
Lacto-ovo	Meat, poultry, fish	Eggs, milk and dairy products, foods of plant origin
Ovo-vegetarian	Meat, poultry, fish, dairy	Eggs, foods of plant origin
Lacto-vegetarian	Meat, poultry, fish, eggs	Milk and dairy products, foods of plant origin
Vegan	Meat, poultry, fish, eggs, and dairy	Only foods of plant origin

Source: Based on "Types of Vegetarian Diets" Pediatric Nutrition Care Manual, American Dietetic Association, 2011, available at https://www.nutritioncaremanual.org.

with the nutrients in cow's milk. To be a creditable milk substitute, soy beverages must contain 8 grams of protein, 100 IU of vitamin D, 500 IU of vitamin A, and 276 mg of calcium per 8 ounces (Murphy et al., 2011). Rice milk and nut milks are generally not acceptable because they are typically lower in protein content.

Several aspects are important to consider when planning menus to meet vegetarian diet needs:

- Select vegetarian protein products that are fortified with calcium, iron, vitamin D, zinc, and vitamin B_{12}.
- Use meat substitutes such as soy burgers, soy cheese, vegetarian deli slices, bean loaves, nut butters, and tofu to maintain variety in the menu.
- Avoid gelatin products made from pork, such as marshmallows, gummy candies, and gelatin desserts, for children following a vegan diet.
- Plan healthy vegetarian snacks such as whole-grain crackers with cheese or nut butters, whole-grain corn tortillas with beans, pita bread triangles with hummus, and yogurt mixed with fresh fruit.

Planning Menus to Reflect Cultural Preferences

The traditions associated with eating are some of the most deeply ingrained behaviors of life. Many cultural traditions, customs, and beliefs are associated with food practices and affect the family's diet preferences. Making menu adjustments to support family cultural practices requires close communication with families.

Each culture's food practices can have health and nutrition advantages and disadvantages for children. For example, traditional Asian meals are low in meats and rich in vegetables, which contribute to a reduced incidence of heart disease, bowel cancer, and breast cancer (Hill & The Ohio State University, 2010). Middle Eastern diets are high in olive oil, which contributes to that population having, in general, lower blood pressures (Nolan & The Ohio State University, 2010). Ethnic and cultural diets also can have negative features. For example, acculturation to mainstream American dietary practices may be less healthful compared with traditional Hispanic diets, which may be higher in fruits, vegetables, and fiber-rich carbohydrates such as beans and corn products (Ghaddar, Brown, Pagán, & Díaz, 2010; Ewing & The Ohio State University, 2010). African American "soul food" is rich in green leafy vegetables such as collards, kale, mustard, and turnip greens and high-fiber beans such as black-eyed peas and red beans. However, the diet also relies on fried and seasoned meats and whole-milk products, resulting in a higher-than-recommended fat and sodium intake (Edwards, 2003; Kulkarni, 2004; The Ohio State University, 2010).

Teachers need to be aware that infant feeding practices vary among cultural and ethnic groups. For example, some cultures give sugar water or tea to infants or add other foods to bottles of formula (Nevin-Folino, 2003, updated 2008; Zhang, Fein, & Fein, 2011). When planning to meet cultural preferences, teachers need to work closely with families to identify foods from the cultural tradition that can be included in the menu while also meeting the goals for healthful menus.

Planning menus that reflect the cultural backgrounds of children in the class or school is one way of demonstrating cultural competency. Cultural competency refers to the respectful understanding and appreciation of cultural differences and similarities among groups and the ability to use this understanding to interact

cultural competency
the respectful understanding and appreciation of cultural differences and similarities among groups and the ability to use this understanding to interact effectively with people across cultures

effectively with people across cultures. Strategies to support cultural sensitivity in the early childhood setting include the following:

- Plan menus that include culturally diverse food options.
- Offer classroom cooking activities for children to prepare and taste foods that represent a variety of traditions.
- Provide information (menus for example) in the various home languages of children in the class.
- Read children's books on eating that reflect culturally diverse settings.
- Conduct field trips to grocery stores, supermarkets, and bakeries, including visits to culturally diverse establishments.

Teachers are sources of information in many cultures and should provide accurate information about diet and heath that is reputable and culturally sensitive.

Planning Menus to Address Religious Beliefs and Practices

Religious beliefs, customs, traditions, and practices hold deep meaning to the families who adhere to them. In some cases, religious belief systems and practices influence the diet choices of children. For example, some religious groups refrain from eating certain meats. People following the Hindu faith do not eat beef, and people of Islamic and Jewish faiths may avoid pork and pork products. Devout Seventh Day Adventists avoid all meats. Teachers need to work closely with families to identify food restrictions and preferences based on religious customs or practices. Table 6-6 summarizes common religious food practices among eight different religious groups.

> **WHAT IF . . .**
> you wanted to include activities in your class curriculum that explored cultural diversity? What themes would you use? What foods could you include on the menu to reinforce your theme?

The Islamic Religion

Adherents to Islam follow religious writings recommending that a mother breastfeed her infant until 2 years of age if possible (Nevin-Folino, 2003, updated 2008). Modesty is an important aspect of this religion. Providing a private location for Islamic mothers who are breastfeeding supports this feeding relationship. The traditional dress and head covering of Islamic women cover most of their body. This puts them and their infants at risk for vitamin D deficiency if the infants are breastfed exclusively.

Many Muslims consume a *halal* diet, which means they consume foods that are lawful or permitted according to the Quran (Islamic Food and Nutrition Council of America, 2011). Only the flesh of animals or poultry killed in a humane way while the name of God is spoken can be eaten, such as beef, veal, turkey, chicken, goat, and lamb. The halal diet avoids pork and pork products such as the gelatin used in marshmallows, gummy candies, and gelatin desserts (American Dietetic Association, 2011c).

The Jewish Religion

The Jewish religion also has rules about how animals are butchered. According to Jewish law, all blood must be drained from the meat for it to be considered *kosher*. Kosher symbols are used on processed foods to designate that they have been prepared in accordance with dietary laws. Milk and meat cannot be consumed at the same meal (American Dietetic Association, 2011c). The term *pareve* on a label indicates foods that contain neither meat nor dairy products. These foods are therefore

TABLE 6-6 Religious Practices That Influence Food Choice

Religious Group	Meat	Poultry	Fish	Shellfish	Dairy	Fruits/Vegetables/Grains	Other
Buddhist	Avoided by most	Avoided by most	Avoided by most	Avoided by most	Permitted	Onion, garlic, chives, or leek or root vegetables are avoided by some. Most but not all are vegetarian.	No set dietary laws. Great variation in customs.
Hindu	Avoided by most. No beef, and pork is often avoided.	Avoided by most	Avoided by most	Avoided by most	Permitted	Use of these foods is encouraged. Some may avoid onions, garlic, and mushrooms. Most but not all are vegetarian.	No set dietary laws. Great variation in customs. No alcohol, coffee, or tea.
Islam	Ritual slaughter laws. No pork.	Ritual slaughter laws	Permitted	Avoided by some	Permitted	Permitted	No alcohol. Coffee and tea avoided by most.
Judaism (kosher diet)	Ritual slaughter laws. No pork.	Ritual slaughter laws	Must have fins and scales	Forbidden	Dairy cannot be served with meat.	Fresh fruits and vegetables are naturally kosher.	Great variation in kosher practice.
Mormonism	Use in moderate amounts	Permitted	Permitted	Permitted	Permitted	Use of these foods is encouraged.	No coffee, tea, or alcohol.
Roman Catholic	Avoided by some on Fridays, especially during certain religious days	Permitted	Permitted	Permitted	Permitted	Permitted	Fish may be consumed when meat is avoided.
Seventh Day Adventist	Avoided by most. No pork.	Avoided by most	Avoided by most	Forbidden	Milk and eggs permitted	Use of these foods is encouraged. Most are vegetarian.	No coffee, tea, or alcohol.

Sources: Framingham State College, Buddhism, 2009, http://www.framingham.edu/food-and-nutrition/documents/buddhism.pdf; KITTLER/SUCHER, Food and Culture, 5e. © 2008 Brooks/Cole, a part of Cengage Learning, Inc.; American Dietetic Association, Cultural Food Practices, Pediatric Nutrition Care Manual, 2011; and FaithandFood.com, 2009, http://www.faithandfood.com/index.php.

considered neutral and can be served with either meat or milk. Pareve foods include eggs, fish, grains, fruits, and vegetables. Pork and pork products are not permitted in the kosher diet. Fish with fins are permissible, but shellfish are not. Eggs and fish can be eaten with milk or meat. During food preparation and service, the cooking and eating utensils are also kept kosher. This means that those of the orthodox faith have two sets of serving ware and cooking utensils available for the separate preparation of meat and milk. The restriction that prohibits drinking milk and eating meat or poultry in the same meal is in conflict with the Child and Adult Care Food Program and the School Lunch Program requirements for milk and meat components served at lunch and supper. To address this, the USDA Food and Nutrition Service provide three options for Jewish schools, institutions, and sponsors to select from and still be in compliance with regulations:

Option I: Serve an equal amount of 100% juice in place of milk with lunch or supper. Programs operating five days per week may substitute juice for milk twice per week for lunches and twice for suppers, but no more than once each day.

Option II: Serve milk at an appropriate time before or after the meal service period, in accordance with applicable Jewish dietary law.

Option III: Serve the supplement (snack) juice component at lunch or supper. Serve the lunch milk component as part of a supplement (snack) (U.S. Department of Agriculture, Food and Nutrition Service, 2006).

The Seventh Day Adventist Religion

This religion encourages the lacto-ovo vegetarian diet. Eggs and dairy are permitted, although egg yolks are limited to three per week. The use of whole grains is encouraged. This diet is healthy for children when adequate calories are consumed. Menu planning for these children follow the guidelines for the lacto-ovo vegetarian diet.

CHECK YOUR UNDERSTANDING 6.4
Click here to check your understanding of managing special dietary considerations.

SUMMARY

- A well-planned menu is the foundation for creating a healthful nutrition environment in early childhood settings. An organized approach to menu planning ensures nutritious meals are created. This involves writing menus that demonstrate understanding of food program requirements and support alternative and special diets. Many resources are available to assist teachers and food service personnel to plan healthful meals that meet the recommendations of health, licensing, accreditation, and funding authorities.

- Menu planning must address the requirements of the child care setting. A cycle menu is typically selected for early childhood settings. This helps organize the process of menu development, purchasing, and food service. It also helps family child care settings, programs, and schools establish and maintain cost-effective practices. The process of menu development includes selecting entrées, side dishes, and beverages that offer variety in taste, texture, and visual appeal. Once established, the basic menu is adjusted to accommodate special dietary needs. Families who send food from home also benefit from the information provided by programs that helps them make healthful choices for children's lunches and snacks.

- Careful menu development is important and is easier when a procedure for building a menu is followed. Children receive a large portion of their daily requirement of nutrients in the early childhood setting. Mealtime offers opportunities for children to participate in relaxed social discussions and guides children in learning self-help skills such as serving their own food and clearing their dishes.

- Children with special dietary considerations or cultural or religious preferences depend on their teachers to ensure they receive the appropriate meal. Careful menu planning contributes to children's health and wellness and establishes healthful eating practices that children can sustain throughout life.

Chapter Quiz 6

Click here to check your understanding of Chapter 6, Menu Planning.

Discussion Starters

1. Discuss the following situations. How would you deal with each scenario in such a way that a child's accidental exposure to an allergen is avoided?
   a. A young child wants to trade or share foods with a child who has allergies.
   b. Food service staff forget to prepare the special diet.
   c. Cross-contamination of foods occurs when some allergen gets into an otherwise acceptable food.
   d. The teacher is absent. How would the substitute know who has allergies and special dietary requirements?
   e. Foods from home are brought in for a celebration, and a toddler with allergies reaches for something he should not have.

2. A group of parents is upset about the school lunch menu. Some are concerned that there are too many processed foods, not enough whole grains, and too much canned fruit instead of fresh fruit. How would you approach this dilemma?

3. A 4-year-old in your program is obese. His mother tells you she has placed him on a diet and he can only eat the foods she packs for him from home. The boy cries during lunch because he can't eat what the other children are eating and he is hungry. How do you handle this situation?

Practice Points

1. You have been asked to join the School Health Advisory Council to develop a new policy that focuses on the development of a more sustainable food service. List the steps you would take to develop and implement the new policy. How would you involve staff, families, and children?

2. Using the Figure 6-4 menu template, develop a weekly menu for 3- to 5-year-old children for breakfast, lunch and snack. Use the Figure 6-9 Sample Menu Evaluation Checklist to check your menu.

3. Using the three phases of menu planning, list important program requirements and develop a one-day breakfast menu that will meet the needs of a preschool Head Start program that includes Hispanic children. Adapt the menu for a child with a milk allergy.

Web Resources

American Academy of Pediatrics: Healthy Children

American Diabetes Association: Diabetes 504 plan

Diabetes Medical Management Plan

Food Allergy and Anaphylaxis Network's Food Allergy Action Plan

Institute of Medicine of the National Academies: Dietary Reference Intakes

National Food Service Management Institute: Measuring Success with Standardized Recipes

USDA recipes for schools

U. S Department of Agriculture and U.S. Department of Health and Human Services

See the *Nutrition and Wellness Tips for Young Children: Provider Handbook for the Child and Adult Care Food Program*

U.S. Department of Agriculture: ChooseMyPlate

U.S. Department of Agriculture Food and Nutrition Service Child Nutrition Programs

Includes links to Child and Adult Care Food Program, National School Lunch Program, and School Breakfast Program

U.S. Department of Health and Human Services: Dietary Guidelines for Americans

Key Terms

anaphylaxis

budget

commercially prepared
entrée

commodity foods

components

creditable food

cultural competency

cycle menu

Head Start Performance
Standards

meal patterns

meal plan

meal requirements

noncreditable food

nutrient dense foods

nutrient targets

refined grains

standardized recipes

sustainable practices

tube feedings

type 1 diabetes

type 2 diabetes

whole grains

CHAPTER 7

Food Safety

After reading this chapter, you should be able to:

1. **Identify the hazards responsible for foodborne illness.**
2. **Define the role of federal, state, and county food safety regulations and guidelines that impact food service in the early childhood setting.**
3. **Explain how to minimize food contamination in the early childhood setting using the principles of the Hazard Analysis and Critical Control Point (HACCP) system and standard operating procedures.**
4. **Explain food safety precautions that need to be considered during an emergency and define strategies for managing food defense.**
5. **Learn how to teach concepts of food safety to young children.**

CASE STUDY

Lacey's class of preschool children enjoys an eventful day. Lacey and Joan, teachers at Sunshine Preschool, have scheduled a field trip for their class groups to an area supermarket. They observe how meat is ground and packaged. They watch as bread and rolls are made and baked in large ovens in the bakery. At the end of the visit, they get to sample fresh warm bread and sliced oranges. When the children return to preschool, they eat lunch (turkey sandwiches, green salad, sliced watermelon, and milk), which was prepared in the school kitchen. Just as lunch is ending, Lacey is surprised by Kimberly's mother who arrives bearing a platter of homemade frosted cupcakes in celebration of Kimberly's fourth birthday.

The next morning Lacey gets the first inkling that something is wrong. A third of the children in the class are absent. Several parents call reporting similar symptoms: vomiting, stomach cramps, and diarrhea. Lacey talks to the director, Jill, who decides to notify the health department of a suspected outbreak of a foodborne illness.

The health sanitarian determines that the trip to the supermarket is not the source of the problem. The supermarket manager and workers have food safety training certification; they follow state and federal food safety guidelines and have consistently passed local sanitation inspections. The children who toured the area where meat was prepared had washed their hands before eating the snacks. Also, the children in Joan's class have not gotten sick.

The food service at the preschool is also reviewed. The director of food service shows the sanitarian their Hazard Analysis and Critical Control Point food safety plan in which documentation confirms that proper safety procedures were used in preparing the lunch. This confirmation and the fact that only the children in Lacey's class are experiencing symptoms similarly rules out the preschool food service as the source of the problem. Next, the sanitarian interviews Kimberly's mother. Ultimately the homemade cupcakes are identified as the culprit in this outbreak of foodborne illness. It is discovered that the frosting on the cupcakes was made with raw egg whites. Salmonella food poisoning was later confirmed by laboratory tests.

Lacey is upset that this occurred in her class. She takes pride in providing a healthy, safe environment for the children in her care. She constantly sanitizes surfaces and carefully supervises children as they wash their hands before meals. She was caught unaware when Kimberly's mother brought in the cupcakes and allowed them to be served against her better judgment. After this event, she learns that serving food made in a home kitchen is against the preschool policy. She decides that she needs to rethink her practices on food safety. She is glad to learn that Jill intends to follow-up by offering a food safety in-service training for both teaching and food service staff.

Food is a source of nutrition; however, in some situations it can also become a source of illness.

Foodborne illness is the sickness that results from the consumption of contaminated foods. It is estimated that foodborne illnesses account for approximately 48 million illnesses per year, which represents about 1 in 6 Americans and results in about 3,000 deaths per year (Centers for Disease Control and Prevention, 2013b). According to the Centers for Disease Control and Prevention (CDC), the incidence of key foodborne diseases is greatest in children less than 5 years of age (Centers for Disease Control and Prevention, 2013c). Understanding how foods become contaminated and the hazards they pose in the early childhood setting helps teachers prevent situations that put children and staff at risk for a foodborne outbreak. Infants and young children are particularly at risk for food poisoning because their immune systems are not yet fully developed (Mayo Clinic, 2015). In addition, their bodies produce fewer stomach acids compared with adults. Stomach acids offer protection from some infectious microorganisms (Pelton, 2011). For these reasons, young children are at greater risk than adults for becoming sick when exposed to contaminated food, and the illness can become severe and even life threatening. In fact, one of the risk factors identified by the CDC for certain specified bacterial illnesses is attendance at a child care center (Centers for Disease Control, 2010; Jones et al., 2007).

Part of teachers' daily routines often involves the handling of food for children. This entails special responsibilities. In the opening case scenario, Lacey followed food-safe practices in the classroom. However, the weak link that resulted in foodborne illness occurred when oversight of food preparation was left to an individual who was outside the umbrella of the program's food safety procedures. The scenario illustrates the importance of the teacher's role in making informed decisions about food preparation within the program setting and with *any* risky situation that may lead to foodborne illness. Children may be at risk when served food prepared by an individual who has not received food safety training in a home kitchen that has not been inspected and approved by an appropriate health regulatory agency.

In this chapter we provide information to help you understand how to effectively manage food safety. We discuss the nature of foodborne illness and describe the food safety requirements mandated by federal and state regulations that provide the foundation you need to develop and implement an

foodborne illness
an illness caused by eating food that has been contaminated by biological, chemical, or physical contaminants

evidence-based food safety program. We also discuss food safety related to emergencies and food defense to help you be prepared to deal with unplanned events. Finally, we discuss how teachers can help young children learn food safety concepts.

IDENTIFYING HAZARDS THAT CAUSE FOODBORNE ILLNESS

contamination
occurs when something hazardous to health is present in food or drink

Contamination occurs when something hazardous to health is present in food or drink. Food and beverages can become contaminated by a variety of agents, including those that are biological in origin, such as germs. Chemical agents such as pesticides and cleansing agents can accidentally end up in food and pose a health risk as well. Physical hazards to food safety include items that fall into foods, such as fingernails, insects, metal shavings, nails, and glass (Environmental Services Department, Maricopa County Arizona, 2011; Wallace, Sperber, & Mortimore, 2010). A review of the different types of food hazards provides insight into the causes of foodborne illness.

Recognizing Biological Hazards

biological hazards
living microorganisms that contaminate food and cause foodborne illness

Biological hazards include microorganisms that contaminate food and cause serious illness when consumed. These germs, which are too small to be seen by the naked eye, include bacteria, viruses, parasites, and fungi. Germs that contaminate food are by far the greatest hazard to health and occur more often than chemical and physical contamination (National Restaurant Association, 2012).

Understanding how microorganisms create illness prepares teachers to identify risky food safety situations and prevent foodborne outbreaks from occurring. Microorganisms damage the human body in three ways: via infection, intoxication, or toxin-mediated infection (Brown, 2011).

Infection

Infection is most familiar because it is a process that occurs routinely in the early childhood setting. Children "catch a cold" or a "flu bug," and the infection runs its course. A foodborne illness that is classified as an infection is similar in that there is an exposure to germs. The exposure, however, occurs via food instead of by coughing or sneezing. The germs grow in the body and create symptoms such as fever, vomiting, and diarrhea until the body's immune system destroys the pathogens and children are once again healthy.

Table 7-1 defines the three categories of foodborne illness and provides examples of microorganisms that cause sickness as well as steps teachers can take to prevent an outbreak from occurring. *Salmonella*, the microorganism responsible for the outbreak in Lacey's class, falls into the infection classification. Because the egg white in the frosting was not cooked, *Salmonella* bacteria were able to grow, especially because the cupcakes were stored at room temperature.

Teachers who work with children often handle food, so they must understand the food safety risks associated with feeding young children.

Suzanne Clouzeau/Pearson Education, Inc.

TABLE 7-1 A Sample of Foodborne Illnesses and Prevention Strategies for Teachers

Pathogen	Type of Illness	Common Sources	Symptoms	Prevention Strategies for Teachers

Campylobacter jejuni	Infection	Raw chicken, unpasteurized (raw) milk	Diarrhea, stomach pain, fever	1. Serve chicken that is thoroughly cooked.
				2. Do not serve raw milk.
				3. Practice good personal hygiene (hand washing).
				4. Avoid cross-contamination.
				  • Keep raw food of animal origin separate from ready-to-eat food.
				  • Use separate cutting boards for foods of animal origin and produce.
				  • Thoroughly clean work area and utensils after preparing raw food of animal origin.

Clostridium botulinum: foodborne	Intoxication: caused by toxin in the food	Home or commercial canned foods that are not processed appropriately, food from damaged cans	Weakness, dizziness, problems with vision, speaking, swallowing, breathing	1. Do not use home canned foods in your program. 2. Do not use food from damaged cans.
Clostridium botulinum: infant botulism (infants less than 12 months of age)	Toxin-mediated infection: caused by spores of the bacteria that grow in the intestine and release toxins	Honey	Constipation, weakness, weak crying, loss of head control	1. Do not feed honey to infants less than 12 months of age. 2. Do not serve food containing honey, such as honey yogurt, to infants less than 12 months of age.
Clostridium perfringens	Toxin-mediated infection	Meat, poultry, gravy, temperature abuse of prepared foods	Severe diarrhea, stomach pain	1. Make sure food is properly cooked, cooled, and reheated. 2. Hold foods at proper temperatures. 3. Divide leftover foods into small quantities and refrigerate promptly.
Escherichia coli, Shiga toxin producing (E. coli O157:H7)	Toxin-mediated infection	Raw or undercooked beef, unpasteurized (raw) milk or apple cider, contaminated foods such as sprouts and leafy greens	Diarrhea (can be bloody), stomach pain, vomiting, kidney failure and death in severe cases	1. Check that meat is thoroughly cooked before serving it. 2. Do not serve raw milk or apple cider or sprouts. 3. Practice good personal hygiene. 4. Avoid cross-contamination (see above).
Norovirus	Infection	Leafy greens, fresh fruits, and shellfish; foods exposed to this virus	Diarrhea, vomiting, stomach pain	1. Do not come to work or handle food if sick. 2. Practice good personal hygiene. 3. Carefully wash fruits and vegetables and cook shellfish.
Salmonella	Infection	Raw or undercooked eggs, poultry, or meat; dairy products; produce such as spinach, sprouts, melon	Diarrhea, vomiting, fever, stomach pain	1. Do not come to work or handle food if sick. 2. Do not serve poultry and meat that is not well-cooked or raw milk products. 3. Use pasteurized eggs in cooking activities. 4. Thoroughly wash produce and avoid raw sprouts. 5. Avoid cross-contamination (see above).
Staphylococcus aureus	Intoxication	Foods contaminated by handling (sliced meat, eggs, tuna, chicken salads, pastries, sandwiches), unpasteurized (raw) milk	Diarrhea, vomiting, stomach pain	1. Practice good personal hygiene. 2. Do not prepare food if you have infection of the nose or eye or on your hands/wrists. 3. Make sure food is properly cooked, cooled, and reheated. 4. Hold foods at proper temperatures. 5. Divide leftover foods into small quantities and refrigerate promptly.

Sources: A–Z Index for Foodborne, Waterborne, and Mycotic Diseases, Centers for Disease Control and Prevention, 2012, from http://www.cdc.gov/nczved/divisions/dfbmd/diseases/index.html; *Essentials of food safety and sanitation*, 4th ed., by D. McSwane, N. R. Rue, and R. Linton, 2005, Upper Saddle River, NJ: Pearson; *Servsafe coursebook*, 5th ed., National Restaurant Association, 2010, Chicago, IL; *Bad bug book: Foodborne pathogenic microorganisms and natural toxins.* 2nd edition. United States Food and Drug Administration, Center for Food Safety and Nutrition, 2012, from http://www.fda.gov/downloads/Food/FoodborneIllnessContaminants/UCM297627.pdf.

Intoxication

Intoxication refers to foodborne illness caused by microorganisms that grow on the food and release toxins (poisons) into it. This in turn produces the symptoms of illness. This type of food poisoning can be very dangerous because the toxin is not destroyed by cooking or the toxin is highly lethal. For example, the microorganism responsible for the foodborne illness called *botulism* creates a toxin that causes paralysis and is considered one of the most dangerous biological hazards known to man (U.S. Department of Agriculture Food Safety and Inspection Service, 2013b). Strategies that teachers can use to avoid the production of toxins in food are listed in Table 7-1.

Toxin-Mediated Infection

The final classification of foodborne illness is the toxin-mediated infection, which has features of both infection and intoxication. When food containing a harmful microorganism is consumed, the germs begin to reproduce and then release toxins in the gastrointestinal tract (Brown, 2011). For example, *Escherichia coli* (*E. coli*) is a diverse group of bacteria that includes both harmless and illness-producing strains. The *E. coli* O157:H7 strain produces a toxin-mediated infection (Shiga toxin) and has gained media attention because of the outbreaks associated with ground beef, spinach, hazelnuts, and Romaine lettuce (Centers for Disease Control and Prevention, 2013a). Another strain of Shiga toxin-producing *E. coli* (*E. coli* O104:H4) resulted in 4,321 cases of illness and 50 deaths in Germany and eventually was linked to the ingestion of raw sprouts (Buchholz et al., 2011). When food containing *E. coli* is cooked to appropriate temperatures, the microorganisms are destroyed and foodborne illness does not occur. The risk of illness, however, remains for food that is not cooked prior to meal service, such as the sprouts.

WHAT IF . . . food arrived in the classroom from the kitchen and you noticed that the hamburgers appeared pink and undone? What would you do to ensure that children do not get a foodborne illness? What would you do if a child has already taken a bite?

Fresh fruits and vegetables have increasingly been identified as sources of foodborne illness. The use of fresh manure for fertilizing, unsanitary water for cleaning, and unsanitary food-processing practices are all factors that increase the risk of foodborne outbreaks from produce (Centers for Disease Control and Prevention, 2013b; Hunting & Gleason, 2012). Although washing produce can help reduce the number of pathogens, it will not completely eliminate the risk.

Food irradiation can be used to control spoilage and eliminate germs that cause foodborne illness (U.S. Environmental Protection Agency, 20141b). The FDA (U.S. Environmental Protection Agency, 20121c) has approved the use of irradiation as a means to make certain fresh produce and meats safer from contamination by microorganisms such as *E. coli*. Labels must indicate when food has been irradiated by displaying the irradiation logo.

Recognizing Chemical Hazards

chemical hazards
unnatural chemicals that are present in foods and pose a health risk when consumed

Chemical hazards are contaminants in foods that pose a health risk when consumed. Chemical contamination can occur during the growing, harvesting, processing, and storage of foods. Examples of chemical contaminants that come in contact with food during growing and harvesting include pesticides and fertilizers. During processing, chemical contaminants in food include lubricants, cleansing detergents, polishes, and sanitizers (National Restaurant Association,

2012). Chemical contamination can also occur when food is not stored appropriately. In the early childhood setting, a potential risk for chemical contamination occurs when cleaning agents are stored near food. Chemical agents can spill onto foods, causing contamination. There is also a chance for mistaken identity when cleaning agents are stored in containers that look similar to items of food (Figure 7-1).

Recognizing Physical Hazards

Physical hazards are items that get into foods that may cause injury or illness. Examples include glass, rocks, metal shavings, staples, bandages, insects, hair, fingernails, and jewelry. In a children's program, physical contaminants might include beads or glitter. On-site strategies that can minimize the risk of physical contamination of foods include wearing caps or hairnets, removing jewelry when preparing and serving food, maintaining kitchen equipment, and practicing pest control. In addition, before and after any type of meal service, teachers should carefully clean tables that are used for both school activities and eating to avoid the chance of introducing physical contaminants to food.

Recognizing Food Allergens and Intolerances as a Special Type of Hazard

Some children face an additional food safety risk that is unique to them and harmless to most others: food allergies. Children with food allergies are at risk for exposure to allergens, which can have life-threatening consequences. In Chapter 6, you learned about the various aspects of food preparation and menu planning that must be taken into consideration for children with food allergies. Food allergies are also a food safety issue. Teachers must read food labels carefully to determine whether the allergens are present in the foods being offered to the child with allergies. Although the Food Allergen Labeling and Consumer Protection Act (FALCPA) requires that the eight major food allergens (milk, wheat, egg, soy, fish, shellfish, peanuts, tree nuts) be listed on food labels, more than 160 known food allergens can trigger allergic reactions (U.S. Food and Drug Administration, 2014a). Careful label reading is especially important for children who suffer less common allergies. For example, consider the following situation:

> *Jan, a teacher in a toddler classroom, discovered how important it is to check on potential food allergens. A 2-year-old in her class has a mild allergy to cranberries. The toddler began to display irritability and stomach discomfort. The child's father believed it was caused by something the toddler ate at school. Jan asked the food service manager to check the labels of all products used to prepare meals for any form of cranberries. The next day the food service manager reported back. In an effort to use up extra cranberry sauce, the cook had been mixing it with grape jelly and serving it with breakfast. The vendor immediately stopped this practice.*

Reading labels is just one aspect of ensuring food safety for children who require special diets. Teachers must also be watchful for **cross-contamination**. Cross-contamination in the context of food allergies occurs when a nonallergenic food comes in contact with an allergen during cooking, baking, or meal service. For example, if ham is sliced on the same machine used to slice cheese, this will create a situation of cross-contamination that puts children who are allergic to

FIGURE 7-1

Food and Cleaning Agents Should Not Be Stored Together Because of the Risk of Chemical Contamination and the Potential for Mistakenly Using the Wrong Product

physical hazards
items that fall into foods that may cause injury or illness

Pearson Education

CLASSROOM CONNECTION

Watch this video to hear teachers describe precautions used in their programs to ensure food safety. What specific steps are taken to protect children with food allergies?

cross-contamination
the transfer of harmful microorganisms from one food to another food or from an infected person to food. It can also refer to food contaminated with an allergen

PROGRESSIVE PROGRAMS & PRACTICES

Addressing Food Allergies

By Sharon Gibson, Corvallis School District Food and Nutrition Services

The Corvallis School District Food and Nutrition Services provide approximately 5,000 meals in 17 schools and an array of other community programs daily. A small, but increasing, percentage of these meals are for children who have food allergies or intolerances.

One major food allergy with significant consequences is associated with peanuts or peanut oil. Even though PB&J sandwiches are served in the cafeterias, special precautions are taken at the Central Kitchen where they are prepared in a secluded area to avoid cross-contamination and then individually wrapped in cellophane. Once they are delivered to the schools, only one student worker is assigned to hand them out and not to touch any other food or area. Many cafeterias designate a peanut-free zone where children can sit without concern. The lunches children choose to bring from home often contain a PB&J sandwich, so the complete elimination of foods containing peanuts in the cafeteria setting is not feasible. There are ways, however, to decrease the likelihood of peanut exposure.

Concerned parents communicate with their child's school about the severity of their allergies and establish a food allergy action plan with input from the child's physician. They also educate their children to be constantly aware of any potential hazards in their environment.

School staff must do their part as well. Carefully scrubbing down lunch tables, prohibiting the sharing of food, and eliminating homemade celebration snacks where ingredients are unknown are the best precautionary practices for decreasing the risk of allergen exposure. When children are offered nutritious, allergen-free meals in a safe school setting, they are less distracted and have the energy and attention they need to learn at school.

Monkey Business Images/Shutterstock

WHAT IF . . .

you had a new child entering your program who needed a gluten-free diet? What information would you need to gather before the child enters your program? What would you do if you were unsure whether a food item contained gluten?

milk at risk when they eat the meat. Cross-contamination can also occur when children share eating utensils, bottles, cups, or food. Teachers who are careful label readers and use safe practices when preparing food for children with allergies create a safe food environment for all children in their care. See the *Progressive Program & Practices* feature that describes how a school district in Corvallis, Oregon, minimizes the risk of cross-contamination of peanut products in its central kitchen and cafeterias.

CHECK YOUR UNDERSTANDING 7.1

Click here to check your understanding of the hazards responsible for foodborne illness.

UNDERSTANDING FOOD SAFETY REGULATIONS AND GUIDELINES

Rules to keep food safe originated in ancient times. For example, some of the religious food laws and practices discussed in the previous chapter may have had their foundation in food safety. Rules and regulations that govern food safety protect children from illness and harm and are especially important in settings that serve this vulnerable age group. Food safety is regulated by federal, state, and county agencies. For example, it is not only convenient but also a requirement that all establishments in which food service occurs have hand washing sinks (National Restaurant Association, 2012).

Federal, State, and County Roles in Food Safety Regulations

Federal food safety laws are established by Congress and implemented through regulations imposed by federal agencies. The FDA Food Safety Modernization Act uses scientific evidence to strengthen food safety systems (that is, producing, processing, transporting, and preparing foods). It also focuses on prevention, more oversight of imported foods, increased inspection of facilities, and a strengthened role of the FDA in food recalls (U.S. Department of Health and Human Services, U.S. Food and Drug Administration, 2014). Food safety regulations outline the specific legal requirements related to various categories of food safety (Marriott & Gravani, 2006; U.S. Department of Agriculture Food Safety and Inspection Service, 2014a). The federal food safety regulations provide the model for state and county guidelines for all establishments that serve food, including early childhood settings. Figure 7-2 summarizes

FIGURE 7-2 The Roles of Federal Programs That Oversee Food Safety

Centers for Disease Control and Prevention (CDC)

- Leads investigations of outbreaks that involve large numbers of the population over multiple states or are foodborne illnesses that are severe or unusual.
- Coordinates PulseNet, a national network of public health and food regulatory agency laboratories that identify foodborne bacteria.

Environmental Protection Agency (EPA)

- Prevents air, water and land pollution.
- Helps avert chemical contamination of food through regulation of pesticide use.
- Sets national standards and develops regulations to support environmental laws.

U.S. Department of Agriculture's (USDA) Food Safety and Inspection Service (FSIS)

- Regulates and sets the standards for the food safety of meats, poultry and egg products.
- Investigates and announces recalls of any outbreak of foodborne illness related to meats, poultry, and egg products.

Food and Drug Administration (FDA)

- Assures that all foods (except meats, poultry and egg products) are safe, wholesome, sanitary and properly labeled.
- Investigates any outbreak of foodborne illness (except meats, poultry and egg products) and issues mandatory recalls of any outbreak of foodborne illness related to all foods except meats, poultry and egg products.
- Regulates the food service industry through the publication and enforcement of the FDA Food Code, a set of national food safety standards.
- Implements the FDA Food Modernization Act of 2011 by creating stronger prevention and regulatory controls for the U.S. food supply as well as imported foods and is mandated to create an integrated national food safety system in partnership with other federal, state and local agencies.

Sources: About Food Safety and Inspection Service, U.S. Department of Agriculture, 2012, from http://www.fsis.usda.gov/about_fsis/index.asp; Foodborne Outbreak Investigations—Key Players in Foodborne Outbreak Response, Centers for Disease Control and Prevention, 2011, from http://www.cdc.gov/foodsafety/outbreaks/investigating -outbreaks/key-players.html; The FDA Food Code, U.S. Food and Drug Administration, 2015, from http://www.fda.gov/Food/GuidanceRegulation/RetailFoodProtection /FoodCode/. About FDA, U.S. Food and Drug Administration, 2015, from http://www.fda.gov/AboutFDA/; Background on the FDA Food Safety Modernization Act (FSMA) U.S. Food and Drug Administration, 2015, from http://www.fda.gov/Food/GuidanceRegulation/FSMA/ucm239907.htm; and U.S. Environmental Protection Agency, 2012, Our Mission and What We Do; U.S. Environmental Protection Agency, 2011, from http://www.epa.gov/aboutepa/whatwedo.html.

the roles of federal agencies in overseeing the safety of the U.S. food supply. The predominant responsibility for monitoring and investigating foodborne illness, however, rests with city or county and state health agencies (Centers for Disease Control and Prevention, 2013a). State agencies work with the FDA and other federal agencies to implement food safety standards for foods produced within the state's borders. State or county health agencies conduct inspections at restaurants, grocery stores, retail food establishments, child care centers, and schools (Orange County North Carolina, 2015).

Impact of Food Safety Regulations

Federal food safety regulations have a direct impact on early childhood programs. For example, the Child Nutrition and WIC Reauthorization Act mandates that all schools participating in the National School Lunch or School Breakfast Program must obtain food safety inspections twice a year (U.S. Department of Agriculture, Food and Nutrition Service, 2014). In addition, funding sources such as Head Start and the Child and Adult Care Food Program have food safety standards in place. If a program receiving their funds does not comply with standards, the program risks losing its funding. Child care licensure by state agencies is contingent on passing health inspections that include an evaluation of food production sites. Efforts such as these implement food safety regulations and improve the quality of food service in children's settings.

Teachers and others who prepare and serve food in school settings must be familiar with the agency that monitors food safety in the child's setting. In most cases, this agency is the local health department. The health department is a program's ally in creating a food safe environment. Creating a strong working relationship with the county health department sanitarians, or workers, has many benefits because they:

- Assist programs in developing effective food safety policies and standard operating procedures.
- Are a resource for food safety and foodborne illness-related questions and issues.
- Conduct inspections that support school goals for promoting food safe environments.
- Investigate foodborne illness outbreaks and assist programs in developing steps to control the spread of infection.
- Help programs identify when a foodborne outbreak needs to be reported to state or federal health agencies (U.S. Department of Agriculture, Food and Nutrition Service, 2014a).

WHAT IF . . .

there was a suspected foodborne illness in your program? Who would you contact? What additional training would you need to be able to identify the signs of a potential foodborne illness? How would you try to minimize the spread of illness?

Teachers and health department personnel have a common goal: children's health and safety. A close working relationship reduces the likelihood of food safety problems. If a concern is identified, health department personnel can provide timely expert advice to limit an illness outbreak. In the opening case scenario, the health department was a key resource. With the sanitarian's help the program was able to identify the source of illness. The *Health Hint* provides another example of the benefits of collaboration between the health department and children's programs or schools when the potential for illness threatens.

MINIMIZING FOOD CONTAMINATION IN THE EARLY CHILDHOOD SETTING

Program inspection by regulatory agencies helps create an environment of knowledge and accountability, which is necessary to support food safety goals. However, an even more important goal for programs is to develop a system of self-inspection that implements the most up-to-date food safety recommendations and monitors the safety of foods. The regulations that pertain to food safety are ever-changing based on new technologies and public demand in response to food safety events. For example, after an *E. coli* O157:H7 outbreak in 1993 that occurred in the Pacific Northwest as a result of hamburgers that were not cooked to proper internal temperatures (the outbreak caused 400 illnesses and 4 deaths), a more evidence-based approach to food safety was demanded, resulting in the development of the Hazard and Analysis Critical Control Point (HACCP) system approach (U.S. Department of Agriculture, Food Safety and Inspection Service, 2014a).

Hazard and Analysis Critical Control Point (HACCP) system
a proactive food safety system that identifies potentially hazardous foods and evaluates food safety risk during food preparation and service

The HACCP is a proactive, preventive system for tracking food through the many phases of production, processing, preparation, and service and evaluating the potential for exposure to contamination. The origin of HACCP has its roots in the U.S. space program where scientific principles were used to ensure that foods fed to astronauts during space missions were absolutely safe (Goodrich, Schneider, Schmidt, & University of Florida, IFAS Extension, 2008). The FDA and the USDA require the use of HACCP procedures in certain food-processing industries. For example, the use of HACCP is mandatory in plants processing seafood, fruit juice, meat, and poultry (U.S. Food and Drug Administration, 2014b).

HACCP procedures can be adapted to any establishment that is involved in food service, including schools. Schools represent the first retail food service establishment in which HACCP was mandated. Currently early childhood programs such as child care centers can voluntarily participate in HACCP food safety programs and use the state and local health departments to understand local food safety requirements (Riggins & Barrett, 2008). Some early childhood programs contract with local

---

HEALTH HINT Managing a Foodborne Illness Outbreak

An outbreak of Norwalk virus was linked to a local fast-food establishment where a recently ill employee had handled lettuce without gloves. Within days, a number of families in the preschool classroom reported their child had been diagnosed with Norwalk virus. One child spent the night in the hospital due to dehydration.

The teacher called the health department for advice. In addition to providing information about the symptoms of Norwalk virus and methods of transmission, the following preventive steps were recommended:

- Inform all staff not to come to work if they are sick.
- Direct food service staff to take extra precautions when handling dirty dishware.
- Wash and sanitize toys and surfaces in the classroom using a chlorine bleach solution.
- Remind teachers, food service staff, and children to wash hands frequently, especially after using the toilet and changing diapers and before eating or preparing food.
- Send home an illness notice explaining the signs and symptoms of Norwalk virus. Notify families that no child or staff should return to the program until 72 hours after his or her last symptoms.

Although a few additional cases occurred in the program, the spread of the illness was limited due to the health department's expert advice and the teacher's quick action.

Sources: *Norovirus: Technical Fact Sheet, Centers for Disease Control and Prevention*, 2010, from http://www.cdc.gov/norovirus/hcp/index.html and *Making the News in Benton County: Norwalk-Like Virus Health Alert*, Benton County Health Department, April 27, 2006, from http://www.co.benton.or.us/read_article.php?d=&p=72.

school districts to provide their food. Food received from public school kitchens has been prepared using HACCP food safety recommendations. Whether a program receives meals through a contracted meal service, prepares food on-site, or serves meals prepared in a home kitchen, it is important to understand and implement HACCP food safety recommendations.

Understanding HACCP Principles

HACCP is a plan for organizing safety measures to ensure that all feasible strategies are used to keep food safe. If a cook called in sick and a teacher was pulled from the classroom to prepare lunch for 50 children, how would the teacher know what to do to make sure food was safely prepared? If a HACCP system is in place, all the procedures involved in preparing a meal (cooking, serving, and cooling foods) have been analyzed and hazardous foods identified. Any risky steps in food preparation have been labeled *critical control points*. This designation is a warning that extra attention is needed to maintain food safety. This warning comes with guidelines, or *critical limits*, that list specific criteria that must be met for food to remain safe. For example, it specifies the temperature a food must reach before it can be served. To make sure the HACCP guidelines are met consistently, a monitoring system must be in place that can be verified as effective. This monitoring system outlines what needs to be done when guidelines are not met (corrective actions) and includes procedures for documentation and record keeping. The HACCP plan of action described above is based on seven basic principles that are summarized in Figure 7-3 and discussed in more detail next (U.S. Food and Drug Administration, 2014b).

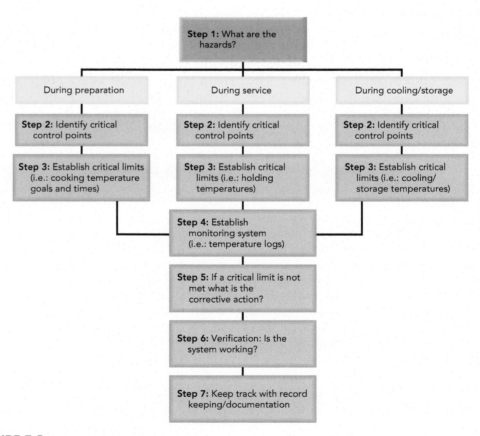

FIGURE 7-3
The Seven Steps of HACCP

It is important to understand these principles because staff who work in early childhood program or school settings are responsible for keeping food safe from the time it enters the program until the time it is served. Teachers are a part of the system of accountability.

Principle 1: Utilizing Hazard Analysis

The first principle of hazard analysis involves evaluating the processes used to prepare foods that might cause safety issues and identifying foods on the menu that are most likely to be hazardous because of their ability to sustain microbial growth if contaminated. Foods that readily support the growth of microorganisms that cause spoilage or illness when improperly handled are called **potentially hazardous foods**. Pathogens such as bacteria need certain conditions to flourish, such as moist foods that are rich in protein and carbohydrates and contain little or no acid. These types of foods support the growth of microorganisms within a certain temperature range and time period of exposure to that temperature range (usually about two to four hours for bacteria) (National Restaurant Association, 2012).

Some potentially hazardous foods are listed in Figure 7-4. Recognizing which foods are potentially hazardous is important so that appropriate management strategies for monitoring food safety can be established. For example, some of the foods served for lunch in Lacey's classroom in the opening case scenario were potentially hazardous. The turkey on the sandwich, the watermelon, and the milk are foods that require careful management. Foods less likely to cause illness are the orange slices and bread served at the supermarket during the field trip because oranges are acidic and bread is low in moisture content. Both time and temperature factors came into play when the cupcakes covered with an egg-based frosting were allowed to sit at room temperature overnight. Potentially hazardous food should not be left at room temperature for more than two hours or one hour if the temperature is 90°F (32°C) or above (American Academy of Pediatrics, American Public Health Association, National Resource Center for Health and Safety in Child Care and Early Education, 2011; U.S. Department of Agriculture, Food Safety and Inspection Service, 2014b). Teachers can prepare to monitor potentially hazardous foods by circling them on the menu so that they can quickly identify which foods need to be observed more closely (Figure 7-5).

potentially hazardous foods
foods that readily support the growth of microorganisms that cause spoilage or illness if food safety practices are not in place and need time and temperature control

---

FIGURE 7-4   Examples of Potentially Hazardous Foods

- Raw or heat-treated foods of animal origin: meat, poultry, fish, shellfish, and crustaceans.
- Milk and egg products (such as custards and cream fillings).
- Leafy greens and tomatoes that have been cut.
- Heat treated foods of vegetable origin: cooked rice, pasta, potatoes, vegetables, and beans.
- Cut or sliced melons.
- Raw sprouts.
- Unprocessed garlic and oil mixtures.
- Any foods with a water, protein, and lower acid content (neutral or slightly acid pH) that make them more likely to support microbial growth.

Sources: The FDA Food Code, U.S. Food and Drug Administration, 2015, from http://www.fda.gov/Food/GuidanceRegulation/Retail FoodProtection/FoodCode/ and *Servsafe coursebook*, 5th edition, 2010, Chicago, IL: National Restaurant Association.

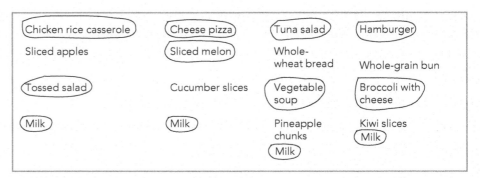

FIGURE 7-5

Lunch Menu with Potentially Hazardous Foods Identified

Once hazardous foods on the menu are identified, it is important to consider how these foods are handled during food preparation. Each food item has a different type of risk associated with its preparation process. Risk is related to the number of times the food item moves through the **temperature danger zone**, the temperature at which microorganisms such as bacteria are more likely to grow—41°F to 135°F (5°C to 57°C) (Figure 7-6) (U.S. Department of Health and Human Services, Public Health Service, U.S. Food and Drug Administration, 2014).

In an effort to promote food safety in all types of establishments where food is consumed, the FDA created a simplified variation of the HACCP food safety system that the USDA promotes for use in schools. It is called the **process approach** (U.S. Department of Health and Human Services Food and Drug Administration Center for Food Safety and Applied Nutrition, 2014). This approach establishes guidelines for the processes that different foods undergo when being prepared. The USDA identifies these food processes as follows:

- *Food preparation with no-cook process:* The food is not cooked and does not enter the temperature danger zone. Examples of foods that are subject to this process include cold cuts, tuna salad, and cheese.

- *Food preparation for same-day service:* The food is heated and served the same day and goes through the temperature danger zone once. Examples include hamburgers, French toast, and scrambled eggs.

- *Food preparation using complex food preparation:* Food is cooked, chilled, and reheated, going through the temperature danger zone two or more times (U.S. Department of Health and Human Services, Food and Drug Administration Center for Food Safety and Applied Nutrition, 2014). Examples include soups, spaghetti sauce, casseroles, and dried beans (that are cooked, chilled, and later used in a burrito recipe).

The overall goal of the process approach is to allow menu planners to group foods according to how they are prepared and served, evaluate the risks, and develop strategies to minimize the time food spends in the temperature danger zone, thereby decreasing the chance of foodborne illness. Food service personnel are responsible for overseeing the process approach for foods served in early childhood centers and schools. Family child care providers (and those serving children in occasional groups) need to identify hazardous foods as well as the process used in preparation to minimize food safety risks when planning

temperature danger zone
the temperature range between 41°F and 135°F (5°C and 57°C) at which microorganisms such as bacteria are likely to grow

process approach
the process of grouping menu items by the method of food preparation into three different processes that are distinguished by the number of times the food item goes through the food temperature danger zone

FIGURE 7-6

Food Temperature Danger Zone

menus and cooking activities that use food in the classroom setting. Teachers also support the process approach by ensuring that food delivered to the classroom has been held at appropriate temperatures prior to service and is served immediately to children.

Principle 2: Identify the Critical Control Points

Critical control points (CCPs) are points in the procedure of food processing, preparation, and service at which food handlers can control or reduce food hazard risks (Schmidt & Newslow, 2009). The points at which control can be established occur during the critical steps in preparing recipes or when holding food prior to meal service. Tools used to manage CCPs include thermometers, refrigerators and refrigeration carts, freezers, ovens, warming carts, and steam tables. For example, a CCP for a program that receives food from an off-site kitchen includes taking the temperature of the delivered food and accepting it only when it is delivered at an appropriate temperature. The temperature of food is measured at the time of delivery to ensure that it is still safe to eat.

critical control points (CCPs)
points in time during food processing, preparation, and service at which control can be exerted to minimize the development of a food hazard risk

Principle 3: Establish Critical Limits

To ensure safety, critical limits (CLs) must be identified for each CCP identified in food processing. The CL is an indicator of whether the control measure is actually managing the identified food safety risk. Critical limits must be measurable, accurate, and realistic and must be based on evidence-based research (Schmidt & Newslow, 2009). CLs include the temperatures and times for cooking, holding, cooling, and reheating foods and ingredients in a recipe. For example, a teacher who has children prepare burritos for a classroom cooking activity needs to know the appropriate temperature to hold this food if the activity includes families joining children later for lunch.

critical limit (CL)
an indicator used to establish whether the control measure identified for a critical control point is actually controlling the food safety risk. Critical limits must be measurable, accurate, and realistic and must be based on evidence-based research

The CL represents the highest and lowest range for a food safety standard established for a critical control point. This information is available in the Food Code. The Food Code is a set of food safety guidelines established by the FDA and the USDA to promote food safety (U.S. Department of Health and Human Services, Public Health Service, U.S. Food and Drug Administration, 2014). For example, the code identifies the critical limit for baking chicken as follows: It must reach an internal temperature of 165°F (74°C) for 15 seconds and maintain a temperature above 135°F (57°C) until the chicken is served (U.S. Department of Health and Human Services, Public Health Service, U.S. Food and Drug Administration, 2014). The USDA website provides standardized recipes for child nutrition programs that offer guidance on food preparation steps and identifies CCPs and their recommended CLs (U.S. Department of Agriculture, Food and Nutrition Service, 2014b). See Figure 7-7.

Food Code
a food safety model developed by the USDA and FDA to be used by state and county regulatory agencies to develop rules to prevent foodborne illness

Principle 4: Establish a Monitoring System

A monitoring system is needed to ensure that food is checked during all aspects of its flow through the processing system—from delivery through storage, food preparation, and service. Examples of monitoring methods include recording the temperature of foods at delivery and during cooking, cooling, and reheating. The temperature maintained by heating and cooling equipment is also measured. A monitoring system is a crucial aspect of the HACCP plan because deviation from an established critical limit, such as food temperatures during cooking, needs to be

FIGURE 7-7   Example of a Bean Burrito Recipe That Uses HACCP with Critical Control Points and Critical Limits

Ingredients	Amounts for 50 Servings
Dried kidney beans	7 pounds
Onions, chopped	¾ cup, 2 Tablespoons
Tomato paste	3 cups, 2 Tablespoons
Granulated garlic	1 Tablespoon
Water	1 quart
Chili powder	3 Tablespoons
Cumin	2 Tablespoons
Pepper	2 teaspoons
Paprika	1 Tablespoon
Onion powder	1 Tablespoon
Low-fat cheese, shredded	3 pounds
Tortillas	50

Directions:

1. Soak beans overnight in 12¼ quarts of water. Cover and refrigerate.
2. Drain beans and add again 12¼ quarts of water and 1 tablespoon salt.
3. Boil gently for 2 hours until tender.
4. Use immediately or cool to 70°F (21°C) within 2 hours and from 70°F (21°C) to 41°F (5°C) or lower within an additional 4 hours.
5. Combine onions, tomato paste, chili powder, cumin, paprika, onion powder, and pepper. Blend and simmer in 1 quart water for 15 minutes.
6. Puree beans until smooth in consistency. Combine with ingredients in step 5 and shredded cheese.
7. Steam tortillas until warm.
8. Place ½ cup beans onto tortilla and fold.
9. Place on a pan, seam side down.
10. Heat to 165°F (74°C) or higher for at least 15 seconds.
11. Hold for hot service at 135°F (57°C) or higher.

Note: Red indicates a critical control point or a step in the recipe that deserves careful attention. Blue indicates a critical limit or standard that must be met for the food to remain safe. If beans are chilled and used at a later time to make the bean burritos, this represents a complex process of food preparation.

Source: USDA Recipes for Child Care by the U.S. Department of Agriculture, Food and Nutrition Service, Child Nutrition Programs June 2009, from http://www.fns.usda.gov/tn/Resources/childcare_recipes.html.

identified and action taken to avoid a potentially hazardous food safety situation. Figure 7-8 shows appropriate cooking temperatures for foods.

Principle 5: Establish a Corrective Action Plan

corrective action plan
a plan of action that must be taken immediately if a lapse occurs in the critical limits established for a critical control point of a menu item

A **corrective action plan** outlines the steps that must be taken immediately if there is a lapse in the identified critical limit for a particular menu item's critical control point. In the early childhood setting, for example, someone might discover that the hot food holding cart had been unplugged and the bean burritos had not been held at the required temperature. The corrective action would be to discard the burritos.

Principle 6: Establish Procedures for Verification

verification procedures
procedures used to determine if a HACCP system is working effectively; can include, for example, a review of records and inspections

Verification procedures are needed to verify, or make sure, that the food has been managed according to the five principles listed above. This step ensures that the

		TEMPERATURE (F/C)	TYPE OF FOOD
		165/74	Ground turkey and chicken Whole turkey, chicken, duck and goose Poultry breasts, thighs, leg, wings Stuffing, soups, stews leftovers and casseroles
		160/71	Ground beef, pork, veal and lamb Egg dishes (cook eggs until yolk and white are firm)
		145/63*	Fresh beef, veal, lamb such as steaks, roasts, chops Fresh pork and raw ham Fish (cook until flesh is opaque and separates easily with a fork)
		140/60	Precooked ham

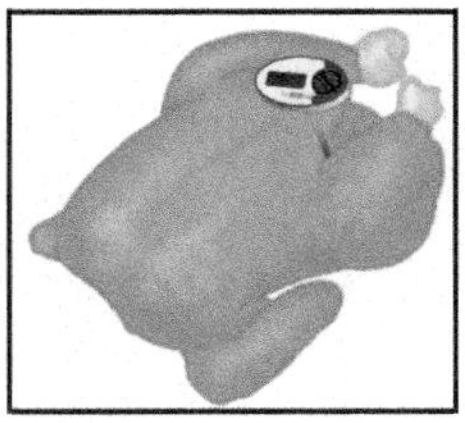

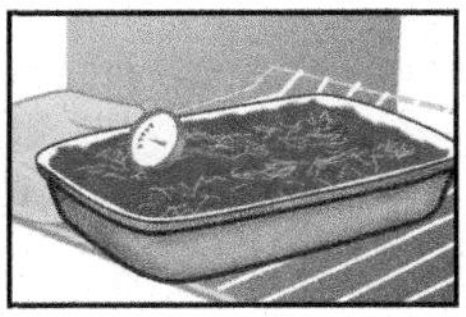

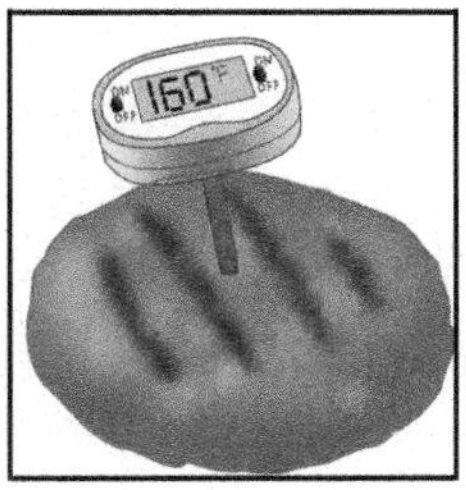

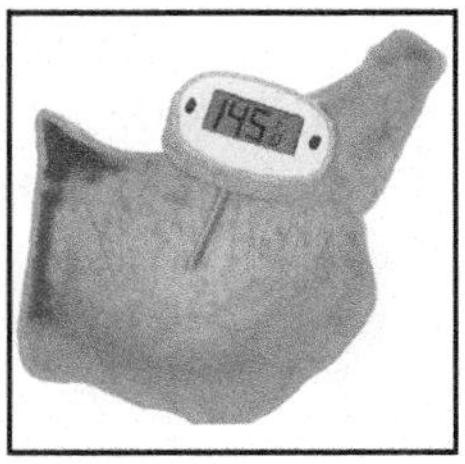

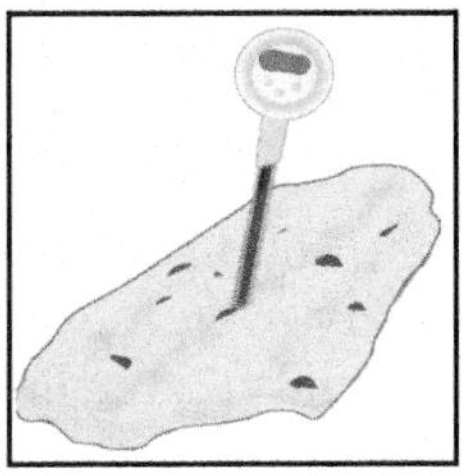

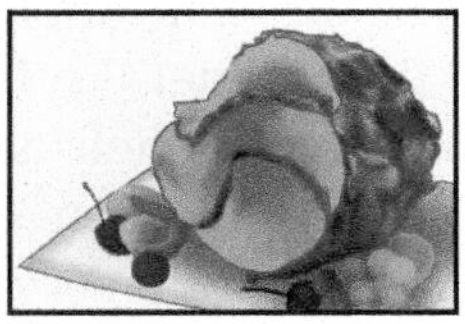

*all meats cooked to 145°F need a rest time 3 minutes which means the temperature either remains constant of increases helping to destroy pathogens

FIGURE 7-8

Recommended Cooking Temperatures for Food

Sources: Use A Food Thermometer U.S. Department of Agriculture & Food Safety and Inspection Service, 2011, from http://www.fsis.usda.gov/wps/portal/fsis/topics/food-safety-education/get-answers/food-safety-fact-sheets/appliances-and-thermometers; Safe Minimum Cooking Temperatures, FoodSafety.gov, 2011, from http://www.foodsafety.gov/keep/charts/mintemp.html and USDA Blog » Cooking Meat? Check the New Recommended Temperatures, U.S. Department of Agriculture, 2011, from http://blogs.usda.gov/2011/05/25/cooking-meat-check-the-new-recommended-temperatures/.

HACCP plan is working. Conducting inspections observing food storage, production, and service procedures are all methods of verification. The program director can accomplish this by doing spot checks when foods are delivered to see if food handlers are taking temperatures or by monitoring temperature logs.

Principle 7: Maintain a System of Record Keeping

Record keeping is an important aspect of the HACCP process. Written records confirm that each required step is conducted appropriately. For example, in the opening case scenario, the sanitarian was able to rule out the school food service as a source of infection in Lacey's class by looking at HACCP logs and records. Taking the temperature of foods at delivery and recording the temperature on a temperature receiving log or on the delivery invoice are other methods that ensure the completion of this step.

Any teacher who consistently handles and prepares food must participate in a food safety plan. In some settings, teachers may not work directly with food and may not need to consider the HACCP procedures routinely. However, understanding how the food safety system works in the early childhood setting or school ensures that teachers are prepared to be a vital link in the chain that supports food safety and protects young children.

Understanding Standard Operating Procedures

Although the HACCP system provides specific strategies for handling foods to prevent foodborne illness, the system cannot be effective if certain general food safety practices are not part of the routine procedures of the food service operation. For example, policies for maintaining a clean kitchen, wearing head coverings during food preparation, sanitizing the kitchen work surfaces and children's eating surfaces, and incorporating basic hand washing guidelines are all examples of general food safety procedures that support safe food handling. In the HACCP food safety system, these are called standard operating procedures (SOPs) (Iowa State University Extension, 2015).

Standard operating procedures are important in early childhood settings. Programs and schools often have policies and procedures based on best practices that address food safety and sanitation. However, SOPs differ from general school policies in that they are written in a consistent HACCP format, which includes a description for monitoring, implementation of corrective action, verification, and record keeping. In a review of trends that affect food safety in retail food service, including schools and child care centers, researchers found that the three most common risk factors for foodborne outbreaks are:

- Improper holding times and temperatures of foods.
- Poor personal hygiene.
- Cross-contamination (the transfer of harmful germs from one food to another, from an infected person to food, or from dirty equipment to food) (U.S. Food and Drug Administration, 2014).

Establishing food safety programs and complying with basic SOPs eliminate these types of risk factors. In the upcoming section, we review general food safety and SOPs that apply to the early child care setting by evaluating the flow of food within a program.

PREVENTING CONTAMINATION AT EACH STAGE OF FOOD HANDLING

Teachers directly involved in the purchase, storage, preparation, and service of foods, such as those who work in the family child care setting, require a detailed commitment to ensuring food safety. All teachers who handle food for young children need to understand the risks associated with each phase of the flow of food.

A Matter of ETHICS

A concerned teacher has been giving leftover food from lunch to needy families in his classroom. Consider this ethical dilemma by reflecting on the risks of food insecurity versus food safety. How does the first principle in the Ethical Responsibilities to Children in the NAEYC Code of Ethical Conduct "Above all, we shall not harm children" guide your thinking?

standard operating procedures (SOPs) written procedures related to food service tasks that help to maintain food safety

CHECK YOUR UNDERSTANDING 7.2

Click here to check your understanding of food safety regulations and guidelines and their impact on food service in the early childhood setting.

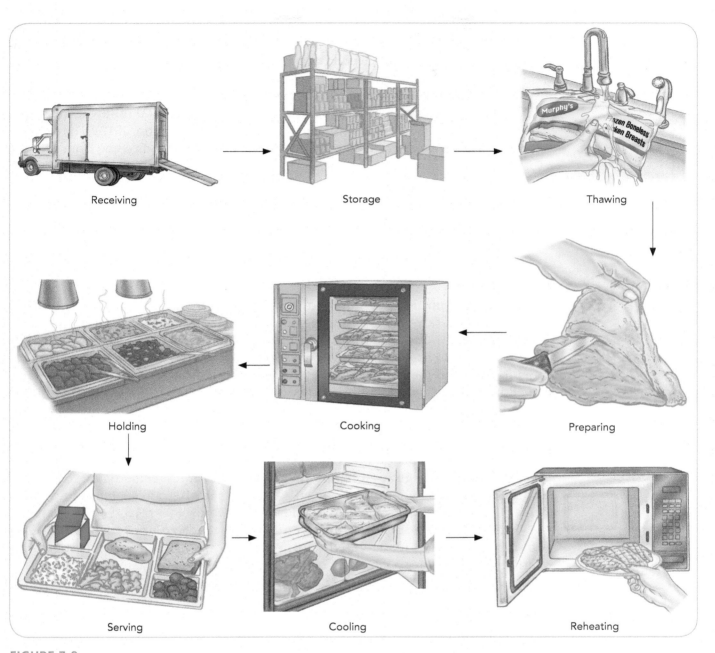

FIGURE 7-9
An Example of Food Flow
Source: Adapted from TrainCan, Inc.: BASICS.fst® *Food Safety Training and Certification*, 2004, http://www.traincan.com.

The flow of food refers to everything that happens to food from the moment it is purchased and delivered to a program until it is ready to be served (Figure 7-9) (National Restaurant Association, 2012).

Minimizing Contamination Risk During Food Purchasing

Purchasing food is the first step in bringing food into the early childhood setting. Although teachers in the family child care setting have more direct responsibility for food safety when purchasing foods for their programs, there may be times

WHAT IF . . .

you observed a staff member who is sick working with food? How would you manage this situation?

when teachers in child care centers or schools also purchase food for classroom cooking activities, snacks, and special social events. All teachers need to consider food safety issues when they buy food for the classroom. A very important consideration is whether the food comes from an approved and reputable source. Reputable suppliers include those that are inspected and follow local, state, and federal laws (National Restaurant Association, 2012). The following tips provide guidance on determining whether foods come from acceptable sources:

- Food must come from a supplier that carries USDA-inspected and USDA-approved meats and poultry and other FDA-approved processed foods.
- Food must be transported in such a way that perishable foods are kept safe.
- Food cannot be home canned.
- Food cannot be prepared in a kitchen that has not been inspected by the health department (U.S. Food and Drug Administration, 2014b).

Allowing families to bring food from home to share with all children introduces a food safety risk because the home kitchen is not an approved source of food. The intentions of families who bring homemade treats to school, such as the mother who brought cupcakes in the case scenario at the beginning of the chapter, are well meaning. However, these foods pose a safety risk and must not be allowed in the early childhood classroom. In addition, these foods can undermine the healthful school food environment that early childhood programs strive to achieve.

Families can be included in the sharing of foods in other ways. Families may offer recipes for inclusion in the program or school menu. In addition, children's programs can arrange for a family member to prepare a recipe using food purchased by the program from approved sources in the program's kitchen under the supervision of a worker who has a food handler's card.

Preventing foodborne illness requires a proactive approach. A variety of strategies assist teachers when purchasing groceries for their programs. Figure 7-10 provides a checklist of safety tips that support safe practices when shopping for food.

FIGURE 7-10   Food Safety Checklist for Purchasing Food

☑ Purchase only the amount that can be safely stored.
☑ Keep raw meats, poultry and seafood separate from other foods in the shopping cart, grocery bag, and refrigerator.
☑ Place foods such as milks, raw meat, poultry, and seafood into the shopping cart last.
☑ Check to make sure eggs aren't cracked and containers and cans aren't damaged.
☑ Select produce that is fresh and free of bruises or cuts.

☑ Carefully evaluate expiration or dates on cans and boxes of food paying special attention to bags or containers of salads or cut fruits and vegetables (select items with the latest date).
☑ Only purchase bagged salads or precut produce that is refrigerated or surrounded by ice.
☑ Use a cooler to store groceries that require refrigeration especially when driving long distances.

Sources: Food Safety for Your Family, Kids Health: The Nemours Foundation, 2014, from http://kidshealth.org/parent/firstaid_safe/home/food_safety.html# and Raw Produce: Selecting and Serving it Safely, U.S. Food and Drug Administration, 2011, from http://www.fda.gov/Food/ResourcesForYou/Consumers/ucm114299.htm.

Minimizing Contamination Risk When Receiving and Storing Food

When food arrives at an early childhood program as a bulk delivery of goods or as cooked meals from a vendor, it must be carefully inspected to determine whether the food is fresh and wholesome and free from spoilage. As discussed earlier, testing the temperature of foods is a critical aspect of this inspection.

A food thermometer is an important tool for food safety. To be effective, the thermometer must be routinely calibrated to ensure that accurate readings are obtained. A thermometer can be calibrated using the ice-point method:

FIGURE 7-11
Calibrating a Thermometer Using the Ice-Point Method

- Insert the thermometer probe into a cup of crushed ice.
- Add enough cold water to remove any air pockets that might remain.
- Allow the temperature reading to stabilize before reading it.
- Remember that temperature measurement should be 32°F (±2°F) (or 0°C (±1°C)).

Figure 7-11 illustrates the ice-point method of calibrating thermometers. Temperatures should be taken as soon as food arrives to ensure that foods sent are heated or chilled to appropriate temperatures.

In early childhood settings and schools, meals are often delivered from a contracted source called a vendor. The food service operations of a school district often act as vendors for early childhood settings in the community, and the school kitchen has the primary cooking responsibility. A key element to ensuring that safe food is sent by the vendor involves creating a detailed contract in which conditions and expectations specify food safety responsibilities, as discussed in the *Policy Point*.

POLICY POINT

Food Safety and Vended Meal Service

An early childhood program that contracts for vended meal service shares responsibility for food safety with the vendors providing the meals. Teachers who work in this setting must support food safety goals to ensure that children are served food that is wholesome. The teacher is the last responsible individual to inspect the food before it is given to children to eat. To ensure that there is a mutual understanding of food safety responsibilities, programs must establish food safety stipulations within the contract. The contract should include the following:

- A specific time and receiving process is designated for delivery of food.
- The conditions for delivery of food are outlined, including the use of a sanitary truck with appropriate warming and chilling containers and the delivery of meals in containers that meet local health standards.

- The vendor is in compliance with all federal, state, and county health and sanitation requirements and HACCP principles.
- Food temperatures at delivery are designated for hot and cold foods.
- Conditions for rejection and substitution of unsafe foods are included in the contract.
- Production records for total amounts and portion sizes are made available.
- Requirements for the accommodation of special diet requests and food labeling of special diets are stipulated.
- Access to the following information is included within the contract:
  - Standardized recipes.
  - Nutrition and CN labels for processed foods.

Sources: Child nutrition and school health CACFP guide for registered food vendors, Nevada Department of Education, 2010, from http://nutrition.nv.gov/Resources/Vendor /Guide_for_Registered_Meal_Vendors/ and Materials & resources for the national school lunch program: Guidelines for contracting vended meals, Wisconsin Department of Public Instruction, 2015, from http://fns.dpi.wi.gov/fns_prvend.

FIGURE 7-12　Food Storage Recommendations

Refrigeration Storage

- Perishable foods should be stored at 41°F (5°C) or colder.
- The temperature in refrigerators should be checked daily and recorded on a temperature log.
- All foods should be labeled and dated.
- Special diet items should be labeled with both the date and the child's name.
- Refrigerator shelves should be cleaned weekly.
- Raw meats and poultry should be stored on the bottom shelves and separate from other foods.
- Medications that require refrigeration should be stored away from food in a locked box within the refrigerator.
- Refrigerators in food service areas should be used exclusively for storing foods for children. (Staff should not store personal foods in the refrigerator.)

Freezer Storage

- Foods that are frozen should be stored in moisture-proof wrap, bags, or containers at temperature of 0°F (−18°C) or colder.
- Freezer temperatures should be measured daily and recorded on a temperature log.
- Frozen food items should be thawed in the refrigerator.

Dry Goods Storage (Canned, Jarred, or Packaged Items)

- Dry storage should be located in a room that is cool, dry, and has a room temperature that is maintained between 50° and 70°F (10°and 21°C).
- Food should be keep 6 to 8 inches off the ground.
- Food should be rotated so oldest items are used first.

Sources: *Caring for Our Children: National Health and Safety Performance Standards: Guidelines for Out-of-Home Child Care Programs,* 3rd edition, 2011, Elk Grove Village, IL: American Academy of Pediatrics; *Essentials of Food Safety and Sanitation,* 4th edition, by D. McSwane, N. R. Rue, and R. Linton, 2005, Upper Saddle River, NJ: Pearson; and *Mealtime Memo for Child Care: Safe Food Storage,* National Food Service Management Institute, 2005, from http://www.nfsmi.org/documentlibraryfiles/PDF/20080610114058.pdf.

In addition, teachers must communicate with vendors about special diet requirements so that children receive the correct menu item. For example, a child in teacher Jaime's class is vegan (eats no animal foods) and another child has a milk and soy allergy. Jaime must make sure the vegan child receives soy milk and the child with allergies is given rice milk. Because both milk products appear the same once they are poured into glasses, Jaime will serve them only if they are clearly labeled.

Once food has arrived, been inspected, and been accepted, staff involved in food preparation must give a high priority to prompt and proper storage. Potentially hazardous foods that sit in the receiving area or a kitchen for an extended period of time can quickly spoil and become unsafe to eat. Such foods must be stored under the correct conditions as soon as possible.

Three types of storage that require special consideration are refrigerator, freezer, and dry goods storage. Figure 7-12 describes food storage recommendations for each of these storage situations. How foods should be stored and at what temperature are important considerations. Germ growth is dependent on the amount of time the food product remains in the temperature danger zone. Consider the thoughtfulness of Shahrnaz, a teacher of 20 preschoolers who does not like to waste food:

The CACFP program guidelines stipulate that ¾ cup milk be served for breakfast. The entire amount must be made available to children at mealtime. Running down the hall to a kitchen to get more milk is not allowable by the CACFP. The milk that is delivered to the classroom is served in 16-ounce pitchers. Not all of the children drink a ¾-cup serving, so a considerable amount of milk is discarded. The CACFP will allow a gallon of milk as a reserve source in the classroom if teachers choose to serve less in the pitchers. Shahrnaz knows, however, that leaving a gallon jug of milk at room temperature for too long is a food safety risk, so this was not a viable option to her. Shahrnaz's solution was to request a small refrigerator for the classroom. She now fills the pitchers with less milk (making it easier for children to pour) and refills with milk as needed from the gallon in the refrigerator. She monitors the temperature in the refrigerator on a daily basis and records this on a temperature log. She accomplished her goal and sets a good example for her preschoolers.

It also is important to monitor the informal storage of foods that are not menu-related. For example, teachers may store crackers, coffee, hot chocolate, non-dairy creamer, and other foods in a cupboard for social events or staff meetings. These foods can pose a risk because there is generally no system for monitoring dates of expiration. Food that sits in cupboards for long periods of time can become a source of rodent or insect infestation.

The amount of time a food is in storage affects both food safety and food quality. A system of food rotation needs to be in place to ensure that previously purchased foods are used first. A common method used in the food service industry is **first in, first out (FIFO)**. Newly purchased foods are stored, and older products are rotated so that they are used first. For example, consider Lewke, a teacher shopping for her family child care program.

first in, first out (FIFO) inventory system in which foods that were previously purchased are rotated and newly purchased foods are stored such that older foods are used first

Lewke has in her cart perishables such as eggs, milk, cheese, and fresh produce. In addition, she has frozen foods such as peas, waffles, juices, canned corn, tomato sauce, and canned fruits. Once she returns home, she evaluates what she currently has on hand and discards any food that is past its expiration date. When storing the newly purchased foods, she labels foods with the date of purchase. She has a food storage rack in her pantry that helps her rotate canned foods. New food is placed behind previously purchased food, making it easy for her to remember which food to use first.

Minimizing Contamination Risk During Food Preparation

Every foodborne illness is preventable. Prevention is a key aspect of keeping food safe during preparation. Three important concepts that support food safety during food preparation and service are maintaining personal hygiene, preventing cross-contamination, and avoiding the temperature danger zone.

Maintaining Personal Hygiene

The human body harbors many microorganisms, which are usually harmless. They live in our lower gastrointestinal tract, mouth, nose, and scalp. These microorganisms usually do not make us sick, but they can contaminate foods and, if conditions are right, grow exponentially to create a foodborne illness. It is very important for teachers who work with food to maintain consistent and scrupulous

Pearson Education

CLASSROOM CONNECTION

Watch this video to see preschoolers washing their hands before a meal. How do the teachers help the children engage in proper hand washing?

personal hygiene. One of the most important aspects of personal hygiene is hand washing.

Hand Washing Hand washing is the simplest and most effective way to decrease the incidence of foodborne illness. A study on the impact of hand washing on the health of school-age children found that washing hands effectively reduced the risk of diarrhea, conjunctivitis (pink eye), and influenza by 30%, 67%, and 50%, respectively, and reduced overall the rate of school absenteeism (Talaat et al., 2011). Teachers also benefit when they wash their hands. For example, a recent study found that there was about a 7% decreased incidence of acute illness in typical work environments when staff was asked to practice good hand washing procedures (Savolainen-Kopra et al., 2012). These findings clearly support the importance of frequent hand washing by both teachers and children as an effective means of reducing the risk of foodborne illness and any infectious disease.

Teachers involved in the care of infants need to be particularly careful with hand hygiene. For example, in a family child care setting, in a short span of time, teachers may change diapers, wipe runny noses, prepare formula, and organize meals for young children. Hands that are not properly washed become a source of biological contamination of food and increase the risk of foodborne illness.

Hand washing specific to food safety is one of the standard operating procedures recommended by health authorities to support HACPP in the school food service environment (National Food Service Management Institute, 2005). Figure 7-13 provides an example of a standard operating procedure for hand washing for staff working with food and children.

In addition, sinks designated for hand washing only are required to minimize the potential for cross-contamination (U.S. Food and Drug Administration, 2014b) (Figure 7-14). For example, consider the potential for contamination if lettuce is washed in the same sink that was just used by a teacher who changed an infant's diaper. Hands should be dried using a single-use (disposable) paper towel or hand dryer. Drying hands on cloth towels or aprons is not acceptable because these can become soiled and are a potential source of cross-contamination.

Wearing Appropriate Attire Appropriate attire is important for maintaining food safety. Teachers who handle food should not wear jewelry, watches, or rings during food preparation because of the risk of biological contamination. Even with proper hand washing, microorganisms remain on the surface and crevices of these personal items. In addition, gemstones, backs of earrings, and jewelry clasps can come apart and become a physical contaminant of food.

Appropriate attire includes easy-to-clean clothes and head coverings such as a cap or hairnet to contain hair. Long hair should be restrained with a clip. An apron can help protect clothing from getting soiled with food or germs from food preparation activities. Ready-to-eat foods should not come in contact with bare hands (U.S. Food and Drug Administration, 2014b). Disposable gloves and serving tongs, ladles, or spoons are appropriate food service tools when working with ready-to-eat foods. Disposable gloves are a useful food safety tool; however, they can become contaminated just as readily as hands and must be changed as often as hands should be washed.

FIGURE 7-13 Standard Operating Procedure for Hand Washing

PURPOSE: To prevent foodborne illness by contaminated hands.

SCOPE: This procedure applies to staff who handle, prepare, and serve food.

INSTRUCTIONS:

1. Train program staff on using the procedures in this SOP.
2. Follow state or local health department requirements.
3. Post hand washing signs or posters in a language understood by all food service staff near all hand washing sinks, in food preparation areas, and in restrooms.
4. Use designated hand washing sinks for hand washing only. Do not use food preparation, utility, and dishwashing sinks for hand washing.
5. Provide warm running water, soap, and a means to dry hands. Provide a waste container at each hand washing sink or near the door in restrooms.
6. Wash hands:
   - Before starting work.
   - During food preparation.
   - Before putting on or changing gloves.
   - After using the toilet.
   - After changing diapers or assisting children with toileting.
   - After sneezing, coughing, or using a handkerchief or tissue or wiping children's noses.
   - After touching hair, face, or body.
   - After smoking, eating, drinking, or chewing gum or tobacco.
   - After handling raw meats, poultry, or fish.
   - After any cleanup activity such as sweeping, mopping, or wiping counters, putting away toys, sanitizing children's tables.
   - After touching dirty dishes, equipment, or utensils.
   - After handling trash.
   - After taking a break.
   - After handling animals.

7. Follow proper hand washing procedures:
   - Wet hands and forearms with warm, running water at least 100°F (38°C) and apply soap.
   - Scrub lathered hands and forearms, under fingernails with a nail brush, and between fingers for at least 20 seconds. Rinse thoroughly under warm running water for 5 to 10 seconds.
   - Dry hands and forearms thoroughly with single-use paper towels.
   - Turn off water at the faucet using paper towels when touching the faucet.
   - Use paper towel to open door when exiting the restroom.
   - Double hand washing by early childhood staff who handle food should occur after coughing, sneezing, having contact with body fluids, or using the bathroom. After using the bathroom or assisting a child in the bathroom, the first hand washing will take place in the restroom; the second at the designated hand washing sink in the work area before continuing work with food.

MONITORING:

Administrative staff will visually observe the hand washing practices of the staff involved in food service during all hours of operation.

CORRECTIVE ACTION:

1. Retrain any staff member found not following the procedures in this SOP.
2. Ask staff members who are observed not washing their hands at the appropriate times or using the proper procedure to wash their hands immediately.

VERIFICATION AND RECORD KEEPING:

The administrator will observe staff and document whether hand washing procedures are being effectively used.

DATE IMPLEMENTED:_____ **BY:**_____

Sources: HACCP-Based Standard Operating Procedures (SOPs), National Food Service Management Institute, U.S. Department of Agriculture and Food and Drug Administration, 2005 http://sop.nfsmi.org/HACCPBasedSOPs/WashingHands.pdf; Food Code 2009, U.S. Department of Health and Human Services, Public Health Service, Food and Drug Administration, 2015 from http://www.fda.gov/Food/GuidanceRegulation/RetailFoodProtection/FoodCode/; and Food Safety Basics: A Reference Guide for Food Service Workers, Julie Garden-Robinson, NDSU Extension Service, January, 2012 from http://www.ag.ndsu.edu/pubs/yf/foods/fn572.pdf.

Reporting Infectious Disease One of the primary methods for cross-contamination or the transferring of germs in food preparation is an infectious staff member who comes to work when sick and contaminates food during the food-handling process. This is an extreme health hazard.

Legal requirements are in place for reporting food service workers who have a confirmed illness or have been exposed to *Salmonella typhi*, *Shigella*, *E. coli* O157:H7,

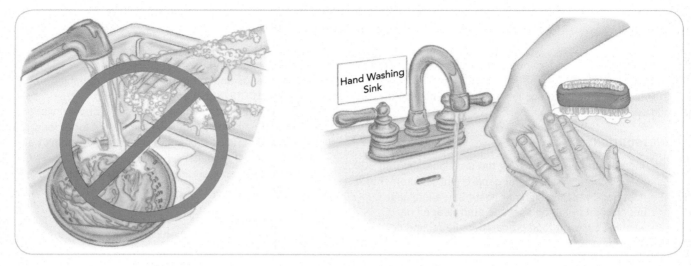

FIGURE 7-14

Teachers Must Wash Hands in Designated Hand Washing Sinks

cleaning
the removal of dirt, grime, and food particles using soap and water and friction with the goal of reducing risk of biological, physical, and chemical contamination

sanitizing
the process used to reduce the risk of contamination by reducing microorganisms to safe levels by heat or sanitizing solutions

Pearson Education

CLASSROOM CONNECTION

Watch this video to see a teacher demonstrate the steps for properly sanitizing the classroom. As you watch, think about why sanitizing is critical in food safety as well as in reducing infectious diseases.

hepatitis A, or norovirus or who have symptoms such as vomiting, diarrhea, jaundice, sore throat, or infected cuts, pimples, or boils (U.S. Food and Drug Administration, 2014b). Food service workers or teachers who have been ill or exposed to the illnesses listed above must report this to the program director, who, depending on state requirements, will share this information with local health authorities. Food service workers and teachers who have contracted the above illnesses should not return to work until they have written approval from a medical provider.

Preventing Cross-Contamination

Using sanitizing methods during food preparation helps to minimize cross-contamination. Cleaning and sanitizing have distinct purposes:

- Cleaning refers to the removal of dirt, grime, and food particles using soap, water, and scrubbing. Although cleaning reduces the risk of biological contamination, it does not destroy all germs.
- Sanitizing involves the use of heat or sanitizing solutions to reduce the risk of contamination by killing microorganisms. After surfaces and equipment have been cleaned, they are ready for sanitizing.

Methods of Sanitizing Typically in the kitchen setting, items sanitized by food handlers include food preparation and service surfaces, dishware, cookware and utensils, thermometers, food service equipment, and doorknobs and handles. Sanitizing is accomplished by:

- Washing dishware, cookware, and utensils in hot water [171°F (77°C) or hotter for at least 30 seconds].
- Using chemical sanitizers such as bleach or other chemical products approved by local regulatory agencies (Garden-Robinson, 2012).

Both sanitizing methods are used when washing dishes in a three-compartment sink. The three-compartment sink procedure is described in Figure 7-15. The three-sink method is used when a facility does not have an appliance that washes and sanitizes dishes.

Preparing and Using Bleach Solutions Sanitizing with bleach solutions is often done because it is inexpensive, kills most germs, can be used in many different situations and in appropriate concentrations, and does not leave a residue that needs to be washed off (American Academy of Pediatrics, American Public Health Association, National Resource Center for Health and Safety in Child Care and Early Education, 2011).

Bleach solution dilutions of between 50 and 200 parts per million or about 1 tablespoon 5.25% sodium hypochlorite unscented bleach per gallon of water are recommended as an option for cleaning food service contact surfaces (countertops, high chair trays, dining tables, and equipment) (American Academy of Pediatrics, American Public Health Association, National Resource Center for Health and Safety in Child Care and Early Education, 2011; U.S. Food and Drug Administration, 2014b). The amount of bleach to add to water, however, is dependent on the temperature, pH, and hardness of the water; therefore, it is important to contact local regulatory agencies for guidance on preparing a solution and to check concentration with chlorine test strips (U.S. Food and Drug Administration, 2014b; National Restaurant Association, 2012). Recently in many states, the concentration of bleach solutions sold in stores has changed to an 8.25% sodium hypochlorite bleach solution. Teachers need to check the bleach bottle labels to determine which concentration they are using. The National Resource Center for Health and Safety in Child Care and Early Education provides guidance for making the correct bleach solution. Health authorities generally agree that leaving the bleach solution on the surface for two minutes significantly reduces microbial contamination. A stronger dilution is recommended for disinfecting spills of body fluids such as blood, feces, and vomit. For this purpose, using about 1 tablespoon of bleach to 1 quart of water with two minutes of contact time is sufficient for disinfecting (American Academy of Pediatrics, American Public Health Association, National Resource Center for Health and Safety in Child Care and Early Education, 2011). Bleach should never be mixed with ammonia or any other cleaning agents because toxic fumes can result. For safety, bottles containing bleach solutions must be clearly labeled and stored out of the reach of children.

A sanitizing routine is needed to ensure that surfaces and equipment are safe for food. It is not sufficient to clean and sanitize when a piece of equipment "looks" soiled. For example, a can opener can appear clean even though the blade may have been exposed to food multiple times during the day. A cleaning schedule such as the one shown in Table 7-2 helps create an appropriate routine.

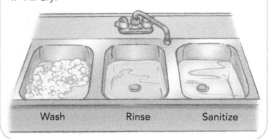

1. Wash items in water that is at least 110°F (43°C).
2. Rinse in water that is at least 110°F (43°C).
3. Sanitize in hot water [171°F (77°C) for 30 seconds or chlorine bleach solution for at least 60 seconds].
4. Air-dry.

Wash   Rinse   Sanitize

FIGURE 7-15

Procedure for Sanitizing Dishware Using the Three-Sink Method

Sources: *HACCP in Your School*, by A. Fraser, October 2007, from http://www.foodsafetysite.com /resources/pdfs/schoolhaccp /SchoolHACCPManual.pdf and *Essentials of Food Safety and Sanitation*, 4th edition, by D. McSwane, N. R. Rue, and R. Linton, 2005, Upper Saddle River, NJ: Pearson.

Safe Food Production at Each Stage of Food Preparation

Biological contamination is a risk during all phases of food preparation such as thawing, cooking, holding, and cooling, and the risk increases substantially when temperature abuse occurs. Once again, temperature control plays an important role in ensuring food safety.

Thawing Food Foods should be thawed overnight in the refrigerator in a drip pan. Food can also be thawed under cool running water of 70°F (21°C) or less or in the microwave but only if it is going to be cooked immediately. Food being thawed should never reach temperatures above 41°F (5°C) (National Food Service Management Institute, 2009).

TABLE 7-2 Sample Cleaning Schedule

Items to Clean	Cleaning Activity	How Often	Mon	Tues	Wed	Thurs	Fri
STOVE	Clean burners	After use	X	X	X	X	X
	Clean outside	Daily	X	X	X	X	X
	Clean inside	Weekly					X
	Clean hood	Weekly					X
REFRIGERATOR AND FREEZER	Defrost/clean	As needed			X		
	Wipe outside	Daily	X	X	X	X	X
	Wipe inside	As needed/weekly					X
FOOD PREP SURFACES	Clean	Before and after use	X	X	X	X	X
	Sanitize	Before and after use	X	X	X	X	X
SINKS	Clean	After use and end of day	X	X	X	X	X
	Sanitize	Before and after use	X	X	X	X	X
CUPBOARDS AND STORAGE AREAS	Wipe and organize	As needed			X		
EATING SURFACES	Clean	Before and after use	X	X	X	X	X
	Sanitize	Before and after use	X	X	X	X	X
EQUIPMENT (can opener, mixer, etc.)	Clean	After use	X	X	X	X	X
DISH MACHINE	Clean	Daily	X	X	X	X	X
TRASH	Nonrecyclables	Daily	X	X	X	X	X
	Recyclables	Daily	X	X	X	X	X
FLOOR	Mop	As needed and at end of day	X	X	X	X	X

Sources: Based on Benjamin, SE, ed. *Making Food Healthy and Safe for Children: How to Meet the National Health and Safety Performance Standards—Guidelines for Early Care and Education Programs*. Second Edition. Chapel Hill, NC: The National Training Institute for Child Care Health Consultants, Department of Maternal and Child Health, The University of North Carolina at Chapel Hill; 2012. Cleaning and Sanitizing for Food Business. Clutha District Council, New Zealand, 2008. Food Code 2015, U. S. Department of Health and Human Services, Food and Drug Administration, http://www.fda.gov/Food/GuidanceRegulation/RetailFoodProtection/FoodCode/.

Preparing Food Food safety relies on careful preparation. Cross-contamination is one critical aspect to avoid. An important strategy is to keep raw meats, poultry, eggs, and seafood separate from ready-to-eat foods. Jan, a teacher who cares for children in her home, uses color-coded cutting boards. She uses a red cutting board for raw meats and a green one for fresh produce. When she prepares salad, she doesn't have to worry that her lettuce will come in contact with bacteria from the hamburger patties she prepares on the red cutting board. She also knows it is not a good idea to "eyeball" a food to see if it looks done. One in four hamburgers turns brown before it reaches an internal temperature that kills germs (U.S. Department of Agriculture Food Safety and Inspection Service, 2014c). Jan uses a thermometer to check the internal temperature of foods. She also refers to the USDA standardized recipes because they tell her what temperatures her foods must reach to minimize the risk of foodborne illness.

Using microwave ovens to cook food may be convenient, but additional factors must be considered. Microwave ovens vary, and heating is not always consistent. To make sure there are no cold spots in food that might harbor bacteria, food should be covered, rotated, and stirred during heating and then allowed to sit for indicated stand times.

Cooling Food Sometimes food is prepared ahead to serve on another day. Food that is prepared in advance must be chilled in a timely manner so that it does not stay in the temperature danger zone for an excessively long period of time. Consider this example:

> Rosalind stays late to prepare soup for the family social event that will be held the following day. Although she uses a USDA-approved standardized recipe, she does not follow proper cooling instructions before refrigerating the soup. The next morning, the health inspector makes an unexpected visit to her children's center. The inspector measures the temperature of the refrigerated soup and finds that it is still 50°F (10°C). The health inspector tells Rosalind that the soup has not been chilled quickly enough for it to be safe and, therefore, the soup must be discarded. The inspector makes some recommendations for the future, telling her that soup can be cooled using shallow 2- to 4-inch-high steam table pans with an ice paddle (a hollow plastic paddle that can be filled with water and frozen and then placed in the soup to chill it quickly).

Reheating Food Methods for reheating foods are also important to food safety. Reheated foods must reach an internal temperature of 165°F (74°C), which should be sustained for at least 15 seconds to kill bacteria (Garden-Robinson, 2012). The time it takes to reheat foods should not exceed two hours. Longer reheating times increase the risk of microorganisms proliferating.

Practices related to keeping and reheating leftover food for service in children's programs is governed by state and local health authorities. If local health regulations allow leftovers to be served, a careful management plan is needed. Any food that is being stored as leftovers should be carefully labeled, including the name of the food, the amount prepared, and the date of preparation. Leftovers should be reheated only once.

Minimizing Contamination Risk During Food Service

Ensuring safety during food service in the children's settings offers special challenges. Keeping heated food sufficiently hot prior to meal service is important. In school settings, children often pass through a lunch line where food is served onto trays by food service workers. This format allows the food in the cafeteria to be held in heating units such as steam tables. This food must be monitored to make sure proper temperatures are maintained. Salad bars also create a food safety risk. Purchasing equipment that contains sneeze guards or food shields reduces the risk of contamination from coughs or sneezes. Salad ingredients are highly perishable and must be kept at 41°F (5°C) or below for proper cold holding.

Children's programs also use family meal–style service, which provides the opportunity for children to gain important self-help skills such as selecting and serving their own food. This approach requires that teachers supervise children to avoid cross-contamination as they serve themselves and pass the serving dishes. It is not unusual for children to want to lick the serving spoon, use the same serving spoon for different menu items, or put their used forks into a serving dish when they want another serving. This can result in biological contamination and put children with food allergies at risk.

It is also important to monitor how long food is maintained at room temperature before it is served. To ensure food safety at the time of service, meals are planned on a regular schedule, with routines that help children to be washed and ready to eat when food is ready, and meal tables are cleaned and sanitized. It is also important to ensure that food is not too hot for consumption. For example, foods that are heated in a microwave oven can have hot spots that may cause burns to the mouth. Soups and stews may be hot and could pose a burning risk if spilled.

Another aspect of food service safety involves ensuring that children on special diets receive the correct meals. Having a system in place for serving children with special diet requirements is helpful because mealtimes can be very busy. For example, Elisa, a preschooler teacher, finds it helpful to serve the children with special diets first. She posts a list in the classroom that includes the children's names and their special diet needs. The program's dietitian has provided a menu that lists special diet substitutions, and Elisa always double-checks to make sure the correct foods are being served.

Understanding the food safety risks related to each phase of the flow of food through a program, from purchasing and storage to food preparation and service, helps teachers to minimize the chances of a foodborne illness. Figure 7-16 provides a checklist that can be used by teachers to make sure that all aspects of food safety are being considered on a routine basis.

Understanding At-Risk Situations in Early Childhood Settings

Although rules and regulations exist that govern food preparation in schools at any age level, feeding young children poses unique challenges. Children's physical and social-emotional development provides the basis for making many decisions that relate to feeding and safe nourishment. In addition, early childhood teachers may work with children from a variety of age groups and must understand children's needs in a variety of settings.

Food Safety and the Feeding of Infants

Infants have a special need for a safe food supply because the immaturity of their immune system puts them at greatest risk for foodborne illness. Infant feeding and handling and storage of breast milk were discussed in earlier chapters. Additional food safety guidelines to consider when feeding infants are listed below.

- Don't leave baby food solids or liquids at room temperature for more than two hours (U.S. Food and Drug Administration, 2014c).
- Check formula and baby food to make sure they have not exceeded their "use by" dates.
- Discard any jar of baby food if the safety button on the lid has popped.
- Do not put an already used bottle back in the refrigerator.
- Do not heat breast milk, formula, or baby food in the microwave oven because uneven heating can lead to hot spots, which can burn the baby's mouth and throat and can destroy protective protein and vitamin components of breast milk (American Academy of Pediatrics, 2014).
- Do not feed baby directly from the jar. This introduces germs from the baby's mouth into the jar of food, creating a food safety risk if food is refrigerated for later use.
- Do not feed babies honey until age 1 and older due to the risk of botulism.

Ensuring that infants receive their own mother's breast milk is another important component of food safety when feeding infants. The *Nutrition Note* discusses this topic and offers guidance on what to do if an infant drinks the wrong milk.

FIGURE 7-16   Sample Food Safety Checklist

Date_____   Reviewer_____

Directions: On a daily basis evaluate food safety by using the following checklist. Record any corrective action taken and file.

HAND HYGIENE	Yes	No	Corrective Action
A standard operating procedure for hand washing is posted.	❏	❏	_____
Teachers ensure children wash hands before and after preparing food and eating meals.	❏	❏	_____

SAFE FOOD PREPARATION	Yes	No	Corrective Action
All food comes from approved sources.	❏	❏	_____
Food is kept out of the temperature danger zone.	❏	❏	_____
• Temperature of hot food being held is at or above 135°F (57°C).	❏	❏	_____
• Temperature of cold food being held is at or below 41°F (5°C).	❏	❏	_____
• Thermometers are available and accurate.	❏	❏	_____
• Food is cooked to the required safe internal temperature for the appropriate time.	❏	❏	_____
Procedures are in place to prevent cross-contamination.	❏	❏	_____
• All equipment, food preparation and service areas are washed, rinsed, and sanitized before and after use.	❏	❏	_____
• Disposable gloves or serving utensils are used to avoid touching ready-to-eat foods with bare hands.	❏	❏	_____
• Raw animal foods are kept separate from ready-to-eat foods.	❏	❏	_____
• Classroom food activities using ready to eat food do not include mixing and consuming ingredients that have been handled by multiple children.	❏	❏	_____
• Cooking activities with children do not include the use of raw egg or other raw animal foods.	❏	❏	_____
• Procedures are in place for handling food allergies.	❏	❏	_____

HOLDING AND STORAGE	Yes	No	Corrective Action
Temperature for refrigerator, freezer, and dry storage area is monitored daily including classroom and staff refrigerators.	❏	❏	_____
All food is properly wrapped, labeled, and dated including special diets.	❏	❏	_____
The FIFO (first in, first out) method of inventory management is used.	❏	❏	_____
All leftover food served to children is discarded after meal service.	❏	❏	_____

CLEANING AND SANITIZING	Yes	No	Corrective Action
Dish machine is working properly.	❏	❏	_____
Water temperatures are correct for wash and rinse and sanitizing.	❏	❏	_____
Tableware and utensils are allowed to air dry.	❏	❏	_____
Children's tables are washed, rinsed, and sanitized before and after meals.	❏	❏	_____
Cleaning cloths are stored in sanitizing solution while in use.	❏	❏	_____

Sources: HACCP-Based SOPs: Food Safety Checklist, by the National Food Service Management Institute, 2005. For a complete list, go to http://sop.nfsmi.org/Records/FoodSafetyChecklist.pdf and Food Safety Basics: A Reference Guide for Foodservice Operators by Julie Garden-Robinson, NDSU Extension Service, 2012, http://www.ag.ndsu.edu/pubs/yf/foods/fn572.pdf.

Food Safety and the Feeding of Toddlers and Preschoolers

Choking is a potential hazard for young children. It is the leading cause of unintentional injury and death of children, especially those under age 3 (American Academy of Pediatrics, 2013). Specific foods introduce safety risks for young children because they have characteristics associated with choking. Foods that can get lodged in the throat or lung are round, hard, small, thick, and sticky (peanut

NUTRITION NOTE   Feeding Breast Milk to Another Mother's Baby

Breast milk is considered the gold standard for infant nutrition. Teachers who support mothers who choose to breast-feed provide an invaluable service to both mother and baby. Breast milk, however, must be handled appropriately to avoid food safety problems.

Teachers who follow proper procedures for handling breast milk rarely feed a baby the wrong bottle of breast milk. However, a bottle can be put down by one infant and picked up by another. If a baby consumes another infant's bottle of breast milk, this must be treated as an accidental exposure to a bodily fluid and a potential exposure to hepatitis B, hepatitis C, or HIV.

The National Resource Center for Health and Safety in Child Care and Early Education and the CDC recommend that the teacher notify the parents of the baby who consumed the wrong milk, the infant's medical provider, and the mother whose breast milk was consumed. The mother whose milk was consumed by the wrong child should be asked if she has had a blood test for hepatitis B, hepatitis C, or HIV test and if she would be willing to share this information with the family whose infant was exposed. If she has not been tested, she should be asked if she would be willing to take a blood test and follow-up test six months later and share the results with the baby's family. Depending on the response to these questions, the medical provider may recommend blood tests for the baby who consumed the wrong milk.

Although the risk of transmission of HIV in breast milk is very low, the follow-up procedures and testing that occur as a result of feeding the wrong breast milk to an infant highlight the importance of following careful food safety procedures when feeding babies breast milk.

Source: American Academy of Pediatrics, American Public Health Association, National Resource Center for Health and Safety in Child Care and Early Education, 2011. Caring for our children: National health and safety performance standards; *Guidelines for early care and education programs*. 3rd edition. Elk Grove Village, IL: American Academy of Pediatrics; Washington, DC: American Public Health Association. Also available at http://nrckids.org.

butter); smooth, compressible, or dense; or slippery and large enough to obstruct an airway (American Academy of Pediatrics, American Public Health Association, National Resource Center for Health and Safety in Child Care and Early Education, 2011). Hot dogs, which are just the right size to lodge in the throat of a child, cause more choking deaths than any other food (American Academy of Pediatrics, 2013). The following foods should not be served to children under age 4 (American Academy of Pediatrics, 2013; American Academy of Pediatrics, American Public Health Association, National Resource Center for Health and Safety in Child Care and Early Education, 2011; Washington State Department of Health, 2011):

- Hot dogs, sausages, and meat sticks
- Nuts and seeds
- Large pieces of meat or cheese
- Beef jerky
- Whole grapes
- Hard, gooey, or sticky candy
- Popcorn
- A large serving size of peanut butter
- Raw vegetables including carrot sticks or rounds and raw peas
- Whole kernel corn
- Hard pretzels, chips
- Small, dried fruits such as raisins
- Rice cakes
- Gum

Food offered to toddlers and preschool-age children should be cut into age-appropriate pieces of ½ inch or less (¼ inch or less for infants). Children should be seated while eating, and teachers should supervise mealtimes closely. NAEYC *Standard 5.B.14* provides guidance on foods that pose a choking risk (National Association for the Education of Young Children, 2012).

Food Safety and Children with Special Needs

Some children with special developmental needs may have food preparation and service requirements that are different from those of other children. These differences may create unique food safety concerns. For example:

- Children with developmental impairments may be at increased risk for choking and require alternative food textures and/or thickeners added to beverages.
- Children with special needs may require tube feeding, which requires careful handling.
- Service of foods to children with special developmental challenges may take longer as the child negotiates the eating process.
- During meal service, temperatures of foods may enter food temperature danger zones longer or more often due to the need to transport special single-serving portions, which are harder to maintain at appropriate temperatures, and prolonged feeding times. Reheating of foods may be more common to support meal service (Krueger, 2008).

As with all food service, specialized equipment used in food preparation for children with special needs, such as blenders and food processors, must be properly cleaned and sanitized. Any special feeding devices such as adaptive eating utensils, plates, and bowls must also be properly cleaned and sanitized.

Some children with identified special developmental needs may require a medical statement or guidance from a medical provider describing the disability and how it affects the child's diet, including what to omit and what to substitute (American Academy of Pediatrics, American Public Health Association, National Resource Center for Health and Safety in Child Care and Early Education, 2011). Teachers may need to obtain training so that they know how to respond if a child's disability interferes with swallowing or if choking is a potential concern. Teachers need to ensure that all children have access to quality, balanced, and wholesome meals that meet their unique requirements. Teachers also need to make sure they understand any required diet modifications.

Food Safety and Food Brought from Home

Some families may ask to bring their child's food from home rather than have meals prepared by the early childhood program. Such a request may be made for children whose diet restrictions are complex. In considering such a request, teachers need to be aware of the health regulations in their area. Many state and local health authorities discourage or prohibit sending meals from home. Foods from home may increase the risk of foodborne illness. Where permitted, a written agreement between families and the children's program should be established (American Academy of Pediatrics, American Public Health Association, National Resource Center for Health and Safety in

WHAT IF . . .
you observed a child sharing food from his lunch box with other children? Isn't a child who shares doing something commendable? How might you explain the safety risks to this child?

Child Care and Early Education, 2011). Guidelines for families who choose to bring food from home include the following:

- Food should always be sent in lunch containers that have frozen ice packs.
- Food should be labeled with the child's name, the date, and the type of food.
- Food should not be shared with other children in the program.

Families may want to share food from home with all children in the program. Programs must carefully weigh the pros and cons of allowing food to be brought from home and be proactive in the prevention of foodborne illness by devising policies that support safe food and meet state and county regulations. As discussed in an earlier chapter, the NAEYC accreditation standards recommend that foods brought from home to share with other children must consist of whole fruits or commercially prepared packaged foods (National Association for the Education of Young Children, 2012). In addition, remember the consequences that occurred in the case scenario when homemade cupcakes were brought into Lacey's classroom.

Food Safety and Cultural Considerations

Teachers who support cultural traditions in the selection of food for early childhood programs create a respectful enriching environment for all children and their families. However, some cultural food traditions may create a dilemma in terms of food safety. For example, some cultural food choices may be associated with increased risk for foodborne illness. For instance, some soft Mexican-style cheeses have been linked to Listeriosis, an uncommon foodborne disease that can cause high fever, severe headache, neck stiffness, nausea, and sometimes death (Centers for Disease Control and Prevention, 2013b). Sushi, a Japanese dish made with rice, seaweed, vegetables, and often raw fish, has also been linked to foodborne illness. If made with raw fish, this menu item should never be served to young children. Teachers can honor cultural food traditions, but this must be done within the context of food safety policies and regulations.

Food Safety on Field Trips

When children go on a field trip, special challenges must be addressed when serving food away from the school program. These challenges have to do with maintaining proper temperatures and personal hygiene. The *Safety Segment* provides advice on acceptable foods for a field trip.

Food Safety and Classroom Cooking Activities

Children learn about food by touching, tasting, and smelling it. They are often more likely to want to try new foods when they have helped with preparation. Safety management considerations for classroom cooking activities include the following:

- *Raw foods:* Avoid handling raw foods that contain infectious microorganisms. Children making cookies using a recipe that calls for eggs are at risk for salmonella food poisoning. Using a pasteurized egg substitute eliminates this problem.
- *Foods that will not be cooked:* If children participate in preparing foods that will not be cooked, they should only eat the food they have prepared and handled. For example, if the teacher plans an activity in which children make salad, each child should be given the ingredients to make his or her own salad.

SAFETY SEGMENT   Food Safety on Field Trips

Taking foods on field trips requires careful planning to keep food safe.

1. *Menu planning:* Field trip menus should include foods with low risk for spoiling. Some safe foods to take along on field trips include the following:

- Boxed juices
- Whole fruit
- Individual canned or plastic fruit cups
- Dried fruit (if age-appropriate)
- Whole-grain crackers, breads, bread sticks, and rolls
- Peanut butter sandwiches (if there are no peanut allergies)
- Nuts (if there are no allergies and this snack is age-appropriate)
- Trail mix (if age-appropriate ingredients are used)
- Dry cereal
- Baked whole-grain chips

2. *Storing food:* Foods must be maintained at proper temperatures. Store foods that need to be chilled in coolers filled with ice or plastic frozen gel packs. Freeze juice boxes and use them to keep other food cold. Place a thermometer in the cooler to make sure temperatures remain under 41°F (5°C). Foods that need to be chilled include the following:

- Meat, poultry, fish, or egg salad sandwiches
- Milk
- Cheese
- Yogurt
- Fruits or vegetables that have been peeled or cut
- Salads

3. *Hand washing:* Remember to wash hands and have children wash hands before eating. Premoistened hand wipes are not a substitute for hand washing, but can be used if no soap and running water are available.

Sources: American Academy of Pediatrics, American Public Health Association, National Resource Center for Health and Safety in Child Care and Early Education, 2011. *Caring for our children: National health and safety performance standards; Guidelines for early care and education programs.* 3rd edition. Elk Grove Village, IL: American Academy of Pediatrics; Washington, DC: American Public Health Association. Also available at http://nrckids.org; American Academy of Pediatrics; *Food Safety Standard Operating Procedures* (SOPs), National Food Service Management Institute, 2005, from http://www.nfsmi.org/ResourceOverview.aspx?ID=75.

- *Potential food allergens:* Teachers must make sure that children with allergies or food intolerances are not involved in activities that lead to exposure. For example, covering a pinecone with peanut butter and birdseed would be a risky project for children with peanut allergies. Making play dough from wheat flour would be hazardous to children with celiac disease.

THE EMERGENCY PLAN AND FOOD DEFENSE

Emergencies cannot be predicted, but children's programs and schools can prepare in advance for potential emergencies. There are two aspects of food safety guide planning for emergencies: (1) ensuring that there is a safe supply of food and water in case of a natural disaster and (2) making sure that foods are not tampered with or intentionally contaminated as an act of terrorism.

Developing an Emergency Food Plan

An emergency food plan is needed in the event an emergency requires that children and teachers cannot return to their homes but must take shelter in the facility. The Federal Emergency Management Agency (Federal Emergency Management Agency, 2014) and the American Red Cross (American Red Cross, 2015) provide guidelines on what foods and how much food and water to store. A three-day supply of food and water is recommended.

CHECK YOUR UNDERSTANDING 7.3
Click here to check your understanding of ways to minimize food contamination in the early childhood setting.

WHAT IF . . .
you were in charge of creating an emergency food plan? How would you plan for children with special diet needs? What might you include in your emergency food supply to address various special diets?

Whereas an effective emergency food plan ensures that children will have access to safe food and water if supplies are interrupted, even an emergency food supply can pose a food safety risk if it is not properly monitored. The FIFO method of food rotation discussed earlier in this chapter is one way to ensure that food on hand is safe. Some examples of emergency foods to store include:

- Canned meats, fish, milk, soup, fruit, juice, and vegetables.
- Ready-to-eat cereals and instant hot cereals.
- Crackers, granola bars, trail mix.
- Peanut butter, jelly.
- Staples such as sugar, salt, and pepper.

The emergency food supply should include foods appropriate for the age group of the children served and should include options for children with food allergies and other food restrictions.

Planning for Food Defense

food defense
practice of ensuring that foods are not tampered with or intentionally contaminated as an act of terrorism

The U.S. Department of Homeland Security has raised awareness that food service establishments may be at risk for intentional contamination of foods by terrorist groups (U.S. Food and Drug Administration, 2014a). To provide **food defense**, which is the assurance that foods are not tampered with or intentionally contaminated as an act of terrorism, food service handlers are the "front line in protecting our food supply" (New York State Department of Health, 2006). For teachers and food services workers, this means being vigilant about who has access to the food that is stored and served to children. Children's programs can implement these strategies:

- Allow only authorized individuals to receive, store, and have access to food preparation areas.
- Know the food delivery personnel and always have someone available to receive food directly.
- Make sure self-service food items are placed in an area that can be supervised by staff.
- Keep buildings and grounds secure by locking doors in delivery, storage, and food preparation areas when not in use and allowing only key or code access.
- Discourage loitering in the program setting or school. Install alarm or video surveillance systems if security problems are an issue.
- Conduct employee background checks to ensure employment of safe teachers and food workers.
- Encourage employees to report suspicious behaviors.
- Train employees on food defense and food safety and on how to recognize potential security risks (New York State Department of Health, 2006; U.S. Food and Drug Administration, 2014a).

CHECK YOUR UNDERSTANDING 7.4

Click here to check your understanding of food safety precautions that should be considered during an emergency.

These recommendations can heighten awareness of threats to food safety, decreasing the risk that early childhood programs will become targets for deliberate contamination. It is unfortunate that issues of this type need to be considered in the early childhood setting. However, children are vulnerable and have been targeted in the past. It is every program's and school's responsibility to consider all aspects of safety.

TEACHING FOOD SAFETY TO CHILDREN

Although program administrators and teachers bear the responsibility of ensuring a safe food supply, children are capable of helping to create a safe food environment. Teaching children about food safety includes a progression of ideas from basic ideas to more advanced concepts.

Routines in the school setting often are established to keep children safe. These routines also teach children expected behaviors that relate to food safety. Children learn about food safety through these every-day practices, especially if teachers explain the rationale behind the routines. Leading questions are appropriate for preschool-age children and older and could include these:

- We wash our hands because. . . .
- We sneeze into our elbow, not our hands, because. . . .
- We pick up the fork by the handle when setting the table because. . . .
- We can put our forks in our mouths but not the serving spoon because. . . .
- We share most things, but we only eat or drink our own food because. . . .
- We put milk in the refrigerator because. . . .
- We wash the tables before and after eating because. . . .

Activity-based exploration of food safety topics is appropriate for all children. For example, teaching food safety tips while preparing and sampling food keeps children interested. Singing the "ABC" song once while washing hands teaches children how long to wash their hands in a way that holds their interest. The *Teaching Wellness* feature offers ideas about how to incorporate food safety lessons such as hand washing into the daily curriculum.

Being a good role model and combining simple explanations with consistent reminders help children establish food safety habits that benefit them now and in the future.

WHAT IF . . .

you were asked to teach food safety topics to children in your class? What topics would you select? How would you create a child-directed activity for a food safety topic?

TEACHING WELLNESS   Washing Hands Keeps Me Healthy

LEARNING OUTCOME   Children will show how to prevent the spread of germs by washing their hands.

Vocabulary focus: Wash, rinse, dry, hand, palm, fingers, wrist, germs, disease.

Safety watch: Ensure that soaps used are allergen-free. Supervise children around water. Monitor the temperature of the water and ensure that the floor near the sinks is kept dry to avoid slipping.

INFANTS AND TODDLERS

- **Goal:** Babies will experience having their hands washed, and toddlers will be able to wash and dry their hands with help.
- **Materials:** Small tub of warm water, gentle soap, paper towels.
- **Activity plan:** For infants, allow babies to touch and splash hands in a shallow tub of lukewarm water. Say words that convey interest and pleasure, such as "That's it. Touch the nice warm water. It feels so nice and clean." Help the baby dip hands in the water and gently stroke hands and between fingers, allowing the infant to touch

and splash about. For toddlers, guide the child to wash under slowly running lukewarm water at a sink. Talk through the process of washing and encourage the child through each step. Say, "First, let's get our hands wet. Next, we add a little bit of soap. That's it. Now we rub the palms, the tops, and between fingers. Now let's rinse away the soap and dry our hands. We turn off the water with this paper towel and throw the towel away. Now we are ready to eat." Reinforce the child's efforts by remarking, "You are scrubbing all parts of your hands. That is how we wash away the germs and make our hands clean."

- **How to adjust the activity:** Post near the sink a picture guide for washing hands. For children who are English learners, learn the words for washing hands, using water, and soap. Assist children with special developmental needs to access water, soap, and towels. Point out the picture

guide to reinforce the steps of hand washing. Allow the child ample time to move through the hand washing process.
- **Did you meet your goal?** Did babies participate in the hand washing process? Can toddlers move through the steps of appropriate hand washing with help?

PRESCHOOLERS AND KINDERGARTNERS

- **Goal:** Children will demonstrate appropriate hand washing techniques and tell when it is important to wash hands.
- **Materials:** The book *Those Mean Nasty Dirty Downright Disgusting But . . . Invisible Germs* by Judith Rice; sink; water; liquid soap; paper towels.
- **Activity plan:** Gather the children and read the book using a variety of fun voices and hand gestures. Talk about germs and explain why it is important to wash them off our hands. Help children to identify the times it is important to wash hands (such as before eating, after sneezing, after going to the bathroom, and after playing in the sensory table). Describe and act out the steps of hand washing. Invite children to practice washing their hands at the sink:
  - Turn on the water and wet hands.
  - Use one squirt of liquid soap.
  - Rub and wash hands for 20 seconds, including between fingers, palms, backs of hands, and wrists. (Count to 20

slowly or sing the *ABC* song once or the *Happy Birthday* song twice.)
- Rinse hands, letting the water run over palms, between fingers, on backs of hands and wrists.
- Dry hands with a paper towel.
- Use the paper towel to turn off the water and then throw the towel away.
- **How to adjust the activity:** As children wash, refer to the posted picture guide for washing hands. For English learners or those whose special developmental need requires repetition and reinforcement, point to each step of the picture and repeat the direction in English. Encourage children's efforts as they move through the process. Make sure the sink, soap, and towels are accessible to all children.
- **Did you meet your goal?** Can children be observed washing hands appropriately? When asked, are children able to identify times when it is important to wash hands?

SCHOOL-AGE CHILDREN

- **Goal:** Children will be able to describe how germs can be spread from one hand to another, demonstrate the steps in hand washing, and explain how washing helps remove germs that can cause illness.
- **Materials:** Magnifying glasses; five small paint cups; five colors of paint (black, brown, red, yellow, blue); five small paint brushes; paper to cover the tabletop; a variety of everyday objects (small empty milk carton, pencils, a small ball, a hairbrush, plastic toys); hand washing sink; liquid soap; paper towels.
- **Activity plan:** Cover a tabletop with paper. Fill each paint cup with a small amount of a different color of paint. Place the filled paint cups, brushes, and objects on the table. Gather a group of five children at the table. Guide them to look at their hands with a magnifying glass and describe what they see. Talk about how you can see skin, wrinkles, and dirt but you cannot see germs with the eyes or a magnifying glass because germs are so small. Explain how germs can hide in the cracks and folds of the skin and describe why germs can be harmful (they carry disease that can make us sick). Offer each child a cup of paint and paint brush and tell them that you are going to pretend that the paint is "germs." Instruct them to dab paint all over the palm of just one hand. Then ask them to shake or grasp their clean hand with their "germy" painted hand. Next, ask them to pick up and move each of the objects to another place on the table for 30 seconds. Now ask them to stop and talk about what you see. Did the (paint) germs spread? How far? Can children detect colors of paint on

their hands that are different from the color they painted on? Remind children that germs spread the same way the paint colors spread around the toys, table, and hands. Guide the children to go the sink and rinse their hands for two to three seconds. Have them inspect their hands under the magnifying glass. Are the (paint) germs gone, or can they still be seen in the cracks of the hand? Guide the children to demonstrate washing their hands using the healthy hand-washing steps described above. Invite them to inspect their hands again when they have washed their hands carefully. Ask the children what they learned from the activity.
- **How to adjust the activity:** Speak clearly and use hand gestures to communicate the steps in the activity. Provide time for each child to describe what they see happening. Adapt the activity for children with special needs by using short paint brushes with wide handles and small shallow saucers of paint for stability. Ensure that students with wheelchairs are able to move up close to the table so that they can reach the objects and move them about on the table. Allow children who choose not to put paint on their hands to sit and watch and participate with others in describing what is happening as the paint "germs" move from place to place.
- **Did you meet your goal?** Are children able to describe how germs are spread? Can they demonstrate healthy hand washing? Can they explain how hand washing helps keep people healthy?

SUMMARY

- Food safety is the responsibility of all staff involved in the purchase, storage, preparation, and service of food to young children. Understanding the sources of food contamination that can cause foodborne illness is the first step in creating a food safe environment.

- Federal, state, and local health authorities are responsible for establishing and regulating food safety in licensed children's programs and schools. Teachers need to understand the food safety requirements that are mandated in their area. The county health department and food safety inspectors are a vital link and valuable resource in maintaining food safety in early childhood programs.

- The Hazard and Analysis Critical Control Point (HACCP) system consists of seven principles that guide the food safety program for any establishment that serves foods and provides strategies for preventing contamination of food at each stage of food handling.

- From the time food is purchased until meals are served, food service workers and teachers have important responsibilities to keep food safe and reduce the risk of foodborne illness.

- Food safety is an important consideration for managing potential emergencies and natural disasters. Teachers should be aware of the need to monitor for food defense and to prevent potential intentional contamination of food.

- Teaching children about food safety helps create a safe food environment. Food safety habits are supported by consistent routines that are offered in age-appropriate and developmentally appropriate ways, with ample opportunity for hands-on exploration.

CHECK YOUR UNDERSTANDING 7.5
Click here to check your understanding of teaching food safety to young children.

Chapter Quiz 7

 Click here to check your understanding of Chapter 7, Food Safety.

Discussion Starters

1. You have been asked by the director of your preschool program to participate on a hazard analysis committee with the goal of developing a food safety system using HACCP. Explain how you would determine the potential hazards and what steps you would take to develop a food safety system.

2. You are preparing a vegetable soup recipe with the preschool-age children in your class. Explain how you would incorporate a food safety message throughout the activity.

3. Explain the precautions and food safety concerns that need to be addressed during the receiving, storing, preparing, and serving of foods in an early child care setting.

Practice Points

1. Using the sample breakfast menu found in Chapter 6 (Figure 6-5), identify the foods that are potentially hazardous and the ideal temperatures at which they should be maintained.

2. Identify the critical control points and critical limits in the following recipe:

Arroz con Queso

Ingredients	Serve 50
Enriched white rice, medium grain	2 lbs. 13 oz.
Water	3½ cups
Fresh onions	1 quart
Canned green chilies, mild	12 oz.
Canned jalapeño pepper, chopped	½ cup
Granulated garlic	1 Tbsp. + 1 tsp.
Low-fat plain yogurt	1 quart +1½ cups
Low-fat milk, 1%	1 quart + 1 cup
Salt	2 tsp.
Reduced-fat Monterey jack cheese, shredded	1 lb.
Reduced-fat cheddar cheese, shredded	1 lb.
Canned pinto beans	2 quarts + 1¼ cups
Fresh tomatoes	1 lb. 8 oz.
Reduced-fat cheddar cheese, shredded	1 lb. 3 oz.

Directions	Critical Control Point (yes or no)	Critical Limit
1. Place rice and water in a stockpot. Bring to a boil. Cover and reduce heat to medium. Simmer for 12 minutes or until tender.		
2. Combine onions, chilies, jalapeños, granulated garlic, yogurt, milk, salt, reduced-fat Monterey jack cheese, reduced-fat cheddar cheese, and pinto beans. Add to rice. Spread 5 lbs. 18 oz. in each steam table pan (12 × 20″ × 2½″) (will need two pans).		
3. Bake in conventional oven at 350°F for 35 minutes.		
4. Sprinkle 12 oz. of diced tomatoes and 9½ oz. of reduced-fat cheddar cheese over the top of each pan and bake for 5 minutes until cheese is melted.		
Bonus question: What if dried pinto beans were used and cooked in advance to be used the next day—would there be any critical control points? If so, what would they be?		

Source: Recipe is from the USDA Recipes for Schools USDA Food and Nutrition Service Team Nutrition Updated November 30, 2011.

Note: For assistance with this practice point, refer to http://teamnutrition.usda.gov/Resources/usda_recipes.html.

3. Your first-grade class is going to the pumpkin patch to select pumpkins. You arranged to have your school food service provide brown bag lunches for this field trip. A mother has volunteered to make pumpkin cookies to bring along. The pumpkin patch farm will demonstrate how apples are turned into fresh cider and will offer children a taste. What are the food safety risks? How would you manage them?

Web Resources

FDA Food Code

Food Safety.Gov

The University of Mississippi National Food Service Management Institute

USDA Team Nutrition Healthy Meals Resource System

Key Terms

biological hazards

chemical hazards

cleaning

contamination

corrective action plan

critical control points (CCPs)

critical limits (CLs)

cross-contamination

first in, first out (FIFO)

food Code

food defense

foodborne illness

Hazard Analysis and Critical Control Point (HACCP) system

physical hazards

potentially hazardous foods

process approach

sanitizing

standard operating procedures (SOPs)

temperature danger zone

verification procedures

PART 3

PROMOTING HEALTHFUL PRACTICES

CHAPTER 8

Creating a Climate of Health and Wellness

learning outcomes

After reading this chapter, you should be able to:

1. Define the *components* of health and wellness, and identify the *determinants* that impact health and illness.

2. Identify resources for creating health policies in children's programs and schools, and describe the components of a written health policy.

3. Describe *health disparities*, and discuss strategies that teachers can use to promote acceptance and tolerance in the early childhood setting.

CASE STUDY

Cooper is a 7-year-old boy who was born with cystic fibrosis, a hereditary disease that affects the lungs and causes progressive disability. He is a pleasant and hard-working child, and his teacher Deanie gets to know him well. She notices in particular that Cooper enjoys drawing pictures of alligators.

Cooper's mother, Alicia, lovingly and tirelessly cares for him. Alicia is a working single mother who cannot afford health insurance for her family. Because she is unable to afford frequent preventive health care visits and medications for Cooper, he does not receive the care he needs. Consequently, he receives minimal routine preventive health care.

Cooper's school environment is one of the most consistent aspects of his life. Alicia often turns to Deanie to help her cope with challenges related to being a low-income single parent. Deanie is glad that Alicia is open to discussing Cooper's needs. It encourages her to learn more about ways she can support Cooper in the classroom. Reflecting on the challenges that Alicia faces, Deanie is inspired to plan a children's art show as part of the school open house. Alicia and Cooper are delighted to see his art on display. Deanie takes advantage of the event to introduce Alicia to other parents during the parent meeting. Deanie presents her plans to conduct special health promotion activities in the classroom and then asks the parents for their ideas.

"Every child deserves to be born well, to be physically fit, and to achieve self-responsibility for good health habits" (Bright Futures at Georgetown University). These goals highlight the importance of creating surroundings that promote and nurture health and wellness in young children. Children spend a large portion of their day under the care and guidance of their teacher, and they rely on teachers not only for significant educational support, but also for attention to their health and well-being. Teachers such as Deanie welcome the opportunity to impact the children's lives by creating healthy classroom environments and by teaching children to establish healthy habits. They also work to establish a positive and accepting atmosphere that helps each child feel valued and welcome.

In this chapter, we introduce the foundations for establishing a climate of wellness. We define health and wellness and discuss the components of health that impact the lives of children. We present strategies for supporting the development of optimal health in young children and explore the influences of health and culture on children's well-being. Creating a climate of health and wellness is an important teaching goal.

HEALTH AND WELLNESS IN EARLY CHILDHOOD

Health and wellness are concepts that together create a complete sense of well-being. They are interrelated but different. Understanding what determines good health helps teachers to recognize that all children do not have the same opportunity for good health.

Defining Health and Wellness

Health is a state of complete physical, mental, and social well-being, not merely the absence of disease or infirmity (World Health Organization, 1948.) Health is influenced by both genetics and environmental influences. Wellness is broader in perspective. It refers to optimal health and the vitality to enjoy life. Wellness is largely determined by lifestyle choices such as selecting healthful foods, obtaining necessary health services, and experiencing safe environments.

Individuals cannot change some aspects of their health, but they can improve their health outcomes by making positive lifestyle choices and focusing on wellness goals. In this way, health and wellness are interrelated, and the words are often used interchangeably to reflect a positive state of well-being.

health
a state of complete physical, mental, and social well-being and not merely the absence of disease or illness

wellness
optimal health and the vitality to enjoy life; is largely determined by lifestyle choices

Components of Health

Health is established through positive growth, development, and well-being in two major areas: physical health and mental health. In young children, both physical and mental health is essential to overall health and wellness. Each of these components influences the other.

Physical Health

Physical health refers to the condition of the body. It is affected by a diet that provides appropriate nutrition, adequate exercise, and sufficient rest. When these conditions are addressed on a daily basis, children are supported in their efforts to develop good physical health.

Children's physical health may be compromised by either acute or chronic conditions. Acute conditions have a sudden onset and short duration. Examples of acute illnesses include infectious diseases, such as the flu or colds, or injuries, such as bone fractures or sprains. Chronic conditions have a long duration and require ongoing evaluation or treatment. Examples include malformations that are present at birth, called congenital conditions—genetic diseases or physical malformations.

physical health
level of functioning and well-being individuals feel with respect to their bodies

acute conditions
medical conditions that have a sudden onset and short duration

chronic conditions
medical conditions that have a long duration and require ongoing evaluation and/or treatment

congenital conditions
physical defects or malformations that are present at birth

Many children with chronic illnesses are also at risk for or prone to acute illnesses. In the opening case scenario, for example, Cooper has a chronic condition called **cystic fibrosis**, which causes inadequate growth, frequent lung infections, and premature death. His physical health is also likely to affect his mental health as well his ability to learn and have healthy relationships in school.

cystic fibrosis
chronic health condition that causes growth retardation and frequent lung infections and premature death

Mental Health

mental health
the ability to function in developmentally appropriate ways with respect to self, family, and peers

Mental health is an essential part of wellness that promotes success in school and in society (American Psychological Association, 2014). Mental health is established in the early childhood years through a process of positive social and emotional development guided by healthy relationships with caregivers and teachers.

Physical and mental health impacts each other. For example, the presence of a special physical need, such as decreased mobility due to an injury or a physical impairment, may influence a child's mental health. On the other hand, children with mental health conditions such as depression may develop unhealthy habits that lead to problems with their physical health. In this chapter's case scenario, Cooper is unable to play actively with his peers because of breathing problems. This separation from typical physical play and interaction may predispose him to depression.

Determinants of Children's Health

Conventionally, we often think of health outcomes as being determined by an individual's characteristics, such as genetics, or as being a condition with a biological cause, such as an infection. However, factors external to an individual have a significant impact on health outcomes as well. For example, in the opening case, Cooper's disease is caused by a genetic defect. However, his health outcomes are dependent on both the course of his disease and external factors such as his relationships with caregivers, family income, and access to adequate housing. Understanding how these factors cause or contribute to disease is important for developing treatment or intervention programs and for promoting health and wellness in the classroom.

determinants of health
factors related to an individual's environment that have an impact on health and wellness

These **determinants of health** can be either **risk factors**, which contribute to illness or disease, or **protective factors**, which support health and wellness. Examples of risk factors include:

risk factors
aspects of health that contribute to illness or disease

- Poverty.
- Inadequate or unsafe housing or neighborhood.
- Poor access to healthy food.
- Dysfunctional family relationships.

protective factors
aspects of health that promote health and wellness

Examples of protective factors include:

- Warm, supportive relationship with family and caregivers.
- Access to wholesome food.
- Positive social support networks.
- Access to high-quality child care and education.

These factors are illustrated in Figure 8-1.

Social and Economic Environment

Social factors that influence health include social support networks and social status. Families who have greater support from other family members, friends, and their community experience better health outcomes. Another important social factor is education level. Lower education levels are associated with adverse health outcomes.

One of the strongest predictors of a child's health is the family's **socioeconomic status**, which includes economic, social, and work status measured by income, education, and occupation (Centers for Disease Control and Prevention, 2014b). An important component of socioeconomic status (SES) is family income because children who live in poverty are at a strong disadvantage with respect to health. Children who live in poverty have higher mortality rates, more frequent and severe diseases such as asthma, inadequate nutrition, less access to quality health care, lower immunization rates, and increased rates of obesity (American Academy of Pediatrics, 2013). When 23% are living in poverty, this is an enormous impact on the health and well-being of children (Annie E. Casey Foundation, 2014). Table 8-1 lists health problems more commonly seen in low-income families and implications for teachers.

Figure 8-1
Determinants of Health
Sources: Pearson Education, Inc., Hoboken, NJ.

socioeconomic status
a measure incorporating income, social, and work status that is a strong predictor of health

Physical Environment

The physical environment refers to where a family lives and visits, the structure of their neighborhood, and any environmental exposures in that space. Specific characteristics of a healthy physical environment include safe water, clean air, safe houses, safe and toxin-free school environments, and safe communities and roads. The physical environment can contribute to a child's health status. For example, certain children are more likely to develop asthma when exposed to toxins such as air pollution or

WHAT IF . . .
You were teaching in an area with families living in poverty? What are some health risks that children in your classroom might encounter? What are two useful activities that you could implement in your setting to contribute positively to their health and well-being?

TABLE 8-1   Health Problems More Commonly Affecting Children Living in Poverty

Common Health Problems	Possible Outcomes	Possible Solutions for Teachers
Exposure to environmental toxins	• Lead poisoning • Increased risk for asthma	• Conduct screenings • Educate families
Inadequate access to health care	• Inadequate immunizations • Lack of preventive health care • At risk for untreated illnesses	• Refer to health department or community health center
Mental health problems	• Emotional and behavioral problems • Learning disabilities	• Refer to available services • Provide support to families
Dental problems and inadequate dental care	• Pain • Problems with self-image	• Teach and promote oral hygiene • Promote screening • Refer to dental programs
Chronic conditions that limit a child's ability to participate fully in activities	• Increased absenteeism • Learning problems	• Refer to community resources • Communicate with families

Source: Seith & Isakson, 2011.

Lucio Rossi/Dorling Kindersley, Ltd.

The environment in which children live, learn, and play contributes to their overall wellness.

cockroaches, and in the opening case, Cooper suffers from a serious health condition that affects his lungs. Certain toxins or germs in his environment could cause him to develop serious infections that impact his overall health and well-being. This chapter's *Health Hint* describes how housing insecurity influences a child's health.

Individual Characteristics and Behaviors

Characteristics that influence health include age, gender, and genetic makeup. For example, infants are more susceptible to certain types of infections. Some diseases afflict only males, such as muscular dystrophy. Genetic defects or hereditary diseases can cause certain health conditions. A child's behavior also influences health. Examples include eating habits, level of physical activity, and hand washing habits.

Influencing Health and Wellness in the Early Childhood Setting

Learning the skills that promote wellness is a lifelong process that begins at birth. Young children depend on adults to make healthy choices for them and to teach them to make choices for themselves. In the early childhood years, children are particularly receptive to aspects in their environment that facilitate learning. They are also vulnerable to forces that obstruct health. Teaching children healthful practices is an investment in a healthy childhood and perpetuates health and wellness into the child's future (American Academy of Pediatrics, American Public Health Association, National Resource Center for Health and Safety in Child Care and Early Education, 2011).

Families and teachers help children establish lifestyles that promote wellness. Children learn habits and behaviors that positively impact health, such as playing actively, getting sufficient sleep, washing hands, and eating a variety of healthy foods. Healthy habits and lifestyle promote healthy outcomes across a lifetime.

In addition, many chronic, or ongoing, conditions seen in adulthood, such as obesity, heart disease, diabetes, and mental health problems, have their roots in

HEALTH HINT   The Effect of Housing Insecurity on Children's Health

Housing insecurity has been strongly associated with poor health outcomes. *Housing insecurity* refers to high housing costs in proportion to income, poor housing quality, unstable neighborhoods, overcrowding, or homelessness. Housing insecurity is also associated with multiple health issues, including growth problems, food insecurity, and developmental delay. In particular, children whose families experience homelessness have higher rates of infections and chronic disease, poor mental health, decreased ability to cope with stress, poor parent-child relationships, poor social relationships, and inadequate sleep. Teachers can support families by screening for these social issues and making appropriate referrals when problems are identified because many families who qualify for housing subsidies do not receive them.

Source: Council on Community Pediatrics, 2013.

early childhood. Parents and teachers play an important role in teaching children lifestyle habits that minimize the potential of such diseases occurring. This is a remarkable and exciting opportunity for teachers to influence children's lifelong development positively. This chapter's *Policy Point* describes how characteristics of the early childhood setting can influence physical activity.

Understanding the determinants of health that impact children guides teachers to establish protective approaches in the classroom. For example, growing up in a poor neighborhood where children often are not free to play outdoors because of unsafe conditions may compromise children's physical health. Teachers address this by providing opportunities for children to play actively in safely supervised outdoor environments. Overall, compared with children living in higher-income neighborhoods, children who live in disadvantaged neighborhoods often benefit more from school health screenings, classroom activities relevant to health promotion, and referral to needed community resources, simply because access to these services outside the school setting is inadequate due to the impacts of poverty and lack of access to usual health care.

Although many factors in a child's life are out of the teacher's control, teachers promote children's health by giving them tools to protect themselves, such as warding off germs, practicing safety procedures, and talking about their worries and frustrations. Teachers observe children throughout the day and are often the first to know when a child's hunger or thirst is getting in the way of learning. They have the authority to make sure children get outside daily to run and be active, and they encourage children to brush their teeth after lunch. These practices counterbalance some of the negative factors existing in children's lives.

POLICY POINT

Physical Activity in Child Care and Preschool Environments

The National Association for Sport and Physical Education recommends that all preschool children (ages 3 to 5 years) participate in up to 60 minutes of structured activities *and* 60 minutes of unstructured play every day. It also recommends that toddlers participate in 30 minutes of structured and 60 minutes of unstructured physical activity per day. Most states have no recommendations or regulations addressing these recommendations. Most children's settings do not provide this level of active play. Characteristics of children's environments influence time spent in moderate and vigorous physical activity. Further recommendations include the following:

- Outdoor active play should be provided at least two times per day.
- An indoor play space should be provided where children can be active.
- Children should not be seated for longer than 30 minutes.
- Staff should encourage and join children in playing actively.
- Denying active playtime should not be used as punishment.

The child care center or preschool a child attends is associated with the child's level of physical activity. Certain policies and environmental characteristics are associated with a healthier level of physical activity, such as the availability of play equipment and activity opportunities, smaller school size, higher education level of staff members, child-initiated play, and an outdoor play area that offers more open areas and the presence of vegetation.

The following characteristics in the center's policies have been noted to increase physical activity:

- Staff education and training.
- Staff behavior on the playground.
- Additional training provided to staff related to physical activity in young children.
- Reaching out to parents supporting physical activity in the home.
- Multiple outdoor recess breaks as opposed to one prolonged break.

Source: Head Start Body Start, 2012.

CHECK YOUR UNDERSTANDING 8.1
Click here to check your understanding of health and wellness in early childhood.

Teachers also contribute to children's healthful development by getting to know each family's social circumstances and the challenges that may impact children's wellness. Teachers arrange opportunities to:

- Promote the development of positive relationships between teachers and parents.
- Increase parental knowledge of children's cognitive and emotional needs.
- Encourage children's healthy social development and behavior.
- Prevent child abuse.

CHILD HEALTH POLICIES

health policies
guidelines that define a desired health outcome, such as promoting healthy behaviors and preventing the spread of disease

A climate of wellness in the early childhood setting is founded on supportive **health policies**. Health policies are guidelines that address common health and safety issues and ensure safe and appropriate health practices, which in turn promote a desired health outcome. They also help to guide decision making about how to manage difficult situations. Specific policies are required by national, state, and local agencies that license early childhood programs. Accrediting organizations also outline minimum standards for programs they endorse.

Resources for Health Policy Development

A variety of resources are available to guide the development of relevant program health policies. The resources discussed next aim to improve services to young children by establishing best practice goals.

National Resource Center for Health and Safety in Child Care and Early Education

The National Resource Center for Health and Safety in Child Care and Early Education (NRC) takes the lead in communicating standards that inform child health policies. The NRC website provides a variety of resources that support health and safety in out-of-home care and education settings:

- *Health and safety standards:* The primary information needed to develop policies that promote health and safety in children's programs is the document called *Caring for Our Children: National Health and Safety Performance Standards; Guidelines for Early Care and Education Settings, 3rd edition*, 2011 (American Academy of Pediatrics, American Public Health Association, National Resource Center for Health and Safety in Child Care and Early Education, 2011). This resource presents the rationale for policies that guide health practices and sets the standards for quality in healthful programming.
- *Licensure regulations:* The licensing regulations of the 50 states, the District of Columbia, Puerto Rico, and the Virgin Islands are available for review and comparison. The minimum policies that must be established in licensed family child care and early education programs are presented.
- *Standards-based resources:* User-friendly materials on specific subjects provide information for developing policies such as how to administer medications in children's settings and when to exclude sick children from care.

Health policies are a requirement for licensed programs. They also describe an early childhood program's commitment to health and safety. While program directors and principals usually manage decisions about policies with input from community health providers, teachers should be familiar with policies that guide health practices in their setting.

Office of Head Start

The Office of Head Start provides the *Head Start Performance Standards* that outline a variety of nutrition, health, and safety policies for Early Head Start, Head Start, American Indian/Alaska Native, and Migrant and Seasonal Head Start programs nationwide (U.S. Department of Health and Human Services, 2011). Head Start programs are required to develop policies and practices related to:

- Child health and development.
- Child health and safety.
- Child nutrition.
- Child mental health.

National Association for the Education of Young Children

The National Association for the Education of Young Children (NAEYC) is a professional organization committed to increasing the quality of programs that serve children from birth through age 8. It offers several systems of **accreditation** (endorsement) to acknowledge programs that meet national standards of quality.

accreditation
endorsement or acknowledgment of programs that meet national standards of quality

NAEYC accreditation assesses quality in 10 children's program standards. Topic areas in the health standards include the following:

- Promote and protect children's health.
- Control spread of infectious diseases.
- Ensure children's nutritional well-being.
- Maintain a healthful environment.

School Wellness Policies

Under the Child Nutrition and Reauthorization Act of 2004 and the Healthy, Hunger-Free Kids Act of 2010, each local education agency is required to develop a wellness policy that includes the following (Centers for Disease Control and Prevention, 2014a):

- Goals for nutrition promotion and education, physical activity, and other school-based activities designed to promote wellness.
- Guidelines to ensure that all food available during the school day is healthy.
- Community involvement in the development of the school wellness policy, including parents, students, and representatives of the school food authority, the school board, school administrators, school health professionals, and the public.
- Plans for measuring implementation of the wellness policies and its effect on school wellness.

Nutrition, health, and safety policies help teachers establish healthful environments and implement safe practices in the classroom.

Johoo/Fotolia

Components of Health Policies

Written health policies need to be clear, brief, and easy to understand. Guidelines for writing health policies include the following:

1. *State prevention goals.* They are usually written in the form of goals that promote positive health outcomes and prevent specific problems. For example: *Health checks will be conducted daily* or *Children will be supervised by sight and sound.*

2. *Identify steps to achieve the policy goals.* List the steps, or procedures, necessary to implement the policy. Procedures should be specific and identify who will do what. For example: *The lead teacher will greet children at the door and conduct a 20-second health check. Identified concerns will be discussed with the parent.*

3. *Guide response to difficult situations.* Policies must also direct appropriate responses to challenging situations. In the health check example, this might include *If signs of illness are observed, communicate kindly but firmly that the parent must take the child home.*

4. *Ensure that procedures are practical and specific to the setting.* Lists of policies established for early childhood and school settings are similar. However, the procedures for implementing each policy may be different to accommodate the particular setting. Health checks in a preschool setting may be conducted as children and parents arrive. Health checks in the school setting may be conducted during an opening circle activity after children are in the classroom.

An important health policy area concerns food allergies. More information is available in this chapter's *Nutrition Note.*

Ensuring That Policies Are Appropriate for the Setting

Some programs serving young children invite local health consultants to advise on the development of health policies. For instance, Head Start programs convene a Health Services Advisory Committee of parents and professionals to participate in developing and reviewing health policies. This ensures that wellness goals are based on current knowledge and practice.

NUTRITION NOTE   Food Allergies in Early Childhood

It is estimated that 5% of children have a food allergy and 88% of schools have at least one child with a food allergy. Allergic reactions to foods are common and can be very severe. Schools can be prepared by developing policies that include the following:

- Ensure the daily management of food allergies in each allergic child by identifying the child and exactly what he or she is allergic to, what the reaction is, and how to treat it. As a first step, make a discreet plan to reduce the risk of food allergy.
- Prepare for food allergy emergencies. Schools should consider having an EpiPen available for emergency use

because in 25% of life-threatening reactions at schools, the child has had no previous history.

- Provide training and education for teachers.
- Teach all children and parents about food allergies.

Teachers should also understand that the parents of children with food allergies often experience constant fear, especially as they transition their child to an environment where they have to trust others. This can be very difficult and stressful. Communication and a clear policy can help reduce this stress for everyone.

Source: Centers for Disease Control and Prevention, 2013.

Obtaining the advice of community health workers also helps to identify policies that are needed to address health and safety concerns unique to a certain community. For example:

- A preschool located in an area where air quality poses a health risk developed a policy related to outdoor play. The policy describes how the program determines when air quality is at an unhealthy level, such as when a smog alert has been issued and where the children will play if an alert has been announced.

- A school in an urban area where violence is frequently reported developed policies related to teaching a violence prevention curriculum. The policy states what curriculum approaches will be used and how often the prevention interventions will be conducted.

Health policies should be reviewed periodically, and new policies should be developed when necessary to improve program services. This chapter's *Progressive Programs & Practices* describes how child care settings can collaborate with public health to promote health and wellness.

PROGRESSIVE PROGRAMS & PRACTICES

Creating a Climate of Health and Wellness

By Kathy Cunningham, Boston Public Health Commission

The Boston Public Health Commission conducted the Wellness in Child Care Initiative that trained Boston family child care providers on strategies to promote healthy weight using the Nutrition and Physical Activity Self-Assessment for Child Care (NAPSACC). The NAPSACC instrument helped to identify strengths and challenges to healthy eating and physical activity within family child care settings. As a result of the trainings, providers implemented wellness action plans to improve nutrition and physical activity at their sites and to engage parents in supporting healthy weight for their children.

Key components of the initiative were to (1) provide free training to family child care providers, with continuing education credits as an incentive for participation; (2) provide resources for providers to assess their own nutrition and physical activity; and (3) make environmental and policy changes to support healthy weight among children.

We offered the training in two 6-hour sessions. The first workshop gave an overview of the obesity issue with modules on ways to improve healthy eating and incorporate 60 minutes of physical activity each day. The second workshop included time for the providers to review their NAPSACC assessment and develop Action Plans for their program. Also discussed was how to communicate with parents about their policy changes for healthy eating, physical activity, and limited television time. Providers had peer-to-peer opportunities to share strategies that worked and to learn about community resources.

The workshops offered child care providers the opportunity to expand their knowledge of healthy foods and ways to offer these foods to children in fun and interactive ways. Providers also received incentives to support indoor physical activity to reach the recommended 60 minutes per day. Finally, they were given the opportunity to work on policies to improve the environments in which children spend a large percentage of their day.

Noah Craigwell/Boston Public Health Commission

CLASSROOM CONNECTION

Watch this video on how services can be provided to families in child care settings. Give three examples of health policies that are important in a child care setting.

dental caries
tooth decay; is the most common and preventable chronic disease in childhood

Policies Promoting Health and Wellness

Policies that promote health in early childhood can meet standards and while being creative and specifically designed to meet the needs of children in the community.

Oral health promotion

Childhood tooth decay, or **dental caries**, is one of the most common and preventable chronic diseases in childhood. Caries can be prevented by proper nutrition, dental hygiene, and early treatment. One of the most important aspects of caries prevention is improving the oral health of mothers through access to dental care.

Schools can promote oral health through education and dental care services. For children who lack health insurance and are unlikely to receive usual, regular dental care, such as Cooper at the beginning of the chapter, school-based oral health promotion is the only access to dental care available to promote dental health. Policies that direct teachers to offer oral hygiene education and encourage toothbrushing after meals contribute to better oral health. Teachers are responsible for planning and implementing these health education activities. The goals for oral health education include helping children understand why their teeth are important and how brushing and seeing a dentist help keep teeth healthy.

Collaboration with community partners is helpful. Programs can collaborate with local dentists or with state dental associations. Teachers of toddlers and preschool-age groups might read books about taking care of teeth or dramatize a trip to the dentist using puppets. Preschool settings may also provide toothbrushes and toothpaste for children.

Oral health promotion begins in infancy. The NAEYC developed a practice guideline that relates to early dental care for infants. The guideline states that infants should have their teeth and gums cleaned with a cloth after each feeding (NAEYC, 2014). Proper nutrition also contributes to the prevention of tooth decay. Teaching proper nutrition and serving meals rich in whole grains, fruits, and vegetables are ways to promote oral health. The *Teaching Wellness* feature describes ways to teach children about the importance of brushing teeth.

WHAT IF . . .

you wanted to teach oral hygiene in your kindergarten class by having the children brush their teeth after their snack each day? What procedures would you need to consider to prevent the spread of germs during toothbrushing? Would you offer toothpaste? Why or why not?

Dental Care Services

Oral health in children has become a priority for early childhood health. The Office of Head Start initiated the Head Start Oral Health Initiative for Young Children in 2005, providing supplemental funding for programs to improve oral health services for enrolled children. School policies that implement dental care services are of great benefit to children. Strategies to provide dental care services in schools include screening for dental problems, collaborating with community members to provide oral health assessments, and promoting school-affiliated or school-based dental care services such as fluoride varnish or dental sealants.

Policies Promoting Physical Activity

The U.S. Department of Health and Human Services recommends that children be physically active for a minimum of 60 minutes per day (Centers for Disease

LEARNING OUTCOME   Children will learn how to brush their teeth.

Vocabulary focus: teeth, gums, germs, plaque, cavity, decay.

Safety watch: Ensure that children sit or stand quietly and use their toothbrushes safely. Watch that toothbrushes are not exchanged. Make sure children drink fresh water and spit appropriately. Use appropriate toothpaste only with children 2 years of age and older.

INFANTS AND TODDLERS

- **Goal:** To encourage children's willingness to have their gums wiped and teeth brushed.
- **Materials:** Damp washcloth or gauze, small toothbrushes, paper cups, fresh water, and paper towels.
- **Activity plan:** For infants without teeth, gently wipe the gums with a clean damp cloth. For infants with teeth and toddlers, use a small, soft toothbrush and fresh water to brush teeth and gums gently. Talk through the process and describe the steps for brushing teeth. Say, "You are keeping your mouth open while I help clean your gums." Say words that teach the steps of brushing, "First, let's rub (or brush) the front of your gums (or teeth) and then the sides, the backs, and the tops." Encourage babies and children to help by placing their hands on yours or by guiding their hands to rub their gums or brush their teeth gently.

Add interest and extend brushing time by singing a song. Try singing this song to the tune of *Row, Row, Row Your Boat*: "Brush, brush, brush, your teeth, brush them twice a day. This will keep them clean and white and help prevent decay." When finished, offer the children a small drink of fresh water.

- **How to adjust the activity:** For children who are not English speakers, post pictures of babies and toddlers having their gums rubbed and teeth brushed. Talk with parents or dentists for recommendations about modified toothbrushes designed to help brush the teeth of children who have special oral health or physical motor needs.
- **Did you meet your goal?** Were babies willing to have their gums wiped or teeth brushed? Were toddlers willing to participate in brushing their teeth?

PRESCHOOLERS AND KINDERGARTNERS

- **Goal:** To learn to brush teeth appropriately and know that toothbrushing is important.
- **Materials:** A children's book about brushing teeth, such as *Clarabella's Teeth* by An Vrombaut; a model of large teeth and a large toothbrush; toothbrushes; paper cups; toothpaste (approved by the American Dental Association); fresh water; sink; paper towels.
- **Activity plan:** Gather a small group at a table. Read a book about brushing teeth. Talk about how brushing teeth removes the food particles that can cause cavities. Demonstrate the steps of brushing teeth using the model teeth and large toothbrush. Provide each child with a toothbrush and a paper cup with a pea-sized dab of toothpaste on the edge. Invite children to practice the steps of toothbrushing:
  - Dab the toothbrush against the toothpaste.
  - Hold the toothbrush at a 45-degree angle; brush front, sides, back, and top of each tooth.

- Gently brush the tongue.
- Spit toothpaste into the cup.
- Rinse toothbrush and return it to the child's place in the toothbrush rack.
- Rinse mouth with water and spit into the sink. Dry mouth on towel and discard towel.

- **How to adjust the activity:** For English learners, read a story in English and in the child's home language. Post pictures as cues for each step in brushing teeth to help all children understand the steps. Assist a child with special physical needs to be successful by providing modified toothbrushes or adjustments to help the child sit at the table or stand at the sink.
- **Did you meet your goal?** Are children able to brush teeth appropriately? When asked, are children able to arrange picture cards to show the steps of toothbrushing, or can they tell why it is important to brush teeth?

SCHOOL-AGE CHILDREN

- **Goal:** To learn how to carefully brush teeth and understand that toothbrushing removes germs that cause cavities.
- **Materials:** Toothbrushes, paper cups with dab of toothpaste, paper cups with water, disposable dentist mirror, plaque-disclosing tablet, sink with running water.
- **Activity plan:** Gather children at a table. Review the steps for brushing teeth. Offer children toothbrushes and cups with toothpaste. Invite them to brush their teeth and spit toothpaste into the cup. Ask the children to look at their

teeth with a disposable mirror and describe what they see. Do they see any germs? Talk about how you cannot see germs because they are so small. Germs can hide on their teeth and cause plaque. Plaque sticks to the teeth and causes holes, or cavities, in the surface of the tooth. It also makes their gums sore. Now ask the children to use the plaque-disclosing tablet. Have the children chew the tablet first on one side of the mouth and then on the other, then spit into a cup. Ask the children to look at their teeth again in their mirror. Do they see red and pink? This shows that the plaque was not brushed away. Encourage children to brush their teeth until the color is brushed away. Offer children a small drink of water to rinse their mouths and guide them to rinse their toothbrushes and return them to the toothbrush rack. Help children explain why it is important to take their time when they brush their teeth.

- **How to adjust the activity:** For English learners, provide a story or information for the child to read in their home language or post pictures that depict and describe the steps of toothbrushing in both English and the children's home languages. Include a picture that shows germs and plaque. For children with special developmental needs, obtain modified toothbrushes, adjust how the child sits or stands to brush teeth, or make other accommodations to assist each child to be successful when brushing teeth.
- **Did you meet your goal?** Are children able to show how to brush teeth carefully and describe why brushing teeth is important?

Ariel Daeschel

CHECK YOUR UNDERSTANDING 8.2

Click here to check your understanding of child health policies.

Control and Prevention and Bridging the Gap Research Program, 2014a). Physical activity promotes many aspects of health, including physical, social, and emotional well-being (Centers for Disease Control and Prevention and Bridging the Gap Research Program, 2014a). Certain characteristics and policies can ensure that early childhood programs promote adequate and safe physical activity, including staff education and training, education of families, multiple outdoor recess breaks, and accessibility to an outdoor play area that offers more open areas and presence of vegetation.

At the district level, 60% of districts had no policy for recess in elementary students. Many districts and states recommended minimum amounts of physical activity but only 22% of districts actually required the standard. States and districts are encouraged to develop thoughtful physical activity policies and provide training to staff. Monitoring and implementing these policies is also needed to ensure that children receive adequate access to physical activity (Centers for Disease Control and Prevention and Bridging the Gap Research Program, 2014b). This chapter's *Policy Point* describes why physical activity guidelines are also important in child care settings.

HEALTH PROMOTION AMONG DIVERSE POPULATIONS

Acknowledging the value and belief systems of children and families from culturally diverse backgrounds is a critical aspect of understanding and promoting health and wellness. An individual's race, culture, and ethnic background influences how they perceive health and illness (Spector, 2012). The demographics of infants and children enrolled in schools and early childhood settings have changed significantly during the past several decades. The cultural composition of families in the United States is increasingly diverse. With more children from a variety of backgrounds in schools today, it is important to understand and acknowledge differing perspectives related to health and health promotion.

Disparities in Quality of Health

Not all families experience the same quality of health. These differences are called **health disparities**, which are differences in quality of health based on social factors such as gender, age, race, ethnicity, socioeconomic status, or geographic location (Flores, 2012). An example of a health disparity is that African American children experience higher rates of certain chronic diseases such as asthma or that children living in rural areas are more likely to be inadequately vaccinated. The reasons health disparities exist are complex. Some families have ready access to health care through insurance programs. Others delay accessing medical treatment until health conditions become dire because they do not know how to access the care or cannot afford the cost. Disparities in physical and mental health also occur due to social reasons such as poverty, unsafe neighborhoods, or inadequate education.

Language may also be a barrier for some families. Teachers gain a perspective about the potential challenges the families face when they build relationships with each child's family. Although teachers are not health professionals, they can provide important links to resources that are available in the community. Health care professionals and teachers should be aware that these disparities exist and help all families access available resources.

Disparities in the quality of health are deeply related to social causes. For example, children's early nutrition can influence health outcomes as they grow. Children who experience malnutrition will have worse health outcomes. Children whose families are exposed to discrimination may have adverse health outcomes. Children living in unsafe neighborhoods or in impoverished living conditions will have a higher risk of health problems. Again, teachers may not be able to influence a child's living conditions or prior history of malnutrition directly, but through family support and health promotion, the chances of the child having better health will be greater.

health disparities differences in health outcomes and quality of health and health care experienced by people of different incomes, races, or education levels

Recognizing Stereotypes and Prejudice

Disparities exist in health but also in other settings that serve diverse racial, cultural, and socioeconomic groups, such as classrooms. Teachers come to classrooms with their own backgrounds, beliefs, and past experiences. Although they may be conscious of discriminatory practices and work to avoid them, there are other subtle ways in which children and families of diverse backgrounds are treated differently. Stereotyping and prejudice often lead to intolerance.

- **Stereotyping** results when individuals are labeled based on certain characteristics such as racial or ethnic heritage, age, gender, or socioeconomic background. An example of stereotyping is evident when teachers make the assumption that "all" boys prefer to play with trucks or "all" children of a particular racial group are good at math or are more expressive. Often individuals are not conscious of the way they stereotype others.

- **Prejudice** refers to an unfounded generalization that is directed toward an individual based on group membership or toward a group (Institute of Medicine, 2003). Prejudice is fueled by intolerance. It is evident when teachers group

stereotyping the labeling of others based on certain characteristics such as racial or ethnic heritage, age, gender, or socioeconomic background

prejudice a negative attitude toward an individual based on group membership

children according to certain characteristics rather than by an understanding of each individual child's skills and needs. For example, the teacher may create a seating arrangement that places the low-income children at the front of the room based on her perception that they will not pay attention if they choose their own seats.

Stereotyping and prejudice can result in discrimination or inequality and unfair treatment. Discrimination exists in health care, education, housing, employment, and other aspects of society. Exposure to discrimination is associated with poor health outcomes (Institute of Medicine, 2003). Besides embracing children and their families' differences, teachers should also ensure that there is acceptance and tolerance among all children in their classrooms.

When teachers notice that families are not treated fairly, they can serve as advocates to support families.

WHAT IF . . .

you are a preschool teacher for a culturally diverse population and you encountered a family that used unusual home remedies to treat a chronic cough? What would be your initial impression of this decision? What health issues would you be concerned about? How would you handle your concerns with the family?

Anadelia, a child in Shauna's first-grade class, is missing a needed immunization. Her mother, Consuelo, tells Shauna that she has taken her daughter to the local clinic twice to obtain the shot. Both times they were told by the receptionist that Anadelia did not need any more shots. Consuelo is concerned because the school nurse has told her that Anadelia will be excluded from class if the immunizations are not brought up to date. Consuelo asks Shauna for help.

Shauna and the school nurse collaborate to help Consuelo obtain an appointment to discuss vaccination details with a nurse or doctor. Consuelo returns to the physician's office where Anadelia receives the needed immunization. Shauna reflects on the situation and feels frustrated that this family was not given sufficient encouragement to sort out the child's needs on the first visit. Was it because the family is Hispanic?

Promoting Acceptance in the Classroom

Teachers set the standard for acceptance and tolerance in the classroom and among children's families. This is demonstrated when teachers interact equitably with all children and families, regardless of their backgrounds and unique characteristics. Teaching children to understand and appreciate differences is one way to promote acceptance. Activities to introduce this complex concept should begin simply and become more detailed, as shown in the following examples.

Pearson Education

CLASSROOM CONNECTION

Watch this video on how a teacher can encourage cooperation and promote acceptance in the classroom. Which strategies are used by this teacher to promote acceptance?

Sandi offers toddlers and preschoolers many opportunities to sort and classify objects while introducing the concepts of "same" and "different." To begin, she offers items that have only one aspect that is different, such as square blocks of the same size in two different colors. Children learn to sort by color. Next, she increases the challenge by offering both square blocks and small balls in two colors. In this task, children are able to sort by color and shape. Activities such as these engage children in interesting discovery of how objects can have characteristics that are the same and at the same time have aspects that are different: Red blocks and red balls are the same color but have different shapes.

Al engages older children in exploration of personal characteristics that may be the same (Who has five fingers?) and those that may be different (Who has brown hair?). He and the children make lists of the many ways children in the class are the same and different. They begin to understand that a large variety of similarities and differences exist among people.

From these activities, children begin to recognize that personal characteristics and personal choices are sometimes the same and sometimes different. Lessons such as these plant the ideas that help children to resist stereotyping: Not all people are the same, and not all people like the same thing. They also help children learn to oppose prejudice as the children begin to see themselves as sometimes members of one group (the group that loves soccer, for example) and sometimes members of another group.

Learning to recognize and enjoy differences and to develop a tolerance of differing points of view is a lifelong process. Teachers who model accepting behaviors and who encourage children to explore these topics offer children the opportunity to develop skills of negotiation, problem solving, and appreciation of the rights of self and others.

Supporting Families Who Do Not Speak English

Communication between teachers and parents is critical to children's well-being. Teachers need to be able to discuss the child's educational progress, describe any observed health concerns, and share information about behavioral or social issues. Likewise parents need to be able to inform teachers of any health issues or other concerns they may have about the child. Because a growing percentage of children come from families whose first language is other than English, teachers need a plan to overcome language barriers when communicating with families.

For casual conversations or communicating with families about everyday classroom activities, teachers may be able to involve other family members or even older children as interpreters. When discussing sensitive or confidential issues, including health issues, however, teachers may need to seek the assistance of interpreters to establish communication with families. Using English-speaking family members may be convenient, but it does have some disadvantages. Family members may not be objective and may filter information instead of translating exactly what has been said. This is particularly troublesome in situations involving details of the child's health or behavior. Confidentiality may be compromised when family members are used as interpreters, and the quality of information obtained may be compromised.

Trained interpreters offer an appropriate but expensive option. When this is a viable option, trained interpreters have skills that are extremely helpful in communicating important information. Trained interpreters demonstrate fluency in both languages and recognize the importance of confidentiality. They also have a clear role, which prevents inaccurate transfer of information. When teachers do not have ready access to the assistance of trained interpreters, alternative strategies are needed. These may include the following:

- To prioritize when trained interpreters are most needed, such as to assist with family conferences or meetings to plan services for children with special health care needs or when situations arise related to challenging behavioral problems or mental health problems.
- To establish connections with community health workers or health navigators with local agencies.

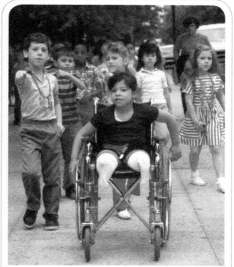

Teachers play an important role in promoting acceptance in early childhood settings.

David Grossman/Alamy

Katie Russell

Pearson Education

CLASSROOM CONNECTION

Watch this video on a how a principal describes techniques used in her school to encourage the involvement of parents who are English language learners. What other strategies would be helpful for schools with diverse classrooms?

A Matter of ETHICS

You are about to start a job teaching in a preschool that is composed predominantly of children from Laos and Cambodia. Most of their families speak only their native language, and few of them speak English. How will you prepare yourself for this experience? What are some ways you can support and maintain the use of the children's home language? How can you facilitate communication with parents?

CHECK YOUR UNDERSTANDING 8.3

Click here to check your understanding of health promotion among diverse populations.

- To create or obtain simple printed bilingual messages related to common early childhood situations to share with parents, such as *Your child appeared ill today* or *Several children in this class have become ill with the flu. Please remember to keep your child home when she is sick.*
- To advocate within the early childhood or school setting for the hiring of bilingual teachers who can assist everyone in improving communication with families who are not English-speaking.

Although using family members or children as interpreters may be appropriate for much of the information that needs to be conveyed to families, such as future early childhood activities and family responsibilities, this practice should be reconsidered when handling information about any aspects of a child's health.

SUMMARY

- Both individual factors *and* a child's social and physical environment contribute to health, whereas lifestyle factors affect wellness.
- Policies that guide health practices in the early childhood settings outline the procedures that create consistency and continuity in health and wellness program services.
- Racial, cultural, and socioeconomic backgrounds influence health, and teachers can plan activities that are culturally sensitive and honor differences.

Chapter Quiz

Click here to check your understanding of Chapter 8, Creating a Climate of Health and Wellness.

Discussion Starters

1. What is your social, cultural, economic, and educational background? How do you think your background has affected your quality of health and your access to health care?
2. How can teachers address health disparities in society?
3. Think about low-income families you have known or worked with in the past. What are some of the challenges they faced? In what ways do you think children from low-income families are at a disadvantage in society? What are some advantages or strengths that children might gain from growing up in a low-income family?

Practice Points

1. Examine the community in which you live. What is the incidence of poverty in your area? What resources are available to families with low incomes? What gaps in local services may limit the involvement of children from low-income families in school activities?

2. Imagine that you are in charge of a dental health promotion event for your school. On what oral health concepts would you focus? What resources would you tap to obtain expertise? What ideas do you have to include both children and parents in this learning experience? How would you ensure that this event reaches non-English-speaking families in your school?

3. Create a lesson that promotes physical activity for preschool-age children. Make adjustments for children who have special needs that pertain to mobility. How would you teach this lesson to children who speak predominantly Spanish? What aspects of the preschool environment might promote physical activity?

Web Resources

Model School Wellness Policies

National Center for Child Poverty

National Resource Center for Health and Safety in Child Care and Early Education

The Annie E. Casey Foundation

Key Terms

accreditation

acute conditions

chronic conditions

congenital conditions

cystic fibrosis

dental caries

determinants of health

health disparities

health policies

health

mental health

physical health

prejudice

protective factors

risk factors

socioeconomic status

stereotyping

wellness

Health Screening and Assessment

After reading this chapter, you should be able to:

1. Describe the components of a comprehensive health history.
2. Explain how to gather and manage confidential health information.
3. Discuss the teacher's role in reviewing immunization records and medical home status in early childhood.
4. Provide examples of health evaluations commonly administered in early childhood settings.

CASE STUDY

Adelina is a bright 9-month-old infant whose family has recently immigrated from Mexico. Adelina is being enrolled in an infant child care program. Her family is pleased to have a chance to visit with the teacher, who explains that during their visit, she will ask some questions to learn about Adelina's health and development. After a few minutes, the family provides the records they brought showing that Adelina received vaccinations in Mexico and additional vaccinations in Texas. As they talk, Maria learns that Adelina had a serious illness at 3 months of age that the family describes as an "infection of the brain." They report that Adelina was hospitalized for several weeks but has otherwise been healthy.

Maria reviews the health history and enrollment materials. Maria asks if the family has concerns about Adelina's development. The family reports that Adelina has not started making sounds or using other vocalizations appropriate for her age. They are worried because this is different from their experiences with their older children. Together Maria and the family decide that this should be evaluated further. The family also reports that they recently moved out of an older home that was very run down. They have heard that a physician can do a simple blood test to determine if the baby was exposed to lead. Maria records these referrals accordingly.

By the end of the visit, Adelina is reaching out to pat Maria's hands and offer her toys. They say good-bye, and the family leaves with instructions on where to follow up on the issues discussed. They are excited about their daughter's new care setting and are pleased that Maria is so helpful and approachable. After they leave, Maria reflects on their conversation. She makes a note to check with the family in a week to see what they learned from their follow-up plan.

Children come to early childhood classrooms with different health and development experiences. Learning about these aspects of a child's history is an important part of the transition into the classroom. Children's health and development information guides the development of the care and education plan. It ensures that teachers are aware of children's individual health needs. It also focuses attention on concerns such as allergies or hearing or vision problems so that children do not miss important opportunities to learn.

In this chapter, we discuss the significance of evaluating children's health to ensure that they are ready to learn. We highlight the importance of managing health information and communicating it appropriately. We explore the common ways in which children are assessed and screened for health and development concerns that might impact learning. Finally, we offer suggestions about how daily health assessments can be conducted in the classroom to monitor and improve children's health and well-being while they are in the classroom.

EVALUATING CHILDREN'S HEALTH AND DEVELOPMENT

Early childhood programs and schools are part of children's health and wellness network. Health evaluation tools are used in early childhood programs and schools because these settings provide an important opportunity to assess children at an early age and determine who needs further assistance or referral for services. The early childhood setting may be the first time some children have had attention given to aspects of health and development that influence learning. In this way, early childhood programs provide an important contribution to children's future development and opportunity to learn.

Understanding Health Evaluations

A **health evaluation** is a comprehensive assessment of a child's health and well-being. It is a multifaceted process that reviews and considers the many factors that influence children's health. Health evaluations are conducted for several specific purposes:

health evaluation
an assessment of a child's overall health and well-being

1. To understand a child's health status or special health-related needs so that teachers can make necessary accommodations.
2. To identify known medical conditions or risk factors for illness or injury.
3. To identify children who benefit from further evaluations or referrals.
4. To help families learn about the health of their child and to understand potential hazards to their child's health.
5. To identify gaps in the family's access to needed resources.

The health evaluation process is an important part of early childhood and school services. In order for children to develop and learn optimally, health problems need to be identified and addressed. The approaches to collecting information for an overall health evaluation are discussed in this chapter. Each approach provides guidance for collecting and managing health information.

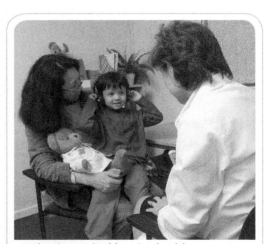

Evaluating and addressing health concerns at an early age sets children on a course for optimal development and learning.

Andy Crawford/Dorling Kindersley, Ltd.

health screenings
evaluations using specific tools to detect potential health problems

Health evaluation involves both initial and ongoing approaches. Initial approaches include health screenings and assessments. Health screenings are specific methods used to identify health conditions or risk factors for health problems. An example is when children's settings and schools offer health fairs or special health screening events where children's hearing, vision, and oral health are evaluated to detect potential problems. Another aspect of screening involves a review of the health history, looking for information that may suggest risk factors associated with diseases such as lead poisoning or dietary habits that put children at risk for anemia or obesity.

health assessment
an evaluation of health or a description of an aspect of health

Health assessment is an evaluation of overall health and includes descriptions of each child's general health. Health assessments also focus on particular aspects of health by evaluating children in relation to others. An example is evaluating children's growth through height and weight measurements that are plotted on growth charts.

daily health checks
visual assessment of a child's apparent health conducted upon arrival

continual observation
consistent observation for signs of impending illness

Ongoing assessment approaches include daily health checks and continual observation for health and illness indicators. Daily health checks involve visual reviews of children soon after they arrive at the classroom. Continual observation refers to consistent and thoughtful evaluations of health. Together these approaches ensure that potential problems are identified and any needed interventions can be implemented.

Managing Health Information Appropriately

Health information is personal and private information. It must be obtained respectfully, used appropriately, and managed confidentially. In 1996, Congress enacted Public Law 104-191, the Health Insurance Portability and Accountability Act, often referred to as HIPAA. The purpose of this legislation was to improve the effectiveness of the health care system and to maintain the privacy of individual health care information. The act requires that safeguards be put in place to ensure that individual health information is managed confidentially and communicated appropriately.

HIPAA requirements are directed primarily to health care providers and insurance agencies. These groups are considered *covered entities*, that is, they are required to follow the HIPAA rules. Child care providers and teachers are not included in the definition of covered entities. However, teachers receive individual health information and may work with health care providers. For example, collecting health history information as part of the enrollment process provides information about the child's past and current health issues. As they receive this information, teachers and their programs interface with HIPAA-covered entities. Because of this, teachers must ensure the privacy of child and family health information. This means that children's settings and schools must have policies that describe how confidential information is to be managed and communicated. Health records should be accurate, complete, confidential, and shared appropriately. Policies should provide details about the safeguards to be put in place to maintain confidentiality. Guidelines for appropriate safeguards includes developing a written policy describing when information should be exchanged and obtaining the proper signatures and information

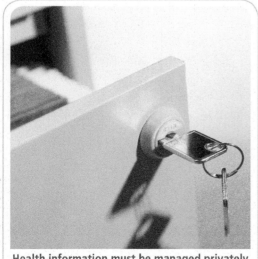

Health information must be managed privately and confidentially.

Stockbyte/Getty Images

from the parent for the release of child's health information (American Academy of Pediatrics, n.d.). A private space should be provided for teachers and families to discuss health issues.

Defining the Health History

Each child's early development and health experiences are unique. A **health history** is a summary of the child's previous health experiences. It includes the child's medical history, immunization records, information about previous injuries, and a history of the child's development. The health history provides an overall view of the child's physical and mental health and development. A comprehensive, or complete, health history includes the following:

health history
a summary of a child's previous health experiences

- Basic details such as the child's name, birth date, names of the parents or guardian, and family contact information.
- List of past major illnesses and recurrent illnesses.
- Summary of any chronic ongoing health conditions.
- Child's record of immunizations given and when.
- History of significant injuries or accidents.
- Summary of the child's behaviors or personal style that might make the child more prone to accidents or may influence his or her ability to learn.
- Information about the health and wellness of the child's family, including medical and mental health conditions and challenges.
- Summary of the child's developmental history, such as a timeline of when the child achieved key **developmental milestones**, which are physical abilities or tasks that most children are able to achieve by a certain age range.
- Information about the child's mental health, including social and emotional well-being
- Information about the child's nutritional background to identify nutritional risks such as over- or undernutrition and access to healthy balanced meals.
- Summary of the child's oral and dental health history.
- Summary of resources the family is currently using and gaps in access to medical care.

developmental milestone
physical abilities or tasks that most children are able to achieve within a certain age range

Knowing these details of children's early life helps teachers to be watchful for aspects that may have negative consequences for growth, development, and learning. Requirements for obtaining health histories in early childhood programs vary according to the type of program and the age of the children in the program. Head Start standards for obtaining health histories represent a comprehensive model that best exemplifies how to obtain information and promote health. Not all teachers will obtain all components of a health history. However, it is important to understand why each component, discussed next, is important to the health and wellness of a child.

A Matter of ETHICS

You are a kindergarten teacher in a public school and have a child enrolled in your class who is prone to frequent skin infections. The child's parents report that he is under the care of a medical provider who confirms that the condition is not contagious. However, some of the other families in the class keep asking you for details and are concerned about their children playing with this boy. They suggest that he should attend a special class. What is the problem that you need to address? How does the NAEYC Code of Ethical Conduct advise you in this situation? What responsibilities do you have to this child, the community, and society in general related to matters such as this?

Early Development

Prenatal and early development set the stage for later development. The health history briefly explores this information, identifying significant aspects that may continue to influence the child's development.

Pregnancy and Birth History Information about the mother's pregnancy and birth history helps identify risks for children's development. Questions include whether the mother had any health problems during the pregnancy or during delivery. Some maternal medical conditions cause congenital defects in children. For example, babies of mothers with diabetes are at risk for heart defects. Mothers who contract rubella, a serious viral infection, during pregnancy are at risk for having a baby with a hearing loss.

rubella
a viral infection that can cause fetal defects when contracted during pregnancy

premature infant
an infant born more than 3 weeks early, or less than 37 weeks' gestation

The health history also explores aspects related to the child's birth to learn if the child was a premature infant (born more than three weeks early) or if the child experienced any problems at birth or during the first few days of life. A child's birth weight is also of interest. Low-birth-weight babies are at risk for developmental delay, poor school performance, seizures, and hearing or visual impairments.

Developmental History A comprehensive health history includes discussions that help teachers learn about the child's progress with respect to developmental milestones. For example, most children are able to walk on their own by age 2. A few children may walk as early as 9 months. Many children are walking at 1 year of age. Some children show a pattern of reaching developmental milestones earlier than the typical age range. Some develop quickly in certain areas of development and more slowly in others. Here are two examples:

- Hal reports that his child began speaking at a very young age but did not begin to walk until well after the child's first birthday. Hal has noticed that his child is more interested in reading and less interested in playing outside.
- Kayla describes her child as very coordinated and active. She remembers that her child was running around the house at 9 months of age and still prefers to play ball games rather than do homework.

Understanding the individual child's pace and pattern of development helps teachers anticipate how to structure learning activities so that each child will thrive in the classroom.

Information from a developmental history also helps detect the possibility of developmental problems or delays. The signs of developmental disability are highly variable depending on cause, type, and severity of the delay. Some developmental delays are apparent soon after birth. Others emerge during early childhood and into the early elementary years. Teachers spend many hours with children. They become acquainted with the range of behaviors that are typical for certain ages, enabling them to recognize gaps in development through observation of the child in the classroom. Using a developmental milestones checklist is another way to engage families in discussion about a child's developmental history. Checklists, like the one shown in Figure 9-1, guide families in recognizing possible indicators of developmental delay.

History of Illness and Disease

The health history helps teachers and families identify and discuss any serious diseases that require special health care or that affect participation in the classroom. Plans for managing chronic illnesses in the classroom can then be developed and discussed.

Illnesses and Hospitalizations Significant illnesses and hospitalizations are important aspects of children's health experiences. Some may have long-term consequences, such as meningitis, which may cause hearing loss or cognitive delays.

FIGURE 9-1   Indicators of Developmental Delay

Age 4 to 7 Months

- Excessive stiffness of muscles.
- Floppy or very loose muscle tone.
- Head falls back when pulled up to sitting position.
- Reaches with one hand rather than both hands.
- Does not show interest in faces.

Age 8 to 12 Months

- No crawl.
- Does not stand with support.
- No babbling by 9 months.
- Has no words such as 'mama' or 'dada'.
- Does not show interest in objects by pointing.

Age 12 to 24 Months

- Does not understand simple instructions by 2 years of age.
- Does not speak at least 15 words by 18 months.
- Not walking by 18 months.
- Does not push a wheeled toy by 2 years of age.
- Does not mimic actions or words by age 2.

Age 24 to 36 Months

- Persistent drooling or unclear speech.
- Little interest in playing with or observing other children.

- Does not point to or show objects of interest to others.
- No pretend play.
- By age 3, has made no progress in self-care or toilet training.
- Frequently falls or has difficulty climbing or descending stairs.

Age 3 to 4 Years

- Cannot jump, ride a tricycle, or throw ball overhand.
- Does not show interest in playing with other children.
- No fantasy play.
- Seems withdrawn on a consistent basis.
- Shows violent behaviors such as hitting or biting.
- Is exceedingly shy or fearful around other children.

Age 4 to 5 Years

- Exhibits overly impulsive behavior when angry or upset.
- Very easily distracted and cannot concentrate on single activity for more than 5 minutes.
- Unable to stack a tower of six to eight blocks.
- Unable to accurately give her first and last name.
- Does not talk about daily activities.
- Exhibits extremely fearful, timid, or aggressive behavior.

Source: Shelov, 2014.

In the opening case scenario, Adelina's mother reported that her child had been hospitalized for an "infection of the brain," which may have been meningitis. The description of this illness along with the mother's report that Adelina made very few vocalizations might indicate that the child suffers from hearing loss. Serious injuries also have the potential to cause developmental problems. For example, a child who has experienced a serious leg fracture may have damaged the growth center in the bone, resulting in growth retardation of the leg and causing physical limitations.

Chronic Health Conditions   The health history should explore chronic or persistent health conditions such as allergies, asthma, or digestive issues. These are important aspects of a child's health that may need special attention in the classroom setting. For example, a teacher could ask if the child was ever diagnosed with **asthma** or has a history of breathing problems or chronic cough. Asthma, one of the most common chronic medical conditions in childhood, causes inflammation in the lungs in response to environmental agents such as cigarette smoke, pollens, or infections. Chronic conditions may require specific treatment plans that involve administering medications in the classroom. Discussing this aspect of the health history helps reveal these needs so that plans can be established. This chapter's *Progressive Programs & Practices* illustrates how chronic health conditions can impact every aspect of the early childhood environment and how teachers can plan the activities of the day appropriately.

asthma
the most common chronic medical condition in childhood, causing chronic inflammation in the lungs in response to environmental agents such as cigarette smoke, pollens, or infections

PROGRESSIVE PROGRAMS & PRACTICES

Giving Caleb a Voice!

By Laurie Katz, The Ohio State University, Franklin County Board of Developmental Disabilities' Early Childhood Education and Family Center

Five-year-old Caleb starts to chuckle and smile as he sees "Curious George," one of his favorite characters, while he plays a game on the computer that moves a school bus to George. Although most young children play this game using their hands to move the mouse, Caleb has limited control of his arms and hands. Caleb plays this game while he sits in his wheelchair with two head switches attached. Caleb uses his switches to "drive" the bus. These switches enable Caleb to take turns and have fun with his classmates at the computer. He also sees that his actions can cause change.

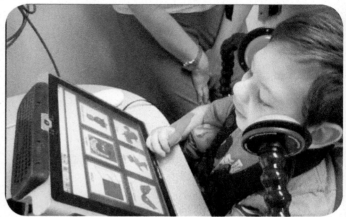

This is no simple task for Caleb, a child born with cerebral palsy and considered medically fragile. While Caleb can vocalize (he cries, laughs, fusses, grunts, and produces some vowel/open sounds such as "ahhhh"), his level of motor involvement limits his ability to produce words. In the past, he communicated his needs primarily by holding his breath when he didn't like something. His family and the professionals at the Franklin County Board of Developmental Disabilities' Early Childhood Education and Family Center located in Columbus, Ohio, have worked together for about four years to give Caleb a voice, control over his environment, and a sense of belonging in his community.

The center is part of an extensive partnership combining numerous agencies that enroll children of all developmental capacities from birth through kindergarten age. The center's philosophy, which is based on *all children* learning together, is influenced by the Reggio Emilia approach and other research-based early childhood practices in which each child is perceived as a unique individual with developmental, family, and cultural histories that shape his or her approach to learning. Important health and wellness programs support each child's growth, such as movement activities including dance, yoga, fitness groups, and jumping for exercise. Whole body activities are used to develop motor skills and self-awareness. Wellness and nutrition are strong features of these programs that involve children in learning about cooking, gardening, and outdoor explorations.

The professionals at the center of Caleb's life at school include a speech and language pathologist (SLP), physical and occupational therapists, classroom teachers and assistants, an adaptive physical educator, and medical personnel who work together to provide Caleb with the education services needed to increase his independence with his peers and the community. His team of professionals is continually challenged to find ways to accommodate Caleb's strengths and needs so that he can access and learn with his peers using the same curriculum. Working together, they help Caleb interact in socially appropriate ways predominantly through nonverbal and augmentative communication to increase his understanding of language and expressive abilities to interact and make choices.

Sandy, (SLP): "Getting to know Caleb and working with him and his family during the past few years has been an amazing adventure! It has both challenged and inspired me to seek further training in augmentative/alternative communication, to find more effective ways to support and expand his communication skills for a wide variety of purposes. Caleb has helped me learn how to really 'listen' to him. I've learned that it's not about what I or someone else thinks he should say, but about providing him a way to have and express his own 'voice.' We are in the process of getting him a new, more sophisticated communication device, but we know that regardless of what he uses (pictures, gestures, facial expressions, or a high-tech speech device), Caleb will always let us know that he has something to say."

Another example of Caleb's use of augmentative communication involved his class making smoothies. Although he was unable to add the ingredients physically, he could assist by giving the directions and pressing another switch to turn on the blender and mix up the smoothies when his classmates asked. By providing simple assistive technology accommodations (such as switches), Caleb was able to engage actively in social interactions with his peers, touch the glass to feel the cold, and smell the smoothies.

Stacy, Caleb's mother, is very grateful for the work of these professionals and believes it's best to have as many professionals as possible working together to help Caleb whether it's in their home or the center.

Medications and Treatments This aspect of the health history directs teachers and families to discuss and document any medications the child is taking. If medications must be given when children are in the classroom, special documentation, training, and procedures are needed. Directions from the child's health care provider must be obtained that outline the timing and dose of medications needed and how the medications are given. Teachers must document what was given, when it was given, and whether there were any side effects. This information should be available to the family.

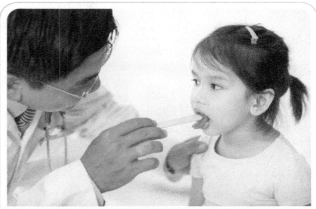

Many states have strict policies regarding children who have not had up-to-date immunizations.

Immunization Status

Immunization records are an important part of the health history. **Immunizations** prevent the incidence and spread of infections. This is of special significance as children enter group settings where transmission of infections frequently occurs.

immunizations
injections that are given to individuals to trigger an immune response and prevent disease if exposed

Immunization Requirements An advisory committee at the government's Centers for Disease Control and Prevention (CDC) outlines the immunizations that are recommended for children and adults. The recommendations include the age at which a vaccine should be given, the number of doses, the time between doses, and safety measures related to the administration of the vaccines. Individual states are responsible for establishing laws that outline the specific immunization requirements for children who participate in child care or school settings. These requirements vary from state to state (Centers for Disease Control and Prevention, 2012). Most routine vaccinations are given during the first six years of life. After age 6, only flu shots may be required until ages 9 through 12, when routine vaccinations are given again. The family should obtain a document of the child's immunization status and provide it to the early childhood program or school well in advance of attendance. Immunization records are then reviewed by the staff to determine whether the child's immunization status meets state requirements and, therefore, whether the child is eligible to begin school.

Family Concerns About Immunizations A small number of families may choose not to vaccinate or only partially vaccinate based on a number of concerns. Parental concerns about vaccines are rising and are affecting immunization rates. Misconceptions can lead to some of these concerns. The following are common misconceptions (American Academy of Pediatrics, 2013):

- Giving too many vaccines at once is harmful to a child's immune system.
- Vaccines cause illnesses such as autism and autoimmune disorders.
- Children get toxic doses of mercury in vaccines. This chapter's *Safety Segment* discusses the use of **thimerosal** in vaccines.
- With respect to hepatitis B, parents believe the vaccine should not be given because it is associated with high-risk behavior (drug use and sexual activity). However, there are other modes of transmission.

thimerosal
a mercury compound that was widely used as a preservative in vaccinations

Families may express their concerns about immunizations to their child's teacher. Teachers should be prepared to refer families to an appropriate resource.

SAFETY SEGMENT   Thimerosal and Vaccines

Thimerosal is a mercury compound that was used in vaccines that came from multidose vials. It is a preservative that prevents bacterial growth and contamination. After 1990, as vaccines were being added to the routine schedule for infants, the amount of total thimerosal given exceeded limits reported by the Environmental Protection Agency. This level that exceeded limits was detected in 1999, but at that time, extensive research has not shown any harm to infants. As a *precaution*, the CDC recommended that vaccine manufacturers eliminate the use of thimerosal in vaccines for children.

Considerable concern has been raised regarding a suspected association between thimerosal and autism. Numerous studies focusing on the relationship between thimerosal and autism and other neurological disorders have not shown any relationship.

Source Centers for Disease Control and Prevention, 2014.

adverse reactions
unintended side effects

local reaction
the most common type of side effect after vaccination; characterized by pain, swelling, and redness at the site of the injection

systemic reaction
a type of reaction following vaccination; characterized by generalized symptoms such as fever, malaise, fatigue, muscle pain, headache, and loss of appetite

allergic reaction
rare but life-threatening reaction following vaccination

Potential Reactions Following Vaccination Some vaccines can produce **adverse reactions**—or side effects. Three types of vaccine side effects have been identified (Centers for Disease Control and Prevention, 2012):

1. **Local reaction:** This is the most common. Local reactions are minor and characterized by pain, swelling, and redness at the site of the injection.

2. **Systemic reaction:** This reaction is characterized by generalized symptoms including fever, malaise, fatigue, muscle pain, headache, and loss of appetite. These symptoms can occur because of the vaccine or because of a concurrent viral infection. Systemic reactions are sometimes seen after immunizations that use components of live viruses, such as MMR and varicella (chicken pox).

3. **Allergic reaction:** Allergic reactions are rare but can be life-threatening. They occur in less than 1 in 500,000 doses. Signs of allergic reaction to immunizations may include trouble breathing, weakness, wheezing, hives, and swelling of the throat. If any of these reactions occur, emergency medical assistance should be obtained immediately.

If a teacher or parent has concerns about any symptoms following a vaccination, a follow-up appointment with the child's health care provider should be scheduled.

Child Safety and Risk-Taking Behaviors

Gathering information about the child's style and behavioral characteristics helps identify the child's potential for injury. Injuries are the single leading cause of death among children. In a classroom setting, it is the teacher's responsibility to ensure that each child is safe and secure. Knowing about the child's safety behaviors aids in planning for the types of activities offered and helps identify any special supervision the child may require. Asking about the child's physical activity habits includes questions such as these: Does the child tend to take risks? Has the child had any major accidents, fractures, or head injuries that were associated with risk-taking behavior? Conversations with families about child safety behaviors also provide an opportunity to talk about ways to promote health and safety at home. Questions to explore with families include the following:

WHAT IF . . .
As a preschool teacher, you welcome a late-enrolling child who arrives with immunization records in hand that were not up to date? How would you handle this situation?

- Is the family car equipped with appropriately installed car seats or booster seats?

- Are all medications and poisons such as cleaning supplies and chemicals stored out of the child's reach?

- Does the home have a swimming pool, a lake, an irrigation canal, or another open water source nearby? Have appropriate measures been taken to prevent unsupervised entry into these areas?
- Does the family feel safe in their neighborhood?
- If the family owns guns, are all guns unloaded, locked, and unavailable? Does the child spend any time where there may be guns, such as homes of family members, caregivers, or friends?

Nutritional History

The nutritional health history identifies aspects of children's dietary habits and special dietary needs. Here are some important aspects of the nutritional health history discussion:

- Are there barriers to providing the child with healthful foods?
- Is the child's diet nutritious and appropriate for the child's age?
- What are the child's eating habits?
- Does the child have any special dietary needs, food restrictions, or food allergies?
- Is the child growing appropriately?

> **WHAT IF . . .**
>
> You are a teacher in a kindergarten class and a mother disclosed to you that her husband sometimes used a back room to cook meth? She says that she doesn't want her child near this, but she doesn't have anywhere else to go. How would you respond? What child health and safety questions might this information suggest? To what resources would you refer this mother?

Discussing the family's ability to provide healthful food for the child may reveal challenges that the family faces. This provides an opportunity for teachers and families to explore community resources that may be supportive. Such conversations also identify whether a child has suffered from periods of malnutrition (overnutrition and undernutrition) that may have interrupted normal growth and development.

Health Issues Related to Nutrition Other health issues related to nutrition are also discussed, such as diabetes and how it should be managed in the class setting. Some children have challenges related to the physical aspects of eating, such as chewing and swallowing. Food allergies are also an important consideration. Food allergies must be carefully explored so that teachers have all the information they need to implement a safe environment. These issues are discussed and strategies are developed for safety at mealtime.

The history also addresses children's individual and age-appropriate feeding needs. It provides an opportunity for families to describe what the child typically eats, how much the child eats, and the child's usual eating schedule. Figure 9-2 provides sample questions to ask when gathering information about children's history and to promote conversations about children's dietary needs.

Special Diets and Food Preferences The nutritional history also informs teachers about family preferences for special diets or food restrictions. Special diets may be followed for religious or cultural reasons. Food preferences may be influenced by a variety of factors, including access to food, presence of food insecurity, ethnicity of family, or level of acculturation. Acculturation refers to the social, psychological, and behavioral changes that are associated with adapting to a new culture. Immigration can influence a family's health behaviors, including the way in which they adjust to dietary changes. Some families may struggle to find familiar foods in the groceries and supermarkets in their new community. They may also be impacted by unhealthy dietary habits of their new environment. For example, young children of

acculturation
the social, psychological, and behavioral changes associated with relocation from one culture to another

FIGURE 9-2   **Sample Nutrition Screening Questions**

For Infants

✓ Is the baby breast- or bottle feeding?
   · If breastfeeding, will you provide breast milk for your baby?
   · If bottle feeding, what type of formula?
✓ How often does your baby eat?
✓ If formula feeding, how much does your baby eat?
✓ If formula feeding, is your baby on a special formula and are there special directions for preparing it?
✓ How long does it usually take to feed your baby?
✓ How does your baby let you know when she is hungry?
✓ How does he let you know when he is full?
✓ Does your baby eat anything other than breast milk or formula? If so, what and how often?
✓ Does your baby have any problems when feeding?
✓ *If age appropriate:* Has your baby had any problems with the introduction of solid foods?

For Preschool and School-Age Children

✓ What foods does your child like? What foods does your child dislike?
✓ Are there any foods your child should not eat for medical, religious, or personal reasons?
✓ Is your child on a special diet?
✓ What is your child's usual meal schedule?
✓ Does your child eat breakfast?
✓ How much and what type of milk does your child drink?
✓ How much juice does your child drink?
✓ Have there been any recent changes in your child's diet?
✓ Does your child have trouble chewing or swallowing?
✓ Does your child eat or chew things that aren't food?
✓ Do you have any concerns about your child's eating?
✓ Do you eat meals at home together as a family?

Source: Head Start Child Health Record, by the U.S. Department of Health and Human Services, Administration of Children and Families, retrieved August 7, 2015, from https://eclkc.ohs.acf.hhs.gov/hslc/hs/resources/ECLKC_Bookstore/PDFs/D54E82AEC0E167A42BFA607F2381960F.pdf.

Hispanic families tend to consume less nutritious diets as they become acculturated to the United States (Wiley et al., 2014).

These discussions are important opportunities not only to learn about a child's habits, but also to promote healthy dietary behaviors. This chapter's *Nutrition Note* discusses the effect of acculturation on families.

Oral Health History

Gathering information about the child's oral health provides an opportunity to identify dental problems by asking the following questions:

- Has the child ever had a dental examination or screening?
- Are the child's teeth brushed regularly?
- Does the child brush her or his own teeth?
- Has the child had any dental surgery or other procedures?

The oral health history also identifies whether the child is at risk for dental disease. For example, infants who are given juice regularly and young children who drink soft drinks are at high risk for developing cavities because of the high sugar content in these beverages. This is especially problematic if babies are put to bed with bottles.

The oral health history also identifies the family's water source and whether the water is a good fluoride source. **Fluoride** is a mineral recommended for children that helps prevent dental disease. Some public water systems have fluoride added to the water system. If the child is drinking well water or water from another non-public source, the child may not be getting the fluoride needed to prevent dental disease. In some cases, a physician will prescribe fluoride drops.

fluoride
a mineral recommended for children 6 months to 6 years of age for the prevention of dental disease

NUTRITION NOTE The Effects of Acculturation on Nutrition in Hispanic Families

Acculturation refers to changes in behaviors, attitudes, and values when families assimilate to a new culture. For example, acculturation impacts eating behaviors and the use of traditional foods. This impact on the diet is more pronounced the longer the family lives outside their native country. Interestingly, research has shown that the health of a recently immigrated Hispanic individual is much better than the typical U.S. Caucasian person. The adoption of the U.S. diet along with other obesity-related behaviors has negative effects as immigrants become more acculturated.

Changes due to acculturation on the diets of Hispanic families who have immigrated to the United States include:

• A decrease in the use of traditional foods.

• An increase in the use of traditional foods in a new way.

• An increase in the use of foods from the host country.

For many Mexican families, dietary acculturation has replaced a diet rich in beans, fruits, vegetables, and grains with a diet composed of highly processed and sugary foods. An acculturated diet leads to higher intake of high-fat milk, soda, and increased fast-food and processed food.

These trends suggest that acculturation can be a risk factor for unhealthy eating behaviors. Early childhood teachers promote healthful nutritional practices by preserving healthy traditional behaviors. They also support children's wellness by assisting families in choosing positive dietary options as they integrate aspects of the American diet.

Source: O'Brien, 2014.

Mental and Emotional Health History

Assessing children's social and emotional development through a mental health history is an important part of ensuring a child's overall health and well-being. Social and emotional problems that go unrecognized can persist into adulthood, interrupting normal development. The mental health history focuses the discussion on a variety of social and emotional health indicators:

• Child's ability to interact positively with others.
• Child's ability to manage emotions such as anger and frustration.
• Child's interest in playing with other children.
• Ways the child copes with change and stress.
• Problems or worries the child may have.
• Presence of mental illness in child's caregivers.

One common topic in the mental health history involves discussing the child's style when transitioning into a new environment. Three behavior styles are often discussed (Thomas, 1977):

• *Easy and adaptable:* Describes children who adapt readily to new situations.
• *Difficult and emotional:* Describes children who display high levels of emotion in new situations.
• *Slow to warm up:* Describes children who withdraw from new situations at first and instead spend time observing before they gradually adapt.

Discussions about these behavior styles help identify the kinds of supports a child may need when beginning in the early childhood setting and when learning the daily classroom routine. Families can also describe other aspects of the child's style or temperament, such as the child's adaptability, typical moods, intensity of reaction, and activity level. These characteristics guide teachers to fit their teaching and management approaches to the individual needs of the child.

The mental health history also includes exploration of ways the family soothes the child when the child is worried or hurt. In programs that care for infants, questions should focus on the infant's patterns, such as whether the child cries frequently

FIGURE 9-3 Sample Questions for a Mental Health History

✔ Does your child sleep less than 8 hours or have trouble sleeping at night?

✔ Is your child learning to use the toilet? Or, does your child manage toileting by herself?

✔ Can your child dress and undress herself?

✔ Does your child have any worries or fears?

✔ Does your child enjoy playing with children her age?

✔ Does your child experience temper tantrums or have any challenges controlling behavior?

✔ Does your child enjoy fantasy play? Is your child able to recognize the difference between fantasy and reality?

✔ Have there been any changes in your child's life in the last 6 months such as a move, family divorce, or death in the family?

✔ Are you or your family having any problems that might affect your child?

✔ Is your child interested in new experiences?

Source: Head Start Child Health Record, by the U.S. Department of Health and Human Services, Administration of Children and Families, retrieved August 7, 2015, from https://eclkc.ohs.acf.hhs.gov/hslc/hs/resources/ECLKC_Bookstore/PDFs/D54E82AEC0E167A42BFA607F2381960F.pdf.

or has fussy periods. Teachers should also ask families about the strategies they use at home. During the mental health history, it is common to ask questions about the child's habits. Examples of questions to spark conversation about social-emotional development are shown in Figure 9-3.

Family Health and Wellness

Health and wellness practices within the family impact children's health. Understanding the context that surrounds the child provides clues to the child's healthful development. It also offers an opportunity for teachers and families to discuss resources the family may need and ways the classroom environment can contribute to the child's healthy development.

Family Medical History It is important to know when a parent has a chronic medical condition because these can be inherited. Teachers should also be aware of situations when parents who are ill have difficulty caring for their child. It may be necessary to provide referrals and support for families to obtain the services they need.

Home Environment Aspects of the home environment help identify conditions that may be unhealthy for children. Children who live with or are exposed to smokers are vulnerable to the effects of secondhand smoke. Drug production and drug use expose children to toxic products and put children in dangerous situations. Older houses introduce risk for lead exposure from paint and other deteriorating building products that contain lead. Unsafe neighborhoods surround children with dangers that may, among other things, limit the child's ability to play outside. The presence of guns in a home puts children at risk for intentional and unintentional injuries and/or death.

CHECK YOUR UNDERSTANDING 9.1

Click here to check your understanding of evaluating children's health and development.

Family Dynamics The relationships that exist among family members impact children's mental health. Dynamics associated with poverty, job loss, single parenthood, and homelessness contribute negatively to children's mental health. For example, parental depression has a negative effect on nurturance and is associated with poor health and developmental outcomes in children (Child Trends Databank, 2014). Teachers are an important component of the family support network and can assist by providing referrals to resources and local support programs.

OBTAINING CHILDREN'S HEALTH HISTORY

Health information is private and sensitive information. It is important for teachers to obtain details with understanding and tact. Information should be gathered efficiently. Questions should be meaningful and useful for the setting. Health histories are used to establish individualized care and service and to aid in the development of wellness activities in the classroom.

Gathering Health History Information

In some settings, families complete a written form. Written forms may be brief and concise or more detailed. In other settings, teachers, health staff, or program directors meet with families to discuss and record health information. Some programs conduct home visits in which teachers and families talk in the home setting. Regardless of how the information is collected, attention to details ensures that an appropriate health history is obtained and that the information is used to improve the child's experience in the classroom. Here is how one teacher prepared for the health history visit:

> Dashay knows that families are sometimes nervous about meeting with the teacher to share health information. He works to create a welcoming environment by moving a small table near the window where a group of houseplants offers home-like comfort. He positions two chairs at the table but has others nearby in case many family members come to participate. On the floor nearby, he places a tub of brightly colored toys. He sets several on the rug with some picture books about "going to school" and some pillows for children to sit on. He is ready when the family arrives and greets them with a big smile.

Often the process of gathering and discussing the child's health history is completed quickly. If a child has no unusual health or development concerns, the discussion may be very brief. Some children may have health issues that are addressed easily and for whom a plan is developed with no further follow-up needed. A few children may have more complex health considerations that require special discussions, planning, and training. For these children, it is important to provide sufficient time to establish a thorough health and safety plan. For each child, the health history sets an important course of action for safe and appropriate services.

Selecting Purposeful Questions

The health history information that is gathered needs to be easy to understand and specific so that useful information is discovered. When only one general question is asked about the child's health, the response may not reveal needed information. For example, if asked, "Does your child have any medical problems?" the parent may simply answer, "No" even when the child has asthma or frequent breathing problems, allergies, or a history of seizures. Because a child with one of these conditions may be stable and not experiencing any current problems, the family may not raise it as a concern.

Using a series of questions can prompt the family to recall past or ongoing health problems. A standard comprehensive health history form is used in many settings, such as Head Start programs, to ensure that specific information is gathered. Children's programs may adapt information to create their own health history format, including special questions that have relevance in the particular community or with the specific group of children and families served.

Pearson Education

CLASSROOM CONNECTION
Watch this video about a parent-teacher conference. What steps has the teacher taken to ensure the mother's comfort and participation during the conference? How might these same strategies be used in a meeting to discuss a child's health history?

Gathering Information Before Children Attend

Ample time should be provided to gather and discuss a child's health history *prior* to the child's attendance. Sometimes this may require additional time for the enrollment process so that important information can be shared and discussed. Families may need to be reminded that the teacher must know about the children's health in advance so that adjustments to the program can be made to ensure safety.

Building Comfortable Relationships

Families need to feel comfortable to fully share information about their child. This is especially true if the child's history is sensitive or if traumatic events occurred in the past. Spending a few minutes explaining the purpose of the health history helps everyone focus on the goals of the discussion:

- To share important information about the child's health.
- To identify whether special arrangements are needed to assist the child in the classroom.
- To ensure that appropriate strategies are planned.

Documenting Information Accurately

Health history information needs to be recorded clearly and objectively. Families may not know the medical name of a condition or an infection. They may use a description rather than a medical term. For instance, in the opening case scenario, Adelina's family reported that the child had an "infection of the brain."

Health information should be recorded exactly as the family reports it. Teachers should not add their own speculation or guesses about the information. This way the health record document the facts as the family understands them. This allows teachers to formulate an understanding of the child's health status based on what is known. Then the teacher may ask the family to obtain additional information from the health care provider to clarify what is not understood.

Asking for Clarifying Information

Teachers should be sure they understand the information that was shared about the child's health. It is important to know if health issues have been resolved or if treatment is continuing. It is helpful to know how a child's chronic health issues are being managed in the home. It is important to know if a food restriction is related to preference or an allergy that could cause a dangerous reaction. Teachers listen carefully to the information that is provided by the family and reflect on how the child's health needs can be managed in the classroom.

Identifying Impacts on the Child's Participation

As the details of the health history are discussed, implications for the child's participation in the classroom are noted and a detailed plan is developed. For example, if the child needs to receive medication during the day, a plan for administering the medication must be developed. This usually involves:

- Obtaining instructions from the child's health care provider.
- Training the teacher to identify when and how to administer the medication.

- Establishing protocols for storing medication and recording when the medicine was given.

Similarly, plans for managing allergies, special health care situations, and emergencies should be discussed.

Confirming Who May Access Health Information

Because children's health information is private, it is important to clarify who is allowed to have access to the records. In children's programs, this typically includes the classroom teachers and appropriate program staff such as the dietitian, the nurse or health consultant, and those who manage children's records. Typically, the appropriate family member signs a consent form, which is stored in the child's file.

Promoting Health and Wellness

Discussing children's health provides a good opportunity for teachers to share information that promotes family well-being and supports children's participation in the setting. Many health promotion topics are appropriate for all families, especially as children prepare to transition into a program or school. Teachers are attuned to the topics that are helpful to address when gathering health history information such as the following:

- Offering healthful food at meals and snack times.
- Feeding children breakfast or arriving early to participate in the school breakfast program.
- Ensuring that children obtain a full night's sleep.
- Providing sufficient opportunity for active play.
- Dressing children appropriately for the weather and for active play.
- Encouraging the use of sunscreen during outside play.
- Decreasing screen time (television, video games, and computers).
- Increasing time spent reading together.
- Teaching children to brush their teeth.
- Teaching children to be safe pedestrians.

Other health promotion topics are situation-specific and emerge during the health history discussions:

- Reducing children's exposure to violence and suggesting ways to accomplish this among families who live in challenging neighborhoods.
- Reducing children's exposure to stress in families where job loss or adult illness adds difficulties.
- Creating smoke-free environments for children if family members smoke.
- Discussing gun safety if guns are present where children live or play.

Health and wellness promotion is accomplished by partnering with families. Teachers and family members are important role models for children. Together they create a team approach to improving health and wellness in the home and classroom.

Identifying Missing Information

The health history discussion between the early childhood program or school staff member and the appropriate family member concludes with a brief referral

CHECK YOUR UNDERSTANDING 9.2

Click here to check your understanding of obtaining aspects of children's health history.

summary that highlights any gaps in needed information. In some cases, the family may need to pursue additional immunizations or obtain directions from the child's medical provider about administering a needed medication in the early childhood setting. The family may need to seek clarification about restrictions for a food allergy or training and guidance about developing a protocol for serving a child with diabetes. The referral summary should clearly list the specific information required and when it is needed.

REVIEWING THE HEALTH HISTORY

After the health history is obtained, it is reviewed to identify aspects that impact the child in the classroom. An individual trained to recognize gaps in information or aspects that need follow-up or further assessment should conduct this review. Some early childhood settings may have a dietitian or health consultant conduct this review. Others may train teachers or program personnel to manage this responsibility.

Screening Immunization Reports

Children's immunization records are compared with the list of vaccinations required for the child's age by the particular state. Figure 9-4 illustrates the standard federal immunization schedule for young children.

If a child is missing a vaccination, the program or school contacts the family and asks them to obtain the immunizations before the child attends the early childhood setting or school. Some immunizations are offered as a series of several shots that must be spaced over specified intervals of time. As guided by the health professional, children may begin receiving a vaccination series before entering the early childhood program and then complete the series at the recommended intervals while attending. The child's immunization record at the school should be updated as additional vaccinations are received to document that the needed series has been completed.

Exclusion Dates

Most states require that all children enrolled in child care and schools have updated immunizations. In an effort to improve compliance, some states establish immunization exclusion dates. If a child's immunization record is incomplete, families receive a warning letter from the state immunization registry. The letter alerts families that the child will be excluded from school on a certain date if documentation of updated immunizations is not provided.

Exemptions

For the vast majority of children, vaccinations are given according to a prescribed schedule. This typical immunization schedule ensures that children will have all the required immunizations in time for early childhood or school entry. However, a small percentage of children may be on a modified immunization plan.

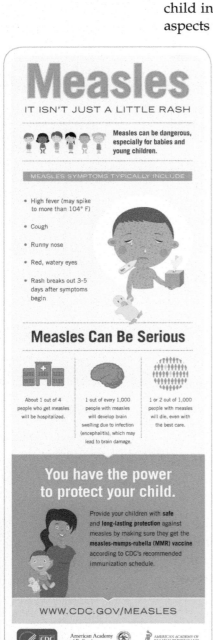

Centers for Disease Control and Prevention

FIGURE 9-4 Childhood Vaccination Schedule

Vaccine ▼ Age ▶	Birth	1 month	2 months	4 months	6 months	9 months	12 months	15 months	18 months	19–23 months	2–3 years	4–6 years	
Hepatitis B[1]	Hep B	HepB	HepB		HepB								Range of recommended ages for all children
Rotavirus[2]			RV	RV	RV[2]								
Diphtheria, tetanus, pertussis[3]			DTaP	DTaP	DTaP		see footnote[3]	DTaP	DTaP			DTaP	
Haemophilus influenzae type b[4]			Hib	Hib	Hib[4]		Hib	Hib					Range of recommended ages for certain high-risk groups
Pneumococcal[5]			PCV	PCV	PCV		PCV	PCV			PPSV		
Inactivated poliovirus[6]			IPV	IPV	IPV		IPV					IPV	
Influenza[7]					Influenza (Yearly)								
Measles, mumps, rubella[8]							MMR	MMR	see footnote[8]			MMR	
Varicella[9]							Varicella	Varicella	see footnote[9]			Varicella	Range of recommended ages for all children and certain high-risk groups
Hepatitis A[10]							Dose 1[10]	Dose 1[10]			HepA Series	HepA Series	
Meningococcal[11]					MCV4 — see footnote[11]								

This schedule includes recommendations in effect as of December 23, 2011. Any dose not administered at the recommended age should be administered at a subsequent visit, when indicated and feasible. The use of a combination vaccine generally is preferred over separate injections of its equivalent component vaccines. Vaccination providers should consult the relevant Advisory Committee on Immunization Practices (ACIP) statement for detailed recommendations, available online at http://www.cdc.gov/vaccines/pubs/acip-list.htm. Clinically significant adverse events that follow vaccination should be reported to the Vaccine Adverse Event Reporting System (VAERS) online (http://www.vaers.hhs.gov) or by telephone (800-822-7967).

State laws also regulate modifications and exemptions to the immunization requirements based on certain circumstances. Three types of immunization exemptions are available: *medical*, *religious*, and *philosophical*. All 50 states allow medical exemptions, all states except West Virginia and Mississippi allow religious exemptions, and only 19 states allow philosophical exemptions. California recently instituted tighter exemption rules. The specifics can be found at the *National Conference of State Legislators website*. Families can request a modification or an exemption from the immunization requirements under these options.

Medical Exemptions Medical exemptions are granted when children have certain medical conditions, have compromised immune systems, or are taking specific medications. A vaccine can also be excluded from a children's immunization schedule if they have had a severe allergic reaction. Modifications or delays in vaccinations for medical reasons are allowed when recommended by a health care provider. Such exemptions should be documented in the child's health record.

Religious Exemptions Some families claim exemption for religious reasons. The religious exemption laws are intended for families who hold sincere objections to vaccinations based on their religious beliefs. Specific religious exemption requirements vary from one state to another. For example, some states require families requesting a religious exemption to be members of the First Church of Christ or Christian Scientists.

Philosophical Exemptions These exemptions are intended for families who have personal or moral beliefs that contradict immunizing their children. States that allow these exemptions have higher rates of vaccine-preventable diseases such as measles and whooping cough, which is a highly contagious respiratory infection that can be fatal to infants and young children (Lee, 2013).

Ensuring That Children Have a Medical Home

The review of the health history may reveal that a child does not have an identified medical home. The term *medical home* refers to an approach to providing comprehensive pediatric care, including regular checkups, immunizations, care

---

WHAT IF . . .

A family in your program has misplaced their child's immunization records. They don't want to bother searching for the documentation, so they tell you they want to claim a religious exemption. What issues does this approach raise? How would you manage this situation?

---

whooping cough
a highly contagious respiratory infection that can be fatal to infants and young children

medical home
a system of preventive health care, sick health care, immunizations, and coordination of medical care

Pearson Education

CLASSROOM CONNECTION

Watch this video about health supervision visits. How can these visits support families, ensure immunizations, and help create safe and healthy home environments?

when the child is sick, and coordination of other vital health care services. Typically the medical home provider is a physician, nurse practitioner, or physician's assistant who works as part of a health care team in partnership with the child and family. The medical home provider offers family-centered services that are accessible and culturally attuned. These services address both medical and nonmedical needs (American Academy of Pediatrics, n.d.).

Under some circumstances, teachers may have the opportunity to assist families in finding a medical home. A list of medical providers or clinics in the community is a helpful resource. In addition, teachers can guide families to overcome any obstacles they may face in trying to obtain necessary health care. Obstacles may include the family's lack of health insurance, cultural and language barriers, or a limited number of providers who serve families with Medicaid.

Many communities have community health centers or clinics that provide comprehensive primary health care regardless of the patient's insurance status or ability to pay. These clinics are often designed to serve a high-need community or a medically underserved population and can be an excellent medical home resource. Teachers may also collaborate with medical consultants, school nurses, or other community resources to help families.

Confirming That Children Have Well-Child Exams

well-child checkups
health care visits provided for children to ensure that health and development are progressing normally

The health history is also reviewed to identify if the child has had regularly scheduled **well-child checkups** with the health care provider. The focus of well-child exams is on preventive health care. Well-child care involves the following:

- A review of the child's health history.
- Screening tests.
- Physical examinations.
- Treatments to prevent disease, including immunizations.
- Education and counseling to promote health and wellness.

Families of children who have not had periodic well-child exams should be encouraged to schedule a checkup as part of the enrollment expectations. Head Start Performance Standards require that programs support families to obtain comprehensive health exams for their child. Table 9-1 lists the recommended timing for well-child visits for all children.

TABLE 9-1 Well-Child Checkup Schedule

Infants (0–12 Months)	Children Older Than 1 Year of Age
✓ Newborn visit	
✓ 2 months	✓ 18 months
✓ 4 months	✓ 2 years
	✓ 2 ½ years
✓ 6 months	✓ 3 years
✓ 9 months	✓ 4 years
✓ 12 months	✓ 5 years and yearly thereafter
✓ 15 months	

Making Referrals

When gaps in the child's health care are discovered, follow-up is initiated through the **referral** process. Referrals are recommendations that direct families to needed resources. Common reasons for making referrals include encouraging the family to get a well-child check, following up on missing immunizations, or obtaining a vision exam. Another frequent referral in the early childhood setting is referring families to agencies that provide early intervention assessment for suspected developmental delays. Families may also raise questions about children's health that are beyond the scope of the teacher's knowledge and expertise. Anytime a concern is identified that requires outside assistance, a referral is appropriate.

Teachers are an important referral resource when families face difficulties providing sufficient health services, housing, food, or transportation. Sharing information about community support services benefits the family and contributes to the child's well-being. In addition, teachers who recognize that families are facing such difficulties are better able to understand how to support the family. Families also benefit from social connections such as a supportive network of family and friends. Teachers help build social networks among families in the class by sponsoring family socials, game days, and parent and child community service activities. These social networking activities contribute to positive outcomes for children.

Referrals are made in collaboration with families. Together the teacher and family member identify and record the specific aspects of concern. A written summary supports families when they take their questions to the health care provider. For example, in the opening case scenario, Maria and the family have identified two areas for possible follow-up. The observation that Adelina is not making vocalizations concerns both Maria and the family, suggesting that an evaluation of Adelina's hearing is needed. The family has also described living in an older home that was in poor condition. They are aware that building materials in older homes often contain lead, a product that is harmful to young children. They decide to ask that Adelina be evaluated for possible lead exposure. Together the teacher and Adelina's family summarize their concerns, and the family is prepared with specific goals as they follow up with their medical provider.

referral
process of obtaining assistance for a family after identifying a need

CHECK YOUR UNDERSTANDING 9.3
Click here to check your understanding of reviewing a child's health history.

CONDUCTING HEALTH EVALUATIONS

In addition to the health history, additional health evaluations are conducted to screen for normal health and development. These include physical health, mental health, and developmental evaluations. Some evaluations are conducted for all children. Others are done to follow up on specific concerns. Teachers or trained volunteers may conduct the evaluations. Some may require the expertise of those with specialized skills, including nurses, dietitians, and counselors. In addition, evaluations of children's health include input through growth measurements, vision screenings, and assessment for risk of lead poisoning. All contribute to understanding the child's health status and the design of the teaching environment.

Growth Measurements

Growth is one of the most important indicators of normal health and development in children. Height, weight, head circumference, and body mass index are the most important growth measurements. A trained person using reliable measuring devices can do these measurements. Because many children lack access to regular health care, the growth measurements obtained in the school may become an essential resource for identifying health concerns.

Growth charts are graphs that demonstrate normal values for children of all ages. Charts published by the CDC consist of a set of percentile curves and are used as a tool to monitor the growth of children over time. In April 2006, the WHO published growth charts that are also now in use. Growth charts published by the WHO should be used for children ages 0 to 2. After age 2, CDC growth charts should be used. See this chapter's *Health Hint* for a summary of the growth charts available.

Height and Weight

The most common measurements taken are height and weight. In infancy, height is often referred to as *length*. Growth is reviewed by plotting height and weight measurements on standard growth charts. These charts are easily obtained from the CDC's website as well as many other online resources.

Standardized growth charts are available for children ages 0 to 36 months and ages 2 to 20 years. Growth charts for boys and girls can be found on the CDC's website. The charts are designed as a tool to determine whether growth is within the normal range. If there is any question that a growth measurement is below or above the normal range, the child should be referred to a health care provider for additional evaluation.

Body Mass Index

Body mass index (BMI) is a measure of body fat. It is calculated based on height and weight. BMI is an inexpensive, reliable method used to screen for underweight or obesity. BMI is calculated by multiplying weight in pounds by 703 and dividing by height in inches squared. This number is then plotted on BMI charts, which are provided for boys and girls ages 2 to 20 years. The chart shows the categories that determine whether the child is underweight, normal weight, overweight, or obese. Children whose BMI falls in the underweight, overweight, or obese categories should be referred for evaluation by a medical professional. BMI charts for boys

HEALTH HINT   Childhood Growth Charts

Monitoring growth in children is an important component of health screenings. Normal growth can be an indicator of health and wellness. Two sets of growth curves exist for children—one published by the CDC and another by the WHO. From the 1970s until 2006, the CDC published the only growth charts available. Although they were widely used, there were concerns that they lacked racial diversity and the infant sample from which the data were extrapolated were almost exclusively formula-fed.

In April 2006, the WHO published growth charts that described the growth of healthy children under optimal environmental conditions. The CDC growth charts were more of a reference, describing how certain children grew in a certain place and time (how children in the United States grew between 1963 and 1994).

Most recent recommendations suggest use of the WHO growth standards for assessing growth in children less than 24 months of age, regardless of type of feeding. After 2 years of age, the CDC growth charts should be used. Data from the WHO growth charts are available only through age 6, whereas CDC growth chart data continue into adulthood. These new recommendations should give health screeners more accurate information and identify children who are truly outside the normal range.

Source: Centers for Disease Control and Prevention.

and girls can be found on the CDC's website. In addition, many BMI calculators for children and adults are available online.

The use of the BMI measurement is being explored as a tool to screen for risk of obesity and to encourage schools to focus on teaching and modeling healthy lifestyles. The AAP and CDC recommend the use of BMI as a screening tool for children beginning at age 2. The *Policy Point* discusses controversies involved with BMI screening in schools.

Oral Health Assessments

Conducting oral health assessments in the early childhood setting or school is highly beneficial for children who do not have access to dental care. Dental caries, or cavities, is one of the most common chronic diseases in childhood. Dental caries is the formation of cavities or tooth decay caused by abnormal growth of bacteria in the mouth. Identification and treatment of dental caries in early life are important to overall physical health. Ideally, children should have a dental visit by their first birthday or within six months of first tooth eruption (American Academy of Pediatrics, 2014).

Many children do not receive these recommended dental examinations. Higher-risk groups include children in low-income families and certain racial/ethnic groups such as blacks and Hispanics (Kawashita, 2011). The federal Head Start program ensures that enrolled children receive comprehensive health care screenings including dental screenings. Head Start serves as a model for supporting early childhood programs to provide needed oral health assessments.

Many children's programs arrange for local dentists or dental hygienists to conduct dental screenings at the children's setting. For some children, these may be the only dental examinations they receive over the course of many years. If additional care is identified, children are referred to their dental provider or community services for further evaluation and intervention.

Accessibility to dental services is often a problem for low-income children. Teachers can help families find options for obtaining dental treatment. For example, "Give Kids a Smile" is an annual component to National Children's Dental Health

POLICY POINT

Controversies Surrounding BMI Screening in Schools

Schools in the United States are mandated to screen for hearing and vision. Many states have added health screenings, including BMI screenings. Currently, seven states require or recommend BMI screening in schools. Perceptions of BMI screening in schools are mixed. Does this promote healthier behaviors or better outcome?

Case studies in Florida demonstrated that many parents were uncomfortable discussing the topic with their child. Some parents of overweight children reported trying to use food restriction to control their child's weight in response to the BMI letter or even increased use of negative comments regarding child's weight.

These unhealthy behaviors could be potentially harmful to the child's emotional development and may not address the underlying problem. It is unclear if these unintended consequences of reporting BMI are due to the way the information was delivered to the parent or to other factors.

Because of lack of clarity regarding the risks and benefits of BMI screening in school, it is important for teachers and other staff to be aware of the unintended consequences and carefully plan on how the information will be delivered to the parents. It may also be helpful to give families specific suggestions regarding follow-up and ensure that children have a medical home where the issue can be evaluated.

Source: Kaczmarski, DeBate, Marhefka, & Dale, 2011; Pietras, Rhodes, Meyers, & Goodman, 2012.

WHAT IF . . .

you discovered that a 5-year-old in your class has never seen a dentist? When you explore this with the family, you learn that it is the parents' fear of the dentist that keeps them from making an appointment. What guidance can you provide to ensure that the child gets the oral health care that is needed?

Month and is officially observed on the first Friday in February. "Give Kids a Smile" is an American Dental Association event that draws on the volunteer services of dentists to provide dental treatment to low-income children who do not have access to care. Many school districts also make arrangements for dental van services where children receive dental examinations and cleanings as well as other forms of treatment for dental caries. More information can be found on the American Dental Association website.

Oral health assessments also provide opportunities to educate children and families about caring for their teeth. Families are notified in advance and permission is obtained for children to participate in dental screenings conducted in the children's setting. Once completed, families are provided a report of the findings. This is a good time to share information with families about how to promote oral health and prevent dental caries.

Hearing and Vision Screenings

Specific tools are also used to screen for hearing and vision disorders. Hearing and vision screenings are often conducted in school settings where large numbers of children can be evaluated. Adequate hearing and vision are critical components of being an effective learner.

Hearing Screening

Permanent hearing loss is the most common congenital condition in the United States, affecting 1 in 500 babies (Chan, 2014). Hearing loss can occur in both ears or just in one ear. It can be mild, moderate, severe, or profound. Milder forms of hearing loss are more difficult to detect because children often compensate by using other sensory stimuli such as watching the environment closely for cues.

Because hearing loss is difficult to detect during the first few months of life, universal hearing screenings for newborns were implemented through the Early Hearing Detection and Intervention (EHDI) program. Newborn hearing screens are now completed 97% of the time (Centers For Disease Control and Prevention, 2013b). Before this program was implemented, many children with hearing loss were not recognized for many months or even years. Children born outside the United States or children born outside a hospital may not have received a hearing screen at birth.

Vision Screening

Vision disorders are common in childhood and can lead to long-term disabilities. It is estimated that 1 in 5 school-age children have some type of vision problem (Basch, 2011). Vision screening is an efficient and cost-effective way to identify children who need further evaluation. For this reason, vision screening has been mandated as a part of federal programs, including the Early Periodic Screening, Diagnosis, and Treatment (EPSDT) Program and Head Start. Early detection of vision problems can promote optimal learning. Vision problems that go untreated can lead to vision loss or blindness. Teachers should also know that the Affordable Care Act has increased access to preventive vision exams and glasses for children with certain health plans. Vision screening can detect the most common vision problems including:

amblyopia
a disorder that involves abnormal interaction between the eyes, causing unfocused vision

strabismus
malalignment of the eyes

- **Amblyopia:** when one eye does not recognize information properly, causing a discrepancy in the visual acuity compared with the other eye.
- **Strabismus:** when the eyes are not aligned with each other.

- **Refractive disorders:** conditions that cause problems with focusing; usually corrected with glasses.
- **Colorblindness:** the inability to distinguish between certain colors.

Vision screening done as part of a health care exam includes assessing how well the child tracks movement, fixates on a point, and responds to light. Familiar methods in the early childhood and school setting include having a child cover one eye while looking at a chart with symbols. The child is asked to match or identify the symbol, such as a letter or picture on the chart. These screening methods include directions for how to conduct the screening and indicators suggesting that the child be referred for additional vision assessment. In addition to this form of vision screening, teachers can detect visual problems by noticing and reporting symptoms of visual disturbances. Signs of visual problems that teachers may notice include the following:

Screenings are highly effective ways to identify children with treatable hearing or vision conditions.

- Eyes don't line up.
- Rubbing eyes frequently.
- Tilting head to look at items.
- Holding objects close to eyes or trouble reading.
- Blinking more than usual.
- Squinting eyes or frowning.

If teachers notice these symptoms, they should refer the child's family to a health care provider for further evaluation. The activities in the *Teaching Wellness* feature contribute to children's learning about hearing and vision.

refractive disorder
visual conditions that cause problems with focusing

colorblindness
the inability to distinguish between some colors

Screening for Communication Disorders

Communication disorders are conditions that cause children to have delays in their speech and language development. Children with communication disorders have better outcomes if they are diagnosed and treated early (Heward, 2013). Formalized screening for communication disorders varies among different types of early childhood programs. Regardless of standard screening practices in early childhood programs, observations by families and teachers is important for identifying children with communication disorders.

For a child whose first language is not English, the teacher must attempt to ascertain if a communication disorder is present or if the child functions normally in his or her native language. When assessing children for disabilities, the Individuals with Disabilities Education Act (IDEA) requires that the assessment be conducted in the child's native language (Heward, 2013).

CLASSROOM CONNECTION

Watch this video about children undergoing hearing and vision screenings. How do the strategies used by the teachers increase children's comfort during these screenings?

communication disorders
conditions that cause children to have delays in their speech and language development

Lead Screening

Lead is a chemical element commonly found in the environment. It has been a component of vehicle emissions and lead paint. Lead poisoning can cause permanent neurological damage and it is entirely preventable. Although the prevalence of lead in the environment has decreased significantly, it is still a public health problem, primarily affecting children in urban settings. There is no safe blood lead level (Centers for Disease Control and Prevention, 2013a).

lead
a chemical element that has been a component of vehicle emissions and lead paint and can cause toxicity in children

TEACHING WELLNESS   Health Care Checkups

LEARNING OUTCOME Children will be more comfortable with the idea of visiting a medical provider and will know what to expect during a checkup.

INFANTS AND TODDLERS

- **Goal:** To introduce information about health care checkups and visits to the doctor.
- **Materials:** *Time to See the Doctor* by Heather Maisner and Kristina Stephenson.
- **Activity plan:** Read the book to the children. Point to aspects of the pictures that show what is found in the doctor's office. Talk about the child who is worried about the

checkup and how he becomes more confident. Talk about what the doctor does and why.

- **Did you meet your goal?** Are the young children interested in the book? Do they follow along and anticipate the story? Do they talk about the activities that occur during the checkup? Can they answer, "What is the doctor doing?"

PRESCHOOLERS AND KINDERGARTNERS

- **Goal:** To reduce children's worries about health care checkups through dramatic play exploration.
- **Materials:** Dramatic play props for the health care setting, including a doctor's kit with stethoscope, thermometer, blood pressure gauge, reflex hammer, bandages, and examination gloves.
- **Activity plan:** Provide the props and space for the children to create a doctor's office and conduct imaginative play. Provide picture books about visiting the doctor, such as:
  - *Biscuit Visits the Doctor*, by Alyssa Satin Capucilli
  - *Corduroy Goes to the Doctor*, by Don Freeman
  - *My Friend the Doctor*, by Joanna Cole
  - *Elmo's World: Doctors!* by Naomi Kleinberg
  - *La Doctora Maisy* (Spanish-language edition), by Lucy Cousins

- *Going to the Doctor*, by Anne Civardi and Michelle Bates
- *Doctor Ted*, by Andrea Beaty
- *Going to the Hospital*, by Fred Rogers
- **How to adjust the activity:** Invite a medical provider to visit the classroom and talk about what to expect. Take pictures of children playing in the dramatic play area. Create a picture board and have children describe what happens when you visit the doctor. Have children talk about their experiences.
- **Did you meet your goal?** Observe children at play in the dramatic play area. Do they dramatize their experiences at the doctor's office? Do you hear them talking about worries or comforting their "patients"? When asked, are children able to describe with accuracy the kinds of things that happen at the exam?

SCHOOL-AGE CHILDREN

- **Goal:** To learn about the work that doctors and other medical providers do and communicate it to others.
- **Materials:** Materials to make posters such as large paper, marking pens, paints. Library books that describe the work of doctors and other medical providers, such as:
  - *What Does a Doctor Do?* by Felicia Lowenstein Niven
  - *A Day in the Life of a Doctor*, by Heather Adamson
  - *Keeping You Healthy: A Book about Doctors*, by Ann Owen
  - *Médico*, by Heather Miller
  - *If You Were a Doctor*, by Virgina Schomp
- **Activity plan:** Provide picture books and other library resources. Ask children to research information about the

different things that doctors do. Have individuals or small groups of children create a poster describing how medical workers help us.

- **How to adjust the activity:** Have children create posters to share with preschool-age children and send them to early childhood programs. Take a field trip to a nearby preschool program. Have the children describe their posters to the preschoolers.
- **Did you meet your goal?** Do children display their knowledge of the work of medical providers through their posters and conversations? Do the posters effectively communicate this information?

The major source of lead exposure is the lead-based paint present in buildings constructed before 1978. Lead-based paint is still present in one-third of the nation's dwellings (Advisory Committee on Childhood Lead Poisoning Prevention of the Centers for Disease Control and Prevention, 2012). Lead-based paint and contaminated dust present in homes with deteriorating surfaces are the most common sources. Lead-based paint is most dangerous when the paint is deteriorating and paint flakes and dust are introduced into the environment. It is ingested via a hand-to-mouth route, or it can be inhaled. Inhalation is especially a problem when homes containing lead are being remodeled. Other sources of lead exposure include (Centers for Disease Control and Prevention, 2013c):

- Artificial turf.
- Imported toys, jewelry, cosmetics, candy.
- Contaminated water pipes, solder, valves, and fixtures containing lead.
- Folk medicine.
- Pottery/ceramics.
- Industrial sources: from parents with occupational exposures such as battery, construction, or ceramics workers or furniture refinishers.

Symptoms of lead poisoning can be nonexistent or vague. Therefore, it is difficult to diagnose based solely on the child's history, making screening important. Screening for lead exposure in the early childhood setting is done as part of the health history using a checklist. Screening for lead toxicity is done in the medical setting using a checklist and possibly a blood test if there are concerns about possible exposure. Children who are enrolled in Medicaid and children who are found to be at risk for lead exposure through use of the checklist are referred to a medical provider to be screened using the blood test. In the past, most children with elevated lead levels were enrolled in Medicaid programs, which is why the CDC recommends screening all Medicaid-eligible children at 1 or 2 years of age. Table 9-2 is an example of a checklist used in screening for lead exposure. If families or caregivers have *any* concerns about possible lead exposure, regardless of the lead screening questions, the child should be referred to a health care provider for lead testing.

Developmental Screening and Assessment

Detecting developmental problems early in life is important so that intervention strategies can be implemented appropriately. **Developmental screening** provides a

developmental screening a type of health screening that provides a single snapshot of a child's status with respect to development

TABLE 9-2 Lead Screening Checklist	
Has the child spent time in a home, school or building built before 1950?	Does the child spend time with anyone whose job or hobby involves working with lead? (examples: painting, remodeling, auto batteries/radiators, smoldering, bullets, pottery, hunting)
Has the child lived in or regularly visited buildings built before 1978 with recent or ongoing remodeling?	Do you have pottery or ceramics made in other countries or pewter used in cooking, storing, or serving food or drink?
Has a sibling, housemate, or playmate being seen or treated for lead poisoning?	Has the child taken any traditional remedies or used imported cosmetics?
Is the child in a Head Start program?	Is the child adopted, or has the child lived in or visited another country?
Are there concerns about the child's development or behavior?	

Source: Oregon Lead Poisoning Prevention Program, 2009.

single snapshot of a child's developmental status and indicates if further evaluation is needed. Important characteristics of developmental screenings include the following (Moodie, 2014):

- It is brief, 30 minutes or less.
- It focuses on developmental skills and abilities in the lower range of performance for the child's age.
- It is designed to detect the possibility of delay but doesn't identify or describe the nature or extent of a developmental problem.
- It is designed to be followed by a more comprehensive evaluation to confirm or rule out a problem.

Screening tools for developmental progress should be considered part of the larger process of evaluation. Teachers have access to another powerful assessment tool: their ability to conduct meaningful observations. The early childhood setting offers an environment in which children's development can be seen in a natural setting. Teachers take advantage of this opportunity by observing children at play and in interactions with others. Knowing about developmental milestones allows teachers to identify behaviors that may benefit from further evaluation.

Both screening and observational assessment are conducted by teachers (or other program personnel) who are familiar to the child and who have received orientation and training on appropriate approaches. Developmental screenings and assessments are conducted using tools that have been validated and are culturally appropriate. The process involves families by first discussing identified concerns. Next, teachers obtain permission from the family to conduct a formal screening and assessment.

When information has been gathered, the teacher and family need to decide how to use the information. They discuss the findings and identify the next step. If a developmental concern is suspected, the child is referred to a developmental specialist for additional evaluation. The screening and assessment process also includes identifying the child's strengths and competencies and ways to promote the next steps in development. In this way, developmental screening serves two purposes:

1. To identify possible developmental delays early so that intervention strategies can be planned and implemented.
2. To identify children's strengths and needs to inform the development of appropriate classroom curriculum.

Recognizing normal developmental patterns and milestones for each child is important for all ages. By knowing and understanding typical developmental patterns, teachers are prepared to recognize abnormal behaviors and patterns that fall outside expected development. Like *red flags*, recognition of behaviors that do not align with expected development attracts the teacher's attention and highlights the need for further exploration.

In many cases, the early childhood teacher is the first person to mention to families that their child may be experiencing a developmental delay or concern. Families may have strong emotional reactions to this information. Teachers should be sensitive to these feelings and prepare carefully for such meetings. Teachers are

WHAT IF . . .

You notice a child who has difficulty speaking so that others can understand him? What kinds of special observations might you make? How would you approach the family with your concerns? What referrals would you make? What resources in your community would you utilize?

partners with families in supporting child development wherever the child is on the continuum of developmental skills and competencies. Developmental screening and assessment provide information for purposeful curriculum planning. Teachers are not responsible for diagnosing developmental delays; however, they are important sources of referral and support for families if developmental concerns are suspected.

Conducting Daily Health Checks

Staying attuned to children's health every day is a part of the teaching process that includes continual observation and reflection. Daily health checks are a natural part of this process. The daily health check is a planned approach to direct teacher attention to the child's health. Teachers conduct these checks to determine whether the child shows signs of illness, injury, or other health concerns. The American Academy of Pediatrics, American Public Health Association, and National Resource Center for Health and Safety in Child Care and Early Education (2011) recommends that daily health checks include the following:

- Changes in behavior or appearance from the previous day.
- Skin rashes, itchy skin or scalp.
- Temperature if the child appears ill.
- Complaints of pain or not feeling well.
- Other signs or symptoms of illness.
- Reports of illness or injury.

Daily health checks can be done efficiently and accurately during the greeting time. The teacher typically conducts these assessments as the child arrives in the classroom. The process involves:

- Stopping briefly to focus attention on the child.
- Looking at the child, observing for signs of illness or disease.
- Listening to the parent and child, paying special attention to information that suggests illness.

A description of this kind of approach is outlined in Figure 9-5.

During the health check, the teacher watches for signs of good health such as pink skin, bright eyes, and easy breathing. The teacher also observes for indications of health problems such as irritability and asks the family if there are any concerns. If the child appears ill, the teacher needs to be prepared to explain to the family members the symptoms that are observed and discuss arrangements for the child to be taken home.

The daily health check and any symptoms of illness or concerns regarding a child's health should be recorded on a tracking chart. The *National Health and Safety Performance Standards* recommends that the daily health check be charted in a way that is convenient for teachers provides a picture of the overall class group's health. Two sample formats are shown in Figure 9-6. These charts make it easy to see the pattern of symptoms of illness and subsequent absences. As total classroom attendance numbers drop due to illness, the chart also demonstrates the rate of disease spread among the children. These charts should be kept for at least three months to help track the spread of communicable diseases. They also provide the teacher and program with information used to reflect on the effectiveness of disease prevention strategies such as extra cleaning and sanitizing of the classroom.

FIGURE 9-5   Stop-Look-Listen Daily Health Check

Stop

Greet each child at arrival and take a moment to really observe the child.
Have a small conversation. Ask kind questions, such as "How are you feeling?" "Did you sleep
well last night?" "Did you eat breakfast today?"

Look

Observe these aspects:

		Signs of Good Health	Possible Signs of Illness
❑	Skin color	Pink and fresh; typical skin color for individual child	Flushed, feverish, or pale?
❑	Skin appearance	Smooth and calm	Rashy with sores or swelling?
❑	Eyes	Bright and alert	Red with discharge or dull with dark circles?
❑	Nose	Clear and clean	Dripping with nasal discharge?
❑	Ears	Does the child look comfortable	Rubbing and holding ears?
❑	Hair	Clean and combed	Unclean and badly tangled?
❑	General appearance	Does the child look interested in play	Droopy, listless, irritable, or restless?

Listen

Pay attention to what you hear:

		Signs of Good Health	Possible Signs of Illness
❑	Breathing pace	Even breathing	Fast breathing or panting?
❑	Breathing sounds	Quiet and smooth	Coughing, spitting, or congested?
❑	Parent reports	No concerns are mentioned	Child has been given medication before school?
			Child would not eat breakfast or has had a stomachache?
			Child has had diarrhea or has vomited recently?
			Child is acting unusually weepy?
			Child has been injured?

FOLLOW UP by asking more about any concerns.

DECIDE if the child is healthy. If signs of illness are present, child should return home.

Ongoing Observation

Observing children and monitoring them for signs of illness is the second part of continual health evaluation in the classroom. Through observation, teachers establish an understanding of each child's typical appearance and style of behavior so that signs of illness are more easily recognized. Signs of illness that are identified through observation include unusual fussiness and crying, listlessness or sleepiness, disinterest in food, paleness, or flushed cheeks. Observation is also important once an illness has been identified. In this situation, the teacher pays special attention to signs of illness spreading to other children.

FIGURE 9-6 Daily Health Check and Attendance Tracking Chart

Option 1: Attendance and daily health check information overlap.

Month: February	Date									
Child's Name	**1**	**2**	**3**	**4**	**5**	**6**	**7**	**8**	**9**	**10**
Asma M.		SL	C,V	A	A					
Shay R.					C			A		
Liliana T.					C,V			A	A	A
Riki H-G.								C,V	A	A

Option 2: Attendance and daily health check are recorded separately.

Month: February	Date									
Child's Name	**1**	**2**	**3**	**4**	**5**	**6**	**7**	**8**	**9**	**10**
Asma M.				A	A					
			SL	C, V						
Shay R.								A		
					C					
Liliana T.								A	A	A
					C, V					
Riki H-G.									A	A
								C, V		

Attendance:

Mark if present

Mark if absent A

Codes for Symptoms:

B = behavior change	I = report of injury	ST = sore throat
CP = chicken pox	L = lice	SR = skin rash
C = coughing	P = complaint of pain	T = suspected temperature
D = diarrhea	SL = sleepy or withdrawn	V = vomiting

Source: American Academy of Pediatrics, American Public Health Association, National Resource Center for Health and Safety in Child Care and Early Education, 2011.

The observations of children's health that teachers provide are important to families. Families rely on teachers to share feedback about how their child is doing in the class group when they are not present. They need to know if the teacher has detected signs of illness. Sometimes signs of illness are sudden and require teachers to contact the family member to take the child home due to illness. Other observations can be shared with families at the time of departure. A clear description of the signs of illness is important so that the family can continue to monitor the child at home. Ongoing observations respect the needs of young children to have teachers who are their advocates for health and wellness.

CHECK YOUR UNDERSTANDING 9.4

Click here to check your understanding of conducting health evaluations in early childhood settings.

SUMMARY

- Health evaluation is an important aspect of early childhood development and education. The teacher–child relationship involves being aware of children's health and wellness.
- Collecting children's health history offers an opportunity to obtain health information in partnership with families. The information that is discussed guides the plan of services for the child in the classroom and provides opportunities to promote wellness in the family setting.
- Understanding the status of children's health, promoting health and wellness in the family, and referring children to needed services improves physical and mental health outcomes for all children.
- Incorporating health screenings such as growth measurements, hearing and vision screening, and developmental screenings into the children's settings is a highly effective and efficient way to access large numbers of children. Identifying and addressing health and development problems early sets children on a course for improved outcomes and optimal learning.

Chapter Quiz 9

 Click here to check your understanding of Chapter 9, Health Screening and Assessment.

Discussion Starters

1. A significant percentage of families in the United States lack affordable health insurance. Even families with public health insurance have difficulty finding regular health care. How might lack of regular medical care influence health screenings in the early childhood setting?

2. Early childhood educators may interact with families who have concerns about vaccinating their children. How might a child who has not been completely vaccinated influence the health of other children in the early childhood setting or the health of the community?

3. As more schools incorporate BMI measurements into health screenings, some children will be identified as overweight or obese. When families are notified about their child's BMI, how might they respond to these screenings? How do you feel about schools using obesity screening tools? What types of unintended consequences should be considered?

Practice Points

1. A 5-year-old child enrolling in kindergarten in your state is unvaccinated. The family has applied for a religious exemption. Find the laws in your state about vaccinations. Determine what vaccinations are required and if religious exemptions are allowable.

2. Various formats are used to obtain health history information. Contact early childhood programs or the school district in your community to learn how they collect this information. Search the Internet for sample health history formats and compare them.

3. Conduct the Stop-Look-Listen Daily Health Check (see Figure 9-5) with a child or peer teacher. Are you able to determine potential health concerns using this format? Why or why not?

4. Research information about conducting classroom vision screenings. What materials are available? What is the cost? Is special training required to use the materials? If possible, obtain vision screening materials and conduct a vision screening with a peer teacher or friend.

Web Resources

American Academy of Pediatrics, Health, Mental Health and Safety Guidelines for Schools

Centers for Disease Control and Prevention, About Child & Teen BMI

Immunization Action Coalition

National Conference of State Legislatures, school immunization exemption laws

Key Terms

acculturation
adverse reactions
allergic reaction
amblyopia
asthma
colorblindness
communication disorder
continual observation

daily health checks
developmental milestone
developmental screening
fluoride
health assessment
health evaluation
health history
health screening

immunizations
lead
local reaction
medical home
premature infant
referral
refractive disorder
rubella

strabismus
systemic reaction
thimerosal
well-child checkups
whooping cough

CHAPTER 10

Managing Infectious Disease

learning outcomes

After reading this chapter, you should be able to:

1. Describe the infectious disease process, including how germs are spread.
2. Describe common symptoms of illness seen in children and how classroom practices can prevent or minimize the spread of infections.
3. Identify some of the more common infectious diseases and describe when children should be excluded from school because of them.
4. Describe how infectious diseases can present unique challenges to internationally adopted children.

CASE STUDY

Mark is a healthy and vibrant 6-year-old who plays actively during recess. Today his first-grade teacher, Mary Beth, notices that Mark is unusually quiet and not playing. She asks him if something is bothering him. He says that he does not feel well and that his "tummy hurts." Mary Beth tells the other playground monitors that she is going to take Mark to the school office. The school nurse evaluates him and finds that he has a fever. She notifies Mark's family, who come to take him home. The nurse recommends that Mark see his primary care provider.

The next day Mark is absent from school. His mother calls and tells Mary Beth that Mark has been diagnosed with strep throat and will be out of school at least another day. Mary Beth knows that strep throat is contagious, but she is not sure if she should report this to the other families in the class. She asks the school nurse for advice. The nurse returns a notice for families alerting them to the signs of strep throat.

At story time, Mary Beth talks with the children about ways to stay healthy. To help explore the topic, she reads *Germs Make Me Sick!* by Melvin Berger. Mary Beth demonstrates how the children can cover their coughs by coughing into the crook of their arms. They also talk about how to wash their hands carefully and when to wash their hands to keep germs away. At the end of the day Mary Beth hears Calvin declare, "When Mark gets back, let's tell him about how to be healthy!"

Children are exposed to many illnesses during the early childhood years. Illness is more common for children who participate in groups because of the potential for spreading germs. Children are naturally curious, and their exploration of the world involves touching and handling toys and surfaces. These behaviors cause them to put their hands and objects in their mouths, creating easy entry for germs. Teaching young children involves caring for them when illness occurs in school and centers as well as being proactive and using strategies to prevent the spread of infection.

Teachers such as Mary Beth become familiar with individual children and are able to recognize changes in the child's behavior or appearance that may be clues to sickness. They also know that they are responsible for assisting children when illness occurs, supporting families to get the medical help the child needs, and teaching children ways to stay healthy. To help in preparing for these important aspects of teaching, this chapter describes the basic process of **disease transmission** and ways to prevent illness from spreading. We discuss some of the symptoms of common diseases and how to manage them in the early childhood setting. Some children such as those who are internationally adopted or who have recently immigrated to the United States may face special health concerns. These needs are also discussed.

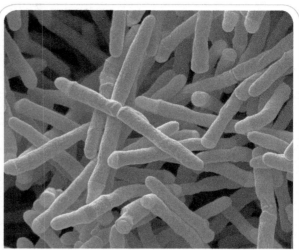

Disease is caused by viruses, bacteria, fungi, and parasites—commonly referred to as germs.

Steve Gschmeissner/Science Photo Library/Getty Images

Throughout the chapter, when we refer to *disease*, we are talking about illnesses, infections, viruses, and other maladies that cause children to get sick. Teachers are not trained medical professionals and should not offer diagnoses or treatment for health care problems. However, the guidance provided here contributes to the skills that prepare teachers to care for children appropriately when illness occurs at school.

disease transmission
process by which infections are spread to individuals

UNDERSTANDING THE INFECTIOUS DISEASE PROCESS

Infectious diseases are illnesses or conditions caused by germs, and they can cause symptoms related to many body systems. Usually, the body's immune system detects and fights off disease. In the process of fighting off infections, a child can become ill and show a wide array of symptoms in response to infections.

Infectious diseases are common in childhood and can interfere with classroom activities. Children rely on their teachers to comfort and nurture them, and their classmates depend on the teacher to help keep them from getting sick. Teachers need to understand the disease process and try to reduce the frequency of disease and minimize its impact.

infectious diseases
diseases caused by microorganisms that are spread from person to person or animal to person

The Causes of Infectious Diseases

Microscopic organisms are present in huge numbers throughout the environment and can cause diseases. These include viruses, bacteria, fungi, and parasites. Each of these organisms exists in one form or another virtually everywhere on earth. In an infectious form, each can cause illness. We commonly refer to these infectious agents as **germs**.

germ
an organism or infectious agent that can potentially cause disease

Viruses

virus
a type of infectious germ that invades human tissue and causes illness

A **virus** is a type of infectious germ that invades human tissue and causes illness. The body's immune system is highly effective at killing off most viruses. Illnesses caused by viruses include chicken pox, measles, the common cold, influenza, and human immunodeficiency virus (HIV). Usually diseases caused by viruses resolve on their own. Through this healing process, the body's systems develop a certain level of immunity to exposure in the future. Most viruses cause mild infections but can rarely cause serious medical complications.

Bacteria

bacteria
infectious germs that invade human tissue and cause illness; sometimes treated with antibiotics

Like viruses, **bacteria** are infectious germs that cause illness. Some bacteria are useful in digestion and in certain familiar processes such as making yogurt from milk, but other bacteria can cause disease. These harmful bacteria are the cause of many respiratory illnesses such as bacterial pneumonia and tuberculosis and other diseases such as pertussis and tetanus. Bacteria are a major cause of disease and death worldwide. Bacterial infections are often treated with antibiotics.

Fungi

fungi
a type of germ that can commonly cause skin infections or allergic reactions

Another germ, **fungi**, is the cause of common illnesses such as ringworm and athlete's foot. Other examples of fungi are mushrooms, mold, and baker's yeast. Other fungi are used to grow special molds for making cheese. The spores of some fungi can cause allergies.

Parasites

parasite
infections that invade the body and live within human tissue for extended periods of time

An infectious agent called **parasites** feed on or enter the body tissue. They can live on and within human tissue for extended periods of time. Examples of parasitic diseases include head lice; scabies; intestinal worms; malaria; and parasites such as *Giardia*, which are contracted from drinking contaminated water.

How Disease Is Spread

communicable diseases
infections that are spread from one person to another

mode of transmission
the route by which an infection is spread

Infectious diseases are spread from person to person or from an animal or insect to a person. The most frequent infections among young children are **communicable diseases**, which are spread from one person to another. The way in which a disease is spread is the **mode of transmission**. (See Figure 10-1.) Most infections are transferred by one of the four common modes of transmission, as discussed next.

Direct or Indirect Contact

This is the most common mode of transmission in the early childhood setting. Direct contact occurs by direct person-to-person contact, whereas indirect refers to transmission via a contaminated object or contaminated hands. This is the most common mode of transmission in early childhood.

Typical actions such as these occur in everyday play and provide the opportunity to spread disease. For example, Cherice, who is coming down with a cold, may sneeze directly on Aiden while they are playing with blocks. Or she may turn away and sneeze on some blocks that Karl, who has just joined the play, touches a few minutes later. When Karl picks up the blocks and later scratches his nose or puts his fingers in his mouth, the germs are indirectly transmitted to him. Most common respiratory and diarrheal infections are spread by direct or indirect contact.

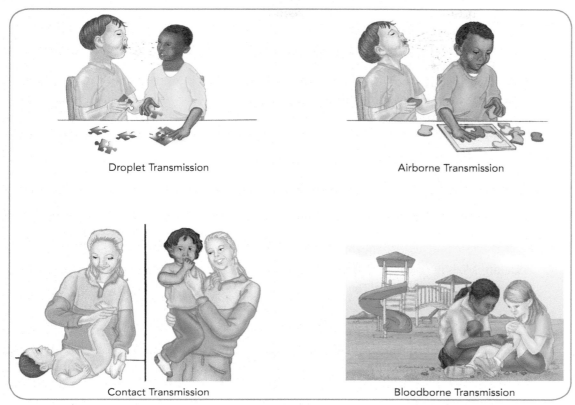

FIGURE 10-1
Common Modes of Transmission

Droplet Transmission

This occurs when a person coughs or sneezes, propelling droplets of contaminated fluid that land on another person's eyes, nose, or mouth. Examples of infections transmitted this way include influenza, whooping cough, and strep throat, which are all discussed later in the chapter.

Airborne Transmission

Similar to droplet transmission, airborne transmission involves much smaller microscopic droplets that travel through the air via air currents and over a longer distance. Examples include chicken pox, measles, and tuberculosis.

airborne transmission
occurs when infected particles are sneezed or coughed into the air and inhaled by another person

Bloodborne Transmission

This type of spread of infection, bloodborne transmission, occurs through contact with contaminated blood or body fluids. In this situation, the infection can be transmitted only if the infected blood comes in contact with an uninfected person's bloodstream through a wound. This might happen if a child comes in contact with infected blood from a wound such as a bite, a nosebleed, blood from excessive scratching of irritated skin, or an injury (American Academy of Pediatrics, 2012). This mode of transmission is very uncommon in early childhood and school settings.

bloodborne transmission
occurs when infections are spread by contamination with blood

The Incubation Period

Illness does not always occur immediately after contact with an infectious germ. Sometimes illness is not evident until a few hours, a few days, or even up to a few

incubation period
period of time between a child's first exposure to an infectious germ and the time the child's first symptom appears

months in rare cases. The time between the child's first exposure to an infectious agent and when the first symptom of illness appears is called the incubation period. Each infectious agent has a typical incubation period. For some diseases, the incubation period is the time when the child can infect others. When an illness has been diagnosed, teachers who are knowledgeable about the illness's incubation period are then able to identify other children who may have been exposed to the disease. Knowing about incubation periods also helps teachers know how long to watch for the spread of the disease and to recognize when the potential risk for additional cases is likely to be over.

In the opening case scenario, Mary Beth understands that other children may have been exposed to strep throat. She takes steps to counteract the possible spread of the disease by teaching the children how to cover their mouths when they cough and wash their hands carefully. She also shares information with parents about the symptoms of strep throat. In addition, Mary Beth will also watch for signs of strep throat over the next two to five days, the typical incubation period for this disease.

The period of contagiousness can also vary and be different from or similar to the incubation period. Local health departments and health care providers can be excellent resources for teachers when potential outbreaks or questions arise. Table 10-1 outlines modes of transmission, incubation periods, and symptoms associated with the infectious diseases discussed in this chapter.

Symptoms of Disease

Understanding symptoms of illness can guide teachers to be watchful and ready to take appropriate action to care for a child. Symptoms that are frequently associated with disease include the following:

- *Fever*, which may be evident by the child's brightly flushed cheeks.
- *Cough*, especially if the cough is new.
- *Rash*, such as a newly emerging flush on the skin.
- *Vomiting*, especially when vomiting occurs with no other likely explanation.
- *Changes in the child's typical behavior*, such as being very quiet or not engaging in typical play.

In the opening scenario, it was Mark's atypical behavior that caught his teacher's attention. Following her observations and after talking with Mark, Mary Beth decided that it was highly likely he was becoming ill. She felt reasonably confident that it was in Mark's best interest to see the school nurse for further assessment.

Pearson Education

CLASSROOM CONNECTION

Watch this video that shows a teacher talking to a young girl who is feeling ill. How does the teacher evaluate the child's symptoms?

Most children's programs do not have a nurse available to assist in determining a course of action for a child who gets sick at school. In these settings, teachers must use their best judgment to determine whether the child can be cared for in the setting or if the parent should be contacted.

A description of the symptoms the teacher observed provides helpful information for families and medical providers. It is not appropriate for the teacher to suggest a medical diagnosis or offer a plan of treatment. However, it is appropriate for

TABLE 10-1 Childhood Infections: Mode of Transmission, Incubation Period, and Symptoms

Infectious Disease	Mode of Transmission	Incubation Period	Symptoms
Chicken pox	Airborne, droplet	10–21 days	Fever, cough, rash
Common colds	Droplet	Variable	Fever, runny nose, cough, congestion
Conjunctivitis (pinkeye)	Droplet	Variable	Eye drainage, redness of eyes
Coxsackie virus (hand, foot, and mouth disease)	Droplet	3–5 days	Fever, blisters in the mouth, refusal to eat, rash on palms and soles, diaper rash
Croup	Droplet	Variable	Fever, barky cough, runny nose
Ear infections	Usually not communicable	Variable	Fever, earache
Fifth disease	Droplet	4–28 days	Fever, headache, muscle aches, rash
Group A strep (strep throat)	Droplet	Several hours to 4 days	Fever, sore throat, rash
Haemophilus influenzae type b (Hib)	Droplet	Unknown	Fever, upper respiratory infection, meningitis
Head lice	Direct contact	10–14 days	Itching of scalp
Hepatitis A	Direct or indirect contact	15–50 days	Fever, nausea, abdominal pain
Hepatitis B	Bloodborne	45–160 days	Inflammation of the liver
Hepatitis C	Bloodborne	6–7 weeks	Inflammation of the liver
Human immunodeficiency virus (HIV)	Bloodborne	12–18 months	Wide range of symptoms
Influenza	Airborne or droplet; depends on the strain	1–4 days	Fever, muscle aches, sore throat, cough, headache
Measles	Airborne, droplet	7–18 days	Fever, pinkeye, runny nose, rash
Methicillin-resistant Staphylococcus aureus (MRSA)	Direct contact	Variable	Skin infections
Pertussis (whooping cough)	Droplet	4–21 days	Initial: fever, runny nose, cough. Later: Numerous bursts of cough, sometimes with the characteristic whoop
Pinworms	Direct or indirect contact	Variable	Itching around anus or genital area
Respiratory syncytial virus (RSV)	Droplet	2–8 days	Fever, runny nose, cough, difficulty breathing
Ringworm	Direct contact	Unknown	Rash
Rotavirus	Direct or indirect contact	1–2 days	Fever, vomiting, diarrhea
Scabies	Direct contact	4–6 weeks	Rash, itching
Streptococcus pneumonia	Droplet	1–3 days	Ear infections, pneumonia, meningitis
Tetanus	Direct contact through open wound	4–21 days	Severe muscle contraction, spasm, seizures
Tuberculosis	Droplet, airborne	2–12 weeks	Chronic cough

Sources: American Academy of Pediatrics, 2012 and Centers for Disease Control and Prevention, 2012.

the teacher to provide a summary of the symptoms that were observed, to inform the family of the intensity of those symptoms, and to recommend that the parent seek medical evaluation. Symptoms provide clues to help medical providers diagnose the disease and create an appropriate treatment plan.

Symptoms of Common Infections

Among the many diseases that children may experience, three groups of infections are most common. These include infections with symptoms of diarrhea, respiratory illness, or skin infections and rashes.

Acute Infectious Diarrhea

diarrhea
the frequent and excessive discharge of watery feces

Diarrhea is the frequent and excessive discharge of watery feces. Young children may have discomfort and soiled diapers and clothing or have a frequent need to use the bathroom. Viruses are the most common cause of infectious diarrhea. The infection is transmitted from person to person usually by direct or indirect contact. Infectious diarrhea outbreaks are more common among children who participate in early childhood group settings than among those who do not, especially in programs that include children in diapers. Therefore, periodic training of staff in hygiene and proper diapering and toileting may reduce the risk of outbreaks.

Because of this frequency of occurrence and the potential for the spread of infectious diarrhea, its management and prevention are especially important. Frequent hand washing is essential for children and teachers. If a child develops diarrhea, the teacher should inform parents how many episodes the child experienced. It is particularly important to notice if any blood is present in the child's stool. Other symptoms such as fever, vomiting, or rash should also be reported.

WHAT IF . . .

several children in your class developed diarrhea? What policies would you implement to minimize further spread of the illness? What resources in your community would you turn to for assistance if it became a large outbreak of infectious diarrhea?

Respiratory Tract Illnesses

Symptoms of respiratory tract illnesses involve the nose, sinuses, ears, throat, and lungs. Respiratory diseases are extremely common in young children. Familiar respiratory infections include the common cold, ear infections, **pharyngitis** (an infection of the throat), **sinusitis** (a sinus infection), and **pneumonia** (a lung infection).

pharyngitis
infection of the throat

sinusitis
sinus infection

pneumonia
lung infection

These illnesses are usually spread by sneezing, coughing, or drainage from the nose. Symptoms of respiratory tract illness include fever, nasal congestion, runny nose, sore throat, ear pain, cough, or difficulty breathing. Some of these infections are associated with skin rashes as well. The incidence of respiratory infections is increased in children attending child care programs but can be reduced with consistent hand washing and appropriate cough etiquette (American Academy of Pediatrics, *Preventing the Spread of Illness in Child Care or School*, 5/5/15, retrieved 8/7/15 from https://www.healthychildren.org/English/health-issues/conditions/prevention/Pages/Prevention-In-Child-Care-or-School.aspx).

Families should be contacted and children should be referred to their medical provider if they exhibit symptoms such as uncontrolled coughing, difficulty breathing, or wheezing (American Academy of Pediatrics, American Public Health Association, National Resource Center for Health and Safety in Child Care and Early Education, 2011). During the initial days of respiratory illness, children may be uncomfortable or in pain. Although they may be receiving treatment and do not have a fever, they should stay home simply because they are not feeling well and are unable to participate in normal school activities.

The symptoms of runny nose and cough are not uncommon in young children, especially during the winter months. These symptoms alone should not exclude children from attending early childhood programs. If teachers have concerns, parents should be notified. Talking with a health care provider may be helpful to determine whether exclusion is necessary. Many of these children can be included safely. See this chapter's *Nutrition Note: Vitamin D and Infectious Diseases* for some interesting information regarding vitamin D and respiratory infections.

NUTRITION NOTE — Vitamin D and Infectious Diseases

Every type of tissue in the body uses vitamin D for various purposes. Although it is not clear what levels of vitamin D are considered normal, it has been shown that low levels of vitamin D are associated with higher risk of respiratory infections, higher rates of asthma, eczema, and food allergies.

Over 90% of vitamin D in the body is produced by exposure to sunlight. It is difficult to ingest enough vitamin D from the diet, so deficiency is common even in children. Because of the widespread deficiency, it is reasonable that all children receive supplementation with vitamin D, especially in areas where there is limited exposure to sunlight during certain seasons. This, of course, must be balanced with the risks of sun exposure: sunburn and skin cancer. Supplementation begins during infancy and should continue throughout the childhood years.

Source: Bozzetto, Carraro, Giordano, Boner, Boraldi, 2012.

Skin Infections and Contagious Rashes

Skin infections are caused by viruses, bacteria, and fungi. They are a common symptom of several diseases. Sometimes respiratory tract infections are associated with skin infections. Chicken pox is one example. Initially, the disease starts with mild respiratory symptoms, then progresses to the characteristic skin rash.

Inclusion or exclusion of children with skin rashes depends on the underlying cause. Teachers may need to rely on recommendations from the child's health care provider when determining whether exclusion is appropriate. Frequent hand washing helps minimize potential spread.

CHECK YOUR UNDERSTANDING 10.1

Click here to check your understanding of the infectious disease process.

PREVENTING AND CONTROLLING INFECTIOUS DISEASE

Because children participating in group settings have the potential to be exposed to a wider range of infections, it is especially important for teachers to be purposeful in implementing strategies to reduce the incidence of illness. Strategies include the following:

- Recognizing national and local public health policies.
- Complying with medical interventions such as required immunizations.
- Following recommended practices for the classroom that are provided by licensing and accreditation agencies.
- Establishing and practicing prevention strategies.

We now look at some of the more common prevention strategies: immunizations, health assessments for teachers, and classroom practices to reduce the spread of disease.

Immunizations

The immunizations that are required for entry and participation in early childhood and school settings are put in place to stop the spread of potentially dangerous diseases. Requirements for children's immunizations are typically regulated by federal or state agencies that have oversight for early childhood settings and schools.

A Matter of ETHICS

One of the families in your class has a philosophical opposition to giving their children vaccinations, so the child in your class has not received any. The family has completed the appropriate paperwork for an exemption. Do you have a personal bias for or against their decision? What specific issues are you be concerned about? How does the Code of Ethical Conduct guide you in this matter? Given your professional responsibilities, what plan might you establish with the family in case the child is exposed to a vaccine-preventable disease at preschool? What steps could you take to minimize exposure to disease for all the children in your class?

Immunization requirements are useful to teachers because they help in establishing healthful environments for young children. Immunizations have been proven to be the most effective method of prevention of infection in children.

Health Assessments for Teachers

Preemployment and ongoing health appraisals for teachers help reduce the potential for spread of disease between teachers and children and assist in keeping teachers healthy. Health assessments assist in detecting infectious disease that teachers may introduce into the classroom. For example, some infectious diseases such as tuberculosis can be "silent," meaning the adult has no symptoms. The *National Health and Safety Performance Standards* recommend that teachers obtain a health assessment before employment, which may include the following items (American Academy of Pediatrics, American Public Health Association, National Resource Center for Health and Safety in Child Care and Early Education, 2011):

- *Health history:* to establish an understanding of the teacher's general state of health.
- *Physical and dental exam:* to screen for illness and to determine if dental decay is evident. The germs that cause dental decay are infectious and can be communicated to young children.
- *Vision and hearing screening:* to identify the need for eyeglasses or hearing assistance.
- *Tuberculosis (TB) screening:* to identify whether the teacher is a potential carrier of TB. Standards related to TB screenings are specific to regional health recommendations depending on the risk of TB in the local area. Many programs require a TB test prior to employment and again if the teacher has a known exposure.
- *Review of occupational health hazards:* to clarify risks to the teacher in the children's setting and to identify any accommodations that might be needed.
- *Assessment of limitations:* to identify issues that may require modifications in the workplace, such as regular break times for a teacher who needs to test and manage her own insulin treatment for diabetes.
- *Review of immunization:* to determine whether any are lacking or needed. Those of particular importance include hepatitis A, hepatitis B, tetanus (Tdap, influenza, chicken pox, measles, and pertussis).

Some infections, such as hepatitis A and chicken pox, are common among children and can easily be spread to an adult. These infections may be more serious for adults than children.

There is an increasing prevalence of whooping cough (pertussis) among older children and individuals whose immunity from previous vaccination is waning. For this reason, the tetanus booster vaccine for adults now includes pertussis vaccination (Tdap). Teachers should receive Tdap instead of the former tetanus booster (dT) (Centers for Disease Control and Prevention, 2012). Yearly influenza vaccination is recommended for staff caring for children of any age (American Academy of Pediatrics, American Public Health Association, National Resource Center for Health and Safety in Child Care and Early Education, 2011).

Teachers need to be concerned about their own health. Teachers who may be pregnant should be aware that some childhood illness can have negative impacts on the unborn child. The *Safety Segment* addresses these situations.

Teachers need to be alert to their own health care. This is especially important for women who become pregnant while teaching young children. Some common infectious diseases introduce risks to the growing fetus, including abnormal development and even death. Infections that spread from the mother to the unborn baby include chicken pox, hepatitis B, coxsackie virus (hand, foot, and mouth disease), herpes, and fifth disease.

Teachers who are pregnant or are planning to become pregnant should consult with their health care provider. A health history and record of immunizations will help the physician evaluate the need to update immunizations such as tetanus, diphtheria, and influenza. Teachers who are exposed to the above infectious diseases during pregnancy should contact their health care provider for guidance.

Finally, teachers not only are susceptible to infection, but also can spread infection, just as children can. When certain symptoms are present, such as fever or vomiting, teachers should stay home and avoid exposing others. If a specific diagnosis has been made, such as strep throat, teachers should follow the same recommendations that are made for children.

Classroom Practices for Controlling the Spread of Disease

Purposeful health practices that are routinely followed in children's settings can significantly decrease the frequency of infections. These include such practices as washing one's hands, conducting daily health checks, sanitizing toys and classrooms, following careful diapering and toileting policies, implementing universal precautions when needed, and teaching children preventive health practices.

Hand Washing

Hand washing is the single most important way to reduce the spread of disease. Unwashed or improperly washed hands are the primary source for the spread of disease. Studies have shown that proper hand washing can significantly reduce the spread of diarrheal and respiratory illnesses in child care programs (American Academy of Pediatrics, American Public Health Association, National Resource Center for Health and Safety in Child Care and Early Education, 2011).

When to Wash Hands All children and teachers should wash their hands at routine times during the day, such as upon arrival or before eating, as well as at other times when germs can be transmitted. Children and teachers should wash their hands at the following times (American Academy of Pediatrics, American Public Health Association, National Resource Center for Health and Safety in Child Care and Early Education, 2011):

- Upon arrival at school or when coming in from outdoor play.
- When moving from one classroom to another (for example, when a teacher moves from leading one group to another).
- Before:
  - Eating or feeding a child.
  - Handling food for a child or for themselves.
  - Giving medication to a child.
  - Playing in the water table or participating in other water play with one or more children.

- After:
  - Using the toilet.
  - Diapering or helping a child use the toilet.
  - Assisting children to wipe or blow their noses.
  - Contacting body fluids such as mucus (from sneezing), blood, and vomit.
  - Handling animals (see the *Health Hint*).
  - Playing in the water table or sandbox.
  - Cleaning or sanitizing.
  - Handling garbage.

Supporting Children to Wash Their Own Hands Children are capable of washing their hands effectively if the appropriate supports are available. This includes providing a child-sized sink or an appropriate step stool so that children can reach the water. Warm running water is needed to encourage scrubbing and to remove soil and germs. Liquid soap should be provided because it is easier for children to use (see Figure 10-2). Disposable towels are recommended to avoid the spread of germs. Children should be taught to turn off the faucet using a paper towel because this helps reduce the spread of germs from the faucet back to the children's hands.

Once children have been taught how to wash their hands effectively, the teacher's role is primarily to supervise for safety. For children who cannot wash their hands independently, a teacher can safely cradle a child in one arm or provide support for a child to stand while the child washes his or her hands. Teachers should wash their own hands after assisting children. For children who cannot be held and cannot stand, it is acceptable to use an alcohol-based hand sanitizer as an alternative (American Academy of Pediatrics, American Public Health Association, National Resource Center for Health and Safety in Child Care and Early Education, 2011).

Conducting Daily Health Checks

Daily health checks are an important way to prevent the spread of disease. Teachers should be prepared to conduct the daily health check as soon as possible after the children arrive. The purpose of the check is to identify children who are ill and who may need to be excluded from participation, which can reduce the transmission

Pearson Education

CLASSROOM CONNECTION

Watch this video in which a teacher giving a lesson on hand washing. What do the children learn from this lesson?

HEALTH HINT   Infections and Animals

Interaction with animals is a fun and valuable teaching tool, but animals can introduce certain types of infections. To minimize risk of infection:

- All animals should be fully vaccinated.
- Teachers and children should wash their hands after handling pets.
- Animal contact should occur in designated areas.
- No food should be allowed in animal contact areas.
- Classroom animals should not be allowed to roam or have contact with wild animals.

- Parents should be informed in advance about the presence of animals. Teachers should consult with parents about children's special health care needs, especially for children with immune problems. Cat allergies are common and can be particularly problematic.
- Aquariums and cages should not be cleaned in sinks that are used for food preparation.
- Children under the age of 5 should not have contact with baby chicks or ducks, reptiles, or ferrets because of increased risk for certain types of infections.

Source: Centers for Disease Control and Prevention, 2012.

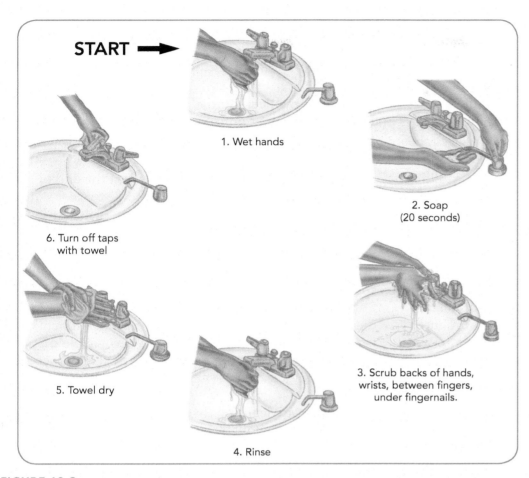

START ➤

1. Wet hands

2. Soap
(20 seconds)

3. Scrub backs of hands,
wrists, between fingers,
under fingernails.

4. Rinse

5. Towel dry

6. Turn off taps
with towel

FIGURE 10-2
Hand Washing Is the Single Most Important Way to Reduce the Spread of Disease
Source: Based on steps from La Crosse County Environmental Health (n.d.).

of infectious diseases (American Academy of Pediatrics, American Public Health Association, National Resource Center for Health and Safety in Child Care and Early Education, 2011). For example, teachers should monitor the class group for two weeks (the incubation period) following a confirmed case of chicken pox. Teachers should document the findings from the daily health checks to assist in tracking and monitoring illnesses in the classroom.

Cleaning and Sanitizing

Cleaning and sanitizing are important actions in preventing the spread of disease. Young children touch and share many objects throughout the day. They deposit germs either directly onto others or indirectly onto surfaces and objects. Because of this, any surface that a child can reach, including floors, should be sanitized regularly to minimize contamination with infectious germs.

Cleaning products should be safe for use in the classroom setting. As discussed elsewhere in this text, the bleach and water solutions used for cleaning and sanitizing are appropriate for use in children's settings. More detailed recommendations for cleaning and sanitizing specific areas and items in early childhood settings are found in the *National Health and Safety Performance Standards*.

Teachers carry the primary responsibility for a healthy classroom environment. This requires teachers' commitment to ensuring clean and sanitary spaces and equipment. It also means that teachers need to have a positive disposition toward what can sometimes be a tedious task: cleaning. Several approaches can help:

- Post a cleaning and sanitizing reminder chart to ensure that the schedule is achieved.
- Provide a "wash me" bucket for collecting toys that have been in children's mouths. The toys in the bucket are then sanitized after class.
- Stock the cupboard with disposable towels for wiping doorknobs and cupboard handles.
- Obtain laundry bags for gathering dramatic play clothing at the end of each week so that the clothing can be laundered.
- Be prepared to increase the frequency of cleaning and sanitizing when the number of children with illness is unusually high.

Diapering and Toileting

Sanitary practices are especially important when changing diapers or assisting children at the toilet. Settings that provide care for children who wear diapers typically require the use of disposable diapers. Exceptions may be made for children who have a medical reason, such as an allergic reaction to disposable diapers. Figure 10-3 describes appropriate diaper-changing procedures. This procedure should be posted in all diaper-changing areas. A child should *never* be left unattended on the changing table.

Settings that serve children who are learning to use the toilet are discouraged from using potty chairs (or non-flushable toilets) because sanitation is difficult. If potty chairs are used, they should be easy to sanitize, used only in the bathroom area, and used on a surface that does not absorb moisture and is easy to clean. They should also be used in areas where toilets and other potty chairs are out of reach and where a sink is designated to sanitize only potty chairs (American Academy of Pediatrics, American Public Health Association, National Resource Center for Health and Safety in Child Care and Early Education, 2011). Ideally, settings serving children ages 2 to 5 should provide child-sized toilets. This makes children more comfortable and helps them learn to manage their own toileting.

When assisting children with toileting, teachers should guide them in removing their garments and help them use the toilet. Teachers should assist with wiping

---

FIGURE 10-3   Diaper-Changing Procedures

1. **NEVER** leave the child unattended at the changing table.
2. Have all needed supplies available at the changing table. Wash hands.
3. Place the child on the changing table, avoiding contact of soiled diaper with surrounding surfaces and clean clothing.
4. Unfasten soiled diaper, leaving it under child. Clean the child's diaper area and genitalia using appropriate wipes. Clean from front to back. Use a fresh wipe each time removing urine or stool.
5. Remove soiled diaper without contaminating surfaces. Enclose the diaper in a disposable bag.
6. Slide the fresh diaper under the child and fasten.
7. Wash the child's hands and return the child to the supervised area.
8. Clean and sanitize the diaper changing area.
9. Wash your hands. Record diaper change in child's daily log.

Sources: American Academy of Pediatrics, American Public Health Association, National Resource Center for Health and Safety in Child Care and Early Education, 2011.

as needed, remembering to wipe from front to back. Young children may need help arranging and fastening their garments. Then both the child and the teacher should thoroughly wash their hands. Sinks and toilets should be cleaned and sanitized daily.

Using Standard Precautions

The **Standard Precautions** are a set of guidelines developed by the CDC for use in health care settings that prevent the spread of infections from exposure to blood and body fluids. The basic principle is that all blood, body fluids, secretions, excretions (except sweat), nonintact skin, and mucous membranes potentially contain germs that can cause infections. Standard Precautions include two important practices relevant to early childhood settings (American Academy of Pediatrics, American Public Health Association, National Resource Center for Health and Safety in Child Care and Early Education, 2011):

1. Using barriers such as disposable gloves when caring for children when blood or body fluids as stated above may be present.
2. Cleaning and sanitizing surfaces to prevent the transmission of infections by touching surfaces that have been contaminated by blood.

Teachers should wear gloves whenever an injury involves blood, such as a cut, scrape, or bloody nose. Once the bleeding has been stopped, any surfaces that have been exposed to blood must be sanitized. Consider this scenario:

Tom is in the play yard bouncing a ball to Lena. He hears a crash and looks to see that Jimmy has tipped over on the trike. Tom moves quickly to Jimmy, who has crawled out from under the trike. He can see that Jimmy's lip is bleeding. As he hurries to Jimmy, Tom reaches into his pocket and pulls out a pair of disposable gloves. He puts them on as he arrives at Jimmy's side. "Hey Jimmy," Tom says as he crouches down to hug Jimmy gently. "That looked like a pretty big bump! Let's go inside and take a good look at it."

Tom was prepared, and he knew immediately to use Standard Precautions. Many teachers find it useful to put a pair of gloves in their pocket for emergencies such as this. Another strategy is to tape pairs of gloves at various locations on the classroom wall and in logical locations in outdoor play areas. Each classroom should have a ready supply of disposable gloves as well as disposable toweling and appropriate sanitizing solutions. Even when gloves are used to manage injuries that involve blood, hand washing is still crucial. After use, the gloves should be removed and discarded in a sanitary manner, and hands should be washed.

Teaching Children Preventive Health Practices

Teachers help children learn disease prevention by guiding them to develop self-help skills and by teaching age-appropriate and developmentally appropriate prevention practices. Teaching disease prevention practices has a dual purpose: It helps to reduce the spread of disease immediately and educates children about ways to improve their wellness in the future. The *Teaching Wellness* feature offers examples for the classroom.

Infusing the daily curriculum with health messages is the best way to engage and educate children about wellness. This includes offering activities that have a health focus. It also means purposefully teaching age-appropriate disease

WHAT IF . . .

a child in your class has just contracted a second bout of illness involving vomiting and diarrhea? The child's parent has called you to ask why her child is sick again. She wants to know why you have not stopped the spread of this illness. How would you respond?

Standard Precautions
a set of guidelines defined by the CDC for use in hospitals and other health care centers to prevent the spread of disease through blood and body fluids

TEACHING WELLNESS   Germ Stoppers

LEARNING OUTCOME   Children will learn how germs spread and how to stop them.

INFANTS AND TODDLERS

- **Goal:** To introduce the child to the concept of germs.
- **Materials:** Paint, paintbrush, and paper; paint smocks.
- **Activity plan:** Make handprints on paper. Have the toddler paint his or her hand and pat it against a piece of paper. Keep making handprints until there is not enough paint to make a mark on the paper. Talk about how germs are so small that we cannot see them but that they stick to our hands like paint and spread to others. Have the child look at his or her hand to see if any paint can still be seen. Talk about how children can wash their hands to take away germs just as washing removes paint.

- **How to adjust the activity:** Have children carry a basket of small blocks ("germs") and "spread" them to places around the room. Tell them these are the germs. When all have been spread around the room, ask the children to "clean" the germs by gathering them back into their baskets.
- **Did you meet your goal?** Were children able to experience how germs can be spread like paint is spread? Listen to what children say about the activity to assess whether children are beginning to discover the concept of germs and their spread.

PRESCHOOLERS, KINDERGARTNERS, AND SCHOOL-AGE CHILDREN

- **Goal:** To learn how germs are spread and ways to stop them.
- **Materials:** Paint, paintbrush, paper towels.
- **Activity plan:** First, talk with children about how germs are spread by touching. Then have a small group of children stand in a line. Have one child paint his or her hand. Then ask that child to shake hands with the next child in line. Have this child shake hands with the third child in line, continuing until each child has shaken hands. Have the children compare their hands to see how many handshakes continued to pass along the paint. Review the concept of spreading germs by touching.

- **How to adjust the activity:** Have the children paint their hands, spreading the paint on generously. Then have the children wash their hands at the sink. Provide paper toweling for each child. Have the child bring their paper towels to the circle. Have each child show their paper towel. Do any show signs of paint? Talk about how much hand washing is needed to wash away germs appropriately and thoroughly.
- **Did you meet your goal?** Were children able to experience and understand how germs are spread through touching? Were children able to experience and understand how hand washing can reduce the spread of germs and that careful and thorough hand washing is needed to completely clean away germs?

prevention practices and ways that children can help reduce the spread of germs. Topics for teaching prevention messages include:

- How and when to wash my hands.
- How to blow my nose.
- How my body gets sick.
- How my body tells me I am sick.
- How to cover my cough.
- How to keep my sickness to myself.
- How to take care of myself when I am sick.

Topics such as these should be explored in different ways through literature and activities. They should be repeated at appropriate intervals to reinforce the ideas.

Partner with Families

Family members and guardians are also important participants in disease prevention and management. To be effective partners, they need teachers to provide them with information about program health practices and ways that parents help keep children and classrooms healthy. Several practices support this effort:

- To begin the partnership, provide preenrollment information about immunization requirements and advise parents to obtain health and dental screenings for their child.
- Communicate the program's commitment to health and wellness in parent handbooks, bulletin boards, etc.
- Ensure that families provide contact information and let them know how they will be contacted in case their child becomes ill at school. This information should be updated regularly.
- Orient families to classroom health practices such as having children wash their hands upon arrival and conducting daily health checks. Tell families how they will be notified of illnesses in the classroom.
- Provide information about when to keep children home from school due to illness.
- Inform families about how the program will care for children who become ill at school.

Managing Challenges

Illness in the classroom can be disruptive as teachers work to continue the daily routine and activities while caring for a sick child. Being prepared for such situations is as important as a management strategy, but also to ensure that germs and disease are not spread unnecessarily. Obtaining supportive supplies in advance and having resources readily available are important ways to prepare to care for sick children appropriately. Programs should have policies that address situations such as epidemics or pandemics as discussed in this chapter's *Policy Point*.

Establish an Isolation Area

Sick children need to be removed from the general class group activities to prevent the spread of germs and to allow them to rest appropriately until a family member or an emergency contact person can come to get them. An isolation area should be identified in the program facility or in a quiet area of the classroom. A pad and blanket should be readily available to provide a comfortable place to rest. These items should be clean and ready for use, and they should be cleaned and sanitized after use. Ill children should be supervised at all times while they are resting. In some settings, this may mean that the isolation area is a corner of the room where the teacher can supervise the ill child as well as other children in the space. When children leave the class, they should be "signed out" on a sign-in/sign-out sheet to document who picked them up and when.

Record Illness Information

It is helpful to have a form available for immediate use that documents the child's illness and release from school. The teacher should follow the program or school protocol for recording the child's illness. Helpful information to record includes:

- Child's name.
- Date and time of day.
- Symptoms observed.

POLICY POINT

Epidemic? Pandemic? Who Sets Policy in Disease Emergencies?

Teachers know to call 911 when there's an emergency in the early childhood setting. But where do teachers get information when disease threat is widespread? Epidemics (situations where the incidence of disease is higher than expected) and pandemics (situations where infectious disease becomes geographically widespread) have the potential to impact programming in children's settings and schools. Emerging diseases can spread across the world with great speed. When this happens, health authorities must work quickly to identify the infectious agent, discover medical treatment to reduce its effect, and communicate methods to prevent spread of disease.

In recent years, concern about avian flu prompted health authorities to plan management strategies for a potential pandemic health crisis. The H1N1 flu (swine flu) outbreak of 2009 tested the strength of such plans. Early childhood programs have taken steps to model their own policies for disease prevention and communication after these efforts. However, when health crises are emerging, teachers and parents need to know where to turn for current information. Several important resources are available:

- The World Health Organization (WHO) monitors the worldwide incidence and spread of disease. The WHO provides updates as emergencies develop and offers guidance for individuals and communities.
- The Centers for Disease Control and Prevention is the national agency for up-to-date information on pandemic

disease. The CDC provides information about how to plan for pandemic health emergencies and guidance about what schools and child care programs need to do when pandemic disease is occurring.

- Local health authorities provide local updates and advice for an emergency response to health crises. During pandemic events, public health agencies make recommendations on prevention strategies and ultimately direct decisions related to program and school closures. Local health authorities also have personnel available to answer questions and provide individualized advice.

Children's programs also need to do their part by establishing program and school-level policies for health emergencies. Policies should include:

- How health crisis information will be communicated to families.
- How program or school-level decisions related to closures will be made.
- How families will be notified in the event of a school closure.
- How decisions related to reopening the program will be made.

Teachers who are prepared become part of the network of disease prevention efforts that is needed to protect the health of young children and their communities.

- Who provided care for the child.
- Who was contacted to pick up the child.
- Who picked up the child from care or school and when.

Be Prepared to Send Sick Children Home

Pearson Education

CLASSROOM CONNECTION

Watch this video to learn more about policies designed to control infections in early childhood settings. How might these policies help control the spread of disease?

A child's illness can cause disruption in the family work schedule. Some families may not have a backup plan to care for an ill child at home or may be stressed about losing their job if they take time off to care for their child. These are realistic concerns that families need to manage. It is helpful to orient families to the program policies related to sick children so that they are alerted in advance to the need to pick up and care for their child if illness occurs.

Teachers should be understanding about the challenges families face, but be firm when children are too ill to attend. If families bring a child back to school too soon following an illness, the daily health check assists teachers in recognizing whether the child is still too ill to attend school. Some programs have sufficient staff to receive children who are no longer contagious but still recovering from illness. Sometimes families request that their child rest in the classroom rather than go outside for recess or playtime. These decisions are made at the program level depending on the capacity to provide individualized supervision.

FIGURE 10-4   Sample Health Alert for Parents

HEALTH ALERT for Parents: Pinkeye

Please observe your child for pinkeye (conjunctivitis).

Pinkeye has been identified in our classrooms. Pinkeye can be alarming because it may make the eyes extremely red and can spread rapidly. Pinkeye (conjunctivitis) can be caused by infections (such as bacteria and viruses), allergies, or substances that irritate the eyes. It is a fairly common condition and usually causes no long-term eye or vision damage. **But if your child shows symptoms of pinkeye, it's important to contact your doctor.**

Avoid the spread of pinkeye at home. Children get pinkeye by touching an infected person or something an infected person has touched, such as a used tissue. If pinkeye is diagnosed in one eye, it can also spread it to the other eye by touching. Teach and help your child to wash his or her hands often with warm water and soap.

If you think your child has pinkeye, it's important to contact your doctor to try to determine what's causing it and to learn how to treat it.

Have Illness Notifications Available

When children are diagnosed with an infectious condition, teachers need to communicate with other families to alert them to the illness. These notices also guide families in how to monitor their own child for symptoms of the disease. Having basic health alert flyers on hand is an important time-saver for teachers who want to distribute correct information as soon as possible. Figure 10-4 provides a sample health alert for pinkeye.

RECOGNIZING AND MANAGING INFECTIOUS DISEASE

Preventing and controlling infections in early childhood settings requires teachers to have a basic understanding of communicable diseases that are common among young children. It is also helpful for teachers to understand the basics of vaccine-preventable diseases even though they are uncommon. Although teachers are not responsible for diagnosing illnesses, those who are able to identify the symptoms of disease are better prepared to understand and control its spread. Rarely, teachers will care for a child who has a bloodborne disease. In this section, we briefly describe these diseases and offer insight into whether children should be excluded from the children's setting.

Vaccine-Preventable Diseases

Vaccine-preventable diseases are prevented by immunization. These diseases have decreased in prevalence during the past several decades because of efforts to increase the number of children who are immunized. For this reason, teachers may never see a child with one of the vaccine-preventable diseases. However, many vaccine-preventable diseases are highly contagious, and some can cause serious disability or death.

CHECK YOUR UNDERSTANDING 10.2

Click here to check your understanding of how to prevent and control the spread of infectious diseases.

Outbreaks of these diseases that do occur may result in clusters of individuals being struck with the illness. More expansive outbreaks are labeled **epidemics**. An epidemic is declared when the number of people with the infection is substantially higher than what would normally be expected in that population. Next, we provide brief summaries of these diseases to help teachers learn to recognize them in the rare event they occur in the children's setting.

Pertussis (Whooping Cough)

epidemics
situations in which the incidence of disease is substantially higher than what is expected in that population

Pertussis, also known as *whooping cough*, is a highly contagious and dangerous bacterial disease, especially for infants. Symptoms include fits of uncontrolled coughing that create the characteristic "whooping" sound. During these coughing spasms, the child may turn blue and have severe respiratory distress.

pertussis
a bacterial respiratory infection that is highly contagious and can be fatal to infants and young children; also called *whooping cough*

The symptoms of pertussis often last several weeks or even months. Children diagnosed with pertussis should be excluded from school, and the community health authority should be notified. Vaccination offers protection against the disease but requires periodic booster shots. Teachers must remain current on vaccinations. Any teacher diagnosed with pertussis should be excluded from the classroom until a course of antibiotics has been completed. Here is an example scenario:

Amy is an observant teacher. She pays close attention to the health and well-being of the children in her class. On this day while working in the teacher's room, she surprises herself as she listens to her coworker cough. She remarks, "Michael, if I didn't know better, I would say that you are suffering from whooping cough!" This remark is enough to send Michael to get a checkup at the Immediate Care Clinic. He calls in later to report that he has been diagnosed with whooping cough.

haemophilus influenzae type b (Hib)
a bacterial infection that can cause severe respiratory problems or meningitis

meningitis
severe infection of the membranes covering the brain

Strong evidence demonstrates that protection provided by the pertussis vaccination wanes over time. In fact, older children or adults who have not received recent boosters are the source of most infections in children.

chicken pox
viral infection that causes fever and rash

Haemophilus influenzae Type b *Haemophilus influenzae* **type b (Hib)** causes **meningitis**, a severe infection of the membranes covering the brain. It occurs most commonly among infants but infected children of any age can pass the infection to others. It can also cause other serious life-threatening respiratory infections.

- If a case of Hib infection is reported within an early childhood program, the families of each child should be notified as well as the local health authorities.
- Children who have not been immunized due to special exceptions should be excluded from school until health authorities determine that there is no longer a risk for infection (American Academy of Pediatrics, American Public Health Association, National Resource Center for Health and Safety in Child Care and Early Education, 2011).

Chicken Pox

Chicken pox is a common childhood condition, especially in unvaccinated children. The chicken pox rash usually progresses from the head to the toes. The majority of the pox, or lesions, appear on the trunk (Centers for Disease

Child with chicken pox.

Dagmara Ponikiewska/Thinkstock/Getty Images

Control and Prevention, 2012). The rash is characterized by itchy red bumps that rapidly progress to fluid-filled lesions. Important points about chicken pox include:

- Children with chicken pox should be excluded from school until all lesions have dried and crusted over and there is no fever.
- Rarely, chicken pox can cause severe complications that require intense medical treatment.
- Teachers should inform parents that *aspirin not be used to treat infants and children for chicken pox influenza (or any other suspected viral illness)*. Aspirin use is associated with a serious complication called **Reye's syndrome**. Reye's syndrome can cause inflammation of the brain and liver and is potentially fatal.

Measles

Measles is an acute, highly contagious infectious disease. It is characterized by cough, runny nose, pinkeye, and rash. The measles rash begins on the face and head and spreads to the body. If a case of measles is confirmed, the child should be excluded from the classroom until a medical provider approves the child's return to the classroom.

Tetanus

The **tetanus** bacteria form spores that are deposited in soil where they can survive for months or even years. The spores are also found in the intestines and feces of many animals, including horses, sheep, cattle, dogs, cats, rats, guinea pigs, and chickens (Centers for Disease Control and Prevention, 2012). The bacteria usually enter the body through a puncture wound caused, for example, by stepping on a contaminated nail.

- Children should be guided to wash their hands after playing in the dirt and after visiting ranches, farms, and fairs where they may come into contact with infected animal feces.
- In case of injuries that cause puncture wounds or cuts, documentation of an updated tetanus vaccine should be confirmed.
- Teachers should periodically receive a tetanus booster to maintain their own immunity.

Influenza (The Flu)

Influenza, also called "the flu," is a highly contagious respiratory disease caused by a virus. Symptoms include fever, sore throat, muscle aches, cough, headache, and fatigue. Although school-aged children (ages 5 to 18) do not have an increased risk of complications of influenza, they have the highest attack rates and serve as a major source of transmission of influenza (Centers for Disease Control and Prevention, 2012).

- Children should be excluded until the symptoms of the flu resolve.
- Hand washing and sanitization practices in the classroom should be monitored.
- All persons older than 6 months of age should be vaccinated. If there is a vaccine shortage, focus will be on children 6 months to 4 years old and household contacts/caregivers of children younger than 5 years old.
- Teachers also should protect themselves from the disease by obtaining a yearly flu vaccination.

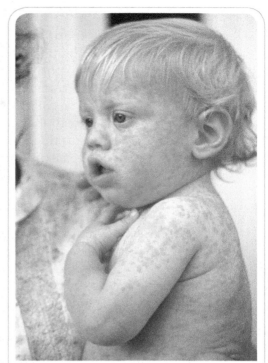

Child with measles.

Lowell Georgia/Science Source

Reye's syndrome
severe inflammation of the brain and liver caused by giving aspirin to children who have certain viral infections

measles
an acute, highly contagious infectious disease that causes fever, rash, and pinkeye

tetanus
a bacterial infection acquired when wounds or lacerations are contaminated with soil that contains the infectious germ

influenza
a highly infectious virus that causes fever, muscle aches, sore throat, cough, and headache

Hepatitis A

Hepatitis A is an acute infection of the liver. Symptoms include fever, diarrhea, abdominal pain, or yellow discoloration of the skin (jaundice). Some children may be exposed and infected with this disease and do not develop symptoms but can still transmit the infection (Centers for Disease Control and Prevention, 2012). These children are called *carriers* because they can expose others to the disease even though they do not display the symptoms. The use of standard policies for diapering and toileting when caring for children and following hand washing procedures helps to interrupt the spread of this hidden disease.

Rotavirus

Rotavirus is a virus that causes infectious diarrhea. Symptoms include fever, vomiting, and watery diarrhea. It is spread through fecal–oral transmission, making it especially contagious among children under the age of 2 and in settings in which children wear diapers. Children infected with rotavirus shed viral particles in the stool beginning 2 days before and during and up to 10 days after the onset of symptoms of the disease (Centers for Disease Control and Prevention, 2012).

Streptococcus Pneumoniae

Streptococcus pneumoniae is a bacterium that commonly causes respiratory infections; ear infections; pneumonia; infection of the bloodstream; and, less commonly, meningitis in young children. The symptoms depend on the type of infection. It is transmitted by direct or indirect contact with respiratory secretions. The prevalence of disease has decreased since widespread vaccination was instituted in children in 2000.

Other Common Communicable and Infectious Diseases of Childhood

Many diseases of childhood are not vaccine-preventable. These infections are common in settings where children have frequent and prolonged contact with one another, such as child care, preschool, and classroom settings. Each of the common infectious diseases has its own set of characteristics and implications for management in the children's setting. Exclusion recommendations vary for each disease, as described in Table 10-2.

Common Colds

Common colds are upper respiratory infections that are caused by more than 100 viruses. Viruses are spread by direct or indirect contact through respiratory secretions. People with colds often carry the virus on their hands and can infect others in this way for up to two hours. Children less than 6 years of age acquire six to eight colds per year. Colds can last up to 14 days. The most contagious period is in the first two to four days. Colds are not caused by cold weather (Pappas, 2013).

Teachers often experience frequent respiratory illnesses during the first few years they teach young children.

- The best way to interrupt the cycle of infection in the classroom is to wash hands frequently and to ensure that toys and surfaces are sanitized.
- Teachers should also wash their hands immediately when they return home to help reduce the spread of the cold virus.

TABLE 10-2 Exclusion Guidelines

Condition	Length of Time Child Should Be Excluded
Fever (>101 orally or >100 axillary)	When fever has ended or when health care provider recommends
Common colds	No exclusion required
Diarrhea not contained by child using toilet	When diarrhea resolves or when health care provider recommends
Cough without a fever and not associated with a communicable disease	No exclusion required
Vomiting illness	24 hours after last bout of vomiting; when health care provider recommends
Persistent or intermittent abdominal pain	When pain resolves; when health care provider recommends
Mouth sores with drooling	When health care provider recommends
Rash with fever or behavior change	When health care provider recommends
Purulent (draining) conjunctivitis (pinkeye)	After treatment is initiated
Head lice	No exclusion required
Scabies	After treatment is completed
Tuberculosis	When health care provider recommends
Impetigo	24 hours after treatment is initiated
Streptococcal infection (strep throat)	24 hours after treatment is initiated
Chicken pox	When all sores are dried and crusted
Pertussis (whooping cough)	5 days after treatment has been completed; when health care provider recommends
Mumps	5 days after onset of salivary gland swelling; when health care provider recommends
Hepatitis A	1 week after onset of jaundice and/or illness; when health care provider recommends
Measles	4 days after onset of rash; when health care provider recommends

Sources: American Academy of Pediatrics, 2012 and American Academy of Pediatrics, American Public Health Association, National Resource Center for Health and Safety in Child Care and Early Education, 2011.

Conjunctivitis (Pinkeye)

Conjunctivitis, also called *pinkeye*, is a condition in which the lining of the eye becomes inflamed. Causes include bacterial and viral infections, allergies, chemicals, or trauma. Bacterial and viral infections usually cause white or yellow discharge from the eye, which may cause the eyelids to stick together in the morning. When a child has symptoms of pinkeye, teachers should:

- Contact the child's parents and refer the child to a health care provider.
- Monitor other children and teachers for signs of pinkeye.
- Disinfect any contaminated articles.
- Notify parents to watch for signs of pinkeye.
- Ensure that proper hand washing procedures are being followed.
- Exclude children with symptoms until they are seen by a health care provider and are approved for readmission.

Croup

Croup is a common upper respiratory infection that causes fever; cough; and, in some cases, difficulty breathing. It can also

conjunctivitis
condition in which the lining of the eye becomes inflamed due to bacterial or viral infections, allergies, chemicals, or trauma; also called *pinkeye*

croup
a viral upper respiratory infection causing fever, runny nose, and barky cough

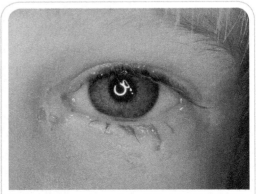

Pinkeye is a common infection among children.

Dorling Kindersley, Ltd.

stridor
noisy breathing

cause noisy breathing, called **stridor**. Many different types of viruses cause croup. Incubation periods vary according to the virus but will be in the typical range of one to three weeks. Its mode of transmission is droplet.

The cough associated with croup is very distinctive and described as *barky* or similar to the sound of a seal. Stridor and difficulty breathing most often occur during the night, but teachers should watch for these symptoms and notify families if they occur. Children should be excluded based only on the presence of fever or other reasons that prevent the child from participating comfortably, such as breathing difficulty.

Group A Strep Infections

group A strep infection
infection with bacteria that causes three common infections in childhood: strep throat, scarlet fever, and impetigo

A **group A strep infection** is caused by bacteria that cause three common infections in childhood: strep throat, scarlet fever, and impetigo. Transmission occurs by contact with infected respiratory secretions. The virus is most contagious when children are acutely ill. Symptoms generally include fever, sore throat, and possibly a rash. Children should be excluded from school until they have been treated with antibiotics for 24 hours and no longer have a fever (American Academy of Pediatrics, 2012). It is especially important to recognize strep throat because if left untreated, other complications can occur, such as **acute rheumatic fever**, a serious complication that affects the heart.

acute rheumatic fever
a serious complication of strep infection that affects the heart

scarlet fever
a type of strep infection characterized by fever, sore throat, and a scarlet rash that has a texture like sandpaper

Scarlet fever is a condition characterized by fever, sore throat, and a scarlet rash that has texture like sandpaper. Scarlet fever is often treated with antibiotics. **Impetigo** is a skin rash composed of blisters with honey-yellow scabs. Impetigo spreads in children's settings through direct contact with infected individuals or from toys. Children with impetigo should be excluded from the classroom or early childhood setting until 24 hours after treatment has started. Exposed lesions should be covered (American Academy of Pediatrics, 2012).

impetigo
a type of strep infection that causes a skin rash marked by pustular lesions

Ear Infections

ear infections
infections of the eardrum

Ear infections are common infectious diseases of childhood. Bacteria or viruses that infect the eardrum cause ear infections. Ear infections are not contagious. However, ear infections are often accompanied by upper respiratory infections, which are contagious. Therefore, children with ear infections do not need to be excluded from school unless they are too ill to participate in normal activities. If other symptoms such as fever are present, the child may have another illness that is contagious. The child should be separated from the group, and parents should be notified.

Fifth Disease

fifth disease
viral illness characterized by fever, headaches, and muscle aches followed by the skin rash

Fifth disease is so called because it is considered the "fifth" of the six common infectious childhood diseases causing a skin rash. The others include measles (first), scarlet fever (second), rubella (third), fourth disease (not recognized today), and roseola (sixth). Symptoms of fifth disease include fever, head and muscle aches, and the characteristic skin rash. Fifth disease is recognized by its intensely red rash, which appears on the cheeks. This is sometimes called "slapped-cheek" rash. As the illness progresses, the rash becomes more diffuse and has a lacy pattern that appears on the trunk. By the time the rash appears, the child is no longer contagious and should not be excluded from the early childhood setting (American Academy of Pediatrics, 2012).

Pinworms

Pinworm infection is a common intestinal parasitic infection in young children. Usually if a child is infected with **pinworms**, others in the family are infected as well. Transmission occurs by ingesting microscopic eggs by the fecal–oral route or by contact with contaminated objects such as toys, bedding, clothing, or toilet seats. Symptoms include itching around the anus, vulva, or genital area, although some children have no symptoms (American Academy of Pediatrics, 2012). Pinworm infections can be difficult to control in early childhood settings. Hand washing is the most effective way to prevent its spread.

Respiratory Syncytial Virus

Respiratory syncytial virus (RSV) is a viral upper respiratory infection that causes fever, runny nose, cough, and possibly wheezing in some children. Transmission is through contact with contaminated secretions. Contaminated droplets can live on surfaces for several hours. The incubation period is two to eight days. Most children have an initial RSV infection during their first year of life. It is common for children to become reinfected later (American Academy of Pediatrics, 2012). RSV in older children and adults looks more like a common cold. Most healthy children with RSV have an uncomplicated upper respiratory infection. Younger infants and premature infants are at higher risk for developing breathing difficulties and requiring hospitalizations for complications.

RSV occurs in epidemics during the winter and spring. Careful cleaning of surfaces and frequent hand washing are the best ways to prevent infection. Exclusion and notification of parents should occur in children with a fever or with breathing difficulties.

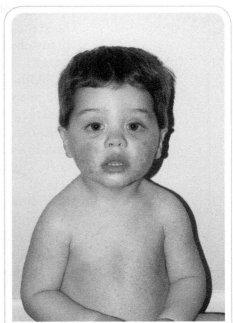

Fifth's disease has a characteristic "slapped-cheek" rash.

John Kaprielian/Science Source

pinworms
a common intestinal parasitic infection in young children

respiratory syncytial virus (RSV)
a common upper respiratory infection that occurs in children and adults most commonly during the winter and spring months

Tuberculosis

Tuberculosis (TB) is a potentially harmful lung infection. It is spread through respiratory and airborne transmission when tiny droplets are propelled through the air from coughing or sneezing. Symptoms include fatigue, fever, and chills. Children are most often exposed to TB from infectious adults. For this reason, many children's programs and schools require that teachers be screened for TB as a requirement of employment. It is a reportable disease, and treatment is often managed by local health authorities.

tuberculosis (TB)
an infection that is transmitted by air droplets and can affect many different parts of the body, most commonly causing lung infections

Infections and Acute Illnesses Involving the Skin

Some infections that are highly contagious in children's settings and schools affect primarily the skin. Head lice, scabies, and ringworm are examples of skin-related infectious diseases. Skin infections are often distinguished by the type and color of the rash they cause.

Head Lice

Head lice is an infestation of the hair and scalp that occasionally causes itching. It is transmitted by close person-to-person contact. It is rare for lice to be transmitted by sharing personal belongings such as combs, hairbrushes, and hats (Centers for Disease Control and Prevention, 2013).

head lice
an infestation of the hair and scalp that is transmitted most commonly by direct contact with the hair of infested people

Adult lice and nits (egg casings) are usually most visible behind the ears and near the nape of the neck. Itching is the most common symptom of head lice, but many children have no symptoms at all. Head lice should not be considered a health hazard and are not responsible for the spread of other diseases.

Although head lice do not represent a serious health problem, this infection often causes disruption in the classroom. When an incidence of head lice is discovered, teachers are faced with trying to contain the spread. Parents may respond with disgust when they learn of the presence of lice. To attain better control of this infection, some health authorities have recommended a *no-nit* policy for early childhood programs. This approach requires that children must stay out of school if they have any lice, eggs, or nits in their hair. Nits are the egg casings that may contain a developing louse, or they may be empty and not infectious. They can remain visible for up to six months on the hair shaft. Consequently, many children have been incorrectly diagnosed with an ongoing head lice infestation and excluded from the classroom. They also may have received unnecessary and potentially toxic repeat treatments of *delousing* pesticides. No-nit policies are ineffective in controlling head lice infestations and are not recommended (American Academy of Pediatrics, 2012). It is also important to remember that over-the-counter and prescription treatments for head lice can be quite toxic and are actually considered pesticides.

Rather than excluding children for head lice, early childhood programs and schools are gaining a new perspective on this annoyance. These thoughts are useful when establishing a policy related to head lice (Centers for Disease Control and Prevention, 2013a):

- Head lice are a health annoyance but do not spread disease.
- Head lice are not associated with poor hygiene and poverty. They are opportunistic, moving from head to head without regard to socioeconomic status.
- If head lice are discovered, children do not need to be sent home immediately; a few hours at school will not make a significant difference.
- Families of infected children should be notified. Treatment should be implemented only after infestation has been confirmed. All other families should be notified so that they can monitor their children for evidence of lice.
- Families can treat head lice with over-the-counter medications, and if problems persist, they can seek care with their health care provider.
- Children can return to school when treatment has been completed.
- Nits that are more than a ¼ inch from the scalp are usually not viable and are unlikely to hatch.

scabies
a skin infection caused by adult female mites that burrow into the skin, causing an intensely itchy, red, bumpy rash that is seen in a snake-like pattern

Scabies

Scabies is a skin infection caused by adult female mites that burrow into the skin, causing an intensely itchy, red, and bumpy rash. The rash typically occurs between the fingers and on wrists and elbows, waistline, thighs, genitalia, and buttocks (American Academy of Pediatrics, 2012). Scabies is transmitted through prolonged personal contact such as household

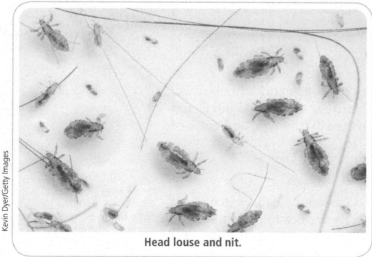

Head louse and nit.

Kevin Dyer/Getty Images

contacts. Children should be excluded until they have received treatment. Any bedding and clothing the child has used should be washed, including dramatic play clothing. Family members often need treatment as well.

Ringworm

Ringworm is a skin infection caused by a common fungus. It appears as a red and scaly skin rash that has a raised circular shape with healthy skin in the middle. No worm is involved in this condition. It is the shape of the rash that gives the infection its name. Ringworm is transmitted by direct contact with infected humans, animals, or objects. It can

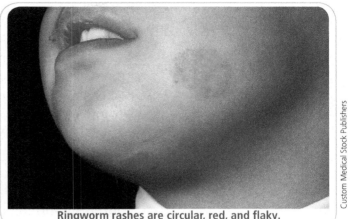

Ringworm rashes are circular, red, and flaky.

occur on the scalp, causing hair loss. Treatment usually involves application of an antifungal cream for several weeks. Children infected with ringworm do not need to stay home from school. Washing hands and maintaining cleanliness in the environment are the most effective ways to prevent spread of the infection.

ringworm
an infection of the skin caused by a fungus

Coxsackie Virus (Hand, Foot, and Mouth Disease)

The **coxsackie virus**, also called *hand, foot, and mouth disease,* causes blisters on the hands, feet, and mouth. It is spread through contact with hands and surfaces that are contaminated with infected droplets from the mouth and nose. Symptoms include fever, loss of appetite, and sore throat, followed by sores in the mouth and gums. A nonitchy rash appears first on the hands and soles of the feet.

The virus spreads easily. Children should stay home if there is a fever of if the symptoms are painful and they are not able to participate fully with the class. Washing hands and sanitizing surfaces are the most important management strategies.

coxsackie virus
a common childhood respiratory virus causing fever, mouth sores, and skin rash

Bite Wounds

Bite wounds are included here because of their potential to cause infection. Bite wounds are relatively common in children's settings. Bites that do not break the skin should be managed with comfort care and guidance to address the cause of the bite. Bites that break the skin are more serious. Around 10% to 15% of human bites become infected (American Academy of Pediatrics, 2012). Teachers should carefully wash the bite wound, using Standard Precautions, and monitor the child's behavior. Parents should be contacted and encouraged to seek medical evaluation. Bite wounds should be monitored for signs of infection, including increasing tenderness, pain, redness, and swelling. In rare cases, bite wounds can also transmit infections such as hepatitis B.

WHAT IF . . .
a child in your toddler group bit another child, creating a bloody wound on the skin? How would you respond to the child who did the biting? What strategies would you use to reduce the risk of this child biting in the future?

staph infection
a potentially dangerous type of bacteria that is normally found in the skin but can cause infections under certain circumstances

Staph Infections

Staph refers to a type of bacteria that can cause infections and disease. Thirty different types of *Staphylococci* (staph) can infect humans. Many of these bacteria are naturally found in the mouth and nose and most often do not cause infection. However, sometimes breaks in the skin allow the bacteria to enter the body and cause a **staph infection. Methicillin-resistant *Staphylococcus aureus* (MRSA)** is a

methicillin-resistant *Staphylococcus aureus* **(MRSA)**
a potentially dangerous type of bacterial skin infection that is resistant to many types of antibiotics

specific type of bacterial skin infection that is resistant to many types of antibiotics. It is spread mostly by having direct contact with an open wound and less commonly by touching items that have touched an infected wound (American Academy of Pediatrics, 2012).

MRSA skin infections are characterized by red, swollen, and painful pimples or boils that usually drain pus. Frequent skin-to-skin contact and potential for children to touch contaminated surfaces makes early childhood classrooms likely settings for the spread of infections such as MRSA.

- Teachers should be watchful for signs of infection on children's hands and arms.
- Any skin cuts and scrapes should be kept clean and dry. Infected wounds should be covered with clean, dry bandages.
- Children should not share clothing or other personal items if an infection is suspected.

Special attention to hand washing practices is important, and disposable towels should be used. Children who have an identified MRSA infection should not be excluded unless it is not possible to cover the wound.

Bloodborne Infections in the Early Childhood Setting

Bloodborne infections such as hepatitis B or C and HIV are not common in early childhood. The risk of transmission even with contact with blood is low. However, because of the seriousness of these diseases, teachers must have a general understanding of precautions for preventing transmission. Consider this scenario:

> *During the middle of the kindergarten year, a new child joins the class. Natasha has been teaching for many years, but this is the first time a child has been accompanied by the school nurse and two other people. They stay through the first full day and tend to drop in to observe the child now and then. The child also has a special health emergency protocol that requires Natasha to contact the school nurse and parents anytime a child in the class is diagnosed with a communicable illness. Natasha wonders if the child has some kind of serious disease. She feels uncomfortable but doesn't know why.*

hepatitis B
a virus that causes chronic inflammation of the liver and can lead to cancer of the liver

Some diseases tend to cause a great deal of alarm. To address such concerns, teachers need to gather information and learn more about the risks of infection. Using Standard Precautions when managing injuries when blood is present is an important way to increase safety and prevent the spread of bloodborne diseases. In this section, we discuss some of the bloodborne diseases that, although uncommon, may occur among young children in child care and school settings.

Hepatitis B

Hepatitis B is a virus that causes chronic inflammation of the liver and can lead to cancer of the liver. Some children who are infected with hepatitis B experience few symptoms but are carriers of the disease. This is more common in children who were not born in the United States.

The virus is spread through contact with blood and body fluids. It can be transmitted from an infected mother to her baby through labor and delivery. Children infected with hepatitis B should not be excluded from the early childhood setting unless they demonstrate high-risk behaviors. Behaviors and situations that may cause spread of the virus include aggressive behaviors (frequent biting or scratching), generalized weeping skin lesions, or bleeding problems (American Academy of Pediatrics, American Public Health Association, National Resource Center for Health and Safety in Child Care and Early Education, 2011).

Parents of children who are infected with hepatitis B are not required to share information about their child's status. If a child is a known carrier or that fact is unknown and the child does exhibit high-risk behaviors, the program director together with a health care provider or local public health authority can determine the appropriateness of having the child participate in the early childhood setting.

Hepatitis C

Hepatitis C infection in children is very rare. It is a virus that causes chronic inflammation of the liver and it is transmitted through blood and body fluids. Exclusion of children from early childhood programs is not recommended (American Academy of Pediatrics, 2012). The risk of transmission by exposure through a skin wound is greater than that of hepatitis B but less than that of HIV (American Academy of Pediatrics, American Public Health Association, National Resource Center for Health and Safety in Child Care and Early Education, 2011).

hepatitis C
a virus that causes chronic inflammation of the liver that is transmitted through blood and body fluids

Human Immunodeficiency Virus

Human immunodeficiency virus (HIV) is a virus that is transmitted through blood and body fluids. Modes of transmission include sexual contact, use of contaminated needles, and mother-to-child transmission during pregnancy or the birth process (American Academy of Pediatrics, 2012). More than 90% of children with HIV in the United States acquired HIV through their mother. Child sexual abuse can be another way children are infected with HIV.

human immunodeficiency virus (HIV)
a virus that is transmitted through blood and body fluids; most common form of transmission in children is from mother to fetus or baby

Children infected with HIV pose a challenge in the early childhood setting because management and treatment of their disease is often complex. The infected child is susceptible to infection, and steps should be taken to ensure the health and safety of all children so that transmission is prevented. The *National Health and Safety Performance Standards* recommend that the admission of children with HIV be considered on a case-by-case basis depending on the health, behavior, development, and immune status of the child (American Academy of Pediatrics, American Public Health Association, National Resource Center for Health and Safety in Child Care and Early Education, 2011). The American Academy of Pediatrics outlines the following specific recommendations for children with HIV in the school setting:

- School-age children should be allowed to participate without restrictions except in rare cases in which the child has an increased likelihood of exposing others. In these situations, children should be evaluated individually.

- The only people who need to know that the child has HIV are the parents, other guardians, and the physician. The number of people who are aware of the child's condition should be kept to a minimum. The parents have the right to decide whether to inform the school.

- All early childhood programs should adopt routine policies for handling blood and blood-contaminated fluids.

**CHECK YOUR
UNDERSTANDING 10.3**
Click here to check your
understanding of common
infectious diseases and
when children should be
excluded from school or
centers because of them.

- Children with HIV are at increased risk for serious infections or complications from infectious diseases. The child's family should be notified immediately if the child is exposed to an infectious illness.
- More specific guidelines exist for children with HIV who participate in athletics.

Although adults with HIV may work with children, Standard Precautions should be taken. The affected adult should also be cautious about possible exposures to infectious diseases.

INFECTIOUS DISEASES IN IMMIGRANT AND INTERNATIONALLY ADOPTED CHILDREN

Each year, families adopt more than 12,000 children from all over the world (Centers for Disease Control and Prevention, 2014c). China is the leading country from which children are adopted, accounting for 30% of international adoptions (Centers for Disease Control and Prevention, 2014c). Other common countries include Ethiopia, South Korea, Ukraine, India, Philippines, Colombia, Taiwan, Uganda, Haiti, and Nigeria (Centers for Disease Control and Prevention, 2014c). In addition, a much smaller group of children came to the United States as **refugees**, immigrants who cannot return to their country due to persecution. Little may be known about the health histories of these children. However, these children may have unique risk factors for infectious disease.

refugees
non-citizen immigrants who cannot return to their country due to persecution

Unknown Health History

Certain infectious diseases and illnesses should be ruled out in children with unknown health histories. Although children born in the United States may also have unknown health histories, the health history of children from international backgrounds is more often incomplete and sometimes unknown. Therefore, these children should have regular medical care during which common diseases can be evaluated and addressed.

Having an unknown health history can complicate entry into early childhood programs. Children who come to the United States through international adoption must have a medical examination in their country of origin before coming to the United States. A physician designated by the U.S. State Department must perform the examination, which screens only for selected infectious diseases and serious physical or mental defects that would prevent the issuing of a permanent visa (American Academy of Pediatrics, 2012). Also, children who are adopted internationally are not required to have documentation showing basic immunizations. Adoptive parents must pledge to obtain basic immunizations for their new children.

Records of immunization and history of family disease may not be available. This lack of information can pose a problem for enrollment in an early childhood setting or school. Parents who are adopting children and those who are supporting refugee families need the support and guidance of a medical provider. The health professional will ensure that the child receives a full medical evaluation and plan for obtaining the immunizations needed for entry into the children's program.

Common Diseases Among Immigrant and Internationally Adopted Children

Many internationally adopted children are diagnosed with infectious diseases. This is due to the wide array of infectious agents and diseases to which children from international backgrounds may have been exposed. Also, other countries do not use the same vaccinations that are required in the United States. Across the world, nutrition, living conditions, prevalence of various diseases, and access to health care vary greatly.

A list of infectious diseases that are seen among children from international backgrounds is shown in Figure 10-5. Descriptions of some of these illnesses are given next to assist teachers in recognizing infections among children from international communities.

Viral Hepatitis

Screening for hepatitis B infection is recommended for internally adopted children. Vaccination is highly recommended unless the child's health care provider has deemed it medically unnecessary. Also, many internationally born children have acquired hepatitis A earlier in life; however, it is recommended that these children also obtain the vaccine unless testing determines that it is not needed.

Intestinal Infections

The prevalence of intestinal infections in recently adopted children has been found to be as high as 74% (Centers for Disease Control and Prevention, 2014c). Screening is recommended after their arrival to the United States. When teachers notice any unusual symptoms related to abdominal pain, abnormal appetite, or abnormal stools, parents should be notified and encouraged to have the child evaluated. For the vast majority of these infections, treatment is effective and simple.

Tuberculosis

The risk of tuberculosis is 4 to 6 times greater in adopted children (Centers for Disease Control and Prevention, 2014b). All children who were not born in the United States should be screened for tuberculosis.

HIV Infections

The risk of HIV among internationally born children depends on the country of origin and individual risk factors. It is recommended that all immigrant children have an HIV test, even if they had one in their country of origin.

Skin Infections

It is not uncommon for children born outside the United States to arrive with various skin infections such as impetigo, scabies, or fungal infections. Teachers should be observant for signs of infection, and children should be referred for medical treatment.

FIGURE 10-5 Common Diseases Among Internationally Adopted Children

Bacterial diseases:
- Salmonella
- Syphilis
- Tuberculosis

Viral diseases:
- Typhoid fever
- Cytomegalovirus
- Hepatitis A, B, and C
- HIV

Other diseases:
- Lice
- Scabies
- Intestinal worms (parasites)
- Giardia
- Malaria
- Impetigo

Source: Centers for Disease Control and Prevention, 2010.

PROGRESSIVE PROGRAMS & PRACTICES

Overcoming Infectious Outbreaks

By Eileen Marma, Public Health Nurse, Benton County Health Department, Corvallis, OR

The primary responsibility of a public health nurse in the communicable disease program is to prevent the spread of infectious diseases and to protect people from exposure. The nurses respond to calls from early childhood teachers who have questions about controlling illness in the early childhood setting. The nurses provide information about what to tell parents and whether a child needs to be excluded from the classroom during the contagious period.

What Challenge Did You Face?

Barbara, a director at an early childhood center that served 72 children, called to report that the number of children who were ill had climbed from 1 to 12 within three days. She wanted to get this situation under control quickly. She described the symptoms of stomach distress with abrupt onset, which sounded like Norovirus. Norovirus is a highly contagious virus that occurs in settings that bring people together, such as classrooms. It causes gastroenteritis, with symptoms of vomiting and diarrhea, cramps, fatigue, and headaches. It often strikes during the fall and winter months. An outbreak involving 30% to 50% of the classroom is not unusual. However, it is often overwhelming for the teacher to deal with children getting sick in the classroom if the teaching assistants are also out sick.

An affected person may be ill for 24 hours but remains contagious for at least 72 hours after the last symptom of vomiting or diarrhea. Thus, if the ill child or adult returns to the classroom before 72 hours (three days) have passed, he or she continues to spread the virus. Without a doctor's diagnosis or laboratory tests, Norovirus is usually suspected as the main cause because it is very common and contagious. Other similar viruses may be stopped using the same precautions.

How Did You Meet the Challenge?
What Was the Teachers' Role?

After Barbara's phone call, I visited the center with an Environmental Health (EH) Specialist who knew the center and made inspections every six months. We brought written information about Norovirus for teachers and all parents, including how to limit its spread, how to clean up areas infected by vomit, and how long to stay home after symptoms stop. Barbara showed us the classrooms; pointed out a couch that a child had vomited on; and described the precautions they had been using, such as washing toys after toddlers had played with them.

We suggested getting rid of the couch, using a strong bleach solution for cleaning all common surfaces, steam cleaning the carpets, having children wash their hands upon arrival at school, and instructing parents to keep ill children at home for 72 hours after the last symptoms had disappeared. We discussed that the teacher's role in such an outbreak is to recognize a child's symptoms early, report this to the supervisor, and ask the parent to get a diagnosis. If no diagnosis or doctor's visit is made, appropriate precautions should still be taken.

What Was the Outcome?

The teachers worked vigilantly on the suggestions and enforced the "stay home for 72 hour" rule. A fact sheet on "Tips for Parents on Coping with Norovirus" was sent home that day. When there have been no new ill persons for four days during an outbreak, it is considered finished. Thus, the teachers and children were back in the classrooms, playing and learning.

Barbara commented that it is very important for the early childhood teacher to develop a comfortable relationship with the EH Specialist. She also noted that it helps when the children's center has developed policies and procedures for the most common infectious diseases among young children. "When a child has symptoms, we quickly turn to the protocol to take appropriate precautions."

Other Infectious Diseases

Outbreaks of certain infections such as measles have been reported among internationally adopted children. Often adoptions from the orphanages where children were living are temporarily suspended until the outbreak is controlled. Typically these illnesses are resolved before these children enroll in child care, preschool, or school.

Culture and Management of Infectious Diseases

Families from diverse cultures often have culturally based perspectives about the cause and treatment of infections and disease. For example, Native American families may view illnesses as a result of a disruption of the spirits and may not identify germs as the cause of infections (Ball, 2012). Families may turn to religion, herbs, acupuncture, and a variety of other traditional healing practices for illnesses. It is important for teachers to communicate with families to protect the health of children, control disease spread, and honor the family's beliefs.

Regardless of race or ethnicity, each family has its own set of personal and philosophical beliefs about treatment of disease. Personal preferences and beliefs may lead families to use nontraditional forms of medicine. **Complementary and alternative medicine (CAM)** refers to the use of healing practices that are not considered part of conventional medical practices. Complementary medicine is treatment used along with conventional medical treatment, whereas alternative medicine is treatment given instead of conventional treatment. Examples include herbs, vitamins, homeopathic remedies, and nutritional supplements. Estimates of the use of CAM practices with children are as high as 60% and are more common in children with special health care needs and children who are partially vaccinated or unvaccinated (Ben-Arye, 2011).

The use of CAM is typically integrated with traditional medical practices. Examples of CAM that teachers may see with respect to infections are the use of herbal remedies such as eardrops for ear infections and supplements such as echinacea and vitamin C for common colds. If families ask teachers to administer any supplement or medications, regardless of the type, the proper procedure for the administration of medicines should be followed in each case.

complementary and alternative medicine (CAM)
healing practices that are not considered part of conventional medical practices

CHECK YOUR UNDERSTANDING 10.4
Click here to check your understanding of infectious diseases in immigrant and internationally adopted children.

SUMMARY

- Common childhood infections are caused by bacteria, viruses, fungi, or parasites. Each infection has its own set of characteristics with respect to mode of transmission, symptoms, and incubation period.
- Infections in the early childhood setting can be prevented by paying careful attention to the immunization status of children and teachers and by supporting classroom practices that prevent disease, such as hand washing.
- Whereas some childhood infections are preventable with vaccinations, others are not. Teachers can become familiar with more common childhood infections and take appropriate measures to exclude children if necessary and notify parents of spreading infections as needed.
- Children born in other countries who immigrate or are adopted here can have a higher risk of certain infections. These children should have appropriate immunizations and health assessments

Chapter Quiz

Click here to check your understanding of Chapter 10, Managing Infectious Disease.

Discussion Starters

1. As discussed in Chapter 1, we know that the quality of child care has an impact on children's overall health and wellness. What impact might the quality of child care have on the control of infectious diseases?

2. Opinions vary related to allowing children to attend school when they have head lice. What are the policies related to head lice in the early childhood and school programs in your area? Do you think a "no-nit" policy should be imposed regarding attendance at schools?

3. HIV is an infectious illness that harbors a significant amount of stigma even in children. Although confidentiality is well established for this illness, a family may choose to be open about their child or a school-age child may discuss his or her infection with friends. How might this influence the child's relationships with his or her peers? How do you think teachers or other staff members would react to the news that a child with HIV is in the classroom?

Practice Points

1. Explore the child care licensing requirements in your area. Are preemployment health assessments required for teachers?

2. Contact the local health authority or access its website to learn about the screening requirements for teachers with respect to tuberculosis. Is the TB skin test required?

3. Imagine that a child in your Head Start classroom has been sent home with a fever and is diagnosed with chicken pox a few days later. Write a written policy that notifies parents and families about the spread of this infectious disease and describes how they can control it.

4. Determine what types of vaccine exemptions are allowed in your state. Ask the local health authority what the exemption rate is for your county. How does it compare with state or national rates?

Web Resources

Healthy Child Care America, American Academy of Pediatrics

Healthy Children, American Academy of Pediatrics

Immunization Action Coalition

Vaccines and Immunizations, Centers for Disease Control and Prevention

Key Terms

acute rheumatic fever

airborne transmission

bacteria

bloodborne transmission

chicken pox

common cold

communicable diseases

complementary and alternative medicine (CAM)

conjunctivitis

coxsackie virus

croup

diarrhea

disease transmission

ear infections

epidemic

fecal–oral transmission

fifth disease

fungi

germ

group A strep infection

head lice

hepatitis A

hepatitis B

hepatitis C

haemophilus influenzae type b (Hib)

human immunodeficiency virus (HIV)

impetigo

incubation period

infectious diseases

influenza

measles

meningitis

methicillin-resistant *Staphylococcus aureus* (MRSA)

mode of transmission

parasite

pertussis

pharyngitis

pinworms

pneumonia

refugees

respiratory syncytial virus (RSV)

Reye's syndrome

ringworm

rotavirus

scabies

scarlet fever

sinusitis

Standard Precautions

staph infections

stridor

Streptococcus pneumoniae

tetanus

tuberculosis (TB)

virus

CHAPTER 11

Teaching Children with Special Health Care Needs

learning outcomes

After reading this chapter, you should be able to:

1. Define and discuss special health needs and how those needs impact children's health, functional status, and education.

2. Identify ways to plan inclusive classrooms that provide a least restrictive environment and meet the goals of inclusion.

3. Explain common health conditions in early childhood and discuss applicable classroom management strategies for these conditions.

CASE STUDY

Jeremy is a 5-year-old African American boy who will join Mary's kindergarten class in the fall. His medical history is complicated. He was born extremely prematurely at 25 weeks gestation, with a birth weight of less than 2 pounds. He stayed in the hospital for nearly two and a half months after his birth. To help him breathe, Jeremy was on a ventilator for six weeks, and he had bleeding around his brain, which was significant but not uncommon for his degree of prematurity. Consequently, Jeremy now has several medical problems that impact his learning. He has cerebral palsy, which mainly affects his lower limbs. He also has asthma and a visual impairment requiring corrective lenses, and he was recently diagnosed with attention deficit disorder.

Mary has had experience with many children who have special developmental needs, but Jeremy's health history is unique. She wonders how his medical problems will impact his learning in the classroom. She looks for resources to learn more about Jeremy so that she can start planning how to help him adjust to the classroom setting. Mary makes notes of her questions. Then she gathers her notebook and walks down the hall to the school library where Jeremy's kindergarten transition meeting is scheduled in a few minutes. One school year is ending, but Mary is already starting to think about next fall and the important experience ahead for this young child.

Teaching young children is an exciting profession that combines the enjoyment of helping young children grow and discover their world with the responsibility of ensuring children's health and well-being. This responsibility adds challenge and focus to teachers' endeavors. For many teachers like Mary, the most rewarding aspect of their work comes from crafting individualized approaches that support the learning of children with unique needs.

In this chapter, we will discuss children's special health care needs and explore ways in which a child's exceptional health needs affect his or her development and the context of the family. We will also discuss laws related to children who have special health needs and briefly explore treatments that are used to improve children's health outcomes. Finally, we will describe the various health needs and discuss some of the ways these conditions are managed in the early childhood setting. Understanding children's special health care needs and making purposeful adjustments to the classroom setting are crucial aspects of teaching that characterize the teacher's role in helping children reach their full potential.

UNDERSTANDING CHILDREN'S SPECIAL HEALTH CARE NEEDS

More than ever before, children with chronic medical conditions are enrolled in early childhood programs and included in school classrooms. Nearly every early childhood classroom includes children with special health care needs. This highlights the need for teachers to be prepared to serve children who have a variety of medical needs and to prepare their classrooms and curriculum to support these learners.

children with special health care needs children who have or are at risk for a chronic physical, developmental, behavioral, or emotional condition and who require health and related services of a type or amount beyond that generally required

Defining Special Health Care Needs

Children with special health care needs "have or are at risk for a chronic physical, developmental, behavioral, or emotional condition and who also require health and related services of a type or amount beyond that required by children generally" (U.S. Department of Health and Human Services, Health Resources and Services Administration, Maternal and Child Health Bureau, 2008). This definition encompasses a wide range of medical conditions that have an impact on education. To support children with special health care needs so that they can develop to their full potential, their health care and educational needs must be addressed at home, at school, and in the community. Children's special health care diagnoses, treatments, and educational interventions and outcomes are unique for each child and change as the child grows and develops.

Teachers make a significant contribution to the education and development of children with special health care needs. They do this by being:

- *Capable and willing*—to learn about the child's unique health care and educational needs.
- *Adaptable and able*—to envision and implement appropriate adjustments in the classroom and curriculum.
- *Reflective and responsive*—to identify successful educational interventions and put them into practice when needed.

In the opening case scenario, Mary demonstrated these engaging and proactive characteristics. As soon as she learned she would be teaching a child with special health care needs, she began to outline the kinds of information she would need to be effective as Jeremy's teacher.

Prevalence of Children with Special Health Care Needs

According to data from surveys in 2011/2012, 19.8%, or 14.6 million, of U.S. children had a special health care need. About 65% of children with special health care needs have more complex needs beyond treatment with prescription medications for management of their condition (U.S. Department of Health and Human Services, Health Resources and Services Administration, 2013). The increase in the number of children with special health care needs in classrooms is due to increased inclusion as well as a growing prevalence of certain conditions. Inclusion of children increased significantly after the Individuals with Disabilities Education Act (IDEA) was adopted.

The incidence of some health conditions has increased as well, such as Jeremy in the opening scenario who was born very premature. Although the survival rates for premature infants are higher, some of these babies are left with medical conditions such as cerebral palsy, intellectual disabilities, or other disabilities that will impact the child's ability to learn.

Children with special health care needs (CSHCN) represent a diverse group. Special health care needs are present in families of all income levels, races, ethnicities, religions, and cultures. Boys have higher rates than girls as do black, non-Hispanic children compared with other races and ethnicities (Child Trends, 2012). Prevalence rates for some health conditions vary according to geographic areas. In the southeastern United States, sickle cell anemia is more common than in West Virginia, where cystic fibrosis is a more prevalent condition.

Functional Status

functional status
characteristics that are most important to parents and teachers: how well a child can function in the community, in the classroom, and in relationships

Functional status describes the characteristics that are most important to parents and teachers: how well a child can function in the community, in the classroom, in relationships and in activities of daily living. The World Health Organization advocates for emphasizing children's functional status and capabilities rather than focusing on children's limitations and disability. This puts the focus on the child and not on the special health care condition or disability. When discussing children who have special medical conditions, the child's name is used first, followed by the identifying characteristic. This is referred to as **people-first language**. The phrase *children with diabetes* reinforces the concept of thinking of children as people with many complexities, qualities, and abilities. The phrase *diabetic children*, by comparison, puts more focus on the medical condition and limitations.

people-first language
Identifying people or children first rather than a health condition

To achieve positive functional status, children with special health care needs may require specialized health care services. These services include prescription medications, special diets, medical equipment, or frequent use of health care services. Specialized services may be offered within the health care system or through special educational services. Following are some examples of specialized health care services:

- Specialist care (pediatric cardiology, pulmonology, neurology).
- Mental health care.
- Dental care.
- Physical therapy, occupational therapy, speech therapy.
- Preventive care.
- Eyeglasses/vision care.
- Prescription medications.

When children have unmet health care needs, many aspects of their lives are affected. A child with Down syndrome, a genetic condition that causes intellectual and physical challenges, needs regular vision care because of the high likelihood of needing corrective lenses or other treatment. Without these interventions, the child's health, wellness, and learning are negatively impacted.

Many CSHCN also have limitations in their ability to participate fully in the activities of daily living. These challenges are called functional limitations and have an impact on educational settings. Over 91% of families of CSHCN report at least one functional limitation. The following are the most common (U.S. Department of Health and Human Services, Health Resources and Services Administration, 2013).

Down syndrome
a genetic condition that causes mental and physical challenges

functional limitations
challenges that limit a child's ability to participate in activities of daily living

- Difficulty breathing or other respiratory problems
- Physical pain that is recurrent or chronic, such as headaches
- Feelings of anxiety or depression
- Problems with learning or sustaining attention
- Behavior problems

Impact on Families

Special health care needs can add complexity to family life depending on the type and degree of the child's challenges. Some families may be better able to cope than others depending on socioeconomic status and other family stressors. Families with children who have special health needs have added financial stress even if health insurance is available.

Financial Issues

Among children with special health care needs, there are higher rates of poverty in African Americans (38.9%) and Hispanic (35.5%) compared with Caucasian (14.1%) (Child and Adolescent Health Measurement Initiative , 2012). Financial problems often pose additional challenges to families with CSHCN. Children living in poverty are more likely to have certain health conditions such as asthma, emotional and behavioral problems, learning disabilities, and obesity (National Center for Child Poverty, 2011).

Over 21% of families of CSHCN identify a significant financial burden. Families of CSHCN may have increased expenses due to health care services, special foods, equipment, utilities (heat, water), clothing, and medications (Parish, Rose, Dababnah, Yoo, & Cassiman, 2012). Parental employment is also affected. Nearly 25% of parents of children with special health care needs report cutting back or quitting their jobs (U.S. Department of Health and Human Services, Health Resources and Services Administration, 2013).

Despite being insured, over 40% of parents with CSHCN still report that their health insurance is inadequate (Child and Adolescent Health Measurement Initiative, 2012). For example, not all prescription medications and therapies are covered by insurance. A child with asthma who does not have an inhaler because the family could not afford it is at risk for having symptoms in school that affect his or her participation and learning.

WHAT IF . . .

a child in your classroom shows symptoms of asthma? The family has not sought medical advice, so you have no guidance about how to manage the child's needs in the classroom. You have called the child's family to pick him up early from school, but this means the family member must leave work, thus losing pay because of the missed time. How will you manage this situation? What resources are available to you?

Educational Impact

Because the health of children is so closely connected to their educational performance, children with special health care needs face unique educational challenges. Identified challenges include more days absent from school, poorer student engagement, behavioral problems, and lower academic achievement (O'Connor, Howell-Meurs, Kvalsvig, & Goldfeld, 2014).

Attendance is also more of a problem for CSHCN. Irregular attendance places children at a disadvantage in the classroom where learning builds on previous lessons the child may have missed. These issues double the negative impact on learning for children with special health care needs: The health challenge itself may impact the child's ability to learn as well as reduce the child's participation and attendance. Special attention is needed to build on the child's capacity to learn and to address gaps that may occur with irregular attendance.

CHECK YOUR UNDERSTANDING 11.1

Click here to check your understanding of children's special health care needs.

PLANNING INCLUSIVE CLASSROOMS

Children with medical conditions bring special health-related issues and needs to the early childhood setting. These needs include a range of activities that necessitate accommodations in the classroom environment. Because children's health care needs permeate all aspects of their lives, it is important for teachers to understand them and learn how best to address each situation so that children will have more positive health outcomes.

Ensuring Access to Education

The federal Individuals with Disabilities Education Act describes the requirements regarding provision of services to children with disabilities across the nation. Children with special health care needs are identified for service through the IDEA when their health condition interrupts their ability to learn. The IDEA ensures that children with disabling conditions are able to participate in and be supported to progress in general education. The IDEA describes other health impairment as follows:

Other health impairment means having limited strength, vitality, or alertness, including a heightened alertness to environmental stimuli, that results in limited alertness with respect to the educational environment, that:

- Is due to chronic or acute health problems such as asthma, attention deficit disorder or attention deficit/hyperactivity disorder, diabetes, epilepsy, a heart condition, hemophilia, lead poisoning, leukemia, nephritis, rheumatic fever, sickle cell anemia, and Tourette syndrome; and
- Adversely affects a child's educational performance.

Three specialized plans describe the services available:
- *Individualized family services plan (IFSP):* This early intervention plan for children ages 0 to 3 years is intended to support and provide services that are targeted to improving the child's developmental progress.
- *Individualized education program (IEP):* This plan is for children in the school setting ages 3 to 21 years who need special education services due to cognitive, motor, social, and communication impairments.
- *Individualized health plan (IHP):* This plan is developed for students who have medical conditions that require management or treatment in the school setting. The IHP may be written as a component of the child's IEP.

Early childhood teachers and schools rely on the support of the local education agency (LEA) charged with administering and overseeing the implementation of the IDEA in the state or locality. This is often the public board of education or another authority that is responsible for evaluating children for participation in early intervention services and for providing needed services. This agency participates with families and schools to create a plan that meets the child's educational needs and addresses the impact of special health conditions.

Some early childhood programs benefit from training provided by the LEA to implement the child's education and health plan. The guidance of a medical consultant is also beneficial. Some school districts have school nurses available to see children and advise teachers in the care of a child with special health needs in the school setting. The *Policy Point* discusses the role of school nurses as a resource for children with special health care needs, their families, and teachers.

Supporting Appropriate Inclusion

Inclusion is the policy that children with disabilities participate in school activities alongside other children without disabilities to the maximum extent possible. This includes academic and extracurricular activities (Turnbull, Turnbull, Wehmeyer, & Shogren, 2013). The principle of *least restrictive* environment supports inclusion. Federal laws do not require inclusion, but the IDEA does require that children be educated in the least restrictive environment appropriate to meet their unique needs (U.S. Department of Education, n.d.). Teachers are important participants in making placement decisions for children with special health care needs. Along with families and the representatives of the LEA, each classroom is evaluated as a potential educational placement. Decisions are based on the needs of the child, her or his peers, and the classroom's ability to meet those needs.

Teachers may be asked to monitor the child's health status and provide individualized care. Some needs may address making relatively minor changes in the environment. Others may include changing diapers; suctioning a **tracheostomy tube**

Pearson Education

CLASSROOM CONNECTION

Watch this video about how a preschool honors and prioritizes inclusion. How is inclusion beneficial to children with special needs as well as children who develop typically?

inclusion
the policy that allows children with disabilities to participate in school activities alongside other children without disabilities to the maximum extent possible

tracheostomy tube
a surgically placed tube that allows air and oxygen to enter the lungs through the neck

POLICY POINT

The Role of School Nurses for Children with Special Health Care Needs

One of the goals of *Healthy People 2020* is to ensure that schools have one school nurse for every 750 students. Even more nurses are recommended for schools enrolling a high number of children with special health care needs. School nurses are directly involved with children's existing and potential health problems. They provide screening and referral for health conditions. School nurses also provide case management services and collaborate with family and community members regarding children's health. Most importantly for children with special health care needs, the school nurse is the health expert for the teams developing the individualized education program (IEP).

School nurses support teachers regarding services for children with special health care needs by:

1. Assessing health complaints. This is particularly important for children who are at risk for acute illnesses such as asthma, cystic fibrosis, and diabetes.

2. Administering medications.

3. Identifying and managing children's health care needs that affect educational achievement.

Recent economic constraints have reduced the number of nurses assigned to schools, hindering the *Healthy People 2020* goal. Early childhood professionals and administrators are important advocates for this service and other forms of school health care support.

Source: Healthy People, n.d.

gastrostomy tube
a tube placed through the abdominal wall into the stomach to feed children who are unable to eat orally

(a surgically placed tube that allows air and oxygen to enter the lungs through the neck); or feeding a child with a **gastrostomy tube**, a tube placed through the abdominal wall into the stomach to feed children who are unable to eat orally.

Teachers are part of a service team that plans, implements, and evaluates the effectiveness of services provided for children with special needs. They follow the guidance provided by the medical professionals and most often have either daily or periodic support of early intervention specialists and therapists. One aspect of inclusion that falls under the teacher's responsibilities is creating an environment in which all children are welcomed and encouraged to thrive.

Administering Medications

Many children with special health care needs are given prescription medications and may require medications during the school day. To manage this safely, early childhood settings should have a written policy describing how medications are to be administered. Persons administering medications should be familiar with the policy and receive appropriate training to ensure safety. Recommended standards are available to guide best practice procedures for medication administration. For example, the *National Health and Safety Performance Standards* recommend that medication administration be allowed when a health care provider orders a prescription or over-the-counter medicine with permission from the parent/guardian.

Because medication errors can occur easily, all schools and child care facilities should use a standard form that explains the details of medication administration. A standard form for this purpose is shown in Figure 11-1. Guidelines for the administration of medications include the following (American Academy of Pediatrics, American Public Health Association, National Resource Center for Health and Safety in Child Care and Early Education, 2011):

- Orders specifying medical need, medication, dosage, and length of time medication is given should be provided by health professional.
- Medications should be labeled and in the original container, and label should include child's name, date filled, prescribing clinician's name, pharmacy name and phone number, dosage instructions, and warnings.
- Observe, report, and document any reactions or side effects from medications.
- Document the time and amount of medicine given and the name of the person administering the medication.

Partnering with Families

Communicating with families is essential to appropriate education and care of children with special medical conditions. Developing partnerships with families has a positive impact on children's education and well-being. When children have special health care needs, communication is of even greater importance. Establishing a good working relationship starts when children with health needs are enrolled and are preparing to join the class. Enrollment materials gather many details about a child's condition and special health considerations. Review of the health history further clarifies aspects of the child's need. However, discussing the plan for the child's entry into the early childhood environment directly with a family member is the most important component of a successful transition.

FIGURE 11-1   Medication Administration Permission Form

Medication Permission and Administration Permission Form

The staff of the King Avenue Child Development Center has been asked by
(Parent/Guardian) _____ to administer medication to
(Child) _____ during the school day.
In order to comply with this request and in accordance with our state law, we need the
following information from you.

MEDICAL PROVIDER INFORMATION

Health care provider signature _____ Date _____
Health care provider name _____
Address _____
Phone _____
Fax _____

DIRECTIONS FOR ADMINISTRATION OF MEDICATION

Child's name _____ Date of birth _____
Name of medication _____
Purpose of medication _____
Starting date _____ Ending date _____
Dosage _____
When to give medication _____
Time(s) to be given _____
How medication is given: By mouth _____ By injection _____ Other _____

Special instructions

_____

Signs or symptom(s) to watch for _____
Possible side effects or reactions _____
Adaptations suggested for the classroom _____

_____

When to call the parent or health care provider regarding symptoms or if the child fails to
respond to treatment

_____

_____

Signs that urgent care is needed _____

_____

PARENT PERMISSION

*I request and authorize the King Avenue Child Development Center to administer this
medication in accordance with the instructions provided by my child's medical provider.*

_____

_____

Parent or Guardian Signature   Date

_____   _____

_____

Parent or Guardian Name   Phone

_____   _____

_____

Dragon Images/Shutterstock

Families need reassurance that their child with special health care needs will be safe in the early childhood setting.

Families may understandably have many worries about their child with special health care needs. They need to feel assured that the teacher is aware of their child's condition and is ready to assume responsibility for the child's safety and well-being. Direct conversation helps to build trust between the family and the teacher. It also contributes to a greater understanding of the relevant issues and strategies. Language and culture are important considerations when building this trusting relationship. Sometimes teachers may tend to communicate less with families who are not English speakers. Some parents may struggle to explain their child's complex health condition and needs. Teachers are responsible for ensuring that every family has the support they need to fully discuss their child's special health care needs. For example, it is not appropriate to use other children in the family as interpreters, so arranging for translation services or encouraging the family to invite a trusted friend to assist with the discussion are examples of ways to ensure full communication and to build an effective partnership.

Once children are enrolled, teacher and family communication focuses on exchanging information about the child's health and well-being during the school day. Families of children with asthma need to know if the child has been coughing, having difficulty with physical activity, or refusing to use the inhaler. A family whose child has **muscular dystrophy**, a genetic condition that causes progressive weakness, needs to know if the child is experiencing emotional problems due to his challenges. Similarly the teacher needs to be informed about any changes in the child's health status or experiences at home that might impact the child's participation in classroom activities.

muscular dystrophy a disease of the muscles causing progressive weakness, susceptibility to pulmonary infections, and premature death

To facilitate communication with families in her preschool, Janna creates a small notebook for each child with special health care needs. The notebook is placed in the child's cubby-locker. At orientation, Janna describes how the notebook is for both the teacher and the family to use in recording notes for the other. When Janna wants to communicate a health-related message, she writes a note in the log. When the family picks up the child, they check the notebook to read the teacher's message. Similarly the family can leave a message for the teacher. This method helps Janna remember to tell the family about important health observations. Karin uses a different approach. The children in her second-grade class ride the bus, so she does not see families very often. Karin uses e-mail to communicate with families about children's special medical needs.

Educating Classmates

Some children's medical conditions are apparent; others may not be obvious. When teachers realize, however, that classmates are aware of a child's special health care needs, they plan activities to educate classmates about the medical condition. Young children may view as "different" or "strange" those unique aspects of a child's appearance, behavior, or interaction in the classroom. This is due to children's natural interest and curiosity in things that are different and the potential to be confused and possibly frightened by new situations. Children may be naturally curious about why a child receives medication or a special diet or why a child does not participate in running games. They may also have fears and wonder, "Could that happen to me?" When curiosity or fear is displayed in a negative way, the child with special health care needs may suffer socially.

The potential for negative social interactions is an important reason for educating classmates about a child's medical condition and special needs in the classroom. Sometimes classmates pester or make fun of children with medical conditions. They might imitate the child's movements or laugh at the child's efforts. Teachers need to be aware of these potential reactions and be prepared with strategies to address them.

Children who begin to wear corrective lenses while they are attending the early childhood program may become the center of interest and attention. Sometimes this interest takes a negative course. For example, another child may reach out to grab at the child's new glasses or children may call the child names or say that the child looks "weird." Teachers must anticipate and intervene in such situations, describing how corrective lenses help the child to see and explaining that the glasses are a precious and important tool for the child. Teachers might have a pair of corrective lenses available to let the other children touch and try on. This approach addresses children's curiosity and invites conversation and questions about vision problems and how they are managed.

In a similar way, young children are capable of learning about other medical conditions. When the mystery is removed, children become accustomed to management of the health need in the classroom; the novelty of the disability wears off, and children are more likely to treat the child with the special health care need in a typical way. Talking with classmates about a child's special health needs helps to address curiosity, lack of understanding, and fear and builds the desired sense of normalcy. This is an important aspect of creating class groups that are caring communities.

Educating classmates about children's special health care needs requires attention to developmentally appropriate messages. Very young children require short and clear explanations such as "I am helping Jax to feel better" or "D'shay needs to take this medicine to help him feel better. You can watch if you want." Older children are capable of learning more details about a condition and the activities that support the child in the classroom. Strategies to support such discussions include the following:

- Begin by discussing experiences that are familiar to the classmates. Ask children if they have ever been sick. Talk about what that felt like. Help children identify ways their family helped them to feel better, such as resting, eating healthy foods, or taking medicine.

- Show the connection between children's common experiences and the child's special health care need. Name the child's medical condition and briefly explain what it is and how it is similar to other children's health experiences. Talk about how the chronic condition is managed or treated. Identify the ways you help the child care for his or her condition in the class. Explain how the treatment helps the child.

- Talk about how the child developed the special medical condition. Explain if the child was born with the condition or if it was the result of an accident. Clarify whether the condition is contagious.

- Invite children to ask questions. Treat each question as an expression of legitimate interest and concern. Help children learn how to form questions about health.

- Discuss inappropriate interactions with the child if any have been observed. Talk about ways that children can advocate for appropriate treatment of those who have special conditions.
- Include the child with the special health care needs as a leader in the discussion if appropriate. Help the child with special health needs gain strategies and skills for describing and talking about her or his medical conditions with others.
- Engage family members in classroom discussions. Many families may choose to lead the discussion about their child's needs. You can assist in this process by ensuring that the family member is familiar with appropriate ways to communicate complex information to the particular age group.
- After holding such discussions, observe children's interactions in the class. Reflect on whether the classroom discussion was helpful in supporting positive interactions among the children with special health care needs and their classmates.

When communicating about a child's special health care need, teachers should avoid drawing undue attention to the child's limitations. Rather, the goal is to reinforce the similarities that help children to befriend one another. For example, Paula has cerebral palsy. In the classroom, she moves with the support of her walker. When the class takes a field trip to the library, Paula's classmates take turns pulling her in a wagon. Paula sits near the back of the wagon to make room for the bag of books the class is returning to the library. As they travel, they talk together about their favorite books and the topics they want to explore next. When they return to the classroom with their new bag of books, Sam turns to Paula and says, "Thanks for carrying the books." The *Teaching Wellness* feature provides other ideas that support recognition of sameness among classmates.

Supports are available to help teachers guide discussions about particular medical conditions. Picture books are a good way to introduce conversations about children's special medical conditions. Reading books such as those suggested below as part of the year-round reading options reinforces the message that special health care needs are part of the everyday world, just like caterpillars and butterflies! Here are some examples of books for young children with special health needs:

- *Lara Takes Charge* (for kids with diabetes, their friends, and siblings) by Rocky Lang and Sally Huss.
- *Taking Asthma to School* (Special Kids in School), 2nd edition, by Kim Gosselin.
- *Taking Food Allergies to School* by Ellen Weiner.

MANAGING SPECIAL HEALTH CARE NEEDS

Learning about chronic health conditions in early childhood equips teachers to be attuned to their impact on children's health and learning. Familiarity with the causes and impacts of special health needs also supports teachers in enrollment conversations with families. It prepares teachers to identify information they need to support the child's positive transition and participation in the classroom.

In the following sections, we provide an overview of a variety of medical conditions that affect young children. Examples of strategies used to manage each medical condition in the classroom are provided as a first step in understanding the many ways teachers support children with special health care needs. These suggestions do not replace the guidance provided by health care providers and early intervention specialists. Because most teachers do not have medical training, teachers

CHECK YOUR UNDERSTANDING 11.2

Click here to check your understanding of planning inclusive classrooms.

TEACHING WELLNESS   Same and Special

LEARNING OUTCOME   Children will be able to identify characteristics of similarity and aspects of uniqueness.

INFANTS AND TODDLERS

- **Goal:** To introduce the concepts of "same" and "different."
- **Materials:** Typical classroom manipulative toys, the book *It's OK to Be Different*, by Todd Parr.
- **Activity plan:** Take advantage of incidental learning opportunities to describe the concepts of "same" and "different." For example, when playing with cube blocks, set aside a pair of green cube blocks and one red cube block. Place the green cube blocks together and say, "Look. These are the same." Then pair a red and green block and say, "These are different. See? One is green, and this one is red."
- **How to adjust the activity:** As children become familiar with the concepts of "same" and "different," ask them to choose a matching item from a group. Hold a blue block and ask the child to find one that is the same. Then ask the child to find one that is different. Read and talk about the book *It's OK to Be Different*.
- **Did you meet your goal?** Did the children listen to the questions? Can the children find objects that match?

PRESCHOOLERS AND KINDERGARTNERS

- **Goal:** To explore the concepts of "same" and "different" and to discuss the concept of "uniqueness" and the notion of being special.
- **Materials:** Provide an array of creative materials such as yarn pieces, fabric scraps, magazine pages, construction paper; scissors; glue; the book *We Are All Alike, We Are All Different*, by the Cheltenham Elementary School Kindergartners and Laura Dwight.
- **Activity plan:** Offer the creative materials during free exploration time. Let children know that you will invite them to show their creations at group time. During group time, ask each child to talk about his or her creation. Then lay the pictures on the floor next to each other. Standing around the pictures, invite the children to talk about what is the same and what is different. Talk about aspects of uniqueness and describe how being different is a way of being unique or special.
- **How to adjust the activity:** Read the book *We Are All Alike, We Are All Different*. Use the book to introduce a discussion about same/special characteristics among people. As children offer suggestions, make lists of all the things children can identify that are the same about people and all the things that are different. Talk about ways that being the same is interesting and ways that being unique is interesting. Use other books to explore more aspects of same and special:
  - *Why Am I Special?* by Melissa Langer
  - *The Family Book*, by Todd Parr
  - *Me I Am!* by Jack Prelutsky and Christine Davenier
  - *I Am Special,* by Charlotte Lisi and David Ortega
- **Did you meet your goal?** Are children able to recognize and identify characteristics that make things the same and different? Are children able to list characteristics of similarity and difference among people?

SCHOOL-AGE CHILDREN

- **Goal:** To explore the concepts of "same" and "different" and to discuss the concept of "uniqueness" and the notion of being special.
- **Materials:** Colored plastic mosaic tiles of various shapes, colors, and sizes; the book *This Is My Hair*, by Todd Parr.
- **Activity plan:** Provide colored plastic mosaic tiles of various shapes. Invite a small group of children to sort all the colored tiles by attribute: all the yellow triangles here, all the blue squares there, and so on. Ask the children to take one of each shape (or two or more of each shape if there are enough) to create a design. When children have finished, ask them to look at each other's designs. Are they the same? Different? Talk about how each child had the same shape, color, and number of tiles but each creation is unique and special.
- **How to adjust the activity:** Read the children's book *This Is My Hair*. Ask the children to draw a picture using the author's illustrative style that depicts their unique style. Display the drawings and conduct an "Illustrator's Interview": Ask each child to describe aspects of their drawing that are similar to others, but also to identify aspects that are unique. Talk about same and special characteristics among children in the class. Provide other books about these concepts to read:
  - *We're Different, We're the Same*, by Bobbi Kates
  - *It's OK to Be Different*, by Todd Parr
  - *I Just Am*, by Tom Lambke and Bryan Lambke
  - *I Am Special,* by Linda Schwartz
- **Did you meet your goal?** Are children able to describe characteristics that make things the same and different? Are they able to discuss aspects of unique and special?

work in partnership with medical providers, early intervention specialists, and families. This partnership carries the responsibility of planning, implementing, and monitoring appropriate management strategies to support the appropriate inclusion of children with special health care needs in the classroom environment and to address health needs that arise in the early childhood setting.

Conditions Related to the Immune System

immune system
the body system responsible for controlling infections and responding to foreign substances that enter the body

Children's **immune systems** are responsible for controlling infections and responding to foreign substances that enter the body. Dental caries, asthma, environmental allergies, and eczema are common health conditions associated with the immune system.

Dental Caries

dental caries
tooth decay or cavities

Dental caries affects 28% of children ages 2 to 5 years, and 72% of tooth decay remains untreated. This condition is a destruction of the tooth enamel caused by an interaction of bacteria, inappropriate feeding practices, lifestyle habits, and individual factors. Both primary and permanent teeth are affected and can be destroyed by the decay. Transmission of the bacteria that causes damage to the teeth is known to be from person to person, most commonly parent to child. The consequences of the disease are not limited to just the teeth, but can have widespread health effects over the course of a lifetime. It is more common in (Çolak, Dülgergil, Dalli, & Hamidi, 2013):

- Families living in poverty.
- Ethnic and racial minority families.
- Single-mother families.
- Families in which parents have low education levels.

fluoride
a mineral that is sometimes found naturally but is also used for prevention and/or treatment of tooth decay

Other more specific risk factors include consumption of sweetened liquids and candy, inadequate **fluoride** exposure, and infrequent toothbrushing. Children whose families live in poverty not only have more caries, but also have more complications such as abscesses (Lewis, 2014).

Fluoride is a mineral that aids in preventing tooth decay and strengthening enamel. Because caries is so common and destructive, many municipal water supplies are supplemented with fluoride as a public health strategy to prevent caries and/or halt the progression of caries. Some children may also be treated with fluoride in early childhood dental programs or schools.

Classroom Management Strategies The early childhood setting is an important place to promote and practice oral health. The following oral hygiene activities should be followed routinely in child care settings (American Academy of Pediatrics, American Public Health Association, National Resource Center for Health and Safety in Child Care and Early Education, 2011):

- All children should have their teeth brushed at least once during their time there.
- Children should be given water after snacks and meals if brushing is not possible.

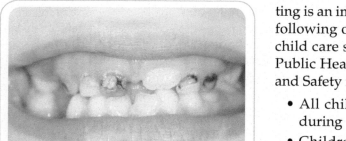
Dental caries are common and an important health condition of early childhood.

Oral health promotion is an important aspect of teaching young children. This can be achieved in the following ways

(American Academy of Pediatrics, American Public Health Association, National Resource Center for Health and Safety in Child Care and Early Education, 2011):

- Teachers can encourage parents to establish dental care within six months of the first tooth erupting.
- Children older than 3 years can be taught about tooth decay and appropriate dietary practices to prevent decay.
- Teachers can educate families about good oral hygiene and avoidance of behaviors that lead to decay.

Asthma

Asthma is a respiratory disease characterized by intermittent attacks of cough or difficult breathing. It causes chronic inflammation of the small airways within the lung, resulting in a narrowing or obstruction of the airways. This narrowing causes children to cough or experience shortness of breath. Children with asthma may also **wheeze**, creating a high-pitched whistling sound typically heard with a stethoscope.

Asthma is the most common chronic disease in childhood, affecting 9% of children (Centers for Disease Control and Prevention, National Center for Health Statistics, 2015). Families living in poverty, minorities (especially African Americans), and children in urban areas have a higher risk of developing severe asthma, experience more hospitalizations from asthma, and have higher death rates due to asthma (Centers for Disease Control and Prevention, 2012). It is one of the leading causes of missed school days and accounts for 14.4 million missed days per year (Meng, Babey, & Wolstein, 2012).

Triggers are specific stimuli that cause an asthma attack (Table 11-1). Some of the most common triggers in children are upper respiratory infections, cigarette smoke, and environmental allergens such as pollens and dust mites. Every child with asthma has different triggers.

Classroom Management Strategies Teachers may be asked to assist children with asthma by administering medications. Two categories of medications are commonly used to treat asthma. One type is used *as needed* to open the airways when

asthma
a condition causing narrowing and obstruction of the airways leading to chronic cough, shortness of breath, and wheezing

wheeze
a high-pitched whistling sound made while breathing; commonly occurs in children with asthma

triggers
stimuli that start an asthma attack

TABLE 11-1 Common Asthma Triggers

Indoor allergens	Animal dander, dust mites, cockroaches, molds Cleaning products
Outdoor allergens	Pollens from trees, grasses, weeds Molds Air pollutants Cold or dry air School bus exhaust
Other irritants	Tobacco smoke Strong odors or fumes from paint, perfumes, or fragrances
Health conditions	Cold, flu, viruses Sinus infections Nasal allergies Reflux
Exercise	More common in cold weather
Foods or food additives	Some children have specific food triggers

Source: American Academy of Pediatrics, 2014.

A nebulizer is used to treat asthma in infants, toddlers, and some older children.

albuterol
medication commonly used to open the airways when children have symptoms of asthma at the onset of an episode or as a rescue medicine

inhaled corticosteroids
a type of medication used to prevent episodes of asthma attacks; is used daily even when the child is not having symptoms

nebulizer
a small electronic device that is used to distribute medication as aerosolized droplets for inhalation by the child

spacer
a hollow plastic tube that attaches to an inhaler and holds aerosolized medication in a confined space while the child inhales the medication

asthma attack
episodes of asthma in which symptoms worsen and require immediate treatment to control breathing; characterized by shortness of breath, fast breathing, or worsening cough

the child has symptoms. **Albuterol** is an example of an as-needed medication. Nearly all children with asthma use this type of medication. The frequency of use depends on the severity and control of the child's illness. The other type of medication, which is used to *prevent* episodes, is given daily even when the child is not having symptoms. **Inhaled corticosteroids** are examples of *prevention* medications.

More common asthma medications are administered as a solution with a nebulizer or with an inhaler and spacer. A **nebulizer** is a small electronic device that distributes a solution into aerosol droplets, or spray, for the child to inhale. An inhaler with a spacer also administers medication to be inhaled but requires more coordination on the part of the recipient. To use an inhaler, the child must be able to put the inhaler in her or his mouth and inhale.

Typically nebulizers are used more often for infants and toddlers and inhalers are used for preschoolers and older children. To ensure that a child receives the medication most effectively, inhalers should *always* be used with a **spacer** regardless of age of the child. A spacer is a plastic tube that attaches to the inhaler and holds the aerosolized medication in a confined space while the child breathes in the droplets. Asthma medications may need to be administered several times a day.

Children with asthma may receive more than one medication, and the frequency of use may change. Periodic communication with the child's family and health care provider may be necessary to understand any changes in the prescribed plan.

Teachers are also important sources of recognizing when a child's asthma is uncontrolled and when a child is experiencing an **asthma attack**. Symptoms of uncontrolled asthma and asthma attacks are similar. Figure 11-2 lists symptoms for both circumstances. Asthma attacks can be life-threatening. Even when receiving treatment for asthma, children can still experience an asthma attack if exposed to a trigger. If symptoms of uncontrolled asthma or an asthma attack

---

FIGURE 11-2   Symptoms of Uncontrolled Asthma and Asthma Attacks

Symptoms of inadequately controlled asthma:

- Persistent cough, especially with physical activity
- Prolonged symptoms after a respiratory tract infections
- Frequent respiratory tract infections
- Need for frequent use of albuterol or rescue inhaler

Symptoms of an asthma attack:

- Frequent or uncontrollable coughing
- Unable to speak in sentences
- Increased use of shoulders or abdominal muscles for breathing
- Audible wheezing
- Shortness of breath, especially if at rest

are observed, emergency treatment as directed by the child's medical provider should be followed immediately, and the family should be notified as soon as possible.

Allergic Conditions

Along with asthma, allergies are one of the most common conditions of childhood. Allergies have many causes and can be manifested in a number of ways. They are categorized as food allergies, skin allergies (eczema), and respiratory allergies (hay fever).

Food Allergies Allergies to foods in children can be very serious and can lead to anaphylaxis, a severe life-threatening allergic reaction. The prevalence is 5.1% and increasing. Hispanic children are less likely to experience a food allergy, and the prevalence increases with higher income levels (Jackson, Howie, & Akinbami, 2013).

Inhalers with spacers are used for preschoolers and older children.

Beneda Miroslav/Shutterstock

anaphylaxis
a severe life-threatening allergic reaction

eczema
a type of reaction seen on the skin that is characterized by red, itchy rash and dry skin

Classroom management strategies should include getting a detailed history from families on known food allergies and documenting the type of reaction the child has as well as the treatment in case of accidental ingestion.

Skin Allergies

Eczema is a condition that causes inflammation and itching of the skin. It is characterized by chronically dry skin with periodic episodes of more intense skin rashes that are red, peeling, and very itchy. The most common areas for the rash are the face, backs of hands and feet, and skinfolds (back of knees and in front of elbows). Children with eczema may scratch constantly and have difficulty sleeping because of itching. Infants with eczema may be irritable and move about as they are trying to fall asleep. Children with eczema are prone to skin infections because the integrity of the skin is compromised.

Eczema varies in severity and tends to come and go. It is quite common, affecting 12.5% of children (Jackson et al., 2013). There are many causes of eczema, including food allergies. However, in most cases, the cause is unknown.

Classroom management strategies involve avoiding known triggers and judiciously keeping the skin moist with lotions recommended by a medical provider. Teachers may be asked to apply creams or lotions if children experience a flare-up. It is also important to reduce children's contact with strong soaps or detergents by selecting appropriate soap for children to use at the sink.

Respiratory Allergies Whereas skin allergies are more common in younger children, respiratory allergies are more common in older children. They are very common and can impact quality of life. Common symptoms of environmental allergies include runny nose, watery eyes, cough, headache, and fatigue.

One of the most important ways teachers can aid children with allergies is to help them avoid known triggers. Adjustments can be made for indoor and outdoor activities. Keeping the indoor environment clean to reduce dust and to discourage mold and mildew reduces these triggers. Children who have an allergy to grass can

A Matter of ETHICS

A 3-year-old child enrolled in your class has moderate to severe asthma. His parents are divorced, and they disagree on the management of the child's asthma in the classroom. The boy's mother wants to use conventional medical treatment, but the father wants to use homeopathic treatments. You get different instructions about what to do depending on who drops the child off at preschool. What are the issues here, and how can the NAEYC Code of Ethical Conduct and your state's program licensing requirements help you determine what to do? How do you think it is best to communicate with the family?

NUTRITION NOTE   Early Dietary Practices and Relationship to Allergies and Asthma in Children

Allergic diseases are becoming more prevalent. During the past several decades, asthma, eczema, and food allergies have increased significantly. To reduce the risk of future allergic disease, the American Academy of Pediatrics recommends breastfeeding exclusively for at least the first 4 to 6 months of life. Other allergic disease prevention practices are being studied. These include:

- Monitoring the diet of the pregnant and lactating mother. The mother's diet may be a factor in the child's future development of allergies. At this time, however, studies do not support the exclusion of certain foods, such as peanuts, during pregnancy or lactation.

- Using specialized "hydrolyzed" formulas in formula-fed children who have a strong family history of allergic

disease. Hydrolyzed formulas are "predigested," meaning the protein content has been broken down to make the product more digestible. There is evidence that allergic disease can be prevented or delayed by using hydrolyzed formulas instead of cow's milk–based formulas. It is still unclear whether this effect is long-lasting.

- Delaying introduction of solid food until at least 4 to 6 months. A variety of fruits and vegetables and, later, eggs, meats, and nuts can be introduced unless there is an indication not to. Choking hazards remain a concern during this time.

- Encouraging exclusive breastfeeding until 4 to 6 months of age. Exclusive breastfeeding has been shown to have the strongest beneficial effect for prevention of allergies and eczema.

Sources: Abrams & Becker, 2013; Duryea & Fleischer, 2014.

---

be encouraged to play in the area of the playground that is covered with mulch and to run and walk in the grassy area rather than sit on or touch the grass.

Conditions Related to the Nervous System

attention deficit disorder/attention deficit/hyperactivity disorder
condition causing inattention, increased distractibility, inability to focus and complete tasks, and sometimes hyperactivity

Many chronic health conditions in childhood affect the nervous system or are caused by disorders of the nervous system. Although the effects of these conditions vary, they all have some effect on health and wellness in childhood.

Attention Deficit Disorder and Attention Deficit/Hyperactivity Disorder

Attention deficit disorder (ADD) and attention deficit/hyperactivity disorder (ADHD) are conditions characterized by inattention, impulsivity, or hyperactivity. The causes are not completely understood. Other health conditions are strongly associated with ADD/ADHD, including structural brain abnormalities, history of prematurity, and prenatal exposure to toxins. ADD/ADHD can interfere with the attainment of academic and fine motor skills as well as social and adaptive skills. As a result, children with ADD/ADHD often experience school failure, poor family and peer relations, low self-esteem, and emotional, behavioral, and learning problems (Turnbull et al., 2013).

Estimates of children with a diagnosis of ADD/ADHD are 11%. Prevalence varies significantly by state. The lowest is 5.6% in Nevada, and the highest is 18.7% in Kentucky. Boys are 2.5 times more likely than girls to be identified (Centers for Disease Control, 2014b). Children born prematurely are also at increased risk for acquiring ADD. This could be due to a brain abnormality, such as the intracranial hemorrhage Jeremy's mother reported in the case scenario, or there could be subtle developmental effects on the infant's neurological system.

Three types of conditions fall under the ADD and ADHD categories: *predominantly inattentive* (ADD), *predominantly hyperactive-impulsive* (HD), and *combined* (ADHD). Behaviors and characteristics of children with ADD/ADHD are described in Table 11-2. In addition

Arkady Chubykin/Fotolia

Children with eczema are more likely to contract skin infections.

TABLE 11-2 Characteristics of ADD and ADHD

Attention Deficit Disorder

Is unable to sustain attention while executing tasks or participating in activities

Appears to not be listening when spoken to

Fails to follow through with instructions frequently

Fails to finish schoolwork

Loses things frequently

Is often forgetful with regard to usual daily activities

Is easily distracted

Makes careless mistakes

Is unable to perform tasks that require sustained mental effort

Hyperactive-Impulsive Type

Fidgets or moves in their seat constantly

Talks excessively

Leaves seat when it is expected that they stay in their seat

Runs or climbs inappropriately

Answers questions before it is time

Cannot wait their turn

Interrupts others constantly

Acts out without thinking

Rushes through activities

Source: American Psychiatric Association, 2013.

to frequently displaying these symptoms, the symptoms should be observed in two or more settings, such as at school and at home. In addition, the symptoms must be seen as impairing social or academic functioning. It can sometimes be difficult to distinguish between normal childhood behaviors and ADHD. Children with ADHD may also share some traits associated with giftedness.

Children with ADD often have symptoms of other conditions that affect learning and behavior, such as learning disabilities, behavioral disorders, conduct disorder, mood disorder, anxiety, or depression. Concerns regarding these health conditions should be communicated to families and health care providers.

Children with ADD are eligible for development of a behavioral management plan under the IEP process. In 1991, the Department of Education confirmed that ADHD is considered within the scope of the IDEA (Turnbull et al., 2013). Children with ADHD may also qualify for special education services under the diagnosis of emotional disturbance, which requires a comprehensive evaluation that meets federal and state requirements. Children who do not qualify for services under the IDEA may be eligible under Section 504 of the Rehabilitation Act. ADHD is considered a disability under Section 504 when the child is substantially limited in a major life activity.

Classroom Management Strategies Teachers provide a variety of supports for children with ADD/ADHD. Teachers may be asked to respond to questionnaires that evaluate the child's symptoms in the classroom setting. Adjustments for children may include seating in a quiet area; more time to complete work; and use of materials to aid in organizing and planning, providing tutoring supports, or modifying homework (Turnbull et al., 2013).

Behavioral therapies may be recommended to assist children in functioning effectively in the classroom. Some children will also be prescribed medications such as **stimulants**, which may need to be administered during the day. These medications can decrease challenge behaviors by increasing focus and decreasing distractibility. The ultimate goal is to improve school performance and relationship building. Although extensive literature demonstrates that the use of these medications is safe and effective, they may not be the most appropriate form of treatment. Several trials of different dosages, medications, and timing intervals may be necessary before the best treatment for an individual child is identified. Modifications made in the classroom and counseling for families to improve parenting strategies are critical in the treatment of this condition.

Autism

Autism is the most common condition in a group of developmental disorders called the *autism spectrum disorders* (ASDs). Autism is a condition that involves impaired social interactions; communication problems; repetitive behaviors; and in some circumstances, a restricted range of interests. Other conditions in the ASDs include Asperger's syndrome and **pervasive developmental disorder (PDD)**. The cause of autism is unknown, although it appears to have a strong genetic component. There has been a steady increase in prevalence, which is now 1% to 2%, and it is more common in boys (Harrington & Allen, 2014).

Symptoms Children with autism exhibit six distinctive characteristics (Turnbull et al., 2013):

- Atypical language development
- Atypical social development
- Repetitive behaviors
- Behavior problems
- Sensory and movement disorders
- Atypical intellectual functioning

Table 11-3 lists more specific characteristics typically seen in children with autism.

One of the ASDs is called **Asperger's syndrome**. Children with Asperger's typically have normal intelligence. They have difficulty establishing peer relationships and lack empathy (similar to but milder than autism). They have language skills that are generally stronger than in other types of PDDs, and tend to perseverate on certain topics or objects.

Controversy exists regarding the cause of the increase in cases diagnosed. Some believe that more frequent diagnosis is due to better recognition of the condition and that children with the condition in the past were misdiagnosed as being mentally retarded. Others are of the opinion that the rates of autism are increasing. The Centers for Disease Control is conducting ongoing surveillance studies to track prevalence rates to better clarify this issue.

The onset of autism occurs during the first three years of life; typically children are diagnosed by age 3. Therefore, many children with autism have been diagnosed by the time they enter the public school system. Children with mild autism or Asperger's syndrome, however, may not be diagnosed until the elementary school years.

stimulants
medications used to increase focus and decrease distractibility for improving school performance and relationship building in children with ADHD

autism
neurological condition characterized by impairments in social interaction and communication as well as restrictive, repetitive, or stereotypical patterns of behavior

pervasive developmental disorder (PDD)
disorder associated with developmental delays; abnormal or delayed social interactions; and in some circumstances, a restricted range of interests

Asperger's syndrome
neurological disorder characterized by normal intelligence, poor peer relationships, lack of empathy (similar to but milder than autism), language skills that are generally stronger than in PDD, and a tendency to overfocus on certain topics or objects (for example, planets and geography)

TABLE 11-3 Characteristics of Children with Autism

Characteristic	Examples
Atypical language development	• Broad range of language abilities • Focusing on one topic • Repeating or echoing • Reversing pronouns
Atypical social development	• Abnormal use of nonverbal language • Lack of relationships with peers • Unable to share enjoyment or interests with others
Repetitive behavior	• Hand and finger mannerisms • Repeating phrases • Persistent attention to parts of objects or toys
Behavior problems	• Self-harm • Aggressive behavior • Tantrums • Destruction of property
Sensory and movement disorders	• Food selectivity • Toe walking • Sleep problems • Abnormal posture
Problems with intellectual functioning	• 75% have intellectual disability

Source: Information from Turnbull, Turnbull, Wehmeyer, & Shogren, 2013.

Classroom Management Strategies The evaluation of autism is often a stressful and anxiety-provoking situation for families. Teachers are part of the support system for families during this evaluation period. Providing information about autism and offering opportunities for families to discuss their concerns are ways in which teachers can lend support. When children are diagnosed, teachers are important partners in developing an effective IEP. The goals of the IEP are to reinforce children's desirable behaviors, improve social skills and communication, and reduce nonadaptive behaviors such as aggression or inappropriate angry outbursts. Providing regular routines and a predictable schedule are important, as is supporting children when schedules vary.

Strategies involve teaching children communication skills, such as helping Mike recognize when Alan is asking to share a toy by saying, "Mike, turn your head to look at Alan. He has a question for you." Teaching children imitation skills is another step in helping them to recognize social cues. Supporting the child to play Follow the Leader games is a familiar example of teaching imitation in the early childhood setting. Providing visual cues such as picture cards or pointing to posters that depict an action are often effective ways to support verbal directions. The greatest success occurs when these strategies are consistently used both at school and at home.

Visual cues are often an effective way to support verbal directions for children with autism.

Monkey Business/Fotolia

Teachers are also an important link in connecting families to resources that help them cope with the challenges of autism. There is no cure for autism. However, strategies are available to reduce the impact of symptoms and to improve children's functioning. Interventions provided during the early childhood years are considered critical to improving the symptoms of autism.

Learning Disabilities

learning disability
term used to describe a condition in which there is a specific and persistent failure to learn age-appropriate academic skills despite normal intelligence, conventional teaching, and adequate sociocultural opportunities

A **learning disability** is a disorder in one or more of the processes in charge of understanding or using spoken or written language (Turnbull et al., 2013). Learning disabilities include a number of specific disabilities reflecting difficulties in learning reading, writing, and/or mathematics skills. The most common is **dyslexia**, a disorder of reading in which children frequently omit, insert, reverse, or substitute words or sounds. The causes are generally unknown, although there is a strong genetic component for certain types of learning disabilities such as dyslexia.

dyslexia
disorder of reading where children frequently omit, insert, reverse, or substitute words or sounds

Problems commonly seen in the classroom in children with learning disabilities include the following (Heward, 2013):

- Reading difficulties or learning how to read later than expected.
- Problems with written language including spelling.
- Problems with math.
- Problems with social skills (occurs in about 75% of children with learning disabilities).
- Problems with attention and hyperactivity.
- Behavioral problems.

Classroom Management Strategies The least restrictive environment as described by IDEA applies to children with learning disabilities. Research demonstrates mixed results with inclusion of children with learning disabilities in the general classroom, and some controversy exists. Generally the quality of education is more important than where the education occurs (Heward, 2013).

Besides specific teaching strategies related to inclusion, teachers' input plays an important role in identifying children with learning disabilities. There is no one test that is diagnostic. Generally it is a compilation of information gained from parents and teachers along with testing done by the school system that aids in the diagnosis made by specialists.

Cerebral Palsy

cerebral palsy
a disability causing problems with motor development

Cerebral palsy (CP) is a condition that permanently affects movement and posture, which cause physical limitations. It is the most common motor disability of childhood, affecting 1.5 to 4 per 1,000 children (Centers for Disease Control and Prevention, 2015b). It is caused by problems that occur in brain development before, during, or after birth. Being born prematurely and being small for gestational age are risk factors for developing CP.

Children with CP have problems with movement that affect muscle tone and with the brain signals that promote movement and coordination. Some children have minimal challenges, whereas others experience extensive challenges. Children with CP often experience developmental delays and frequently have other health conditions such as visual problems, hearing loss, speech problems, seizures, feeding difficulties, learning disabilities, and intellectual disability. Children with CP may move with a walker or use a wheelchair. They may have trouble with small motor coordination, making it difficult to hold small items and to learn to write. Children with CP may experience difficulties with speech. Different classifications of CP are based on the type of movement difficulties and the part of the body that is affected. Over half of children with CP can walk independently (Centers for Disease Control and Prevention, 2015b).

Classroom Management Strategies Children with cerebral palsy experience a wide variety of type and severity of symptoms. Teachers should learn about the child's needs for adjustments in the classroom environment to accommodate the child's movement in the setting. Understanding how the child communicates is also important because children with CP may use various communication methods, such as a picture board, digital communication device, or keyboard. An educational assistant who works with the lead teacher to manage any medical interventions and to modify the learning environment appropriately supports many children with CP in the classroom. Speech and physical therapists are usually partners in supporting the child's educational plan.

Fetal Alcohol Spectrum Disorder

Fetal alcohol syndrome (FAS), now identified as fetal alcohol spectrum disorder, is set of neurological conditions caused by exposure to alcohol during pregnancy. The prevalence is largely unknown. Reported alcohol consumption during pregnancy is common, occurring in 1 in 8 pregnancies, and 2% of pregnant women report heavy drinking during pregnancy (Centers for Disease Control and Prevention, 2015a). This condition has lifelong, severe effects on the fetus, affecting a child's physical, emotional, and neurological development. The following are characteristics of the disorder (May et al., 2014):

fetal alcohol syndrome (FAS)
neurological condition causing a range of physical and developmental outcomes that occur as a result of fetal exposure to alcohol

- Abnormalities in the structure of the face.
- Growth deficiency.
- Central nervous system abnormalities, including small head circumference, neurological problems, cognitive/developmental deficits, and behavioral/emotional deficits.

The facial abnormalities seen in FAS include a smooth **philtrum** (the fold typically seen between the nose and upper lip), a thin upper lip, and small eyes, all of which may be obvious in some individuals and subtle in others. Central nervous system abnormalities range from severe structural abnormalities of the brain to mild cognitive deficits.

philtrum
the fold typically seen between the nose and upper lip

Some children exposed to alcohol do not meet the full criteria for FAS. The term *fetal alcohol spectrum disorders* encompasses the range of disabilities associated with exposure to alcohol *in utero* and includes the diagnosis **alcohol-related neurodevelopmental disorder (ARND)**. The ARND diagnosis is often used when there is a history of alcohol exposure but the child does not meet all of the official criteria for FAS.

alcohol-related neurodevelopmental disorder (ARND)
neurological condition covering a spectrum of symptoms that can occur with fetal exposure to alcohol; diagnosis is often used when there is a history of alcohol exposure, but the child does not meet all of the official criteria for FAS

Children with FAS often struggle with attention, memory, and learning, which leads to difficulties in school. It is common to see other health conditions such as hearing and vision disorders, seizures, intellectual disability, abnormal relationships with peers, and deficits in judgment and decision making (May et al., 2014).

Classroom Management Strategies In spite of the wide range of potential behavioral challenges, many children with FAS are described as outgoing, friendly, and socially engaging. Most children with FAS do not qualify for special education services.

Rick's Photography/Shutterstock

Children with FAS often have subtle characteristics such as a smooth philtrum and a thin upper lip.

As they plan to teach children with FAS successfully, many teachers find evaluation of children's **executive functioning** to be helpful. Executive functioning refers to children's ability to function in a school setting with respect to planning, organization, and attention.

Teachers focus on teaching skills that build children's self-help skills to navigate the daily routines of the classroom. Detailed visual cues and prompts are used to make abstract concepts more concrete and to reinforce directions such as "Time to clean up" and "Time to wash hands." Teachers work to reduce distractions and to help children with FAS focus on tasks and skill-building activities. Teachers also provide immediate feedback for appropriate and inappropriate behaviors.

Intellectual Disability

Intellectual disability is the most common developmental disability. This condition was previously referred to as cognitive disability or mental retardation, a term that is no longer used because of stigmatization. It is characterized by a significantly below-average score on a test of intellectual ability and by limited ability to function in the tasks of daily life such as caring for oneself, communicating, and managing social interactions.

Intellectual disability can result from genetic conditions and developmental causes before birth, as well as injury, infection, or illness occurring at birth or during childhood. The most common causes of intellectual disability are Down syndrome, fetal alcohol syndrome, and fragile X syndrome. These are examples of prenatal influences leading to the condition.

Intellectual disabilities are often associated with environmental or biological causes. Environmental causes tend to be exhibited through mild expressions of disability, whereas severe disease is more likely linked to biological causes. Risk factors also exist. Children with mild intellectual disability are more likely to have mothers who did not complete high school, linking the disability to genetics and to environmental influences such as poverty and other social issues. Poverty is more highly associated with intellectual disability than is any other social factor (Turnbull et al., 2013).

Children with intellectual disabilities exhibit a wide range of challenges. **Adaptive behaviors** are challenging for children with intellectual disabilities. Adaptive behaviors refer to the skills children learn to function in everyday life. These include language skills; social skills such as taking turns and sharing; and self-help skills relevant to activities of daily living, such as dressing, bathing, and brushing teeth. There are three aspects of adaptive behaviors (Turnbull et al., 2013):

Conceptual skills such as language, reading, writing, understanding of money, and self-direction.

- Social skills, including following rules, being responsible, and having self-esteem.
- Activities of daily living.

Many children with intellectual disabilities also have problems with **short-term memory**, the information that is stored for a few seconds to a few hours. For example, in the kindergarten classroom, Rachel has been teaching 5-year-old Zane to count by pointing to each block and saying the counting words, "One, two, three,

executive functioning
a set of cognitive skills involved in planning, inhibition, concept formation, and reasoning

intellectual disability
significantly subaverage intellectual functioning existing concurrently with deficits in adaptive behavior and manifested during the developmental period; adversely affects a child's educational performance; term used previously was *mental retardation*

adaptive behavior
skills children learn to function in everyday life, including language, social skills, and skills relevant to activities of daily living

short-term memory
information stored for a few seconds to a few hours

four, five." At the end of the counting session, Zane is able to point and count to five. When asked, "How many blocks all together?" Zane responds, "Five!" The next day when Rachel prepares to practice the counting lesson using toy animals, she discovers that Zane is unable to repeat the counting task from the previous day. She recognizes that Zane associates the counting task with blocks, but he cannot generalize the process when using new props.

Classroom Management Strategies Children with intellectual disabilities vary greatly in the supports needed for successful inclusion in the classroom. Some children may need assistance with many aspects of their participation and to ensure that they are sufficiently supervised for safety. A classroom education assistant may be needed to support and teach the child individually in the larger class group. Children with milder intellectual disabilities may require more modest assistance and can be supported by adapting the typical curriculum. Adaptations may include offering a slower pace so that children can explore and try new concepts and providing more specific guidance to ensure that children understand directions.

For very young children, the focus in the classroom is on developing social interaction and self-help skills. This includes providing specific guidance or age-appropriate modeling and "lessons" about topics such as how to ask for help, how to express needs, how to share a toy, and how to wash hands and serve food. For older children, the focus in the class moves toward developing communication and personal care skills and academic skills such as reading, writing, and basic math.

Lead Exposure and Poisoning

Lead poisoning is a condition caused by ingestion or inhalation of lead. Lead is toxic to most body systems especially the nervous system. Lead can build up in the body over time, causing lead poisoning that can lead to cognitive impairment in young children. Most children with lead exposure or poisoning do not have symptoms. But if they do, symptoms include gastrointestinal complaints such as loss of appetite, nausea, vomiting, abdominal pain, or constipation. At high levels of exposure, lead poisoning can be lethal and result in **encephalopathy**, brain injury due to a toxin or an infection.

encephalopathy
brain injury due to a toxin or an infection

The most adverse effect of lead poisoning is on cognition and intelligence. However, lead can have adverse effects on multiple systems in the body. Lead poisoning is preventable. During the past few decades, the Centers for Disease Control has lowered the acceptable threshold of levels of lead in the blood, stating that no level of lead in blood is safe and the primary focus should be on prevention.

Young children are at risk for lead exposure because of their mouthing behaviors and because they absorb and retain more lead relative to their body weight compared with adults. Children who are not well nourished and have nutritional deficiencies, such as a child with an iron deficiency, may be at increased risk for lead poisoning. Lead poisoning is diagnosed through blood testing that is obtained because of concern that the child was at risk for exposure. The prevalence of high lead levels in children ages 1 to 5 is about 1.6%. The primary sources of lead are the following (Ball, Bindler, & Cowen, 2012):

- Lead paint (banned in 1978) present in buildings or homes. Paint may chip, and children can ingest or inhale particles.
- Airborne lead from gasoline that has contaminated soil.

- Parental occupations/hobbies (plumbing, battery manufacturing, furniture refinishing, pottery).
- Water from lead pipes.
- Toys.

Classroom Management Strategies Early childhood settings can contribute to prevention of lead poisoning primarily by:

- Establishing classroom environments that reduce exposure to lead.
- Administering lead exposure questionnaires to identify children who may be at risk for lead exposure.
- Educating families about the dangers of lead exposure.

Children who may have been exposed to lead sources should be referred to their primary care provider or public health department for further evaluation.

Spina Bifida

spina bifida
a defect of the vertebral column or spine causing the contents of the spinal cord/nervous tissue to protrude

Spina bifida is a defect of the vertebral column, or spine, that causes the contents of the spinal cord nervous tissue to protrude and consequently fail to develop normally. This is also known as neural tube defects. It occurs very early in prenatal development, just weeks after conception. Folic acid deficiency is thought to be associated with spina bifida, and in 1998, the U.S. Department of Agriculture mandated adding folic acid to enriched cereal grain products. Subsequent to fortification, the prevalence rate decreased by 31% and is now about 5 per 10,000 births (Centers for Disease Control and Prevention, 2014a). The degree to which spina bifida affects children's overall health depends on the location of the defect: The higher the defect in the spinal column, the more severe the effects.

Common health issues associated with spina bifida include (Heward, 2013):

hydrocephalus
too much fluid in the chambers of the brain, requiring a shunt

- **Hydrocephalus** (too much fluid around the brain, requiring a shunt).
- Seizures.
- Varying degrees of paralysis of lower limbs.

catheterization
process of placing a small tube through the urethra into the bladder for the removal of urine

- Varying degrees of bladder and bowel control; some children may require intermittent **catheterization** of the bladder, a process by which a small tube is placed by the caregiver or child through the urethra into the bladder to remove urine.

Children may require surgery soon after birth to close the gap in the spine. Surgery may also be needed to manage problems with the feet, hips, or spine. Some children may need assistive supports for walking, such as crutches, leg braces, or wheelchairs. It is common to have trouble with bladder and bowel control. They may experience problems with perceptual motor skills; cognitive skills such as attention, memory, sequencing, and organization; and hyperactivity or impulse control.

Classroom Management Strategies Supporting children with spina bifida in the classroom requires that teachers have an understanding of the child's strengths and needs, medical support requirements, and strategies that support inclusion. Details of a child's condition are often determined through psychological and neuropsychological evaluations. Findings of these assessments guide the development of the child's IEP. Teachers work in partnership with the child's medical provider, early interventionists, and families to identify goals and to plan adjustments in the classroom.

The physical spaces need to be reviewed to ensure that children will be able to move throughout the classroom and access the outdoor play area. Children may need to be oriented carefully to the schedule and routines and provided extra time and support when changes in the routine must be made. Some medical supports may be required, such as periodic catheterization to ensure children's bladder health. More than half of children with spina bifida will develop a latex allergy, so it is important to keep the classroom latex free, including gloves, balloons, and other toys (Ball et al., 2012).

The IEP provides focus for teaching, such as needed skills in verbal communication, social skills and behavior management, motor skills, and academic areas. As with all children with special health needs, the focus in the classroom is on assisting the child to experience positive social interactions with other children and to be a part of all classroom activities.

CLASSROOM CONNECTION

Watch this video about Carly, a young child born with a genetic condition. What kinds of accommodations could be used in the classroom to promote Carly's health and wellness?

Conditions That Are Genetic

Genes influence most aspects of health. For example, children with certain genes are more prone to develop allergies or asthma. Other health conditions are caused by defects in specific genes. These conditions may or may not be inherited. In this section, we discuss some of the conditions that have strong genetic connections, including cystic fibrosis, sickle cell anemia, diabetes mellitus, and others.

Cystic Fibrosis

Cystic fibrosis (CF) is an inherited disease that affects the lungs and digestive system. A defective gene causes the body to create thick, sticky mucus that clogs the lungs and obstructs the digestive process. This results in progressive respiratory and nutritional problems that lead to severe respiratory infections and premature death. In addition to the chronic respiratory problems, children with CF tend to exhibit poor growth and malnutrition due in part to insufficient pancreatic function.

cystic fibrosis
a genetic condition causing chronic pulmonary infections, growth failure, and premature death

CF is most common among Caucasians, occurring in 1 in 3,200 live births. Among African Americans, CF occurs in 1 in 15,000 births; among Asians, the rate is 1 in 31,000; and in Hispanics, it is 1 in 7,000 (Ball et al., 2012). Cystic fibrosis is often diagnosed before age 2, largely because of newborn screening (Paranjape & Mogayzel, 2014).

Children with CF display a number of symptoms:

- Persistent coughing, occasionally spitting up thick mucus.
- Shortness of breath and wheezing.
- Frequent lung infections.
- Poor growth and delayed weight gain.
- Difficulty with bowel movements or frequent greasy stools.

Children with CF typically undergo therapy during which the chest is vigorously thumped to dislodge mucus. This kind of treatment may be required during the day. They may also require frequent courses of antibiotics that are sometimes given intravenously. This may or may not require hospitalizations.

In spite of a good appetite, children with CF need to consume a large number of calories to keep up with nutritional requirements because they have significantly increased energy expenditures from respiratory effort. They are typically treated with medications, including inhalers to improve breathing and pills that help them digest food.

Classroom Management Strategies Most children with CF are eligible for services under the IDEA. Teachers work in partnership with medical providers, early interventionists, and parents to support the inclusion of children with CF in the classroom. Understanding the effects of the disease helps to identify appropriate supports. For example, it is important to recognize that children with CF need to cough frequently and are highly susceptible to respiratory infections.

Administration of medication may be required. Time should be provided to administer or allow the child to take the medication and to conduct activities or treatments to clear the airway. An appropriate space should be identified to help the child feel comfortable.

An emergency medical response plan should be drafted to provide appropriate response when needed. Regular attendance may be an issue for children with CF depending on the severity of the disease. For school-age children, teachers work with families to optimize learning by arranging appropriate homework so that the children can make up the work they missed.

Sickle Cell Anemia

sickle cell anemia
an inherited disorder of red blood cells that causes chronic anemia, pain, and susceptibility to infection

Sickle cell anemia is a genetic condition that is inherited from both parents. It affects the integrity of red blood cells, causing them to have a much shorter life span than they would normally and to be *sickle*-shaped, hence the name of the condition. The condition leads to anemia, chronic pain, and susceptibility to infections. It is most common in African American children.

The severity of the disease varies and has improved with earlier diagnosis due to newborn screening, antibiotics, and parent education. The chronic anemia that occurs with sickle cell anemia can lead to developmental delays if not carefully managed. The disease is also characterized by acute pain crises that can be precipitated by dehydration and cold weather. The symptoms include pain, swelling of joints, or abdominal pain. A child with a sickle cell crisis needs urgent medical attention. Many children require blood transfusions and hospitalizations to treat complications of the condition.

Classroom Management Strategies The teacher's main role will be to report any complaints of pain or other physical health problems to the parents and school nurse, if appropriate. Children with sickle cell anemia may also miss school days due to illness or hospitalizations, and special considerations should be made to help them make up work. In addition, chronic pain can cause poor peer relationships and problems with self-esteem. Teachers can be an important support system for children and families.

Diabetes Mellitus

diabetes mellitus
a disorder of insulin metabolism causing long-term health problems

insulin
hormone secreted by the pancreas that is essential for the metabolism of glucose and fat

Diabetes mellitus is a chronic medical condition that occurs when the body does not produce or appropriately use **insulin**. Insulin is a hormone that breaks down sugars, starches, and fats into food energy. The body's failure to produce insulin results in elevated blood glucose levels, which has detrimental impacts on the body's organ systems. Left untreated or poorly managed, diabetes can result in many long-term health consequences, including nerve damage, loss of vision, kidney failure, heart problems, circulatory problems that may require amputation, and early death.

Type 1 Diabetes Type 1 diabetes is brought about by a combination of genetics and immunity. Individuals with certain types of genes are prone to develop diabetes. The condition develops when these individuals experience an **autoimmune condition** that causes them to develop antibodies against their own pancreas, resulting in the destruction of cells that produce and secrete insulin. Without sufficient insulin, body cells are not able to use glucose (sugar) to fuel the body. Children with Type 1 diabetes require administration of insulin through injection or through an insulin pump.

Children who develop diabetes tend to become ill very quickly. Symptoms include:

- Frequent urination.
- Excessive thirst.
- Fatigue.
- Irritability.
- Blurred vision.

In the early childhood setting, children with diabetes may have a noticeable increase in frequency of urination, requiring more frequent diaper changes, or urinary accidents.

Careful management of diabetes and a healthy lifestyle reduce the impact of the disease and improve children's long-term outlook. Treatment involves testing blood sugar levels, administering injections of insulin, and offering a specialized diet and exercise program. Eliminating the need to administer injections, many children now wear an insulin pump that injects insulin. A nutritionally balanced diet is needed, and aspects of the diet must be monitored, such as the kinds and amounts of foods eaten and the timing of meals and administration of insulin injections.

After diagnosis, children with diabetes and their families require a good deal of support and education about the disease. It can sometimes take several weeks to months to establish a treatment regimen, which may be frustrating for families and caregivers. In addition, as children grow, their regimen will change based on changes in caloric intake, physical activity, and rate of growth. For these reasons, children with diabetes require careful monitoring by their medical provider as well as a specialist in diabetes management. See this chapter's *Progressive Programs & Practices* feature for an interesting case scenario involving a child with Type I diabetes.

Type 2 Diabetes Type 2 diabetes results from the body's inability to use insulin properly so that the body becomes resistant to insulin. Compared with Type 1, this type of diabetes is less common among young children. Type 2 diabetes typically occurs in later childhood and among older people who are obese and who have a strong family tendency toward Type 2 diabetes. Type 2 diabetes is influenced by a family history of diabetes, obesity, and sedentary lifestyle. Some racial groups are at greater risk for developing Type 2 diabetes, including African Americans, Hispanic/Latino Americans, American Indians, and some Asian Americans and Native Hawaiians or other Pacific Islanders.

Establishing healthy nutritional and physical activity habits early are prevention efforts that may reduce the incidence of Type 2 diabetes. Although this condition is uncommon during the early childhood years, it is important for teachers to understand that the habits and sequence of events leading to the condition begin in early childhood. Besides the prevalence of Type 2 diabetes increasing in children, the average age of onset is becoming younger and disproportionately affects minorities (Dileepan & Feldt, 2013).

autoimmune condition causes individuals to secrete antibodies against their own organs

PROGRESSIVE PROGRAMS & PRACTICES

Accommodating Nate (Type 1 Diabetes)

By Jamie M. Wincovitch, Classroom Teacher at the University Child Development Center, University of Pittsburgh

The University Child Development Center (UCDC), a laboratory school at the University of Pittsburgh, serves children from birth to 5 years of age. We have approximately 160 families at any given time with 12 classrooms.

What challenge did you face?

We had a 2-year-old enrolled who was energetic, full of life, and an amazing communicator. While in a toddler classroom, he started to show symptoms uncharacteristic of his typical behavior. He was easily fatigued, was using the bathroom excessively, and had excessive thirst. Soon after, Nate was diagnosed with Type I diabetes.

How did you meet the challenge? What was the teachers' role?

Nate used an insulin pump (a small battery-operated insulin-delivering device, worn on a belt or in a pocket, with a narrow plastic tube inserted just under the skin and taped in place). All carbohydrates he consumed had to be counted. Although the pump then calculated how much insulin to deliver, a teacher had to decide how much would be delivered immediately and how much would be distributed over time, depending on the fat content and nutritional makeup of the food consumed. The classroom teachers were trained extensively by the parents and the Children's Hospital of Pittsburgh on how to make these decisions and care for a child with these diverse needs.

Initially, teachers were nervous about this responsibility, but over time, the process of caring for Nate became second nature.

I actually prided myself in my newfound ability to know the carbohydrate count of almost any amount of any food.

To create a classroom climate that was inclusive, we aimed to provide Nate with care that didn't make him feel "different." For example, we put Velcro name stickers on chairs for assigned seating that changed daily. This ensured, discreetly, that Nate was always near a teacher so that she could monitor food intake without forcing him to sit by a teacher every day while other children had free choice. We eat family style, so children are able to scoop their own food onto their plates. We replaced all serving spoons with measuring cups so that Nate didn't feel isolated when a teacher recorded how much he consumed.

Nate's blood sugar level had to be tested every few hours (typically five or six times a day), which required pricking his finger with a pin, squeezing a small amount of blood onto a glucose testing strip, and inserting it into a blood glucose meter. Nate was very cooperative and verbal, excellent at telling us how he was feeling, which helped notify us of his changing needs.

What was the outcome?

This all sounds so intense and medical, but in reality, Nate was a typical preschool child with typical preschool needs. He sometimes struggled resting quietly at nap time, he loved anything math, and he loved being silly. Yes, the medical part was always present, but as teachers, we worked really hard at making sure Nate was thought of as a preschooler (with Type 1 diabetes), *not* a diabetic kid. It makes a *big* difference!

Classroom Management Strategies Children with diabetes typically require no special adjustments for participation in the classroom and academic success. The medical management of the disease in the classroom is the most important area of focus. Management of diabetes requires a clear understanding of the child's medical protocols. Teachers require training on how to test blood sugar levels, how to adjust the kinds and quantities of food served, how to administer insulin injections, and how to recognize and manage emergencies such as administering glucagon treatments. A medical provider directs these practices. Teachers should receive formal training and supervision as they implement the child's medical plan. Two complications are important to recognize for management of diabetes:

hypoglycemia
a low blood glucose level measuring less than 50 to 60 mg/dl

- **Hypoglycemia** occurs when the blood sugar level is low (less than 50 to 60 mg/dL). It can be caused by missing or delaying meals, taking too much insulin, or exercising strenuously (Heward, 2013). Symptoms include faintness, dizziness, blurred vision, drowsiness, nausea, and irritability. Treatment entails giving the child concentrated sugar such as a sugar cube or a glass of fruit juice.

- **Diabetic ketoacidosis (DKA)** is a common but life-threatening complication of diabetes. It occurs when blood sugar levels remain high over a period of time as a result of insufficient insulin or sometimes due to illnesses. Symptoms include elevated blood sugars, excessive thirst and urination, unusual odor to breath (smells like acetone/nail polish remover), and lethargy or weakness. Emergency medical personnel should be contacted immediately if DKA is suspected.

The demands of diabetes often influence children's social and emotional well-being, affecting their learning and peer relationships. Table 11-4 shows guidelines that were established by the American Diabetes Association to optimize diabetes care in schools.

Down Syndrome

Down syndrome is one of the most common causes of intellectual disability. Down syndrome is also known as trisomy 21 because it occurs when the child has an extra 21st chromosome. Children with this condition usually have some degree of cognitive impairment; reduced muscle tone; and characteristic facial features such as almond-shaped eyes, small chin, and flat nasal bridge. Children with Down syndrome often suffer from associated health problems, including:

- Congenital heart disease.
- Gastrointestinal abnormalities.
- Leukemia.

diabetic ketoacidosis (DKA)
a life-threatening complication of diabetes that occurs when blood sugar levels remain high over some period of time

Down syndrome
a genetic condition whereby an individual's 21st chromosome has an extra segment, causing increased risk of heart problems, cognitive impairment, and short stature

TABLE 11-4 Diabetes in the Early Childhood Setting

Guideline	Details
Medical Management Plan	• Developed by the child's personal diabetes health care team along with parents • Provides instructions for glucose monitoring; insulin administration; and amount, type, and frequency of meals and snacks • Defines symptoms and treatment for hypoglycemia and hyperglycemia • Provides guidelines for physical activity • Provides instructions for emergencies
Parent Responsibilities	• Provide materials such as insulin, other medications, equipment needed for glucose monitoring, etc. • Provide supplies to treat hypoglycemia • Provide emergency phone numbers • Provide information about meals and snacks
School/Teacher Responsibilities	• Provide appropriate training for persons responsible for child • Ensure accessibility to insulin and meals/snacks as defined in medical plan • Ensure accessibility to trained individual in the case of hypoglycemia • Have backup staff available who are trained to assist child in case the usual teacher or nurse is not available • Allow student to see nurse upon request • Provide opportunity for child to eat snack anywhere if necessary to prevent hypoglycemia • Allow student to go to bathroom or get water if necessary • Provide a plan for disposal of needles
Student Responsibilities	• Toddlers/Preschool age: Need an adult to provide all aspects of diabetes care. Involve the child in decisions such as which finger to poke • Elementary age: May be able to check their own glucose but need supervision. Some older children may be able to give themselves insulin

Source: American Diabetes Association, 2013.

Children with Down syndrome have characteristic facial features.

- Alzheimer's disease at an early age.
- Immune problems.
- Thyroid problems.
- Problems with hearing and vision.

Children with Down syndrome are typically social and friendly. They usually experience delays in speech and communication. Although children may understand much of what they hear, their ability to articulate a response and produce understandable speech may be impaired. Motor skill development is also typically delayed. Cognitive challenges related to problem solving and reasoning are evident.

Classroom Management Strategies Children with Down syndrome are eligible for services through the IDEA. Often an educational assistant is assigned to support the child with Down syndrome along with other children with special needs in the classroom. Teachers should be well oriented to the child's IEP goals and strategies for successful inclusion. Children with Down syndrome benefit from inclusive learning activities. The use of visual cues is another important strategy to guide children to develop self-help skills and to reinforce verbal messages. Activities should be planned to help children build fine motor skills and to improve gross motor coordination.

Children with Down syndrome are often exceptionally sensitive to the visual cues and responses of others. They may be quick to recognize disapproval and are sensitive to failure, which may cause them to avoid situations that may be difficult. Teachers should provide tasks with appropriate challenge and supportive encouragement.

Muscular Dystrophy

Muscular dystrophy (MD) refers to a group of genetic diseases that cause deterioration of the muscles resulting in progressive weakness, susceptibility to pulmonary infections, and premature death. It is a relatively rare disease that is diagnosed in 500 to 600 newborns each year. The most common type of MD is Duchenne's. It results from a genetic mutation that is linked to the X chromosome, causing the absence of a protein needed to maintain the integrity of muscle. It only affects males, although females can be carriers of this gene defect.

Initial symptoms of MD are weakness of the lower extremities, which becomes evident in early childhood, usually by 2 to 6 years of age (Heward, 2013). Families or teachers may notice that the child has enlarged calf muscles, walks on his toes, falls more than other children his age, or has difficulty climbing stairs (Ball et al., 2012; Heward, 2013). Typically by the middle of the teenage years, the child is unable to walk. Life expectancy is in the twenties.

Treatment for MD focuses on maintaining as much function as possible. Physical, respiratory, and speech therapies may be offered. Assistive devices are used to support mobility. Some drug therapies may be used.

Classroom Management Strategies Teachers work with early intervention specialists and families to identify the IEP goals for children with MD. Attention to

WHAT IF . . .

a child in your classroom has Down syndrome? How would you plan ways to educate the class about this child's condition? What resources would you use to guide your planning? What would be your goals for this activity?

the physical environment is important to allow the child to move easily about the classroom and play yard. Adaptive equipment may be used to support the child's movement. Here is an example:

Lyle moves with the assistance of an electronic wheelchair. His teacher, Nancy, rear-ranges the furnishings in her classroom to open pathways for Lyle to move to each activity area. She creates a large open area in the center of the classroom so that he can participate easily at group time. At age 3, he is very efficient navigating through the space. His wheelchair has a special attribute that allows him to lower the seat so that he is sitting on the floor. This makes it easy for him to build block structures with his friends and to be at the same height as the other children during group time.

Despite physical health problems, children with MD should receive regular physical therapy and exercise. Outdoor play areas that have firm surfacing are especially important for children who have mobility problems. Teachers are cautioned never to lift these children by the arms because of the increased likelihood of joint dislocations (Heward, 2013). The teacher should provide small motor activities with pieces that come in a range of sizes. This allows the child to select the objects that best fit his ability to grasp and move. Encouraging activities such as washing hands, brushing teeth, and gathering pictures and personal belongings at the end of the day helps the child develop organizational and self-help skills.

Seizure Disorders

Seizures are a sign of a brain problem. They occur when the electrical activity in the brain is abnormal. Seizures are the most common pediatric neurological disorder, and they are caused by high fevers, medicines, injuries to the head, and some diseases. Most seizures are relatively harmless, lasting from a few seconds up to two minutes. Seizures that last more than five minutes are a medical emergency. The types of seizures vary as follows (Ball et al., 2012):

- **Partial seizures** are caused by abnormal activation of a limited number of neurons. Children may have twitching or jerking of only part of their body, one extremity, or the face. These seizures may or may not impair consciousness.
- **Generalized seizures** involve a global, or total, abnormal activation of all neurons. These seizures do impair consciousness. In the past, these were called *grand mal seizures.*
- **Absence seizures** cause frequent, abrupt, but brief losses of consciousness often accompanied by eyelid flickering. In the past, these were referred to as *petit mal seizures.*

Febrile Seizures Some seizures such as **febrile seizures** may not represent a seizure disorder. They are caused by fever and occur with the sudden rise in body temperature associated with acute illness. They are usually brief, lasting one to two minutes, and are more common among children between 6 months and 3 years of age with a peak incidence of 18 to 24 months. One-third of children who experience a febrile seizure will have another one (Ball et al., 2012).

Although most febrile seizures do not indicate an underlying problem or a serious infection, they can be a frightening experience for teachers and families. Families should be notified immediately if a child experiences a febrile seizure. A clear description of the event is important for families and medical providers. Because of the risk of recurrence, it is important to control any future fevers. Febrile seizures tend to diminish with age, and prognosis is excellent.

partial seizures
seizures caused by abnormal activation of a limited number of neurons; symptoms typically are related to where the focus is located

generalized seizures
seizures caused by global abnormal activation of all neurons

absence seizures
frequent, brief, abrupt losses of consciousness

febrile seizures
seizures caused by fever

HEALTH HINT   Chronic Medical Conditions Have an Impact on Children's Lives

Chronic medical conditions such as epilepsy can have a strong impact on the life of families. For example, children with epilepsy have a higher risk of mental health conditions, including behavioral disorders, anxiety, and depression. Epilepsy is stressful for families, especially at onset. Parents report a high level of stress and worry associated with watching their child seize. In addition, the unpredictable nature of epilepsy can add to the worry. Families may wonder what would happen if their child had a seizure at school.

Children with epilepsy also have more problems with academics, even children with normal intelligence. Medications have been proposed as a possible cause, but this theory has not been substantiated by research. Families of children with special health care needs must have support and understanding from teachers to assure them that their child is safe and secure. Teachers can carefully document the child's history and indicate what to do if the child experiences an event or worsening of the condition at school. This not only ensures that proper treatment is given, but also comforts the family and helps relieve their stress.

epilepsy
a chronic seizure disorder that is defined by having two or more unprovoked (not febrile) seizures

Epilepsy A chronic seizure disorder known as **epilepsy** is defined by having two or more unprovoked, not febrile (fever), seizures. Epilepsy may be caused by problems in brain development, illness, or injury, but in some cases, the cause is not known. Epilepsy occurs in about 1% of the population. This chapter's *Health Hint* discusses how epilepsy and other chronic health conditions can have an impact on children's lives and be associated with psychosocial issues.

Classroom Management Strategies A seizure care plan needs to be in place for any child with seizure disorders. Chapter16 discusses the management of seizures in the classroom. A seizure care plan should include the following information:

- Type and description of the child's seizures.
- Current treatment regimen including medications, schedule, doses, route of administration, and side effects.
- Restrictions from activities including those that could be dangerous to the child should the child have a seizure during the activity and any activities that could precipitate a seizure.
- How to recognize a seizure and recommendations for first aid should a seizure occur.
- Guidelines on when emergency medical help should be obtained for the child.
- Plan to document seizures if they occur, including type/frequency of seizures, how the seizure was managed, any relevant observations.
- Plan to support the family of a child with epilepsy.

Teachers also need to be oriented to any medications that need to be given, and a medication administration plan must be in place. Often medication is not given unless the seizure lasts a certain amount of time, typically minutes. This should be defined by the child's health care provider.

valium
a medication that can be given rectally in the case of acute seizures

Valium is a medication that is often used for acute seizures. It is administered rectally. Teachers follow the protocol for contacting emergency medical services as directed by the medical provider. Management of a seizure disorder may change frequently, especially in young children, requiring the care plan to be reviewed and updated.

Conditions Affecting Communication, Hearing, and Vision

communication
the exchange of ideas, feelings, needs, and desires

Some medical conditions involve the ability to communicate and the use of the hearing and vision sensory systems. **Communication** refers to the exchange of ideas, feelings, needs, and desires (Heward, 2013). It occurs through a variety of avenues including verbal language, facial expressions, written language, body language, and sign language. Effective communication is necessary for all aspects of daily life. Children begin communicating as young infants and progress rapidly in the first few years of life. It is during this time that communication disorders may become apparent.

A **communication disorder**, as defined by the American Speech-Language-Hearing Association (ASHA), is "an impairment in the ability to receive, send, process, and comprehend concepts or verbal, nonverbal, and graphic symbols systems" (Heward, 2013, p. 283). Conditions affecting hearing and vision can have an adverse impact on aspects of communication. A child born with hearing loss may have difficulty with normal language development. A child with visual problems may not be able to express some forms of nonverbal language effectively. Although many conditions discussed in other sections of this chapter, such as Down syndrome, may involve communication problems, here we focus on children who have disorders specifically affecting communication, hearing, and vision.

communication disorder
an impairment in the ability to verbally or nonverbally exchange ideas, desires, or needs

Speech and Language Impairments

Speech is the aspect of language that is produced verbally. **Language** is a formal code developed by groups of people for the purpose of communication. Impairments in the speech and language systems interfere with communication. Communication disorders can be caused by damage to a specific organ or part of the body. More commonly, the cause cannot be attributed to any physical condition, and some researchers believe that environmental influences may play a role in some communication disorders (Heward, 2013).

speech
the aspect of language produced verbally

language
a formal code developed by groups of people for the purpose of communication

Estimates of the prevalence of speech and language impairments vary widely. Current estimates suggest that 2.5% of school-age children receive special education services for speech and language impairment. In addition, more than half of children receiving special education services for other diagnoses also receive speech and language services (Heward, 2013).

Speech Impairments The term *speech impairment* refers to problems in producing verbal speech. Three types of speech impairments are recognized (Turnbull et al., 2013):

- *Articulation disorders* affect the production of specific speech sounds. Articulation problems make it difficult to understand children's speech.
- *Fluency disorders* affect the rhythm or flow of speech. Stuttering is an example of a fluency disorder.
- *Voice disorders* cause problems with the quality or use of the voice. Voice disorders can cause chronic hoarseness or abnormalities in the air coming through the nasal passage. These disorders are less common in young children.

Language Impairments Language impairments are typically classified as receptive or expressive:

- **Receptive language disorders** are impairments in understanding language. Children with receptive language disorders may have difficulties following directions or understanding spoken language.
- **Expressive language disorders** are impairments in the expression of language, or the use of language to communicate. Expressive language disorders may cause children to use words or phrases incorrectly.

receptive language disorders
impairments in the understanding of language

expressive language disorders
impairments in the expression of language

Children with language impairments often have difficulty in school and with social development and peer relationships. They also tend to have more difficulties reading and writing (Heward, 2013).

FIGURE 11-3   Identifying Speech and Language Problems

The following indicate that a child needs further evaluation for a speech and language problem:

At < 12 months:
- Rarely requests attention or objects
- Does not use more than one consonant or vowel

12–18 months:
- Does not take turns using vocalizations or utterances
- Does not comprehend single words
- Does not follow one-step commands

18–24 months:
- Does not speak or sign 50 words by age 2
- By age 2, does not begin to use ≥2 word utterances
- Rarely initiates his own language (as opposed to imitating or echoing)

2–3 years:
- Does not engage in small conversations
- Uses only one verb

3–4 years:
- Persons outside the family unable to understand spoken language
- Little or no growth of vocabulary

5 years:
- Has deficits in intelligibility, simple communication with others
- Not interested in learning about printed concepts

Source: Wankoff, 2011.

CLASSROOM CONNECTION

Watch this video to see how a teacher works with a child who has speech and language delays. What strategies does she use to keep the child focused on the task?

Classroom Management Strategies Teachers play an important role in identifying children with speech and language impairments. Through interaction and observation, teachers are often able to identify speech and language problems that families may not recognize. In the home, it is not unusual for family members to understand the meaning of children's communication by using contextual cues and nonverbal styles of communication. In the classroom setting, a child's challenges with communication may be more evident. Figure 11-3 lists a number of red flags that cue teachers to recommend that children receive further evaluation for potential communication disorders.

Children with speech and language problems may be eligible to receive early intervention services. Teachers can integrate speech and language goals into the daily curriculum with the help of speech-language pathologists. Consider this example:

Nephi sets out a display of plastic snakes on the table. He invites Angie to inspect the toy snakes. First, they count the snakes, discovering that there are "seven snakes." Next, they inspect the designs on the toy snakes. Some have stripes and some have spots. They count the striped and spotted snakes and find that there are "four striped snakes and three spotted snakes." Through this game, Nephi helps Angie practice articulating the s sounds. They continue to add descriptive words that use the letter s sounds, such as "slithering snakes and silly snakes." As other children join the group, Nephi suggests that Angie tell the others how to play the counting game using the toy snakes.

Hearing Impairment

hearing impairment
a condition causing partial or complete loss of hearing

Hearing impairment is a general term that describes a decrease in ability to hear and discriminate among sounds. Although it is a frequently used term, many people in the Deaf community prefer *deaf* or *hard of hearing*. Two kinds of hearing impairment are most common:

conductive hearing loss
hearing impairment caused by damage to the middle ear or eardrum

- **Conductive hearing loss** refers to the type of hearing loss resulting from problems with the middle ear or eardrum and is usually milder than a sensorineural hearing loss.

SAFETY SEGMENT   Noise-Induced Hearing Loss in Children

Noise is an important preventable cause of hearing loss in children. Noise exposure destroys cells in the ear that are essential for hearing. Once lost, these cells cannot be regenerated. Noise is a growing concern because of the increasing prevalence of portable music and gaming devices used by children. Other sources of noise include concerts, airplanes, tools, power equipment, and guns. There is even more concern now with extended use of earpieces for iPods and other similar devices.

Research demonstrates that school-age children are at risk for some degree of hearing loss due to noise exposure. Although the degree of the hearing loss tends to be mild to moderate, it can create challenges for school-age children, particularly in noisy settings such as classrooms. In classrooms, even mild hearing loss may reduce how much a child hears and understands directions and lessons. Teachers can make an impact by:

- Recognizing when a child may be having trouble hearing and referring the child for evaluation.
- Advocating for and implementing policies restricting the use of portable devices and the use of earphones at school.
- Educating parents about noise as a prevalent and preventable cause of hearing loss.

Source: Ball, 2012.

- **Sensorineural hearing loss** refers to damage to the acoustic nerves that connect the ear to the brain or to damage to the inner ear organ called the cochlea. The cochlea is the organ responsible for hearing. This type of hearing loss is permanent and more difficult to treat. The sound of speech from children who have sensorineural hearing loss is often distorted.

sensorineural hearing loss damage to the acoustic nerves that connect the ear to the brain or damage to the inner ear organ called the cochlea

Hearing impairment is one of the most common birth defects. Three in 1,000 babies born in America are diagnosed with permanent hearing loss (Heward, 2013). Hearing loss can also develop during childhood and later in life. Hearing impairment can be caused by various factors including genetics, illness experienced by the mother during pregnancy, illness during childhood, and injuries. The use of certain medications may cause hearing loss, and some environmental conditions can negatively impact hearing. The *Safety Segment* discusses noise-induced hearing loss.

Early identification of hearing loss is important. Research demonstrates that children who are identified with hearing impairment prior to 6 months of age and who receive appropriate interventions have a better chance of developing normal speech and language. Because the early years are so important for the development of speech and language, all states are required to offer a **universal newborn hearing screen** prior to hospital discharge.

universal newborn hearing screen hearing test done soon after birth that detects hearing loss in newborns

Medical definitions of hearing impairment classify the degree of hearing loss on a spectrum from mild to profound. The following degrees of hearing loss describe the lowest range a child can hear. The following decibel level ranges describe degrees of hearing loss (Ball et al., 2012):

- 0–25 decibels (dB): No hearing loss.
- 26–40 dB: Mild hearing loss.
- 41–60 dB: Moderate hearing loss; most conversational speech sounds are missed.
- 61–80 dB: Severe hearing loss; no speech sounds can be heard at conversational levels.
- 81–90 dB: Profound hearing loss; no speech sounds are heard.
- >90 dB: Deaf; no sounds are heard.

After the newborn period, children typically do not receive a hearing screen at preventive health care visits until 4 or 5 years of age. Some early childhood programs incorporate hearing screenings as part of their health services for children and families.

Observation in the early childhood classroom is another way children may be identified. Teachers may notice symptoms of hearing loss or difficulties in the child's speech development that may suggest hearing impairment. Some children with hearing impairments may not manifest symptoms early in life and can exhibit typical development. This is why screenings are so important. Following are examples of behaviors according to age that may be of concern with regard to hearing impairment (Ball et al., 2012):

In young infants, teachers and families should be concerned if:

- There is no startle reflex or it is diminished.
- Child vocalizes very little or not at all.
- Child doesn't turn head toward sound by 3 to 4 months of age.

In preschool-age children, teachers and families should be concerned if:

- Child doesn't speak or cannot be understood.
- Child communicates mainly through gestures rather than speech.
- Child does not appear to be interested in playing with other children.

In school-age children, teachers and families should be concerned if:

- Child needs words to be repeated frequently.
- Child has problems speaking or has a monotone voice.
- Child prefers that music and TV be very loud.

Classroom Management Strategies Educational definitions of hearing impairment focus on the impact the hearing loss has on the development and use of speech and language as well as its effects on educational performance. The IDEA identifies two categories under which children may be eligible for services:

- "*Hearing impairment* means impairment in hearing, whether permanent or fluctuating, that adversely affects a child's educational performance but that is not included under the definition of deafness" (U.S. Department of Education, n.d.). A child with a hearing impairment can usually hear and respond to auditory stimuli including speech.
- "*Deafness* means a hearing impairment that is so severe that the child is impaired in processing linguistic information through hearing, with or without amplification, and that adversely affects a child's educational performance" (U.S. Department of Education, n.d.). A child with deafness is prevented from receiving nearly all forms of sound.

Children identified for services by the local education agency may enter the early childhood program with an outline of goals identified in the IEP. The child's IEP and the early intervention team will outline the focus for services in the classroom. The teacher needs to know the style of communication the child is using. Oral approaches include Listening and Spoken Language; visual and gestural systems include Cued Speech and American Sign Language. Some children use a total communication method that combines spoken language and American Sign Language. The use of sign language also supports the language development of typically developing children.

Families often have strong preferences for a particular mode of communication. Some may prefer the Total Communication method, when a child communicates with both spoken and signed language (Heward, 2013). Sometimes the disability of the child with hearing impairment can be "invisible." Hearing loss cannot be seen, and often children with hearing impairments blend into the classroom so easily that the teacher may forget the child's special health care need. Common strategies used to teach all young children are also appropriate for teaching children with hearing impairments. The focus on seeing and doing and engaging in activity-based learning are characteristic learning modes in early childhood that are also appropriate for children with hearing impairments.

Children with hearing impairments rely on their other senses, such as vision, to support learning. Because of their reduced ability to hear, they do not benefit from incidental conversations in the room. A review of the classroom noise level may be necessary to identify ways to reduce background noises. Facing the child when speaking and getting the child's attention before giving directions help to address this challenge. Speaking clearly and simply in a usual tone and volume and avoiding overly long and complex sentences are useful tactics when giving directions. Using appropriate facial expressions and gestures also helps to reinforce verbal messages, as do real-life pictures. The teacher's face and mouth should be clearly visible to the child who may support understanding by reading lips. Teachers also need to know how to check the child's amplification system (hearing aids), doing it *daily*, to ensure that it is working appropriately.

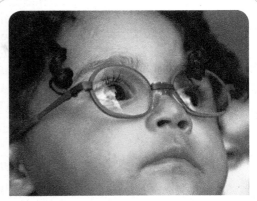

Children with visual impairments rely on their tactile and auditory senses to support learning.

Vision Impairments

The term *vision impairments* refers to conditions in which vision is reduced even when corrected with glasses or contact lenses. Genetics, birth defects, and eye disorders, as well as age-related eye disease, can cause vision impairments. Some of the common causes are refractory errors (nearsightedness and farsightedness), amblyopia, and strabismus. About 2.5% of preschoolers and over 3% of school-age children have vision problems (Ball et al., 2012).

Two kinds of vision impairment are typically recognized: low vision and blindness. These are identified using a test of **visual acuity**, a measure of how well a child can distinguish forms or discriminate details. This is typically assessed by having a child read letters, numbers, or symbols on an eye chart. The measure provides a pair of numbers that compare what the child can see against what a normal eye can see at 20 feet.

visual acuity
a measure of how well a child can distinguish forms or discriminate details

- A *normal eye* is scored at 20/20.
- *Low vision* is the term used for measures between 20/70 and 20/400.
- **Blindness** is identified at measures of 20/400.
- *Legal blindness* is measured at 20/200.

For example, a child with low vision (20/70) must stand 20 feet away from an object that a child with normal vision could see clearly at a distance of 70 feet.

blindness
vision of 20/200 or worse even with the best possible correction

Classroom Management Strategies Children with low vision may not be identified for services by the local education agency. Children with more significant vision loss and blindness are likely to be identified for service and will enter the early childhood classroom with an IEP. These children are likely to receive support services from a vision specialist in addition to the early childhood program, and the specialist may serve as a consultant for the child's teacher.

Children with visual impairments rely on their other senses to support learning. Children with low vision are able to use sight for some activities as well as sound and tactile exploration. For these children, it may be useful to assess the lighting in the classroom. Reducing glare and providing color contrasts in some materials may assist the child to discriminate among objects visually. Children who are blind rely primarily on tactile and auditory stimuli.

For children with both types of vision challenges, direct interaction with materials and objects is important to support learning. Sensory activities that allow them to gain vocabulary based on tactile stimuli are good choices. Placing ice cubes in the sensory table where children can feel them melting in warm water is a good way to introduce a discussion of temperature, melting and freezing, solids and liquids, and floating. It is important to maintain appropriate expectations for children with vision impairments so that they can be as independent as possible. Other ideas for support include these:

- Speak the child's name when addressing him or her in the classroom. Children with visual impairments may have a difficult time noticing eye contact.
- Name specific items and events rather than using pronouns such as *this* or *that*.
- Give verbal warnings prior to handing something to the child.
- Provide appropriate supports for mobility in the classroom.
- When physically showing a child how to do something, put the child's hand over yours rather than the other way around.
- Assign the child appropriate and meaningful classroom "jobs."
- Encourage cooperative group activities so that peer socialization skills can be learned.
- Remember safety while being careful not to overprotect the child.

Children with vision impairments may begin learning tactile codes such as Braille along with their early reading activities in elementary school. Specialized instruction of this kind is usually done by a teaching specialist.

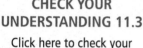

CHECK YOUR UNDERSTANDING 11.3

Click here to check your understanding of managing special health care needs.

SUMMARY

- The range of health care needs is broad and can impact many aspects of health, including activities of daily living, learning, and socialization. By understanding each child's special health care needs and planning strategies to maximize the child's functional status and capabilities, teachers can help children with special health care needs succeed in the classroom.
- Teachers are a critical part of identifying goals for inclusion and planning strategies to address these goals in the classroom.
- Because health care needs are so broad and each child has specific capacities, teachers many need to gain a renewed understanding of conditions as each classroom develops.
- Having a basic understanding of health care needs and planning classroom management strategies will enable teachers and families to enhance learning in the early childhood setting.

Chapter Quiz

 Click here to check your understanding of Chapter 11, Teaching Children with Special Health Care Needs.

Discussion Starters

1. How might teachers alleviate stressors that families experience when their children are enrolling in an early childhood program?

2. As a teacher of a toddler-age group, you notice a child displaying possible symptoms of autism. How do you approach the family with your concerns? How do you prepare for the meeting? To whom do you make a referral?

3. As a teacher in a second-grade classroom, you are teaching a child with a hearing impairment who requires hearing aids. He is able to speak, but the quality of his voice is obviously affected. Other children notice and ask why he sounds different than they do. How do you handle this situation?

Practice Points

1. Imagine that a child with Type 1 diabetes has enrolled in your third-grade classroom. You know that she checks her blood sugar during the day and receives insulin injections. What other information do you need as she begins attending? With whom might you collaborate in addition to her parents?

2. Often children who are suspected as having ADHD are evaluated by the school system before being evaluated by a medical professional. Who evaluates children in your school district? How is the diagnosis made?

3. Call your local health department and ask about the prevalence of lead poisoning in your area. Do preschools in your area conduct lead screening? If so, how?

Web Resources

Children and Adults with Attention Deficit/ Hyperactivity Disorder

Identify the Signs of Communication Disorders (American Speech-Language-Hearing Association)

Managing Asthma in the School Environment

National Survey of Children with Special Health Care Needs

Key Terms

absence seizures
adaptive behavior
albuterol
alcohol-related neurodevelopmental disorder (ARND)
anaphylaxis
Asperger's syndrome
asthma
asthma attack
attention deficit disorder
attention deficit/ hyperactivity disorder
autism
autoimmune condition
blindness
catheterization
cerebral palsy
children with special health care needs

communication
communication disorder
conductive hearing loss
cystic fibrosis
dental caries
diabetic ketoacidosis (DKA)
diabetes
Down syndrome
dyslexia
eczema
encephalopathy
executive functioning
expressive language disorders
cerebral palsy
fetal alcohol syndrome (FAS)
fluoride
functional limitations

functional status
gastrostomy tube
generalized seizures
hearing impairment
hydrocephalus
spina bifida
hydrocephalus
hypoglycemia
immune system
inclusion
inhaled corticosteroids
insulin
intellectual disability
language
learning disabilities
muscular dystrophy
nebulizer
partial seizures
people-first language

pervasive developmental disorder (PDD)
philtrum
receptive language disorders
sensorineural hearing loss
short-term memory
sickle cell anemia
spacer
speech
spina bifida
stimulants
tracheostomy tube
trigger
universal newborn hearing screen
valium
vision impairment
visual acuity
wheeze

Children's Mental Health

After reading this chapter, you should be able to:

1. Define mental health and discuss the biological, environmental, and developmental factors that influence mental health in young children.
2. Describe what skills are important for healthy social and emotional development and how early childhood programs can promote these skills.
3. Understand the prevalence, consequences, and academic characteristics of childhood mental health problems.
4. Discuss mental health disorders in children and identify teaching strategies for these children.

CASE STUDY

Parent and teacher conferences have been scheduled for the 2- to 3-year-old class group. Meegan is preparing to meet with Heather's parents. She has made a special effort to schedule the conference late in the day to be sure there will be enough time to discuss her concerns. Meegan is worried about how to talk about the behavior concerns she has observed. Heather's aggressive behavior against other children has not stopped in spite of Meegan's efforts to guide and teach her. Meegan has intervened more than once when Heather grabbed another child around the neck. One time Heather picked up a large block and hit the assistant teacher on the head, and during

group time, Meegan saw Heather hit Arturo in the face with her hand, without even turning to look at him.

Meegan believes the parents have also been experiencing difficult behaviors at home because they shared with her that they take the baby to the grandmother's house when they need to leave Heather at home with a caregiver. To prepare for the conference, Meegan has done some reading about social and emotional development and behavior and explored some of the services that are available in the community. She is uncomfortable about sharing the unpleasant observations she has made, but she is prepared and hopes that the conversation will go well so that she and the family can develop a plan to help Heather.

In this chapter, the terms *social and emotional development* and *mental health* are used interchangeably to represent a *positive* state of mental and emotional wellness in children. This highlights the understanding that just as teachers support children's physical health through purposeful practices, teachers also foster children's mental and emotional health through intentionally established environments and positive relationships and experiences that encourage healthy social and emotional development.

In this chapter, we focus on ways that teachers contribute to children's mental health. First, we define the terminology we will use to discuss children's mental health. We then provide an overview of healthy and typical social and emotional development. Next, we describe how healthy social and emotional development can be promoted in the classroom. Finally, we review some of the more common mental health disorders and provide guidance for partnering with families and mental health professionals to design successful interventions when children need special help. Focusing on children's mental health is an important teacher responsibility that builds foundations for children's future success and happiness.

UNDERSTANDING MENTAL HEALTH

The early years are a significant period for establishing wellness habits and patterns, including children's emotional health. Teachers are best prepared to impact children's emotional health positively by understanding mental health, what influences it, how it develops across the early years, and how to recognize typical social and emotional development.

Defining Mental Health

Mental health refers to children's abilities to understand and manage their emotions and behaviors and to have healthy relationships with others in age-appropriate and developmentally appropriate ways. Children attain mental health and wellness by reaching typical social and emotional developmental milestones, exhibiting healthy social skills, and demonstrating ability to cope with stress or problems (Centers for Disease Control and Prevention, 2015). Mental health is a positive term that refers to the presence of mental or emotional wellness and the absence of mental illness.

Social and emotional development is a part of human development. It is also linked to and is considered part of the **continuum of mental health**. Most early childhood sources consider social and emotional development and mental health to be synonymous, or one and the same. The promotion of mental health and the prevention of mental health problems begin in infancy or even earlier. Teachers should recognize, however, that poor social and emotional development does not automatically suggest that children have mental illness. However, children with atypical social and emotional development have a higher rate of poor health outcomes and higher rates of mental illness. The continuum of mental health includes behaviors that:

- *Demonstrate positive social and emotional development*, suggesting that the child is on course for positive outcomes.
- *Indicate problems with social and emotional development*, also called *mental health problems*, suggesting that further attention is needed to guide the child to more positive mental health habits.

mental health
the capacity to experience and manage emotions, form close and secure relationships, and learn and experience life in a healthy way

continuum of mental health
range of behaviors associated with positive social and emotional development, mental health problems, and mental illness

Paul Miller

Children benefit from learning adaptability, resilience, and flexibility in the early childhood years.

Positive experiences and interactions in the early years help children to form close and secure interpersonal relationships.

- *Imply potential underlying mental disorders*, or *illness*, suggesting that the child should be evaluated by a medical professional for possible mental health diagnosis and services.

When children exhibit behaviors that are typical for the child's age and developmental level, social and emotional development is usually on course. Behaviors that are not typical are more challenging to understand. They may indicate that a child is simply slower in this area of development at that particular time or that the child has not had sufficient experiences to practice and attain typical social and emotional skills. These challenging behaviors may also be a sign that the child is *at risk* for more serious problems over time. The most important point is that challenging behaviors be identified and managed early to prevent more serious problems later. The boundaries of what behaviors constitute appropriate and inappropriate development are further clouded based on the expectations of social behaviors in different cultures and neighborhoods. For example, behaviors that one group considers aggressive may be viewed by another group as a sign of strength.

In spite of the difficulties associated with defining what behaviors suggest mental health problems, teachers are responsible for managing children's behavior and advancing children's development. In this chapter, we explore these issues and offer a range of ways teachers play a role in fostering children's social and emotional development. As professionals, teachers remain informed of emerging information, partner with families, collaborate with mental health specialists if needed, and design and implement interventions to promote positive mental health.

Current Focus on Children's Mental Health

Mental health problems are an important health issue because of the prevalence and early onset. There is also a long-term impact on the child and family's well-being and an impact on community. Between 13% and 20% of families have a child with a mental health problem within a given year (Perou et al., 2013).

Data demonstrates an increase in the use of services for mental health disorders in children, indicating an increase in prevalence. The long-term impact involves very serious health issues, including suicide, substance abuse, criminal behavior, and inability to function effectively in society. Children with mental disorders typically have serious challenges at home, with peers, and at school (Perou et al., 2013). Early childhood teachers interact with many children and need special understanding about how mental health develops and how to support positive outcomes.

Influences on Children's Mental Health

Children's mental health is influenced by a variety of dynamics that can be apparent even in infancy. These include biological and environmental factors, which in turn impact social and emotional development.

Biological Factors

Biological factors are traits or characteristics that are specific to the individual child and are related to genetics and proper development of the brain. The importance of these factors begins in utero. Biological factors include:

- *Genetics,* or hereditary factors such as those that influence physical size and appearance and pace of development.
- *Temperament,* or the child's style and personality, often described as "easy," "slow to warm up," or "difficult."
- *Physical and health attributes,* such as physical anomalies and prematurity.
- *Type of nutrition,* including quality of food.
- *Brain development,* which is growth and development of the brain.

Brain development significantly influences children's mental health. Although the development of the brain begins at conception and does not end until adulthood, the fastest rate of growth is in utero and during the first few years of life. During this period, an incredible amount of information is learned and the structures for future learning are established.

Brain development is also strongly influenced by experiences with people and the environment. Interactions that are nurturing encourage brain cell development and refine brain cell connections, which set the foundation for positive social and emotional health. Persistent stressful experiences damage normal brain development, causing problems with learning, behavior, and physical and emotional health (Harvard University, n.d.).

These biological factors interact with environmental factors described below, creating either positive or negative influences on social and emotional development.

Environmental Factors

Children's social and emotional development is extremely vulnerable to environmental factors such as these:

- Family life situations, including stress, domestic violence, poverty, abuse, neglect, parental drug use or mental illness, quality of the nurturing relationship, and cultural influences on parenting.
- Community well-being, including community violence, accessible health care, and social service resources.
- Environmental toxins including chemicals such as mercury and secondhand smoke.
- Emotional and social influences such as quality of caregiver bonding and family interactions. Caregivers include parents and other family members such as grandparents, child care providers, and teachers.

Environmental factors such as adverse childhood experiences can exert a strong negative influence on children's social and emotional development. Adverse childhood experiences (ACEs) are events or stressors that infants and young children experience that later contribute to illness, poor quality of life, and death. The experiences are categorized as abuse, neglect, and household dysfunction. The more ACEs an individual has, the higher the likelihood of poor health outcomes, which include physical and mental health disorders. Figure 12-1 illustrates the ACEs

caregiver
persons who care for children, such as parents, family members, and child care providers

adverse childhood experiences (ACEs)
significant events or stressors that infants and young children experience that later contribute to physical and mental illness, poor quality of life, and premature death

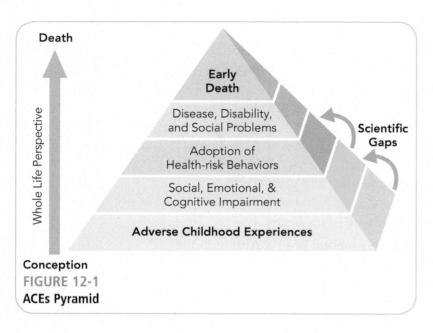

Death

Whole Life Perspective

Early Death

Disease, Disability, and Social Problems

Adoption of Health-risk Behaviors

Social, Emotional, & Cognitive Impairment

Adverse Childhood Experiences

Scientific Gaps

Conception

FIGURE 12-1
ACEs Pyramid

pyramid, which demonstrates how ACEs early in life leads to a number of consequences throughout the lifespan. This chapter's *Safety Segment* has more information about the effects of stress on the developing brain. Healthy interactions and relationships with teachers provide important opportunities for children to develop socially and emotionally.

Amaya, who teaches infants, knows that some people get frustrated with babies who cry. But she has a special affinity for infants and enjoys trying a variety of approaches to create a strong and positive bond with each child. She is usually highly successful in helping babies establish a strong attachment and develop alternative ways of communicating.

Characteristics of Healthy Social and Emotional Development

Social and emotional development begins at birth and progresses actively during the childhood and adolescent years. It is highly dependent on healthy interactions and relationships with people, including family members, teachers, and peers.

Children's social and emotional development occurs in a predictable pattern across the early years. They emerge through children's many interactions with their family, teachers, and classmates and according to their developmental readiness. Table 12-1 lists social and emotional milestones of infants from birth to 12 months of age. Characteristics of children 1 to 8 years of age are listed in Table 12-2. Overall, social and emotional development shows a progression from self-centered thinking to a greater understanding of being in relationships with others. Understanding the characteristic steps of social and emotional

toxic stress
stress that is strong, frequent and prolonged

SAFETY SEGMENT   The Role of Stress on the Developing Brain

Extensive research now demonstrates how stress can change the normal development of the brain and the body, leading to harmful effects on learning, behavior, and health. When children are exposed to stress, there are known physiological effects such as an increase in heart rate, increase in blood pressure, and increase in the secretion of stress hormones. The harmful effects of stress are diminished when the child has healthy, supportive relationships with adults.

Different kinds of stress have been described: positive stress, tolerable stress, and toxic stress. Positive stress is short-lived and moderate and gives the child an opportunity to practice how to manage stress. Stress can be positive when children have nurturing relationships with adults who support them. Tolerable stress is more significant and could cause harm if there

is no supportive relationship available to the child. Examples include death of a family member, a bad accident, or parental divorce. **Toxic stress** is strong, frequent, and prolonged. It occurs in situations when children do not have access to supportive relationships. When children experience toxic stress, it is thought that the neurons in the brain involved with fear, anxiety, and impulsivity are overproduced and neurons responsible for reasoning, planning, and control of behavior form fewer connections. This effect on the brain causes lifelong effects on mental health.

The most important aspect of preventing toxic stress or dealing with stress is the presence of positive relationships with caregivers. The effect of high-quality child care and caring teachers can also mitigate the stress that children experience in the early years.

Sources: National Scientific Council on the Developing Child, 2014; Shonkoff, 2012.

TABLE 12-1 Social and Emotional Characteristics of Infants Birth to 12 Months

Age	Characteristics
By 6 months	• Focuses on sights, sounds, interactions • Communicates needs through expressions, sounds, movements • Smiles and enjoys playful interaction • Develops attachment when needs are met
6 to 12 months	• Seeks interaction • Enjoys initiating and imitating sounds and actions • Responds positively to encouragement • Prefers familiar routines • Has preference for parent and regular caregivers • May be shy or anxious with strangers

Sources: Gerber et al., 2011; Trubo, 2014.

development helps teachers recognize behaviors that are age-appropriate and developmentally appropriate, providing information to guide the creation of focused and purposeful activities in the classroom.

Infants

Most healthy children are born with the drive to connect with others. The most critical earliest social milestone is bonding with a caregiver. **Attachment theory** refers to the process that occurs when an infant cries and the caregiver responds, resulting in the baby gaining confidence in the caregiver's ability to care for and respond to the

attachment theory process that occurs when an infant cries and the caregiver responds, resulting in the baby gaining confidence in the caregiver's ability to care for and respond to the child

TABLE 12-2 Social and Emotional Characteristics of Children Ages 1 to 8 Years

Age	Characteristics
1 to 2 years	• Communicates through both words and actions • Uses increasingly complex vocabulary • Identifies and communicates likes and dislikes • Expresses wide range of emotions • May struggle with emotions and behaviors in new settings • Enjoys interacting with toys • Sometimes cooperates; sometimes seeks to be independent • Plays alone and alongside others • Develops joint attention
3 to 5 years	• Begins to identify and talk about own emotions • May express fears or be concerned about "monsters" • Enjoys humor, including silly words and word games • May be self-centered but begins to show empathy for others • Responds well to routines; may need support to make changes • Engages in detailed make-believe play; may struggle with fantasy and reality • Expresses self through singing, dancing, arts and crafts • Seeks interaction with other children
6 to 8 years	• Uses language to share information and describe stories and events • Seeks independence, but still has fears • Develops a sense of right and wrong • Enjoys companionship with adults but prefers to play with other children • Wants to be liked and accepted by peers • Expresses personal interests and preferred play • Develops and repeats intricate play themes and rules of play • Plays cooperative games with designated rules

child (Gerber, Wilks, & Erdie-Lalena, 2011). Characteristics typical of the first year of life include:

- Developing a social smile.
- Imitating movements and facial expressions.
- Expressing communication with face and body.
- Responding to others' emotions and expressing joy often.

After 3 to 4 months of age, infants start becoming less interested in basic needs such as eating and sleeping and more interested in the world around them, providing more opportunities to strengthen relationships with caregivers. These signs of healthy development evolve from children's sense of safety and security. A sense of security emerges from the consistent caregiver's warm, affectionate tone; familiar routines; and positive social interactions.

joint attention
when a baby indicates that he or she wants to share an experience with the caregiver by pointing or drawing attention to something

During infancy, differences in children's temperaments may become more apparent and require that caregivers adjust their interactions for each child. Babies of all temperaments need to experience loving, responsive adults, but the manner in which the adults interact with them may be slightly different. For example, more energetic babies may need more patience and gentle guidance from caregivers, whereas calm, sensitive babies may need to be eased into contact with adults and other children (Trubo, 2014). By 12 months of age, most babies have developed **joint attention**, which is when a baby indicates that he or she wants to share an experience with the caregiver by pointing or drawing attention to something (Gerber et al., 2011).

Interruptions in normal development can result in significant problems during infancy. For example, infants who experience hardships or difficulties in attachment with the caregiver during this critical period are more likely to demonstrate abnormal expressions of emotions, inattention, and distractibility, disruptions in feeding and sleeping patterns, developmental delays, and abnormal relationships with their peers and caregivers as they grow older (National Scientific Council on the Developing Child, 2015). This highlights the need to focus on ensuring that infants establish a sense of safety, trust, and security as crucial elements of social and emotional development during the first year of life and beyond.

One to Two Years

During the second year of life, children develop an image of their social world, which includes family, friends, caregivers, and acquaintances. Children at this age view themselves to be at the center of the world. This view is described as being **egocentric**. Although other people interest them, children at this age have no idea how these people think or feel (Trubo, 2014). For example, 1- to 2-year-old children may play alongside others, but they do not yet interact with purpose or play cooperatively. Characteristics of social and emotional development during the second year of life include (Trubo, 2014):

egocentric
the perspective of viewing oneself as the center of the world

- Imitating behaviors of others.
- Being increasingly aware of self as separate from others.
- Being increasingly excited about being around other children.
- Demonstrating increasing independence.
- Beginning to show defiant behaviors.
- Showing more separation anxiety until midyear, when it fades.

Interest in exploration is a characteristic of children in the toddler years, creating a "pushing and pulling" situation that can seem confusing. These children desire more independence and may express defiance when exploration is hindered, while at the same time needing to be confident in the caregiver as a source of security. Exploration in toddlers can be encouraged by providing safe, adequate play areas; encouraging children's participation; and using language to label objects, pictures, and ideas. It is important to invite these young children into free exploration within established limits.

Children in this age group need clear and consistent guidance. Typical 2-year-old behavior includes challenges such as aggression. However, these interactions need to be redirected appropriately so that children learn how to manage their emotions. Focused approaches to guidance build on children's natural curiosity and tendency to explore while teaching appropriate boundaries. Teaching children the parameters for play, establishing clear limits for behavior, and guiding children appropriately without harsh punishment or scolding are important strategies that enhance social and emotional development.

Two to Three Years

During the third year of life, children continue to be concerned about their own needs. They are still developing awareness of others and may not understand how others feel. Characteristics of social and emotional development for this age group include:

- Exhibiting more sense of individuality.
- Demonstrating more advanced memory in certain areas.
- Growing in emotional understanding.
- Increasing interest in friendships.
- Increasing development of conscience (sense of right and wrong).

Playing imitation and pretend games are important to social development for this age group. Children 2 to 3 years of age tend to participate in parallel, or side-by-side, play unless they want to play with a toy that is being used by another child. However, it is common for 2-year-olds to look at their playmates and imitate them. These situations create important opportunities for children in this age group to explore concepts such as sharing, taking turns, and cooperating (Gerber et al., 2011). By 2½ years of age, they begin to use much more pretend play in their daily living.

Children at this developmental age seek autonomy and exhibit self-assertion. They are most concerned about their own needs and mostly cannot understand how others feel. These are complex challenges, and it is natural for children to struggle to maintain emotional balance. Negotiating a plan to share a toy may begin well, but when it comes to deciding who gets the toy first, the negotiation may result in frustration and impatience. A child might exclaim, "I *am* sharing, but I want to play with the truck first!" Emotionally, the 2- to 3-year-old period is characterized by mood swings, which are an indication that the child is trying to learn how to control actions, impulses, and feelings (Trubo, 2014).

It is natural for children in this age group to test limits and occasionally lose control. Managing their emotional impulses is difficult; thus, anger and frustration may quickly turn into crying, hitting, or screaming (Trubo, 2014). Understanding that such behaviors are part of children's natural struggle to gain social and emotional resiliency and competency in difficult situations is important as teachers implement guidance strategies.

Teachers can help children of this age develop healthy emotional skills by setting reasonable and consistent limits that allow children to understand the boundaries for actions and behaviors and begin to take charge of their actions. Offering appropriate encouragement and reinforcement for appropriate behaviors is important. Teachers also need to be prepared to redirect inappropriate behaviors and to

Learning to share is a stage in social and emotional development. Even when very young children agree to share, they may want the toy first.

Stockbyte/Getty Images

help children begin to understand how negative behaviors affect the children around them.

In the opening scenario, Meegan knows that Heather's aggressive behaviors in the classroom won't just go away. She understands that it is her responsibility to identify specific strategies to guide Heather to more appropriate behaviors. At the same time, Meegan knows that she must try to recognize and understand the challenges that may be limiting Heather's healthful development.

Three to Four Years

At ages 3 to 4 years, children's sense of identity and security is stronger and they become more interested in developing relationships with others. Characteristics of social and emotional development for 3- and 4-year-olds include:

- Exhibiting increased interest in interacting with others.
- Using language to communicate wants, needs, and ideas.
- Demonstrating greater ability to manage emotions and regulate behavior.
- Following rules and showing an interest in pleasing others.
- Taking part in more play that involves fantasy and pretend.
- Continuing to be interested in having a strong relationship with the teacher.

Children in this age group are increasingly interested in associative play, or playing alongside other children and engaging in a similar focus. For example, 3-year-olds might be observed building blocks side by side. They share the same materials and talk about what they are doing, but their play is essentially individual. During this time, children start to become more aware of the feelings and actions of others. They notice if another child is upset and can begin to recognize the consequences of their actions.

For example, when Lindsay asks Ben what will happen if he keeps pushing his truck against Karen's block tower, Ben is able to say, "It will fall down." Lindsay follows up by asking, "What do you think Karen thinks about that?" Three-year-olds are becoming more able to take turns; trade toys; and use fewer tactics such as grabbing, whining, and screaming to get what they want (Trubo, 2014). A vivid imagination begins to develop during this period, enabling children to explore a wide range of emotions including love, anger, protest, and fear. Imaginary friends are common, and children may shift rapidly from fantasy to reality. Children continue to need the support of teachers to understand the expectations of behavior and to help them learn ways of managing relationships and emotions.

Four to Five Years

Children become very social at ages 4 to 5 years. They begin to enjoy an active social life and may even have a *best* friend (Gerber et al., 2011). Friendships should be encouraged because these are key opportunities for children to practice the social and emotional skills that are involved in building and maintaining relationships. Characteristics of social and emotional development for this age group include:

- Focusing on social interactions.
- Practicing taking leadership roles.

- Exhibiting an increasing ability to understand the perspective of others.
- Demonstrating ability to focus on projects.
- Being literal with rules and needing support to understand flexibility.
- Taking part in more complex imaginary play.

Four- and five-year-old children begin to engage in cooperative play in which elaborate games and rules are established, roles are assigned, and the course of play involves negotiation and give-and-take situations. During this time, children develop increased sensitivity for the feelings of others. They are increasingly able to identify feelings and recognize the impact of their behaviors. Self-confidence is also developing, and children are ready for responsibilities that build their sense of competence, such as setting a table or cleaning a play area. This age group continues to need the support and guidance of teachers to ensure that all children are included in play and to find security in consistent expectations about behavior.

Five to Eight Years

Children in kindergarten and elementary school enter a time of industrious exploration of their world and interest in greater independence. Characteristics of social and emotional development for this age group include:

- Increasing interest in autonomy and independence.
- Continuing to judge self on how adults value and respond to what they do.
- Beginning to rely on peers for feedback about what is good and bad.
- Demonstrating individual skills and competencies.
- Communicating emotions, ideas, wants, and needs.

Children in this age group tend to become involved in projects and enjoy working on them over a period of days, seeing them through to completion. Children also begin to build friendships and social connections outside the family, developing friends in the neighborhood and class group.

Cooperative play evolves to a high level as 5- to 8-year-old children carry over play themes from one day to the next. A child may have several good friends, most often children of the same sex, and enjoy frequent contact and "play dates." This is also a time during which children may have heated disagreements that emerge and "blow over" quickly; the child who is an "enemy" on one day may be a "best friend" the next. Children are growing in their ability to understand the feelings of others. They are able to nurture younger children while looking up to older children as role models.

This age range is also a challenging "between" age. On the one hand, children ages 5 to 8 years are seeking greater independence and find pride in their emergent skills, which may be displayed by tattling when others break the rules or "pushing back" and showing resistance when given guidance. At the same time, they may still have youthful fears such as death, rejection, or failure, and they can be very sensitive to feedback.

PROMOTING SOCIAL AND EMOTIONAL DEVELOPMENT

Growing numbers of children spend many hours in early childhood settings during their early years, providing significant opportunities for teachers to promote positive social and emotional development. Programs that plan on supporting social

Pearson Education

CLASSROOM CONNECTION

Watch this video of young children displaying aspects of emotional development. How does the characteristic of self-awareness evident in this video contribute to mental health?

CHECK YOUR UNDERSTANDING 12.1

Click here to check your understanding of the biological, environmental, and developmental factors that influence mental health in young children.

and emotional development can contribute to better social skills and behaviors, fewer conduct problems, and improved academic performance (Kendziora, 2011). Creating appropriate environments, establishing positive relationships, and implementing strategies that specifically encourage social and emotional development equip children with the skills they need to be successful in school and in life.

Contributing to Healthy Social Emotional Development

Early childhood programs have an increased focus on learning skills that promote social and emotional development because these skills, in turn, promote future success in all aspects of life. These skills include but are not limited to establishing healthy relationships; self-concept; or self-awareness, self-regulation, and resilience.

Building Healthy Relationships

The relationships children have with their caregivers are critical, and to a large extent, they determine how children flourish later. As discussed previously, these relationships modulate stress hormones in the child. In addition to these relationships, the quality of early child care and education also play important roles in the stress hormone response (National Scientific Council on the Developing Child, 2014). As children enter and learn to participate in early childhood classrooms, they have opportunities to practice their social skills with people outside their families. Committed teachers such as Meegan in the opening case recognize the importance of these relationships and guide children in a way that enables them to grow and thrive. Teachers are also important observers and can communicate with families about the child's ability to form and negotiate friendships.

The Collaborative for Academic, Social, and Emotional Learning (CASEL) identifies relationship skills as one of the core competencies for health development. The goal is to help children maintain health and rewarding relationships by (Kendziora, 2011):

- Teaching cooperation.
- Teaching children to resist social pressure that is inappropriate.
- Prevent conflict in the classroom as much as possible.
- Help children manage and resolve conflict.
- Teach children to ask for help when needed.

Finally, skills and trust that children learn from healthy relationships help them acquire important skills, which are discussed in the next section.

Developing Self-Concept and Self-Efficacy

self-concept
awareness or idea of one's self

self-efficacy
set of beliefs an individual has about his or her capacity to pursue and complete tasks, activities, or other attainments

Self-concept is an awareness or idea of one's self. **Self-efficacy** is the set of beliefs an individual has about his or her capacity to pursue and complete tasks, activities, or other attainments. For children, it is the concept of *I can do it!* Together self-concept and self-efficacy help children develop a sense of who they are and what their purpose in the world is (a sense of identity).

Each day, children practice skills that can promote their sense of self. Teachers can contribute to these skills. Here are a few general concepts related to self concept and self-efficacy (U.S. Department of Health and Human Services, Administration for Children & Families, 2014):

- Develop a classroom that is welcoming for each child.
- Give children opportunities to share aspects of themselves and their families.

- Teach children independence with respect to activities of daily living.
- Help children develop a sense of accomplishment.

When children develop a positive self-concept, they can use other important skills more readily and they will exhibit greater success in both school and community. The *Teaching Wellness* activities provide ideas for setting the stage for children's understanding of their own competencies.

Teachers help young children gain social and emotional skills by setting reasonable limits and providing clear guidelines for behavior.

Developing Self-Regulation

Self-regulation is the ability to control one's emotions and to handle stress, the ability to develop impulse control, and the ability to develop perseverance. It is a process for young children to develop these skills, and as they enter kindergarten, they are expected to develop the capacity to regulate their impulses and emotions according to the rules of the new setting. For example, with a few gentle reminders, children in kindergarten are expected to learn to raise their hands and wait to be called on rather than calling out an answer to a question. Learning in the school setting relies on children being able to listen to and follow directions given by the teacher rather than rushing forward with the task.

Early childhood teachers can plan many activities to help children learn and practice self-regulation skills during the preschool years. For example, Su Lin recognized at the beginning of the year that many children in her class would run with excitement from one activity to another. She found that providing clear instructions and a predictable daily routine helped the children understand expectations. When they heard the five-minute warning bell, they were more able to stop their play and participate in cleanup time before moving on to the next activity of the day. Su Lin continued to offer specific instructions about appropriate behaviors to reinforce her expectations. Over the year, she noticed remarkable improvement. Children's ability to self-regulate enabled them to manage the tasks associated with learning and to develop positive social relationships successfully.

Developing Resilience

Resilience is an individual's ability to overcome stress and to adapt effectively to stress, adversity, or threats. It can also be defined as the ability to change toxic stress into tolerable stress (National Scientific Council on the Developing Child, 2015). As with other skills, resilience is acquired by experiencing supportive relationships early in life and is mitigated by intrinsic factors such as personality and temperament.

Despite adversity, many children still overcome and thrive and demonstrate resilience. Studies have shown that there are some common characteristics among those who overcome major challenges. These positive factors include (National Scientific Council on the Developing Child, 2015):

- Having at least one stable, nurturing relationship with a caregiver. Examples include parent, teacher, neighbor, and social workers.
- Helping children develop a sense of accomplishment.
- Helping children attain self-regulation and executive skills.
- Believing in cultural traditions or faiths.

CLASSROOM CONNECTION

Watch this video of a teacher helping Alec learn how to use an eyedropper. How do her skills help him develop self-efficacy?

self-regulation
the ability to control one's emotions and to handle stress, the ability to develop impulse control, and the ability to develop perseverance

resilience
individual's ability to overcome stress and to adapt effectively to stress, adversity, or threats.

TEACHING WELLNESS   I Can Do Things

LEARNING OUTCOME   To develop children's recognition of their own competence by guiding them to identify themselves realistically as people who can do things.

INFANTS AND TODDLERS

- **Goal:** Children experience the teacher describing the child's abilities.
- **Materials:** No materials are needed.
- **Activity plan:** Use everyday activities and experiences to encourage, name, and describe the infant and toddler's emergent skills. Use phrases such as "You are drinking milk from the bottle. You know how to drink milk!" or "I see you are looking at the book. You know how to turn the pages."
- **How to adjust the activity:** Describe the actions of adults, pointing out what the grown-up can do, such as

"Your mommy knows how to pack your lunch" or "Your dada knows how to zip your coat." As children begin to develop language, spend some quiet time talking with the child and remembering all the things the child did during the day. Summarize the list, saying, "You colored on some paper; you ate your snack; you took your nap. You know how to do many things."

- **Did you meet your goal?** Does the infant enjoy the friendly conversation? Does the toddler begin to respond when the teacher describes "what" the child can do? Does the child provide examples when asked, "Sasha, what do you know how to do?"

PRESCHOOLERS AND KINDERGARTNERS

- **Goal:** Children can identify skills they have and skills they desire.
- **Materials:** Magazine pictures or clip art showing people doing many different activities, some of which depict skills children can typically accomplish and some that take training or practice. Select pictures that show a range of skill activities, people of various ages, people with special developmental needs, and other features that would be familiar to the children in the group.
- **Activity plan:** Guide the child to look at each picture and place it in the "I can do this now" pile or the "I would like

to learn to do this" pile. Invite the child to describe one of his or her skills in detail (such as brushing teeth or cutting a banana slice). Help the child imagine how he or she could learn a skill that is in the "like to learn" pile (such as riding a bicycle or baking muffins).

- **How to adjust the activity:** Play a "Can you do this?" game. Take turns asking, "Do you know how to … jump?" or "… take care of a goat?" Add some silly options: "… how to give a hippopotamus a bath?"
- **Did you meet your goal?** Can children realistically identify their current skills?

SCHOOL-AGE CHILDREN

- **Goal:** Children are able to identify many personal skills.
- **Materials:** Paper, pens, stapler.
- **Activity plan:** Guide the children to construct an *I Can Do Things* book that includes drawings and stories about skills they have.

- **How to adjust the activity:** Work with the children to identify different kinds of skill "chapters" for their book, such as Caring for Myself, Caring for Others, and Caring for My World. Periodically encourage children to add to their book.
- **Did you meet your goal?** Is each child able to draw and write about many skills?

Other important aspects of resilience are that although some children are particularly vulnerable to stress, they can have a strongly positive response to positive factors. Also, how well a child copes with stress can be specific to situations. A child may cope well with being bullied but not as well with being separated from a parent. Most importantly, promoting resilience requires the presence of supportive relationships (National Scientific Council on the Developing Child, 2015).

Creating Supportive Environments

Establishing environments that are welcoming and attuned to children's development sets the stage for appropriate social and emotional development. Many studies have suggested that children's social and emotional development is encouraged in early childhood environments that have specific characteristics such as these (Biringen et al., 2012; National Scientific Council on the Developing Child, 2014):

- High quality teacher–child relationships with low ratios.
- High classroom quality.
- Quality of attachment relationship between teachers and infants/toddlers.

The characteristics of the school that are most important in mental health promotion include the following (Bershad & Blaber, 2011):

- Caring and healthy teacher–student relationships, especially respecting ethnic, cultural, and racial aspects of families.
- Maintaining expectations that are high and age-appropriate.
- Clearly written standards that are implemented throughout the entire school.
- Using strategies and interventions that are effective and sensitive to children's needs, including social and emotional needs.
- Creating an environment of safety—emotional and physical.

Teachers create welcoming spaces where children play, learn, and thrive by developing a sense of safety and security and by helping children manage their emotions and get along with others. An example is providing space for block play and construction that is not in the walkway of the dramatic play center. Other aspects include creating social and quiet areas that allow children to select the setting that meets their needs and encouraging self-sufficiency by providing toileting areas that allow children to be self-sufficient when it is age-appropriate and labeling tubs and shelves for toys so that children can help at cleanup time. Young children recognize environments that are child-oriented and child friendly. These attentions to the physical space communicate that children are welcomed and valued.

Establishing Caring Relationships

During the early years, the child–caregiver relationship has the most important environmental influence on a children's mental health. Recent research has also highlighted the value of the teacher–child relationship as making unique contributions to children's social and emotional development (National Scientific Council on the Developing Child, 2014). This relationship exerts a positive influence on a child's development when the relationship is responsive and nurturing. In the classroom, these contributions are put into action through close and nurturing interactions between children and their teachers that demonstrate commitment to building strong and positive reciprocal relationships.

Nurturing Relationships

Building nurturing relationships is a primary component of healthy teacher–child interaction. It encompasses the essential elements of the teacher's contribution to children's positive mental health: respect, responsiveness, appropriate guidance, and positive expectations. For example:

- Providing interesting challenges and encouraging children's natural interests to explore and discover communicates respect, which enhances each child's feeling of worth.

- Recognizing children's strengths and needs and responding by purposefully planning activities and experiences to meet those needs shows value for children and promotes a mutually trusting relationship.
- Communicating appropriate limits and guiding children to positive interactions help children learn how to be positive members of the group and how to build friendships, demonstrating faith in their capabilities.
- Supporting and caring for children through challenging circumstances and persisting in helping children to learn expresses confidence in children's competency.
- Assisting children with stressful circumstances helps children develop resilience.

Teachers also serve as models for children regarding how to manage difficult situations. When teachers face challenges with ease, children learn coping strategies rather than defeat. Some children are born with conditions that influence their overall health, such as prematurity or heart defects, and may challenge their social and emotional development. The teacher–child relationship can mitigate the effect of these conditions on children's mental health. If a child is born very prematurely, the teacher can provide high-quality stimulation and attention to maximize that child's potential. This focused interaction communicates to the infant a sense of being valued, demonstrates commitment and love for the child, and models a positive approach to managing challenges. For teachers to provide caring relationships with children, they must also be attuned to their own **social and emotional competencies**. These are a set of skills that allow an individual to process, understand, and regulate emotions; develop interpersonal skills; and use cognitive skills so that he or she can be attentive and focused. Teaching can be a stressful and demanding job. Managing stress and emotions is needed to support children in stressful circumstances. See this chapter's *Policy Point* for a discussion on the importance of social and emotional skills for teachers.

In her Head Start classroom, Jan tries to model appropriate interactions when she conducts home visits for families of toddlers who have identified special developmental needs. She helps families recognize their child's abilities and accomplishments as they unfold and encourages them to enjoy their child's unique personality.

social and emotional competencies
set of skills that allow an individual to process, understand, and regulate emotions, to develop interpersonal skills, and to use cognitive skills so that he or she can be attentive and focused

POLICY POINT

Teachers Use Social and Emotional Skills to Manage Healthy Classrooms

Teachers must use many skills to manage a classroom effectively and to promote healthy development. Surveys have demonstrated unfortunate increases in teachers' level of stress and dissatisfaction. Social and emotional competencies affect the quality of the teacher–student relationship, influence what behavior is modeled for children, and influence teachers' classroom organization and management.

Stress on teachers also influences learning in the classroom and relationships with children. When teachers and caregivers are stressed, the quality of the interaction with children becomes less warm and nurturing. Some interventions for teachers have been designed, such as training in emotional regulation, relationship building interventions, and integration of structure and routines that remind teachers of position social and emotional skill strategies. Other recommendations include daily practices such as building emotional awareness, using reflection as a daily practice, managing professional and personal stress, and creating a culture of improvement and learning. Teachers and other school staff can develop strategies together to incorporate these practices.

Source: Jones, Bouffard, & Weissbourd, 2013.

Building Attachment

Attachment refers to the bonds of trust, care, understanding, and safety that develop between children and their caregivers. The ability to develop an attachment relationship is considered a hallmark of emotional wellness. Attachment is a springboard for exploration and future learning. Children who experience the positive bonds of attachment are able to explore and learn with confidence. They know that their caretaker is close and accessible if needed. Children who form strong attachment relationships are better able to manage separation from their families as they enter the early childhood setting and ultimately are supported to understand themselves as unique human beings (Bowlby, 1969; Biringen et al., 2012). The quality of the relationship with teachers is associated with academic achievement and social competence (Biringen et al., 2012).

Positive social-emotional development helps children approach learning with curiosity and enthusiasm.

Syda Productions/Fotolia

attachment
bonds of trust, care, understanding, and safety that develop between children and their caregivers

Secure attachments also build children's perceptions of trust, value, and self-worth, which are components of personal safety. For example, children who feel valued are better able to understand the concept of safety rules for themselves and others.

Providing Appropriate Play

Free and unstructured play contributes to children's cognitive, physical, creative, expressive, and social and emotional development. It is considered so important to childhood that the United Nations Commission on Human Rights has identified play as a *right* of childhood (Committee on the Rights of the Child, 1991). Children's involvement in play is one aspect of social and emotional development that is easily observed. Through play, children are immersed in dynamic interaction and exploration with the objects and people of their world. Play provides opportunities for children to participate in enjoyable activities, use their imaginations, test ideas, practice dexterity, explore outcomes, and gain mastery. Unstructured play, or play that is not directed by adults, is especially important. It allows children to be self-directed in determining the rules and procedures involved in their play themes. This inspires an individual experience of direction and mastery and encourages social interaction and problem solving. These activities result in a sense of accomplishment and cooperation by using skills that teach resilience and negotiation (Milteer & Ginsburg, 2012). The confidence and resiliency that children develop through child-directed play builds capacities that support them in new situations and challenges. They learn of their abilities to impact the world and apply decision making to outcomes.

Play also brings children into contact with other people and provides opportunities for them to experience useful social skills such as taking turns, waiting, negotiating, compromising, and sharing (Milteer & Ginsburg, 2012). Unstructured play allows children to explore according to their own interests and at their own pace. Children who are less verbal, who are learning English, or who have special developmental needs are equally able to engage in and benefit from play when they are allowed to set their own pace and follow their own interests.

Through play, children learn to use words to express emotion and experience the reactions of others. For example, two 4-year-old girls might begin their friendship this way:

Sophia hears the teacher introduce Althea. "Hey!" said Sophia. "Althea! That sounds like Sophia! I could be your friend!" Althea thinks for a minute and says, "Sometimes my mom calls me 'Thea.'" Sophia exclaims, "Sometimes my mom calls me 'Phia!' I could be your friend forever!"

From individual exploration to games that involve rules and negotiation, children practice and learn many social skills through different types of age-appropriate play.

Open and unstructured playtime is important throughout the early years. In some settings, however, free playtime is being reduced due to pressures to promote academic skills both in the home and in the early childhood and school setting. Academically oriented activities have clear benefits for children's learning. When adult-planned and academically focused activities dominate, children's days may become overscheduled, causing children to feel hurried. The trends that promote attention to academic learning rather than play and social interaction are problematic. Free and unstructured play provides many stress-reducing benefits that contribute to children's resilience and help build social and emotional wellness.

CHECK YOUR UNDERSTANDING 12.2
Click here to check your understanding of healthy social and emotional development.

UNDERSTANDING MENTAL HEALTH PROBLEMS

Many children experience normal social and emotional development. They gradually develop interpersonal skills and learn to manage their emotions within the broad range of typical development. However, growing numbers of children are experiencing delays and challenges in social and emotional development that are exhibited through significant behavior problems in the classroom. Teachers are better able to understand and address children's needs by understanding the prevalence of these concerns and how they are identified and by being familiar with the types of mental health problems that young children may experience.

Understanding prevalence of Mental Health Problems

Most studies of the prevalence of mental health disorders focus on specific disorders. For example, the prevalence of depression is 4% (Harrison, Vannest, Davis, & Reynolds, 2012). More generalized studies indicate that between 13% and 20% of children under the age of 6 experience emotional, behavioral, or other mental health problems. This includes a wide spectrum of conditions that include emotional and behavioral disorders as well as mental health disorders. Based on a number of reporting methods, the prevalence is increasing (Perou, 2013). Children from low-income families have higher rates of mental health problems.

The most common mental health disorder is ADD/ADHD at 6.8%, followed by behavioral/conduct disorders (3.5%), anxiety (3.0%), and depression (2.1%) (Perou, 2013). Also of growing concern is the relationship between mental health disorders in youth and the risk of suicide later. Adolescents with mental health disorders usually exhibit signs of behavior problems or maladjustment in earlier years.

In very young children, before a diagnosis is made, teachers and caregivers are observing for signs of atypical social or emotional development that is usually manifested as significant behavioral challenges, extreme difficulty forming relationships with peers, or difficulty understanding authority or following common classroom rules even after behavior modification strategies have been employed. As with any health problem, identifying problems as early as possible will result in better outcomes.

Recognizing Consequences

Mental health problems that begin in early childhood can develop into serious disorders as children age. Over half of lifetime mental health disorders begin in childhood. Children with mental health disorders have problems at home, in peer relationships, and in school, affecting all aspects of their lives. Mental health problems in childhood can lead to substance abuse, criminal behavior, and other serious risk-taking behaviors (Perou, 2013).

Even seemingly minor mental health problems can impact children and families. Children with mental health problems often have problems with self-esteem, learning, and relationships with others. They are more likely to experience other health conditions that impact their daily activities and increase their absence from school.

WHAT IF . . .

you were asked to be on an early childhood advisory committee for your community? What ideas could you offer to help promote children's success in school? What strategies might you suggest to address the gap in social and emotional development that some children experience?

Understanding Socioeconomic Factors

Social and emotional development and mental health outcomes are closely tied to social, cultural, and economic factors. One important and well-documented example is the increase in mental health disorders in children living in poverty. This also is consistent with the increase in other physical health problems. Other trends that are seen include (National Center for Children in Poverty, 2012):

- Increased visits to the emergency room by children with mental health problems.
- Inadequate access to affordable care for mental health problems.
- Less likelihood of Hispanic children having reported a mental health problem.
- Treatment received by about half of children with mental health problems.

Characteristics of a child's family can also influence mental health and wellness. Children with mental health problems have higher rates of single-parent households, of parents who are unemployed, and of families living in poverty. Unfortunately, many of these families believe that they are being blamed for the problem. They are also less likely to be involved parents and to be satisfied with their child's education, further complicating the circumstances (Turnbull, Turnbull, Wehmeyer, & Sogren, 2013). Teachers are encouraged to offer support without judgment and to tap into resources in the community to assist with these circumstances. This chapter's *Health Hint* discusses how maternal depression can be associated with mental health problems in children.

Using Teachers' Observations

Enhancing children's social and emotional skills is important to academic success. During the early years, teachers help children develop foundational skills for learning and healthy development. Teachers spend many hours with children, and they have an important perspective on children's social and emotional skills and development.

Pearson Education

CLASSROOM CONNECTION

Watch this video of teachers discussing children who exhibit attention-seeking behaviors. What are some observations and strategies the teacher uses to deal with these behaviors?

HEALTH HINT   Parental mental health impacts children

Children are vulnerable to people and circumstances around them in both positive and negative ways. Conditions such as depression can have an impact on how well parents or primary caregivers establish attachment, manage emotions, and manage conflict within their families. Maternal depression can have both physical and mental health effects on the child. Having a parent with major depression is a significant stressor for a child, essentially an adverse childhood experience, and can have both short-term and long-term impacts.

The best strategy for these stressors is prevention and early recognition. Parental depression, in particular, is more common than previously thought. There is a significant stigma associated with mental health problems in parents, and it is far too easy for parents to think that they will harm their child. Although parental mental health problems are associated with challenging childhood behaviors, teachers should offer assistance to these families that is appropriate and nonjudgmental. Interventions during a child's early years will prevent more significant problems later.

Sources: Turnbull, Turnbill, Wehmeyer, & Shogren, 2013; Rahman, Surkan, Cayetano, Rwagatare, & Dickson, 2013.

Observing for Positive Development

Children who approach learning with interest and enthusiasm and who are comfortable forming questions and focusing on outcomes are better able to acquire new information and apply new concepts to future settings. These are signs of positive social and emotional adjustment that contribute to children's success in school. The competencies associated with mental health are observable. For example, in her infant and toddler class, Sharina recognizes healthy social and emotional development, or "good" mental health, when she observes Caitlin laughing and crawling over to interact with Lin Lin. Caitlin shows appropriate interest, enjoyment, and curiosity and expresses this through developmentally appropriate emotions and actions. To Sharina, this observation is similar to the height and weight measurements she takes to understand children's physical health. While physical measurements give clues to physical health, observations of children's interactions with their peers and with adults help teachers understand children's mental health.

Observing for Atypical Development

To establish successful class groups, teachers must develop a wide range of behavior management approaches and techniques. Sometimes challenging or atypical behaviors can be a sign that children are at risk for more significant problems. To assist teachers in recognizing behaviors that have an understandable cause and those that suggest the potential for social and emotional problems, special focus must be given to observing the child's behavior in the classroom setting. Through careful observation, teachers look for behaviors that are extreme, such as excessively aggressive or withdrawn behaviors, and for emotional responses that are not age-appropriate or that seem atypical. Signs of problems in social and emotional development are demonstrated through behaviors that are:

- Inappropriate or dangerous.
- Frequent and reoccurring.
- Persistent.

Children's difficult behaviors are often the first indication that a problem with social and emotional development exists. But recognizing behaviors that suggest a mental health problem may not be straightforward. For example, Bob, a teacher in the young preschool room, frequently observes 3-year-old Sasha acting aggressively, such as pushing other children in the play yard and knocking over other children's block structures. Bob has been unsuccessful in managing these behaviors and is unsure whether they indicate a lack of communication skills or are signs of more serious mental health concerns. He is not alone in wondering how to interpret such behaviors.

Difficult behaviors are a common and natural experience in early childhood classrooms. Even typical behaviors can be difficult to manage, and most children display inappropriate behaviors at one time or another. For young children, understanding how to participate appropriately in the group setting requires learning the rules and cues for appropriate social interaction. Testing limits as children gain this social knowledge is normal. A core responsibility of early childhood teaching involves guiding children through these aspects of social and emotional development and helping them learn to interact appropriately.

Appropriate behaviors are related to normal growth and development; they are behaviors that are expected of most children based on their age and developmental maturity. Behaviors that are considered appropriate change as children age. What is understandable behavior for a 2-year-old is not expected behavior for a 5-year-old. In addition, children who experience special developmental delays may demonstrate behaviors that are understandable given their developmental maturity but are not age-appropriate. For example, 6-year-old Sam, who has a developmental disability, may kick another child who is taking a turn on the bicycle—a behavior commensurate with Sam's special developmental condition but not typically expected of a 6-year-old. Teachers need to weigh the behaviors that are observed with children's individual age and maturity. Other aspects such as children's culture and nutritional health can also impact behavior. There are common behavioral patterns in children with mental health problems that teachers can look for, such as internalizing and externalizing behaviors.

externalizing behaviors negative behaviors that are directed against others or things in the environment (for example, displaying atypical aggression, acting out, and being persistently noncompliant)

bullying externalizing behavior when children use physical or verbal aggression to intimidate others

internalizing behaviors problems related to mood or emotions such as sadness, depression, or worthlessness

Externalizing Behaviors

Externalizing behaviors are negative behaviors that are directed against others or things in the environment. Examples are displaying atypical aggression, acting out, and being persistently noncompliant. **Bullying** is an externalizing behavior when children use physical or verbal aggression to intimidate others. These behaviors are most common in children with conduct disorder or oppositional defiant disorder, as described in the next section (Turnbull et al., 2013).

Internalizing Behaviors

Internalizing behaviors are problems related to mood or emotions such as sadness, depression, or worthlessness. Children with internalizing behaviors tend to be referred less to specialists because their behavior is less disruptive in a group or toward others (Turnbull et al., 2013).

Observing for Mental Health Problems That Impact Academics

As with physical health, mental health impacts how well a child learns and succeeds in the classroom. There can be a wide range of expectations for these children academically, but it is more common for them to have

A Matter of ETHICS

A 6-year-old girl has joined your first-grade class. You learn that she recently came to live with her grandparents for an indefinite period of time while her mom starts a new job in another state. You notice that the girl is shy and quiet and seems sad and lonely. She has had difficulty making friends and rarely plays outside during recess. You have tried to talk with the grandparents about your observations, but they are not concerned and do not want the child to be referred for any "help." You recognize that you have an ethical commitment to support the child, but you don't want to upset the family. What ideas for managing this situation can you glean from the NAEYC Code of Ethical Conduct? What will be your next step? What resources in your community might you investigate for information and assistance?

low-average IQs. A significant percentage can have low reading and math achievement. Nearly two-thirds of students with mental health problems also have language delays. Ultimately children with mental illness have much higher rates of dropping out of school altogether (Turnbull et al., 2013).

To improve outcome, the stress that causes or contributes to mental health problems in early childhood can be mitigated in the early years. Teachers are important sources of information for caregivers, are critical role models, and can be a positive influence in the life of a child with mental health problems.

Understanding Cultural Influences

Children's cultural backgrounds can impact the kinds of behaviors that are considered appropriate. What might be considered appropriate behavior in one culture may not be understood in another. For example, a Korean American child may be taught to hide his or her emotions, causing the teacher to worry that the child is not capable of expressing and managing emotions, a possible sign of problems in social and emotional development.

Cultural values also influence family reactions to children's behaviors. For example, parents may allow certain behaviors in the home environment that are not considered appropriate in the early childhood setting. To better understand the cultural framework that influences children's behavior, teachers should discuss these issues with families. This helps everyone understand whether particular behaviors have a recognizable source or indicate signs of problems.

Acknowledging the Role of Sleeping and Eating Habits

Behaviors can also be influenced by children's sleeping and eating patterns. Children who do not receive sufficient rest may show behavior extremes in the classroom. Difficulties with sleep are far more common in children with mental health problems. Children with sleep problems tend to show more externalizing behaviors and have higher rates of mental health conditions such as ADHD (Armstrong, Ruttle, Klein, Essex, & Benca, 2014).

What children eat can also influence the way they behave in the classroom. For example, children who have not eaten breakfast or who receive a poor diet may demonstrate behaviors such as inability to concentrate, lethargy, and persistent fatigue. Understanding children's sleeping and eating routines can help teachers understand the source of behavioral issues. This chapter's *Nutrition Note* discusses how obesity is related to childhood mental health.

NUTRITION NOTE   Childhood Obesity and Mental Health

While obesity is not technically considered a psychological condition, many agree that is has a significant psychological impact, especially on children. Children with obesity have increased rates of depression and anxiety, but it is not known whether this association is a cause for obesity or a consequence of obesity. Children also have more problems with self-esteem, body dissatisfaction, emotional problems, and resilience. These problems can further complicate the condition. When a child has poor self-esteem, it may be difficult for them to be confident in making healthy choices and in being more physically active.

Caregivers and teachers are encouraged to take the focus off weight by emphasizing a healthy body image and healthy choices and providing opportunities for increased physical activities. Teachers are also encouraged to promote healthy relationships in the classroom by not allowing children to target other children who are overweight.

Source: Russell-Mayhew, McVey, Bardick, & Ireland, 2012.

Using Community Resources

A small percentage of children may experience significant behaviors that persist in spite of efforts to guide and manage the behavior concerns. These children may benefit from assessment and evaluation by a behavior specialist or mental health consultant. However, determining when efforts to manage children's behaviors are not making progress and when additional support is needed can be difficult. For example, Hal feels as though he is not doing his job as a teacher when Mandy's behavior does not show signs of improving despite his careful efforts. He thinks the principal will question his teaching skills because the problems persist—in fact, they may be increasing—but he is also struggling because every day is getting harder.

When well-planned intervention strategies are not successful in redirecting children to more positive behaviors, additional supports are needed for both the child and the teacher. To evaluate progress, teachers, families, and others who may be teaming to address the child's needs discuss questions such as these:

- Have the frequency and intensity of the child's behaviors improved?
- Is the child able to navigate most of the activities successfully during the day with relatively little support, or does a teacher need to be nearby to prevent aggressive acts or injury?
- Is the child demonstrating more positive behaviors?
- Is growth evident?

Responses indicating that problems are continuing mean that more information and support is needed. Referring the child to special services is the next step. Some schools may have counselors or behavior management specialists who help with classroom management strategies while they find other resources.

The teacher's role in making referrals is to provide concrete descriptions of the behaviors that are problematic and information about what is working. Even after referrals are made, the teacher's responsibility to the child continues through additional efforts to manage and guide behavior. In the example above, Hal finds that talking with other teachers about strategies and support resources is one way for him to boost his confidence and maintain his motivation. Advocating for additional training or the temporary assistance of an aide is another way that teachers obtain support to better teach children with mental health problems.

CHECK YOUR UNDERSTANDING 12.3

Click here to check your understanding of the prevalence, consequences, and academic characteristics of childhood mental health problems.

MENTAL HEALTH DISORDERS IN EARLY CHILDHOOD

Children who experience mental health problems sometimes display significant behavior challenges. These are behaviors that are problematic, out of the ordinary, frequent, persistent, and sometimes dangerous. Teachers are an important source of information for parents and health care providers regarding the child's social behaviors and/or symptoms of mental health problems. However, medical professionals make the diagnosis of mental health disorders. Making a definitive diagnosis of mental health problems is complex. It involves a broad review of biological and environmental factors, children's age and development, and assessments of how children function in the school and home environments. Sometimes these diagnoses are made over time.

Understanding some of the mental health disorders that may occur during children's early years provides teachers with a general understanding of the range of conditions that may affect children's mental health and behaviors in the classroom. Under the Individuals with Disabilities Education Act (IDEA), the term *emotional disturbance* is used to refer to mental health conditions. The more common mental health disorders identified among young children are discussed in the following sections.

Reactive Attachment Disorder

reactive attachment disorder
condition that occurs when a child's basic needs for attachment have been denied or neglected, resulting in severe problems with social interactions

Reactive attachment disorder occurs when a child's basic needs for attachment have been denied or neglected, resulting in severe problems with sense of self and with establishing healthy relationships. It can be caused by child abuse or neglect. Children at high risk for attachment disorder are (National Institutes of Health, U.S. National Library of Medicine, 2014b):

- Children of parents who are intellectually disabled.
- Children whose parents have very poor parenting skills.
- Children who have had frequent changes in primary caregivers, such as living in multiple foster homes in early years.
- Children separated from primary caregivers or placed in orphanages.

Symptoms of attachment disorder include avoiding contact with caregiver, having difficulty with being comforted, and showing no interest in social interactions. Early diagnosis and treatment is essential and requires counseling for both the child and caregiver and reinforcement of healthy relationships.

Behavioral Disorders of Childhood

Some mental health conditions fall under a behavioral category simply because many of the manifestations are related to the child's behavior in a group setting, in relationships with teachers, or in relationships with peers. All children misbehave, but behavior disorders are more serious and are manifested by symptoms that are more severe and last longer than would typically be expected in normal development.

Attention Deficit/Hyperactivity Disorder

attention deficit/ hyperactivity disorder(ADHD)
condition characterized by restlessness, persistent lack of attention, impulsiveness, and hyperactivity

Attention deficit/hyperactivity disorder (ADHD) is a condition characterized by distractibility, persistent lack of attention, impulsiveness, and hyperactivity. The most important characteristics of this condition are (Efron et al., 2014):

- Difficulties in social interactions.
- Academic underachievement.
- Association with other mental health problems.

ADHD affects a small percentage of very young children. Prevalence rates and more discussion of symptoms and treatment are included in Chapter 11. Treatment for ADHD includes classroom modifications and medications; however, the appropriateness and effectiveness of treatment strategies continues to be researched.

Teachers may be asked by parents, providers, medical specialists, or mental health providers to describe their observations of the child. This is important in diagnosis and treatment. ADHD is associated not only with other mental health conditions such as depression, but also with other behavioral conditions such as conduct disorder.

Oppositional Defiant Disorder

Symptoms of **oppositional defiant disorder** usually start by age 8. The most common characteristics include propensity to argue with people in authority, abnormal outbursts of anger, a bad temper, and difficulty making and keeping friends. These children are frequently in trouble. It is caused by a combination of factors related to biology and social and psychological circumstances (National Institutes of Health, U.S. National Library of Medicine, 2014a).

The most important form of treatment is mental health referral involving counseling and possibly psychiatry and medication. The best form of prevention is for a child to have caregivers who offer consistent and reasonable rules while avoiding harsh or inappropriate punishments. Children who are abused or neglected are at high risk for developing this condition.

oppositional defiant disorder
behavioral condition characterized by a propensity to argue with people in authority, abnormal outbursts of anger, a bad temper, and difficulty making and keeping friends

Conduct Disorder

Conduct disorder is characterized by impulsivity and lack of empathy. Symptoms include breaking rules frequently, being aggressive or cruel toward other people and animals, lying, setting fires, or vandalizing. This disorder has been associated with child abuse, parental substance abuse, and poverty. As in oppositional defiant disorder, conduct disorder is more common in boys (National Institutes of Health, U.S. National Library of Medicine, 2013). These children have a high risk of developing other mental health problems such as depression and personality disorders. Early recognition and treatment is imperative.

conduct disorder
behavioral disorder characterized by impulsivity and lack of empathy. Symptoms include breaking rules frequently, being aggressive or cruel toward other people and animals, lying, setting fires, or vandalizing

Implications for Teachers

Behavioral disorders can be some of the most difficult disorders to manage in a group setting. Often a behavioral specialist or mental health consultant is needed to develop appropriate behavioral management strategies. Children often need frequent and recurrent reminders of how to behave and how to manage their emotions. Communication with parents is important. When the parents understand the behavior management plan and can replicate it at home, children often have better outcomes. Children should understand expectations clearly and be reminded of them repeatedly.

Anxiety Disorders

This is another category of mental health disorders that includes generalized anxiety disorder, separation anxiety, obsessive-compulsive disorder, and post-traumatic stress disorder.

Generalized Anxiety Disorder

Anxiety is a common emotional response, but when it is persistent and experienced with great intensity, it is considered a problem. Anxiety disorder is characterized by excessive worry and/or fear (Turnbull et al., 2013). Treatment for anxiety disorders may include cognitive problem solving, behavioral therapy, or medications. Cognitive problem solving might include discussing the potential realities of a fear and identifying ways children can manage them, such as helping a child explore a fear of the red light on the smoke detector. Behavioral therapy involves having children gradually face their fears, such as helping a child practice making changes in routines.

generalized anxiety disorder
a mental health disorder causing excessive worry and/or fear

Children with generalized anxiety disorder express excessive worry about many things, including future events, potential dangers such as earthquakes, and promptness. In the early childhood setting, this may be seen when the class is practicing for a fire drill. For example, Cathy, a 4-year-old, may begin displaying anxiety as soon as she sees her teacher bring out the home-style smoke alarm that he will use at group time when they practice evacuating the classroom. Cathy worries about the loud noise the smoke alarm makes. Her teacher notices her discomfort and sets the alarm in a cupboard until group time. Then he asks Cathy if she would like to push the button to make the alarm sound, putting her in control of the situation, or if she would like to cover her ears, giving her an option to reduce the sound of the alarm.

Separation Anxiety Although common in infants and children up to 18 months of age, separation anxiety diminishes as children age and is not considered typical of older children. It is characterized by an extreme need to be near the parent or home. Behaviors may include inability to sleep alone or fear associated with separating from the parent when being left in the early childhood setting.

separation anxiety
inability to sleep alone or fear associated with separating from the parent when being left with other caregivers or teachers

obsessive-compulsive disorder
a type of anxiety disorder causing obsessive and repetitive behaviors such as repeated hand washing and/or insistence on routines atypical for age

Obsessive-Compulsive Disorder Children with obsessive-compulsive disorder (OCD) display obsessive and repetitive behaviors such as repeated hand washing, insistence on routines such as having the teacher stand in a certain place at the door during arrival and departure, and insistence on having things in their place. Teachers may also notice that children use nonsense words or sounds and that they describe recurring thoughts and themes much longer than would be of interest to most children.

post-traumatic stress disorder
a disorder that occurs after children have experienced or been exposed to a traumatic experience such as extreme violence in the home or neighborhood or frequent instances of maltreatment, resulting in extreme worry, vigilance, and inability to manage normal stress

Post-Traumatic Stress Disorder Post-traumatic stress disorder (PTSD) occurs after children have experienced or been exposed to a traumatic experience such as extreme violence in the home or neighborhood or frequent instances of maltreatment. As a result, children may be extremely worried, vigilant, and tense. This can be observed as the child watches others from the edge of play. The teacher might also notice that the child constantly keeps an eye on the teachers and parents as they come and go, noticing the details of what everyone is doing. Children who suffer from PTSD have difficulty relaxing and enjoying their play. Teachers assist by building children's sense of security, as in this example:

> Helena, teacher of the class for 3-year-olds, knows that Zack has experienced violence in his home. Zack and his mother now live in a "safe" house for women and children who have suffered from domestic violence, and he does not get to play outside very often due to their current living situation. Zack appears tense and is unable to enjoy playing in the preschool. Helena makes arrangements with her coteachers to take Zack outside to play for 10 minutes on his own at the beginning of every day. She runs and plays ball with him and encourages him to climb and swing. After a few days of this routine, she sees that Zack is relaxing. They agree to invite a small group of children outside to play with him the following day.

Approaches such as this acknowledge children's struggles and provide an option for working through fears in acceptable ways.

Implications for Teachers

Teachers can use a number of strategies on children with anxiety to minimize their symptoms. Children with anxiety disorders are more likely to worry and are less able to regulate their emotions. They can also become easily frustrated.

Teachers can do the following (Minnesota Association for Children's Mental Health, n.d.):

- When students worry about deadlines, offer some flexibility.
- Ask parents what works for their child.
- Keep a routine/schedule.
- Ask children to complete their work, but balance that with flexibility.
- Offer clear expectations and check in with students to make sure they understand the expectations.

Mood Disorders

Mood disorders are characterized by significant changes in mood—depressed or elevated or both (Turnbull et al., 2013). They are complex and are treated with a variety of therapies. Mood disorders include bipolar disorders and depression.

mood disorders
disorders causing abnormal fluctuations in mood

Bipolar Disorder Extreme fluctuations in mood and energy are characteristics of **bipolar disorder**. Children with bipolar disorder may have long periods of normal behavior and then swing to highly depressive behaviors and then to extreme manic episodes (high-energy swings) (Ball, Bindler, & Cowen, 2013). The types of behaviors and how they may be exhibited in the classroom are described in Table 12-3.

Bipolar disorder is very rare in the early childhood years, and it is thought to be associated with an underlying biological condition; however, it is difficult to pinpoint a specific cause. Although it is rare, its symptoms often begin in early childhood as significant behavioral challenges. Treatment for bipolar disorder includes medication and various therapies such as cognitive and behavior therapies and family therapy, which are often combined with medications.

bipolar disorder
mood disorder characterized by long periods of normal behavior and then swings to highly depressive behaviors and then to extreme manic episodes

Depression A mental health disorder that causes disturbances in mood is known as **depression**. Children with depression can display a wide range of behaviors including sadness, irritability, anger, changes in appetite, fatigue, problems sleeping, and recurring physical complaints. Depression can affect many aspects of health and wellness, including growth and development, behavioral problems, academic performance, and relationships. It is more commonly associated with other mental health diagnoses such as ADHD.

Determining the actual cause of depression in young children can be very difficult because no definitive test is available. Evidence suggests that underlying

depression
a mood disorder causing a wide range of behaviors including sadness, irritability, anger, changes in appetite, fatigue, problems sleeping, and recurring physical complaints

TABLE 12-3 Behaviors Associated with Bipolar Disorder

Behaviors	Description	Classroom Examples
Depressive behaviors	<ul><li>Passivity.</li><li>Difficulty sleeping or eating.</li><li>Feeling worthless.</li><li>Unpredictably switching to manic behavior.</li></ul>	<ul><li>Child shows little interest in toys or other children.</li><li>Child appears excessively tired; is not interested in snacks or meals.</li><li>Child expresses self-doubt; can't be encouraged to participate.</li></ul>
Manic behaviors	<ul><li>Excessive high energy.</li><li>Risky behavior.</li><li>Unpredictably switching to depressive behavior.</li></ul>	<ul><li>Child makes unusual movements, wildly running, jumping, calling out, moving from activity to activity.</li><li>Child is unusually aggressive.</li><li>Child is not sleeping much.</li><li>Child tests boundaries; climbs and uses toys and equipment without regard to safety.</li></ul>

Sources: Ball, Bindler, & Cowen, 2013; Heward, 2013.

biological causes such as changes in brain chemistry might affect a child's mood. Depression can also occur in response to environmental situations such as parental depression, child abuse or neglect, parental substance abuse, family problems, low socioeconomic or education levels, and loss of a parent or sibling (Tang & Pinsky, 2015).

Medical professionals diagnose depression, giving careful attention to the child's medical history as well as details related to behavior, peer relationships, and behavioral symptoms. The length of time the child's daily functioning has been impaired and the presence of specific symptoms such as sleep disturbances, change in appetite, or thoughts of death are also considered. Sometimes families ask teachers for input regarding their observations when they have worries about a child's behaviors, such as the potential for depression.

Implications for Teachers

Teachers may be involved in logging children's classroom behaviors to help inform medical providers and mental health specialists about the child's participation. Teachers also support children with bipolar disorder by establishing familiar routines and guiding them to manage extreme behaviors by offering appropriate choices. Figure 12-2 shows an example of a child's drawing that should raise red flags for a teacher. Although teachers do not make diagnoses, they do have a responsibility to support families by discussing their concerns, referring them to professional assistance, and working to address children's issues in the classroom.

FIGURE 12-2
Children's drawings may provide clues to how they are feeling. Other observations are needed to determine whether this is a sign of depression or another mood disorder.

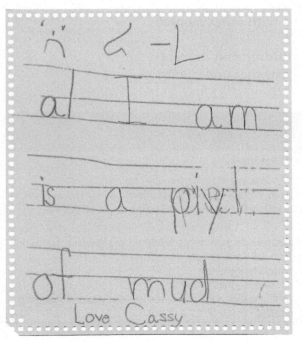

Teachers' Role in Children with Mental Health Disorders

Children who are preschool age and younger may demonstrate frequent and persistent behaviors such as hitting, kicking, biting, and throwing toys or furnishings at other children and teachers. School-age children may display aggressive behaviors such as harming animals; starting fires; or fighting, bullying, and showing other forms of hostile physical or emotional interactions. Teaching children with these behaviors can be very difficult because they introduce distress, discord, and upset in the classroom.

Significant behavior challenges require a great deal of the teacher's attention and energy to manage while at the same time trying to maintain a learning environment for the larger group of children. Sometimes teachers believe that they are only "containing" children's behaviors and not helping them to move on to more positive ways of showing emotions and interacting. Teachers need a range of supports including ways to promote appropriate behaviors, approaches to manage them when they occur, and strategies to direct children from inappropriate to appropriate behaviors. They need to understand the resources that are available to them, such as families and mental health professionals.

Demonstrating Sensitivity

This is an important aspect of all early childhood programs, but is especially needed when addressing mental health issues. Parents are often hesitant to discuss mental health issues. Some may think that mental health issues are not as "real" as physical health issues and believe that people should be able to "fix" their own problems. Families want their children to be accepted by others; they may feel dismayed and embarrassed when their child displays behaviors that are out of the ordinary, aggressive, or problematic. If a mental health issue is identified, parents may wonder if they are to blame. They may find it difficult to reveal this situation to others, and they may not know what to do about it.

Active and supportive communication that includes being sensitive to unique family experiences and perspectives is key to navigating discussions of children's mental health challenges successfully. At times, special creativity and problem-solving strategies are needed. For example, language barriers can make communication about children's mental health problems more complex. Discussions may use words and language that are not typically part of everyday communication. Special efforts are needed to ensure clear communication, such as obtaining the support of bilingual family members or qualified interpreters.

At other times, teachers may need to approach situations with flexibility, good humor, and understanding. Some children with mental health problems have difficulty being flexible or adapting to rules that are different in different settings. For example, a child may arrive at class wearing a Halloween costume even though the teacher has specifically asked families *not* to send their child to school in costume. The parent may report that the child insisted on wearing the costume, stating that this was the only way he or she could get the child to school. It is easy to be frustrated when it seems that parents, too, are not "following the rules." However, in this situation, recognizing the challenges the family faces in managing the child's difficult behaviors (and drawing on good humor and understanding rather than frustration) helps the teacher and family negotiate the issue together. This builds a bond of mutual understanding and joint problem solving.

WHAT IF . . .

a mother of a child in your care blamed family problems on her child's poor social development? How might you explain more healthful ways to approach the child and family's challenge? What ideas do you have to help the parent find support for the family problems mentioned?

Understanding Successful Integration

Many children with mental health problems participate successfully in early childhood classrooms. This success is founded on the attitudes and supports provided by the early childhood setting and teachers as well as the candid involvement of families.

Successfully including children with mental health problems also requires that teachers, families, and program staff all see value in the participation of such children. This requires special efforts to create a common commitment to all children. Teachers are important in promoting this sense of community and acceptance among all children in the class. To accomplish this, they must address two issues: They must establish open and candid communication with the families of children who have mental health problems, and they must encourage other families to be welcoming to children with social and emotional concerns.

Supports Needed from Families

Teachers need the support of families whose children are experiencing mental health problems. These families must be openly communicative and candid about their child's strengths and challenges so that teachers will know how to plan for successful integration and how to manage potential challenges in the classroom. Both teachers

WHAT IF . . .

a parent did not disclose that her child had a mental health disorder until after the child was enrolled in your class? Would this influence your relationship with the child or parent? Upon learning of the disorder, how would you respond?

and parents may have fears related to the child's participation in the classroom. They may worry about difficult behaviors that will be hard to manage or that the child will be unsafe or not accepted by other children.

Other issues to keep in mind are cultural diversity and how it relates to mental health as well as stigma which may often be associated with mental health problems.. Parenting styles, expectations of personal boundaries, and gender roles are all aspects that influence cultural and family expectations for children's behaviors. These need to be carefully explored and understood to facilitate an appropriate interpretation of behaviors. It can be challenging to navigate situations where the teacher observes problematic and possibly dangerous behaviors that the family views as "typical" and appropriate. Consider this example:

Hector has been teaching 3-year-old Davonne to interact with the other children in the class without pushing and hitting. Davonne is beginning to control his impulse to hit by using his words. Davonne's dad arrives to pick him up from the play yard. Davonne's friend Karl runs by and pushes Davonne saying, "Try to catch me!" Davonne clenches his fists and says, "No pushing!" Hector is sorry that Davonne has been pushed, but he is happy to see that Davonne responded appropriately. Before he can get close enough to comfort and encourage Davonne, Davonne's dad grabs his son and gives him a shake, saying, "When someone hits you, you hit him back!" As Hector approaches the pair, quickly trying to summon the words to explain the behavior plan he has been working on, he realizes that Davonne's dad has been left out of the discussion.

The successful involvement of children with mental health problems also relies on the positive attitudes of families whose children are typically developing. Creating a classroom motto that "everyone is welcome" is one way to introduce the concept that all children have a place in the early childhood setting. Offering social events that focus on helping families get acquainted builds a sense of common experience and togetherness. Families may be more resilient or "forgiving" when they occasionally observe a child displaying challenging behaviors if they know and appreciate one another.

Finally, all families need to be able to see the concrete ways in which teachers are working to build cooperation and harmony in the classroom. Age-appropriate class group meetings where children discuss classroom rules or make a list of appropriate behaviors demonstrate that teachers are working to educate all children about how to be an appropriate member of a community.

Conducting a functional assessment

When a child's behavioral challenges are recognized as atypical, teachers use a focused process to reflect on, describe, and define what is occurring. This is called **functional behavioral assessment**. Features of functional assessment include (Turnbull et al., 2013):

functional behavioral assessment
a focused process to reflect on, describe, and define what is occurring with respect to challenging behaviors in the early childhood setting

- *Describing the child's behaviors:* What? When? Where? How often? Intensity?
- *Recognizing events surrounding the behavior:* What tends to affect the behavior, such as changes in the routine and schedule, sleep challenges, or medical needs?
- *Identifying predictable events:* In what situations are the problem behaviors likely to occur?
- *Summarizing the child's play abilities:* What successes and difficulties does the child experience in play?

- *Understanding the function of problem behaviors:* What does the child get (or avoid doing) because of the behavior?
- *Reflecting on the effectiveness of the problem behavior:* What response does the child get? How quickly?

The goal of functional assessment is to determine the purpose of the problematic behavior, to design interventions to prevent the problem behavior, and to teach the child appropriate skills or alternative behaviors.

A functional assessment may be conducted individually by the teacher or with a team that may include family members, behavior specialists, and counselors. Teachers conduct and record observations of the child's behavior and keep data to look for patterns of behavior. The team meets to learn about the family's experiences with the child's behavior, to discuss what was observed in the classroom, and to plan appropriate interventions.

This approach is successful in helping teachers and families work together to plan ways to prevent problem behaviors and to increase the effectiveness of managing the behaviors in the early childhood setting and home. In the opening case scenario, Meegan may find that the functional assessment process would be a good next step to explore with Heather's family to address Heather's behavior concerns.

Mental Health Consultants in Early Childhood Programs

Collaboration with mental health professionals such as behavior specialists, counselors, nurses, or physicians provides an important benefit to children who are at risk for or have been diagnosed with a mental health disorder. Consultation supports teachers and families when they are not able to understand children's behaviors and symptoms and need help managing concerns in the school and home. Together teachers, families, and mental health professionals can usually design an appropriate management plan to address the challenges and assist children in developing coping strategies. This chapter's *Progressive Programs & Practices* feature describes how mental health consultants can be utilized.

Services provided by mental health consultants include conducting observations of children in the classroom and home setting. Consultation is provided to sort out ways to foster healthy social and emotional development and to manage behavior challenges. The consultant is also an important resource for understanding services that may be available to the child and family in the community, such as public or private family counseling and behavior management safety net programs that teach parenting skills and provide respite for families as needed. The mental health consultant may also play a role in helping children's programs establish an environment that promotes social and emotional development as well as develop policies and procedures to promote children's mental health (Heller et al., 2011).

Many consultants can observe classroom environments and offer recommendations to improve the program. They may also offer training for teachers that address the following topics (Heller et al., 2011):

- Establishing positive relationships with children, families, and other staff.
- Creating supportive environments, including schedules/routines and successful transitions, and designing appropriate rules.
- Teaching socioemotional skills to young children.
- Developing strategies to address challenging behaviors.

PROGRESSIVE PROGRAMS & PRACTICES

Promoting Social Emotional Development

By Allison Boothe and Angela Keyes, Tulane University Institute of Infant and Early Childhood Mental Health

The Tulane University Institute of Infant and Early Childhood Mental Health uses a unique model of early childhood mental health consultation (ECMHC). ECMHC is embedded within Louisiana's Quality Rating and Improvement System, Quality Start, which focuses on children's social and emotional development. The approach is designed to assist all children, staff, and families involved in center-based child care with the goal of achieving healthy behavioral, social, and emotional development for young children.

Through the ECMHC model, mental health consultants provide services across the state, working with individual centers every other week for six months. The mental health consultants strive to form relationships with teachers and directors to assist them in creating supportive environments for young children and building strong teacher–child relationships. With this foundation in place, the mental health consultant works with center staff to design specific interventions for children who exhibit challenging behaviors and provide referrals for families if needed.

Program evaluation has demonstrated that teachers who received the Tulane model of ECMHC believe that they are more efficacious as teachers (Heller et al., 2011). Observation showed that teachers provided increased emotional support for children (e.g., they were more sensitive and showed greater regard for the student's perspective) and increased classroom organization skills (e.g., behavior management) (Heller et al., in press).

The ECMHC model works at two levels: program-wide and child-specific. For example, one center requested ECMHC to assist in the 2-year-old classroom. The teacher, Ms. Jenny, was struggling with the aggressive behaviors of three children in her class. The mental health consultant spent time in the classroom and worked with Ms. Jenny to create visual schedules and visual class rules to help all children in the class know what to expect during the day. The mental health consultant encouraged Ms. Jenny to discuss the visual schedule and the three simple rules with the children individually and during small and large group activities to help children to learn and remember the rules. Verbal reinforcement was given throughout the day when children followed the rules (e.g., "Wow, Kwan, you used your gentle hands while playing with Esme. You should be really proud of yourself!").

After these supports were in place, one child, Jackson, continued to display aggressive behaviors. The mental health consultant observed Jackson closely and met with Ms. Jenny and Jackson's parents. Together they created a behavior management plan for school and home. Jackson's family also acted on a referral provided by the mental health consultant to help Jackson get a behavioral evaluation.

Teachers who have worked with mental health consultants in their classrooms using the Tulane model have said:

"It is always nice to have a fresh pair of eyes to see things that I may have missed … just to see the same situation in a different perspective … the idea that all situations have a solution. You just have to figure it out!"

"I had a challenging child in my class, and she and I worked together to find solutions to help him. She was very encouraging to me. She taught me to praise good behavior and other children will follow."

Source: Heller, S. S., Boothe, A., Keyes, A., Nagle, G., Sidell, M., & Rice, J. (2011). Implementation of a mental health consultation model and its impact on early childhood teachers' efficacy and competence. *Infant Mental Health Journal, 32,* 143–164. doi:10.1002/imhj.20289.

CHECK YOUR UNDERSTANDING 12.4

Click here to check your understanding of mental health disorders in children and the teaching strategies for those children.

Providing mental health services in the early childhood setting is a prevention effort that benefits all children who are enrolled. In this way, early childhood teachers and their programs contribute to public health by ensuring that children's social and emotional needs are recognized and addressed.

Unfortunately, few early childhood teachers have access to mental health consultants and not all schools have counselors or behavior specialists on staff. Community resources may be available to provide some assistance. Local early intervention services for children with special developmental needs or community health services may offer some supports.

Pursuing professional development training related to children's mental health and advocating for resources to use in accessing occasional mental health consultations are other important ways teachers build skills and raise awareness of the importance of children's mental health. Teachers are in a good position to engage in advocacy efforts that bring attention to the need for mental health services for young children.

SUMMARY

- Children's mental health refers to children's capacities to manage and express appropriate emotional responses and behaviors, to form close relationships, and to explore and learn. Children who are supported to develop these capabilities are able to adjust successfully to new situations and build positive future relationships.
- There are key skills in childhood that promote social and emotional wellness: forming healthy relationships and developing self-concept, self-efficacy, self-regulation, and resilience. Teachers can promote these skills by creating supportive environments, establishing caring relationships, and realizing the importance of play.
- Teachers can better manage mental health problems by understanding prevalence, consequences, cultural influences, and relationship to physical health and by recognizing atypical behaviors in the classroom.
- Mental health disorders in childhood include behavioral, anxiety, and mood disorders. The teacher's role is a critical component in diagnosis and management of these conditions.

Chapter Quiz

 Click here to check your understanding of Chapter 12, Children's Mental Health.

Discussion Starters

1. Think of a child of any age you know or have worked with who exhibited difficult behaviors. Discuss any risk factors the child had, such as living in poverty or in a single-parent household? Discuss any specific warning signs?
2. Consider a child in the early childhood setting who has been exposed to a significant amount of violence and is displaying severe aggression in the classroom. Can you apply the principles of inclusion described in the chapter? How do you feel about including these children in the classroom? Describe some advantages and disadvantages to inclusion.
3. Based on what you have read about risk factors that contribute to poor mental health in children, what national policies contribute to these risk factors? What national policies help alleviate the stress of these factors on children? What services available in your community help families who are at risk?

Practice Points

1. Teachers have many opportunities in the classroom to promote social and emotional development by establishing healthy relationships and promoting healthy play activities. How can teachers engage families in promoting healthy social and emotional development?

2. Mood disorders can interfere with healthy social and emotional development. How can teachers help children with mood disorders establish healthy relationships with their peers in the classroom?

3. Develop a list of resources and agencies in your community that can help early childhood programs manage challenging behaviors.

Web Resources

Georgetown University Center for the Early Childhood Mental Health Consultant

Harvard Howard University Center for the Developing Child

Tulane University Institute of Infant and Early Childhood Mental Health

Zero to Three: Early Childhood Mental Health

Key Terms

ADHD

adverse childhood experiences (ACEs)

attachment

attachment theory

bipolar disorder

bullying

caregiver

conduct disorder

continuum of mental health

depression

egocentric

externalizing behaviors

functional behavioral assessment

generalized anxiety disorder

internalizing behaviors

joint attention

mental health

mood disorder

obsessive-compulsive disorder

oppositional defiant disorder

post-traumatic stress disorder

reactive attachment disorder

resilience

self-concept

self-efficacy

self-regulation

separation anxiety

toxic stress

PART

4

PROMOTING SAFETY

CHAPTER 13

Enhancing Safety Through Appropriate Environments

learning outcomes

After reading this chapter, you should be able to:

1. Identify how safety impacts children's physical and emotional development and list the most frequent causes of unintentional injury.

2. Describe the purpose of regulations and licensing and discuss how program administrators and teachers use those regulations in planning.

3. Identify the factors that guide planning and development of the aspects of a safe facility for young children.

4. Discuss the ways teachers create safe indoor classroom environments for young children.

5. Explain the characteristics of toys that are safe and appropriate for early childhood settings.

6. Describe the considerations that are important when creating safe outdoor environments for young children.

CASE STUDY

Cass and Everett are looking for child care for their 2-year-old son, Caden. They have heard good things about Sunshine Child Development Center, so they schedule a visit and prepare a list of questions. Barb, the classroom teacher, greets them, gives them a tour of the classrooms and play yard, and describes the curriculum.

Cass likes the colorful environment and the energetic involvement of the children. Everett is impressed by the pretend tide pool touch table and the way the children and teacher are exploring the materials and talking about the oceans. Even so, they have concerns. They have never left Caden in a setting without individual attention, and

they worry about whether he will be safe. They ask about the teachers, wanting to know about their education and whether they are trained in first aid.

Barb realizes that this family needs reassurance that their son will be well cared for. Barb describes the program's safety policies. She talks about how the room arrangement helps the children play safely while being supervised by the teachers. As they watch, Cass and Everett observe a teacher holding a child who has fallen down. They like the way she comforts the child and then treats the hurt using gloves and speaking calmly. When they leave, the parents feel confident that they have found a setting that will be a good fit for Caden and for them.

safety
protection from harm or danger

Ensuring children's **safety** is a fundamental responsibility of early childhood teachers. Because potential threats to children's safety are present in all parts of the physical and emotional environment, achieving safety is not something that can happen by accident. Safety is established when teachers merge their knowledge of child growth and development with recognition of the potential risks for harm. Hazards such as accidents caused by risks in the environment, poor supervision or safety management practices, weather and other natural disasters, and violence in the community or children's homes are all aspects that early childhood teachers must consider. Teachers are called on to be aware of potential safety risks and capable of addressing them through careful planning of indoor and outdoor play and learning environments.

In this chapter, we describe the importance of safety to children's healthy growth and development and discuss the accidental injuries that occur most frequently during childhood. We explore the safety standards and regulations that guide the creation of safe early childhood environments. Finally we identify the characteristics of safe indoor and outdoor classrooms and provide guidance about selecting toys and equipment that are safe and developmentally appropriate for young children.

ENSURING PHYSICAL AND EMOTIONAL SAFETY

During the early years, growth and development occur at a rapid pace. Because of this, teachers need to understand the role of safety in children's typical growth and development. Attention to both physical and emotional safety is important. Teachers also need to recognize the influence of development on children's physical ability to navigate safely in the world and their emotional maturity to make safe decisions.

Understanding the Impact of Safety on Healthy Development

Safe environments support children's healthy development.

Ensuring safety is naturally focused on avoiding harm and pain. However, it is also a foundational requirement for children's healthy development. For children to grow, thrive, and develop to their fullest potential, their physical and emotional safety requirements must be recognized. Children's basic needs must be met, and the classroom must be created as a safe refuge.

Attending to Physical Safety Needs

Physical safety involves freedom from real or threatened bodily harm. Children's physical safety is achieved by considering safety in all aspects of early childhood program planning.

Teachers promote physical safety by arranging environments to protect children from injuries such as bumps, bruises, cuts, and scrapes. Teachers select toys and equipment that offer safe and appropriate challenge for children's capabilities. Teachers consider safety when selecting appropriate food and determining how to offer it at meals to prevent choking. Safety guides the implementation of practices to avoid the spread of germs that

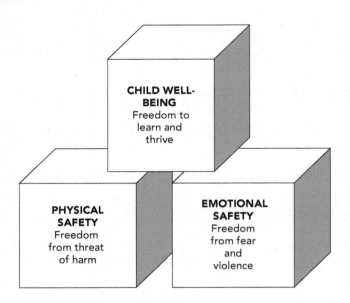

FIGURE 13-1

Physical and Emotional Safety Serve as Supports for a Child's Well-Being

may lead to disease and illness. As a result, children are able to explore, focus, be active, rest, and learn—free from the threat of harm.

Teachers are generally accustomed to these essential teaching responsibilities. But physical safety is only one important aspect of a child's well-being that must be considered. Emotional safety is another significant element of a child-safe environment.

Supporting Emotional Safety Needs

Emotional safety refers to children's internal sense of security. It includes the sense of being protected, sheltered, and free from fear and violence. Emotional safety is achieved by protecting children from experiences that cause anxiety or fear or that damage their spirit and sense of personal worth.

Teachers accomplish this by providing children with experiences where they are free to develop trust and confidence. Emotional safety is supported by a favorable teacher-to-child ratio, predictable routines, and developmentally appropriate activities. For infants, emotional safety is provided through responsive and caring relationships where voices are soothing, touch is kind, and the child's needs are met. Preschoolers and older children experience emotional safety when teachers guide them to learn appropriate ways of interacting and when teacher's step in to ensure that no child experiences bullying or intimidation (National Association for the Education of Young Children [NAEYC], 2011; Shonkoff & Phillips, 2000).

Children who feel emotionally safe are able to be responsive to the guidance of the teacher and more capable of following safety rules. They are able to be attentive to their environment and open to learning from experiences. This emotional comfort supports development of *executive functioning skills* such as remembering directions, controlling reactions, and being flexible, aspects that form the foundation for cognitive and social abilities (Center on The Developing Child at Harvard University, 2012; Shonkoff & Phillips, 2000). Emotional safety is a component of positive mental health that enables children to establish a sense of personal value or worthiness (Cohen, Onunaku, Cothier, & Poppe, 2005). (See Figure 13-1.)

Addressing Basic Needs

Children's growth and development rely on having their basic needs met. These basic needs are thought to exist in a hierarchy, or ladder, of levels (Maslow, 1954). First on the ladder, are the foundational needs—those that are crucial for basic survival, including physical or bodily needs (air, food, water, and shelter) and safety needs (including the physical and emotional safety needs of protection from violence and aggression). Next

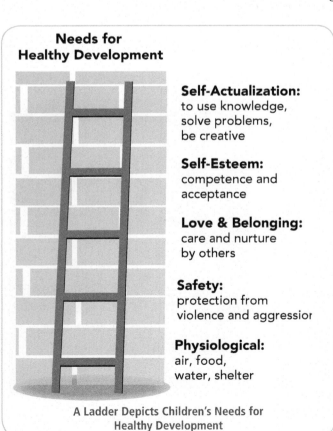

Needs for Healthy Development

Self-Actualization: to use knowledge, solve problems, be creative

Self-Esteem: competence and acceptance

Love & Belonging: care and nurture by others

Safety: protection from violence and aggression

Physiological: air, food, water, shelter

A Ladder Depicts Children's Needs for Healthy Development

are needs related to love and belonging (the need to be cared for and nurtured by others), self-esteem (the need to feel competent and socially acceptable), and self-actualization (the need to use and apply knowledge, be able to solve problems, and express oneself creatively). Children's needs at each step of the ladder must be met before the child can grow, develop, and move to the next level of the hierarchy ladder. Safety is an important first step.

When children are in out-of-home care settings, the important task of meeting these needs falls to the teachers and early childhood program. This is a reminder of the important contribution that teachers make to young children's physical and emotional safety, essential aspects of well-being.

Creating the Classroom as Refuge for Children

Some children face many challenges in their daily lives outside the early childhood classroom. As depicted in Figure 13-2, some of these challenges involve negative experiences that can harm children's brain development, such as violence, abuse, and unsafe living conditions (Shonkoff & Phillips, 2000). Early childhood classrooms offer a time and space in which children can be free from worry about their physical and emotional safety, allowing them to relax and learn.

Teachers who create classroom environments that protect children from threats and ensure their physical and emotional safety introduce a vision of a healthy lifestyle that supports children in two ways. First, children are provided a direct opportunity to rest, be nurtured, and learn within the secure environment. Second, seeds are planted for the future; children are given concrete experiences of safe and

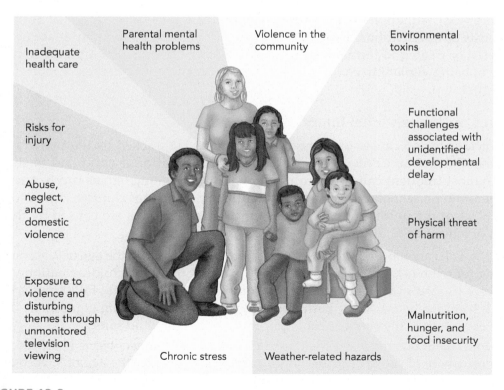

FIGURE 13-2

The Classroom Is a Refuge from Threats to Children's Physical and Emotional Safety

Source: Based on *From neurons to neighborhoods: The science of early childhood development*, edited by J. P. Shonkoff and D. A. Phillips, 2000, Washington, DC: National Academy Press, retrieved July 30, 2015, from http://www.nap.edu/openbook .php?isbn=0309069882.

healthy living that give them hope and broaden their understanding of what their futures can be.

Parents such as Cass and Everett in the opening case scenario may not specifically ask how the program addresses physical and emotional safety or basic needs. Instead they may ask, "What do you do if a child hits?" or "How will you be sure our child is picked up only by our child care provider or us?" Teachers can offer confident descriptions of how they ensure that children's physical and emotional safety needs are met.

Identifying Unintentional Injuries

Injuries during the early years range from the familiar bumps, scrapes, and bruises that are common among young children, to significant injuries that may lead to lifelong disability or death. These are called unintentional injuries. Unintentional injuries are often referred to as "accidents." However, the Centers for Disease Control and Prevention (Centers for Disease Control and Prevention [CDC], 2013a) has chosen to move away from this definition. Instead it defines unintentional injuries as predictable and preventable events that result in harm, not accidents. In this way, the focus is on injury prevention through the use of appropriate safety precautions.

unintentional injuries
predictable and preventable injuries from accidents

Many children suffer from unintentional injuries each year. It is estimated that nearly 9 million children under the age of 19 are seen in hospital emergency departments every year due to unintentional injury, and more than 225,000 are hospitalized due to their injuries (CDC, 2013a). The costs related to treatment of these injuries are estimated at $87 billion a year for medical costs and related costs such as loss of family income when wage earners must stay home to care for children (CDC, 2013a). Although these numbers are large, it is likely that the actual number and costs of unintentional injuries is even higher because many injuries are never reported or treated in formal settings. Even so, these figures highlight the importance of being vigilant to children's safety. Knowing about the causes of injury is a good first step.

Causes of Unintentional Injury

The incidence and causes of unintentional injuries are tracked by the Centers for Disease Control and Prevention (Table 13-1). Information is compiled to show the 10 most frequent causes of unintentional injury among babies (up to age 1), toddlers and preschoolers (ages 1 to 4), and primary school-age children (ages 5 to 9). Over 73% of the unintentional injuries for these age groups are caused by three types of injury (CDC, 2013a):

falls
the leading cause of injury that occurs when a person descends abruptly due to the force of gravity and strikes a surface at the same or a lower level

- *Falls:* Falls are the leading cause of injury in children under the age of 9, accounting for over 44% of total injuries. In 2013, over 1.6 million children nationwide were treated in hospital emergency rooms due to accidental falls from cribs, high chairs, beds, chairs, bathtubs, and playground climbing equipment. The risk for falls is the single most important concern for child safety.

struck by or against injury
resulting from being hit or by hitting against an object

- *Struck by or against injury:* Being struck or striking against objects is the second most frequent cause of treated injury for children under the age of 9, accounting for over 21% of the unintentional injuries for the age group. Injuries of this kind occur when babies pull objects over onto themselves, toddlers wobble into the edge of tabletops, or preschoolers and elementary school-aged children accidentally hit each other with toys or sports equipment. The world is full of risks for this kind of injury.

TABLE 13-1 National Estimates of the 10 Leading Causes of Nonfatal Injuries, United States, 2013

Rank	Birth–1 year	1–4 Years	5–9 Years
1	Fall 134,229	Fall 852,884	Fall 624,890
2	Struck by/against 28,786	Struck by/against 336,917	Struck by/against 403,522
3	Bite or sting 12,186	Bite or sting 158,587	Cut or pierce 112,633
4	Foreign body 10,650	Foreign body 139,597	Bite or sting 107,975
5	Other 10,511	Cut/pierce 85,575	Overexertion 93,612
6	Fire/burn 9,816	Overexertion 81,588	Pedal cyclist 74,831
7	Inhalation/suffocation 8,294	Other specified 65,120	Foreign body 63,450
8	Cut/pierce 7,139	Fire/burn 52,884	Motor vehicle occupant 58,114
9	Unspecified 5,735	Unspecified 41,297	Dog bite 43,499
10	Overexertion 4,985	Poisoning 32,443	Unspecified 35,303
Total	**232,331**	**1,846,892**	**1,617,829**

Based on *National Estimates of the 10 Leading Causes of Nonfatal Injuries Treated in Hospital Emergency Departments, United States, 2013*, by the Centers for Disease Control and Prevention, National Center for Injury Prevention and Control, Office of Statistics and Programming, retrieved March 2015, from http://www.cdc.gov/injury/wisqars/pdf/leading_cause_of_nonfatal _injury_2013-a.pdf.

- *Bite or sting injury:* Bites and stings are the third most frequent cause of injury for children age 4 and under and the fourth cause of injury for children ages 5 to 9. This type of injury accounts for over 8% of the unintentional injuries among children under the age of 9. Bites or stings include human, animal, or insect bites and insect, jellyfish, or plant stings.

bite or sting injury includes human, animal, or insect bites or stings from jellyfish, insects, or plants

Teachers need to be keenly aware of these most frequent causes of unintentional injuries and generally knowledgeable about the range of types of unintentional injury for each age group. This information helps to focus attention on preventive actions.

Defining Fatal Injuries

Some unintentional injuries ultimately lead to death. These are called **fatal injuries**. Table 13-2 depicts the most frequent causes of fatal injuries among young children. For teachers, the possibility of a child dying from an injury sustained while in the early childhood setting is unthinkable. But the early years are a time of fast growth and rapid change that increase children's vulnerability. Children's ability to put themselves at risk can outpace their judgment. They rely on the adults in their lives—families and teachers—to keep them safe. Being aware of the most common causes of fatal injuries helps teachers to take action to reduce children's risk.

fatal injuries unintentional injuries that ultimately lead to death

Falls are the leading cause of injury among young children.

Incidence of Fatal Injuries

Unintentional injuries are the leading cause of death among children and teens. In 2013, nearly 3,600 children died from unintentional injuries (Centers for Disease Control and Prevention [CDC], National Center for Injury Prevention and Control, Office of Statistics and Programming, 2013). Death due to injury was highest in the 1- to 4-year-old age group (toddlers and preschoolers), followed by infants (birth to 1 year) and school-age children (5 to 9 years of age) (CDC, 2013b).

Causes of Fatal Injury

The four primary causes of death due to injury among young children in 2012 have been identified by the CDC (2013b):

- **Suffocation** was the leading cause of death due to injury for children under the age of 9 years, accounting for 1,184 deaths in 2013. Nearly 83% of child deaths caused by suffocation occurred among infants.
- **Motor vehicle and traffic accidents** ranked second in 2013, causing the death of 735 children. This category was the leading cause of injury death among children ages 5 to 9 years old.

TABLE 13-2   Ten Leading Causes of Injury Death by Age Group, United States, 2013

Rank	Birth–1 Year	1–4 Years	5–9 Years
1	Suffocation 979	Drowning 393	Motor vehicle/traffic 342
2	Homicide: unspecified 139	Motor vehicle/traffic 327	Drowning 116
3	Homicide: other 74	Suffocation 161	Fire/burns 87
4	Motor vehicle/traffic 66	Homicide: unspecified 153	Homicide: firearm 48
5	Undetermined: suffocation 43	Fire/burns 129	Suffocation 44
6	Undetermined 28	Pedestrian 90	Other land transport 29
7	Drowning 23	Homicide: other 71	Natural/environmental 22
8	Homicide: suffocation 22	Natural/environment 43	Pedestrian 18
9	Natural/environment 19	Homicide: firearm 39	Homicide: other 15
10	Fire/burn 17	Struck by/against 33	Unintentional: firearm 15
Total	**1,410**	**1.439**	**736**

Based on: *10 Leading Causes of Injury Death by Age Group Highlighting Unintentional Injury Deaths, United States, 2013b*, Centers for Disease Control and Prevention, National Center for Injury Prevention and Control, Office of Statistics and Programming, retrieved March 2015, from http://www.cdc.gov/injury/images/lc-charts/leading_causes_of_injury_deaths_highlighting _unintentional_injury_2013-a.gif; http://www.cdc.gov/injury/wisqars/pdf/leading_cause_of_nonfatal_injury_2013-a.pdf.

Jupiterimages/Stockbyte/Getty Images

- **Drowning** ranked third, causing 532 child deaths in 2013. This was the leading cause of injury death among children ages 1 to 4 years old.
- **Burns** ranked fourth for non-homicide-related deaths, causing 233 child deaths in 2013. The highest number of burn injury deaths occurred among 1- to 4-year-olds.

While the ranking of these four causes of fatal injury tends to vary from year to year among the age groups, suffocation, vehicle accidents, drowning, and burns persist as the most significant dangers to young children.

Understanding Risk Factors for Unintentional Injury and Death

A variety of factors influence the incidence of injuries and fatalities due to injury among children (Borse et al., 2008; Danseco, Miller, & Spicer, 2000). These include children's age, developmental maturity, sex, race/ethnicity, socioeconomic status, location of residence, and the child's individual risk profile. The association of these factors to actual risk for injury for a particular child is a matter of speculation, as described next.

Child Age

The number of unintentional injuries tends to be higher among preschoolers and young primary school-age children; however, the number of deaths due to injury is highest among infants and preschoolers (CDC, 2013). The high unintentional death rate among children under the age of 1 is due primarily to unintentional suffocation or accidental strangulation. Unintentional suffocation includes **sudden infant death syndrome (SIDS)**. SIDS, the sudden and unexplainable death of a young child, is the leading cause of death of children under the age of 1 year (CDC, 2013; National Institute of Child Health and Human Development [NICHD], 2012).

Child's Developmental Maturity

Developmental maturity also influences risk. For example, infants who are less mobile may be unable to move away from the dangers that lead to suffocation. On-the-other-hand, as children grow and mature, they gain new motor skills and can more easily move themselves into dangerous situations. Their newfound mobility may exceed their ability to recognize danger. For example, physically adept 1- to 4-year-olds may put themselves in danger of drowning by exploring water sources. Children in the 5- to 9-year-old age group may be allowed to move about more freely, such as walking and bicycling near traffic, which can put them at risk for motor vehicle and traffic injuries. These examples highlight the importance of adult supervision across the early childhood age range.

At the same time, the risks for some injuries decrease as children age and mature. For example, the number of deaths from pedestrian causes drops as children age (CDC, 2013b). This suggests that children become more able to understand the dangers, and be responsive to educational guidance about staying away from traffic.

Child's Sex

Death rates due to injury are higher in boys than girls (CDC, 2012). This may be because boys are often encouraged to take risks and may be allowed to test their skills more freely, or they may receive less supervision.

suffocation
inhalation, aspiration, or ingestion of food or other object that blocks the airway

motor vehicle and traffic accidents
death due to injuries sustained when riding as a passenger in a vehicle

drowning
suffocation (asphyxia) resulting from submersion in water or another liquid

burns
severe exposure to flames, heat, or chemicals that leads to tissue damage in the skin or deeper in the body; injury from smoke inhalation to the upper airway, lower airway, or lungs

sudden infant death syndrome (SIDS)
the sudden and unexplainable death of a young child

WHAT IF . . .

A parent told you that her 3-year-old son had been treated in the emergency room because of falls from climbing on high shelves at home? What steps would you take to increase the safety of this child in your classroom?

Child's Race/ethnicity

Death due to injury occurs with about the same frequency among white and African American children, but more often among American Indian and Alaskan Native children (CDC, 2012). These higher mortality rates due to injury may suggest exposure to more severe injuries or less access to follow-up health care or both.

Child's Individual Potential for Risk

Individual children also have unique characteristics that may put them at risk for injury. Aspects such as how the child approaches a new situation or responds to directions may affect their safety in the early childhood setting. Teachers can use information that parents may share, such as statements that a child "Always climbs on things" or "Puts things in her mouth," as well as direct observation to recognize risky behaviors that require focused supervision.

Family Socioeconomic Status

A variety of socioeconomic factors are associated with higher rates of unintentional injuries (CDC, 2012). These include low family income, younger and less educated mothers, higher numbers of people in the household, single parenting, and low-income neighborhoods with crowded multifamily dwellings.

Location of Child's Residence

Children who live, work on, or visit farms are considered at special risk for injury or death. Risks are related to child involvement with machinery, including riding all-terrain vehicles (ATVs), and interaction with large animals. Although the numbers of child injuries in agricultural settings has decreased in recent years due to special injury prevention initiatives, the number of unintentional injuries among children under the age of 10 has increased (National Children's Center for Rural and Agricultural Health and Safety, 2013). Issues related to providing insufficient supervision or allowing children to assume responsibilities that exceed their developmental maturity for understanding safety risks may be aspects that put children at risk.

Acknowledging Risk for Injury in Early Childhood Settings

Unfortunately, only 38 states require licensed early childhood programs to report child fatalities that occur in child care (Child Care Aware of America, 2014). The most recent study of child injury and fatality in child care settings was conducted in 2005 by Wrigley and Dreby. Their study suggests that out-of-home early childhood settings are generally safe environments for young children; however, accidents do occur and some children's settings are safer than others (Wrigley & Dreby, 2005). The study examined the numbers of fatal injuries reported in three types of early childhood settings: child care centers, family child care

The risk for injury is high among children who live in rural areas.

Vstock LLC/Thinkstock/Getty Images

homes (care for small groups of children in the provider's home), and in-home child care (care provided for children in the child's home). Of the nearly 1,400 fatal injuries reviewed, the fewest (110) occurred in child care centers. In-home child care reported 320 deaths. The most fatalities occurred in family child care homes where more than 700 child deaths were reported.

It was postulated that fewer fatalities occurred in child care centers because of the more open nature of the environment and the presence of two or more teachers. Teachers in child care centers are also easily observed, which may allow supervisors and other teachers to provide advice regarding safety practices, assist with challenges, and offer support when needed. The safety standards required for licensed children's centers are also likely to reduce the frequency of child injury and death. By contrast, teachers in family child care homes and in-home settings usually work alone or with relatively little support. Family child care and in-home settings may also have environmental dangers that are not present in center-based settings.

Implications for Teachers

Even though the numbers of child fatalities in child care appear to be relatively low, teachers must maintain vigilance for safety. Child Care Aware of America (2014) points out that given the numbers of infants in child care, less than 9 % of SIDS deaths should be occurring in those settings. However, data suggests that 20 % of SIDS deaths are occurring while children are in child care. In addition, increasing numbers of 3- to 5-year-old children in the general population and a continued focus on the importance of early childhood education indicate that more children under the age of 5 will participate in out-of-home care and education settings in the next decade (Bureau of Labor Statistics, U.S. Department of Labor, 2014). These trends highlight the need for teachers to be aware of emerging safety trends and learn to be proactive in keeping children safe. Understanding and following safety standards and regulations are important support resources in this effort.

CHECK YOUR UNDERSTANDING 13.1
Click here to check your understanding of ensuring physical and emotional safety.

USING REGULATIONS TO IMPROVE SAFETY

Early childhood programs and teachers have access to a variety of resources that guide the development of safety policies and practices. These include professional organizations, research institutes, and the state and local regulatory agencies that oversee the safety standards that guide programs serving young children. Licensing requirements and accreditation standards help teachers implement the essential elements of safe early childhood classrooms.

Implementing Safety Regulations

A primary resource for safety in early childhood programs is the publication *Caring for Our Children: National Health and Safety Performance Standards: Guidelines for Out-of-Home Child Care Programs*. This publication is a joint effort of the American Academy of Pediatrics, the American Public Health Association, and the National Resource Center for Health and Safety in Child Care and Early Education.

It provides a comprehensive list of safety standards and recommendations developed from reviews of research and the debates and discussions of individuals and associations concerned for child safety. A key recommendation directs each state to establish by law a regulatory agency with authority to protect children through mandatory licensing of all out-of-home care settings. The recommendation advocates for mandatory licensing of all children's programs, including both part-time and full-time settings.

The Role of the Regulatory Agency

Each state has a regulatory agency that is responsible for creating minimum health and safety standards for child care settings to protect children from harm and to enhance children's learning and development. All 50 states and the District of Columbia regulate child care to some extent, although the structure of oversight varies from state to state. The child care regulatory agencies are directed by legislation to:

- Establish standards for out-of-home child care.
- Monitor for compliance.
- Enforce the child care regulations.

Licensing Criteria

The criteria that identify which programs must be licensed vary from state to state. Most regulatory agencies use the following factors to determine which programs must be licensed:

- *Group size:* the number of children to be served.
- *Length of the service day:* to separate child care from residential or 24-hour care.
- *Location of care:* centers, family child care homes, and in-home child care.

Regulated child care settings typically include child care centers, school-based child care settings, and family child care homes (home settings where a provider cares for a small group of children that are not the provider's own). Some children's settings may be exempt from the regulatory requirements. These include child care provided in the child's own home (in-home child care); recreation programs; day camps; and programs where the child's parent is on site, such as child care at sports clubs and in faith-group settings.

The National Association for Regulatory Administration (NARA) (2013) estimates that there are more than 10 million licensed child care slots nationwide. These are located in approximately 312,254 licensed child care facilities and 45,244 group child care homes. Of the children who participate in out-of-home child care, 75% attend center-based settings and 12% participate in group child care homes.

Understanding Common Licensing Requirements

Licensing covers a range of requirements that create the minimum foundation for health and safety in out-of-home care settings. Child care licensing requirements address licensing applications and fees, facilities, program design and practices, teacher qualifications and orientation, health and nutrition, and the children's educational program.

Licensing Application and Fees

Child care programs that are regulated must apply for a license before starting services. About half of the states require a fee for the license. The fee for center-based care programs is usually based on the number of children in care. Family child care or group child care homes are most often charged a flat licensing fee. Most licenses are valid for a one- to two-year period (NARA, 2013).

Facility Requirements

Facility inspections are conducted by a designated agency such as the city or county fire inspector or health department sanitarian. The children's environments are reviewed to identify fire hazards (blocked evacuation route, too much paper on the walls), health and sanitation concerns (water, heat, toileting facilities), emergency facility supports (emergency lighting, exits, evacuation plans), and adherence to local building codes. Minimum square footage requirements, cleanliness, durability and appropriateness of furnishings, food preparation, and service areas are also inspected.

Program Design and Practices

Licensing requirements include expectations for program design and operation. Guidance is provided for determining child age groupings, class group size, and teacher-to-child ratios. Table 13-3 describes recommendations for maximum group size and teacher-to-child ratios for licensed early childhood programs.

TABLE 13-3 Class Size and Teacher-to-Child Ratios for NAEYC-Accredited Programs		
Child Age Groups	**Maximum Class Size**	**Teacher-to-Child Ratio**
Infants (birth to 15 months)	6 8	1:3 1:4
Toddlers (12 to 38 months)	6 8 10 12	1:3 1:4 1:4 1:4
Toddlers and Twos (21 to 36 months)	8 10 12	1:4 1:5 1:6
Preschoolers (2.5- and 3-year-olds)	12 14 16 18	1:6 1:7 1:8 1:9
Preschoolers (4- and 5-year-olds)	16 18 20	1:8 1:9 1:10
Kindergartners and young school-age children (5- to 9-year-olds)	20 22 24	1:10 1:11 1:12

Sources: Based on *Leadership & management: A guide to the NAEYC early childhood program standards and related accreditation criteria*, (p. 29), edited by S. Ritchie and B. Willer, 2005, Washington, DC: National Association for the Education of Young Children and American Academy of Pediatrics, American Public Health Association, National Resource Center for Health and Safety in Child Care and Early Education, 2011 and *Caring for our children: National health and safety performance standards; Guidelines for early care and education programs*. 3rd edition. Elk Grove Village, IL: American Academy of Pediatrics; Washington, DC: American Public Health Association.

A variety of safety procedures are mandated, such as maintaining child attendance records, planning secure arrival and departure practices, supervising children, managing guidance and discipline, conducting emergency evacuation drills, and planning for child safety in special settings such as field trips, transportation, water activities, and nap time.

Teacher Qualifications and Requirements at Hire

Licensing regulations outline the required qualifications for teachers and program directors, including minimum age, education, and experience. A criminal background screening and reference checks are required before hire. Many states require a preemployment health assessment to rule out the presence of a communicable disease or conditions that cannot be managed through safety practices. Orientation to program safety procedures, emergency response, and child abuse reporting are often requirements for preemployment training.

Children's Health and Nutrition

Regulations also mandate health practices used to reduce the spread of disease and ensure child safety in the program setting. These include following recommendations for child health exams before enrollment; gathering information about a child's special health, nutrition, and feeding needs; and ensuring that children have required immunizations before they participate. The *Health Hint* describes the ways in which immunizations protect children in care and education settings from the effects of disease. A variety of other guidelines promote children's health and safety in child care.

Children's Programming

Licensing standards describe expectations for the design of the children's program. These include expectations for the use of developmentally appropriate activities, communicating with families, and always allowing families to access their child and the classroom.

HEALTH HINT   Immunizations Keep Children Safe from Disease

The National Vaccine Program Office in the U.S. Department of Health and Human Services has developed a website to provide information and resources about vaccines and immunizations for infants, children, teens, adults, and seniors. It offers these important reasons to vaccinate children.

Immunizations can save a child's life. Some childhood diseases once killed or injured millions of children. Vaccination has eliminated these risks for many diseases.

Vaccination is safe and effective. Immunizations are given only after careful review by scientists and medical professionals. The benefits of vaccination are greater than possible side effects for most children.

Immunizations protect other loved ones. Immunizing children helps stop the spread of disease to others, including babies, other family members, and friends.

Immunizations can save time and money. Childhood diseases can cause suffering and disability. Illness associated with childhood diseases may involve costly medical assistance or require a family member to stay home from work to care for a child. Because most insurance companies cover the cost of immunization, families are supported in keeping their child well and healthy.

Immunization protects future generations. Vaccines have reduced or eliminated many diseases, such as smallpox, that killed or disabled people in the past. Immunizing children helps ensure that the diseases of today are not around in the future.

U.S. Department of Health and Human Services. vaccines.gov. *Five Important Reasons to Vaccinate Your Child*. Washington DC. Retrieved March 2015 from http://www.vaccines.gov/more_info/features/five-important-reasons-to-vaccinate-your-child.html

Monitoring for Compliance

Regulatory agencies must ensure that licensed programs meet the mandatory requirements at the time the license is approved and that compliance is maintained on an ongoing basis. Monitoring for compliance and instituting clear sanctions for noncompliance are important aspects of health and safety in early childhood programs.

Conducting Site Visits

Regulatory agencies monitor programs through both prearranged and unannounced site inspections, classroom observations, and review of records. Inspections focus on identifying problems that put children at risk for injury or disease. The most commonly identified licensing violations identified during monitoring visits include (NARA, 2013):

- *Supervision gaps* such as putting children at risk through inconsistent or incomplete supervision practices.
- *Staff-to-child ratio violations* such as having too few teachers for the group size or age of children or exceeding the required maximum group size.
- *Health/safety/cleanliness/nutrition issues* such as poor program practices or lack of adherence to program policies.
- *Discipline/behavior management problems,* including providing inappropriate activities.

Site visits are also used as opportunities to provide technical assistance to help program staff meet and exceed the minimum licensing requirements for keeping children safe.

Investigating Complaints

Child care regulatory agencies may receive complaints about licensed child care settings from the general public or families of children in care. The licensing agency documents all complaints and decides how to follow up based on knowledge of the early childhood setting and the immediacy of the concern. Unannounced visits and interviews with the program director may be conducted to explore the validity of the complaint.

Some regulatory agencies now make information about verified complaints and the agency's actions available to the general public through the agency website. This step confirms the seriousness with which regulatory agencies view their role in increasing safety in early childhood settings and reminds teachers to ensure that licensing regulations are put into practice every day.

Responding to Licensing Violations

If licensing violations are discovered, the regulatory agency must determine a course of action. Some violations can be remedied quickly, such as posting emergency procedures. Others may constitute a serious problem that threatens child safety, such as not conducting criminal background checks on program staff. Once the nature of the violation is understood, the regulatory agency determines the appropriate consequence.

Enforcing Consequences

Repercussions are determined based on the severity of the violation. They might include putting the program on probation until the violation has been remedied, withholding licensing, or closing the facility. In some cases, programs may have to pay a fine.

In a few cases, the violation may be of significant severity that criminal prosecution and imprisonment are the outcome (NARA, 2013). Enforcing health and safety standards is an important way in which the regulatory agency provides for the safety of young children in out-of-home care and education settings.

Moving Beyond Minimum Standards

Public systems to ensure the safety of children in out-of-home care settings are still evolving, and current licensing and regulatory activities still fall short of the goals for thorough and effective licensing systems. Not all states systematically implement regulatory rules for programs serving children in out-of-home settings, and many children's programs are not licensed. And although information on strategies that improve child safety are becoming more readily available, regulatory standards do not always keep up. For example, the "Safe to Sleep" campaign has reduced death due to SIDS by 50% for infants below the age of 1 (Eunice Kennedy Shriver National Institute of Child Health and Development, NIH, DHHS, 2012). New recommendations for a *safe infant sleep environment* include using no soft bedding such as blankets in infant sleep spaces (American Academy of Pediatrics, 2011). Although evidence shows that the states are making positive efforts to improve licensing requirements and policies which ensure the health and safety in care (NARA 2013), progress is still needed. Improvements might include:

- Mandatory licensing for all programs that serve young children in out-of-home care.
- More complete regulations regarding the skills and education of childhood teachers.
- More focus on research-guided policies.
- More vigorous enforcement of mandatory requirements.

Individual programs can choose to move beyond the minimum regulations. One way is to achieve program accreditation by the NAEYC.

Program Accreditation

Accreditation by entities such as the NAEYC guides early childhood programs through a process of self-study and improvement to increase the quality of their program of care and education. Achieving accreditation shows that a program has met important quality standards. All children's settings can voluntarily use the materials provided by the NAEYC to set a course of action to identify aspects of service that need improvement and to take steps to enhance program quality.

Increasing Quality in Other Ways

Quality rating and improvement systems (QRIS) are being developed by many states to increase the quality

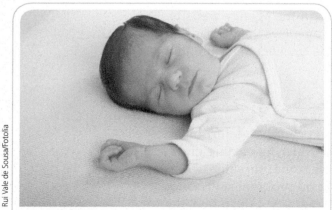

Placing infants on their backs in safe sleep environments has greatly reduced the incidence of SIDS.

Rui Vale de Sousa/Fotolia

of child care. Most often the process is being offered as voluntary way for programs to move beyond minimum standards of care. A variety of indicators such as the following are being implemented (Caronongan, Kirby, Malone, & Boller, 2011):

- Improving Teacher-to-Child Ratio and Class Size—by adding another teacher to the classroom or limiting the total size of the group to increase the opportunity for child and teacher interaction and to improve supervision.

- Improving Teacher Qualifications—by increasing qualifications in educational background for teachers and expecting more specific educational qualifications for administrators. A teacher's educational background and experience teaching in the specific age group are often associated with better educational outcomes for children.

- Enhancing Health and Safety—by offering health and safety training beyond the minimum requirement of infant and child first aid and CPR (cardiopulmonary resuscitation). For example, training on when and how to use an epinephrine autoinjection (EpiPen) to treat anaphylactic shock from bee stings is reasonable given the number of unintentional injuries due to bites and stings. Knowing how to respond to seizures and asthma attacks are other beneficial training topics that may enhance a teacher's ability to keep children safe.

- Building Collaborative Systems—by encouraging the development of commonly used program quality indicators that enhance the quality of services provided to young children across program types (such as family child care, center-based child care, Head Start, and state prekindergarten programs) and agencies (including state Child Nutrition Programs and health care) to improve and streamline services.

Exploring the Implications of Increasing Safety Regulations

Mandatory licensing and regulations governing the care of young children are designed foremost to improve the health and safety of children in out-of-home care settings, reduce disease and injury, and increase child well-being. It is particularly difficult then to recognize that stricter standards designed to achieve these goals has the potential to push some children into more risky situations. How does this happen?

Implementing more rigorous safety standards carries hidden costs. Improving teacher-to-child ratios, increasing teacher education requirements, and providing safety training are all projected to improve children's safety. But these steps ultimately increase the cost of child care. Consequently, some families may no longer be able to afford to enroll their children in licensed care settings. They may be compelled to seek alternative settings that cost less, which may include settings that are not licensed or regulated. Children's risk for injury may be greater in these unregulated settings (Currie & Hotz, 2004). As a result, the efforts made to increase safety for children in child care may result in more children being placed in unsafe settings.

This also aggravates a current social problem. Affluent families may be able to afford the more costly, higher-quality early childhood settings, while lower-income families may have to settle for less costly, lower-quality settings. As regulatory agencies consider stricter standards and programs work to achieve higher quality, the relative costs and benefits must be explored and reasonable changes implemented so that high-quality early childhood settings are available to all.

Understanding Program Responsibilities

Early childhood program leaders, including owners of family child care settings, program directors, coordinators, and principals, are responsible for implementing the regulations and systems that support the health and safety of children and staff in the early childhood setting or school. They attend to the overarching, or program-level decision making, that addresses physical facilities and program services, policies, and practices.

Providing Safe Facilities

Children's facilities must be safe, secure, and accessible. They must meet local building construction and safety codes and be appropriate for the age groups served and the kinds of services provided, such as infant care or after-school programs.

Developing Safety Policies and Procedures

Program safety policies and procedures must be relevant and appropriate guides for teachers as they do their work. For example, if a classroom is supervised by two teachers, the procedures must be designed to be accomplished successfully by two people. Procedures must also be responsive to current issues. If a particularly contagious flu virus has emerged as a health concern, a new safety procedure may need to be developed. The *Policy Point* describes the process of drafting a policy for an emergent issue.

POLICY POINT

Emerging Safety Practices—Do We Need a Policy?

Sometimes early childhood settings are challenged to make policy decisions when the best practice approaches are not yet clear. Developing a new policy and putting it into practice require a thoughtful team approach:

1. **Define the question or problem**.

   Helmets versus head lice: Which is a more significant risk to health and safety?

   - Head injuries due to bicycle accidents are a significant safety concern.
   - Sharing helmets may increase the risk of spreading head lice.

2. **Get others involved.**
   - Teachers, family members, informed community partners.

3. **Identify the anticipated problems and the potential benefits.**
   - **Problems:** Cost of helmets and cleaning supplies; cleaning helmets between uses may be hard; more

head lice means more program cleaning and management.
   - **Benefits:** Teaches children a safe habit; might avoid injury now and in the future; although head lice are a health annoyance, they are not deadly.

4. **Draft a plan.**
   - Children will wear helmets when riding tricycles or scooters at preschool.
   - We will provide four helmets to share, a cleaning protocol, and supplies.

5. **Implement the new plan for a defined trial period.**
   - We will try the new plan for six months.

6. **Reflect on progress and revise the policy.**
   - The children are wearing the helmets; no lice so far; we will check back in six months.

Hiring Safe Personnel

Program leaders ensure that all the people who work in the setting are safe, appropriate, and capable of performing their roles. Making certain that staff have appropriate qualifications and conducting a criminal background screening are ways program leaders address children's safety during the hiring process.

Providing Orientation

Before new staff assume their responsibilities, program leaders provide orientation about the program's safety procedures. This ensures that all staff members are aware of their role in implementing safety protocols and assisting in emergencies.

Monitoring for Compliance with Safety Rules

Ensuring that the policies and procedures designed to increase health and safety are effectively implemented is crucial. It is accomplished through periodic review. Program leaders may use monitoring activities such as observing classrooms and using facility safety checklists. They use this information to create program and individual action plans for improving health and safety.

Building Collaborations with Others

Early childhood programs and schools do not work alone to ensure the health and safety of young children. Program administrators; principals; teachers; families; and community safety workers such as firefighters, police, protective service personnel, and social service workers are all partners in the effort to keep children safe. Child health and safety concerns are best addressed through collaboration with community partners, thus building a system of strategies to support children wherever they are in the community.

Obtaining Insurance and Legal Counsel

Early childhood program leaders are also accountable for anticipating events that may negatively impact child and program health and safety. Having accident and liability insurance and seeking the assistance of a legal counselor can be important support in times of need.

Insurance for Accidental Injury and Death Accident insurance provides backup coverage for some of the medical costs involved in treating injuries that children experience while at the early childhood program. Depending on the details of the selected plan, accident insurance assists families in paying medical costs as a backup to the family's insurance. In some cases, the program accident insurance may be the child's only accident insurance coverage. Obtaining basic accident insurance coverage is a part of the program leader's safety plan.

Liability insurance Liability insurance supports the program and teachers in the event a court of law determines they have been negligent in the care and supervision of children. In the event of a tragic injury or death of a child, parents or their insurance agencies may present claims against the program or individual teachers asserting that the program or teacher was careless or negligent in his or her duties. Programs should purchase the most insurance coverage they can afford. Lawsuits have been known to award large amounts of money in response to credible suits for loss of a child's life or disability due to injury. Claims related to child care can be made years after the child was enrolled in the program.

Legal Counsel Making arrangements for legal counsel provides program leaders the opportunity to obtain advice that can be helpful in creating safe policies and in knowing how to respond in case of tragic events. This also provides program leaders with confidence, knowing that legal guidance is only a phone call away.

Clarifying Teacher Responsibilities

Children and the classroom are the teacher's specific sphere of influence. Teachers are responsible for ensuring children's safety during all class activities. The various steps described below show how teachers link classroom-level actions with program-level safety procedures. These actions build a strong system of safety to surround the children.

Making a Professional Commitment to Safety

Teachers make a professional commitment to keep children safe. Many join the NAEYC, the National Association for the Education of Young Children, which is the professional organization for those who teach children ages birth to 9 years. Members of NAEYC follow the guidelines of the NAEYC Code of Ethical Conduct and Statement of Commitment (National Association for the Education of Young Children [NAEYC], 2011), which guides teachers to, "above all," not harm children (NAEYC, 2011, p. 3).

Teachers put this ethic into practice by structuring their teaching and care on sound safety principles. They study the recommendations of reputable resources and stay current about the most frequent causes of injury to young children. They use this information to identify safety strategies proactively to reduce the risk of harm.

Implementing Program Safety Practices

Teachers learn and follow the safety procedures of their school or program. Without this commitment, program-level policies and procedures are useless. A true children's safety team blends the administrative design of policies with thoughtful implementation by teaching professionals.

Putting program guidelines into practice requires unique decision making. Following are two examples:

Scenario 1: Kyra, a first-grade teacher, is given specific evacuation procedures about who does what and when during a fire drill. She is notified to prepare the children to respond to the school fire alarm when it sounds. She is directed to lead the children to a designated gathering spot, count the children to determine whether all are accounted for, and return to the building when the all-clear bell rings. At the end of the day, Kyra is required to record information about the drill on a prescribed form and return it to the office. These steps are conducted by all teachers and classes. This approach ensures that the safety procedure is systematically practiced and provides an opportunity for program leaders to confirm that the evacuation plan works for large groups of children.

Scenario 2: Talea has been guided by her director to plan a fire drill for her preschool class once each month. She is allowed to decide when the drill will occur and how it will be introduced and carried out. She must also keep a record of each drill to document that she has met the monthly practice requirement. Talea imbeds the fire drill in a teaching unit. For example, one month Talea plans the drill as part of a larger unit on safety. She invites the local firefighter education team to visit her class. The firefighters show children the fire truck, talk about the safety equipment, and teach children to "get out and stay out" in case of fire. Then Talea guides the children to pair off and follow the assistant teacher while she activates a home smoke alarm. This approach provides an appropriate mechanism for teachers of very young children to design a drill format that fits the children's developmental understanding.

Modeling Safe Behaviors

Teachers are important role models for children and are careful that their actions demonstrate appropriate health and safety behaviors. This includes doing what they expect children to do. For example, teachers respond appropriately during emergency drills, use appropriate ladders rather than a chair to reach objects on high shelves, sit down and chew foods carefully at meals, and use words to demonstrate how to ask for help.

A Matter of ETHICS

Emergency drills are important but can sometimes frighten children. Some teachers may be tempted to skip the drill or not use the loud smoke alarm during the practice. What aspects of the code of ethics should teachers consider as they plan for a fire drill?

Teaching Safety Skills

Teachers are purposeful about teaching developmentally appropriate safety messages. With very young children, this includes redirecting a child to keep him from hitting the window with a block while saying, "Blocks are for building, not for hitting. Show me how you can build with blocks." Teachers are intentional about teaching children how to use materials safely and how to play safely on equipment. They imbed safety lessons in the curriculum for all age groups. The *Teaching Wellness* feature provides examples of ways to teach children about pedestrian safety.

CLASSROOM CONNECTION

Watch this video showing how the teachers and parents of young elementary children create an experiential lesson on walking safely near the street and crossing the street safely. Watch how the teachers point out cues in the environment and use both words and actions to reinforce the safety messages. Consider the small-group activities they implement after practicing outdoors.

Supervising Children and Taking Action When Needed

Teachers supervise children without fail. They recognize supervision as a core teacher responsibility and keep children within sight and sound at all times. If teachers see a child in a dangerous situation, such as using a toy inappropriately

TEACHING WELLNESS   Pedestrian Safety

LEARNING OUTCOME   Children will be able to move along the sidewalk safely and demonstrate the safety skills of stop, look, listen, and cross with an adult.
VOCABULARY FOCUS: Walking, safety, sidewalk, pedestrian, crosswalk, crossing lights.
SAFETY WATCH: Supervise children carefully on all neighborhood walks.

INFANTS AND TODDLERS

- **Goal:** Infants and toddlers will experience the rhythm associated with walking safely along the sidewalk and safely crossing the street with an adult.
- **Materials:** Baby carrier, backpack, or stroller.
- **Activity plan:** Take a walk in a nearby neighborhood that is not too busy or noisy. Have toddlers hold hands with a teacher. Walk along the sidewalk. Describe what you are doing and use your body movements to reinforce the messages. Say, "The children are walking safely along the sidewalk with their grown-ups. The sidewalk is the place for people to move along the street." Stop at a crosswalk. Say, "We are getting ready to cross the street. First, we stop. We look at the light to know when it is time to move. Do you see the green 'Walk' sign glowing? That

means it is time for us to walk across. We hold hands, and we look and listen for cars. We keep watching to make sure it is safe while we walk across. There, we are across the street. That was a safe way to cross."
- **How to adjust the activity:** Use a puppet and pictures to convey the safety message. Learn the words for stop, go, and safety in the languages of children in the class. Reinforce the message often. Give pedestrian safety information to families so that they can reinforce the messages at home.
- **Did you meet your goal?** Did children listen to the words and follow directions? Did the toddlers stop, look, and listen?

PRESCHOOLERS AND KINDERGARTNERS

- **Goal:** Children will be able to name the safety cues: stop, look, listen, cross with an adult.
- **Materials:** Toy vehicles, people figures, small street signs, blocks, masking tape.
- **Activity plan:** Create a "neighborhood." Place masking tape on the floor in rectangular shapes to resemble neighborhood blocks. Place other materials nearby. Introduce the activity: Talk about the safety rules for crossing the street: stop, look for the crossing sign, watch and listen for cars, cross when it is clear, always cross with a grown-up. Invite the children to create a town. Ask them to teach the people how to cross the street safely. Watch as children play. Ask questions such as "How will this child get to the

store? Does she know to stop-look-listen? Does she have a grown-up to hold her hand?" If a child in the class uses a wheelchair, use inclusive words such as *move* instead of *walk*. At group time, review the safety message.
- **How to adjust the activity:** Take a neighborhood walk with the children and families. Demonstrate the steps of stop–look–listen–cross with an adult. Guide families to support safety message at home. Learn how families teach such messages to their child with special developmental needs.
- **Did you meet your goal?** Can children identify the steps for safely crossing the street? Are they able to say why it is important to cross with a grown-up?

SCHOOL-AGE CHILDREN

- **Goal:** Children will be able to name the safety cues—stop, look, listen when crossing the street—and to describe how to walk along the sidewalk safely, cross at the crosswalk, and use pedestrian crossing lights.
- **Materials:** Construction paper, scissors, pens, glue, tape.
- **Activity plan:** Provide materials for making pedestrian safety books. Introduce the activity. Discuss the safety cues stop–look–listen, walk along the sidewalk away from the traffic, cross at the crosswalk, and obey the crossing signals. Invite children to create a character (a person or

an animal). Ask them to write and illustrate a book about pedestrian safety to read to the others in the class.
- **How to adjust the activity:** Arrange an opportunity for the children to read their books to younger children. Provide materials for the children to draw bookmarks communicating the pedestrian safety messages.
- **Did you meet your goal?** Are children able to identify the safety cues? Can you observe from their stories that children understand the safety concepts?

or climbing unsafely on outdoor equipment, they take action immediately. Teachers prepare in advance to implement first aid or take action in emergencies if needed.

Sharing Safety Messages with Families

Teachers also communicate with families about the safety lessons being taught at school and ways families can reinforce these messages at home. Teachers also share information about important topics such as supervising children on playgrounds and using safe practices in parking lots. They also connect families to information about toy recalls or other emergent topics to extend the teaching of safety to the home setting.

CHECK YOUR UNDERSTANDING 13.2
Click here to check your understanding of using regulations to improve safety.

CREATING SAFE AND APPROPRIATE FACILITIES

Establishing settings that support children's physical and emotional health and safety is an important task of teaching. To meet this challenge, many thoughtful decisions must be made to address safety in the children's environment, which includes the physical facilities and the materials used to facilitate learning. This includes selecting appropriate locations for children's programs, establishing safe classrooms and outdoor facilities, and providing safe toys and equipment. The task can be challenging, given the variety of facilities and schools where young children are typically served. Several aspects guide decision making when creating spaces to care for and educate young children: meeting family and community needs, creating spaces that value the developmental needs of young children, and making a commitment to address safety standards in facility development.

children's environment
the physical facilities and materials used to facilitate learning

Meeting the Need for Safe Spaces

Early education facilities currently provide out-of-home care and education for a large number of young children. According to the U.S. Census Bureau, in 2011, more than 12.5 million (61%) of the children under the age of 5 participated in some kind of organized child care and education arrangement and 40.5 million (50%) of the children ages 5 to 14 years received some kind of regular care in addition to their school attendance (Laughlin, L., 2013). Families need child care, but state and community goals also impact the need for early childhood spaces.

The importance of early education as a step in closing educational achievement gaps is receiving a great deal of attention. Many states are exploring how to provide *universal prekindergarten*, publicly supported early childhood education programs offered to all 4-year-old children. Such initiatives increase the need for safe and secure early childhood classroom spaces, but there are challenges to be addressed.

Recognizing Challenges

Addressing the need for facilities to serve young children is complicated. Several aspects contribute to this challenge:

- A variety of spaces are needed to address the range of services required and the unique needs of each age group.

- Many early childhood settings must make do with borrowed, rented, or renovated spaces that were not designed to serve young children and are often inadequate.
- Existing early childhood programs usually do not realize sufficient profit to build new facilities.
- Few early childhood professionals have the training to make the important decisions needed to design appropriate facilities or manage the real estate and loan decisions needed to finance the construction of a new facility.

National facility development policies and supports are needed to help guide the creation of safe and appropriate early childhood facilities.

Accessing Guidance for Facility Development

A few resources are available to help guide the planning and development of early childhood facilities that meet the needs of young children and that address health and safety standards. Two resources may offer some guidance:

- Guidance for the construction of federally funded child care settings can be accessed from the U.S. Department of Education's National Clearinghouse for Educational Facilities and the U.S. General Services Administration's (GSA's) Public Buildings Service, Office of Childcare (U.S. General Services Administration, 2003).
- Guidelines for spaces serving young children are provided by the NAEYC's accreditation standards and the National Resource Center for Health and Safety in Child Care and Early Education.

In the long run, for the benefit of young children in the future, early childhood professionals need to advocate for policies and initiatives that develop spaces for early childhood care and education.

Designing Appropriate Spaces for Children

The child should be the primary consideration in the design and arrangement of safe and appropriate early childhood environments (NAEYC, 2008). A child-centered approach to design emerges from the perspective that the early years of development are unique and that the spaces that serve young children should reflect this importance. Commitment to this approach is demonstrated by embracing a belief that young children are valued members of society. It is informed by considering the shortcomings of many early childhood environments and envisioning appropriate settings that offer sufficient space, are accessible, and reflect cultural values.

Demonstrating Value for Young Children

Decisions made about the design and arrangement of children's spaces are influenced by beliefs regarding the value of children, the way children learn, and the role of the teacher and environment in promoting growth and development. These beliefs are based on a philosophical perspective that considers the connection of the space to the activities, experiences, and learning that will occur there. Two approaches provide examples of ways the philosophical perspective about young children influences the development of spaces that serve them.

Maria Montessori Dr. Maria Montessori (1870–1952) believed that children are capable learners and that careful attention should be paid to the arrangement of early childhood environments (Montessori, 1966). As a result, Montessori-oriented classrooms are orderly environments that promote children's independent learning and invite both individual and group exploration. Toys and materials are carefully arranged on low, open shelving, allowing children to choose what they need and to be responsible for returning materials to their place after use. The use of child-sized furnishings is central to this child-centered approach.

Reggio Emilia The Reggio Emilia approach emerged from the village of Reggio Emilia, Italy, where beliefs embrace the ideal that children are of equal value to others in the community and are the responsibility of the collective group (New, 1993). The value for community is evident in facility design that links children to each other by providing common spaces and plazas, as well as to the larger community and world through the use of carefully placed windows and classroom doorways that connect children to the outdoors (New, 1993). Displays of children's artwork, lovely furnishings, and mirrors are used to promote enjoyment of the indoor and outdoor environments and to invite exploration (Edwards, Gandini, & Forman, 1993; Katz & Cesarone, 1994). In this way, the Reggio Emilia approach promotes the idea that the environment is an additional teacher (New, 1993).

The design and arrangement of the environment send the message that young children are valued.

Learning from Criticism

Children's environments in the United States are sometimes criticized for showing limited expression of value for the work of young children. Most children's programs are housed in adapted spaces, and programs often do not have the funds to create innovative and beautiful environments. One report claims that early childhood classrooms in the United States tend to be overly busy and crowded spaces (Tarr, 2001) where children are separated from each other and disconnected from the outside world (Greenman, 2005). Some spaces that serve children under the age of 5 are thought to have the look of miniature elementary school classrooms with rows of desks or tables, where the focus appears to be on what teachers do in the setting rather than what children experience (Tarr, 2001). These criticisms invite teachers to revitalize their energy around creating safe environments that demonstrate value for young children and nurture children's emotional well-being, as well as keeping them safe.

Envisioning Appropriate Environments

Appropriate environments are established with consideration for children's age, size, and developmental needs. They recognize the ways in which children use their senses to experience and learn from the visual, auditory, aromatic, and tactile attributes of their surroundings. They are also welcoming, comfortable, beautiful, and inspirational. Appropriate environments encourage creativity and exploration and build children's confidence to learn. In sum, appropriate children's spaces:

- Support physical safety and emotional security.
- Convey a sense of welcome and familiarity.
- Provide space for children to ease gradually into the classroom.
- Address children's age, developmental, and educational needs.
- Are culturally appropriate and developmentally accessible.

CLASSROOM CONNECTION

Watch this video describing a children's classroom that follows the Montessori design. Notice how toys are displayed and how they are used for specific purposes. Even though you may not work in a Montessori program, what ideas from this approach might you choose to use in your classroom?

- Inspire exploration and discovery.
- Support teaching and learning.

Environments that are appropriate for children offer important attributes that are good for teachers too. Teachers need comfortable spaces that provide flexibility for creative room arrangement, support curriculum delivery, and offer adequate storage. Appropriate environments for teachers contribute to teacher satisfaction, which may reduce the rate of teacher turnover and thus improve the quality of programs for young children. A list of space needs in appropriate early childhood environments is shown in Figure 13-3.

Providing Sufficient Space

usable square footage the amount of floor space that is not covered by furniture but is open and accessible to children

Classroom square footage is considered to be the single most important characteristic of a safe and appropriate children's environment. Usable square footage refers to the floor space in a classroom that is not covered by furnishings but is open and accessible. This measurement is used as a basic guide to determine the number of children that may be present in the space at one time. As a result, classroom square footage, along with the furnishings plan, determines the group size for any room in the early childhood setting.

State licensing standards and NAEYC accreditation standards have traditionally identified that each indoor classroom should provide a minimum of 35 usable square feet per child. This is equivalent to a space 5 feet by 7 feet in dimension, or only slightly more than the square footage of two playpens, causing concern that the small spaces may be stressful for young children. As a result, efforts are under way

---

FIGURE 13-3   Typical Space Needs for Early Childhood Settings

Teacher and General Classroom Space Needs
- ✓ Sufficient square footage for group size
- ✓ Durable and easy-to-clean floors, walls, and counters
- ✓ Emergency exits in two directions
- ✓ Child-sized and adult toileting and hand washing areas
- ✓ Water fountain or access to fresh drinking water
- ✓ Food storage, preparation, and service areas
- ✓ Locked storage and refrigeration for medications
- ✓ General storage space

Infant Classroom Space Needs
- ✓ Space for children's belongings (diapers, clothing)
- ✓ Sufficient space for cribs and high chairs
- ✓ Movable dividers to separate mobile and nonmobile infants
- ✓ Diaper changing and hand washing area
- ✓ Refrigeration for breast milk, infant formula, medications

Toddler Classroom Space Needs
- ✓ Storage for children's belongings (diapers, clothing, blanket)
- ✓ Diaper changing and toileting area

- ✓ Hand washing area near diapering area
- ✓ Refrigeration for breast milk, infant formula, medications

Preschooler Classroom Space Needs
- ✓ Coat cubbies; space for child belongings
- ✓ Space to store cots for napping
- ✓ Access to child-sized toilets and hand washing
- ✓ Space to store projects

School-Age Child Space Needs
- ✓ Lockers for belongings
- ✓ Appropriate access to gender-specific toilets
- ✓ Space to store projects

Children with Special Developmental Needs
- ✓ Accessible toilets, sinks, and furniture
- ✓ Appropriate floor surfacing, acoustics, and lighting
- ✓ Storage for adaptive equipment
- ✓ Sound and light-flashing alarm system

to increase the recommended square footage per child. The GSA (2003) requires a minimum of 45 square feet of usable floor space per child for federally constructed early childhood facilities. The Head Start Technical Assistance Center (National Head Start Facilities Information Services, 2002) and the *National Health and Safety Performance Standards* (American Academy of Pediatrics [AAP], American Public Health Association, National Resource Center for Health and Safety in Child Care and Early Education, 2014) recommends a minimum of 42 (preferably 50) square feet per child. These highlight the trend toward larger space requirements per child.

The goal of providing more square footage per child also creates some challenges:

- Increasing square footage per child adds to the cost of new facility construction.
- Current early childhood settings would need to reduce the number of children served in a particular space, which would decrease the program's income or require the program to increase the cost of care.
- Increased costs might push some children out of the quality care setting.

It is important for teachers to be aware of quality standards discussions and to contribute ideas for reaching health and safety goals.

Ensuring Accessibility

Spaces used to provide care and education for young children need to be accessible to all children, including those with special developmental needs as described in the requirements of Section 504 of the Rehabilitation Act of 1973 and the Americans with Disabilities Act (ADA). These guidelines ensure that people with disabilities have access to the buildings, classrooms, play areas, and toilets and sinks. Consideration should also be given to meeting the needs of persons who have special health or developmental needs. For example, children who have hearing impairments are supported when classrooms are constructed with soft surfaces to control for noise and are equipped with fire alarms that signal emergencies with a flashing light in addition to the sound of the alarm. Accessibility guidelines are best addressed as facilities are developed and classrooms are furnished. This way the environment is prepared beforehand to include all children.

Creating Spaces That Are Culturally Relevant

Environments send a message about who and what is valued by what is and is not in the space. Including aspects of culture in children's spaces is important to send the appropriate message, but it can be a challenge. Teachers have their own experience and knowledge to draw on, but it is easy to overlook ways the environment can reflect the cultural traditions of the children and families who are participating. Teachers need to work together with families to gather ideas and put them into action.

Ideas may include selecting colors for walls and furnishings and choosing work from local artists to display, such as paintings, weavings, pottery, and tile work. Displaying children's artwork adds another unique expression. The arrangement of furnishings can also help support local customs. For example, placing benches in the lobby or chairs near the door creates a place for families to gather and visit, acknowledging customs that view arrival and departure as important social times. Partnering with families to create culturally relevant spaces communicates that all children and families are welcomed and valued.

WHAT IF . . .
You were new to the community and wanted to learn more about the cultural backgrounds and interest of the children and families you were going to serve? How would you gather this information?

Understanding Building Codes and Facility Requirements

Local building codes specify the requirements for safe facility construction and renovation. Regulations address choice of building materials, construction techniques, and requirements for appropriate handrails and barriers around porches and decks to avoid potential falls. Certain restrictions must be addressed for spaces that serve young children in group care settings. Examples include the following (American Academy of Pediatrics, American Public Health Association, National Resource Center for Health and Safety in Child Care and Early Education, 2014):

- Building materials must be free from hazardous products such as mold and toxic products.
- Basement spaces may be used only by children 2 years of age and older who are able to walk on their own.
- Only ground floor spaces may be used if the building is constructed of wood.
- Safety glass must be used for windows and doors, or they must be covered with metal mesh safety guards that extend at least 36 inches from the floor.

Any repairs or renovations must also follow appropriate safety codes.

Providing Appropriate Utility Services

Programs that serve young children are required to ensure that utility services are safe. These services are typically reviewed during child care licensing site visits and must be monitored to ensure continued safety:

- *Water:* An approved water supply, such as a public water system or well water that has been tested periodically, must be provided to ensure that children are safe from waterborne illnesses caused by bacteria, parasites, or other infectious agents. Salmonella, *E. coli*, and dysentery are three bacterial agents that can be found in contaminated water.
- *Sewer:* A reliable sewer system is important to avoid contaminating the facility and grounds with sewer seepage that can introduce disease.
- *Electrical services:* Sufficient electrical outlets are required to avoid overloading the electrical system. This ensures that teachers do not use electrical extension cords, which can cause a tripping hazard. Emergency lighting is needed in hallways, in stairways, and at exits to guide evacuation, if needed.
- *Heating, cooling, and airflow systems:* A system that maintains appropriate temperature and humidity and controls for air pollution is important for health and safety. Fresh air is needed to maintain healthy indoor air quality and to reduce the incidence of respiratory problems (AAP et al., 2014).
- *Garbage services:* Periodic removal of garbage is needed to control for insects, rodents, and other pests that may introduce disease in the children's environment.
- *Communication systems:* Telephones or other communication systems are needed to contact emergency services or families in case of child illness or injury.

Providing these utility services is a safety issue. If services fail due to mechanical failure, weather, or other conditions, children are put at risk and program services may need to be suspended.

Creating Safe Areas Around the Building

A safety zone around the building supports safe access. Safe entrances and exits, bicycle parking, and loading zones all contribute to safety as children come to school.

Providing Safe Entrances and Exits Clearly identified walkways into the building and marked exits increase safety as children move in and out of the building, as well as during emergency evacuation. Walkways must protect children from areas used by cars. Pathways need to accommodate strollers, baby carriages, and wheelchairs and must be kept clear.

Addressing Parking Lot Safety Parking areas are a significant source of danger to young children. Nearly one-third of child pedestrian deaths occur when a child darts into the street or parking lot from between two cars (Savage, Kawanabe, Mejeur, Goehring, & Reed, 2002). Parking areas need to be kept visually open by trimming shrubs and marking walkways through the parking lot with painted stripes, brightly colored traffic cones, flags, or signs.

Marking Emergency Exits Emergency exits are passageways to the outdoors. They should be clearly marked and visible from all areas of the classroom. Access to the exit doors should be kept clear and open at all times. In settings where the exit doors open into a parking lot or another potentially dangerous area, door alarms should be installed to alert the teacher if a child tries to open the door (AAP et al., 2011).

Offering Bicycle Parking Bicycle parking racks encourage a healthy form of transportation and help keep bikes from being propped near the doors, which can cause a tripping hazard.

Creating Bus Lanes and Passenger Loading Areas Safe bus loading areas ensure that children move directly from the bus onto a sidewalk rather than into a parking lot, which is dangerous.

Marking Emergency Vehicle Parking Zones Programs may be required to designate parking zones for emergency vehicles. These spaces are identified with painted stripes and are usually located directly outside an entrance.

Designating School Zones Elementary schools often mark the nearby streets as a *school zone* to warn drivers of the presence of young children. This is a good idea near preschool and child care centers too. If this formal designation is not available, the presence of children can be communicated by placing signs or decorative flags to mark the site as a children's area.

WHAT IF . . .

You observed a child running in and out of parked cars in the parking lot while the child's parent was talking with another parent? What would you do?

Managing Security

The security of children in the early childhood facility is an important aspect of overall safety. Security refers to keeping children safe from contact with inappropriate or unsafe persons. Families want assurance that teachers are going to keep their children safe from intruders, and teachers want support in case an intruder enters the facility. Security plans help to address these concerns.

Significant attention has been given to ensure that children *stay in* the early childhood facility—that they are protected from being able to wander off. Focus must also be directed to ensure that potential intruders *stay out*—that only approved persons have access to the children's facility and classrooms. Security approaches seek to address both of these concerns without unduly constricting children's opportunities to explore, take on challenges, and learn (Greenman, 2005).

To avoid barricading children from the outside world, teachers look to strategies that are appropriate for the setting. These include identifying security concerns in the local neighborhood, recognizing family issues that may introduce security concerns, and controlling access to the building and classroom. Even with these approaches, it is important to remain alert to the activities and people in the children's environment and supervise children at all times.

Identifying Neighborhood Security Concerns and Resources

While safety is a common theme in creating children's classrooms, what works in one neighborhood may not be appropriate or safe in another. Neighborhood factors to consider include nearby traffic patterns, the availability of community services such as police and emergency medical care, the presence of drug- and gang-related issues, and the general crime rate. Being aware of such issues helps to prioritize facility and classroom safety goals and the strategies needed to address security concerns.

Understanding Family Concerns and Issues

Sometimes families have circumstances that threaten the security of the child or another family member, and that spills over into the classroom. Domestic violence or the presence of a restraining order for a family member are issues that may require a special plan for arrival and departure, space for private conversations, and cues about when to call for support for a security concern.

Controlling Facility Access

Controlling access involves managing who comes in and out of the facility and who has access to the classroom, as well as controlling for perceived threats such as harassment and views of violence. Managing access is a familiar security management approach, but it can be complicated because early childhood programs have a responsibility to ensure that parents and legal guardians have access to their children at any time. This requires a confident understanding of who is approved to enter.

Approaches used to control access depend on the style of the facility and the types of security concerns that may be present in the local neighborhood. Strategies include:

- Restricting entry to one doorway and providing a lobby with locked doors into the program service areas beyond which only approved individuals may enter.
- Requiring employees to wear identifying uniforms.
- Requiring all persons in the facility to wear employee or visitor identification tags.
- Installing an electronic keyless entry system with passkeys or passwords available only to approved individuals.

Systems such as these communicate attentiveness to security and build a climate of watchfulness. However, it is difficult to determine whether they are as effective as hoped in improving security. When the security system relies heavily on one identified entryway for the building, attention might be diverted from other potential access areas, such as doors that are propped open as supplies are moved in and out or windows that provide access into the building. It is important to identify the level of security that is reasonable for the setting. Here are some examples:

- *Setting 1:* A 4-foot-tall play yard fence meets licensing requirements and adequately prevents children from leaving the play area. In this neighborhood, the threat of intruders is considered to be low, so the 4-foot fence is sufficient. Teachers pay special attention to supervision at the periphery of the play yard.

- *Setting 2:* A 6-foot-tall solid fence is needed to screen out views of gang activity on the street. Although the solid fence closes off visual access, it also limits the teacher's ability to see if potential intruders are loitering on the other side of the fence. Teachers consider this as they supervise in the play yard.

- *Setting 3:* Special barriers are planned to screen out the high-rise buildings that surround the play area and overlook the space. Teachers advocate for covered areas to be constructed at strategic locations to screen children from view and from the potential of being hit by objects tossed from the buildings. They conduct a walk-through of the playground each day before it is used to ensure that the space is clean and that no hazardous debris has been introduced.

Security in children's spaces is reinforced by teachers, families, and program staff who continually observe the children's areas for inappropriate people or potential threats.

Implications for Teachers

Teachers may not be in charge of facility design and management, but they do interface with all aspects of facility safety when teaching young children. This knowledge is also important when creating safe indoor and outdoor environments.

ESTABLISHING SAFE INDOOR ENVIRONMENTS

Teachers create and maintain safe classrooms where children can learn and thrive. This is accomplished through careful arrangement of the space, selection of furniture that supports children's developmental needs, thoughtful storage of toys and equipment, and continual monitoring to remove potential hazards.

Organizing the Classroom

Classroom organization begins with a planning process that identifies conceptually the activities and goals for space use. In this stage, each part of the available space is assigned to support an important classroom activity, such as arrival and departure, toileting and hand washing, and snack and meal service. Areas are also defined to support developmental goals, such as a reading area to support early literacy or a creative/expressive area where easels and paints are located. It is recognized that some spaces will overlap, and furnishings may be adjusted during the day to allow flexibility.

Next, a space use plan, or map of the children's environment, can be created to show how the space will be arranged to accommodate the desired activities and developmental goals. The basic layout of the space is drawn on a large piece of paper, and small circles of paper are used to identify program activity areas. These can be moved around as the space use plan develops. Figure 13-4 provides an example of a preschool or kindergarten classroom space use plan.

Safety aspects to consider when creating a space use plan vary depending on the size of the space and services to be provided. Examples include the following:

- *Identify a doorway for arrival and emergency exits.* Create open areas inside the entry and exit doors where families can gather and teachers can greet and supervise children appropriately at arrival and departure.

CHECK YOUR UNDERSTANDING 13.3
Click here to check your understanding of creating safe and appropriate facilities.

space use plan
a map or diagram of a children's space showing how the space will be used and the locations of desired activities, furniture, entrances, and exits

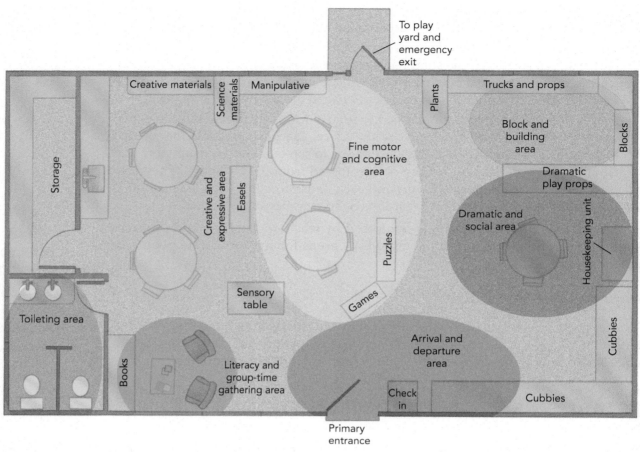

FIGURE 13-4
Preschool or Kindergarten Classroom Space Use Plan

- *Arrange pathways through the room.* Plan logical walkways to ensure clear evacuation routes and to support services such as moving lunch into the classroom.
- *Provide space for small- and large-group activities.* Plan enough open space for children to gather and move safely during games and dancing.
- *Locate activity areas logically.* Position activity centers to avoid unnecessary conflicts—for example, by separating active block play from the quieter reading corner.
- *Take advantage of windows.* Use natural light to its best advantage. Place the creative arts areas near a window to encourage themes related to the natural environment.
- *Locate furniture thoughtfully.* Use low shelves to create play areas and to provide easy access to toys. Position tall furniture where it can be attached to the wall to prevent tipping hazards. Use area rugs to designate play spaces.

Furnishing the Classroom

Furniture is an important part of the children's environment. It needs to be inviting, durable, and appropriate to support children's needs. Furniture should be selected to support appropriate exploration and learning, and address safety.

Choosing Child-Sized Furniture

Child-sized furniture is furniture that "fits" young children. Options typically include:

- Chairs that children can back up to and sit in without climbing.
- Tables that are approximately waist–high, allowing children to stand and play with toys without straining.
- Shelves that allow children to reach toys without stretching.
- Toilets that are low and easy for children to sit on unaided.
- Sinks that are sized so that children can reach the water faucets without needing a stool or step.

Providing furniture that is child-sized has several benefits. It helps children know that they are in a space made for kids, which may smooth the child's transition into the classroom and set the tone for a positive experience. And safety is increased as children are able to use the furniture easily while keeping their feet on the floor. This helps children be more self-sufficient and encourages exploration and the development of self-care skills.

Meeting the Needs of Each Age Group

Each age group has special requirements for the kinds of furniture that supports children's size and developmental needs. For safety, it is best if furnishings are chosen to meet specific needs rather than trying to "make do" with less appropriate options.

Infants Furnishings for infant spaces include a crib and high chair for each baby and sturdy changing tables that safely secure the infant, are easy to sanitize, and are comfortable for teachers to use. Two comfortable adult-sized chairs are useful when feeding babies. Rocking chairs should be selected to avoid pinch hazards. Carpeting or area rugs that are firm and easy to clean can add color and softness to the environment. Small tubs are helpful for assembling toys. Low room dividers may be useful for dividing spaces for mobile and nonmobile infants.

Mobile Infants and Toddlers Furniture for toddlers and newly mobile infants needs to be low, solid, and sturdy. It should not slip as children pull themselves to a standing position. For example, shelves with rolling casters on the legs should be avoided unless the casters can be locked to keep the shelves in place and prevent them from rolling. Chairs for toddlers are typically 10 inches high at the seat. Chairs should have a wide base to avoid the potential of them slipping away as the toddler attempts to sit down. Table height should match the toddler-sized chairs. Play kitchens and cubbies with coat hooks should be low and sturdy. Individual cots for naptime should be comfortable, easy to sanitize, and stackable for efficient storage.

Preschoolers Furniture for preschool classrooms should fit children of various sizes. A selection of chairs ranging from 10 to 14 inches hig at the seat and tables of varying heights or with adjustable legs offer flexibility. Shelves should be sturdy and should not exceed children's eye height to allow safe access to toys. Other furnishings may include cots; water or sensory tables; painting easels; cubbies for coats; workbenches; small tables for listening centers or science activities; kitchen and dramatic play units; and comfy chairs, cushions, and pillows.

Kindergarten and Elementary Children Chairs for kindergarten and elementary classrooms are usually 16 to 18 inches high. A sufficient number of tables or desks are needed to ensure that each child has a place to sit and work. Tables of various

Pearson Education

CLASSROOM CONNECTION

Watch this video to see how one classroom creates the environment for mobile infants and toddlers. What, if any, aspects of this environment surprise you? What is provided in this classroom that you would want to adopt in your own teaching?

sizes are useful for projects and small-group activities. Other furnishings may include water and sensory tables, easels, tub-style shelving units, open shelves, bookshelves, area rugs, cubbies, and lockers or coat hooks.

Evaluating Furniture for Safety

Children's furniture should be strong, durable, and free from splinters or sharp edges. There should be no gaps that could pinch or entrap fingers. No lead-based paint or other toxic products should be used in construction. Soft-surfaced furniture such as child-sized couches and chairs should be covered with material that is easy to clean. Furniture for children's environments must be obtained from reputable sources. Furniture purchased from import suppliers should be reviewed to determine whether it meets U.S. product safety standards.

Safely Storing Classroom Supplies

Most early childhood teachers report that there is never enough storage. It seems that creative teaching goes hand in hand with collecting teaching materials. Storage must be carefully managed to prevent toys and materials from overflowing into the classroom and hallways, creating an appearance of disorganization and lowering the professional appearance of the environment, or to avoid a safety hazard as materials slide off overloaded shelves or topple when closet doors are opened. Ideally, storage should provide space in the classroom for materials used every day, a common storage space for shared materials, and cupboards or file cabinets for a teacher's personal teaching materials. Special attention must be given to organizing materials, storing medications, restricting access to cleaning supplies, and avoiding infestation.

WHAT IF . . .

You noticed children climbing on a tall shelf to reach the paper supplies? You already reported the tippy shelf to your director, but no one has come to attach it to the wall. What would you do?

Organizing Materials

Many storage systems are available to help teachers organize materials. Using labeled boxes or transparent plastic tubs allows teachers and children to identify needed items and helps in returning materials to the shelves. Organization helps prolong the considerable investment that is made in curriculum materials and makes it more likely that toys will be returned to their storage space, helping prevent a tripping hazard if toys are left in walkways.

WHAT IF . . .

A parent asked you to store her child's EpiPen in the classroom so that you can access it quickly in case of emergency? Is this request legitimate? How would you manage this situation to ensure safety for all children?

Securing Medications

Medications that are to be administered to children need to be safely stored in a medication lockbox or locking cupboard. This allows the medication to be easily accessible to the teacher but out of the reach of children. A lockbox may also be needed to store medications in the refrigerator.

Storing Cleaning Supplies

All cleaning supplies, lotions, bleach, and other potentially toxic materials must be stored outside the children's space or in a locked cabinet (AAP et al., 2011). Careful organization of such supplies keeps inappropriate materials from ending up in the children's space, which could be dangerous.

Avoiding Infestation of Insects and Rodents

Dried food-related products such as rice, cornmeal, and birdseed are often used in sensory bins. Such items should be stored in containers with tight-fitting lids to avoid spoilage or infestation by insects or rodents. These materials should be discarded periodically so that the bins and storage area can be cleaned thoroughly.

Controlling for Hazards

Managing children's safety also involves making careful decisions about materials that could introduce dangers into the environment, such as plants, wall displays, electrical appliances, and recycling bins. Conducting periodic safety checks is an important way to identify and correct potential hazards.

Choosing Appropriate Plants for the Classroom

Teachers often include softening materials such as flowers and plants to enhance the environment. However, not all plants and plant materials are appropriate for children's spaces. Figure 13-5 lists plants that are appropriate choices for children's settings and those that should not be used because of their poisonous properties.

FIGURE 13-5   Safe and Poisonous Plants

Safe House Plants to Use in Children's Settings

African violet	Christmas cactus	Jade plant	Spider plant
Aluminum plant	Coleus	Peperomia	Swedish ivy
Anthurium	Corn plant	Prayer plant	Velvet, purple passion
Aphelandra	Dracaena	Rubber plant	Wandering Jew
Baby tears	Emerald ripple	Schefflera	Wax plant
Begonia	Hen-and-chickens	Sensitive plant	Weeping fig
Boston fern	Impatiens	Snake plant	Yellow day lily

Poisonous Plants – DO NOT Use in Children's Settings

House Plants	Flowers & Shrubs	Vegetables	Wild Plants
Bird of paradise	Autumn crocus	Asparagus	Belladonna
Castor bean	Bleeding heart	Potato (green parts)	Bittersweet
Dieffenbachia	Boxwood	Rhubarb leaves	Buttercups
English ivy	Chrysanthemum	Tomato (green parts)	Indian hemp
Holly	Daffodil	**Trees and Shrubs**	Jack-in-the-pulpit
Jequirity bean	Four-o'clocks	Black locust	Jimson weed
Jerusalem cherry	Foxglove	Chokecherry	Larkspur
Mistletoe	Hyacinth	Elderberry	Monkshood
Mother-in-law	Hydrangea	English yew	Mushrooms (some)
Oleander	Iris	Ground ivy	Nightshade
Philodendron	Lily of the valley	Horse chestnut, buckeye	Poison hemlock
Poinsettia	Morning glory	Juniper	Poison oak & ivy
	Rhododendron	Oak	Poison sumac

Sources: Based on: Caring for Our Children: National Health and Safety Performance Standards (Appendix Y), *Non-poisonous and Poisonous Plants*; University of California Agriculture and Natural Resources, and *Safe and Poisonous Garden Plants*; Texas A&M *Common Poisonous Plants and Plant Parts*, retrieved August 2015, from www.ct.gove/caes.

Creating Safe Wall Displays

Early childhood classrooms are typically bright with children's artwork and posters displayed on bulletin boards and walls. However, posting a large amount of paper can be a fire hazard. Many fire districts do not allow flammable products to be suspended from the ceiling. The local fire department can provide guidance about the appropriate amount of paper to use in displays. It is also best to attach materials to the wall using tape rather than staples, tacks, or pins that can fall to the floor and be discovered by young children.

Managing Electrical Outlets and Appliances

Electrical outlets can be a shock hazard if a curious child pokes a finger or toy into the socket. This can be avoided by installing child-proof electrical outlets or outlet covers that close off the outlet when not in use. Classrooms should also be equipped with a sufficient number of electrical outlets. This supports the occasional use of electrical appliances as allowed by licensing requirements and avoids overuse of electrical cords that can cause a trip hazard.

Organizing Recycling and Composting Bins

To support recycling and conservation efforts, many teachers provide collection bins in the classroom. The bins need to be placed out of the walkways and emptied periodically to avoid creating trip or fire hazards.

Conducting Classroom Safety Reviews

Teachers constantly monitor their classrooms to keep them safe. As part of this process, they periodically step outside their teaching roles to take a critical look at the children's environments for potential hazards. Figure 13-6 provides a sample checklist to use when conducting a safety review of the children's environments. Recording the details of the problem and following through until the problem has been resolved completes the safety review process.

Providing Safe Indoor Areas for Active Play

For many years, attention to creating indoor spaces where children could be physically active diminished. In addition, research suggests that over time, early childhood programs have tended to provide fewer opportunities for children to play outdoors while focusing more on sedentary activities indoors (Pate, Pfeiffer, Trost, Ziegler, & Dowda, 2004). Teachers may also place restrictions on the activity level and intensity of play indoors because of the crowded nature of the classroom space and concerns for safety. It is common to hear teachers say, "Remember to use your walking feet!" This needs to be balanced with plenty of opportunity for children to use their "running feet" while engaged in active play both indoors and outdoors.

Whenever possible, indoor active play spaces should be provided to offer:

- Sufficient space for the age of the children and the size of the group.
- Space for a variety of movements such as running, playing catch, riding tricycles, dancing, and jumping, as well as taking part in group and individual activities.

FIGURE 13-6 Safety Checklist for Children's Environments

Safety Feature General Facility Overview	Details and Follow-Up	Initial When Corrected
❑ Entrance and exit routes are clear and open.		
❑ Electrical outlets are covered when not in use.		
❑ All light bulbs are covered.		
❑ Water source is approved and properly maintained.		
❑ Drinking fountains are clean with adequate water pressure.		
❑ Sewage system is in good working order.		
❑ Garbage is collected at least weekly.		
❑ Classrooms receive fresh air; air flow is satisfactory.		
❑ Heating and cooling systems are in good repair.		
❑ Smoke detectors and fire alarms are in working order.		
❑ Storage is free from rodent, insect, and vermin infestation.		
❑ Windows and doors are screened.		
❑ Other:		

Safety Feature Children's Spaces	Details and Follow-Up	Initial When Corrected
❑ Space provides at least 35 usable square feet per child.		
❑ Space is clean and orderly.		
❑ First-aid supplies are properly stored. Location is marked.		
❑ Exits are clearly marked; passageway is clear.		
❑ Telephone numbers for emergency medical care, fire, and poison control are posted by each telephone.		
❑ Classroom equipment is clean and in good repair.		
❑ Classroom cabinets contain no hazardous substances.		
❑ Furniture is sturdy and stable, or attached to the walls.		
❑ Diapering area keeps children safe; area is easy to clean.		
❑ Toilet rooms are clean, well lighted, well ventilated.		
❑ Hand washing sinks are near diapering and toileting areas.		
❑ Soap and paper towels are available.		
❑ Other:		

Source: *Based on Health and Safety Checklist for Early Care and Education Programs;* Caring for Our Children National Health and Safety Performance Standards, Third Edition; developed by the California Childcare Health Program, UCSF School of Nursing 2014.

- Separate spaces for mobile infants, active toddlers, and older children.
- Spaces that are easy to supervise and manage.
- Appropriate storage for equipment, such as a rolling cart for balls so that children can access the toys on their own.
- Access to drinking water from a water fountain or a tray with cups of water.

Figure 13-7 provides a list of needed features for safe indoor active play environments.

Providing many opportunities for active play in both indoor and outdoor spaces naturally directs children's energies in appropriate ways. As a result, active play may reduce the frequency of roughhousing that can lead to unsafe behaviors in the classroom.

> **FIGURE 13-7   Attributes of Safe Indoor Active Play Areas**
>
> - The space has appropriate boundaries and separation from nonactive play areas, cupboards, closets, tables or other protrusions that might have corners children could run against.
> - Area is clean and clear of hazards; materials are stored appropriately.
> - Walls are relatively smooth.
> - The floor surface is relatively smooth and even.
> - All windows are screened for safety.
> - Area is well lighted; lightbulbs are covered to avoid danger from shattering.
>
> - There are no entrapment or entanglement hazards.
> - Equipment and other toys are appropriate for the age of the children.
> - Indoor climbing equipment is positioned over safety-approved resilient surfacing mats that extend at least 6 feet beyond the structure.
> - Indoor equipment has a maximum height equal to 1 foot per year of age, such as 2 feet for 2-year-olds, 3 feet for 3-year-olds.

Sources: Based on *Handbook for Public Playground Safety* (Publication No. 325), by the U.S. Consumer Product Safety Commission, 2010, retrieved March 2015.

SELECTING SAFE TOYS

Choosing safe toys for the classroom is both exciting and challenging. A wide variety of interesting options is available, and marketing efforts are rigorous. Sorting through the options and making informed selections for young children is a significant aspect of safety management. Toys should be appropriate and meet strict safety standards.

Ensuring That Toys Are Appropriate

Toys are children's learning tools, representing more than just a fun pastime. Interaction with interesting toys allows children to act on, construct knowledge from, and make discoveries about their world. Toys need to offer developmental challenges and be reviewed to ensure that they include appropriate learning characteristics. Toys should be developmentally appropriate, be available in sufficient quantity, and help teach wellness concepts.

Providing Appropriate Developmental Challenge

To be appropriate, toys should attract children's interest, invite safe interaction, and match children's need for challenge. Teachers work to understand children's capabilities and emerging interests so that they can provide toys that will help each child move from one skill level to the next.

Infants   Children ages birth to 1 year are interested in color contrast, design, and patterns, as well as interesting sounds and textures. Soft toys, rattles, simple musical toys, and board books are good choices. Infants naturally explore toys with their mouths, so toys should not have small parts that can come loose and cause choking. Toys should also be easy to clean.

Toddlers   Children ages 1 to 3 years tend to explore toys with their mouths, hands, and toes, and they are becoming more mobile. They enjoy hand-sized blocks, nesting toys and shape-sorters, puzzles with one to four large pieces, and sturdy push toys. Toys that could introduce dangers to this age group include those that can be pulled over on top of the child; toys with strings that can cause strangulation; and toys with small parts such as beads, marbles, or magnets that are choking hazards.

Preschoolers Children ages 3 to 5 years are eager to try new things and take on new challenges. They enjoy puzzles with increasingly more pieces, blocks and construction toys, dolls and housekeeping, toy vehicles, manipulative toys of all kinds, and riding toys. Children in this age group may display curiosity that exceeds their abilities. Potential hazards include toys that use electricity; toys with strings; toys that shoot small parts; and hard toys that may be swung about, potentially harming others.

Kindergarten and Elementary Children ages 5 to 8 years have a wide range of interests and are able to explore topics with detail. Their growing capabilities can be supported with increasingly complex puzzles, board games, manipulative building sets, hobbies and collections, and sturdy bikes and scooters. Children in this age group are also eager to test their skills, sometimes beyond their understanding of impacts. Toys to avoid include lawn darts, toys that shoot small parts (including water guns that shoot more than 3 feet), and bikes and sports equipment that are too big. Electrical toys should be closely supervised.

Judging Toy Characteristics

Interesting toys promote child-directed play and self-directed learning. Toys that are self-explanatory allow children to explore and figure out what to do on their own. Toys can also offer attributes of self-correction, meaning they have pieces designed to fit in specific ways so that children can understand the concept the toy presents.

Toys that promote skills in several developmental areas are also ideal. Small blocks that encourage fine motor skills offer exploration of spatial awareness and can be used for counting and color and shape recognition and for sorting and making patterns; they also can become part of a dramatic play theme when matched with trucks or people figures. Figure 13-8 provides a list of characteristics to consider when selecting toys.

Offering Enough Toys

Toys need to be available in sufficient quantities so that all children can be actively involved in constructive play without undue competition. This is especially important for toddlers and very young children who are still learning to wait for a turn to play. Having a variety of interesting toys available allows teachers to redirect toddlers to appealing alternatives while they are waiting for a turn with the specially desired toy.

Positive social interactions are promoted when several children are able to play side by side with similar toys. For example, a good quantity of blocks moves the play from a solitary activity to a more social activity as children see one another's structures, participate in give and take, talk about what they are building, and perhaps cooperate on group structures.

Supporting Children's Special Developmental Needs

Every child needs to be able to access the learning environment through the available toys and materials. To accomplish this, teachers must recognize barriers that keep some children from full participation. Sometimes simply noticing a child's

CLASSROOM CONNECTION

Watch this video to see and hear one teacher's ideas about providing books for infants and toddlers. Do you agree with her thinking? What other toys do you see displayed for this age group?

Pearson Education

FIGURE 13-8 Toy Characteristics Checklist

Size and shape of parts	❑ Are the attributes of the toy safe, suitable, and appealing for the age group?
Number of parts	❑ Does the number of parts suit the ability of the intended age group?
	❑ Does the toy provide appropriate challenge?
Interlocking nature of parts	❑ Does the connection of the parts suit the interest and ability level of the age group?
Materials	❑ Are the materials the toy is made of suitable for the age group?
Developmental skill needed to play	❑ Do the motor and cognitive skills needed fit the intended age group?
Color/contrast	❑ Does the appearance of the toy invite the child to engage in play?
Cause and effect	❑ Does the toy respond in some way to the child's actions?
Sensory contribution	❑ Does the toy offer unique sensory experiences appropriate for the age group?
Level of realism	❑ Does the toy suit the maturity level of the age group?
Licensing	❑ Is the toy marketed to encourage a licensed product or character?
	❑ Does the licensing interest suit the age group and program goals?
Classic aspects	❑ Does the toy have long-lasting appeal? Will it maintain interest over time?
Robotic or smart features	❑ Does the toy have electronic or robotic appeal? Is it easy to use?
	❑ Does it encourage appropriate cognitive reasoning?
Educational	❑ Does the toy have an educational or cognitive goal that is achievable by the age group and appropriate to the program philosophy?

Source: Based on *Age Determinant Guidelines: Relating Children's Ages to Toy Characteristics and Play Behavior*, edited by T. P. Smith, September 2002, Bethesda, MD: U.S. Consumer Product Safety Commission. Retrieved March 2015; and *Which toy for which child: a consumer's guide for selecting suitable toys, ages birth through 5*. Pub. No. 285, by Barbara Goodson and Martha Bronson. U.S. Consumer Product Safety Commission, retrieved March 2015.

struggles will highlight a need, such as the need to provide "lefty" scissors for a child who is left-handed. Providing a particular toy with a range of attributes helps make an activity easier or more challenging so that children with varying skills can participate. For example, paintbrushes with chubby rather than skinny handles may be easier for children whose hand strength and coordination skills are just emerging.

Some toy attributes are especially appropriate for children with special developmental needs:

- Toys with texture and color contrasts and realistic and recognizable designs help children visually focus on the object and persist with play.
- Toys with large components or raised parts are easier for children with motor challenges to grasp.
- Toys that are sturdy and have nonskid bases will hold still as children play, an attribute that supports children with coordination challenges.

Some toys and equipment are designed to allow the teacher to offer specific assistance. For example, adaptive scissors provide spaces for both the teacher and child to position their fingers as they practice the cutting movements together. This supports the child while she builds hand strength and coordination and teaches the rhythm of cutting. Adaptations can also be made to typical equipment. For example, attaching a wooden block to a tricycle pedal helps a child with low muscle tone learn to push effectively against the pedal to ride the tricycle. Developmentally appropriate toys, adaptive equipment, and adaptations made to typical equipment enhance safety by fitting the challenge of the materials to the child's capabilities. This allows all children to use the toys safely and appropriately.

WHAT IF . . .

A parent asked why you do not have more popular fashion dolls or electronic toys in your classroom? How would you explain how toys are chosen for your classroom?

Choosing Toys That Encourage Active Play

Teachers also need to select toys that encourage children to be active both inside and outside. Active play toys include balls, hoops, large blocks, and rolling toys such as tricycles and wagons. Seasonal toys such as child-sized rakes and tubs with handles invite children to gather and move leaves in the fall. Providing ready access to such toys helps children choose to be active and energetic in positive and appropriate ways.

Using Toys to Teach Wellness Concepts

Safety concepts are naturally promoted by using traffic signs near the tricycle path in the play yard. Figures and trucks that depict emergency personnel provide opportunities to discuss topics such as fire safety and people who help in emergencies. Medical equipment props in the dramatic play area encourage children to explore health care concepts. The *Nutrition Note* provides ideas of toys and equipment that help children explore important nutrition lessons.

Ensuring That Toys are Safe

Teachers are responsible for ensuring that all toys provided to children are safe. This involves reviewing each toy against strict safety guidelines, evaluating toys for potential choking hazards, keeping toys clean, and checking periodically to make sure the toys are still safe for use.

Meeting Safety Guidelines

The U.S. Consumer Product Safety Commission (CPSC) is charged with establishing safety requirements and testing strategies to ensure toy safety and communicating toy safety labeling requirements. These requirements dictate that toys for young children must not contain lead paint, have small parts that could be swallowed, or present other hazards. Toys used with young children must be in good repair and durable for use in the busy children's setting. They should have no sharp edges or protrusions and no splinters or chipped paint. They should be constructed of nontoxic materials. When working with a mixed-age group of children, teachers must be especially vigilant about the toys that are accessible to the very youngest child. Older children should be taught about the safety hazard and the importance of keeping toys with small parts away from the younger children.

    The CPSC prohibits the sale of toys designed for use by children under the age of 3 if the toy contains small parts or is easily broken into pieces that form small parts. However, even with toy labeling laws, unsafe toys still find their way into

---

NUTRITION NOTE   Toys That Teach Nutrition Concepts

- Play foods representative of many cultures
- Measuring cups and spoons, bowls, whisks, pancake turners, pots, pans, funnels
- Specialty equipment: butter churn, hand-operated food grinder, pasta maker, crank-style apple peeler, tortilla press

- Books with food themes
- Puzzles and matching games with pictures of food
- Posters of food, crops, children cooking, and children eating

SAFETY SEGMENT   Toy Labeling Troubles

The U.S. Consumer Product Safety Commission requires that toys designed for use by children under the age of 3 be banned from the market if they contain small parts or are easily broken into pieces. Toys intended for children ages 3 to 6 that contain small parts must be specifically labeled with a choke hazard warning. However, some manufacturers appear to misuse the labeling laws, allowing unsafe toys to enter the market. This is done by marking toys with the choke hazard warning for children ages 3 to 6 even though the toy is typically associated with the play of infants and toddlers. This effectively gets around the ban on small parts in toys for children under the age of 3 through "creative" labeling. For example:

- A series of small-sized children's foam fabric books, with titles such as *I Love My Puppy*, look like board books typically suitable for children as young as 7 months even though they are marked for children ages 3 to 6. The books have Velcro tabs that tear off easily, posing a choking hazard.

- A plastic tea party set looks suitable for children who are 18 months of age, but the package is marked for children ages 3 to 6. The small plastic utensils are easily broken into small parts, presenting a choking hazard.

Source: Based on *Small Parts for Toys and Children's Products Business Guidance*. U. S. Consumer Products Safety Commission. Retrieved July 29, 2015 from http://www.cpsc.gov/en/Business--Manufacturing/Business-Education/Business-Guidance/Small-Parts-for-Toys-and-Childrens-Products.

stores. The *Safety Segment* describes how manufacturers can mislead consumers through misuse of labeling laws.

Some imported toys are not constructed for U.S. markets and are not reviewed against the safety guidelines before they are made available for sale. Imported toys should be evaluated carefully and removed from the classroom if there is concern. In some instances, imported toys have been discovered to contain lead and other materials that are toxic to young children. The CPSC provides lists of toys and equipment that have been recalled or pulled off the market due to child injury. This information can be accessed on the CPSC website. Teachers can also register to receive e-mail notification about toy recalls.

Toys purchased at garage sales, flea markets, and thrift shops and those donated to the children's program should be reviewed carefully. Toys that have been recalled due to safety hazards may have been donated for sale in these settings, unknowingly putting new buyers at risk for purchasing dangerous products. In addition, older toys may not have been constructed to meet the current safety standards. Teachers need to be smart by checking any purchase against the guidelines and toy recall information provided by the CPSC and by carefully reviewing the condition and appearance of each toy. If a toy does not meet a high standard for safety, cleanliness, and appropriateness, it should be discarded.

WHAT IF . . .

A family brought you a gift of toys from their country for use in the classroom? You know the potential hazards, but how will you respect the generous gesture while also ensuring children's safety?

Avoiding Choking Hazards

Toys provided for babies and very young children should not have small parts that can be swallowed, causing a choking hazard. Toys commonly associated with choking include:

- Marbles, small balls, and beads.
- Toys with small parts, such as wheels on toy cars that can be chewed off.
- Coins and buttons, often used for sorting and counting activities.
- Balloons used in celebrations and games. An uninflated balloon or pieces of popped balloons can cause choking.

- Small magnets on toys that may pose a choking hazard and, if swallowed, can attach to one another inside the body, causing internal damage.

Choke testing devices that are designed to resemble the size of a child's throat are available to test toys for dangerous small parts. The CPSC tests toys and toy parts using a device that is 1³⁄₁₆ inches deep with an oval-shaped opening measuring approximately 1⅜ inches by 2 inches. If any part of a toy fits into the testing device, the toy is considered too small for use with babies and toddlers. This includes toys and rattles that have handles or other protruding parts. If the protruding parts can fit into the space created by the testing device, they can also be inserted far into the child's mouth and cause choking.

Providing Clean and Sanitary Toys

Everyday play naturally results in children putting toys in their mouths and sand and dirt sticking to sensory bin toys. Choosing toys that are easy to clean and sanitize is wise, especially for use with children under the age of 5. Toys made of plastic that can be washed in the dishwasher or sanitized in tubs are good choices. The NAEYC has identified periodic cleaning and sanitizing of toys as an emerging practice for accredited programs. This means that the importance of sanitizing toys is moving toward the level of a policy requirement, something to keep in mind when making purchases.

Keeping Toys Safe

Toys should be evaluated frequently for safety. Checking toys as they are put away at cleanup time is a good time to notice if parts are coming loose, which could cause a safety hazard. Toys that are broken, worn out, or have missing parts should be discarded.

Storing Toys Appropriately

Each toy should have a specific storage place on a shelf or in a tub. Teachers often use a photograph or line drawing to indicate where each toy should be stored, both in the classroom and in the storage areas. Proper storage helps keep the parts of toys together, prolonging the usable life of the toy. Caring for toys in this way sends a message of respect for the materials that children use for learning and enhances safety by avoiding breakage and by keeping the toys from being a trip hazard.

CHECK YOUR UNDERSTANDING 13.5
Click here to check your understanding of selecting safe toys.

CREATING SAFE OUTDOOR ENVIRONMENTS

Outdoor environments bring children into contact with the natural world and provide space for energetic and active play. They include formally designed spaces such as school yards and public playgrounds, as well as backyards used by family child care homes. Creating safe outdoor play spaces requires attention to many details. These include appreciating the contributions of outdoor play settings to children's development, recognizing potential hazards, organizing the environment, designing appropriate spaces, attending to safety details, choosing safe equipment, storing outdoor materials safely, and monitoring play equipment.

Appreciating the Importance of Outdoor Play Spaces

Outdoor environments offer children opportunities to play and explore in ways that are not available indoors. Play outdoors allows children to feel the seasons, experience the climate where they live, and come into contact with nature and a variety of living things (Greenman, 2005; Rivkin, 1995). These experiences help children develop competencies and comfort in moving safely in the larger world (Trancik & Evans, 1995). They form the foundation of the child's appreciation of the natural world and the role people play in it.

Many children have few opportunities to play outdoors. Neighborhood parks and community outdoor spaces may have been lost due to expansion of housing and development. Some public outdoor sites are not safe for children because they are located too close to traffic or too far from family homes. Some families simply do not plan time for children to play outside. For many children, the opportunity to play outdoors at the early childhood program or school is the only time they are able to move freely outside.

Teachers who understand this believe that outdoor environments are extensions of the classroom that provide unique resources and tools for learning. Astute teachers plan outdoor activities in the daily schedule just as they do for the indoor environment.

Considering Injury Hazards

Teachers need to consider the potential hazards that may be associated with injuries in outdoor settings when they develop the outdoor play setting. The most frequent injuries that occur in the early childhood playground environment involve (CPSC, 1999, 2010):

- Falls—from platforms, slides, swings.
- Collisions—from children running into equipment or being struck by moving equipment.
- Entrapment— gaps that allow the child's head or other body part to enter and get stuck.
- Entanglement—getting caught on protruding components, S-style hooks, and ropes or straps that children bring into the environment.
- Pinching or crushing—as fingers and other body parts get caught in the equipment.

Awareness of these potential hazards must guide decision making whenever play areas are being constructed or rearranged. It is also important for teachers to stay current about safety recommendations for outdoor play and use of play equipment because restrictions and recommendations continue to evolve and change.

Organizing the Outdoor Environment

Safe outdoor play environments address children's developmental needs, support appropriate supervision, and provide accessible and safe opportunities for active and energetic play. These goals are accomplished by reviewing the site and correcting safety problems, establishing an appropriately sized space with appropriate fencing, and designating spaces for a range of play activities while ensuring needed setbacks for safety.

This drawing provides a glimpse into the child's vision of a play area that offers a variety of equipment challenges as well as a row of pleasing trees.

Reviewing the Site

Teachers assess the outdoor play space to identify hazards, plan for safety, and recognize play opportunities. Potential hazards may include nearby traffic, standing water, poor soil drainage, and exposure to sun and wind. Safety plans could include identifying the direction to locate slides to avoid the heat of afternoon sun. Opportunities might involve noticing natural pathways that could be used to move children around the area where swings could be placed.

Correcting Safety Problems

The outdoor play area should have no dangerous materials such as garbage, rubbish, metal scraps, or broken glass. The space should be well drained with no standing water. Plants, shrubs, or trees that have poisonous parts should be removed. The soil should be free of toxic materials such as paint chips that may contain lead.

Establishing Spaces of Sufficient Size

The NAEYC (2008) recommends that outdoor areas provide a minimum of 75 square feet of usable space per child. The space should be open for active play and provide visibility for adult supervision.

> **WHAT IF . . .**
> Your family child care has only a small space for outdoor play? How will you create play areas for children of different ages? What safety aspects will you consider?

Fencing the Play Space

Outdoor play spaces should be fenced or have other appropriate barriers to prevent children from wandering into the street, the parking lot, or other unsafe locations. Fences should be a minimum of 4 feet in height. Gate latches should be self-closing and childproof. Fenced play areas should have at least two exits.

Designating Activity Areas

Defining, clustering, and linking activity areas helps to establish the space as a learning environment while avoiding unnecessary conflicts or hazards.

Defining Learning Spaces Spaces are needed to support all types of active play such as running, climbing, riding, carrying, and building. Open areas for group games and spaces for individual play are ideal. Natural areas and vegetable gardens offer opportunity for exploration and discovery. Strategies to address competing needs include grouping activities and planning transition areas.

Clustering Activities Grouping climbing equipment and swings in one area and planning open space for running games in another area is desirable because it provides the opportunity to organize playground surfacing needs and focus areas for teacher supervision.

Providing Transition Zones Transition zones, which are the entry and exit routes between play areas, provide helpful cues for children. For example, a concrete walkway that divides the grassy area from the climbing equipment surrounded by wood chips provides a physical reminder that children are moving from one zone to another. This helps children predict the kinds of activities and behaviors that are expected or allowed in each area.

Arranging Safe Setbacks

A setback, or safety zone, is needed around playground equipment. Equipment should be set back from fences and walkways. Climbing and play structures more than 30 inches high should be separated by a space of at least 9 feet to avoid creating overlapping danger zones. Because swings are a significant source of childhood injuries from moving play equipment, they should be made of rubber, plastic, or another soft material and be located away from other play areas. Slides need to be appropriate for the size of children using them. They should face away from busy play areas so that children exiting the bottom of the slide do not hit others. Slides should also be positioned so that they are not pointing directly south or west where the sun may overheat the surface, causing potential for burns.

Planning Appropriate Spaces

Developmentally appropriate outdoor play areas address the needs of each age group. They support the needs of children with disabilities and invite socialization while also offering semiprivate spaces.

Meeting the Needs of Each Age Group

Outdoor play environments should be appropriate for children's developmental capabilities and offer a series of gradually increasing challenges. In shared-use spaces, this may require establishing a separate area in which each age group can play actively, providing safety for younger children who are easily bumped and knocked over by older children running by. Pathways, shrubs, and benches are options for separating age group play areas.

Infants Outdoor spaces for infants should provide many sensory experiences without overexposure to sun and wind. Pathways with surface variations add interest as children are pushed over them in strollers. Mobile infants enjoy surfaces that are interesting and safe for crawling, such as concrete aggregate pathways that incorporate rounded stones, areas with rubber mat surfacing, and grassy areas.

Toddlers Spaces for toddlers should offer a variety of walking surfaces, allowing the children to practice walking on regular and less regular surfaces such as grass, concrete, and rubber mats. Loose-fill surfacing materials such as pea gravel, wood mulch, and shredded rubber mulch should not be used in toddler playgrounds because they introduce hazards for eating or aspirating small pieces (CPSC, 2010).

Preschoolers and School-Age Children Outdoor spaces for preschool and older children can offer variety in textures and colors through surfacing materials, trees, plants, and shrubs. This age group enjoys the challenges of sloped areas for running and rolling and hills and dips in tricycle and bicycle pathways to challenge their riding skills.

Making Spaces Accessible

Children with special developmental needs are more able to participate actively if the outdoor environment has enough space to move safely. Walkways that accommodate wheelchairs and children on crutches should be at least 44 inches wide, and the surfacing should be firm and sturdy (Rivkin, 1995). Teachers should assess ramps and slopes to ensure that children can negotiate them.

Encouraging Socialization

Outdoor playtime is an important opportunity for socializing. Equipping the environment to encourage this is a natural way to bring children together. For example, a large grassy area invites a group of children to play running or ball games. Planning space for a tire swing invites the participation of two to four children, which meets the needs of a small group better than a single swing.

Offering Semiprivate Spaces

Opportunities to enjoy semiprivate spaces in the outdoor environment are also important. Planning space for a playhouse, tunnel, or bench provides an area that is visually open to facilitate supervision while offering a sense of privacy for child-directed make-believe play. These spaces also contribute to a child's sense of peacefulness and well-being as they offer respite from the noise and action.

Outdoor equipment supports social interactions as well as active play.

Addressing Safety Details

Establishing outdoor play areas requires a variety of safety decisions, including the choice of safe surfacing materials, the choice of planting materials, and attention to air quality and sun exposure.

Selecting Appropriate Surfacing Materials

Falls are the primary concern for injury in outdoor play spaces, making the selection of protective surfacing under climbing equipment an important safety decision. Some products that are *not* approved for surfacing under playground equipment are asphalt, concrete, dirt, grass, or wood mulch that has been treated with chromate copper arsenate (CCA). For safety, surfacing materials should meet American Society for Testing and Materials guidelines, ASTM F1292 (CPSC, 2010). The two types of approved protective surfacing materials are:

- Unitary surfacing materials that include rubber mats and tiles that are installed in place. Safety-tested rubber mats support access for wheelchairs.
- Loose-fill surfacing materials such as sand, pea gravel, and wood chips. These products are often less expensive but require more maintenance.

Each type of surfacing material has been tested to identify potential product toxicity (such as treated wood or recycled products) and accessibility for wheelchairs and to understand the minimum amount of depth of loose-fill surfacing materials needed to protect children in case of a fall (CPSC, 2010). Table 13-4 describes the minimum

TABLE 13-4   Minimum Compressed Loose-Fill Surfacing Depths

Inches	Of Loose-Fill Material	Protects to a Fall Height of (feet)
9	Wood chips	10
9	Shredded/recycled rubber	10
9	Wood mulch (non-CCA)	7
9	Pea gravel	5
9	Sand	4

Source: *Public Playground Safety Handbook* (Publication No. 325), by the U.S. Consumer Product Safety Commission, 2010, retrieved March 2015, from http://www.cpsc.gov/PageFiles/122149/325.pdf.

Cascade Sorte and Matt Bracken

depths of various loose-fill surfacing materials to protect children in case of falls from different heights. The selected surfacing material should extend at least 6 feet beyond the play equipment.

Including Plants, Shrubs, and Trees

Plants, shrubs, and trees contribute to the beauty and natural appeal of the outdoor environment. They offer variety in color and texture, teach about the seasons, and can be used to guide travel and designate play spaces. It is important to select plant materials that are safe for young children. Some bulbs, roots, leaves, seed pods, berries, and bark are unsafe for young children.

Considering Air Quality and Sun Exposure

Outdoor play spaces should be located where air quality meets safety levels. Air quality should be checked daily to ensure that pollution levels are low enough for safe outdoor play. Exposure to direct sunlight should be minimized as overexposure can cause painful sunburn and puts children at risk for developing skin cancer later in life (American Academy of Dermatology, 2005). Babies in particular should be kept out of direct sunlight at all times. If natural shade is not available, awnings or covered areas should be used.

Choosing Outdoor Play Equipment

Play equipment in outdoor environments invites children to try new challenges and develop new skills. Two types of equipment should be offered: *fixed equipment* such as climbing structures, swings, and slides and *movable equipment* such as balls, cones, and hoops. Providing both fixed and movable equipment establishes the space as an outdoor classroom. For safety, outdoor equipment must be developmentally appropriate, offer options for children with special needs, be durable, meet safety requirements, and be installed properly.

Making Developmentally Appropriate Choices

Many fun and challenging options are available for fixed equipment. However, some introduce risk for impact injuries and strangulation. These include trampolines, swinging gates, ropes that are not attached at both ends, heavy metal swings, rope swings, swinging rings, and trapeze bars, all of which should be avoided (CPSC, 2010).

Equipment to be used by children of various age groups should reflect each age group's emerging skills in balance, coordination, and reaction time, as well as arm and upper body strength. There should also be sufficient equipment for children at each developmental skill level. This ensures that younger children are not playing on equipment that is too large for them, which exposes them to challenges beyond their abilities (Nemours Foundation, 2012).

Offering Options for Children with Special Developmental Needs

Some play structures provide attributes that are inviting to all children while being especially suitable for children with physical challenges. Interest areas that can be reached from a wheelchair, such as steering wheels and sand and water trays, are safe options. Some swings provide wheelchair access or have seats in which children can be secured as they enjoy the fun. Sufficient space around accessible equipment is needed so that adults can assist children as needed.

Selecting Durable Equipment

It is important to refer to resources that provide guidance for selecting durable equipment, such as the *Public Playground Safety Handbook* published by the U.S. Consumer Product Safety Commission (2010). Equipment should be constructed of materials that have been used in similar playground settings and have a demonstrated history of durability and safety. The equipment should not contain any products that are known to be toxic. Painted or coated metal options are good choices. Wood used in the construction of play equipment should be naturally resistant to insects and deterioration, such as cedar or redwood, or it should be treated with an appropriate product. Equipment made from wood is resilient and natural but is harder to maintain because of the potential to splinter. Fasteners and connectors should be secure with no protruding hardware that can cause cuts. Moving parts should be covered with shields to avoid entrapment.

Addressing Fall and Entrapment Hazards

The equipment design should include required guardrails and barriers and avoid potential pinch hazards.

Guardrails Guardrails are required on all play equipment platforms, landings, and stairs. They reduce the likelihood of accidental falls, but do not prevent children from purposefully climbing through them.

Barriers Barriers are required on any elevated walking surface above 18 inches for toddlers, 30 inches for preschoolers, and 48 inches for school-age children (CPSC, 2010). Barriers are designed to prevent children from climbing over or through them.

Entrapment and Pinch or Crush Points Play equipment, handrails, guardrails, and fences need to be carefully designed to avoid entrapment and pinch or crush points. Entrapment can occur if a child's body part becomes lodged between nonmovable parts. Head entrapment can put the child at risk for strangulation. Pinch and crush points refer to openings that could entangle arms, legs, fingers, toes, and clothing. To avoid these hazards, openings should measure less than 3½ inches or be wider than 9 inches. Equipment should also be monitored to make sure surfaces are smooth with no snag areas that could catch fingers and clothing (CPSC, 2010).

Purchasing and Installing Equipment

Play equipment should be purchased from and installed by an experienced and reputable vendor. The vendor should be able to confirm that the product meets CPSC safety guidelines for children's equipment. The manufacturer's directions for assembly and installation should be strictly followed, and all instructions should be kept on file (CPSC, 2010). The equipment should be evaluated periodically to ensure continued safety, and any problems should be corrected immediately. Teachers are in a good position to monitor playground equipment and to notice and report any problems.

Pearson Education

CLASSROOM CONNECTION

Watch this video to see how the outdoor equipment at this preschool supports play year-round. Notice the material used to construct this equipment. Why might this program's leaders and teachers have chosen this material? What special approaches may be needed to maintain this equipment?

Monkey Business/Shutterstock

Monitoring for Safety

Ongoing monitoring of the outdoor environment ensures that emergent and incidental dangers are recognized and managed appropriately. Seasonal plant materials, the entry of potential hazards, and the effects of weather can introduce problems on a daily basis. Periodic safety checks of the play space help teachers identify and address these and other safety issues.

Providing Safe Storage

It is important to keep outdoor toys and movable equipment in the best condition possible. This ensures that they continue to provide for safe play, and it protects the investment made in the materials. Weatherproof storage sheds located near the play areas are ideal. This protects equipment made of metal from rusting or deteriorating, which are safety hazards.

Storage units should be organized, easy to access, and large enough to contain the equipment. This helps avoid safety hazards that could occur from the storage area being overfilled. Tubs of toys positioned on shelves and tricycles hung on the wall may be too heavy for children to access safely. For these reasons, the outdoor storage spaces should be used only by adults and should lock securely.

Child-accessible shelving such as a hinged shelving unit that opens and can be locked when folded closed is useful for smaller equipment. This allows children to be self-directed as they access the toys they need to develop their play themes.

Supervising Children Near Plant Materials

It is important for children to have access to growing things, but even play near safe plants, shrubs, and trees needs to be supervised. Small seeds can be interesting, but if poked in the nose or ears, they can be very difficult to dislodge. Mushrooms and toadstools in the play area should be removed on a daily basis if needed, even though not all of them are poisonous. Gloves should be worn to avoid physical contact with the plant and to demonstrate to children that mushrooms and toadstools may be dangerous and should not be touched.

Teachers who engage children in planting gardens should be aware of the parts of fruits or vegetables that might be dangerous. Both safe and unsafe plants can have attractive berries and seed pods that may tempt children to taste them. Teachers need to help children learn to look at but never eat any part of a plant that has not been served to them by their teacher or family.

The *Progressive Programs & Practices* feature, Safety Measures in a Gardening Experience, offers ideas about how the University of Louisiana, Lafayette, Child and Family Studies Early Childhood Lab implemented a special garden project to help children learn to enjoy vegetables by growing their own.

Watching for Incidental Entry of Hazardous Materials

Teachers need to monitor the outdoor environment for hazards every day. The nests of wasps or hornets must be removed to reduce the potential for stings. If a bat is

PROGRESSIVE PROGRAMS & PRACTICES

Safety Measures in a Gardening Experience

By Mary Sciaraffa, University of Louisiana, Lafayette, Child and Family Studies Early Childhood Lab

In response to the high rate of childhood obesity in Louisiana, a garden project was implemented at the University of Louisiana, Lafayette, Child and Family Studies Early Childhood Lab in collaboration with the UL Dietetics department and the UL Renewable Resource department. The primary educational significance of the garden project, which incorporates life science standards, is to provide children and their families with the knowledge of how to grow their own vegetable garden and to adopt healthier eating habits for a lifetime.

The children learn about the process of growing food and the importance of consuming a variety of vegetables. They learn about planning, planting, caring for (feeding, watering), harvesting, preparing, cooking, tasting, and the importance of eating these "home-grown" vegetables. The children's educational experiences are furthered as they are given a home garden to share with their families.

Ensure a safe gardening experience with children.

- Place the garden away from potential contamination sources as well as any gas or electric lines. Consider fencing in the garden to assist teachers in monitoring children.
- Make sure the soil and water sources are free of contaminants (lead, mold, algae). Contact local extension agents to discuss soil and water tests and help ensure that water containers and procedures are appropriate.

- If using raised garden beds, note that cedar, untreated pine, or fir are naturally durable, weatherproof, and pest-resistant building materials. Do not use nonresidential pressure-treated lumber, used tires, or railroad ties because these contain arsenic, petroleum, and creosote, which are not safe for children's settings.
- Be aware that some plants are naturally poisonous when consumed raw (rhubarb leaves, lima beans and red kidney beans, potato and tomato leaves and vines, green tomatoes, eggplant). Check on children's allergies before planting. Teach children never to eat any plant or seed without adult permission.
- Use sturdy child-sized garden tools. Show children the proper use of tools and how to move them safely. For example, when laying tools down, teach children to place rakes and other pointed tools with the tines down and put the tools away when they are no longer needed. If stakes are used, make sure they are taller than the children to avoid eye injuries.
- Avoid chemicals and pesticides. Local extension agents can assist in determining child-appropriate pest control methods.

The outdoor garden area provides a wonderful learning opportunity for children. Adults need to pay careful attention to the children and take appropriate safety precautions just as they do in the indoor classroom.

---

found hanging under a covered area, children should be kept at a distance until the bat is removed by an appropriate naturalist. Animal excrement should be removed immediately. Teachers should also look over the area to ensure that no garbage, beverage cups, needles, broken glass, or other hazards have been brought into the environment.

Recognizing the Effects of the Weather

The weather can also cause safety hazards. Long periods of hot sun can cause drying and splintering of wooden structures. A hot sunny day can raise the temperature of the slide, making it an unsafe burn hazard. Freezes and wind can damage trees and shrubs, causing hazards from falling limbs. Teachers need to be ready to correct or report problems, and to adapt children's play as needed.

Conducting Periodic Safety Checks

Regular inspection of the outdoor environment and equipment is important to ensure that the play area continues to meet safety expectations. Periodic monitoring helps teachers recognize and correct safety hazards. Table 13-5 provides a checklist that teachers can use to monitor the safety of the outdoor setting.

CHECK YOUR UNDERSTANDING 13.6

Click here to check your understanding of creating safe outdoor environments.

TABLE 13-5 Playground Maintenance Checklist

Maintenance Problems	Details and Follow-Up	Initial When Corrected
Play Area Review		
☐ Garbage, debris, broken glass, other hazardous materials		
☐ Gaps in fencing or other safety barriers (entrapment hazards)		
☐ Broken gate latches; latches that do not work		
☐ Cables, ropes, wires in the area (entanglement hazards)		
☐ Decayed or splintered wooden structures, benches, tables		
☐ Trip hazards		
☐ Rust or chipped paint exposing metal on toys, trikes, wagons		
☐ Standing water; problem with drainage		
☐ Sandbox cover is missing; sand is not protected from animals		
☐ Cracks in plastic equipment		
Play Equipment Assessment		
☐ Sharp points, corners, edges		
☐ Head entrapment areas		
☐ Crush or shear points		
☐ Corrosion, rust, deterioration on structural components that connect to the ground		
☐ Damaged equipment or missing components		
☐ Equipment footings are exposed		
☐ Surfacing under equipment is not sufficient		
☐ Other		

Source: Based on *Public Playground Safety Handbook* (Publication No. 325), U.S. Consumer Product Safety Commission, 2010, retrieved March 2015, from http://www.cpsc.gov/PageFiles/122149/325.pdf.

SUMMARY

- Ensuring children's physical and emotional safety by protecting them from the threat of harm and violence allows children to relax, grow, develop, and learn. Creating the classroom as such a refuge relies on teachers who predict and prevent unintentional injuries such as falling, being struck by or striking against objects, and being bitten or stung.

- Child care regulations and licensing assist teachers in creating safe settings for learning by establishing a basic level of health and safety for children in out-of-home care settings. Early childhood program leaders assume responsibility for the program systems that support health and safety in the setting, and teachers are responsible for the actions that keep children safe in the classroom and all class-related activities.

- Safe facilities for early childhood care and education meet common building codes and safety regulations and include welcoming and developmentally appropriate environments that provide sufficient space for the number of children, are accessible for everyone, and reflect the cultural traditions of the families served.

- Teachers create safe classroom environments by organizing the space to reduce conflicts, furnishing the classroom with durable and child appropriate furniture, storing materials and supplies safely, and controlling for hazards that may emerge during play.
- Teachers select toys based on their ability to support developmentally appropriate exploration and interaction while ensuring that safety guidelines are followed and hazards are avoided.
- Safe outdoor play environments are created by organizing the spaces to maximize developmentally appropriate play value while avoiding hazards that may cause falls, collisions, or entrapment and pinch injuries.

Chapter Quiz

Click here to check your understanding of Chapter 13, Enhancing Safety Through Appropriate Environments.

Discussion Starters

1. Consider the aspects of children's age and developmental maturity that influence children's risk for injury. Discuss ways teachers should adapt their supervision practices for each of the following age groups: infants, children ages 1 to 4 years, and children ages 5 to 9 years. Because of the differences in developmental skills, should children be grouped by age? Can a mixed-age class group be safe? Explain your answers.

2. Reflect on a children's classroom you have taught in or observed. What policies and actions were in place to ensure children's safety? How would you describe these to prospective parents to help them feel that their child would be secure in the environment?

3. Review the various responsibilities teachers have for children's safety. Which responsibility is most central to ensuring that children are safe? Which responsibility is most important to families?

4. Consider the developmental characteristics of each age group: infants, toddlers, preschoolers, and school-age children. Discuss ways you would arrange an appropriate indoor environment for each age group, Explain how your choices address age-specific safety risks.

5. Recall early childhood settings where you have worked or classrooms you have observed. Describe the potential safety hazards of each environment and how they were addressed (or not addressed) by the teacher in charge. What aspects of children's safety would you find most challenging to correct?

Practice Points

1. Go to the Centers for Disease Control and Prevention web page. Select three topics relevant to child safety to explore. Discuss how this information can guide you as you plan your classroom environment and establish safe supervision practices.

2. Log on to the National Child Care Resource and Referral Agency's Child Care Aware website. Explore the section, *About Child Care*. Review the *State Child Care Fact Sheet* for your state. Read the *We Can Do Better* section to identify the strengths, weaknesses, and recommendations for improvement of child care in your state. Discuss how this information can help you be a better teacher.

3. Consider your responsibilities as a teacher for children's safety. Create a list of safety practices that you believe you are ready to assume. Identify at least three concerns you have related to keeping children safe in your classroom. Find two resources that can help you gain the information and skills you need. What actions will you take to improve your competencies and confidence in each of these areas?

4. Go to the U.S. Consumer Product Safety Commission's website and access the *Public Playground Safety Handbook*. Use the Suggested General Maintenance Checklist in Appendix A to conduct a safety review of a playground in your community. Forward your recommendations to the school or public parks office.

5. Explore the types of toys and children's equipment that have been recalled recently due to safety hazards. Click the Safety Education tab on the U.S. Consumer Product Safety Commission's website to view toy recall statistics. Summarize the types of hazards that were identified in the 15 most recent toy recalls. Describe how this information helps you with your teaching.

Web Resources

Centers for Disease Control and Prevention

Head Start Design Guide, Second Edition

National Association for the Education of Young Children

National Child Care Information and Technical Assistance Center

National Clearinghouse for Educational Facilities

National Resource Center for Health and Safety in Child Care and Early Education

U.S. Consumer Product Safety Commission

U.S. Department of Justice, ADA Standards for Accessible Design

Key Terms

bite or sting injury

burns

children's environment

drowning

falls

fatal injury

fatal injuries

motor vehicle and traffic accidents

safety

space use plan

struck by or against injury

sudden infant death syndrome (SIDS)

suffocation

unintentional injuries

usable square footage

CHAPTER 14

Promoting Safe Practices Through Effective Classroom Management

learning outcomes

After reading this chapter, you should be able to:

1. Name and describe classroom routines that teachers use to enhance safety in the early childhood classroom.
2. Discuss safe supervision strategies and identify situations that require special attention to safety.
3. Compare the unique safety needs of children of different age groups and describe ways to teach children to be safe.

CASE STUDY

After teaching third grade for four years, Jean was assigned to teach full-day kindergarten. She was enthusiastic about starting the school year, but after three weeks, she is exhausted and disheartened.

Her class has taken a toll on her confidence. One child still cries well into the first hour of the day. Two have gotten hurt at recess. Manny pushes Sasha and pulls her hair. Candida and Sebastian are learning English but tend to fade into the background. Kellis and Mohammed finish their work quickly and start bothering the other children. Sam, who has Down syndrome, was found by another teacher sitting in the hallway outside the classroom door. Yesterday, Jean discovered that Emma was trading her lunch with Angie, who has a food allergy. And this morning, Malcomb's mom called and said that she doesn't believe he is being challenged enough.

Jean is an experienced teacher, but her class seems unmanageable. She is unsure if the children are safe, and she certainly is not making progress on her lesson plans! Jean doesn't know where to turn for help. If she contacts her principal, he may think that she is not doing her job.

Every group of children can present teachers with a variety of individual needs and classroom challenges. How teachers such as Jean address these challenges determines the effectiveness of the learning environment and children's safety. Jean is faced with a range of issues that cause her to question her ability to provide a safe class experience. Some are safety issues that should be her first priority; others are educational and organizational concerns that require thoughtful intervention. What management approaches will assist teachers such as Jean to develop strategies to ensure children's safety?

In this chapter, we present a variety of methods that contribute to safety in the early childhood setting. We start by exploring routines that set the stage for safety. Next, we describe supervision strategies to use in indoor and outdoor environments. Finally, we discuss ways teachers address children's individual safety needs and teach developmentally appropriate safety messages.

DEVELOPING SAFE CLASSROOM ROUTINES

Teachers are responsible for ensuring that children are safe in the classroom and during all class activities. They prepare by setting the stage for safety, establishing a daily schedule, planning secure arrival and departure procedures, and supporting safe transportation. Together these approaches create a proactive management plan that places children's safety at the core.

Setting the Stage for Safety

The strategies that build safety in the classroom occur before children arrive. Setting up the environment with appropriate toys and equipment is one example. Other examples include reflecting on evidence-based safety practices, gathering enrollment information, and orienting families to the classroom's safety procedures.

Using Evidence-Based Safety Practices

Information about the frequency of unintentional injuries and death in young children guides the development of strategies that are effective in reducing disease, injury, disability, and death in children's settings (American Academy of Pediatrics [AAP], American Public Health Association, and National Resource Center for Health and Safety in Child Care and Early Education, 2011). Staying alert to these trends and guidelines helps teachers know what to do to keep children safe, how to do it, and why.

Most states require that early childhood teachers stay current on recommended safety practices through yearly training and professional development activities. This ensures that classroom safety practices continue to address emerging issues. Teachers who understand and use evidence-based safety practices can feel confident that they are teaching in ways that are consistent with the recommendations of the field (Strain & Dunlap, 2006).

Gathering Information at Enrollment

Information collected when children enroll provides the details that teachers need to make appropriate safety plans and prepare to supervise children effectively. Beyond learning about the child's daily rhythms and feeding and nap schedules, teachers need to know about any situations that require special attention to safety and how to contact the family if needed. Ideally, teachers have the opportunity to review enrollment materials and meet with families before children attend so that everyone who cares for the child understands any special safety needs. Figure 14-1 provides examples of information that helps teachers support children's safe participation. In the opening scenario, Jean could have benefited from this information as a guide to developing supportive classroom practices.

Orienting Families

Teachers often invite families and children to visit the classroom before the child attends. This supports a smooth transition and offers the opportunity to

FIGURE 14-1   Enrollment Information That Supports Child Safety

Child Information

- ✓ Child's name and nickname
- ✓ Child's birth date
- ✓ Arrival and departure plan

Contact Information

- ✓ Contact information for custodial parent(s) or guardian(s): name, address, daytime phone numbers, email
- ✓ Emergency contacts: at least one person who lives locally but is not of the immediate family
- ✓ Secondary emergency contact: include a family member or friend that lives outside the community (in community-wide emergencies local communication may be jammed but individuals at a distance may be available to contact)
- ✓ Names of any persons who should never pick up the child from care

Health Information

- ✓ Record of child's immunizations
- ✓ Special health considerations including allergies

- ✓ Food or other restrictions due to religious, cultural, or family practice
- ✓ Information about identified or suspected developmental needs
- ✓ Child's healthcare providers and contact information (medical, dental, other)
- ✓ Child's insurance provider (name of the primary insured, policy or member number)
- ✓ Statement of program emergency medical response plan signed by the parent

Child Comfort Information

- ✓ Feeding and toileting practices (especially for infants and toddlers)
- ✓ Child information to support transition into care:
  - · Favorite toys or games
  - · Child's words for routines
  - · Names of siblings or close friends
  - · Child's comfort strategies
- ✓ Other information (family information that may affect the child in care such as illness of parent or close relative, incarcerated parent)

Sources: American Academy of Pediatrics, 2011; National Association for the Education of Young Children, 2009.

introduce classroom safety practices and the role families have in supporting them (National Association for the Education of Young Children [NAEYC], 2009). During the visit, safety topics are discussed naturally as children and parents tour the setting. For example, the importance of staying with the group is introduced as children walk into the classroom. Safety rules related to use of the swing and slide can be discussed while walking through the playground. Teachers use this time to remind families to dress children in clothes suitable for the weather so that outdoor play will be comfortable and safe (AAP et al., 2011; NAEYC, 2009).

Families that do not speak English should be encouraged to bring a trusted family member or friend to assist if a translator is not available. This helps teachers convey the basic safety rules and allows families to ask questions, increasing everyone's confidence about security in the setting. When a large percentage of children in the group speaks a language other than English, the program should, for safety and as a matter of good practice, provide at least one teacher who speaks that language.

Establishing a Daily Schedule

A familiar schedule guides the flow of daily activities and supports an organized approach to safe group management. The schedule should offer a predictable plan of activities, create familiar routines, support smooth transitions, and be flexible enough to accommodate disruptions.

Designing a Schedule of Activities

The daily schedule is a general timeline that organizes the day's activities. In early childhood settings, the daily schedule is usually created around time periods for meals, group activities, outdoor play, free-choice play, and rest times. The schedule addresses children's age and needs. For infants, the daily schedule is individualized as teachers follow each child's familiar eating and sleeping patterns (Wittmer & Petersen, 2008). The schedule for toddlers begins to introduce longer blocks of playtime. As children mature, they are more able to accommodate a schedule that is designed for the group.

Children quickly learn the daily schedule and are able to anticipate what will happen next. They learn that when they arrive, they wash their hands and sit down to breakfast. They know that after cleanup, they will go outside to play and that after story time, they will go home. This awareness allows children to engage in productive play and become more self-directed and competent moving through the familiar steps. This helps the teacher focus on supervising the group for safety (Alter & Conroy, 2007).

A predictable schedule helps children know what to expect and encourages cooperation.

Suzanne Clouzeau/Pearson Education

Creating Familiar Routines

Each day children have many opportunities to practice and become familiar with *routines*. Routines are rhythms and habits that help children "know how" to do what is expected within each segment of the daily schedule. For example, at mealtimes, children become familiar with the routines of washing their hands before they eat and clearing their plates when they are done with a meal. They learn the routines of getting toys off the shelves to play and putting them back when they are done. Children contribute to classroom organization and safety through their engagement in these routines. Figure 14-2 offers examples of routines that become familiar to children in the early childhood setting.

FIGURE 14-2   Sample Daily Routines

- Arrival: greet the teacher; hang up coat; wash hands before play.
- Free play: choose an activity; put toys away when done; choose another activity.
- Clean-up time: listen for the 5 minute warning; put toys in their tub and place tub on the shelf; go to circle.
- Circle time: Sit on the circle marker; listen for directions; raise hand and wait to be called on before talking.
- Going to meals: Listen for the transition song; wash hands; sit at the table; wait for everyone to sit before starting.
- During meals: take turns passing the food; serve myself; wait till the food has been passed to everyone before eating.
- Emergency drills: Listen for the alarm; stop playing; listen and follow the teacher's directions.
- Departure: Wait to be excused; put on coat and get artwork from cubby; wait until a grown-up checks you out; walk out together.

Source: Sorte (from practice).

CLASSROOM CONNECTION

Watch this video on how the teacher uses a song as she excuses children to line up. What ideas do you have to create a smooth transition?

Implementing Smooth Transitions

Transitions refer to the movement from one activity to another, such as ending free-choice play and beginning to clean up or ending story time and preparing to go outside to play. Transitions can be disruptive. What was a calm group of busy children one minute can become a whirlwind the next if the transition is unexpected or poorly managed. These ideas help avoid such safety concerns (Alter & Conroy, 2007):

- Keep the number of transitions to a minimum by planning large blocks of playtime.
- Give children a five-minute warning to prepare them for a change of activity.
- Ease into the transition by directing small groups of children to the next activity.

These approaches show respect for the importance of children's focus on their play. They teach children to navigate successfully through the change of activities, which keeps the group on track.

In the opening scenario, Jean might benefit from reviewing her approach to transitions. The ideas above might help address some of her classroom management challenges.

Addressing Schedule Disruptions

Disruption of the daily schedule is an unwelcome event. Late lunch delivery or loss of electricity can cause confusion and safety concerns in the classroom. Effective teachers reassure the children while swiftly assessing the situation: Is child safety threatened? What response strategies are needed? The teacher could read a story while waiting for lunch or take charge during the electrical outage by saying "1-2-3, eyes on me" to gain children's attention and give directions. Child security and safety depend on the teacher's ability to take the lead during unanticipated situations: conveying confidence and making reasonable adjustments until the familiar schedule can be restored.

Creating Secure Arrival and Departure Procedures

Children arrive and depart from early childhood classrooms in many ways. Younger children are usually delivered directly to the teacher at arrival and picked up directly from the teacher at departure. Children may be transported by a bus. School-age children may travel to school on their own. Teachers need to understand the plan for each child. They need to know how and when the child will arrive, who will be bringing the child, and who is authorized to pick up the child. This information helps teachers ensure that children are received and released appropriately.

Ensuring Safety at Arrival and Departure

For safety, teachers are present to supervise and greet children at arrival and to say good-bye at departure. Clear policies are needed to support safety during this exchange (AAP et al., 2011). For example:

- Young children must be delivered directly to the teacher and not be dropped off outside the building and allowed to "run in" to the classroom.
- Children may not be dropped off or picked up when the program is conducting an emergency evacuation or lockdown except under the direction of a public safety official.
- Children may not be released to go home with other children without written consent from parents or other authorized individuals.

Planning child-directed activities at arrival and departure times allows teachers to be more accessible to families and to monitor for safety. For example, setting out puzzles at arrival and books at departure engages children's attention and helps create organized transitions (Hemmeter, Ostrosky, Artman, & Kinder, 2008).

Signing In and Out Most early childhood settings for infants through preschool age require that children be "signed in" upon arrival and "signed out" at departure. This routine documents who delivered and received the child and creates a record of the exchange if there is any confusion. Figure 14-3 provides a sample sign-in and sign-out sheet. Arrival and departure routines can be complicated, especially if several adults participate in transporting the child. A system is needed to record arrival and departure if families arrive while the class is in the play yard or away from the classroom. Teachers might carry a small notebook for parents to sign.

Releasing Children to Appropriate Adults Teachers are responsible for releasing children only to the custodial parent or other authorized adult. The identification of anyone who is authorized to pick up the child but is unknown to the teacher must be checked. Children should not be released to anyone who displays behaviors that could endanger the child due to debilitation by alcohol, drugs, or other impairing conditions (AAP et al., 2011). State requirements differ about how such situations should be managed. At a minimum, teachers should have a plan in place to delay the release of the child while other arrangements are made, such as calling an alternate authorized adult. Teachers may also need to contact the police for advice. Sometimes families authorize an older sibling to pick up a younger child from the classroom. Rules regarding the ages of children who are allowed to pick up younger children from care and the ages of children who can be released to a minor are not universal. Teachers should consult with their local child care licensing authority for guidance. In addition, teachers should have a plan in the event that no authorized adult comes to pick up a child. The local child protective services agency is a resource for helping design a protocol for this situation.

CLASSROOM CONNECTION

Watch this video on how the teacher engages with children and families at arrival. How does she position her body and what does she say and do to support the child's safety and comfort?

FIGURE 14-3   Arrival and Departure Sign-In and Sign-Out Sheet

Note to Families: Please include time of arrival/departure and sign or initial below.

CHILD'S NAME	Monday, October 20		Tuesday, October 21	
	Arrive	Depart	Arrive	Depart
Annette	7:50	5:25	7:45	5:15
	Alice Yates	*Ben Yates*	*Ben Yates*	*Alice Yates*
Arturo	7:45	12:15	7:45	5:45
	Belinda Dee	*Belinda Dee*	*Belinda Dee*	*Belinda Dee*
Maria D.	7:45	12:15	7:45	5:45
	Belinda Dee	*Belinda Dee*	*Belinda Dee*	*Belinda Dee*
Maria M.	7:55	5:15	7:55	5:15
	Marc Mitchel	*Mike Robinson*	*Marc Mitchel*	*Mike Robinson*
Su Lin	7:55	5:25	7:55	5:45
	Seong Yun	*Joon Lee Yun*	*Seong Yun*	*Joon Lee Yun*

Monitoring Child Attendance

Taking attendance is a familiar safety practice in early childhood classrooms. Teachers need to know who is present and how many total children are in attendance at all times (AAP et al., 2011). To avoid confusion, attendance should be recorded immediately as each child arrives and as soon as each child departs. Throughout the day, teachers should periodically count the number of children to confirm that all are present. This is especially important anytime the group moves from one location to another, such as to and from the play yard, during an emergency drill, after the class gets on and off the bus for a field trip, or after walking down the hallway to and from the school restroom.

Contacting Parents About Child Absence Monitoring children's absence is also an important health and safety practice. Teachers inform families about how to communicate when children are absent and follow up as needed. For example, families should call or e-mail the teacher if a child will be absent and explain if it is due to a planned event or if the child is sick. If a child is absent without notification, the teacher should call the family to learn the reason. This is especially important to ensure the safety of school-aged children who travel to school on their own.

Attendance should be recorded as children arrive and checked periodically to make sure all children are present.

Knowing if children are sick helps teachers track the spread of communicable disease. If several children are sick, teachers can notify other families to watch for signs of illness, conduct additional sanitizing, and take other precautions to prevent spread of disease in the classroom.

Tracking Midday Variations in Attendance Not all children arrive and depart at the beginning and end of the class day. Some may arrive late or go home early. A child might leave for a dental appointment but return again before the school day is complete. Or a child who receives speech services might be taken to another room to participate in activities. Writing the number of children in attendance on a whiteboard and changing the total as children arrive late or leave early is one way teachers can remain aware of the total number of children that should be present (AAP et al., 2011).

Transporting Children Safely

Transportation services are provided for many school-age children, those with special developmental needs, and some Head Start and child care programs. Teachers are often assigned to supervise child transportation activities. They should understand transportation rules, know how to support safe transportation practices, and safely arrange transportation for field trips.

Understanding Child Transportation Regulations

WHAT IF . . .
you wanted to arrange bus transportation for a field trip? Who would you contact to learn about the regulations in your area?

Children are safer being transported in school buses than in any other form of motor vehicle (National Highway Traffic Safety Administration , 2011). The strict requirements for school bus construction and people's familiarity with the bright yellow buses used to transport children are two reasons given for the high safety rating.

The use of vans to transport young children is highly discouraged, and in many areas, it is strictly forbidden because of a variety of dangers, such as fewer regulations for vehicle construction, no requirements that vans stop at train crossings, and the fact that other drivers do not recognize vans as transportation sources for children.

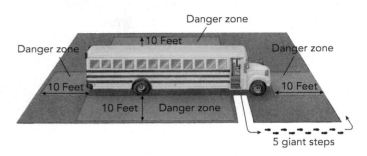

Although federal guidelines direct the safe transportation of young children, each state establishes the specific requirements for transporting children to and from public schools. Some state regulations identify guidelines specific to transporting children younger than 5 years of age, such as (NHTSA, 2011; Savage, Kawanabe, Mejeur, Goehring, & Reed, 2002):

FIGURE 14-4
School Bus Danger Zone

- The kinds of child safety restraint systems to be used.
- The maximum number of children that may be transported on a bus (based on age).
- The number of adult monitors required to maintain appropriate supervision and their qualifications.
- The procedures used for pickup and drop-off.

Teachers can learn more about these regulations from each state's director of pupil transportation services.

Supporting Safe Transportation Practices

Teachers have an especially important role at bus arrival and departure times. Each year on average, 19 school-aged children are killed in school transportation-related traffic crashes (NHTSA, 2011). The majority of these fatalities involve children between 5 and 7 years of age who are hit in the *bus danger zone*, the space within 10 feet surrounding the bus, as shown in Figure 14-4. Teachers need to be extra vigilant to supervise children as they pass through this danger zone and ensure that the children do not loiter in this space.

Arranging Transportation for Field Trips

Private early childhood programs may not be governed by federal guidelines, but should draft policies that meet state and local requirements to guide safe field trip transportation. Central to such policies should be the requirement that each child weighing less than 50 pounds must ride in an appropriately installed *child safety seat* and that adult supervision is appropriate for the group (National Safety Council, 2009; NHTSA, 1999).

Communication with families about transportation for field trips is very important. Families need to know:

- Where the group is going—the site and address.
- When the child will be transported—departure and return times.
- How the child will be transported—mode of transportation.
- Who will be driving—describing the qualifications of the drivers.
- Who will be supervising the children and monitoring for safety.

Teachers must ensure compliance with program transportation safety rules. In practice, this means that if safe, appropriate transportation cannot be achieved, the trip must be canceled.

CHECK YOUR UNDERSTANDING 14.1

Click here to check your understanding of developing safe classroom routines.

IMPLEMENTING SAFE SUPERVISION PRACTICES

Supervision is key to effective teaching. It is the most important way that teachers ensure the safe physical interactions and secure emotional environments that allow children to thrive in the setting. To prepare, teachers must understand what constitutes effective supervision, know how to supervise children in various settings, and be able to enforce program safety rules as needed.

Understanding Appropriate Supervision

Supervising children's safety requires deliberate planning and consistent and careful attention. Teachers must supervise children appropriately, know their supervisory responsibilities, coordinate with team teachers, reassure children that they are safe, and maintain children's attention and focus.

Supervising by Sight and Sound

Supervision is basic. It is what teachers *do* and *don't do* on a daily basis that makes the most difference in keeping children secure from harm. The *Code of Ethical Conduct* of the NAEYC (2011a) calls for teachers to supervise children by sight and sound:

- Infants and toddlers must be supervised by sight and sound at all times.
- Preschoolers must be supervised by sight at all times. Preschoolers may be out of sound supervision for short periods of time.
- Kindergartners, in a safe environment, may be out of sight and sound supervision for short periods of time if they are checked on regularly.

The arrangement of the physical environment can support supervision. Infant rooms typically create spaces for sleeping, diapering, feeding, and play. The room is arranged so that teachers can see and hear children who are participating in each activity. Spaces used by toddlers and older children are usually equipped with low shelving, allowing the teacher to monitor activity by moving about the room. Some states have specific requirements related to supervision of children when they are sleeping. Regulations for registered family child care homes may address whether children can sleep on a different floor from where the teacher is working.

Teachers must be continually alert to keeping all children in view and paying attention to the sounds of children at play. They must also know how to position themselves in the space, such as (NAEYC, 2009):

- Standing or sitting where the majority of children are easily in view.
- Being in a position to see the door to prevent a child from walking out.
- Scanning the environment and moving about to remain aware of the group.

Supervision also extends to knowing when special awareness is needed. Table 14-1 describes a variety of supervision scenarios and provides teachers with ideas of what to do and what to avoid.

Assigning Children to Specific Teachers

To increase safety, children in early childhood settings are assigned to a specific teacher who carries primary responsibility for knowing where that child is and what that child is doing at all times. Ideally, children are assigned to the same teacher and the same group of children every day (NAEYC, 2009). This supports bonding and

TABLE 14-1 Supervision Practices	
DO THIS	**NOT THIS**
DO – Check the environment every day for potential hazards.	DO NOT – Assume that someone else will do this.
DO – Keep children in direct sight and sound at all times.	DO NOT – Leave children unattended.
DO – Teach children to stay with the group.	DO NOT – Assume that children will remember to watch for the group.
DO – Teach children safety rules for relevant situations.	DO NOT – Transfer inappropriate worry or concern to children.
DO – Learn about children's special family situations (custody issues, people who should not have access to the child).	DO NOT – Assume that a child's family members or friends are safe people.
DO – Know whom the parent has approved to pick up the child.	DO NOT – Release the child to anyone who has not been approved.
DO – Require photo identification for approved persons you do not know.	DO NOT – Ask the child to tell you if the person is "okay."
DO – Understand your role in the security plan for your program.	DO NOT – Assume that security is being taken care of by other people.
DO – Know what to be concerned about; anticipate potential security risks; take appropriate precautions.	DO NOT – Ignore issues that you read about happening "somewhere else."
DO – Step in immediately if you see a person you do not know in the facility.	DO NOT – Assume that it is all right for people you don't know to be in the classroom or any part of your secure environment.

Source: Sorte (from practice).

allows parents to communicate directly with their child's assigned teacher when changes are needed in the child's care routine.

Infants and Toddlers Consistent teacher assignments ensure that the infant's and toddler's feeding and sleeping routines are understood and that their emotional and comfort needs are supported. This is called *continuity of care*. Typically in infant and toddler settings, each teacher is assigned to three or four children. For example, a group of eight infants and toddlers is led by two teachers. Each teacher is ultimately responsible for the care and security of the assigned children.

Preschoolers Preschool children in class groups of 16 to 18 are usually led by two or more teachers. The teachers work together to provide consistent supervision of the class. Teachers set up the classroom so that children can be easily viewed and heard from all areas of the room.

School-Age Children Kindergarten and elementary school class groups vary greatly in size, ranging from 18 to 24 or more children. Classes are often led by one teacher who is responsible for providing safe activities and consistent supervision. The teacher plans activities and lessons that allow children to be self-directed while the teacher supervises by moving around the room and addressing the needs of individual children.

Children with Special Needs Each child who has a disability or another special need should be assigned to a specific teacher. This increases the likelihood that the child's special educational supports, language assistance, and allergy or other medical needs are understood and managed consistently and safely (NAEYC, 2009). The *Health Hint* provides an example of the information that a teacher needs to provide safe services for a child with diabetes. Although one teacher would be assigned to supervise this child's care, it improves safety in case a teacher is absent when more than one teacher receives the training to address the child's needs. An educational assistant may be assigned to support a child's special needs in the classroom. Educational assistants are part of the teaching team and need to understand their supervision responsibilities.

HEALTH HINT Information Teachers Need to Serve Children with Diabetes

✓ General orientation about what diabetes is and how it can be effectively managed in the early childhood and school setting

✓ Detailed training on the child's specific medical plan for daily support

✓ Training on the administration of glucagon and other emergency care steps

✓ Resources to contact for more information, such as those provided by the American Diabetes Association:
- *Diabetes Medical Management Plan*
- *Tips to Help Teachers Keep Kids with Diabetes Safe at School*
- *Solutions for Common Diabetes Management Concerns in the Classroom*

Sources: The American Diabetes Association: Living with Diabetes: *Diabetes medical management plan*. Retrieved August 2015 from: http://www.diabetes.org/living -with-diabetes/parents-and-kids/diabetes-care-at-school/written-care-plans/diabetes-medical-management.html *Safe at School*. Retrieved August 2015, from http://www.diabetes.org/living-with-diabetes/parents-and-kids/diabetes-care-at-school/?loc=lwd-slabnav

Temporary Groupings Sometimes children are gathered in temporary groups, such as in before- and after-school care or when classes are merged as children depart at the end of the day. Temporary groups may include children of different ages, and the membership of the group may vary from day to day. Assigning teachers to specific children helps teachers recognize their responsibilities and focuses the teachers' attention on learning if one of their children has special safety needs.

Coordinating Supervision with Team Teachers

Groups of children younger than kindergarten age are most often led by a *teaching team* of two or more teachers. Teaching as part of a team requires a deliberate plan for sharing the responsibility of supervision (Kern & Wakeford, 2007). For example, one teacher might supervise the water play activity while the other moves about the room supervising in a general way. Or each teacher could assume responsibility to supervise in a particular zone of the room. Tasks could be divided so that one teacher is observing the entire group while the other attends to a child's need or sets up lunch. Clarifying the supervision plan helps teachers focus on their assigned responsibility and prevents teachers from thinking that "someone else" is watching (Kern & Wakeford, 2007).

Reassuring Children That They Are Safe

Children find comfort in knowing that the teacher is there to keep them safe. Children who feel safe and secure are able to move out into the play setting and enjoy and learn from their interactions in the environment (Bowlby, 1982). They are also more likely to seek the teacher for help if a safety issue arises.

The amount of reassurance required depends on the children's age and maturity and their need at a particular time. For example:

- Infants benefit from being able to see and hear the teacher and knowing that the teacher will attend to their needs.
- Toddlers need reassurance that the teacher is nearby as a physical and emotional safety base.
- Preschool children like to know that the teacher is available to listen to their ideas and concerns and to respond when they have a need.
- School-age children like to know what the rules are and whom to go to if they need help.

The reassurance that teachers provide includes being *accessible* (physically near and attentive) and *responsive* (approachable and easy to talk to). This is demonstrated when teachers position themselves physically near and when they engage with children by talking or smiling to show that they are available and ready to help if children need them.

Keeping Focused and Remaining Alert

Maintaining attention and focus is critical to safe supervision. This means that teachers must avoid boredom and distractions such as the following (AAP et al., 2011):

- Daydreaming.
- Talking together or talking or texting on the telephone.
- Cleaning or performing tasks that interrupt appropriate supervision.
- Being overly involved in children's play so that group supervision is forgotten.

Teachers learn to balance interacting with one child while observing the entire classroom. For example, when helping a toddler assemble a puzzle, the teacher periodically looks up to scan the room, making eye contact, smiling, and ensuring that all children are playing safely.

Supervising Classroom Activities

Supervision is an essential aspect of safe classroom management. Effective supervision in the classroom is supported by planning developmentally appropriate activities, paying attention to activities that offer special risks, and purposefully monitoring the environment for safety.

Planning Appropriate Activities

Balancing the number of activities that require direct teacher involvement with the number of activities that children can participate in on their own is one way to ensure that teachers have time to monitor children's play carefully (Alter & Conroy, 2007). Interesting activities draw children into focused play and increase their opportunity to be self-directed. This frees teachers to scan and move about the room observing for safety.

Managing Interactions with Animals

Children are very interested in and excited about animals. This makes special planning important to ensure the safety of children and the visiting animal. Child care regulations may limit the types of animals that are allowed in children's settings because of safety concerns (AAP et al., 2011). For example, birds with hooked beaks and animals that may carry salmonella (lizards, frogs, turtles, baby chicks) are typically not allowed. Any visiting animals should be healthy and not aggressive with children.

To increase safety, teachers carefully arrange interactions between children and animals. For example, as the children sit in a circle on the floor, the teacher may say:

Today Sally's dog, Bess, is coming to visit. We don't want to frighten Bess, so we will sit in a circle quietly while Sally introduces her to us. Sally will invite each of you to come up one at a time to pet Bess.

A Matter of ETHICS

Children often look to teachers to provide reassurance about their worries. How does the NAEYC Code of Ethical Conduct guide you when a child clings to you and says that she does not want to go home?

This approach provides children with the information they need. It communicates:

- What children should do (sit quietly in the circle; watch and listen).
- What will happen (your name will be called when it is your turn to pet Bess).
- Who will get to participate (everyone).

When children know what is expected and receive confirmation that each of them will be able to participate, the experience is more enjoyable and safe for the children and the animal.

Supervising Activities That Involve Water

Water activities can present significant safety concerns, including the dangers of slipping and drowning. Careful planning and supervision is essential. Offering clean water in shallow trays is a good choice for infants and toddlers. This allows children to play while reducing the likelihood that a child might "tip" over into the water, which could be dangerous. For preschoolers and older, water play may be offered in shallow tubs or sensory tables where they can stand and play. Teachers ensure appropriate play and watch that the floor does not become wet and slippery. They also guide children to wash their hands when they are done to avoid spreading germs (U.S. Consumer Products Safety Commission, 2012).

The use of wading pools should be done in compliance with the regulations governing child care in the local area. Some states do not allow wading pools in children's programs.

Monitoring the Environment

Classroom supervision involves continually observing the environment to identify and correct safety hazards. Manipulative toys left in the walkway could cause tripping or block emergency exits. Sand spilled from the sensory bin could cause children to slip. Safety issues such as these can be addressed by anticipating the problem and providing supports to avoid or address them. For example, the manipulative toys could be located away from the walkway and a mat could be placed under the sensory bin. Careful monitoring ensures that unanticipated safety problems are corrected right away.

Safety hazards, such as materials spilled from the sensory table, should be cleared away as soon as they are noticed.

Suzanne Clouzeau/Pearson Education

Supervising Outdoor Activities

Special attention is needed when supervising children in outdoor play areas because injuries can happen quickly and have the potential to be severe. Children must be visible at all times, and teachers must be able to hear them to know if they are in danger or if they are being harassed or bullied. A well-designed outdoor environment should work "with" teachers, supporting the teachers' ability to scan the near and far environments to track for safety (Kern & Wakeford, 2007). Supervising children effectively in outdoor play areas involves planning appropriate activities, using supervision zones to ensure appropriate oversight, and teaching actively.

Planning Outdoor Playtime

Outdoor playtime is learning time. It is not enough simply to give children the opportunity to be outdoors; the playtime must be planned and prepared to make sure children have the freedom to move safely and be active. Teachers organize the activities and identify where each activity will take place to avoid conflicts or hazards. For example, playing ball games away from the swings reduces the likelihood that a child will run under a moving swing to retrieve a rolling ball.

Establishing expectations about safe use of the toys and equipment also helps children be active within the boundaries of acceptable play. A good time to share this information is during the transition as children prepare to go outside. While children gather, teachers talk about the activities and equipment that are available and remind children of the rules for safe play. Overall, when planning outdoor play activities teachers are responsible for:

- Selecting appropriate and interesting activities that offer challenges and build skills.
- Arranging the needed equipment and supplies.
- Teaching children the rules for safe and acceptable play.
- Encouraging children to be highly active at least part of the time.
- Supervising children for safety at all times.

These purposeful planning activities set the stage for safe play. They also reduce the likelihood of bullying and rough play that may emerge due to boredom.

WHAT IF . . .

You found yourself daydreaming about what you needed to buy at the grocery store when you were supposed to be supervising children at the slide? What could you do to improve your supervision in this important area?

Using Supervision Zones

During outdoor play, teachers need to allow children to explore and discover without undue intervention, but they must be ready to intervene immediately if they observe unsafe behavior. Teachers should avoid thinking of outdoor playtime or recess as "break time." Clustering at the periphery of the play area, and supervising from a distance but not engaging with children except when needed, are distracting and harmful practices.

Outdoor play areas are usually large spaces where trees and equipment may block teachers' view, and the sounds of play can make supervision by sight and sound more challenging. Dividing the outdoor play area into "zones" and assigning each teacher to supervise a zone is a good strategy for improving safety (Kern & Wakeford, 2007). This approach helps teachers focus their attention on the specific activities occurring in their zone and increases their attentiveness in guiding children to play appropriately. Periodically rotating teachers to new supervision zones helps refresh their attention and reduce supervision boredom.

Teaching Actively

Active teaching is purposeful and engaged. Teachers move about the room observing children's skill development and encouraging active play. They ask questions to introduce ideas and spark children's interest. They are also alert and attuned to the tone of the play. Teachers show by this presence that they are watching to make sure the rules of safety are being followed and that interactions are positive. This prompts children to play appropriately and sends a message that bullying will be noticed and stopped.

Supervising Special Situations

Many special situations require that teachers be ready to use their professional experience and common sense to supervise children appropriately. Examples include field trips; the presence of substitutes, visitors, and strangers; complicated family issues; and special family events. Teachers need to be ready to enforce rules and address unsafe behaviors.

Staying Alert on Field Trips

Moving out of the familiar environment into new settings on field trips can distract children's attention. Teachers reduce the possibility of unintentional injury by selecting appropriate destinations and by visiting the field trip site in advance to assess for safety concerns. Orienting children and adult volunteers about the safety rules and assigning each child to an adult leader are important strategies for safe supervision.

Ensuring Safety When Substitutes Are Assigned

A change in group leadership might introduce safety concerns. Substitute teachers must quickly adjust to the classroom schedule and may not know individual children's needs. An appropriate orientation can address these concerns. Introducing the substitute teacher and explaining why the regular teacher is absent helps children understand that the substitute is a leader and person of safety in the class. It is helpful to adjust the day's plan so that the majority of activities are child-directed. This allows the new teacher to focus on interacting with the children and supervising for safety. Having a "substitute day" lesson plan prepared in advance can help support substitute teachers and improve safety.

Supervising Visitors

Visitors bring welcome assistance and special skills to the class, but they can also disrupt safety routines. Visitors need to be oriented to the classroom safety routines. Teachers should introduce the visitors to the children, confirming that they are "teacher-approved" members of the class. It is best if visitors have clear assignments, such as reading to children or supervising the block corner. Visitors should never be left alone with the children, and teachers should supervise their interactions at all times.

Visitors in uniform, such as firefighters or costumed characters, are sometimes invited to visit. Adults may see these visitors as fun, but children can find them frightening. Teachers can help by inviting appropriate visitors and giving them ideas in advance about how best to interact with the children. Teachers should stay close to ensure children's comfort and safety.

Confronting Strangers

Teachers need to be prepared to approach any unknown person in the children's environments. They need to learn the purpose of the person's presence and be ready to direct the person to leave if needed. A backup plan should be in place if the teacher requires assistance, such as calling for support from other teachers or the program director or principal.

Navigating Complicated Family Issues

Teachers sometimes need to handle complex family or child custody issues that can include safety concerns. For example, a parent might report that the noncustodial parent has a court-ordered temporary restraining order and is not allowed to have contact with the child. The temporary restraining order should be reviewed and the limits of the exclusion understood. This is done so that the teacher does not restrict access to the child by one parent simply on the direction of the other parent.

Teachers also need to avoid being drawn into family disagreements. Parents involved in custody battles sometimes ask teachers to record observations about the other parent's behavior with the child. Teachers should explain that the school is a safe and neutral place for the child and that recording observations is not an appropriate teacher activity. Developing a relationship of collaboration with families helps when it is necessary to communicate about difficult issues like these (Olson, 2007).

Families need to know about classroom safety policies.

Suzanne Clouzeau/Pearson Education, Inc.

Guiding Family Events

Gathering families for special events is a common way to encourage family engagement, yet even such welcome activities can introduce safety concerns. For example, there may be confusion about who is supervising the children—the teacher or the family? Clarifying this confusion can be accomplished in the invitation:

- If the teacher will supervise the children, parents could be invited to "Please come watch the class dance and sing their favorite songs."
- If parents are to supervise their children, the invitation could say, "Please supervise your children while you enjoy walking together through the classroom art show."

Even when families are expected to supervise their children, teachers should be aware of safety and be ready to enforce safety rules if needed.

Enforcing Program Safety Rules

Teachers are responsible for ensuring that program safety rules are followed during all program and school activities. When necessary, teachers must step forward to kindly but firmly enforce the program safety rule. Teachers should persist until unsafe activities stop and safety is restored. Table 14-2 provides examples of potential situations and ideas for responsive action.

Intervening When Families Are Unsafe

Teachers need to act immediately and decisively if they observe families using unsafe practices. The *Safety Segment* provides information for families about the dangers of leaving children unattended in cars, a practice that has led to the deaths of many children due to heat suffocation. Families are most often appreciative of guidance that helps them keep their child safe. If families are resistant and the dangerous behavior is repeated, teachers may need to contact the police.

CHECK YOUR UNDERSTANDING 14.2

Click here to check your understanding of implementing safe supervision practices.

TABLE 14-2 Situations That Require Responsive Action

Potential Safety Hazard	Responsive Action
A parent parks her bicycle in the walkway to the classroom.	Tell the parent how the bicycle is a safety hazard. Identify a safe place to park the bike.
A child brings in a favorite toy, but it is unsafe for toddlers in the family care home.	Allow the child to enjoy telling you about the toy. Talk about the dangers for the young children; choose a safe place to store the toy until the end of the day.
A pet is brought into the classroom unannounced.	Inform the pet owner that the pet must be kept outside. Schedule a pet visit following program policies.
A person walks by the play yard and stops to talk with a child at the fence.	Intervene immediately. Redirect the child and ask the person not to talk to children at play. Increase supervision along the fence.
After pick-up, parents stay to talk in the play yard. They do not monitor their children or enforce safety rules.	Approach the parents and explain the safety concerns; ask for their help. Suggest that they come early to visit before pick-up.
A parent sends an unfamiliar person to preschool to pick up a child.	Keep the child in care. Contact the parent. Obtain verbal permission to release to the unfamiliar adult. Make a note of the conversation. Require a new person to show photo identification.
A parent calls in and asks the teacher to send his child out to the car where he is waiting.	Remind the parent that the child can only be released directly to the parent. Work with the parent to create a workable pick-up plan.

Source: Sorte (from practice).

SAFETY SEGMENT Don't Leave Children in Motor Vehicles

Leaving children alone in motor vehicles is dangerous. A vehicle parked in the sun traps the heat and can reach an internal temperature of up to 131° in only 10 minutes. Even on mild overcast days, the interior of the vehicle can reach 110°. Orient families to these safety rules:

- Never leave a child in an unattended vehicle even with the windows down.

- Don't forget a sleeping child in the vehicle. Place a needed item such as a purse or backpack in the backseat so that you see the child when you retrieve the item as you get out.
- Always lock vehicle doors when not in use so that children do not enter and accidentally lock themselves in.
- Teach children never to play in a vehicle.
- Call 911 if you see a child left unattended in a vehicle.

Based on National Highway Traffic Safety Association. *Children and Cars: A Potentially Lethal Combination*. Retrieved August 2015, from www.nhtsa.dot.gov/people/injury/enforce/ChildrenAndCars/pages/Unattend-HotCars.htm and Safe Kids Worldwide. *Preventing Injuries, at home, at play, and on the way: Safety in and around cars*. Retrieved August 2015, from www.safekids.org/safety-basics/safety-resources-by-risk-area/in-and-around-cars/.

IMPLEMENTING SAFE MANAGEMENT PRACTICES

The early childhood years are a time of rapid change. Children grow from being vulnerable infants to active young children whose greater skills and maturity help them begin to learn how to recognize dangers and stay safe. Teachers support this process by understanding appropriate safety management practices, being attuned to the safety needs of each age group, and equipping themselves with strategies to teach all children safely.

Identifying Appropriate Safety Management Practices

Children's physical skills may develop more rapidly than their knowledge about danger, which can draw them into dangerous situations. A toddler who has just learned to walk might try to walk down the stairs or move in the direction of the street. It is a mistake to "blame" very young children for acting in unsafe ways simply because they are young and inexperienced. Similarly, it is not helpful to "allow" older children to behave in unsafe ways assuming that they should "know better." Management strategies need to keep pace with these changes.

The functions that guide appropriate safety management practices in the classroom are planning, modeling, and teaching about safety.

1. *Planning for safety* includes ensuring that selected activities are suitable for children's physical capabilities and that the environment is set up to support safe active play.

2. *Modeling safety practices* occurs when teachers show children how to interact appropriately with materials and each other, such as how to put toys away safely or how to take turns.

3. *Teaching safety messages* is done gradually and appropriately for each age group. The safety message is introduced in a simple way that focuses on concrete safety actions rather than danger. Then the message is repeated with more detail as children mature and is reinforced through practice. The *Teaching Wellness* feature shows how safety messages are introduced and reinforced.

Understanding the Safety Needs of Infants

During the first year of life, infants become enthusiastic crawling or walking explorers. Safety management should encourage and not get in the way of this normal development. Exploration is the way children gain practical abilities, knowledge, and confidence that the environment is safe and inviting.

Using Infant-Appropriate Safety Practices

Safety for infants involves individualized care rhythms such as a familiar schedule for eating and sleeping, a safe environment, a kind and caring touch, and appropriate encouraging conversation (NAEYC, 2009). Teachers use these infant care practices to:

- Check the environment every day to ensure clean floors, covered electrical outlets, sturdy furnishings, no choking hazards, no rough or sharp surfaces, no blinds with pull strings, no bibs except during feeding, and no pacifiers on strings around necks.
- Label and store the infant's food, personal belongings, high chair, and crib appropriately.
- Place infants on their backs to sleep alone in cribs with no toys, blankets, or bumper pads.
- Talk and sing to help infants associate the sound and feel of language with positive social connection and safe relationships.

Managing for Safety

Guiding the explorations and interactions of infants is the primary goal of safety management for this age group. Teaching approaches for safety include the following:

- Supervise play with materials. Sanitize dropped toys and pacifiers. Make sure toys that have been in babies' mouths are not exchanged with other babies.
- Guide interactions. Help children touch without grabbing. Say, "Pat Lin-Lin's cheek gently like this."
- Protect infants from more mobile children. Teach older children how to interact safely with the baby.

TEACHING WELLNESS   Class Safety Rules

LEARNING OUTCOME   Children will name and describe safety rules.

Vocabulary focus: Safety, rules, be careful.

Safety watch: Select appropriate toys and materials for use with each age group. Be alert to safe play; appropriately reinforce the safety rules.

INFANTS AND TODDLERS

- **Goal:** Babies and toddlers will experience the safety rule of "Be gentle with one another to keep from getting hurt."
- **Materials:** Play space, appropriate toys including people figures and toy animals.
- **Activity plan:** Place toys in a comfortable play space. Invite children to play. Demonstrate with words and gestures that convey caring and kindness. Say, "You are touching the toy doggie very gently. See how you can pet the toy doggie with no hurting? That's how we take care of him." Redirect rough touching by guiding the child's hands to touch gently.
- **How to adjust the activity:** As needed, assist children by moving their hands to stroke a stuffed animal. Repeat the message in both English and the child's home language. Share the class safety rules with families so that they can reinforce the concepts at home.
- **Did you meet your goal?** Did children hear kind words and practice caring touch with the toys?

PRESCHOOLERS AND KINDERGARTNERS

- **Goal:** Children will identify activity safety rules and tell how the rules help keep them safe.
- **Materials:** Photos of children at play in different school activities (cutting, eating, climbing steps on the slide) taped on a large sheet of paper.
- **Activity plan:** Gather children. Tell them that rules are made to keep them safe from getting hurt. Show each picture. Ask, "Is there a way a person could get hurt when doing this activity?" Ask them to think of a rule that could help children stay safe. For example, "The rule is to sit down when cutting. We have this rule so that no one gets poked by the scissors." Write the rule on the poster and place it where children can see and talk about the rules at mealtimes.
- **How to adjust the activity:** Ask the children to act out the safety rule for each activity. Allow time for children to respond. Reinforce all efforts. Learn the safety words in the home languages of the children. Post the safety rules in multiple languages as appropriate.
- **Did you meet your goal?** Are children able to identify safety rules? Can they explain how the rules help keep children safe?

YOUNG SCHOOL-AGE CHILDREN

- **Goal:** Children will identify rules for the classroom, the cafeteria, the bus, outdoors, and field trips. They will be able to explain the rules to others.
- **Materials:** Poster-sized paper, marking pens, tape.
- **Activity plan:** Talk about how rules help people remember to be safe. Create small groups. Ask each group to create a poster listing two to four safety rules for one of the school settings. Invite children to illustrate their poster. Gather together and ask each group to report on the rules they developed and explain how the rules keep children safe. Invite the rest of the class to offer feedback and ideas. Place the posters where others can see them and learn the safety rules.
- **How to adjust the activity:** Monitor the small groups as they work to ensure that each child has a chance to participate. Provide support and extra time if needed. Reinforce each child's efforts when they present to the class.
- **Did you meet your goal?** Are children able to identify rules for school settings and explain the rules to others?

Amelia Cobarrubias

Petee reminds his friends to hold hands and stay together when they go on field trips.

Teaching Safety Messages

Important safety messages are conveyed to infants by establishing a comfortable and relaxed environment. Teachers reinforce safety and trust when they:

- Respond to the infant's needs.
- Place the infant in safe positions to eat and sleep.
- Use gentle touching and comforting sounds.

Understanding the Safety Needs of Toddlers

The toddler years (from walking to age 3) are a time of increasingly active exploration and interest in independence. Teachers take advantage of this enthusiasm through responsive guidance.

Guide babies to touch each other gently.

Using Toddler-Appropriate Safety Practices

Teachers of toddlers address safety by recognizing that the toddlers' greater mobility may lead them to climb higher, toddle further, and engage with materials in new and inventive ways. Important safety practices for toddlers include the following:

- Review the environment for safety. Make sure child safety locks are used on cupboards and furniture is sturdy so that children can pull themselves up to standing and balance without worry of furniture tipping over.
- Provide toileting supports, including potty chairs, child-sized toilets, child-accessible sinks, or sturdy step stools, so that children can gain skills while being closely monitored.
- Arrange open spaces for play and provide plenty of time for toddlers to move and explore without undue restrictions.
- Monitor toys, sensory bin materials, and food for potential choking hazards.
- Offer finger-food options that promote independence but do not present choking hazards.
- Label and store children's personal items and sleeping mat or cot.

CLASSROOM CONNECTION

Watch this video of a teacher using conversation to safely manage the diaper changing routine with a young child. What approaches might you use?

Managing for Safety

Toddlers need close supervision. They have discovered the joys of movement, but may have limited ability to communicate and sometimes are not able to achieve the goals they are aiming for. A child might move the helpful teacher's hand away saying, "Alex do it!" Or a child might respond to frustration through familiar toddler behaviors such as scratching or biting, behaviors that cause grief for children, teachers, and parents. The teacher should stay as close as necessary to recognize when such behaviors are about to occur and be ready to intervene immediately to prevent the problem behavior and redirect the child to productive play. Communication should be clear and direct (NAEYC, 2009):

WHAT IF . . .

A toddler you were playing and laughing with suddenly grabbed your glasses? How would you respond?

- Firmly state what the child should do: "No biting!" or "No running to the street!"
- Briefly state why: "Biting hurts." or "Streets are dangerous!"
- Provide an alternative: "Let's play with these blocks. At snack time, you can bite an apple" or "Here is the safe place to run. Let's go!"

Teaching Safety Messages

Safety messages for toddlers are taught by modeling and using words that describe safe play. This approach helps toddlers see appropriate behavior and connect words with their meaning. For example, the teacher might guide a child's hand to poke a tofu cube with a small fork while saying, "Use the fork to poke the tofu. No poking people." Adding facial expressions that reinforce the "yes" and "no" part of the message increases the likelihood of correct communication. The toddler might repeat the message, "Poke fu," while nodding his or her head up and down in affirmation. Other toddler-relevant safety messages taught through modeling actions and words include these:

- *Use gentle touch:* Keep from poking or scratching eyes and faces or pulling earrings.
- *Stay back from dangers:* Beware of hot stoves, broken glass, unknown animals, and swings.
- *Eat and drink safely:* Sit while eating and drinking; eat slowly and remember to chew.
- *Move safely:* Watch out for tabletops that stick out at eye level; go down slides feet first.
- *Be safe in the environment:* Show and say, "The flower is for touching and smelling but not eating" or, "The window is just for looking, not hitting."
- *Play safely:* Show and say, "Look Jenna, hold the truck down here where it is away from Leon's eyes. Down here is the safe place for your truck."

Storybooks and puppets can teach safety messages. Facial expressions help reinforce meaning.

Understanding the Safety Needs of Preschoolers

Preschool children (ages 3 to 5 years) mature from playing individually or alongside other children to being highly interested in interactive play. They are increasingly able to run and climb quickly and are capable of sustained involvement with activities and inventive dramatic play. Preschool children are also able to learn, implement, and teach others important safety routines. Safety management strategies should respect these increasing capabilities while empowering children with knowledge to recognize dangers and ways to keep safe.

Using Preschooler Appropriate Safety Practices

Teachers enhance safety for active preschoolers by creating environments where children can test their skills in appropriate ways, encouraging children to try solving problems, and supporting the development of self-help skills (NAEYC, 2009). Safety practices for preschool-age children include the following:

- Arrange the environment so that children can be self-directed. Ensure that furniture is stable and toys are organized on low shelves within easy reach. Store large toys on the floor or bottom shelf to avoid danger of children pulling heavy toys down on themselves.
- Encourage the development of safe self-help skills. Set out tubs for toys or dirty dishes so that children can pick up after playtime and clear their spaces after meals. The *Progressive Programs & Practices* feature describes how one program works to encourage children's self-help skills by offering snack during choice time.

PROGRESSIVE PROGRAMS & PRACTICES

Managing Hunger with the Smart Snack Area

By Roni Cohen Leiderman, Dean, Mailman Segal Center for Human Development of Nova Southeastern University

The Mailman Segal Center for Human Development of Nova Southeastern University, in Fort Lauderdale, Florida, houses preschool, infant/toddler, and parenting programs. We have 43 classrooms with over 1,000 participating children and families. Our nationally accredited preschool programs and clinical services serve the community and offer a learning laboratory for professional training and development in a variety of fields.

What Challenge Did You Face?

Unlike a home environment, where a young child can request food or drink, children in group care often are on regimented schedules without easy access to snacks and meals. The challenge we saw with this typical setup was twofold. First, we were not teaching children to pay attention to their body's signals. Very young children modulate their hunger and thirst via signals, but as they mature, their food intake is controlled by schedules. The second challenge was how to incorporate healthy eating habits whereby children could have access to healthy food choices throughout the day within the confines of a classic preschool program schedule.

How Did You Meet This Challenge?

We generated possible solutions with parents and staff before deciding on a plan of action. Families in our program take turns being the "snack parent or grandparent" and bring sufficient food items for all the children in their class. We have always given families clear guidelines for healthy snack foods and drinks and ask that sugary, artificially flavored, or high-sodium foods be replaced with whole grains, natural foods, and fresh fruits and vegetables.

After considerable discussion and research, staff suggested a unique snack program to implement quality effective teaching practices that would simultaneously support children's well-being from a nutritional perspective. The idea was to set up a snack table known as the Smart Snack area that would function similarly to other areas of interest (art, manipulatives, imaginative play, etc.). Each day the family responsible for the snack would work with their child and the classroom staff to put the food, drink, napkins, utensils, and plates on the table. The area would be located near the sink so that children would wash their hands before eating. The snack area would be open during self-selected play and small-group time. Visuals with pictures and simple words would be displayed reminding children to wash their hands, throw out their trash, and clean their area when done, in addition to offering suggested "recipes." For example, when Maya's mom brought strawberries, whole-grain crackers, and cream cheese, sturdy cardboard cards showed step-by-step how to make a cream cheese and strawberry sandwich. Child-sized pitchers with water and cups would always be available.

Imagesab/Fotolia

At first, parents and teachers had some concerns about the approach: Would children sit and spend too much time eating in preference to using other learning and play areas in the classroom? Would the setting be difficult to monitor?

What Was the Outcome?

During the first few weeks, the children spent a lot of time at the snack table, but as time went on, the approach developed a rhythm of its own. Children began using the snack table less often, an indication that they were eating less for the novelty and were better able to tune into their individual body signals indicating that they were hungry or thirsty. While at the Smart Snack table, rich language developed as did fine motor skills for pouring and spreading. Independence and cooperative skills increased as children shared, negotiated for chairs, and used proper hygiene as modeled by the teachers and posted on the displays. The preschoolers developed an illustrated cookbook of their favorite recipes, and the children began to recognize the sight words that were matched to the pictures of the daily snack suggestions.

Even with the success of the Smart Snack program, some teachers would like to return to scheduled snack times. We continue to dialogue and discover ways to handle logistical challenges while maintaining the program. We have a commitment to the children who spend long hours away from home and family. We aim to nurture, protect, teach, and play with the children in our care in ways that foster beneficial habits and pave the way for a healthy future.

Young children are able to understand safety messages such as look but do not touch.

- Label a cubby or hook for the child's coat and a cot or sleeping mat for each child's consistent use. Create labels in the language the child speaks to encourage literacy awareness.
- Provide access to toileting at will, if possible. Supervise children when they are toileting.

Managing for Safety

Preschool-age children can develop intense play themes that may introduce dangers, such as making and eating "stew" from leaves and mushrooms during outdoor play. Or they may follow the unsafe behaviors of other children, such as running up the slide, climbing around equipment and barriers, and jumping from high platforms. Here are some strategies for managing safety for preschoolers:

- Teach children the boundaries for activity and safety.
- Recognize and reinforce safe behaviors with a smile, a wink, or a whisper.
- Guide children to recognize the effect of their unsafe actions. Say, "If you keep riding your tricycle toward the hopscotch area, someone may get hurt."
- Teach children strategies to assert and communicate their needs in unsafe settings. Say, "Tell her you don't want to do that. It's not safe."
- Supervise children's social interactions and intervene in bullying situations.
- Move actively and confidently to correct unsafe behaviors.

Teaching Safety Messages

Preschool children are growing in their ability to understand the cause and effects of behaviors and are able to understand and learn safety messages. For example, by about age 3, most typically developing children understand that going down the slide is fun, but for safety, they need to take turns and "Go down the slide feet first." However, teaching preschool children about dangers has the possibility of introducing worries, and ultimately such discussions may convey the message that sometimes things occur that adults cannot control. For example, teaching children to evacuate for a fire drill introduces the concept that fires might happen. Safety messages need to be presented in ways that are appropriate for the child to understand and that avoid overdramatizing worrisome events. Typical safety messages for preschool children include:

- Follow the teacher's directions to leave the classroom in case of emergency.
- Get down, take cover, and hold on in case of a tornado or an earthquake.
- Stay away from dangerous materials (matches and lighters, paints, cleaning supplies, poisons, hot beverages), strange animals, and strangers.
- Eat only the foods given to you by your family or teacher.
- Play safely outdoors and follow the rules of games.

Safety messages can be taught through books and flannel board stories that depict children responding appropriately in potentially dangerous situations. Visits by safety officers such as firefighters and police officers and field trips to locations such as swimming pools where safety lessons can be discussed in context are also effective ways to teach about safety.

Teaching safety messages to preschoolers can also begin to introduce self-awareness concepts. For example, as preschool children develop greater language skills, they become more able to communicate worries, fears, or experiences that threaten them. Teachers support this process by helping children learn to recognize and name their emotions. Pictures showing various facial expressions, such as those in Figure 14-5, can help children identify and learn to express how they feel. Learning to recognize and understand their emotions and those of others is a developmental task of early childhood.

FIGURE 14-5

Helping Children Identify Emotions

Understanding the Safety Needs of School-Age Children

School-age children (ages 5 and older) are more mobile and often are allowed to move independently in their neighborhood and travel on their own to school (Centers for Disease Control and Prevention, National Center for Injury Prevention and Control, 2006). This is an impressionable age group where heroic television characters and other media-driven images are infused into their experience, potentially confusing children's understanding about realistic abilities. Greater independence can place school-age children in unsupervised settings, increasing the potential for unintentional injury. At the same time, these children are capable of learning and following safety rules and telling others about safety. Teachers need to remain alert to safety practices while focusing more on teaching children how to stay safe and supervising from a greater distance.

Using School-Age Appropriate Safety Practices

Safety practices for school-age children continue to focus on safe environments and appropriate activities. Teachers need to avoid thinking that children's greater maturity and capability suggest that they know how to stay safe. Safety practices for school-age children include the following:

- Model safe behaviors and establish boundaries for movement and behavior.
- Plan activities that provide appropriate challenge as well as opportunities to learn about safety hazards and ways to stay safe.
- Ensure that children do not have access to dangerous items such as matches, lighters, harmful cleaning products, poisons, alcohol, drugs, firearms, and sharp knives.
- Be aware of peer pressure and the influences of older children who may be intrigued by dangerous items; listen for interest in fire, smoking, firearms, explosives, drugs, alcohol, and other dangerous products, which may be signs of inappropriate interactions.
- Recognize when children are becoming tired and need guidance to stop and rest.

Managing for Safety

Various unsafe behaviors may be exhibited and boundaries may be tested with intensity during the school-age years, making managing for safety a challenge. Behaviors teachers may confront include children using materials inventively but unsafely, trying "daredevil" behaviors, and bullying other children by telling them they "can't play." Although these may be typical ways in which children test their skills, they are also examples of times when teachers must help children identify boundaries (Gartrell & Gartrell, 2008). Teachers should reaffirm that dangerous behaviors will not be allowed. Safety management strategies include the following:

- Focus on behaviors and provide clear messages that communicate the problem and confirm that unsafe behaviors are not allowed. Say, "That tree is dangerous to climb; you need to come down."
- Direct the industriousness and productivity of this age; provide new challenges and opportunities for children to explore.
- Help children build leadership skills; guide them to resolve conflicts and identify safe alternatives.

Teachers redirect unsafe behaviors by planning activities that appeal to everyone, such as crafts, hobbies, information about collecting, and photography.

Teaching Safety Messages

Safety messages for school-age children focus on preventive safety themes. Safety topics for this age group include:

- How to ride a bicycle safely (wear a helmet; follow the rules of the road).
- How to be a safe passenger in the car (keeping hands and head inside the car, not distracting the driver) and in the bus (getting on and off the bus safely).
- How to call 911 for help in case of an emergency.
- How to respond if a stranger approaches and who to go to for help.
- Staying away from sick or injured animals.
- Staying away from guns, knives, and other sharp objects.
- Staying away from deep water; don't go swimming without an adult.
- How to safely use e-mail and the Internet.
- How to stay home alone for short periods of time (for older school-age children).

Preventive messages can be more abstract than with younger children because this age group is increasingly able to discuss dangers they may not have experienced. For example, children are capable of learning how to stay away from matches and other things that are hot using the "I Spy Something Hot" plan (Start Safe Kids USA, 2009).

Group problem-solving approaches such as classroom meetings are effective in helping school-age children gain skills to address safety issues (Nast, 2012). Teachers who hold regular classroom meetings can use this opportunity to discuss problems such as bullying or unsafe behaviors (Utah Education Network [UEN], 2003). The group process could unfold like this: Children gather in a circle, discuss the problem, and offer solutions by following simple rules such as letting everyone speak, listening, and being respectful (Gartrell, 2006; UEN, 2003). The teacher should guide the process, providing sufficient time for children to have their point of view heard while moving children through the process of negotiation. The use of drawn-out problem-solving meetings to help children resolve small issues is counterproductive and often ends up with children forgetting what the issue was about. An example of group problem solving is provided in Figure 14-6.

WHAT IF . . .
you overheard a small group of children in your class talking about a gun they had been looking at the previous afternoon? What would you do with this information?

FIGURE 14-6   **Sample Group Problem Solving Process**

1. Identify the issue. [Tricycles are parked in front of the door.]
2. Talk about why the issue is a safety problem. [The tricycles block the door so people can not come in; people might trip over the tricycles.]
3. Think about ways the problem could be solved. [Not let children ride tricycles? Park the tricycles against the wall? Make "no tricycle parking" signs?]
4. Choose one or two resolutions to try. [Park tricycles against the wall and make "no parking" signs for the door.]
5. Agree on the plan. [Heather and Connor will make signs.]
6. Implement the resolution. [Try it for a few days.]
7. Do a check-up. [Is it working?]

Source: Sorte (from practice).

Understanding the Safety Needs of Children with Special Needs

Teachers might be hesitant about how to ensure the safety of children with special developmental needs in the classroom. The Americans with Disabilities Act (ADA) guides teachers not to make assumptions about how a child will behave or what the child can learn simply because the child has an identified disability or special health care need. Instead, it is important to consider children's individual safety needs related to the potential of the program to meet those needs reasonably. A child may need adaptive supports or special assistance to increase safety outdoors, or a child with a seizure disorder may require a special health and safety routine. Understanding the child's capabilities, identifying support strategies, and drafting an action plan are logical steps for meeting the child's unique safety needs.

Implementing Appropriate Safety Practices

Safety routines for children with special needs are created in collaboration with families, early interventionists, medical providers, and others who advise the teacher about safety accommodations (AAP et al., 2011). Safety routines include:

- Addressing children's need for physical supports by acquiring special equipment such as adaptive scissors or chairs with seat belts for security.
- Supporting children's behavior needs using extra guidance during playtime and using a variety of communication methods such as gestures to reinforce spoken language or picture schedules to depict what children should do during transition time (Hanline, Nunes, & Worthy, 2007).
- Creating a health management plan for each child who has special health needs or allergies.

Monitoring for Food Allergies

The impacts of food allergies extend beyond careful menu planning. Curriculum activities also need to be monitored to ensure that they do not introduce food allergens. The *Nutrition Note* explores some common food allergens and ways they might be brought into the classroom through curriculum activities. Planning cooking activities that are safe for all children is supported by creating a cookbook in which recipes are labeled as nut-free, egg-free, and milk-free.

NUTRITION NOTE   Classroom Activities That Can Introduce Food Allergens

Food allergies are the most common cause of anaphylactic shock, which if untreated can lead to death. To keep children safe, early childhood teachers need to be cautious that they don't introduce food allergens through curriculum activities.

Common Food Allergens	Activities That May Bring These Allergens into the Classroom
Eggs	• Cooking activities that include eggs (muffins or pancakes) • Egg cartons used for craft activities
Cow's milk	• Cooking activities that use milk (bread or smoothies) • Finger painting using pudding made with milk
Peanuts	• Pinecone bird feeders made with peanut butter and birdseed • Peanuts used in the sensory table or for counting games
Wheat	• Baking activities and play dough made with wheat flour • Noodle necklaces made with wheat-based pasta
Soy	• Mosaics made with soybeans • Tambourines or maracas made using soybeans for "sound"

Source: Based on "Symposium: Pediatric Food Allergy," by S. H. Sicherer et al., 2003, *Pediatrics*, 111(6), 1591–1594.

Managing for Safety

Safety management for children with special needs focuses on the individual child's maturity and ability to understand and recognize danger and to follow safety guidance. Teachers need to think about each child's unique situation and implement focused strategies that are clear and straightforward. In practice, many of these strategies are appropriate to use with all children. Some examples are listed next.

For children with special developmental needs:

• Use direct and clear language supplemented by gestures or photographs to communicate and reinforce sequenced responses where appropriate.

• Place danger picture codes or "Stop" signs near boundaries or areas of danger.

For children with specific health concerns:

• Clearly state the safety concern: "You have a special condition called diabetes."

• Describe the purpose of any safety measures: "We need to test your blood sugar levels and choose the right foods for your snack."

• Help the child know what to expect: "After group time, we will go to the quiet corner where we can concentrate while we test your blood. Then we will join the other children at snack."

• Teach the child to explain his or her health condition to others as a way of fostering normal conversation about the child's specific health safety need: "I have to eat a snack that is just right for my body."

For children who are learning English:

• Talk with families or others who can provide safety words in the child's home language. Create note cards with the directions written phonetically.

- Provide books that present safety issues and are written in the child's home language. Request that the family assist you in teaching the safety message.

Guidance reminders should be presented clearly, repeated frequently, and followed consistently to avoid confusion. Reminding children of rules that have been discussed previously can seem frustrating to teachers, but it should be done kindly and with a steady voice, remembering that for some children, learning the safety rules will take longer.

Teaching Safety Messages

Safety messages for children with special needs should be appropriate for the child's developmental ability to understand and accomplish and should be relevant to the child's special situation. The teacher also needs to be able to assess the degree to which the child can recognize, understand, and respond appropriately to danger. Each child's needs may be unique. For this reason, teachers should seek guidance and assess the effectiveness of strategies as they are tried. Examples of safety messages for children who have special needs include the following:

- *Children with physical disabilities:* Guide children to recognize and avoid safety hazards, such as learning to look for uneven pavement that may cause tripping.
- *Children who have hearing impairments:* Teach children to look at the teacher when she gives safety directions because not doing so might be dangerous. Help children recognize the flashing lights or vibrations of the emergency alarm and learn to watch for environmental cues such as other people lining up at the door during evacuation drills.
- *Children who have vision impairments:* Teach children where to find the emergency exit and how to recognize the smell of smoke. Keep the furniture pattern consistent and the pathway to the emergency exit clear, as this provides cues that help the child find the exit.
- *Children who move in wheelchairs:* Ensure that the emergency exit is wheelchair-accessible. Teach children how to use the emergency exit during an evacuation drill.
- *Children with ADHD:* Teach children to use visual cues such as a picture of a stop sign on the door or, for an older child, a sign that says "Wait for the teacher" to remind children what to do to be safe. Post rules where children see them easily. Rehearse emergency scenarios.
- *Children with diabetes:* Help the child begin to recognize the warning signs of low blood sugar levels so that they can tell you, "I feel low." Manage the use of glucose tablets or gel and other emergency foods as indicated in the diabetes medical management plan. Explain how the foods are used in case of low blood sugar levels.
- *Children with special health concerns:* Help children learn to recognize personal safety hazards and, when age appropriate, how to monitor personal safety, such as teaching a child with asthma to wear a dust mask when sanding wood at the workbench or guiding and supporting a child with food allergies not to eat certain foods.
- *Children who are learning English:* Teach children the words and gestures for safety, including *stop* and *dangerous*. Enlist the support of the family to help you reinforce the meanings of these safety words.

Managing Challenging Behaviors

Sometimes children's behaviors are intense and dangerous. Children may interact in socially harmful ways such as biting, scratching, kicking, or bullying others. Such behaviors can be damaging for the child who is out of control, the child or teacher who is the target of the behavior, and all the children of the group who are at risk for feeling insecure and unsafe in the setting. One report identifies the expulsion rate due to behavior challenges as three times higher among prekindergarten aged children than among children in the K-12 setting (Gillian, W.S., 2005).

Teachers use guidance strategies to help children be safe and appropriate in the social setting (NAEYC, 2011b; Fox & Garrison, 2009). *Guidance* is a method of teaching that promotes children's understanding and ability to manage their behaviors appropriately. Guidance is different from *discipline*, which tends to be associated with punitive approaches used to enforce acceptable behavior.

Teachers work closely with families to identify guidance approaches that can be reinforced in both the school and home environments (Alter & Conroy, 2007). Such interventions help children learn to manage their behaviors and become more able to listen to and follow directions, both of which are crucial responses in emergency situations. In the opening scenario, Jean was very discouraged due to a variety of challenging behaviors. She needed to summon the courage to reflect on her guidance strategies and seek support to create a plan for improvement.

Reinforcing Safety Messages

As with any kind of learning, safety messages need to be reinforced. Recognizing the safety lessons in daily activities and helping children understand safety as being important in their lives are ways teachers reinforce safety messages and prepare children for the future.

Infusing Safety Messages in Everyday Lessons

Reinforcing safety messages through everyday activities helps children begin to recognize that they deserve—and can achieve—safety and security in their lives (Bales, Wallinga, & Coleman, 2005). Learning to stack blocks so that the tower does not fall over teaches children about careful touch and the consequences of being rough. Achieving success by carrying a cup of water without spilling, teaches children the benefits of practice. Teachers support these lessons by helping children recognize the safety skills they are developing.

Using Teachable Moments

Unplanned situations can provide useful teaching opportunities. For example, although the teacher's first response to an accident is to care for the injury and comfort the child, these situations can also be learning moments if they are handled with understanding. After administering needed first aid, the teacher could hug the child and state, "Bumping heads hurts! Next time if you walk slowly around the corner, it will help you see the bookshelf and so that you don't bump your head." This acknowledges the hurt while offering the child a strategy to avoid the accident in the future.

Making Safety Relevant to Children's Lives

Safety messages are most effective if they are meaningful to children's experiences. If children experience events that make them feel unsafe, teachers can help them discover ways to address their worries, such as telling their family when they are scared. Some children witness acts of violence through the media or in their neighborhoods. Storybooks that describe how a character demonstrates strength and resilience in a difficult situation can encourage conversation about how children can manage their worries.

Safety messages should also be relevant to the dangers children might find in or around their home or community. Children in rural settings may benefit from safety messages that relate to farm animals, use of farm equipment, and irrigation canals. Children in urban areas should be taught about how to ride on the subway or use elevators safely.

Although teachers impart safety knowledge of many kinds, they often do not know if the safety lessons they teach will keep children safe in the future. By using effective management practices, teachers provide a place and a period of time where children can be secure and have a chance to learn and where the ideas of a safe environment and safe and positive interactions are planted.

CHECK YOUR UNDERSTANDING 14.3
Click here to check your understanding of implementing safe management practices.

SUMMARY

- Effective classroom management relies on carefully established routines that when used systematically, increase children's safety.
- Sight and sound observation that is appropriate for the age group and the setting is the foundation of safe supervision.
- Recognizing and addressing the safety needs of each age group and offering information to make safety relevant to children's lives are approaches that help children establish patterns of safety that benefit them now and in the future.

Chapter Quiz 14

 Click here to check your understanding of Chapter 14, Promoting Safe Practices Through Effective Classroom Management.

Discussion Starters

1. Identify a classroom routine and explain how it contributes to children's safety.
2. Select a setting (indoors, outdoors, or another special situation) and describe safe supervision practices appropriate for the setting.
3. Describe how the safety needs of toddlers are different from the safety needs of preschoolers, and discuss the management approaches you would use for each age group.

Practice Points

1. Using the online resources as a guide, search the Internet for an article that discusses safe practices for early childhood classrooms.
2. Identify a field trip destination for a kindergarten class. Visit the site and make a list of potential safety hazards. Explain how you would ensure children's safety at the location.
3. Create a newsletter article for families that communicates the safety rules for a particular age group. Provide an explanation for each safety rule that describes how the rule improves safety while also allowing children to explore and learn.

Web Resources

Child Care Aware

National Association for the Education of Young Children (NAEYC)

National Education Association (NEA)

National Infant & Toddler Child Care Initiative

Safe Kids Worldwide

CHAPTER 15

Child Abuse and Neglect

After reading this chapter, you should be able to:

1. Define child maltreatment and describe the four most common types.
2. Describe some of the physical and behavioral signs that suggest a child may have been abused or neglected.
3. Explain the term *mandated reporter* and describe the steps in reporting suspected child maltreatment.
4. Identify some of the strategies that teachers can use to support children's recovery from abusive or violent experiences and take steps to prevent child maltreatment.

CASE STUDY

Min Jee teaches a small group of children ages 2 to 5 years who are gathered together from several class groups at the end of the program's service day. The children are involved and busy, and she notices with pleasure that Katherine is drawing with marking pens. Katherine usually spends the end of the day alone in the book corner. Min Jee watches as Katherine carefully outlines a figure of a girl in a pink dress who has curly hair just like her own. Min Jee encourages Katherine by saying softly, "Tell me about your picture." Katherine pauses and then speaks slowly, "This girl is a special princess. She has a beautiful dress, and she likes to dance." Then Katherine looks intensely at Min Jee and says very solemnly, "But I smell and I'm dirty." Leaving her picture on the table, Katherine gets up and walks to the book corner where she curls up against a pillow.

Min Jee is bothered by this statement, but it seems to summarize the concerns she has about Katherine. The other children do not want to sit beside Katherine because she smells bad. Although Katherine is anxious to eat at afternoon snack, she struggles to chew and sometimes gives up. Min Jee learns that Katherine's full-day teacher has been concerned about the child's teeth and has provided the child's mother with information about a once-a-month free dental clinic. Min Jee decides to follow up and offers to help the mother by calling to schedule an appointment. But Katherine's mother responds by saying, "That girl is always causing me trouble. She's just too dumb to brush her teeth." Min Jee reflects on all of these observations and makes a decision. She calls the child protective services hotline to report child maltreatment due to neglect.

Child abuse, neglect, and violence are serious threats to children's safety. They interfere with healthful development by eroding children's trust in others and in their world. Maltreatment and violence inflict cruel injuries, scarring children physically and emotionally, and can cause disability and death (U.S. Department of Health and Human Services, Administration for Children and Families, Administration on Children,

Youth and Families [HHS/ACF], Children's Bureau, 2014). However, in spite of these overwhelming negative impacts, maltreatment of children is sometimes disregarded by those who confuse maltreatment with parental discipline practices or is overlooked by those who believe that child maltreatment "doesn't happen here." Young children are vulnerable, unable to defend or protect themselves, and may not know where to go for help. Teachers play an important role in keeping children safe by reporting suspected maltreatment. In this chapter, we discuss the different types of child maltreatment and violence that impact children, provide guidance for teachers to recognize the signs of maltreatment, and outline the steps to take if maltreatment is suspected. We also present strategies to prevent and reduce maltreatment and to address the effects of all forms of violence in children's lives.

UNDERSTANDING CHILD MALTREATMENT

Childhood is a special period of development. Because of their vulnerability, young children have the right to expect safe and kind care to meet their basic needs. In turn, the child's "task" during childhood is to explore the world, grow, develop, and learn. During the early years of development, young children are particularly impressionable and can be seriously affected by negative experiences. Many behaviors of parents, teachers, caregivers, and others enhance the child's development, but sometimes these people mistreat children or fail to protect them from sources of violence. In this section, we define child maltreatment, discuss the history that brought child maltreatment to the public's attention, and describe the different kinds of maltreatment and the risk factors that are associated with them.

Defining Child Maltreatment

Child maltreatment is a collective term that encompasses all aspects of harmful or injurious behaviors toward children, including abuse and neglect. **Child abuse** specifically involves *harmful acts*, whereas **child neglect** refers to *failure to protect* a child from harm. A formal definition of child maltreatment was first established by the federal government in 1974 through legislation called the Child Abuse Prevention and Treatment Act (CAPTA) and was reaffirmed through the CAPTA Reauthorization Act of 2010. The law defines child maltreatment as follows:

> *Any recent act or failure to act on the part of a parent or caretaker which results in death, serious physical or emotional harm, sexual abuse or exploitation, or an act or failure to act which presents an imminent risk of serious harm. (Administration for Children and Families [ACF], 2011)*

The federal definition is considered a minimum explanation of acts or behaviors that constitute maltreatment. Each state is allowed to further define child maltreatment in state law. This means that the actual definition of child maltreatment may vary from state to state and that the state definition may be stricter and more detailed than the federal definition.

Teachers must know the laws for the state in which they work to assume their professional responsibilities effectively. In the opening scenario, Min Jee had

child maltreatment
a collective term that encompasses all aspects of harmful or injurious behaviors toward children, including abuse and neglect

child abuse
child maltreatment that involves harmful *acts* toward children

child neglect
child maltreatment that refers to failure to protect a child from harm

reviewed the statutes for her state when she was hired, so she knew what to watch for and what to do. State-specific information is available through the State Statutes Search provided online by the Child Welfare Information Gateway, a service of the U.S. Department of Health and Human Services.

The History of Child Abuse Prevention

Throughout history children have been used and exploited, suffering the cruelty of forced labor, long work days, and dangerous environments. Early on, the treatment of children was considered a family matter and there was no formal recognition of child maltreatment. Efforts to protect children from abuse first emerged from the success of the Society for the Prevention of Cruelty to Animals (SPCA). In 1874, Henry Bergh, who had founded the SPCA, was approached about a little girl named Mary Ellen who was being severely beaten. The hope was that his work with the SPCA could be used to help the child. Bergh was successful in bringing the case to court. The seriousness of the abuse caused the jurors to weep aloud at the sight of the girl, and as a result, the New York Society for the Prevention of Cruelty to Children was founded (New York Society for the Prevention of Cruelty to Children, 2008).

The frequency and severity of nonaccidental injuries to children caused by their parents and other adults was not fully understood until Henry Kempe, a physician, changed the course of history with his articles describing maltreatment as "the battered child syndrome" (Kempe, Silverman, Steele, Droegemueller, & Silver, 1962). Subsequently the landmark Child Abuse Prevention and Treatment Act of 1974 (Public Law 93-247) was written into law. The act provided federal funding for research and a variety of prevention and treatment services that are in place today. The act also sparked greater attention to children's safety, such as protecting children from environmental hazards.

Over time, child maltreatment has become better understood. This has led to more specific definitions for each type of maltreatment and the expectation that state and local agencies should investigate and manage reports of abuse. However, historic tensions continue. Some people deny that child maltreatment is a concern in their community or consider it a problem of "other" economic or cultural groups. Others believe their communities are doing too little to protect children from maltreatment. Even as these tensions persist, the reports of child maltreatment continue to increase, and the ill treatment of children continues to threaten children's growth and development.

Types of Child Maltreatment

The formal definitions of child maltreatment vary from state to state. However, four primary types of child maltreatment are typically identified (Centers for Disease Control and Prevention [CDC], 2014):

1. Physical abuse.
2. Neglect.
3. Sexual abuse and exploitation.
4. Emotional abuse.

Physical Abuse

Physical abuse includes any injury that is caused by physical force, including hitting, kicking, shaking, burning, or using other kinds of force against a child (CDC, 2014). Other injuries caused by physical abuse may include welts, cuts, bruises, broken bones, sprains, and bites that are inflicted on a child. Physical abuse can also include poisoning by forcing children to drink huge quantities of water or laxatives. Patterns of particular kinds of physical abuse have been assigned specific names:

- *Battered child syndrome:* Battered child syndrome refers to the physical signs indicating that a pattern of abuse has occurred over a period of time (Kaneshiro, 2014). The child may demonstrate injuries at various stages of healing.

- *Shaken baby syndrome:* Shaken baby syndrome refers to a type of traumatic brain injury that is caused by intentional and violent shaking, hitting, or impacting a child's head (National Institute of Neurological Disorders and Stroke, National Institutes of Health, 2010). Injuries associated with shaken baby syndrome include internal bleeding, blood clots, injury to the brain, blindness, and death. Children of any age can be damaged by being shaken or hit on the head.

- *Munchausen's syndrome by proxy:* This type of maltreatment occurs when the parent, usually the mother, causes the child to become ill, induces the symptoms of disease, or fabricates illness claiming that the child has symptoms that do not exist. The child may undergo frequent medical procedures to address the false symptoms. This form of abuse is usually identified by medical personnel who notice variations from typical disease characteristics (Kaneshiro & Dugdale, 2011).

Neglect is the most frequent form of child maltreatment.

Neglect

Neglect is defined as a failure to meet the child's basic needs, including food, housing, clothing, medical care, and education (CDC, 2014). When identifying neglect, the focus is on what the responsible adult does *not* do to care for the child appropriately. Neglect is further clarified through four distinct categories:

- *Physical neglect:* Physical neglect refers to depriving the child of the basic necessities of food, clothing, and shelter or not providing sufficient supervision such that the child's safety and health are compromised (Child Welfare Information Gateway [CWIG], 2013a; Children's Bureau & DePanfilis, 2006).

- *Medical neglect:* Medical neglect involves failure to provide for the medical and health care needs of a child in spite of having sufficient resources to do so or refusing care for the child when medical help is offered (CWIG, 2013a; U.S. Health and Human Services, Administration for Children and Families, Administration on Children, Youth, and Families, Children's Bureau [HHS/ACF/ACYF/Children's Bureau, 2015). This is the type of neglect that Min Jee recognized when she noticed Katherine's unmet need for dental care and saw how it was interfering with both her ability to eat and her overall health. Medical neglect also refers to cases where parents do not access medical care for their child due to religious beliefs. Religious beliefs are typically honored and are not considered neglect except in cases where the child's life is in danger. A checklist of signs of medical neglect is provided in the *Health Hint*.

WHAT IF . . .
you were told by another parent that a family was restricting a child's food because of religious or cultural practices such as fasting? How would you explore this with the family to learn more?

HEALTH HINT   Signs of Medical Neglect

- Child has chronic and severe diaper rash or infections that are not treated.
- Child's injury is not cared for; for example, a child who experiences a fall or blow to the head that could typically cause a fracture or concussion is not taken for medical assessment.
- Child is medicated inappropriately without guidance from a medical professional.
- Child's special health needs such as diabetes or allergies are not addressed.

- *Educational neglect:* Educational neglect includes failure to provide for the basic education or special education needs of a child (CWIG, 2013a).
- *Emotional neglect:* Emotional neglect encompasses failure to act on behalf of the child's emotional needs. It includes not interacting with or being responsive to a child's needs and not protecting a child from threats, bullying, or other fearful situations. It also includes ignoring a child's use of alcohol or drugs (CWIG, 2013a).

Sexual Abuse and Exploitation

Sexual abuse refers to engaging an infant or a child in any sexual act including fondling, raping, or exposing a child to sexual activities (CDC, 2014). It also includes indecently exposing one's self to a child and showing a child pornographic materials. Exploitation involves actions that take advantage of a child in a sexual manner, such as coercion to participate in prostitution or pornography (CWIG, 2013a).

Emotional Abuse

Emotional abuse refers to acts that cause injury to a child's self-worth or emotional, psychological, or mental stability. It includes verbal abuse such as threatening, ridiculing, calling names, shaming, and withholding love (CDC, 2014). Emotional abuse also includes making demands that are beyond the child's ability or developmental level to achieve; threat of harm such as exposure to or involvement in domestic violence; patterns of terrorizing, isolating, or rejecting a child; selling a child for sexual purposes; and deserting or abandoning a child (CWIG, 2013a; HHS/ACYF/ACF/Children's Bureau, 2015).

Maltreatment may also include overlapping kinds of abuse and neglect. For example, physical abuse, emotional abuse, and emotional neglect may occur together. Some states use an "other" category to describe situations in which several kinds of abuse occur in combination, and some identify additional categories such as parental substance abuse and abandonment as specific categories of child maltreatment (CWIG, 2013a).

Incidence of Child Maltreatment

The National Child Abuse and Neglect Data System collects and summarizes reported cases of child abuse and neglect and examines the findings made by state child protective agency investigations (HHS/ACF/ACYF/Children's Bureau, 2015). This information is used to track trends in child maltreatment across the country. In 2013, 3.5 million referrals of suspected maltreatment were made. Of these, 679,000 children were identified as suffering maltreatment (HHS/ACF/ACYF/Children's Bureau, 2015). The following details further describe the incidence of maltreatment among young children:

- Neglect is the most frequently occurring form of child maltreatment. In 2013, neglect was the cause of 79% of the confirmed cases. Physical abuse was the second (18%), followed by sexual abuse (9%), and emotional (or psychological) abuse (8.7%) (HHS/ACF/ACYF/Children's Bureau, 2015). This total exceeds 100% because some cases of abuse are attributed to more than one cause.
- Child maltreatment can cause permanent disability and death. In 2013, 1,520 children died from maltreatment (HHS/ACF/ACYF/Children's Bureau, 2015). Of these more than 71% of the deaths were due to neglect; 47% died from physical abuse or physical abuse in combination with other types of maltreatment. It is thought that many child deaths are not recognized correctly as being caused by maltreatment.

These are sobering statistics. Even so, there is doubt that the magnitude of the problem is sufficiently understood. Several reasons are cited for this challenge (HHS/ACF/ACYF/Children's Bureau, 2015; Chalk, Gibbons, & Scarupa, 2002):

- Many instances of abuse are never reported to child protective agencies.
- Only a small percentage of the incidents that are reported are actually substantiated due to lack of follow-up or insufficient evidence.
- States' definitions of maltreatment vary, making it difficult to compare data at a national level.

The actual numbers of children who have suffered maltreatment is probably much higher than current estimates. More reliable methods are needed to fully understand the scope of the problem of abuse and neglect and to address their impacts.

Being Aware of Other Forms of Violence in Children's Lives

In addition to the formally defined types of maltreatment, other sources of violence impact children's experience. Violence is evident in nearly every part of the child's environment: the home, school, and community. In fact, violence in the lives of children is so prevalent that some experts consider violence to be a "public health epidemic" (Dahlberg & Mercy, 2009; Mitchum, 2011).

Domestic Violence

Domestic violence is the term used to describe a pattern of abusive behavior used by one partner in an intimate relationship to gain power and control over the other partner. It includes verbal and physical abuse and may involve insults, intimidation, threats, hitting, and fatal assault with weapons. Domestic violence is the most prevalent form of violence to which children are exposed (U.S. Department of Justice, 2011; Swaner et al., 2011). It is estimated that 3 million to 10 million children witness domestic violence each year (Child Welfare Information Gateway, 2014). Children who witness domestic violence are at high risk for maltreatment.

Media Violence

The violence depicted through media sources such as television, movies, the Internet, electronic games, and music touches nearly every child in the United States today. It is estimated that a typical child watches television 28 hours per week and by the age of 18 has seen 200,000 acts of violence and 16,000 dramatized murders (Beresin, 2014; American Psychological Association [APA], 2013). Studies have found that television programs may depict over 800 acts of aggression or cruelty in

CLASSROOM CONNECTION

Watch this video on the impacts of media violence on children's play. Notice how the restaurant play theme is influenced by the child who gives the others girls "power things" and talks about "bad guys." Should the teacher intervene? What ideas do you have for helping the children keep the play positive while allowing the child who enjoys the "power things" to participate?

an hour and that up to 15% of musical videos include acts of interpersonal violence (Beresin, 2014). Media violence is especially damaging because most of the acts of violence depicted go unaddressed and are not corrected. Even children as young as 14 months are more likely to imitate the violent and aggressive behaviors they view on TV because punishment is not shown as a consequence.

Research links exposure to violence from media sources with increased aggression and antisocial behaviors (Fitzpatrick, Barnett, & Pagani, 2012), desensitization to both fantasy and real violence, and identification of violence as a desirable reflection of power (Beresin, 2014). Claire encourages the families of her second graders, to limit screen time, turn off violent television shows, and talk disapprovingly of violent depictions, teaching children that such behaviors in real life cause pain and injury.

Community Violence

Some children live in neighborhoods that exhibit high levels of community violence and frequent exposure to the use of guns, knives, drugs, and random violence (Cooley-Strickland et al., 2009). These children are able to describe witnessing shootings and beatings and may see them as everyday and ordinary events (Osofsky, 1999). Community violence also includes the signs of aggression and vandalism that children see, such as broken windows, and the sounds associated with violence, such as yelling in the street and police sirens. These kinds of exposure may result in psychological trauma that can persist into adulthood (Luthar & Goldstein, 2004). To direct children's attention away from the sounds outside that may disturb them, Teacher Karl plays soft music from different cultures in his kindergarten class.

Gang- and Drug-Related Violence

Gang violence, drug use, and assault may also be part of a child's environment while growing up. Young children may witness gang violence in the neighborhood or be the unintended victims of violence associated with drug use. Children may become involved in gangs or social groups that are founded on violence, especially if they have older siblings who participate in these activities. They may be trained by older children to threaten or inflict violence on younger children. Teachers need to be aware that these kinds of violence and maltreatment can directly and indirectly inflict harm on young children.

Perpetrators of Maltreatment

perpetrators
people who commit acts of abuse or harm children by neglecting them

The people who commit acts of abuse, harm children through neglect, or fail to keep children safe from violence are called **perpetrators**. Perpetrators can include parents, other immediate family members, relatives, the unmarried partner of a parent, foster parents, child care providers, family friends, and other children (HHS/ACF/ACYF/Children's Bureau, 2015). Perpetrators of child maltreatment are most often the adults who have the most frequent contact with the child. Trends found in 2013 identify the following (HHS/ACF?ACYF/Children's Bureau, 2015).

The child's parents, acting together, alone, or with others, were the most common perpetrators of child maltreatment (91%). The perpetrators in 13% of maltreatment cases included male relatives, the unmarried male partner of a parent, and "others" (HHS/ACF/ACYF/Children's Bureau, 2015):

- More women (54%) than men (45%) were identified as the perpetrators of maltreatment.

It is important for teachers to remain aware that parents and family members are frequently the perpetrators of maltreatment and to serve as healthy role models for adult and child interactions.

Risk Factors Associated with Maltreatment

Various factors are associated with the likelihood that a child will be maltreated. These include children's age, gender, race, disability, and family factors. Certain factors have also been identified as associated with the likelihood that an adult will inflict abuse or commit acts of neglect. These include personal and situational factors and triggers that may spark acts of maltreatment.

Child Risk Factors for Maltreatment

A review of the confirmed cases of child maltreatment identifies the factors discussed next as being associated with a greater likelihood that a child will suffer from abuse or neglect.

Age Younger children have the highest risk for maltreatment and death due to maltreatment. Of the children who died from maltreatment in 2013, 70% were younger than 3 years of age (HHS/ACF/ACYF/Children's Bureau, 2015). Being born prematurely may put a child at greater risk for abuse.

Gender Of the children who suffer from maltreatment, more are girls (51%). However, the fatality rate due to maltreatment is higher among boys (nearly 58%) (HHS/ACF/ACYF/Children's Bureau, 2015).

Race and Culture Racial disparities are evident among children who suffer maltreatment and die from its effects. The incidence of maltreatment is highest for African Americans and American Indian/Alaska Natives. The death rate due to maltreatment is highest for African Americans and Pacific Islanders (HHS/ACF/ACYF/Children's Bureau, 2015).

Disability and Special Developmental Needs Children with a disability, including behavior problems, emotional disturbance, or medical conditions, or with a chronic illness are at greater risk for being the victim of abuse (CDC, 2014).

Adult Risk Factors for Maltreating Children

Factors that may put adults at risk for committing violent acts against children include personal attributes, stresses or situations that increase the risk for abuse, and susceptibility to triggers that might set off abusive events. The impact of these factors can compound; when more risks are present, the likelihood for maltreatment increases.

Personal Risk Factors A personal history of having been abused as a child, a lack of understanding of child development or a lack of parenting knowledge, depression, substance abuse, or thinking patterns that justify abusive behaviors are adult risk factors associated with perpetration of abuse.

Situational Risk Factors Situational factors include being socially isolated, being a young or single parent, or being a victim of domestic violence. These stressful circumstances may cause an adult to be cut off from positive social connections. Without access to advice or help to address challenging conditions, an adult's

FIGURE 15-1   Risk for Maltreatment Among the Families of Enlisted Soldiers

Military families face a variety of challenges including making frequent moves, experiencing times of single parenting while the soldier parent is being trained or is on assignment, and managing the impacts of combat-related deployment.

A research investigation explored the incidence of parent-perpetrated child maltreatment among families of enlisted U.S. Army soldiers during combat-related deployment and times when the parent soldier was not deployed. When soldier-fathers were deployed, the incidence of physical abuse doubled and the rate of neglect was four times greater than when the soldier father was not deployed. To address these challenges, the army provides support services for families affected by combat deployment including assistance centers that link families to support agencies.

Source: Based on "Child Maltreatment in Enlisted Soldiers' Families during Combat-Related Deployments," by D. Gibbs, S. Martin, L. Kupper, and R. Johnson, 2007 (August), *Journal of the American Medical Association*, *298*(5). Retrieved November 20, 2014, from http://jama .jamanetwork.com/article.aspx?articleid=208223.

CHECK YOUR UNDERSTANDING 15.1

Click here to check your understanding of child maltreatment.

violent and abusive behaviors may escalate. Figure 15-1 describes the risk for maltreatment among military families who face long periods of time when one parent is absent during deployment.

Triggering Factors Triggers are conditions that set off a series of events leading to an increased risk for abuse. Triggers can include difficult child behaviors such as excessive crying, discipline, or teaching situations (such as pressuring a child during toilet training) that have gotten out of control or adult arguments that carry over to behaviors acted out against a child.

IDENTIFYING CHILD MALTREATMENT

Teachers such as Min Jee in the opening scenario interact closely with children, observing their growth and development and building relationships of trust that allow children to bring their worries and concerns forward. Teachers must be intentional about watching for the physical and behavioral signs of maltreatment.

Recognizing the Signs of Child Maltreatment

Children display the signs of child maltreatment in various ways that astute teachers learn to recognize. The signs may be obvious and observable or exhibited through subtle changes in the child's behavior. The behaviors of the parent may also be signs that maltreatment is occurring (Crosson-Tower, 2002).

Teachers need to consider all the ways in which maltreatment may be evident and use this information to determine whether there is reasonable cause to suspect that abuse has occurred. For example, at a Head Start teachers' meeting, Celia just shared her frustrations about working with a child whose behavior has regressed. Some of the other teachers respond to her descriptions saying, "That sounds like neglect!" When Celia reflects on it, she decides that they are right. How did she miss it? Figure 15-2 lists child and parent behaviors that may signal maltreatment.

FIGURE 15-2 Signs of Maltreatment

Physical Abuse

Child PHYSICAL Signs

- ✓ Bruises, welts, and marks, possibly in varying stages of healing
- ✓ Burns and marks in the shape of objects: cigarette, handprints, wooden spoons
- ✓ Bald spots from severe hair pulling
- ✓ Unexplained or recurrent injuries
- ✓ Unexplained broken bones
- ✓ Child reports being hit by parent

Child BEHAVIOR Signs

- ✓ Limping or protecting body parts
- ✓ Recurrent complaints of headache or belly ache or other pains
- ✓ Child protests when it is time to go home; seems frightened of the parent
- ✓ Child's behavior changes; is more withdrawn or aggressive

Parent BEHAVIOR Signs

- ✓ Parent cannot explain child's injuries or offers unconvincing or conflicting explanations
- ✓ Parent reports that child harmed self
- ✓ Parent shows little interest or concern for child
- ✓ Parent instructs teacher to use harsh discipline with child

Emotional Abuse

Child PHYSICAL Signs

- ✓ Unexplained delayed physical, intellectual, or emotional development
- ✓ Otherwise unexplained persistent habits such as rocking, sucking on fingers, head banging
- ✓ Self-destructive actions (hitting self)
- ✓ General destructive actions

Child BEHAVIOR Signs

- ✓ Apathy and depression: low affect, empty facial expression
- ✓ Fear of parent
- ✓ Extreme fears or phobias
- ✓ Extreme behavior: overly passive or aggressive
- ✓ Cruelty to others; laughing at others' pain

Parent BEHAVIOR Signs

- ✓ Parent belittles the child
- ✓ Parent rejects the child
- ✓ Parent minimizes concerns for the child

Sexual Abuse

Child PHYSICAL Signs

- ✓ Pain, itching, bruises, or bleeding around the genitalia
- ✓ Stained or bloody underclothing
- ✓ Discharge from vagina or urinary openings
- ✓ Difficulty walking or sitting

Child BEHAVIOR Signs

- ✓ Acting out sexual behaviors that are too sophisticated for age
- ✓ Asking others to do sexual acts
- ✓ Acting in a sexual or seductive manner
- ✓ Showing an inordinate fear of males (or females)
- ✓ Child reports sexual abuse

Parent BEHAVIOR Signs

- ✓ Parent is controlling and jealous of others
- ✓ Parent is isolated or secretive

Neglect

Child PHYSICAL Signs

- ✓ Poor hygiene such as dirty hair, skin, and clothes; smells of urine or feces
- ✓ Unaddressed medical or dental needs
- ✓ Dress that is inappropriate for the weather
- ✓ Failure to grow and thrive

Child BEHAVIOR Signs

- ✓ Begging for food
- ✓ Hoarding food
- ✓ Fatigue or listlessness
- ✓ Child craves attention, even eliciting negative attention

Parent BEHAVIOR Signs

- ✓ Parent is indifferent and uninterested in the child
- ✓ Parent is depressed or seems apathetic
- ✓ Parent does not provide age-appropriate supervision for long periods of time

Source: Based on Child Welfare Information Gateway. (2013). *What is child abuse and neglect? Recognizing the signs and symptoms.* Washington, DC: U.S. Department of Health and Human Services, Children's Bureau. Retrieved November 20, 2014, from https://www.childwelfare.gov/pubs/factsheets/whatiscan.cfm.

Physical Signs

Some signs of maltreatment are definite and unambiguous. Teachers are able to observe marks, movements, or other visible signs that signal that abuse or neglect are occurring. Special attention should be given to details.

Observable Marks Some signs of maltreatment can be observed during the teacher's daily interactions with children. The marks of physical abuse may be evident in the form of bruises, burns, or scalds. They might be seen on the child's face, neck, or hands; revealed on the legs and torso when changing a baby's diaper; or noticed on the arms when children pull up their sleeves to play in the sensory bin. Signs to watch for:

- Marks that are unusual or different from the injuries a child might logically receive during the course of everyday play, such as a series of circular marks on the leg.
- Marks that are patterned, such as in the shape of a hand or an object or a series of striped marks caused by being hit with a strap.
- Marks in various stages of healing, suggesting the possibility of repeated physical abuse (CWIG, 2013a).

For example, Teacher Mandy is alarmed to notice dark bruise-colored marks all over Krissy's arms. They look as though Krissy was poked repeatedly with a blunt object. As Mandy studies the marks closely, Krissy says, "See! I was playing 101 Dalmatians, and those are my spots. I made them with markers, but they are hard to wash off." In this case, the spots are harmless.

Observable Movements The child's movements might also suggest abuse. Teachers may observe a child limping or protecting a sore arm, or the child might complain of a headache or other soreness. Teachers should not investigate or try to "prove" that maltreatment has occurred. However, it is within the realm of a teacher's responsibility to show sympathy for a child's injury and to ask, "How did it happen?" or say, "Show me where it hurts." For example when Teacher Carolyn first notices 6-year-old Ennis limping, she asks him what happened. Looking down he answers, "Um, I fell down." Soreness and some injuries may be easily explained by overexertion or typical accidents, but a child's unlikely explanation may be a signal that maltreatment has occurred (CWIG, 2013a).

Visible Signs of Neglect Neglect can be observed through recognizable patterns that suggest that the parent is ignoring a child's needs. The child may be consistently hungry, dirty, or dressed inappropriately for the weather (even when the family has resources for appropriate garments), or the child may have unaddressed medical or dental needs, such as Katherine in the opening case scenario (CWIG, 2013a).

Child Statements A child might tell the teacher directly about an incident of maltreatment. Trina might say, "I don't want to go home; my mom hits me with a spoon." Dustin, her teacher, should believe what she says. Young children are considered to be very reliable sources for reporting abusive situations, and at the very minimum, the child is expressing worry or fear. It is best if Dustin responds to Trina's statement without shock. He should reassure her that the incident was not her fault and tell her that there are people who can help. When she returns to play, Dustin should immediately report Trina's statement to the appropriate child protective services or law enforcement agency and make special efforts to demonstrate support and understanding to Trina.

Hiding Signs of Maltreatment It is important to be alert for indications that a parent or child is trying to hide the signs of maltreatment. For example, Brandie might dress her son Jacob in excessive layers of clothing to cover the marks of abuse, or William might report that he does not know how his daughter Sophia's injury occurred. In some cases, a child may be coached to explain marks of abuse through unlikely stories, or the child may be threatened that their pet or a family member will be hurt if they tell what happened. Children who have been sexually abused are often caught up in a web of secrecy and threats that lead them to hide the signs of abuse.

Child Behavioral Signs

Maltreatment can also be expressed through a child's behavior, for example, in the themes of play or by changes in the child's mood and level of activity (CWIG, 2013a). Behavioral indicators are sometimes more ambiguous and harder to connect clearly to maltreatment. These signs should be considered together with other observations of the child and parent when considering whether abuse is occurring. Some behavioral indicators are discussed next.

Communicating Through Play A child might reveal signs of maltreatment through play, for example, by repeatedly acting out abusive situations in the housekeeping area or dollhouse. Sami might hit and spank the dolls excessively or make cruel threats that reflect the violence he witnesses in his neighborhood. Laurie may not understand the sexual abuse she has experienced; sometimes it is not until years later when children's greater maturity helps them understand the meaning of the actions they have experienced (London, Bruck, Ceci, & Shuman, 2005). However, Laurie may demonstrate signs of sexual abuse by showing physical discomfort when walking or sitting or by inviting others to engage in secretive games that suggest awareness of sexual actions beyond her maturity. A child might also demonstrate his or her experiences by depicting the abuse in drawings or by building clay structures that communicate situations of maltreatment.

Change in Mood A child's change in mood may be a signal. A typically happy child who suddenly becomes excessively withdrawn and sad or a typically congenial child who suddenly becomes overly aggressive, argumentative, or resistant may be experiencing abuse or neglect (CWIG, 2013a).

Change in Activity Level A change in the child's typical level or style of activity should also raise concern (CWIG, 2013a). For example, Madison, who is usually a leader, might suddenly prefer to play alone. Or Logan, who is typically very active, may lose interest in the games he used to enjoy and appear listless and lethargic. These changes may be signs of abuse or neglect.

Parent Behaviors

The daily interactions that teachers observe between parents and their children may reveal behaviors or a style of interaction that, when consistently demonstrated, suggests risk for abuse. These include negative interactions such as (CWIG, 2013a):

- Belittling the child.
- Describing the child in negative ways, such as "evil," "bad," or "worthless."

Children sometimes communicate signs of maltreatment through play.

Stockxpert/Getty Images

- Ignoring the child and showing lack of interest or concern.
- Not attending to the child's needs when they have been identified.
- Having unreasonable expectations for the child's behavior or performance.

The suspicion of child maltreatment is often based on not just one signal, but on a combination of indications, including observable signs, behaviors of the child or parent, and interactions between the child and parent (CWIG, 2013a). Teachers need to be alert to the many ways in which maltreatment is communicated and the signs that it is being hidden and then reflect on everything they know about the child and family when determining whether there is reasonable cause to suspect maltreatment.

Considering Cultural Perspectives

WHAT IF . . .
you were teaching full-time during the day and taking classes at a community college in the evening? How would you ensure that you have the time to reflect appropriately on your observations for the day and still remain alert to the signs of maltreatment?

Definitions of child abuse, perspectives about the vulnerability of children, and child-rearing practices are highly influenced by culture (Children's Bureau & DePanfilis, 2006). There is no common international standard regarding child maltreatment by which cultural practices are judged. This may leave teachers wondering about their role in identifying signs of maltreatment when they teach children from diverse cultural backgrounds. For example, some cultures tend to use mild physical punishment such as spanking with more frequency than other cultures. Parents in some cultures allow young children more freedom and autonomy than do parents in typical Western cultures. They may permit their young child to move about freely with little supervision or allow the child to stay home alone. In the United States, these practices might be viewed as signs of neglect. In turn, the Western practice of placing an infant in his or her own bed to sleep might be considered cruel by some cultures.

A practice called "coin rubbing" is used by Southeast Asian families as a traditional cure for fevers, chills, and headaches (Renteln, 2010). Heated metal coins are rubbed against the child's body, typically leaving circular bruises or scrape marks. A teacher might view the marks as signs of abuse, yet the family's purpose is to enhance the child's health. Although the practice causes bruises to the child, the intent is different from what is typically considered abuse.

When Teacher Jessica is confused about how to interpret such issues, she makes a call to the child protective services agency to discuss her concern. The protective services worker can help clarify steps to take when the parenting practices are unfamiliar and the potential for child maltreatment is not easily understood. Being culturally sensitive is appropriate and important, but it does not mean overlooking signs of possible child maltreatment (Renteln, 2010).

Reflecting on Family Disciplinary Practices

Child guidance and disciplinary practices are heavily influenced by regional, cultural, and religious perspectives. Some approaches are permissive; others are stricter than typical practices used in the early childhood classroom. Some parents may use spanking as a disciplinary approach, whereas others consider spanking to be inappropriate. While spanking is not recommended, it is not generally defined as child maltreatment unless it is frequent, out of proportion to the situation, or intense. Examples of inappropriate spanking include spanking with a solid object such as a belt or hairbrush. Teachers strive to be supportive of families, but this does not mean overlooking parental use of disciplinary actions that are detrimental to a child's health and well-being. A child protective services worker is an important resource when teachers find it difficult to interpret harsh family disciplinary practices.

A Matter of ETHICS

If you were at a teacher's meeting and one of the teachers remarked that parents have the right to manage their children however they want, how would you respond? What aspect of the NAEYC Code of Ethical Conduct would you reference? What aspect of your state's laws would you refer to?

Evaluating the Effects of Maltreatment and Violence

The negative impacts of child maltreatment do not end when the abuse ends. The effects are measurable and long-lasting (CWIG, 2013b; APA, 2013; Luthar & Goldstein, 2004), and they impact everyone: children, families, teachers, and society.

Impacts on Children

Some effects of maltreatment, such as bruises, are temporary and brief, whereas other experiences cause permanent physical and emotional scars. Child age and the type, frequency, and duration of the maltreatment are factors associated with long-term effects.

Frequent and continual exposure to maltreatment and violence significantly increase a child's experience of a form of stress called *toxic stress*. Toxic stress disrupts the body's hormones and brain chemical systems. This negatively impacts brain development, impairing learning, behavior, and health (National Scientific Council on the Developing Child, 2005/2014, 2010). Toxic stress is especially alarming when it is experienced by infants and toddlers, who are most vulnerable, are at greatest risk for maltreatment, and consequently are in the greatest danger for long-term damage.

Children who have suffered brain injuries, such as those seen in cases of shaken baby syndrome, may suffer permanent brain damage or death because of bruising of the brain and intracranial bleeding (CWIG, 2013b). Long-term impacts on children who experience maltreatment include being more likely to suffer as adults from depression and having physical health concerns such as allergies, arthritis, asthma, high blood pressure, and ulcers (CWIG, 2013b).

The effects of witnessing violence on very young children's behavior and development are just beginning to be understood. Research has revealed that experiencing violence directly or indirectly affects children of all ages (Shonkoff & Phillips, 2000). Even before children can talk, the negative consequences of witnessing domestic or community violence are demonstrated through children's temper tantrums, fears, and difficulty separating from parents (Osofsky, 2004). Sleep disturbances such as fear of going to bed, aggressive or withdrawn behaviors, and disruption in parent and child attachment are also associated with exposure to violence (Rice & Groves, 2005). Some children who witness violence in the community even show symptoms of posttraumatic stress disorder similar to the responses of those who experience violence in war zones (National Center for Posttraumatic Stress Disorder, 2007).

Kindergarten and school-age children, who are able to understand the intentionality of acts of violence, often have trouble concentrating and paying attention due to fears and intrusive thoughts. Children who are not able to trust in the safety of their surroundings may withdraw and have trouble building social attachments. They may also become disassociated with their surroundings, eventually losing the ability to develop care and empathy for others (APA, 2013). These experiences take

WHAT IF . . .

you have experienced abuse or neglect person-
ally? How might reading about maltreatment be
difficult for you? Where could you get support if
reading this information is difficult for you
to handle?

social and emotional development off course and ultimately negatively
impact the child's ability to learn.

Marion, a teacher of 3-year-olds, remembers two brothers who
attended her class. They had been so traumatized by violence in
their neighborhood that when they first joined her class, they
would lie on the floor in front of the door. They didn't cry, but
they didn't play. She helped them transition into typical play
by bringing toys to them and allowing them to gain trust slowly.
Sonya uses storyboards to help her first graders review the actions
of the characters in a story. She teaches words to describe inappropriate
behaviors and provides opportunities for the children to offer creative alternatives for the poor decisions or aggressive actions of the characters.

Impacts on Families

Domestic and community violence traumatize parents as well as children. Parents
who witness or experience such violence are challenged to cope and manage their
own fears while at the same time realizing that they might not be able to keep their
child safe (Osofsky, 1999; Margolin & Gordis, 2004). These parents may respond
by becoming overprotective, not allowing the child to be away from them. They
may become numb to the effects of violence and may experience extreme sadness
and depression. This can create an overwhelming sense of helplessness and hope-
lessness that is unavoidably communicated to the child. Over time, the parent may
become emotionally unavailable, less responsive to the child's needs, and unable to
be a source of comfort to the child (Osofsky, 1999). As a result, the parent becomes
unable to provide supportive care for the child, which disrupts the parent–child
relationship.

Parents living in violent environments need to find ways to manage their own
trauma before they are able to support their children. Teachers play an important
role in this effort by offering information to parents about social service supports
and by strengthening the parent–child relationship through positive experiences in
the early childhood setting. Maria keeps a stack of information cards on her desk
that provide information for social service supports in her community. Because she
has these readily available, parents recognize that many people need extra support
now and then.

Impacts on Teachers

Adults who work with young children who have been impacted by violence also
experience its negative effects. Learning about a child's tragic stories can evoke
many feelings, including anger, fear, and anxiety. Teachers may express these
"secondhand" effects of violence through physical symptoms such as headaches
and stomach upsets, as well as emotional distress, exhaustion, and sadness (Rice
& Groves, 2005). In addition, teachers are called on to help children cope with
their negative experiences while also managing the child's expressions of distress
through behaviors such as aggression toward others, fears and clinginess, or regres-
sion in toileting or language development.

Teachers may need extra support and assistance from their supervisors to help
them manage children's needs while coping with their own stresses (Osofsky, 1999;
Rice & Groves, 2005). In the opening case scenario, Min Jee recognizes the signs
of maltreatment and knows how to make a report. However, after doing so, she
reflects on her actions and wonders if she should have noticed and addressed her

concerns sooner. She feels guilty thinking that she should have been able to protect Katherine. Min Jee may need to seek support from others to help resolve her feelings about this situation before she can focus on supporting Katherine and her mother in the future.

Impacts on Society

The negative impacts of child maltreatment and violence are not limited to individual children or families; communities suffer as well. Negative impacts on the community include higher rates of crime, juvenile delinquency, disability, and mental illness in those who have suffered maltreatment. As an example, children who have been abused are 11 times more likely to be arrested for juvenile crime and nearly 3 times more likely to be arrested for violence when they are adults (CWIG, 2013b; English, Widom, & Brandford, 2004). Addressing these issues, as well as funding child welfare agencies, investigating reports, and providing social services for children and families, affects communities both socially and economically (Children's Bureau & DePanfilis, 2006). It is sobering to learn that the estimated economic impact of child maltreatment and violence in the United States is $124 billion (Fang, Brown, Florence, & Mercy, 2012).

CHECK YOUR UNDERSTANDING 15.2
Click here to check your understanding of how to identify child maltreatment.

REPORTING CHILD MALTREATMENT

It is standard practice in early childhood classrooms for teachers to observe children on a daily basis, looking for signs of general health, illness, or stress. These observations may also reveal the possibility that abuse or neglect is occurring. Teachers need to be prepared to report maltreatment as soon as it is suspected.

Understanding Reporting Responsibilities

Teachers become children's trusted friend and may be the first to become aware that maltreatment could be occurring. By the nature of the profession, teachers have a legal obligation and professional and ethical duty to report suspected child abuse and neglect.

Legally Mandated Reporters

Teachers and others employed in positions that have close and frequent contact with children are identified legally as **mandatory reporters**. Mandatory reporters are required by law to immediately report their "reasonable suspicions" of child maltreatment to law enforcement or the local child protective services agency. Each state identifies the professions that are mandatory reporters. They typically include (CWIG, 2013a):

- Medical personnel such as physicians, nurses, dentists, optometrists, and psychologists.
- Law enforcement personnel.
- Employees in licensed child care and early education programs.
- Teachers and other school employees.
- Social workers, counselors, and therapists.
- Clergy.

mandatory reporters persons who because of the nature of their employment have close and frequent contact with young children are required by state law to report suspected child maltreatment

- Attorneys.
- Firefighters.

More than three-fifths of the reports of child maltreatment are made by mandatory reporters, most by education and law enforcement professionals (HHS/ACF/ACYF/Children's Bureau, 2015). Another 28% of cases are reported by nonprofessional sources such as parents, relatives, friends, neighbors, and sports coaches. The involvement of "everyday citizens" is important in reporting and stopping child maltreatment.

Stressors can compound, increasing the potential for abuse.

Professional and Ethical Responsibilities

Teachers have a *professional and ethical responsibility* to protect children in their care. That is, they have a duty to take honest and moral action to protect a child from further abuse. The Code of Ethical Conduct and Statement of Commitment of the NAEYC (2011) confirms this ethical responsibility by noting that teachers who commit to ethical practice, "shall not harm children" and highlighting the need to stay current on the signs, symptoms, and risk factors for child maltreatment. By taking on the responsibility to care for and educate children, teachers pledge themselves to advocate for the health and safety of each child by reporting suspected cases of abuse. This is an important aspect of professionalism.

Sometimes teachers may struggle with their own discomfort in discussing or addressing child abuse and neglect. Teachers cite various reasons for having difficulty in reporting suspected maltreatment (Kenny, 2001):

- Worry about retribution from the family if they learn that the teacher has made a report.
- Concern that they will disrupt the family by reporting suspected maltreatment.
- A mistaken and dangerous notion that they can "help" the family better by withholding information or delaying such a report.
- Lack of trust in child protective services.
- Lack of knowledge about the signs of child maltreatment or how to report suspected abuse.
- Worry about making a mistake or being wrong, especially when there are no observable signs of abuse.

Not reporting suspected child maltreatment is harmful to children, and it is against the law. It abandons children to the despair of neglect and abuse and the long-term negative effects they create, and it may even jeopardize the child's life. Teachers can gain confidence in their ability to participate appropriately in protecting children by knowing the signs of maltreatment, whom to contact, and how to make a report.

Responding Appropriately When Abuse Is Suspected

When observations suggest that maltreatment has occurred or when a child reveals that abuse is happening, teachers need to be ready to respond with calm confidence. Teachers can provide reassurance that the child will be kept safe and allow the child to fully express worry, fear, and any other emotions that surround the experience.

Photos to go/Getty Images

FIGURE 15-3   What Should Teachers Do When a Child Discloses Abuse?

Do this:

Be prepared:
- ✓ Understand your responsibility as a reporter.
- ✓ Know your program policy about reporting.
- ✓ Know the signs of child maltreatment.
- ✓ Know who to call for help.

Take action if needed.

Allow the child to talk or show what happened without interruption or questions.

Believe what the child says.

Reassure the child that it was a good thing to come to you and that you will find the right people to help.

Redirect the child to play.

Report immediately by calling child protective services or law enforcement.

Keep the child with you unless authorities agree the child may be released to the parent.

Write down what the child told you as soon as possible.

Continue to support the child.

Do NOT do this:

Do not ignore a child's report of abuse.

Do not promise not to tell. You must report abuse. Tell the child you will find people to help.

Do not act shocked. Don't correct or criticize the child's choice of words or language. Just receive the information with confidence.

Do not express doubt or disbelief or try to talk the child out of what he or she is saying.

Do not ask a lot of questions. Act quickly to mobilize the system that will investigate and protect the child.

Do not entice the child to disclose. Do not offer rewards or suggest negative consequences if the child does not tell.

Do not conduct an investigation. Document the information and investigators will take over from there.

Do not call the child's parents. Let law enforcement or child protective services decide at what point the parents should be involved. Investigations can be ruined and children endangered by informing family members.

Source: Based on practice (author).

The teacher's response should be warm and encouraging, and it should clearly communicate that the teacher believes what is being said. It is important to avoid showing alarm or dismay about anything the child says. Figure 15-3 provides guidance for teachers regarding what they should and should not do when a child discloses situations of maltreatment.

Reporting Suspected Abuse and Neglect

Teachers need to be ready to make a report and assume their responsibilities in the protective services process as soon as they have reasonable suspicion that a child is being maltreated.

Making a Report

A call to the appropriate child protective services agency should be made as soon as possible. The teacher should summarize what was observed and what the child said that led to the suspicion of maltreatment. The teacher may be asked for basic information about the child and family. Figure 15-4 provides an example of information typically included when making a protective services call. Teachers can

> **FIGURE 15-4 Steps in Reporting Suspected Maltreatment**
>
> 1. Provide your name and contact information.
>   Say: *My name is Min Jee Kim. I am a teacher at the Northside Child Development Center. My phone number is XXX-XXX-XXXX.*
> 2. State the purpose for your call and what maltreatment you suspect has occurred.
>   Say: *I'm calling to make a report. I suspect a child is being neglected.*
> 3. Give the name of child, age, and birth date if known.
>   Say: *The child's name is Katherine Goss. She is four years old. Her birthday is March 4, 2012.*
> 4. Give the name and address of the family.
>   Say: *Her parents are Lynn and Calvin Goss. They live at 3579 Canal Street, Our City and State.*
> 5. Tell what you observed.
>   Say: *This child is consistently dirty and has severe dental needs, and Katherine told me she does not want to go home because her mom hits her when she wets her pants.*
> 6. Provide other relevant information.
>   Say: *We referred the mom to community dental services to help the child, but she won't go. The dad recently lost his job and I think that he may have an alcohol problem. I know that toilet training has been a challenge for this child.*

Source: Based on practice (author).

contact the National Child Abuse Hotline (1-800-4-A-CHILD) to learn more about making a child abuse report.

Steps in Protective Service

Once a report has been made, the protective services or law enforcement agency will determine whether the situation warrants investigation and follow-up. An investigation may include interviews with the child, teacher, and family (Children's Bureau & DePanfilis, 2006). Sometimes teachers are asked to participate in the interview with the child to provide familiarity and support. For example, Abby participated with law enforcement when Leon was being interviewed about injuries he obtained during a weekend visit to his dad's house. Her presence helped Leon talk about the experience. The information gathered through the assessment process determines whether there is reasonable cause to believe that maltreatment has occurred and whether there is continuing threat of harm.

When Maltreatment Is Confirmed

If it is established that maltreatment has occurred, the protective and law enforcement workers move quickly to protect the child from immediate harm. Child protection workers consider whether the child can remain in the family home safely. If it is determined that the child's safety is at risk by remaining in the home, an out-of-home placement is identified and temporary shelter may be arranged with a safe relative or an appropriate foster family. Meanwhile, the child protective services agency creates a service plan with the child's family. Goals are outlined to provide support and training for the parents, to address the issues that contributed to the maltreatment, and to improve the parents' capacity to care for the child's well-being safely in the future.

Guidance for Teachers

Teachers should not contact parents or other family members to inform them that a report has been made. This is important for several reasons (Office on Child Abuse and Neglect, Caliber Associates, & Crosson-Tower, 2003):

- Doing so may put the child in danger of retribution, especially if the child is the one who disclosed the abuse.
- The parent may flee with the child.
- The parent may try to coach the child to deny the abuse.
- The perpetrator may be at risk for suicide following reports of sexual abuse.

The child protective or law enforcement agency will direct teachers about how to interact with the family appropriately immediately following a maltreatment report. Although reports to law enforcement and child protective services are confidential, a parent may suspect that the report came from the teacher. If approached, teachers should be prepared to discuss the situation with the parent in a calm and professional manner. Teachers do not need to specifically acknowledge that they made the report. Rather, the focus of the conversation should be on establishing the understanding that teachers want to help families keep children healthy and safe and that teachers have a responsibility to make a report if they suspect abuse.

If a discussion with a parent feels threatening in any way, teachers should know whom in their school or program they can contact to provide support. Likewise, a family child care provider should have a neighbor or nearby friend or family member to call on for support. Usually, listening to the parent's concerns and treating the parent with respect helps to diffuse difficult situations such as these and can be crucial in building a relationship of support to help keep the child safe in the future.

> **WHAT IF . . .**
> you suspected that a child was being maltreated? What aspects of reporting abuse do you believe would be most challenging? How would you overcome these worries?

CHECK YOUR UNDERSTANDING 15.3
Click here to check your understanding of how to report child maltreatment.

SUPPORTING FAMILIES AND PREVENTING MALTREATMENT

Teachers are important resources for helping children and families manage traumatic events. Teachers can be a source of safety, offering caring support and providing reassurance for the child and family (Office on Child Abuse and Neglect et al., 2003). Teachers are adept at creating classroom environments and offering activities that help children and families cope with negative experiences and build skills to prevent maltreatment.

Creating Safe Environments for Children and Teachers

Children who are surrounded by warm and reassuring environments fare better than those who are isolated or not supported (CWIG, 2004). The extended family members, caring and responsive teachers, and other positive models can assist the child to form an optimistic vision of the future. Teachers contribute by recognizing their role in prevention efforts.

Being Aware of a Teacher's Potential for Abuse

Even though early education teachers make up a small percentage (less than 0.5%) of those who abuse children (HHS/ACF/ACYF/Children's Bureau, 2015), it is alarming to note that maltreatment does occur in early childhood settings. On occasion, even well-seasoned teachers may experience frustration and find it difficult to manage children's behaviors. Teachers who frequently exhibit frustration and poor management may be showing signs that they could abuse children, such as (Karageorge & Kendall, 2008):

- Yelling at or belittling children for mistakes.
- Responding inappropriately to challenging behaviors such as grabbing or jerking the child.
- Expressing personal frustrations to a child.
- Showing unusual or inappropriate interest in a particular child or seeking to be alone with a child.

WHAT IF . . .

you witnessed another teacher threatening, belittling, or yelling at a child? What would you do?

Supervisors watch for these kinds of behaviors as signs of inappropriateness for working with children and intervene as needed. It is also important for teachers to be aware of their own behaviors and recognize when they may need additional supports, such as rest breaks and new strategies to ensure that they can keep children safe.

Improving Child and Teacher Safety Through Arrangement of the Environment

The way the classroom or home care environment is arranged helps reduce the chance of abuse and protects teachers from claims of suspected abuse (Rice & Groves, 2005). Furniture and equipment should be positioned to provide a clear view of all the indoor and outdoor spaces, with no hidden areas. Diaper-changing and toileting areas should be open so that adults can be observed for appropriate interaction.

Following Safety Guidelines

Program and school safety policies are designed to keep children safe and to eliminate the possibility that abuse will occur. Teachers need to understand and follow these guidelines. For example, some settings may require that teachers and volunteers never be alone with children. The *Safety Segment* provides examples of program policies and practices that should be in place to ensure children's safety from maltreatment and to protect teachers from potential allegations of abuse.

SAFETY SEGMENT   Practices That Reduce Risk of Abuse by Teachers

- Policies allowing parents access to their children at all times.
- Procedures for diapering, assisting children with toileting, and changing clothes.
- Policies restricting teachers from taking children away from the center without a parent's permission.
- Procedures describing appropriate methods for managing challenging behaviors.

- Field trip procedures that minimize opportunities for adults to be alone with children.
- Procedures for reporting accidents and recording responsive actions to mitigate possible allegations of abuse in the early childhood setting.
- Procedures for responding if an allegation of maltreatment by a teacher or staff member is made.

Source: Based on *The role of professional child care providers in preventing and responding to child abuse and neglect*, by K. Karageorge & R. Kendall, 2008. U.S. Department of Health & Human Services, retrieved from https://www.childwelfare.gov/pubs/usermanuals/childcare/childcare.pdf and *Building Circles—Breaking Cycles* (Publication DD2), 2004, Washington, DC: National Association for the Education of Young Children.

Touching Children Appropriately

Many early childhood settings have policies related to touching children. Some prohibit teachers from holding children on their laps or hugging a child; others may have "no-touch" policies. Implementing "no-touch" policies to reduce the risk of abuse is an extreme measure, especially because touch is an essential component of interaction and responsive care for very young children. More appropriate approaches guide teachers to touch children in ways that are suitable for the setting. Holding hands, patting a child on the back, or putting an arm around a child's shoulder are ways teachers can show care through safe touch. Teachers must also be mindful of cultural variations in acceptable ways to touch. It is important to recognize and respect that children always have the right to say that they do not want to be touched (Karageorge & Kendall, 2008; National Association for the Education of Young Children [NAEYC], 2004).

Implementing Supportive Strategies for Children

To improve children's positive long-term outcomes after negative experiences, teachers focus special attention on supports for the child in the classroom. This includes focusing on children's needs and assisting children to manage their emotions in appropriate ways.

Focusing on Individual Child Needs

Not all children who experience maltreatment or violence respond the same way. Teachers learn to support children's coping strategies by acknowledging each child's individual needs and challenges. Children may need to:

- Overcome fear and regain the ability to trust.
- Dispel a sense of helplessness.
- Regain self-esteem.
- Feel safe and supported.
- Build a sense of autonomy, or independence.
- Feel in control and competent.

These needs can be addressed through interventions offered by skilled practitioners as well as through the child's participation in a high-quality early childhood education program (Finkelhor et al., 2009). Caring teachers work to address children's needs in ways that are developmentally appropriate.

The Infant Teachers provide extra time for holding and rocking infants who have experienced maltreatment or violence. They smile and speak kindly and gently when playing. They pay special attention to the infant's cues for hunger, need to sleep, or interest in play, helping to reestablish the baby's trust.

The Toddler Toddlers may need extra support to experience positive interactions. Allowing the toddler to play without having to share a toy for an extended period of time may help the child relax, boosting the child's sense of autonomy and control. Teachers might encourage the child to explore a new task, such as crawling through an interesting obstacle course, to help the child regain interest in play and develop a refreshed sense of competence.

The Preschooler Preschoolers might benefit from opportunities to immerse themselves in positive play, where they can retreat from their fears, relax, and pursue their own interests. Interesting dramatic play settings, extended play periods in the sensory bin materials or sandbox, and positive interest from the teacher are ways to build the child's sense of safety and personal control.

The Kindergarten and School-Age Child Teachers can support school-age children in two somewhat opposing ways. On the one hand, children in this age group may be interested in expressing and discussing their fears and feelings of violation from maltreatment or exposure to violence. Inviting children to share their concerns with the teacher at appropriate times is one approach. At the same time, children in this age group may want to retreat from the experience and simply immerse themselves in play and exploration. In the opening case scenario, Min Jee noticed that Katherine recognized that she was dirty. Min Jee helped Katherine gain self-care skills by presenting activities in group time about how to brush your teeth, how to wash your hands and face, and how to comb your hair. Activities such as these help children to gain awareness of ways they can impact their future positively.

The *Progressive Programs & Practices* feature describes an innovative effort initiated by an Early Head Start Program at a women's correctional institution. The approach addresses the baby's need to bond with the mother and focuses on the child and family's needs even when mom is incarcerated.

Reducing the Child's Sense of Isolation

Children who have experienced maltreatment or violence often feel set apart or emotionally isolated from other children. Supportive approaches include offering activities that encourage interactive play and that build social skills, such as group games, team projects, and dramatic play. For example, when Min Jee sees Katherine alone in the library corner, she invites her to join the children who are playing with play dough. Min Jee offers Katherine a basket of cookie cutters to share with other children at the table.

Creating Opportunities for Appropriate Problem Solving

Children who have been victimized may have experienced feelings of being trapped or not being in control. They need support to regain a sense of confidence and competence. Teachers encourage this by offering the child appropriate opportunities to make choices and by guiding the child through reasonable problem-solving situations that build a sense of accomplishment. Activities to accomplish this include:

- Providing new physical challenges such as offering the toddler an interesting new target for beanbags or presenting a preschooler with a variety of appropriate challenges on the child-sized balance beam.
- Involving the preschool child in selecting the snack menu or the books for story time for the following week.
- Creating opportunities for school-age children to assist in making decisions for the classroom, such as choosing books to purchase or selecting games for gym time.

Addressing Violence in Children's Play Themes

Children may engage in play about violence, especially if this has been a part of their experience. Children are also easily attracted to strong characters depicted in the media, such as superheroes, and are interested in the excitement of games that involve chasing others and using pretend weapons. Children use play to explore

Pearson Education

CLASSROOM CONNECTION

Watch this video about a hospital project that a group of children helped to develop following the teacher's foot injury. How do you think a project such as this allows children to process feelings while experiencing a sense of control as they design the details of the project?

PROGRESSIVE PROGRAMS & PRACTICES

Building Bonds by Supporting Breastfeeding Behind Bars

By Farzana Siddiqui, Community Action Head Start, Washington County, OR

Community Action of Washington County, Oregon, operates an innovative Early Head Start program at Coffee Creek Correctional Facility. Over 75% of inmates at this women's prison have children, and some inmates are pregnant when they enter the facility. Through a partnership with the Oregon Department of Corrections (DOC), eight children under age 3 and their incarcerated mothers meet for two half-day classes each week in an Early Head Start classroom on the prison grounds. Qualified teachers help mothers bond with their children and learn parenting skills to prepare for parenting after prison. The teachers also conduct monthly visits with the children's caregivers. Through the partnership, a Prenatal Services Group[1] was formed.

Working together, Early Head Start, DOC, and Health Department staff reviewed the system that was in place for incarcerated mothers and identified some gaps. They found that prenatal and labor and delivery services were provided. The incarcerated mothers would deliver their babies at a community hospital and then return to prison while their infants were cared for by family members or foster parents. Breastfeeding and expressing breast milk was allowed, but was logistically difficult. To breast-feed, mothers had to visit with their babies during normal visiting hours, but these visits counted against the mother's monthly allowance of visit points. The mothers were forced to choose between bonding with their babies during visiting hours or visiting with other family members. Mothers who expressed breast milk were only allowed to use hand pumps, and family members had to supply coolers and cold packs for transporting the breast milk.

Through the Early Head Start partnership, new mothers were provided machine breast pumps supplied by the Women, Infants, and Children (WIC) program, and Baby Bonding visits to breast-feed no longer counted against the mother's total visit

Oksana Kuzmina/Fotolia

points. This support resulted in positive outcomes for incarcerated mothers and their babies. For example, one mother entered prison early in her pregnancy. After she delivered her son, a volunteer brought him to the prison to visit her, affirming her role as a mother. A Department of Homeland Security (DHS) worker brought the incarcerated mother's son to the Coffee Creek Child Development Center Early Head Start class, where mother and child established their relationship and the mother was able to breast-feed her baby. The mother is now out of prison, she has been reunited with her son, and they have a strong parent–child relationship.

[1]This group included Sharon Bolmeier, Community Head Start Family Support Teacher; Sue Omel, RN, MS, MTH, Washington County Department of Health and Human Services Supervisor; Cally Wolery, Nurse Manager at Coffee Creek; Becky Wiggin, Executive Support at Coffee Creek; and Carol Thompson, RN, Nurse at Coffee Creek.

---

and understand events, and play involving violent themes may have value in therapeutic settings (Levin, 2003). However, in the early childhood setting, teachers worry that engaging in play that has violent themes may be detrimental. Teachers are concerned that:

- Once violent play gets started, it is hard to stop; children get out of control.
- Other children may be scared or traumatized by watching the play violence.
- Acting out violent acts reinforces violent behaviors and may teach children to be violent.
- Playing the same fantasy role over and over may interrupt children's social connection with other children and distracts children from other skill development.

There is no simple solution to meeting both children's needs and teacher concerns. However, some basic strategies can be implemented for all age groups of young children (Levin, 2003).

Recognizing Violent Themes in Play Teachers should be observant and try to understand the topic children are exploring through play. Simply banning such play denies children the opportunity to process difficult topics in a developmentally appropriate way; also, doing so rarely works and is often counterproductive because children may respond by hiding the play themes and perhaps even lying about their play (Levin, 2003). Instead, teachers should offer interesting challenges to divert interest away from violent play and explore alternative ways to meet children's needs. For example, Noemi recognizes that Aaron and Kip tend to act out shooting themes in their play. She brings a variety of beanbags out to the play yard and helps the boys create targets for a challenge course. Later Noemi guides the children to write creative stories and draw pictures about events that interest them. In this way, Aaron and Kip are provided an active alternative in the play yard and an opportunity to explore the violent themes that interest them in ways that do not disturb the other children.

Ensuring That Everyone Is Safe Children engaged in play with violent themes may frighten others. Safety limits are needed to address the concerns of the other children. Involving all children in the development of the safety limits is a useful teaching approach. Noemi plans a group time for the discussion and guides the children to identify what to say when they don't want to play the scary games.

Meeting Children's Needs Teachers need to be purposeful in planning activities that provide alternative and appropriate ways for children to explore frightening topics. Through painting, drawing, building with clay, and dictating stories, children who have experienced trauma are able to express emotions outwardly in ways that are less threatening than speaking about them (Malchiodi, 2001, 2008). It is also important to rotate the toys and materials that are available for play to ensure that children have interesting alternatives and are not falling back on violent play themes as a sign of boredom.

Promoting Healthy Play Violent play themes sometimes emerge as children imitate the violent actions they have experienced. This is called *imitative play*. Children involved in imitative play act out the same violent events and themes over and over again. For example, Warren and Kyle might persist in play in which one child pretends to be waiting for a bus while the other sneaks up behind him and "shoots" him. Children engaged in imitative play seem stuck and unable to move beyond these repetitious themes. If these play themes persist in their focus on violence and death, the special assistance of a counselor or mental health specialist might be helpful. Teachers should work closely with families to share strategies for managing a child's worries and guiding the child to engage in *imaginative play*.

Imaginative play explores a variety of scenarios, with the play partners demonstrating creative ways for staying safe or withstanding the effects of violence. Tony, Karen, and Enrique pick up their play theme each day at recess, but the ideas and activities change. What began as play focused on police and shootings evolves to firefighters saving people and animals and then changes to play about being a veterinarian. Teachers can encourage these empowering themes by offering ideas for resolving conflicts and giving suggestions about how the "characters" might take charge and manage the dramatic theme in appropriate ways. This approach guides children in continuing to move on to new play themes.

WHAT IF . . .
a small group of parents approached you with a complaint that they had observed children acting out violent themes in the play yard? How would you respond?

Building Conflict Resolution Skills

Learning to resolve disagreements in positive and productive ways helps children build the skills they need to cope with and resolve future difficulties. Conflict resolution approaches offer concrete alternatives to using force or violence to address problems. Lessons learned through these approaches may mediate children's tendencies to play out the abuse they have suffered by acting violently against others. Activities that help children develop these negotiation skills include:

- Reading books about children who solve problems.
- Using puppets to act out a challenge, such as figuring out how to divide an apple.
- Planning activities that require problem solving, such as setting out cut-and-paste activities for four children while providing only two pairs of scissors and two glue sticks.
- Teaching children the language of conflict resolution and modeling how to solve a problem, such as naming the problem, identifying possible solutions, and selecting a mutually agreeable result (Office on Child Abuse and Neglect et al., 2003).

Reinforcing Resilience and Building Protective Factors.

In spite of the serious effects of child maltreatment and violence, not all children demonstrate poor development. Some children who have suffered from these negative events display considerable ability to cope and are able to thrive following interventions that restore their sense of confidence. This characteristic is called **resilience** (Children's Bureau & DePanfilis, 2006). Some children may need extra assistance to develop **protective factors**. Protective factors are buffers that reduce the potential for abuse or neglect. These factors are associated with a decreased incidence of child maltreatment, making them important contributors to abuse prevention (CWIG, 2004). High-quality early childhood settings help children develop protective factors by providing opportunities for children to experience safety and security in an environment where all people are treated with respect and dignity (Cohen & Knitzer, 2004). Such experiences help children form secure relationships; increase their interest in problem solving; and promote the development of language, healthy physical development, and positive social skills (Cohen, Onunaku, Clothier, & Poppe, 2006). These protective factors also enhance children's abilities to develop interests and hobbies, practice self-control, and learn to seek help and gain independence and autonomy (CWIG, 2004).

As children grow through the preschool and elementary school years, they can also learn personal safety skills through appropriate and purposefully planned activities. Activities might focus on lessons such as:

- Don't go with strangers.
- Whom to go to for help.
- What are "good" secrets and what are "bad" secrets.
- Safe touch—it's okay to say "don't touch me."

The *Teaching Wellness* feature provides examples of ways to teach children about safe touch and how to say "Stop!"

Supporting Families

Teachers are an important source of information and social support for families who have been affected by maltreatment and other forms of violence. Teachers'

CLASSROOM CONNECTION

Watch this video about helping children to develop conflict resolution skills. Notice how the teacher guides the children through discussion to identify the problem and create solutions. What kinds of situations have you experienced that required you to help children work through a problem?

resilience
the ability to cope with negative experiences

protective factors
buffers that reduce the potential for abuse or neglect

LEARNING OUTCOME   Children will know the concepts of friendly and not friendly touch and know that they can choose if they want to be touched.

Safety watch: Observe children's feelings. Listen if they want to tell about a time they were hurt or not touched in a friendly way. Provide reassurance and guide the conversation back to the group discussion as needed. Follow up if children's behaviors suggest possible maltreatment.

INFANTS AND TODDLERS

- **Goal:** Children will imitate gentle touch.
- **Materials:** Small doll or stuffed animal.
- **Vocabulary focus:** Words that convey friendly touch (gentle, soft, kind, nice) and unfriendly touch (too hard, hurts, not nice).
- **Activity plan:** Sit together on the floor. Create play inter-actions between the child and the doll or animal. Hold the prop kindly and demonstrate gentle touching. Point to the eyes, ears, and nose. Say, "This is how I touch gently" or "This hug is my friendly touch."

- **How to adjust the activity:** Reinforce these concepts during everyday play. Use body language; smile and pro-vide positive encouragement when a child demonstrates friendly touching. Make a frowning face if unfriendly touching of toys or people is demonstrated and say, "We don't hit; hitting hurts." Then smile and use a friendly voice and gestures demonstrating "This is the way to be gentle. See, this is a friendly way to touch."
- **Did you meet your goal?** Do children begin to imitate the gentle touching that you model? Do toddlers begin to use words such as *gentle, kind, nice, friendly*?

PRESCHOOLERS AND KINDERGARTNERS

- **Goal:** Children will describe friendly and unfriendly touch and know how to respond appropriately when they do not want to be touched.
- **Materials:** Paper cut into 5" × 8" card; marking pen; two boxes or containers, one labeled with a smiling face and one with a frowning face.
- **Vocabulary focus:** Words that convey friendly touch (gen-tle, kind, reassuring, friendly); words that describe hurtful and unfriendly touch (pain, uncomfortable, scary); phrases that communicate dislike and stop (I don't like that, stop that, go away!).
- **Activity plan:** Gather the children. Introduce the defi-nitions of *friendly* and *unfriendly touch*. Say, "Friendly touching is touch that cares for us and make us feel good, such as hugging or patting or giving a high five." Talk about unfriendly touching, the kind that hurts—such as hitting or kicking. Ask the children to suggest words that describe friendly touch. Write each word on a card. Ask the children to give examples of unfriendly touching words and write each example on a card. Lay the cards facedown and give each child a turn to pick up a card. Read the word and ask if the word describes friendly or unfriendly

touch. Show the child how to place friendly words or scenarios in the "smiling face" box and unfriendly words or scenarios in the "frowning face" box. Tell children that unfriendly touching is not okay and that children can say "no" if they do not want to be touched by saying, "You need to stop. I don't like that. That hurts!" Tell children that they can go to their teacher or parents to tell them about the unfriendly touching. Invite each child to show how they could say "no" to unfriendly touching. Close the activity by reminding children about friendly and unfriendly touching and telling them that it is okay to say "no" if they do not want to be touched.

- **How to adjust the activity:** Ask parents to help you teach the words for friendly and unfriendly touching in each child's language. Observe children as they use friendly and unfriendly touching during their everyday play. Repeat the words for friendly and unfriendly touch. Repeat the activity periodically to support children with special learn-ing needs.
- **Did you meet your goal?** Are children able to describe friendly and unfriendly touch? Can they use words appro-priately to convey that they don't want to be touched?

SCHOOL-AGE CHILDREN

- **Goal:** Children will be able to describe a variety of friendly and unfriendly touches and give an example of when a friendly touch might become an unfriendly touch.
- **Materials:** Small pieces of paper, marking pens.
- **Vocabulary focus:** Words that describe friendly (kind, car-ing, nice, gentle, tender, soft, good) and unfriendly (harsh, hard, rough, mean, bad, hurtful) touch.
- **Activity plan:** Create game cards by having children write down different friendly and unfriendly kinds of touch on small pieces of paper. Fold the pieces of paper and place

them in the middle of the group. Tell the children take turns selecting and reading from one of the pieces of paper. Ask the other children to "vote" by raising their hands if the word describes a friendly or unfriendly touch. Ask the children to explain why they voted the way they did. Explain that some kinds of touching can be friendly, but if it is done too hard, it can be unfriendly or hurtful, such as hugging or tickling too hard. Guide discussion about friendly touching that might become unfriendly touching if it is too hard or too rough.

- **How to adjust the activity:** Invite children to take turns using a puppet to tell the others what kind of touch they think is friendly and give an example of what might happen if the friendly touch was done too hard. Encourage the children to think of many different friendly touch words. Make sure that each child has the opportunity to participate fully.
- **Did you meet your goal?** Are children able to describe friendly and unfriendly touch? Can they tell when a friendly touch begins to feel like an unfriendly touch?

positive contributions include demonstrating awareness, creating welcoming environments, and offering activities that teach important lessons and connect families with positive experiences. Sometimes simply being friendly can offer the encouragement that families need to face the process of healing from traumatic events (NAEYC, 2004).

Recognizing Overlooked Victims

When violence occurs in the family there may be overlooked victims. Children may have witnessed the abuse of a sibling, or they may have been made to participate in the abuse in some way. Children may have been coached to cover up the abuse, or they may feel guilty that they were not able to protect the other child from maltreatment. Similarly a parent may suffer from guilt, feeling that he or she should have recognized and protected the child from maltreatment. In homes where abuse or violence has occurred, everyone in the family has been impacted in some way.

Domestic and community violence disrupt a basic function of the family by challenging a mother's ability to keep her child safe.

Photos to go/Getty Images

Building Networks of Support.

Many early childhood programs such as Head Start have a specific commitment to supporting families through parenting education and family service approaches. Schools may have a family social service worker who assists families in accessing resources that help to bolster these protective factors, However, often the early childhood teacher is seen as the most accessible and trusted resource for families. A variety of family support strategies can be developed to build family protective factors and reduce the future potential for maltreatment. These include (HHS et al., 2015; Children's Bureau & DePanfilis, 2006):

- Arranging times to talk with families to explore, recognize, and use their strengths as the foundation for future growth.
- Guiding families to identify their needs, recognize their current network of supports and resources, and engage in problem solving about how to address challenges.
- Linking parents to available resources and guiding them to access these supports.
- Modeling and offering guidance techniques to address children's challenging behaviors.
- Helping families know whom to call in times of crisis.
- Encouraging families to be involved in community service projects to help develop a sense of contribution, confidence, and connection to the community in which they live.

Teachers should focus on linking families to services in the community that the families will be able to access long after the child has moved along in the school setting. By building collaborative relationships with community health and social services providers, teachers also guide those agencies to be receptive to families in need. The *Nutrition Note* describes an example in which collaboration with a local dietitian helps families develop protective factors while addressing a situation of potential medical neglect.

Contributing to Community Abuse Prevention Efforts

Positive Community Influences

Aspects of the broader community also support children and families. These include access to health care, social service resources, stable neighborhoods, and safe schools (Fraser & Terzian, 2005). Children in communities that have accessible resources such as these are more likely to have their physical and emotional health needs met, thus reducing the long-term negative effects of maltreatment and contributing to prevention efforts.

In spite of this knowledge, however, and the increasing scientific evidence about the long-term negative impacts of child maltreatment, little is being done to systematically provide the resources or strategies needed to reduce maltreatment or address its consequences (Center on the Developing Child at Harvard University, 2007). The *Policy Point* provides examples of public policies that could improve this situation.

Mobilizing Abuse Prevention Efforts.

Effective child abuse prevention relies on community efforts. However, sometimes energizing the public around the topic of abuse is difficult because it requires people to think about an uncomfortable subject. A lack of common understanding about the prevalence of abuse in the community and disagreement about appropriate parenting practices can also hinder community efforts. Early childhood teachers are logical partners for contributing to such initiatives because they have knowledge and experience that equip them to speak strongly about the challenges that families face and the negative effects of maltreatment and violence (Kracke & Cohen, 2008).

A positive approach to child abuse prevention is often the best approach. This involves placing the focus on supporting and strengthening all families and raising healthy children (Washington Council for Prevention of Child Abuse, 2005). Successful child abuse prevention efforts focus on (Thomas, Leicht, Hughes, Madigan, & Dowell, 2003):

- Providing access to emergency care and shelter for domestic violence protection.
- Providing support programs for parents, especially first-time parents.

NUTRITION NOTE Community Partners Help Develop Protective Factors

Teachers play an important role in linking families to community support agencies. Programs such as the Women, Infants, and Children (WIC) program can help families access food and support them in addressing a child's special nutritional needs. For example, a child with an iron deficiency is at risk for poor growth and learning challenges. A parent who offers the child a vegetarian diet may not be aware of the growing child's need for an iron-rich diet, resulting in anemia. WIC dietitians teach the parent how to offer a diet that will address the child's need for iron-rich foods. This knowledge builds protective factors that reduce the potential for medical neglect.

POLICY POINT

Public Policy Strategies to Reduce Child Maltreatment

- Enact policies that allow parents to take leave from work after the birth or adoption of a child and provide financial supports for those who want to stay home with their newborn but are not financially able to do so.
- Provide supports for parents who struggle with the challenges of working and raising their children, especially those who hold low-paying jobs or work irregular hours, and

those whose children have special health or developmental challenges.
- Increase access to mental health care for young children and families.
- Provide resources for parents and early childhood teachers to manage children's challenging behaviors.
- Make quality early childhood programs accessible for all families.

Source: Based on *Excessive Stress Disrupts the Architecture of the Developing Brain: Working Paper 3. Updated Edition.* National Scientific Council on the Developing Child. (2005/2014). Retrieved from www.developingchild.harvard.edu.

- Enhancing family relationships.
- Teaching parenting skills.

It is important to frame the actions of child abuse prevention as part of the many ways in which communities contribute to the positive growth and development of children. When communities work to provide libraries, parks, schools, and youth sports and recreation programs that all members of the community can access, everyone participates in the goal to raise safe and healthy children and to prevent child maltreatment.

CHECK YOUR UNDERSTANDING 15.4

Click here to check your understanding of how to support families and take steps to prevent maltreatment.

SUMMARY

- Many young children suffer from harmful acts of abuse or neglect. Teachers need to recognize the different types of maltreatment and violence children may experience and understand that the negative effects of such events can be long-lasting.
- To support children's healthy development, teachers must be able to recognize the signs of abuse or neglect.
- Teachers are ethically and legally mandated to report when child abuse or neglect is suspected. They must be prepared to call the appropriate authorities and know how to make a report.
- Teachers play a supportive role in helping children who have experienced maltreatment or have witnessed violence to regain confidence and interest in play. Teachers also contribute to their communities when they convey the importance of child abuse prevention as a foundation for building safe communities and enhancing the development of healthy children and families.

Chapter Quiz

Click here to check your understanding of Chapter 15, Child Abuse and Neglect.

Discussion Starters

1. Scan the local media in your area to identify a case of child maltreatment in the news. Discuss the case with others in your class. Identify supports or strategies that might have helped prevent the maltreatment from occurring.

2. Most teachers find some children's styles or behaviors to be annoying and frustrating, such as clinging, whining, having a runny nose, or demonstrating aggressive behaviors. Identify the style or behavior that you find most frustrating. What steps have you taken (or would you take) to learn how to better manage these frustrating behaviors? Talk with others about your ideas and supports that may be available.

3. Making reports of suspected abuse or neglect can be stressful for teachers because it means that they must recognize when they have reasonable suspicion that maltreatment has occurred. What aspects of child maltreatment would be the most difficult to recognize? For you, what would be the most difficult part of making a report? What agency would you call to make a report?

Practice Points

1. Go online to find the laws that govern child maltreatment in your community or state. Read about the types of maltreatment under your state's definition and clarify who is considered a mandatory reporter by the laws of your state or community.

2. Spend time reviewing the children's television programming that is available in your area. What aspects of violence stand out to you? Are the characters that perform the aggressive or violent acts held accountable for their behaviors? What lessons about violence are communicated in the programs you reviewed? What activities would you implement in your early childhood classroom to reduce the impact of such messages?

3. Gather information about the incidence and prevalence of abuse and neglect in your community. Identify the resources that are available to support children who are victims of maltreatment and their families. What specific services are available to children and parents? What cost is associated with getting this help? What other barriers might keep families from benefiting?

Web Resources

Child Trends

Child Welfare Information Gateway

Family Violence Prevention Fund

National Center on Shaken Baby Syndrome

New York Society for the Prevention of Cruelty to Children

U.S. Department of Health and Human Services, Administration for Children and Families

Key Terms

child abuse

child maltreatment

child neglect

mandatory reporters

perpetrators

protective factors

resilience

CHAPTER 16

Managing Emergencies

learning outcomes

After reading this chapter, you should be able to:

1. Define emergencies and describe the components that are part of emergency management planning.
2. Explain the goals of first aid and describe the use of universal precautions and steps taken to assess injuries.
3. Discuss basic first aid approaches used when caring for a variety of common injuries in early childhood settings.
4. Identify appropriate responses to various types of disasters and describe ways that teachers help children cope with the effects of disaster events.

CASE STUDY

Jamal runs a family child care program that serves five children ages 2 to 5 years. At outdoor playtime, the children select balls from the equipment cart. They begin to toss the balls and laugh as the brightly colored balls bump across the yard. Jamal smiles as he watches. Then he hears a crash and turns to discover that 2-year-old Kevin has pulled the cart over on top of himself.

Jamal quickly removes the cart. He sees a bright red welt running from Kevin's forehead across his eyebrow and cheek, and blood is pouring out of his nose and mouth. Kevin's eyes are open and staring, but he is completely silent. Jamal crouches down to assess the situation and puts on the plastic gloves that he always carries in his pocket. The other children gather about him. He calls out to Kevin saying, "Hey, Kevin. Hey, buddy! Are you okay?" Kevin blinks and looks at Jamal. Then he takes in a big breath, begins to cry, and reaches out to Jamal.

Jamal gently picks Kevin up and, calling for the other children to follow, carries him to the kitchen where the first aid supplies are stored. He shifts Kevin to his hip and directs Callie and Ahmed to entertain the younger children in the book corner. Jamal opens sterile gauze pads and presses them to Kevin's nose and mouth. He rocks his body back and forth saying, "I'm here, Kevin. We're going to make it better." Kevin is whimpering but settles against Jamal. Jamal can see that the other children are comfortable looking at books. He calls Kevin's mother, Mimi, who is at work. She says that she will come as soon as she can.

When Mimi arrives, she is alarmed by Kevin's appearance. The bleeding has stopped, but Kevin is still groggy. Jamal encourages Mimi to take Kevin to the doctor.

After they leave, Jamal ties the soiled gauze and latex gloves in a plastic bag, disinfects the nearby surfaces, and washes his hands. Then he helps the other children get ready for nap time. That evening Jamal checks the ball cart and sees that a protective cover for one of the supports has fallen off. It looks as though it can be repaired, but he sets the cart in the garage until he can work on it carefully. Then he calls Mimi and learns that Kevin needed stitches but he should be fine.

Early childhood teachers assume a complex range of responsibilities when caring for and educating young children. They must attend to the small injuries that occur and sometimes must manage more serious emergencies. For teachers such as Jamal to respond efficiently, they must have an emergency management plan in place and have the skills and confidence necessary to manage small injuries and take action in emergency. Teachers must also be prepared for disaster situations and have a plan to supervise children until they can be released to their families.

In this chapter, we discuss the planning processes that help teachers take effective action to care for small injuries and seek help in case of emergency. This review highlights the need for teachers to obtain first aid and emergency response training from credible authorities. Together emergency preparedness and formal training assist teachers to respond effectively and help keep children safe.

PREPARING FOR EMERGENCIES

Emergencies are shocking to witness and challenging to experience. Emergencies may occur from unintentional injury or disasters that cause unimaginable destruction. In these difficult moments, teachers are called on to assess what has happened, respond quickly, and ensure that safety is restored and children receive care. Steps in preparing to assume these responsibilities confidently include recognizing what an emergency is, developing an emergency management plan, conducting practice drills with children, and obtaining appropriate training.

Defining Emergencies

Serious situations can occur even when teachers are doing all they can to keep children safe from harm. An incident is called an emergency if the situation threatens the life of a child or that presents risk for permanent injury or disability (National Association of Child Care Resource and Referral Agencies [NACCRRA] and Save the Children, 2010). When the situation involves an event or a combination of events that overwhelm the ability to restore safety and order in a short period of time, the emergency is referred to as a disaster.

Several types of emergency situations may threaten children's safety (American Academy of Pediatrics [AAP], American Public Health Association, National Resource Center for Health and Safety in Child Care and Early Education, 2011; NACCRRA and Save the Children, 2010). These include:

- *Health emergencies.* These are caused by serious injury, severe health concerns, or potentially deadly disease epidemics such as Ebola virus, H1N1, or other pandemic flu illnesses.
- *Natural disasters.* These include events caused by nature, such as hurricanes, tornadoes, wildfires, or floods. They are sometimes referred to as "acts of God."
- *Technological disasters.* These are caused by industrial sources and exposure to hazardous materials. Examples include loss of electricity or water, fires, and chemical or oil spills.

emergency
any situation that threatens the life of a child or that presents risk for permanent injury or disability

disaster
an event that overwhelms available community emergency response resources and often results in widespread injury, death, and destruction of property

FIGURE 16-1   When Is It an Emergency?

An emergency exists if the child:
- Loses consciousness or becomes less and less responsive.
- Has trouble breathing or cannot speak.
- Has confusion, headache, or vomiting after a head injury.
- Has signs of a broken bone.
- Has bleeding that won't stop.
- Is vomiting blood or passing large quantities of blood in the stool.
- Shows signs of shock.
- Has increasingly severe pain.
- Shows signs of dehydration: sunken eyes, lethargy.

Sources: Based on *Caring for Our Children: National Health and Safety Performance Standards: Guidelines for Out-of-Home Child Care Programs*, 3rd ed., 2011, by American Academy of Pediatrics, American Public Health Association, and National Resource Center for Health and Safety in Child Care and Early Education, retrieved August 2015, from http://nrckids.org/CFOC3/index.html and *Is it a Medical Emergency?* 2009, by KidsHealth, Nemours, retrieved August 2015, from http://kidshealth.org/parent/general/aches/emergencies.html?tracking=P_RelatedArticle#.

- *Attacks and threats to personal safety.* These acts of violence include threats from guns, sniper fire, bomb threats, kidnapping (missing child), intruders, and acts of terrorism.

All describe situations that require the assistance of specially trained and equipped emergency response and medically trained personnel. As an example, Figure 16-1 lists some of the signs that cue teachers that a child is experiencing a health emergency. Emergency assistance must be obtained as soon as a teacher recognizes that an event threatens life or has potential to result in disability.

Creating an Emergency Management Plan

The National Commission on Children and Disasters *2010 Report to the President and Congress* recommends that disaster training and emergency preparedness be required as part of the minimum safety requirements of licensed child care programs. Teachers are the first responders when it comes to managing the effects of emergencies and disasters on the children in their care. They must be ready to take the lead in managing emergencies that happen in the classroom and work as part of a team in addressing emergency situations in their center or school. To provide the support that teachers need, various agencies have established websites to help teachers plan and practice appropriate emergency responses. The *Policy Point* provides a list of resources to help create an emergency management plan (EMP).

An EMP is a written document developed through a process of careful discussion among teachers, families, and community emergency responders. The process helps to connect the early childhood program to the greater community, which ensures that the needs of very young children are considered at both the program and community planning levels. This work is done proactively, before an emergency occurs. The emergency management plan anticipates potential threats to the program, outlines steps to take to mitigate the potential hazard, identifies how to access emergency resources, addresses site-specific characteristics as well as the special needs of children enrolled, outlines options for taking shelter, and proposes a plan for transporting children if evacuation is required. Each program's EMP will have similar components but will be unique to the setting.

POLICY POINT

Early Childhood Programs Need Emergency Preparedness Plans

The National Commission on Children and Disasters *2010 Report to the President and Congress* highlighted the need for early childhood educators to develop emergency and disaster preparedness plans. Resources that were developed to address this need include the following, which can be found online:

The Office of Head Start offers tools to support program planning for emergencies, including tools on how to plan for specific emergencies in the *Head Start Emergency Preparedness Manual* (ACF-IM-09-09).

The Office of Child Care provides emergency preparedness information and resources to guide emergency response at the *Child Care Resources for Disasters and Emergencies* website.

The National Association of Child Care Resource and Referral Agencies provides a variety of resources for disaster planning and preparation for teachers in child care centers and family child care homes at the NACCRRA website. Search for NACCRRA, then Disaster Planning and Recovery Basics.

Source: Based on National Commission on Children and Disasters. *2010 Report to the President and Congress.* AHRQ Publication No. 10-M037. Rockville, MD: Agency for Healthcare Research and Quality. October 2010.

Analyzing Potential Emergency Threats

An effective emergency management plan starts with an analysis of potential emergency threats. Health emergencies resulting from sudden injuries such as falls are the most familiar crisis situation in early childhood settings. Pandemic health issues are detected at the public level, and in most cases, warnings are communicated as the issue is recognized.

Threats that may cause natural disasters in particular geographic areas can sometimes be anticipated. For example, natural disasters often occur in a rhythm related to seasons, such as tornadoes and hurricanes, or wildfires caused by drought (NACCRRA, 2010). Areas with industrial plants and major transportation routes for industrial materials have increased potential for chemical or oil spills. Disasters situations can also be linked. For example, earthquakes often cause fires, severe storms can cause mudslides and power outages, and spills of toxic materials may bring on acute illness (NACCRRA, 2010). These situations can create barriers to effective response. Road closures may block safe evacuation routes or stop families from being able to retrieve children from school or care. As a result, the emergency management plan must consider both the potential for disaster and the possibilities that could threaten children.

Various resources help with planning. The Federal Emergency Management Agency (FEMA) provides information about the types and dates of disasters that have been declared for each state. This information can be helpful in planning for the types of disasters that might occur. The National Weather Service provides a Storm Watch, Warning, and Advisory map that can be accessed electronically. Local emergency personnel are another good resource for learning about the types of dangers that may threaten the community.

Removing Potential Hazards

Preventive actions work to mitigate or reduce the potential for harm. Teachers look closely at the children's environment to identify possible hazards and make needed adjustments. Ensuring that light fixtures are well secured to the ceiling, tall furniture is attached to the wall, and heavy items are stored on the floor all help to avoid the danger of falling if an earthquake occurs. Knowing how to turn off gas, water, and electricity helps avoid dangers to the facility during severe storms. Removing dangerous tree branches reduces the likelihood that they will be blown into windows in the event of high winds. These actions contribute to positive outcomes.

Identifying How to Access Emergency Resources

The effectiveness of the emergency management plan relies on the teacher's ability to connect with emergency responders as quickly as possible. Various aspects ensure quick response, including the ability to:

- *Know whom to contact in case of an emergency.* Emergency phone numbers for fire, ambulance, and poison control should be posted by each phone and entered into cell phone emergency contact lists.
- *Recognize how quickly emergency personnel are likely to respond.* When support is readily available and quick to respond, teachers can focus on implementing basic first aid and keeping children stable for a shorter period of time. When emergency personnel are at a greater distance, response will take longer and teachers must be prepared to provide care for a longer period of time.
- *Identify options for transporting children to emergency services.* Some communities may have readily accessible medical transport. In other settings, teachers may need to rely on air transport to get children to more distant medical centers, or teachers may need to be ready with a plan to transport the child themselves.
- *Create formal arrangements with medical providers for over-the-phone consultation if needed.* When emergency personnel are at a distance or when immediate response is crucial, teachers need to know whom to call for guidance. Posting the contact information of a medical advisor in an easily accessed location is an important support in such situations.

Addressing Site-Specific Characteristics

Each early childhood setting has specific needs that must be addressed in the emergency management plan. Child care centers and school-based programs usually have a variety of personnel who can assist with emergency response. In family child care or short-term child care settings, individual teachers such as Jamal may be responsible for managing emergencies while at the same time supervising the group of children.

Attributes of the facility also contribute to the EMP. Designating a space where an injured or ill child can be isolated (and equipping the space ahead of time with a cot or sleeping pad, a blanket, and first aid supplies) adds to a coordinated response during the first minutes of an injury emergency. Access to both a telephone (landline) and cell phone is advisable to provide options if the electricity is out or the cell phone batteries are dead.

The EMP should also address emergency procedures for each part of the classroom day, such as when children are playing inside and outside, are at lunch, are napping, or are on a field trip. The pattern of supervision and location of the children need to be considered.

Planning for Children's Special Needs

Children's age, special medical conditions, or developmental needs must be considered when developing the EMP. Specific evacuation plans are needed for infants and toddlers and children with mobility challenges. First aid kits need to be equipped with copies of individual emergency medical protocols for children who have special health needs. Medications approved for administration to individual children should be readily available for teachers to access during an emergency. This may require special planning to ensure that these items are accessible to the teacher but out of the reach of children. Foods stored for emergencies need to be selected with children's food restrictions or allergies in mind.

WHAT IF . . .

a child in your class is known to have an allergy to bee stings? What extra items might you need in your first aid kit to support this child in case of an emergency?

Understanding Options for Taking Shelter

Some emergencies require that teachers and children leave the facility. In other situations, staying inside is the safest choice. Knowing when to leave and when to stay is a key element in safety management. Common shelter options are as follows:

- *Sheltering-in-place* refers to remaining within the early childhood facility until the emergency is over or until help can arrive. This option is used when the facility is essentially safe and secure and when leaving the facility is unsafe or is not an option due to outside dangers or blocked evacuation routes. Taking shelter-in-place is an appropriate choice if exit routes are blocked by floods or downed power lines, for example.

- *Lockdown* refers to sheltering with children in a secure location within the early childhood facility. This option is used when danger from the outside is present and children are threatened even in their own classroom. Lockdown is put into action when the threat is imminent and leaving the facility is unsafe—for example, if there is danger from an intruder in the building or gunfire near the school.

- *Evacuation and Relocation* refer to leaving the facility and traveling to an alternative assembly location. Evacuation is required when it is not safe to remain in the children's facility. Evacuation is used in response to a sudden emergency such as a fire in the facility.

The EMP describes appropriate preparations and the procedures for managing children in each shelter option.

Transporting Children

The emergency management plan guides the options for relocating children to both nearby and distant evacuation sites and describes how children will be transported during evacuation. A nearby assembly location that can be reached easily by walking is a good choice when the emergency is related to the children's facility, such as a fire. The nearby location should provide shelter from the weather and be appropriate for a stay of a few hours.

When the emergency requires moving children a good distance from the children's setting, teachers need to consider the number of children to be transported and ways to address children's special mobility needs. Some programs may have vehicles that are always present and available for use in emergencies. Others may rely on the presence of teacher and staff vehicles. It is recommended that vehicles identified as part of the relocation plan contain at least ½ tank of gas at all times (Schwartz, 2009). Alternative methods of transportation could also be considered, including using strollers, carts, wagons, wheelchairs, or cribs equipped with wheels.

Preparing for Action

A variety of familiar aspects are involved in preparing to take action in case of injury. These include identifying roles and responsibilities, assembling emergency

CLASSROOM CONNECTION

Watch this video on evacuation plans. Notice the narrator's suggestions about the distance to the evacuation site from the children's setting and the type of shelter it should provide. For a children's program, what would be a potential evacuation site with which you are familiar?

shelter-in-place
tactic of taking shelter in the early childhood setting if the facility is secure and if leaving the facility would put children at risk

lockdown
taking shelter in the children's facility while stopping the access and entry of an intruder

evacuation
leaving the children's facility when it is not safe to remain and traveling to an alternative assembly location

Pearson Education

supplies, compiling children's emergency information, communicating the plan to families, and posting the emergency procedures.

Identifying Roles and Responsibilities

To ensure purposeful and organized action, it is essential that teachers understand their role and the activities for which they are responsible. Each teacher should know:

- Who will call for emergency assistance.
- Who will provide emergency care for an injured child.
- Who will supervise the remaining children.
- Who will assume leadership if taking shelter or evacuating is required.
- Who will contact the parents.
- Who will document and report the emergency to appropriate supervisors or emergency responders.

In group settings, teachers share the emergency response responsibilities. This inspires confidence among the teaching team and contributes to children's safety during emergencies. Family child care workers need to develop supports in advance, such as identifying a neighbor who will help during a crisis. Teachers in elementary school settings may need to know whom to call for backup assistance in the classroom in case of an emergency.

Assembling First Aid Kits

The AAP, American Public Health Association, and National Resource Center for Health and Safety in Child Care and Early Education (2011) recommend that children's programs maintain at least one first aid kit to keep at the facility and one to take along on field trips. The AAP and child care licensing agencies specify the first aid supplies that are required for children's settings. Figure 16-2 provides a sample checklist.

Teachers locate the classroom first aid kit in a place that is out of the reach of children but easily accessible. The kit is labeled so that it is easy to identify. A "traveling" first aid kit is also needed to take along on trips away from the facility. This first aid kit should include children's emergency contact information and any special medical protocols and supplies for children with special health needs. A backpack that can be hung near the door is a good container for a traveling first aid kit. In addition, first aid kits are located in any vehicles used to transport children. The first aid kits should be checked at least monthly and restocked after use.

In the opening case scenario, Jamal was able to attend to Kevin's cut quickly because the emergency supplies he needed were readily available. This supported effective management of the injury and reduced confusion while he supervised the remaining children.

Creating a Blood Spill Cleanup Kit

Careful cleanup of blood spills or splashes is important to avoid possible exposure to bloodborne diseases. A well-equipped blood spill kit includes protective equipment such as gloves and goggles or other eye protection. Paper towels to absorb the spill and bags to dispose of soiled materials safely should also be included, as should soap or antibacterial gel for

Children's programs need at least one first aid kit that stays in the facility and one that is taken on field trips.

Dorling Kindersley, Ltd.

FIGURE 16-2 First Aid Supplies Checklist

- ☐ Telephone numbers for community emergency care providers and Poison Control center
- ☐ Emergency contact information for children's families
- ☐ Guide to standard first aid care
- ☐ Emergency medications for children with special medical needs
- ☐ Disposable plastic gloves (latex free preferred)
- ☐ Scissors
- ☐ Tweezers
- ☐ Thermometer (non-glass and mercury free)
- ☐ Adhesive-style strip bandages
- ☐ Sterile gauze pads and rolls
- ☐ Adhesive bandage tape
- ☐ Safety pins
- ☐ Triangular bandages
- ☐ Eye dressing
- ☐ Cold pack
- ☐ Water
- ☐ Small plastic or metal splints
- ☐ Liquid soap
- ☐ Flashlight (and working batteries)
- ☐ Pen/pencil and note pad
- ☐ First aid chart or booklet
- ☐ Plastic bags for disposing of soiled materials
- ☐ Cell phone

Source: Based on *Emergency/Disaster Preparedness for Child Care Programs: Applicable Standards from "Caring for Our Children,"* American Academy of Pediatrics, American Public Health Association, and National Resource Center for Health and Safety in Child Care and Early Education, 2011. Retrieved August 2015, from http://nrckids.org/CFOC3/PDFVersion/PDF_Color/CFOC3_ch5.pdf.

washing hands after cleanup. A spray bottle or bucket is needed to mix disinfectant products such as the bleach and water solution used to sanitize soiled surfaces.

Assembling Emergency Supplies

Emergency supplies are stored in case sheltering-in-place or evacuating to another location is required. Enough supplies should be ready to support care for 48 to 72 hours. The *Safety Segment* provides a sample checklist to assist in gathering disaster emergency supplies. Large plastic tubs or rolling garbage cans with lids are good choices for containing disaster emergency supplies. These supplies should be checked periodically, and stored food and water should be rotated every six months.

Compiling Children's Emergency Information

Emergency files and information need to be readily accessible in case evacuation is required. Needed information includes:

- *Attendance roster for the day* to ensure that all children are accounted for.
- *Child and teacher emergency contact information* to support communication with families.
- *Emergency medical plans for children and staff* to ensure that special health or medical needs are addressed appropriately.

Maintaining emergency information in a current, readily accessible, and portable format takes special attention. Teachers might e-mail the information to a secure

SAFETY SEGMENT   Disaster Emergency Supplies Checklist

Assemble supplies in backpacks, rolling luggage, or large plastic crates with handles.

✓ First aid supplies: first aid kit, hand sanitizers, antiseptic wipes.

✓ Clothing and bedding: extra clothing, rain gear, hats, gloves, blankets, or sleeping bags.

✓ Tools and supplies: paper cups and plates, utensils, manual can opener, plastic sheeting, duct tape, scissors, battery-operated radio, extra batteries, flashlight, cash, tool kit, matches (in a waterproof container), signal flare, whistle, map of the local area, emergency preparedness handbook.

✓ Personal care and sanitation supplies: toilet paper, towels, soap, plastic garbage bags, disinfectant, or bleach.

✓ Special items: formula, bottles, diapers, special medications, games, books, telephone, emergency contact information for children and adults, telephone numbers of local and state emergency agencies.

✓ Water: enough for three days (at least 1 gallon of water per person per day).

✓ Food: enough for three days. Choose nonperishable foods that are lightweight, are compact, and do not need refrigeration or cooking, such as canned fruits and meats, high-energy and comfort foods, and infant foods.

• Package foods in clean plastic containers with lids.

• Rotate supplies every six months.

Source: Based on *Preparing for Disaster* (FEMA 475; A4600), August 2004, Jessup, MD: FEMA and Washington, DC: American Red Cross, retrieved August 2015, from www.fema.gov/pdf/library/pfd.pdf and *Emergency Preparedness and Response: Chemical Agents: Facts about Sheltering in Place*, May 21, 2013, Atlanta, GA: Centers for Disease Control and Prevention, retrieved August 2015, from www.bt.cdc.gov/planning/shelteringfacts.asp.

location so that it is available electronically or place paper copies in a resealable plastic bag in the traveling first aid kit.

Communicating the Plan to Families

Communicating with families once children have taken shelter or have been evacuated is crucial, but the process of communication begins during the planning and preparation process. To begin, teachers invite families to participate in developing the emergency management plan. Once the plan is established, they acquaint families with the emergency plans through program orientation meetings, handbooks, newsletters, the program website, and posted emergency procedures. Families want to know:

• Who will care for their children during an emergency.

• Where children will be sheltered in case of evacuation and relocation (address and telephone number).

• How families will be contacted.

Families need to be assured that in emergency situations, teachers will give their attention first to the safe care and supervision of children and that communication with families will be a later step in emergency management. This can sometimes be a topic of dispute. In some scenarios, a family member may learn from a news report that a fire or another problem occurred at the school or children's site before teachers have the opportunity to communicate with families. Sharing information with families is very important, but children's safety always comes first.

Posting Emergency Procedures

Emergency procedures provide clear and straightforward directions about what actions to take; telephone numbers for emergency services; and a statement that teachers can read, including the name of the program or school, the address and driving directions to the location, and the telephone number of the classroom. The

FIGURE 16-3   **Sample Emergency Procedures Poster**

Head Teacher:

- Administer emergency first aid and CPR.
- Provide child's medical information to emergency personnel.
- Stay with the child at all times.
- Travel with the child to the hospital if needed.
- Transfer responsibility directly to parent or other authorized adult.

Assistant Teacher:

- Call 911. Report the emergency. Give directions.
- Provide supervision for remaining children.
- Contact other program staff for backup.
- Contact the child's family.

Emergency Telephone Numbers

FIRE - AMBULANCE - POLICE: Call 911
POISON CONTROL: Call 9-1-800-222-1222
Emergency Room at Good Health Medical Center: Call XXX-XXXX
Electricity: Call XXX-XXXX Water: Call XXX-XXXX Gas: Call XXX-XXXX
Say, "I'm calling from Kennedy School at 567 NW 160th Street, at the corner of 160th and Adams Boulevard. Take Main Street to Adams, turn north and travel one mile to 160th Street. The building is on the right side of the street. We are in room 107. Our phone number is XXX-XXX-XXXX."

procedures are written in all languages spoken by the teachers or any volunteers who might be assisting. Using large bold print is helpful for reading from a distance. The emergency procedures should be posted where everyone will know where to look, such as on the wall near the first aid kit and beside each telephone. This ensures that the information is readily available to support teachers during a stressful emergency. Figure 16-3 provides an example of an emergency procedures poster.

It is also helpful to post directions for common first aid procedures on the inside of a cupboard door where the first aid kit is stored or on the wall in the area where first aid might be provided. This way the information can be a reminder for a teacher who is working quickly to put on gloves, access supplies, and administer first aid.

Accessing Emergency Response Training

Training by credible authorities is an essential part of managing emergencies. Infant and child first aid and cardiopulmonary resuscitation (CPR) are the most common training topics for appropriate emergency response. These trainings offer specific information about the injuries and emergency situations that might involve young children and up-to-date guidelines for addressing injuries.

Obtaining First Aid and CPR Training

Dependable first aid and CPR training is conducted by trained personnel from organizations such as the American Red Cross, the American Heart Association, and hospitals. Under the guidance of certified trainers, teachers have the opportunity to practice identifying first aid concerns and implementing rescue procedures such as applying bandages and conducting CPR for infants, children, and adults. Teachers learn that changing a child's position to open a blocked airway or stopping blood flow by applying pressure are examples of first aid actions that can save a child's life. Training helps teachers learn ways to get past the fear of doing something wrong by helping them recognize that in an emergency, the consequence of *not* responding may be death or serious disability.

Most states require that teachers maintain certification in infant and child first aid and CPR through renewal classes every two years. This ensures that teachers refresh their skills and learn about new and emerging safety practices. Sometimes well-learned lessons become outdated as new information is discovered and safety practices are improved.

Larger child care centers or schools may schedule periodic training for staff, but ultimately it is the responsibility of individual teachers to maintain their certification as a part of their professional commitment to keep their skills current.

Accessing Specialized Training

Specialized training may be needed to support children who have health concerns during an emergency event. Such training may include:

- Use of glucagon for children with diabetes.
- Use of epinephrine autoinjectors (EpiPens) for children with sensitive allergies.
- Appropriate response for children with seizure disorder.
- Emergency response for children with specific developmental concerns such as potential for choking.

Participating in Community Disaster Response Training

Participating in community disaster preparedness training is a good way for teachers to gain a perspective of the kinds of actions and supports that can be expected in a community-wide emergency event and the roles and responsibilities of emergency responders. These activities also help teachers recognize the ways that early childhood facilities and schools can support their communities in times of disaster by serving as potential evacuation sites or by providing child care for emergency personnel who are working to address the effects of the disaster. When teachers participate in disaster planning, they help raise awareness that children and early childhood programs are vulnerable parts of the population that should be considered in community emergency management plans (National Association of Child Care Resource and Referral Agencies [NACCRRA] and Save the Children, 2010).

Conducting Emergency Drills

Practicing the planned response steps for emergencies is a useful way to determine whether the emergency management plan is realistic. It builds teachers' familiarity with the actions that will support them in case of an emergency and helps them identify possible barriers. Managing simulated emergency scenarios also builds a sense of teamwork among staff as they work together to solve the problem scenario, an aspect that is crucial to effective response. Through practice, teachers are able to recognize how their own personal or family lives could be impacted by an emergency at school. For example, teachers may need to travel with an injured child to obtain emergency medical care and, as a result, should have a backup plan for their own children and families. Advance planning helps teachers avoid being distracted by competing responsibilities.

Practicing Emergency Drills with Children

Familiar emergency drills in early childhood and school settings include fire, earthquake, tornado, and lockdown drills. It is also important to practice response drills with children, using injury or medical scenarios. One way to conduct such a drill is for the director to enter the play yard and hand a note to a teacher indicating the beginning of an "Injury Drill." Following the directions on the note, the teachers could select a child to pretend to be injured and then act through the appropriate response steps. Questions to consider during a medical emergency drill such as this include the following:

- Is at least one communication source available to call for emergency aid?
- Are first aid supplies and family emergency contact information easily accessible?
- Does the plan provide sufficient supervision for both the "injured" and remaining children?
- Would a report identify additional safety precautions needed to reduce danger in the future?

Emergency procedures should be reviewed periodically to make sure barriers and problems have been corrected and all supports remain available. An emergency is no time to learn that bandages were "borrowed" from the first aid kit for use in dramatic play.

Testing Disaster Emergency Response

One way to practice for a potential disaster is to identify a scenario in which teachers must determine the appropriate shelter or evacuation plan and simulate the action steps of the plan. This also helps children gain familiarity with following the teachers' directions for responding to a variety of emergencies. The *Teaching Wellness* feature offers ideas about how to help children develop skills in focusing on the teacher and following directions.

Practicing disaster emergency response also offers opportunities to review the emergency supplies and test whether emergency foods and water have been rotated, batteries for flashlights have been replaced, and emergency information is readily available if evacuation is needed. These actions help ensure that disaster preparations are organized and useful.

RESPONDING TO EMERGENCIES

Teachers have a strong commitment to children's safety. Even so, taking action in emergencies is not always easy or natural. Being familiar with basic and emergency first aid, understanding volunteer protection laws, knowing how to assess an emergency, and using universal precautions when responding to emergencies are

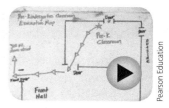

Pearson Education

CLASSROOM CONNECTION

Watch this video on conducting fire drills with children. Consider the director's dilemma about the new requirement to plan fire drills during nap time. How would you implement this new plan?

CHECK YOUR UNDERSTANDING 16.1

Click here to check your understanding of how to prepare for emergencies and how to create an emergency response plan.

TEACHING WELLNESS   Sometimes I Lead—Sometimes I Follow

LEARNING OUTCOME   Children will be able to show what it means to follow directions (look at the teacher, listen to the words, do what is asked) and tell why following directions is important in emergencies.
VOCABULARY FOCUS: Follow, leader, copy, look, listen, do, safety.
SAFETY WATCH: Use motions appropriate for babies to follow.

INFANTS AND TODDLERS

- **Goal:** Babies and toddlers will play follow-me copying activities.
- **Materials:** Play space, colored blocks, two small tubs or containers.
- **Activity plan:** Sit with the child to play copying games. Make motions, facial expressions, or sounds. Encourage the baby to follow you; then follow movements and sounds the baby makes.
- **How to adjust the activity:** Help all children focus by using clear and repetitive movements. Encourage the child with words and gestures to look and follow.
- **Did you meet your goal?** Did children copy and follow actions in play?

PRESCHOOLERS AND KINDERGARTNERS

- **Goal:** Children will show and tell what it means to be the leader and the follower.
- **Materials:** A variety of small toys (five of each selected toy) such as small blocks, beads, manipulative and sorting toys, construction paper.
- **Activity plan:** Place a piece of construction paper in front of each child. Put the toys in the center of a table. Ask the children to watch and then copy what you do. Choose two toys and place them on your paper. Position the toys in obvious locations such as near each other in the center, at the edges, or at opposing corners. Ask the children to follow by finding the same toys and placing them on their paper in the same way. As children work, talk through the steps of what it means to follow: Listen and look, think about the directions, and copy the placement. Can they do it? Repeat the game, inviting a child to be the leader. Give each child a turn to lead. Ask children to tell you what it means to lead and to follow. Reinforce the concepts of listening, watching, and following.
- **How to adjust the activity:** Increase visual contrast by using white construction paper so that children with vision impairment can see and focus more easily on copying the placement of the toys. Verbally describe each step of the activity to reinforce listening, watching, and following. Offer toys that all children are able to pick up and position the toys within easy reach. Learn the vocabulary words for listen, watch, and follow in the home language of children in the class and use them with the English words to reinforce the concepts.
- **Did you meet your goal?** Are children able to copy the placement of the toys? Do they demonstrate understanding of lead and follow? When asked, can they define the words?

SCHOOL-AGE CHILDREN

- **Goal:** Children will explain what it means to follow directions and tell why it is important to follow directions during an emergency.
- **Materials:** 1-inch-cube blocks, 12-inch × 18-inch poster board pieces (one for each pair of children), current events article from the newspaper describing an emergency or a disaster.
- **Activity plan:** Gather children and introduce the topic of the importance of listening and following directions in emergencies. Ask children to pair with another child to practice an activity involving giving and following directions. Give each pair a piece of poster board and ask them to fold it in half and stand it on a table like a screen. Ask the children to sit one child on each side of the screen where they cannot see what the other child is building. Give each child five blocks. Identify one child in each pair to be the leader and one to be the follower. Ask the leader to build a three-block structure and then give instructions guiding the follower to build one just like it. Allow time for the follower to complete his or her structure. Ask the children to remove the poster board and compare the structures. Are they the same? Why would they be the same, and why would they be different? Reverse the roles, increasing the number of blocks. Finish the activity and assemble as a group. Read about an emergency event that has occurred in your community. Talk about how following directions in emergencies is similar to this game; some people must be the leaders, and some must be the followers. Identify the leaders and the followers in an emergency. Discuss why following directions during an emergency is important.
- **How to adjust the activity:** Ensure that all children can grasp and build with the selected blocks. Position an adult near children who may have coordination, hearing, or focus challenges to repeat the lead child's directions and guide the follower to listen, think, and do what is directed. Ensure that all children are supported and have a chance to be the leader.
- **Did you meet your goal?** Can children describe what it means to follow directions? Are they able to explain why it is important to follow directions during an emergency?

all aspects that prepare teachers to respond with confidence and knowledge when emergency action is needed. Obtaining formal training in emergency response procedures from credible sources such as certified trainers of the American Heart Association and the American Red Cross is the most important way for teachers to learn to recognize the signs that emergency medical assistance is needed and to be prepared to take appropriate action until emergency help arrives.

Defining First Aid

The care that teachers offer when a child is injured or ill is called first aid. **First aid** refers to the set of actions taken to address injury or illness. First aid has three primary goals:

first aid
the actions taken to address illness or injury

1. To preserve life.
2. To avoid additional injury.
3. To assist with recovery.

Most first aid offered in the early childhood setting involves uncomplicated, commonsense procedures such as cleaning and bandaging a small cut or placing a cold compress on a bump or bruise. These are examples of *basic first aid* that in most cases do not require formal medical assistance. Even so, the child's family should be contacted so that parents can participate in determining whether they will seek additional medical assistance.

Some situations are more complex, requiring additional and advanced actions such as providing CPR or wrapping a body part to immobilize an injured area in case of a broken bone. These are examples of injuries that require *emergency first aid*. If an injury requires emergency first aid, teachers should call for professional medical assistance right away, while providing basic first aid assistance until help arrives. The interventions of trained medical personnel are needed in emergency situations to reduce further injury to the child and to avoid the risk of disability or death.

Understanding Volunteer Protection Laws

To encourage people to help in emergencies, all states and the District of Columbia include protections in their common laws for those who voluntarily provide first aid and assist with rescue efforts. These protections are referred to as the **Good Samaritan doctrine**. The laws protect rescuers from being sued for wrongdoing when they provide emergency help as long as the care is considered reasonable and prudent and the volunteer uses all the resources available at the time (Rosenbaum, Harty, & Sheer, 2008).

Good Samaritan doctrine
laws designed to encourage people to help in emergencies by protecting rescuers from being sued for providing emergency help

For emergency assistance to be covered by the Good Samaritan doctrine:

- The help must be a volunteer act.
- The person receiving the help must not object.
- The actions of the helper must be a good faith effort to provide help.

The Good Samaritan doctrine does not provide protection for rescue acts that are unreasonable, careless, or negligent. In the teaching setting, this means that teachers are expected to provide appropriate first aid to address the child's immediate needs, but that this care is administered only as a substitute until professional emergency medical help can be obtained. Calling for medical assistance and ensuring that the child receives professional care are part of the expectations of teachers under the Good Samaritan doctrine.

Assessing for Injury

The first few minutes after an injury occurs are of crucial importance. For example, brain death begins within four to six minutes after sudden cardiac arrest if air and circulation are not restored (Heller & Zieve, 2011a). Providing effective CPR chest compressions within minutes of cardiac arrest greatly increases the chances of survival (Berg et al., 2010). When accidents happen, teachers need to be ready to evaluate what has happened and take appropriate action quickly.

Sometimes the accident may be observed, but often the teacher will need to conduct a quick review to understand what happened. A great deal of information must be gathered quickly even while preparing to respond (Berg et al., 2010). The following steps guide appropriate response:

Assess the situation. Put on protective gloves while you look for signs of the type of injury that may have occurred. For example:

- Is the child lying under climbing equipment that might suggest a fall? If so, the head or back may be injured and the child should not be moved.
- Is furniture tipped over? If so, was the child hit or cut?
- Could electricity be involved? If so, do not touch the child until the electricity is turned off.
- Are sharp objects such as broken glass present? If so, look for ways to avoid danger while approaching and assisting the child.

Notice the child's behavior. Look for signs of distress. For example:

- Is the child crying or moving? If not, say the child's name and ask, "Are you all right?"

Observe the child's physical appearance. Quickly inspect the child from head to toe, looking for problems or signs of injury. For example:

- Is the child breathing? If not, call for emergency assistance and immediately begin CPR.
- Is the child bleeding profusely? If so, call for emergency assistance and conduct first aid to stop the bleeding.
- Is the child's body position abnormal or distorted? If so, do not move the child. Call for emergency assistance. Keep the child evenly warm and speak calmly to reassure the child.

Table 16-1 provides additional guidance about how a review of the situation can help teachers consider the context of the accident as they determine the types of injuries that may have occurred and begin to put a response plan into action.

The attending teacher stays with the child at all times until emergency medical personnel take over. At that time, the teacher can provide the child's medical information and verbally describe any allergies, medications the child is taking, or health concerns such as diabetes or asthma the child may have. It is appropriate for the teacher to travel to and stay at the emergency medical facility until the child's parent or guardian assumes responsibility.

An assistant teacher should contact the child's parent or guardian as soon as possible. Family child care providers might need to make this call after emergency personnel arrive. The cause of the accident and the first aid and medical care that has been provided should be shared with the family, as well as information about who is providing emergency care and where the child has been transported for medical assistance. Teachers must not attempt to diagnose the situation or offer

TABLE 16-1 ACCIDENT SETTINGS AND POTENTIAL INJURIES

Setting	Types of Injuries
Climbing equipment	• Fall from equipment (head injury, broken bone?)
	• Climbing (pinched fingers?)
Tricycle	• Striking against objects (bumps, bruises?)
	• Falling over in motion (bump to head?)
Outdoor play area	• Trip or fall (skinned knee, bumps, bruises?)
	• Insects (bites or stings?)
	• Children running into others or against equipment (bumps, scrapes?)
	• Excessive heat (heat exhaustion or heatstroke?)
Sandbox	• Sand (foreign object in the eye?)
Workbench	• Hammer, nails (crushed finger, cut or pierced?)
Indoor play	• Striking against objects (bumps and bruises?)
	• Objects falling against child (bumps, bruises, cuts?)
Craft materials	• Exposure to allergens (acute illness or anaphylaxis?)

medical advice to the family. Instead, they should direct the family to the medical provider for professional assistance and follow-up.

In the opening scenario, Jamal was able to recognize quickly that Kevin's wound was the result of being struck by the ball cart and that there was low likelihood of broken bones. By the time he reached Kevin, Jamal had determined that the child could be moved without worry. But even though the bleeding was managed with bandaging, Jamal encouraged the mother to seek medical advice because a head injury was involved.

Using Universal Precautions

Many emergencies involve bleeding injuries that require use of special precautions when providing assistance. Universal precautions are a set of safety measures used when managing bleeding injuries or providing rescue breathing. These steps are designed to prevent the transmission of bloodborne diseases such as human immunodeficiency virus (HIV), hepatitis B virus (HBV), and other bloodborne pathogens (Siegel, Rhinehart, Jackson, Chiarello, & the Healthcare Infection Control Practices Advisory Committee, 2007). Universal precautions help ensure that health care workers and emergency responders are not harmed when they provide first aid assistance. Universal precautions include the following practices:

universal precautions a set of precautions designed to prevent transmission of human immunodeficiency virus (HIV), hepatitis B virus (HBV), and other bloodborne pathogens when providing first aid or health care

- Wear gloves whenever providing care for any injury involving blood or other body fluids containing visible signs of blood.
- Use a one-way mask when offering rescue breathing.
- Watch for sharp objects, electricity, toxic fumes, and other hazards at the site of the accident.
- Use appropriate hand washing when providing medical assistance.
- Dispose of contaminated materials appropriately.

Universal precautions guide practices both during and after emergency help has been offered.

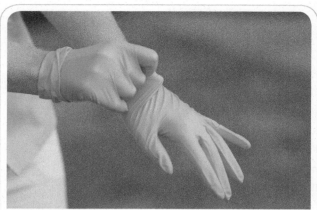

photoniko/Fotolia

Universal precautions include wearing protective gloves when caring for any injury that involves blood or body fluids containing visible signs of blood.

Conducting CPR

The first assessment in case of an injury is to check that the child is breathing. If a child stops breathing, CPR must be administered immediately to ensure a continued flow of air to the brain and the body's vital organs. The most common reasons a child might stop breathing are cardiac arrest due to SIDS, congenital malformations, injuries from motor vehicle accidents, choking, and drowning. First aid treatment for a child who is not breathing follows a sequenced approach called CAB: chest compressions, airway, and breathing/ventilation (Berg et al., 2010).

C = Chest Compressions

Chest compressions help oxygen-rich blood flow and circulate to the body's vital organs. If a child or an infant is unresponsive and not breathing, the American Heart Association (AHA) (Berg et al., 2010) recommends giving 30 chest compressions right away, followed by two breaths (and repeat). If the teacher is not trained in rescue breathing or is unable to do so, the chest compressions should be continued in what is called "hands only" CPR (Berg et al., 2010). Certified instructors will prepare teachers to administer chest compressions using the general process described below.

For a child (Berg et al., 2010):

- Place the child on a hard surface such as the floor. Call out to another teacher or child to call 911.
- Kneel over the child, placing the heel of one hand at the midpoint of the child's breast.
- Keeping the elbows locked, apply 30 downward compressions. Depress the chest hard, about 2 inches, and fast, at a rate of at least 100 compressions per minute.
- After each compression, allow the chest to recoil as the heart fills with blood.

For infants (Berg et al., 2010):

- Lay the baby on a hard surface. Call out to another teacher or child to call 911.
- Position two fingers on the center of the chest just below an imaginary "line" between the two nipples.
- Give 30 downward compressions. Depress the chest hard, about 1½ inches, at a fast rate of 100 compressions per minute.
- After each compression, allow the heart to refill with blood as the chest recoils.

A = Airway

After giving the 30 chest compressions, ensure that the child or infant's airway is open. Lift the child's chin and gently press back on the forehead to tip the child's head back naturally. This lifts the tongue off the throat, opening the airway (Berg et al., 2010; Heller & Zieve, 2011b).

If the child or baby is unconscious, these moves often correct the cause of stopped breathing.

B = Breathing/Ventilation

If breathing does not start when the airway is opened, give two rescue breaths (ventilations).

For a child:

- Keeping the child's chin tilted upward, gently pinch the nose closed to ensure that air is guided into the child's lungs.
- Lay a one-way mask across the child's mouth and give two rescue breaths (Berg et al., 2010). At each breath, the rise in the chest should be visible.

For an infant:

- Place mouth over the baby's nose and mouth. Give two small rescue breaths by offering a puff-breath, or small "mouthful" of air, at a rate of about one breath per second.
- Reposition the baby if needed to ensure that the breaths are effective.

For both children and infants:

- Repeat the 30 compressions and 2 rescue breaths cycle for two minutes. Then if you are alone, call 911.
- Continue the "30 and 2" cycle until emergency help arrives.

If a rescue breath does not go in, check that the airway is sufficiently opened and try again.

If breath still does not go in, the airway may be obstructed and must be cleared. Do not give up! Your efforts may save the child's life.

Clearing the Airway

Choking from obstructions in the airway occurs when a child swallows or aspirates (breathes in) a small object such as food or a toy that gets stuck in the throat. The blockage stops the flow of air, which cuts off oxygen to the brain. First aid is required as soon as possible.

Watch for a child who is:

- Clutching the throat.
- Unable to talk or cough.
- Turning blue—look at skin, lips, nails.
- Unconscious.

Perform emergency actions to clear the airway.

For children (Heller & Zieve, 2011a):

- Stand or kneel behind the child.
- Wrap arms around the child's waist.
- Make a fist with one hand over the other.
- Position the hands just above the navel but below the breastbone.
- Press hard giving quick thrusts inward and upward.
- Continue until the object is dislodged or the child becomes unconscious.
- If the child becomes unconscious, lower the child to the floor, call 911, and begin CPR.
- If the object is visible, try to remove it.

- Continue giving CPR until emergency help arrives.

  For infants (Heller & Zieve, 2011b):

- Sit down. Place the infant facedown along your forearm. Rest your forearm on your thigh. Hold the infant's jaw with your fingers and support the chest with your hand to stabilize the neck. Keep the head lower than the body.
- Using the heel of your hand give five firm thumps on the middle of the back. Check to see if the item has been dislodged.
- If not, "sandwich" the child between both forearms. Roll the child face up on one forearm, keeping the head lower than the body. Place two fingers just below the nipple line on the middle of the breastbone. Give five quick chest compressions, thrusting in one-third to one-half of the depth of the chest.
- Continue giving five back thumps and five chest thrusts until the object is dislodged or emergency personnel arrive.
- If the baby becomes unconscious, administer CPR for two minutes and then call 911.
- If the object blocking the airway is visible, try to remove it.
- Continue giving CPR until emergency help arrives.

Stopping Bleeding

Follow these steps when treating a child who is bleeding:

- Wear vinyl or nonlatex gloves.
- Cover the wound with a sterile gauze pad and apply direct pressure on the wound.
- If possible, lay the child down to address shock and hold the bleeding area higher than the heart to slow blood flow.
- If blood fills the gauze, add more layers of gauze. Do not remove the gauze because this will disturb the natural blood clot that is forming.
- If bleeding is excessive, hold firmly against pressure points. Call for immediate medical help.
- When the bleeding stops, wash the wound with water and cover with a clean bandage.

Seek medical help if the wound is dirty or deep, if you cannot stop the bleeding, if any blood seeps from the ears, or if the child vomits blood (Dowshen, 2013; Heller, Zieve, Black, Slon, & Wang, 2013a). The *Health Hint* provides suggestions about how to ensure that teachers have protective gloves readily available.

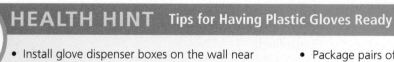

HEALTH HINT   Tips for Having Plastic Gloves Ready

- Install glove dispenser boxes on the wall near the emergency first aid supplies and in the diapering and toileting areas.
- Place a pair of gloves in a plastic bag and carry them in a pocket.
- Package pairs of gloves inside several plastic bags. Tape the bags at various locations around the children's indoor and outdoor spaces where they can be easily seen and readily accessed.
- Include several pairs of gloves in the traveling first aid kit.

Cleaning Blood Spills

Cleaning up blood spills is important to prevent the possibility of transmitting communicable disease. The U.S. Occupational Safety and Health Administration and the *National Health and Safety Performance Standards* (AAP et al., 2011) are good sources of information for managing blood spills at the worksite and in the early childhood setting.

Cleaning Blood Spills Indoors

Wear gloves and other appropriate protection (apron, eye covering) depending on the extent of the blood spill. Do not step on the contaminated area and avoid splashing the spill into eyes, mouth, and nose and onto unprotected skin. Spray the area thoroughly with disinfecting solution (1 tablespoon of bleach to 1 quart of water) and wipe with absorbent paper towels. Repeat a second time. Then wash the area with soap and water and wipe with paper towels. Place soiled paper towels in a leakproof plastic bag, being careful not to touch the outside of the bag. Close the bag securely and discard. Figure 16-4 provides guidance for removing and discarding protective gloves safely. When done, wash hands thoroughly (AAP et al., 2011).

Cleaning Blood Spills Outdoors

Wear appropriate protection and avoid stepping on or splashing the spill. Spray the grass, sand, bark, or sidewalk areas thoroughly with disinfecting solution (mix 2 quarts of bleach with 5 gallons of water). Let stand for 15 minutes and then spray the area thoroughly with a hose to disperse the solution (Purdue University, 2014).

Cleaning Large Blood Spills

Clean large spills using absorbent pellet materials. Allow the pellets to absorb the spill. Then collect and discard them along with other contaminated materials.

Cleaning Upholstery and Carpeting

Spot clean upholstery and carpeting using a disinfectant product designed for fabrics. Let the solution set for 15 minutes (or as directed) and then blot the area dry. Repeat until the spill is no longer visible on the surface (AAP et al., 2011).

FIGURE 16-4 Procedure for Safely Discarding Protective Gloves

1. Grasp the palm of the left-hand glove with the fingers of the right-gloved hand. Pull outward and remove the left-hand glove from the hand. Do not reach inside the opposite glove—let only the dirty surfaces touch each other.
2. Grasp the left-hand glove in a ball inside the palm of the gloved right hand.
3. Use a finger of the left hand to reach inside the wrist of the right-hand glove, and peel the right-hand glove off inside out encasing the dirty surfaces of both gloves.
4. Drop the soiled gloves inside a plastic bag. Seal the bag and discard it in an appropriate location.
5. Wash your hands thoroughly.

Source: Based on *Sequence for Removing Personal Protective Equipment: Gloves*, Centers for Disease Control and Prevention. (2012). Retrieved August 2015, from http://www.cdc.gov/sars/downloads/ppeposter148.pdf.

CHECK YOUR UNDERSTANDING 16.2

Click here to check your understanding of how to respond in emergencies.

Addressing Blood Spill Splatters

Flush eyes thoroughly with clean water. Wash skin with soap and water as soon as possible. If there are cuts or open sores on the skin, wash thoroughly; then contact a medical provider for follow-up (AAP et al., 2011).

ADMINISTERING BASIC FIRST AID CARE

Teachers of young children are likely to be involved in providing basic first aid care for a variety of injuries. In this section, we offer descriptions of familiar injuries and illnesses and provide common approaches to address them.

Falls

Falls are a primary cause of injury in young children. Some falls can cause significant injury, including broken bones or head injuries. If a fall is witnessed or suspected:

- Do not move the child.
- Check to ensure that the airway is open and the child is breathing.
- Notice the height of the fall and the hardness of the surface on which the child landed.
- Seek immediate medical help for any suspected head injury or broken bones.
- Treat minor wounds with basic first aid.
- Inform the family of the fall right away, even if the injury appears minor. This way the family can determine the next step of action and the child can be monitored for any unrecognized injuries (Cronan, 2011).

Head Injury

Any injury to the head could be serious and should be reported to the child's family as soon as possible. A severe head injury can cause bleeding inside the skull, which can result in brain damage or death. Even if the child wants to play again soon after the accident, the child should be kept calm and be monitored closely until the parent arrives and can participate directly in determining whether medical care is needed. Take these care steps:

- Lay the child down, positioning the head higher than the feet.
- Keep the child calm.

Seek immediate medical assistance if the child is unconscious or if any signs of concussion are evident such as drowsiness; nausea and vomiting; slurred speech; disorientation; fluid seeping from nose, ears, and mouth; or headache (Centers for Disease Control and Prevention [CDC], 2013; Heller, Zieve, & Black, 2014).

Asthma

The most common symptoms of asthma attack in children are a wheezing sound when breathing and frequent episodes of coughing or coughing spasms. In some cases, asthma attacks can be acute and life-threatening (CDC, 2014a). Watch for:

In an emergency, first aid is administered until professional medical help can be obtained.

Ryan McVay/Getty Images

- Increasing shortness of breath or wheezing.
- Chest tightness or pain.
- High level of distress.

For children with a known asthma condition, treat according to the child's asthma emergency medical plan using the child's nebulizer. Contact the family to report the child's condition. Seek medical help immediately if the asthma attack is acute and resembles anaphylaxis (Ben-Joseph, 2011; Kaneshiro & Zieve, 2012).

Anaphylactic Shock: Severe Allergic Reaction

Anaphylactic shock is a life-threatening allergic reaction that causes respiratory distress or circulatory collapse. Severe allergic reactions may result from a wide range of causes including allergy to foods or drugs, insect venom (from bites), pollen, latex, and other possibly unknown causes (Dugdale, Henochowicz, & Zieve, 2012). Reaction can occur quickly or a few hours after exposure. Signs of anaphylactic shock include:

- Hives that spread.
- Swelling of the eyes or mouth.
- Difficulty breathing and talking.
- Dizziness or mental confusion.
- Abdominal cramping, nausea, and vomiting.

  Treat anaphylaxis as follows:

- Call 911 immediately.
- Administer epinephrine injection (EpiPen).
- Lay the child down on her or his back.
- Do not offer any food or drink.
- Monitor the child carefully.
- If breathing stops, administer CPR.

Seek medical assistance immediately. Epinephrine treatment is only temporary. A second injection may be needed if signs of anaphylaxis return (Defelice & Stewart, 2011; Dugdale et al., 2012).

A Matter of ETHICS

Sarah and Erin have just attended training on how to use an EpiPen. They have a child in their class who has a known allergic reaction to peanut butter. Sarah is uncomfortable because Erin, her assistant teacher, left the training and was gone for over 30 minutes, missing much of the demonstration and practice. Sarah knows that if she reports this to her director, it will likely disrupt her relationship with Erin. But she is also worried that Erin won't be able to help in case of a child's allergic reaction. What are the issues here, and what course of action would you recommend?

Nosebleeds

Nosebleeds can be quite common in the early childhood setting. Treat them as follows:

- Have the child sit down and lean forward.
- Use a sterile gauze pad to pinch the nose between the thumb and index finger and guide the child to breathe through the mouth.
- Hold this position for 10 minutes or until bleeding stops.

Seek medical help if the nosebleed is the result of an injury to the head or if the bleeding does not stop (Cronan, 2011; Cunah & Shiel, 2014).

Bites

Bites from animals, humans, or spiders are one of the top causes of unintentional injury in young children.

Animal Bites

Teachers should closely supervise children with any animal in the early childhood setting. If injury occurs:

- Apply direct pressure to stop the bleeding if needed.
- Wash the wound for three to five minutes using gentle soap and water.
- Cover the wound with a bandage.

Seek medical help immediately if the bite was caused by an animal with unknown immunization for rabies; if the wound is deep and the skin is torn; if the injuries are on the head, face, or hands; or if there is sign of infection (Green, 2014).

Human Bites

The human mouth can contain dangerous bacteria and viruses that present a high risk for infection. Human bites can also transmit bloodborne pathogens. If the bite breaks the skin:

- Apply direct pressure to the wound, using a sterile gauze pad, until the bleeding stops.
- Wash the bite area with soap and water for three to five minutes.
- Apply a clean bandage.

Contact the child's family and recommend that the family seek medical advice if the bite is on the face, neck, hands, or feet (Heller & Zieve, 2012b).

Spider Bites

Usually spider bites are just an annoyance, but brown recluse (violin shape on back) and black widow (red hourglass shape on back) spider bites can be dangerous. If possible, capture or try to identify the spider. To treat a spider bite:

- Clean the bite area with soap and water.
- Apply a cool compress.
- Watch for signs of chills, fever, nausea, or abdominal pain, which may indicate a serious spider bite reaction.

Seek immediate medical assistance if the bite is known to be from a brown recluse or black widow spider or if signs of a serious bite are observed (Ben-Joseph, 2010; Heller & Zieve, 2014a).

Bruises and Bumps

Good comfort care is often the best first aid for bruises and bumps.

- Raise the injured area.
- Wrap a cold pack in cloth; hold it against the bruised area. Do not place the cold pack directly against the skin because this may cause damage by freezing.
- Cover the bruise with a bandage only if the skin is broken and bleeding.

Seek medical assistance if the bruised area is extensive or if there is sign of infection (Gavin, 2014; Vorvick & Zieve, 2013).

Zulufoto/Shutterstock

A cool cloth and comfort care may be the best first aid for bumps and bruises.

Burns

Burns are classified according to the severity of the wound (Heller & Zieve, 2012a):

- **First-degree burn:** The skin looks red.
- **Second-degree burn:** The skin is red, blotchy, and blistered.
- **Third-degree burn:** The skin is charred; it may be black or ash white.

What to do:

- Cool the burned area under cool running water for five minutes.
- Cover with a light dry sterile gauze bandage.
- Do not use ice, apply oils or ointment, or pop any blisters.
- Monitor breathing and treat for shock as needed.

Seek medical assistance for any burn on an infant. For toddlers and older children, seek medical help if the burned area is larger than 3 inches in diameter or if the burn is on the hands, feet, face, groin, or buttocks; if the burn is over a major joint; or if signs of infection appear (National Institute of General Medicine Sciences, 2012). Notify the child's family as soon as possible.

Drowning

Call for emergency assistance and begin these steps of first aid as soon as possible:

- Remove the child from the water without endangering yourself.
- Check for breathing and heartbeat. Begin CPR and rescue breathing as soon as possible.
- Keep the child warm and treat for hypothermia and shock.

Don't give up. Some children have been successfully resuscitated after being in cold water for up to an hour. Seek medical help right away. Even if resuscitation revives the child, medical help is needed to ensure that infection, respiratory problems, or other complications do not occur.

Electrical Shock

If a child is severely shocked by electricity:

- Do *not* touch the child. Assess the situation.
- If possible, turn off the electricity or move the electrical source away from the child and yourself using a nonconductive product such as cardboard or plastic.
- Call 911 for emergency assistance if the electrical source is a high-voltage wire or if you cannot turn off the electrical source.
- If the child is no longer touching the electrical source, observe the child for heartbeat and breathing. Administer CPR and rescue breathing.
- Treat for shock: Lay the child down and elevate the child's legs.

Call 911 for emergency assistance and continue to monitor the child (Heller & Zieve, 2014b).

Foreign Objects

The goal of first aid for foreign objects in the eyes and nose is to remove any object carefully but only if this can be done without causing harm.

Pearson Education

CLASSROOM CONNECTION

Watch this video on how to teach children to stay away from things that can cause burns and what to do if a child gets a burn. What are the main messages that teachers should instill in children about fire?

To remove a foreign object from an eye:

- Wash hands carefully.
- Have the child sit down and look upward.
- Lift the eyelid away from the eye and look for the object.
- If the object is visible, try gently flushing the eye with water to wash it out.
- *Do not* rub the eye or try to remove items that are lodged in the eyeball.

Seek medical assistance if the object is not removed through tears, if the object is large, or if vision is impaired (Lusby, Zieve, & Black, 2013).

To remove a foreign object from the nose:

- Determine which nostril holds the foreign object.
- Gently pinch in the other (unobstructed) nostril and have the child blow the nose gently to dislodge the object.
- Do not probe the nose—this may move the object in deeper.

Seek medical assistance if these steps do not dislodge the object (Lusby et al., 2013).

Tooth Injury

WHAT IF . . .

you were administering first aid for a child's injury, when a parent arrived and told you that you were doing something wrong? You are trained in first aid and know your approach is appropriate. How would you respond to the concerned parent?

If a child's baby tooth is injured, apply pressure to stop bleeding and offer comfort. Call for medical guidance. If a child's permanent tooth is knocked out, careful treatment can sometimes restore it.

- Find the tooth and gently rinse it in a bowl of water; do not rub or scrape it.
- Place the tooth in the tooth socket in the child's mouth; cover with gauze and hold in place or have the child bite down gently on the gauze. If the tooth cannot be replaced in the socket, place it in a cup of whole milk and immediately contact a dentist for guidance (Hirsch, 2014).

Heat Exhaustion

Heat exhaustion is a moderate heat-related illness. It may occur due to highly active play on very warm days. Dehydration may be a cause. Signs of heat exhaustion include dizziness, nausea, rapid heartbeat, fast shallow breathing, and cramps. To address heat exhaustion:

- Lay the child down in a shady area and remove extra clothing.
- Sponge or spray the child's skin with cool water and offer the child cool water to drink.

Seek medical assistance if symptoms increase (CDC, 2014b, 2012).

Heatstroke

Heatstroke is a severe heat-related illness. Without aid, heat stroke can lead to death. Signs of heatstroke include elevated body temperature (above 104°F [40°C]), hot dry skin, rapid heartbeat, confusion, dizziness, fainting, or coma. To address heatstroke:

- Move the child to a cool and shady place.
- Call 911 for emergency medical assistance.

- Lay child down and remove extra clothing.
- Cover child with moist cloth or spray the child with cool water.
- Fan the child to help with cooling.

Seek medical assistance immediately (CDC, 2014b, 2012).

Seizure

Seizures are the result of abnormal activity in the brain. The goal of first aid is to prevent the child from being hurt during a seizure. Signs include showing temporary confusion or losing consciousness; uncontrollably jerking arms, legs, and head; and staring straight ahead and showing no signs of recognition.

If a seizure occurs:

- Protect the child from harm: Ease the child down to the floor. Clear the area around the child. Gently roll the child onto one side and place something soft under the child's head.
- Do not put anything in the child's mouth or restrain the child.
- Let the seizure take its course.
- Call the child's family immediately to report the seizure event.

Seek immediate medical help if the seizure lasts more than five minutes or the child is slow to improve or has trouble breathing (Kaneshiro, Zieve, & Ogilvie, 2014; Filloux & Goodman, 2010).

Shock

Shock is often associated with injury but can also occur with heatstroke, allergic reactions, infections, poisoning, or other causes. Shock is a sign that the body is struggling. Watch for cool and clammy skin, a weak but rapid pulse, faintness, or confusion. To care for shock:

- Lay the child down with feet elevated, if this does not contribute to injury.
- Check for an open airway, regular breathing, and circulation.
- Keep the child calm, comfortable, and warm.
- Do not give the child anything to eat or drink.
- Provide first aid for any injuries.

Seek medical assistance if these actions do not resolve the concern or if shock is associated with significant injury (Heller & Zieve, 2014b).

CHECK YOUR UNDERSTANDING 16.3

Click here to check your understanding of common approaches to take to address familiar injuries and illnesses.

TAKING ACTION IN DISASTERS

Whether disaster strikes suddenly or through a series of events, teachers must be ready to take decisive steps to ensure children's safety. These include the following:

- Remain calm.
- Review the facility for immediate danger and assemble children is a safe area.
- Provide first aid for any injury.
- Listen to the radio for reports and guidance.
- Decide whether to shelter-in-place, lockdown, or evacuate.
- Take action.

Teachers should follow their emergency management plan while remaining alert to the directions of emergency personnel. Teachers must make informed decisions based on the availability of support resources and opportunities to increase children's safety.

Sheltering-in-Place

Taking shelter involves staying inside the facility as required by the threat of harm. For tornadoes, take shelter in the lowest area in the building, such as a basement or an interior room or hallway. For chemical spills or airborne hazards, cover doors, windows, and any air vents with plastic and seal them shut with duct tape (CDC, 2006; Federal Emergency Management Agency [FEMA] 2013a). When taking shelter, teachers should:

- Assemble children and visitors in the identified shelter space as quickly as possible.
- Take the first aid kit and emergency food and water.
- Lock windows and exterior doors to seal them. Cover air vents with plastic if necessary.
- Engage children in calm and quiet games: reading, playing with manipulative toys.
- Watch TV, check the Internet news, or listen to the radio for information.
- Stay in shelter until word is received that it is safe to leave.

Usually, the need to shelter-in-place exists for only a few hours. If it is necessary to take shelter for a longer period of time, use the emergency supplies to care for and comfort children. The *Nutrition Note* provides guidance for using stored food and water.

Implementing Lockdown

Lockdown refers to taking shelter within the classroom or children's facility to avoid harm when there is a danger from entry of an intruder, a shooting, or a hostage situation, when evacuation is not possible If lockdown is needed:

NUTRITION NOTE   Using Emergency Food and Water

- Take an inventory of the kinds and quantity of food you have.
- Throw away any foods that are spoiled and cans that are swollen or corroded.
- Create a plan to portion out the foods. Aim to provide fully balanced meals.
- Use any perishable foods in the refrigerator, freezer, and cupboards first.
- Open stored foods carefully. Store leftover food in resealable bags or containers.
- Canned food can be eaten right out of the can (no heating is required).

- Water in the hot water heater can be used as needed. Make sure the gas or electric power is turned off. Turn off the water intake valve at the water heater tank. Open the drain at the bottom of the water heater. Place a container below it to collect the water. Turn on a hot water faucet somewhere in the building. This will start the water flowing from the water heater drain.
- If needed, boil stream, pond, spring, or rainwater for one full minute and let cool or treat with 1/8 teaspoon of newly opened unscented household bleach (that contains 6.0% sodium hypochlorite). Stir and let stand for 30 minutes. The water should smell slightly of bleach. If it doesn't, repeat the process.

Source: Based on *Food and Water in an Emergency* (FEMA 447; A5055), August 2004, Jessup, MD: FEMA and Washington, DC: American Red Cross. Retrieved August 2015, from http://www.fema.gov/pdf/library/f&web.pdf.

- Respond to the program's code word or other way of signaling the need for lockdown.
- Assemble children in an interior room or corner of the children's classroom.
- Create a protective barrier behind a shelf or table turned on its side.
- If possible, lock doors and windows; close blinds and turn off lights.
- Stay quiet and still.
- Call 911 to report what was seen or heard.
- Count children to make sure all are present.
- Stay in lockdown until informed that it is "all clear" by emergency personnel.

Teachers may need to shelter with children for several hours. Locating bottled water and small comfort toys in the designated space can support teachers and children until the lockdown is lifted (American Red Cross, 2012a). Gathering courage to remain calm is essential.

Evacuating and Relocating

Evacuation requires that children be assembled and moved safely to a previously identified location (IEMSC, 2006). Follow the emergency management plan unless guided otherwise by emergency personnel. If evacuation is needed (FEMA, 2013a):

- Gather children and exit the classroom safely to the designated assembly location.
- Count to ensure that all children and staff are present. Assign each child to an adult.
- If time permits, place a sticker label on each child's coat with the child's name, family name, address, and phone number.
- Take emergency kit, child and staff emergency contact records, and supplies.
- Post a sign identifying where you are going.
- Travel to the emergency evacuation spot along a predetermined route.
- Make contact with emergency personnel if possible and follow their directions.
- Listen to the radio for instructions as appropriate.

Because disaster emergencies are unpredictable, the timing for emergency assistance is hard to anticipate. Teachers may find that their informed care and management makes the difference between life and death for the children and themselves. Preparation, practice, and courage are the resources that teachers carry with them to make a positive impact in such significant situations.

Responding to Natural Disasters

Disasters can be caused by a wide range of natural causes, including tornadoes, hurricanes, earthquakes, storms, floods, and fires. The plan for response is unique to each situation.

Tornadoes

Weather radar warning systems can be installed in facilities whose area has the potential for tornadoes. Teachers remain aware by listening for storm watch warnings on the radio and modifying activities in case safety actions are needed

(FEMA, 2013b; IEMSC, 2006). If a tornado warning is announced, take the following action as recommended:

- Move children to shelter in an underground space, an interior room, or a hallway away from windows.
- Take cover under tables or desks.
- If a mobile home is used for family child care, leave and take shelter in a safe location.
- Take a cell phone or cordless phone.
- Remain in the shelter until the warning has ended.

Hurricanes

Teachers remain alert for hurricane warnings on storm watch systems on the radio, TV, or Internet. If enough time is available, cancel school in advance or try to return children to their families. If not, follow these precautions (FEMA, 2013b):

- Close windows and secure the facility as much as possible.
- Turn off propane tanks and unplug unneeded appliances.
- Gather water containers and emergency supplies at the ready.
- Take cover in an interior room or hallway away from windows.
- Lay down on the floor under a table or other sturdy furniture.
- Remain indoors until the hurricane has passed over.
- Evacuate as directed by emergency personnel.

Earthquakes

Earthquakes usually occur without warning. Teachers and children must be prepared to take cover immediately (FEMA, 2013b).

- If indoors, drop to the ground and take cover against an interior wall or under tables or desks. Hold on until shaking stops.
- After shaking stops, evacuate if the facility is unsafe. Be aware that aftershocks may occur.
- If outside when the earthquake occurs, move to an open area away from walls, windows, or electric wires.

Storms

Check emergency broadcasts for storm warnings and travel advisories. Close the children's program if recommended. Return children to families if time allows. If the children must remain at the school or care facility (FEMA, 2013b):

- Gather emergency supplies if a storm warning is issued.
- Move to an interior space away from windows if high winds are a concern.
- Stay in shelter until the storm is passed.
- Evacuate if needed.

Floods

Remain aware of flood warnings. Close the facility and return children to families if time allows. Otherwise (FEMA, 2012b):

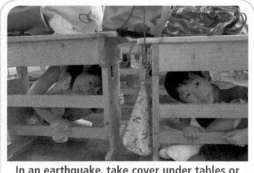

In an earthquake, take cover under tables or desks and hold on until shaking stops.

Peter Essick/Aurora Photos/Alamy

- If there is time, secure the facility: Forward electronic records to a recipient outside the area, move equipment to a higher location, and turn off gas and utilities.
- Evacuate from the facility if there is any chance of flooding or flash flooding.

Wildfires and Forest Fires

Stay aware of active fires in the area. Follow the guidance of emergency management personnel regarding closure or evacuation. Close the facility and return children to families if time allows. If a fire approaches near the children's setting (FEMA, 2013b):

- Gather all children inside.
- Close doors and windows.
- Turn off gas and electricity.
- Position sprinklers to spray water against the building and roof.
- Evacuate as soon as possible.

Responding to Technological Hazards

Technological hazards that are a danger to children's settings include disruption of utilities, chemical spills or explosions involving toxic materials, and threats to personal safety.

Disruption of Utilities

The children's program should be closed if water, electricity, heat, or the ability to communicate by telephone are disrupted for more than a short time. When utility disruption occurs without warning:

- Gather children in a secure location that has sufficient light and heat.
- Help children feel secure and comfortable.
- Contact families by cell phone or wireless e-mail to pick up children as needed.

Chemical Spills and Explosions of Hazardous Materials

Assess the situation to determine a plan for shelter and then follow these steps (CDC, 2006; IEMSC, 2006):

- Do not turn any electrical switches on or off.
- Evacuate immediately, moving upwind from the hazard if it is safe to do so.
- Otherwise, shelter-in-place: Assemble children in an interior room and cover windows, doors, and air vents.
- Use cell phones or wireless e-mail to communicate with emergency personnel.
- Stay in the shelter until advised by emergency personnel that it is safe to leave.

Attacks and Threats to Personal Safety

Attacks and threats usually occur without warning. Teachers need to be prepared to take appropriate and responsive actions such as:

- *Explosions:* Take cover from falling debris. Evacuate quickly and calmly.

Pearson Education

CLASSROOM CONNECTION

Watch this video on using a fire extinguisher. Notice the way the firefighter moves the fire extinguisher in a sweeping motion at the base of the fire. When would it be logical for a teacher to use a fire extinguisher to fight a fire while ensuring that the children are being evacuated from the facility?

Sheri Armstrong/Shutterstock

Nearby industrial activities can introduce chemical or explosive hazards.

- *Fire:* Stay low. Get out and stay out. If clothes catch on fire, stop-drop-roll and cover eyes with hands.
- *Missing child or kidnapping:* Call 911 immediately to report a missing child. Provide information about when and where the child was last seen and what the child was wearing. Follow the guidance of emergency personnel.
- *Bomb threat:* Report bomb threats to emergency personnel immediately. Provide details about the threat. Evacuate quickly and calmly.
- *Person with firearms:* Call 911. Implement lockdown procedures. Stay in lockdown until emergency personnel direct that it is safe and lockdown has ended.

Addressing Disease Emergencies

Health emergencies include the threat of widespread communicable disease that challenges the ability of public health organizations to administer aid to victims and to stop the spread of disease. Some health emergencies, including pandemic flu and illness due to viruses such as Ebola, may unfold gradually as health professionals recognize the outbreak and monitor the spread of disease across the world. Other health emergencies are discovered when unusual numbers of people are suddenly struck with acute illness, as may occur with severe acute respiratory syndrome (SARS). Although pandemic disease disasters are rare, teachers must pay special attention to taking steps such as sanitizing the environment, teaching children ways to reduce the spread of disease, and monitoring children's health. Teachers themselves are threatened with contracting disease during health emergencies and must take precautions such as obtaining special immunizations. Teachers remain aware of diseases under emergency watch and are prepared to (FEMA, 2014):

- Follow the guidance of medical personnel to reduce the exchange and spread of disease.
- Communicate closely with families about symptoms of disease.
- Report identified cases as directed.
- Close the children's program as directed by community health personnel.

Reflecting on and Evaluating Emergency Response

After the trauma and drama of the emergency has passed, teachers continue to have responsibilities related to management of the event. It is common for teachers to be asked to complete an injury or incident report. The report is a summary of what happened, when it happened, and what emergency response steps were taken during the event. It is also an analysis of whether the emergency management plan served as a support for effective action. Such information is used to reflect on what worked and what changes could be made to guide future program emergency management planning. Disaster emergency response is also evaluated at the federal and policy levels. For example, the *Progressive Programs & Practices* feature describes how lessons learned from Hurricane Katrina raised awareness of the need for emergency preparedness planning in early childhood settings, promoted the development of resources for teachers, and influenced federal policies.

Supporting Children After Emergencies

After traumatic events, children may need to regain their confidence that things will be "all right again." Teachers are important resources for helping children and

PROGRESSIVE PROGRAMS & PRACTICES

Lessons Learned from Hurricane Katrina

By Cathy Grace, Director (Retired), The Early Childhood Institute, Mississippi State University (MSU)

The Early Childhood Institute (ECI) is a unit of the College of Education at Mississippi State University. The institute was established in 1999 by Cathy Grace, Ed.D., to provide training, technical assistance, and applied research for improved quality and accessibility of early care and education across Mississippi. The institute serves communities statewide through programs that focus on improving the quality of early childhood education, providing professional development for early childhood professionals, and engaging the community in supporting young children.

What Challenge Did You Face?

After Hurricane Katrina hit the Mississippi Gulf Coast in 2005, close to 90% of the early care and education programs were inoperable. At the request of Chevron and state government agencies, ECI spearheaded an early care and education program recovery effort like none ever attempted in the country.

How Did You Meet the Challenge? What Was the Institute's Role?

Given the degree of community devastation in the coastal communities and extending 200 miles northward, ECI staff went to each licensed early care and education center and assessed its operational condition. The information gathered was transformed via spatial mapping to communicate to government agencies and potential funders the degree of need that existed. Working with Chevron, Save the Children, the MSU Extension Service, and a small foundation based in South Mississippi, ECI enlisted the support of numerous foundations, donors, and businesses to provide funds and other resources to reconstruct and refurnish over 200 programs and conduct training for hundreds of staff members.

The work, which lasted over two years, moved from repairing and equipping the buildings to providing support to the adult staff members and children suffering from post-traumatic stress syndrome as a result of hurricane Katrina. Through this process, national awareness was raised with regard to the failure of federal agencies to address early care and education programs in emergency planning at the state and local level, to provide mental health counseling to small children and their families, and to provide simple and accessible procedures so that program owners could file claims for disaster relief funding.

Although the repair to the facilities has been completed, the emotional stress and trauma is still present for some. Recovery may take many more years as residents work to heal fully. Some early care and education teachers on the Gulf Coast lost their homes and, in some cases, family members. This created challenges as to how to support the mental health of those who had suffered great loss but had no time to grieve and recover.

VStock/Alamy

In emergency situations such as the one Katrina created, early care and education teachers should be considered as first responders and afforded the necessary training and support. When communities are in disarray and families are in the midst of attempting to secure financial assistance and social services, individuals charged with the care of young children should be supported and given first priority for their own needs being met so that they can meet the needs of children and families in trauma. To address this, ECI contracted with national experts to provide mental health assistance to teachers in early care and education facilities. The support extended to classroom strategies for teachers to use with preschoolers to help the children heal and move forward.

Classroom teachers, depending on the age of children they teach, can do the following to help children cope with unexpected life events:

- Provide problem-solving activities as part of daily instruction.
- Read books that highlight how children, when faced with a problem, determined solutions and resolved the issue.
- Encourage the children to talk to their parents about developing an escape plan in the event of a fire or natural disaster.
- Invite emergency personnel to the classroom so that the children can meet them and better understand their jobs.
- Practice emergency drills in a calm and controlled manner so that the children will gain confidence and knowledge of what to do in the event of an emergency.

What Was the Outcome?

As a result of the work, by March 2006, 251 centers out of a total of 291 were operational in new or renovated facilities and had materials of a higher quality than before Hurricane Katrina. A partnership with the National Association of Child Care Resource and Referral Agencies resulted in the development of a resource book for early care and education programs that is used across the country to support emergency planning in all types of early childhood programs. Approximately 100 playgrounds were provided to early care programs on the coast, and training materials were developed that supported staff in using the newly purchased materials. Changes in federal policies regarding emergency preparedness for children in out-of-home settings have occurred, but further revisions are needed to ensure that children and families who are displaced receive the services to which they are entitled. The original reporting of the physical condition of the program facilities and use of spatial mapping and color coding has been replicated in other natural disasters after facility assessments were conducted.

WHAT IF . . .

you had managed an emergency in your classroom effectively, like Jamal in the opening scenario. How would you tell the other families about the event now that it is over? Do you think the families will blame you for "allowing" the accident to happen? Explain.

families cope with their feelings of loss so that they can reconstruct a positive vision of the future. Strategies to help after emergency events include the approaches listed below.

Being a Confident Role Model

Children are reassured when they observe their teachers managing situations calmly and positively and showing appropriate optimism (American Red Cross, 2012b; CDC, 2014c). This is demonstrated by moving with confidence rather than appearing disorganized.

Returning to Familiar Routines

Children may feel hopeless when routines are disrupted; they may think that no one is in control. Returning to familiar routines as quickly as possible is one way to begin the process of healing (American Red Cross, 2012b; CDC, 2014c). Once children are surrounded by their familiar world, they are better able to work through the stresses of the unusual events, helping them regain a sense of safety and well-being.

Acknowledging Children's Feelings

After a difficult experience, a child might wonder: *Can it happen again? Could someone I love be hurt? Could I be left alone?* (FEMA, 2010). These concerns need to be validated and addressed with brief and correct information. Teachers should not avoid talking about the event. It is okay to say, "That was scary, wasn't it?" At the same time, teachers must not use frightening descriptions when talking about the emergency with the children and with one another or when talking on the phone in the presence of children.

Focusing on the Positive Actions That Were Taken

Teachers should help the child change from thinking from the difficult details of the emergency to the actions children, teachers, and others performed to address the emergency situation. For example, teachers might say, "I'm glad we had our bandages ready." or "Wasn't it good that we knew to move up the hill to the community center until the moms and dads could come?" This addresses feelings of powerlessness by conveying the positive message that children and teachers are capable of taking appropriate actions in difficult events (International Save the Children Alliance, 2006).

Addressing Tragedies

If the emergency had a tragic outcome such as the death of a playmate or teacher, everyone may need the opportunity to process feelings of loss. One approach is to invite families to join their child while the teacher explains in simple terms what happened. Describing how much the child or teacher was loved and talking about how the group will miss that person offers the opportunity for children and teachers to tell their stories of love and loss.

Turning sad thoughts to productive actions and expressions is a positive next step. Decorating a special remembrance poster with drawings or planting a special tree "for Teacher Karla" are options that allow children to express their feelings through action.

Planting a tree empowers children and helps them look to the future.

Offering Empowering Activities

Children are often able to cope better when they feel the sense of being prepared (FEMA, 2010). One approach is to engage children in appropriate emergency response preparation. For example, teachers and children could review together the contents of the first aid kit and make a shopping list of items needed to replenish it. Helping to restore the outdoor play area by planting a tree helps children engage in reconstruction and builds hope for the future. Activities such as these allow children to experience the power of planning together.

Continuing to Monitor the Effects on Children

Each child copes with extraordinary events in unique and personal ways. Some children may be outward in their expression of worry or sadness, whereas others may seem uninterested and unaffected by the events. Children need many opportunities to express their concerns safely. This support should be provided over a long period of time because a child may express worry many weeks after the event. Tips for helping children cope after distressing situations are provided in Figure 16-5. If the worries interrupt the child's daily behavior, a referral for special counseling support may be needed (CDC, 2014c; FEMA, 2010).

FIGURE 16-5 Tips for Helping Children Cope After Disasters

❑ Protect children from graphic images—limit television and keep from talking about the event when children can hear.
❑ Offer reassurance—let children know that everyone is working to keep them safe.
❑ Provide children extra time and attention—be available, accessible, and close.
❑ Model positive coping—explain your feelings as appropriate and help children recognize how you are managing your emotions.
❑ Reestablish normal routines and activities—surround the child with familiar activity.
❑ Pay attention to what children say—learn what they are worried about.
❑ Find ways for children to engage in helpful action—have them draw pictures, or send cards or books to share with others.
❑ Recognize different responses—children do not experience events in the same way.
❑ Watch for changes that might signal emotional stress—seek professional counseling for the child, if needed.

Source: Based on *Emergency Preparedness and Response: Coping with Disaster or Traumatic Events*, Centers for Disease Control and Prevention. (2014). Retrieved August 2015, from http://emergency.cdc.gov/mentalhealth/.

CHECK YOUR UNDERSTANDING 16.4

Click here to check your understanding of the steps to take to ensure children's safety in case of disaster.

Recognizing That Teachers Need Support Too

Teachers, like parents, carry the dual responsibilities of emergency responder and care provider for children, which can be extremely stressful. Some teachers may feel responsible for injuries, thinking they should have protected the children in some way, or they may wonder if they made the right decisions during an emergency situation (CDC, 2012c). Unsettling events may cause teachers to feel unsafe in the environment. It is important for teachers to be aware of these concerns and access needed supports to help resolve their feelings and regain their sense of personal confidence and well-being (Government Services Agency, Child Care Division, 2011).

SUMMARY

- Developing an emergency management plan, assembling emergency supplies, and obtaining training from credible sources prepare teachers to take effective action when injuries or emergencies occur.
- Teachers use their emergency training to respond confidently in emergency situations by conducting CPR chest compressions, providing rescue breathing, or stopping blood flow until emergency medical assistance is obtained.
- Prepared teachers are also equipped to care for a variety of small injuries using basic first aid approaches and communicating with families when injuries occur.
- If disaster strikes, prepared teachers care for and lead children to safety and support children in coping and regaining hope for the future.

Chapter Quiz

 Click here to check your understanding of Chapter 16, Managing Emergencies.

Discussion Starters

1. Think about a children's classroom you have observed. Describe the setting and propose an emergency management plan for the classroom. Discuss some of the supports available for the classroom and identify challenges.
2. Consider a rural and urban community in your state. Identify and compare some of the similarities and differences in challenges that teachers in those areas may face in accessing emergency assistance.
3. Imagine that you manage a small child care program in a rural area. You know that first aid training is important, but you work every weekday and no training is available in your small town. What other options for training can you identify?
4. Select an age group—infants, toddlers, preschoolers, or school-age children—and develop activities for teaching the children the appropriate emergency response for different disaster events.

Practice Points

1. Create a list of emergency supplies needed to support a class group of 18 children and 2 adults for three days. Use the Selected Websites as resources to guide your planning. Draft a budget for the needed supplies. Explain how the supplies can be assembled and stored in readiness for emergency evacuation.

2. Interview a teacher in a family child care home setting to learn about how she will manage an injury emergency if she is the only adult caring for the children.

3. Access information from credible sources to create a basic first aid poster for common injuries and illnesses in early childhood settings.

4. Go to the Federal Emergency Management Agency (FEMA) website to learn about disaster emergencies that have been recorded for your area. How will you use this information to prepare yourself and the children in your class for such emergencies?

Selected Websites

American Academy of Pediatrics

American Red Cross

Federal Emergency Management Agency

Mayo Clinic, First Aid Information

National Oceanic and Atmospheric Administration's National Weather Service

National Resource Center for Health and Safety in Child Care and Early Education

Key Terms

disaster

emergency

evacuation

first aid

Good Samaritan doctrine

lockdown

shelter-in-place

universal precautions

REFERENCES

Chapter 1

Alemango, S., Niles, S., Shafer-King, P., & Miller, W. (2008). Promoting health and preventing injury among preschool children: The role of parenting stress. *Early Childhood Research & Practice, 10*(2).

Allard, P., & Greene, J. (2011). *Children on the outside: Voicing the pain and human costs of parental incarceration. Justice strategies.* Retrieved March 2015, from http://www.justicestrategies.org/sites/default/files/publications/JS-COIP-1-13-11.pdf

American Academy of Pediatrics, American Public Health Association, National Resource Center for Health and Safety in Child Care and Early Education. (2011). *Caring for our children: National health and safety performance standards; Guidelines for early care and education programs* (3rd ed.). Elk Grove Village, IL: American Academy of Pediatrics; Washington, DC: American Public Health Association. Also available at http://nrckids.org

American Academy of Pediatrics. (2007, April). *AAP: Healthy Child Care America: Health and Safety E-news for caregivers and teachers.* Retrieved April 2015, from http://www.healthychildcare.org/ENewsApr07.html#habits

American Academy of Pediatrics. *Healthy Child Care America.* Retrieved April 2015, from http://www.healthychildcare.org/about.html#1

American Association for Health Education. (2007). Health Education Standards.

American Psychological Association. (2012). *Changing diet and exercise for kids.* Retrieved April 2015, from http://www.apa.org/topics/children/healthy-eating.aspx#

Bloom, B., Cohen, R. A., & Freeman, G. (2011). Summary health statistics for U.S. children: National Health Interview Survey, 2010. National Center for Health Statistics. *Vital Health Stat, 10*(250).

Bronfenbrenner, U. 1979. *The ecology of human development: Experiments by nature and design.* Cambridge, MA: Harvard University Press. ISBN 0-674-22457-4

Center on the Developing Child at Harvard University. (2007). *A science-based framework for early childhood policy: Using evidence to improve outcomes in learning, behavior, and health for vulnerable children.* http://www.developingchild.harvard.edu

Centers for Disease Control and Prevention. (2014). Childhood Obesity Facts. *Prevalence of Childhood Obesity in the United States, 2011–2012.* Retrieved April 2015 from http://www.cdc.gov/obesity/data/childhood.html

Centers for Disease Control and Prevention. (August 2013). Vital Signs: Obesity Among Low-Income, Preschool-Aged Children—United States, 2008–2011. *Morbidity and Mortality Weekly report. 62*(31), 629-634.

Coleman-Jensen, A., Gregory, C., & Singh, A. (2014). *Household Food Security in the United States in 2013,* ERR-173, U.S. Department of Agriculture, Economic Research Service. http://www.ers.usda.gov/publications/err-economic-research-report/err173.aspx

Copple, C., & Bredekamp, S. eds. (2009). *Developmentally Appropriate Practice in Early Childhood Programs Serving Children From Birth Through Age 8* (3rd ed.). National Association for the Education of Young Children.

Council on Communications and Media. (2011). Children, adolescents, obesity, and the media. *Pediatrics, 128*(1), 201–208.

Dolinoy, D. C., Das, R., Weidman, J. R., & Jirtle, R. L. (2007). Metastable epialleles, imprinting, and the fetal origins of adult diseases. *Pediatric Research, 61*(5 Pt 2), 30R–37R.

Douglas-Hall, A., & Chau, M. (2008). *Basic facts about low-income children birth to age 6.* New York: National Center for Children in Poverty, Mailman School of Public Health, Columbia University. Retrieved April 2015 from http://www.nccp.org/publications/pdf/download_215.pdf

Faulk, C., & Dolinoy, D. C. (2011). Timing is everything: The when and how of environmentally induced changes in the epigenome of animals. *Epigenetics, 6*(7), 791–797.

Federal Interagency Forum on Child and Family Statistics, *America's children: Key national indicators of wellbeing, 2011; Immunizations.* Retrieved December 2012, from http://www.childstats.gov/pubs/pubs.asp?PlacementID=2&SlpgID=22

Federal Interagency Forum on Child and Family Statistics. *America's children: key national indicators of wellbeing, 2012; Demographic background.* Retrieved July 2015, from http://www.childstats.gov/pdf/ac2012/ac_12.pdf

Federal Interagency Forum on Child and Family Statistics. *America's children: Key national indicators of wellbeing, 2013.* Retrieved March 2015, from http://www.childstats.gov/pdf/ac2013/ac_13.pdf

Federal Interagency Forum on Child and Family Statistics. *America's children: Key national indicators of wellbeing, 2014.* Retrieved March 2015, from http://www.childstats.gov/pdf/ac2014/ac_14.pdf

Food Research and Action Center (FRAC). (April 2015). *How Hungry is America? FRAC's National, State and Local Index of Food Hardship.* Available at http://www.frac.org

Fox, S. E., Levitt, P., & Nelson, C.A. (January/February 2010). How the timing and quality of early experiences influence the development of brain architecture. *Child Development.* Volume 81, Issue 1, pages 28–40. Society for Research in Child Development. Retrieved March 2015 from http://www.ncbi.nlm.nih.gov/pubmed/20331653

Glaze, L. E., & Maruschak, L. M. (2010). Parents in Prison and Their Minor Children. *Bureau of Justice Report.* Retrieved March 2015, from http://www.bjs.gov/content/pub/pdf/pptmc.pdf

Hawley, T. (2000). *Starting smart: How early experiences influence brain development.* Ounce of Prevention Fund and ZERO TO THREE. Retrieved July 2015, from www.theounce.org/pubs/Starting_Smart.pdf?v=1

Howes, C., Burchinal, M., Pianta, R., Bryant, D., Early, D., Clifford, R., & Barbarin, O. (2008). Ready to learn? Children's pre-academic achievement in pre-kindergarten programs. *Early Childhood Research Quarterly, 23*(3), 27–50.

Let's Move. (2012). Retrieved April 2015, from http://www.letsmove.gov/

Massachusetts Institute of Technology. (2006). Researchers provide first evidence for learning mechanism in brain. *ScienceDaily.* Retrieved April 2015, from http://www.sciencedaily.com/releases/2006/08/060824222608.htm

National Academy of Medicine. (2015). Background Information: Dietary Reference Intakes Tables and Applications. National Academies of Sciences. Retrieved April 2015 from http://www.iom.edu/Activities/Nutrition/SummaryDRIs/DRI-Tables.aspx

National Academy of Medicine (NAM) and National Research Council (NRC). (April 1, 2015). Transforming the Workforce for Children Birth Through Age 8: A Unifying Foundation. Retrieved April 2015 from http://iom.edu/Reports/2015/Birth-To-Eight.aspx

National Association for the Education of Young Children. (2011). *Code of ethical conduct and statement of commitment.* Retrieved April 2015, from http://www.naeyc.org/positionstatements/ethical_conduct

National Association for the Education of Young Children & National Association of Early Childhood Specialists in State Departments of Education. (2002). *Early learning standards: Creating the conditions for success.* Retrieved April 2015, from http://www.naeyc.org/files/naeyc/file/positions/position_statement.pdf

National Governors Association Center for Best Practices & Council of Chief State School Officers. (2015). *Common Core State Standards Initiative.* National Governors Association Center for Best Practices, Council of Chief State School Officers, Washington DC. Retrieved March 2015 from http://www.corestandards.org/

National Institute of Mental Health. (2011). *Child Mental Health Awareness: Brain DevelopmentDuring Childhood and Adolescence (Fact Sheet).* Retrieved April 2015, from http://www.nimh.nih.gov/health/publications/brain-development-during-childhood-and-adolescence/index.shtml

National Scientific Council on the Developing Child. (2006). *Early exposure to toxic substances damages brain architecture: Working Paper No. 4.* Retrieved April 2015, from http://www.developingchild.harvard.edu

National Scientific Council on the Developing Child. (2007). *The timing and quality of early experiences combine to shape brain architecture: Working Paper No. 5.* Retrieved April 2015 from http://www.developingchild.harvard.edu

National Scientific Council on the Developing Child. (2010). *Early experiences can alter gene expression and affect long-term development: Working Paper No. 10.* Retrieved April 2015, from http://www.developingchild.harvard.edu

Noble, K. G., Houston, S. M., Brito, N. H., Bartsch, H., Kan, E., Kuperman, J. M., et al. (March 30, 2015). Family income, parental education and brain structure in children and adolescents. *Nature Neuroscience.* Retrieved April 2015 from http://www.nature.com/neuro/journal/vaop/ncurrent/full/nn.3983.html

Nutrition and the epigenome. 2012. Retrieved April 2015, from http://learn.genetics.utah.edu/content/epigenetics/nutrition/

Ogden, C., & Carroll, M. (2010). *Prevalence of obesity among children and adolescents: United States, trends 1963–1965 through 2007–2008.* NCHS Health E-Stat. Retrieved April 2015, from http://www.cdc.gov/nchs/data/hestat/obesity_child_07_08/obesity_child_07_08.htm#table1

Ogden C., Carroll, M., Kit, B., & Flegal, K. (2012). *Prevalence of obesity in the United States, 2009–2010.* NCHS data brief, no 82. Hyattsville, MD: National Center for Health Statistics.

Partnership for 21st Century Skills. (2011). Retrieved June 2012, from http://www.p21.org/index.php

Piaget, J. (1929). *The child's conception of the world.* New York: Harcourt, Brace Jovanovich.

Simopoulos, A. P., & Milner, J. (2010). Personalized nutrition: Translating nutrigenetic/nutrigenomic research into dietary guidelines. *World Review of Nutrition and Dietetics Volume 101,* Switzerland: S. Karger AG. Retrieved April 2015, from http://content.karger.com/ProdukteDB/produkte.asp?Aktion=showproducts&searchWhat=books&ProduktNr=253821

Robert Wood Johnson Foundation. (February 2015). *Declining childhood obesity rates: Where are we seeing signs of progress?* Retrieved April 2015 from http://www.rwjf.org/content/dam/farm/reports/reports/2015/rwjf417749

Sorte, J., & Daeschel, I. (2006). Health in Action: A program approach to fighting obesity in young children. *Young Children, 61*(3), 40–48.

U.S. Department of Agriculture. (2011). *USDA's MyPlate—home page.* Retrieved April 2015, from http://www.choosemyplate.gov/

U.S. Department of Agriculture Food & Nutrition Service. (2012). *Child Nutrition Reauthorization: The Healthy, Hunger Free Kids Act of 2010.* (PL111-296). Retrieved March 2015, from http://www.fns.usda.gov/school-meals/healthy-hunger-free-kids-act

U.S. Department of Education. (2001). No Child Left Behind Act of 2001 (Public Law 107-110). Retrieved April 2015 from http://www2.ed.gov/policy/elsec/leg/esea02/beginning.html#sec1

U.S. Department of Education. (2007). *History: Twenty-five years of progress in educating children with disabilities through IDEA.* Retrieved April 2015, from http://www.ed.gov/policy/speced/leg/idea/history.html

U.S. Department of Education, Building the Legacy: IDEA 2004; Individuals with Disabilities Education Act. http://idea.ed.gov/

U.S. Department of Education. (2015). Elementary and Secondary Education Act: History of ESEA. Retrieved March 2015 from http://www.ed.gov/esea

U.S. Department of Health & Human Services. (2003). *A national call to action to promote oral health.* Rockville, MD: U.S. Department of Health and Human Services, Public Health Service, Centers for Disease Control and Prevention, National Institutes of Health, National Institute of Dental and Craniofacial Research. NIH Publication No. 03-5303, May 2003. Retrieved March 2015, from http://www.nidcr.nih.gov/DataStatistics/SurgeonGeneral/NationalCalltoAction/nationalcalltoaction.htm

U.S. Department of Health & Human Services. (2012). *Healthy people 2020.* Retrieved April 2015, from http://www.healthypeople.gov

U.S. Department of Health & Human Services, & U.S. Department of Agriculture. (2015). *Dietary guidelines for Americans, 2015.* Retrieved April 2015, from http://www.health.gov/dietaryguidelines/2015.asp

Vygotsky, L. S. (1962). *Thought and language.* Cambridge, MA: MIT Press.

Wang, J., Wu, Z., Li, D., Li, N., Dindot, S. V., Satterfield, M. C., et al. (2012). Nutrition, epigenetics, and metabolic syndrome. *Antioxidants and Redox Signaling,* March 9, 2012.

World Health Organization. (2014). *Mental health: A state of well-being. Fact file: 10 facts on mental health.* Retrieved April 2015, from http://www.who.int/features/factfiles/mental_health/en/

Chapter 2

Academy of Nutrition and Dietetics. (2011). *Family nutrition and physical activity report from the Academy of Nutrition and Dietetics.* Retrieved March 2012, from http://www.eatright.org/foundation/fnpa/

Academy of Nutrition and Dietetics. (2011). Position of the American Dietetic Association: Benchmarks for nutrition in child care. *111*(4), 607–615.

Academy of Nutrition and Dietetics. (2012). *Pediatric nutrition care manual.* Retrieved February 2012, from http://peds.nutritioncaremanual.org

Adams, I. (2011). Family mealtimes: A wealth of benefits. *Cooperative Extension Service, University of Kentucky College of Agriculture, FCS3-552,* March 6, 2012.

Baker, R. D., Greer, F. R., & The Committee on Nutrition. (2010). Diagnosis and prevention of iron deficiency and iron-deficiency anemia in infants and young children (0–3 years of age). *Pediatrics, 126*(5), 1040–1050.

Beard, J. L. (2008). Why iron deficiency is important in infant development. *Journal of Nutrition, 138*(12), 2534–2536.

Bernal, A. J., & Jirtle, R. L. (2010). Epigenomic disruption: The effects of early developmental exposures. *Birth Defects Research. Part A, Clinical and Molecular Teratology, 88*(10), 938–944.

Boone-Heinonen, J., Gordon-Larsen, P., Kiefe, C. I., Shikany, J. M., Lewis, C. E., & Popkin, B. M. (2011). Fast food restaurants and food stores: Longitudinal associations with diet in young to middle-aged adults: The CARDIA study. *Archives of Internal Medicine, 171*(13), 1162–1170.

Brotanek, J. M., Gosz, J., Weitzman, M., & Flores, G. (2008). Secular trends in the prevalence of iron deficiency among U.S. toddlers, 1976–2002. *Archives of Pediatric Adolescent Medicine, 162*(4), 374–381.

Centers for Disease Control and Prevention. (2010). *Growth charts.* Retrieved March 2012, from http://www.cdc.gov/growthcharts

Cepeda-Lopez, A. C., Aeberli, I., & Zimmermann, M. B. (2010). Does obesity increase risk for iron deficiency? A review of the literature and the potential mechanisms. *International Journal for Vitamin and Nutrition Research, 80*(4–5), 263–270.

Chenhall, C. (2010). *Improving cooking and food preparation skills: A synthesis of the evidence to inform program and policy development.* Government of Canada.

Coleman-Jensen, A., Gregory, C., Singh, A. (2014). Household food security in the United States in 2013. U.S. Department of Agriculture, Economic Research Service (ERR-173).

Committee to Review Dietary Reference Intakes for Vitamin D Food and Nutrition Board & Institute of Medicine of the National Academies. (2011). In C. Taylor, A. L. Yaktine, & H. B. Del Valle (Eds.), *Dietary reference intakes for calcium and vitamin D.* Washington, DC: National Academies Press.

Faulk, C., & Dolinoy, D. C. (2011). Timing is everything: The when and how of environmentally induced changes in the epigenome of animals. *Epigenetics, 6*(7), 791–797.

Food Research and Action Center. (2011). *FRAC brief: Food insecurity and obesity understanding the connections.* Retrieved April 2012, from http://frac.org/pdf/frac_brief_understanding_the_connections.pdf

Food Research and Action Center. (2012). *Food hardship in America 2011.* Retrieved March 2012, from http://frac.org/pdf/food_hardship_2011_report.pdf

Fretham, S. J., Carlson, E. S., & Georgieff, M. K. (2011). The role of iron in learning and memory. *Advances in Nutrition (Bethesda, Md.), 2*(2), 112–121.

Georgieff, M. K. (2011). Long-term brain and behavioral consequences of early iron deficiency. *Nutrition Reviews, 69,* S43–S48.

Health Canada. (2011). Canada's food guide. Retrieved April 2012, from http://www.hc-sc.gc.ca/fn-an/food-guide-aliment/order-commander/index-eng.php

Hubbard, K. L., Must, A., Eliasziw, M., Folta, S. C., & Goldberg, J. (2014). What's in children's backpacks: Foods brought from home. *Journal of the Academy of Nutrition and Dietetics, 114*(9), 1424–1231.

Holick, M. F. (2010). The vitamin D deficiency pandemic: A forgotten hormone important for health. *Public Health Reviews, 32,* 267.

Institute of Medicine. (2009). *Use of dietary reference intakes in nutrition labeling-Institute of Medicine.* Retrieved April 2012, from http://www.iom.edu/Activities/Nutrition/DRINutritionLabeling.aspx

Institute of Medicine. (2011). *Dietary reference intakes for calcium and vitamin D.* Washington, DC: The National Academies Press.

Jarratt, J., & Mahaffie, J. B. (2007). The profession of dietetics at a critical juncture: A report on the 2006 environmental scan for the American Dietetic Association. *Journal of the American Dietetic Association, 107*(7), S39.

Johns Hopkins Children's Center. (2012a). *Failure to thrive.* Retrieved March 2012, from http://www.hopkinschildrens.org/tpl_rlinks_nav1up.aspx?id=5112

Johns Hopkins Children's Center. (2012b). *Failure to thrive.* Retrieved March 2012, from http://www.hopkinsmedicine.org/health-library/conditions/adult/pediatrics/failure_to_thrive_90,P02297/

Kenney, E. L., Henderson, K. E., Humphries, D., & Schwartz, M. B. (2011). Practice-based research to engage teachers and improve nutrition in the preschool setting. *Childhood Obesity, 7*(6), 475–479.

Kraak, V. I., Story, M., & Wartella, E. A. (2012). Government and school progress to promote a healthful diet to American children and adolescents: A comprehensive review of the available evidence. *American Journal of Preventive Medicine, 42*(3), 250–262.

Krukowski, R. A., Eddings, K., & West, D. S. (2011). The children's menu assessment: Development, evaluation, and relevance of a tool for evaluating children's menus. *Journal of the American Dietetic Association, 111*(6), 884–888.

Larson, N., MacLehose, R., Fulkerson, J. A., Berge, J. M., Story, M., & Neumark-Sztainer, D. (2013). Eating breakfast and dinner together as a family: Associations with sociodemographic characteristics and implications for diet quality and weight status. *Journal of the Academy of Nutrition and Dietetics, 113* (12), 1601–1609.

Lee, V., Srikantharajah, J., & Mikkelsen, L. (2010). *Fostering physical activity for children and youth: Opportunities for a lifetime of health.* Retrieved April 2012, from http://www.convergencepartnership.org/atf/cf/{245A9B44-6DED-4ABD-A392-AE583809E350}/Convergence_Physical_Activity_final.pdf

Looker, A. C., Johnson, C. L., Lacher, D. A., Pfeiffer, C. M., Schleicher, R. L., & Sempos, C. T. (2011). *Vitamin D status: United States, 2001–2006.* NCBI (NCHS Data Brief. 2011 No. 59). Hyattsville, MD 20782, USA: Centers for Disease Control and Prevention's National Center for Health Statistics, Division of Health and Nutrition Examination Surveys.

McDonald's Corporation. (2012). *McDonald's momentum delivers another year of strong results for 2011 press release.* Retrieved March 2012, from http://phx.corporate-ir.net/phoenix.zhtml?c=97876&p=irol-newsArticle&ID=1651870&highlight=

Murphy, D. (2012). The more we eat together: State data on frequency of family meals. *Child Trends Fact Sheet, Publication # 2012–03*(January), March 6, 2012.

National Association for Sport and Physical Education. (2009). *Active start: A statement of physical activity guidelines for children from birth to age 5.* Retrieved January 2011, from http://journal.naeyc.org/btj/200605/NASPEGuidelinesBTJ.pdf

National Institutes of Health, Office of Dietary Supplements. (2011). *Vitamin D—health professional fact sheet.* Retrieved March 2012, from http://ods.od.nih.gov/factsheets/VitaminD-HealthProfessional/

Nevin-Folino, N. L. (2008). *Pediatric manual of clinical dietetics* (2nd ed.). United States of America: American Dietetic Association.

Nutrition and the epigenome. (2012). Retrieved March 2012, from http://learn.genetics.utah.edu/content/epigenetics/nutrition/

O'Dea J. A., & Eriksen M. P. (Eds.). (2010). *Childhood obesity prevention: International research, controversies and interventions.* New York: Oxford University Press.

Odgen, C., Carroll, M., & Centers for Disease Control and Prevention. (2010). *Prevalence of obesity among children and adolescents: United States, trends 1963–1965 through 2007–2008.* Retrieved March 2012, from http://www.cdc.gov/nchs/data/hestat/obesity_child_07_08/obesity_child_07_08.htm#figure1

Ogden, C. L., Carroll, M. D., Kit, B. K., & Flegal, K. M. (2012). Prevalence of obesity and trends in body mass index among U.S. children and adolescents, 1999–2010. *The Journal of the American Medical Association, 307*(5), 483–490.

Olshansky, S. J., Passaro, D. J., Hershow, R. C., Laydon, J., Brody, J., Carnes, B. J., et al. (2005). Peering into the future of American longevity. *Discovery Medicine, 5*(26), 130–134.

Piernas, C., Mendez, M. A., Ng, S. W., Gordon-Larsen, P., & Popkin, B. M. (2014). Low-calorie- and calorie-sweetened beverages: Diet quality, food intake, and purchase patterns of US household consumers. *American Journal of Clinical Nutrition, 99*(3), 567–577.

Otten, J. J., Pitzi-Hellwig, J., & Meyers, L. D. (Ed.). (2006). *Dietary reference intakes, the essential guide to nutrient requirements.* Washington, DC: National Academies Press.

Queen Samour, P., & King, K. (2012). *Pediatric nutrition* (4th ed.). Sudbury, MA: Jones & Bartlett Learning, LLC.

Quets, G., & Spota, A. (2011). *NYC Hunger experience: Sacrifice and support.* New York: Food Bank for New York City.

Reedy, J., Krebs-Smith, S. M., & Bosire, C. (2010). Evaluating the food environment: Application of the healthy eating index-2005. *American Journal of Preventive Medicine, 38*(5), 465–471.

Schneeman, B., Trumbo, P., Ellwood, K., & Satchell, F. (2006). The regulatory process to revise nutrient labeling relative to the dietary reference intakes. *The American Journal of Clinical Nutrition, 83*(5), 1228S–1230S.

Schwimmer, J. B., Burwinkle, T. M., & Varni, J. W. (2003). Health-related quality of life of severely obese children and adolescents. *The Journal of the American Medical Association, 289*(14), 1813–1819.

Shine Dyer, J., & Rosenfeld, C. R. (2011). Metabolic imprinting by prenatal and postnatal overnutrition. *Seminars in Reproductive Medicine, 29,* 266–277.

Sloan, E. (2012). What, when, and where America eats. *Food Technology, 66*(1), 21–32.

Spruyt, K., & Gozal, D. (2012). A mediation model linking body weight, cognition, and sleep-disordered breathing. *American Journal of Respiratory and Critical Care Medicine, 185*(2), 199–205.

Story, M. (2009). The third school nutrition dietary assessment study: Findings and policy implications for improving the health of U.S. children. *Journal of the American Dietetic Association, 109*(2), S7.

Sweitzer, S. J., Briley, M. E., Roberts-Gray, C., Hoelscher, D. M., Harrist, R. B., Staskel, D. M., et al. (2010). Lunch is in the bag: Increasing fruits, vegetables, and whole grains in sack lunches of preschool-aged children. *Journal of the American Dietetic Association, 110*(7), 1058–1064. doi:10.1016/j.jada.2010.04.010

Sweltzer, S. J., Briley, M. E., & Robert-Grey, C. (2009). Do sack lunches provided by parents meet the nutritional needs of young children who attend child care? *Journal of the American Dietetic Association, 109*(1), 141–144.

University of Washington. (2012). *Childhood obesity FAQs*. Retrieved April 2012, from http://www.washington.edu/earlychildhood/faqs/childhood-obesity-faqs

U.S. Department of Agriculture. (2011). *ChooseMyPlate.gov choking hazards*. Retrieved October 2011, from http://www.choosemyplate.gov/preschoolers/food-safety/choking-hazards.html

U.S. Department of Agriculture. (2015). *MyPlate in Multiple Languages*. Retrieved June 2015, from http://www.choosemyplate.gov/print-materials-ordering/MultipleLanguages.html

U.S. Department of Agriculture. (2012). *ChooseMyPlate.gov*. Retrieved April 2012, from http://www.choosemyplate.gov/

U.S. Department of Agriculture, Economic Research Service. (2011). *ERS/USDA child nutrition programs*. Retrieved March 2012, from http://www.ers.usda.gov/topics/food-nutrition-assistance/child-nutrition-programs.aspx

U.S. Department of Agriculture, Food and Nutrition Service. (2012a). *FNS supplemental nutrition assistance program (SNAP)*. Retrieved March 2012, from http://www.fns.usda.gov/snap/

U.S. Department of Agriculture, Food and Nutrition Service. (2012b). *Links to state agency (WIC) approved food lists*. Retrieved March 2012, from http://www.fns.usda.gov/wic/Contacts/stateagencyfoodlists.htm

U.S. Department of Agriculture, Food and Nutrition Service. (2012c). Nutrition standards in the national school lunch and breakfast programs. *Federal Register, 77*(17).

U.S. Department of Health and Human Services. (2012). *Nutrition and weight status—Healthy People 2020*. Retrieved March 2012, from http://www.healthypeople.gov/2020/topics-objectives/topic/nutrition-and-weight-status

U.S. Department of Health and Human Services, & U.S. Department of Agriculture. (2011). *Dietary guidelines for Americans, 2010*. Retrieved April 2012, from http://www.health.gov/dietaryguidelines/2010.asp

U.S. Department of Labor U.S. Bureau of Labor Statistics. (2014). *Women in the labor force: A databook (2014 edition)*. Retrieved November 2014, from http://www.bls.gov/cps/wlf-databook-2013.pdf

U.S. Food and Drug Administration (2011a). Consumer updates: A glimpse at 'gluten-free' food labeling. Retrieved April 2012, from http://www.fda.gov/ForConsumers/ConsumerUpdates/ucm265212.htm

U.S. Food and Drug Administration. (2011b). *Food labeling guide: Appendix G: Daily values for infants, children less than 4 years of age, and pregnant and lactating women*. Retrieved April 2012, from http://www.fda.gov/Food/GuidanceRegulation/GuidanceDocumentsRegulatoryInformation/LabelingNutrition/ucm064930.htm

U.S. Food and Drug Administration. (2011c). Food labeling guide: Nutrition labeling; questions L1 through L153. Retrieved April 2012, from http://www.fda.gov/Food/GuidanceRegulation/GuidanceDocumentsRegulatoryInformation/LabelingNutrition/ucm064904.htm

U.S. Food and Drug Administration. (2012). *How to understand and use the nutrition facts label*. Retrieved April 2012, from http://www.fda.gov/Food/IngredientsPackagingLabeling/LabelingNutrition/ucm274593.htm

U.S. Food and Drug Administration. (2013). Labeling & nutrition: New menu and vending machines labeling requirements. Retrieved November 2014, from http://www.fda.gov/Food/GuidanceRegulation/GuidanceDocumentsRegulatoryInformation/LabelingNutrition/ucm2006828.htm

U.S. National Library of Medicine, National Institutes of Health. (2010). *Anemia caused by low iron-children: MedlinePlus medical encyclopedia*. Retrieved March 2012, from http://www.nlm.nih.gov/medlineplus/ency/article/007134.htm

U.S. National Library of Medicine, National Institutes of Health. (2012). *Slipped capital femoral epiphysis: MedlinePlus medical encyclopedia*. Retrieved April 2012, from http://www.nlm.nih.gov/medlineplus/ency/article/000972.htm

Wood, Y., & Child and Nutrition Division, Food and Nutrition Service. (2008). *Strategies for creating a healthier school environment*. Retrieved April 2012, from http://www.extension.iastate.edu/NR/rdonlyres/1EF27C-B93E0C-4875-A232-47BFDA05E296/76661/ICNsessionSchoolHealthEnvironment1.pdf

Ziegler, E. E. (2011). Consumption of cow's milk as a cause of iron deficiency in infants and toddlers. *Nutrition Reviews, 69* (Supplement), S37–S42.

Chapter 3

American Academy of Nutrition and Dietetics. (2011). *Pediatric Nutrition Care Manual*. Retrieved May 2012, from http://peds.nutritioncaremanual.org

American Academy of Nutrition and Dietetics. (2012a). *Nutrition Care Manual*. Retrieved May 2012, from http://www.nutritioncaremanual.org

American Academy of Nutrition and Dietetics. (2012b). Use of nutritive and nonnutritive sweeteners. *Journal of the Academy of Nutrition and Dietetics, 112*(5), 739–758.

American Academy of Nutrition and Dietetics. (2008). Position of the American Dietetic Association: Nutrition guidance for healthy children ages 2 to 11 years. *Journal of the American Dietetic Association, 108*(6), 1038–1047.

American Academy of Pediatrics, American Public Health Association, National Resource Center for Health and Safety in Child Care and Early Education. (2011). *Caring for Our Children Third Edition, National Resource Center for Health and Safety in Child Care and Early Education, American Academy of Pediatrics*, Elk Grove Village, IL, 3rd edition.

American Academy of Pediatrics, Hassink, S. (2014). *Low fat diets for babies*. Retrieved February 2015, from http://www.healthychildren.org/English/ages-stages/baby/feeding-nutrition/Pages/Low-Fat-Diets-For-Babies.aspx

American Dental Association. (2014). *Baby bottle tooth decay—American Dental Association*. Retrieved February 2015, from http://www.mouthhealthy.org/en/az-topics/b/baby-bottle-tooth-decay

American Dietetic Association. (2008). Position of the American Dietetic Association: Nutrition guidance for healthy children ages 2 to 11 years. *Journal of the American Dietetic Association, 108*(6), 1038–1047.

American Heart Association. (2014a). *About cholesterol*. Retrieved February 2015, from http://www.heart.org/HEARTORG/Conditions/Cholesterol/AboutCholesterol/About Cholesterol_UCM_001220_Article.jsp

American Heart Association. (2014b). *Dietary recommendations for healthy children*. Retrieved February 2015, from http://www.heart.org/HEARTORG/GettingHealthy/NutritionCenter/Dietary-Recommendations-for-Healthy Children_UCM_303886_Article.jsp

Anderson, J., & Young, L. (2012). *Water-soluble vitamins*. Retrieved February 2015, from http://www.ext.colostate.edu/pubs/foodnut/09312.html

Ball, J. W., Bindler, R., & Cowen, K. J. (2010). *Child health nursing: Partnering with children and families* (2nd ed.). Upper Saddle River, NJ: Pearson Education, Inc.

Berg, J. M., Tymoczko, J. L., & Stryer, L. (2010). *Biochemistry* (7th ed.). New York: W. H. Freeman and Company.

Birch, E. E., Carlson, S. E., Hoffman, D. R., Fitzgerald Gustafson, K. M., Fu, V. L., Drover, J. R., et al. (2010). The DIAMOND (DHA intake and measurement of neural development) study: A double-masked, randomized controlled clinical trial of the maturation of infant visual acuity as a function of the dietary level of docosahexaenoic acid. *American Journal of Clinical Nutrition, 91*(4), 848–859.

California Department of Education. (2014). *Nutrition education resource guide—healthy eating & nutrition education.* Retrieved February 2015, from http://www.cde.ca.gov/ls/nu/he/nerg.asp

Campanozzi, A., Boccia, G., Pensabene, L., Panetta, F., Marseglia, A., Strisciuglio, P., et al. (2009). Prevalence and natural history of gastroesophageal reflux: Pediatric prospective survey. *Pediatrics, 123*(3), 779–783.

Centers for Disease Control and Prevention. (2013). *Q & A's—fact sheets—community water fluoridation—oral health.* Retrieved February 2015, from http://www.cdc.gov/fluoridation/fact_sheets/cwf_qa.htm#3

Centers for Disease Control and Prevention Division of Oral Health. (2014). *Children's oral health.* Retrieved February 2015, from http://www.cdc.gov/oralhealth/children_adults/child.htm

Dee, D. L., Sharma, A. J., Cogswell, M. E., Grummer Strawn, L. M., Fein, S. B., & Scanlon, K. S. (2008). Sources of supplemental iron among breastfed infants during the first year of life. *Pediatrics, 122*(Supplement 2), 98–104.

Drake, V. J. (2011). *Linus Pauling Institute at Oregon State University: Multivitamin/mineral supplements.* Retrieved February 2015, from http://lpi.oregonstate.edu/infocenter/multivitamin-mineral.html

Goodman, B. E. (2010). Insights into digestion and absorption of major nutrients in humans. *Advances in Physiology Education, 34*(2), 44–53.

Harvard School of Public Health. (2015). *Fats and cholesterol: Out with the bad, in with the good—what should I eat?* Retrieved February 2015, from http://www.hsph.harvard.edu/nutritionsource/what-should-you-eat/fats-and-cholesterol/

Higdon, J., & Drake, V. J. (2012). *An evidence-based approach to vitamins and minerals* (2nd ed.). New York: Thieme Publishing Group.

Hirsch, G., Edelstein, B., Frosh, M., & Anselmo, T. (2012). A simulation model for designing effective interventions in early childhood caries. *Preventing Chronic Disease.* doi: 9:110219

Hurrell, R., & Egli, I. (2010). Iron bioavailability and dietary reference values. *The American Journal of Clinical Nutrition, 91*(5), 1461S–1467S.

Jonnalagadda, S. S., Harnack, L., Hai Liu, R., McKeown, N., Seal, C., Liu, S., et al. (2011). Putting the whole grain puzzle together: Health benefits associated with whole grains—summary of American Society for Nutrition 2010 satellite symposium. *Journal of Nutrition, 141*(5), 1011S–1022S. doi: 10.3945/jn.110.132944

Kleinman, R. K. (Ed.). (2009). *Pediatric nutrition handbook* (6th ed.). United States: American Academy of Pediatrics.

Linus Pauling Institute at Oregon State University. (2014). *Essential fatty acids.* Retrieved February 2015, from http://lpi.oregonstate.edu/infocenter/othernuts/omega3fa/index.html#activities

Mahan, L., Escott-Stump, S., & Raymond, J. L. (Eds.). (2012). *Krause's food and the nutrition care process* (13th ed.). St. Louis: Elsevier Saunders.

Mayo Clinic. (2014). *Cavities/tooth decay: Prevention.* Retrieved February 2015, from http://www.mayoclinic.com/health/cavities/DS00896/DSECTION=prevention

Mennella, J. A., Ziegler, P., Briefel, R., & Novak, T. (2006). Feeding infants and toddlers study: The types of foods fed to Hispanic infants and toddlers. *Journal of the American Dietetic Association, 106*(Supplement 1), 96–106.

National Institute of Diabetes and Digestive and Kidney Diseases, National Institutes of Health. (2013). *National digestive diseases information clearinghouse: Your digestive system and how it works.* Retrieved February 2015, from http://digestive.niddk.nih.gov/ddiseases/pubs/yrdd/

Oregon Department of Education. (2012). *CACFP memos.* Retrieved May 2012, from http://www.ode.state.or.us/search/page/?id=3282

Otten, J. J., Pitzi-Hellwig, J., & Meyers, L. D. (Ed.). (2006). *Dietary Reference Intakes, the essential guide to nutrient requirements.* Washington, DC: National Academies Press.

Queen Samour, P., & King, K. (2012). *Pediatric nutrition* (4th ed.). Sudbury, MA: Jones & Bartlett Learning, LLC.

Reed, K. A., Warburton, D., & McKay, H. A. (2007). Determining cardiovascular disease risk in elementary school children: Developing a healthy heart score. *Journal of Sports Science and Medicine, 6*(1), 142.

Reuter-Rice, K., & Bolick, B. (2012). *Pediatric acute care: A guide for interprofessional practice.* Burlington MA: Jones & Bartlett Publishers.

Ridker, P. M. (2012). Hyperlipidemia as an instigator of inflammation: Inaugurating new approaches to vascular prevention. *Journal of the American Heart Association, 1*(1), 3–5.

Roberts, M. W., & Wright, J. T. (2012). Nonnutritive, low caloric substitutes for food sugars: Clinical implications for addressing the incidence of dental caries and overweight/obesity. *International Journal of Dentistry, 2012.*

Shills, M., Shike, M., Ross, A., Caballero, B., & Cousins, R. (Eds.). (2006). *Modern nutrition in health and disease* (10th ed.). Baltimore, MD: Lippincott Williams & Wilkins.

Simopoulos, A. P. (2011). Evolutionary aspects of diet: The omega-6/omega-3 ratio and the brain. *Molecular Neurobiology, 44*(2), 303–315. doi: 10.1007/s12035-010-8162-0

Sizer, F., & Whitney, E. (2011). *Nutrition concepts and controversy* (12th ed.). Belmont CA: Wadsworth Cengage Learning.

U.S. Department of Agriculture. (2010). *Conclusion statement: Is intake of sugar sweetened beverages associated with adiposity in children? (DGAC 2010).* Retrieved February 2015, from http://www.nel.gov/conclusion.cfm?conclusion_statement_id=250242

U.S. Department of Agriculture. (2014). School Meals: Healthy Hunger-Free Kids Act. Retrieved July 2015 from http://www.fns.usda.gov/school-meals/healthy-hunger-free-kids-act.

U.S. Department of Agriculture. (2015). *Choose MyPlate.gov.* Retrieved February 2015, from http://www.choosemyplate.gov/

U.S. Department of Health and Human Services & U.S. Department of Agriculture. (2015). *Dietary Guidelines for Americans 2010.* Retrieved February 2015, from http://www.health.gov/dietaryguidelines/2010.asp

U.S. Geological Survey. (2014). *Water properties: The water in you.* Retrieved February 2015, from http://ga.water.usgs.gov/edu/propertyyou.html

U.S. National Library of Medicine & National Institutes of Health. (2015). *Fat: MedlinePlus medical encyclopedia.* Retrieved February 2015, from http://www.nlm.nih.gov/medlineplus/ency/patientinstructions/000104.htm

U.S. National Library of Medicine National Institutes of Health. (2013). *Amino acids: MedlinePlus medical encyclopedia.* Retrieved February 2015, from http://www.nlm.nih.gov/medlineplus/ency/article/002222.htm

U.S. National Library of Medicine, National Institutes of Health. (2014). *Small intestine disorders: MedlinePlus.* Retrieved February 2015, from http://www.nlm.nih.gov/medlineplus/smallintestinedisorders.html

Weber, C., & Noels, H. (2011). Atherosclerosis: Current pathogenesis and therapeutic options. *Nature Medicine, 17*(11), 1410–1422. doi: 10.1038/nm.2538

World Health Organization. (2015). *Micronutrient deficiencies.* Retrieved February 2015, from http://www.who.int/nutrition/topics/vad/en/

Yang, Y., Lucas, B., & Feucht, S., (Eds.). (2010). *Nutrition interventions for children with special health care needs* (3rd ed.). Olympia, WA: Washington State Department of Health.

Chapter 4

Academy of Nutrition and Dietetics. (2012). *Pediatric Nutrition Care Manual.* Retrieved June 2012, from http://peds.nutritioncare-manual.org

Allali, F., El Aichaoui, S., Saoud, B., Maaroufi, H., Abouqal, R., & Hajjaj-Hassouni, N. (2006). The impact of clothing style on bone mineral density among postmenopausal women in Morocco: A case-control study. *BMC Public Health, 6.*

Al-Oballi Kridli, S. (2011). Health beliefs and practices of Muslim women during Ramadan. *American Journal of Maternal/Child Nursing, 36*(4), 216–224.

American Academy of Pediatrics. (2011). *Vitamins for breastfed babies.* Retrieved June 2012, from http://www.healthychildren.org/English/agesstages/baby/breastfeeding/pages/Vitamins-for-Breastfed-Babies.aspx

American Academy of Pediatrics. (2012a). Breastfeeding and the use of human milk. *Pediatrics, 129*(3), e827–e841.

American Academy of Pediatrics. (2012b). *Ages and stages baby 0–12 months: Feeding and nutrition—water and juice.* Retrieved June 2012, from http://www.healthychildren.org/English/ages-stages/baby/feeding-nutrition/Pages/default.aspx

American Academy of Pediatrics. (2012c). *Health Issues: Botulism.* Retrieved June 2012, from http://www.healthychildren.org/English/healthissues/conditions/infections/Pages/Botulism.aspx

American Academy of Pediatrics. (2012d). *Ages and stages baby 0–12 months: Feeding and nutrition—Cereal in a bottle: Solid food shortcuts to avoid.* Retrieved June 2012, from http://www.healthychildren.org/English/ages-stages/baby/feeding-nutrition/pages/Cereal-in-a-Bottle-Solid-Food-Shortcuts-to-Avoid.aspx

American Academy of Pediatrics. (2012e). *Childhood nutrition.* Retrieved July 2012, from http://www.healthychildren.org/English/healthy-living/nutrition/Pages/Childhood-Nutrition.aspx

American Academy of Pediatrics. (2012f). Policy statement: Breastfeeding and the use of human milk. *Pediatrics, 129*(3), e827–e841.

American Academy of Pediatrics. (2012g). *Press release: Low-income moms under stress may overfeed infants.* Retrieved June 2012, from http://www.aap.org/en-us/about-the-aap/aap-press-room/Pages/Low-Income-Moms-Under-Stress-May-Overfeed-Infants.aspx

American Academy of Pediatrics, American Public Health Association, and National Resource Center for Health and Safety in Child Care and Early Education. (2011). *Caring for our children: National health and safety performance standards; guidelines for early care and education programs* (3rd ed.). Elk Grove Village, IL: American Academy of Pediatrics.

American Dietetic Association. (2009). Position of the American Dietetic Association: Promoting and supporting breastfeeding. *Journal of the American Dietetic Association, 109*(11), 1926–1942.

Avery, A., Zimmermann, K., Underwood, P. W., & Magnus, J. H. (2009). Confident commitment is a key factor for sustained breastfeeding. *Birth (Berkeley, Calif.), 36*(2), 141–148.

Berseth, C. L., Mitmesser, S. H., Ziegler, E. E., Marunycz, J. D., & Vanderhoof, J. (2009). Tolerance of a standard intact protein formula versus a partially hydrolyzed formula in healthy, term infants. *Nutrition Journal, 8,* 27.

Bhatia, J., & Greer, F. (2008). Use of soy protein-based formulas in infant feeding. *Pediatrics, 121*(5), 1062–1068.

Black, M. M., & Aboud, F. E. (2011). Responsive feeding is embedded in a theoretical framework of responsive parenting. *The Journal of Nutrition, 141*(3), 490–494.

Blossfied, I., Collins, A., & Delahunty, C. (2007). Texture preferences of 12-month-old infants and the role of early experiences. *Food Quality and Preference, 18*(2), 396.

Butte, N., Cobb, K., Dwyer, J., Graney, L., Heird, W., & Rickard, K. (2004). The start healthy feeding guidelines for infants and toddlers. *Journal of the American Dietetic Association, 104,* 442–454.

Cattaneo, A., Williams, C., Pallás-Alonso, C. R., Hernández-Aguilar, M. T., Lasarte-Velillas, J. J., Landa-Rivera, L., … Oudesluys-Murphy, A. M. (2011). ESPGHAN's 2008 recommendation for early introduction of complementary foods: How good is the evidence? *Maternal & Child Nutrition, 7*(4), 335–343.

Centers for Disease Control and Prevention. (2010). *Breastfeeding: Frequently asked questions (FAQs)* Retrieved June 2012, from http://www.cdc.gov/breastfeeding/faq/

Centers for Disease Control and Prevention. (2011a). *Breastfeeding Report Card—United States, 2011.* Retrieved June 2012, from http://www.cdc.gov/breastfeeding/data/reportcard.htm

Centers for Disease Control and Prevention. (2011b). *Breastfeeding: Data: Breastfeeding among U.S. children born 2000–2008, CDC national immunization survey.* Retrieved June 2012, from http://www.cdc.gov/breastfeeding/data/NIS_data/index.htm

Chapman, D. J., & Perez-Escamilla, R. (2012). Breastfeeding among minority women: Moving from risk factors to interventions. *Advances in Nutrition, 3,* 95–104.

Coulthard, H., Harris, G., & Emmett, P. (2009). Delayed introduction of lumpy foods to children during the complementary feeding period affects child's food acceptance and feeding at 7 years of age. *Maternal & Child Nutrition, 5*(1), 75–85.

Dattilo, A. M., Birch, L., Krebs, N. F., Lake, A., Taveras, E. M., & Saavedra, J. M. (2012). Need for early interventions in the prevention of pediatric overweight: A review and upcoming directions. *Journal of Obesity, 2012,* 123023. doi:10.1155/2012/123023

Dee, D. L., Li, R., Lee, L., & Grummer-Strawn, L. M. (2007). Associations between breast-feeding practices and young children's language and motor skill development. *Pediatrics, 119*(Supplement 1), S92–S98.

Dellwo Houghton, M., & Graybeal, T. E. (2001). Breast-feeding practices of Native American mothers participating in WIC. *Journal of the American Dietetic Association, 101*(2), 245–247.

Diamant, A. (2005). *The new Jewish baby book: Names, ceremonies, & customs—A guide for today's families* (2nd ed.). Woodstock, Vermont: Jewish Lights Publishing.

Division of Communicable Disease Control, California Department of Public Health. (2010). *Infant botulism treatment and prevention program.* Retrieved June 2012, from http://www.infantbotulism.org/

Division of Communicable Disease Control, Center for Infectious Diseases, California Department of Public Health. (2011). *Epidemiological summaries of selected general communicable disease in California 2001–2008.* Retrieved June 2012, from http://www.cdph.ca.gov/programs/sss/Documents/Epi-Summaries-CA-2001-2008-083111.pdf

Eidelman, A. I., Schandler, R. J., & American Academy of Pediatrics. (2012). Executive summary: Breastfeeding and the use of human milk. *Pediatrics, 129*(2), 600–603.

Fischer, T. P., & Olson, B. H. (2014). A qualitative study to understand cultural factors affecting a mother's decision to breast or formula feed. *Journal of Human Lactation, 30*(2), 209–216.

Food and Drug Administration. (2011). *Infant formula.* Retrieved June 2012, from http://www.fda.gov/food/foodsafety/productspecificinformation/infantformula/default.htm

Gill, S. L. (2009). Breastfeeding by Hispanic women. *Journal of Obstetric, Gynecologic, and Neonatal Nursing, 38*(2), 244–252.

Grummer-Strawn, L. M., Scanlon, K. S., & Fein, S. B. (2008). Infant feeding and feeding transitions during the first year of life. *Pediatrics, 122*(2), S36.

Guxens, M., Mendez, M. A., Moltó-Puigmarti, C., Julvez, J., Garcia-Esteban, R., Forns, J., … Sunyer, J. (2011). Breastfeeding, long-chain polyunsaturated fatty acids in colostrum, and infant mental development. *Pediatrics, 128*(4), e880–889. doi:10.1542/peds.2010-1633

Haggerty, L. L. (2011). Maternal supplementation for prevention and treatment of vitamin D deficiency in exclusively breastfed infants. *Breastfeeding Medicine, 6*(3), 137–144.

Heinig, M. J., Follett, J. R., Ishii, K. D., Kavanagh-Prochaska, K., Cohen, R., & Panchula, J. (2006). Barriers to compliance with infant-feeding recommendations among low-income women. *Journal of Human Lactation, 22*(1), 27–38.

Holmes, A.V. (2013). Establishing successful breastfeeding in the newborn period. *Pediatric Clinics of North America*, 60(1), 147–168.

Horodynskia, M. A., Calcaterab, M., & Carpenter, A. (2012). Infant feeding practices: Perceptions of Native American mothers and health paraprofessionals. *Health Education Journal*, 71(3), 327–339.

Huh, S. Y., Rifas-Shiman, S. L., Taveras, E. M., Oken, E., & Gillman, M. W. (2011). Timing of solid food introduction and risk of obesity in preschool-aged children. *Pediatrics*, 127(3), e544–551.

Hurley, K. M., & Black, M. M. (2011). Introduction to a supplement on responsive feeding: Promoting healthy growth and development for infants and toddlers. *The Journal of Nutrition*, 141(3), 489.

Hurley, K. M., Cross, M. B., & Hughes, S. O. (2011). A systematic review of responsive feeding and child obesity in high-income countries. *The Journal of Nutrition*, doi:10.3945/jn.110.130047

Ip, S., Chung, M., Raman, G., Chew, P., Magula, N., DeVine, D., Trikalinos, T., & Lau, J. (2007). *Breastfeeding and maternal and infant health outcomes in developed countries.*

Isaacs, E. B., Fischl, B. R., Quinn, B. T., Chong, W. K., Gadian, D. G., & Lucas, A. (2010). Impact of breast milk on IQ, brain size and white matter development. *Pediatric Research*, 67(4), 357–362. doi:10.1203/PDR.0b013e3181d026da

Johnson, S. L., Ramsay, S. A., Armstrong Shultz, J., Branen, L. J., & Fletcher, J. W. (2013). Creating potential for common ground and communication between early child care program staff and parents about young children's eating. *Journal of Nutrition Education and Behavior*, 45 (6), 558–570.

Katz, S. H. (Ed.). (2003). *Baby food: Encyclopedia of food & culture*. New York: Charles Scribner's Sons.

Kittler, P. G., Sucher, K., & Nelms, M. (2012). *Food and culture* (6th ed.). Belmont, CA: Wadsworth Publishing.

Kleinman, R. K. (Ed.). (2009). *Pediatric nutrition handbook* (6th ed.). Elk Grove Village, IL: American Academy of Pediatrics.

Koletzko, B., von Kries, R., Monasterolo, R. C., Subías, J. E., Scaglioni, S., Giovannini, M., ... Grote, V. (2009). Can infant feeding choices modulate later obesity risk? *The American Journal of Clinical Nutrition*, 89(5), 1502S–1508S.

Kramer M. S., Aboud, F., Mironova, E., Vanilovich, I., Platt, R. W., Matush, L., ... Shapiro, S. (2008). Breastfeeding and child cognitive development: New evidence from a large randomized trial. *Archives of General Psychiatry*, 65(5), 578–584.

Li, M., Bauer, L. L., Chen, X., Wang, M., Kuhlenschmidt, T. B., Kuhlenschmidt, M. S., ... Donovan, S. M. (2012). Microbial composition and in vitro fermentation patterns of human milk oligosaccharides and

prebiotics differ between formula-fed and sow-reared piglets. *The Journal of Nutrition*, 142(4), 681–689.

Mahan, L., Escott-Stump, S., & Raymond, J. L. (Eds.). (2012). *Krause's food and the nutrition care process* (13th ed.). St. Louis: Elsevier Saunders.

Mayo Clinic. (2011). *Infant choking: How to keep your baby safe.* Retrieved July 2012, from http://www.mayoclinic.com/health/infant-choking/MY01224/

McDowell, M. M., Wang, C., & Kennedy-Stephenson, J. (2008). Breastfeeding in the United States: Findings from the national health and nutrition examination survey, 1999–2006. *NCHS Data Brief*, 2009(No.5).

Mennella, J. A., Ziegler, P., Briefel, R., & Novak, T. (2006). Feeding infants and toddlers study: The types of foods fed to Hispanic infants and toddlers *Journal of the American Dietetic Association*, 106(1 Suppl 1), S96–106.

Mirkovic, K. R., Perrine, C. G., Scanlon, K. S., & Grummer-Strawn, L. M. (2014). Maternity leave duration and full-time/part-time work status are associated with US mothers' ability to meet breastfeeding intentions. *Journal of Human Lactation*, 30(4), 416–419.

National Association for the Education of Young Children. (2012). *Academy for early childhood program accreditation: Standard 5: NAEYC accreditation criteria for health standard.* Retrieved June 2012, from http://www.naeyc.org/files/academy/file/All-CriteriaDocument.pdf

National Institute of Dental and Craniofacial Research & National Institute of Health. (2011). *A healthy mouth for your baby.* Retrieved June 2012, from http://www.nidcr.nih.gov/OralHealth/Topics/ToothDecay/AHealthyMouthforYourBaby.htm

National Resource Center for Health and Safety in Child Care and Early Education, University of Colorado Denver. (2011). *National resource center for health and safety in child care and early education: Achieving a state of healthy weight: A national assessment of obesity prevention terminology in child care regulations 2010.* Aurora, CO. Retrieved June 2012, from http://nrckids.org/regulations_report_2010.pdf

Nemours. (2012). *Formula feeding FAQs: Starting solids and milk.* Retrieved June 2012, from http://kidshealth.org/parent/pregnancy_newborn/formulafeed/formulafeed_solids.html

Ogbuanu, C., Glover, S., Probst, J., Liu, J., & Hussey, J. (2011). The effect of maternity leave length and time of return to work on breastfeeding. *Pediatrics*, 127(6), e1414–e1427.

Oregon Department of Education. (2009). *USDA child and adult care food program child care center manual.* Salem, Oregon.

Pak-Gorstein, S., Haq, A., & Graham, E. A. (2009). Cultural influences on infant feeding practices. *Pediatrics in Review*, 30(3), e11–21.

Perneczky, R., Wagenpfeil, S., Lunetta, K. L., Cupples, L. A., Green, R. C., DeCarli, C., ... Kurz, A. (2010). Head circumference, atrophy, and cognition: Implications for brain reserve in Alzheimer disease. *Neurology*, 75(2), 137–142. doi:10.1212/WNL.0b013e3181e7ca97

Przyrembel, H. (2012). Timing of introduction of complementary food: Short- and long-term health consequences. *Annals of Nutrition and Metabolism*, 60(Supplement 2), 8–20.

Queen Samour, P., & King, K. (2012). *Pediatric nutrition* (4th ed.). Sudbury, MA: Jones & Bartlett Learning, LLC.

Rajendran, A. (2011). *Annaprashana in Bengali culture—rice eating ceremony.* Retrieved June 2012, from http://www.hindu-blog.com/2010/05/annaprashana-in-bengali-culture-rice.html

Ramachandran, A. (2004). *Congee: Asia's comfort food: Things Asian.* Retrieved July 2009, from http://www.thingsasian.com/stories-photos/2953

Retnakaran, R., Ye, C., Hanley, A. J. G., Connelly, P. W., Sermer, M., Zinman, B., & Hamilton, J. K. (2012). Effect of maternal weight, adipokines, glucose intolerance and lipids on infant birth weight among women without gestational diabetes mellitus. *Canadian Medical Association Journal*, doi:10.1111/j.1463-1326.2012.01607

Roed, C., Skovby, F., & Lund, A. M. (2009). Severe vitamin B12 deficiency in infants breastfed by vegans [Abstract]. *Ugeskr Laeger*, 171(43), 3099–3101.

Ruowei, L., Scanlon, K., May, A., Rose, C., & Birch, L. (2014). Bottle feeding practices during early infancy and eating behaviors at 6 years of age. *Pediatrics*, 134(1), S70–S77.

Shaikh, U., & Ahmed, O. (2006). Islam and infant feeding. *Breastfeeding Medicine*, 1(3), 164.

Sinclair, D., & Dangerfield, S. D. (1998). *Human growth after birth* (6th ed.). Oxford: Oxford University Press.

Sparks, P. J. (2011). Racial/Ethnic differences in breastfeeding duration among WIC-eligible families. *Women's Health Issues*, 21(5), 374–382.

United States Breastfeeding Committee. (2011). *Workplace support in federal law: Breastfeeding Promotion Act 2011.* Retrieved June 2012, from http://www.usbreastfeeding.org/Employment/WorkplaceSupport/WorkplaceSupportinFederalLaw/tabid/175/Default.aspx

U.S. Department of Agriculture. (2009). *Infant nutrition and feeding: A guide for use in the WIC and CSF programs.* Retrieved February 2012, from http://www.nal.usda.gov/wicworks/Topics/FG/CompleteIFG.pdf

U.S. Department of Agriculture, Food and Nutrition Service. (2000). *Issues related to feeding infants in the CACFP.* Retrieved May 2012, from http://www.fns.usda.gov/cnd/Care/Regs-Policy/InfantMeals/2000-04-20.htm

U.S. Department of Agriculture, Food and Nutrition Service. (2012). *WIC food package regulatory requirements* Retrieved June 2012, from http://www.fns.usda.gov/wic/benefitsandservices/foodpkgregs.htm#INFANT_FOOD_FRUITS_and_VEGETABLES

U.S. Department of Health and Human Services. (2012). *Affordable care act rules on expanding access to preventive services for women*. Retrieved June 2012, from http://www.healthcare.gov/news/factsheets/2011/08/womensprevention08012011a.html

University of Illinois College of Agricultural, Consumer and Environmental Sciences. (2012). *New infant formula ingredients boost babies' immunity by feeding their gut bacteria*. Retrieved May 2012, from http://nutrsci.illinois.edu/content/new-infant-formula-ingredients-boost-babiesimmunity-feeding-their-gut-bacteria

World Health Organization. (2010). *Infant and Young Child Feeding Fact Sheet*. Retrieved July 2012, from http://www.who.int/mediacentre/news/statements/2011/breastfeeding_20110115/en/index.html

World Health Organization. (2011). *Exclusive breastfeeding for six months best for babies everywhere*. Retrieved June 2012, from http://www.who.int/mediacentre/news/statements/2011/breastfeeding_20110115/en/index.html

World Health Organization. (2013). Long-term effects of breastfeeding: A systematic review. WHO Library Cataloguing-in-Publication Data. ISBN 978 92 4 150530 7

World Health Organization & UNICEF. (2003). *Global strategy for infant and young child feeding*. Geneva, Switzerland: World Health Organization.

Worobey, J., Lopez, M. I., & Hoffman, D. J. (2009). Maternal behavior and infant weight gain in the first year. *Journal of Nutrition Education and Behavior, 41*(3), 169–175.

Yang Y., Lucas B., & Feucht S. (Ed.). (2010). *Nutrition interventions for children with special health care needs* (3rd ed.). Olympia, WA: Washington State Department of Health.

Chapter 5

Academy of Nutrition and Dietetics. (2014). *Pediatric nutrition care manual*. Retrieved June 2012, from http://peds.nutritioncaremanual.org

American Dietetic Association. (2011). Position of the American Dietetic Association: Benchmarks for nutrition in child care. *Journal of the American Dietetic Association, 111*(4), 607–615.

American Dietetic Association and the American Dietetic Association Foundation. (2011). The state of family nutrition and physical activity: Are we making progress? *Journal of the American Dietetic Association, 111*(4), F1–F30.

Anderson, S. E., & Whitaker, R. C. (2009). Prevalence of obesity among U.S. preschool children in different racial and ethnic groups. *Archives of Pediatrics Adolescent Medicine, 163*(4), 344–348.

Andreyeva, T., Luedicke, J., Henderson, K. E., & Schwartz, M. B. (2014). The positive effects of the revised milk and cheese allowances in the special supplemental nutrition program for women, infants, and children. *Journal of the Academy of Nutrition and Dietetics, 114*(4), 622–630.

Ball, S. C., Benjamin, S. E., & Ward, D. S. (2008). Dietary intakes in North Carolina child-care centers: Are children meeting current recommendations? *Journal of the American Dietetic Association, 108*(4), 718–721.

Benjamin Neelon, S. E., Vaughn, A., Ball, S. C., McWilliams, C., & Ward, D. S. (2012). Nutrition practices and mealtime environments of North Carolina child care centers. *Childhood Obesity, 8*(3), 216–223.

Benton, D., & Jarvis, M. (2007). The role of breakfast and a mid-morning snack on the ability of children to concentrate at school. *Physiology & Behavior, 90*(2–3), 382–385.

Birch, L. L., Fisher, J. O., & Davison, K. K. (2003). Learning to overeat: Maternal use of restrictive feeding practices promotes girls' eating in the absence of hunger. *The American Journal of Clinical Nutrition, 78*(2), 215–220.

Branen L., & Fletcher, J. (1997). Effect of pre-portioned and family style service on preschool children's food intake and waste at snack time. *Journal of Research Childhood Education, 12*(1), 88–95.

Branen, L. J., & Fletcher, J. (2015) Feeding Young Children in Group Settings. Retrieved February 2015, from http://www.cals.uidaho.edu/feeding/

Brotanek, J. M., Schroer, D., Valentyn, L., Tomany-Korman, S., & Flores, G. (2009). Reasons for prolonged bottle-feeding and iron deficiency among Mexican-American toddlers: An ethnographic study. *Academic Pediatrics, 9*(1), 17–25.

Burger, K. S., Fisher, J. O., & Johnson, S. L. (2011). Mechanisms behind the portion size effect: Visibility and bite size. *Obesity, 19*(3), 546–551. doi:10.1038/oby.2010.233

Butte, N. F., Fox, M. K., Briefel, R., R., Siega-Riz, A. M., Dwyer, J. T., Deming, D. M., & Reidy, K. C. (2010). Nutrient intakes of U.S. infants, toddlers, and preschoolers meet or exceed dietary reference intakes. *Journal of the American Dietetic Association, 110*(12, Supplement), S27–S37.

Centers for Disease Control and Prevention. (2012). *Nutrition-facts—adolescent and school health*. Retrieved July 2012, from http://www.cdc.gov/healthyyouth/nutrition/facts.htm

Chefs Move to Schools. (2012). *Chefs move to schools*. Retrieved July 2012, from http://www.chefsmovetoschools.org/

Committee to Review Child and Adult Care Food Program Meal Requirements & Institute of Medicine. (2011). In S. P. Murphy, A. L. Yaktine, C. W Suitor, & S. Moats, *Child and Adult Care Food Program: Aligning dietary guidance for all*. Washington DC: National Academies Press.

Cooke, L. J., Haworth, C., & Wardle, J. (2007). Genetic and environmental influences on children's food neophobia. *American Journal of Clinical Nutrition, 86*(2), 428–433.

Coppinger, T., Jeanes, Y. M., Hardwick, J., & Reeves, S. (2012). Body mass, frequency of eating and breakfast consumption in 9–13-year-olds. *Journal of Human Nutrition and Dietetics, 25*(1), 43–49.

Davis, A. M., Cocjin, J., Mousa, H., & Hyman, P. (2010). Empirically supported treatments for feeding difficulties in young children. *Current Gastroenterology Reports, 12*(3), 189–194.

Deshmukh-Taskar, P. R., Nicklas, T. A., O'Neil, C. E., Keast, D. R., Radcliffe, J. D., & Cho, S. (2010). The relationship of breakfast skipping and type of breakfast consumption with nutrient intake and weight status in children and adolescents: The national health and nutrition examination survey 1999–2006. *Journal of the American Dietetic Association, 110*(6), 869–878. doi:10.1016/j.jada.2010.03.023

Dipti, A. D., Speirs, K. E., McBride, B. A., Donovan, S. M., & Chapman-Novakofski, K. (2014). Head Start and child care providers' motivators, barriers, and facilitators to practicing family-style meal service. *Early Childhood Research Quarterly, 29*(4), 649–659.

Dwyer, J. T., Butte, N. F., Deming, D. M., Siega-Riz, A. M., & Reidy, K. C. (2010). Feeding infants and toddlers study 2008: Progress, continuing concerns, and implications. *Journal of the American Dietetic Association, 110*(12(Supplement)), S60–S67.

Erinosho, T. O., Hales, D. P., McWilliams, C. P., Emunah, J., & Ward, D. S. (2012). Nutrition policies at child-care centers and impact on role modeling of healthy eating behaviors of caregivers. *Journal of the Academy of Nutrition and Dietetics, 112*(1), 119–124. doi:10.1016/j.jada.2011.08.048

Fishel, A. (2010). *The power of table talk*. Retrieved July 2012, from http://thefamilydinnerproject.org/the-power-of-table-talk/

Fisher, J. O., Liu, Y., Birch, L. L., & Rolls, B. J. (2007). Effects of portion size and energy density on young children's intake at a meal. *American Journal of Clinical Nutrition, 86*(1), 174–179.

Fisher, J. O., Wright, G., Herman, A. N., Malhotra, K., Serrano, E. L., Foster, G. D., & Whitaker, R. C. (2015). "Snacks are not food". Low-income, urban mothers' perceptions of feeding snacks to their preschool-aged children. *Appetite, 84*(1), 61–67.

Food Research & Action Center. (2010). *School breakfast program*. Retrieved July 2012, from http://www.frac.org/html/federal_food_programs/programs/sbp.html

Fox, M., Devaney, B., Reidy, K., Razafindrakoto, C., & Ziegler, P. (2006). Relationship between portion size and energy intake among infants and toddlers: Evidence of self-regulation. *The Journal of American Dietetic Association, 106*(1 Suppl 1), S77–S83.

Frankel, L. A., Hughes, S. O., O'Connor, T. M., Power, T. G., Fisher, J. O., & Hazen, N. L. (2012). Parental influences on children's self-regulation of energy intake: Insights from developmental literature on emotion regulation. *Journal of Obesity, 2012.* doi:10.1155/2012/327259

Harding, C., Faiman, A., & Wright, J. (2010). Evaluation of an intensive desensitization, oral tolerance therapy and hunger provocation program for children who have had prolonged periods of tube feeds. *International Journal of Evidence Based Health Care, 8*(4), 268–276.

Hayes, J. E., Wallace, M. R., Knopik, V. S., Herbstman, D. M., Bartoshuk, L. M., & Duffy, V. B. (2015). Allelic variation in TAS2R bitter receptor genes associates with variation in sensations from and ingestive behaviors toward common bitter beverages in adults. *Chemical Senses, 36*(3), 311–319.

Huber, D. (2009). Making a difference in early childhood obesity. *Child Care Exchange.*

Ishige, R. (2012). *The dietary culture of Asia.* Retrieved July 2012, from http://asiasociety.org/print/1646

Johnson, L., van Jaarsveld, C. H. M., & Wardle, J. (2011). Individual and family environment correlates differ for consumption of core and non-core foods in children. *British Journal of Nutrition, 105*(6), 950–959.

Kaar, J., Buti, A., & Johnson, S. (2014). Food neophobia and food preference concordance among parent-child dyads and parents' offering of new foods. *The Journal of the Federation of American Societies for Experimental Biology, 28*(1)(Supplement 252.1).

Kleinman, R. K. (Ed.). (2009). *Pediatric nutrition handbook* (6th ed.). United States: American Academy of Pediatrics.

Knaapila, A., Silventoinen, K., Broms, U., Rose, R. J., Perola, M., & Kaprioand, J. T. (2011). Food neophobia in young adults: Genetic architecture and relation to personality, pleasantness and use frequency of foods, and body mass index—A twin study. *Behavior Genetics, 2012*(7/7/2012), 512–521.

Knaapila, A., Tuorila, H., Silventoinen, K., Keskitalo, K., Kallela, M., Wessman, M., … Perola, M. (2007). Food neophobia shows heritable variation in humans. *Physiology & Behavior, 91*(5), 573–578.

Let's Move. (2010). *Let's move!* Retrieved July 2012, from http://www.letsmove.gov/

Luitel, A. (2006). Food and eating customs differ around the world. *Silver International Newspaper*, retrieved July 2012, from http://silverinternational.mbhs.edu/v202/V20.2.05a.eatingcustoms.html

Lyn, R., Evers, S., Davis, J., Maalouf, J., & Griffin, M. (2014). Barriers and supports to implementing a nutrition and physical activity intervention in child care: Directors' perspectives. *Journal of Nutrition Education and Behavior, 46*(3), 171–180.

Mahan, L., Escott-Stump, S., & Raymond, J. L. (Eds.). (2012). *Krause's food and the nutrition care process* (13th ed.). St. Louis, MO: Elsevier Saunders.

Maritz, J. (2011). *Parmalat pushing into Africa; powdered milk remains a challenge.* Retrieved July 2012, from http://www.howwemadeitinafrica.com/parmalat-pushing-into-africa-powderedmilk-remains-a-challenge/8475/

Martinez, J. M., & Shelnutt, K. P. (2010). *FCS8902/FY1154: Raising healthy children: The role of snacking.* Retrieved July 2012, from http://edis.ifas.ufl.edu/fy1154

McConahy, K., Smiciklas-Wright, H., Mitchell, D., & Picciano, M. (2004). Portion size of common foods predicts energy intake among preschool-aged children. *Journal of the American Dietetic Association, 104*(6), 975–979.

Monneuse, M., Hladik, C. M., Simmen, B., & Pasquet, P. (2011). Changes in food neophobia and food preferences during a weight reduction session: Influence of taste acuity on the individual trajectory. In V. R. Preedy, R. R. Watson, & C. R. Martin (Eds.), *Handbook of behavior, food and nutrition* (chapter 111). New York: Springer.

Montana Team Nutrition Program. (2009). *Challenges, benefits and essential factors for success in implementing a recess before lunch schedules in Montana elementary schools.* Retrieved July 2012, from http://www.opi.mt.gov/pdf/SchoolFood/RBL/08RBLSurveySumRpt.pdf

Muthayya, S., Thomas, T., Srinivasan, K., Rao, K., Kurpad, A. V., van Klinken, J. W., … Bruin, E. A. (2007). Consumption of a mid-morning snack improves memory but not attention in school children. *Physiology & Behavior, 90*(1), 142–150.

Natale, R., Messiah, S. E., Asfour, L., Uhlhorn, S. B., Delamater, A., & Arheart, K. (2014). Role modeling as an early childhood obesity prevention strategy: Effect of parents and teachers on preschool children's healthy lifestyle habits. *Journal of Developmental & Behavioral Pediatrics, 35*(6), 378–387.

National Association for the Education of Young Children. (2012). *Academy for early childhood program accreditation: Standard 5: NAEYC accreditation criteria for health standard.* Retrieved June 2012, from http://www.naeyc.org/files/academy/file/AllCriteriaDocument.pdf

National Food Service Management Institute. (2012). *New meal pattern.* Retrieved July 2012, from http://nfsmi.org/ResourceOverview.aspx?ID=425

Nederkoom, C., Jansen, A., & Havermans, R. C. (2015). Feel your food. The influence of tactile sensitivity on picky eating in children. *Appetite, 84*(1), 7–10.

NOVA. (2009). *The science of picky eaters.* Retrieved July 2012, from http://www.pbs.org/wgbh/nova/body/science-picky-eaters.html

Ochs, E. S., & Shohet, M. (2006). The cultural structuring of mealtime socialization. *New Directions for Child and Adolescent Development, 111*, 35–49.

O'Connell, M. L., Henderson, K. E., Luedicke, J., & Schwartz, M. B. (2012). Repeated exposure in a natural setting: A preschool intervention to increase vegetable consumption. *Journal of the Academy of Nutrition and Dietetics, 112*(2), 230–234. doi:10.1016/j.jada.2011.10.003

Ogata, B. N., & Hayes, D. (2014). Position of the Academy of Nutrition and Dietetics: Nutrition Guidance for Healthy Children Ages 2 to 11 Years. *Journal of the Academy of Nutrition and Dietetics, 114*(8), 1257–1276.

Orlet Fisher, J., Rolls, B. J., & Birch, L. L. (2003). Children's bite size and intake of an entrée are greater with large portions than with age-appropriate or self-selected portions. *The American Journal of Clinical Nutrition, 77*(5), 1164–1170.

Piernas, C., & Popkin, B. M. (2011). Increased portion sizes from energy-dense foods affect total energy intake at eating occasions in US children and adolescents: Patterns and trends by age group and sociodemographic characteristics, 1977–2006. *The American Journal of Clinical Nutrition, 94*(5), 1324–1332.

Pinhas, L., Morris, A., Crosby, R. D., & Katzman, D. K. (2011). Incidence and age-specific presentation of restrictive eating disorders in children: A Canadian paediatric surveillance program study. *Archives of Pediatrics & Adolescent Medicine, 165*(10), 895–899.

Queen Samour, P., & King, K. (2012). *Pediatric nutrition* (4th ed.). Sudbury, MA: Jones & Bartlett Learning, LLC.

Rainville. A. Wolf, K. N., & Carr, D. H. (2006). Recess placement prior to lunch in elementary schools: What are the barriers? *Journal of Child Nutrition & Management—School Nutrition Association, 30*(2).

Rampersaud, G. C. (2009). Benefits of breakfast for children and adolescents: Update and recommendations for practitioners. *American Journal of Lifestyle Medicine, 3*(2), 86.

Rampersaud, G. C., Pereira, M. A., Girard, B. L., Adams, J., & Metzl, J. D. (2005). Breakfast habits, nutritional status, body weight, and academic performance in children and adolescents. *Journal of the American Dietetic Association, 105*(5), 743.

Ramsay, S. A., Branen, L. J., Fletcher, J., Price, E., Johnson, S. L., & Sigman-Grant, M. (2010). "Are you done?" child care providers' verbal communication at mealtimes that reinforce or hinder children's internal cues of hunger and satiation. *Journal of Nutrition Education and Behavior, 42*(4), 265–270.

Ramsay, S. A., Branen, L. J., & Johnson, S. L. (2012). How much is enough? Tablespoon per year of age approach meets nutrient needs for children. *Appetite, 58,* 163–167.

Ritchie, L. D., Boyle, M., Chandran, K., Spector, P., Whaley, S. E., James, P., ... Crawford, P. (2012). Participation in the child and adult care food program is associated with more nutritious foods and beverages in child care. *Childhood Obesity, 8*(3), 224–229.

Rolls, B., Engell, D., & Birch, L. (2000). Serving portion size influences 5-year-old but not 3-year-old children's food intakes. *The Journal of the American Dietetic Association, 100*(2), 232–234.

Satter, E. (2008). *Secrets of feeding a healthy family: How to eat, how to raise good eaters, how to cook* (2nd ed.). Madison: Kelsey Press.

Satter, E. (2012a). *The picky eater.* Retrieved July 2012, from http://www.ellynsatter.com/the-pickyeater-i-43.html

Satter, E. (2012b). *3 to 5 years: Feeding your preschooler.* Retrieved July 2012, from http://www.ellynsatter.com/to-years-feeding-yourpreschooler-i-32.html

Satter, E. (2012c). *Children know how much they need to eat.* Retrieved July 2012, from http://www.ellynsatter.com/children-know-howmuch-they-need-to-eat-i-36.html

Savage, J. S., Haisfield, L., Fisher, J. O., Marini, M., & Birch, L. L. (2012). Do children eat less at meals when allowed to serve themselves? *Journal of Clinical Nutrition, 96,* 36–43.

Schwartz, C., Issanchou, S., & Nicklaus, S. (2009). Developmental changes in the acceptance of the five basic tastes in the first year of life. *The British Journal of Nutrition, 102*(9), 1375–1385.

Snow, C. E., & Beals, D. E. (2006). Mealtime talk that supports literacy development. *New Directions for Child and Adolescent Development,* (111), 51–66.

Tan, C. C., & Holub, S. C. (2011). Children's self-regulation in eating: Associations with inhibitory control and parents' feeding behavior. *Journal of Pediatric Psychology, 36*(3), 340–345.

U.S. Department of Agriculture Food and Nutrition Service. (2011a). (CACFP Memo No. 21-2011 revised). Retrieved July 2012, from http://www.fns.usda.gov/cnd/care/regs-policy/policymemo/2011/CACFP-21-2011.pdf

U.S. Department of Agriculture Food and Nutrition Service. (2011b). *Child and Adult Care Food Program.* Retrieved September 2011, from http://www.fns.usda.gov/cnd/care/cacfp/aboutcacfp.htm

U.S. Department of Agriculture Food and Nutrition Service. (2012). *Summer food service program.* Retrieved July 2012, from http://www.fns.usda.gov/cnd/summer/sponsors/waiver.html

U.S. Department of Agriculture. (2012a). *ChooseMyPlate.gov.* Retrieved April 2012, from http://www.choosemyplate.gov/

U.S. Department of Agriculture Food and Nutrition Service. (2012b). *Healthier US school challenge.* Retrieved July 2012, from http://www.fns.usda.gov/tn/HealthierUS/index.html

U.S. Department of Agriculture Food and Nutrition Service. (2012c). *Team nutrition homepage.* Retrieved July 28, 2012, from http://www.fns.usda.gov/tn/

U.S. Department of Health and Human Services & U.S. Department of Agriculture. (2011). *Dietary Guidelines for Americans, 2010.* Retrieved April 2012, from http://www.health.gov/dietaryguidelines/2010.asp

U.S. Food and Drug Administration. (2012a). *Final rule: Nutrition standards in the national school lunch and school breakfast programs* Retrieved July 2012, from http://www.fns.usda.gov/cnd/Governance/Legislation/nutritionstandards.htm

U.S. Food and Drug Administration. (2012b). *Healthy meals resource system.* Retrieved July 2012, from http://healthymeals.nal.usda.gov/

U.S. Food and Drug Administration. (2012c). *School breakfast program.* Retrieved July 2012, from http://www.fns.usda.gov/cnd/breakfast/

U.S. Food and Drug Administration Food and Nutrition Service. (2009). *WICworks sharing gallery—overview of the new food packages.* Retrieved July 2012, from http://www.nal.usda.gov/wicworks/Sharing_Center/CO/Overview.pdf

U.S. Food and Drug Administration Food and Nutrition Service. (2012). *USDA farm to school.* Retrieved July 2012, from http://www.fns.usda.gov/cnd/F2S/Default.htm

U.S. Food and Drug Administration Food and Nutrition Service. (2015). *Local school wellness policy.* Retrieved July 2012, from http://www.fns.usda.gov/tn/healthy/wellnesspolicy.html

Wells, N. M., Myers, B. M., & Henderson, C. R. (2014). School gardens and physical activity: A randomized controlled trial of low-income elementary schools. *Preventative Medicine, 69,* S27–S33.

Zero to Three. (n.d.). *It's too mushy! It's too spicy! The peas are touching the chicken! (or, how to handle your picky eater).* Retrieved July 2012, from http://www.zerotothree.org/site/PageServer?pagename=ter_key_health_picky

Zuercher, J. L., & Kranz, S. (2012). Toddlers and preschoolers consume more dietary fiber when high-fiber lunch menus are served. *Childhood Obesity, 8*(1), 71–75.

Chapter 6

Academy of Nutrition and Dietetics. (2012). *Pediatric Nutrition Care Manual.* Retrieved February 2012, from http://peds.nutritioncaremanual.org

Affenito, S. (2007). Breakfast: A missed opportunity. *Journal of the American Dietetic Association, 107*(4), 565–569.

Allen, J. H., Benson, C., Shuman, M., & Skees-Gregory, D. (2011). *Making food service sustainable: Portland State University's experience.* Retrieved October 2011, from http://www.pdx.edu/sites/www.pdx.edu.sustainability/files/sus_sustainable_food_service.pdf

American Diabetes Association. (2011a). Diabetes care in the school and day care setting. *Diabetes Care, 34*(1), S70–74.

American Diabetes Association. (2011b). *Food and fitness.* Retrieved October 2011, from http://www.diabetes.org/food-and-fitness/food/

American Diabetes Association. (2012). Diabetes care in the school and day care setting. *Diabetes Care, 35*(1), S76–S80.

American Dietetic Association. (2004). *Conclusion statement: Is intake of fruits and vegetables related to adiposity in children?* Retrieved October 2011, from http://www.andeal.org

American Dietetic Association. (2010). *Executive summary of recommendations: Pediatric weight management.* Retrieved October 2011, from http://www.andeal.org

American Dietetic Association. (2011a). *Pediatric Nutrition Care Manual.* Retrieved October 2011, from http://www.nutritioncaremanual.org/auth.cfm

American Dietetic Association. (2011b). Position of the American Dietetic Association: Benchmarks for nutrition in child care. *Journal of the American Dietetic Association, 111*(4), 607–615.

American Dietetic Association. (2011c). *Cultural food practices. Pediatric Nutrition Care Manual.* Retrieved from http://peds.nutritioncaremanual.org

Anderson, J. (2009). *Birthing green students.* Retrieved October 2011, from http://www.sherwoodgazette.com/sustainable/story.php?story_id=124456510676248000

Annema, N., Heyworth, J. S., McNaughton, S. A., Iacopetta, B., & Fritschi, L. (2011). Fruit and vegetable consumption and the risk of proximal colon, distal colon, and rectal cancers in a case-control study in Western Australia. *Journal of the American Dietetic Association, 111*(10), 1479–1490.

August, G. P., Caprio, S., Fennoy, I., Freemark, M., Kaufman, F. R., Lustig, R. H., ... Montori, V. M. (2008). Prevention and treatment of pediatric obesity: An endocrine society clinical practice guideline based on expert opinion. *Journal of Clinical Endocrinology and Metabolism, 93*(12), 45–76.

Beauchamp, G. K., & Mennella, J. A. (2011). Flavor perception in human infants: Development and functional significance. *Digestion, 83 Supplement* 1, 1–6.

Berni Canani, R., Di Costanzo, M., & Troncone, R. (2011). The optimal diagnostic workup for children with suspected food allergy. *Nutrition, 27*(10), 983–987.

Birch, L. L., & Anzman-Frasca, S. (2011). Promoting children's healthy eating in obesogenic environments: Lessons learned from the rat. *Physiology & Behavior, 104*(4), 641–645.

Carlsen, M. H., Halvorsen, B. L., Holte, K., Bøhn, S. K., Dragland, S., Sampson, L., … Blomhoff, R. (2010). The total antioxidant content of more than 3100 foods, beverages, spices, herbs and supplements used worldwide. *Nutrition Journal, 9*(3). doi:10.1186/1475-2891-9-3 or retrieved January 2013 from http://www.nutritionj.com/content/9/1/3

Connecticut State Department of Education, Bureau of Health/Nutrition, Family Services and Adult Education. (2010). *Action guide for child care nutrition and physical activity policies.* Retrieved October 2011, from http://www.sde.ct.gov/sde/cwp/view.asp?a=2678&Q=322594

Correia, D. C. S., O'Connell, M., Irwin, M. L., & Henderson, K. E. (2014). Pairing vegetables with a like food and visually appealing presentation: Promising strategies for increased vegetable consumption among preschoolers. *Childhood Obesity, 10*(1), 72–76.

Davis, M. M., Gance-Cleveland, B., Hassink, S., Johnson, R., Paradis, G., & Resnicow, K. (2007). Recommendations for prevention of childhood obesity. *Pediatrics, 120*(Supplement 4), S229–S253.

Edwards, G. M. (2003). The health cost of soul food: Introduction. *Topic in Advanced Practice Nursing, 3*(2). Retrieved from http://www.medscape.com/viewarticle/453335

Ewing, J. & The Ohio State University. (2010). *The Ohio State University fact sheet: Cultural diversity: Eating in America—African American HYG-5250-95-R10.* Retrieved October 2011, from http://ohioline.osu.edu/hyg-fact/5000/pdf/5250.pdf

Ferdman, R., McClenahan, J. M., & Falco, J. (2010). Food allergy prevention: To eat or not to eat. *Infant, Child, & Adolescent Nutrition, 2*(6), 340.

Flock, M. R., & Kris-Etherton, P. M. (2011). Dietary guidelines for Americans 2010: Implications for cardiovascular disease. *Current Atherosclerosis Reports, 13*(6), 499.

Food Allergy Anaphylaxis Network. (2011). *About food allergy—FAAN.* Retrieved October 2011, from http://www.foodallergy.org/section/about-food-allergy

Food and Nutrition Service & United States Department of Agriculture. (2001). Accommodating children with special dietary needs in the school nutrition programs: Guidance for school food service staff. Retrieved February 2012, from http://www.fns.usda.gov/cnd/guidance/special_dietary_needs.pdf

Forestell, C. A., & Mennella, J. A. (2007). Early determinants of fruit and vegetable acceptance. *Pediatrics, 120*(6), 1247–1254.

Ghaddar, S., Brown, C. J., Pagán, J. A., & Díaz, V. (2010). Acculturation and healthy lifestyle habits among Hispanics in United States-Mexico border communities. *Revista Panamericana De Salud Pública, 28*(3).

Guidetti, M., & Cavazza, N. (2008). Structure of the relationship between parents' and children's food preferences and avoidances: An explorative study. *Appetite, 50*(1), 83–90.

Gupta, R. S., Springston, E. E., Warrier, M. R., Smith, B., Kumar, R., Pongracic, J., & Holl, J. L. (2011). The prevalence, severity, and distribution of childhood food allergy in the United States. *Pediatrics, 128*(1) e9–e17. Retrieved from http://pediatrics.aappublications.org/content/128/1/e9.full

Harvard School of Public Health. (2011a). *Health gains from whole grains—what should I eat?—the nutrition source.* Retrieved October 2011, from http://www.hsph.harvard.edu/nutritionsource/what-should-you-eat/healthgains-from-whole-grains/

Harvard School of Public Health. (2011b). *The nutrition source—vegetables and fruits: Get plenty every day—what should I eat?* Retrieved October 2011, from http://www.hsph.harvard.edu/nutritionsource/what-should-you-eat/vegetables-full-story/index.html

Hesketh, K. D., & Campbell, K. J. (2010). Interventions to prevent obesity in 0–5 year olds: An updated systematic review of the literature. *Obesity, 18 Supplement* 1, S27–S35.

Hill, P., & The Ohio State University. (2010). *The Ohio State University fact sheet: Cultural diversity: Eating in America—Asian HYG-5253-95-R10.* Retrieved October 2011, from http://ohioline.osu.edu/hyg-fact/5000/pdf/5253.pdf

Hoyland, A., Dye, L., & Lawton, C. L. (2009). A systematic review of the effect of breakfast on the cognitive performance of children and adolescents. *Nutrition Research Reviews, 22*(2), 220–243.

Institute of Medicine. (2008). *Nutrition standards and meal requirements for national school lunch and breakfast programs phase I. Proposed approach for recommending revisions.* Washington, DC: National Academies Press.

Islamic Food and Nutrition Council of America. (2011). *IFANCA: What is halal?* Retrieved October 2011, from http://www.ifanca.org/halal/

Kleinman, R. K. (Ed.). (2009). *Pediatric nutrition handbook* (6th ed.). Elk Grove Village, IL: American Academy of Pediatrics.

Kulkarni, K. D. (2004). Food, culture, and diabetes in the United States. *Clinical Diabetes, 22*(4), 190–192.

Liu, R. H. (2003). Health benefits of fruit and vegetables are from additive and synergistic combinations of phytochemicals. *The American Journal of Clinical Nutrition, 78*(3), 517S–520S.

Llargues, E., Franco, R., Recasens, A., Nadal, A., Vila, M., Perez, M. J., … Castells, C. (2011). Assessment of a school-based intervention in eating habits and physical activity in school children: The AVall study. *Journal of Epidemiology and Community Health, 65*(10), 896–901.

Martinez, S., Hand, M., Da Pra, M., Pollack, S., Ralston, K., Smith, T., … Newman, C. (2010). *Local food systems: Concepts, impacts, and issues,* No. 97, U.S. Department of Agriculture Economic Research Service.

Middleton, A. E., Henderson, K. E., & Schwartz, M. B. (2013). From policy to practice: Implementation of water policies in child care centers in Connecticut. *Journal of Nutrition Education and Behavior, 45*(2), 119–125.

Murphy, S. P., Yaktine, A. L., Suitor, C. W., & Moats, S. (Eds.) (2011). Committee to Review Child and Adult Care Food Program Meal Requirements, Institute of Medicine. *Child and Adult Care Food Program: Aligning dietary guidance for all.* Washington, DC: National Academies Press.

National Association for the Education of Young Children. (2012). *Academy for early childhood program accreditation: Standard 5: NAEYC accreditation criteria for health standard.* Retrieved September 2012, from http://lms.naeyc.org/icohere/custompages/naeycsearch/search_framer.cfm?t=1319069982686

National Association for the Education of Young Children (2015). Access the NAEYC Accreditation Standards and Criteria. Retrieved March 2015, from http://www.naeyc.org/academy/primary/viewstandards

National Diabetes Education Program. (2011). *Overview of diabetes in children and adolescents* Retrieved February 2012, from http://ndep.nih.gov/media/youth_factsheet.pdf

National Resource Center for Health and Safety in Child Care and Early Education, University of Colorado Denver. (2011). *Achieving a state of healthy weight: A national assessment of obesity prevention terminology in child care regulations 2010.* Retrieved October 2011, from http://nrckids.org/regulations_report_2010.pdf

Nemours. (2011). *All about allergies.* Retrieved October 2011, from http://kidshealth.org/parent/medical/allergies/allergy.html

Nevin-Folino, N. L. (2003; updated 2008). *Pediatric manual of clinical dietetics* (2nd ed.). United States of America: American Dietetic Association.

NIAID-sponsored expert panel, Boyce, J. A., Assa'ad, A., Burks, A. W., Jones, S. M., Sampson, H. A., … Schwaninger, J. M. (2010). Guidelines for the diagnosis and management of food allergy in the United States: Report of the NIAID-sponsored expert panel. *Journal of Allergy and Clinical Immunology*, 126(6 Suppl), S1–S58.

Nicklas, T. A., Liu, Y., Stuff, J. E., Fisher, J. O., Mendoza, J. A., & O'Neil, C. E. (2013). Characterizing lunch meals served and consumed by pre-school children in Head Start. *Public Health Nutrition*, 16(13), 2169–2177.

Nolan, J. E., & The Ohio State University. (2010). *The Ohio State University fact sheet: Cultural diversity: Eating in America—Middle Eastern HYG-5256-95-R10*. Retrieved October 2011, from http://ohioline.osu.edu/hyg-fact/5000/pdf/5256.pdf

The Ohio State University. (2010). *The Ohio State University fact sheet: Cultural diversity: Eating in America—Mexican American HYG-5255-R10*. Retrieved October 2011, from http://ohioline.osu.edu/hyg-fact/5000/pdf/5255.pdf

Oliveira, P. (2005). *Connecticut child care center operating budget basics: Calculating your bottom line*. Retrieved October 2011, from http://www.ctkidslink.org/publications/ece05operating06.pdf

Rampersaud, G. C. (2008). Benefits of breakfast for children and adolescents: Update and recommendations for practitioners. *American Journal of Lifestyle Medicine*, 3(2), 86.

Ramsay, et al., (2010).

Ramsay, S. A., Eskelsen, A., Branen, L. J., & Armstrong Shultz, J. (2014). Nutrient Consumption of Fruit and Vegetables in Young Children. *Infant Child and Adolescent Nutritio*, 2014, 6, 6:, 332–344.

Samour, P. Q., & King, K. (Eds.) (2012). *Pediatric nutrition* (4th ed.). Sudbury, MA: Jones & Bartlett Learning, LLC.

Satter, E. (2011). *The child who doesn't eat fruits and vegetables*. Retrieved October 2011, from http://www.ellynsatter.com/the-child-who-doesnt-eat-fruits-and-vegetables-i-42.html

Schwartz, C., Chabanet, C., Lange, C., Issanchou, S., & Nicklaus, S. (2011). The role of taste in food acceptance at the beginning of complementary feeding. *Physiology & Behavior*, 104(4), 646–652.

Siminerio, L. M., Albanese-O'Neill, A., Chiang, J. L., Hathaway, K., Jackson, C. C., Weissberg-Benchell, J., … Deeb, L. C. (2014). Care of young children with diabetes in the child care setting: A position statement of the American Diabetes Association. *Diabetes Care*, 37(10), 2834–2842.

Skelton, J. A., & Beech, B. M. (2011). Attrition in paediatric weight management: A review of the literature and new directions. *Obesity Reviews*, 12(5), e273–e281.

Stallings, V. A., Suitor, C. W., & Taylor, C. (Eds.). Food and Nutrition Board, Institute of Medicine. (2010). *School meals: Building blocks for healthy children*. Washington, DC: National Academies Press.

United Nations Department of Social and Economic Affairs Division for Sustainable Development. (2009). *UN division for sustainable development—initiative details page*. Retrieved July 2009, from http://webapps01.un.org/dsd/caseStudy/public/displayDetailsAction.do?code=8

U.S. Department of Agriculture. (2009). *Infant nutrition and feeding: A guide for use in the WIC and CSF programs*. Retrieved February 2012, from http://www.nal.usda.gov/wicworks/Topics/FG/CompleteIFG.pdf

U.S. Department of Agriculture. (2010). *Topic: Dietary intake and childhood adiposity*. Retrieved October 2011, from http://www.nel.gov/topic.cfm?cat=3068

U.S. Department of Agriculture. (2012). Health and Nutrition Information for preschoolers. Retrieved December 2012, from http://www.choosemyplate.gov/preschoolers.html

U.S. Department of Agriculture (2015a). Child and adult care food program proposed rule. Retrieved March 29, 2015, from http://www.fns.usda.gov/cacfp/meals-and-snacks

U.S. Department of Agriculture. (2015b). MyPlate. Retrieved March 2015, from http://www.choosemyplate.gov/

U.S. Department of Agriculture (2015c). Child and Adult Care Food Program. Retrieved March 2015, from http://www.fns.usda.gov/cacfp/child-and-adult-care-food-program

U.S. Department of Agriculture (2015d). U.S. Department of Health and Human Services and U.S. Department of Agriculture. (2015). Dietary Guidelines for Americans. Retrieved March 29, 2015, from http://www.health.gov/dietaryguidelines/

U.S. Department of Agriculture, Food and Nutrition Service. (2006). *Healthy school meals resource system: Special diets—vegetarian diets and other variations—Jewish schools and institutions*. Retrieved November 1, 2011, from http://healthymeals.nal.usda.gov/hsmrs/Special_Diets_jewish_for_print.htm

U.S. Department of Agriculture, Food and Nutrition Service. (2011). Nutrition standards in the national school lunch and school breakfast programs. *Federal Register*, 76(9), Retrieved September 2011, from http://www.fns.usda.gov/cnd/governance/regulations/2011-01-13.pdf

U.S. Department of Agriculture, Food and Nutrition Service. (2012a). *Final rule: Nutrition standards in the national school lunch and school breakfast programs*. Retrieved February 2012, from http://www.fns.usda.gov/school-meals/nutrition-standards-school-meals

U.S. Department of Agriculture, Food and Nutrition Service. (2012b). *National School Lunch Program*. Retrieved September 2012, from http://www.fns.usda.gov/nslp/national-school-lunch-program-snlp

U.S. Department of Agriculture, Food and Nutrition Service. (2015a). *CACFP policy memos*. Retrieved September 2011, from http://www.fns.usda.gov/cnd/care/regs-policy/policymemoranda.htm

U.S. Department of Agriculture, Food and Nutrition Service. (2015b). *Child and adult care food program*. Retrieved September 2011, from http://www.fns.usda.gov/cnd/care/cacfp/aboutcacfp.htm

U.S. Department of Agriculture, Food and Nutrition Service. (2015c). *Child nutrition labeling*. Retrieved October 2011, from http://www.fns.usda.gov/cnlabeling/child-nutrition-cn-labeling-program

U.S. Department of Agriculture Nutrition Evidence Library. (2010). *Evidence summary: In adults, what is the relationship between the intake of vegetables and fruits, not including juice, and cardiovascular disease?* Retrieved October 2011, from http://www.nel.gov/evidence.cfm?evidence_summary_id=250366&highlight=fruits andvegetables&home=1

U.S. Department of Health and Human Services Food and Nutrition Service & Administration for Children and Families. (2008). *Head Start program performance standards and other regulations–Head Start*. Retrieved September 2012, from http://eclkc.ohs.acf.hhs.gov/hslc/Head Start Program/

U.S. Department of Health and Human Services & U.S. Department of Agriculture. (2015). *Dietary Guidelines for Americans, 2010*. Retrieved September 2011, from http://health.gov/dietaryguidelines/2010.asp#overview

U.S. National Library of Medicine, the National Institutes of Health. (2010). *Allergic reactions: MedlinePlus medical encyclopedia*. Retrieved October 2011, from http://www.nlm.nih.gov/medlineplus/ency/article/000005.htm

Vos, M. B., & Welsh, J. (2010). Childhood obesity: Update on predisposing factors and prevention strategies. *Current Gastroenterology Reports*, 12(4), 280–287.

Weight realities division of the Society of Nutrition Education, Center for Weight and Health, U.C. Berkeley. (2003). Guidelines for obesity prevention programs: Promoting healthy weight in children. *Journal of Nutrition Education and Behavior*, 35(1), 1–4.

WIC Works Resource Team. (2010). *WIC works resource system*. Retrieved October 2011, from http://wicworks.nal.usda.gov

Zhang, Y., Fein, E. B., & Fein, S. B. (2011). Feeding of dietary botanical supplements and teas to infants in the United States. *Pediatrics*, 127(6), 1060–1066.

Chapter 7

American Academy of Pediatrics. (2013). *Health issues: Choking prevention*. Retrieved March 2015, from http://www.healthychildren.org/English/health-issues/injuries-emergencies/pages/Choking-Prevention.aspx

American Academy of Pediatrics. (2014). *Storing and preparing expressed breast milk*. Retrieved March 2015, from http://www.healthychildren.org/English/ages-stages/baby/breastfeeding/pages/Storing-and-Preparing-Expressed-Breast-Milk.aspx

American Academy of Pediatrics, American Public Health Association, National Resource Center for Health and Safety in Child Care and Early Education. (2011). *Caring for our children: National health and safety performance standards; guidelines for early care and education programs* (3rd ed.). Elk Grove Village, IL: American Academy of Pediatrics.

American Red Cross. (2015). *Be red cross ready—get a kit, make a plan, be informed.* Retrieved March 2015, from http://www.red-cross.org/prepare/disaster-safety-library

Brown, A. L. (2011). *Understanding food: Principles and preparation* (4th ed.). Belmont, CA: Wadsworth Cengage Learning.

Buchholz, U., Bernard, H., Werber, D., Böhmer, M. M., Remschmidt, C., Wilking, H., … Kühne, M. (2011). German outbreak of Escherichia coli O104:H4 associated with sprouts. *New England Journal of Medicine, 365*(19), 1763–1770.

Centers for Disease Control and Prevention. (2010). Preliminary FoodNet data on the incidence of infection with pathogens transmitted commonly through food—10 states, 2009. *Morbidity and Mortality Weekly Report, 59*(14).

Centers for Disease Control and Prevention. (2013a). *CDC—foodborne outbreak investigations—key players in foodborne outbreak response.* Retrieved March 2015, from http://www.cdc.gov/foodsafety/outbreaks/investigating-outbreaks/key-players.html

Centers for Disease Control and Prevention. (2013b). *Prevention—listeriosis.* Retrieved March 2015, from http://www.cdc.gov/listeria/prevention.html

Centers for Disease Control and Prevention. (2013c). Vital signs: Incidence and trends of infection with pathogens transmitted commonly through food—foodborne diseases active surveillance network, 10 U.S. sites, 1996–2010. *Morbidity and Mortality Weekly Report, 60*(22).

Environmental Services Department, Maricopa County Arizona. (2011). *Food safety manual for the food service worker.* Retrieved March 2015, from http://www.azgfd.gov/pdfs/hahwg/2012summer/04b-Food%20Safety%20Manual.pdf

Federal Emergency Management Agency. (2014). *Build a kit.* Retrieved March 2015, from http://www.ready.gov/build-a-kit

Garden-Robinson, J. (2012). *Food safety basics: A reference guide for foodservice operators—FN572: NDSU.* Retrieved March2015, from http://www.ag.ndsu.edu/publications/landing-pages/food-and-nutrition/food-safety-basics-fn572

Goodrich, R. M., Schneider, K. R., Schmidt, R. H. & University of Florida, IFAS Extension. (2008). *HACCP: An overview.* Retrieved March 2015, from http://edis.ifas.ufl.edu/fs122

Hunting, K. L., & Gleason, B. L. (2012). *Essential case studies in public health, putting public health into practice.* Burlington, MA: Jones & Bartlett Learning.

Iowa State University Extension. (2015). *HACCP—School Foodservice.* Retrieved March 2015, from http://www.extension.iastate.edu/foodsafety/content/haccp-school-foodservice

Jones, T. F., Ingram, L. A., Fullerton, K. E., Marcus, R., Anderson, B. J., McCarthy, P. V., … Angulo, F. J. (2007). A case-control study of the epidemiology of sporadic salmonella infection in infants. *Pediatrics, 118*(6), 23–80.

Kids Health: The Nemours Foundation. (2014). *Food safety for your family.* Retrieved March 2015, from http://kidshealth.org/parent/firstaid_safe/home/food_safety.html#

Krueger, L. (2008). *Working together to accommodate children with special needs.* Retrieved March 2015, from fns.dpi.wi.gov/sites/default/files/imce/fns/ppt/ms_sdn_2.ppt

Marriott, N. G., & Gravani, R. B. (2006). *Principles of food sanitation* (5th ed.). New York: Springer Science+Business, Media, Inc.

Mayo Clinic. (2015). *Food-borne illness: First aid.* Retrieved March 2015, from http://www.mayoclinic.com/health/first-aid-food-borne-illness/FA00043

National Association for the Education of Young Children. (2012). *Standard 5: NAEYC accreditation criteria for health standard.* Retrieved March 2015, from http://www.naeyc.org/files/academy/file/AllCriteriaDocument.pdf

National Food Service Management Institute. (2005). *Food safety standard operating procedures (SOPs)*. Retrieved March 2015, from http://www.nfsmi.org/documentlibrary-files/PDF/20080213012315.pdf

National Food Service Management Institute. (2009). *Food safety fact sheet: Thawing foods.* Retrieved March 2015, from http://www.nfsmi.org/DocumentSearch.aspx?q=thawing food

National Restaurant Association. (2012). *Servsafe coursebook* (6th ed.). Chicago, IL: National Restaurant Association Educational Foundation.

Nevada Department of Education. (2010). *Child nutrition and school health CACFP guide for registered food vendors.* Retrieved March 2015, from nutrition.nv.gov/Resources/Vendor/Guide_for_Registered_Meal_Vendors/

New York State Department of Health. (2006). *Food defense strategies—A self-assessment guide for food service operators.* Retrieved March 2015, from https://www.health.ny.gov/publications/7079/

Orange County North Carolina. (2015). *Environmental health inspection services FAQ.* Retrieved March 2015, from http://www.orangecountync.gov/departments/health/inspection_services_frequently_asked_questions.php

Pelton, S. I. (2011). *Watch for foodborne illness. Pediatric News, 45*(7), 4–5.

Riggins, L. D., & Barrett, B. (2008). Benefits and barriers to following HACCP-based food safety programs in childcare centers. *Food Protection Trends, 28*(1), 12/10/11-37-44. Foodsafety.gov. Safe minimum cooking temperatures. Retrieved January 2015, from http://www.foodsafety.gov/keep/charts/mintemp.html

Savolainen-Kopra, C., Haapakoski, J., Peltola, P. A., Ziegler, T., Korpela, T., Anttila, P., … Hovi, T. (2012). Hand washing with soap and water together with behavioral recommendation prevents infection in common work environment: An open cluster-randomized trial. *Trials, 13*(1).

Schmidt, R. H., & Newslow, D. L. (2009). *Hazard analysis critical control points (HACCP)—principle 3: Establish critical limits and principle 4: Monitoring critical control points (CCPs).* Retrieved March 2015, from http://edis.ifas.ufl.edu/FS141

Talaat, M., Afifi, S., Dueger, E., El-Ashry, N., Martin, A., Kandeel, A., El-Sayed, N. (2011). Effects of hand hygiene campaigns on incidence of laboratory-confirmed influenza and absenteeism in schoolchildren, Cairo, Eygpt. *Emerging Infectious Disease Journal, 17*(4), 619–625.

U.S. Department of Agriculture, Food and Nutrition Service. (2014a). *Food safety.* Retrieved March 2015, from http://www.fns.usda.gov/food-safety/food-safety

U.S. Department of Agriculture, Food and Nutrition Service. (2014b). *USDA recipes for child care.* Retrieved March 2015, from http://www.fns.usda.gov/tn/Resources/childcare_recipes.html

U.S. Department of Agriculture, Food Safety and Inspection Service. (2013). *Cleanliness helps prevent foodborne illness.* Retrieved March 2015, from

U.S. Department of Agriculture, Food Safety and Inspection Service. (2014a). *About FSIS: Agency history.* Retrieved March 2015, from http://www.fsis.usda.gov/wps/portal/informational/aboutfsis/history/history

U.S. Department of Agriculture, Food Safety and Inspection Service. (2013b). *Fact sheet on clostridium botulinum.* Retrieved March 2015, from http://www.fsis.usda.gov/wps/portal/fsis/topics/food-safety-education/get-answers/food-safety-fact-sheets/foodborne-illness-and-disease/clostridium-botulinum/ct_index

U.S. Department of Agriculture, Food Safety and Inspection Service. (2014a). *Fact sheet: Safe food handling.* Retrieved March 2015, from http://www.fsis.usda.gov/wps/portal/fsis/topics/food-safety-education/get-answers/food-safety-fact-sheets/safe-food-handling

U.S. Department of Agriculture, Food Safety and Inspection Service. (2014b). *Is it done yet? recommended internal temperatures.* Retrieved March 2015, from http://www.fsis.usda.gov/wps/portal/fsis/topics/

food-safety-education/teach-others/
fsis-educational-campaigns/is-it-done-yet

U.S. Department of Health and Human Services, Food and Drug Administration. (2014). *Federal Register, 76*(149). Retrieved March 2015, from http://www.gpo.gov/fdsys/pkg/FR-2011-08-03/pdf/2011-19620.pdf

U.S. Department of Health and Human Services, Food and Drug Administration Center for Food Safety and Applied Nutrition. (2014). *A manual for the voluntary use of HACCP principles for operators of food service and retail establishments. Chapter 2—the process approach for managing food safety.* Retrieved March 2015, from http://www.fda.gov/Food/GuidanceRegulation/HACCP/ucm2006811.htm

U.S. Department of Health and Human Services, Public Health Service, U.S. Food and Drug Administration. (2014). *Food code 201309.* Retrieved December 13, 2011 March 8, 2015, from http://www.fda.gov/Food/GuidanceRegulation/RetailFoodProtection/FoodCode/ucm374275.htm-http://www.fda.gov/Food/FoodSafety/RetailFoodProtection/FoodCode/FoodCode2009/ucm186451.htm#part3-5

U.S. Department of Health and Human Services, U.S. Food and Drug Administration. (2014). *Consumer updates: Food bill aims to improve safety.* Retrieved March 2015, from http://www.fda.gov/ForConsumers/ConsumerUpdates/ucm237758.htm

U.S. Food and Drug Administration. (2014a). *Consumers: Food allergies: What you need to know.* Retrieved March 2015, from http://www.fda.gov/food/resourcesforyou/consumers/ucm079311.htm

U.S. Food and Drug Administration. (2014b). *Guidance for industry, retail food stores and food service establishments: Food security preventive measures guidance.* Retrieved March 2015, from http://www.fda.gov/Food/GuidanceRegulation/GuidanceDocuments-RegulatoryInformation/FoodDefense/ucm083075.htm

U.S. Food and Drug Administration. (2014c). *Hazard analysis and critical control point principles and application guidelines.* Retrieved March 2015, from http://www.fda.gov/Food/GuidanceRegulation/HACCP/ucm2006801.htm

U.S. Food and Drug Administration. (2014d). *Once baby arrives: Food safety for mothers to be.* Retrieved March 2015, from http://www.fda.gov/food/resourcesforyou/healtheducators/ucm089629.htm

U.S. Food and Drug Administration. (2014e). *Retail food risk factor studies: FDA trend analysis report on the occurrence of foodborne illness risk factors in selected institutional food-service, restaurant, and retail food store facility types (1998–2008).* Retrieved March 2015, from http://www.fda.gov/Food/GuidanceRegulation/RetailFoodProtection/FoodborneIllnessRiskFactorReduction/ucm223293.htm

U.S. Food and Drug Administration, Center for Food Safety and Nutrition. (2012). *Bad bug book: Introduction to foodborne pathogenic microorganisms and natural toxins,* 2nd edition. Retrieved March 2015, from http://www.fda.gov/downloads/Food/FoodborneIllnessContaminants/UCM297627.pdf

Wallace, C. A., Sperber, W. H., & Mortimore, S. E. (2010). *Food safety for the 21st century: Managing HACCP and food safety throughout the global supply chain.* United Kingdom: Wiley-Blackwell.

Washington State Department of Health. (2011). *BE AWARE these foods may cause choking in toddlers—health education resource exchange (H.E.R.E.).* Retrieved March 2015, from http://here.doh.wa.gov/materials/prevent-choking-intoddlers/12_Foods CCsm_E13L.pdf

Wisconsin Department of Public Instruction. (2011). *Materials & resources for the national school lunch program: Guidelines for contracting vended meals.* Retrieved June 2015, from http://fns.dpi.wi.gov/fns_prvend

Chapter 8

American Academy of Pediatrics. (2013, May 4). Poverty threatens health of US children. *Science Daily.*

American Academy of Pediatrics, American Public Health Association, National Resource Center for Health and Safety in Child Care and Early Education. (2011). *Caring for Our Children: National Health and Safety Performance Standards: Guidelines for Out-of-Home Childcare Programs* (3rd ed.). Elk Grove Village, IL.

American Psychological Association. (2014). Retrieved September 2015, from http://www.apa.org/pi/families/children-mental-health.aspx

Annie E. Casey Foundation. (2014). *2014 Kids Count Data Book.* Retrieved August 2015, from http://www.aecf.org/resources/the-2014-kids-count-data-book

Bright Futures at Georgetown University. (n.d.). *Bright futures.* Retrieved September 2015, from https://brightfutures.org/physicalactivity/frontmatter/index.html

Centers for Disease Control and Prevention. (2013). *Voluntary Guidelines for Managing Food Allergies in Schools and Early Care and Education Programs.* U.S. Department of Health and Human Services, Washington, DC.

Centers for Disease Control and Prevention. (2014a). *Local school wellness policy.* Retrieved September 2015, from www.cdc.gov/healthyyouth/npao/wellness.htm

Centers for Disease Control and Prevention. (2014b). *Social determinants of health.* Retrieved August 2015, from www.cdc.gov/socialdeterminants/definitions.html

Centers for Disease Control and Prevention and Bridging the Gap Research Program. (2014a). *Strategies for Supporting Quality Physical Education and Physical Activity in Schools.* U.S. Department of Health and Human Services, Atlanta.

Centers for Disease Control and Prevention and Briding the Gap Research Program. (2014b). *Strategies for Supporting Recess in Elementary Schools.* Department of Health and Human Services, Atlanta.

Council on Community Pediatrics. (2013). Providing care for children and adolescents facing homelessness and housing insecurity. *Pediatrics, 131*(6), 1206–1210.

Flores, R. (2012, July). Poverty, health disparities and the nation's children. *Children, Youth, and Families.*

Head Start Body Start. (2012). *Just the Facts. Evidence Base and Policy Overview. Physical Activity and Nutrition in Early Childhood Settings.* American Alliance for Health, Physical Education, Recreation, and Dance.

Institute of Medicine. (2003). *In Unequal Treatment. Confronting Racial and Ethnic Disparities in Healthcare* (p. 524). Washington, DC.

NAEYC. (2014, April 1). *Access the NAEYC Accreditation Standards and Criteria.* Retrieved March 2015, from http://www.naeyc.org/academy/primary/viewstandards.

Seith, D., & Isakson, E. (2011). Who are America's poor children? Examining the health disparities among children in the United States. National Center for Children in Poverty, Mailman School of Public Health, Columbia University.

Spector, R. (2012). *Cultural Diversity in Health and Illness* (8th ed.). Upper Saddle River, NJ: Pearson.

U.S. Department of Health and Human Services. (2011). *Head Start program performance standards and other regulations.* Retrieved September 2015, from http://eclkc.ohs.acf.hhs.gov/hslc/standards/hspps

World Health Organization. (1948). *Preamble to the Constitution of the World Health Organization as adopted by the International Health Conference, New York, 19 June–22 July 1946 by the representatives of 61 states (Official records of the World Health Organization, no. 2, p. 100) and entered into force on 7 April 1948.* Retrieved September 2014, from www.who.int/about/definition/en/print.html

Chapter 9

Advisory Committee on Childhood Lead Poisoning Prevention of the Centers for Disease Control and Prevention. (2012). Retrieved October 2015, from www.cdc.gov/nceh/lead/acclpp/final_document_030712.pdf

American Academy of Pediatrics. (n.d.). *Confidential health records.* Retrieved October 2015, from www.nationalguidelines.org/guideline.cfm?guideNum=4-25

American Academy of Pediatrics. (n.d.). *National Center for Medical Home Implementation.* Retrieved October 2015, from www.medicalhomeinfo.org

American Academy of Pediatrics. (2013). *American Academy of Pediatrics.* Retrieved October 2015, from www2.aap.org/immunization/pediatricians/pdf/vaccine-hesitant%20parent-final.pdf

American Academy of Pediatrics. (2014). *Healthy living.* Retrieved October 2015, from https://www.healthychildren.org/English/healthy-living/Pages/default.aspx

American Academy of Pediatrics, American Public Health Association, National Resource Center for Health and Safety in Child Care and Early Education. (2011). *Caring for Our Children: National Health and Safety Performance Standards: Guidelines for Out-of-Home Childcare Programs* (3rd ed.). Elk Grove Village, IL.

Basch, C. (2011). Vision and the achievement gap among urban minority youth. *Journal of School Health, 81*(10), 599–605.

Centers for Disease Control and Prevention. (2012). *Epidemiology and Prevention of Vaccine-Preventable Diseases* (12th ed.). (W. W. Atkinson, Ed.). Washington, DC: Public Health Foundation.

Centers for Disease Control and Prevention. (2013a). Blood lead levels in children aged 1–5 years—United States, 1999–2010. *Morbidity and Mortality Weekly Report, 62*(13), 245–248.

Centers For Disease Control and Prevention. (2013b). *Hearing loss in children.* Retrieved October2014, from www.cdc.gov/ncddd/hearingloss/data.htm

Centers for Disease Control and Prevention. (2013c). *Sources of lead.* Retrieved October 2014, from www.cdc.gov/nceh/lead/tips/sources.htm

Centers for Disease Control and Prevention. (2014). *Thimerosal.* Retrieved October 2014, from www.cdc.gov/vaccinesafety/concerns/thimerosal/index.html

Centers for Disease Control and Prevention. (XXXX). Use of World Health Organization and CDC growth charts for children ages 0–59 months in the United States. *Morbidity and Mortality Weekly Report, 59*(RR-9), 1–13.

Chan, D. (2014). *Congenital hearing loss: A silent epidemic.* Retrieved October 2015, from http://pediatrics.ucsf.edu/blog/congenital-hearing-loss-silent-epidemic#.VFVSlb7DOJU

Child Trends Databank. (2014). *Parental depression.* Available at http://www.childtrends.org/?indicators=parental-depression

Heward, W. (2013). *Exceptional Children: An Introduction to Special Education* (10th ed.). Upper Saddle River, NJ: Pearson.

Kaczmarski, J., DeBate, R., Marhefka, S., & Daley, E. (2011). State-mandated school-based BMI screening and parent notification: A descriptive case study. *Health Promotion Practice, 12*, 797–801.

Kawashita, Y., Kitamura, M., & Saito, T. (2011). Early childhood caries. *International Journal of Dentistry, 2011*, 1–7.

Lee, E., Rosenthal, L., & Scheffler, G. (2013). *The Effect of Childhood Vaccine Exemptions on Disease Outbreaks.* Center for American Progress.

Moodie, S., Daneri, P., Goldhagen, S., Halle, T., Green, K., & LaMonte, L. (2014). *Early childhood developmental screening: A compendium of measures for children ages birth to five (OPRE Report 2014-11)* . U.S. Department of Health and Human Services, Office of Planning, Research and Evaluation, Administration for Children and Families, Washington, DC.

O'Brien, M., Alos, V., Davey, A., Bueno, A., & Whitaker, R. (2014). Acculturation and the prevalence of diabetes in US Latino adults, National Health and Nutrition Examination Survey 2007–2010. *Preventing Chronic Disease, 11*, 140–142.

Oregon Lead Poisoning Prevention Program. (2009). *Lead screening protocols for children.* Retrieved October 2015, from https://public.health.oregon.gov/HealthyEnvironments/HealthyNeighborhoods/LeadPoisoning/MedicalProvidersLaboratories/Documents/screenprotocolschild.pdf

Pietras, S., Rhodes, E., Meyers, A., & Goodman, E. (2012). Understanding pediatricians' views toward school-based BMI screening in Massachussetts: A pilot study. *Journal of School Health, 82*(3), 107–114.

Shelov, S. A. (2014). *Caring for Your Baby and Young Child: Birth to Age 5* (5th ed.). Elk Grove, IL: Bantam.

Thomas, A. C., & Chess, S. (1977). *Temperament and Development.* New York: Brunner-Mazel.

U.S. Department of Health and Human Services, Administration of Children and Families. (n.d.). Retrieved October 2015, from eclkc.ohs.acr.hhs.gov/hslc/hs/resources/ECLKC_Bookstore/pdfs/d54e82aec0e-167a42bfa607f2381960f.pdf

Wiley, J., Cloutier, M., Wakefield, D., Hernandez, D., Grant, A., Beaulieu, A., … Gorin, A. (2014). Acculturation Determines BMI Percentile and Noncore Food Intake in Hispanic Children. *Journal of Nutrition, 144*(3), 305–310.

Chapter 10

American Academy of Pediatrics. (2012). *Red Book 2012 Report of the Committee on Infectious Diseases* (29th ed.). (L. B. Pickering, Ed.). Elk Grove Village, IL.

American Academy of Pediatrics, American Public Health Association, National Resource Center for Health and Safety in Child Care and Early Education. (2011). *Caring for Our Children: National Health and Safety Performance Standards: Guidelines for Out-of-Home Childcare Programs* (3rd ed.). Elk Grove Village, IL.

American Academy of Pediatrics, *Preventing the Spread of Illness in Child Care or School,* 5/5/15, retrieved 8/7/15 from https://

www.healthychildren.org/English/health-issues/conditions/prevention/Pages/Prevention-In-Child-Care-or-School.aspx

Ball, J. B. (2012). Chapter 19: Infectious and communicable diseases. In Principles of Pediatric Nursing Upper Saddle River, NJ.

Ben-Arye, E. T., Traube, Z., Schachter, L., Haimi, M., Levy, M., Schiff, E., & Lev, E. (2011). Integrative pediatric care: Parents' attitudes toward communication of physicians and CAM practitioners. *Pediatrics, 1,* e84–e95.

Bozzetto, S. C., Carraro, S., Giordano, G., Boner, A., & Baraldi, E. (2012). Asthma, allergy and respiratory infections: The vitamin D hypothesis. *Allergy, 67*(1), 10–17.

Centers for Disease Control and Prevention. (2012). *Epidemiology and prevention of vaccine-preventable diseases.* Washington DC: Public Health Foundation.

Centers for Disease Control and Prevention. (2013a, September 24). *Head lice.* Retrieved September 2015, from www.cdc.gov/parasites/lice/head/

Centers for Disease Control and Prevention. (2013b, September 24). *Head lice Information for Schools.* Retrieved September 2015, from http://www.cdc.gov/parasites/lice/head/schools.html

Centers for Disease Control and Prevention. (2014a). *CDC Health Information for International Travel 2014.* New York: Oxford University Press.

Centers for Disease Control and Prevention. (2014b). Measles outbreak associated with adopted children from China—Missouri, Minnesota, and Washington, July 2013. *Morbidity and Mortality Weekly Report, 63*(14), 301–304.

Centers for Disease Control and Prevention. (2014c). *International adoption: Health guidance and the immigration process.* Retrieved September 2015, from www.cdc.gov/immigrantrefugeehealth/adoption/

Pappas, D. H. (2013, May 3). *Patient information: The common cold in children.* Retrieved September 2015, from http://www.uptodate.com/contents/the-common-cold-in-children-beyond-the-basics

Chapter 11

Abrams, E., & Becker. A. (2013). Introducing solid food. *Canadian Family Physician, 59*(7), 721–722.

American Academy of Pediatrics. (2014). *Asthma triggers and what to do about them.* Retrieved February 2015, from www.healthychildren.org/English/health-issues/conditions/allergies-asthma/Pages/Asthma-Triggers-and-What-to-do-About-Them.aspx

American Academy of Pediatrics, American Public Health Association, National Resource Center for Health and Safety in Child Care and Early Education. (2011).

Caring for our children: National health and safety performance standards; Guidelines for early care and education programs. Retrieved from http://nrckids.org

American Diabetes Association. (2013). Diabetes care in the school and day care setting. *Diabetes Care, 36*(1), S75–S79.

American Psychiatric Association. (2013). *Diagnostic and Statistical Manual of Mental Disorders* (5th ed.). Arlington, VA: American Psychiatric Association.

Ball, J. W., Bindler, R. C., & Cowen, K. J. (2012). *Principles of Pediatric Nursing* (5th ed.). Upper Saddle River, NJ: Pearson.

Centers for Disease Control and Prevention. (2012). *Trends in asthma prevalence, health care use, and mortality in the United States, 2001–2010*. Retrieved February 2015, from www.cdc.gov/nchs/data/databriefs/db94.htm

Centers for Disease Control and Prevention. (2014a). *Data and statistics*. Retrieved February 2015, from www.cdc.gov/ncbddd/spinabifida/data.html

Centers for Disease Control. (2014b). *Data & statistics*. Retrieved February 2015, from www.cdc.gov/ncbddd/adhd/data.html

Centers for Disease Control and Prevention. (2015a). *Data & statistics*. Retrieved February 2015, from www.cdc.gov/ncbddd/fasd/data.html

Centers for Disease Control and Prevention. (2015b). *Data & statistics for cerebral palsy*. Retrieved February 2015, from www.cdc.gov/ncbddd/cp/data.html

Centers for Disease Control and Prevention, National Center for Health Statistics. (2015). *FastStats*. Retrieved February 2015, from www.cdc.gov/nchs/fastats/asthma/htm

Child and Adolescent Health Measurement Initiative. (2012). *National survey of children with special health care needs*. Retrieved February 2015, from www.childhealthdata.org/learn/NS-CSHCN

Child Trends. (2012). *Children with special health care needs*. Retrieved February 2015, from http://www.childtrends.org/?indicators=children-with-spcial-health-care-needs

Çolak, H. D., Dülgergil, C. T., Dalli, M., & Hamidi, M. M. (2013). Early childhood caries update: A review of causes, diagnoses, and treatments. *Journal of Natural Science, Biology and Medicine, 4*(1), 29–38.

Dileepan, K. F., & Feldt, M. M. (2013). Type 2 diabetes mellitus in children and adolescents. *Pediatrics in Review, 34*(12), 541–548.

Duryea, T. F., & Fleischer, D. M. (2014). *Patient information: Starting solid foods during infancy (Beyond the Basics)*. Retrieved February 2015, from www.uptodate.com/contents/starting-solid-foods-during-infancy-beyond-the-basics

Harrington, J., & Allen, K. (2014). The clinician's guide to autism. *Pediatrics in Review, 35*(2), 62–78.

Healthy People. (n.d.). *Educational and community-based programs*. Retrieved February 2015, from Healthy People 2020.

Heward, W. (2013). *Exceptional Children: An Introduction to Special Education* (10th ed.). Upper Saddle River, NJ: Pearson.

Jackson, K. D., Howie, L. D., & Akinbami, J. L. (2013). Trends in allergic conditions among children: United States 1997–2011. *NCHS data brief, no 121*.

Lewis, C. (2014). Fluoride and dental caries prevention in children. *Pediatrics in Review, 35*(1), 3–15.

May, P., Baete, A., Russo, J., Elliott, A., Blankenship, J., Kalberg, W., … Hoyme, H. (2014). Prevalence and characteristics of fetal alcohol spectrum disorders. *Pediatrics, 134*(5), 855–866.

Meng, Y., Babey, S. H., & Wolstein, J. (2012). Asthma-related school absenteeism and school concentration of low-income students in California. *Preventing Chronic Disease, 9*.

National Center for Child Poverty. (2011). *Who are America's poor children? Examining health disparities by race and ethnicity*.

O'Connor, M., Howell-Meurs, S., Kvalsvig, A., & Goldfeld, S. (2014). Understanding the impact of special health care needs on early school functioning: A conceptual model. *Child Care Health and Development, 41*(1), 15–22.

Paranjape, S. M., & Mogayzel, P. J. (2014). Cystic fibrosis. *Pediatrics in Review, 35*(5), 194–205.

Parish, S. L., Rose, R. A., Dababnah, S., Yoo, J., & Cassiman, S. A. (2012). State-level income inequality and family burden of U.S. families raising children with special health care needs. *Social Science & Medicine, 74*, 399–407.

Turnbull A., Turnbull, R., Wehmeyer, M., & Shogren, K. (2013). *Exceptional Lives. Special Education in Today's Schools* (7th ed.). Upper Saddle River, NJ: Pearson.

U.S. Department of Education. (n.d.). *Building the Legacy: IDEA 2004*. Retrieved February 2015, from http://idea.ed.gov/explore/home

U.S. Department of Education. (n.d.). *Sec. 300.8 Child with a disability*. Retrieved February 2015, from http://idea.ed.gov/explore/view/p/,-root,regs,300,A,300%252E8

U.S. Department of Health and Human Services, Health Resources and Services Administration. (2013). *Child and adolescent health measurement initiative. Who are children with special*http://idea.ed.gov/explore/view/p/,root,regs,300,A,300%252E8,health-careneeds. Retrieved February 2015, from http://www.childhealthdata.org/learn/NS-CSHCN

U.S. Department of Health and Human Services, Health Resources and Services Administration, Maternal and Child Health

Bureau. (2008). *The national survey of children with special health care needs. Chartbook 2005–2006*. Retrieved February 2015, from http://mchb.hrsa.gov/cshcn05/

Wankoff, L. (2011). Warning signs in the development of speech, language, and communication: When to refer to a speech-language pathologist. *Journal of Child and Adolescent Psychiatric Nursing, 24*(3), 175–184.

Chapter 12

Armstrong, J. M., Ruttle, P. L., Klein, M. H., Essex, M. J., & Benca, R. M. (2014). Assocations of child insomnia, sleep movement, and their persistence with mental health symptoms in childhood and adolescence. *Sleep, 37*(5) 901–909.

Ball, J. B., Bindler, R. C., & Cowen, K. J. (2013). *Principles of Pediatric Nursing. Caring for Children* (6th ed.). Upper Saddle River, NJ: Pearson.

Bershad, C., & Blaber, C. (2011). *Realizing the promise of the whole-school approach to children's mental health. A practical guide for schools*. National Center for Mental Health Promotion and Youth Violence Prevention. Education Development Center.

Biringen, Z., Altenhofen, S., Aberle, J., Baker, M., Brosal, A., Bennett, S., … Swaim, R. (2012). Emotional availability, attachment, and intervention in center-based child care for infants and toddlers. *Development and Psychopathology, 24*, 23–34.

Bowlby, J. (1969). *Attachment and Loss: Volume 1: Attachment*. New York: Basic Books.

Centers for Disease Control and Prevention. (2015). *Children's mental health*. Retrieved March 2015, from www.cdc.gov/ncbddd/childdevelopment/mentalhealth.html

Committee on the Rights of the Child. (1991). *Official Records of the General Assembly, Forty-Seventh Session, Supplement No. 41*. Retrieved March 2015, from

https://www.iom.int/jahia/webdav/shared/shared/mainsite/policy_and_research/un/63/A_63_41.pdf

Efron, D., Sciberras, E., Anderson, V., Hazell, P., Ukoumunne, O. C., Jongeling, B., … Nicholson, J. M. (2014). Functional status in children with ADHD at age 6–8: A controlled community study. *Pediatrics, 134*(4), e992–e1000.

Gerber, R., Wilks, T., & Erdie-Lalena, C. (2011). Developmental milestones 3: Social-emotional development. *Pediatrics in Review, 32*(12), 533–535.

Harrison, J. R., Vannest, K., Davis, J., & Reynolds, C. (2012). Common problem behaviors of children and adolescents in general education classrooms in the United States. *Journal of Emotional and Behavioral Disorders, 20*(1), 55–64.

Harvard University. (n.d.). *InBrief: The impact of early adversity on children's development*.

Retrieved March 2015, from http://developingchild.harvard.edu

Heller, S. S., Boothe, A., Keyes, A., Nagle, G., Sidell, M., & Rice, J. (2011). Implementation of a mental health consultation model and its impact on early childhood teachers' efficacy and competence. *Infant Mental Health Journal, 32,* 143–164.

Heward, W. (2013). *Exceptional Children. An Introduction to Special Education* (10th ed.). Upper Saddle River, NJ: Pearson.

Jones, S. M., Bouffard, S. M., & Weissbourd, R. (2013). Educators' social and emotional skills vital to learning. *Kappan, 94*(8), 62–65.

Kendziora, K. W. (2011). *Strategies for Social and Emotional Learning: Preschool and Elementary Grade Student Learning Standards and Assessment.* National Center for Mental Health Promotion and Youth Violence Prevention, Newton, MA.

Milteer, R. G., & Ginsburg, K. R. (2012). The importance of play in promoting healthy child development and maintaining strong parent-child bond: Focus on children in poverty. *Pediatrics, 129*(1), e204–e213.

Minnesota Association for Children's Mental Health. (n.d.). *Children's mental health disorder fact sheet for the classroom.* Retrieved March 2015, from http://www.macmh.org/publications/fact_sheets/Anxiety.pdf

National Center for Children in Poverty. (2012). *Mental Health Chartbook. Tracking the Well-being of People with Mental Health Challenges.* Mailman School of Public Health, Columbia University.

National Institutes of Health, U.S. National Library of Medicine. (2013). *Conduct disorder.* Retrieved March 2015, from www.nlm.nih.gov/medlineplus/ency/article/000919.htm

National Institutes of Health, U.S. National Library of Medicine. (2014a). *Oppositional defiant disorder.* Retrieved March 2015, from www.nlm.nih.gov/medlineplus/ency/article/001537.htm

National Institutes of Health, U.S. National Library of Medicine. (2014b). *Reactive attachment disorder of infancy or early childhood.* Retrieved March 2015, fromwww.nlm.nih.gov/medlineplus/ency/article/001547.htm

National Scientific Council on the Developing Child. (2014). *Excessive Stress Disrupts the Architecture of the Developing Brain: Working Paper 3.* Center on the Developing Child at Harvard University. http:developingchild.harvard.edu

National Scientific Council on the Developing Child. (2015). *Supportive Relationships and Active Skill-Building Strengthen the Foundations of Resilience: Working Paper 13.* Center on the Developing Child at Harvard University. http:developingchild.harvard.edu

Perou, R. Bitsko, R., Blumberg, S., Pastor, P., Ghandour, R., Gfroerer, J., ... Huang, L. (2013). Mental health surveillance among

c—United States, 2005–2011. *Morbidity and Mortality Weekly Report, 62*(2), 1–35.

Rahman, A. S., Surkan, P. J., Cayetano, C. E., Rwagatare, P., & Dickson, K. E. (2013). Grand challenges: Integrating maternal mental hHealth into maternal and child health programmes. *PLOS Medicine, 10*(5).

Russell-Mayhew, S., McVey, G., Bardick, A., & Ireland, A. (2012). Mental health, wellness, and childhood overweight/obesity. *Journal of Obesity, 2012.*

Shonkoff, J. G. (2012). The lifelong effects of early childhood adversity and toxic stress. *Pediatrics, 129*(1), e232–e246.

Tang, M. H., & Pinsky, E. G. (2015). Mood and affect disorders. *Pediatrics in Review, 36*(2), 52–61.

Trubo, R. (2014). *Caring for Your Baby and Young Child.* New York: Bantam Books.

Turnbull, A. T., Turnbill, R., Wehmeyer, M. L., & Shogren, K. (2013). *Exceptional Lives. Special Education in Today's Schools* (7th ed.). Upper Saddle River, NJ: Pearson.

U.S. Department of Health and Human Services, Administration for Children and Families. (2014). *Social & emotional development.* Retrieved March 2015, from eclkc.ohs.acf.hhs.gov/hslc/hs/sr/approach/cdelf/se_dev.html

Chapter 13

American Academy of Dermatology. (2005). *Sun protection for children.* Schaumburg, IL: Author. Retrieved September 2012, from http://www.aad.org/public/publications/pamphlets/sun_sunprotection.html

American Academy of Pediatrics. (2001). Prevention of agricultural injuries among children and adolescents. *Pediatrics, 108*(4), 1016–1019.

American Academy of Pediatrics, American Public Health Association, National Resource Center for Health and Safety in Child Care and Early Education. (2011). *Caring for our children: National health and safety performance standards; Guidelines for early care and education programs* (3rd ed.). Elk Grove Village, IL: American Academy of Pediatrics; Washington, DC: American Public Health Association. Also available at http://nrckids.org.

American Academy of Pediatrics, American Public Health Association, National Resource Center for Health and Safety in Child Care and Early Education. 2014. *Caring for our children: Environmental health in early care and education.* Applicable standards from: *Caring for our children: National health and safety performance standards; Guidelines for early care and education programs* (3rd ed.). Elk Grove Village, IL: American Academy of Pediatrics; Washington, DC.

Borse, N., Gilchrist, J., Dellinger, A., Rudd, R., Ballesteros, M., & Sleet, D. (2008). *CDC childhood injury report: patterns of unintentional injuries among 0–19 year olds in the United States, 2000–2006.* U.S. Department of Health and Human Services, Centers for Disease Control and Prevention, National Center for Injury Prevention and Control, Division of Unintentional Injury Prevention. Atlanta, GA.

Bureau of Labor Statistics, U.S. Department of Labor. (2014). *Occupational outlook handbook: 2014–15 edition, Preschool Teachers.* Retrieved March 2015, from http://www.bls.gov/ooh/education-training-and-library/preschool-teachers.htm

Caronongan, P., Kirby, G., Malone, L., & Boller, K. (2011). *Defining and measuring quality: An in-depth study of five child care quality rating and improvement systems.* OPRE Report #2011-29. Washington, DC: Office of Planning, Research and Evaluation, Administration for Children and Families, U.S. Department of Health and Human Services. Retrieved July 2012, from http://www.acf.hhs.gov/programs/opre/cc/childcare_quality/five_childcare/five_childcare.pdf

Center on the Developing Child at Harvard University. (2012). *The science of neglect: The persistent absence of responsive care disrupts the developing brain: working paper 12.* Retrieved from www.developingchild.harvard.edu

Centers for Disease Control and Prevention. (2012b). *Protect the Ones You Love: Child Injuries are Preventable.* Retrieved August 2015 from http://www.cdc.gov/safechild/NAP/background.html

Centers for Disease Control and Prevention, National Center for Injury Prevention and Control, Office of Statistics and Programming. (2013a). *National Estimates of the 10 Leading Causes of Nonfatal Injuries Treated in Hospital Emergency Departments, United States, 2013.* Retrieved March 2015, from http://www.cdc.gov/injury/wisqars/pdf/leading_cause_of_nonfatal_injury_2013-a.pdf

Centers for Disease Control and Prevention, National Center for Injury Prevention and Control, Office of Statistics and Programming. (2013b). *10 Leading Causes of Injury Death by Age Group Highlighting Unintentional Injury Deaths, United States, 2012,* retrieved March 2015, from http://www.cdc.gov/injury/images/lc-charts/leading_causes_of_injury_deaths_highlighting_unintentional_injury_2013-a.gif

Child Care Aware of America. (2014) *Child Fatalities and Severe Injuries in Child Care Centers and Family Child Care Homes in America.* Retrieved March 2015 from https://usa.childcareaware.org/sites/default/files/default_site_pages/2014/one-pager_-_child_fatalities_and_severe_injuries_-_june_2014.pdf

Cohen, J., Onunaku, N., Clothier, S., & Poppe, J. (2005). *Helping young children succeed: Strategies to promote early childhood social and*

emotional development. Retrieved May 2007, from the National Conference of State Legislatures website: http://www.zerotothree. org/site/DocServer/helping_young_children_succeed_final.pdf?docID=1725&AddInterest=1157

Currie, J. M., & Hotz, V.J. (2004). Accidents will happen? Unintentional injury, maternal employment, and child care policy. *Journal of Health Economics, 23*, 25–59.

Danesco, E.R., Miller, T.R., & Spicer, R.S. (2000). Incidence and costs of 1987-1994 childhood injuries: Demographic breakdowns. *Pediatrics, 105(2)*, e27. Online at: http://pediatrics.aappublications.org/cgi/content/full/105/2/e27

Edwards, C., Gandini, L., & Forman, G. (1993). *The hundred languages of children: The Reggio Emilia approach to early childhood education.* Norwood, NJ: Ablex Publishing.

Eunice Kennedy Shriver National Institute of Child Health and Human Development, NIH, DHHS. (2012). *Safe Sleep for Your Baby: Reduce the Risk of Sudden Infant Death Syndrome (SIDS) and Other Sleep-Related Causes of Infant Death* (12-7040). Washington, DC: U.S. Government Printing Office. Retrieved July 28, 2015 from: https://www.nichd. nih.gov/publications/pages/pubs_details. aspx?pubs_id=5807

Greenman, J. B. (2005). Places for childhood in the 21st century: A conceptual framework. In *Young children: Beyond the journal*.

Katz, L. G., & Cesarone, B. (Eds.). (1994). *Reflections on the Reggio Emilia approach.* Urbana, IL: ERIC Clearinghouse on Elementary and Early Childhood Education.

Laughlin, L. (2013). *Who's Minding the Kids? Child Care Arrangements*: Spring 2011. Current Population Reports, P70-135. U.S. Census Bureau, Washington, DC. Retrieved August 2015 from: www.census.gov/prod/2013pubs/p70-135.pdf

Maslow, A. (1954). *Motivation and personality*. New York: Harper & Row.

Montessori, M. (1966). *The secret of childhood*. Notre Dame, IN: Fides.

National Association for the Education of Young Children (NAEYC). (2008). *Overview of the NAEYC Early Childhood Program Standards*. Retrieved January 2012, from http://www.naeyc.org/files/academy/file/OverviewStandards.pdf

National Association for the Education of Young Children. (2011). *Code of ethical conduct and statement of commitment.* Retrieved July 2012, from http://www.naeyc.org/positionstatements/ethical_conduct

National Association for Regulatory Administration (NARA). (2013). *The 50-State child care licensing study, 2011–2013 edition.* Retrieved March 2015 from http://www.naralicensing.org/Resources/Documents/2011-2013_CCLS.pdf

National Children's Center for Rural and Agricultural Health and Safety. (2013). *2014 Fact Sheet Childhood Agricultural Injuries in*

the U. S. Retrieved March 2015 from http://www3.marshfieldclinic.org/proxy/MCRF-Centers-NFMC-NCCRAHS-2014_Child_Ag_Injury_FactSheet.1.pdf

National Head Start Facilities Information Services. (2002). *Region IV Head Start quality improvement center.* Bowling Green, KY: Author.

Nemours Foundation. (2012). *KidsHealth for parents: Playground safety*. Retrieved July 2012, from http://www.kidshealth.org/parent/firstaid_safe/outdoor/playground.html

New, R. S. (1993). *Reggio Emilia: Some lessons for U.S. educators.* Retrieved August 2015 from http://eric.ed.gov/?id=ED354988.

Pate, R., Pfeiffer, K. A., Trost, S. G., Ziegler, P., & Dowda, M. (2004). Physical activity among children attending preschools. *Pediatrics, 114(5)*, 1258–1263.

Ritchie, S., & Weller, B. (Eds.). (2005). *Physical environment: A guide to the NAEYC early childhood program standard and related accreditation criteria.* Washington, DC: National Association for the Education of Young Children.

Rivkin, M. S. (1995). *The great outdoors: Restoring children's right to play outside.* Washington, DC: National Association for the Education of Young Children.

Savage, M. A., Kawanabe, I. T., Mejeur, J., Goehring, J. B., & Reed, J. B. (2002). *Protecting children: A guide to child traffic safety laws.* Washington, DC: National Conference of State Legislatures.

Shonkoff, J. P., & Phillips, D. A. (Eds.). (2000). *From neurons to neighborhoods: The science of early childhood development*. National Research Council and Institute of Medicine. Committee on Integrating the Science of Early Childhood Development. Board on Children, Youth, and Families, Commission on Behavioral and Social Sciences and Education. Washington, DC: National Academy Press.

Tarr, P. (2001). Aesthetic codes in early childhood classrooms: What art educators can learn from Reggio Emilia. *Art Education, 54(3)* 33–39.

Trancik, A. M., & Evans, G. W. (1995). Spaces fit for children: Competency in the design of daycare center environments. *Children's Environments, 12(3)*, 43–58.

U.S. Consumer Product Safety Commission. (1999). *Consumer product safety commission staff study of safety hazards in child care settings.* Washington, DC: Author. Retrieved July 2012, from http://www.cpsc.gov/library/ccstudy.html

U.S. Consumer Product Safety Commission. (2010). *Public playground safety handbook* (Publication No. 325). Retrieved March 2015, from http://www.cpsc.gov/PageFiles/122149/325.pdf

U.S. Department of Health & Human Services. vaccines.gov. *Five Important Reasons to Vaccinate Your Child.* Washington DC. Retrieved March 2015 from http://www.vaccines.

gov/more_info/features/five-important-reasons-to-vaccinate-your-child.html

U.S. General Services Administration. (2003). *Child care center design guide.* Washington, DC: Author. Retrieved July 2012, from http://www.gsa.gov/graphics/pbs/designguidesmall.pdf

Wrigley, J., & J. Dreby. (2005). Fatalities and the Organization of Child Care in the United States, 1985–2003. *American Sociological Review, 70*, 729–757. Retrieved July 2012, from http://fcd-us.org/resources/fatalities-and-organization-child-care-united-states-1985-2003?destination=resources%2Fsearch%3Fpage%3D23

Chapter 14

Alter, P. J., & Conroy, M. (2007). *Recommended practices: Preventing challenging behavior in young children: Effective practices.* Center for Evidence-Based Practice. Retrieved from www.challengingbehavior.org

American Academy of Pediatrics, American Public Health Association, and National Resource Center for Health and Safety in Child Care and Early Education. (2011). *Caring for our children: National Health and Safety Performance Standards: Guidelines for out-of-home child care programs* (2nd ed.). Elk Grove Village, IL: American Academy of Pediatrics and Washington, DC: American Public Health Association. Also available at http://cfoc.nrckids.org/

Bales, D., Wallinga, C., & Coleman, M. (2005). *The teaching basic health and safety in the early childhood classroom curriculum.* University of Georgia.

Bowlby, J. (1982). *Attachment and loss: Vol. 1. Attachment* (2nd ed.). New York: Basic Books.

Centers for Disease Control and Prevention, National Center for Injury Prevention and Control. (2006). *Web-based injury statistics query and reporting system (WISQARS).* Available online at http://www.cdc.gov/injury/wisqars

Fox, L., & Garrison, S. (2009). Helping children learn to manage their own behavior: What Works Brief #7. Center for Social and Emotional Foundations for Early Learning. Retrieved June 2014, from http://csefel.vanderbilt.edu/resources/what_works.html

Gartrell, D. (2006). Guidance matters: The beauty of class meetings. *Young Children, 61(6)* 1–3.

Gartrell, D., & Gartrell, J. J. (2008). Guidance matters: Understanding bullying. *Young Children. 63(3)*, 54–57.

Gilliam, W. S. (2005). Prekindergartners left behind: Expulsion rates in state prekindergarten programs. *Policy Briefs*. Foundation for Child Development. Retrieved June 2014, from http://www.challengingbehavior.org/explore/policy_docs/prek_expulsion.pdf

Hanline, M. F., Nunes, D., & Worthy, M. B. (2007). Augmentative and alternative communication in the early childhood years. *Young Children*, 62(4), 78–82.

Hemmeter, M., Ostrosky, M., Artman, K., & Kinder, K. (2008, May). Planning transitions to prevent challenging behavior. Beyond the Journal: *Young Children* on the Web. National Association for the Education of Young Children. Retrieved June 2014, from http://journal.naeyc.org/btj/200805/pdf/BTJ_Hemmeter_Transitions.pdf

Kern, P., & Wakeford, L. (2007). Supporting outdoor play for young children: The zone model of playground supervision. *Young Children*. 62(5), 12–18.

Nast, P. (2012). Establishing classroom rules. *Classroom Management*. National Education Association. Retrieved June 2014, from http://www.nea.org/tools/establishing-classroom-rules.html

National Association for the Education of Young Children. (2009). *Developmentally appropriate practice in early childhood programs serving children birth through 8*. Washington DC: NAEYC.

National Association for the Education of Young Children (NAEYC). (2011a). *Code of ethical conduct and statement of commitment*. Retrieved June 2014, from http://www.naeyc.org/positionstatements/ethical_conduct

National Association for the Education of Young Children (NAEYC). (2011b). *Q & A highlights: What can I do when a child bites?* Retrieved June 2014, from http://www.naeyc.org/event/challenging-behaviors/highlights

National Highway Traffic Safety Administration. (1999, February). *Guidelines for the safe transportation of pre-school age children in school buses*. Retrieved June 2014, from http://www.nhtsa.dot.gov/people/injury/buses/Guide1999/prekfinal.htm

National Highway Traffic Safety Administration. (2011). School transportation related crashes. *Traffic safety facts: 2009 data*. NHTSA National Center for Statistics and Analysis. Publication 811396. Retrieved June 2014, from http://www-nrd.nhtsa.dot.gov/Pubs/811396.pdf

National Safety Council. (2009). *School bus safety: Infants, toddlers, and preschoolers*. Retrieved June 2014, from http://www.nsc.org/news_resources/Resources/Documents/School_Bus_Safety_Infants_Toddlers_and_Pre-schoolers.pdf

Olson, M. (2007). Strengthening families: Community strategies that work. *Young Children*, 62(2), 26–32.

Savage, M., Kawanabe, I., Mejeur, J., Goehring, J., & Reed, J. (2002). *Protecting children: A guide to traffic safety laws*. National Conference of State Legislatures. Retrieved August 2015, from www.nhtsa.gov/staticfiles/nti/enforcement/pdf/ProtectingChildren.pdf

Start Safe Kids USA. (2009). *Start safe fire safety. Start safe fire: A fire and burn prevention safety program for preschoolers and their families*. Retrieved June 2014, from http://www.safekids.org/educators/Start-safe/fire-safety/

Strain, P. S., & Dunlap, G. 2006. *Recommended practices: Being an evidence-based practitioner*. Tampa: University of South Florida, Louis de la Parte Florida Mental Health Institute, Center for Evidence-based Practice: Young Children with Challenging Behavior.

U.S. Consumer Products Safety Commission. (2012). *Water safety tips*. Publication 210. Retrieved January 2014, from http://www.cpsc.gov/cpscpub/pubs/210.pdf

Utah Education Network. (2003). *The Classroom – A Caring Community*. Retrieved August 2015 from: http://www.uen.org/k-2educator/classroom.shtml

Wittmer, D. S., & Petersen, S. H. (2008). Issues in infant/toddler programs. In S. Feeney, (Ed.), *Issues in Early Childhood Education*. Upper Saddle River, NJ: Merrill Prentice Hall.

Chapter 15

Administration for Children and Families. (2010). The Child Abuse and Prevention and Treatment Act. (PL 111-320) Reauthorization of CAPTA, 2012. U.S. Department of Health and Human Services, Retrieved December 2014, from http://www.acf.hhs.gov/programs/cb/resources/capta2010.pdf

American Psychological Association. (2013). *Violence in the Media—Psychologists Study TV and Video Game Violence for Potential Harmful Effects*. Retrieved December 2014, from http://www.apa.org/research/action/protect.aspx

Beresin, E. (2014) The Impact of Media Violence on Children and Adolescents: Opportunities for Clinical Intervention. American Academy of Child & Adolescent Psychiatry. Retrieved November 2014, from www.aacap.org/aacap/Medical_Students_and_Residents/Mentorship_Matters/DevelopMentor/The_Impact_of_Media_Violence_on_Children_and_Adolescents_Opportunities_for_Clinical_Interventions.aspx

Center on the Developing Child at Harvard University. (2007, August). *A science-based framework for early childhood policy: Using evidence to improve outcomes in learning, behavior and health for vulnerable children*. Cambridge, MA: Author. Retrieved December 2014, from http://developingchild.harvard.edu

Centers for Disease Control and Prevention. (2014). National Center for Injury Prevention and Control. *Child Maltreatment: Risk and Protective Factors*. Retrieved November 2014, from http://www.cdc.gov/violenceprevention/childmaltreatment/riskprotectivefactors.html

Chalk, R., Gibbons, A., & Scarupa, H. J. (2002). The multiple dimensions of child abuse and neglect: New insights into an old problem (Child Trends Research Brief). Washington, DC: Child Trends. Retrieved August 2015, from www.childtrends.org/wp-content/uploads/2013/05/childabuserb.pdf

Child Welfare Information Gateway (2004). *Risk and protective factors for child abuse and neglect*. Washington, DC: Author. Retrieved August 2015, from http://www.childwelfare.gov/can/factors

Child Welfare Information Gateway. (2014). Domestic violence and the child welfare system. Washington, DC: U.S. Department of Health and Human Services, Children's Bureau.

Child Welfare Information Gateway. (2013a). *What is child abuse and neglect? Recognizing the signs and symptoms*. Washington, DC: U.S. Department of Health and Human Services, Children's Bureau. Retrieved August 2015 from www.childwelfare.gov/pubpdfs/whatiscan.pdf

Child Welfare Information Gateway. (2013b). Long-term consequences of child abuse and neglect. Washington, DC: U.S. Department of Health and Human Services, Children's Bureau. Retrieved August 2015 from www.childwelfare.gov/pubpdfs/long_term_consequences.pdf

Children's Bureau & DePanfilis, D. (2006). *Child neglect: A guide for prevention, assessment and intervention*. User Manual Series. Retrieved December 2014, from https://www.childwelfare.gov/pubs/usermanuals/neglect/chaptersix.cfm

Cohen, E., & Knitzer, J. (2004, January). *Young children living with domestic violence: The role of early childhood programs*. Iowa City: University of Iowa.

Cohen, J., Onunaku, N., Clothier, S., & Poppe, J. (2006). *Helping young children succeed: Strategies to promote early childhood social and emotional development* (Early Childhood Research and Policy Report). Washington, DC: National Conference of State Legislatures and Zero to Three.

Cooley-Strickland, M., Quilee, T. J., Griffin, R. S., Stuart, E., Bradshaw, C., & Furr-Holden, D. (2009). National Institutes of Health. Community Violence and Youth: Affect, Behavior, Substance Use, and Academics. *Clinical Child and Family Psychology Review*, 12(2), 127–156. Retrieved November 2014 from: www.ncbi.nlm.nih.gov/pmc/articles/PMC2700237/

Crosson-Tower, C. (2002). How can we recognize child abuse and neglect? In *When children are abused: An educator's guide to intervention* (pp. 8–34). Boston, MA: Allyn & Bacon.

Dahlberg L. L., & Mercy, J. A. (2009, February). History of violence as a public health problem. *AMA Journal of Ethics*, 11(2), 167–172.

English, D. J., Widom, C. S., & Brandford, C. (2004). Another look at the effects of child abuse. *National Institute of Justice Journal*, 251, 23–24.

Fang, X., Brown, D. S., Florence, C. S., & Mercy, J. A. (2012). The economic burden of child maltreatment in the United States and implications for prevention. *Child Abuse and Neglect*, 36(2), 156–165.

Finkelhor, D., Turner, H., Ormrod, R., Hamby, S., & Kracke, K. (2009). Children's exposure to violence: A comprehensive national survey. *Juvenile Justice Bulletin*. Office of Justice Programs. U.S. Department of Justice. Retrieved June 2012, from https://www.ncjrs.gov/pdffiles1/ojjdp/227744.pdf

Fitzpatrick, C., Barnett, T., & Pagani, L. S. (2012). Early exposure to media violence and later child adjustment. *Journal of Development and Behavioral Pediatrics*, 33(4), 291–297. Retrieved June 2012, from http://www.ncbi.nlm.nih.gov/pubmed/22481072

Fraser, M. W., & Terzian, M. A. (2005). Risk and resilience in child development: Principles and strategies of practice. In G. P. Mallon & P. M. Hess (Eds.), *Child welfare for the 21st century: A handbook of practices, policies, and programs* (pp. 55–71) New York: Columbia University Press.

Kaneshiro, N. (2014). *Child abuse: Physical*. PubMed. National Institutes of Health. Retrieved August 2015, from http://www.nlm.nih.gov/medlineplus/ency/article/001552.htm

Kaneshiro, N. K., & Dugdale, D. C. (2011). *Munchausen syndrome by proxy*. MedlinePlus. National Institutes of Health. Retrieved August 2015, from http://www.nlm.nih.gov/medlineplus/ency/article/001555.htm

Karageorge, K., & Kendall, R. (2008). *The role of professional child care providers in preventing and responding to child abuse and neglect*. U.S. Department of Health and Human Services, Administration for Children & Families. Administration on Children, Youth, and Families, Children's Bureau. Office on Child Abuse and Neglect. Retrieved from https://www.childwelfare.gov/pubs/usermanuals/childcare/childcare.pdf

Kempe, C. H., Silverman, F. N., Steele, B. F. Droegemueller, W., & Silver, H. K. (1962). The battered-child syndrome. *Journal of the American Medical Association*, 181(1), 17–24.

Kenny, M. C. (2001). Child abuse reporting: Teachers' perceived deterrents. *Child Abuse and Neglect*, 25(1), 81–92.

Kracke, K., & Cohen, E. P. (2008). The Safe Start Initiative: Building and disseminating knowledge to support children exposed to violence. *Journal of Emotional Abuse*, 1(2), 155–174.

Levin, D. (2003, March). *Beyond banning war and superhero play: Meeting children's needs in violent times*. Washington, DC: National Association for the Education of Young Children.

London, K., Bruck, M., Ceci, S., & Shuman, D. (2005). Disclosure of child sexual abuse: What does research tell us about the ways the children tell? *Psychology, Public Policy, and Law*, 11(1), 194–226.

Luthar, S., & Goldstein, A. (2004). Children's exposure to community violence: Implications for understanding risk and resilience. *Journal of Clinical Child and Adolescent Psychology*, 33(3), 499–505. Retrieved August 2015, from http://www.ncbi.nlm.nih.gov/pubmed/15271607

Malchiodi, C. A. (2001). Using drawing as intervention with traumatized children. *Trauma and Loss: Research and Interventions*, 1(1). Gross Pointe Woods, MI: National Institute of Trauma and Loss in Children. Retrieved August 2015, from http://www.starr.org/training/tlc/resources-for-parents

Malchiodi, C. A. (2008). When trauma happens, children draw. The healing arts: The restoring power of imagination. *Psychology Today*. Retrieved August 2015, from http://www.psychologytoday.com/blog/arts-and-health/200805/when-trauma-happens-children-draw-part-i

Margolin, G., & Gordis, E. (2004). Children's Exposure to Violence in the Family and Community. *Current Directions in Psychological Science*, 13(4). American Psychological Society. Retrieved August 2015, from http://www.psy.miami.edu/faculty/dmessinger/c_c/rsrcs/rdgs/peers_social_general/margolin.exposure2violence.curdir.04.pdf

Mitchum, R. (2011). Public health epidemics without diseases. *Science Life*. University of Chicago. Retrieved August 2015, from http://sciencelife.uchospitals.edu/2011/02/03/public-health-epidemics-without-diseases/

National Association for the Education of Young Children. (2004). *Building circles—Breaking Cycles* (Publication DD2). Author.

National Association for the Education of Young Children. (2011). *Code of ethical conduct and statement of commitment*. Retrieved August 2015, from http://www.naeyc.org/files/naeyc/file/positions/Ethics%20Position%20Statement2011.pdf

National Center for Posttraumatic Stress Disorder. (2007). *Community violence: The effects on children and teens*. U.S. Department of Veteran's Affairs. Retrieved August 2015, from www.ptsd.va.gov

National Institute of Neurological Disorders and Stroke, National Institutes of Health. (2010). *NINDS Shaken baby syndrome information page*. Retrieved August 2015, from http://www.ninds.nih.gov/disorders/shakenbaby/shakenbaby.htm

National Scientific Council on the Developing Child. (2005/2014). *Excessive Stress Disrupts the Architecture of the Developing Brain: Working Paper 3*. Updated Edition. Retrieved from www.developingchild.harvard.edu

National Scientific Council on the Developing Child. (2010). *Persistent fear and anxiety can affect young children's learning and development: Working paper no. 9*. Retrieved from www.developingchild.harvard.edu

New York Society for the Prevention of Cruelty to Children. (2008). *The catalyst: 1870–1874*. New York: Author. Retrieved August 2015, from http://www.nyspcc.org/about-the-new-york-society-for-the-prevention-of-cruelty-to-children/history/

Office on Child Abuse and Neglect, Caliber Associates, & Crosson-Tower, C. (2003). *The role of educators in preventing and responding to child abuse and neglect*. User manual series. Retrieved August 2015, from https://www.childwelfare.gov/pubs/usermanuals/educator/index.cfm

Osofsky, J. (1999). The impact of violence on children. *The Future of Children*, 9(3), 33–49.

Osofsky, J. (Ed.). (2004). *Young children and trauma: Intervention and treatment*. New York: Guilford Publications.

Renteln, A. D. (2010). *Corporal punishment and the cultural defense*. Retrieved December 2014, from http://scholarship.law.duke.edu/lcp/vol73/iss2/10

Rice, K., & Groves, B. (2005). *Hope & healing; A caregivers' guide to helping young children affected by trauma*. Washington, DC: Zero to Three.

Shonkoff, J., & Phillips, D. (Eds.). (2000). *From neurons to neighborhoods: The science of early childhood development*. Washington DC: National Academy Press.

Swaner, R., Kohn, J. Rempel, M., Campbell, M., Jaffe, P., & Wolfe, D. (2011). *The U.S. Attorney General's Defending Childhood Initiative: Formative evaluation of the Phase I Demonstration Program*. Retrieved August 2015, from https://www.ncjrs.gov/pdffiles1/nij/grants/236563.pdf

Thomas, D., Leicht, D., Hughes, C., Madigan, A., & Dowell., K. (2003). *Emerging practices in the prevention of child abuse and neglect*. Wayne, PA: Caliber Associates. Retrieved August 2015, from http://www.childwelfare.gov/pubPDFs/emerging_practices_report.pdf

U.S. Department of Health and Human Services, Administration for Children and Families, Administration on Children, Youth and Families, Children's Bureau. (2015). *Child maltreatment 2013*. Available at http://www.acf.hhs.gov/programs/cb/research-data-technology/statistics-research/child-maltreatment

U.S. Department of Health and Human Services' Children's Bureau (HHS), Office on Child Abuse and Neglect, Child Welfare Information Gateway, FRIENDS National Resource Center for Community-Based Child Abuse Prevention, and the Center for the Study of Social Policy—Strengthening Families. (2015). *The 2015 Prevention Resource Guide: Making Meaningful Connections*. Retrieved August 2015, from https://www.childwelfare.gov/preventing/

U.S. Department of Justice. (2011). *Fact Sheets: Domestic violence*. Retrieved August 2015, from http://www.ojp.usdoj.gov/newsroom/factsheets/ojpfs_domesticviolence.html

Washington Council for Prevention of Child Abuse. (2005). *Reframing child abuse messages*. Seattle: Author.

Chapter 16

American Academy of Pediatrics, American Public Health Association, National Resource Center for Health and Safety in Child Care and Early Education. (2011). *Caring for our children: National health and safety performance standards; Guidelines for early care and education programs* (3rd ed.). Elk Grove Village, IL: American Academy of Pediatrics; Washington, DC: American Public Health Association. Also available at http://nrckids.org

American Red Cross. (2012a). *Red Cross helps kids build preparedness backpacks*. Retrieved August 2015, from www.redcross.org

American Red Cross. (2012b). *Recovering after disaster: Recovering emotionally*. Retrieved August 2015, from www.redcross.org

Ben-Joseph, E. P. (2010). Hey! A black widow spider bit me! *KidsHealth*. Nemours Foundation. Retrieved August 2015, from http://kidshealth.org/kid/ill_injure/bugs/black_widow.html#

Ben-Joseph, E. P. (2011). Asthma. *KidsHealth*. Nemours Foundation. Retrieved August 2015, from http://kidshealth.org/kid/asthma_basics/what/asthma.html#

Berg, M. D., Schexnayder, S. M., Chameides, L., Terry, M., Donoghue, A., Hickey, R. W., ... Hazinski, M. F. (2010). Part 13: Pediatric basic life support: 2010 American Heart Association Guidelines for Cardiopulmonary Resuscitation and Emergency Cardiovascular Care. *Circulation, 122*(suppl 3), S862–S875.

Centers for Disease Control and Prevention. (2006). *Emergency preparedness: Chemical agents: facts about sheltering in place*. Retrieved August 2015, from http://www.bt.cdc.gov/planning/shelteringfacts.asp

Centers for Disease Control and Prevention. (2013). *Traumatic brain injury: Prevention*. Retrieved August 2015, from http://www.cdc.gov/traumaticbraininjury/prevention.html

Centers for Disease Control and Prevention. (2014a). *Learn How to Control Asthma.*. Retrieved August 2015, from http://www.cdc.gov/asthma/faqs.htm

Centers for Disease Control and Prevention. (2014b). *NIOSH workplace safety and health topics: Heat stress*. Retrieved August 2015, from http://www.cdc.gov/niosh/topics/heatstress/

Centers for Disease Control and Prevention. (2014c). *Emergency preparedness and response: Coping with disaster or traumatic events*. CDC Emergency Risk Communication Branch (ERCB), Division of Emergency Operations (DEO), Office of Public Health Preparedness and Response (OPHPR). Retrieved August 2015, from http://emergency.cdc.gov/mentalhealth/

Centers for Disease Control and Prevention. (2012). *Emergency Preparedness and Response. Frequently Asked Questions (FAQ) About Extreme Heat*. Retrieved August 2015, from http://www.bt.cdc.gov/disasters/extremeheat/faq.asp

Cronan, K. M. (2011). Nosebleeds. *KidsHealth*. Nemours Foundation. Retrieved August 2015, from http://kidshealth.org/parent/firstaid_safe/emergencies/nose_bleed.html#

Cunah, J. P., & Shiel, W. C. (2014). *Nosebleed*. Retrieved August 2015, from http://www.medicinenet.com/nosebleed/article.htm

Defelice, M., & Stewart, S. M. (2011). Nut or peanut allergy. *KidsHealth*. Nemours Foundation. Retrieved August 2015, from http://kidshealth.org/kid/nutrition/diets/nut_allergy.html#

Dowshen, S. (2013). Dealing with cuts. *KidsHealth*. Nemours Foundation. Retrieved August 2015, from http://kidshealth.org/parent/firstaid_safe/emergencies/bleeding.html

Dugdale, D. C., Henochowicz, S. L., & Zieve, D. (2012). *Anaphylaxes*. MedlinePlus. U.S. National Library of Medicine & National Institutes of Health. Retrieved August 2015, from http://www.nlm.nih.gov/medlineplus/ency/article/000844.htm

Federal Emergency Management Agency. (2010). *Helping children cope*. Retrieved August 2015, from http://www.ready.gov/kids/parents/coping

Federal Emergency Management Agency. (2013a). *Terrorist hazards*. Retrieved August 2015, from http://www.ready.gov/terrorist-hazards

Federal Emergency Management Agency. (2013b). *Natural disasters*. Retrieved August 2015er , from http://www.ready.gov/natural-disasters

Federal Emergency Management Agency. (2014). *Pandemic*. Retrieved August 2015, from http://www.ready.gov/pandemic

Filloux, F., & Goodman, M. (2010). Seizures. KidsHealth. Nemours Foundation. Retrieved August 2015, from http://kidshealth.org/parent/firstaid_safe/emergencies/seizure.html#

Gavin, M. L. (2014). What's a bruise? *KidsHealth*. Nemours Foundation. Retrieved August 2015, from http://kidshealth.org/kid/talk/qa/bruise.html

Government Services Agency, Child Care Division. (2011). *Child Care Emergency Preparedness Toolbox*. Retrieved August 2015, from http://www.gsa.gov/graphics/pbs/Child_Care_Emergency_Preparedness_Toolbox.pdf

Green, N. A. (2014). Rabies. *KidsHealth*. Nemours Foundation. Retrieved August 2015, from http://kidshealth.org/kid/health_problems/infection/rabies.html

Heller, J. L., & Zieve, D. (2011a). *Choking first aid—adult or child over 1 year—series*. MedlinePlus. U.S. National Library of Medicine & National Institutes of Health. Retrieved August 2015, from http://www.nlm.nih.gov/medlineplus/ency/presentations/100222_5.htm

Heller, J. L., & Zieve, D. (2011b). *Choking first aid—infant under 1 year—series*. MedlinePlus. U.S. National Library of Medicine & National Institutes of Health. Retrieved August 2015, from http://www.nlm.nih.gov/medlineplus/ency/presentations/100221_3.htm

Heller, J. L., & Zieve, D. (2012a). *Burns*. MedLinePlus. U.S. National Library of Medicine & National Institutes of Health. Retrieved August 2015, from http://www.nlm.nih.gov/medlineplus/ency/article/000030.htm

Heller, J. L., & Zieve, D. (2012b). *Human bites*. Medline Plus. U.S. National Library of Medicine & National Institutes of Health. Retrieved August 2015, from http://www.nlm.nih.gov/medlineplus/ency/article/000035.htm

Heller, J. L., & Zieve, D. (2014a). *Insect bites and stings*. Medline Plus. U.S. National Library of Medicine & National Institutes of Health. Retrieved August 2015, from http://www.nlm.nih.gov/medlineplus/ency/article/000033.htm

Heller, J. L., & Zieve, D. (2014b). *Shock*. MedLinePlus. U.S. National Library of Medicine & National Institutes of Health. Retrieved August 2015, from http://www.nlm.nih.gov/medlineplus/ency/article/000039.htm

Heller, J. L., Zieve, D., & Black, B. (2014). *Head injury—first aid*. MedlinePlus. U.S. National Library of Medicine & National Institutes of Health. Retrieved August 2015, from http://www.nlm.nih.gov/medlineplus/ency/article/000028.htm

Heller, J. L., Zieve, D., Black, B., Slon, S., & Wang, N. (2013a). *Bleeding*. MedlinePlus. U.S. National Library of Medicine & National Institutes of Health. Retrieved August 2015, from http://www.nlm.nih.gov/medlineplus/ency/article/000045.htm

Heller, J. L., Zieve, D., Black, B., Slon, S., & Wang, N. (2013b) *Electrical injury*. MedlinePlus. U.S. National Library of Medicine & National Institutes of Health. Retrieved August 2015, from http://www.nlm.nih.gov/medlineplus/ency/article/000053.htm

Hirsch, L. (2014). First Aid: Teeth injuries. *KidsHealth*. Nemours Foundation. Retrieved August 2015, from http://kidshealth.org/parent/firstaid_safe/sheets/tooth_sheet.html

Homeier, B. P. (2005). Falls. KidsHealth. Nemours Foundation. Retrieved August 2015, from http://kidshealth.org/teen/safety/first_aid/falls_sheet.html

International Save the Children Alliance. (2006). *Two years later: Rebuilding lives after the tsunami: The children's road to recovery*. London: Author. Retrieved August 2015, from http://www.savethechildren.org/atf/

cf/%7B9def2ebe-10ae-432c-9bd0-df91d2e-ba74a%7D/savechild_tsunami_report.pdf

Kaneshiro, N. K., & Zieve, D. (2012). *Signs of an asthma attack*. MedlinePlus. U.S. National Library of Medicine & National Institutes of Health. Retrieved August 2015, from http://www.nlm.nih.gov/medlineplus/ency/patientinstructions/000062.htm

Kaneshiro, N. K., Zieve, D., Ogilvie, I. (2014) Febrile Seizures. Medline Plus. U.S. National Library of Medicine & National Institutes of Health. Retrieved August 2015, from http://www.nlm.nih.gov/medlineplus/ency/article/000980.htm

Lusby, F. W., Zieve, D., & Black, B. (2013). *Eye—foreign object in*. MedlinePlus. U.S. National Library of Medicine & National Institutes of Health. Retrieved August 2015, from http://www.nlm.nih.gov/medlineplus/ency/article/002084.htm

National Association of Child Care Resource and Referral Agencies and Save the Children. (2010). *Protecting children in child care during emergencies*. Retrieved August 2015, from http://www.naccrra.org/sites/default/files/publications/naccrra_publications/2012/protectingchildreninchildcareemergencies.pdf

National Commission on Children and Disasters. *2010 Report to the President and Congress*. Retrieved August 2015, from http://archive.ahrq.gov/prep/nccdreport/

National Institute of General Medical Sciences. (2012). *Burns fact sheet*. Retrieved August 2015, from http://www.nigms.nih.gov/Education/Pages/Factsheet_Burns.aspx

Purdue University. (2014). *Radiological and environmental management: Blood spill procedures*. West Lafayette, IN: Author. Retrieved August 2015, from http://www.purdue.edu/rem/eh/bsp.htm

Rosenbaum, S., Harty, M., & Sheer, J. (2008, March–April). State laws extending comprehensive legal liability protections for professional health-care volunteers during public health emergencies. *Public Health Report, 123*(2), 238–241. PMC2239336. Association of Schools of Public Health.

Retrieved August 2015, from http://www.ncbi.nlm.nih.gov/pmc/articles/PMC2239336/

Schwartz, A. (2009). *Head Start Emergency Preparedness Manual*. Office of Head Start, Administration for Children and Families, U.S. Department of Health and Human Services. Retrieved August 2015, from http://eclkc.ohs.acf.hhs.gov/hslc/tta-system/health/ep/Head_Start_Emergency_Preparedness_Manual.pdf

Siegel, J. D., Rhinehart, E., Jackson, M., Chiarello, L., & the Healthcare Infection Control Practices Advisory Committee. (2007). *Guideline for isolation precautions: Preventing transmission of infectious agents in healthcare settings*. Retrieved August 2015, from http://www.cdc.gov/hicpac/2007IP/2007isolationPrecautions.html

Vorvick, L. J., Zieve, D. (2013). *Bruise*. Medline Plus. U.S. National Library of Medicine & National Institutes of Health. Retrieved August 2015, from http://www.nlm.nih.gov/medlineplus/ency/article/007213.htm

NAME INDEX

SUBJECT INDEX

Note: Page numbers follow by "b" indicate boxed material; "f " for illustrations and "t" for tables.